CLYDE
FANS

Moir 4-1516
Ombrd 0955
nwd 9143
ydbk 2778
Curtains
.MIdwy
Enwood
Mayor
uette 8681

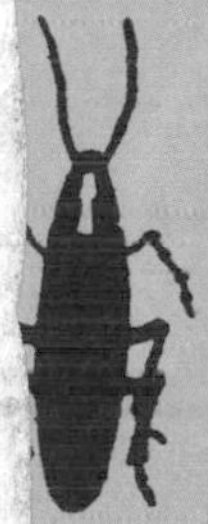

LE
RS
SECTS
RVICE
ANCE
51
CIATION

ook 0733
gdl 2215
th 5-5251
st 1-2008
ivr 4041
TD

Ventilating Equipment
717Church..............................Klingdl 5129

ARNOLDI MANUFACTURING
1136Davenport....**OL**ivr 1433

BEVERLY FANS
IMPERIAL ELECTRIC MOTORS *Commercial, Industrial, Domestic*
785QueenW................**EM**pir 8-3127

Sloan Ha
Sullivan
Temple J
Vitafeed

F
GAL
LINK
PLA
FEN
PR
PL5

FE
WI
CHA
FEN
L55

PEER J
RISEBR
Sloan Ha
Sillivan E
Temple J
Vitafeed

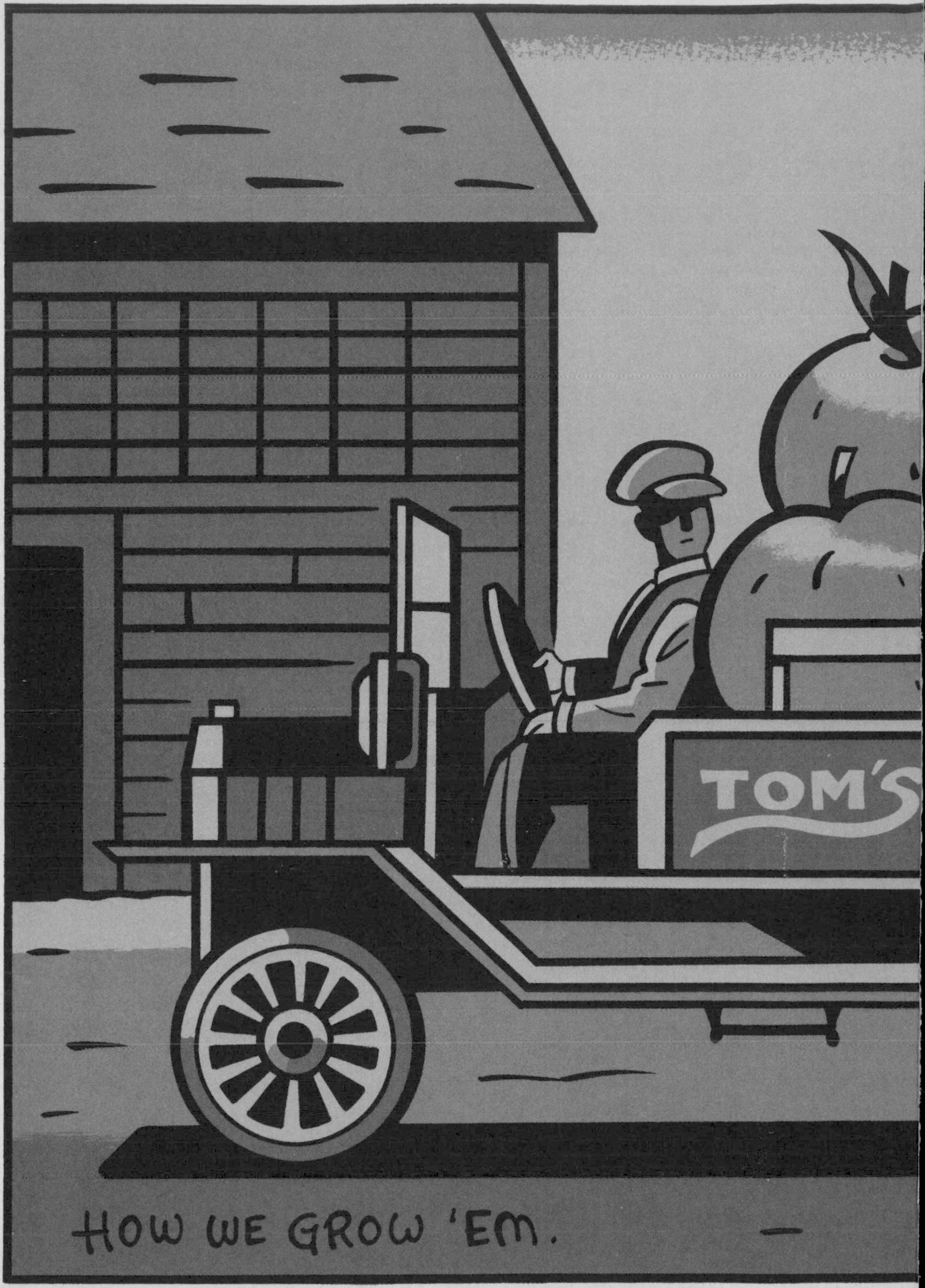
TOM'S
HOW WE GROW 'EM.

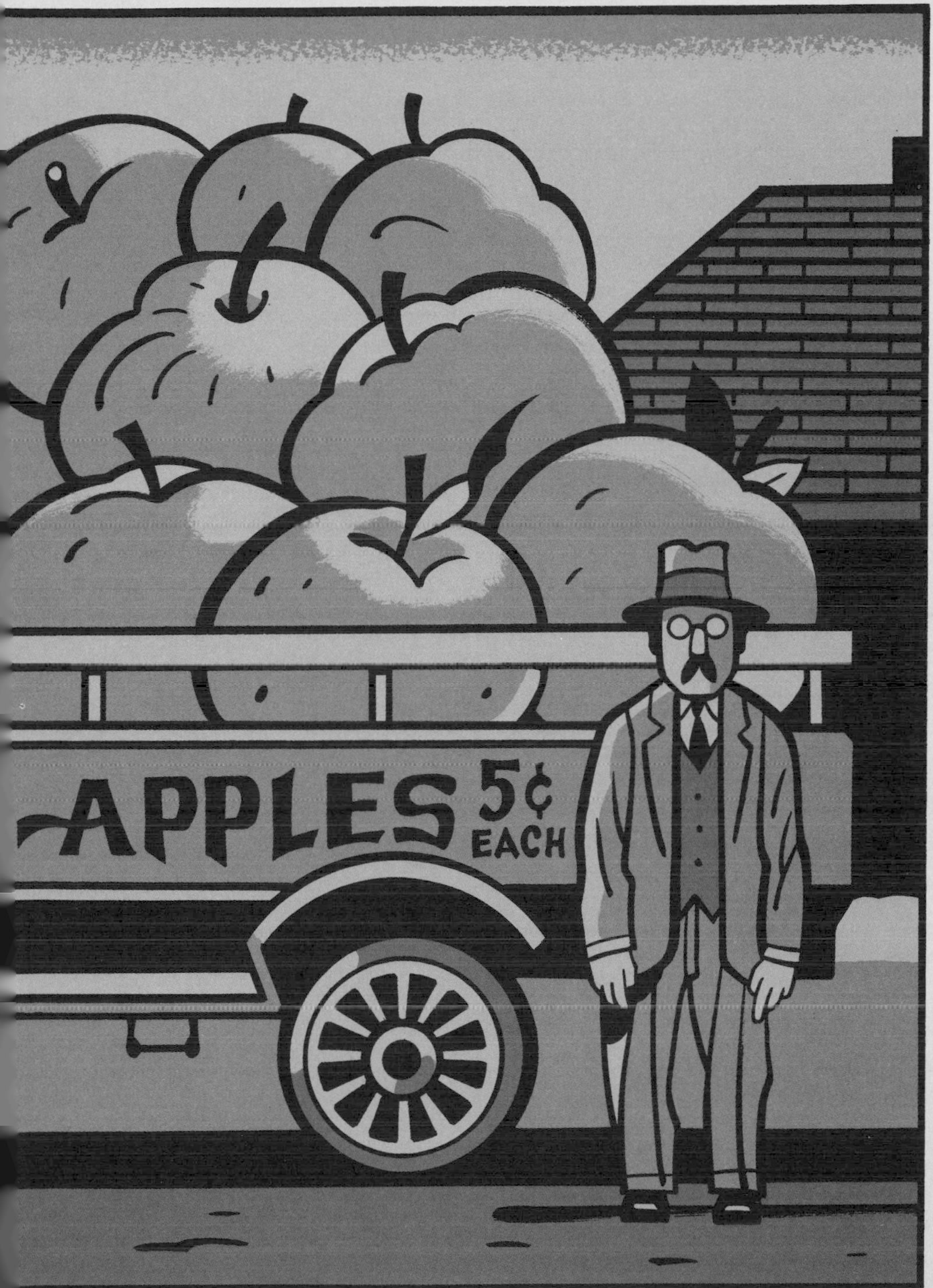
APPLES 5¢ EACH

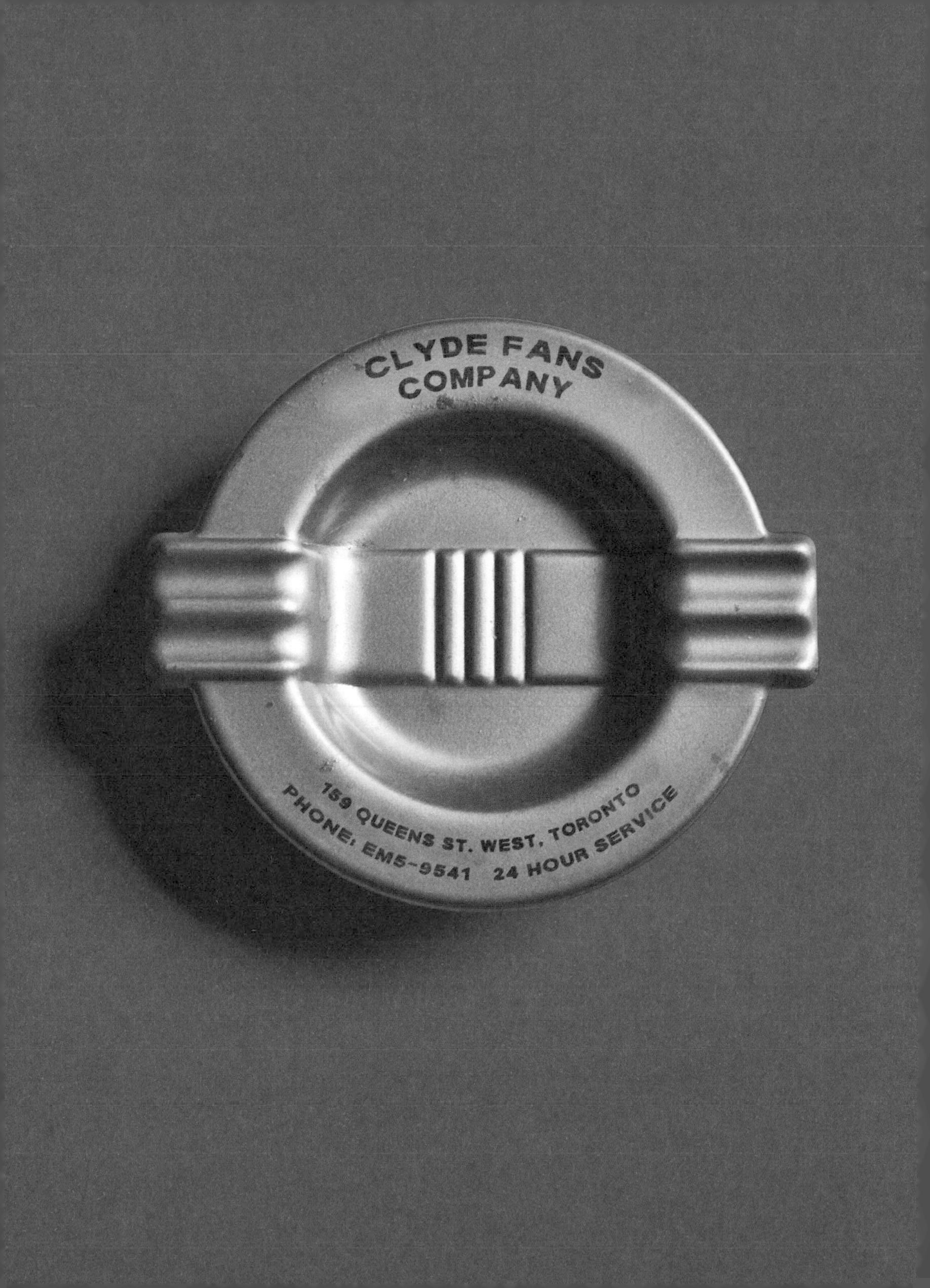
CLYDE FANS
COMPANY
159 QUEENS ST. WEST, TORONTO
PHONE: EM5-9541 24 HOUR SERVICE

CLYDE FANS

159 QUEENS STREET W.

TORONTO, ONTARIO

PHONE: EM5-9541

INSTALLATION
AND SERVICE
24 HOUR SERVICE

FOR OFFICES,
FACTORIES, STORES,
HOUSES, BARNS,
APARTMENTS, ETC.

CLYDE FANS

Last Month

JANUARY

S	M	T	W	T	F	S
		1	2	3	4	5	6	7
8	9	10	11	12	13	14
15	16	17	18	19	20	21
22	23	24	25	26	27	28
29	30	31				

1957 **FEBRUARY** 1957

SUN	MON	TUE	WED	THU	FRI	SAT
			1	2	3	4
5	6	7	8	9	10	11
12	13	14	15	16	17	18
19	20	21	22	23	24	25
26	27	28				

Next Month

MARCH

S	M	T	W	T	F	S
					1	2	3
4	5	6	7	8	9	10
11	12	13	14	15	16	17
18	19	20	21	22	23	24
25	26	27	28	29	30	31

CLYDE CO FANS

CLYDE CO FANS

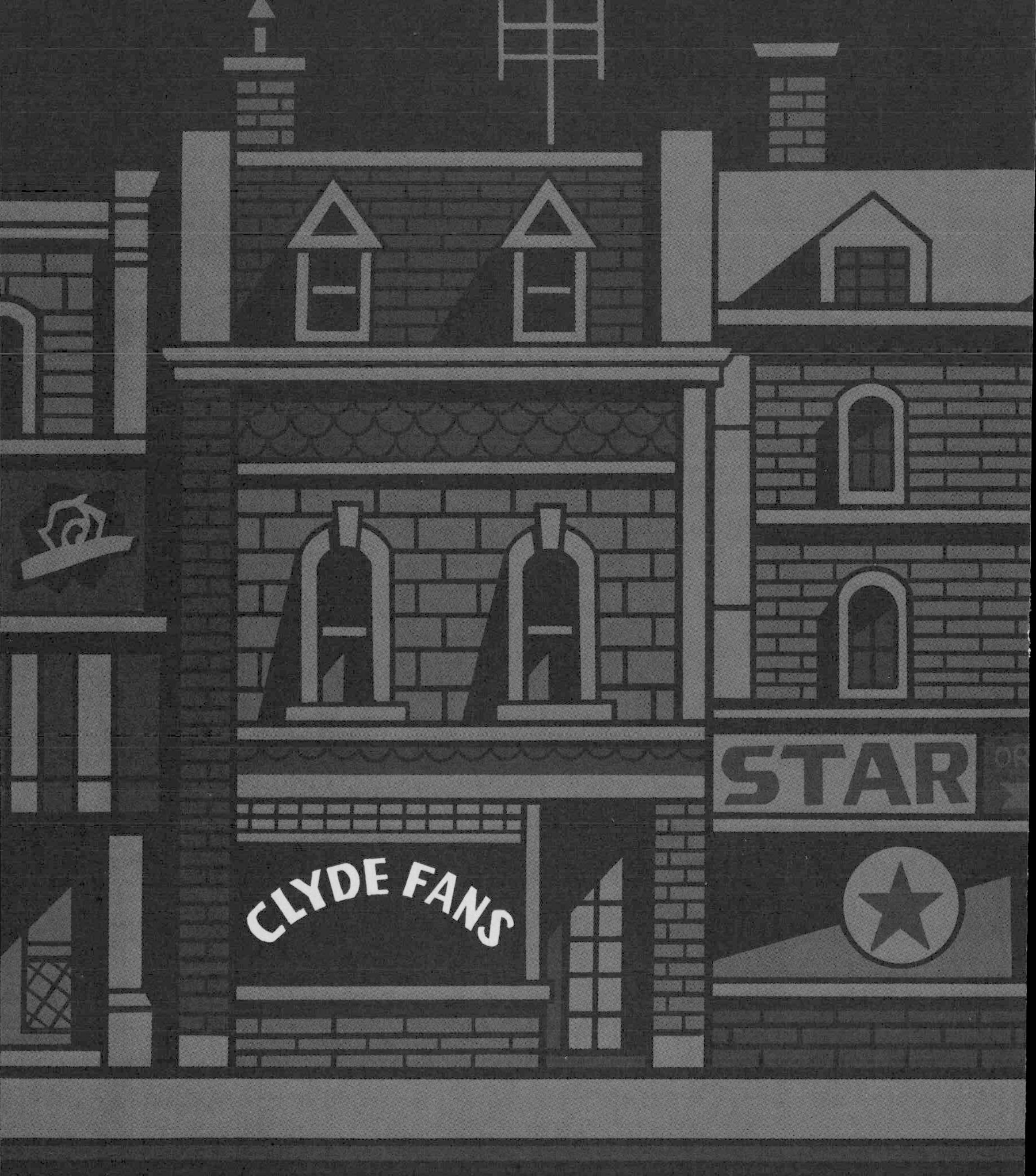
STAR
CLYDE FANS

A PICTURE

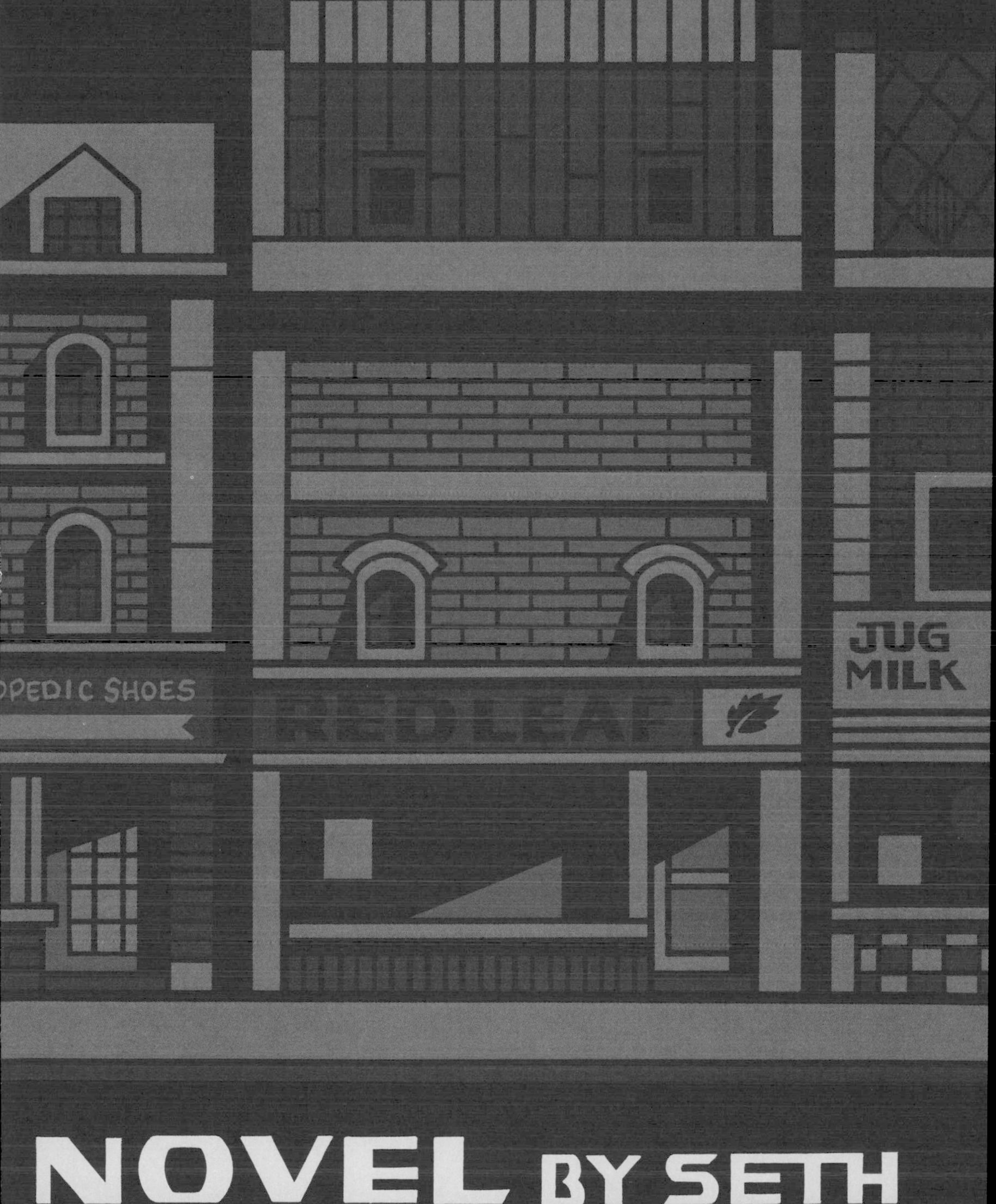
OPEDIC SHOES
REDLEAF
JUG
MILK
NOVEL BY SETH

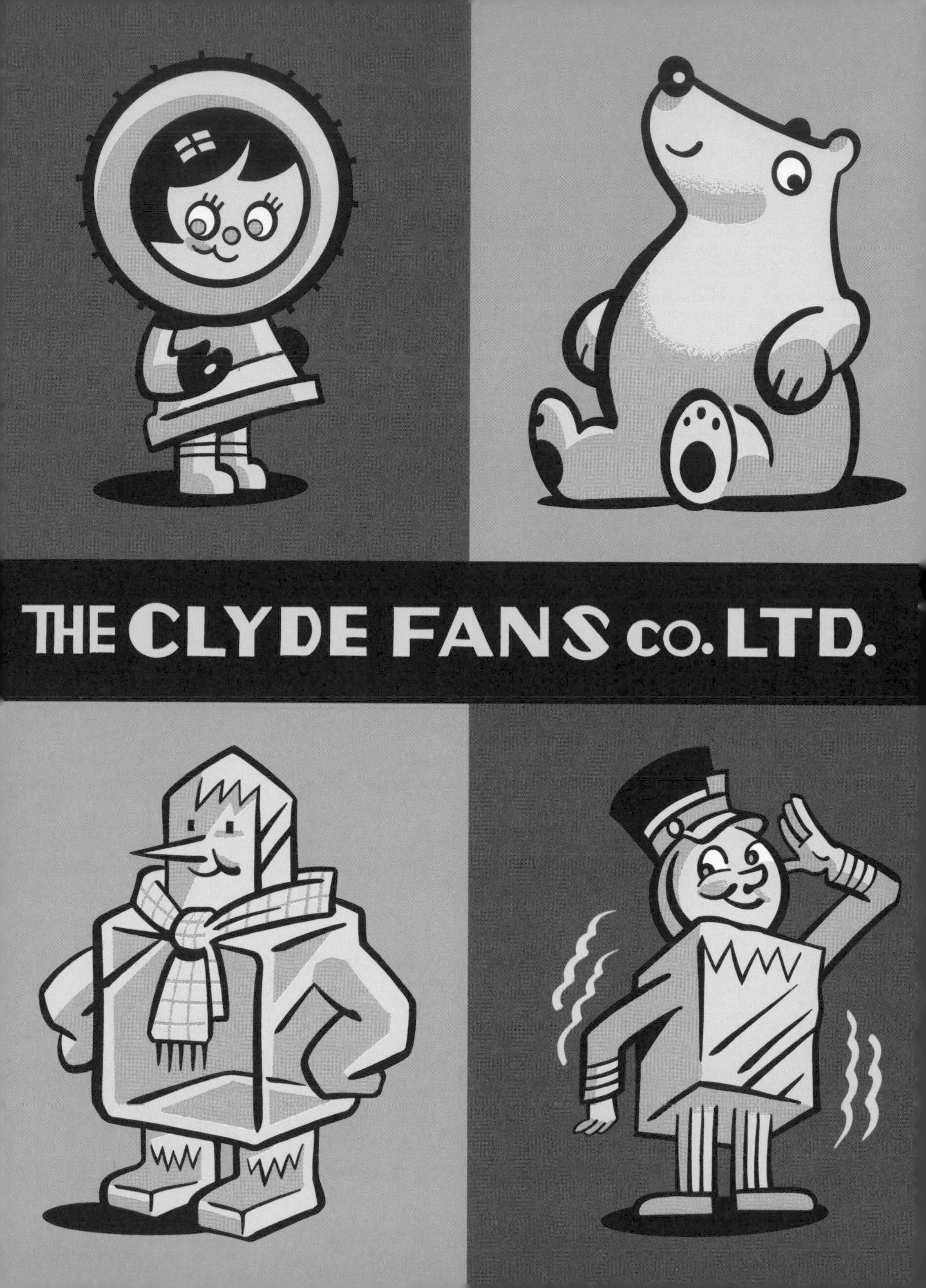
THE CLYDE FANS CO. LTD.

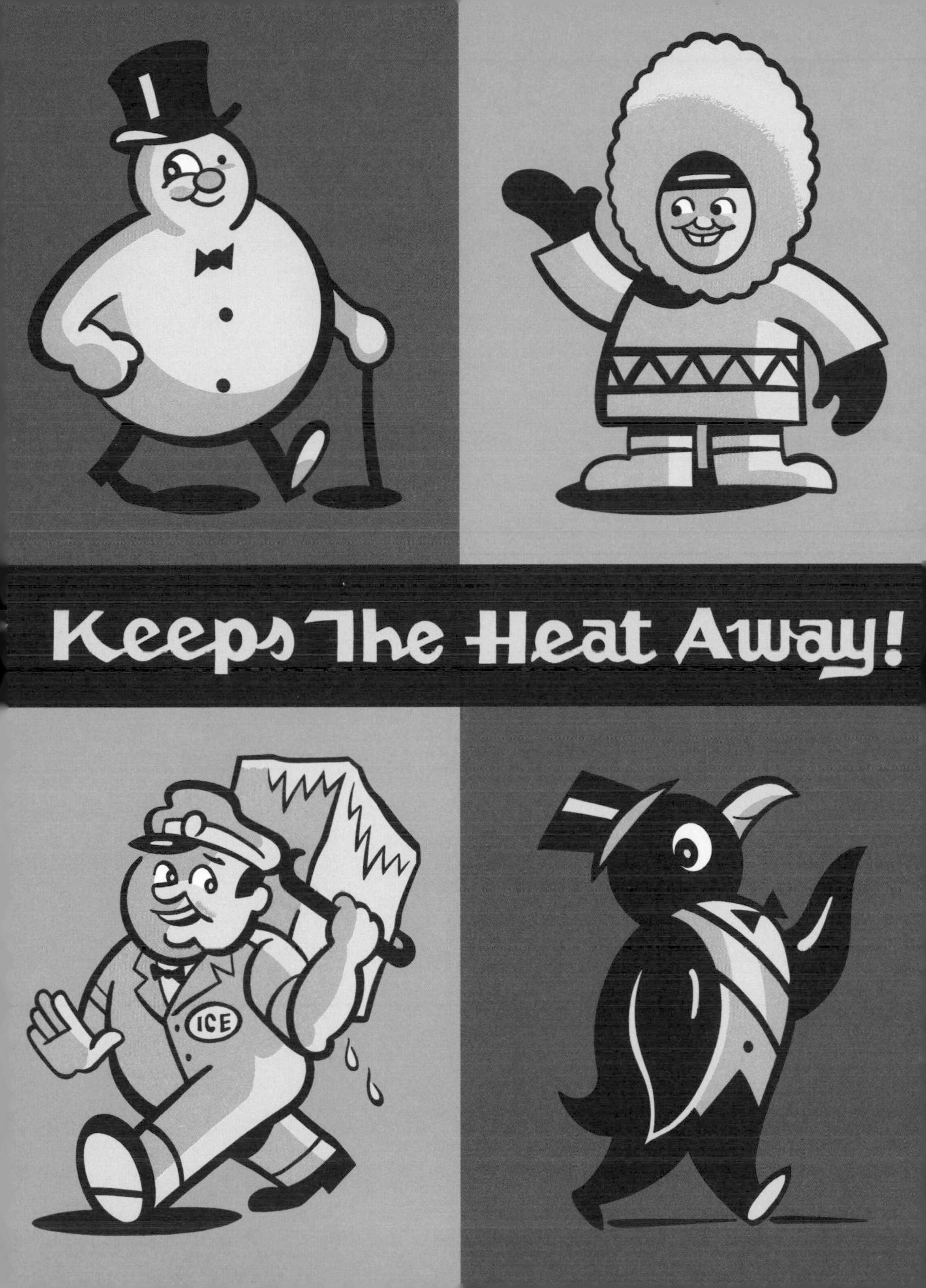
Keeps The Heat Away!
ICE

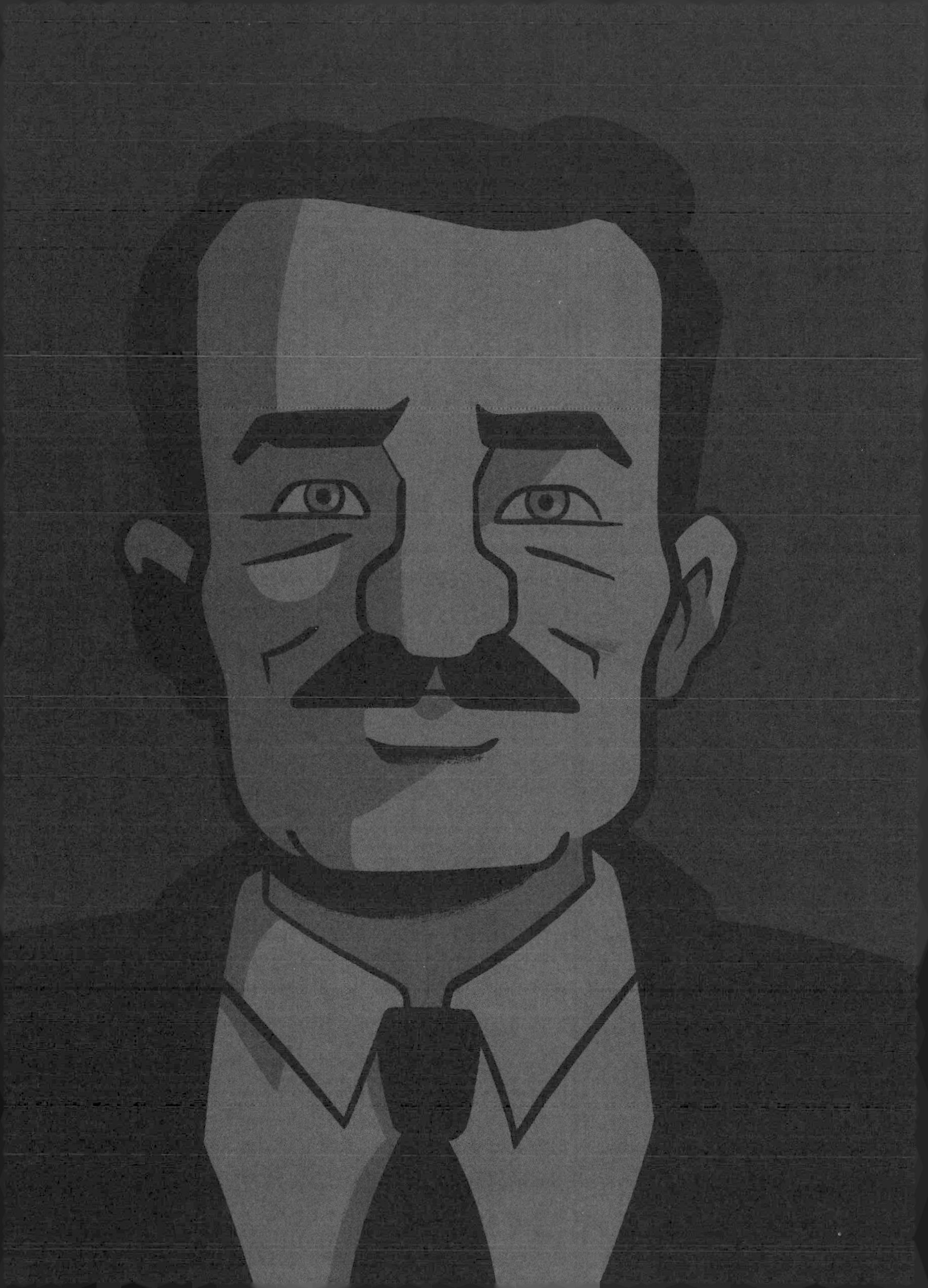

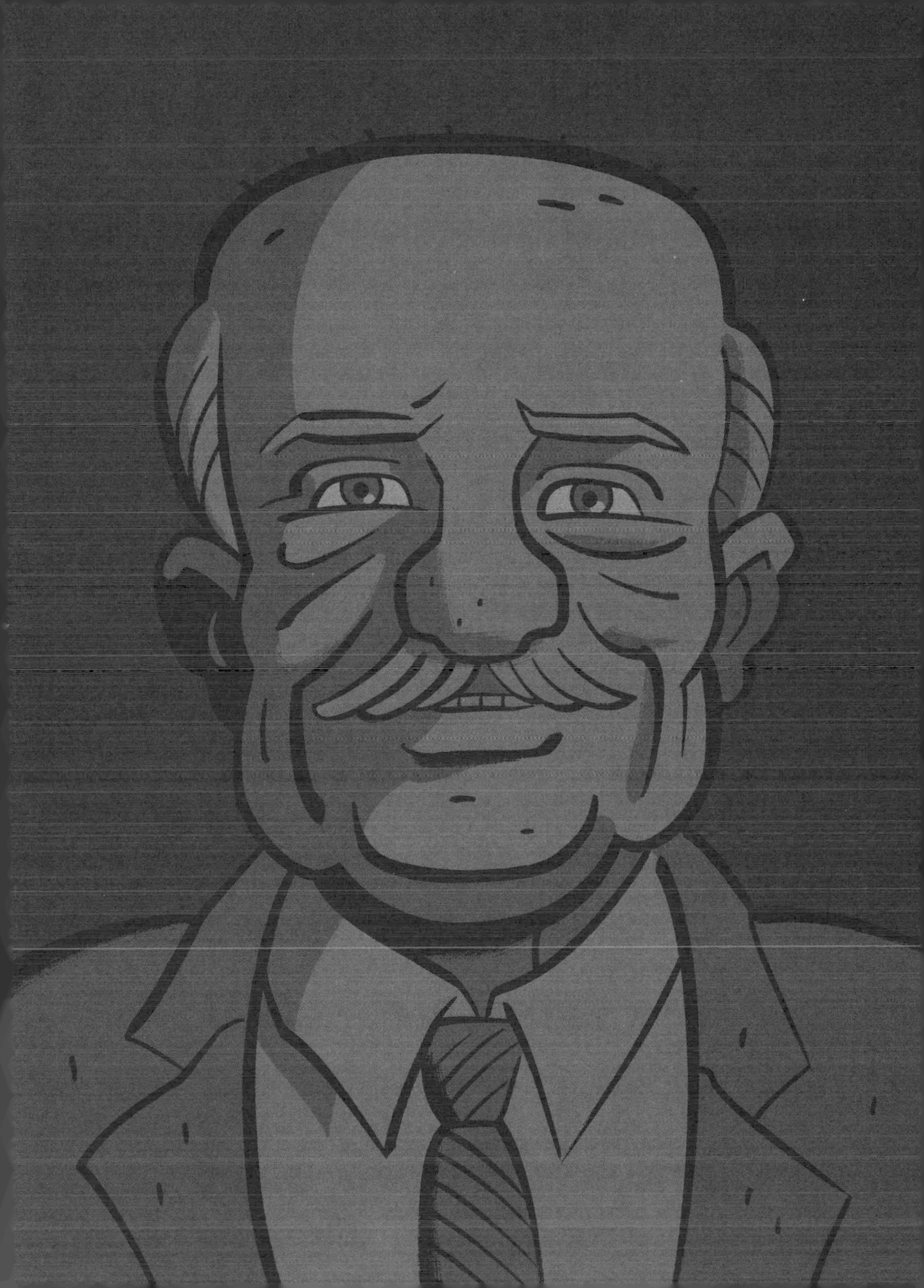

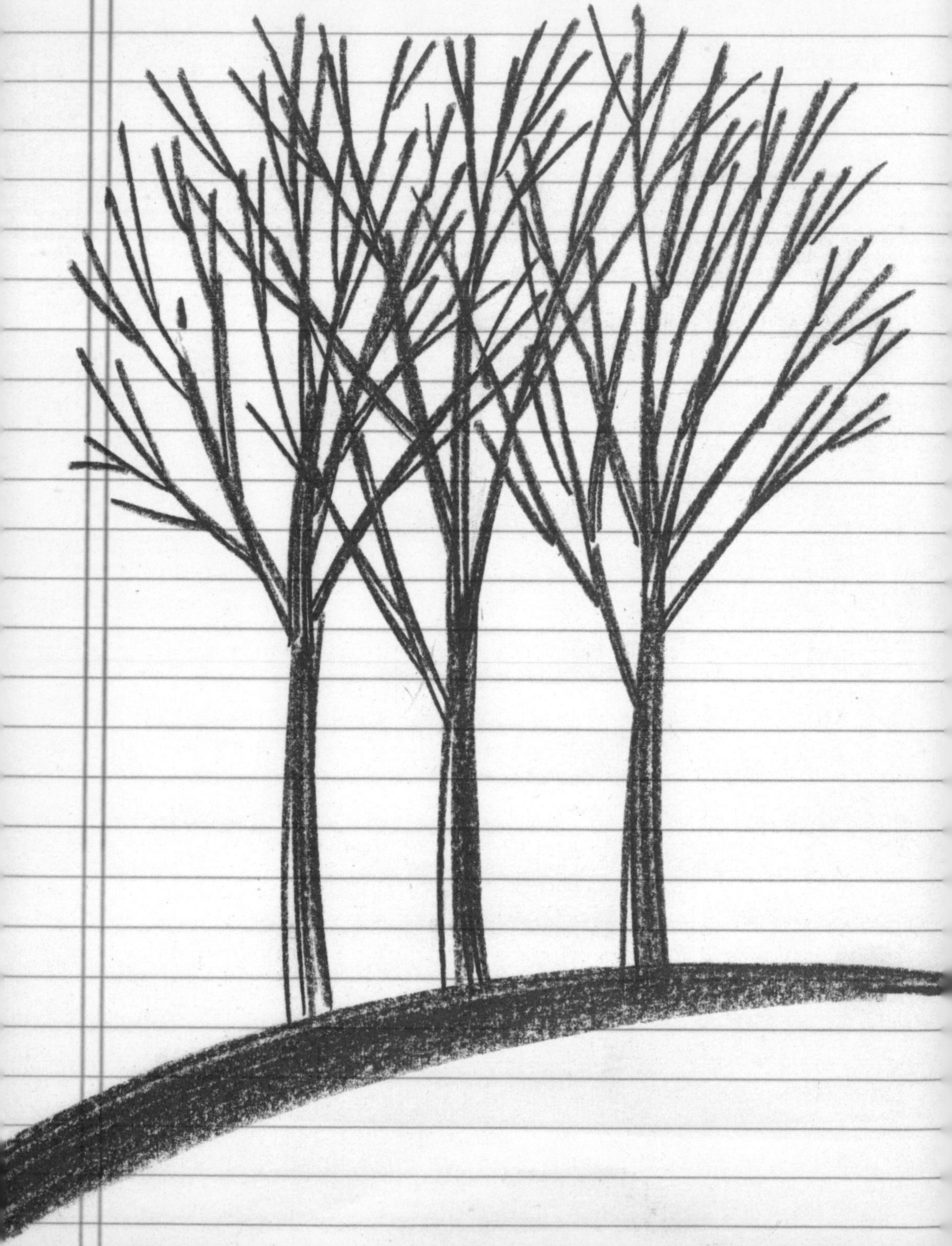

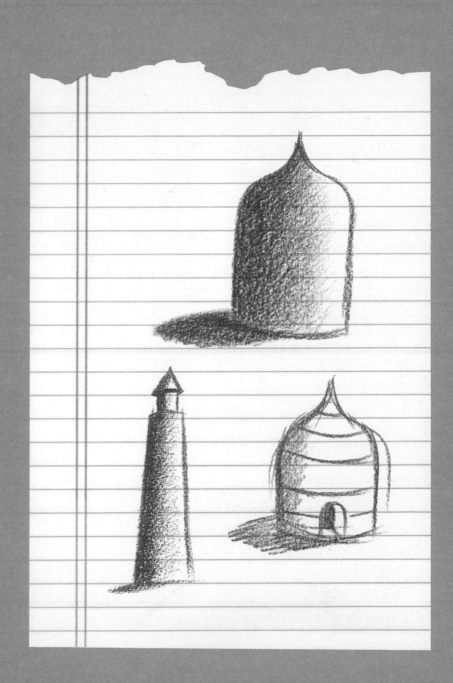

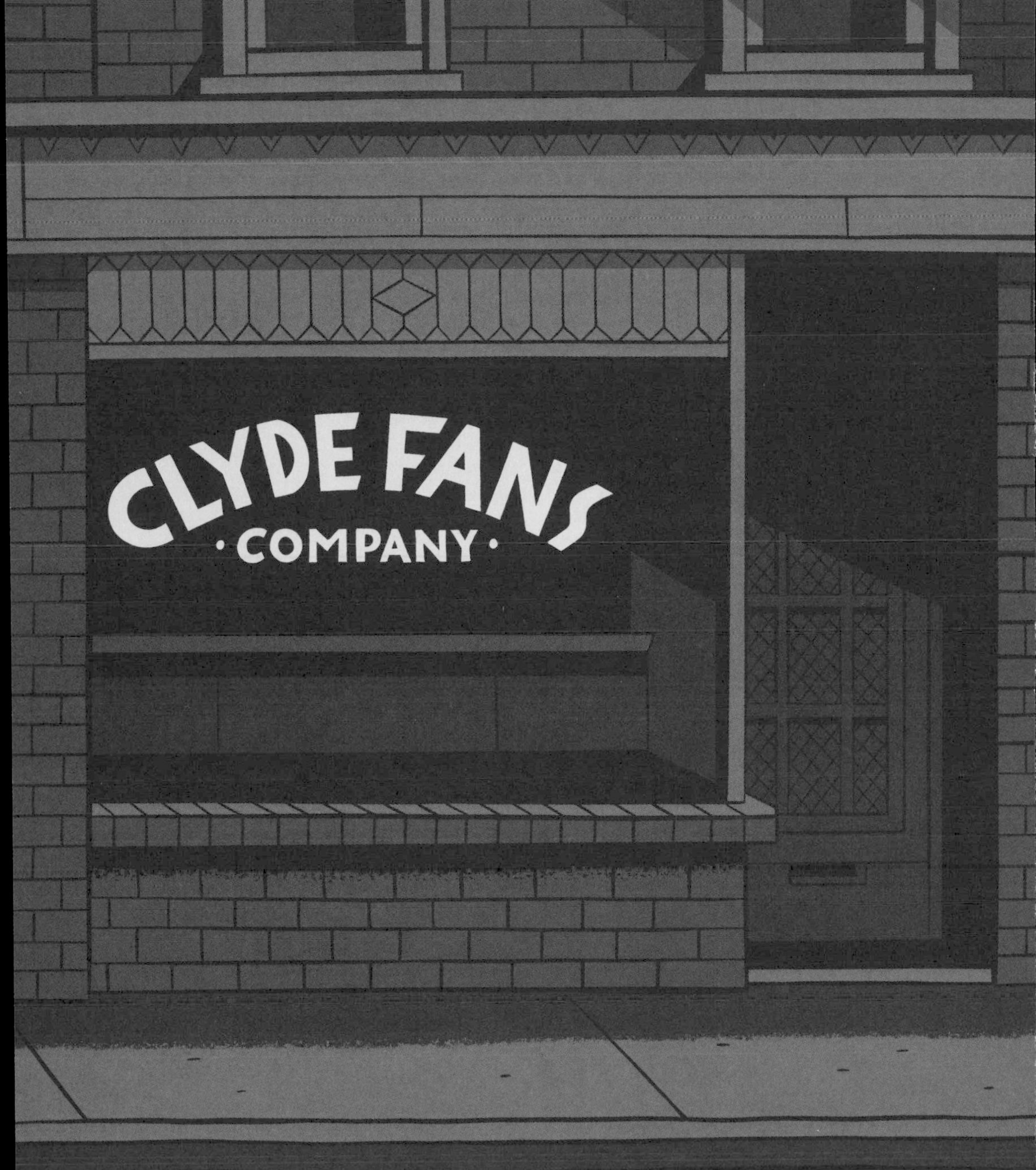
CLYDE FANS
·COMPANY·

CLYDE FANS

A PICTURE·NOVEL IN FIVE PARTS

SETH

DRAWN & QUARTERLY
MONTREAL

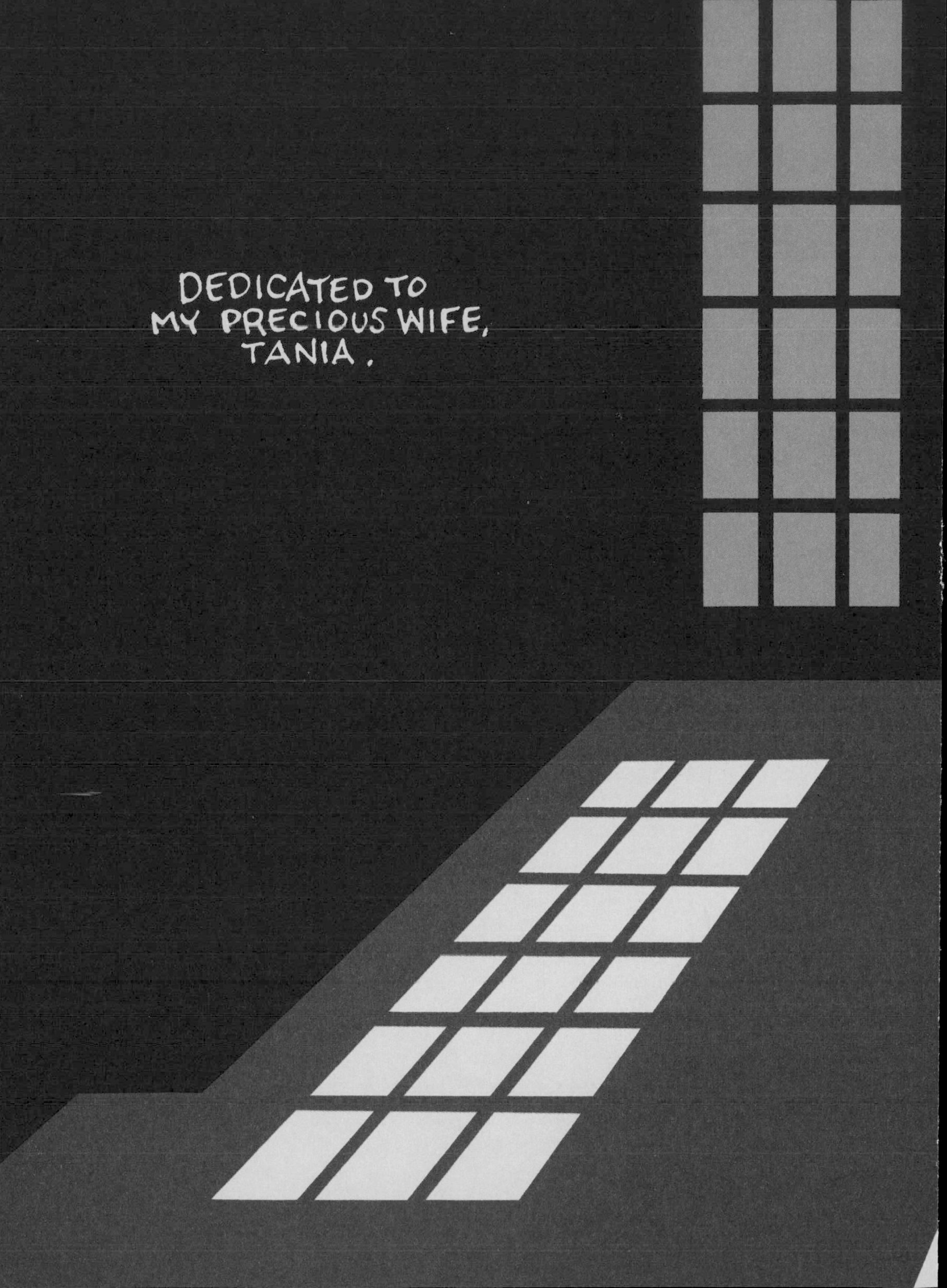
DEDICATED TO
MY PRECIOUS WIFE,
TANIA.

CLYDE
FANS

FANS
CLYDE

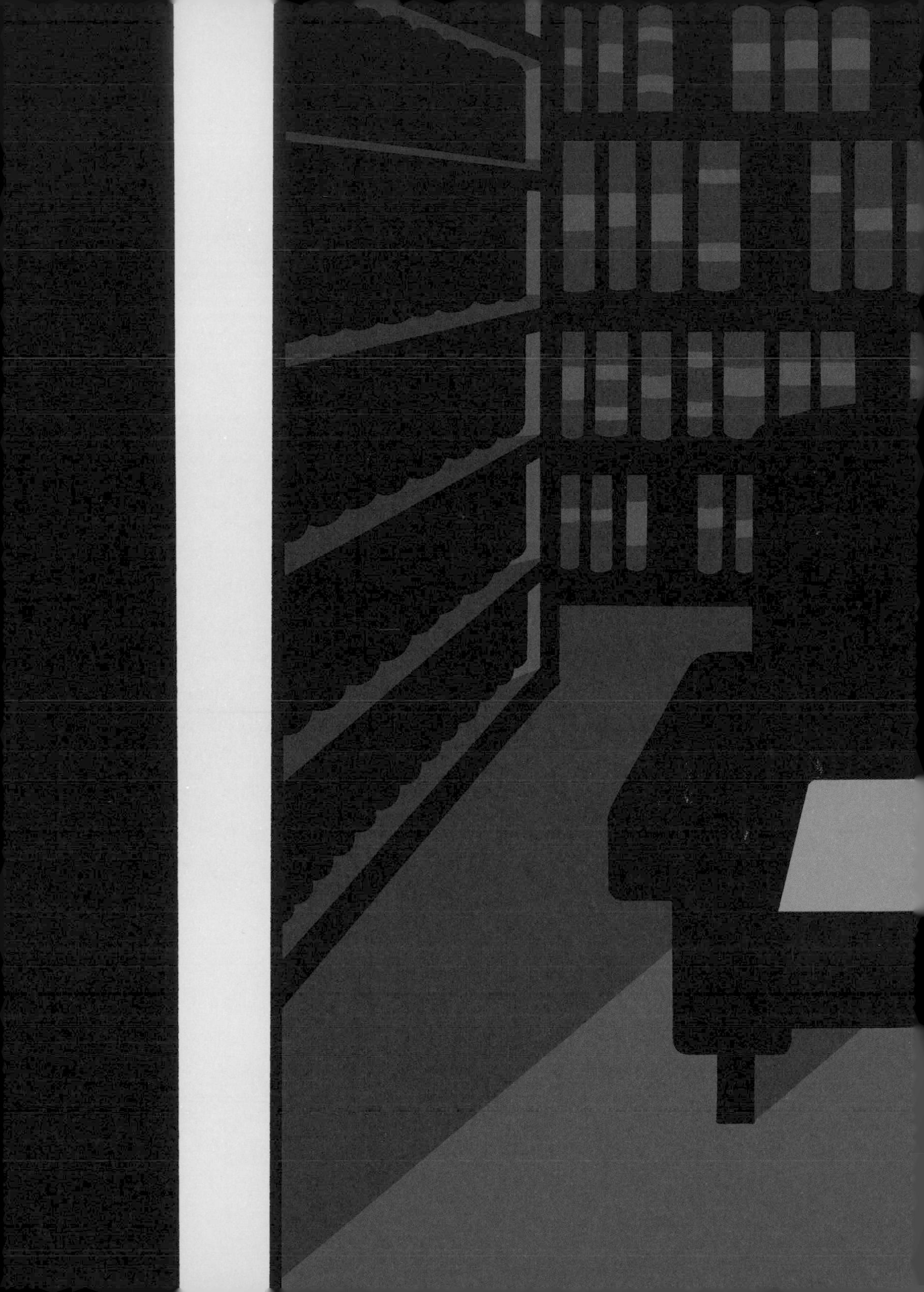

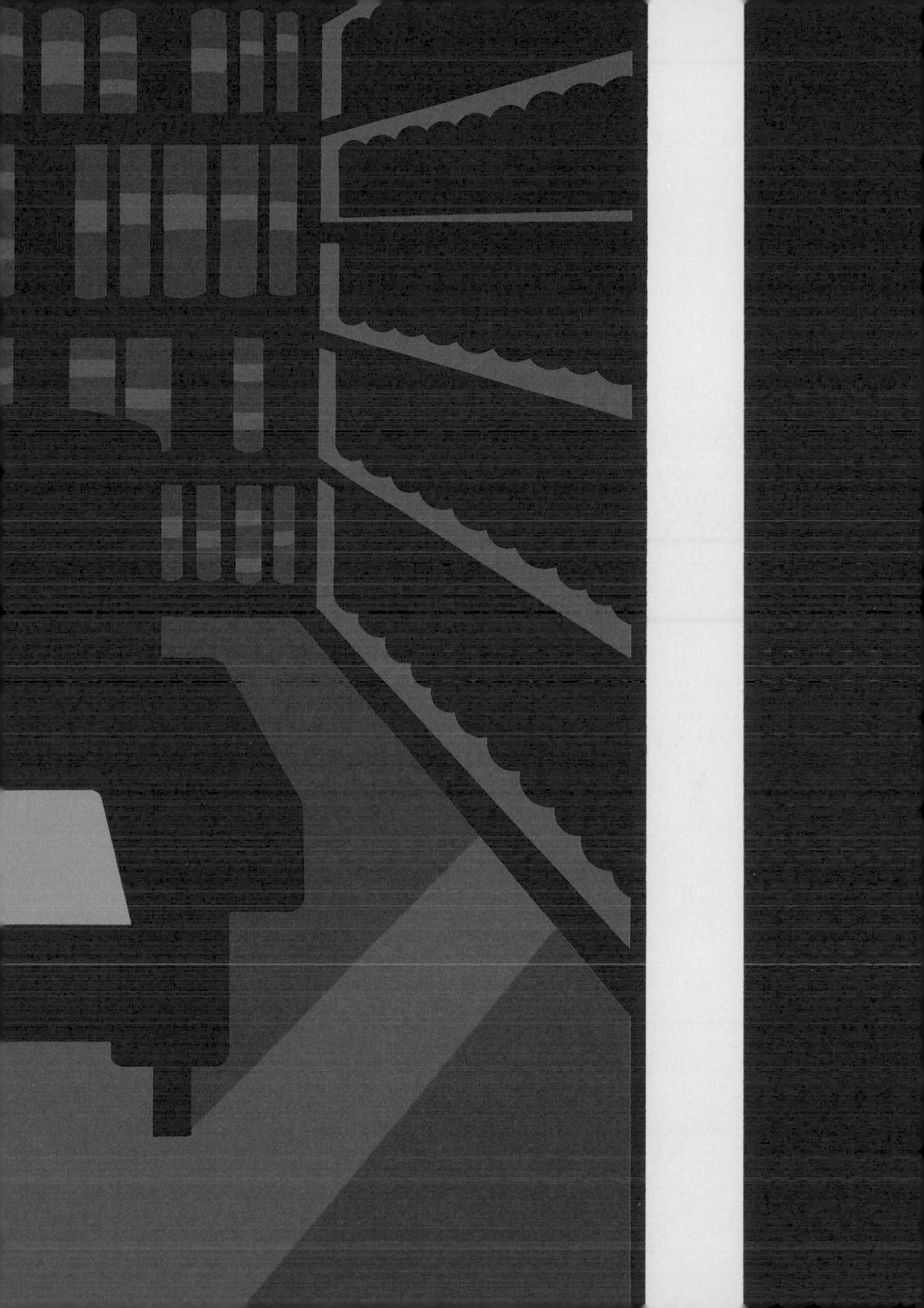

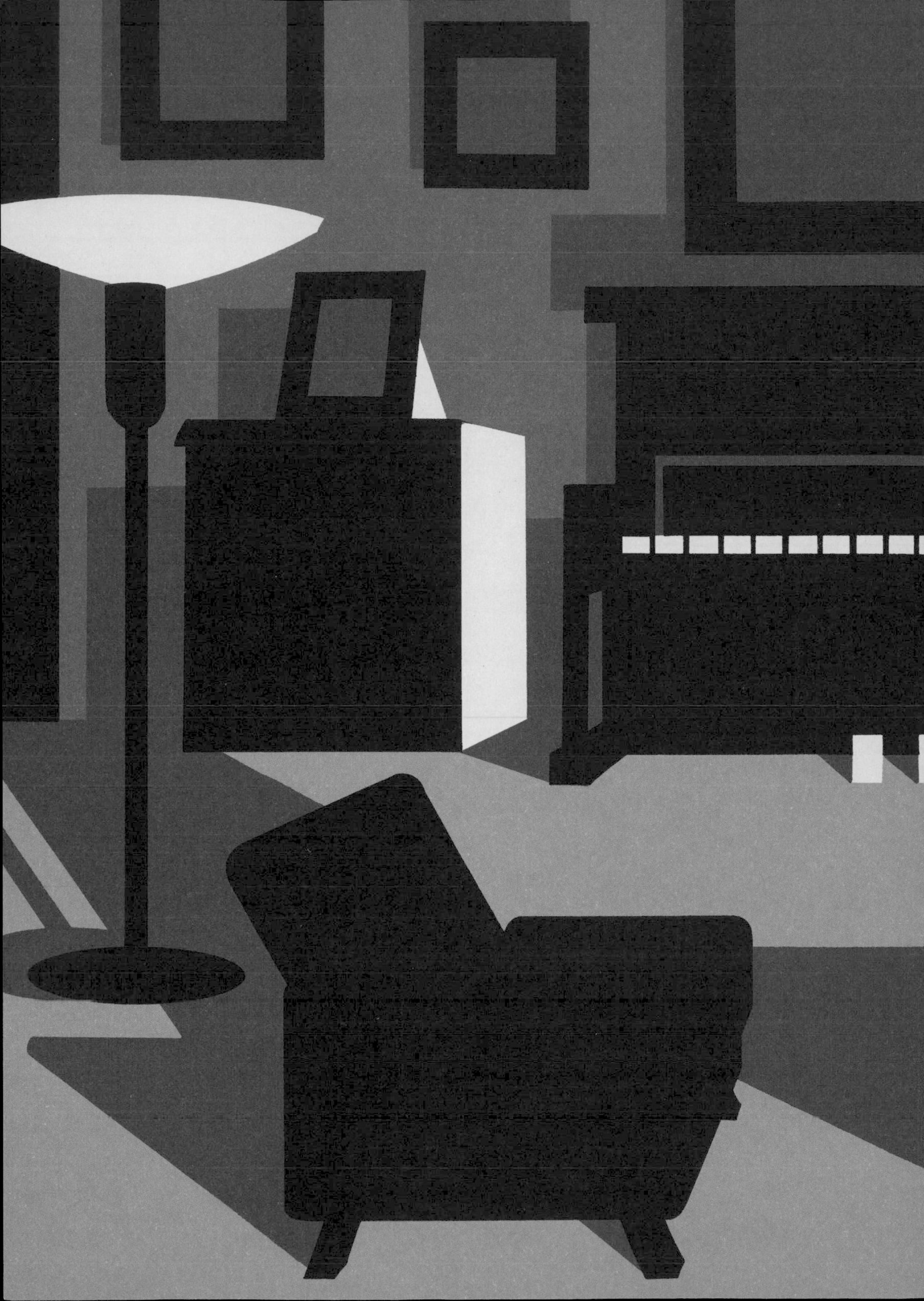

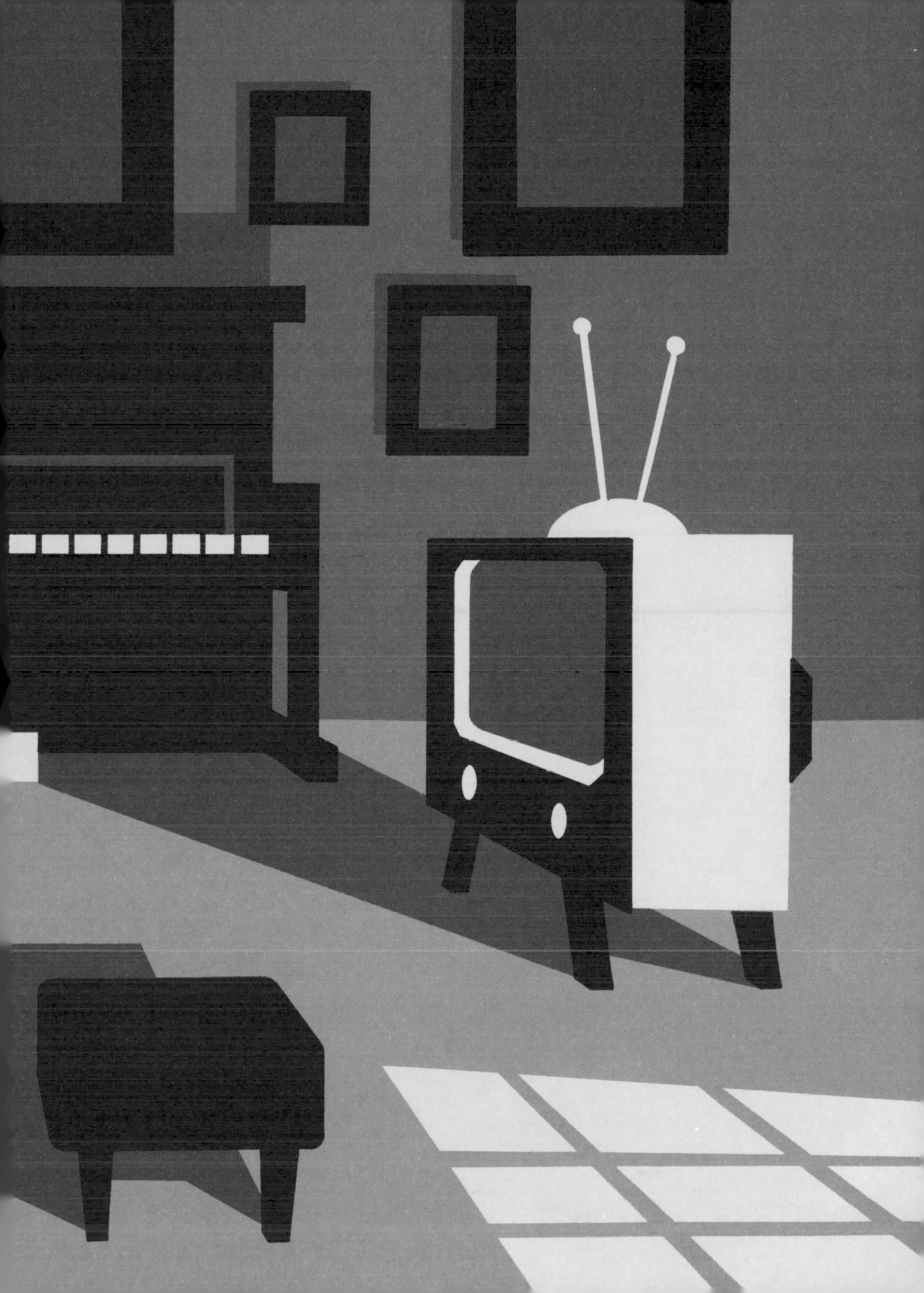

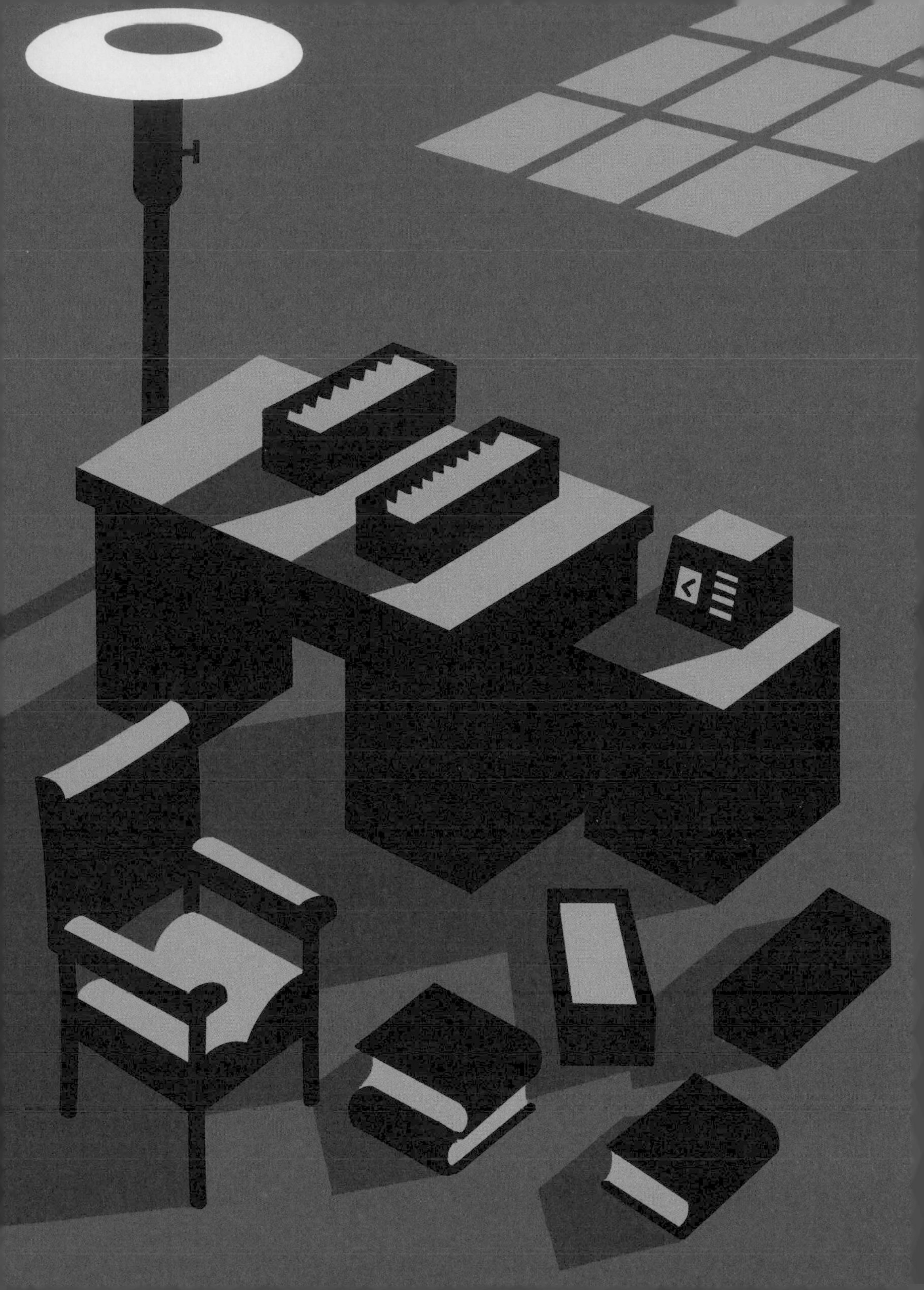

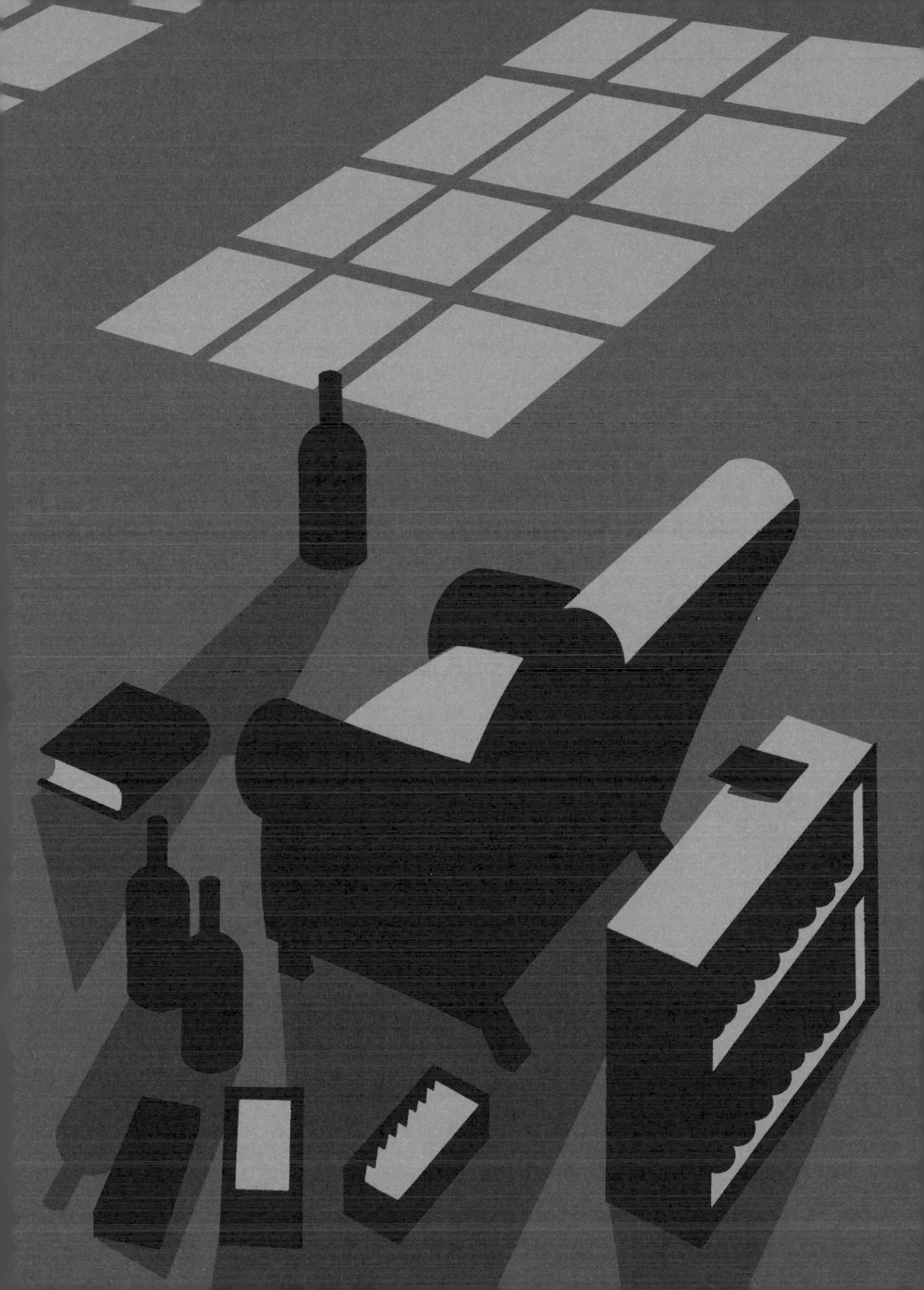

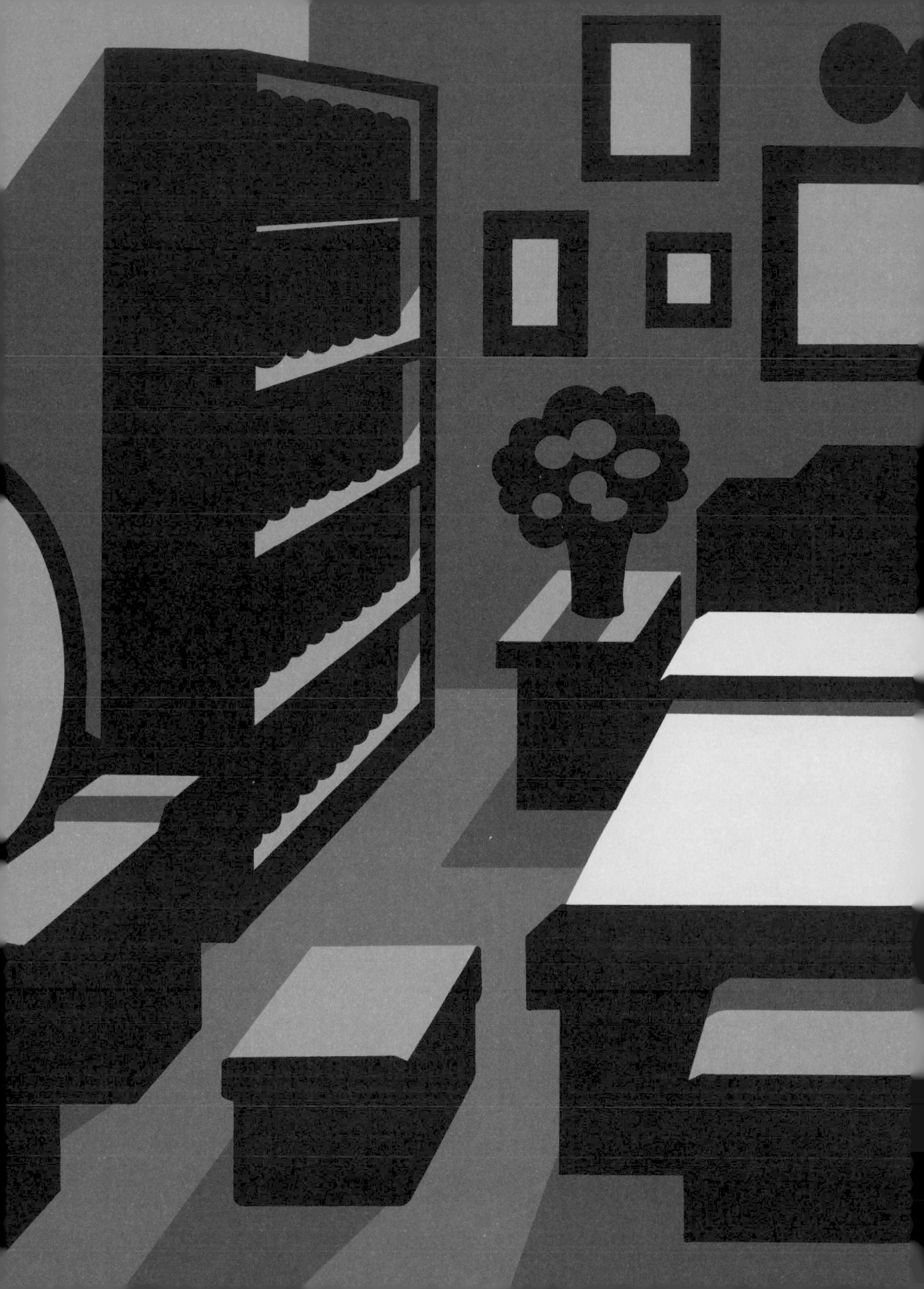

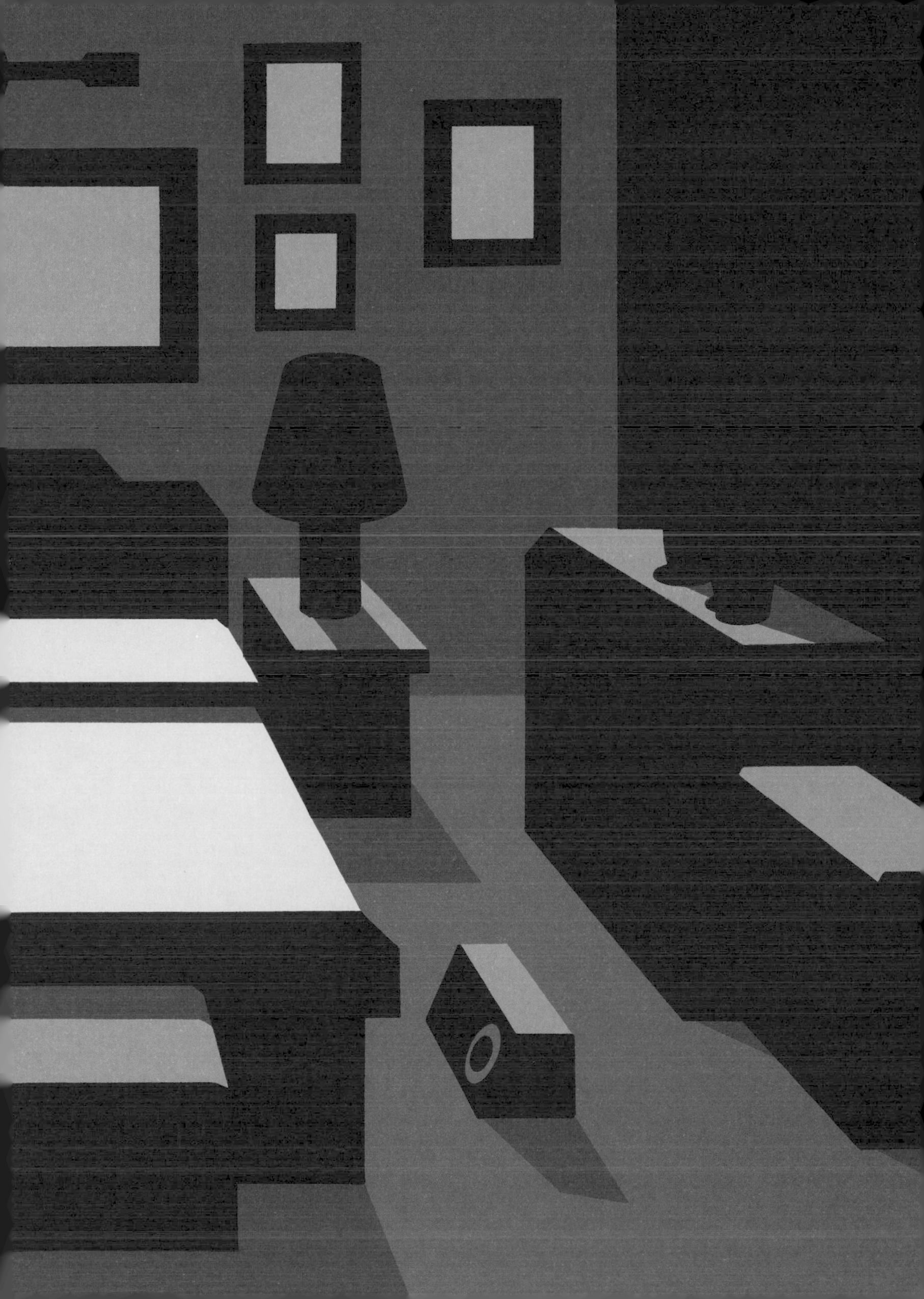

1997

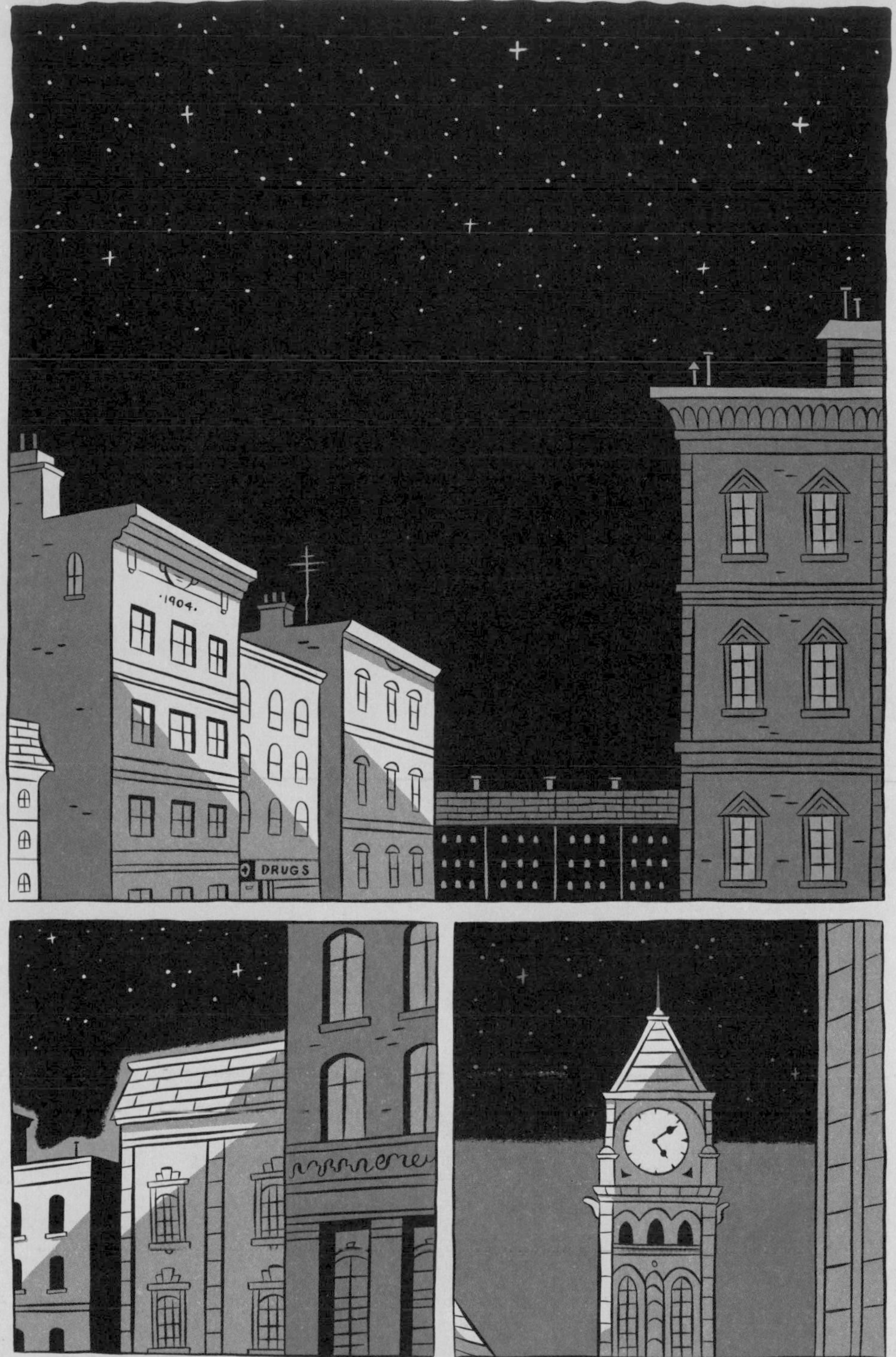
·1904·
DRUGS

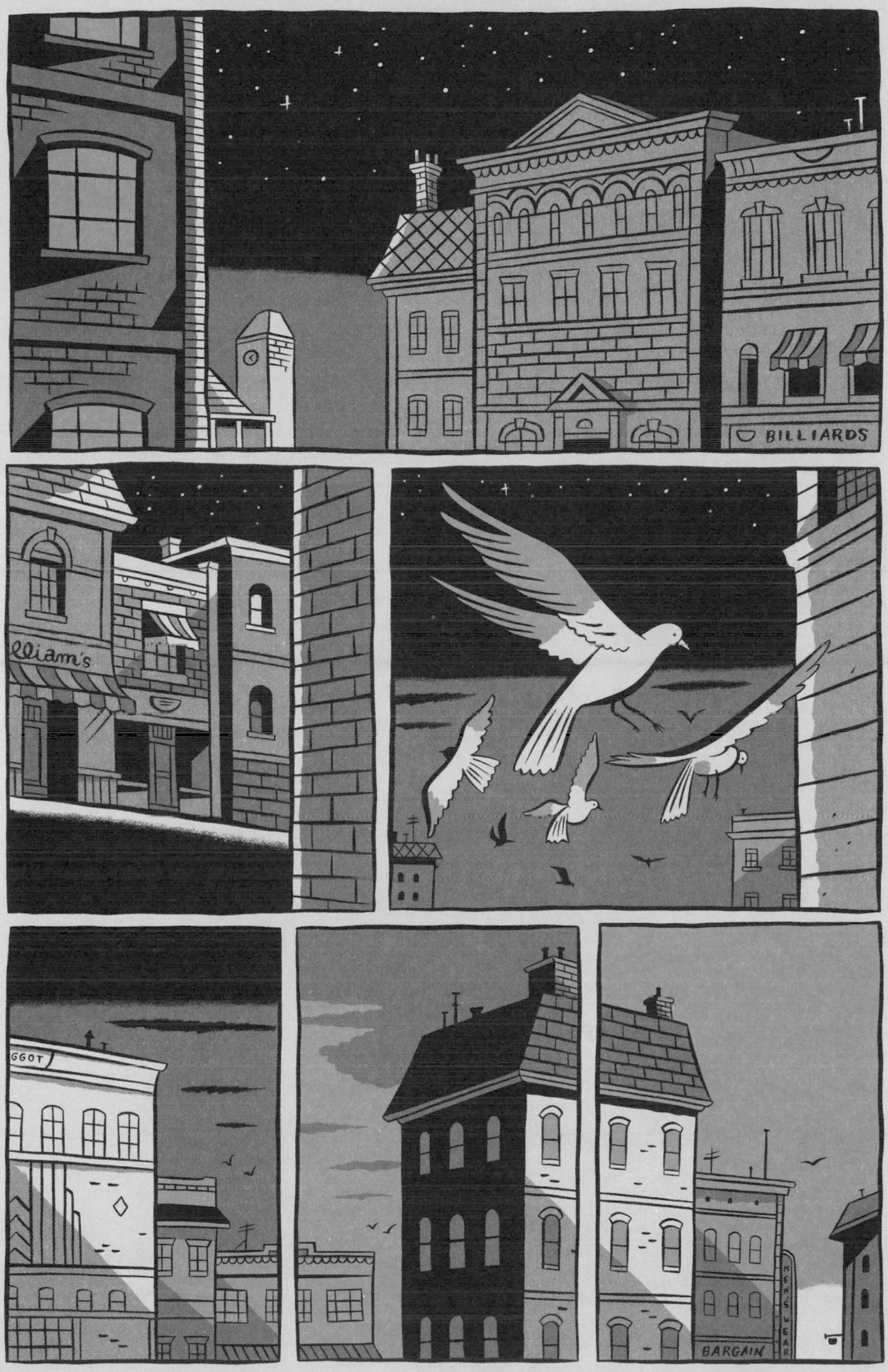
BILLIARDS
lliam's
GGOT
MEN'S WEAR
BARGAIN

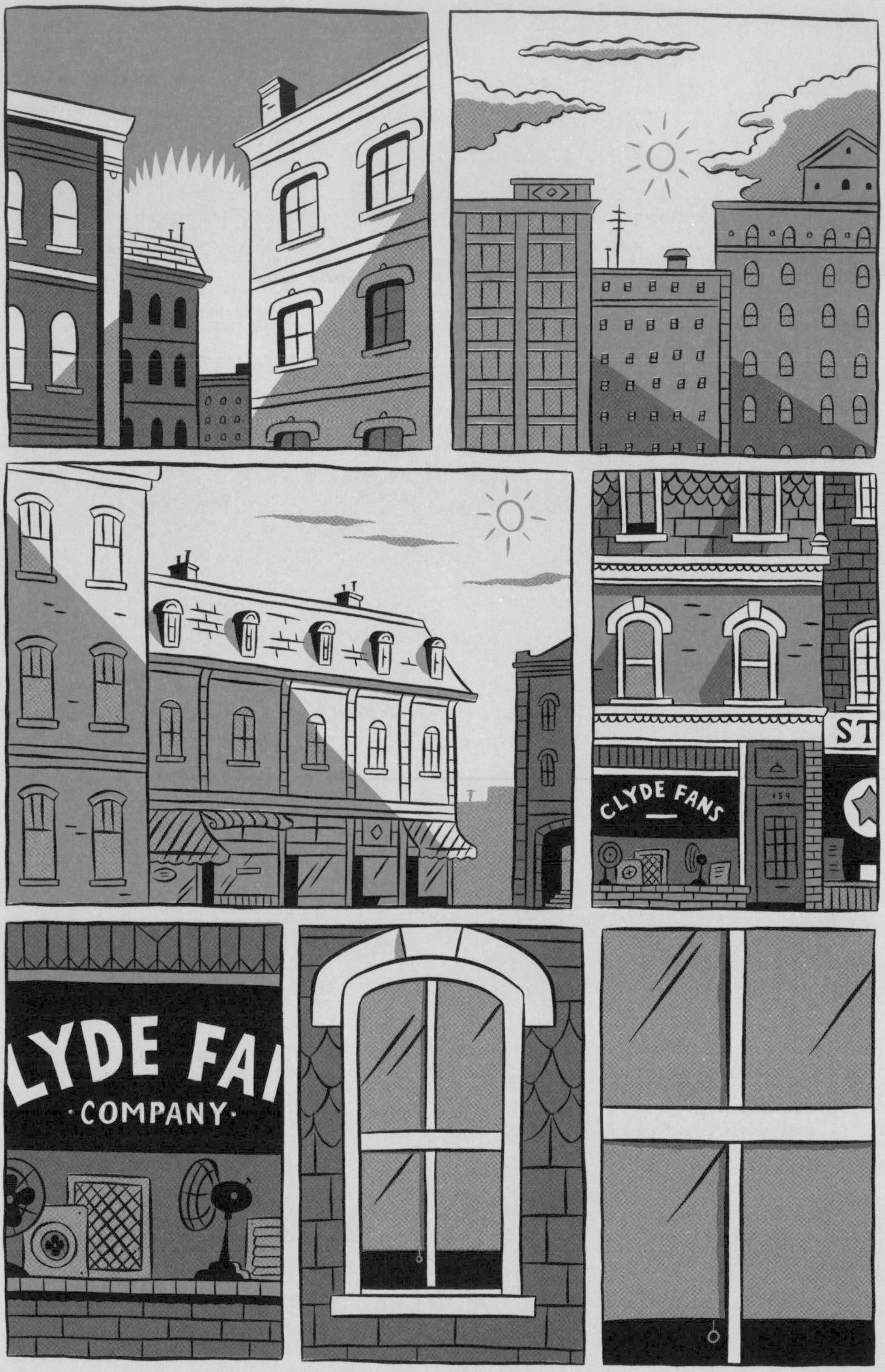
CLYDE FANS
ST
LYDE FA
·COMPANY·

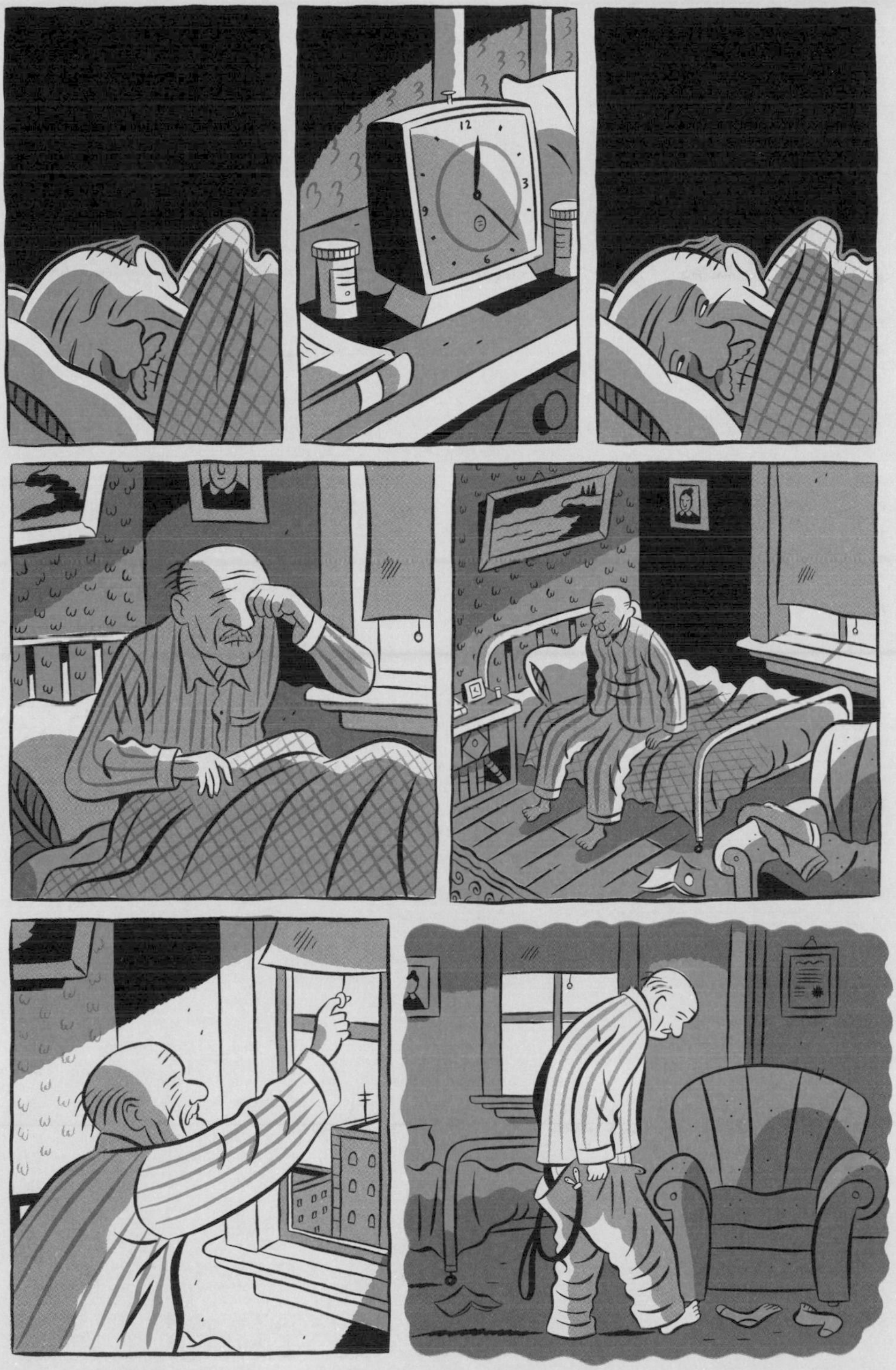

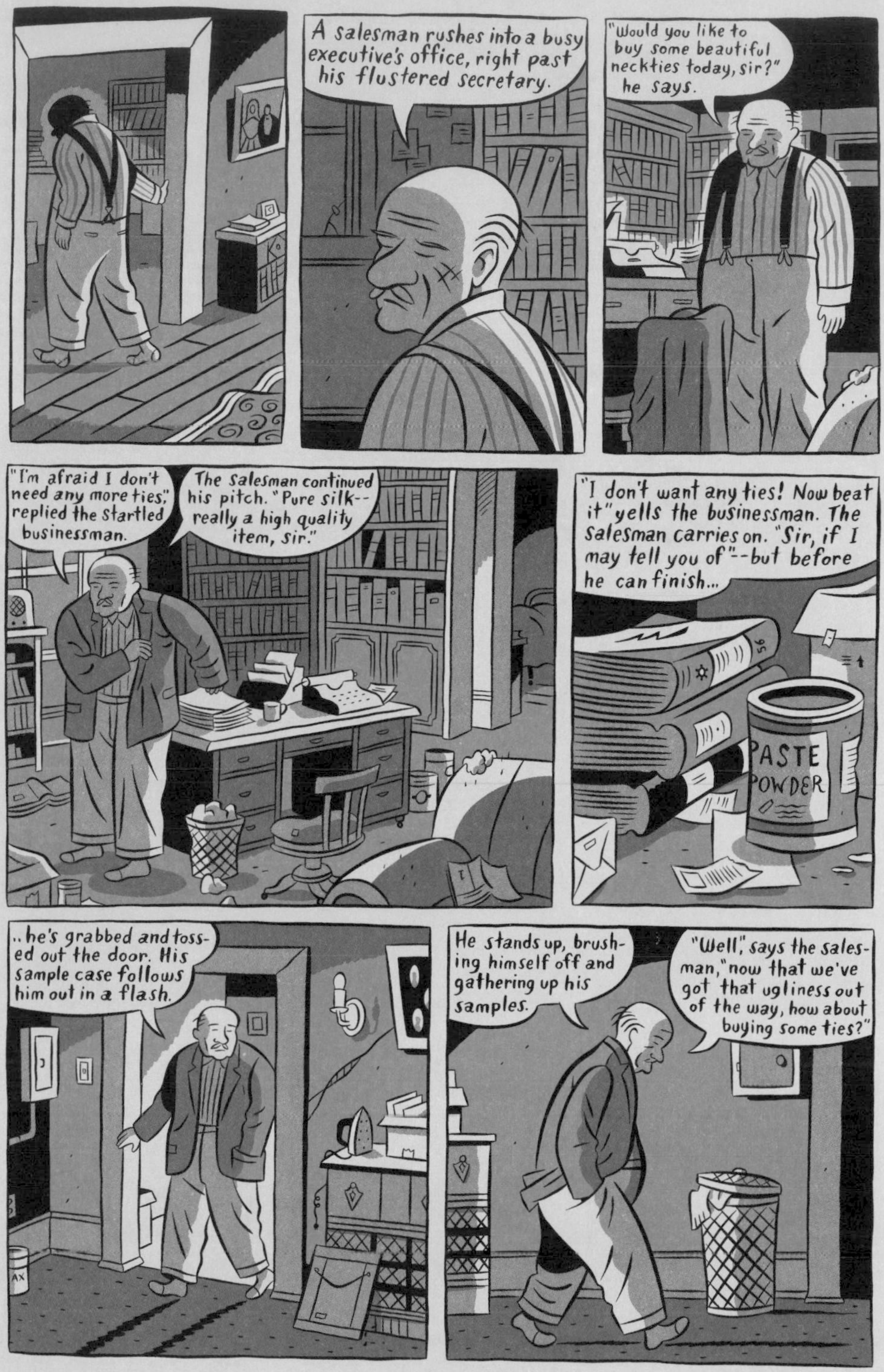

A salesman rushes into a busy executive's office, right past his flustered secretary.
"Would you like to buy some beautiful neckties today, sir?" he says.
"I'm afraid I don't need any more ties," replied the startled businessman.
The salesman continued his pitch. "Pure silk--really a high quality item, sir."
"I don't want any ties! Now beat it" yells the businessman. The salesman carries on. "Sir, if I may tell you of"--but before he can finish...
PASTE POWDER
..he's grabbed and tossed out the door. His sample case follows him out in a flash.
He stands up, brushing himself off and gathering up his samples.
"Well," says the salesman, "now that we've got that ugliness out of the way, how about buying some ties?"

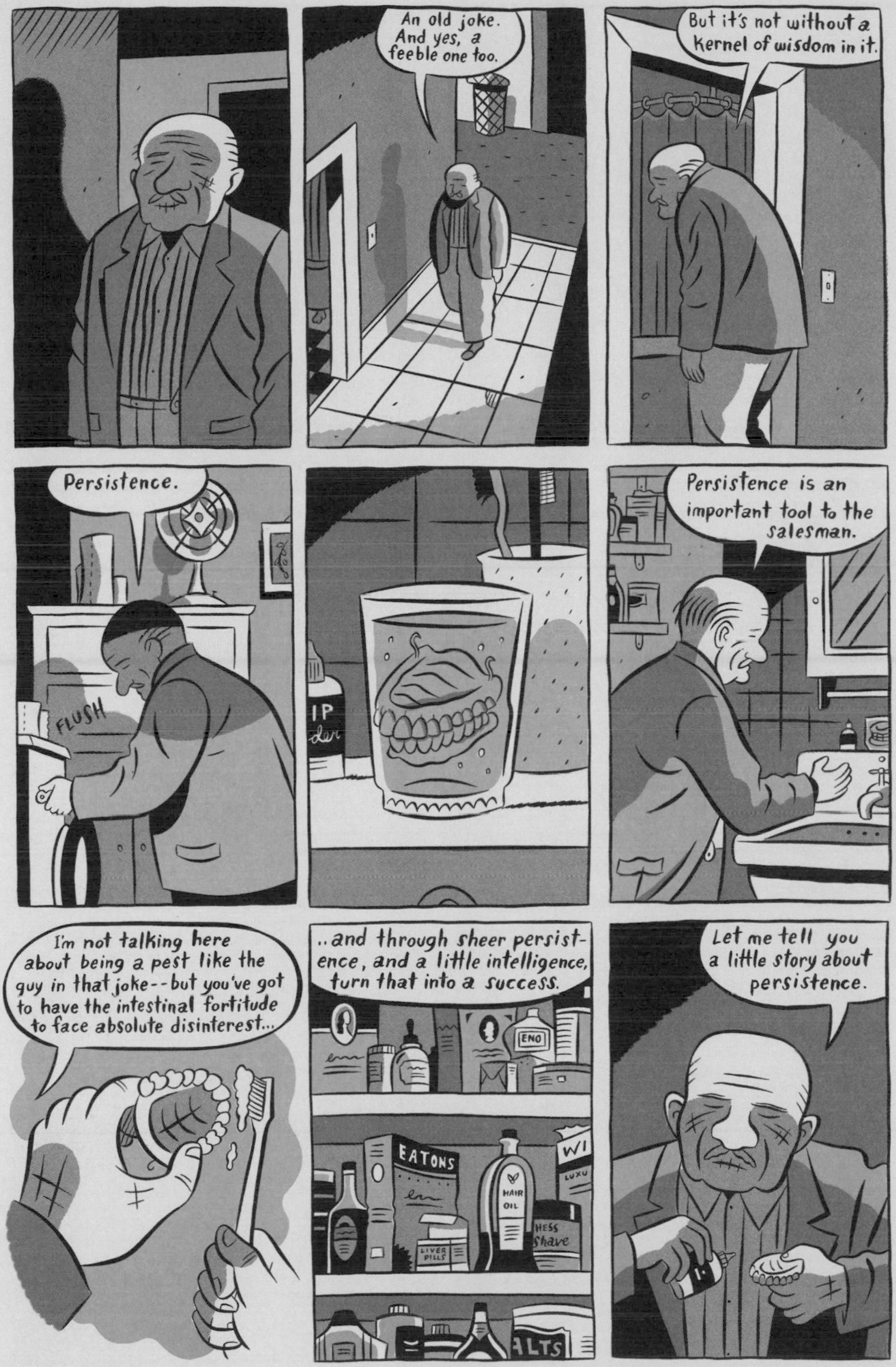
An old joke. And yes, a feeble one too.
But it's not without a kernel of wisdom in it.
Persistence.
FLUSH
Persistence is an important tool to the salesman.
I'm not talking here about being a pest like the guy in that joke--but you've got to have the intestinal fortitude to face absolute disinterest...
..and through sheer persist-ence, and a little intelligence, turn that into a success.
ENO
EATONS
HAIR OIL
LIVER PILLS
HESS Shave
Let me tell you a little story about persistence.

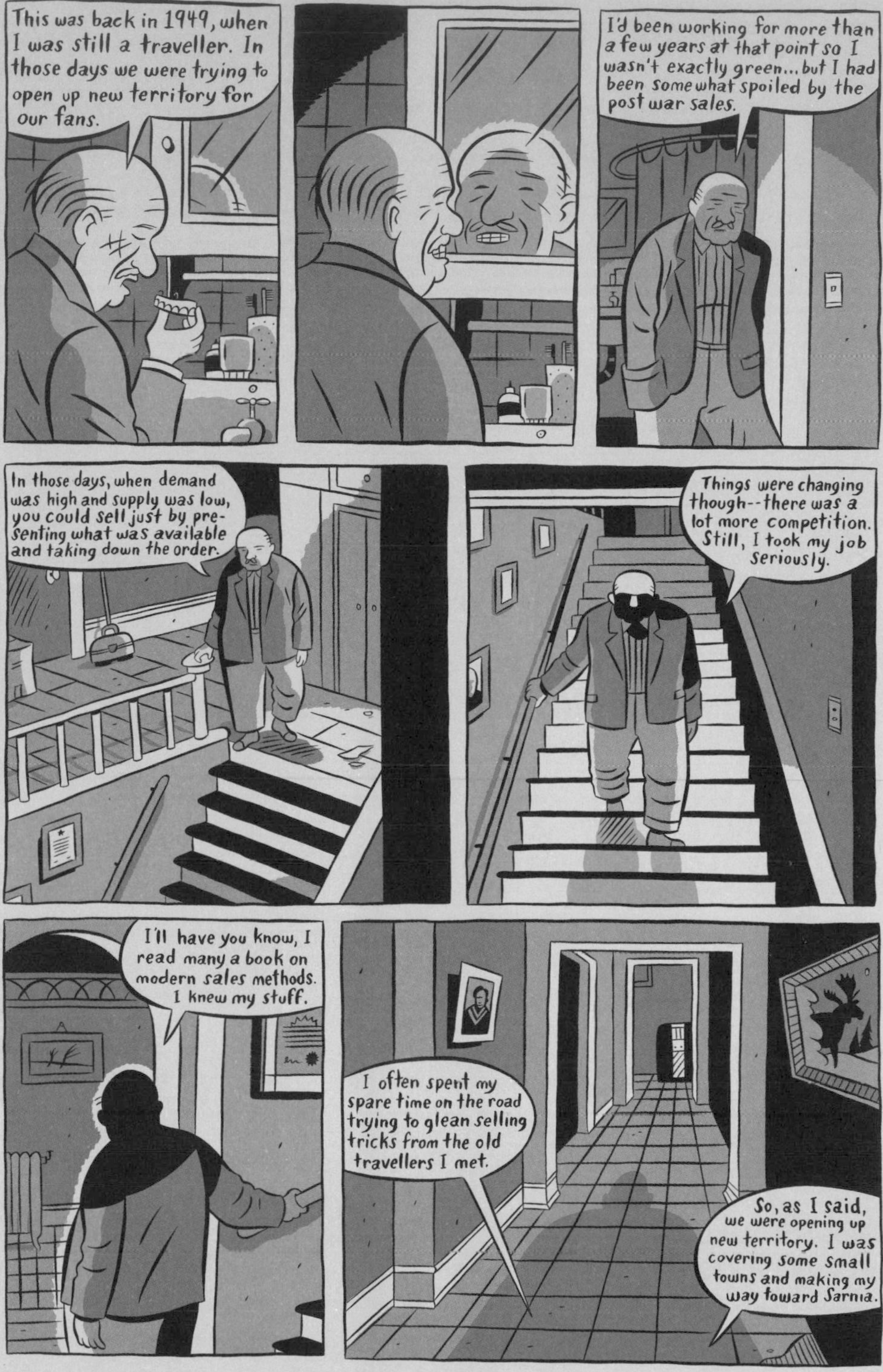
This was back in 1949, when I was still a traveller. In those days we were trying to open up new territory for our fans.
I'd been working for more than a few years at that point so I wasn't exactly green... but I had been somewhat spoiled by the post war sales.
In those days, when demand was high and supply was low, you could sell just by presenting what was available and taking down the order.
Things were changing though--there was a lot more competition. Still, I took my job seriously.
I'll have you know, I read many a book on modern sales methods. I knew my stuff.
I often spent my spare time on the road trying to glean selling tricks from the old travellers I met.
So, as I said, we were opening up new territory. I was covering some small towns and making my way toward Sarnia.

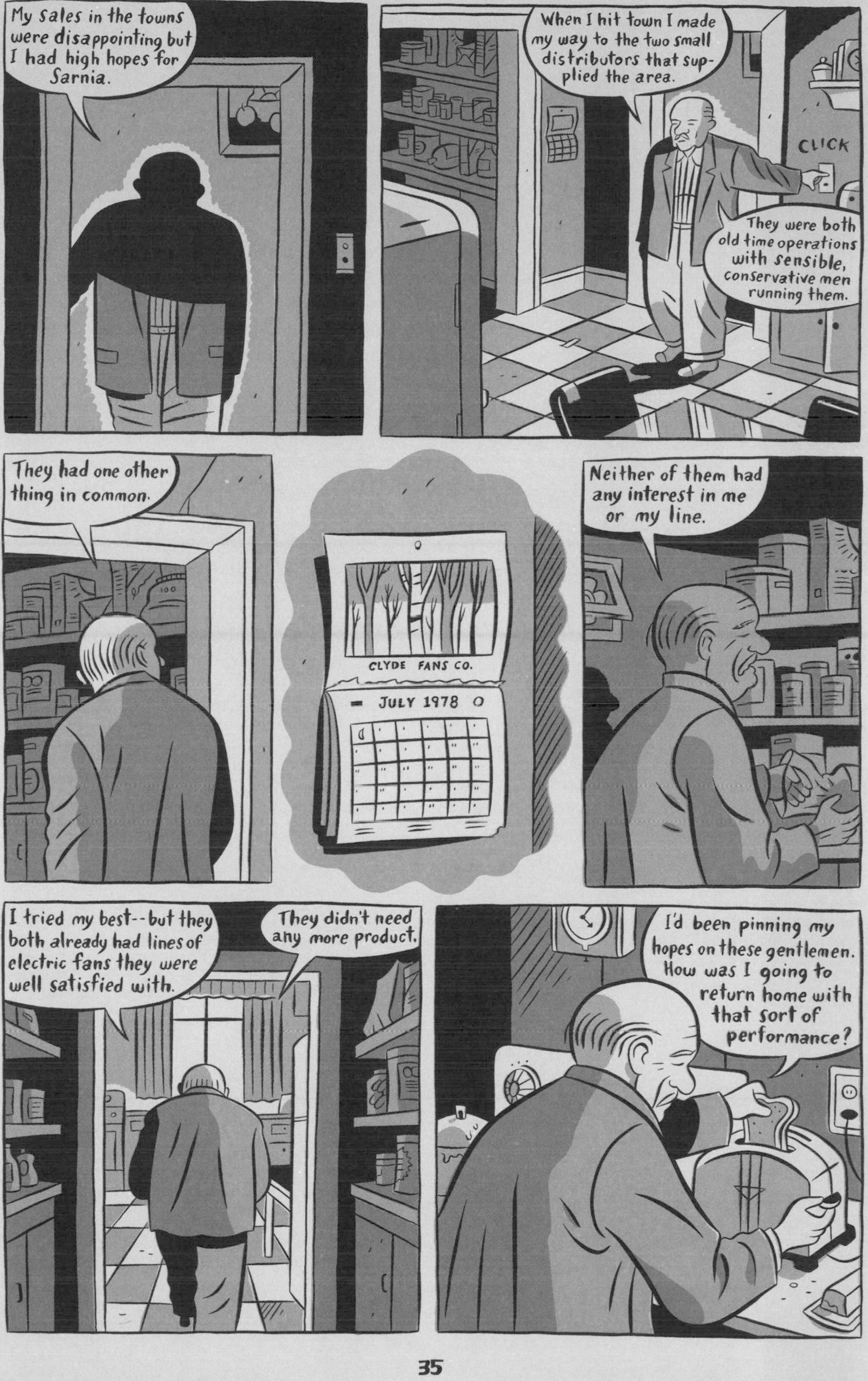
My sales in the towns were disappointing but I had high hopes for Sarnia.
When I hit town I made my way to the two small distributors that supplied the area.
CLICK
They were both old time operations with sensible, conservative men running them.
They had one other thing in common.
CLYDE FANS CO.
JULY 1978
Neither of them had any interest in me or my line.
I tried my best--but they both already had lines of electric fans they were well satisfied with.
They didn't need any more product.
I'd been pinning my hopes on these gentlemen. How was I going to return home with that sort of performance?

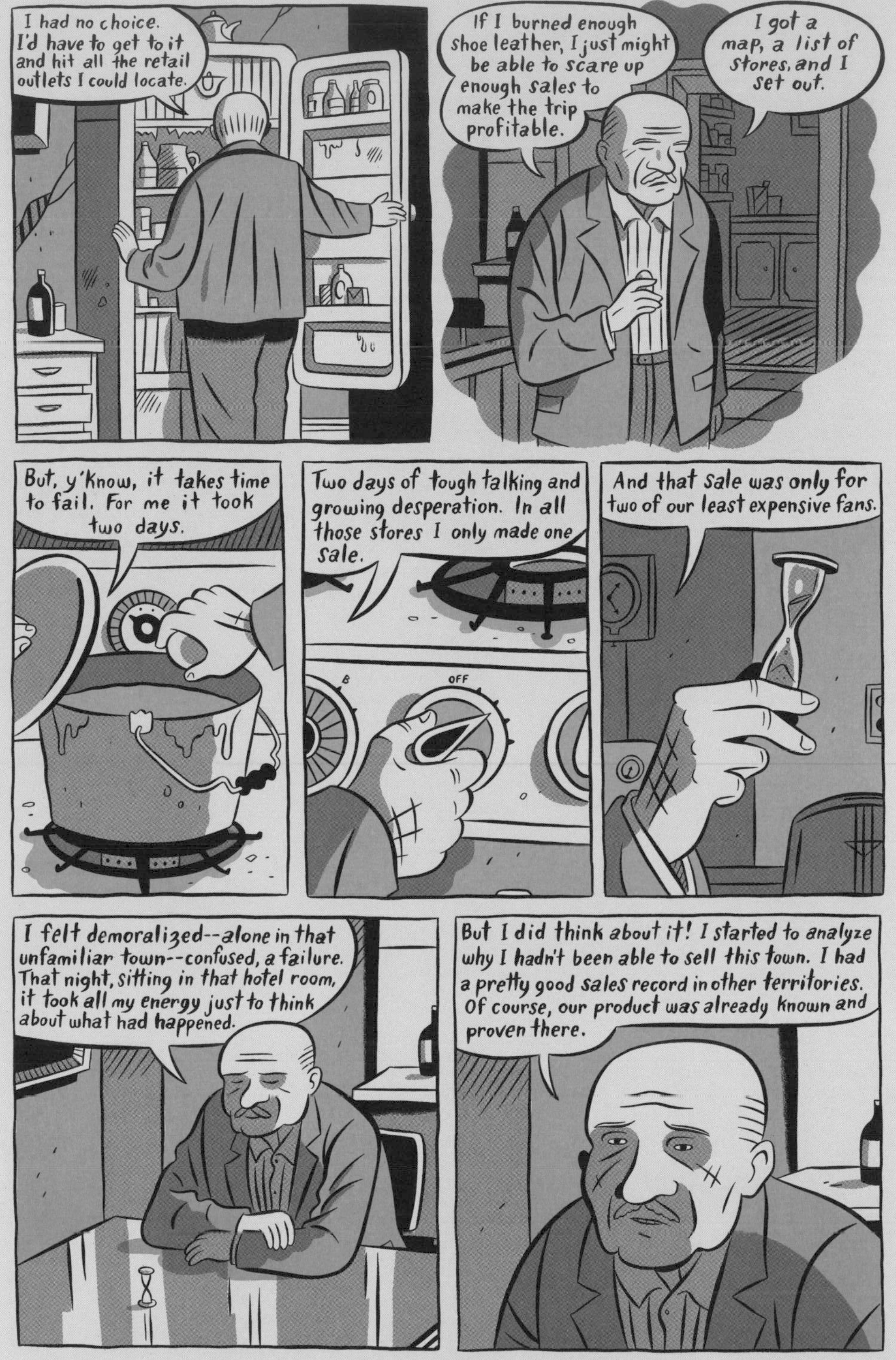
I had no choice. I'd have to get to it and hit all the retail outlets I could locate.
If I burned enough shoe leather, I just might be able to scare up enough sales to make the trip profitable.
I got a map, a list of stores, and I set out.
But, y'know, it takes time to fail. For me it took two days.
Two days of tough talking and growing desperation. In all those stores I only made one sale.
And that sale was only for two of our least expensive fans.
B
OFF
I felt demoralized--alone in that unfamiliar town--confused, a failure. That night, sitting in that hotel room, it took all my energy just to think about what had happened.
But I did think about it! I started to analyze why I hadn't been able to sell this town. I had a pretty good sales record in other territories. Of course, our product was already known and proven there.

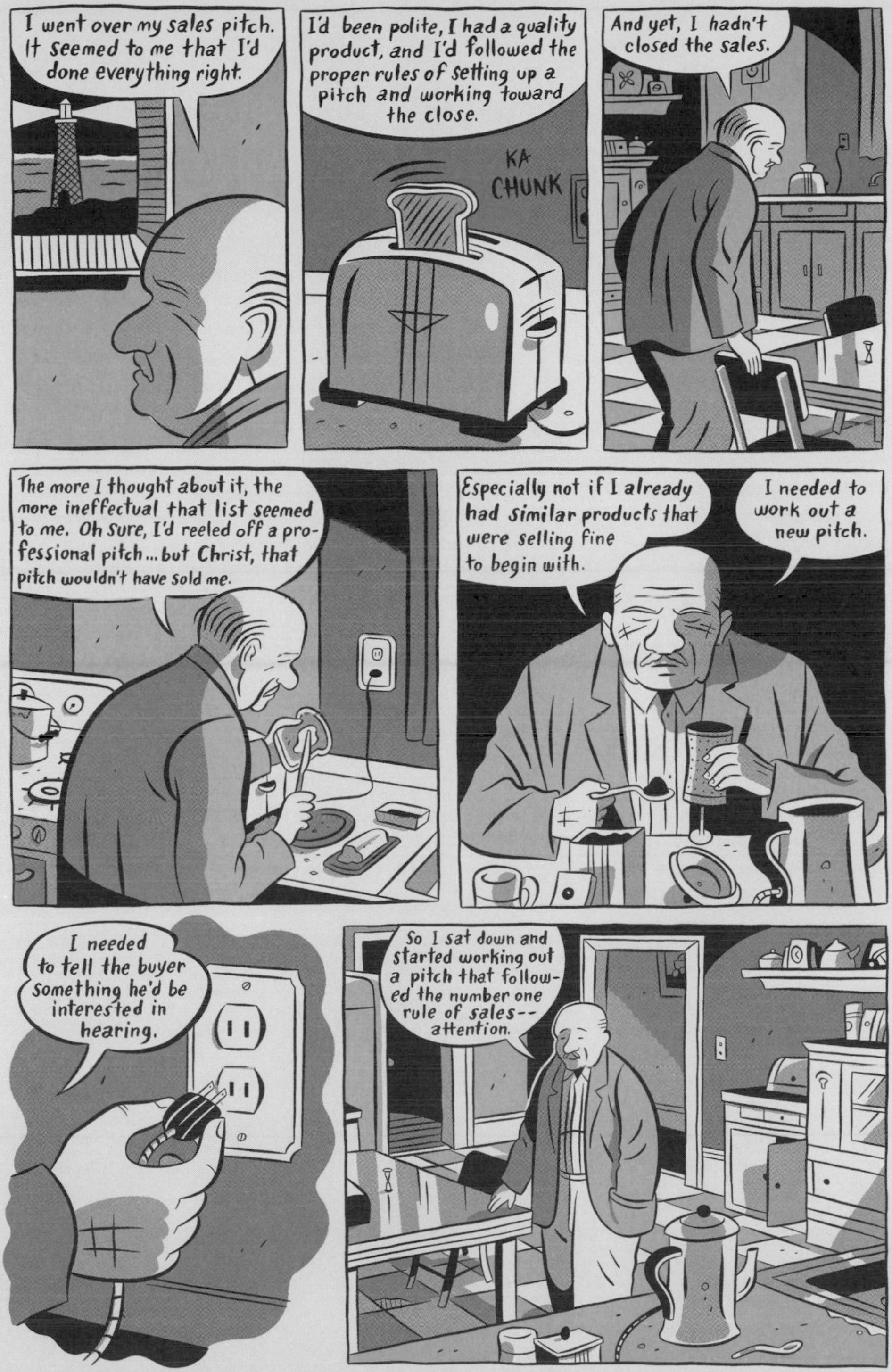
I went over my sales pitch. It seemed to me that I'd done everything right.
I'd been polite, I had a quality product, and I'd followed the proper rules of setting up a pitch and working toward the close.
KA CHUNK
And yet, I hadn't closed the sales.
The more I thought about it, the more ineffectual that list seemed to me. Oh sure, I'd reeled off a professional pitch... but Christ, that pitch wouldn't have sold me.
Especially not if I already had similar products that were selling fine to begin with.
I needed to work out a new pitch.
I needed to tell the buyer something he'd be interested in hearing.
So I sat down and started working out a pitch that followed the number one rule of sales-- attention.

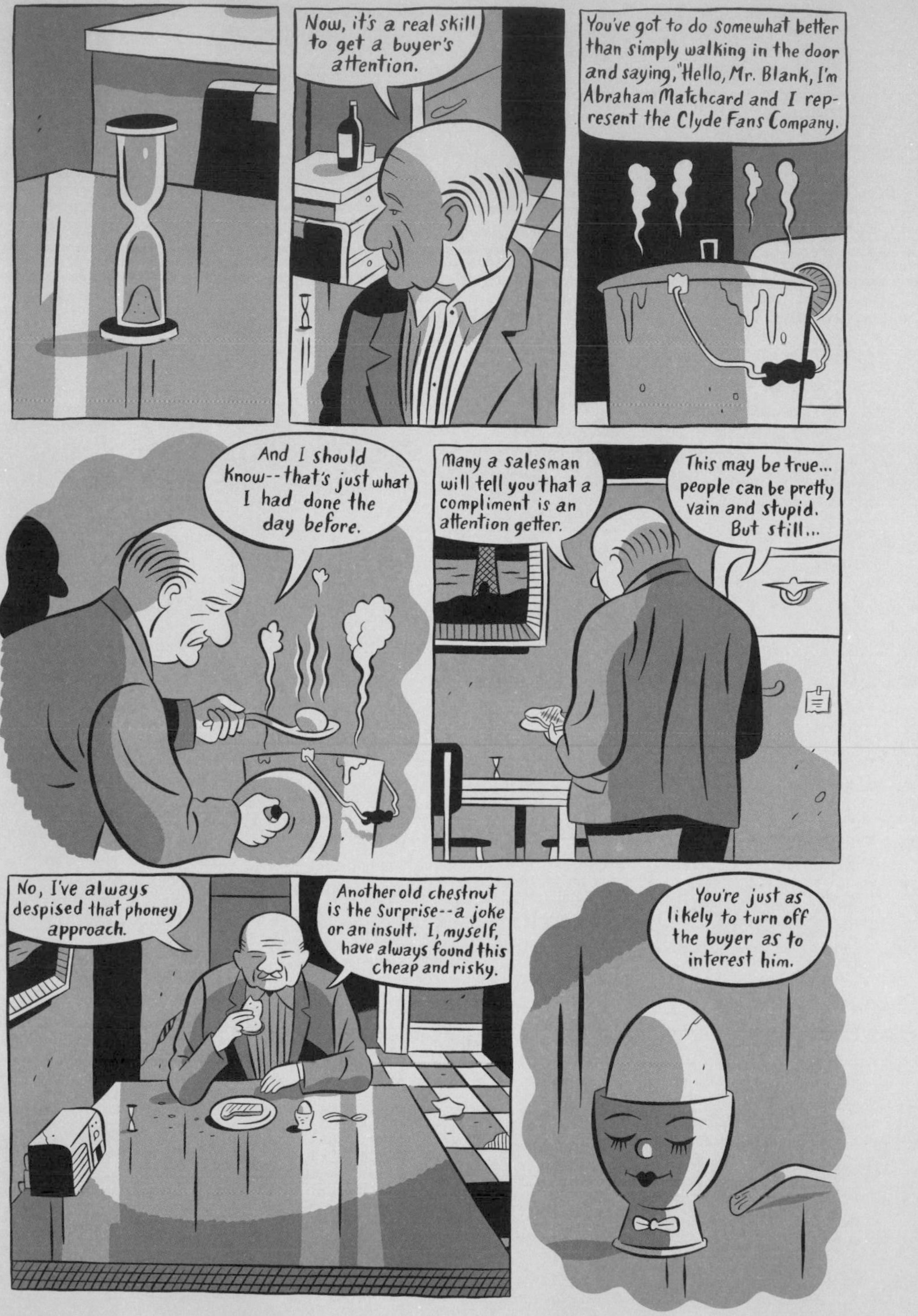
Now, it's a real skill to get a buyer's attention.
You've got to do somewhat better than simply walking in the door and saying, "Hello, Mr. Blank, I'm Abraham Matchcard and I represent the Clyde Fans Company.
And I should know--that's just what I had done the day before.
Many a salesman will tell you that a compliment is an attention getter.
This may be true... people can be pretty vain and stupid. But still...
No, I've always despised that phoney approach.
Another old chestnut is the surprise--a joke or an insult. I, myself, have always found this cheap and risky.
You're just as likely to turn off the buyer as to interest him.

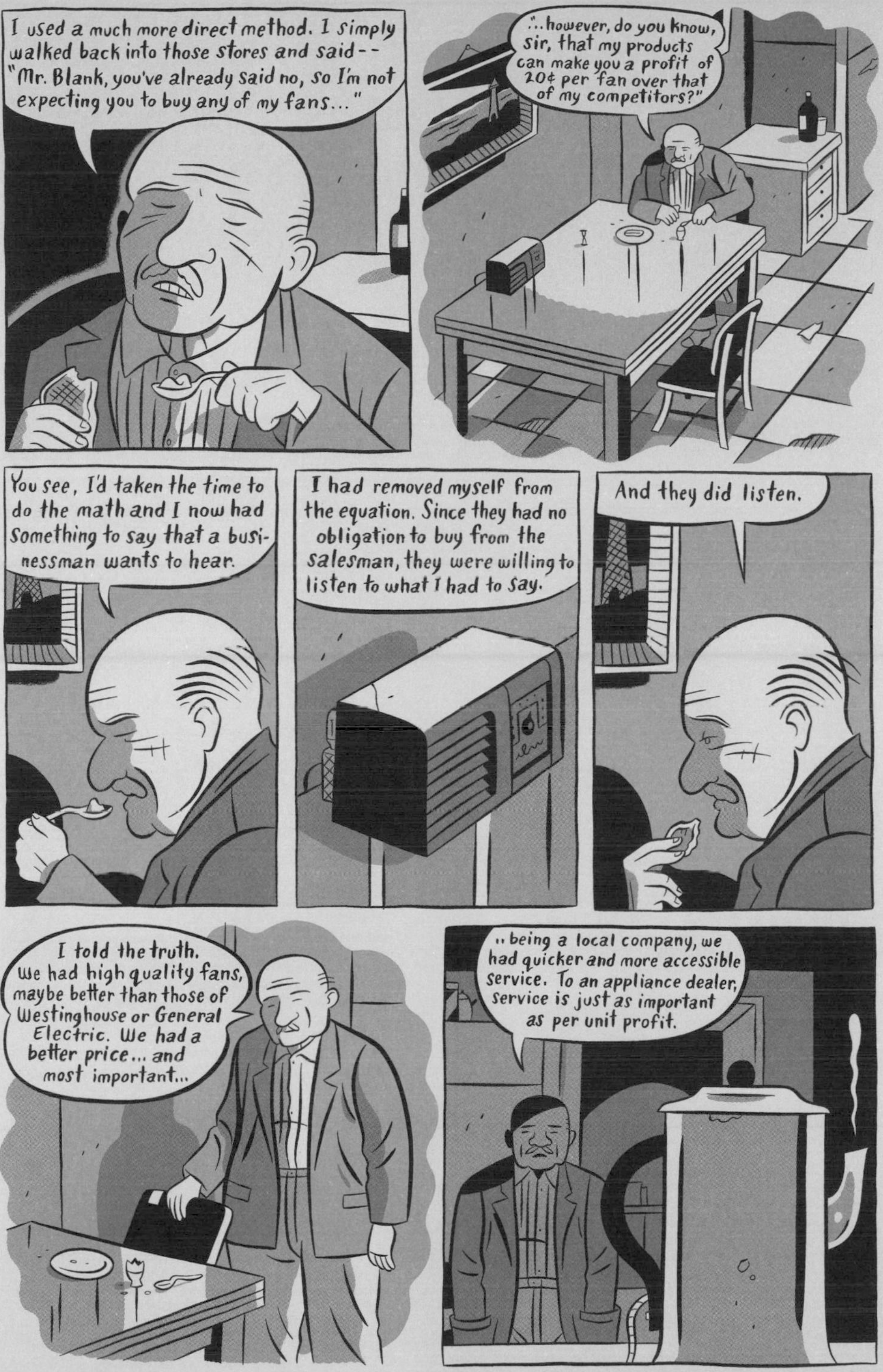
I used a much more direct method. I simply walked back into those stores and said-- "Mr. Blank, you've already said no, so I'm not expecting you to buy any of my fans..."
"...however, do you know, sir, that my products can make you a profit of 20¢ per fan over that of my competitors?"
You see, I'd taken the time to do the math and I now had something to say that a businessman wants to hear.
I had removed myself from the equation. Since they had no obligation to buy from the salesman, they were willing to listen to what I had to say.
And they did listen.
I told the truth. We had high quality fans, maybe better than those of Westinghouse or General Electric. We had a better price... and most important...
..being a local company, we had quicker and more accessible service. To an appliance dealer, service is just as important as per unit profit.

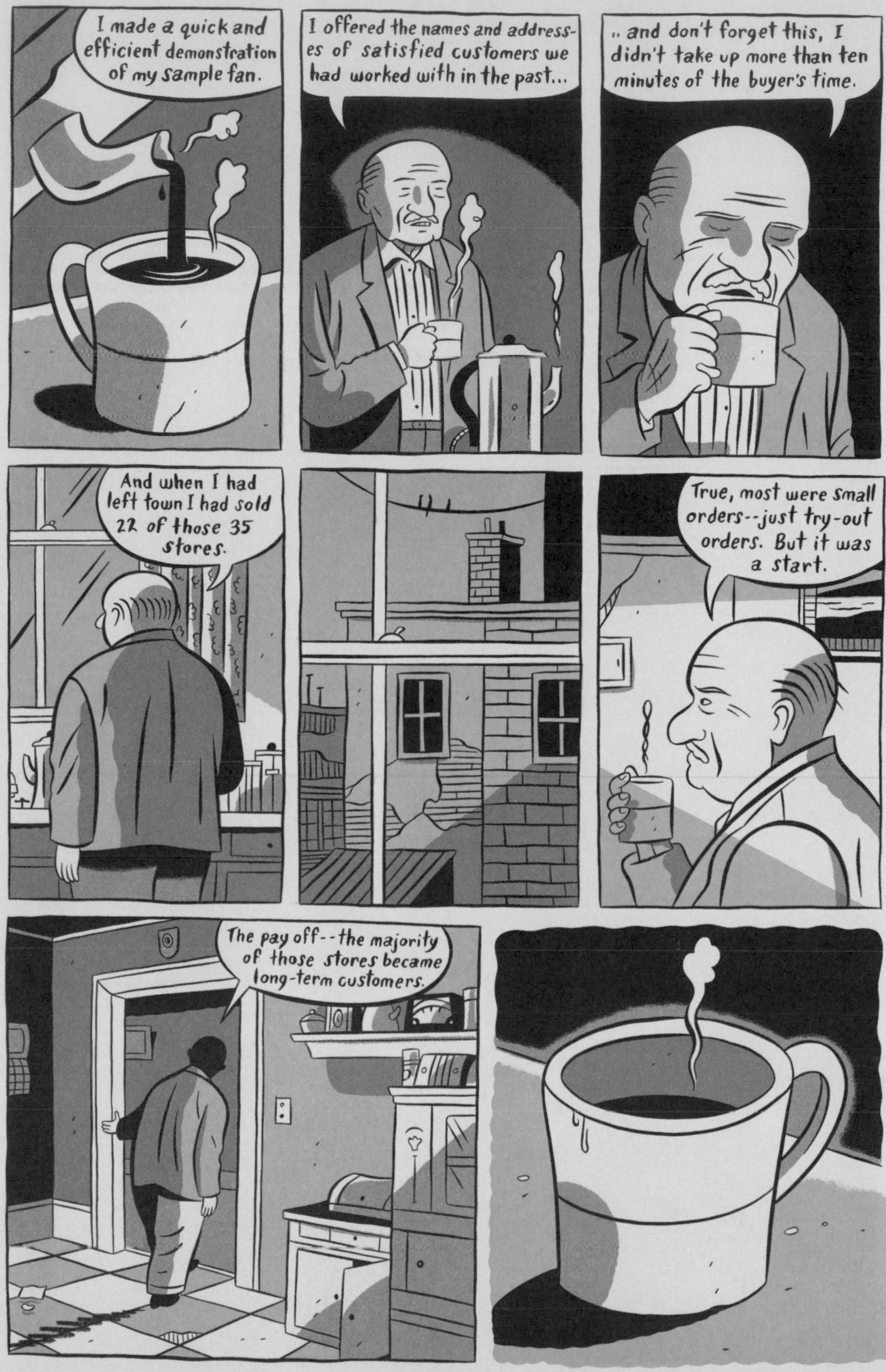
I made a quick and efficient demonstration of my sample fan.
I offered the names and addresses of satisfied customers we had worked with in the past...
.. and don't forget this, I didn't take up more than ten minutes of the buyer's time.
And when I had left town I had sold 22 of those 35 stores.
True, most were small orders--just try-out orders. But it was a start.
The pay off--the majority of those stores became long-term customers.

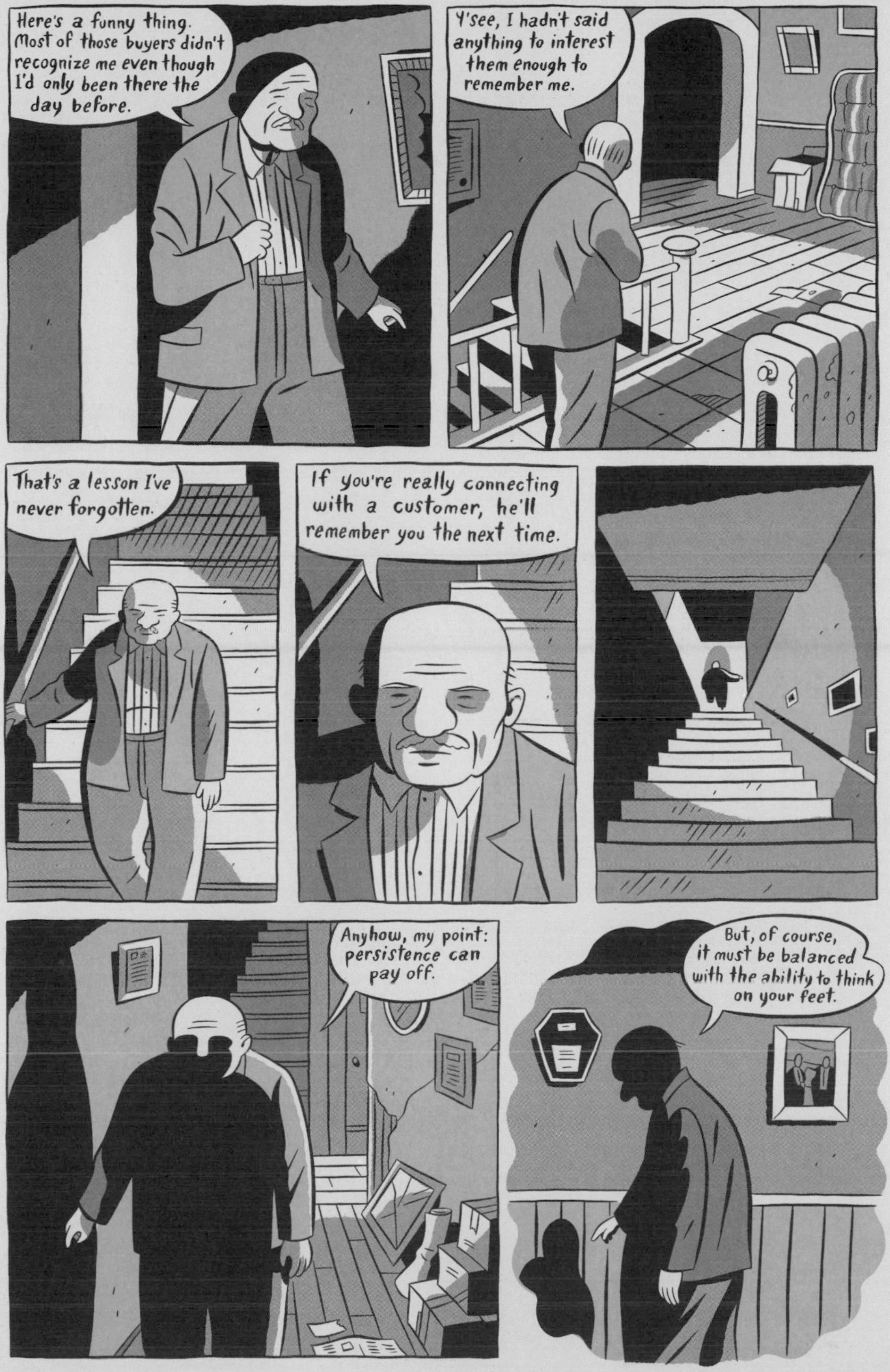
Here's a funny thing. Most of those buyers didn't recognize me even though I'd only been there the day before.
Y'see, I hadn't said anything to interest them enough to remember me.
That's a lesson I've never forgotten.
If you're really connecting with a customer, he'll remember you the next time.
Anyhow, my point: persistence can pay off.
But, of course, it must be balanced with the ability to think on your feet.

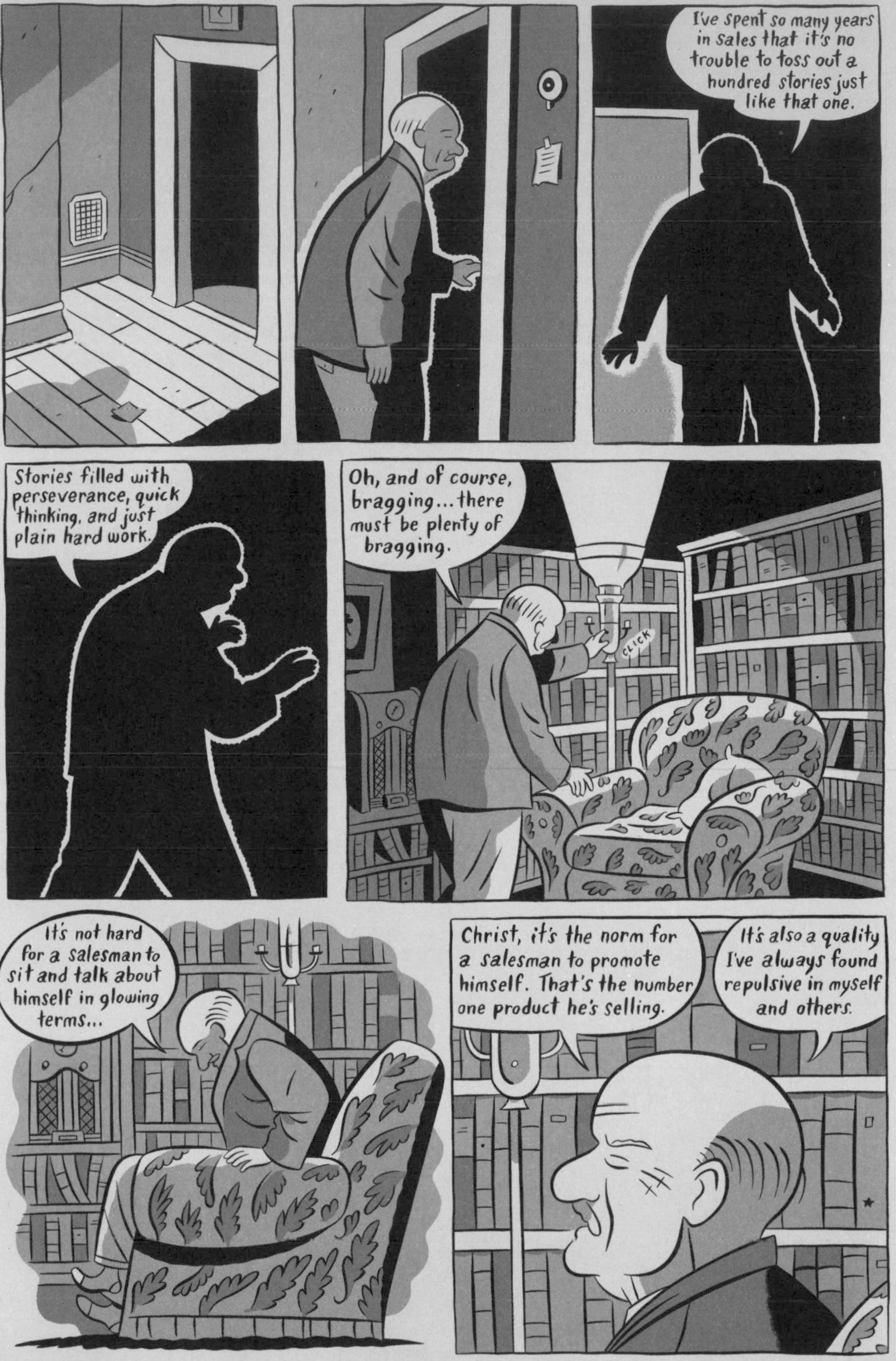
I've spent so many years in sales that it's no trouble to toss out a hundred stories just like that one.
Stories filled with perseverance, quick thinking, and just plain hard work.
Oh, and of course, bragging... there must be plenty of bragging.
CLICK
It's not hard for a salesman to sit and talk about himself in glowing terms...
Christ, it's the norm for a salesman to promote himself. That's the number one product he's selling.
It's also a quality I've always found repulsive in myself and others.

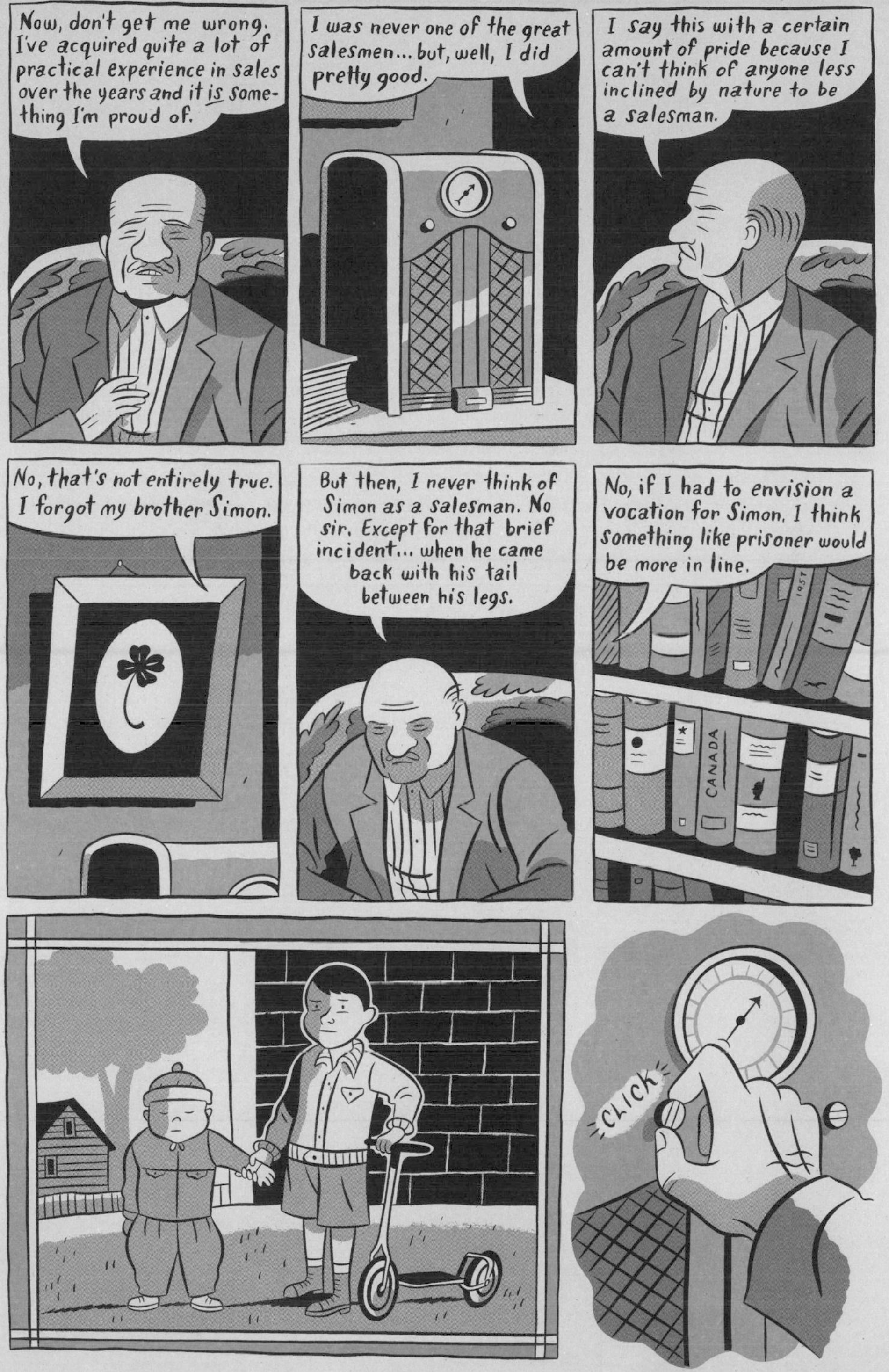
Now, don't get me wrong. I've acquired quite a lot of practical experience in sales over the years and it is something I'm proud of.
I was never one of the great salesmen... but, well, I did pretty good.
I say this with a certain amount of pride because I can't think of anyone less inclined by nature to be a salesman.
No, that's not entirely true. I forgot my brother Simon.
But then, I never think of Simon as a salesman. No sir. Except for that brief incident... when he came back with his tail between his legs.
No, if I had to envision a vocation for Simon, I think something like prisoner would be more in line.
1957
CANADA
CLICK

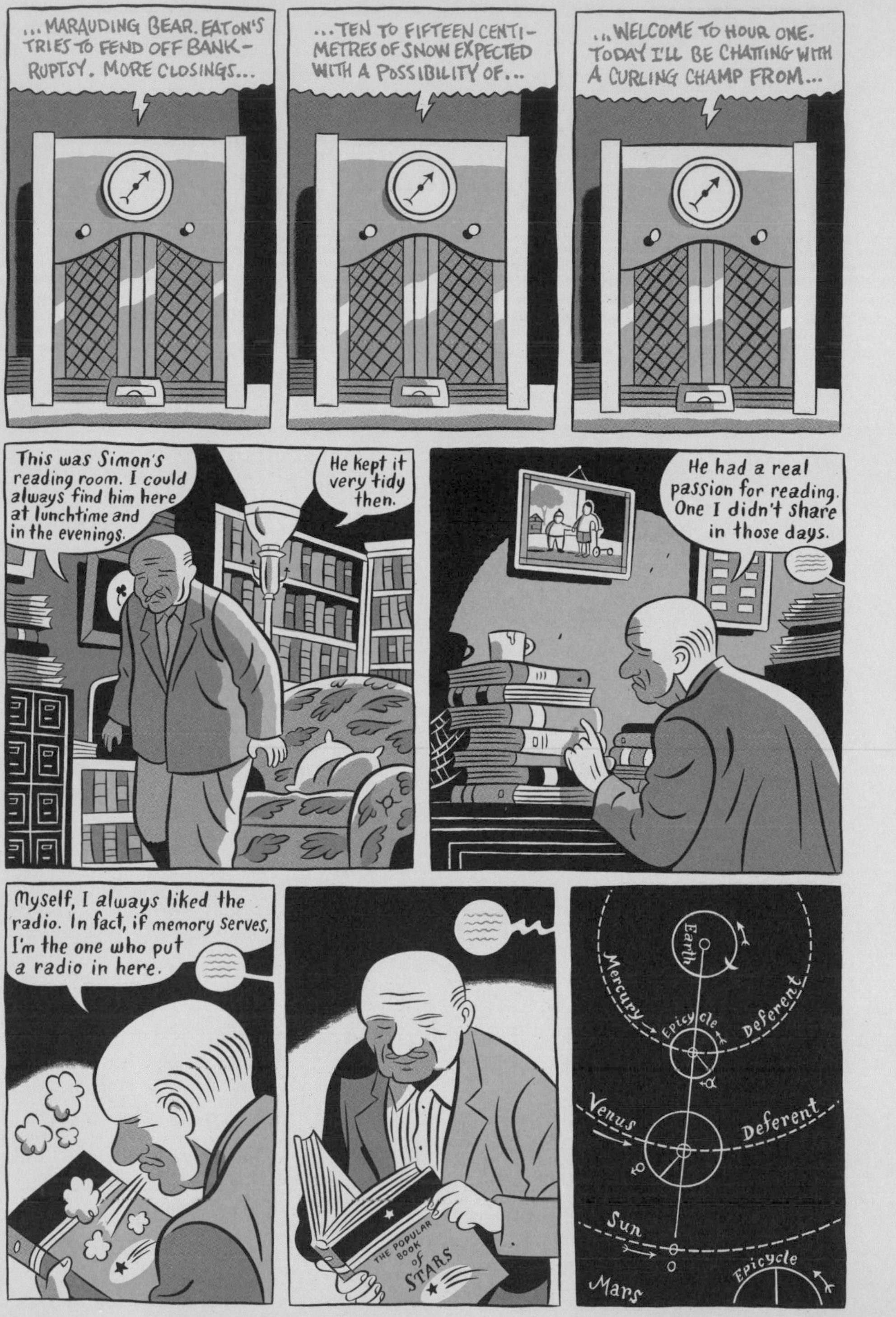
...MARAUDING BEAR. EATON'S TRIES TO FEND OFF BANK-RUPTSY. MORE CLOSINGS...
...TEN TO FIFTEEN CENTI-METRES OF SNOW EXPECTED WITH A POSSIBILITY OF...
...WELCOME TO HOUR ONE. TODAY I'LL BE CHATTING WITH A CURLING CHAMP FROM...
This was Simon's reading room. I could always find him here at lunchtime and in the evenings.
He kept it very tidy then.
He had a real passion for reading. One I didn't share in those days.
Myself, I always liked the radio. In fact, if memory serves, I'm the one who put a radio in here.
THE POPULAR BOOK of STARS
Earth
Mercury
Epicycle
Deferent
Venus
Deferent
Sun
Mars
Epicycle

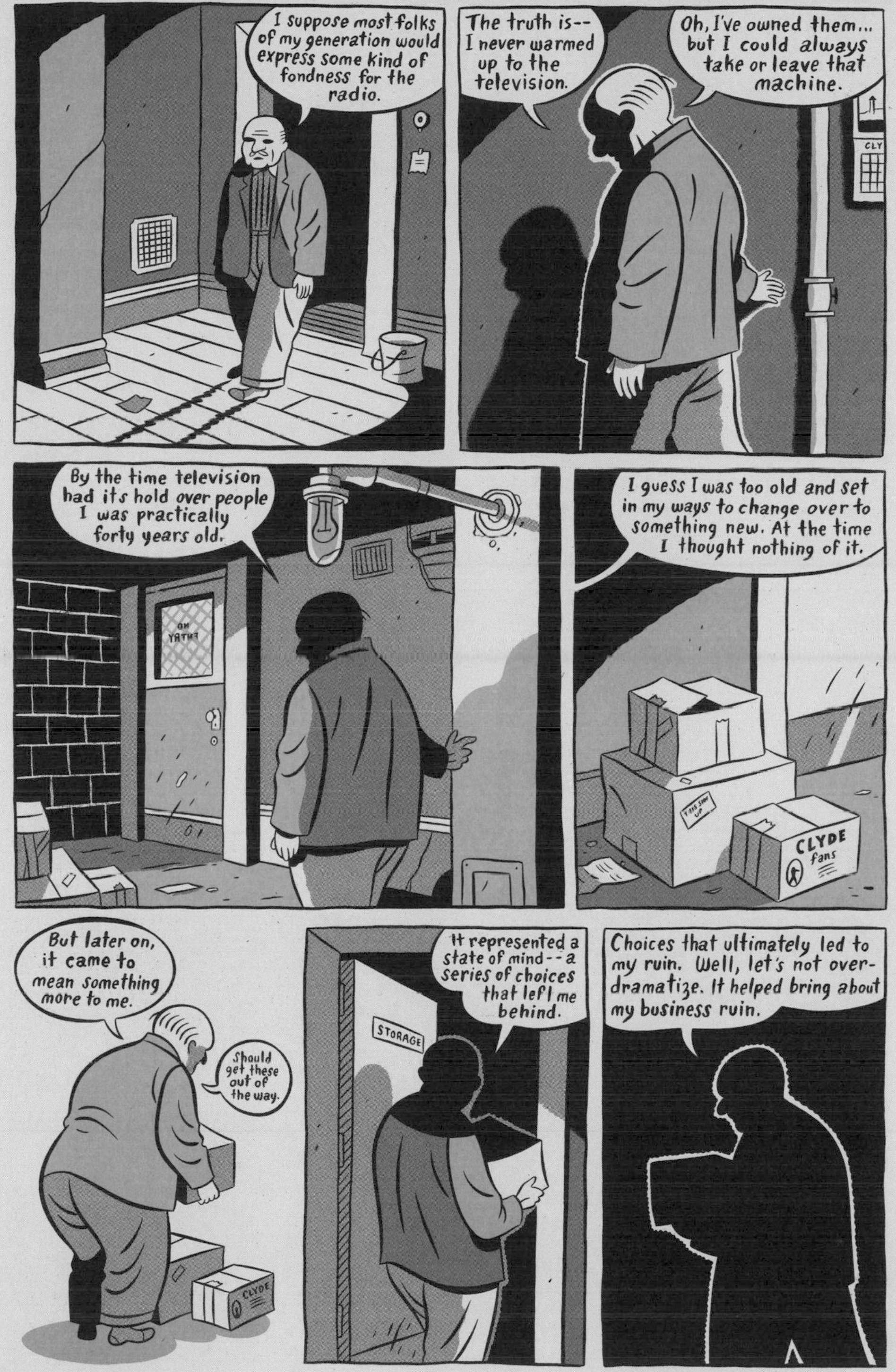
I suppose most folks of my generation would express some kind of fondness for the radio.
The truth is-- I never warmed up to the television.
Oh, I've owned them... but I could always take or leave that machine.
By the time television had its hold over people I was practically forty years old.
I guess I was too old and set in my ways to change over to something new. At the time I thought nothing of it.
CLYDE fans
But later on, it came to mean something more to me.
Should get these out of the way.
CLYDE
STORAGE
It represented a state of mind-- a series of choices that left me behind.
Choices that ultimately led to my ruin. Well, let's not over-dramatize. It helped bring about my business ruin.

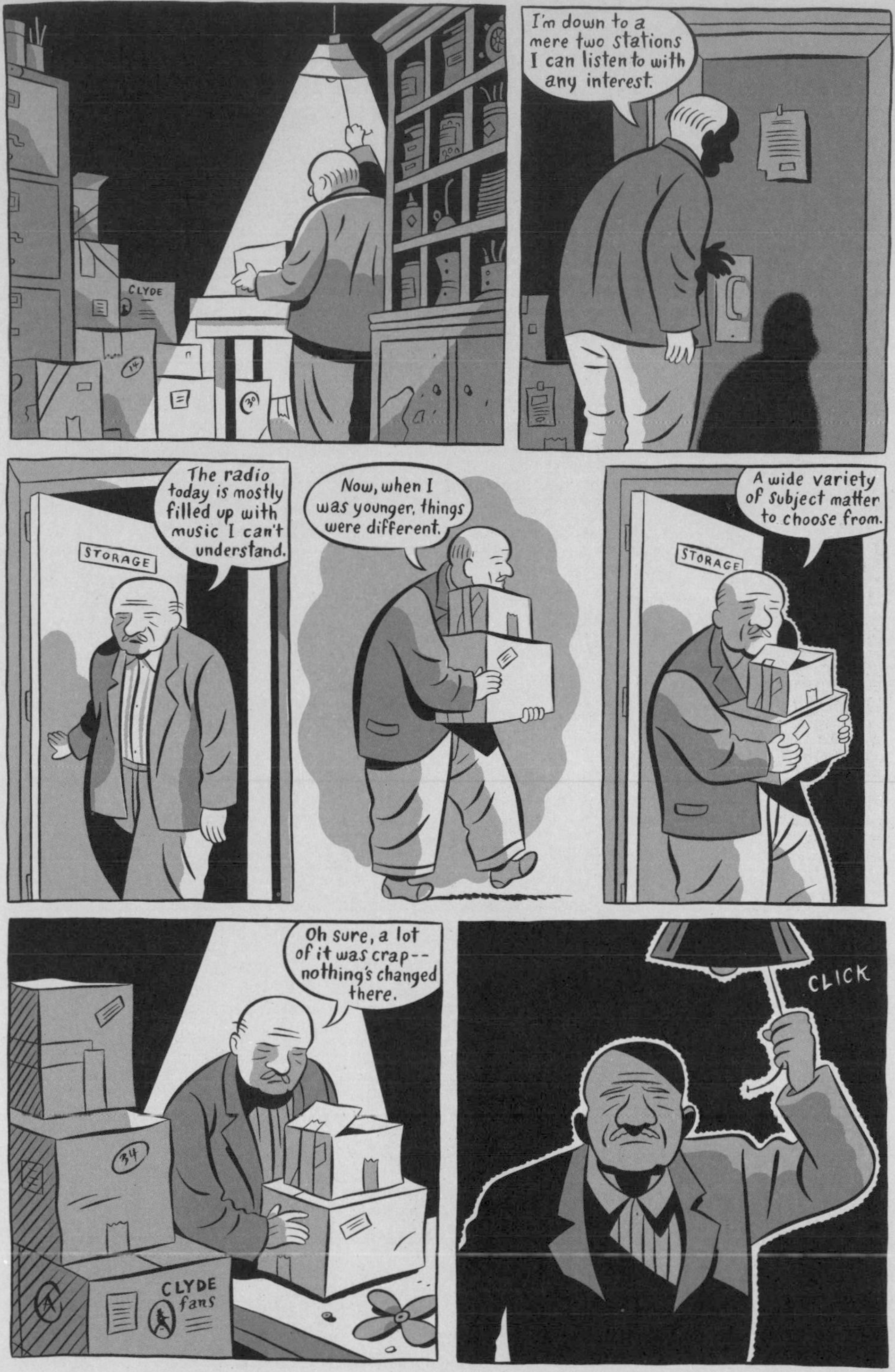
CLYDE
I'm down to a mere two stations I can listen to with any interest.
STORAGE
The radio today is mostly filled up with music I can't understand.
Now, when I was younger, things were different.
STORAGE
A wide variety of subject matter to choose from.
Oh sure, a lot of it was crap-- nothing's changed there.
CLYDE fans
CLICK

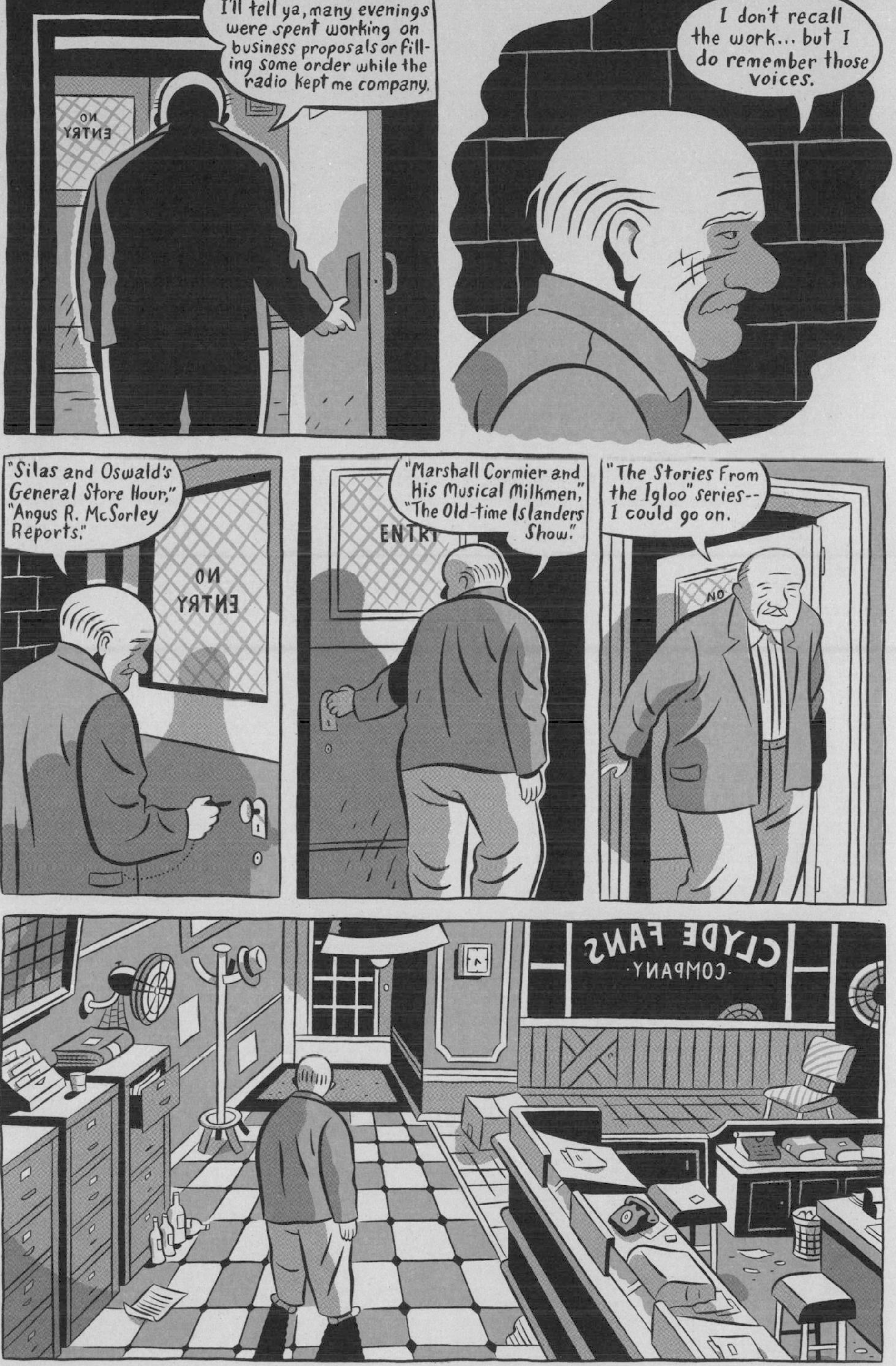
I'll tell ya, many evenings were spent working on business proposals or filling some order while the radio kept me company.
NO ENTRY
I don't recall the work... but I do remember those voices.
"Silas and Oswald's General Store Hour," "Angus R. McSorley Reports."
NO ENTRY
"Marshall Cormier and His Musical Milkmen," "The Old-time Islanders Show."
"The Stories From the Igloo" series-- I could go on.
CLYDE FANS COMPANY

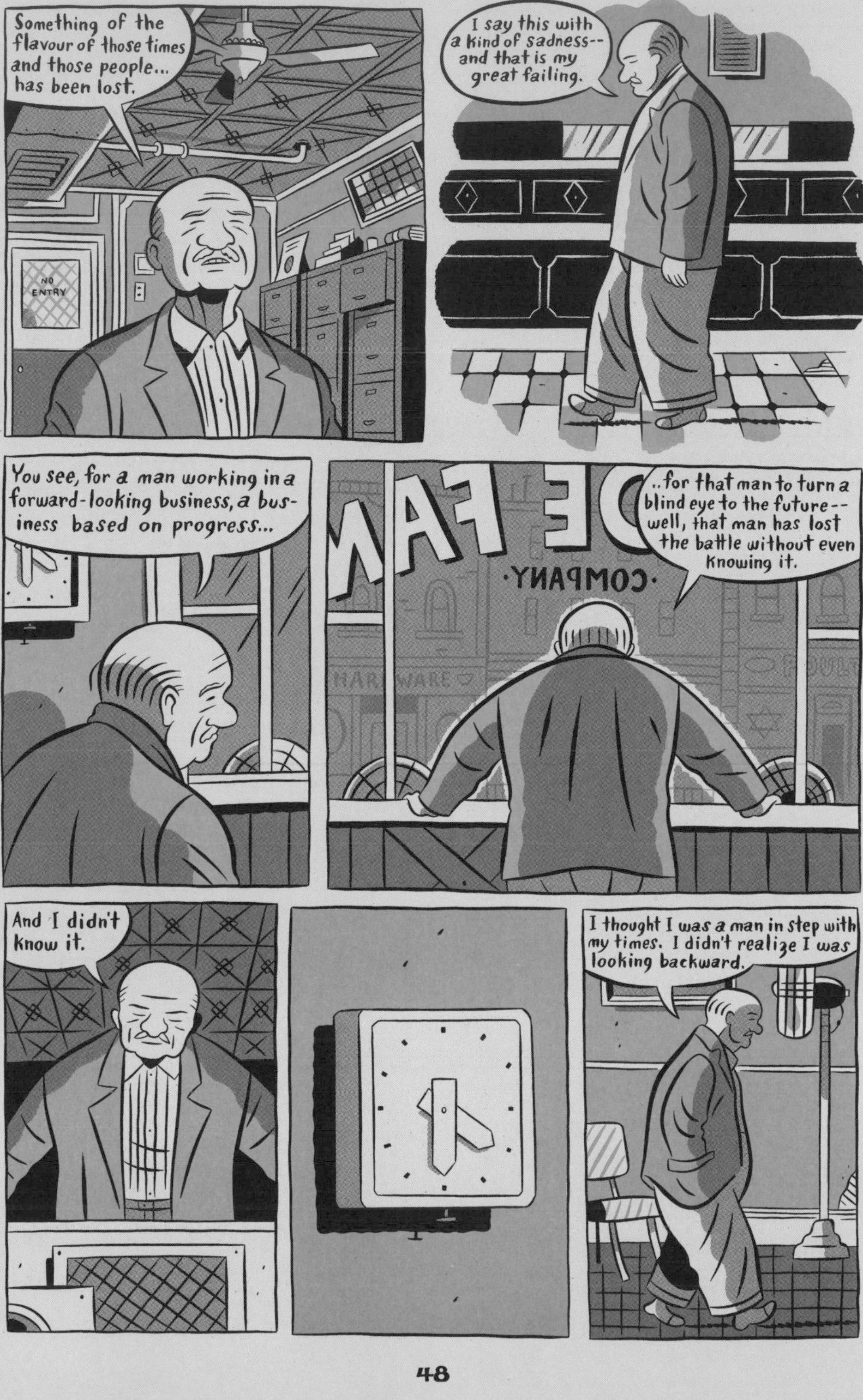
Something of the flavour of those times and those people... has been lost.
NO ENTRY
I say this with a kind of sadness-- and that is my great failing.
You see, for a man working in a forward-looking business, a business based on progress...
·COMPANY·
HARDWARE
..for that man to turn a blind eye to the future-- well, that man has lost the battle without even knowing it.
And I didn't know it.
I thought I was a man in step with my times. I didn't realize I was looking backward.

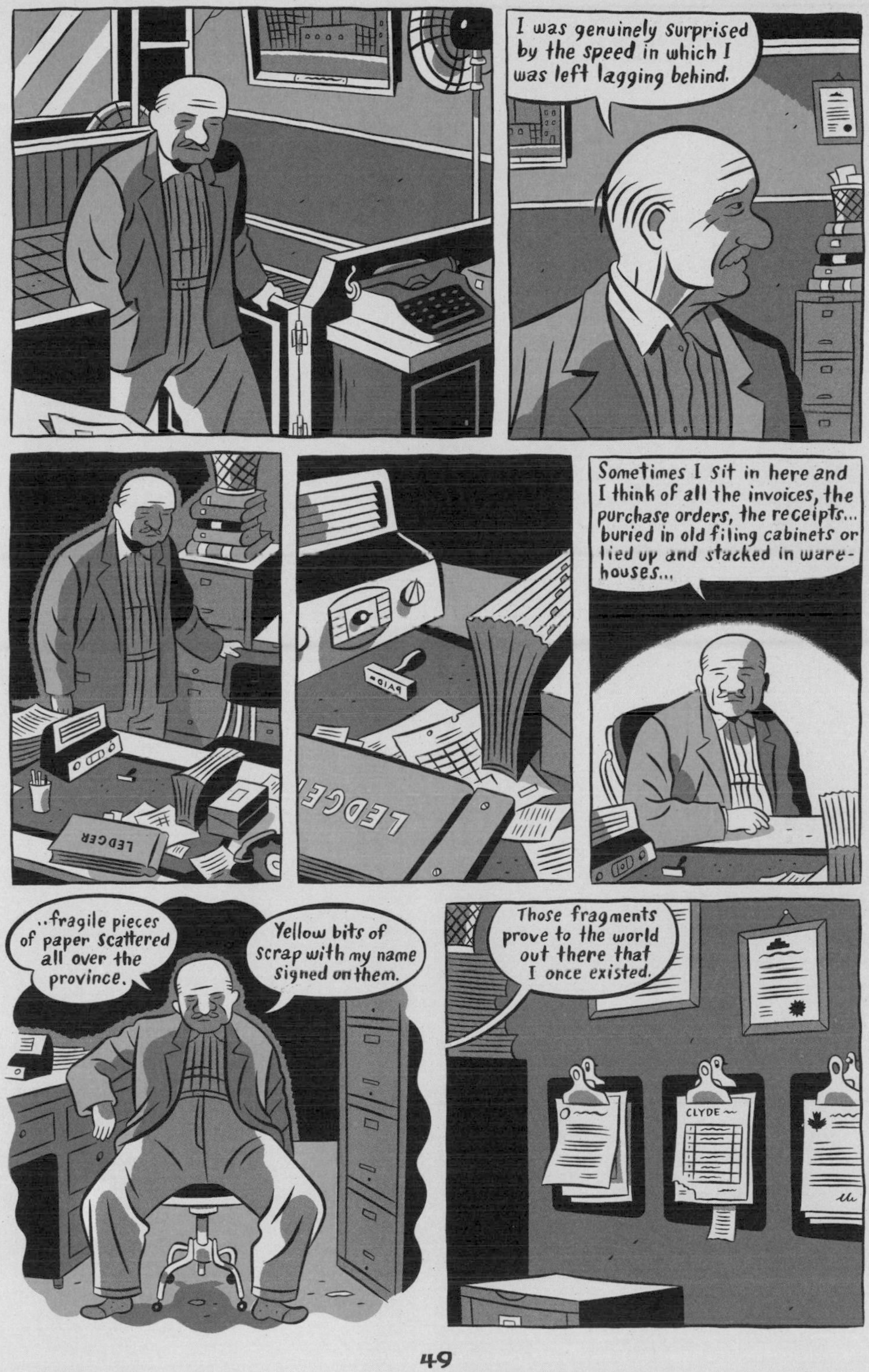
I was genuinely surprised by the speed in which I was left lagging behind.
Sometimes I sit in here and I think of all the invoices, the purchase orders, the receipts... buried in old filing cabinets or tied up and stacked in warehouses...
PAID
LEDGER
LEDGER
..fragile pieces of paper scattered all over the province.
Yellow bits of scrap with my name signed on them.
Those fragments prove to the world out there that I once existed.
CLYDE

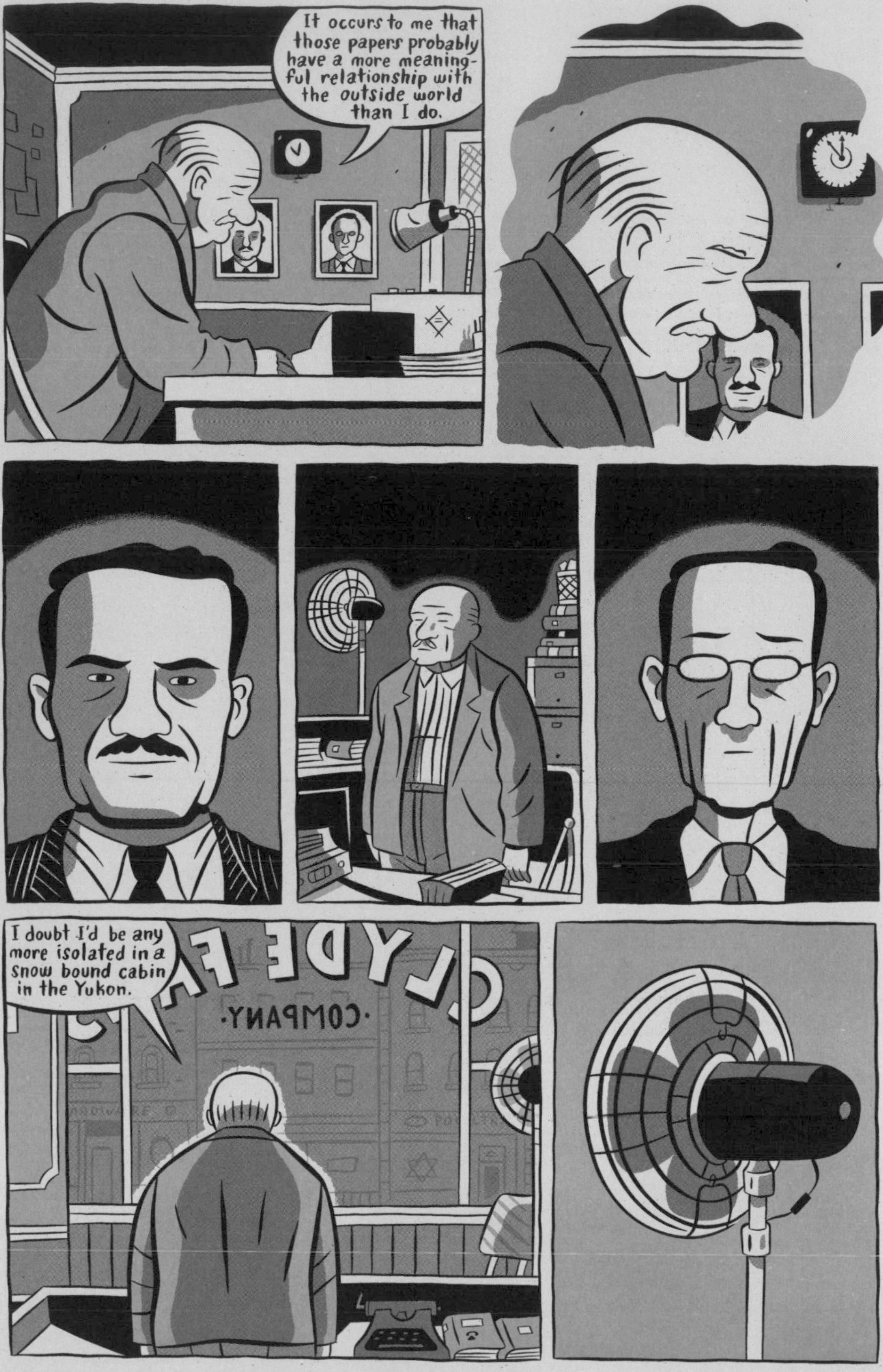
It occurs to me that those papers probably have a more meaning-ful relationship with the outside world than I do.
I doubt I'd be any more isolated in a snow bound cabin in the Yukon.
CLYDE F
·COMPANY·

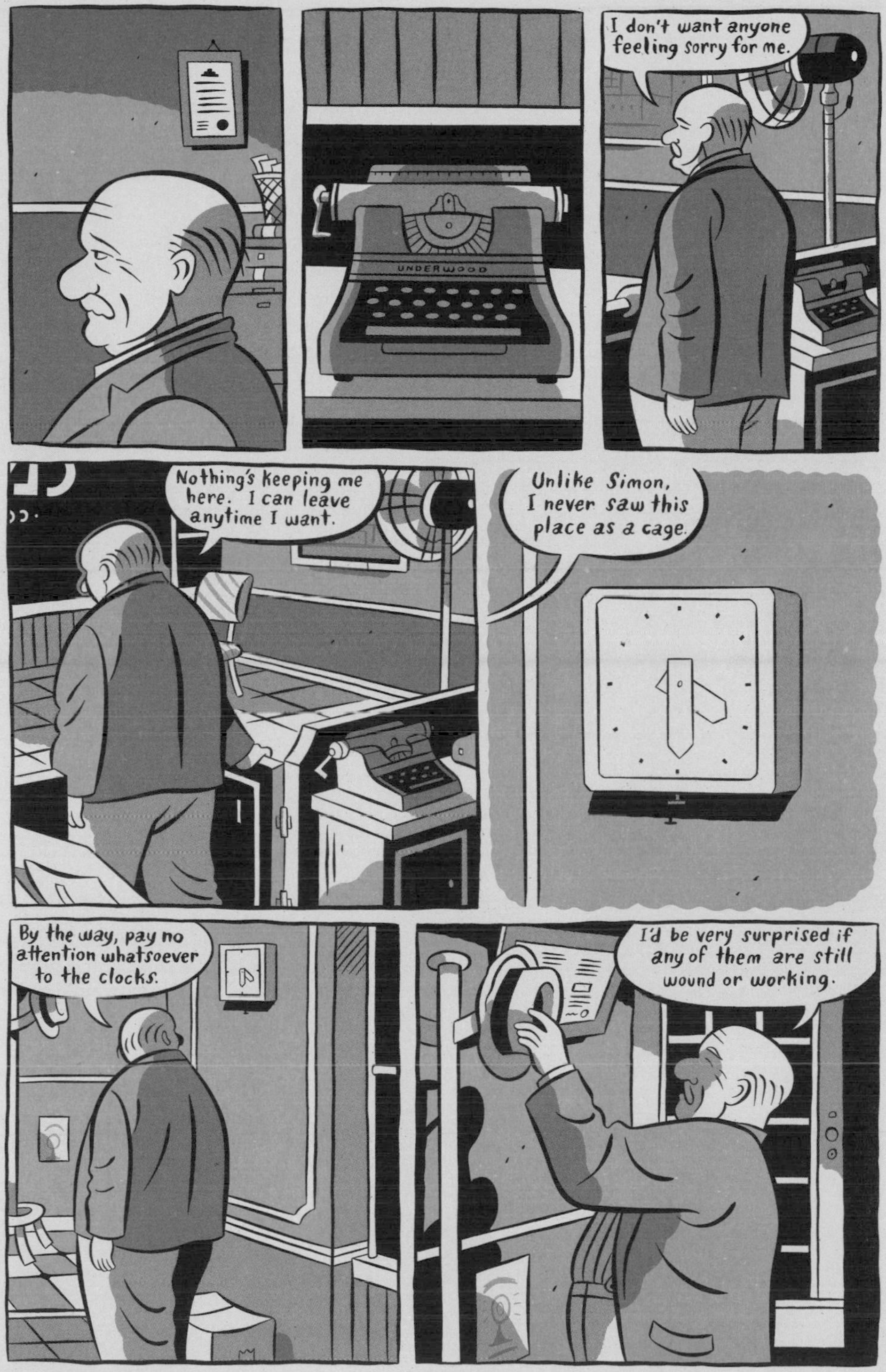
I don't want anyone feeling sorry for me.
Nothing's keeping me here. I can leave anytime I want.
Unlike Simon, I never saw this place as a cage.
By the way, pay no attention whatsoever to the clocks.
I'd be very surprised if any of them are still wound or working.

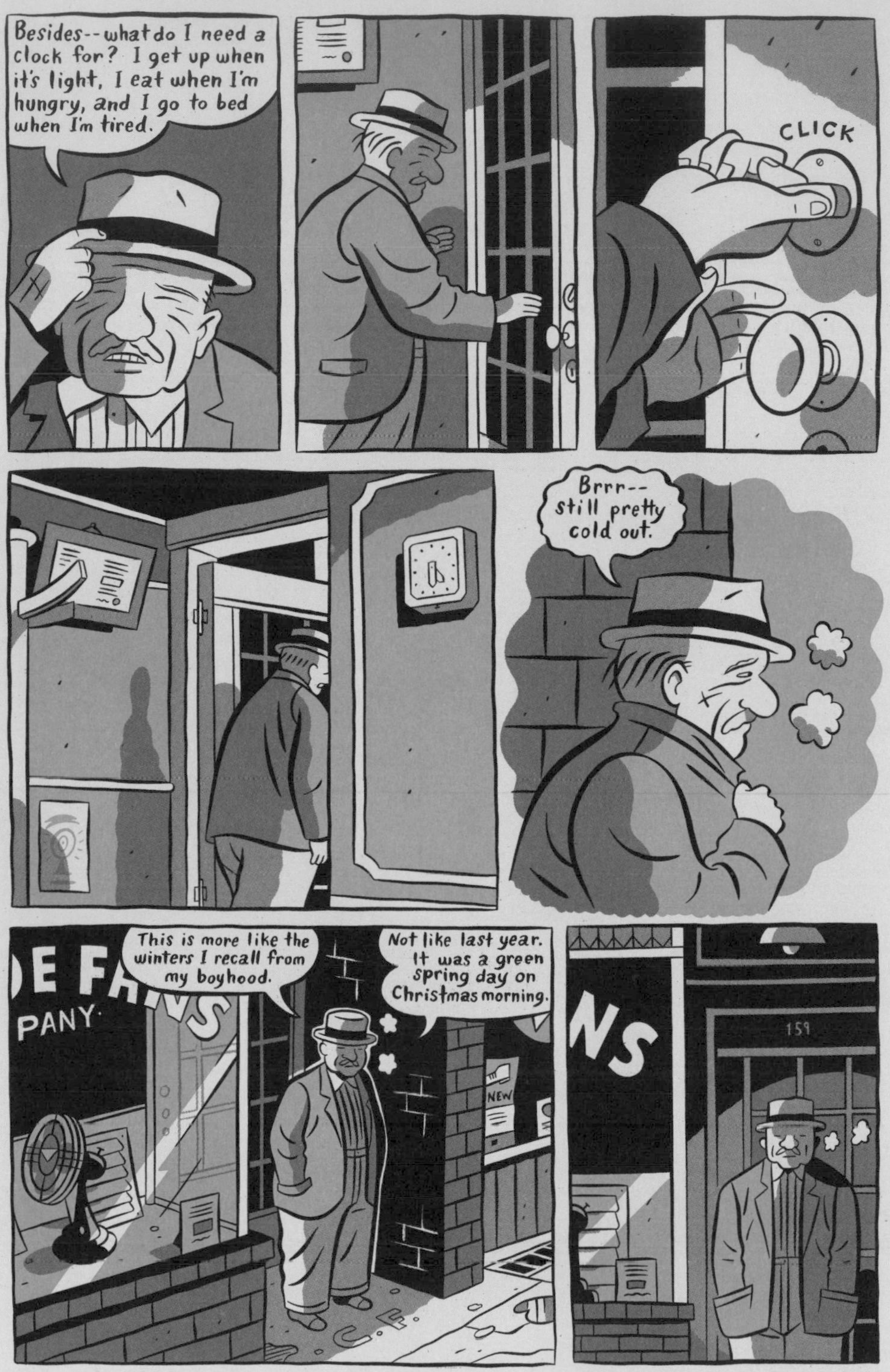
Besides--what do I need a clock for? I get up when it's light, I eat when I'm hungry, and I go to bed when I'm tired.
CLICK
Brrr-- still pretty cold out.
This is more like the winters I recall from my boyhood.
Not like last year. It was a green spring day on Christmas morning.
PANY
NEW
NS
159

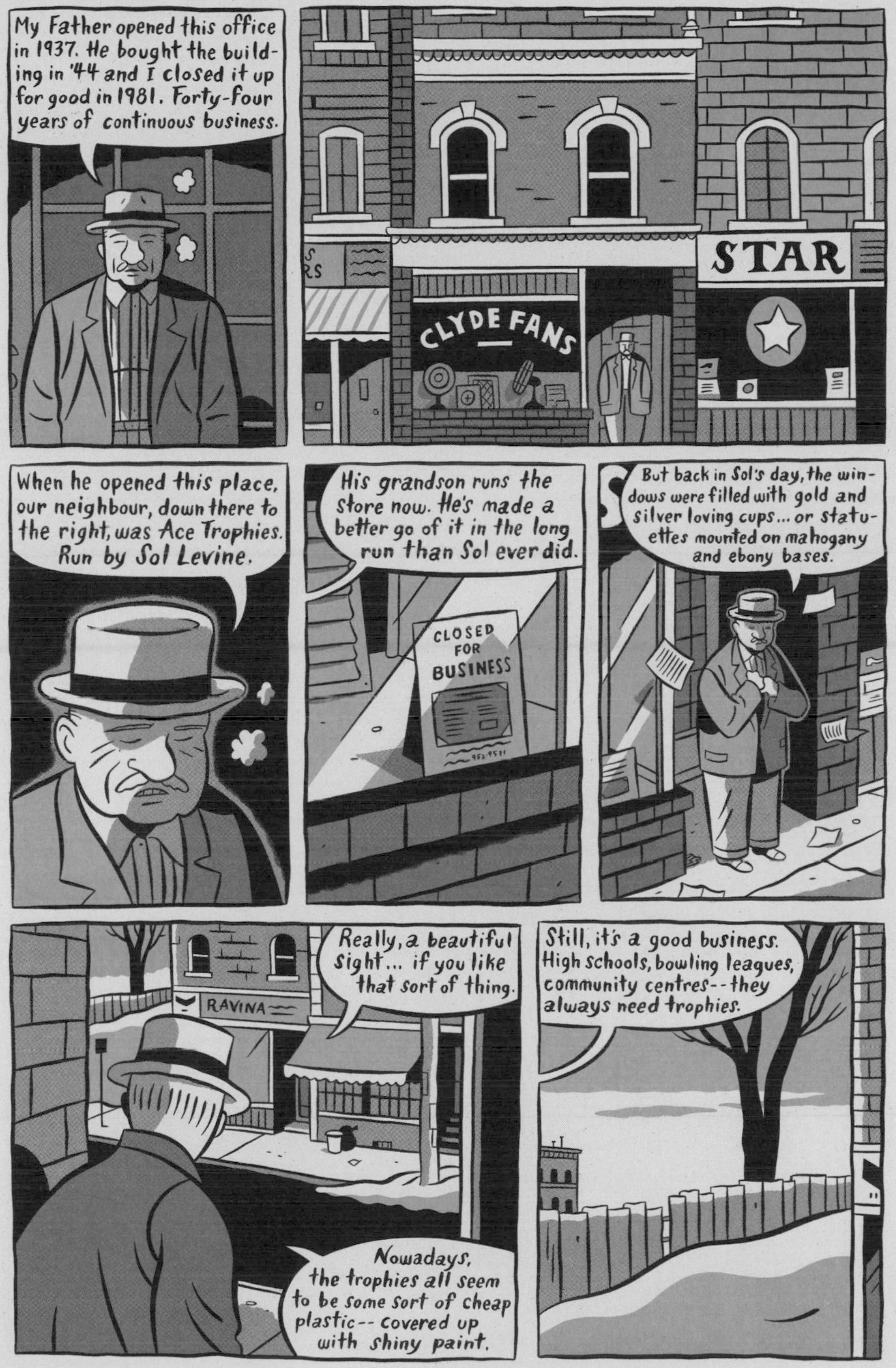
My Father opened this office in 1937. He bought the building in '44 and I closed it up for good in 1981. Forty-four years of continuous business.
CLYDE FANS
STAR
When he opened this place, our neighbour, down there to the right, was Ace Trophies. Run by Sol Levine.
His grandson runs the store now. He's made a better go of it in the long run than Sol ever did.
CLOSED FOR BUSINESS
But back in Sol's day, the windows were filled with gold and silver loving cups... or statuettes mounted on mahogany and ebony bases.
Really, a beautiful sight... if you like that sort of thing.
RAVINA
Nowadays, the trophies all seem to be some sort of cheap plastic-- covered up with shiny paint.
Still, it's a good business. High schools, bowling leagues, community centres--they always need trophies.

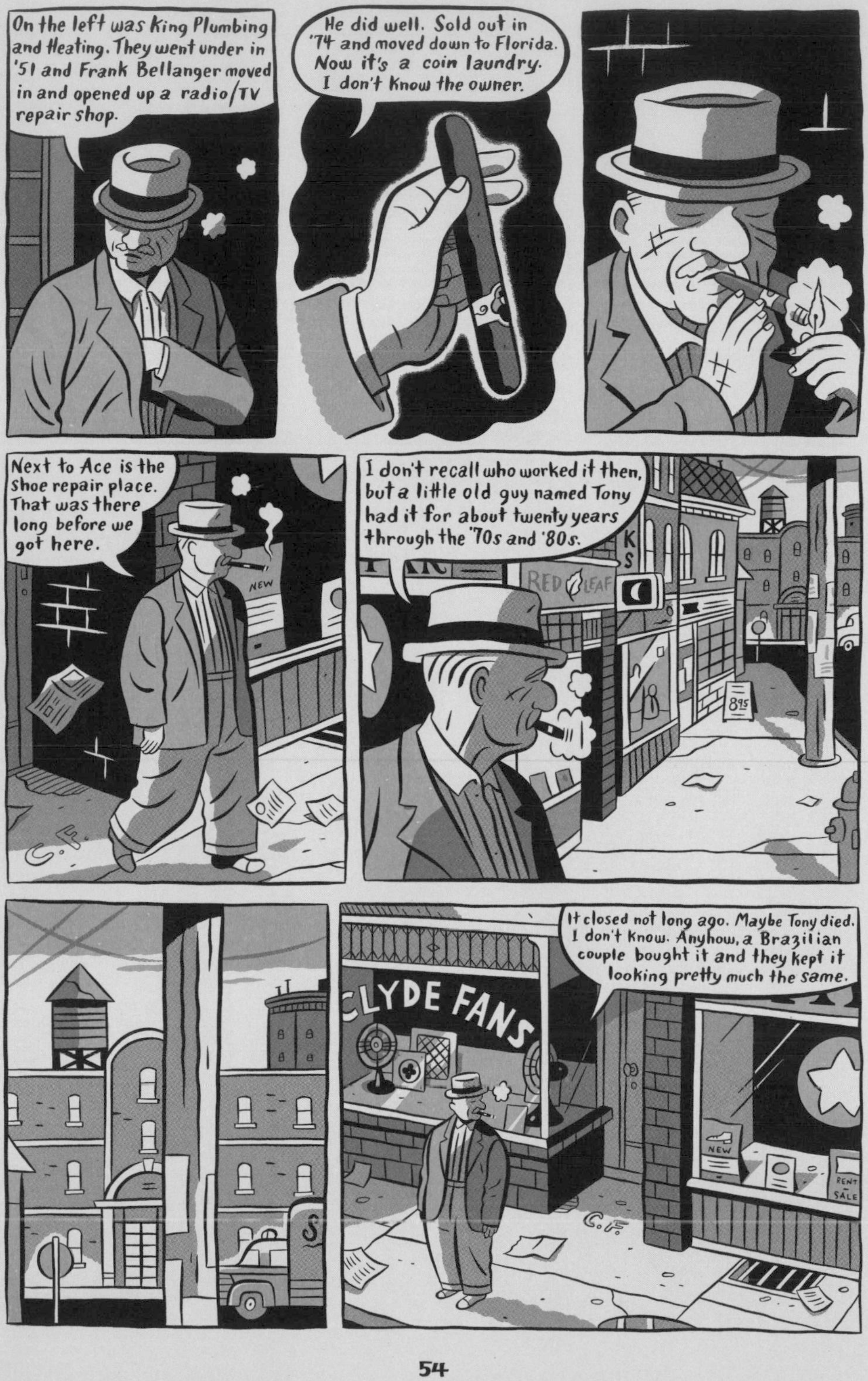
On the left was King Plumbing and Heating. They went under in '51 and Frank Bellanger moved in and opened up a radio/TV repair shop.
He did well. Sold out in '74 and moved down to Florida. Now it's a coin laundry. I don't know the owner.
Next to Ace is the shoe repair place. That was there long before we got here.
NEW
C.F.
I don't recall who worked it then, but a little old guy named Tony had it for about twenty years through the '70s and '80s.
RED LEAF
8.95
It closed not long ago. Maybe Tony died. I don't know. Anyhow, a Brazilian couple bought it and they kept it looking pretty much the same.
CLYDE FANS
NEW
RENT SALE
C.F.

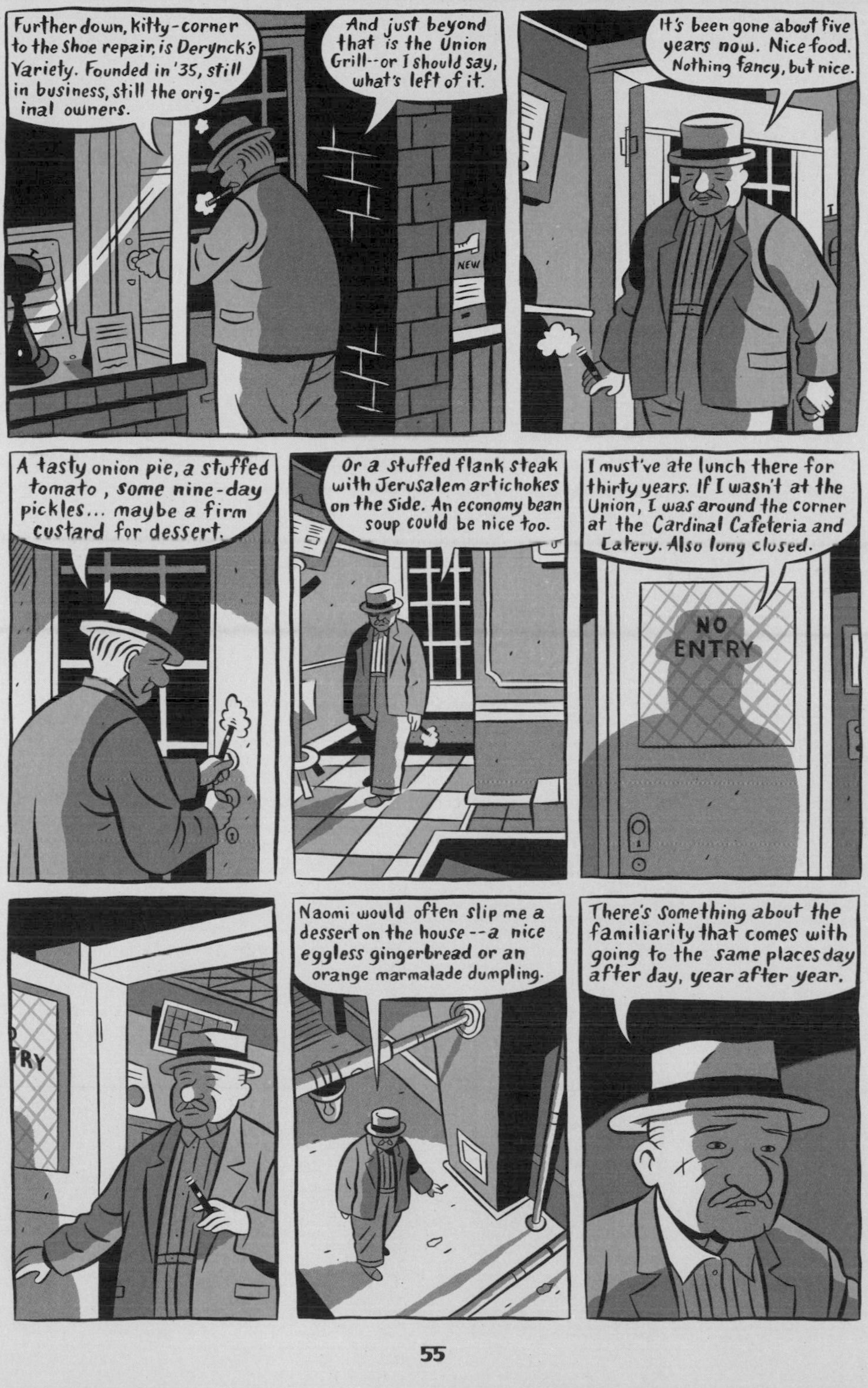

Further down, kitty-corner to the shoe repair, is Deryncк's Variety. Founded in '35, still in business, still the original owners.
And just beyond that is the Union Grill--or I should say, what's left of it.
NEW
It's been gone about five years now. Nice food. Nothing fancy, but nice.
A tasty onion pie, a stuffed tomato, some nine-day pickles... maybe a firm custard for dessert.
Or a stuffed flank steak with Jerusalem artichokes on the side. An economy bean soup could be nice too.
I must've ate lunch there for thirty years. If I wasn't at the Union, I was around the corner at the Cardinal Cafeteria and Eatery. Also long closed.
NO ENTRY
TRY
Naomi would often slip me a dessert on the house--a nice eggless gingerbread or an orange marmalade dumpling.
There's something about the familiarity that comes with going to the same places day after day, year after year.

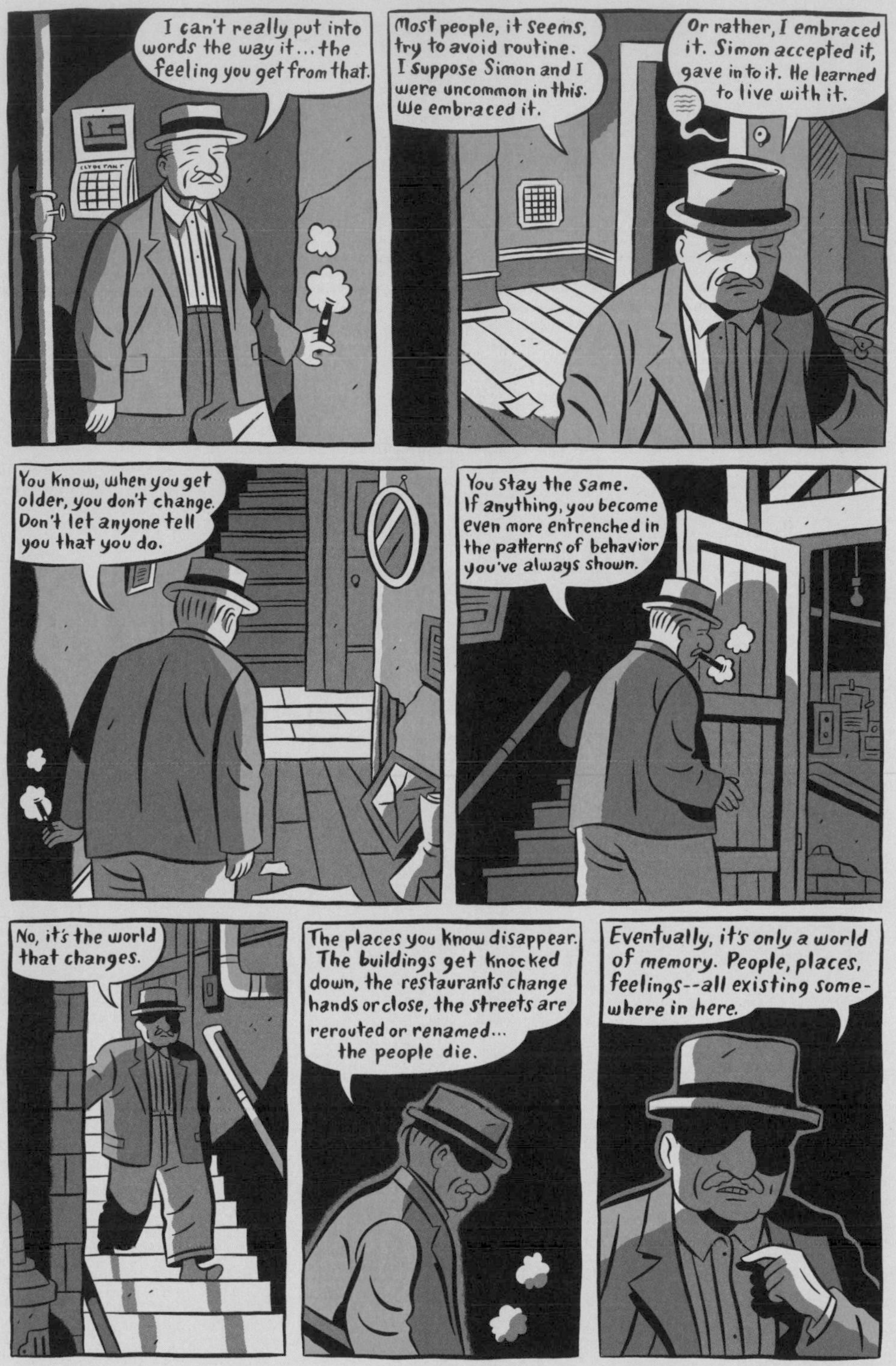
I can't really put into words the way it... the feeling you get from that.
Most people, it seems, try to avoid routine. I suppose Simon and I were uncommon in this. We embraced it.
Or rather, I embraced it. Simon accepted it, gave in to it. He learned to live with it.
You know, when you get older, you don't change. Don't let anyone tell you that you do.
You stay the same. If anything, you become even more entrenched in the patterns of behavior you've always shown.
No, it's the world that changes.
The places you know disappear. The buildings get knocked down, the restaurants change hands or close, the streets are rerouted or renamed... the people die.
Eventually, it's only a world of memory. People, places, feelings--all existing somewhere in here.

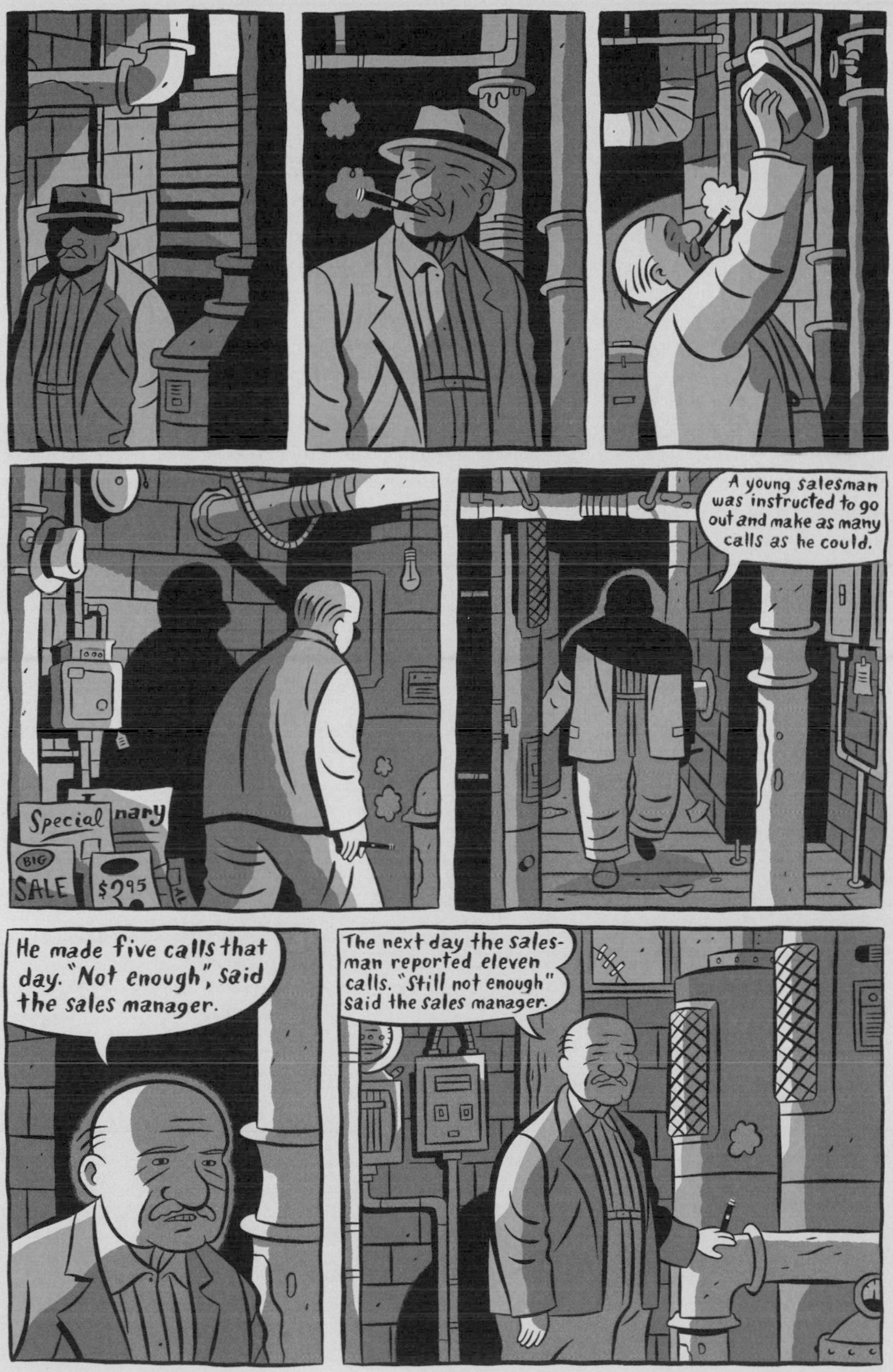
Special
nary
BIG
SALE
$2.95
A young salesman was instructed to go out and make as many calls as he could.
He made five calls that day. "Not enough", said the sales manager.
The next day the salesman reported eleven calls. "Still not enough" said the sales manager.

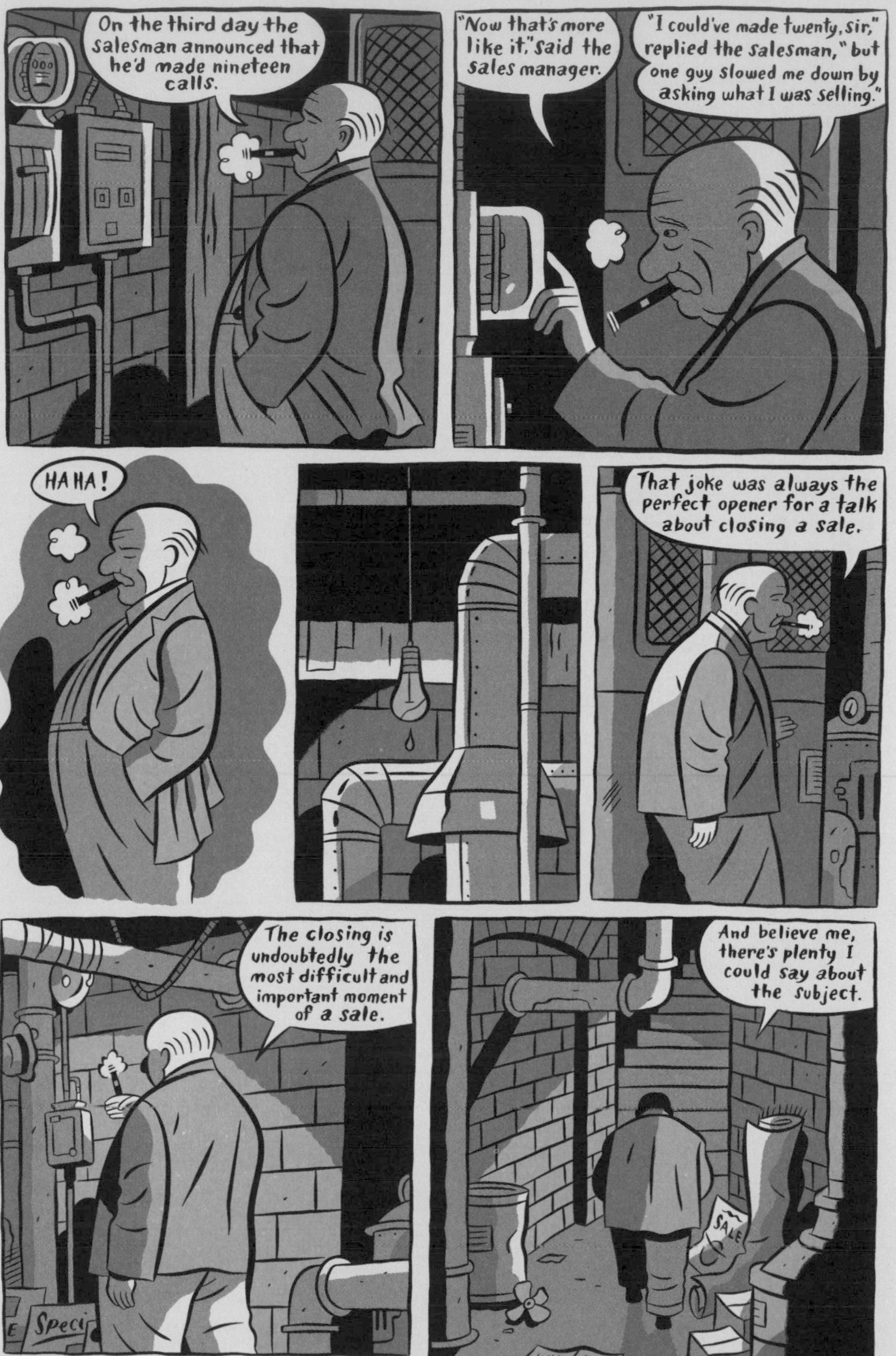
On the third day the salesman announced that he'd made nineteen calls.
"Now that's more like it," said the sales manager.
"I could've made twenty, sir," replied the salesman, "but one guy slowed me down by asking what I was selling."
HA HA!
That joke was always the perfect opener for a talk about closing a sale.
The closing is undoubtedly the most difficult and important moment of a sale.
And believe me, there's plenty I could say about the subject.
SALE

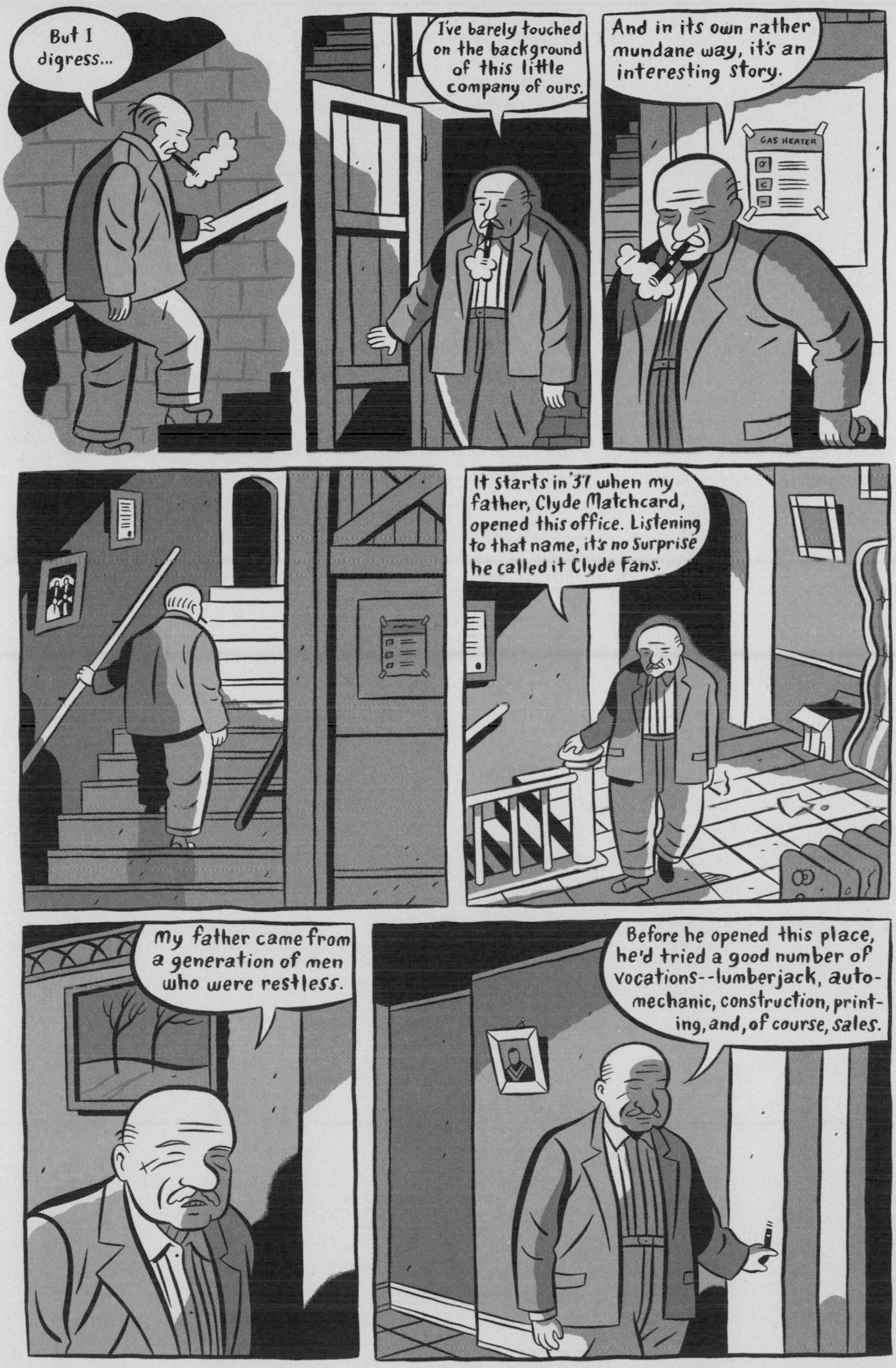
But I digress...
I've barely touched on the background of this little company of ours.
And in its own rather mundane way, it's an interesting story.
GAS HEATER
It starts in '37 when my father, Clyde Matchcard, opened this office. Listening to that name, it's no surprise he called it Clyde Fans.
My father came from a generation of men who were restless.
Before he opened this place, he'd tried a good number of vocations--lumberjack, auto-mechanic, construction, printing, and, of course, sales.

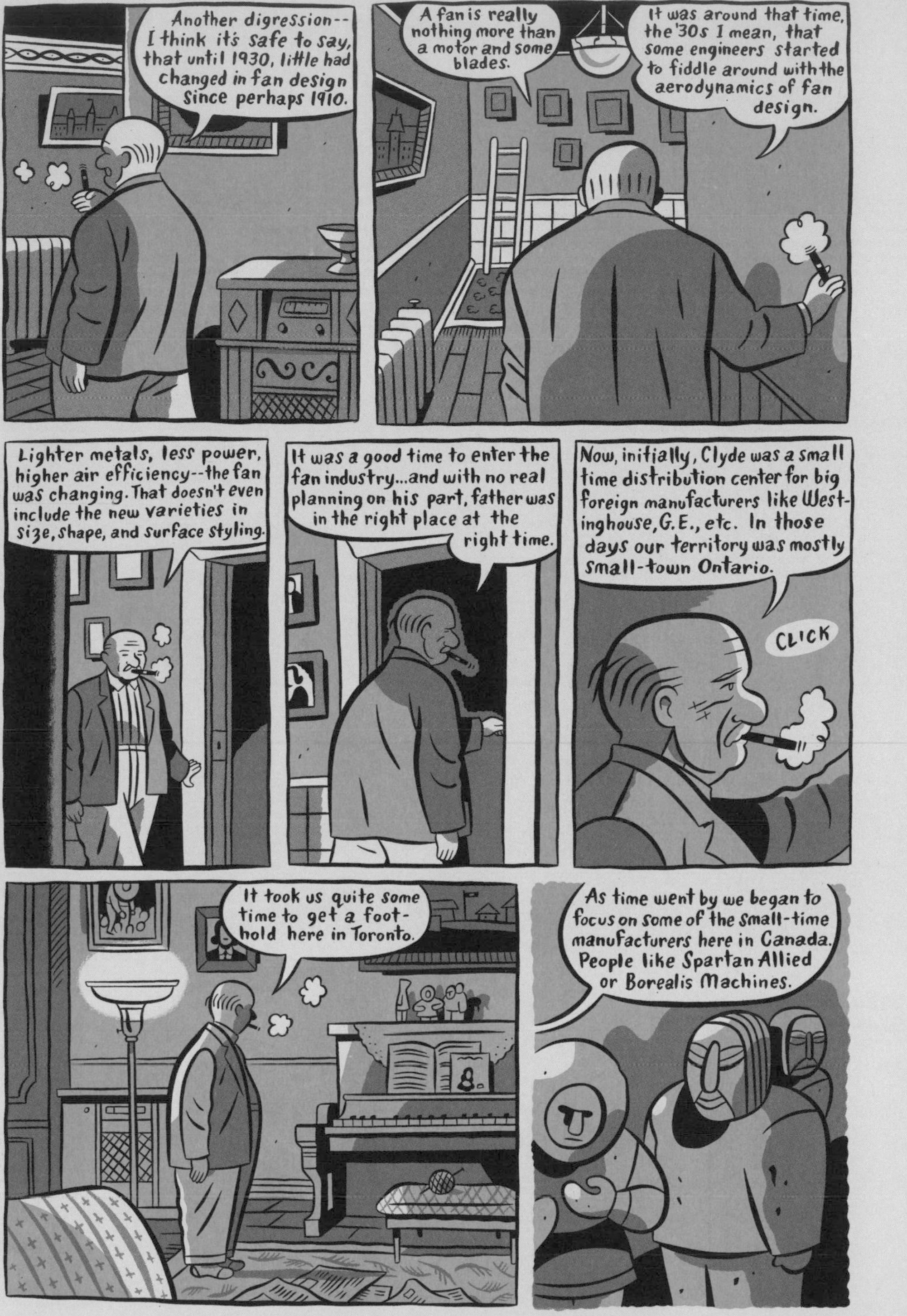
Another digression--
I think it's safe to say, that until 1930, little had changed in fan design since perhaps 1910.
A fan is really nothing more than a motor and some blades.
It was around that time, the '30s I mean, that some engineers started to fiddle around with the aerodynamics of fan design.
Lighter metals, less power, higher air efficiency--the fan was changing. That doesn't even include the new varieties in size, shape, and surface styling.
It was a good time to enter the fan industry...and with no real planning on his part, father was in the right place at the right time.
Now, initially, Clyde was a small time distribution center for big foreign manufacturers like Westinghouse, G.E., etc. In those days our territory was mostly small-town Ontario.
CLICK
It took us quite some time to get a foothold here in Toronto.
As time went by we began to focus on some of the small-time manufacturers here in Canada. People like Spartan Allied or Borealis Machines.

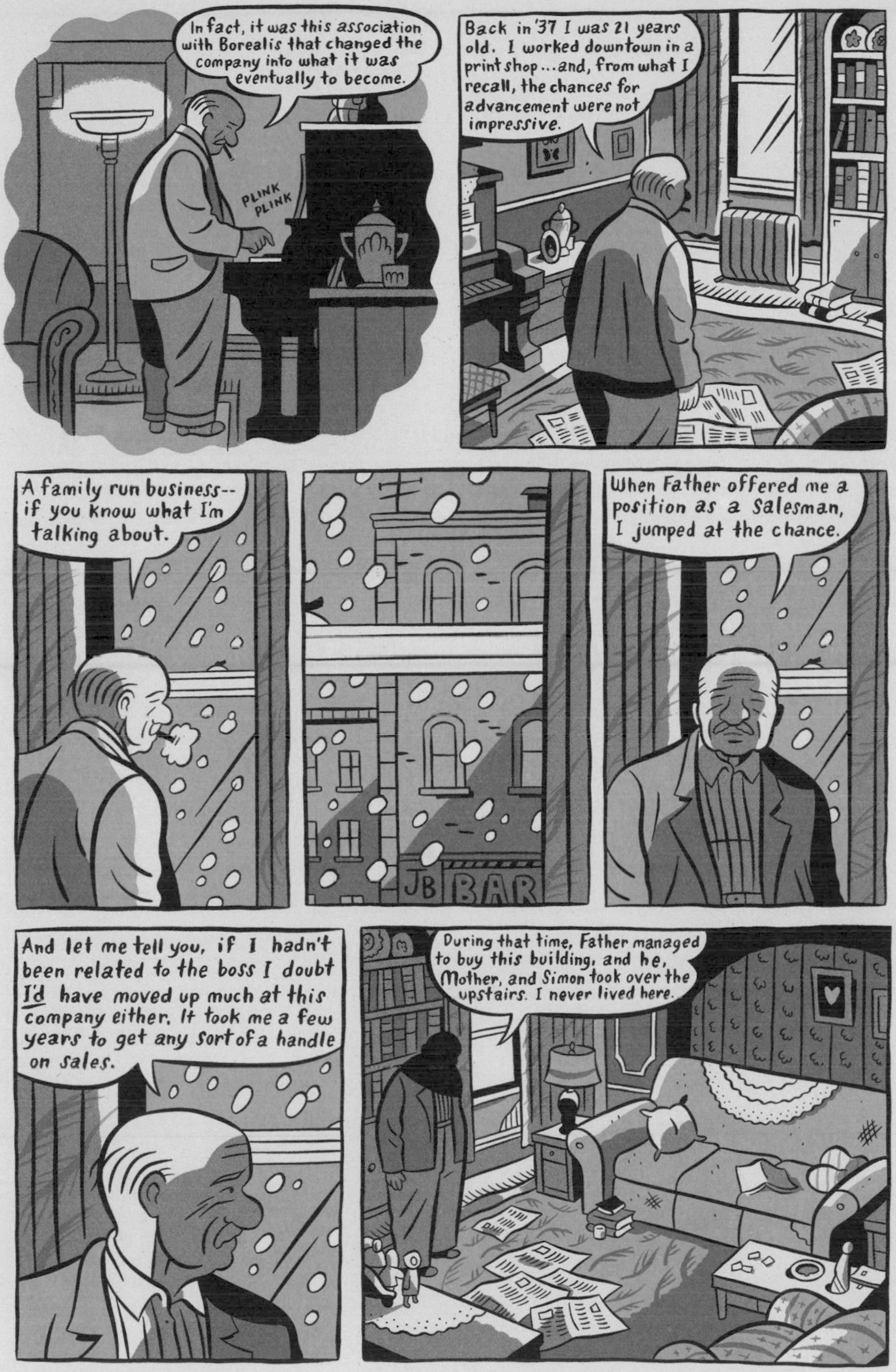
In fact, it was this association with Borealis that changed the company into what it was eventually to become.
PLINK PLINK
Back in '37 I was 21 years old. I worked downtown in a print shop ...and, from what I recall, the chances for advancement were not impressive.
A family run business-- if you know what I'm talking about.
JB BAR
When Father offered me a position as a salesman, I jumped at the chance.
And let me tell you, if I hadn't been related to the boss I doubt I'd have moved up much at this company either. It took me a few years to get any sort of a handle on sales.
During that time, Father managed to buy this building, and he, Mother, and Simon took over the upstairs. I never lived here.

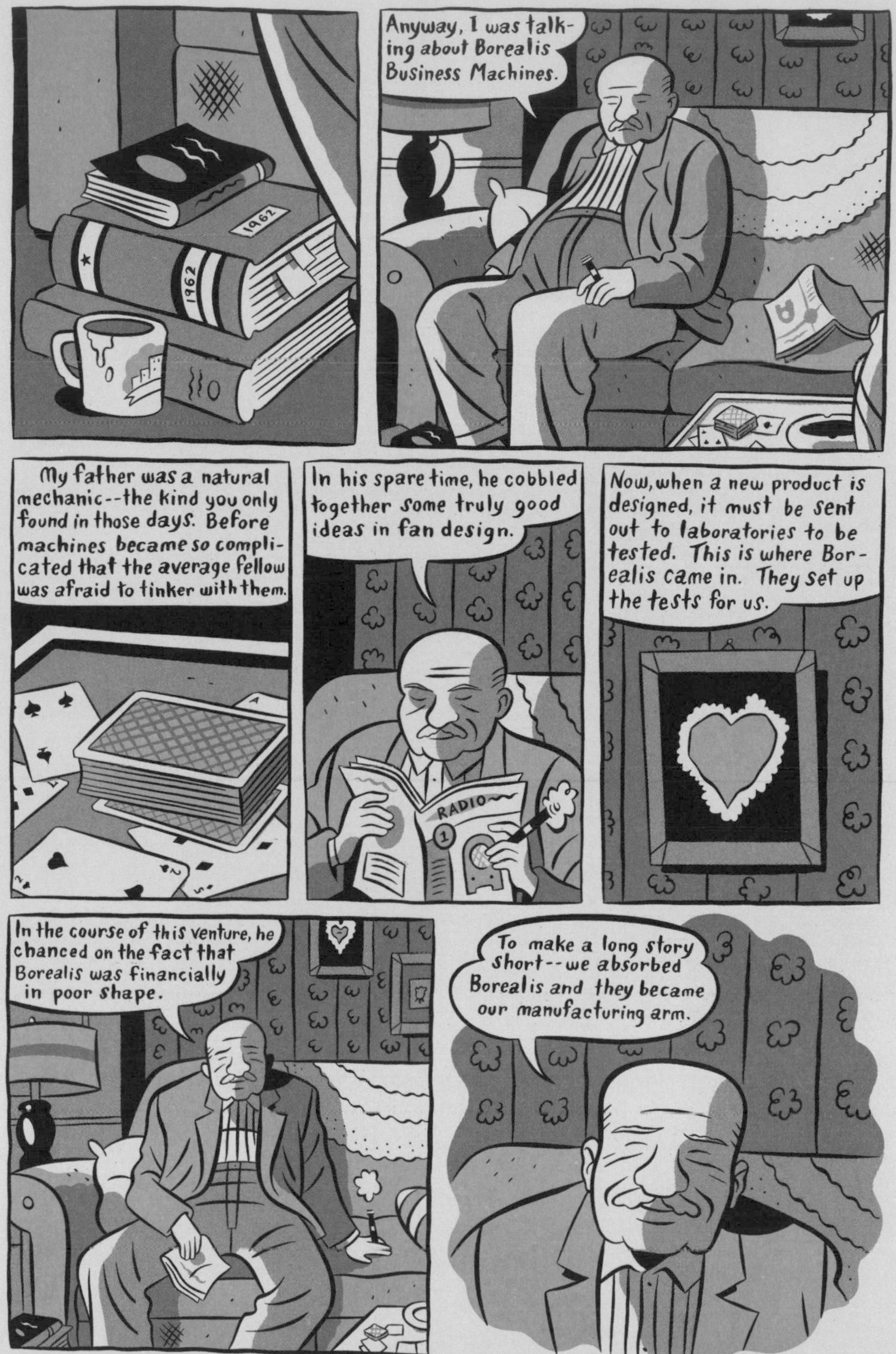

Anyway, I was talking about Borealis Business Machines.
1962
1962
My father was a natural mechanic--the kind you only found in those days. Before machines became so complicated that the average fellow was afraid to tinker with them.
In his spare time, he cobbled together some truly good ideas in fan design.
RADIO
Now, when a new product is designed, it must be sent out to laboratories to be tested. This is where Borealis came in. They set up the tests for us.
In the course of this venture, he chanced on the fact that Borealis was financially in poor shape.
To make a long story short--we absorbed Borealis and they became our manufacturing arm.

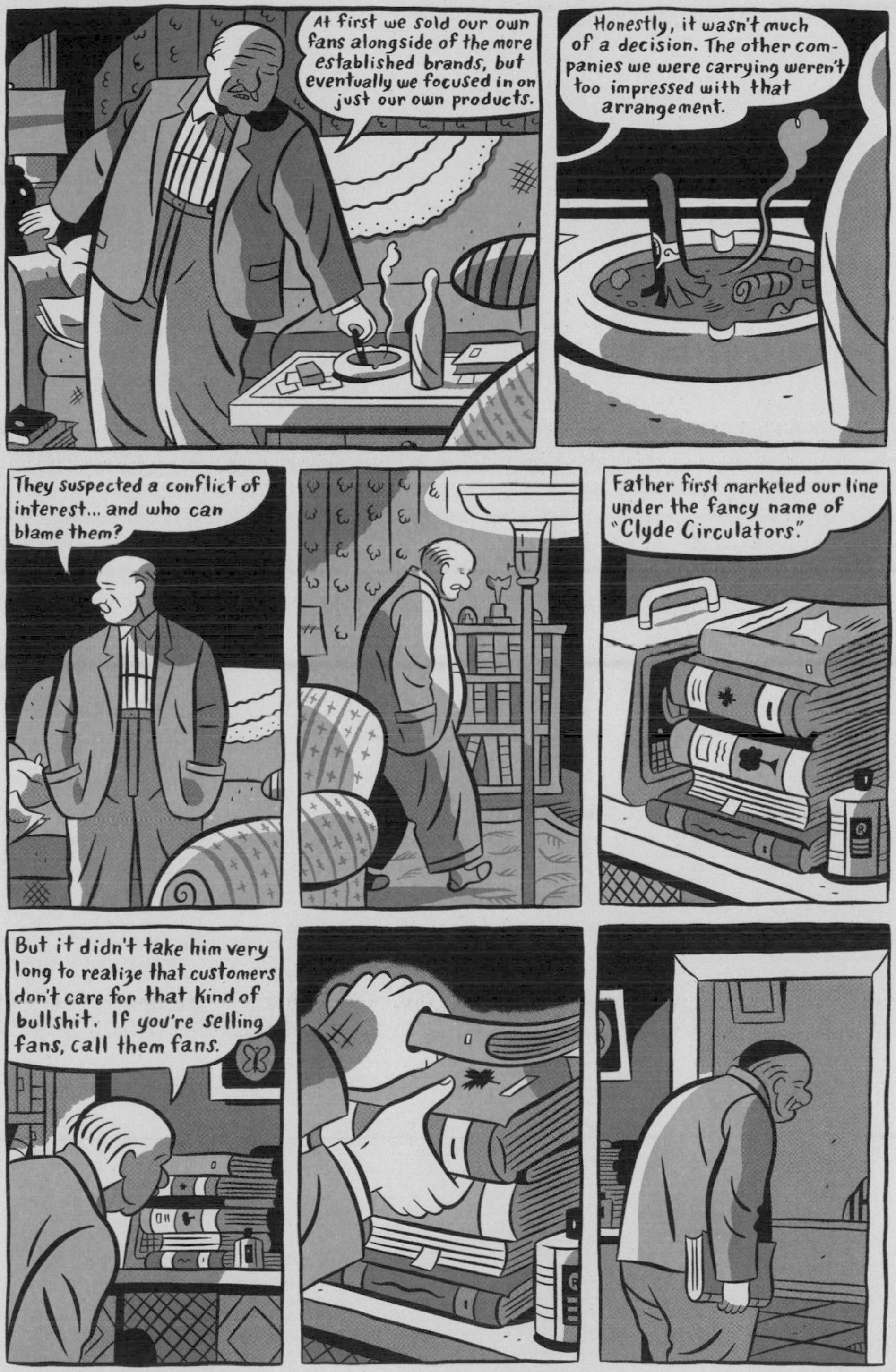
At first we sold our own fans alongside of the more established brands, but eventually we focused in on just our own products.
Honestly, it wasn't much of a decision. The other companies we were carrying weren't too impressed with that arrangement.
They suspected a conflict of interest... and who can blame them?
Father first marketed our line under the fancy name of "Clyde Circulators."
But it didn't take him very long to realize that customers don't care for that kind of bullshit. If you're selling fans, call them fans.

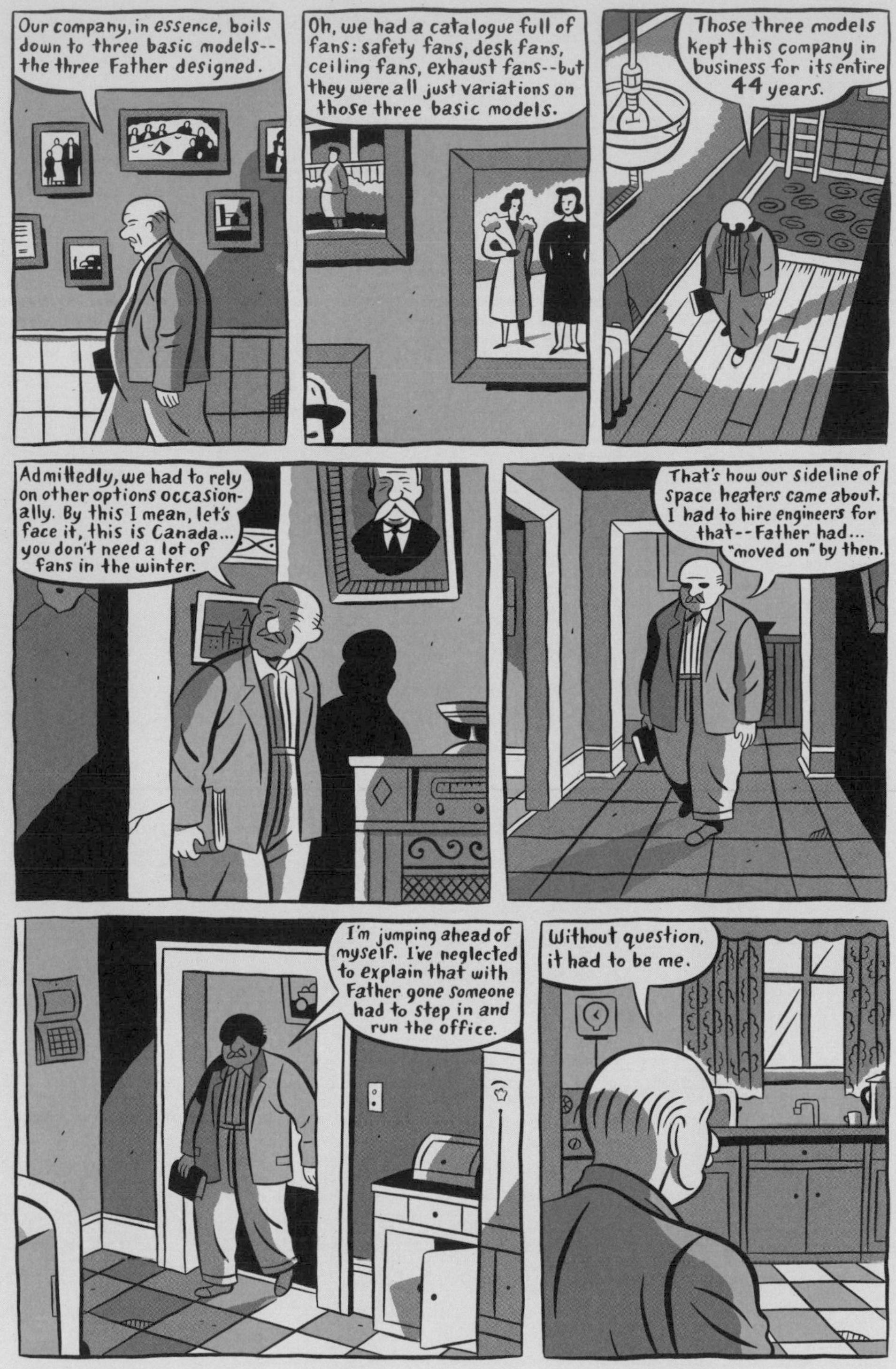
Our company, in essence, boils down to three basic models--the three Father designed.
Oh, we had a catalogue full of fans: safety fans, desk fans, ceiling fans, exhaust fans--but they were all just variations on those three basic models.
Those three models kept this company in business for its entire 44 years.
Admittedly, we had to rely on other options occasionally. By this I mean, let's face it, this is Canada... you don't need a lot of fans in the winter.
That's how our sideline of space heaters came about. I had to hire engineers for that--Father had... "moved on" by then.
I'm jumping ahead of myself. I've neglected to explain that with Father gone someone had to step in and run the office.
Without question, it had to be me.

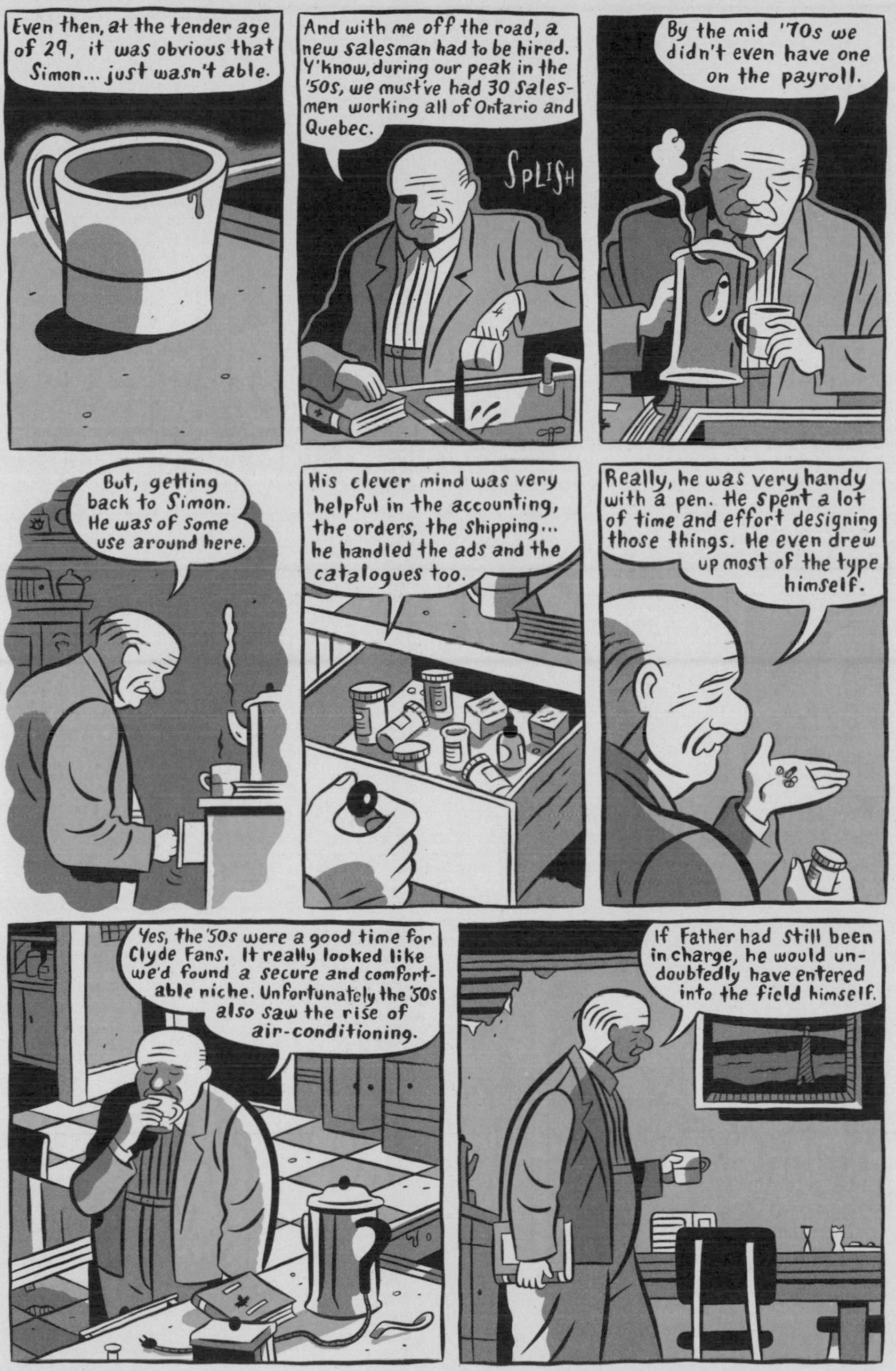

Even then, at the tender age of 29, it was obvious that Simon... just wasn't able.
And with me off the road, a new salesman had to be hired. Y'know, during our peak in the '50s, we must've had 30 salesmen working all of Ontario and Quebec.
SPLISH
By the mid '70s we didn't even have one on the payroll.
But, getting back to Simon. He was of some use around here.
His clever mind was very helpful in the accounting, the orders, the shipping... he handled the ads and the catalogues too.
Really, he was very handy with a pen. He spent a lot of time and effort designing those things. He even drew up most of the type himself.
Yes, the '50s were a good time for Clyde Fans. It really looked like we'd found a secure and comfortable niche. Unfortunately the '50s also saw the rise of air-conditioning.
If Father had still been in charge, he would undoubtedly have entered into the field himself.

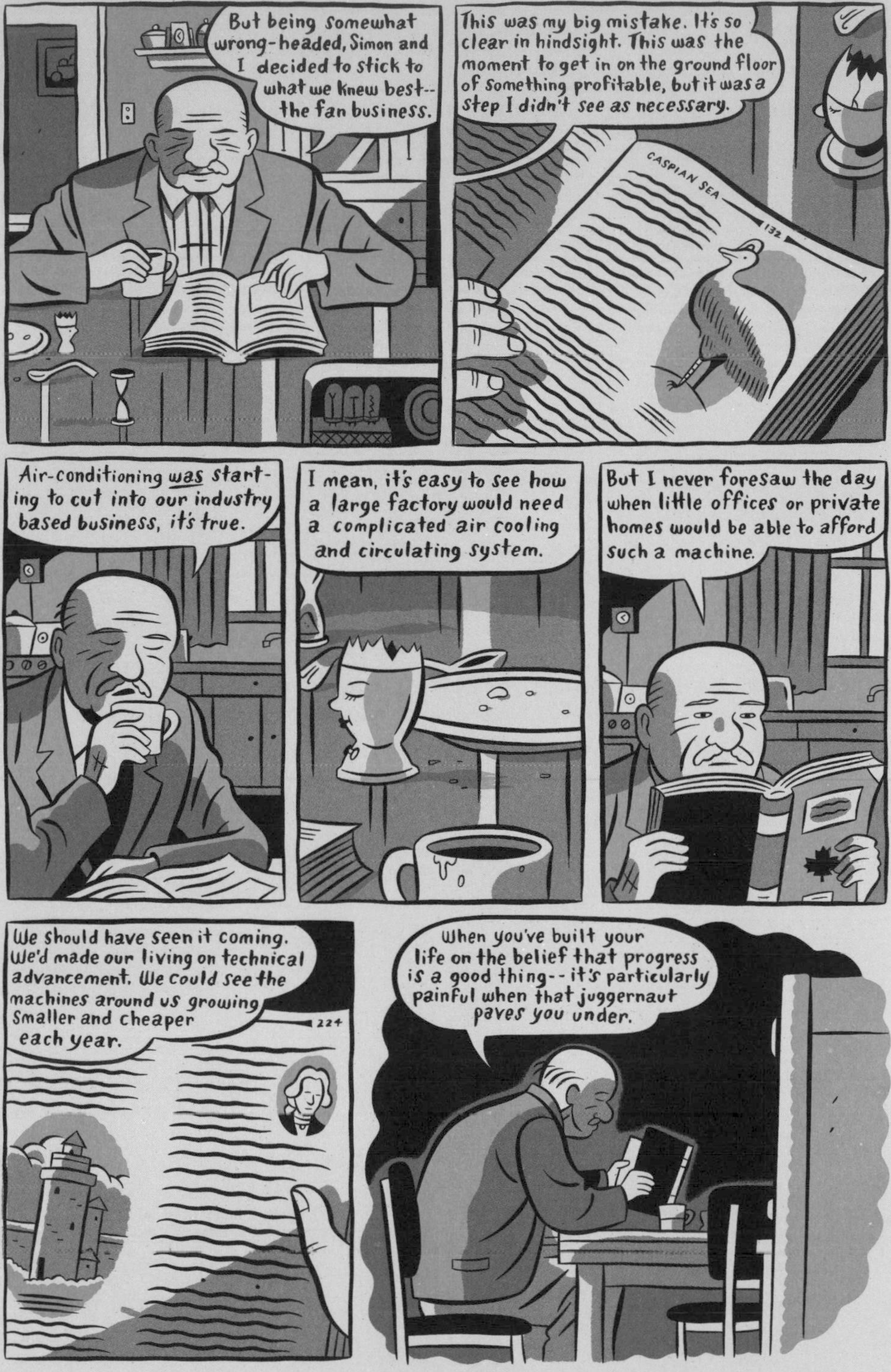

But being somewhat wrong-headed, Simon and I decided to stick to what we knew best-- the fan business.
This was my big mistake. It's so clear in hindsight. This was the moment to get in on the ground floor of something profitable, but it was a step I didn't see as necessary.
CASPIAN SEA
132
Air-conditioning was starting to cut into our industry based business, it's true.
I mean, it's easy to see how a large factory would need a complicated air cooling and circulating system.
But I never foresaw the day when little offices or private homes would be able to afford such a machine.
We should have seen it coming. We'd made our living on technical advancement. We could see the machines around us growing smaller and cheaper each year.
224
When you've built your life on the belief that progress is a good thing-- it's particularly painful when that juggernaut paves you under.

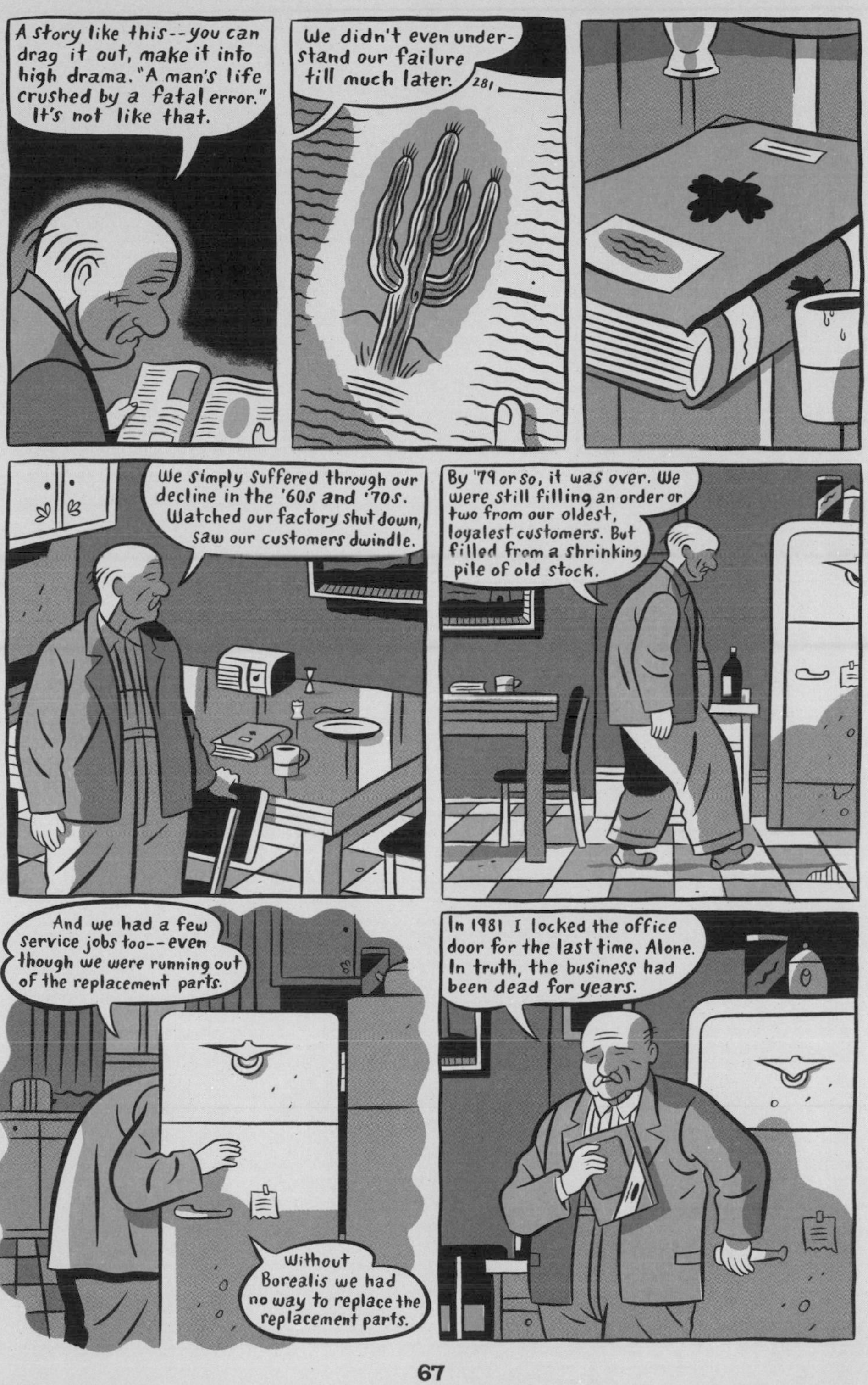
A story like this--you can drag it out, make it into high drama. "A man's life crushed by a fatal error." It's not like that.
We didn't even understand our failure till much later.
281
We simply suffered through our decline in the '60s and '70s. Watched our factory shut down, saw our customers dwindle.
By '79 or so, it was over. We were still filling an order or two from our oldest, loyalest customers. But filled from a shrinking pile of old stock.
And we had a few service jobs too--even though we were running out of the replacement parts.
Without Borealis we had no way to replace the replacement parts.
In 1981 I locked the office door for the last time. Alone. In truth, the business had been dead for years.

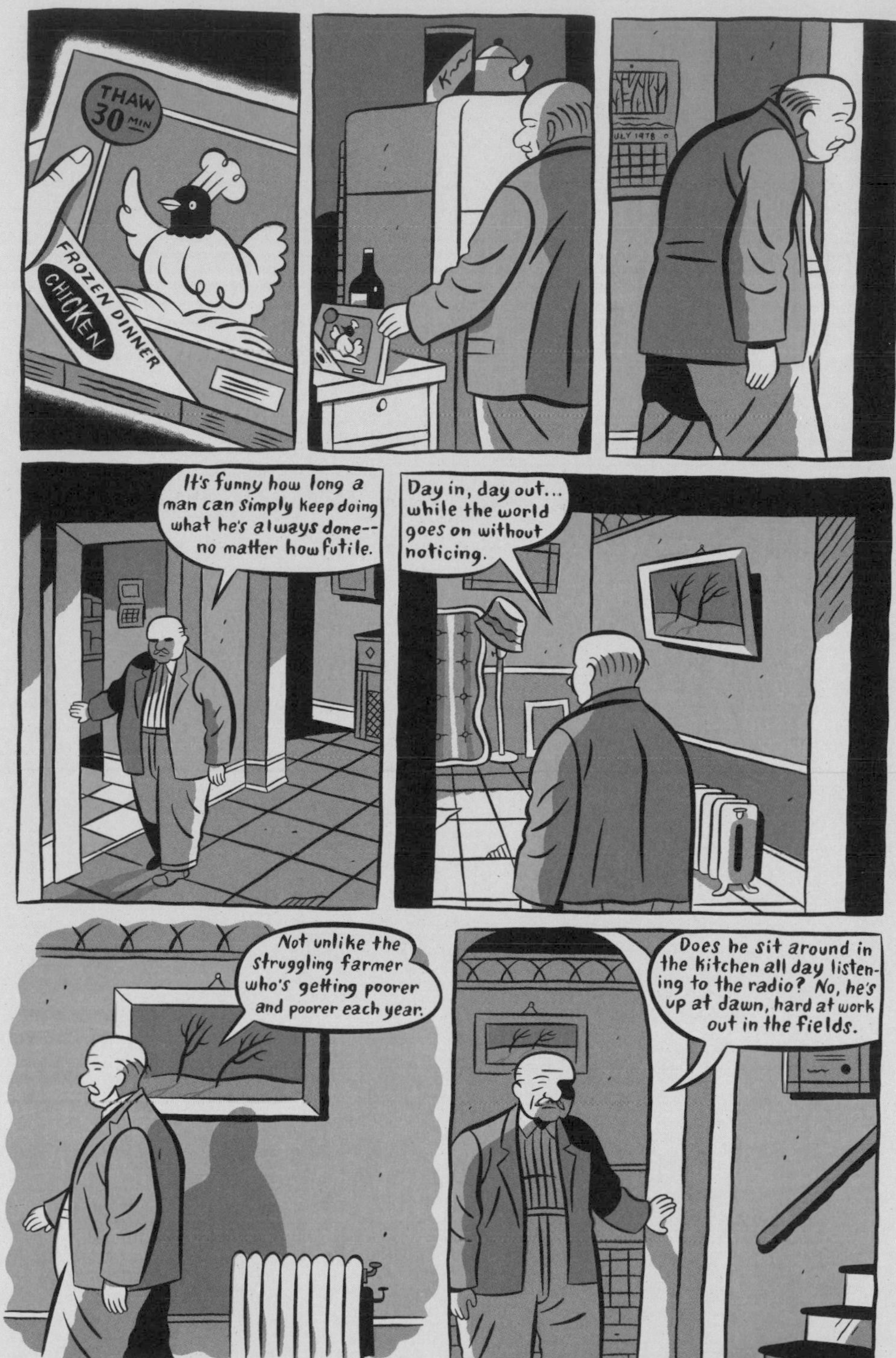
THAW 30 MIN
FROZEN DINNER
CHICKEN
JULY 1978
It's funny how long a man can simply keep doing what he's always done-- no matter how futile.
Day in, day out... while the world goes on without noticing.
Not unlike the struggling farmer who's getting poorer and poorer each year.
Does he sit around in the kitchen all day listening to the radio? No, he's up at dawn, hard at work out in the fields.

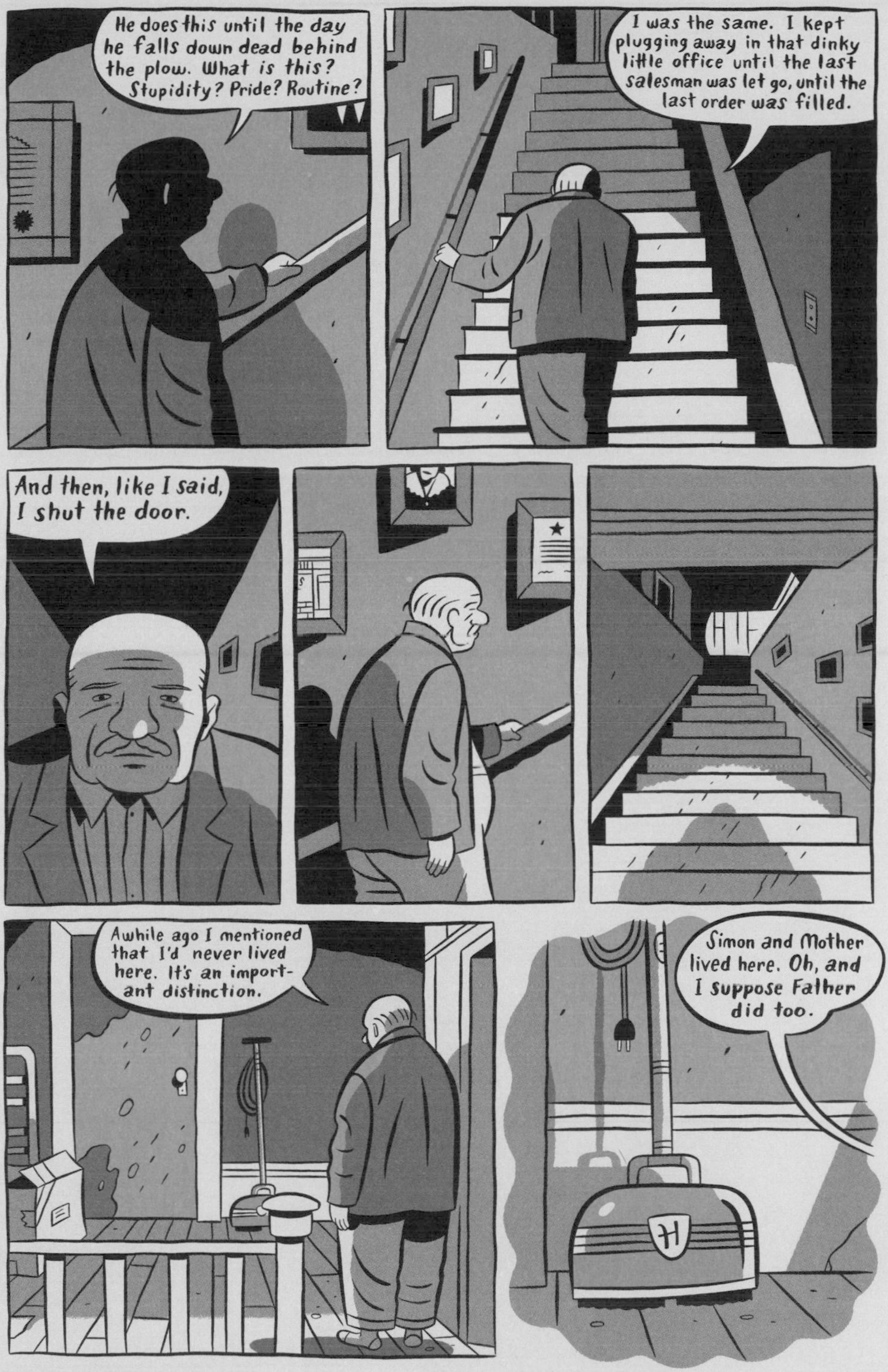
He does this until the day he falls down dead behind the plow. What is this? Stupidity? Pride? Routine?
I was the same. I kept plugging away in that dinky little office until the last salesman was let go, until the last order was filled.
And then, like I said, I shut the door.
Awhile ago I mentioned that I'd never lived here. It's an important distinction.
Simon and Mother lived here. Oh, and I suppose Father did too.

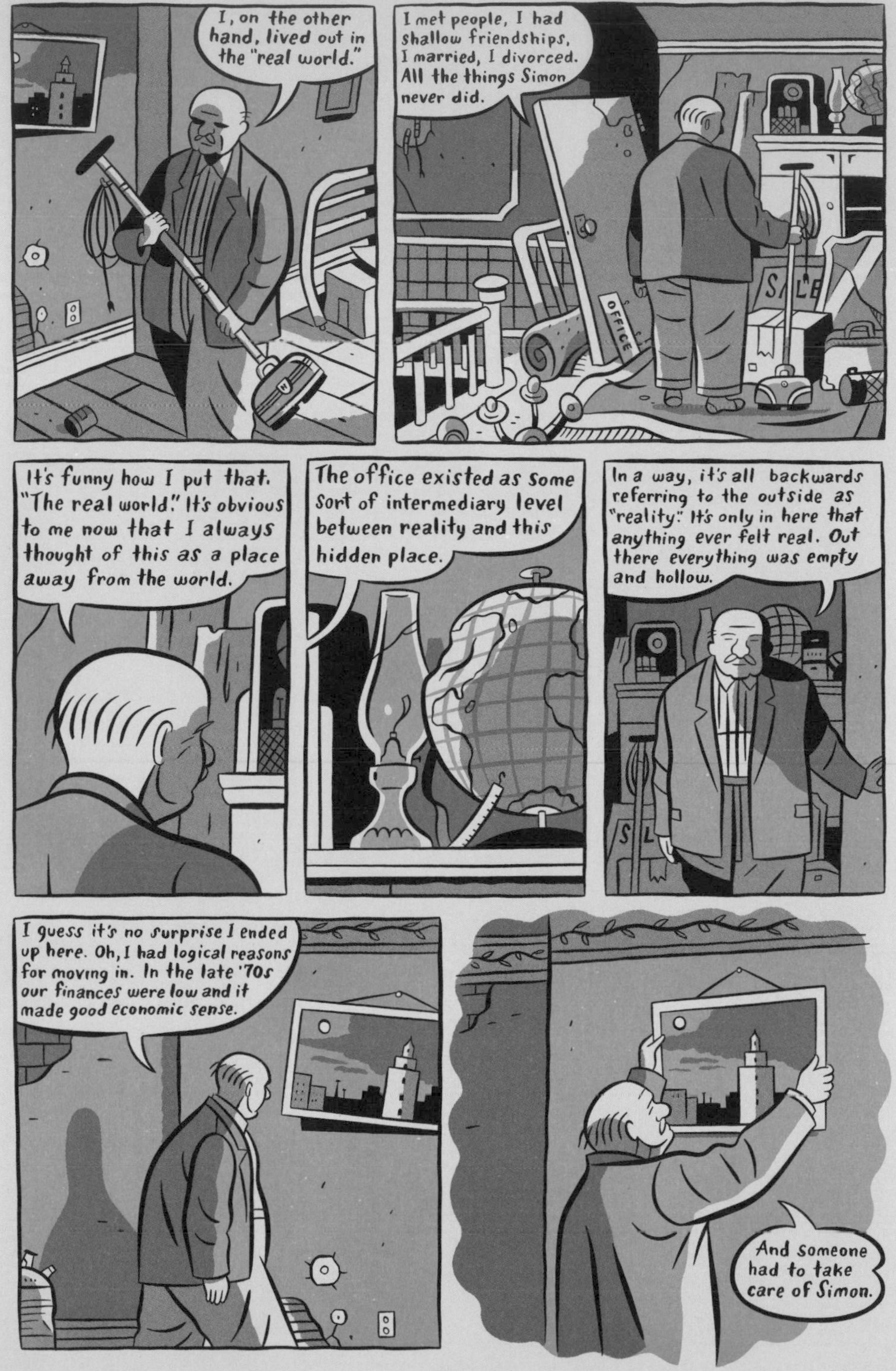
I, on the other hand, lived out in the "real world."
I met people, I had shallow friendships, I married, I divorced. All the things Simon never did.
OFFICE
SALE
It's funny how I put that. "The real world." It's obvious to me now that I always thought of this as a place away from the world.
The office existed as some sort of intermediary level between reality and this hidden place.
In a way, it's all backwards referring to the outside as "reality." It's only in here that anything ever felt real. Out there everything was empty and hollow.
I guess it's no surprise I ended up here. Oh, I had logical reasons for moving in. In the late '70s our finances were low and it made good economic sense.
And someone had to take care of Simon.

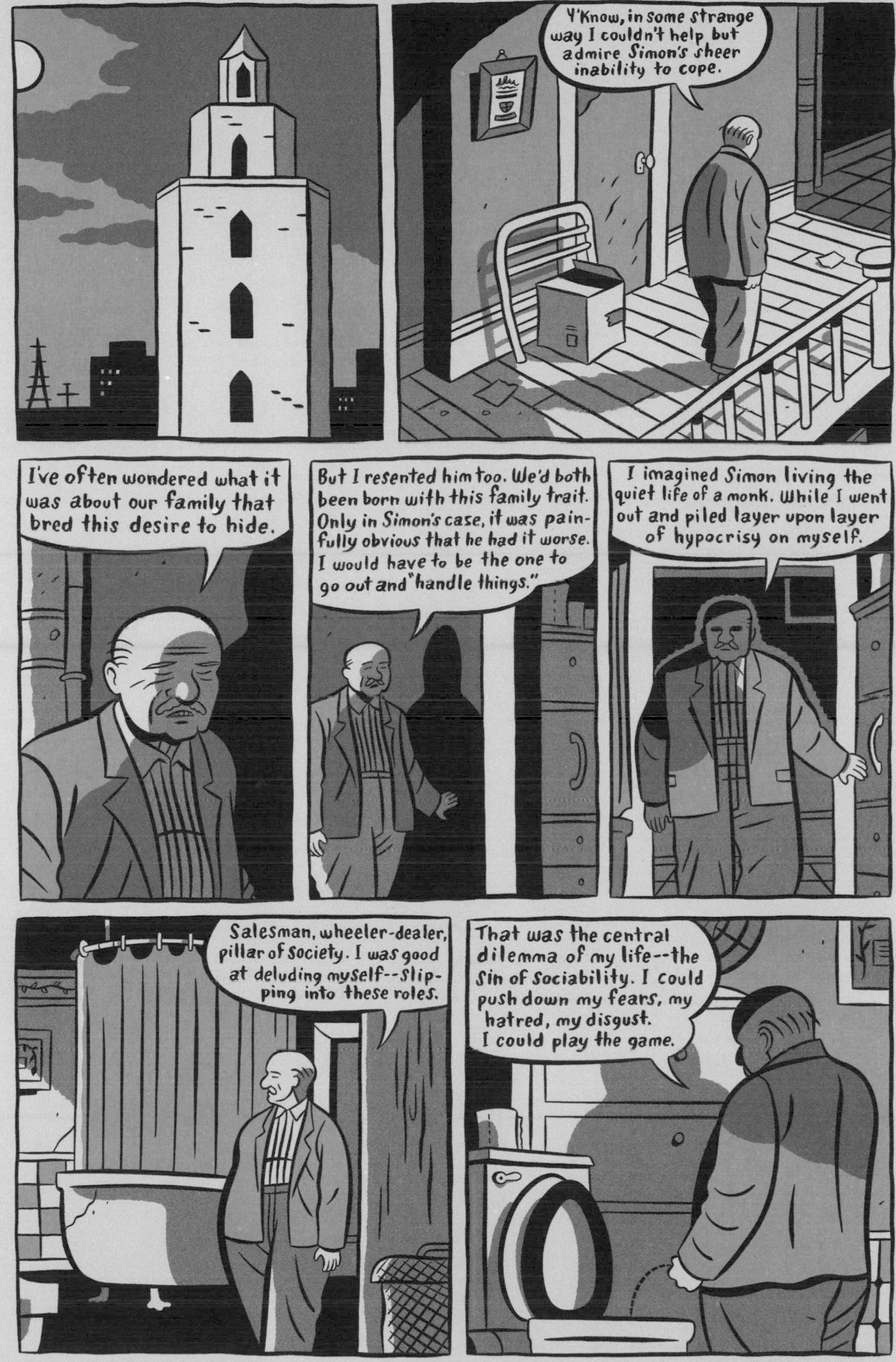
Y'Know, in some strange way I couldn't help but admire Simon's sheer inability to cope.
I've often wondered what it was about our family that bred this desire to hide.
But I resented him too. We'd both been born with this family trait. Only in Simon's case, it was painfully obvious that he had it worse. I would have to be the one to go out and "handle things."
I imagined Simon living the quiet life of a monk. While I went out and piled layer upon layer of hypocrisy on myself.
Salesman, wheeler-dealer, pillar of society. I was good at deluding myself--slipping into these roles.
That was the central dilemma of my life--the Sin of Sociability. I could push down my fears, my hatred, my disgust. I could play the game.

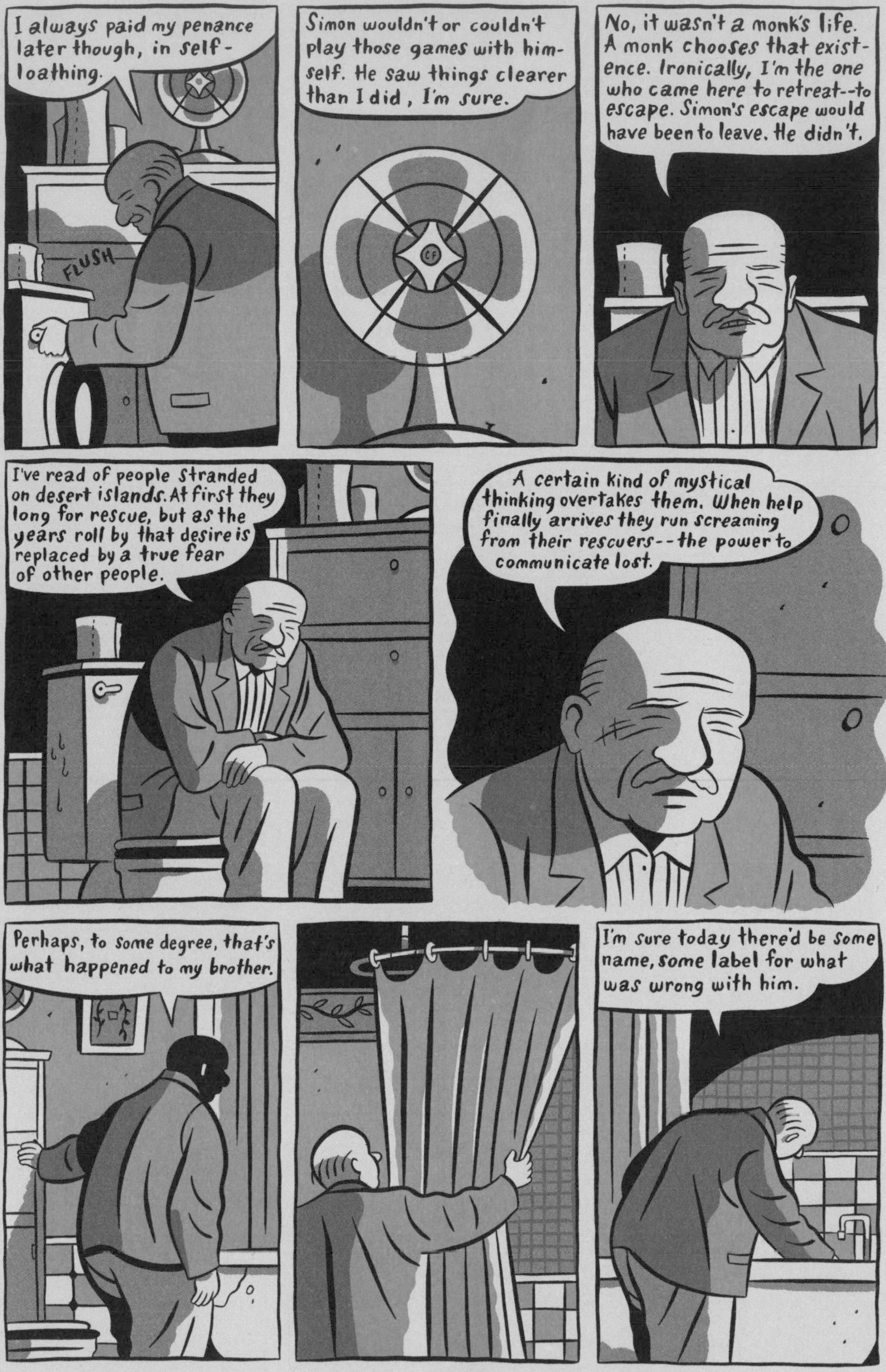
I always paid my penance later though, in self-loathing.
FLUSH
Simon wouldn't or couldn't play those games with himself. He saw things clearer than I did, I'm sure.
No, it wasn't a monk's life. A monk chooses that existence. Ironically, I'm the one who came here to retreat--to escape. Simon's escape would have been to leave. He didn't.
I've read of people stranded on desert islands. At first they long for rescue, but as the years roll by that desire is replaced by a true fear of other people.
A certain kind of mystical thinking overtakes them. When help finally arrives they run screaming from their rescuers--the power to communicate lost.
Perhaps, to some degree, that's what happened to my brother.
I'm sure today there'd be some name, some label for what was wrong with him.

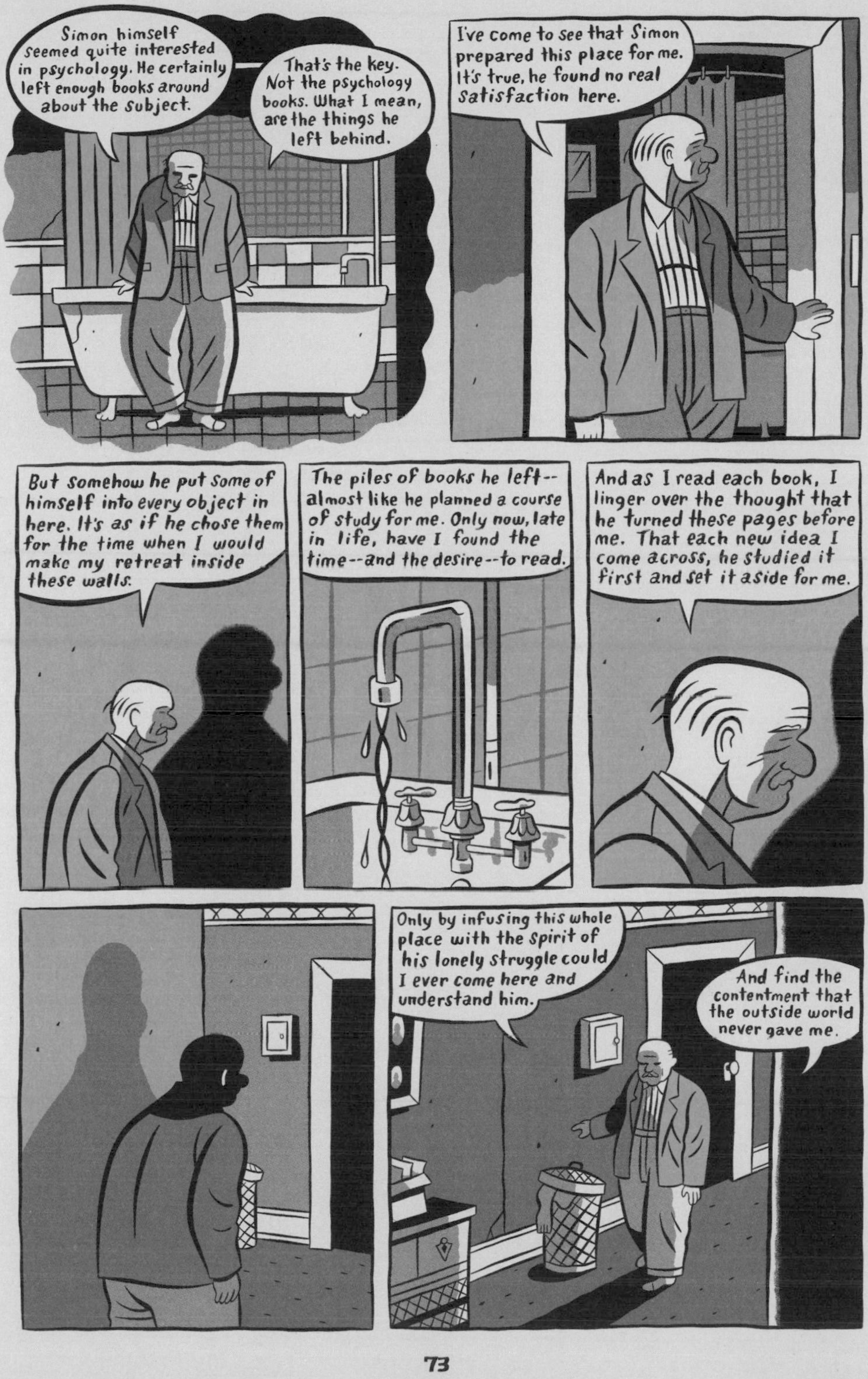
Simon himself seemed quite interested in psychology. He certainly left enough books around about the subject.
That's the key. Not the psychology books. What I mean, are the things he left behind.
I've come to see that Simon prepared this place for me. It's true, he found no real satisfaction here.
But somehow he put some of himself into every object in here. It's as if he chose them for the time when I would make my retreat inside these walls.
The piles of books he left--almost like he planned a course of study for me. Only now, late in life, have I found the time--and the desire--to read.
And as I read each book, I linger over the thought that he turned these pages before me. That each new idea I come across, he studied it first and set it aside for me.
Only by infusing this whole place with the spirit of his lonely struggle could I ever come here and understand him.
And find the contentment that the outside world never gave me.

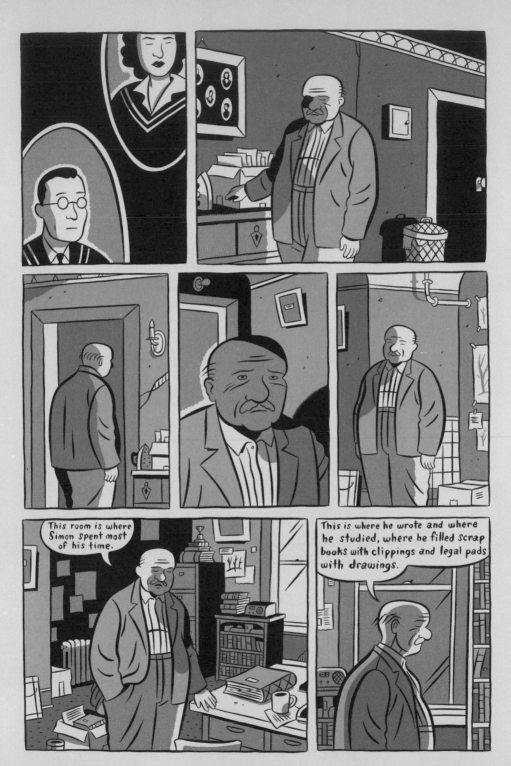

This room is where Simon spent most of his time.

This is where he wrote and where he studied, where he filled scrap books with clippings and legal pads with drawings.

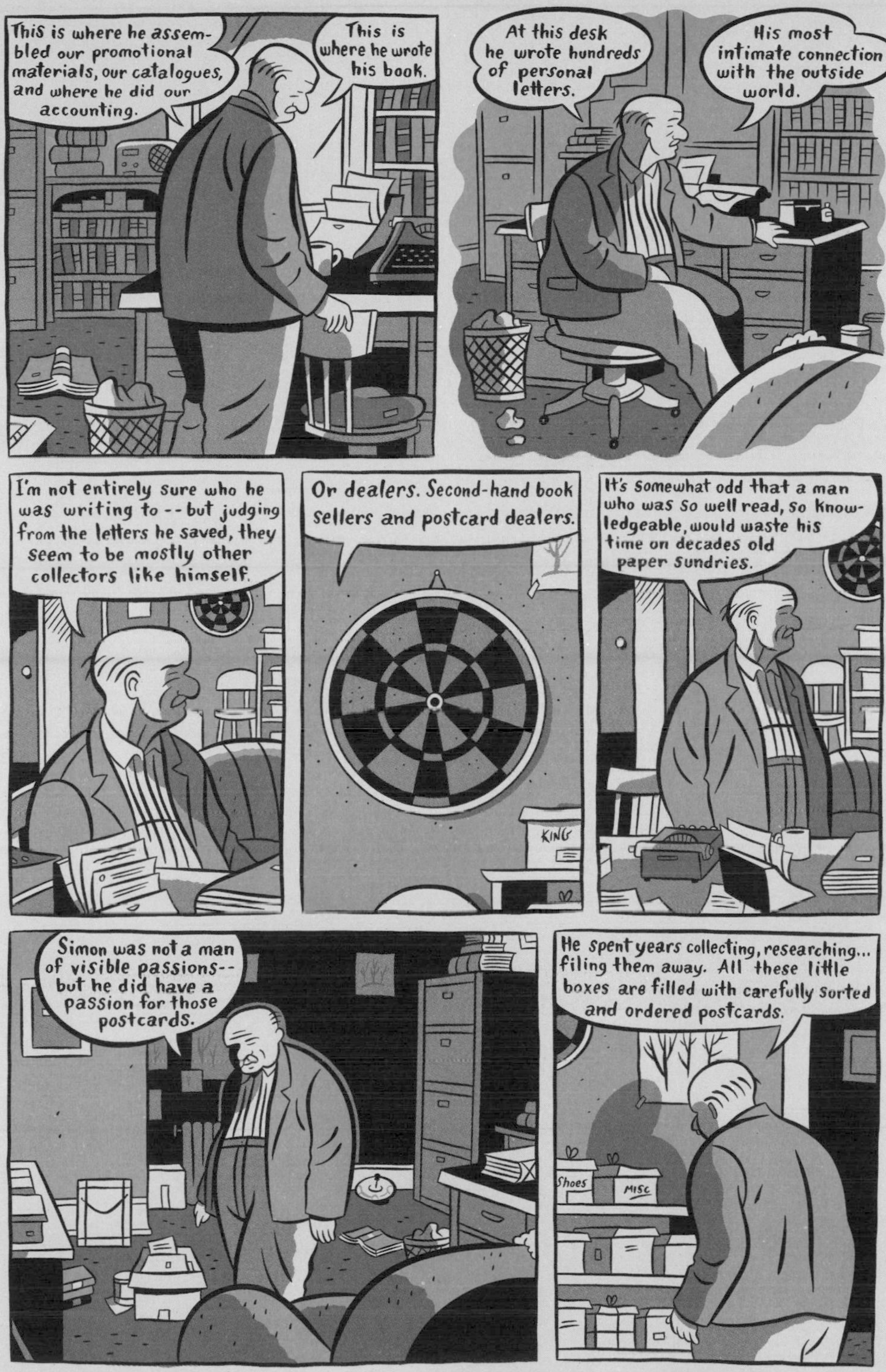
This is where he assembled our promotional materials, our catalogues, and where he did our accounting.
This is where he wrote his book.
At this desk he wrote hundreds of personal letters.
His most intimate connection with the outside world.
I'm not entirely sure who he was writing to -- but judging from the letters he saved, they seem to be mostly other collectors like himself.
Or dealers. Second-hand book sellers and postcard dealers.
KING
It's somewhat odd that a man who was so well read, so knowledgeable, would waste his time on decades old paper sundries.
Simon was not a man of visible passions-- but he did have a passion for those postcards.
He spent years collecting, researching... filing them away. All these little boxes are filled with carefully sorted and ordered postcards.
Shoes
MISC

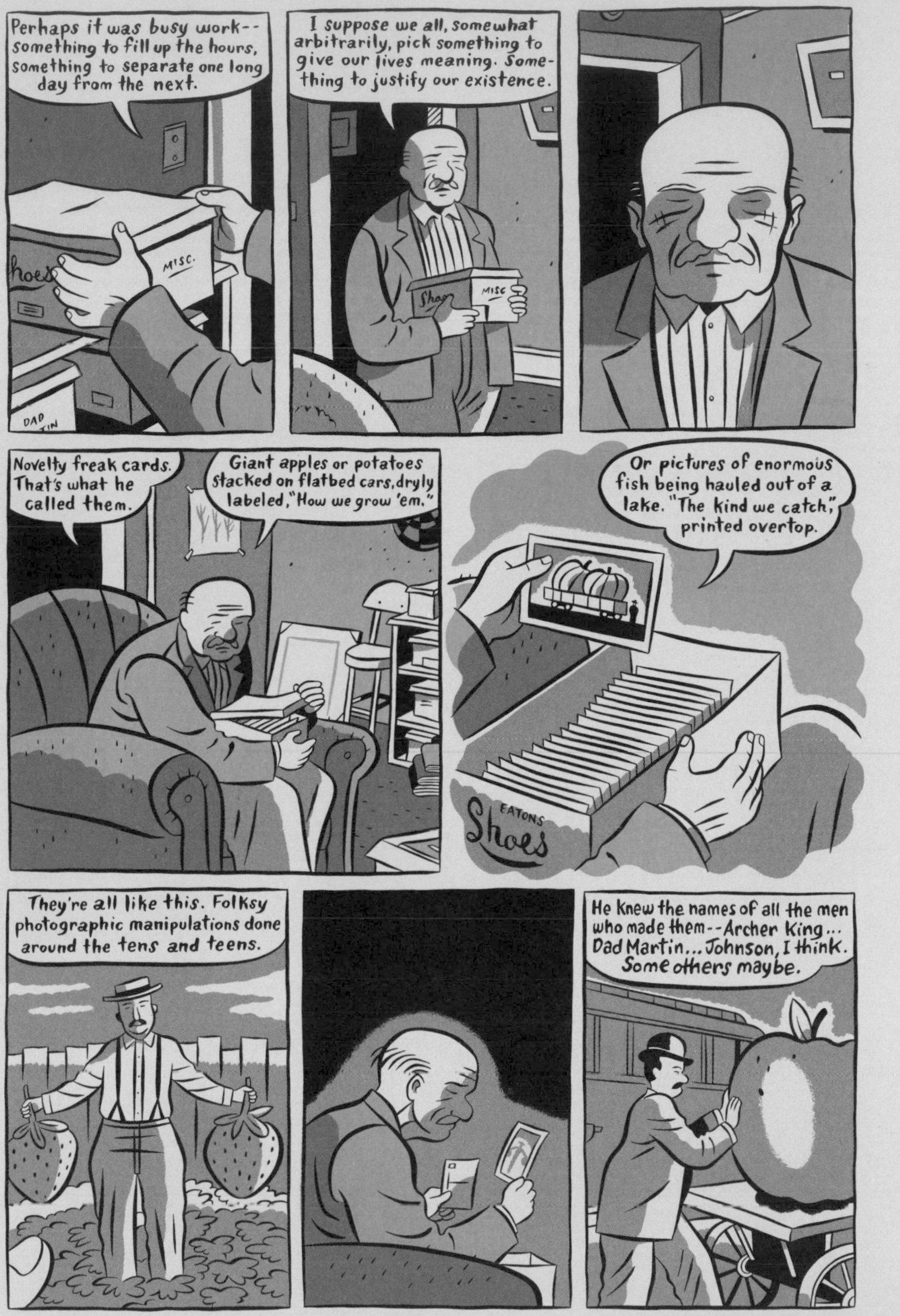
Perhaps it was busy work--something to fill up the hours, something to separate one long day from the next.
Shoes
MISC.
DAD
I suppose we all, somewhat arbitrarily, pick something to give our lives meaning. Something to justify our existence.
Shoes
MISC
Novelty freak cards. That's what he called them.
Giant apples or potatoes stacked on flatbed cars, dryly labeled, "How we grow 'em."
Or pictures of enormous fish being hauled out of a lake. "The kind we catch," printed overtop.
EATONS
Shoes
They're all like this. Folksy photographic manipulations done around the tens and teens.
He knew the names of all the men who made them--Archer King... Dad Martin... Johnson, I think. Some others maybe.

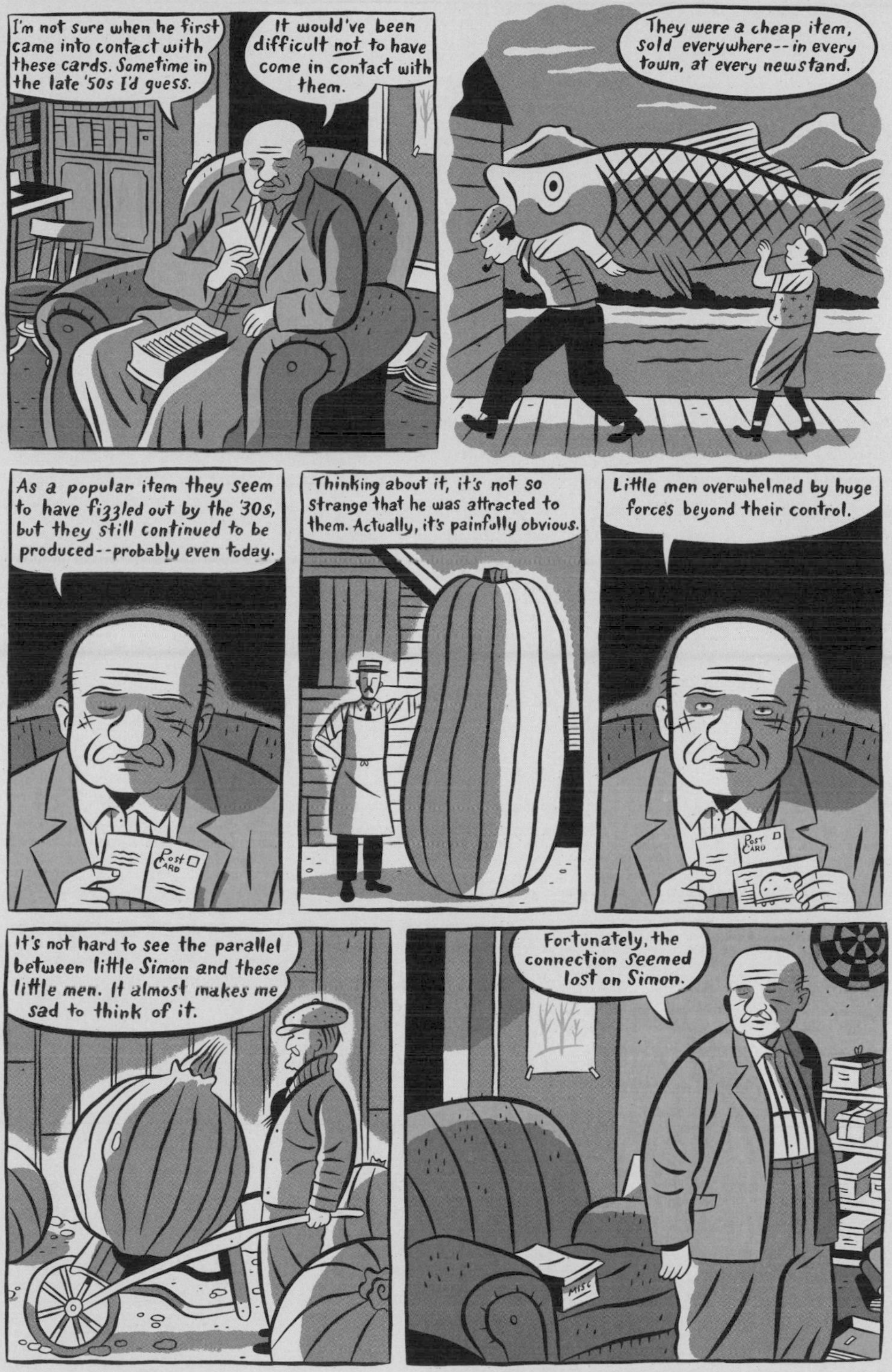
I'm not sure when he first came into contact with these cards. Sometime in the late '50s I'd guess.
It would've been difficult not to have come in contact with them.
They were a cheap item, sold everywhere--in every town, at every newstand.
As a popular item they seem to have fizzled out by the '30s, but they still continued to be produced--probably even today.
Post Card
Thinking about it, it's not so strange that he was attracted to them. Actually, it's painfully obvious.
Little men overwhelmed by huge forces beyond their control.
Post Card
It's not hard to see the parallel between little Simon and these little men. It almost makes me sad to think of it.
Fortunately, the connection seemed lost on Simon.
MISC

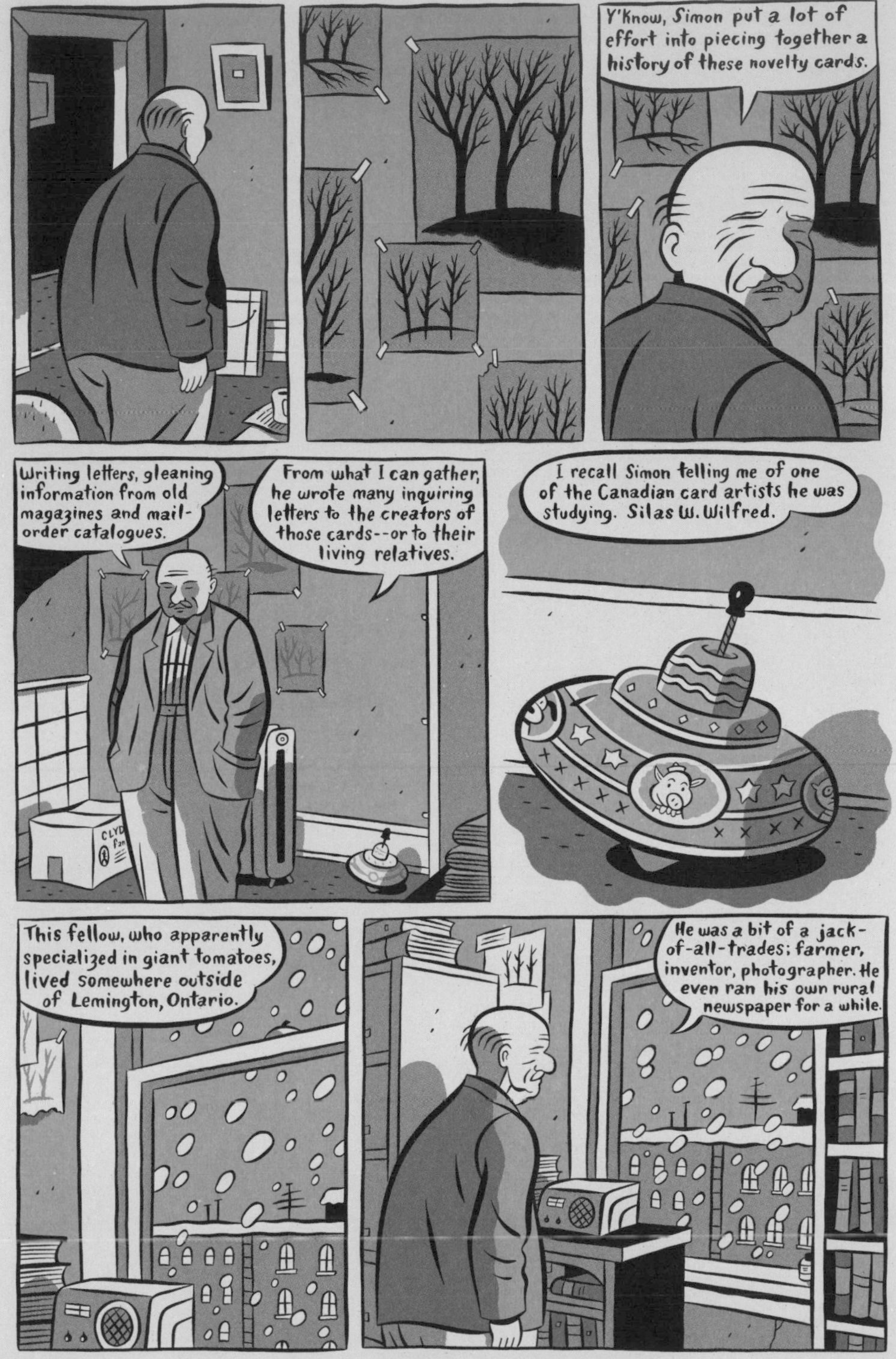
Y'Know, Simon put a lot of effort into piecing together a history of these novelty cards.
Writing letters, gleaning information from old magazines and mail-order catalogues.
From what I can gather, he wrote many inquiring letters to the creators of those cards--or to their living relatives.
I recall Simon telling me of one of the Canadian card artists he was studying. Silas W. Wilfred.
This fellow, who apparently specialized in giant tomatoes, lived somewhere outside of Lemington, Ontario.
He was a bit of a jack-of-all-trades; farmer, inventor, photographer. He even ran his own rural newspaper for a while.

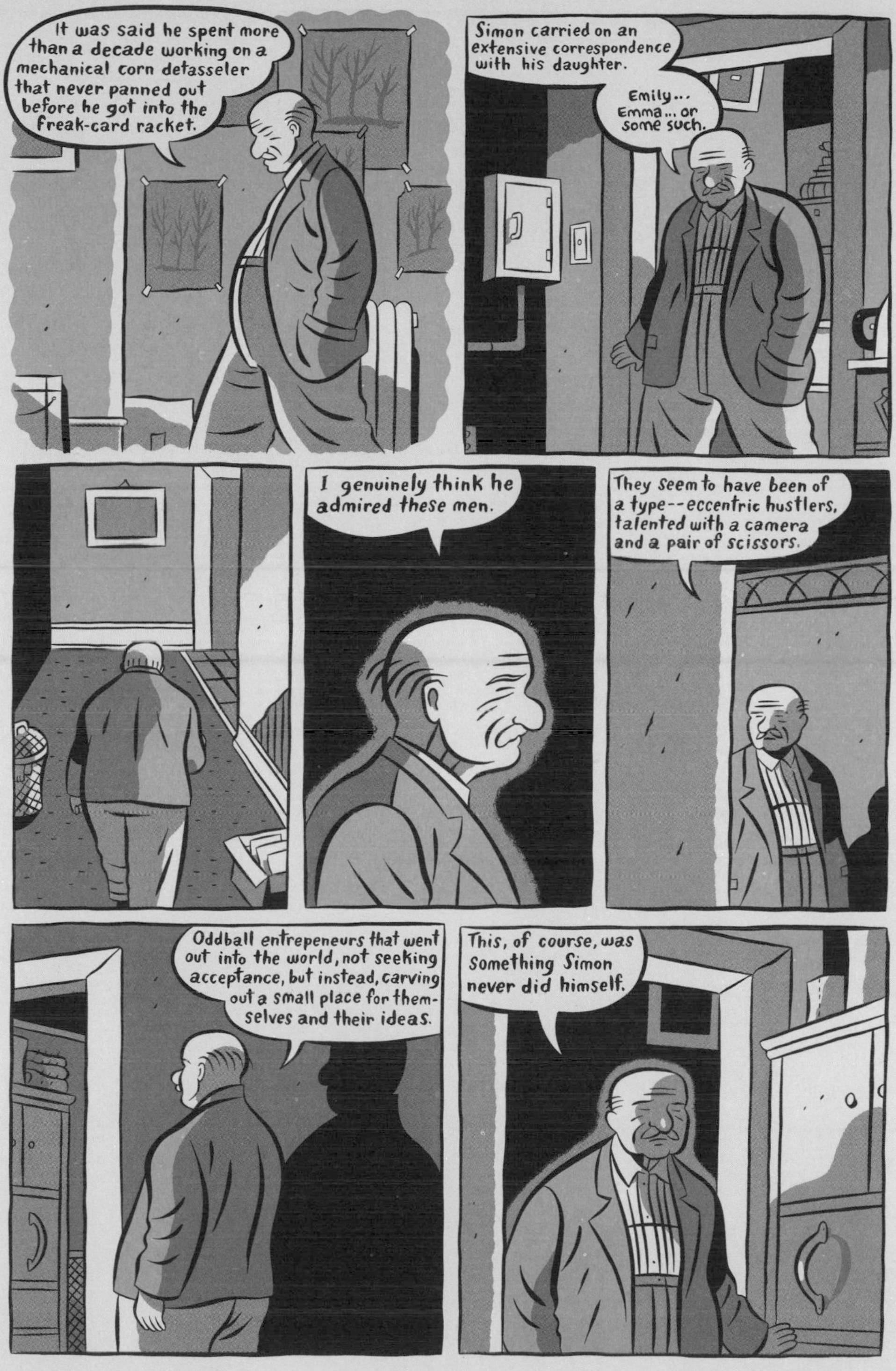

It was said he spent more than a decade working on a mechanical corn detasseler that never panned out before he got into the freak-card racket.
Simon carried on an extensive correspondence with his daughter.
Emily... Emma... or some such.
I genuinely think he admired these men.
They seem to have been of a type--eccentric hustlers, talented with a camera and a pair of scissors.
Oddball entrepeneurs that went out into the world, not seeking acceptance, but instead, carving out a small place for themselves and their ideas.
This, of course, was something Simon never did himself.

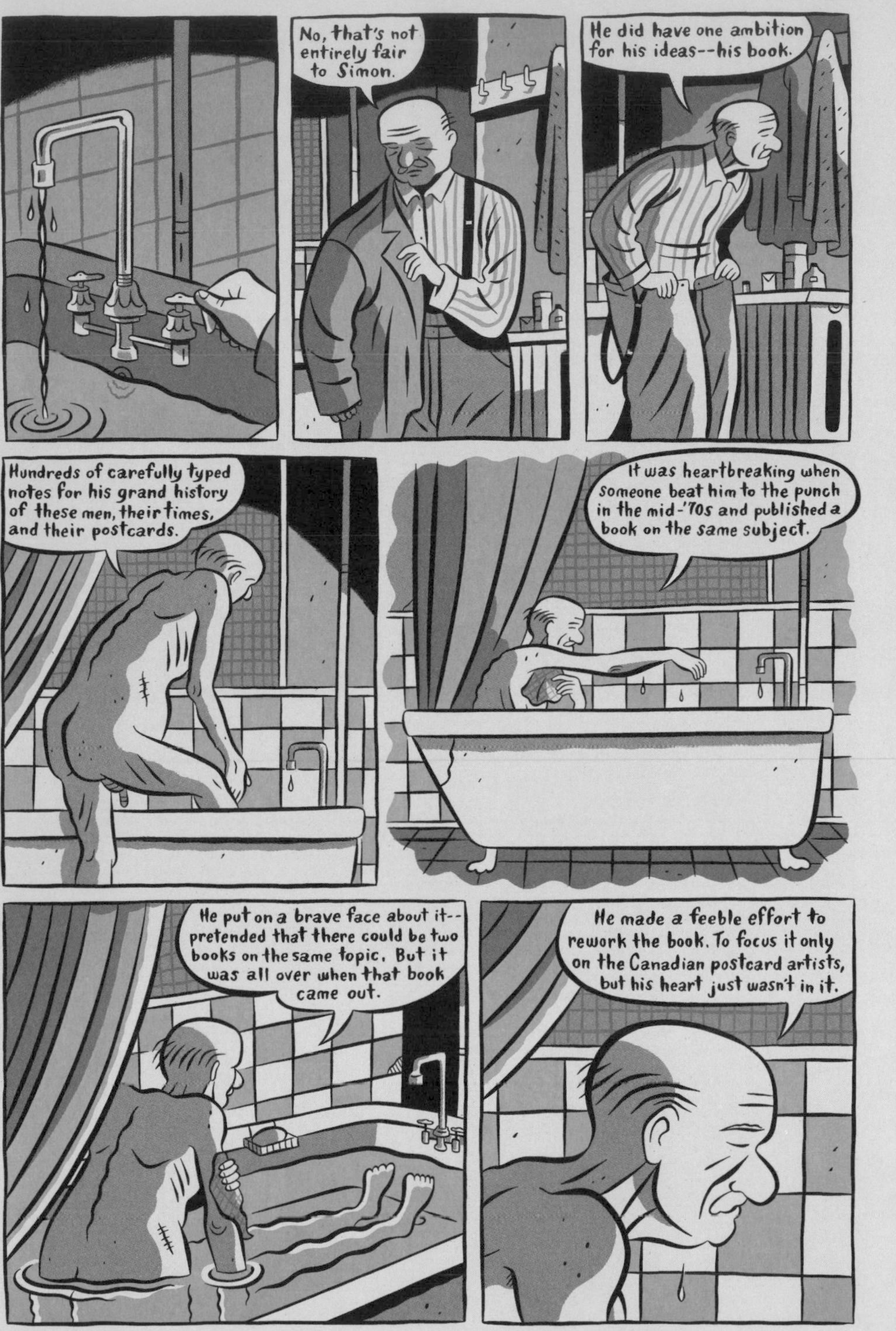
No, that's not entirely fair to Simon.
He did have one ambition for his ideas--his book.
Hundreds of carefully typed notes for his grand history of these men, their times, and their postcards.
It was heartbreaking when someone beat him to the punch in the mid-'70s and published a book on the same subject.
He put on a brave face about it--pretended that there could be two books on the same topic. But it was all over when that book came out.
He made a feeble effort to rework the book. To focus it only on the Canadian postcard artists, but his heart just wasn't in it.

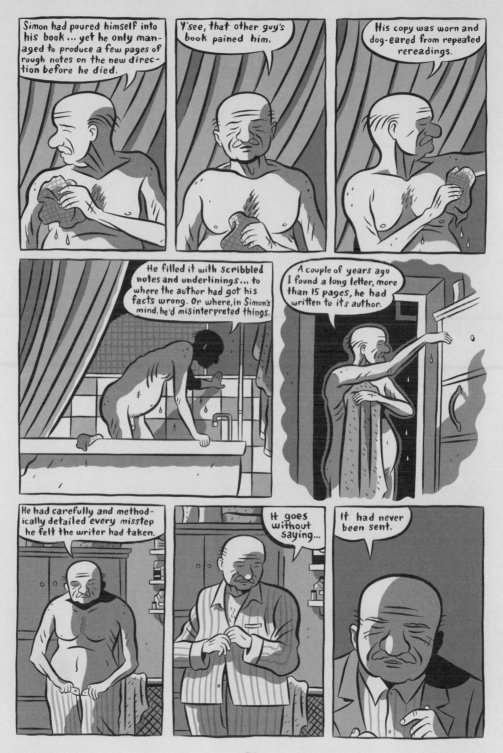

Simon had poured himself into his book... yet he only managed to produce a few pages of rough notes on the new direction before he died.

Y'see, that other guy's book pained him.

His copy was worn and dog-eared from repeated rereadings.

He filled it with scribbled notes and underlinings... to where the author had got his facts wrong. Or where, in Simon's mind, he'd misinterpreted things.

A couple of years ago I found a long letter, more than 15 pages, he had written to its author.

He had carefully and methodically detailed every misstep he felt the writer had taken.

It goes without saying...

It had never been sent.

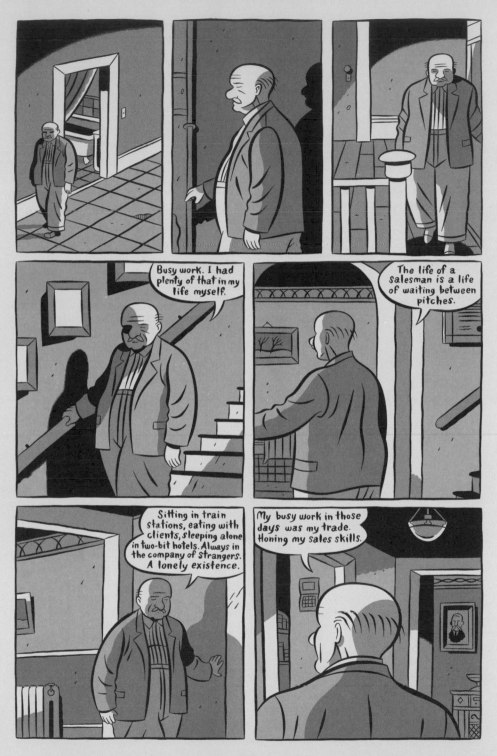

Busy work. I had plenty of that in my life myself.

The life of a salesman is a life of waiting between pitches.

Sitting in train stations, eating with clients, sleeping alone in two-bit hotels. Always in the company of strangers. A lonely existence.

My busy work in those days was my trade. Honing my sales skills.

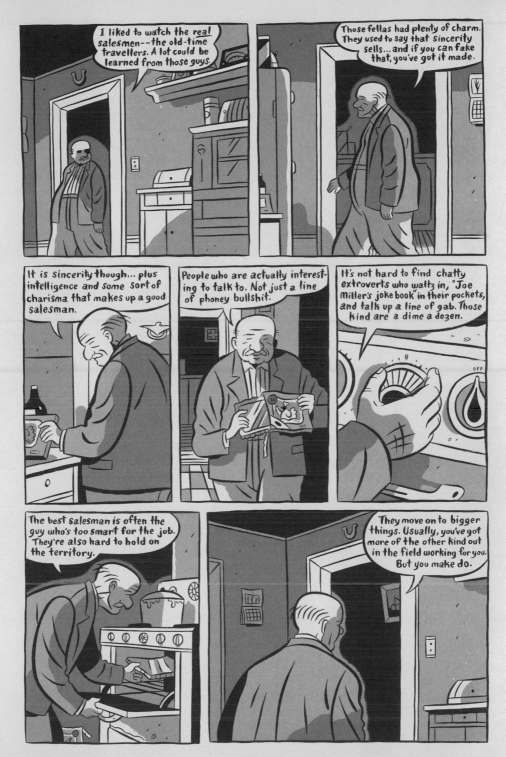

I liked to watch the _real_ salesmen—the old-time travellers. A lot could be learned from those guys.

Those fellas had plenty of charm. They used to say that sincerity sells...and if you can fake that, you've got it made.

It is sincerity though... plus intelligence and some sort of charisma that makes up a good salesman.

People who are actually interesting to talk to. Not just a line of phoney bullshit.

It's not hard to find chatty extroverts who waltz in, "Joe Miller's joke book" in their pockets, and talk up a line of gab. Those kind are a dime a dozen.

The best salesman is often the guy who's too smart for the job. They're also hard to hold on the territory.

They move on to bigger things. Usually, you've got more of the other kind out in the field working for you. But you make do.

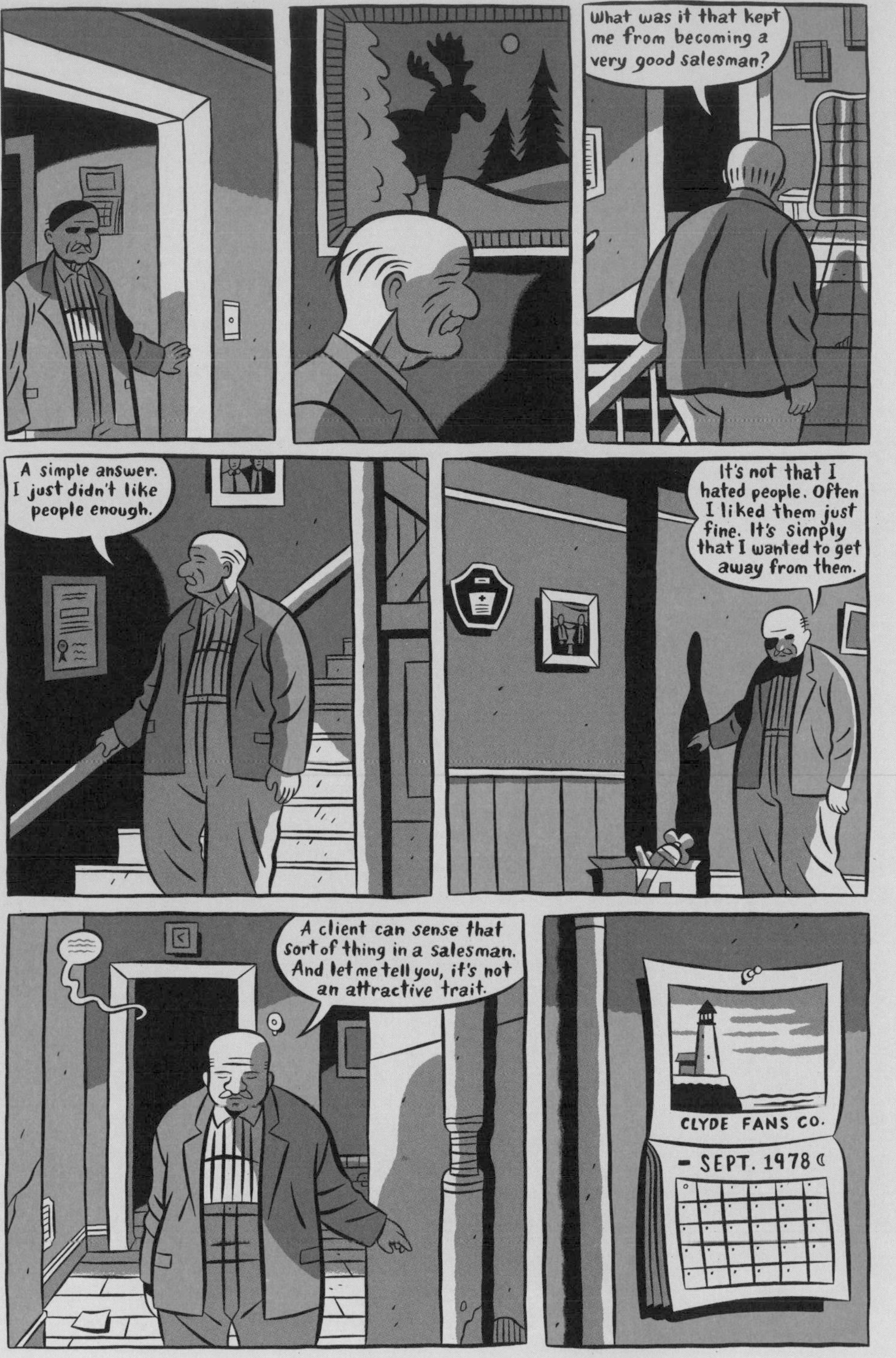
What was it that kept me from becoming a very good salesman?
A simple answer. I just didn't like people enough.
It's not that I hated people. Often I liked them just fine. It's simply that I wanted to get away from them.
A client can sense that sort of thing in a salesman. And let me tell you, it's not an attractive trait.
CLYDE FANS CO.
SEPT. 1978

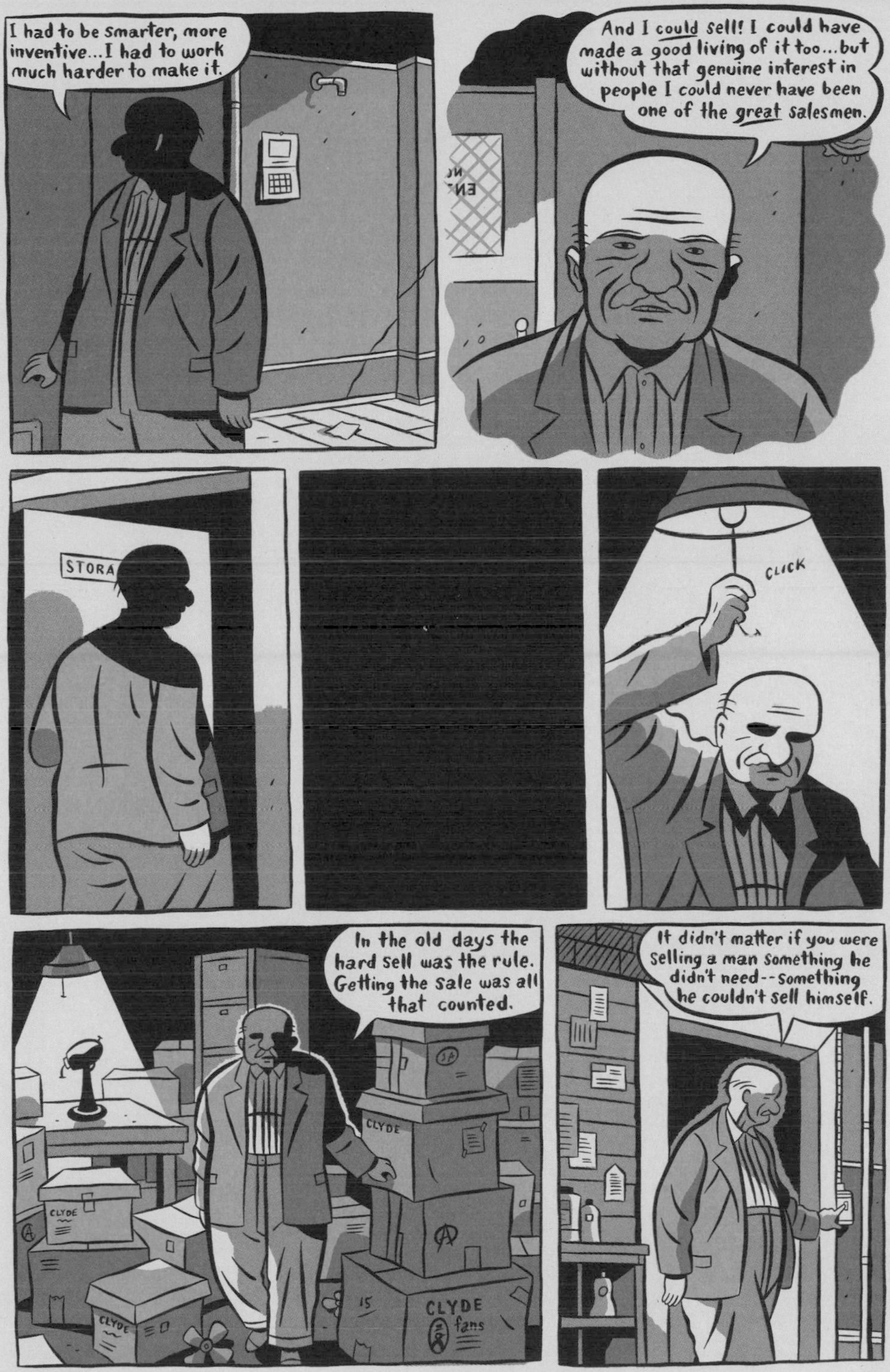
I had to be smarter, more inventive...I had to work much harder to make it.
And I could sell! I could have made a good living of it too...but without that genuine interest in people I could never have been one of the great salesmen.
STORA
CLICK
In the old days the hard sell was the rule. Getting the sale was all that counted.
CLYDE
CLYDE
CLYDE fans
It didn't matter if you were selling a man something he didn't need--something he couldn't sell himself.

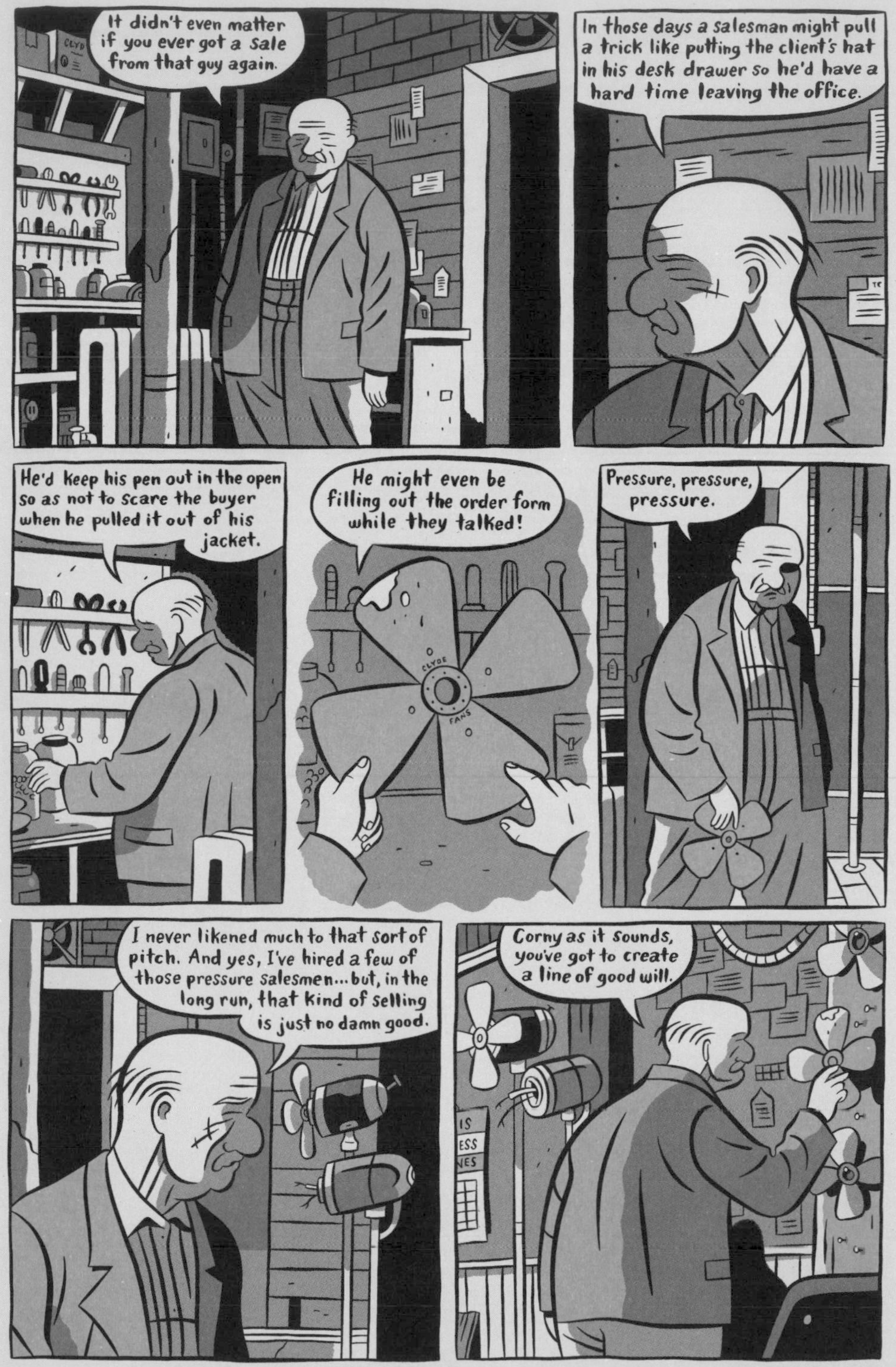
It didn't even matter if you ever got a sale from that guy again.
In those days a salesman might pull a trick like putting the client's hat in his desk drawer so he'd have a hard time leaving the office.
He'd keep his pen out in the open so as not to scare the buyer when he pulled it out of his jacket.
He might even be filling out the order form while they talked!
CLYDE FANS
Pressure, pressure, pressure.
I never likened much to that sort of pitch. And yes, I've hired a few of those pressure salesmen... but, in the long run, that kind of selling is just no damn good.
Corny as it sounds, you've got to create a line of good will.

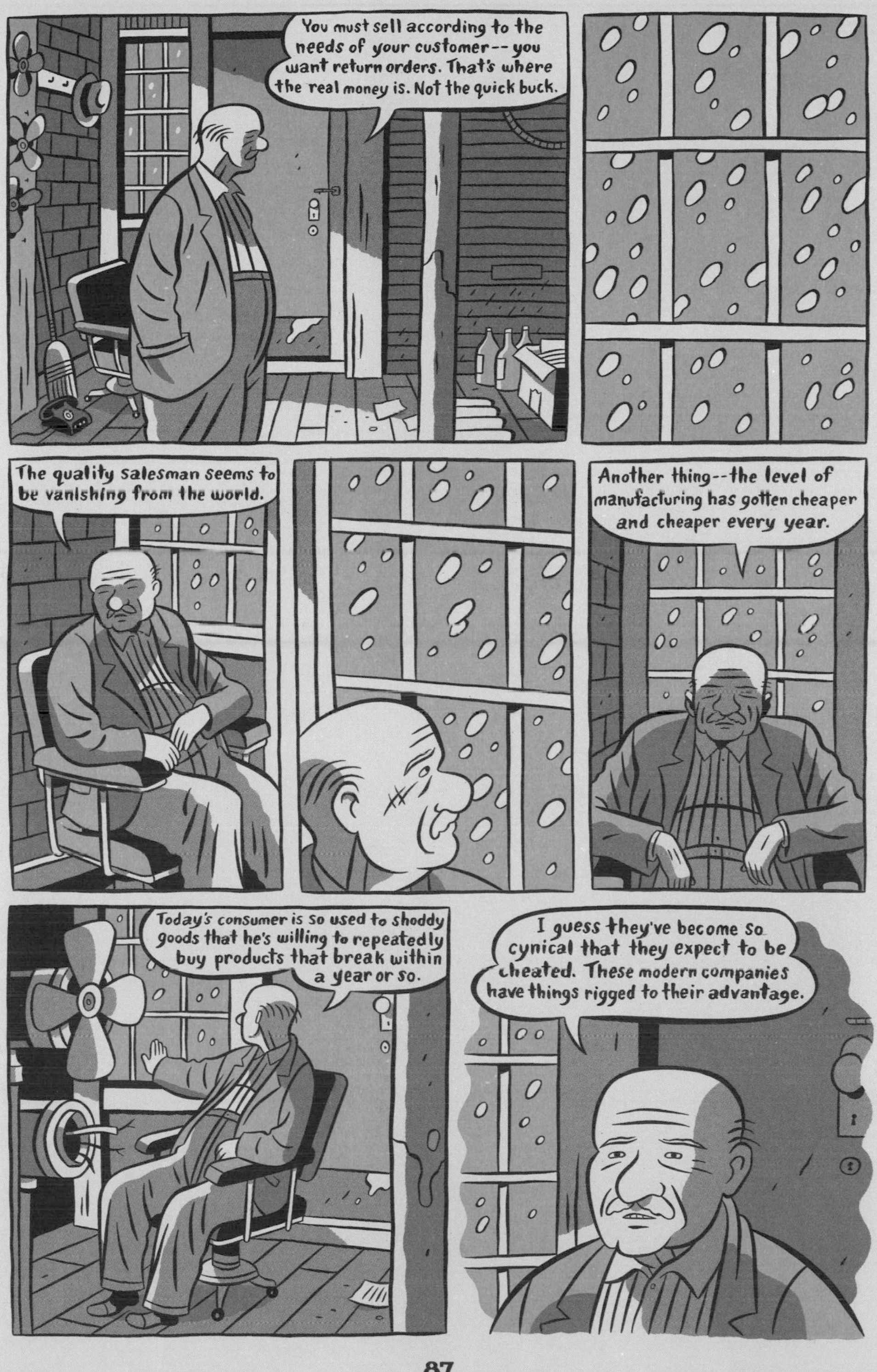
You must sell according to the needs of your customer-- you want return orders. That's where the real money is. Not the quick buck.
The quality salesman seems to be vanishing from the world.
Another thing--the level of manufacturing has gotten cheaper and cheaper every year.
Today's consumer is so used to shoddy goods that he's willing to repeatedly buy products that break within a year or so.
I guess they've become so cynical that they expect to be cheated. These modern companies have things rigged to their advantage.

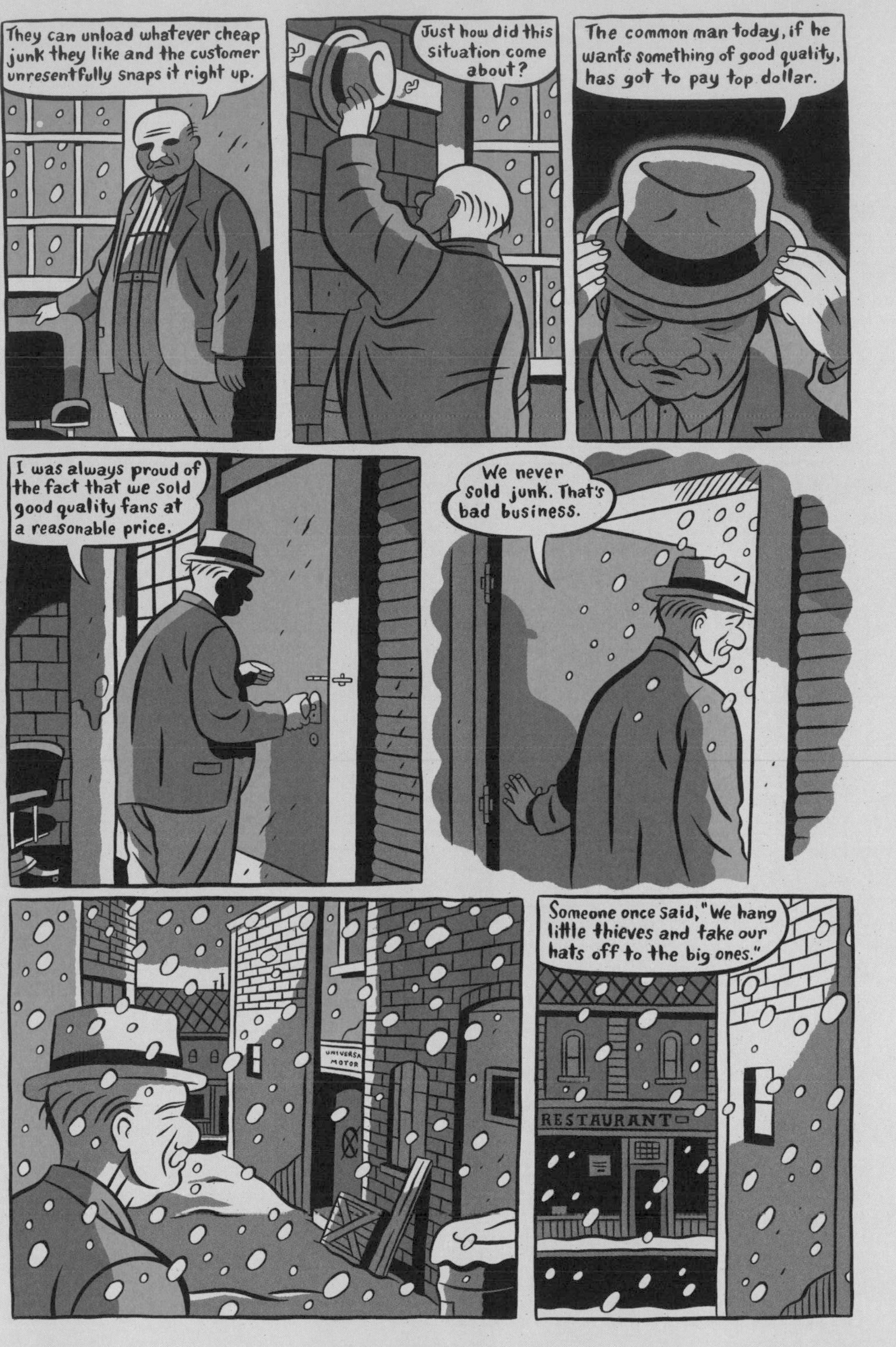
They can unload whatever cheap junk they like and the customer unresentfully snaps it right up.
Just how did this situation come about?
The common man today, if he wants something of good quality, has got to pay top dollar.
I was always proud of the fact that we sold good quality fans at a reasonable price.
We never sold junk. That's bad business.
UNIVERSA MOTOR
Someone once said, "We hang little thieves and take our hats off to the big ones."
RESTAURANT

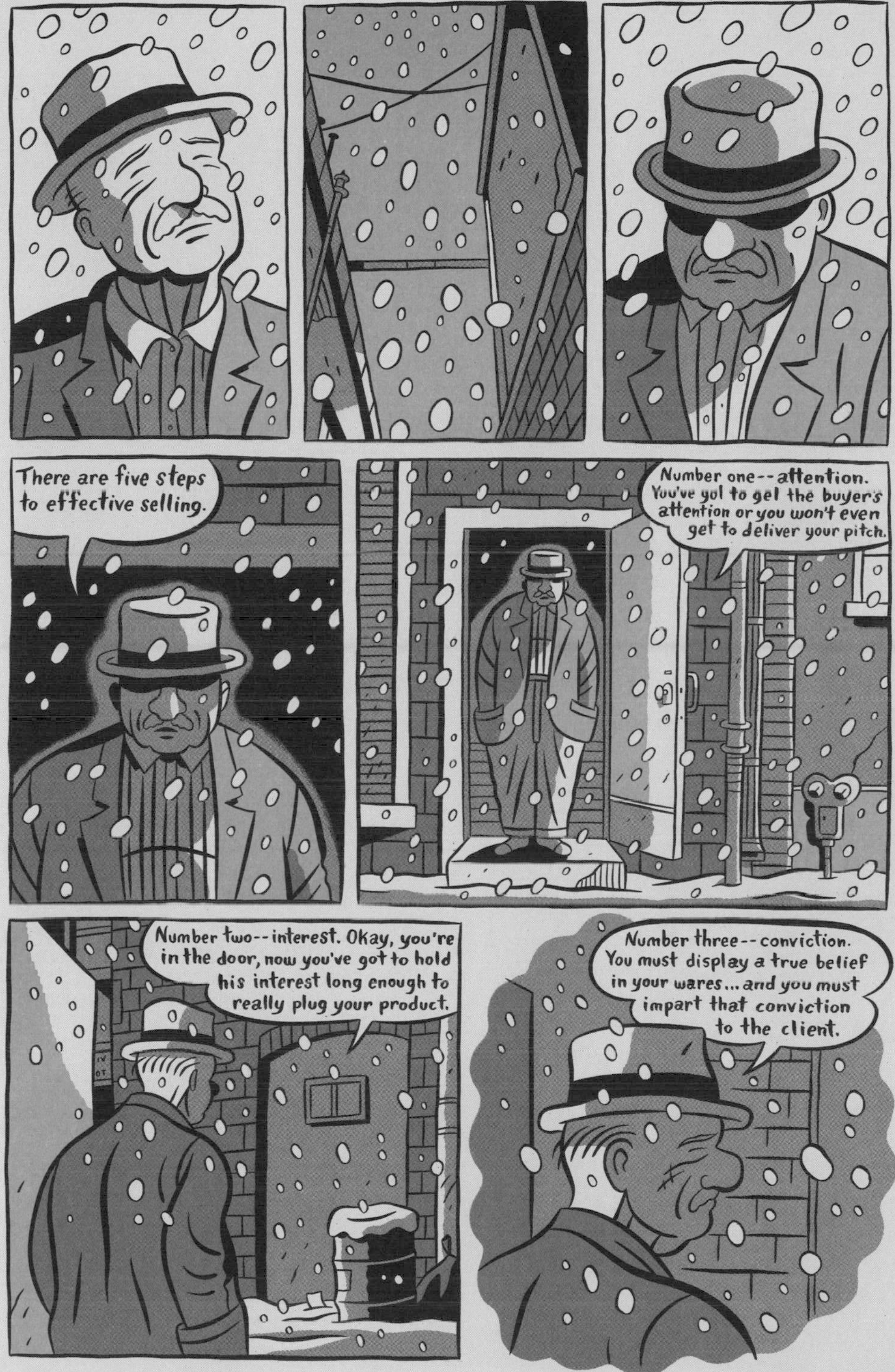
There are five steps to effective selling.
Number one--attention. You've got to get the buyer's attention or you won't even get to deliver your pitch.
Number two--interest. Okay, you're in the door, now you've got to hold his interest long enough to really plug your product.
Number three--conviction. You must display a true belief in your wares... and you must impart that conviction to the client.

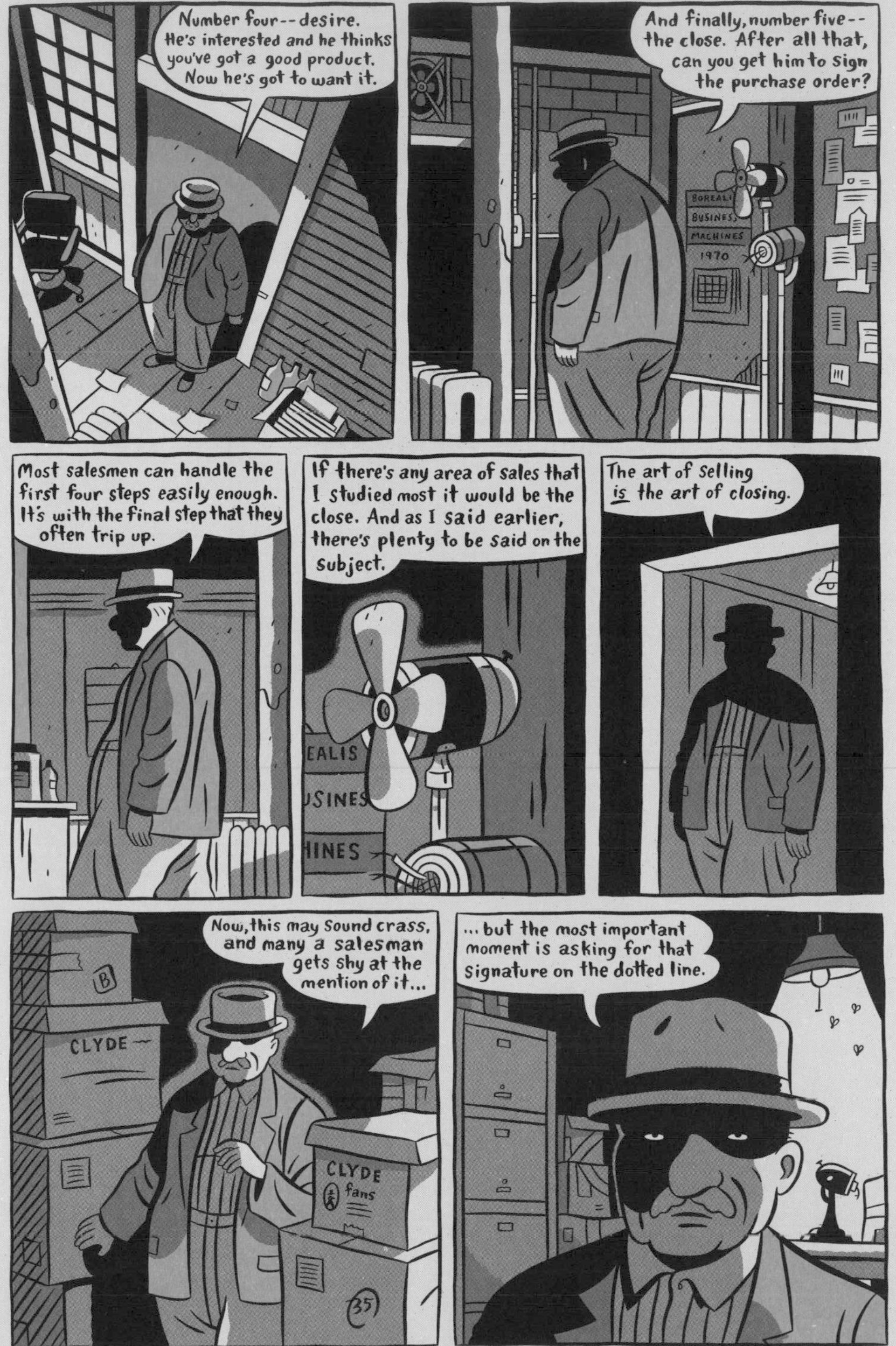
Number four--desire. He's interested and he thinks you've got a good product. Now he's got to want it.
And finally, number five--the close. After all that, can you get him to sign the purchase order?
BOREALIS
BUSINESS
MACHINES
1970
Most salesmen can handle the first four steps easily enough. It's with the final step that they often trip up.
If there's any area of sales that I studied most it would be the close. And as I said earlier, there's plenty to be said on the subject.
EALIS
USINES
HINES
The art of selling is the art of closing.
Now, this may sound crass, and many a salesman gets shy at the mention of it...
B
CLYDE
CLYDE fans
35
...but the most important moment is asking for that signature on the dotted line.

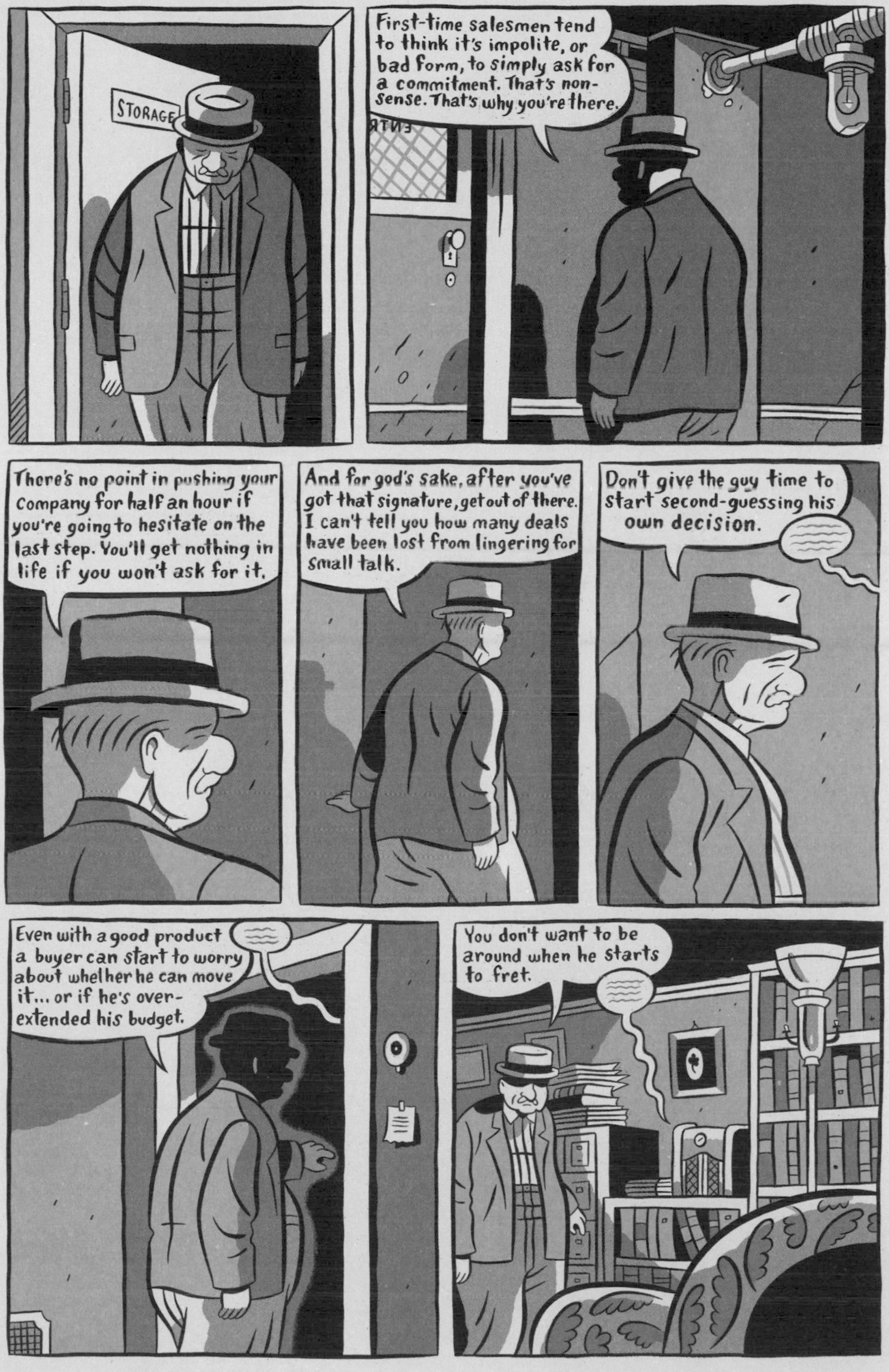
STORAGE
First-time salesmen tend to think it's impolite, or bad form, to simply ask for a commitment. That's non-sense. That's why you're there.
There's no point in pushing your Company for half an hour if you're going to hesitate on the last step. You'll get nothing in life if you won't ask for it.
And for god's sake, after you've got that signature, get out of there. I can't tell you how many deals have been lost from lingering for small talk.
Don't give the guy time to start second-guessing his own decision.
Even with a good product a buyer can start to worry about whether he can move it... or if he's over-extended his budget.
You don't want to be around when he starts to fret.

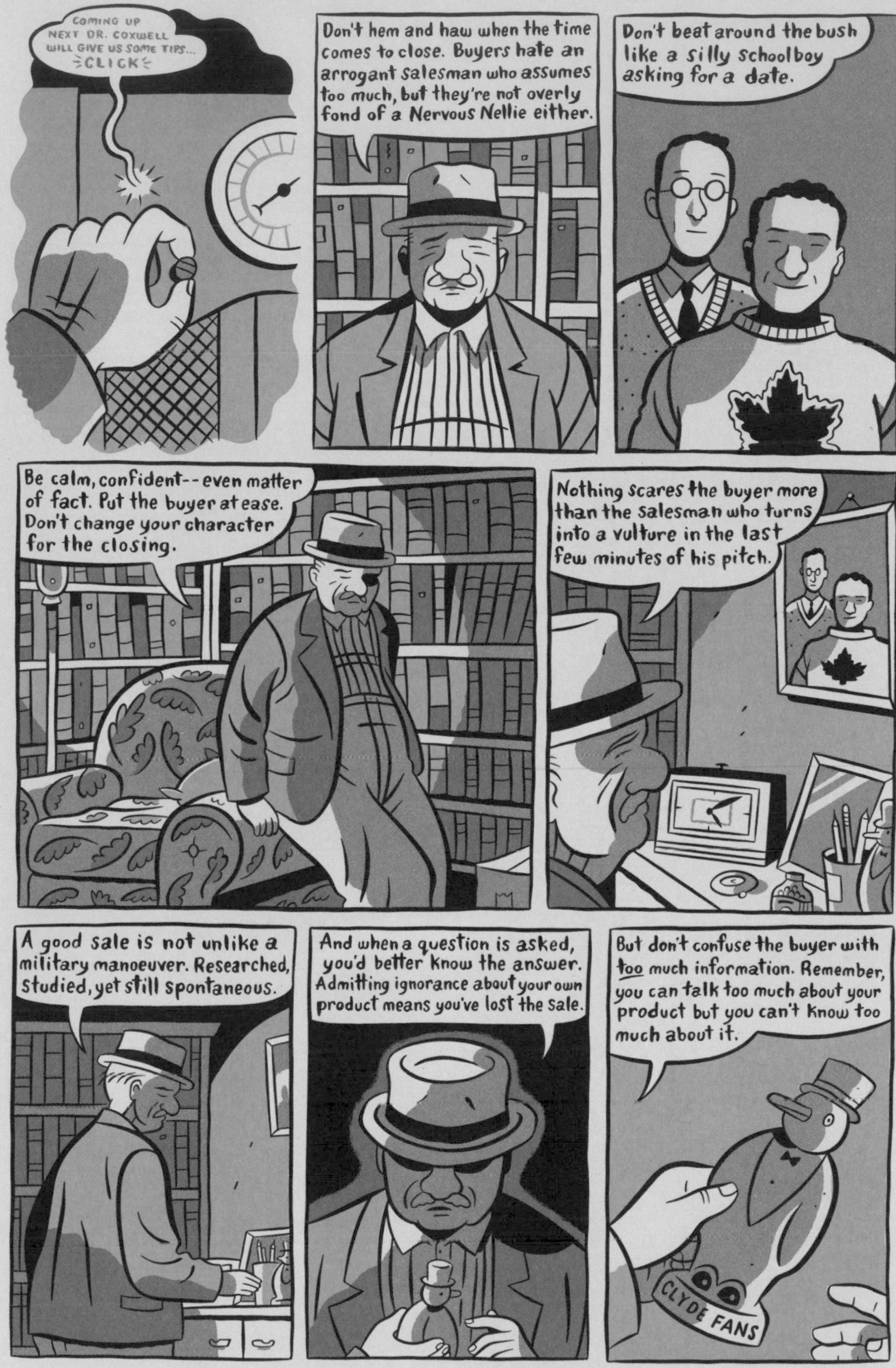
COMING UP NEXT DR. COXWELL WILL GIVE US SOME TIPS...
CLICK
Don't hem and haw when the time comes to close. Buyers hate an arrogant salesman who assumes too much, but they're not overly fond of a Nervous Nellie either.
Don't beat around the bush like a silly schoolboy asking for a date.
Be calm, confident--even matter of fact. Put the buyer at ease. Don't change your character for the closing.
Nothing scares the buyer more than the salesman who turns into a vulture in the last few minutes of his pitch.
A good sale is not unlike a military manoeuver. Researched, studied, yet still spontaneous.
And when a question is asked, you'd better know the answer. Admitting ignorance about your own product means you've lost the sale.
But don't confuse the buyer with too much information. Remember, you can talk too much about your product but you can't know too much about it.
CLYDE FANS

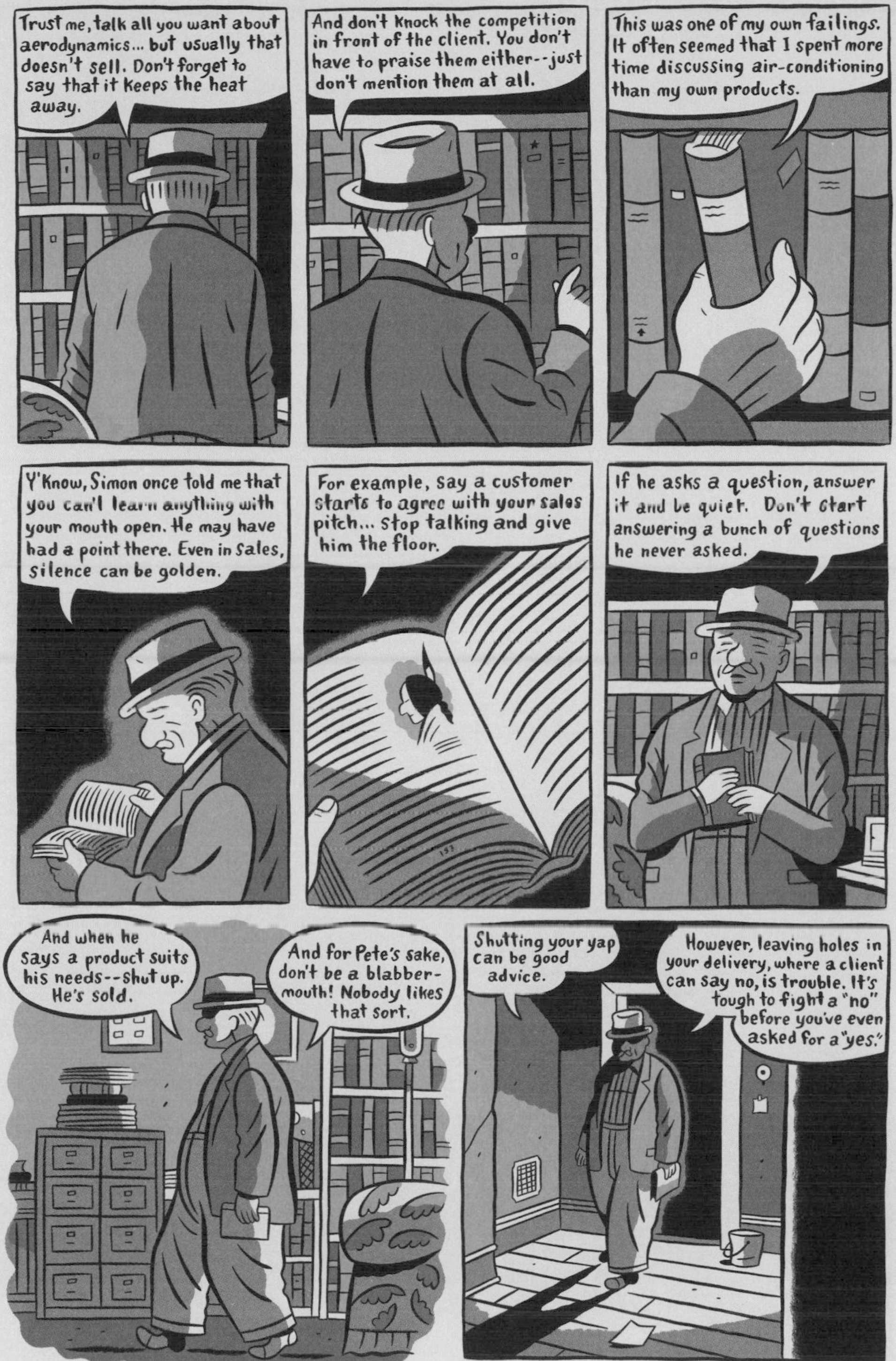

Trust me, talk all you want about aerodynamics... but usually that doesn't sell. Don't forget to say that it keeps the heat away.
And don't knock the competition in front of the client. You don't have to praise them either--just don't mention them at all.
This was one of my own failings. It often seemed that I spent more time discussing air-conditioning than my own products.
Y'Know, Simon once told me that you can't learn anything with your mouth open. He may have had a point there. Even in Sales, silence can be golden.
For example, say a customer starts to agree with your sales pitch... stop talking and give him the floor.
If he asks a question, answer it and be quiet. Don't start answering a bunch of questions he never asked.
And when he says a product suits his needs--shut up. He's sold.
And for Pete's sake, don't be a blabbermouth! Nobody likes that sort.
Shutting your yap can be good advice.
However, leaving holes in your delivery, where a client can say no, is trouble. It's tough to fight a "no" before you've even asked for a "yes."

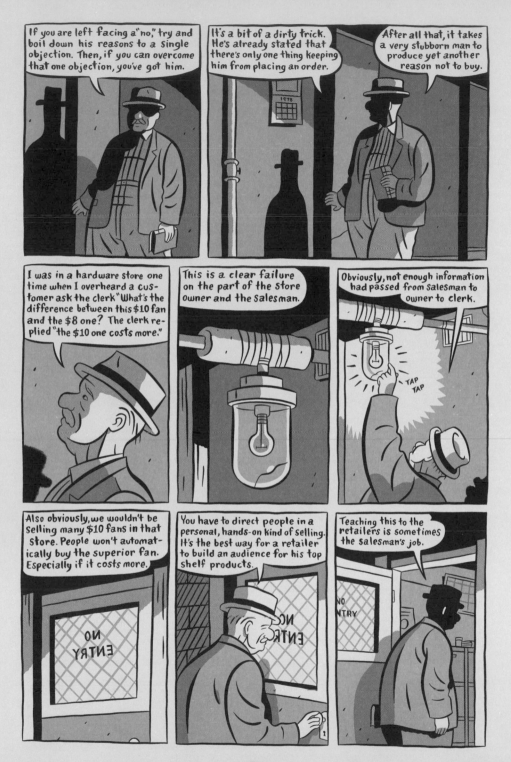

If you are left facing a "no," try and boil down his reasons to a single objection. Then, if you can overcome that one objection, you've got him.

It's a bit of a dirty trick. He's already stated that there's only one thing keeping him from placing an order.

After all that, it takes a very stubborn man to produce yet another reason not to buy.

I was in a hardware store one time when I overheard a customer ask the clerk "What's the difference between this $10 fan and the $8 one? The clerk replied "the $10 one costs more."

This is a clear failure on the part of the store owner and the salesman.

Obviously, not enough information had passed from salesman to owner to clerk.

TAP TAP

Also obviously, we wouldn't be selling many $10 fans in that store. People won't automatically buy the superior fan. Especially if it costs more.

You have to direct people in a personal, hands-on kind of selling. It's the best way for a retailer to build an audience for his top shelf products.

Teaching this to the retailers is sometimes the salesman's job.

NO ENTRY

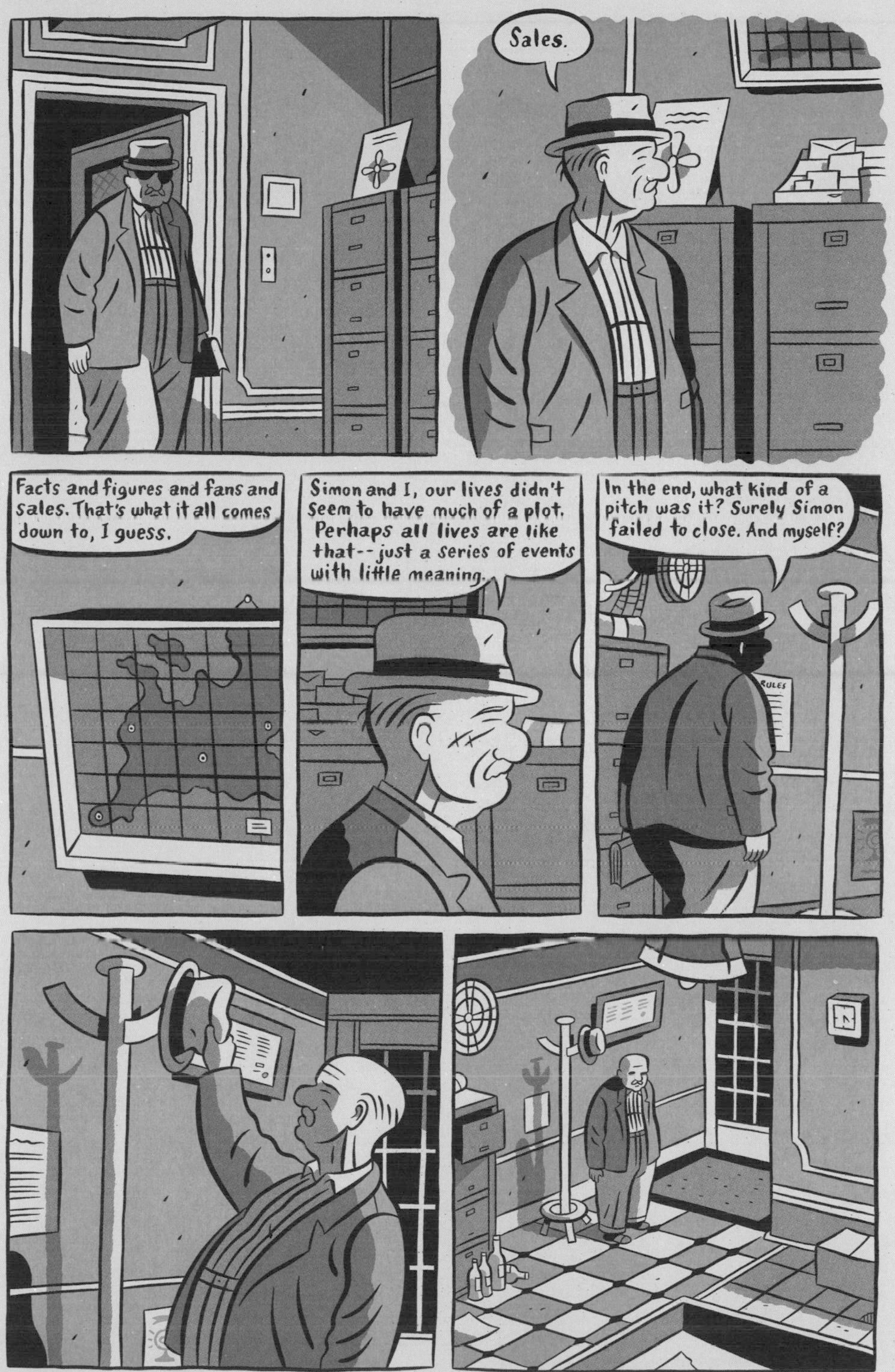
Sales.
Facts and figures and fans and sales. That's what it all comes down to, I guess.
Simon and I, our lives didn't seem to have much of a plot. Perhaps all lives are like that--just a series of events with little meaning.
In the end, what kind of a pitch was it? Surely Simon failed to close. And myself?
RULES

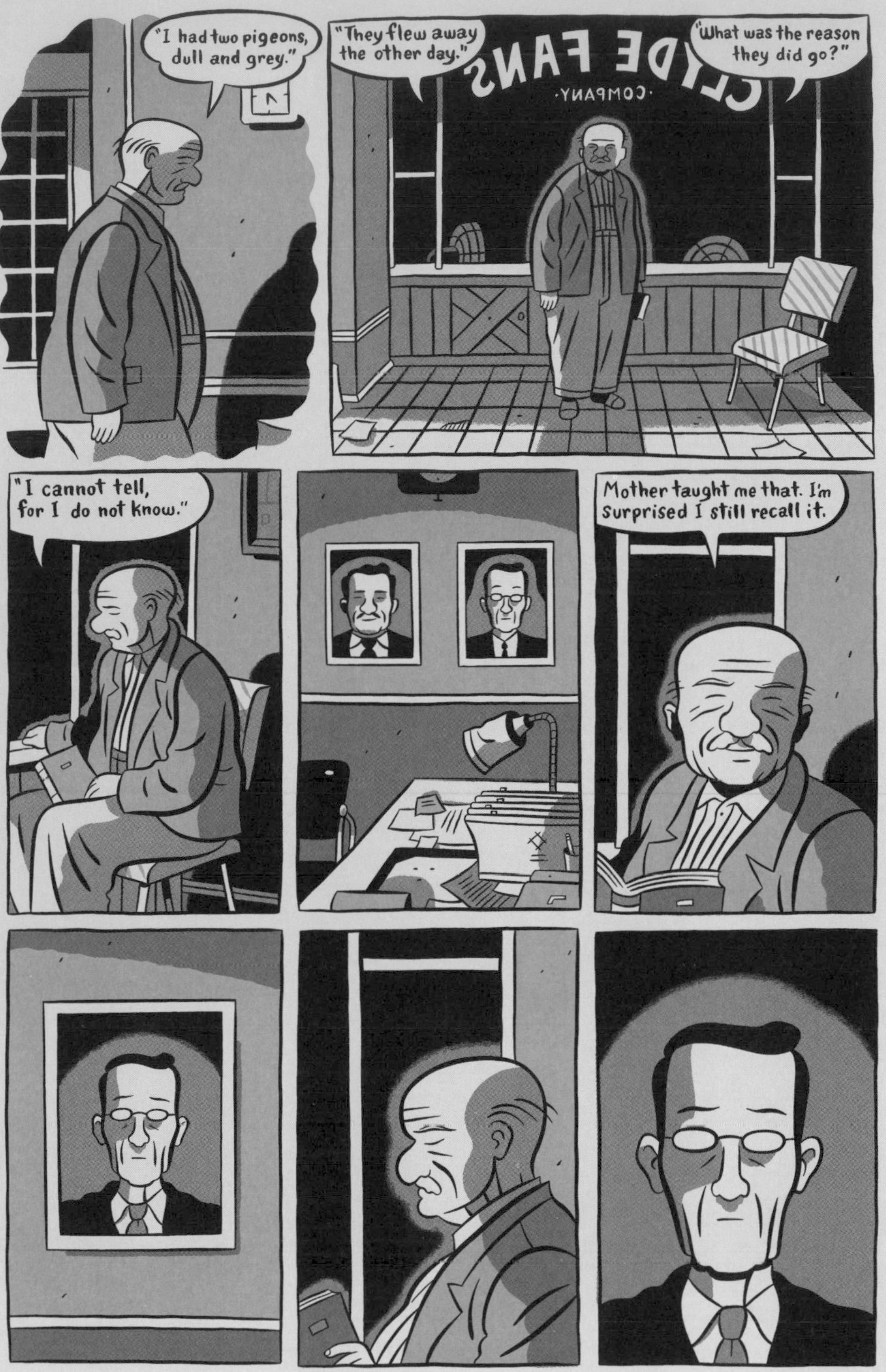
"I had two pigeons, dull and grey."
"They flew away the other day."
CLYDE FANS
·COMPANY·
"What was the reason they did go?"
"I cannot tell, for I do not know."
Mother taught me that. I'm surprised I still recall it.

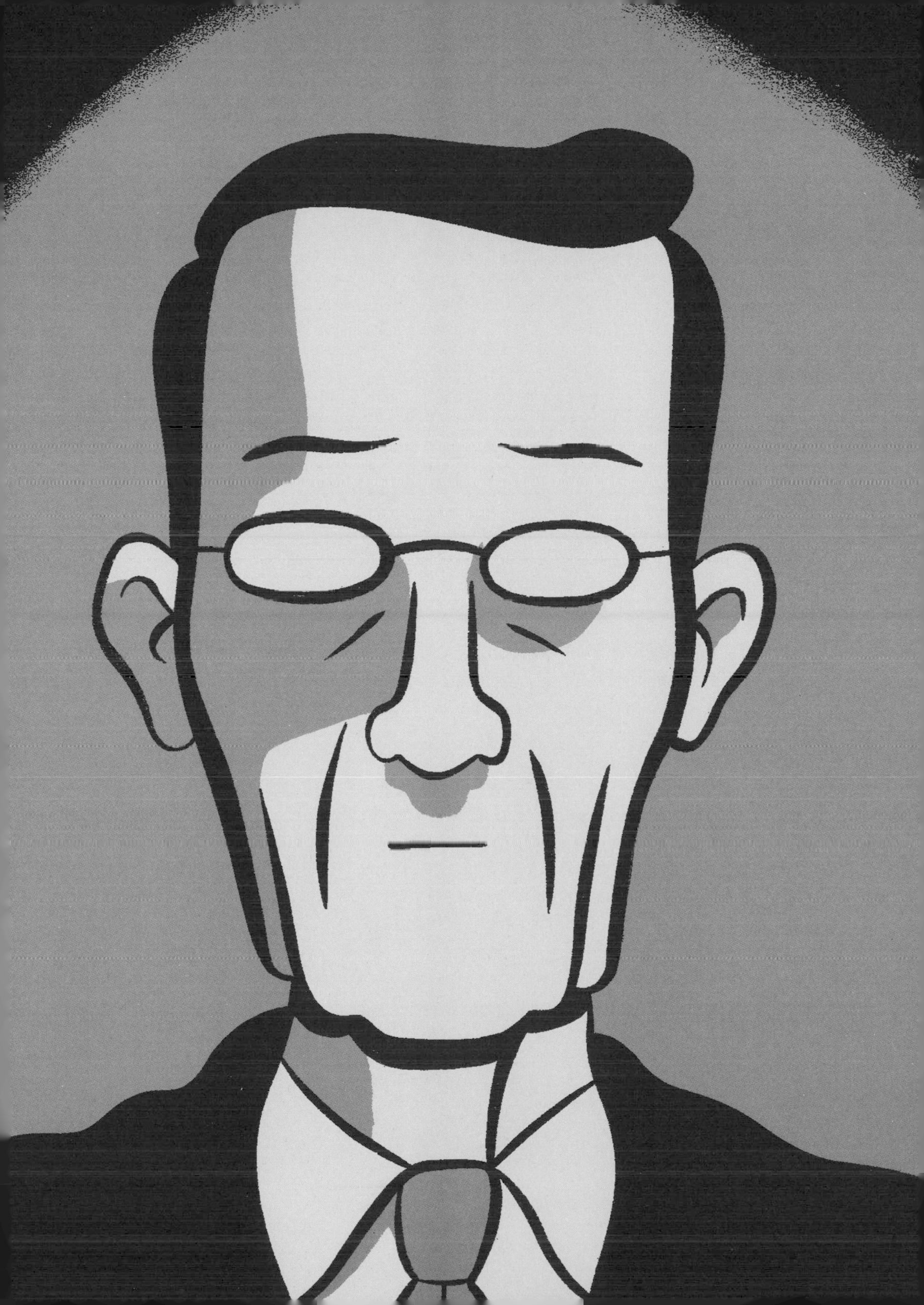

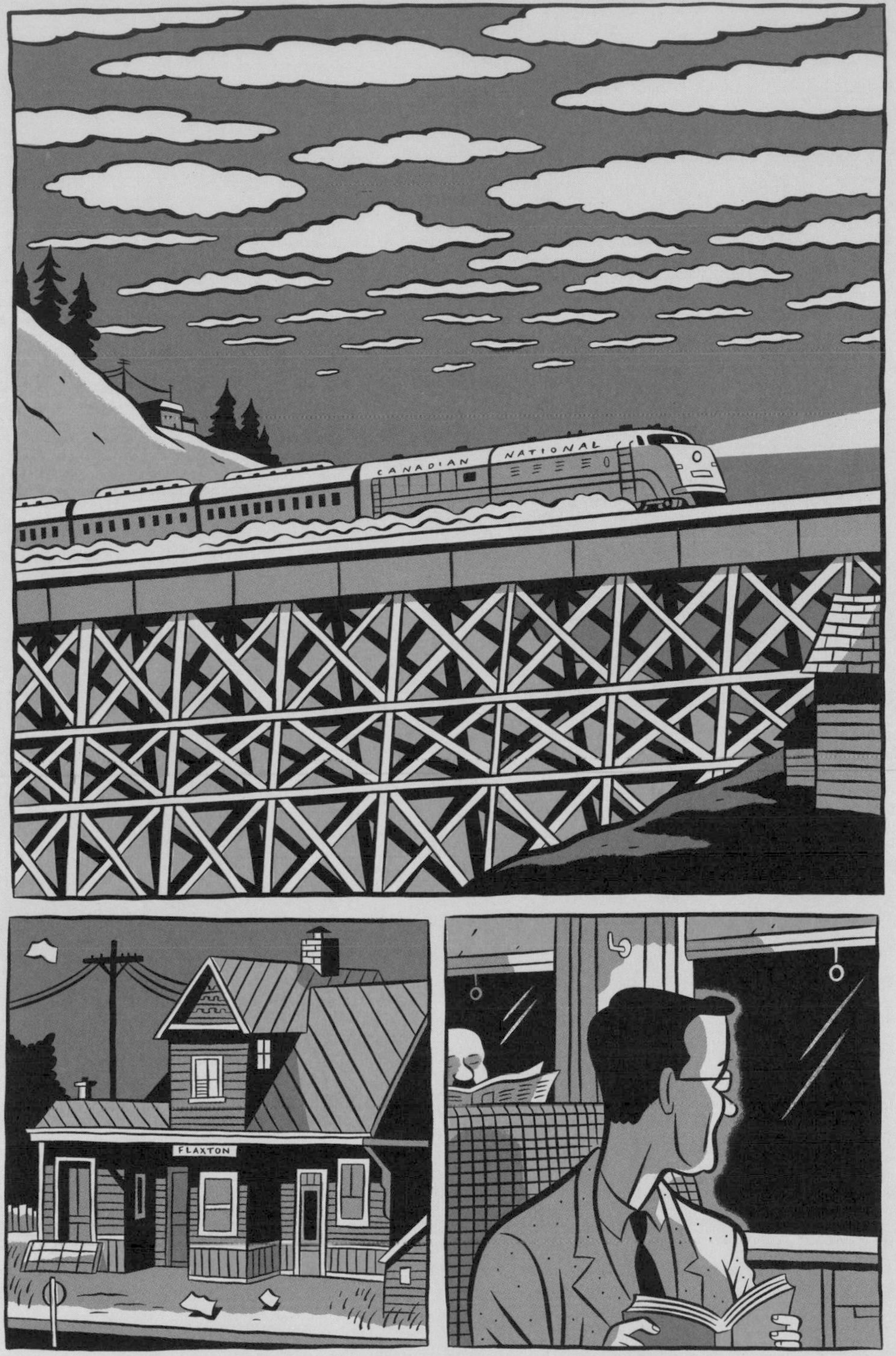
CANADIAN NATIONAL
FLAXTON

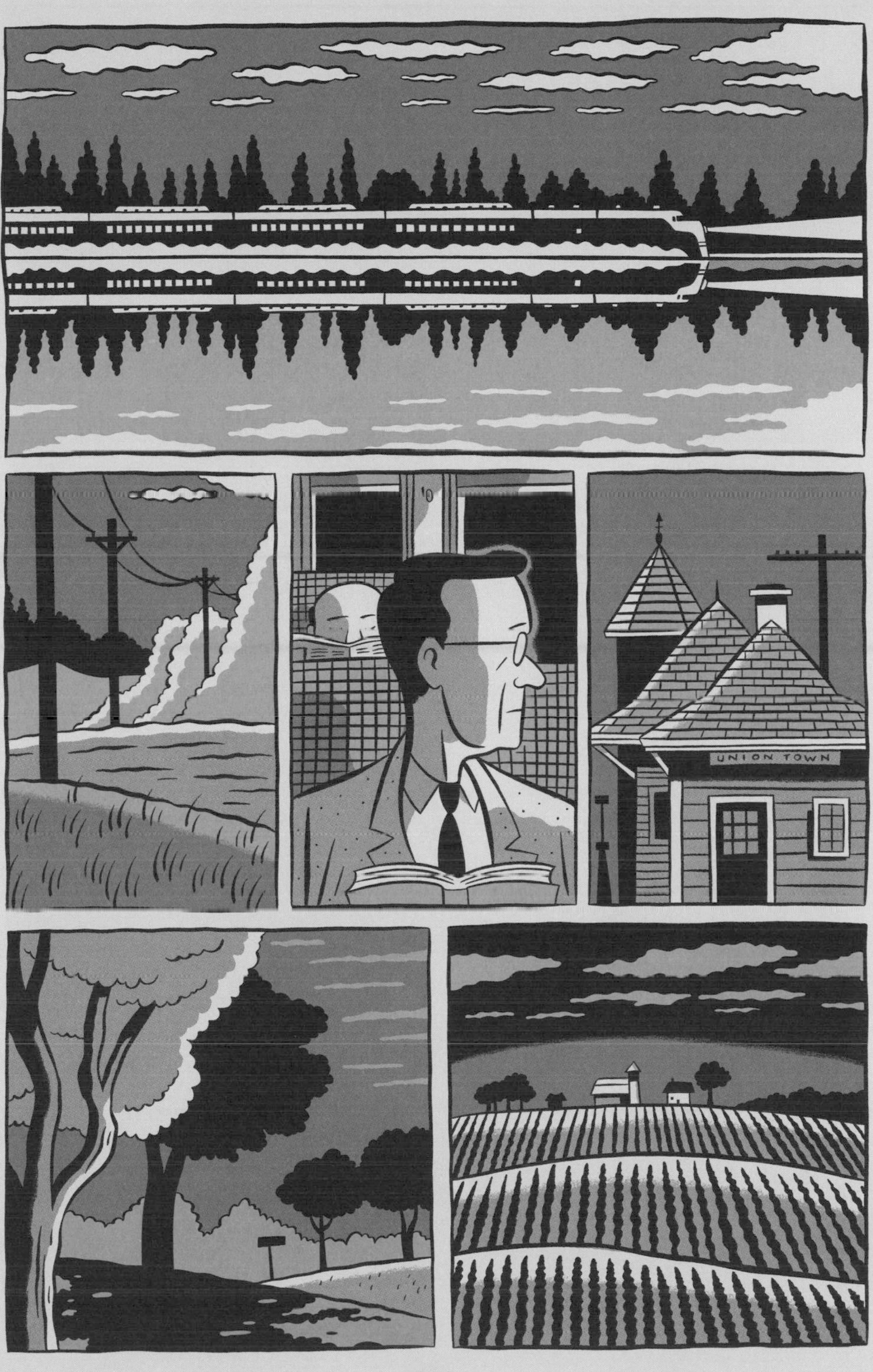
UNION TOWN

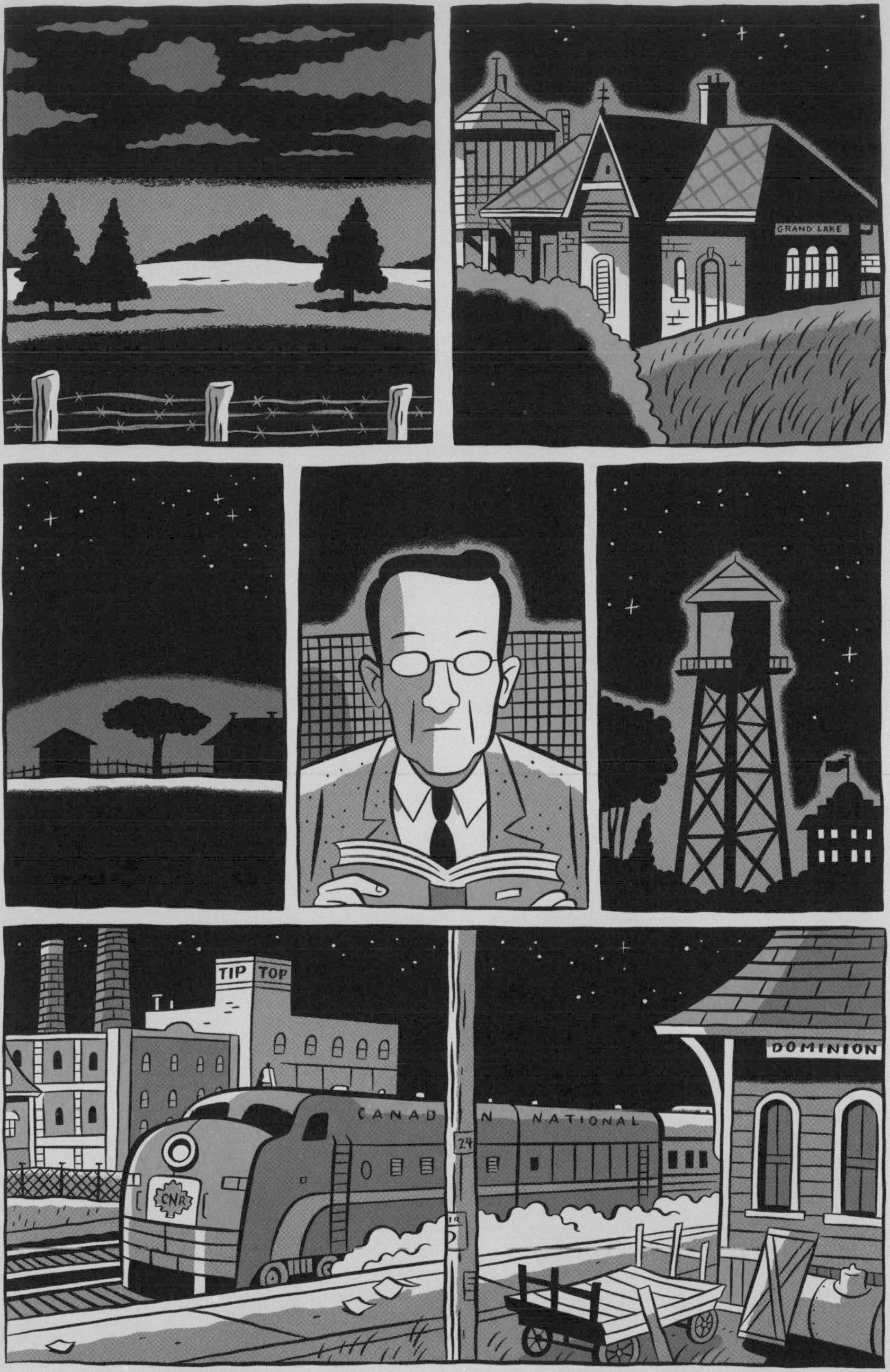
GRAND LAKE
TIP TOP
DOMINION
CANAD N NATIONAL
CNR
24

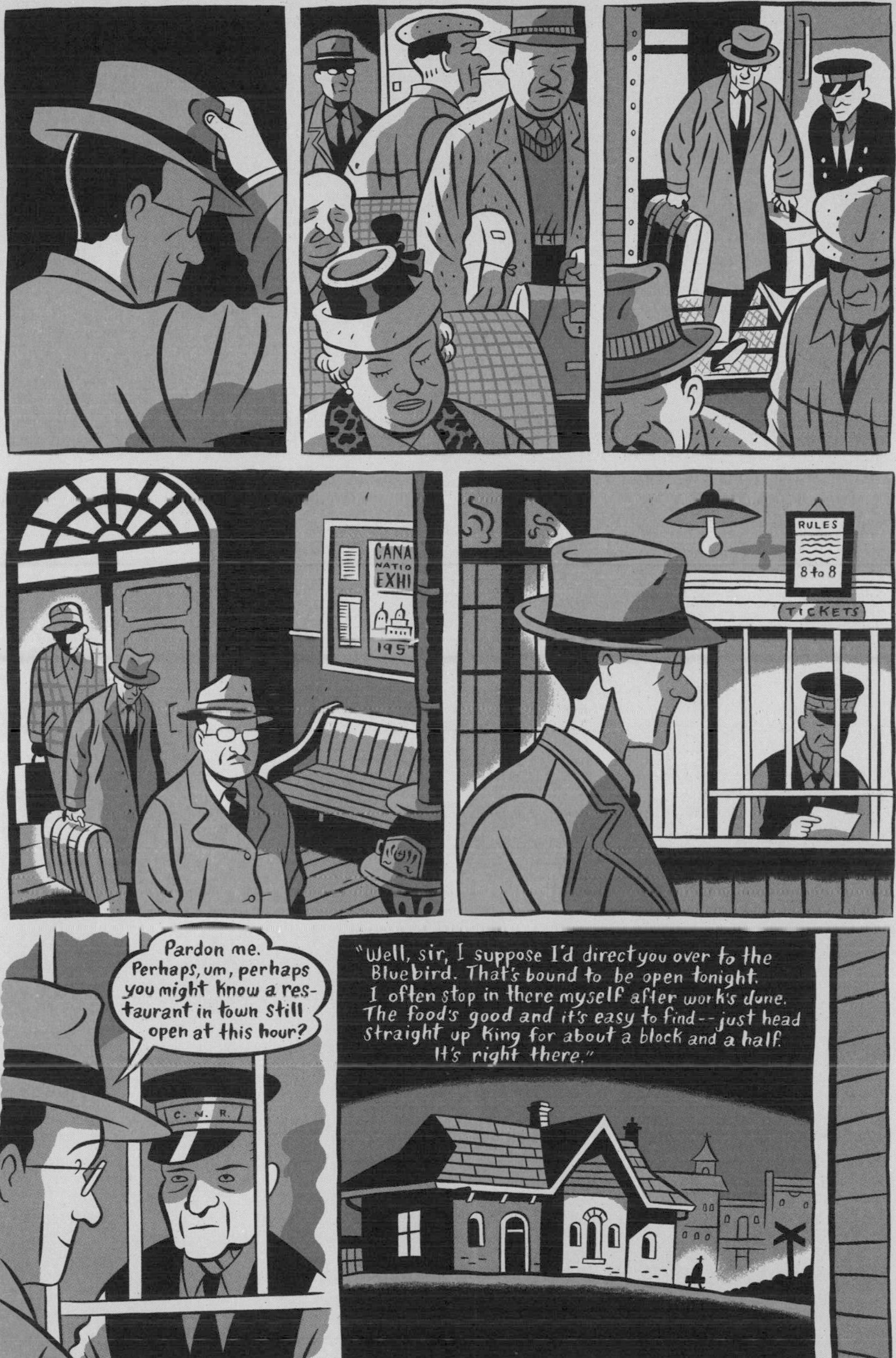
CANA
NATIO
EXHI
195
RULES
8 to 8
TICKETS
Pardon me. Perhaps, um, perhaps you might know a restaurant in town still open at this hour?
C. N. R.
"Well, sir, I suppose I'd direct you over to the Bluebird. That's bound to be open tonight. I often stop in there myself after work's done. The food's good and it's easy to find--just head straight up King for about a block and a half. It's right there."

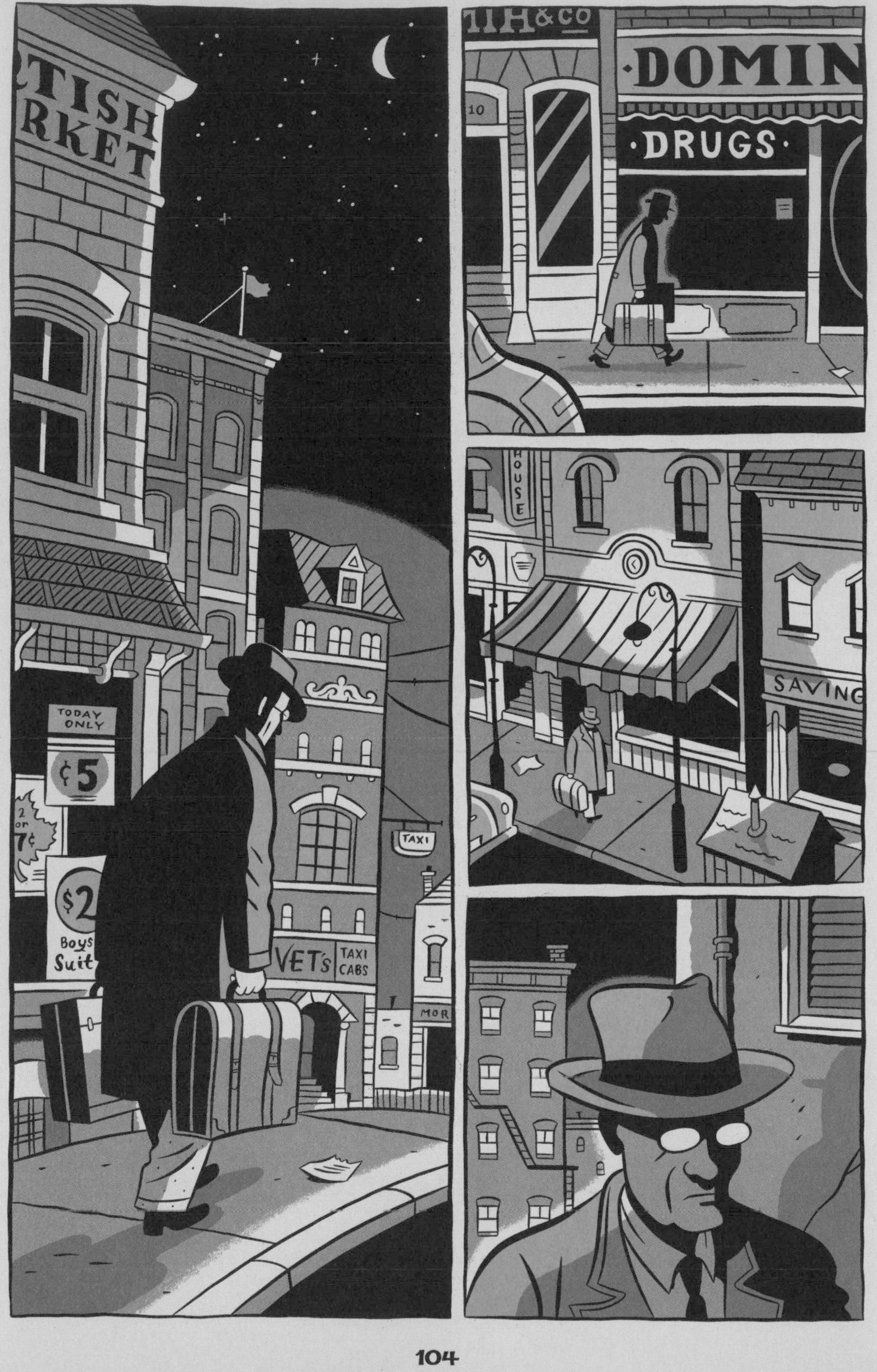
TISH
RKET
TODAY ONLY
¢5
2 for 7¢
$2
Boys Suit
TAXI
VET's
TAXI CABS
MOR
IH&CO
DOMIN
DRUGS
10
HOUSE
SAVING

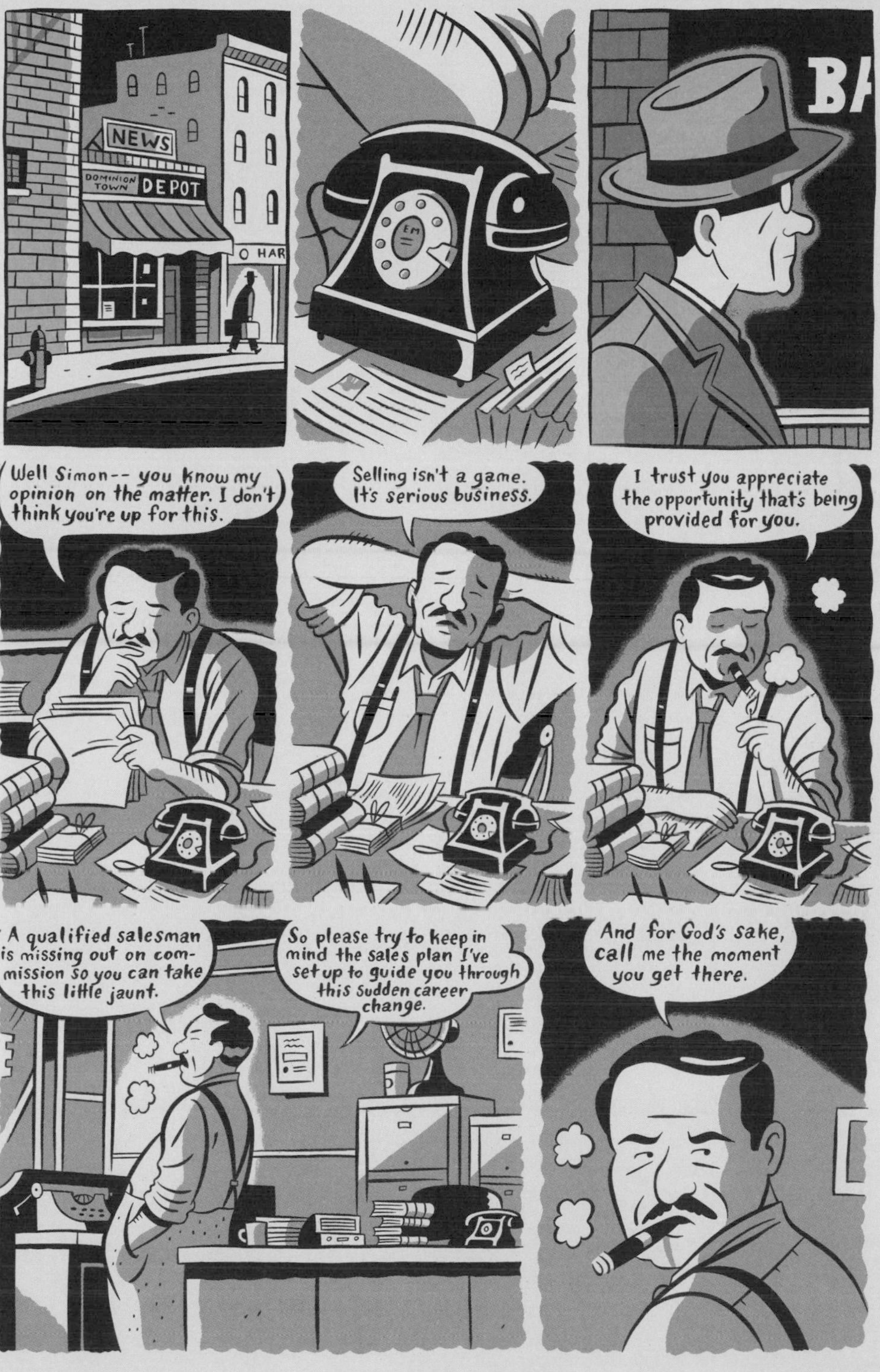
NEWS
DOMINION TOWN
DEPOT
O HAR
BA
Well Simon-- you know my opinion on the matter. I don't think you're up for this.
Selling isn't a game. It's serious business.
I trust you appreciate the opportunity that's being provided for you.
A qualified salesman is missing out on commission so you can take this little jaunt.
So please try to keep in mind the sales plan I've set up to guide you through this sudden career change.
And for God's sake, call me the moment you get there.

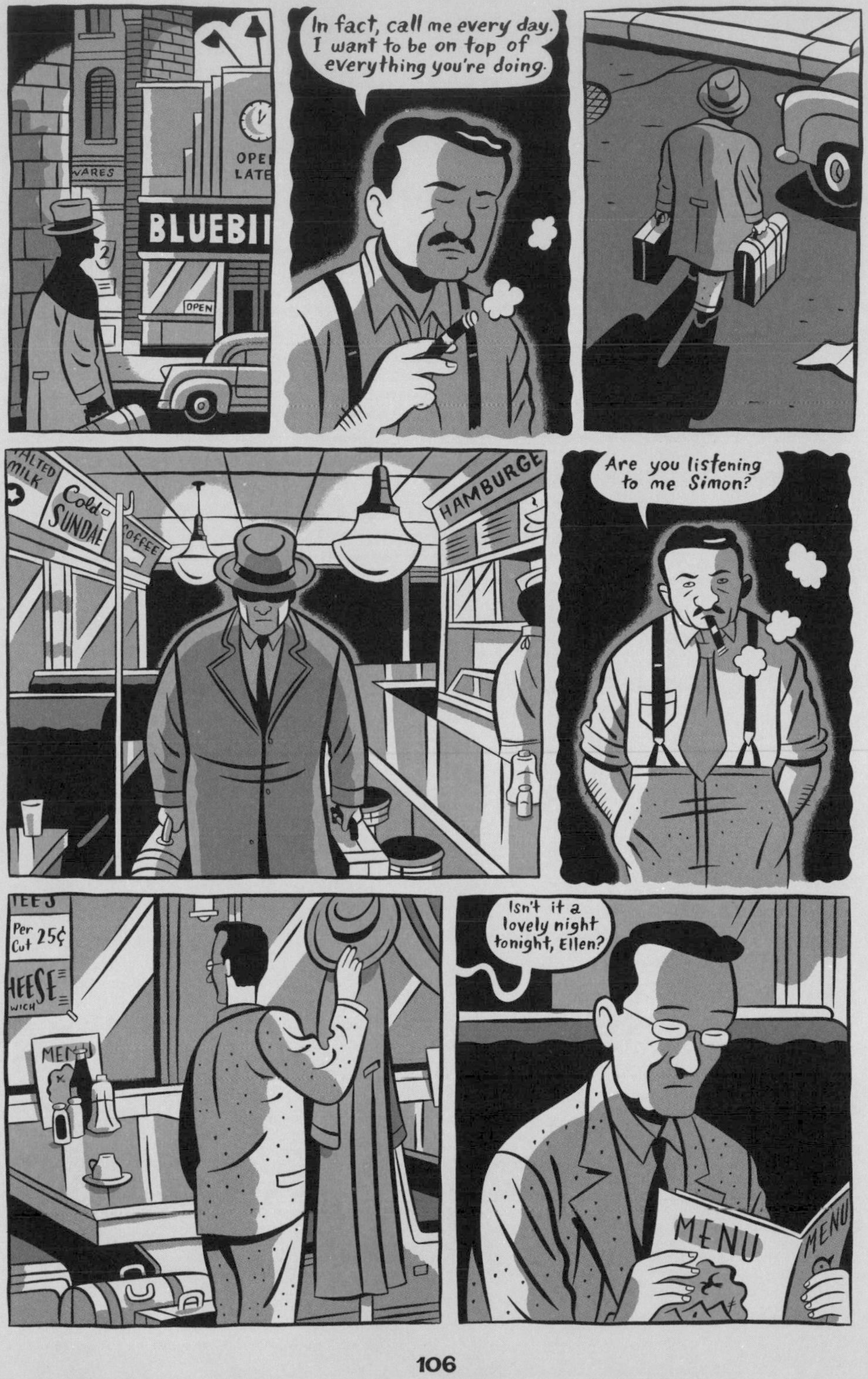
WARES
OPE
LATE
BLUEBI
OPEN
In fact, call me every day. I want to be on top of everything you're doing.
MILK
Cold SUNDAE
COFFEE
HAMBURGE
Are you listening to me Simon?
Per Cut 25¢
HEESE WICH
MENU
Isn't it a lovely night tonight, Ellen?
MENU
MENU

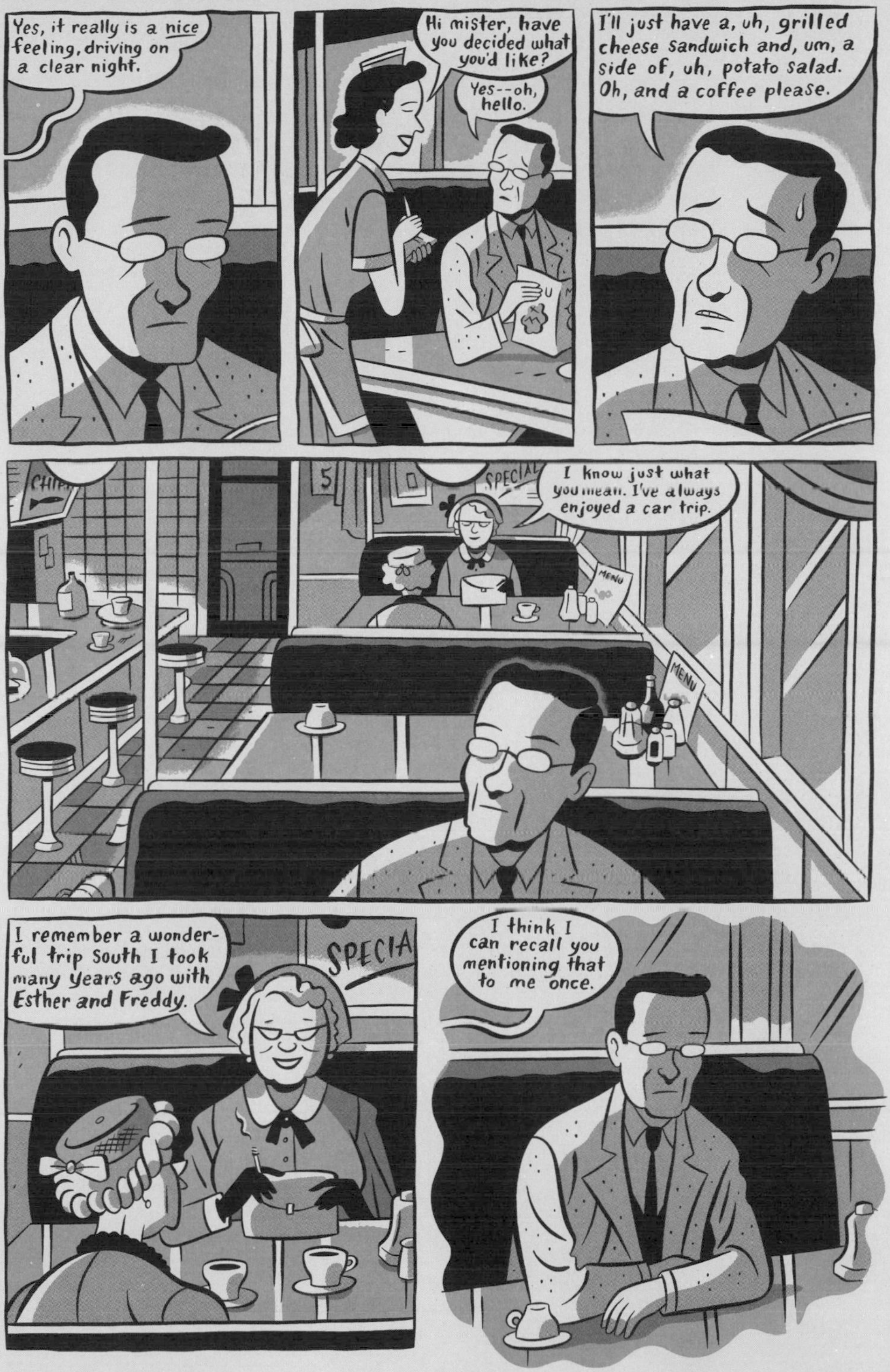
Yes, it really is a nice feeling, driving on a clear night.
Hi mister, have you decided what you'd like?
Yes--oh, hello.
I'll just have a, uh, grilled cheese sandwich and, um, a side of, uh, potato salad. Oh, and a coffee please.
SPECIAL
MENU
MENU
I know just what you mean. I've always enjoyed a car trip.
I remember a wonderful trip South I took many years ago with Esther and Freddy.
SPECIA
I think I can recall you mentioning that to me once.

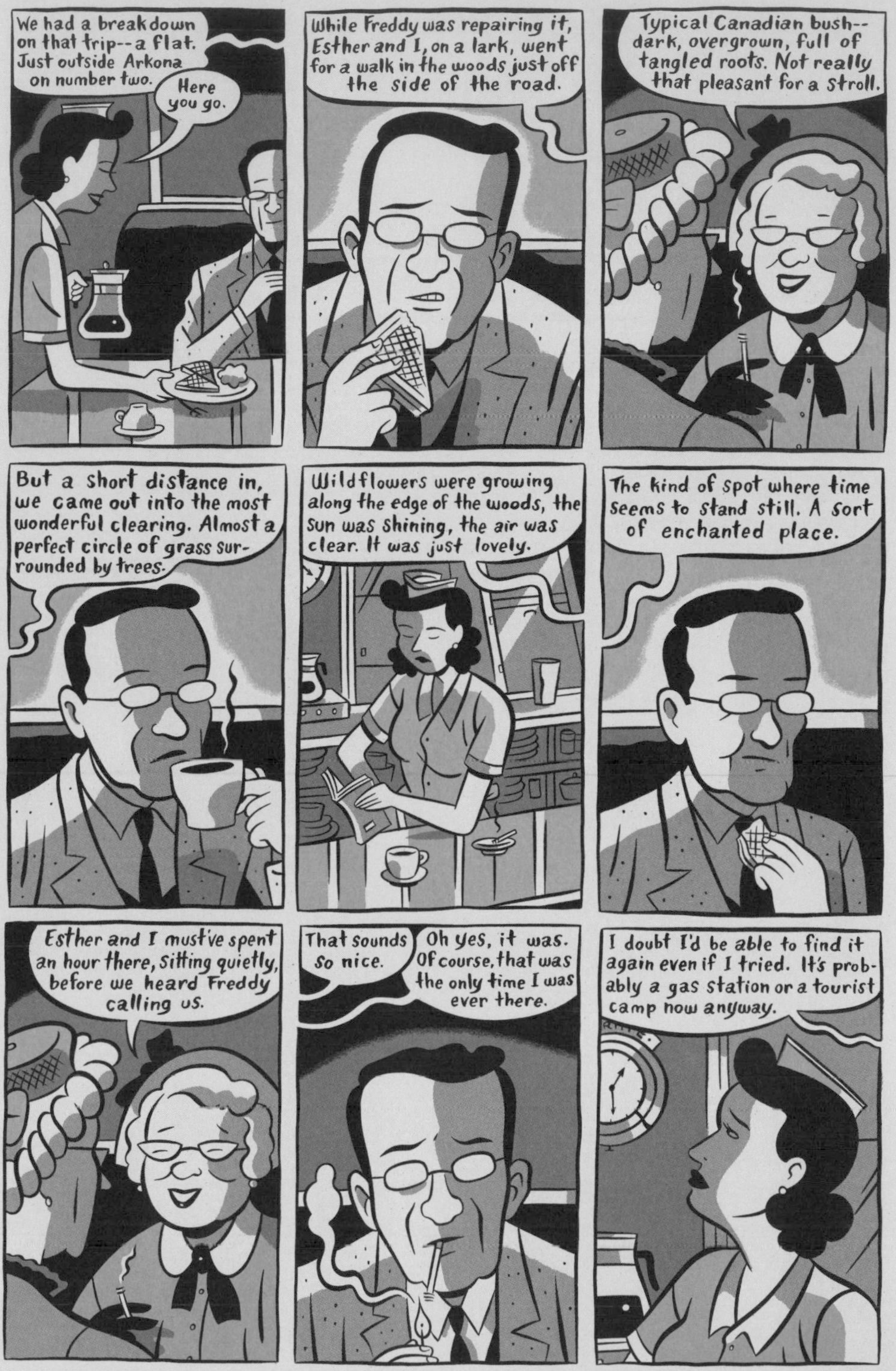
We had a breakdown on that trip--a flat. Just outside Arkona on number two.
Here you go.
While Freddy was repairing it, Esther and I, on a lark, went for a walk in the woods just off the side of the road.
Typical Canadian bush--dark, overgrown, full of tangled roots. Not really that pleasant for a stroll.
But a short distance in, we came out into the most wonderful clearing. Almost a perfect circle of grass surrounded by trees.
Wildflowers were growing along the edge of the woods, the sun was shining, the air was clear. It was just lovely.
The kind of spot where time seems to stand still. A sort of enchanted place.
Esther and I must've spent an hour there, sitting quietly, before we heard Freddy calling us.
That sounds so nice.
Oh yes, it was. Of course, that was the only time I was ever there.
I doubt I'd be able to find it again even if I tried. It's probably a gas station or a tourist camp now anyway.

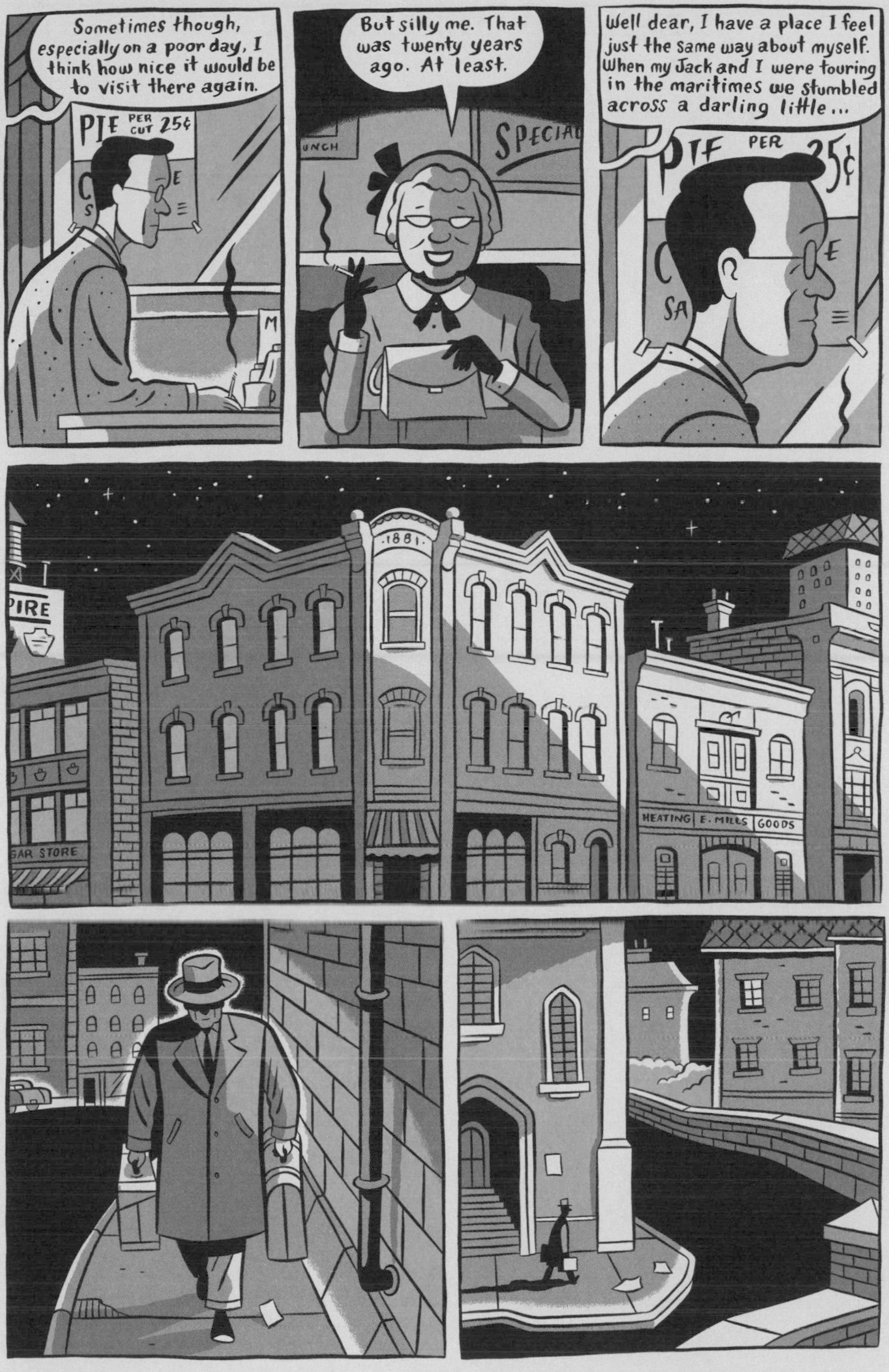
Sometimes though, especially on a poor day, I think how nice it would be to visit there again.
PIE PER CUT 25¢
But silly me. That was twenty years ago. At least.
SPECIAL
Well dear, I have a place I feel just the same way about myself. When my Jack and I were touring in the maritimes we stumbled across a darling little...
PIE PER 25¢
·1881·
PIRE
HEATING
E. MILLS
GOODS
GAR STORE

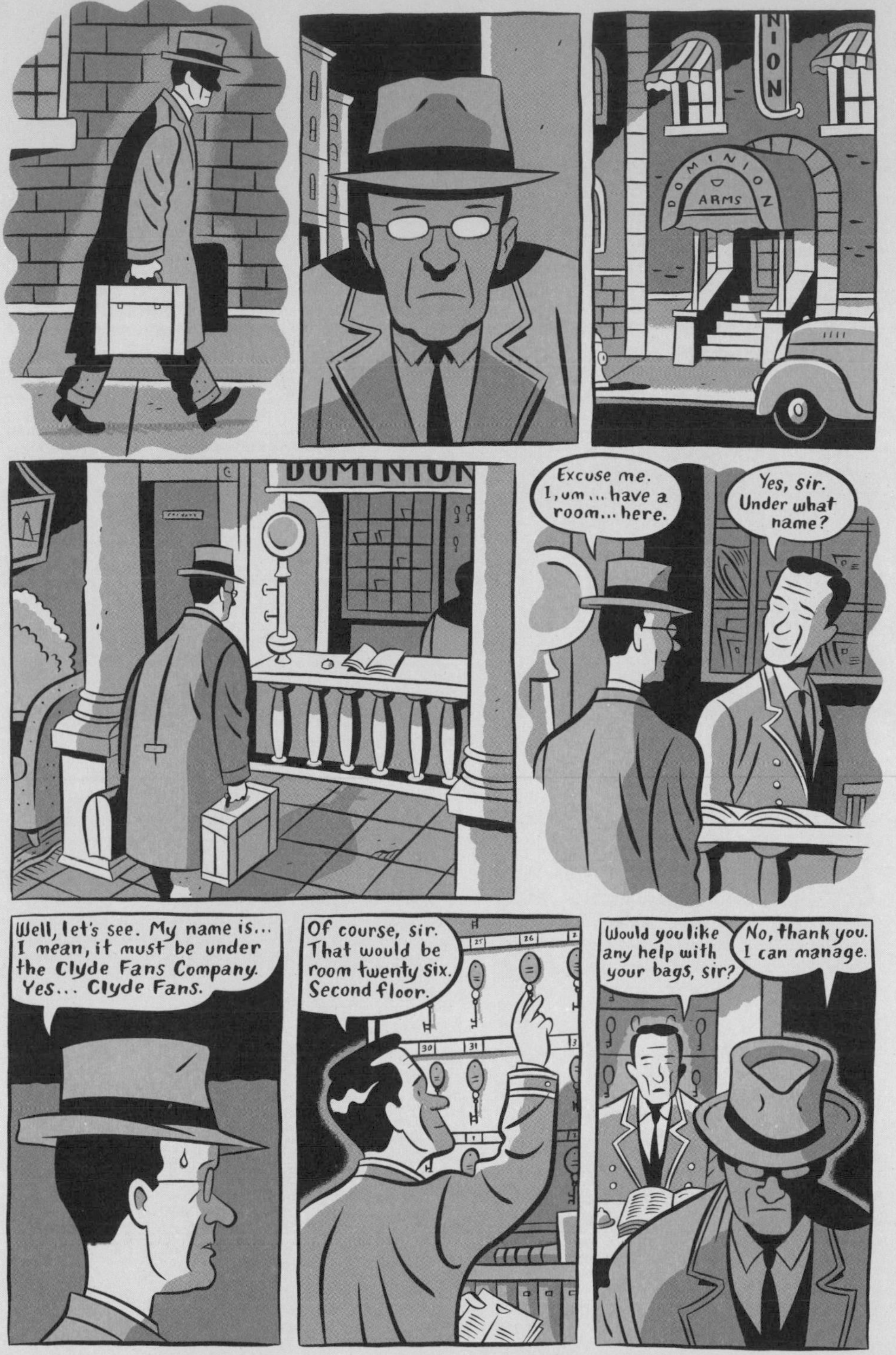

NION
DOMINION ARMS
DOMINION
Excuse me. I, um... have a room... here.
Yes, sir. Under what name?
Well, let's see. My name is... I mean, it must be under the Clyde Fans Company. Yes... Clyde Fans.
Of course, sir. That would be room twenty six. Second floor.
Would you like any help with your bags, sir?
No, thank you. I can manage.

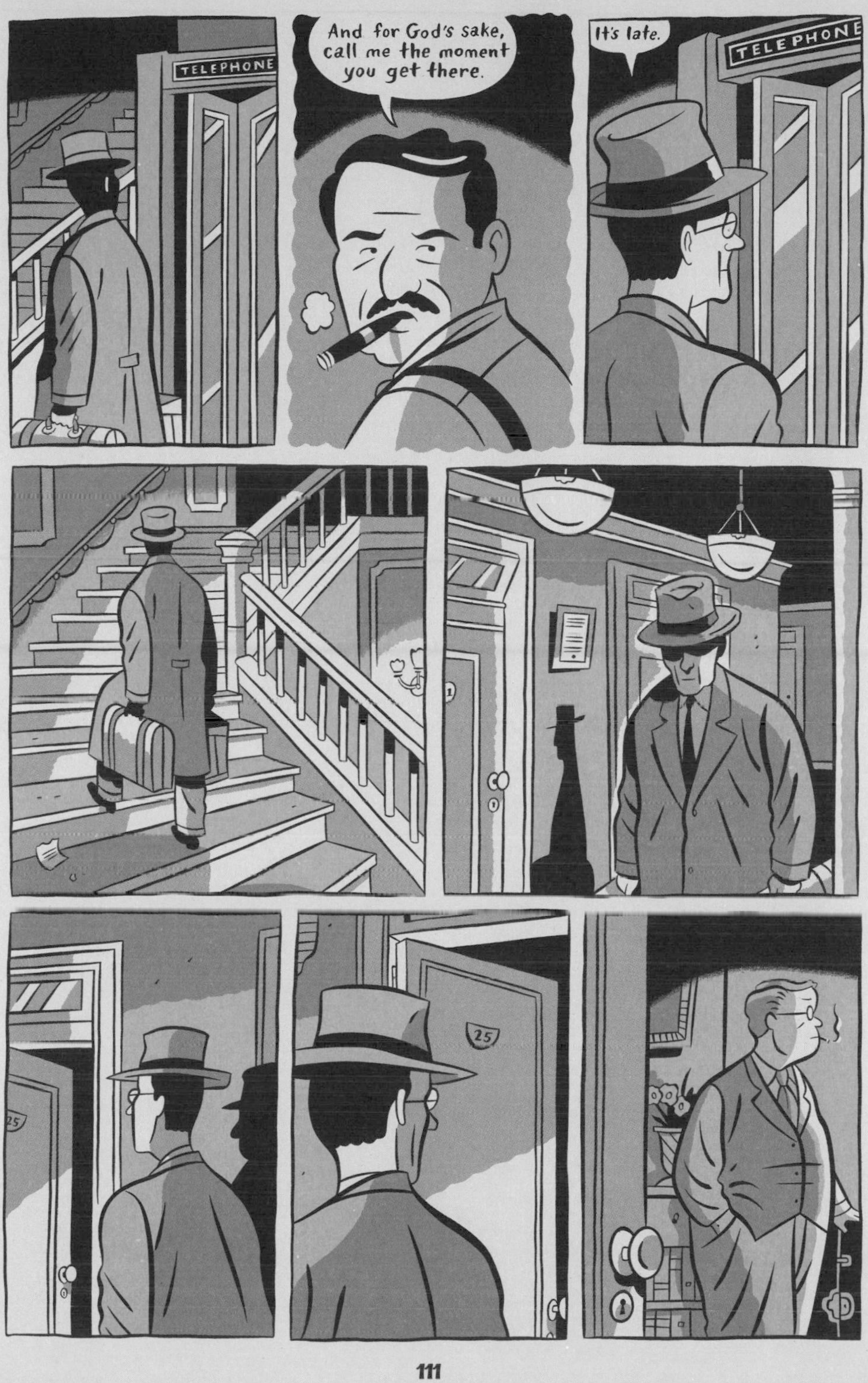
TELEPHONE
And for God's sake, call me the moment you get there.
It's late.
TELEPHONE
25
25

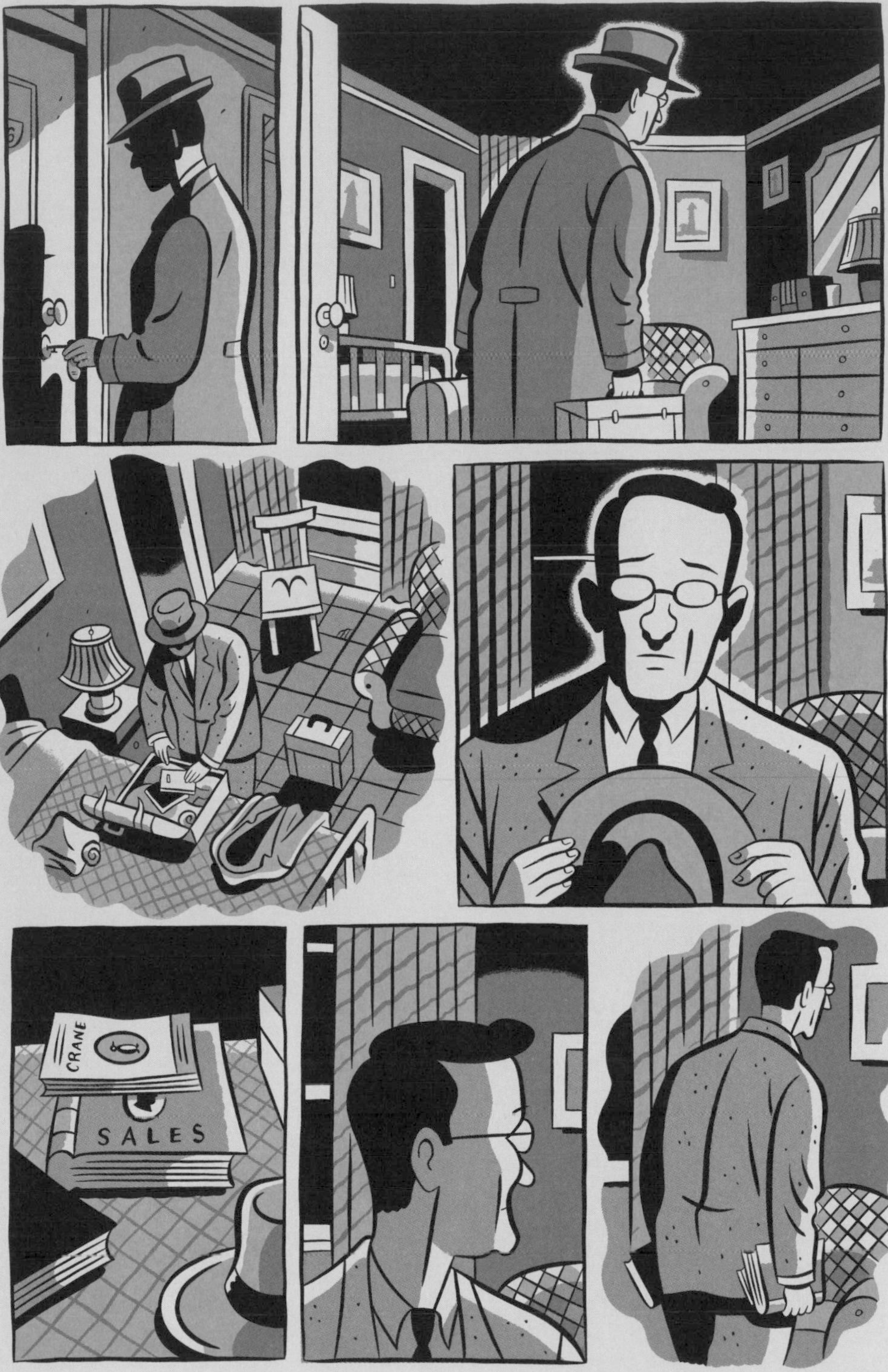
CRANE
SALES

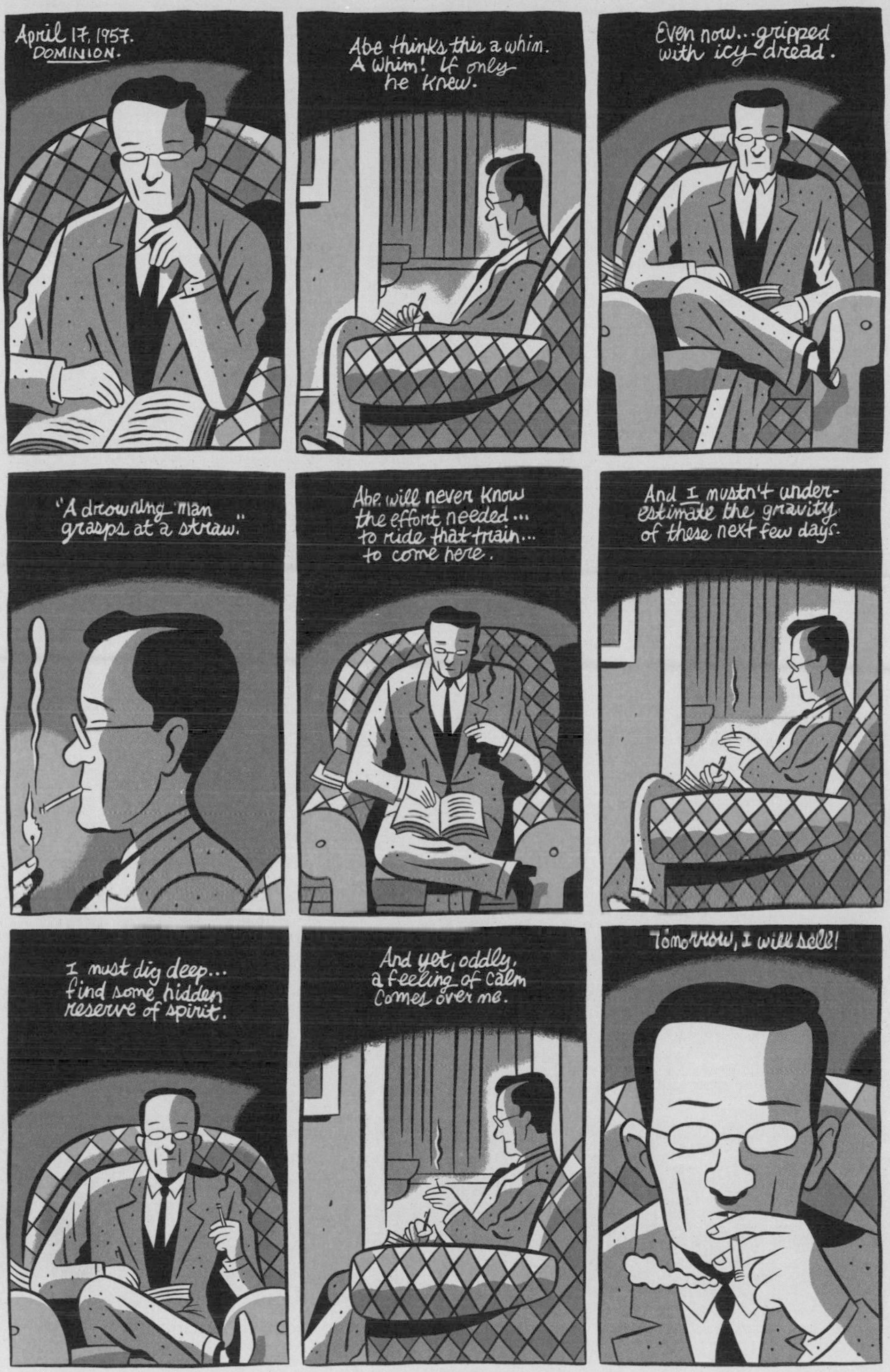
April 17, 1957.
DOMINION.
Abe thinks this a whim. A whim! If only he knew.
Even now... gripped with icy dread.
"A drowning man grasps at a straw."
Abe will never know the effort needed... to ride that train... to come here.
And I mustn't under-estimate the gravity of these next few days.
I must dig deep... find some hidden reserve of spirit.
And yet, oddly, a feeling of calm comes over me.
Tomorrow, I will sell!

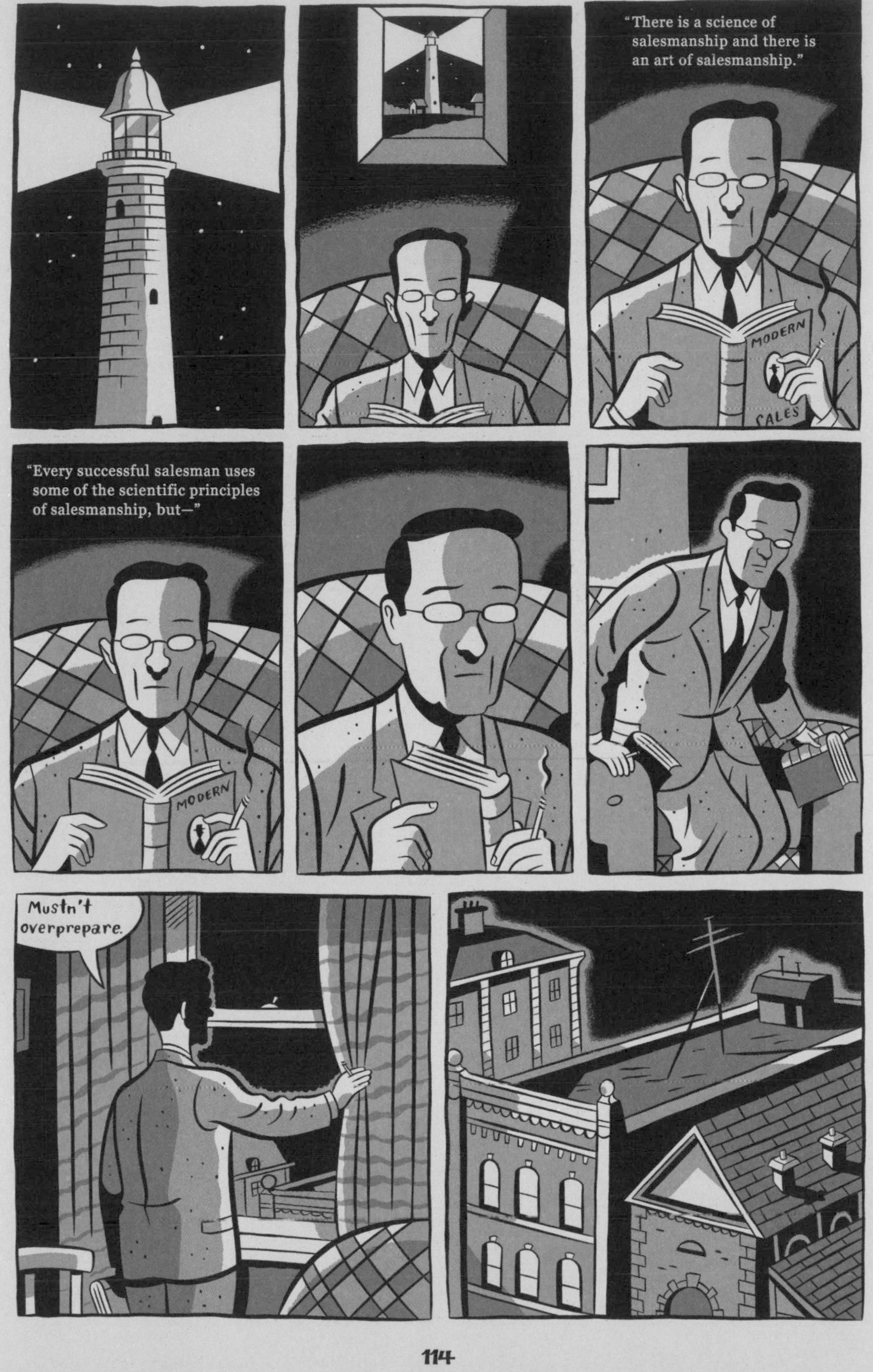
"There is a science of salesmanship and there is an art of salesmanship."
MODERN
SALES
"Every successful salesman uses some of the scientific principles of salesmanship, but—"
MODERN
Mustn't overprepare.

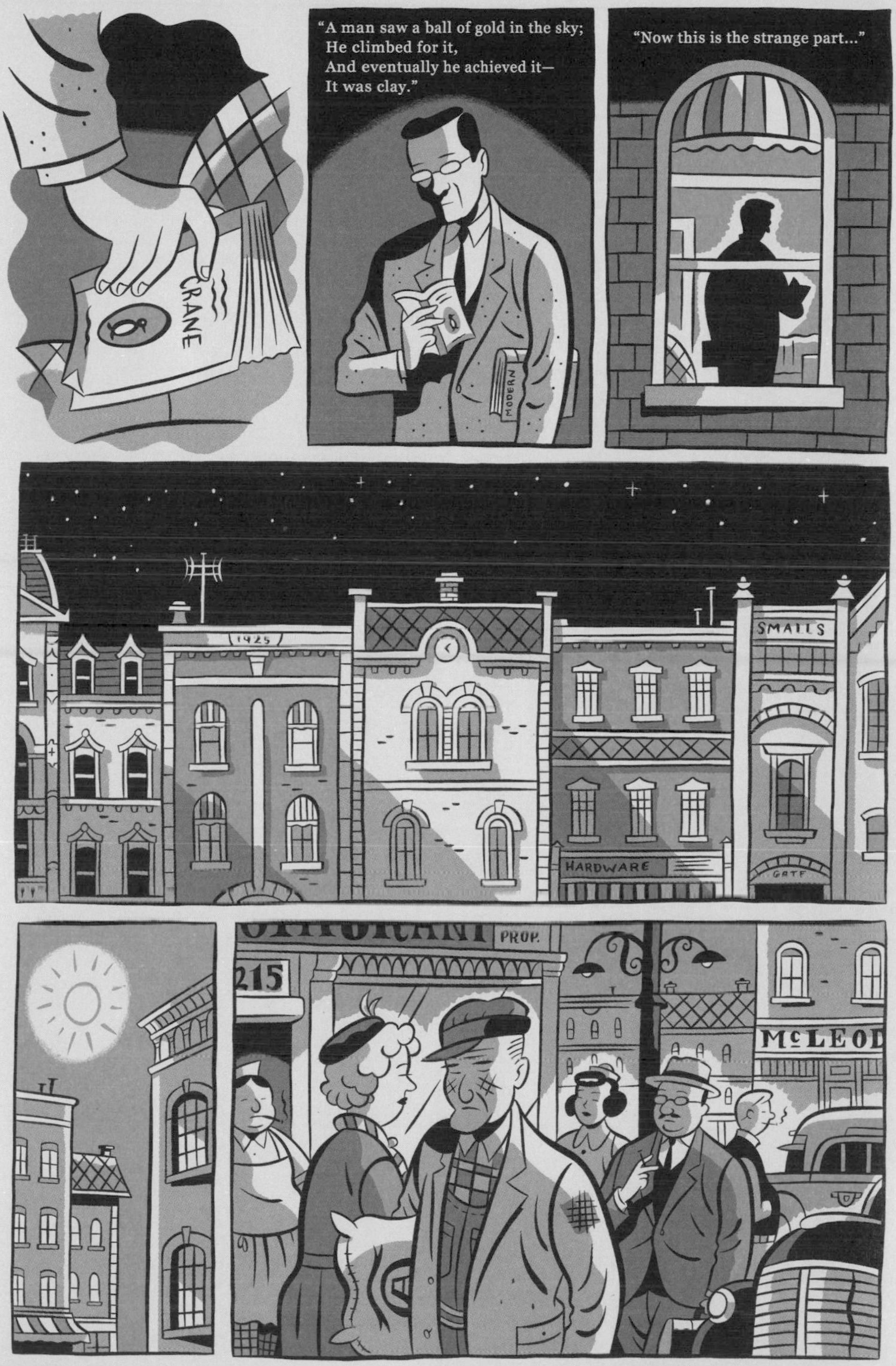
CRANE
"A man saw a ball of gold in the sky;
He climbed for it,
And eventually he achieved it—
It was clay."
MODERN
"Now this is the strange part..."
1925
SMALLS
HARDWARE
PROP.
215
McLEOD

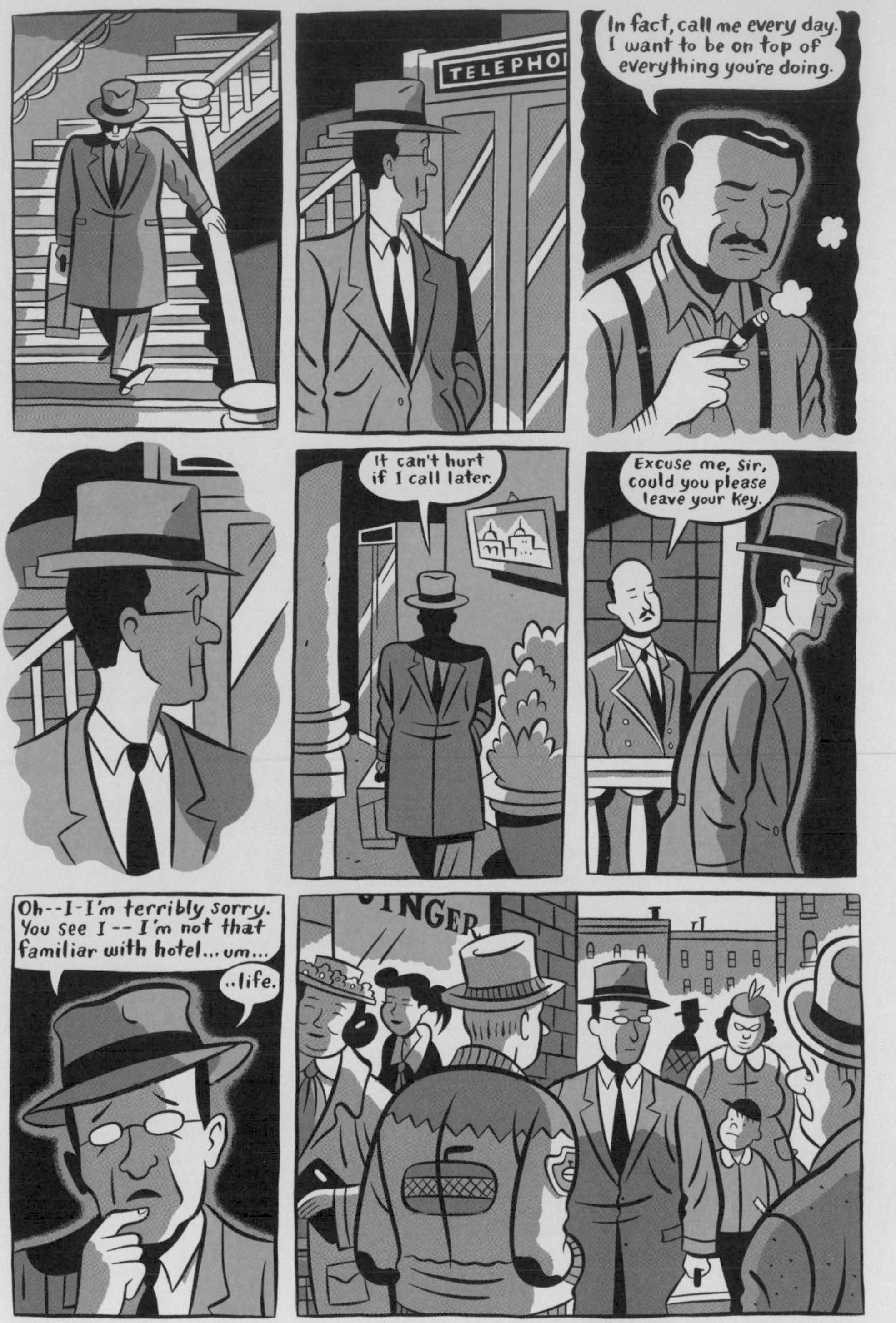
TELEPHO
In fact, call me every day. I want to be on top of everything you're doing.
It can't hurt if I call later.
Excuse me, sir, could you please leave your key.
Oh--I-I'm terribly sorry. You see I -- I'm not that familiar with hotel... um...
..life.
INGER

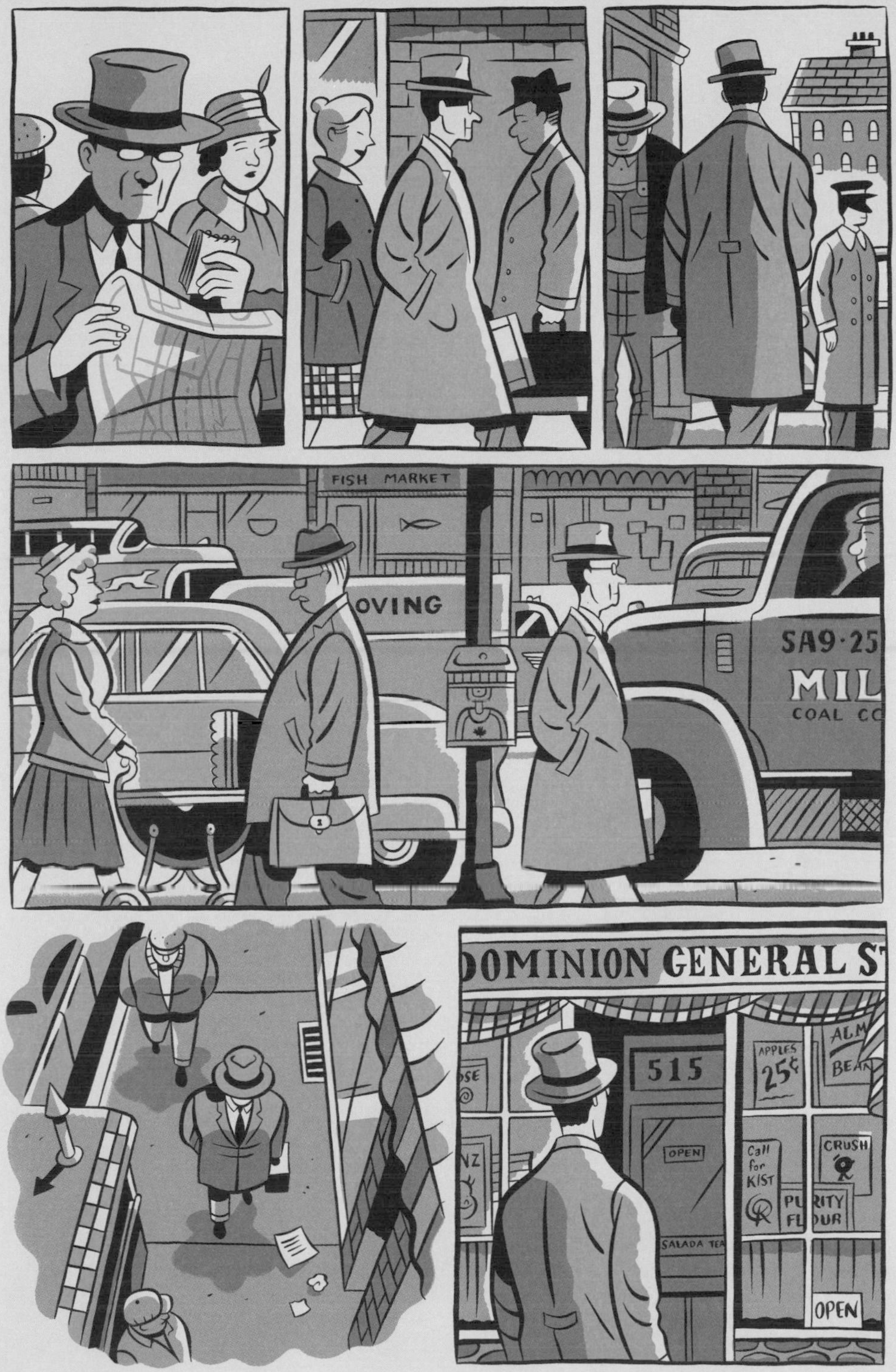
FISH MARKET
OVING
SA9·25
MIL
COAL CO
DOMINION GENERAL ST
515
APPLES 25¢
OPEN
Call for KIST
CRUSH
PURITY FLOUR
SALADA TEA
OPEN

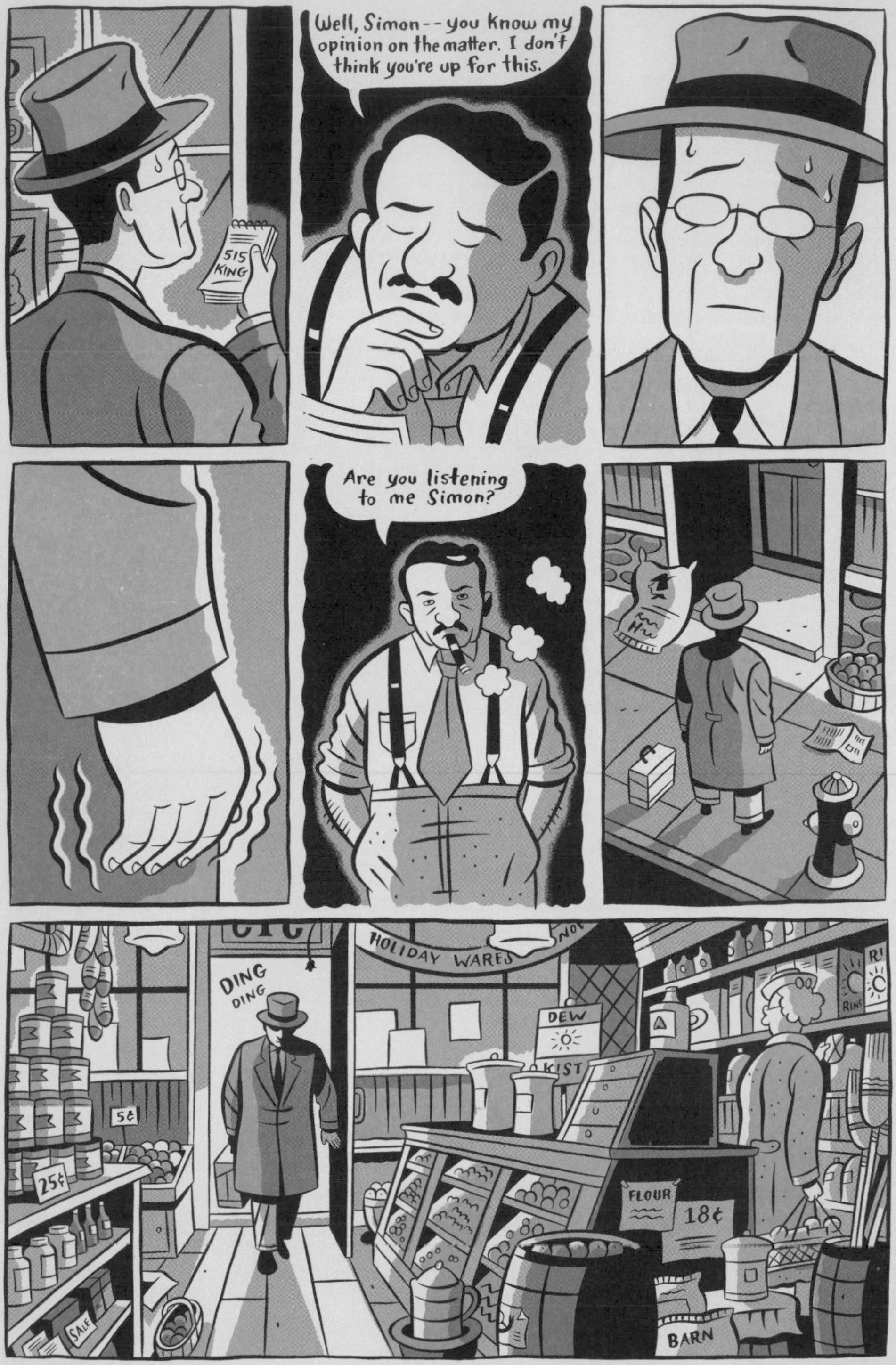
515 KING
Well, Simon-- you know my opinion on the matter. I don't think you're up for this.
Are you listening to me Simon?
HOLIDAY WARES
DING DING
DEW
KIST
5¢
25¢
FLOUR
18¢
SALE
BARN

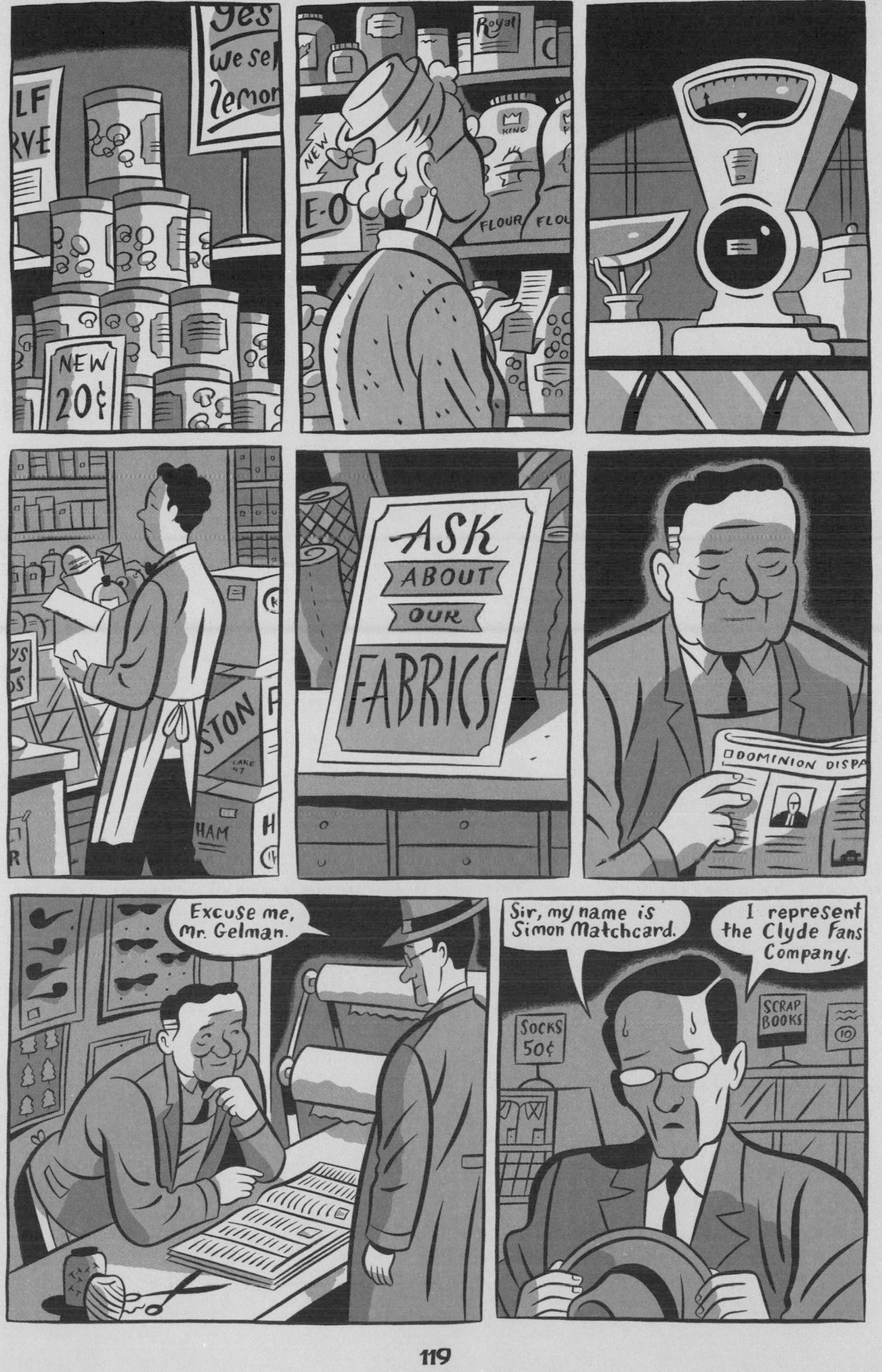
Yes
NEW 20¢
Royal
NEW
KING
FLOUR
ASK ABOUT OUR FABRICS
Excuse me, Mr. Gelman.
Sir, my name is Simon Matchcard.
I represent the Clyde Fans Company.
SOCKS 50¢
SCRAP BOOKS

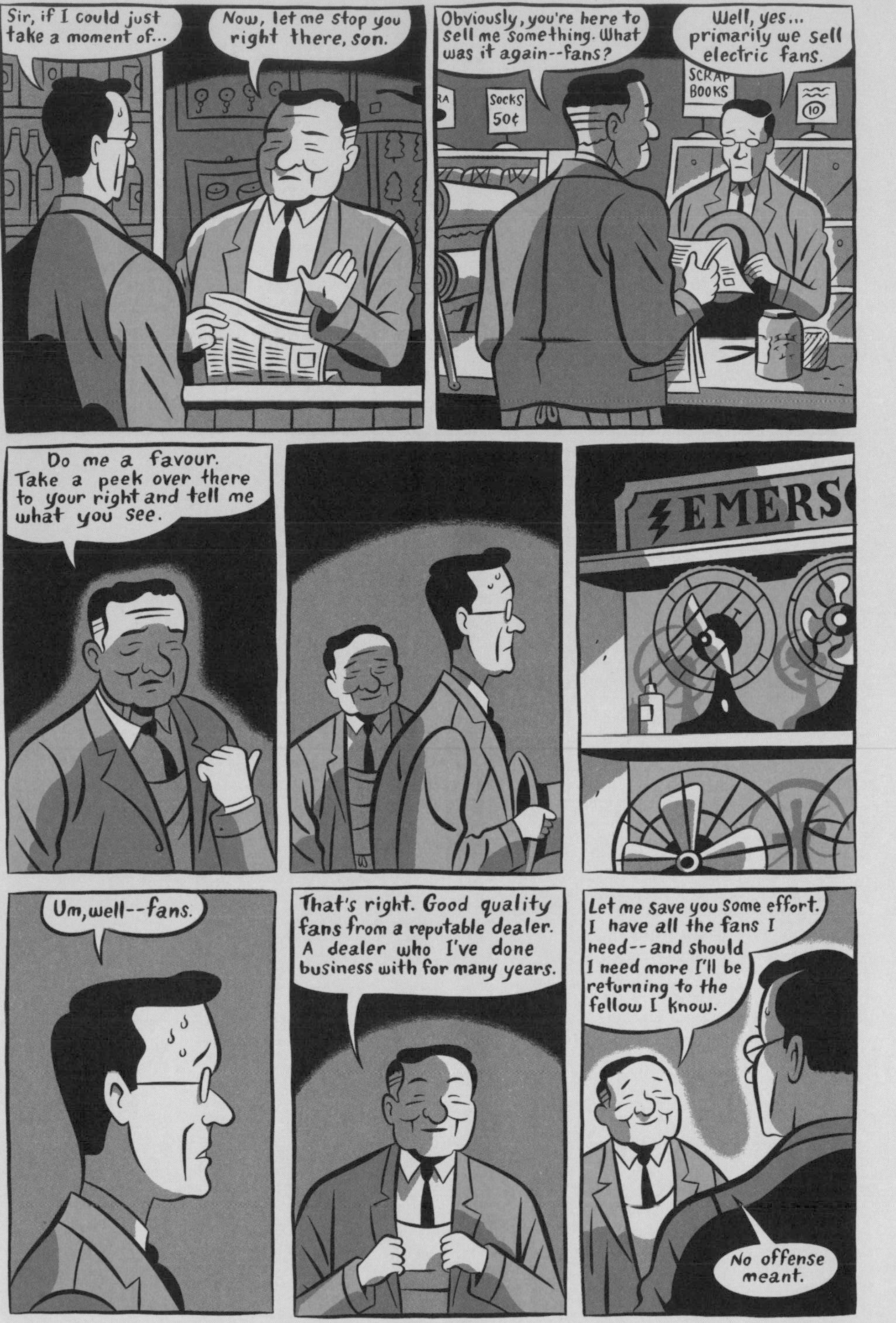

Sir, if I could just take a moment of...
Now, let me stop you right there, son.
Obviously, you're here to sell me something. What was it again--fans?
Well, yes... primarily we sell electric fans.
SOCKS 50¢
SCRAP BOOKS
Do me a favour. Take a peek over there to your right and tell me what you see.
EMERS
Um, well--fans.
That's right. Good quality fans from a reputable dealer. A dealer who I've done business with for many years.
Let me save you some effort. I have all the fans I need--and should I need more I'll be returning to the fellow I know.
No offense meant.

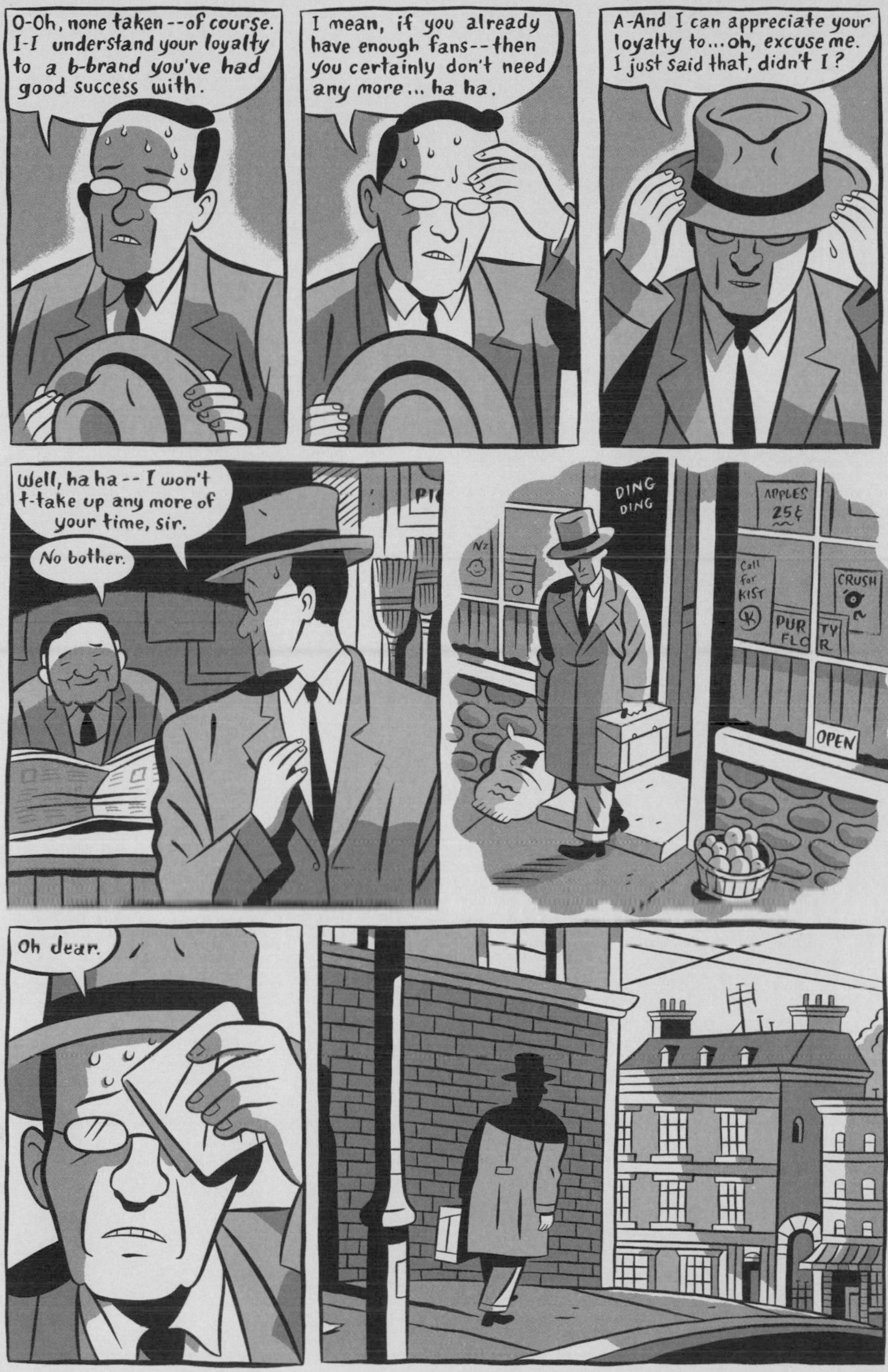
O-Oh, none taken--of course. I-I understand your loyalty to a b-brand you've had good success with.
I mean, if you already have enough fans--then you certainly don't need any more... ha ha.
A-And I can appreciate your loyalty to...oh, excuse me. I just said that, didn't I?
Well, ha ha-- I won't t-take up any more of your time, sir.
No bother.
DING DING
APPLES 25¢
Call for KIST
CRUSH
PUR TY FLO R
OPEN
Oh dear.

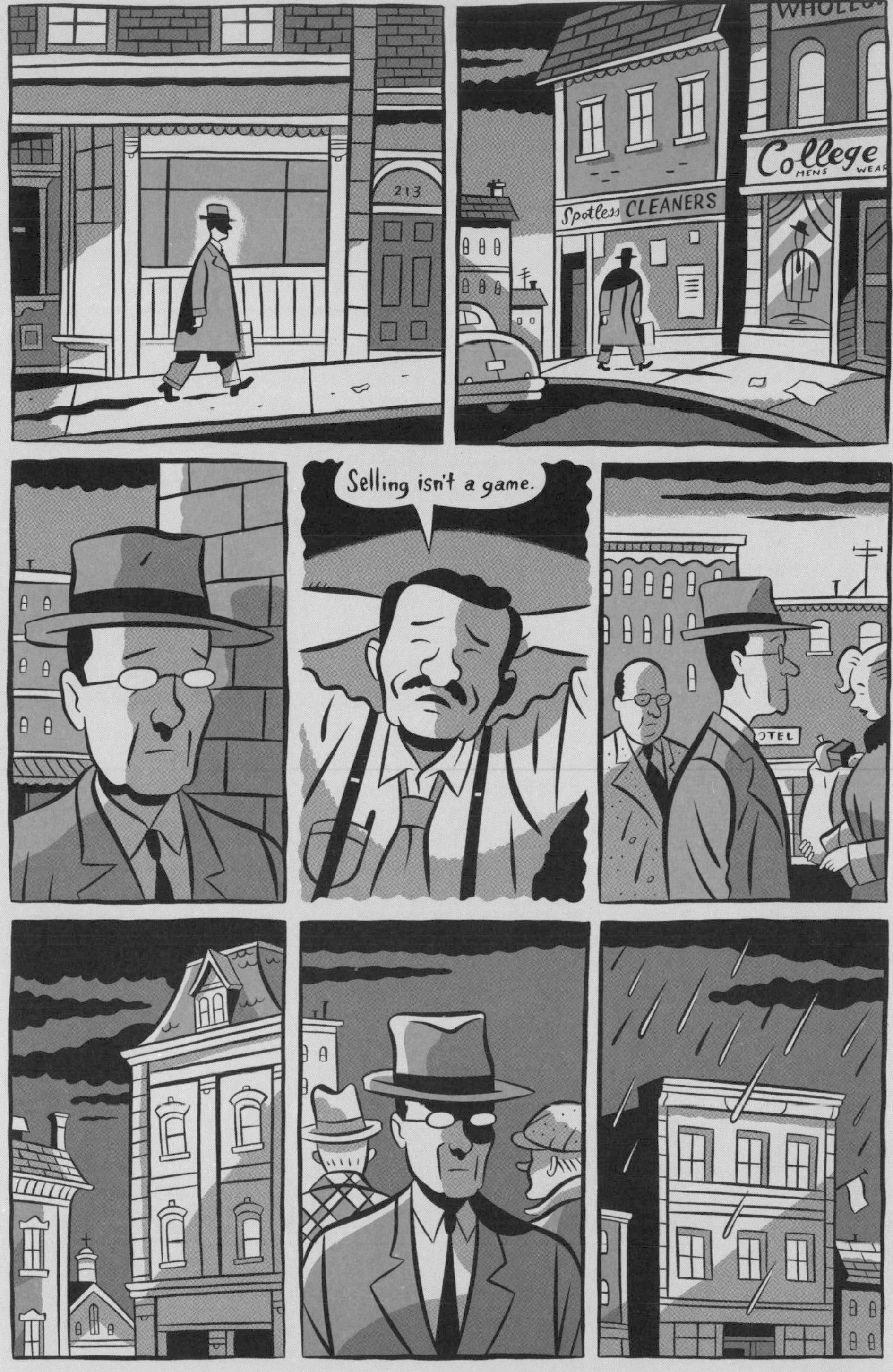
213
WHOLE
College
MENS WEAR
Spotless CLEANERS
Selling isn't a game.
OTEL

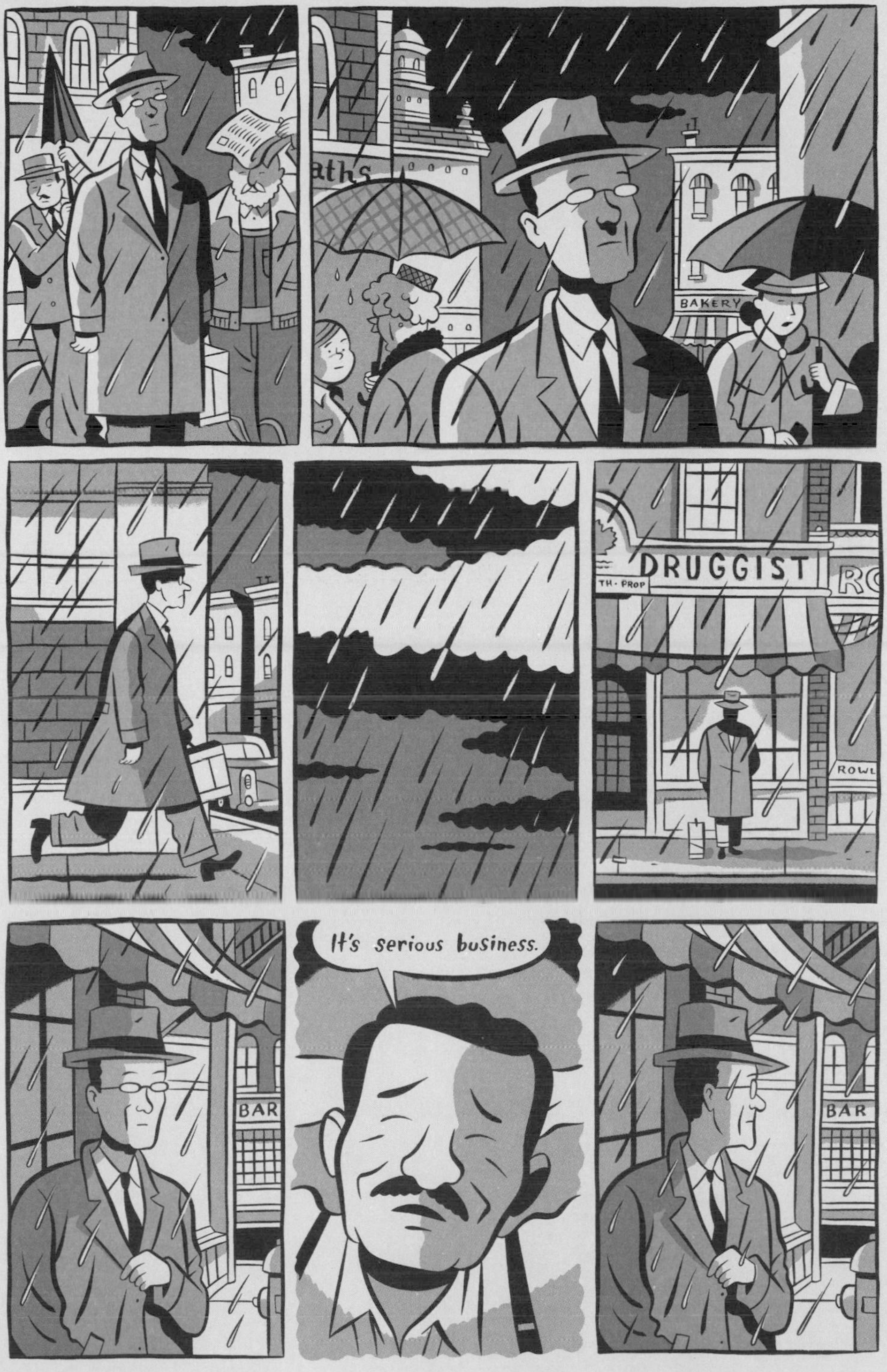
ath's
BAKERY
DRUGGIST
TH. PROP
ROWL
BAR
It's serious business.
BAR

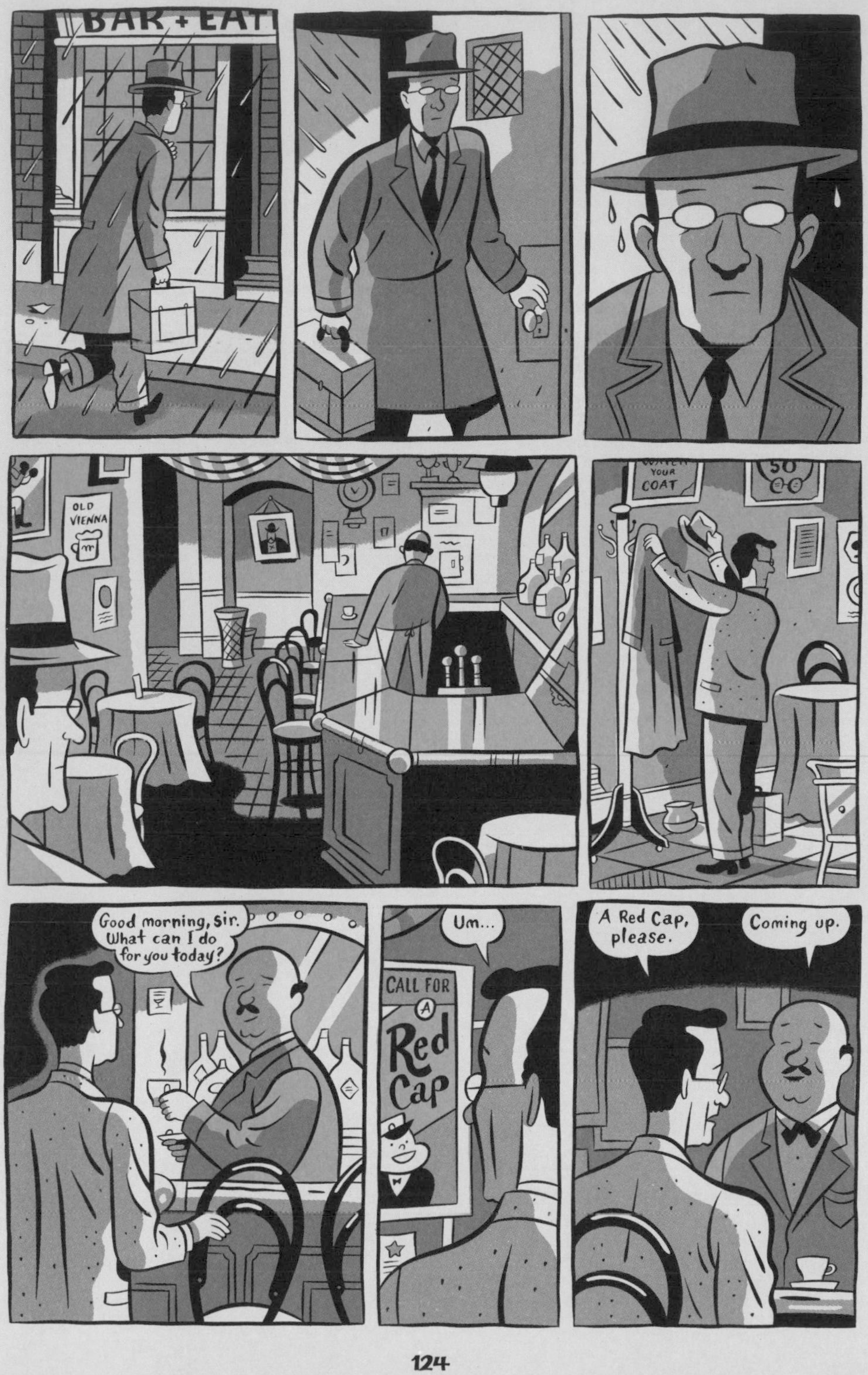
BAR + EAT
OLD VIENNA
YOUR COAT
50
Good morning, sir. What can I do for you today?
Um...
CALL FOR A Red Cap
A Red Cap, please.
Coming up.

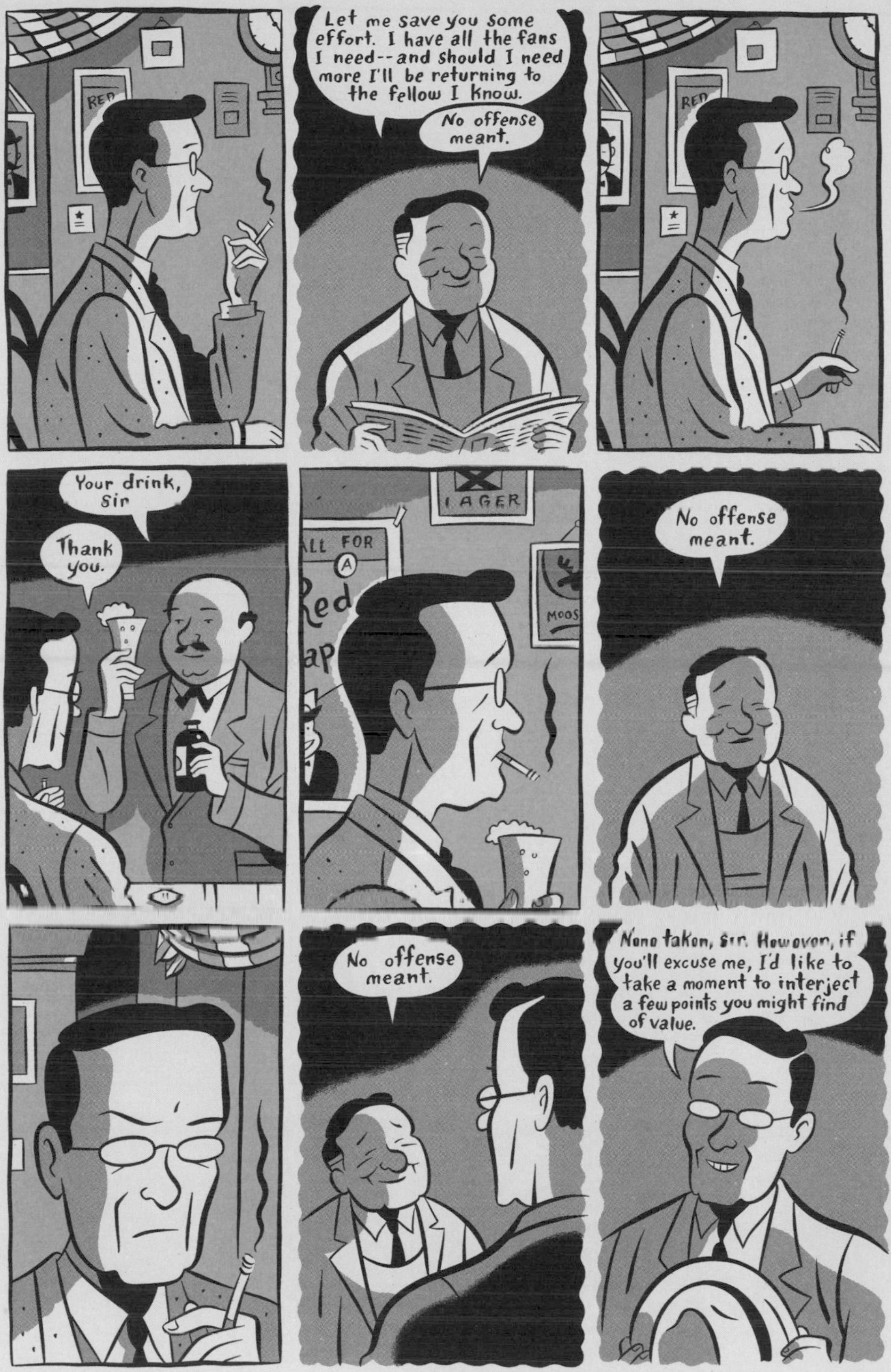
Let me save you some effort. I have all the fans I need--and should I need more I'll be returning to the fellow I know.
No offense meant.
RED
Your drink, sir
Thank you.
LAGER
ALL FOR
A
Red
MOOS
No offense meant.
No offense meant.
None taken, sir. However, if you'll excuse me, I'd like to take a moment to interject a few points you might find of value.

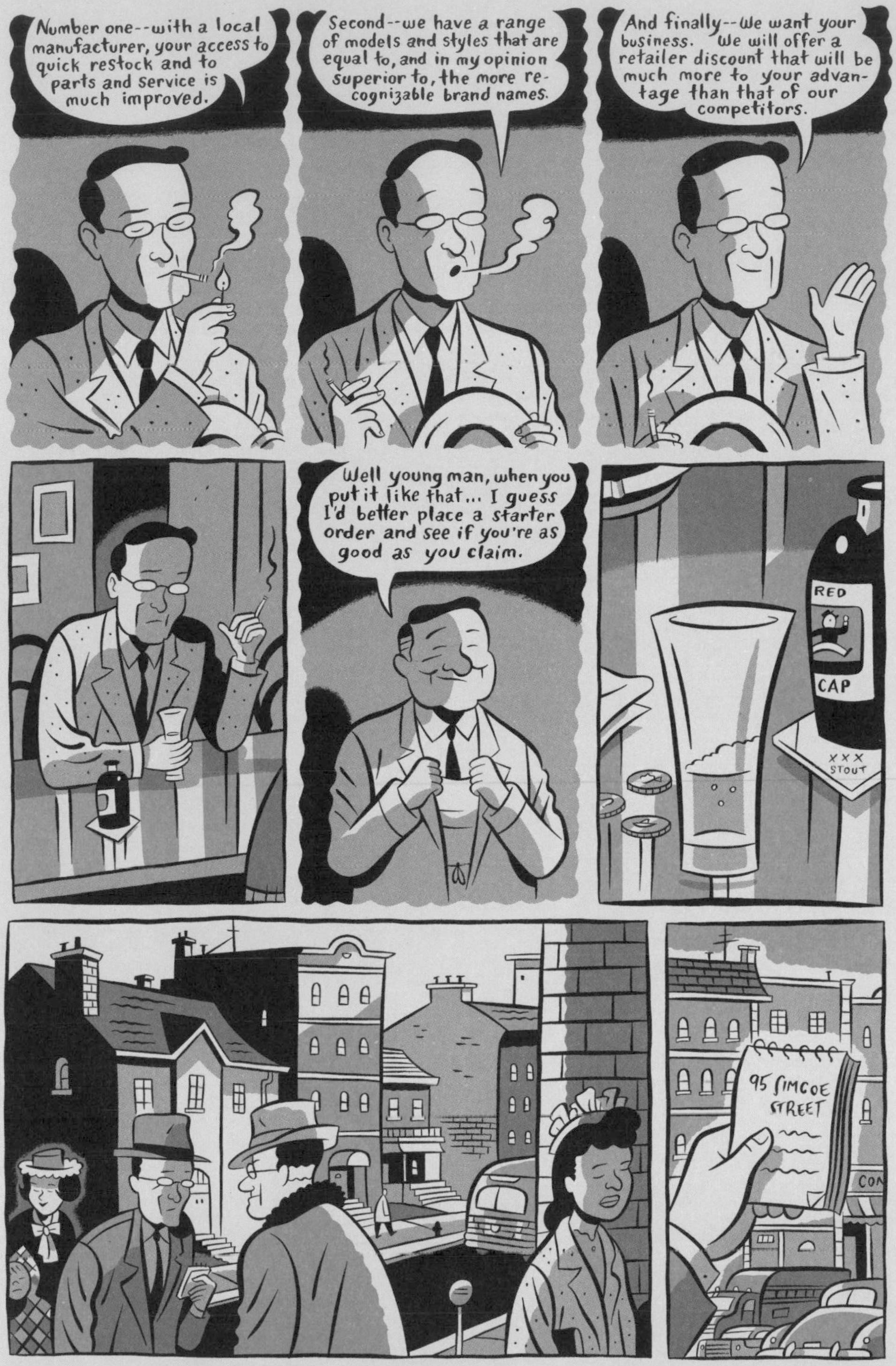

Number one--with a local manufacturer, your access to quick restock and to parts and service is much improved.
Second--we have a range of models and styles that are equal to, and in my opinion superior to, the more recognizable brand names.
And finally--We want your business. We will offer a retailer discount that will be much more to your advantage than that of our competitors.
Well young man, when you put it like that... I guess I'd better place a starter order and see if you're as good as you claim.
RED CAP
XXX STOUT
95 SIMCOE STREET

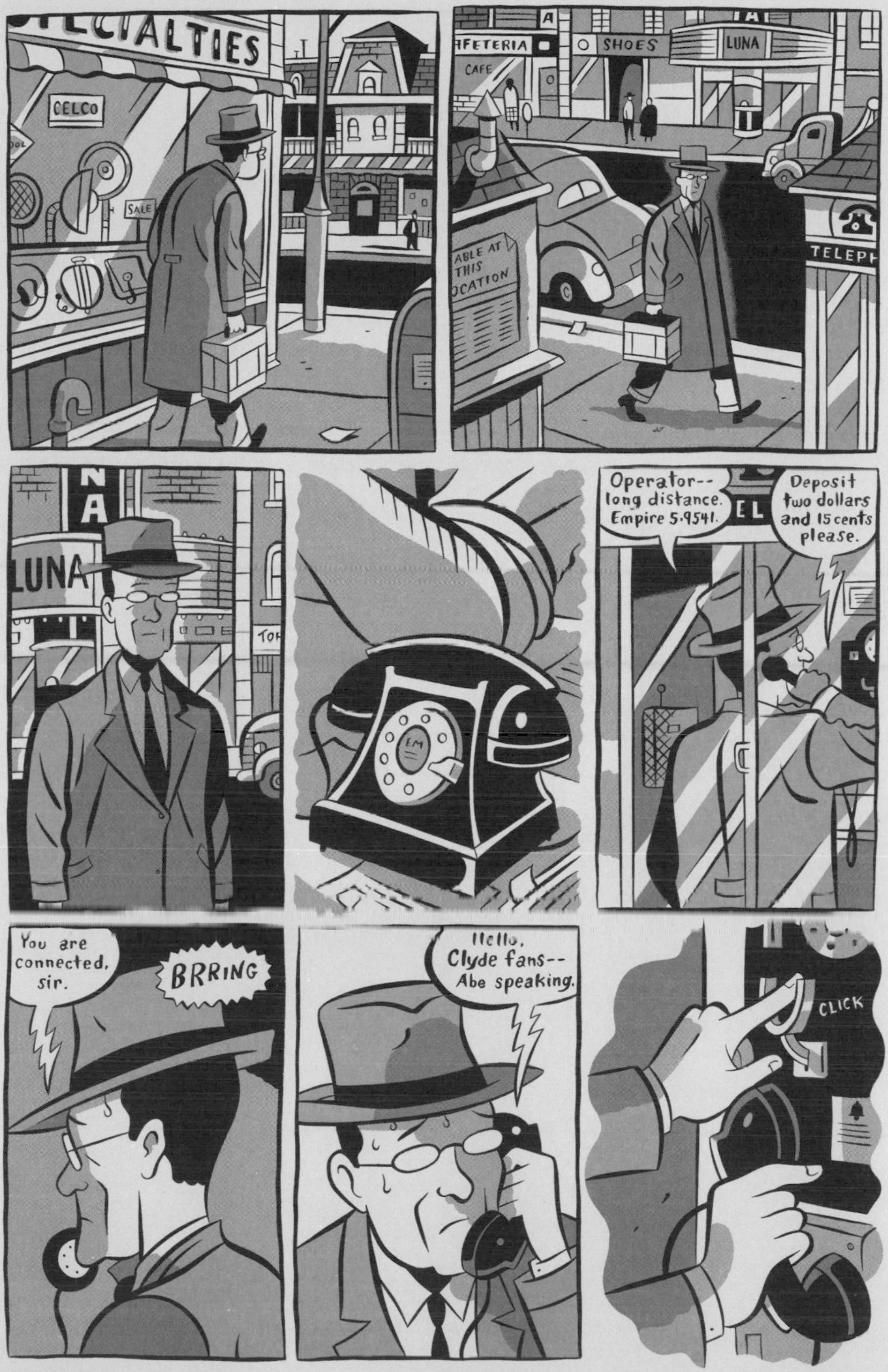
SPECIALTIES
CELCO
SALE
AFETERIA
CAFE
SHOES
LUNA
ABLE AT
THIS
OCATION
TELEPH
LUNA
Operator--
long distance.
Empire 5.9541.
Deposit
two dollars
and 15 cents
please.
You are
connected,
sir.
BRRING
Hello,
Clyde fans--
Abe speaking.
CLICK

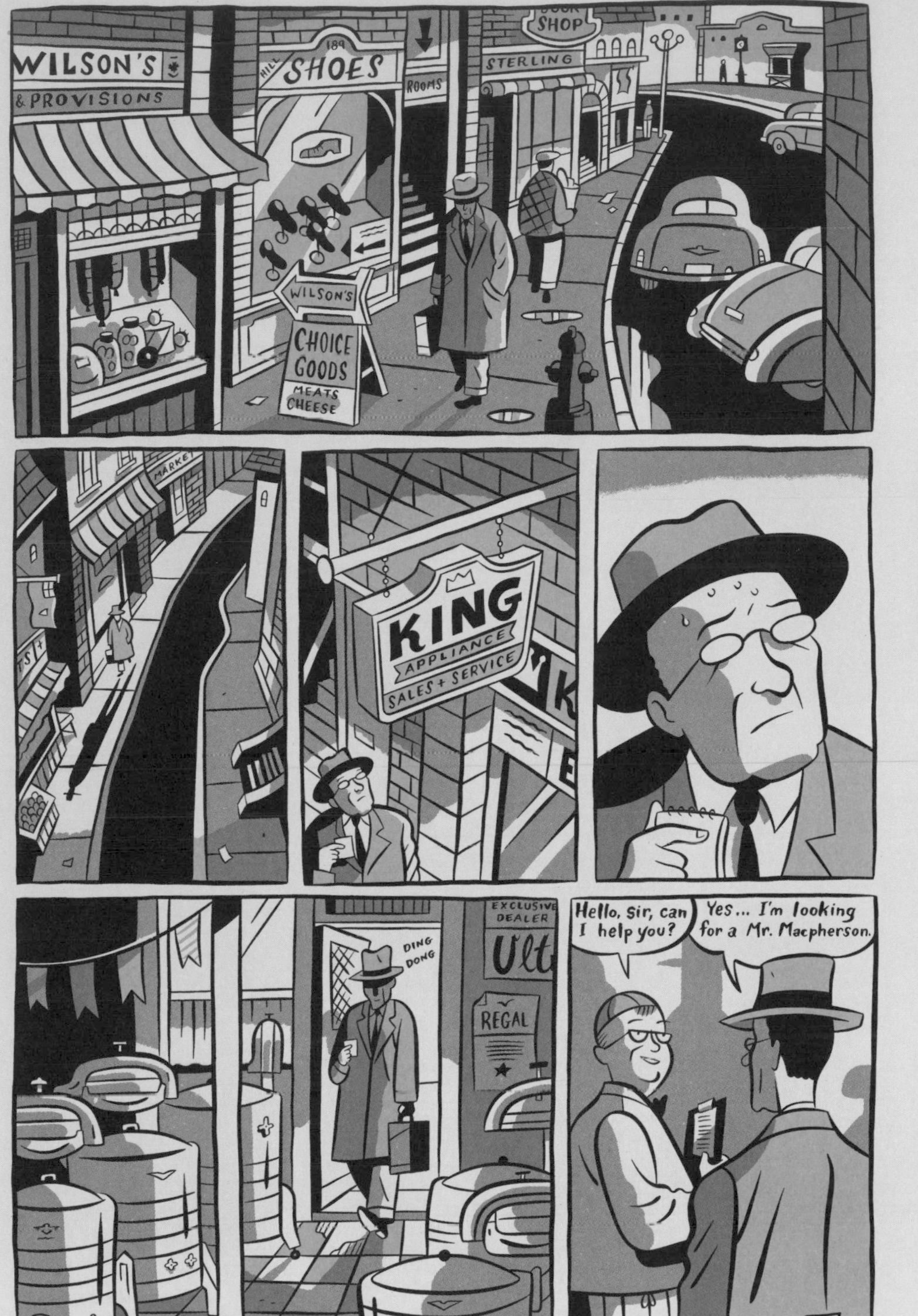
WILSON'S
& PROVISIONS
189
HILL SHOES
ROOMS
SHOP
STERLING
WILSON'S
CHOICE GOODS
MEATS
CHEESE
KING
APPLIANCE
SALES + SERVICE
EXCLUSIVE DEALER
DING DONG
REGAL
Hello, sir, can I help you?
Yes... I'm looking for a Mr. Macpherson.

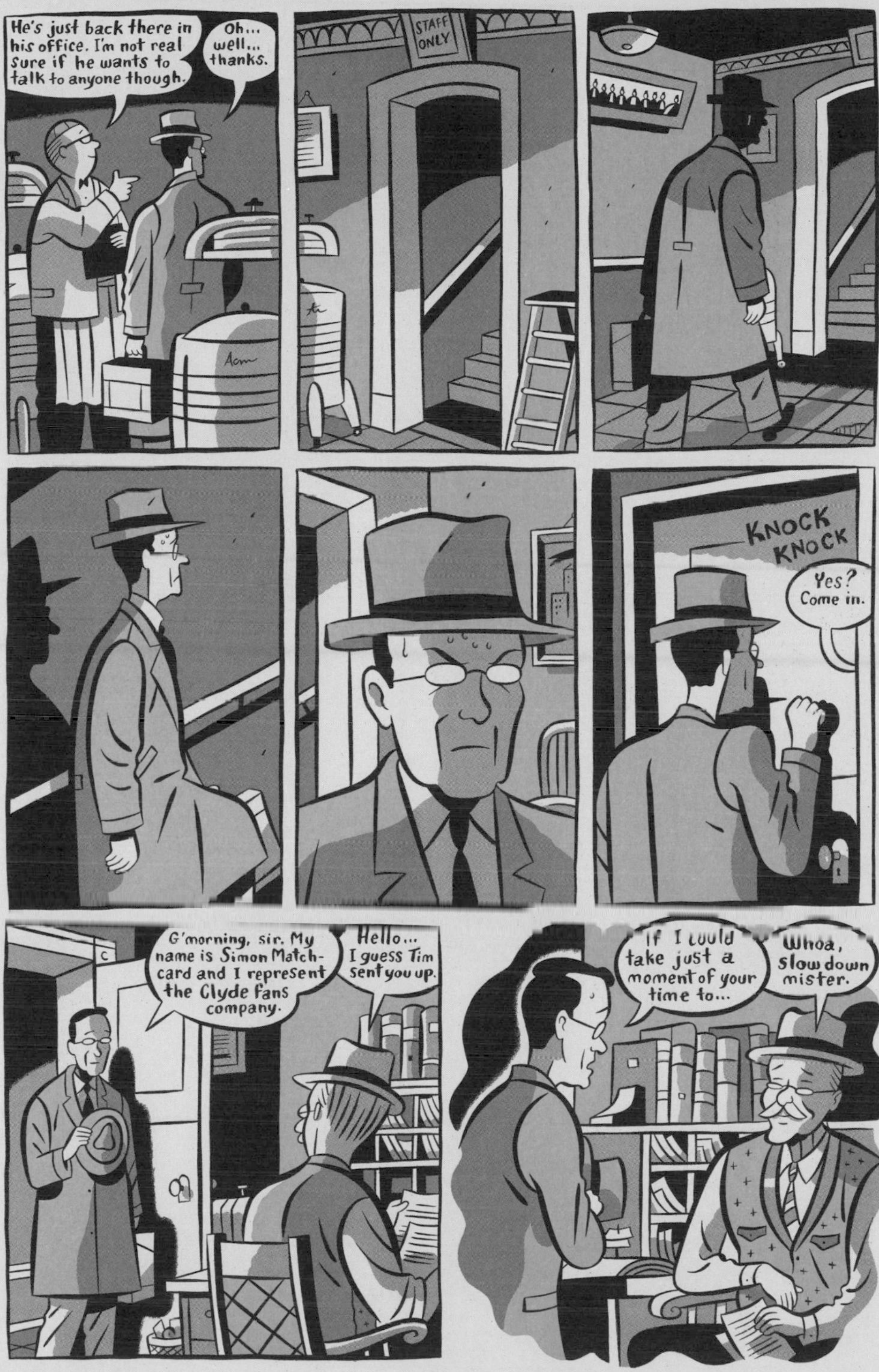
He's just back there in his office. I'm not real sure if he wants to talk to anyone though.
Oh... well... thanks.
STAFF ONLY
KNOCK KNOCK
Yes? Come in.
G'morning, sir. My name is Simon Matchcard and I represent the Clyde fans company.
Hello... I guess Tim sent you up.
If I could take just a moment of your time to...
Whoa, slow down mister.

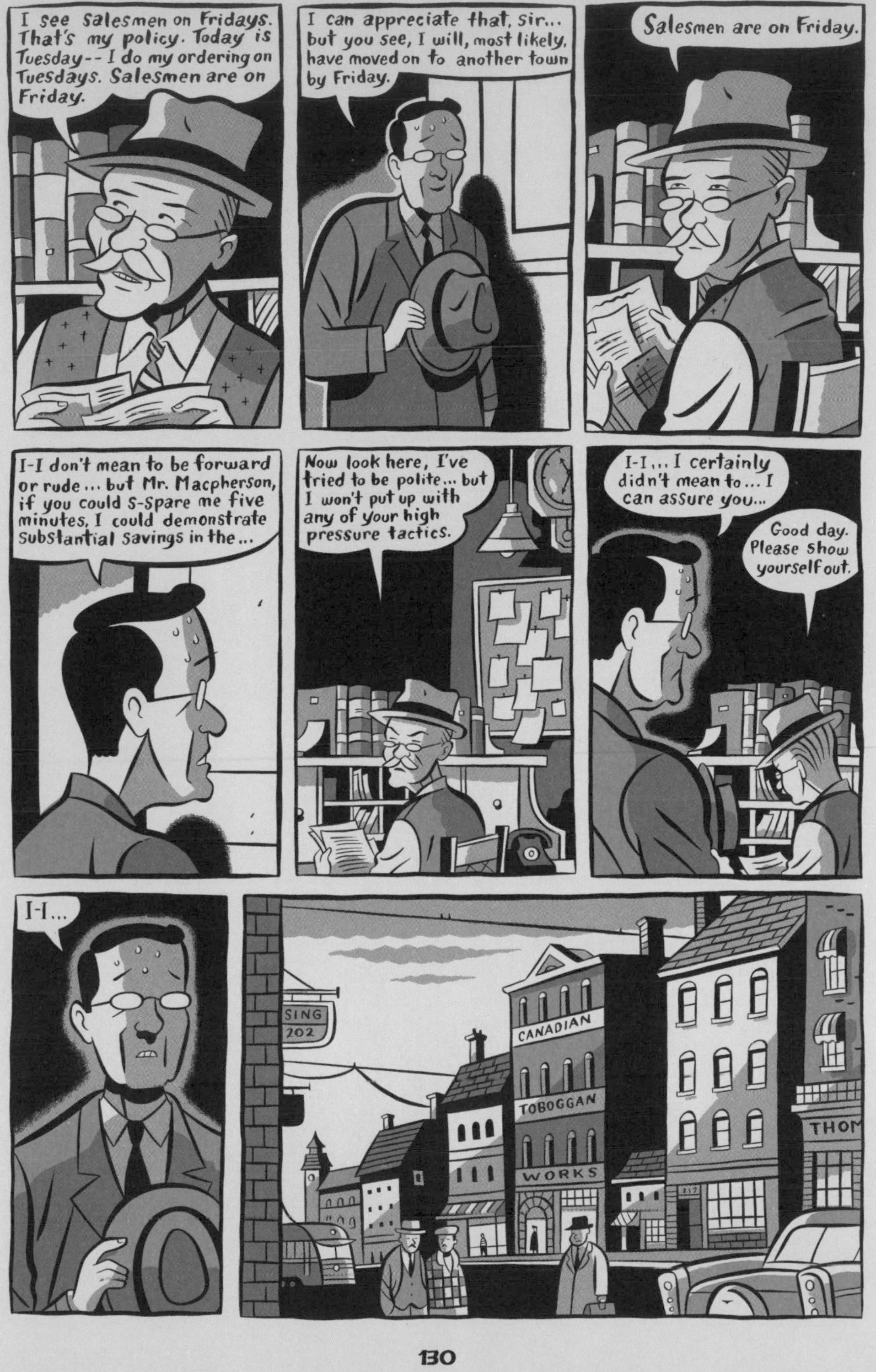
I see salesmen on Fridays. That's my policy. Today is Tuesday-- I do my ordering on Tuesdays. Salesmen are on Friday.
I can appreciate that, sir... but you see, I will, most likely, have moved on to another town by Friday.
Salesmen are on Friday.
I-I don't mean to be forward or rude... but Mr. Macpherson, if you could s-spare me five minutes, I could demonstrate substantial savings in the...
Now look here, I've tried to be polite... but I won't put up with any of your high pressure tactics.
I-I... I certainly didn't mean to... I can assure you...
Good day. Please show yourself out.
I-I...
SING
202
CANADIAN
TOBOGGAN
WORKS
THOM

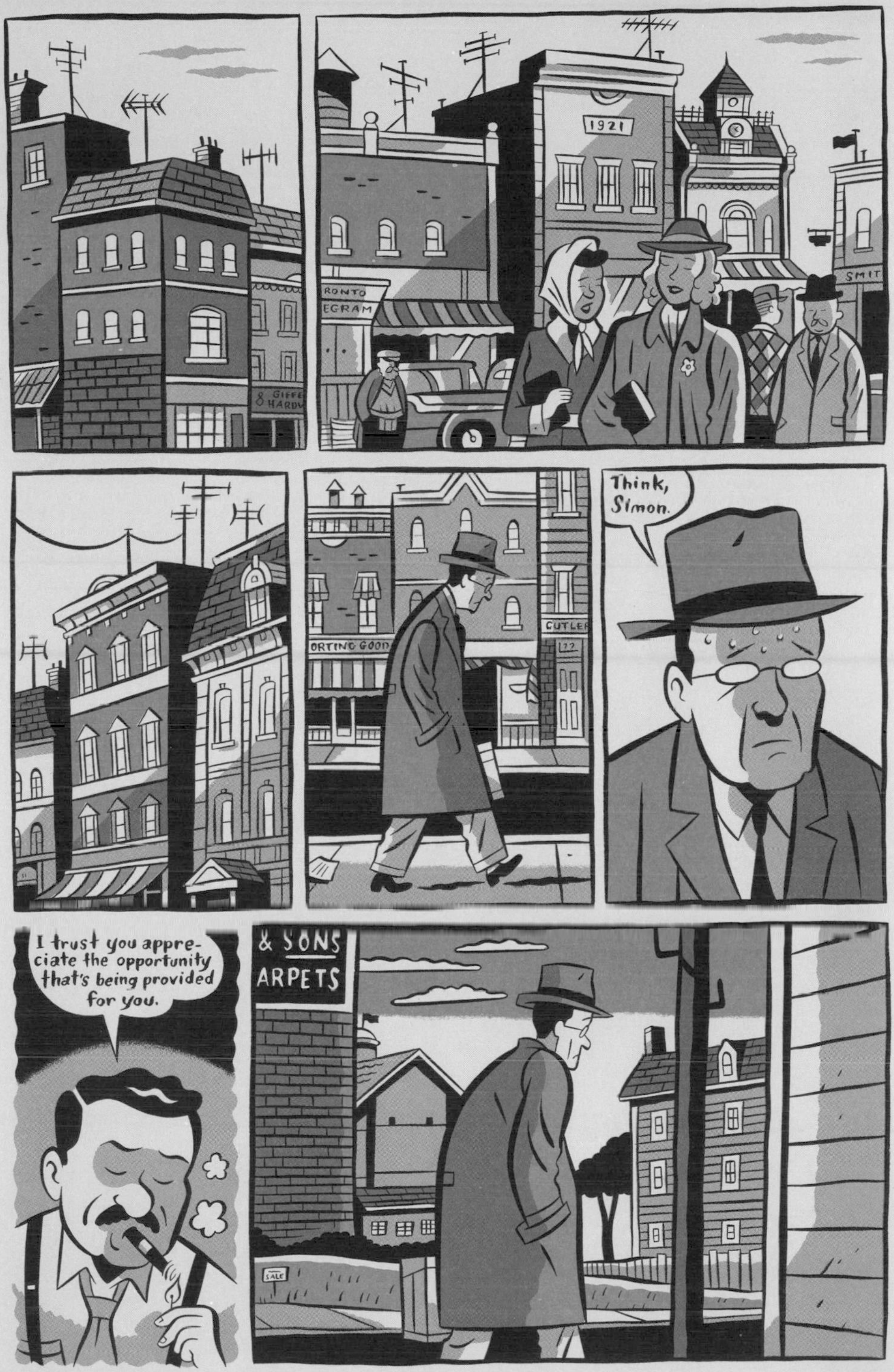
1921
RONTO
EGRAM
SMIT
GIFFE
HARDW
ORTING GOOD
CUTLER
Think, Simon.
I trust you appreciate the opportunity that's being provided for you.
& SONS
ARPETS
SALE

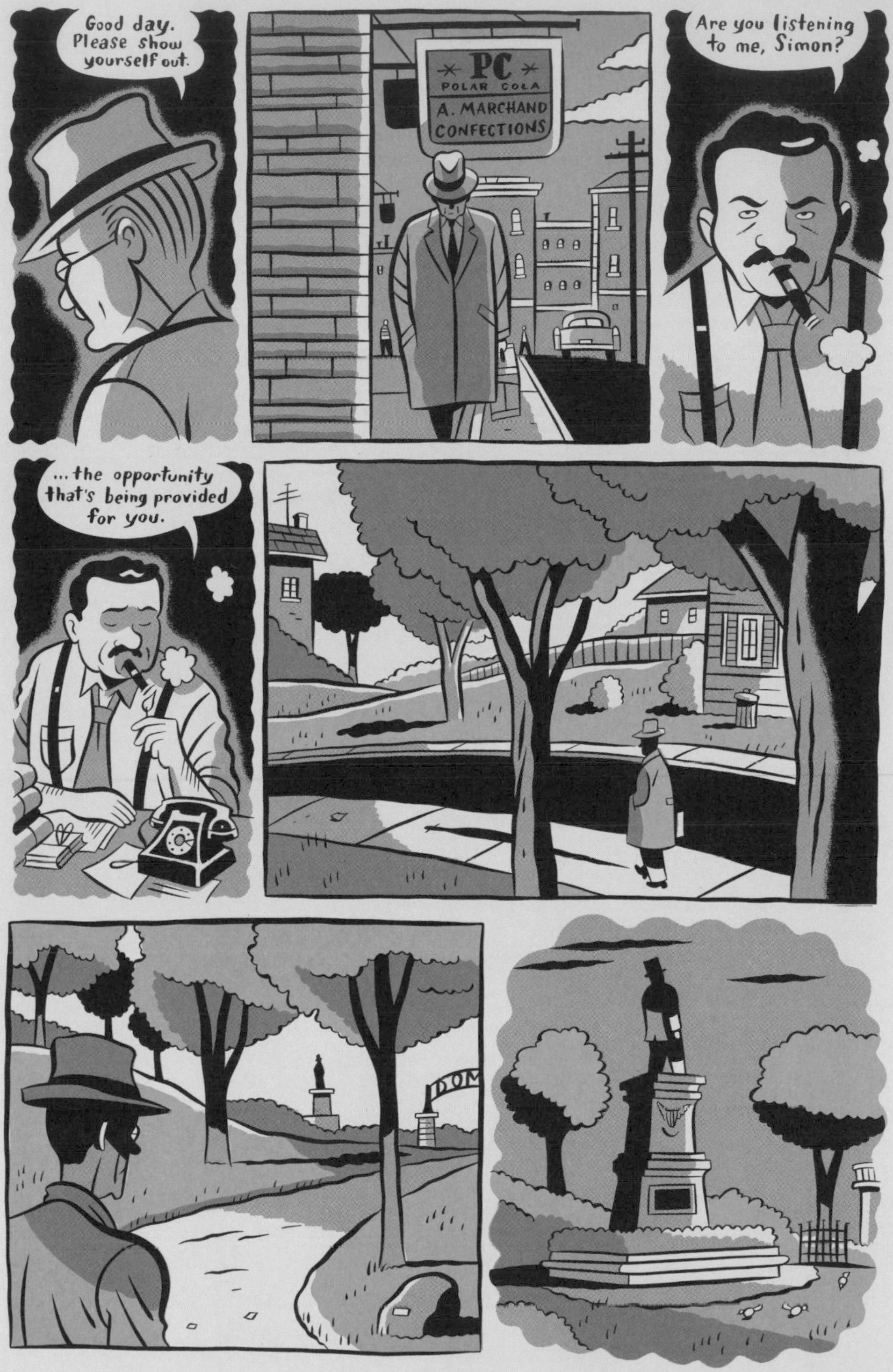
Good day. Please show yourself out.
PC
POLAR COLA
A. MARCHAND CONFECTIONS
Are you listening to me, Simon?
...the opportunity that's being provided for you.
DOM

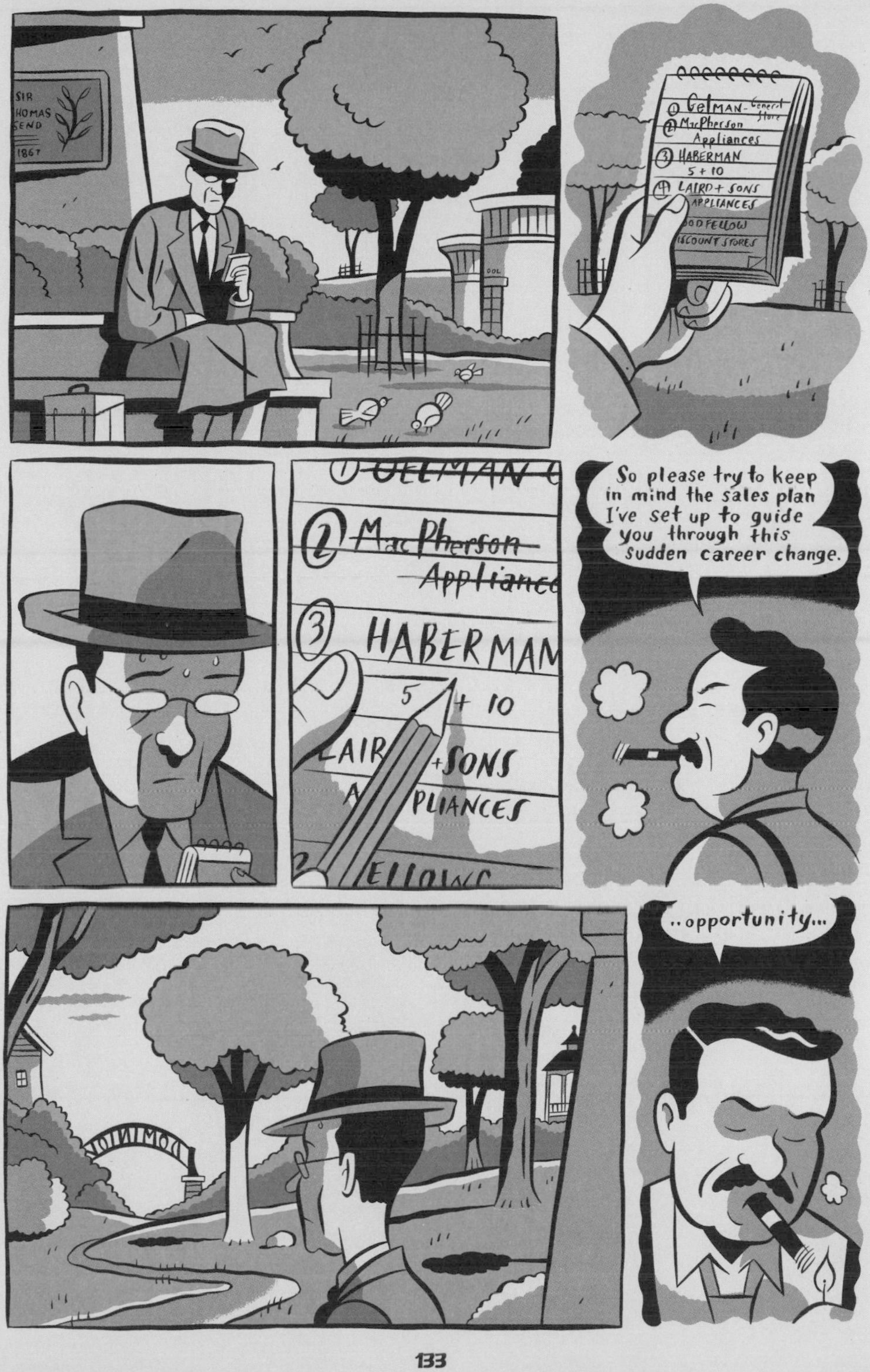

1 Gelman - General Store
2 MacPherson Appliances
3 HABERMAN 5 + 10
4 LAIRD + SONS APPLIANCES
So please try to keep in mind the sales plan I've set up to guide you through this sudden career change.
..opportunity...

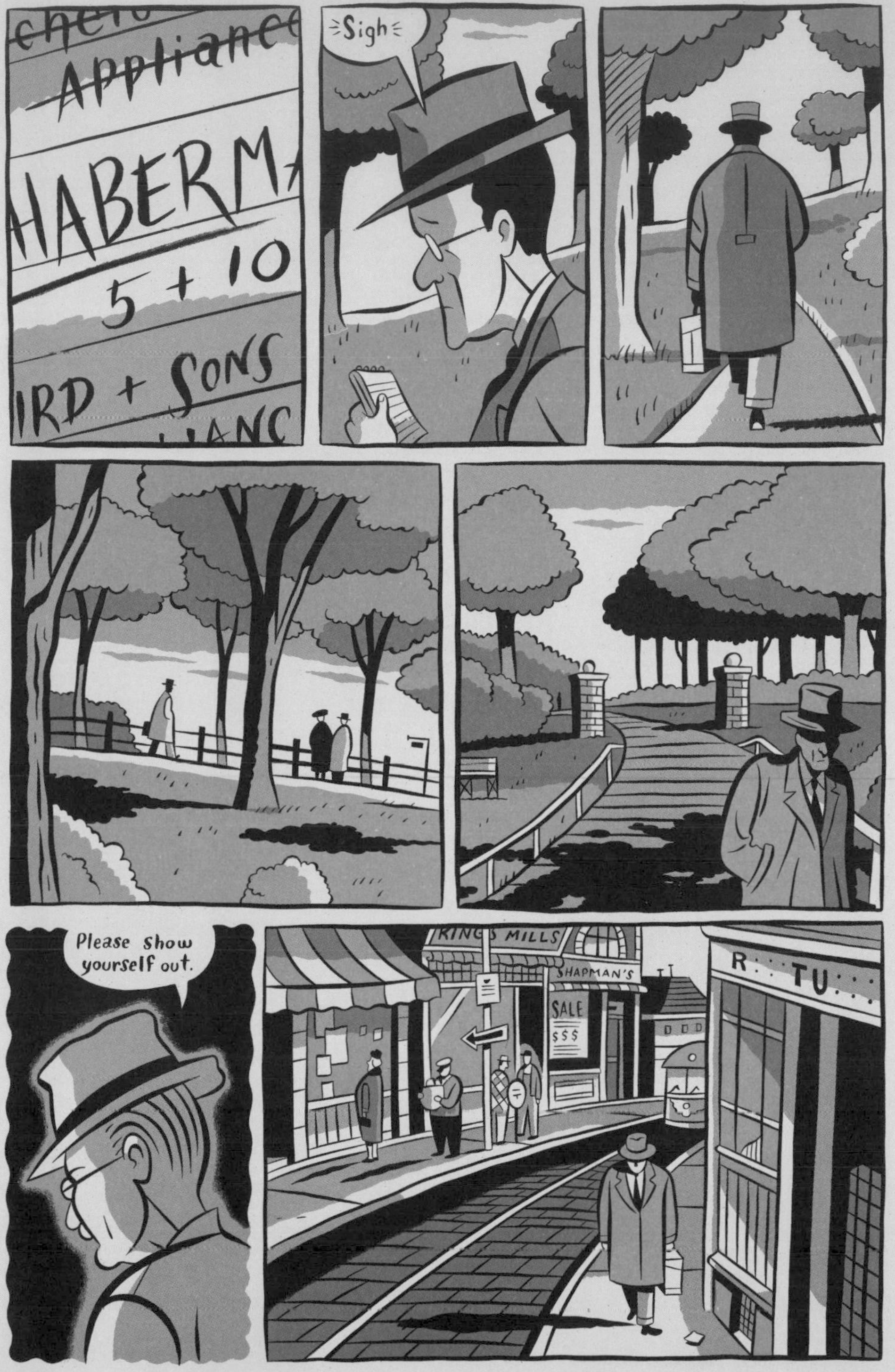
Appliance
HABERM
5 + 10
IRD + SONS
Sigh
Please show yourself out.
SHAPMAN'S
SALE
$$$

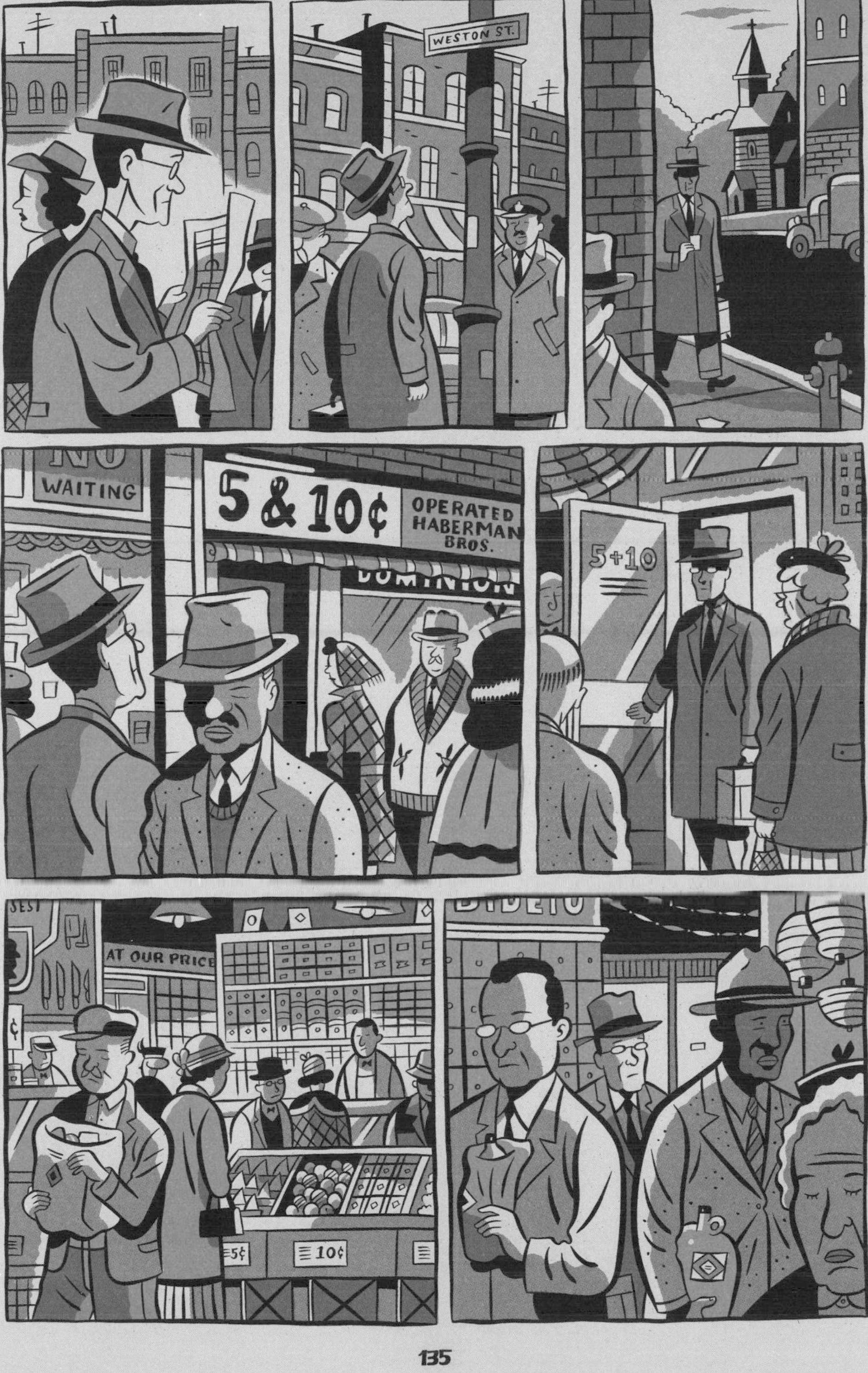
WESTON ST.
WAITING
5 & 10¢
OPERATED HABERMAN BROS.
DOMINION
5+10
AT OUR PRICE
5¢
10¢

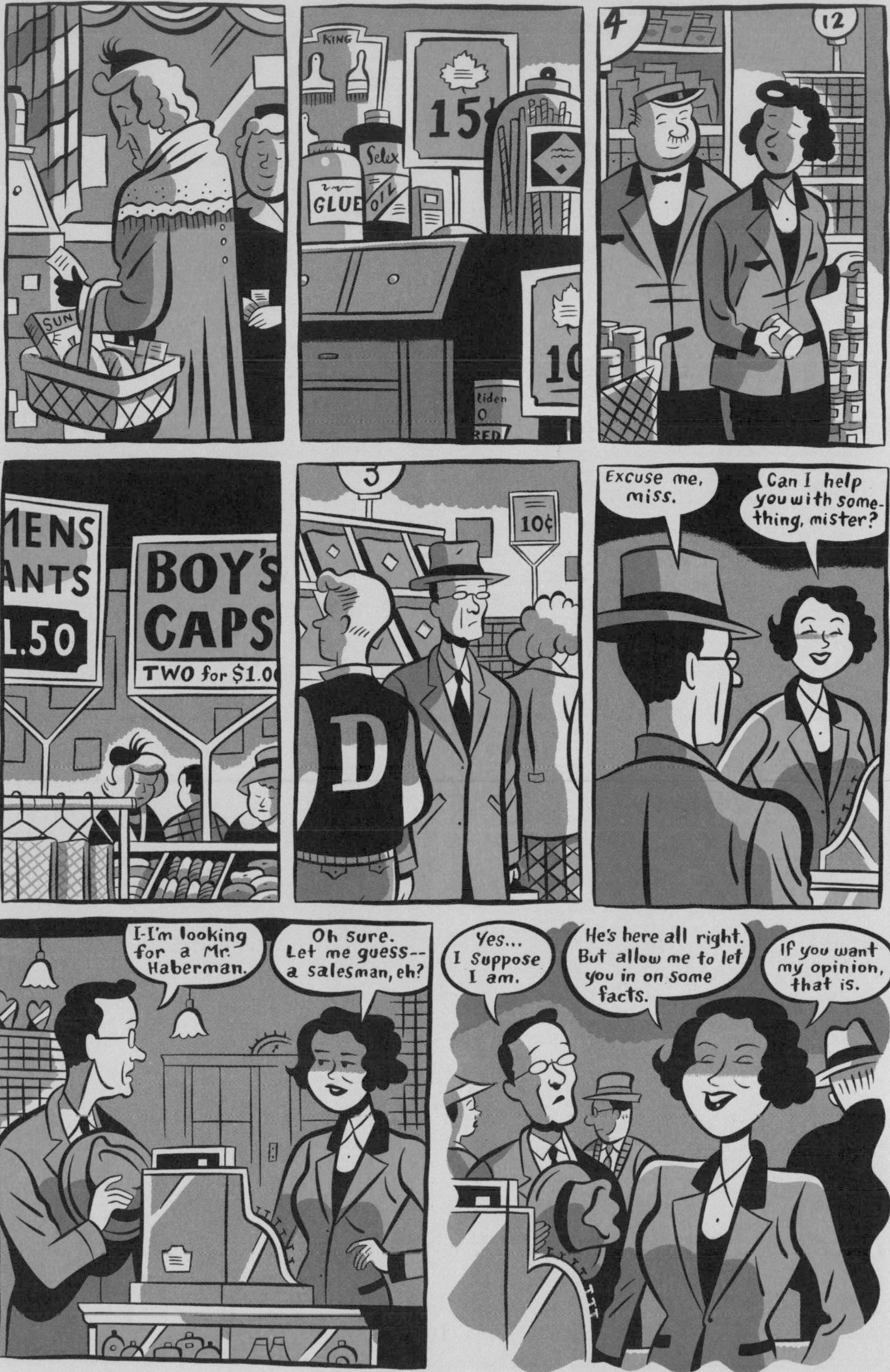
KING
15¢
Selex
GLUE
OIL
4
12
MENS
ANTS
.50
BOY'S
CAPS
TWO for $1.0
10¢
D
Excuse me, miss.
Can I help you with something, mister?
I-I'm looking for a Mr. Haberman.
Oh sure. Let me guess-- a salesman, eh?
Yes... I suppose I am.
He's here all right. But allow me to let you in on some facts.
If you want my opinion, that is.

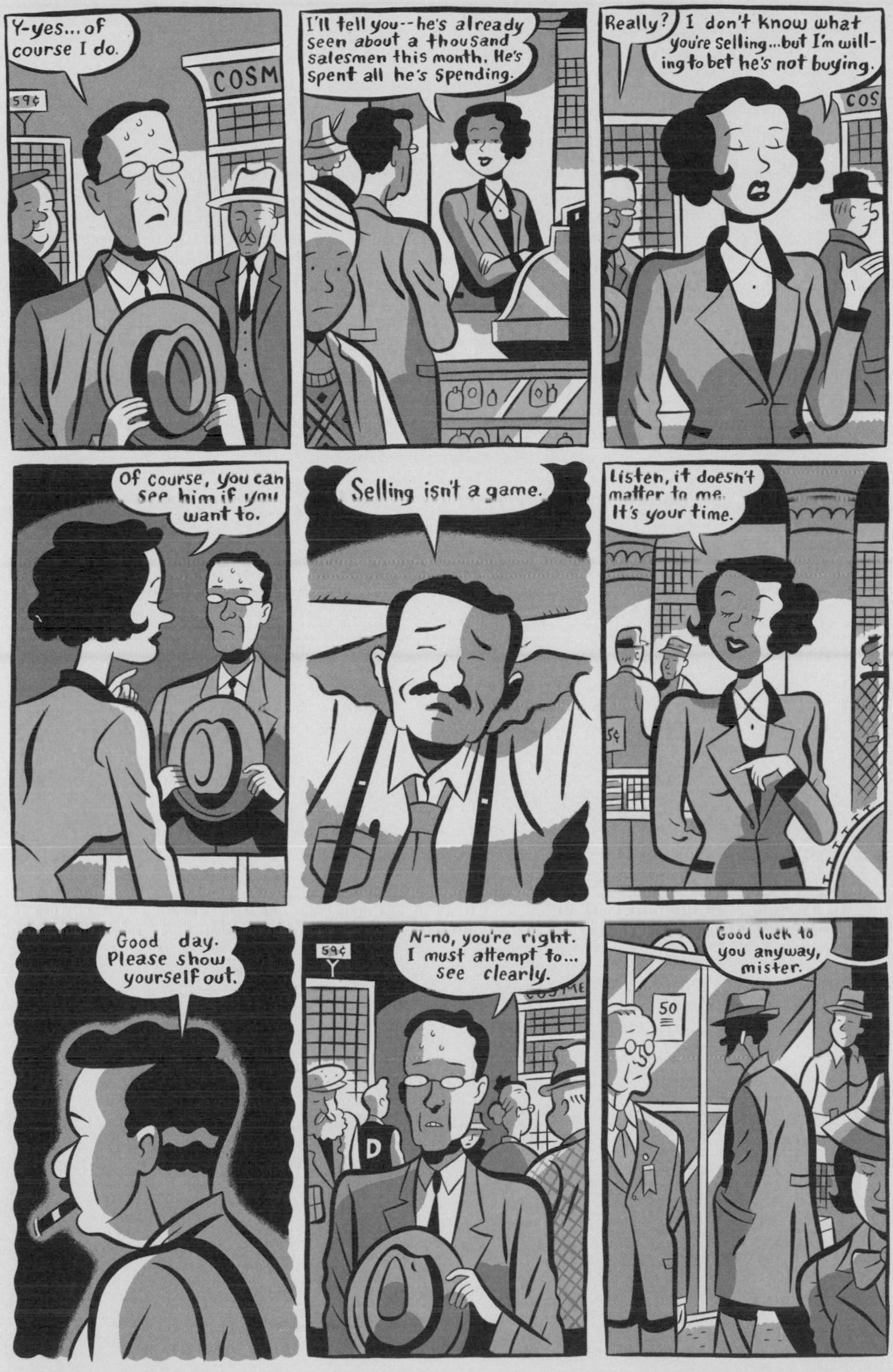
Y-yes... of course I do.
COSM
59¢
I'll tell you--he's already seen about a thousand salesmen this month. He's spent all he's spending.
Really?
I don't know what you're selling...but I'm willing to bet he's not buying.
COS
Of course, you can see him if you want to.
Selling isn't a game.
Listen, it doesn't matter to me. It's your time.
5¢
Good day. Please show yourself out.
59¢
N-no, you're right. I must attempt to... see clearly.
D
Good luck to you anyway, mister.
50

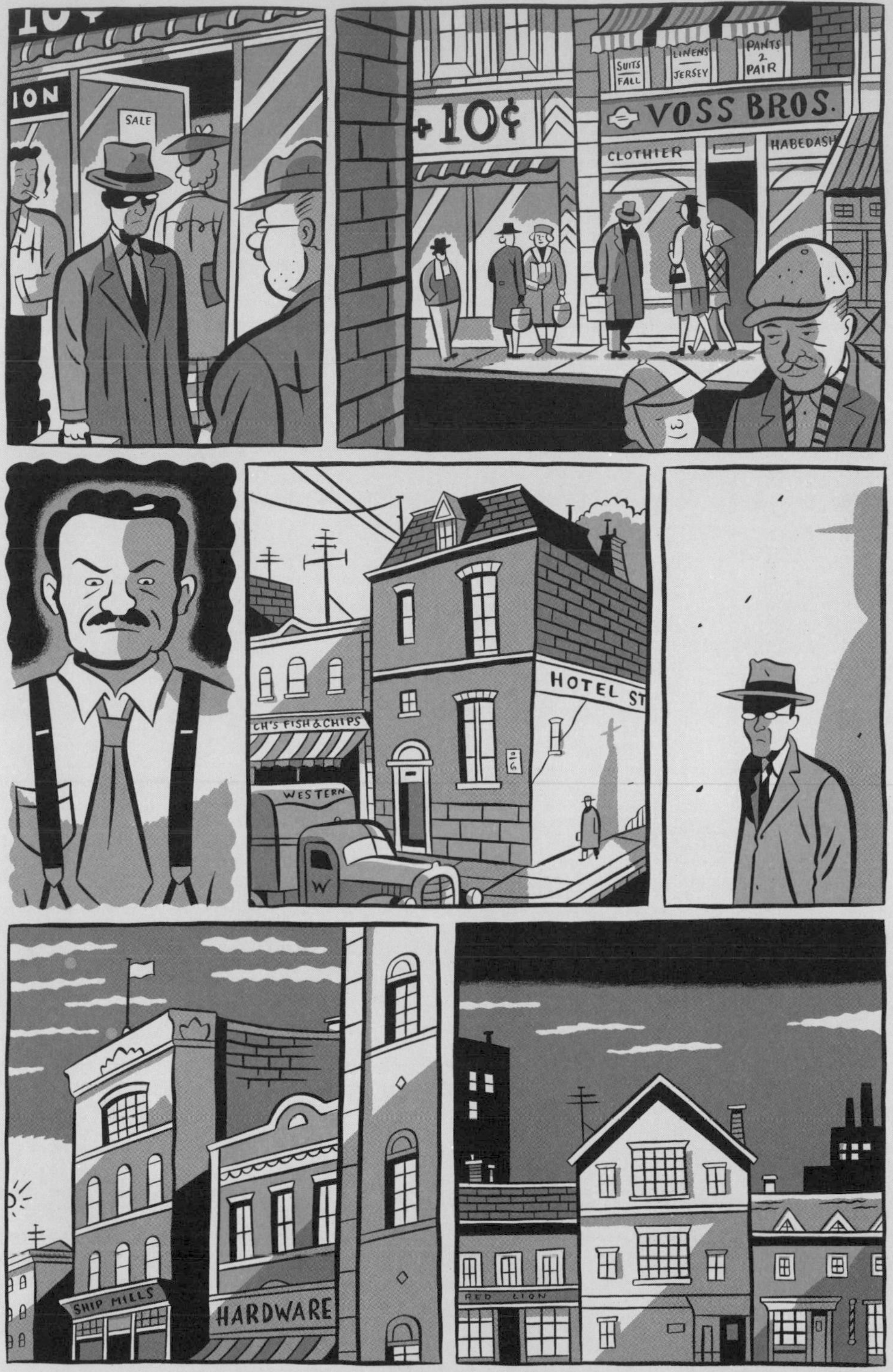
SALE
SUITS FALL
LINENS JERSEY
PANTS 2 PAIR
+10¢
VOSS BROS.
CLOTHIER
HOTEL ST
WESTERN
SHIP MILLS
HARDWARE
RED LION

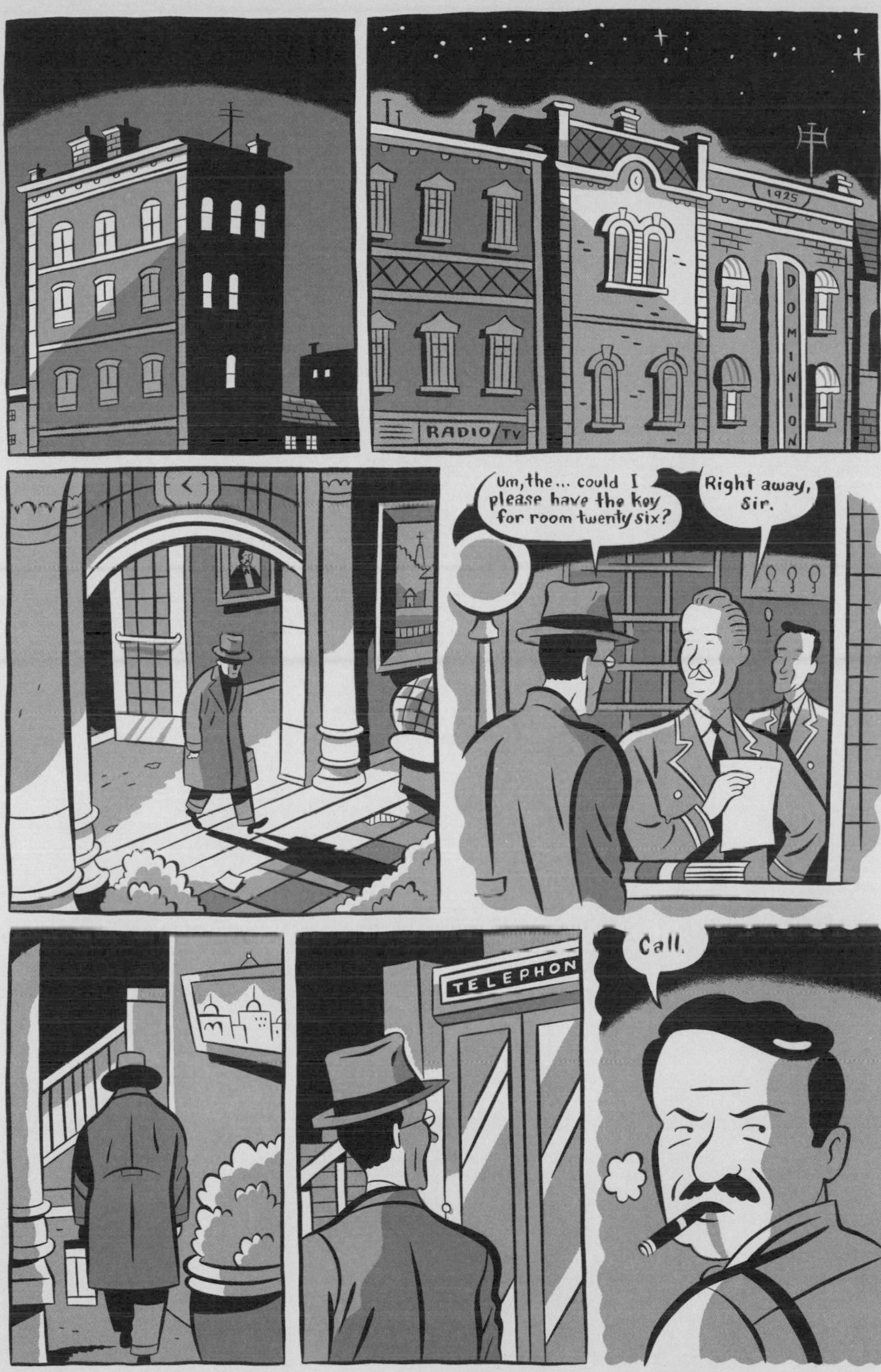
1925
DOMINION
RADIO/TV
Um, the... could I please have the key for room twenty six?
Right away, sir.
TELEPHON
Call.

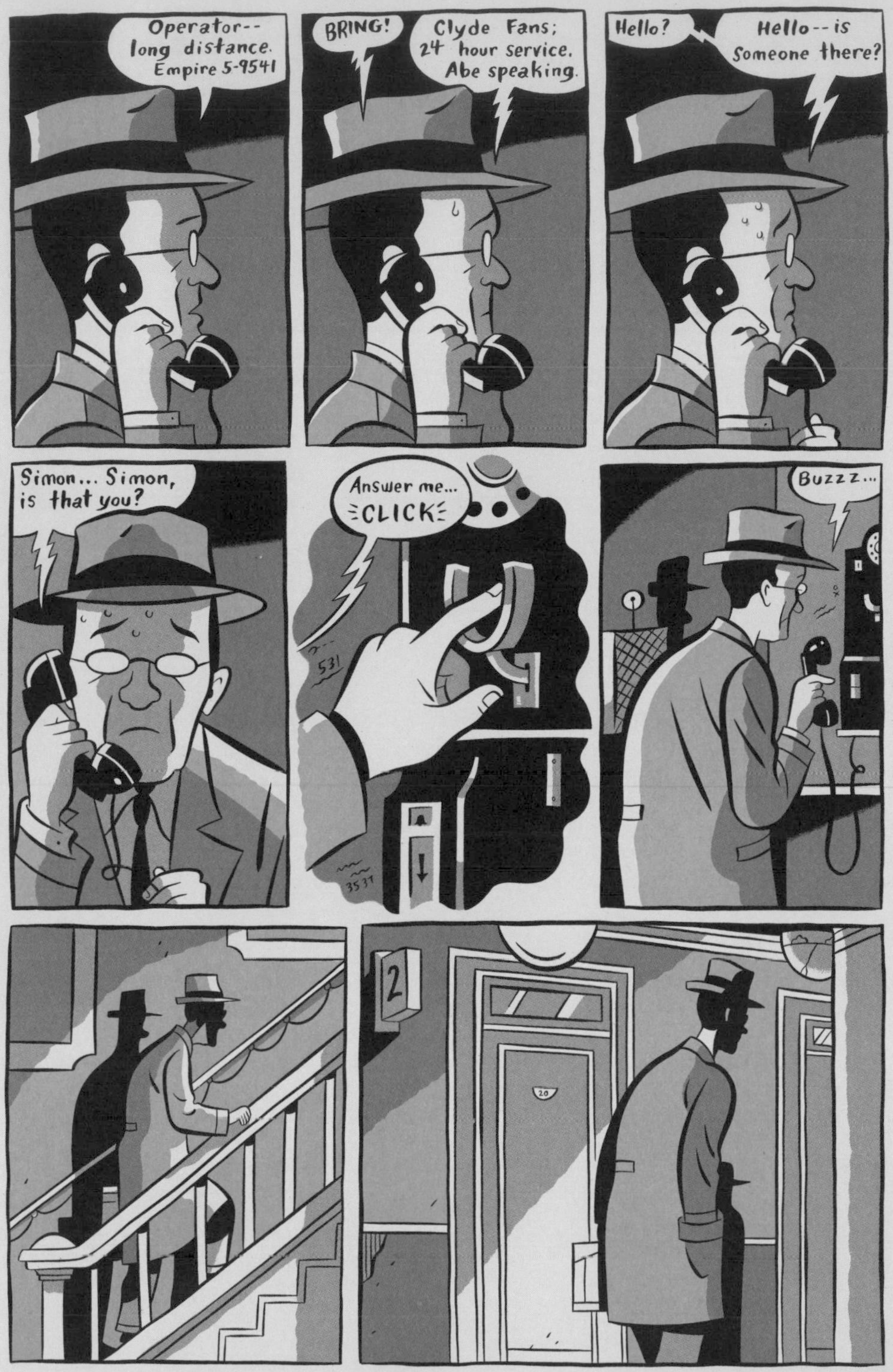
Operator-- long distance. Empire 5-9541
BRING!
Clyde Fans; 24 hour service. Abe speaking.
Hello?
Hello--is Someone there?
Simon... Simon, is that you?
Answer me...
CLICK
Buzzz...
531
3537
2
20

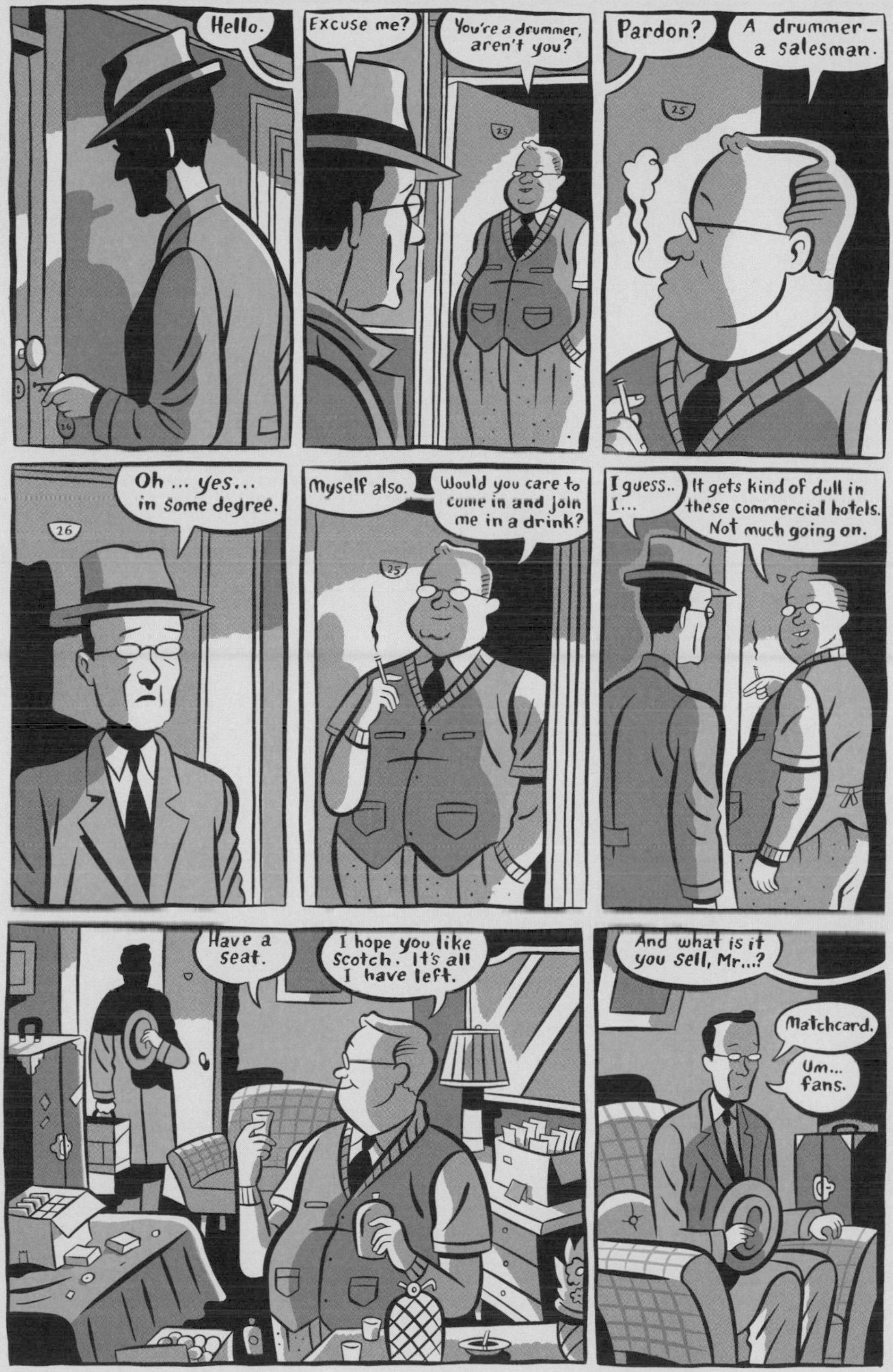
Hello.
Excuse me?
You're a drummer, aren't you?
Pardon?
A drummer - a salesman.
Oh ... yes... in some degree.
Myself also.
Would you care to come in and join me in a drink?
I guess.. I...
It gets kind of dull in these commercial hotels. Not much going on.
Have a seat.
I hope you like Scotch. It's all I have left.
And what is it you sell, Mr...?
Matchcard.
Um... fans.

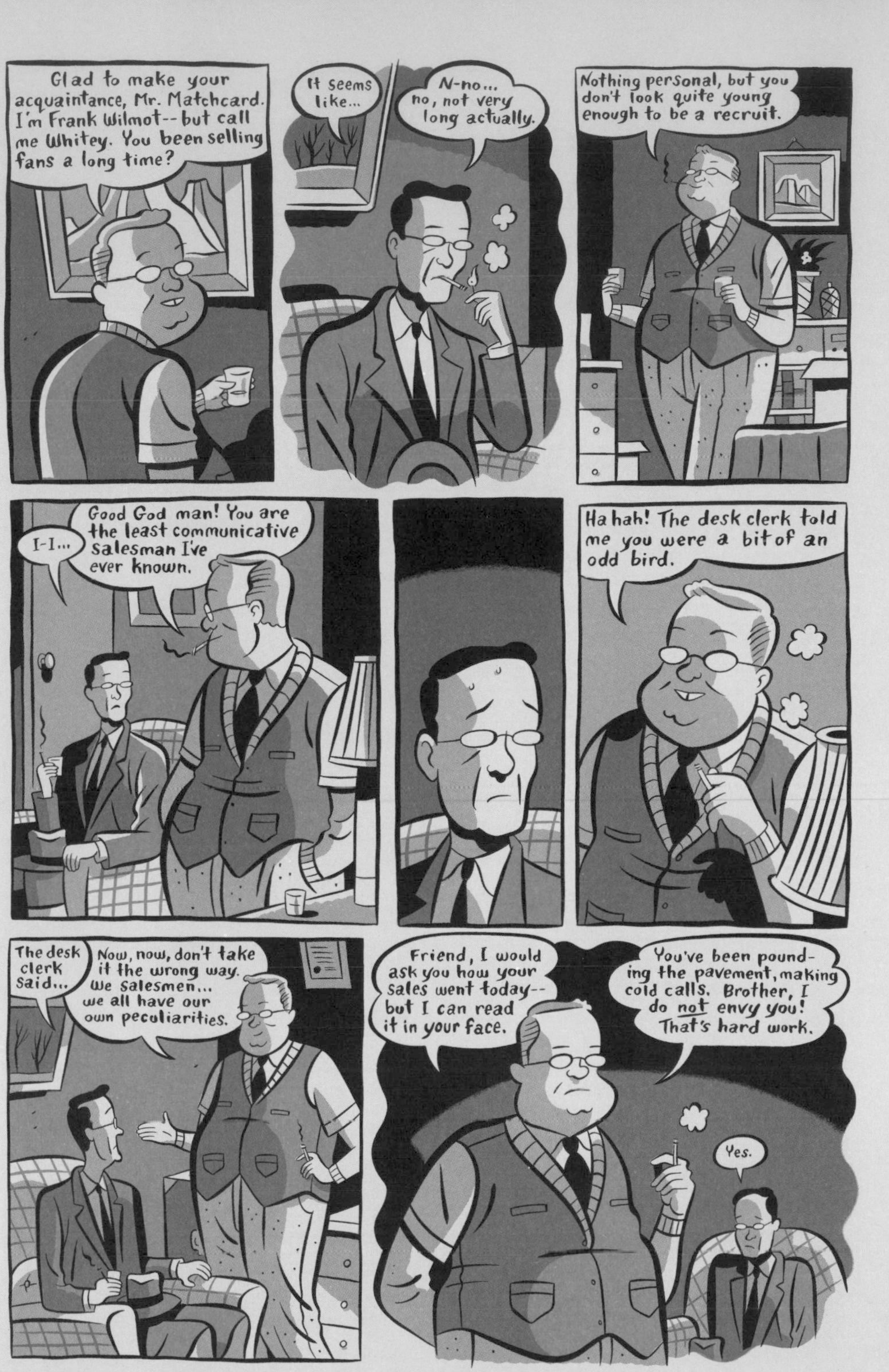
Glad to make your acquaintance, Mr. Matchcard. I'm Frank Wilmot--but call me Whitey. You been selling fans a long time?
It seems like...
N-no... no, not very long actually.
Nothing personal, but you don't look quite young enough to be a recruit.
I-I...
Good God man! You are the least communicative salesman I've ever known.
Ha hah! The desk clerk told me you were a bit of an odd bird.
The desk clerk said...
Now, now, don't take it the wrong way. We salesmen... we all have our own peculiarities.
Friend, I would ask you how your sales went today--but I can read it in your face.
You've been pounding the pavement, making cold calls. Brother, I do not envy you! That's hard work.
Yes.

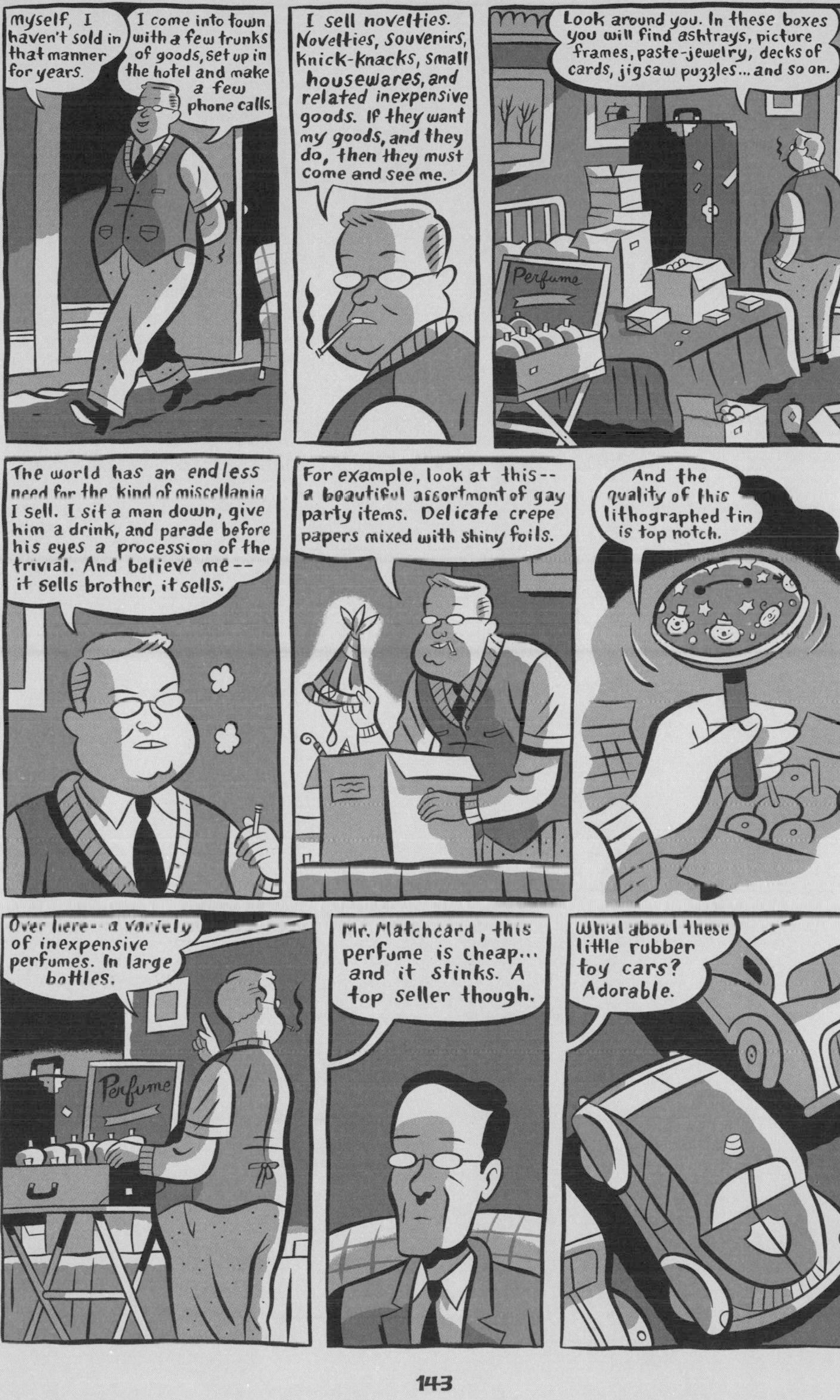

myself, I haven't sold in that manner for years.
I come into town with a few trunks of goods, set up in the hotel and make a few phone calls.
I sell novelties. Novelties, souvenirs, knick-knacks, small housewares, and related inexpensive goods. If they want my goods, and they do, then they must come and see me.
Look around you. In these boxes you will find ashtrays, picture frames, paste-jewelry, decks of cards, jigsaw puzzles... and so on.
Perfume
The world has an endless need for the kind of miscellania I sell. I sit a man down, give him a drink, and parade before his eyes a procession of the trivial. And believe me -- it sells brother, it sells.
For example, look at this -- a beautiful assortment of gay party items. Delicate crepe papers mixed with shiny foils.
And the quality of this lithographed tin is top notch.
Over here -- a variety of inexpensive perfumes. In large bottles.
Perfume
Mr. Matchcard, this perfume is cheap... and it stinks. A top seller though.
What about these little rubber toy cars? Adorable.

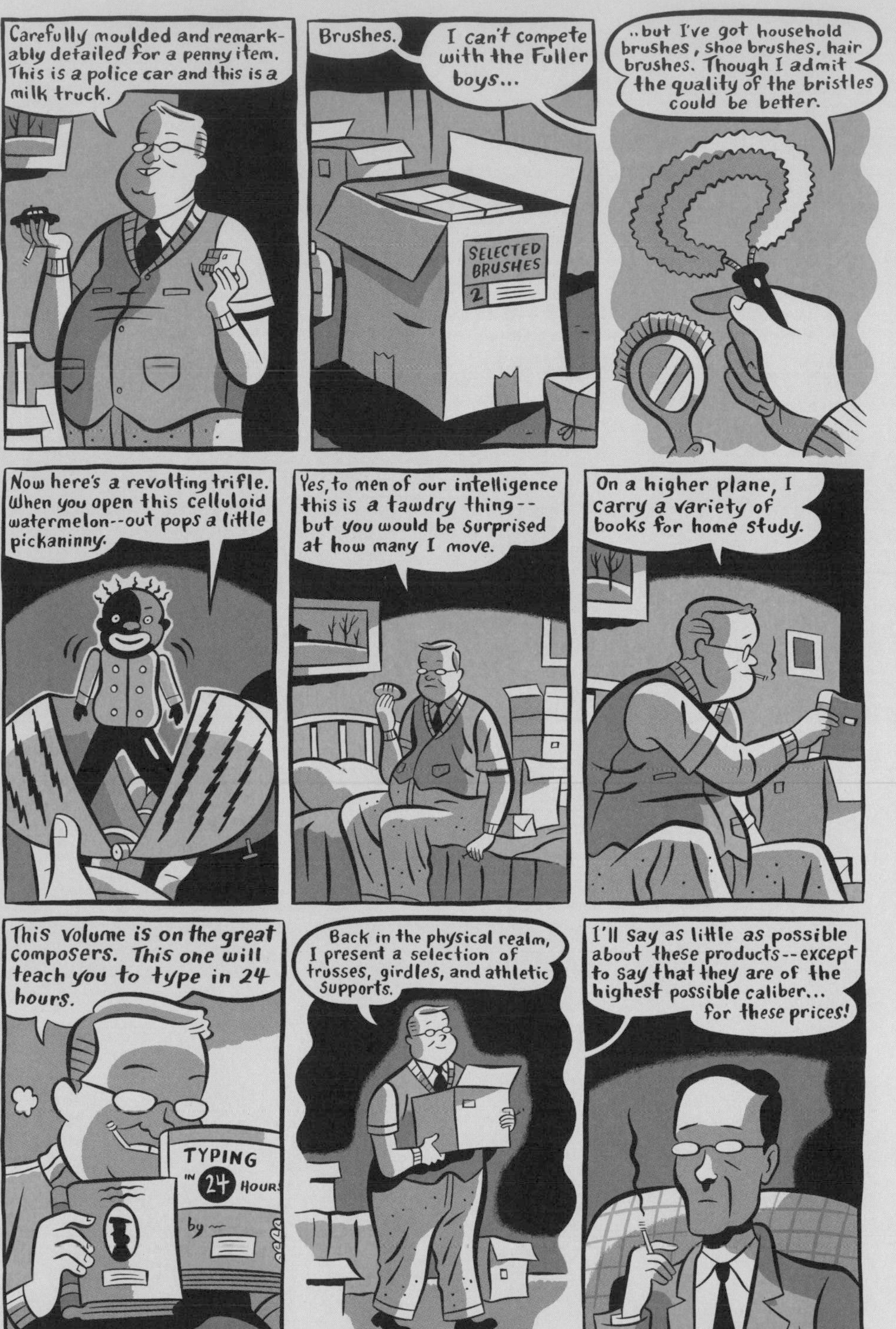
Carefully moulded and remarkably detailed for a penny item. This is a police car and this is a milk truck.
Brushes.
I can't compete with the Fuller boys...
SELECTED BRUSHES
2
..but I've got household brushes, shoe brushes, hair brushes. Though I admit the quality of the bristles could be better.
Now here's a revolting trifle. When you open this celluloid watermelon--out pops a little pickaninny.
Yes, to men of our intelligence this is a tawdry thing--but you would be surprised at how many I move.
On a higher plane, I carry a variety of books for home study.
This volume is on the great composers. This one will teach you to type in 24 hours.
TYPING IN 24 HOURS
by ~
Back in the physical realm, I present a selection of trusses, girdles, and athletic supports.
I'll say as little as possible about these products--except to say that they are of the highest possible caliber... for these prices!

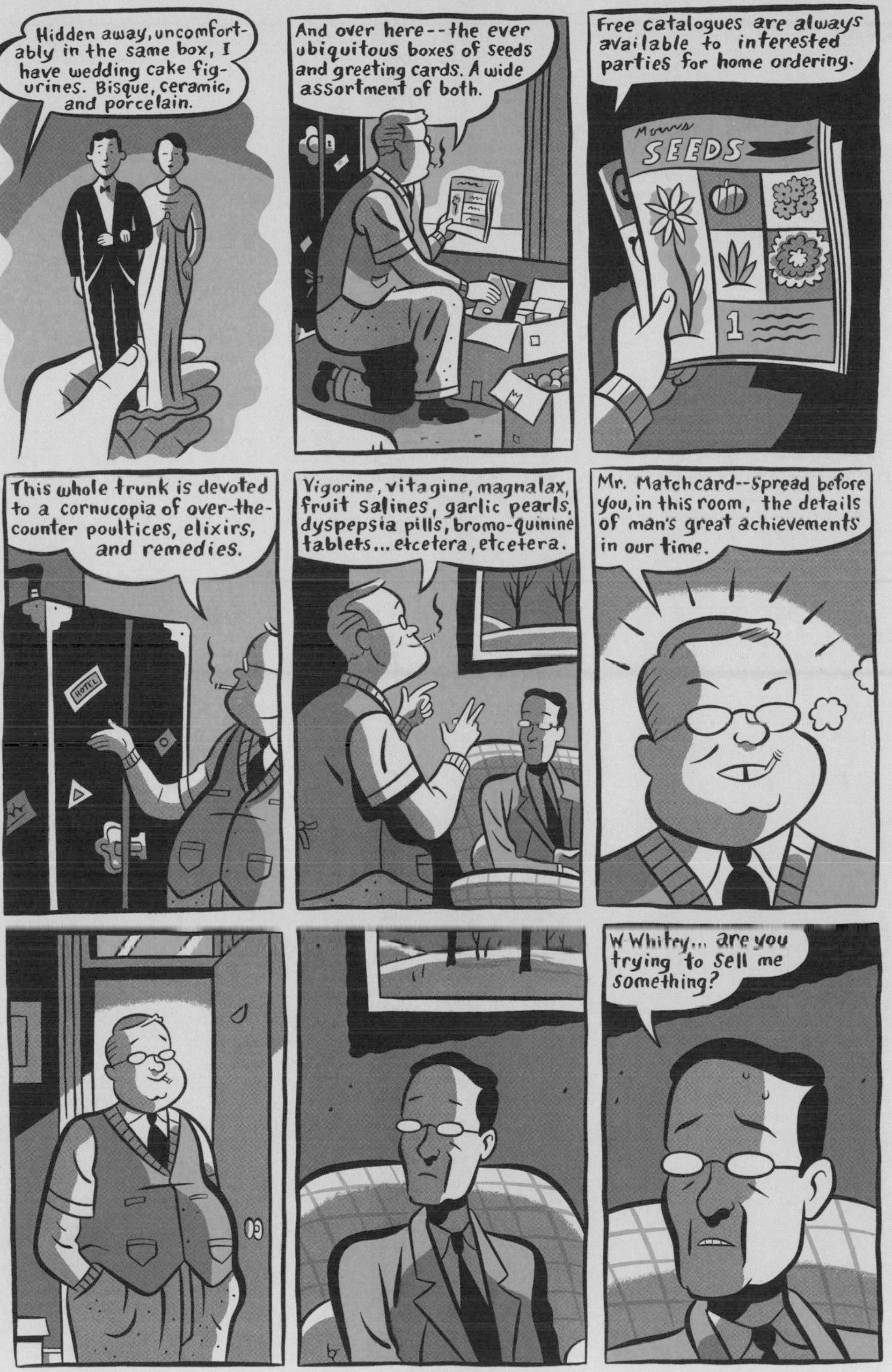
Hidden away, uncomfortably in the same box, I have wedding cake figurines. Bisque, ceramic, and porcelain.
And over here--the ever ubiquitous boxes of seeds and greeting cards. A wide assortment of both.
Free catalogues are always available to interested parties for home ordering.
SEEDS
This whole trunk is devoted to a cornucopia of over-the-counter poultices, elixirs, and remedies.
HOTEL
Vigorine, vitagine, magnalax, fruit salines, garlic pearls, dyspepsia pills, bromo-quinine tablets... etcetera, etcetera.
Mr. Matchcard--Spread before you, in this room, the details of man's great achievements in our time.
W-Whitey... are you trying to sell me something?

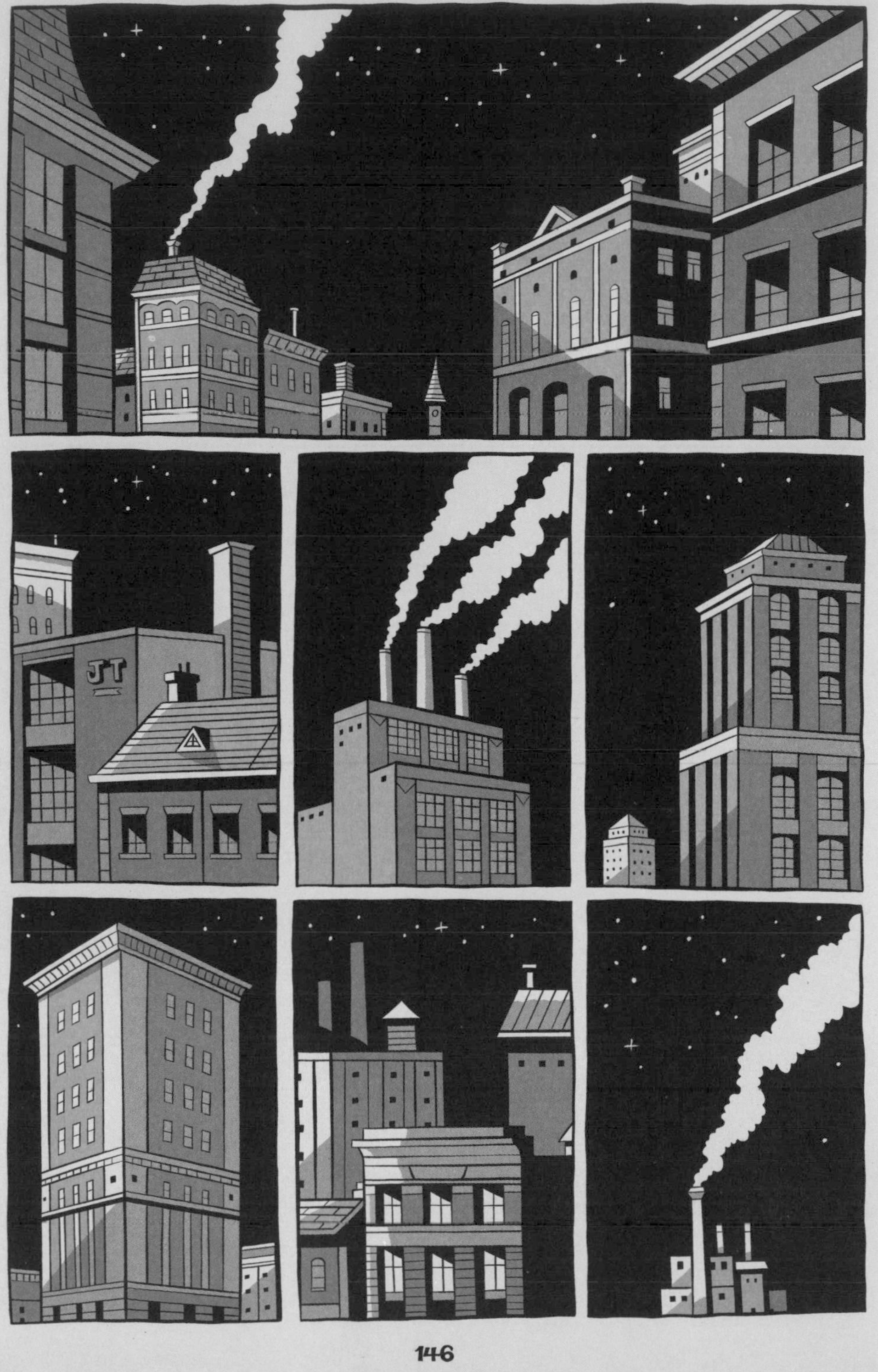
JT

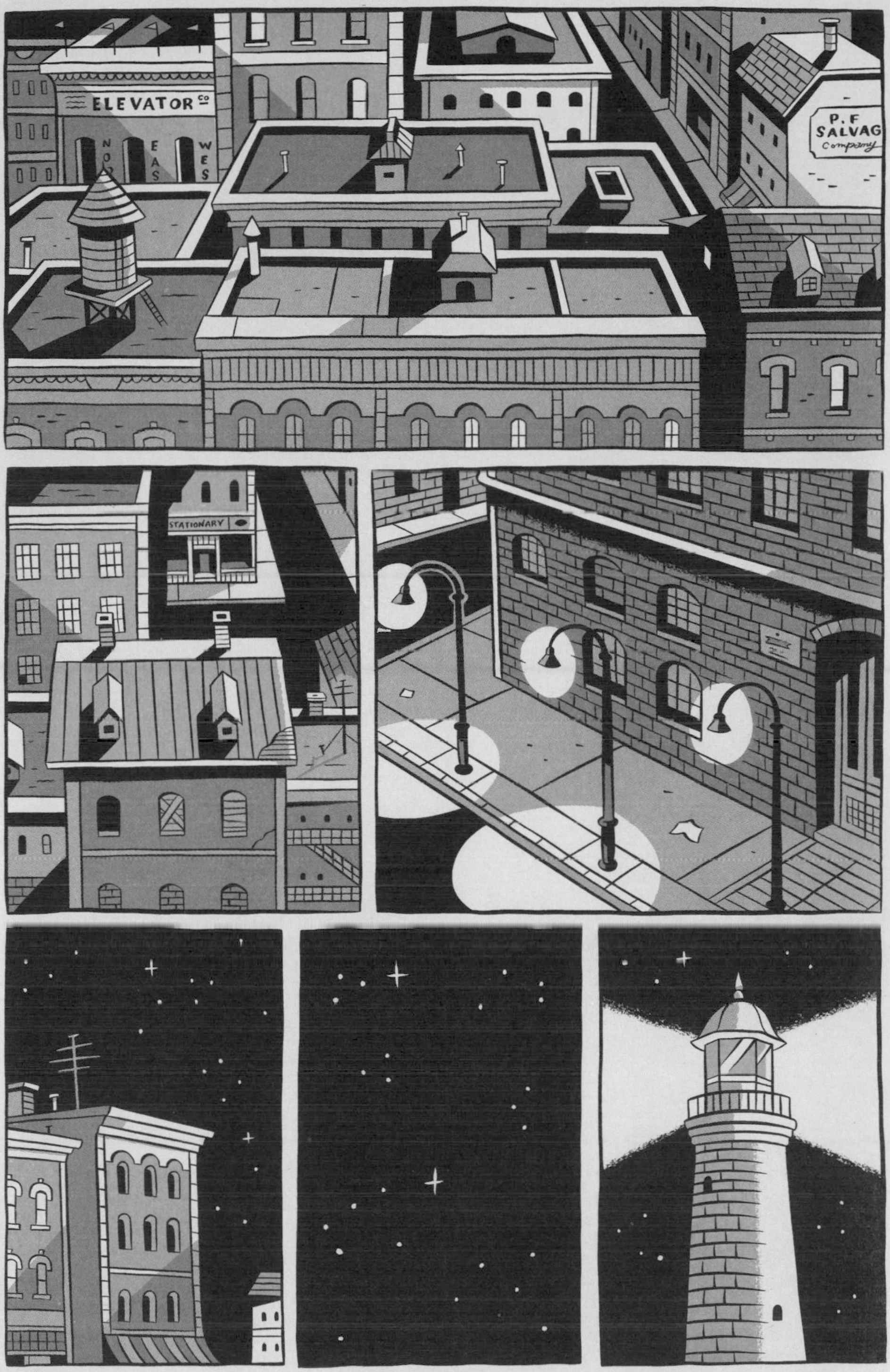
ELEVATOR Co
P.F
SALVAG
Company
STATIONARY

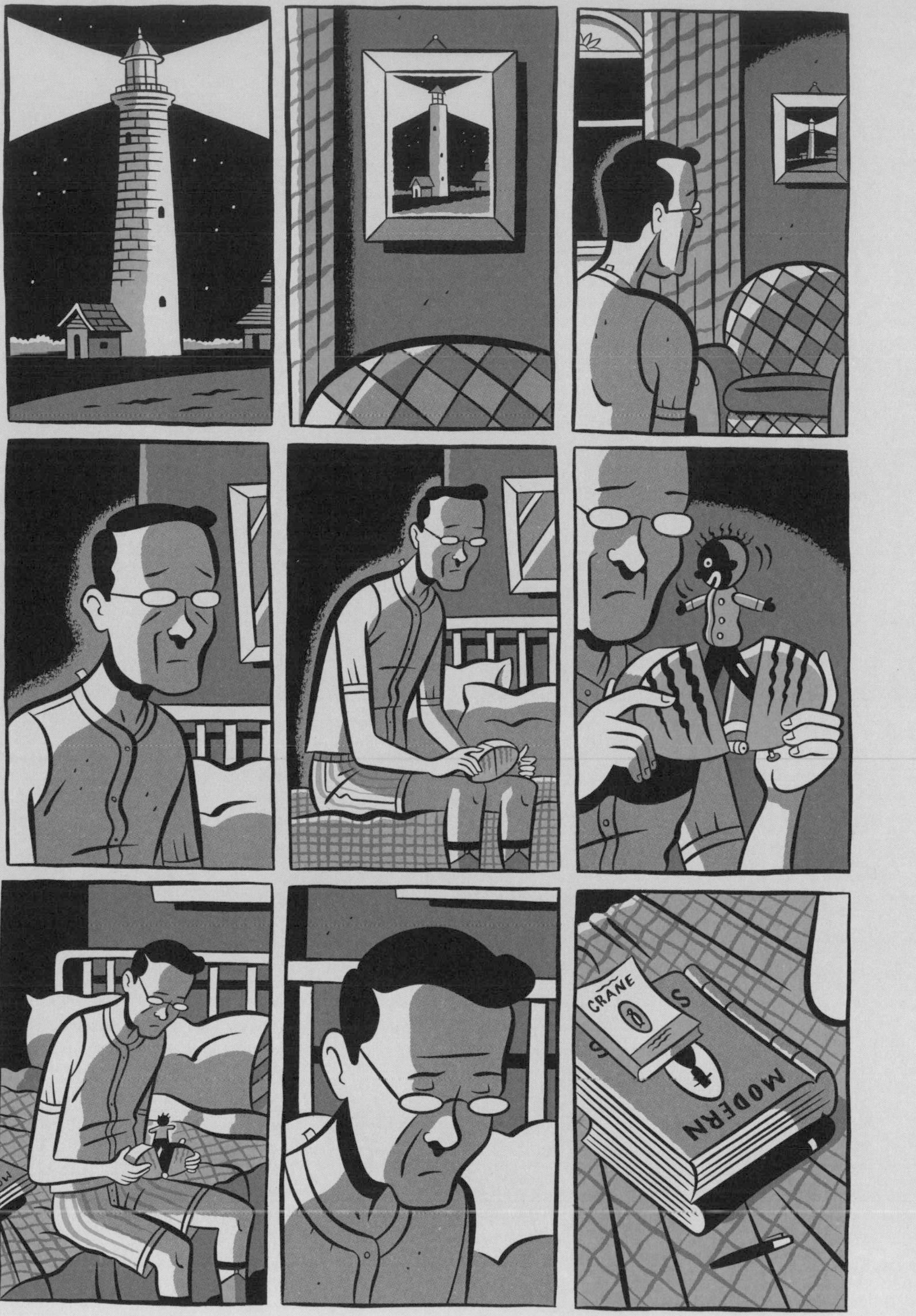
CRANE
MODERN

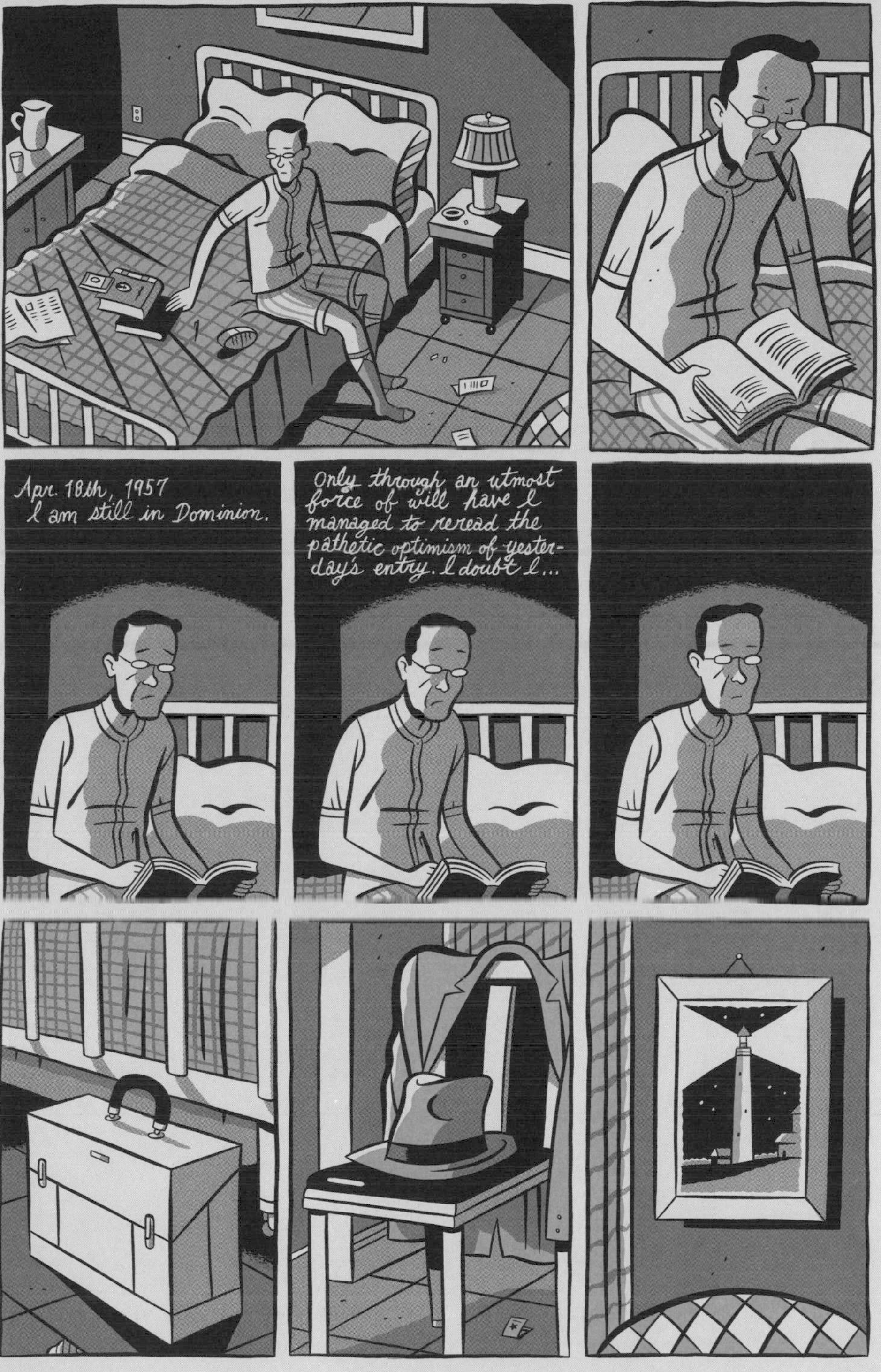
Apr. 18th, 1957
I am still in Dominion.
Only through an utmost force of will have I managed to reread the pathetic optimism of yesterday's entry. I doubt I...

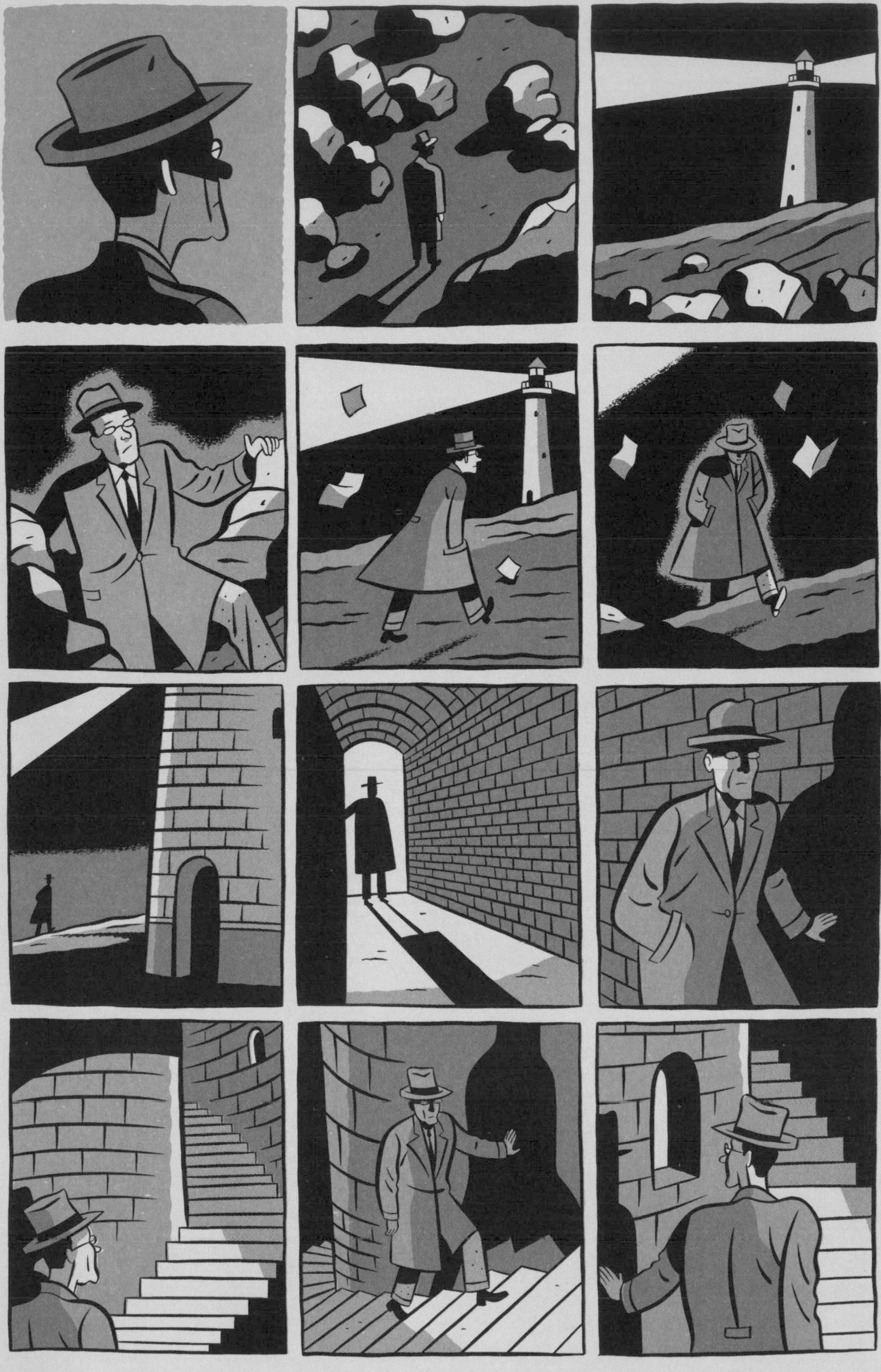

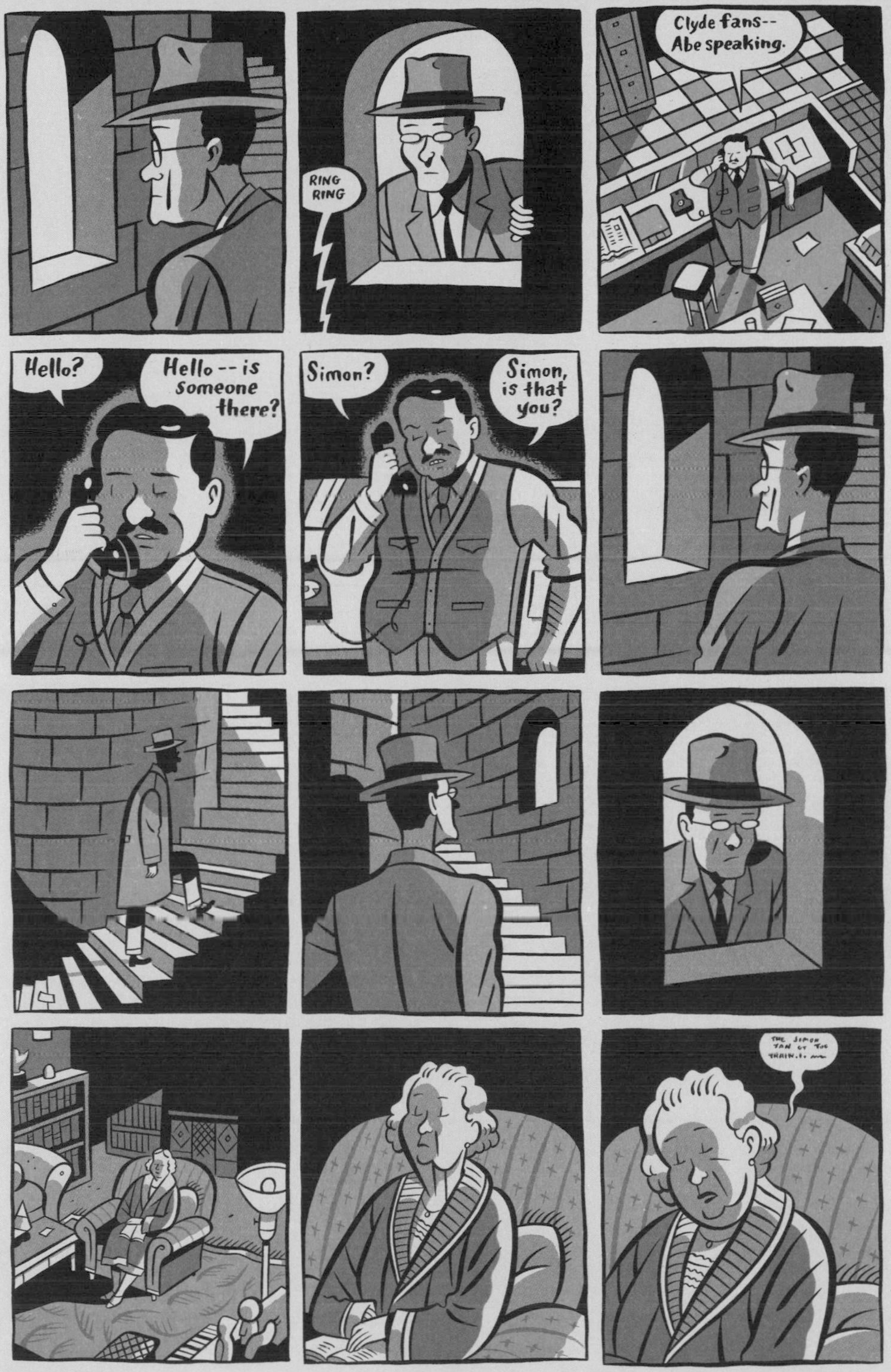
RING
RING
Clyde fans--
Abe speaking.
Hello?
Hello -- is someone there?
Simon?
Simon, is that you?

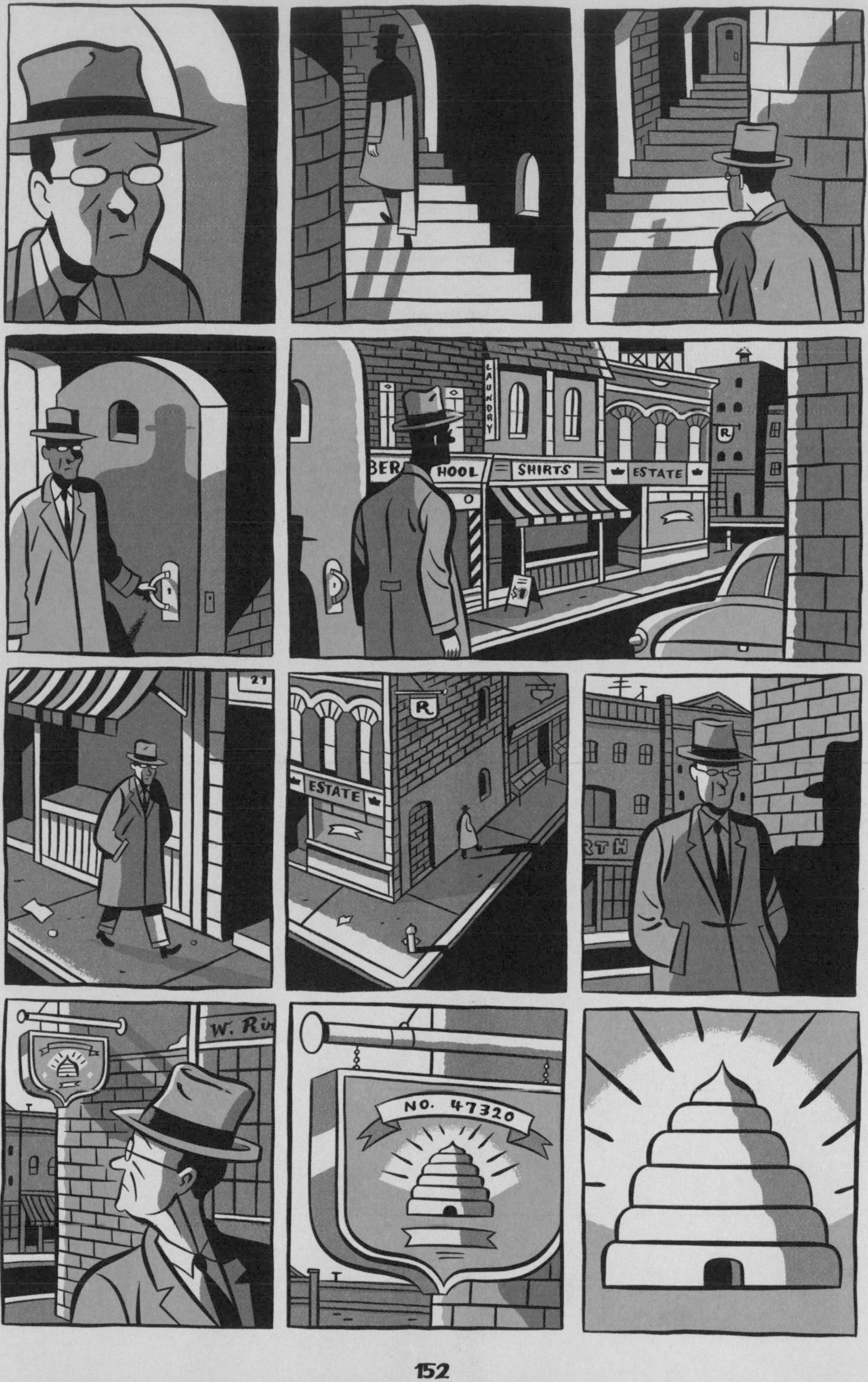
LAUNDRY
BER
HOOL
SHIRTS
ESTATE
R
21
ESTATE
R
RTH
W. Ri
NO. 47320

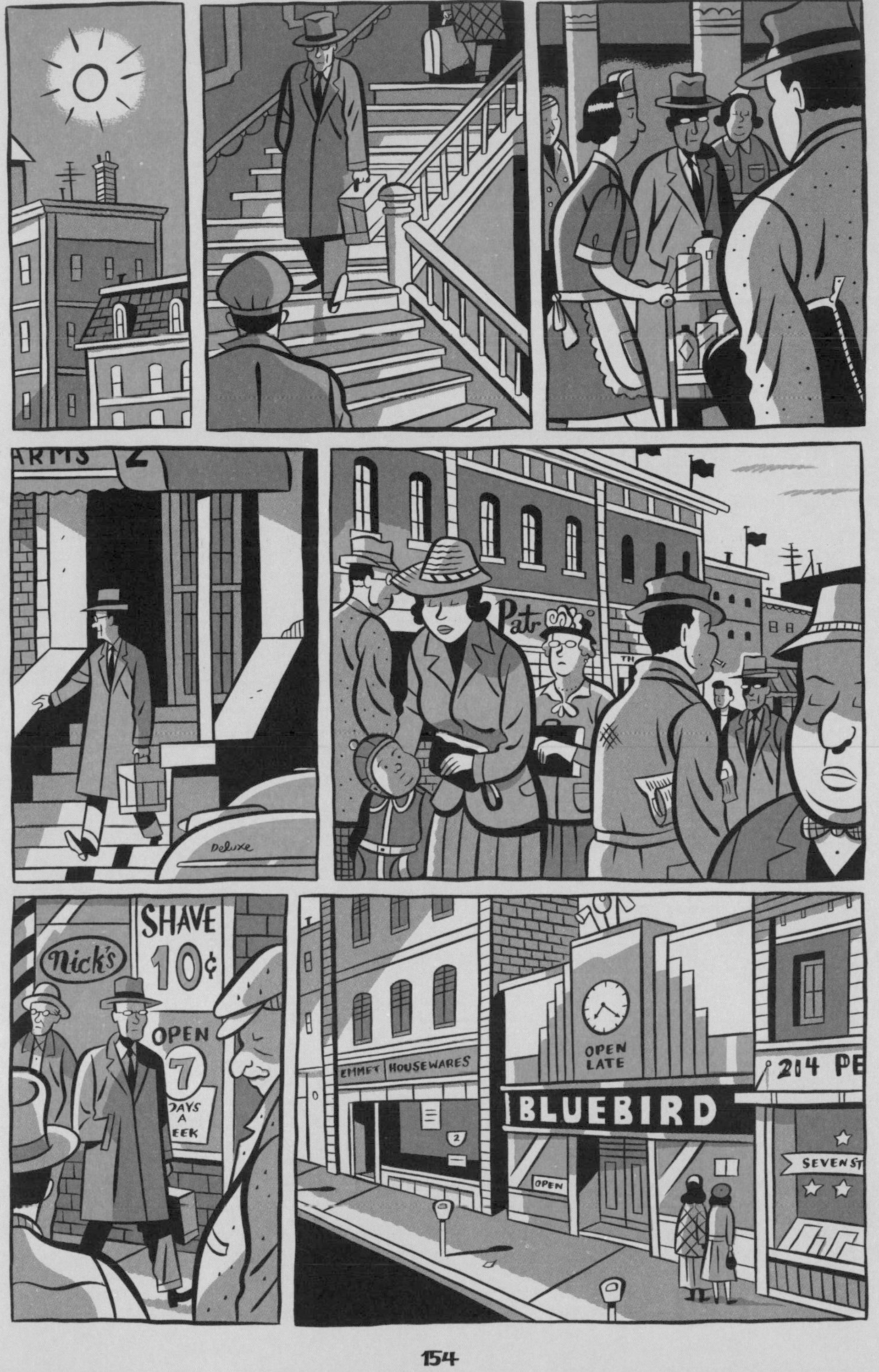
ARMS
2
DeLuxe
SHAVE
10¢
Nick's
OPEN
7
EMMET
HOUSEWARES
OPEN LATE
BLUEBIRD
OPEN
204 PE
SEVEN ST

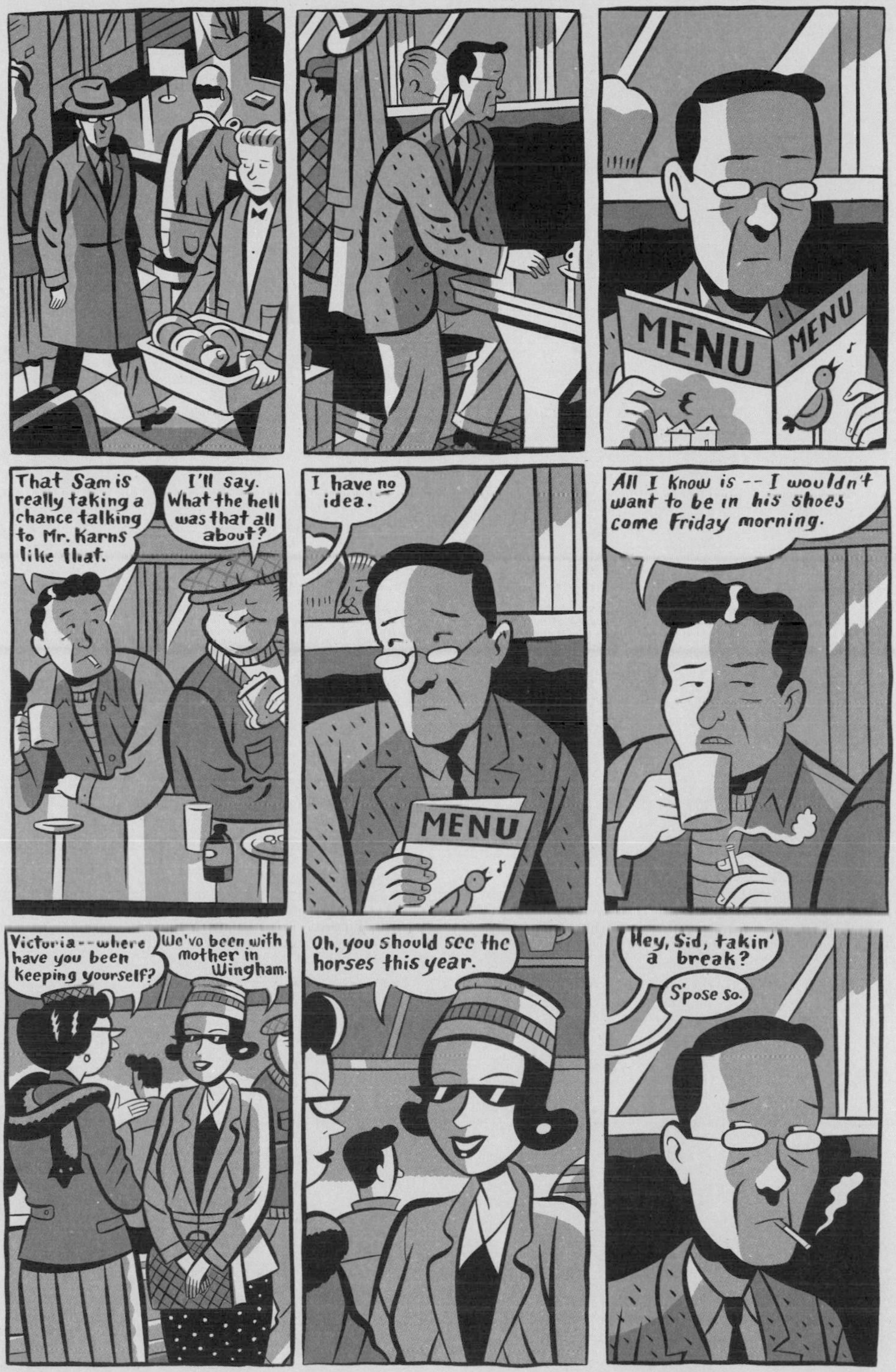
MENU
MENU
That Sam is really taking a chance talking to Mr. Karns like that.
I'll say. What the hell was that all about?
I have no idea.
MENU
All I know is -- I wouldn't want to be in his shoes come Friday morning.
Victoria--where have you been keeping yourself?
We've been with mother in Wingham.
Oh, you should see the horses this year.
Hey, Sid, takin' a break?
S'pose so.

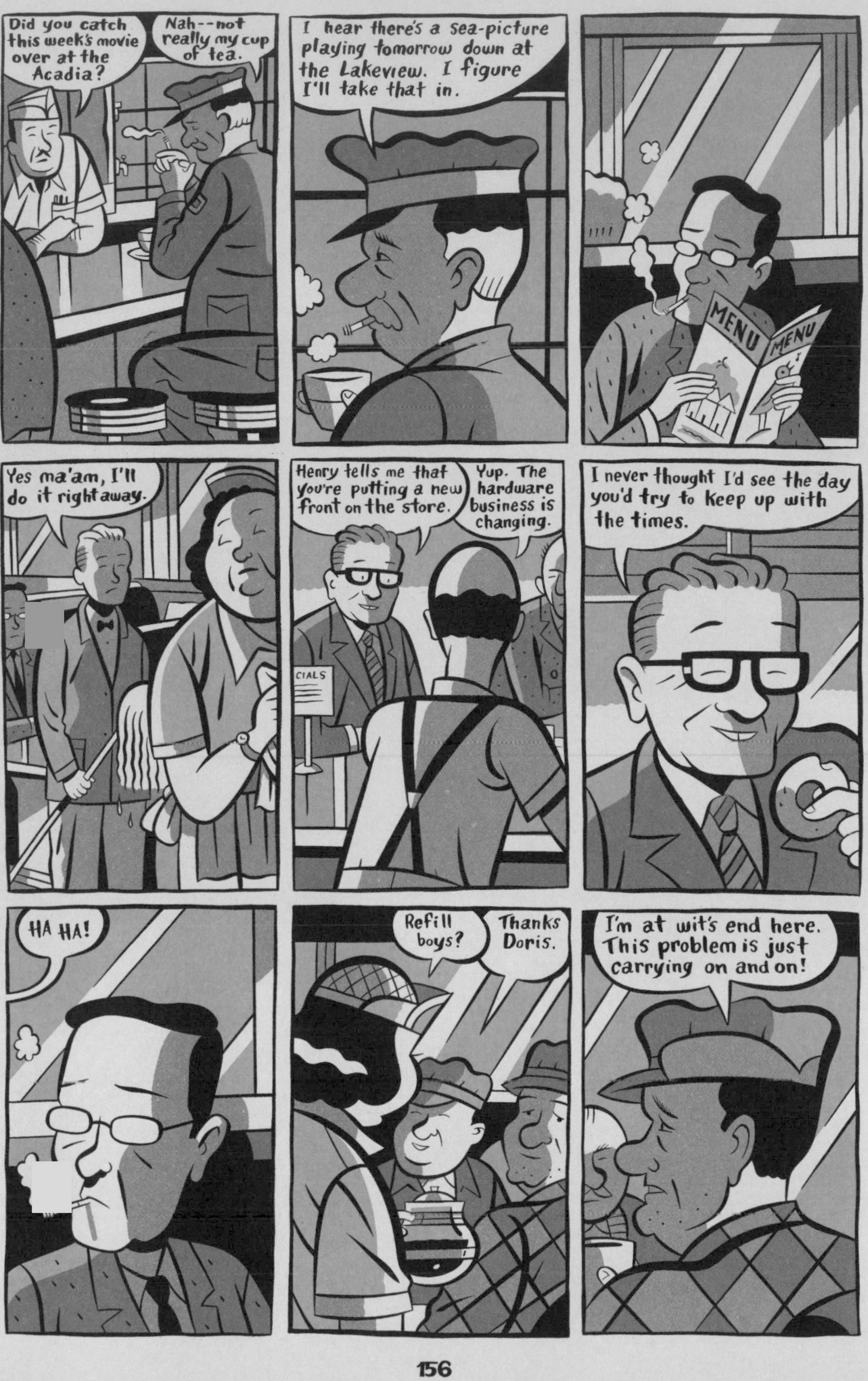

Did you catch this week's movie over at the Acadia?
Nah--not really my cup of tea.
I hear there's a sea-picture playing tomorrow down at the Lakeview. I figure I'll take that in.
MENU
MENU
Yes ma'am, I'll do it right away.
Henry tells me that you're putting a new front on the store.
Yup. The hardware business is changing.
CIALS
I never thought I'd see the day you'd try to keep up with the times.
HA HA!
Refill boys?
Thanks Doris.
I'm at wit's end here. This problem is just carrying on and on!

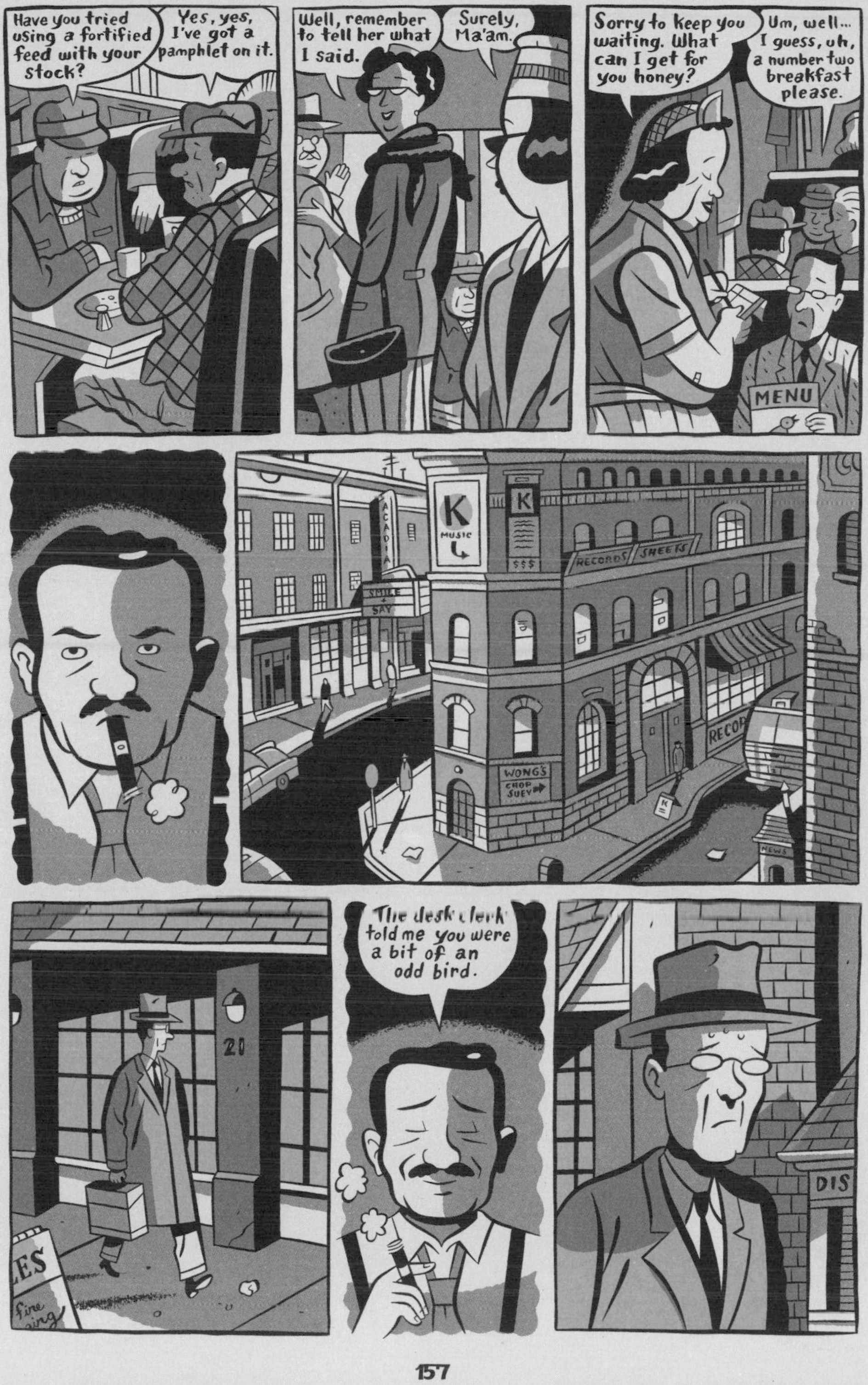
Have you tried using a fortified feed with your stock?
Yes, yes, I've got a pamphlet on it.
Well, remember to tell her what I said.
Surely, Ma'am.
Sorry to keep you waiting. What can I get for you honey?
Um, well... I guess, uh, a number two breakfast please.
MENU
ACADIA
MUSIC
RECORDS
SHEETS
WONG'S CHOP SUEY
21
The desk clerk told me you were a bit of an odd bird.
DIS

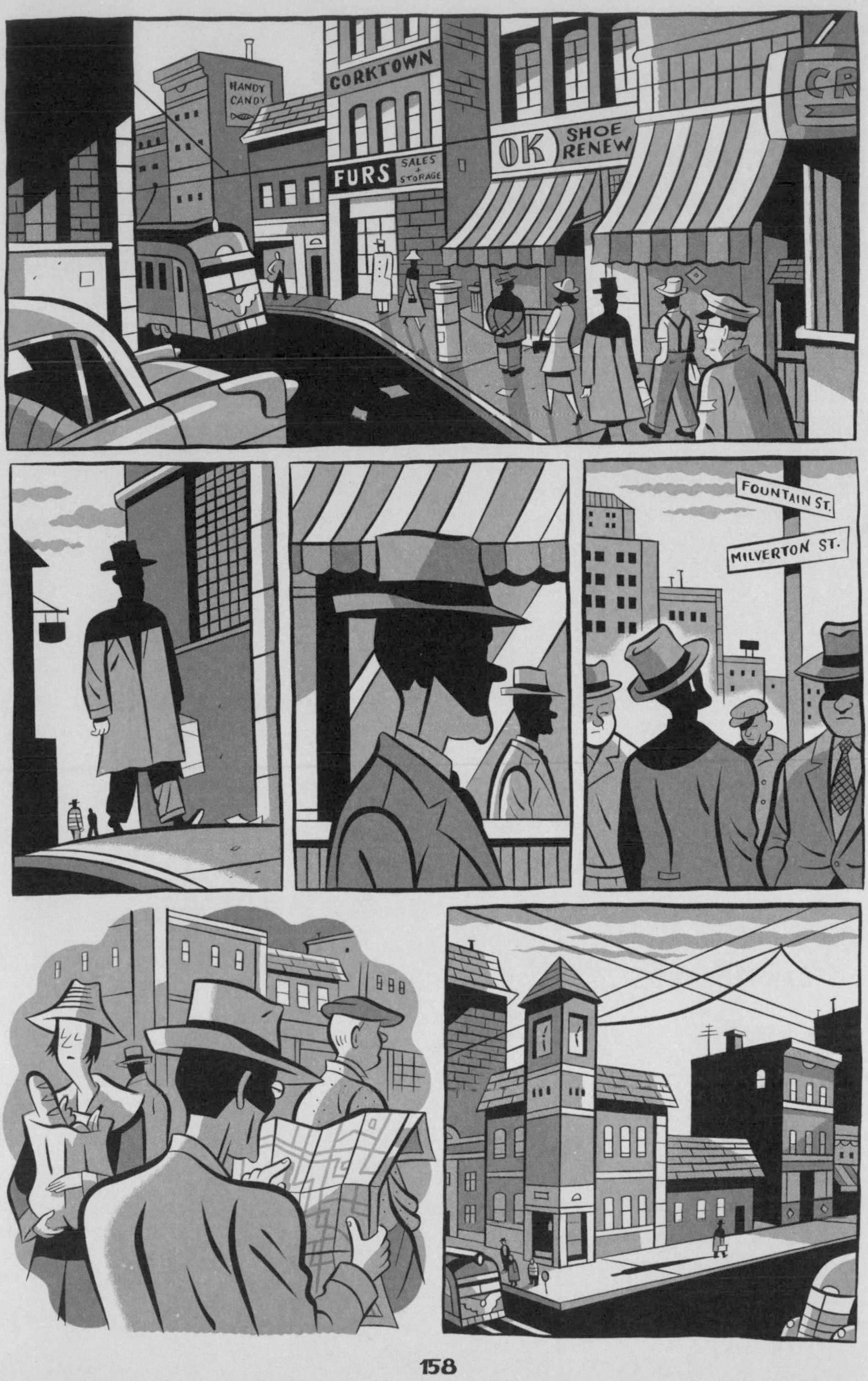
HANDY CANDY
CORKTOWN
FURS
SALES + STORAGE
OK
SHOE RENEW
FOUNTAIN ST.
MILVERTON ST.

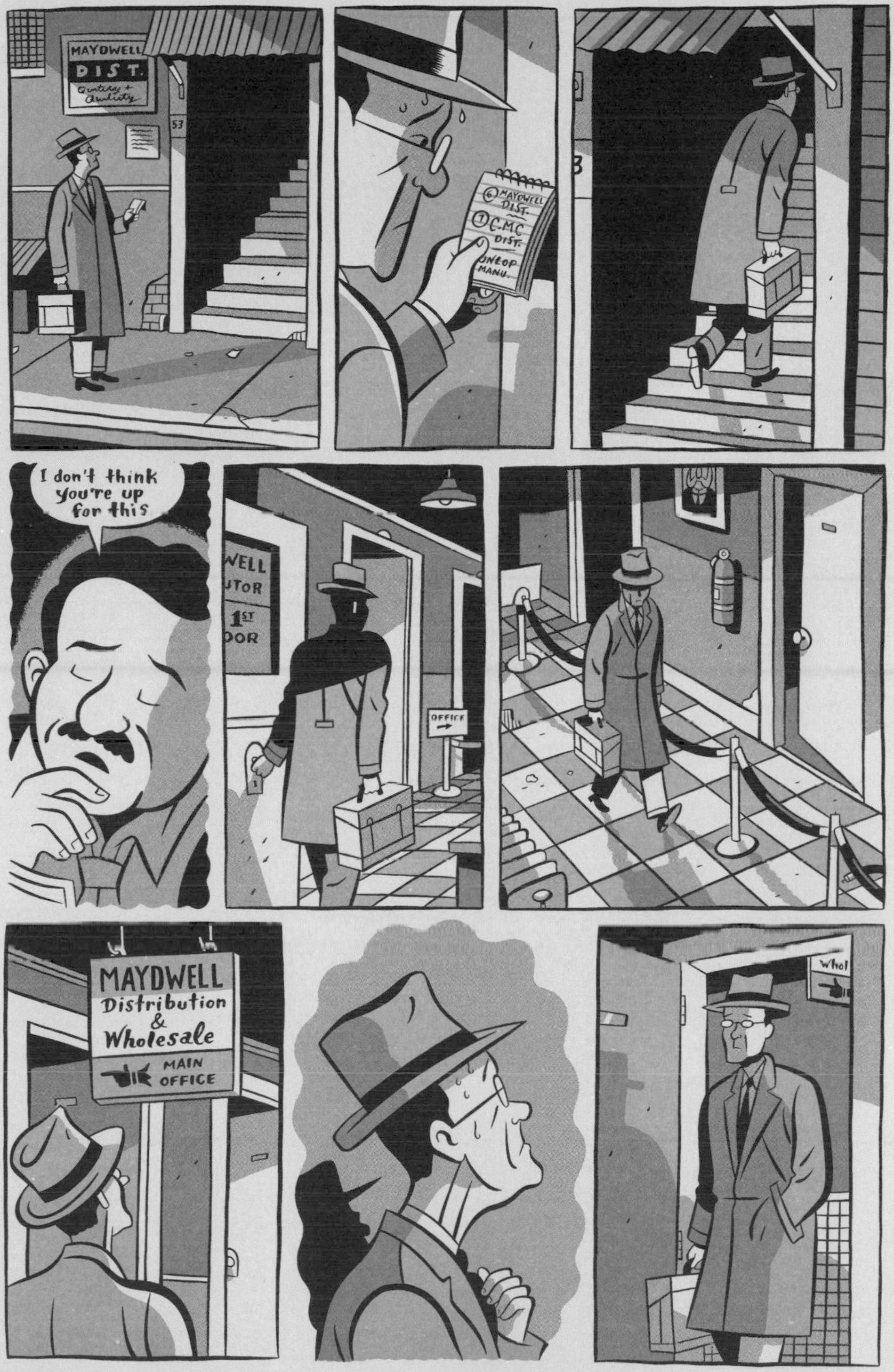
MAYDWELL
DIST.
I don't think you're up for this
OFFICE
MAYDWELL
Distribution
&
Wholesale
MAIN OFFICE

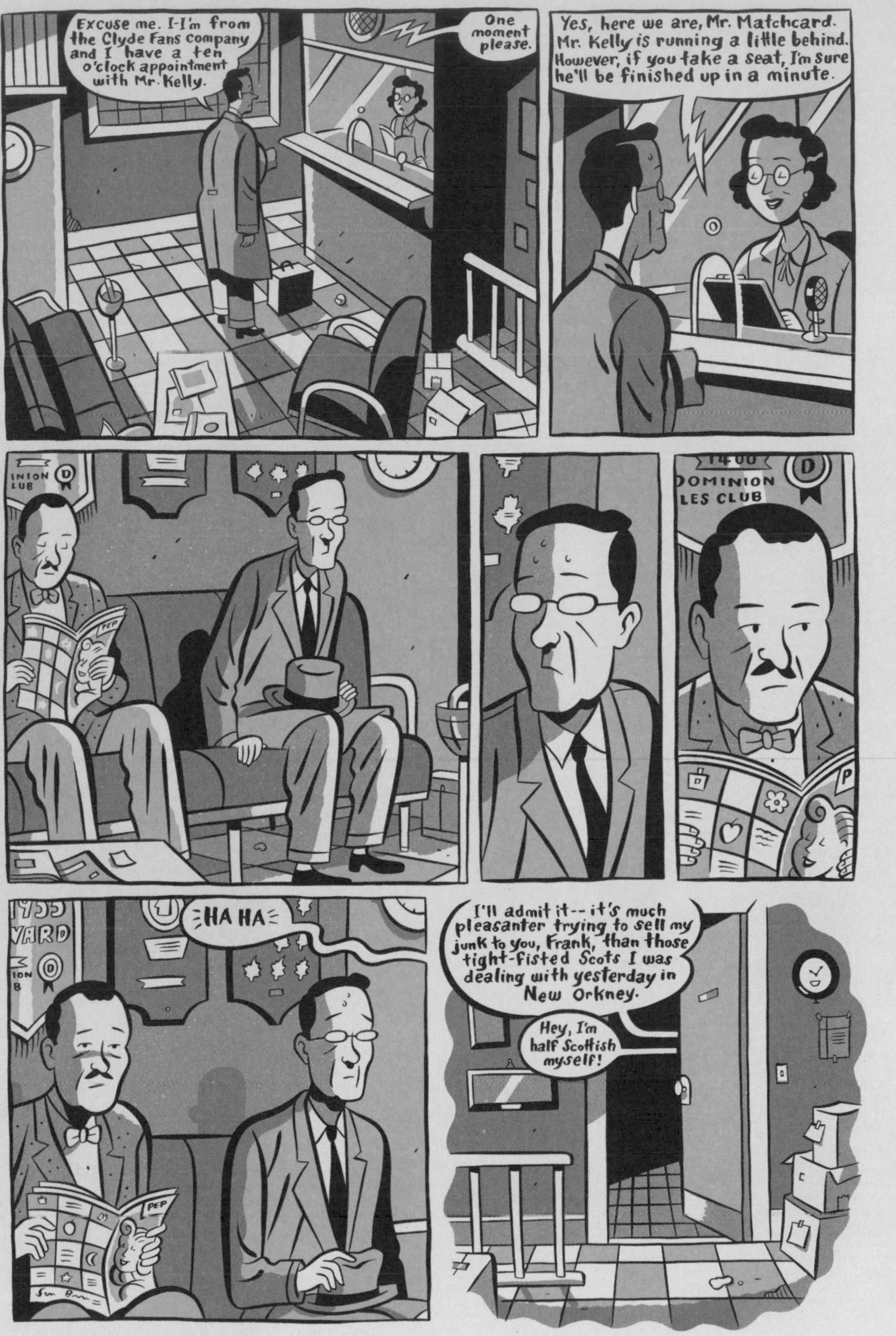
Excuse me. I-I'm from the Clyde Fans company and I have a ten o'clock appointment with Mr. Kelly.
One moment please.
Yes, here we are, Mr. Matchcard. Mr. Kelly is running a little behind. However, if you take a seat, I'm sure he'll be finished up in a minute.
DOMINION
LES CLUB
HA HA
I'll admit it-- it's much pleasanter trying to sell my junk to you, Frank, than those tight-fisted Scots I was dealing with yesterday in New Orkney.
Hey, I'm half Scottish myself!

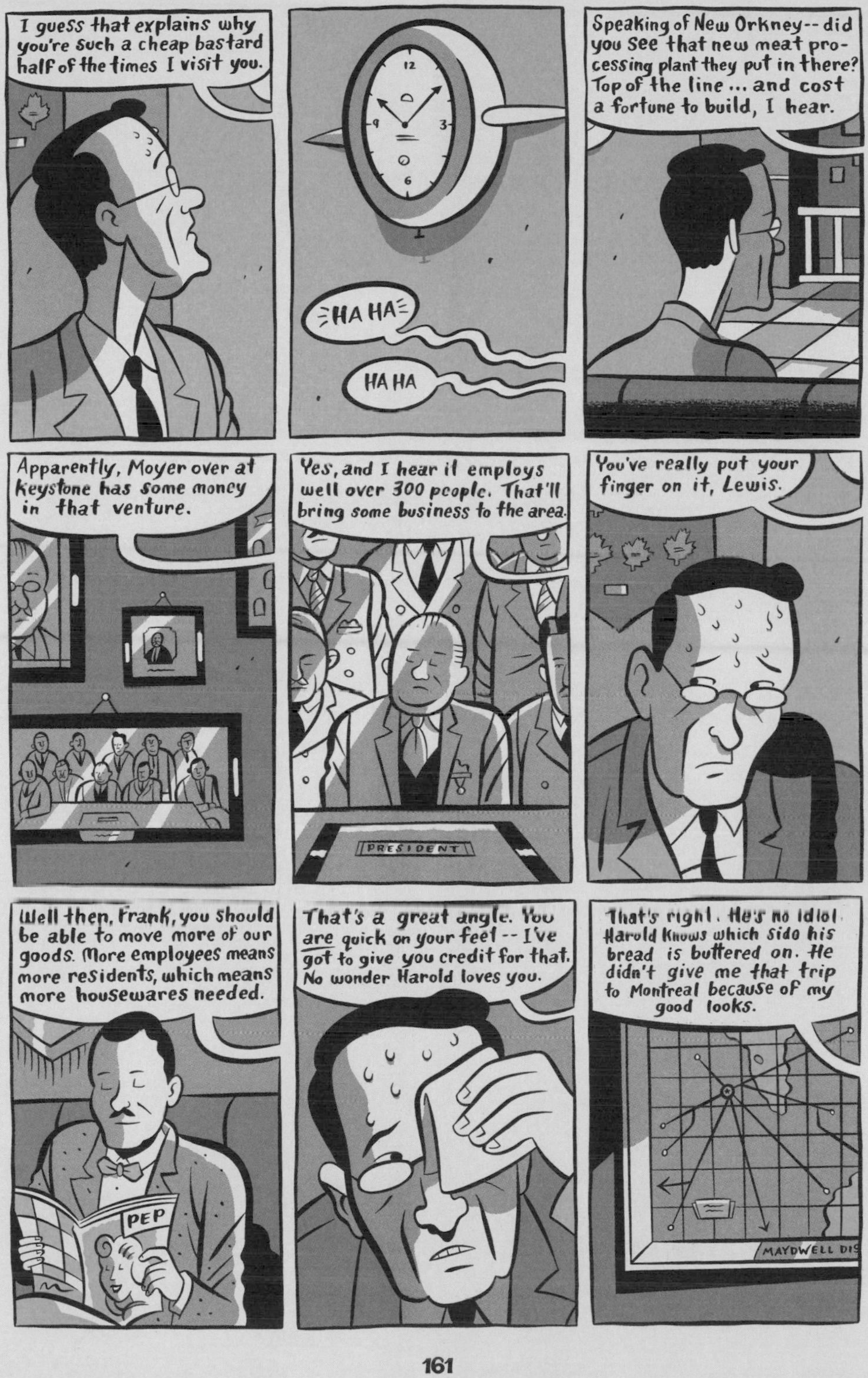
I guess that explains why you're such a cheap bastard half of the times I visit you.
HA HA
HA HA
Speaking of New Orkney-- did you see that new meat processing plant they put in there? Top of the line ... and cost a fortune to build, I hear.
Apparently, Moyer over at Keystone has some money in that venture.
Yes, and I hear it employs well over 300 people. That'll bring some business to the area.
PRESIDENT
You've really put your finger on it, Lewis.
Well then, Frank, you should be able to move more of our goods. More employees means more residents, which means more housewares needed.
PEP
That's a great angle. You are quick on your feet -- I've got to give you credit for that. No wonder Harold loves you.
That's right. He's no idiot. Harold knows which side his bread is buttered on. He didn't give me that trip to Montreal because of my good looks.
MAYDWELL DIS

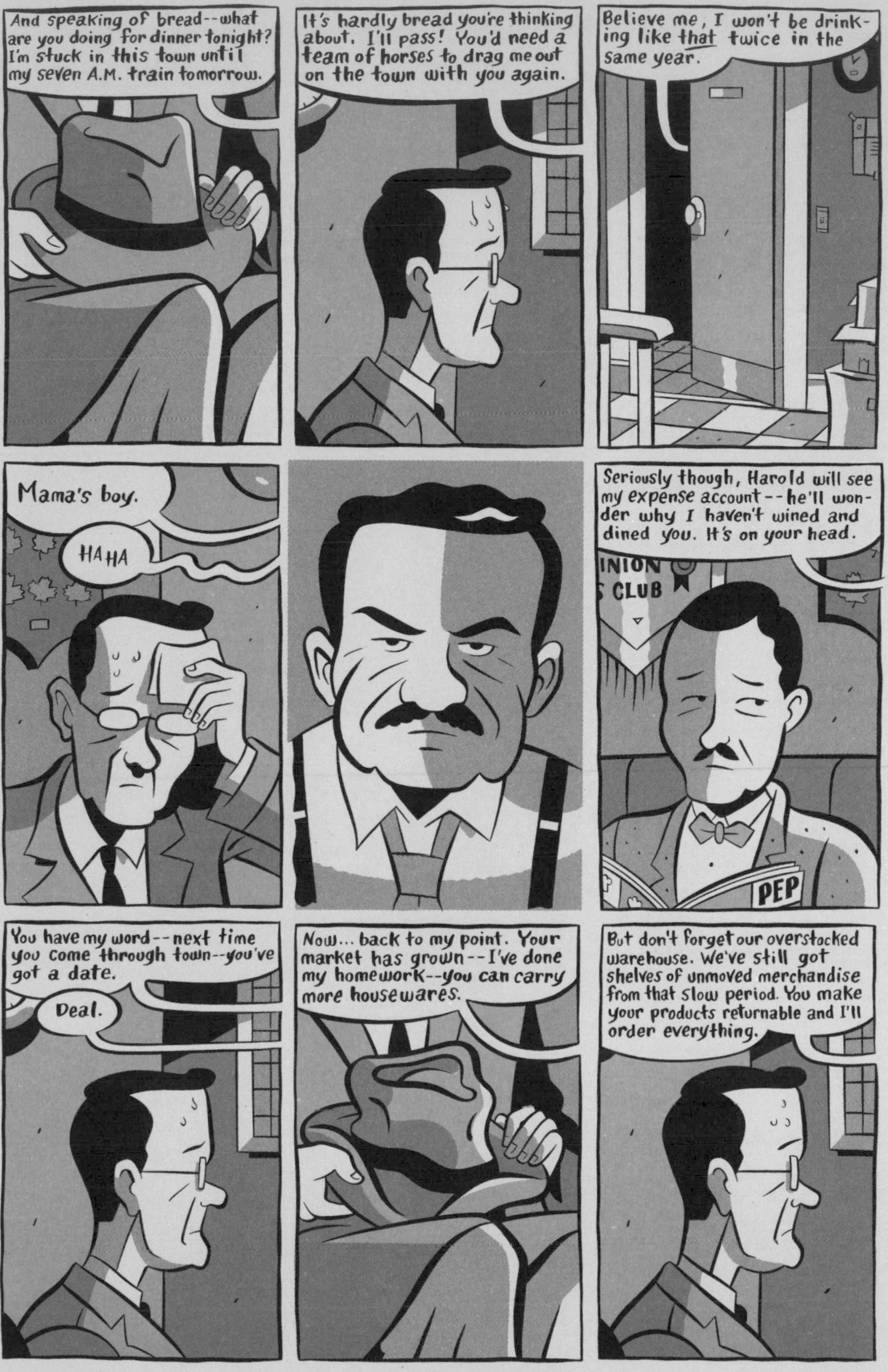
And speaking of bread--what are you doing for dinner tonight? I'm stuck in this town until my seven A.M. train tomorrow.
It's hardly bread you're thinking about. I'll pass! You'd need a team of horses to drag me out on the town with you again.
Believe me, I won't be drinking like that twice in the same year.
Mama's boy.
HAHA
Seriously though, Harold will see my expense account--he'll wonder why I haven't wined and dined you. It's on your head.
INION
CLUB
PEP
You have my word--next time you come through town--you've got a date.
Deal.
Now... back to my point. Your market has grown--I've done my homework--you can carry more housewares.
But don't forget our overstocked warehouse. We've still got shelves of unmoved merchandise from that slow period. You make your products returnable and I'll order everything.

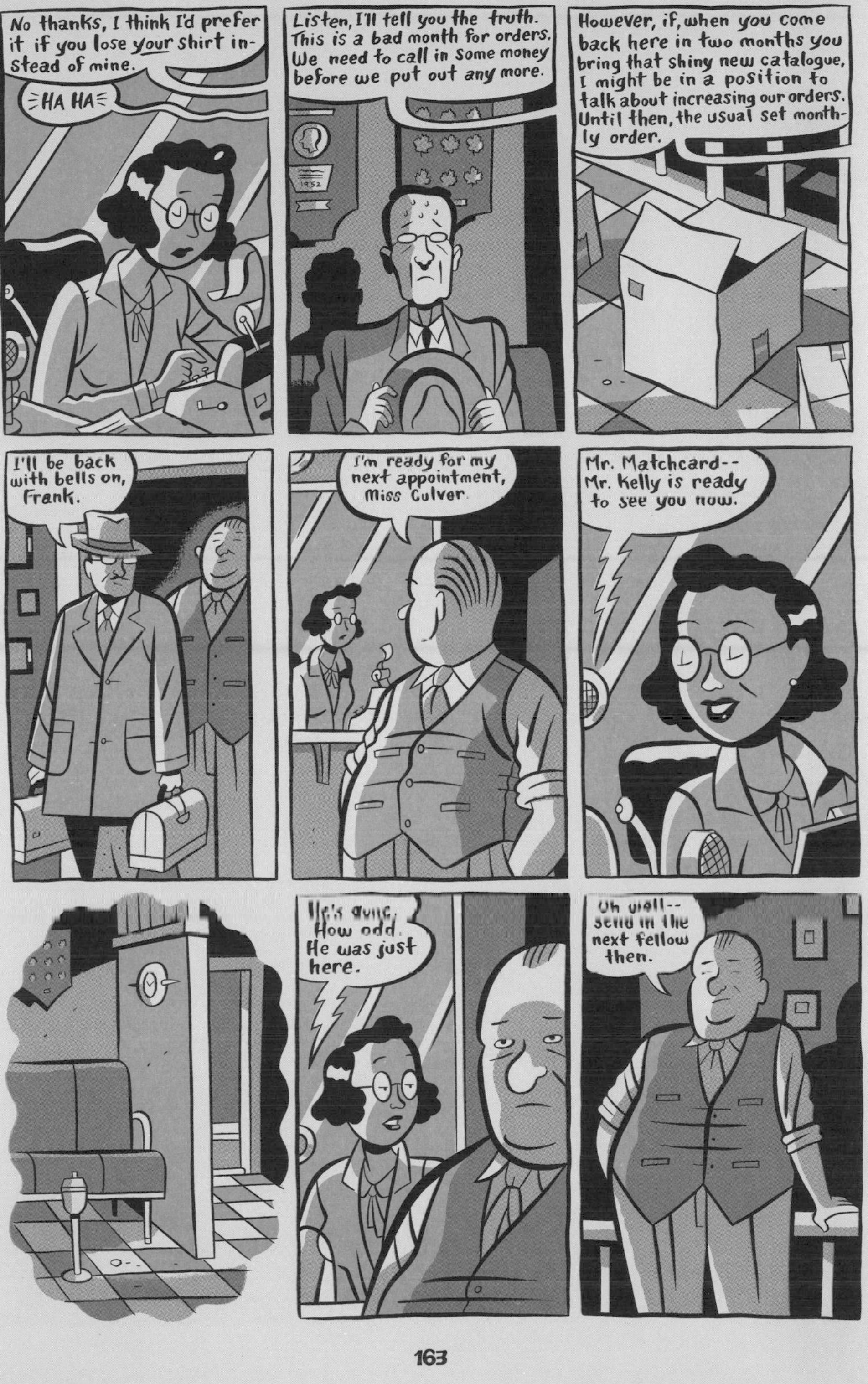
No thanks, I think I'd prefer it if you lose your shirt instead of mine.
HA HA
Listen, I'll tell you the truth. This is a bad month for orders. We need to call in some money before we put out any more.
However, if, when you come back here in two months you bring that shiny new catalogue, I might be in a position to talk about increasing our orders. Until then, the usual set monthly order.
I'll be back with bells on, Frank.
I'm ready for my next appointment, Miss Culver.
Mr. Matchcard-- Mr. Kelly is ready to see you now.
He's gone. How odd. He was just here.
Oh well-- send in the next fellow then.

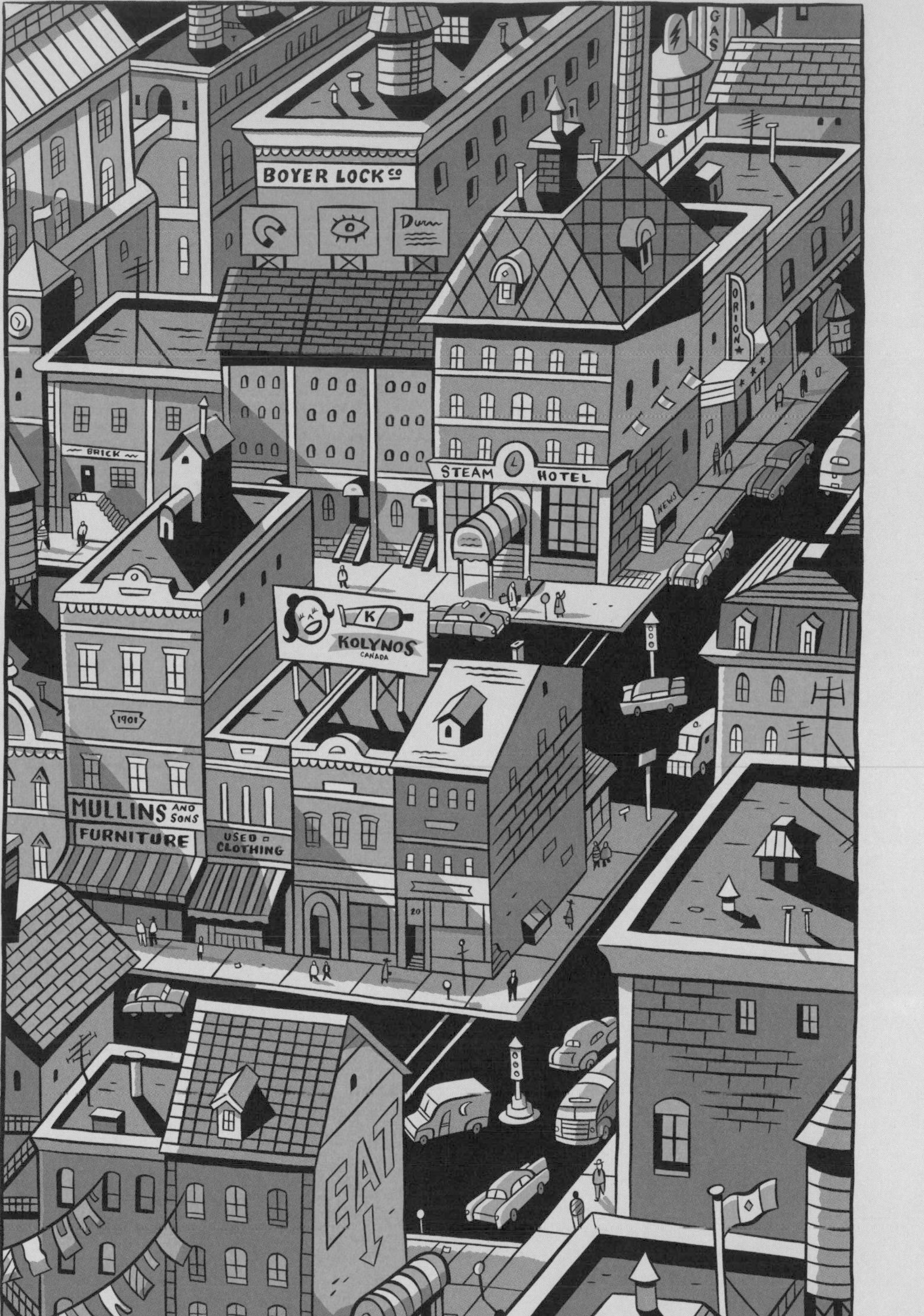
GAS
BOYER LOCK CO
ORION
BRICK
STEAM HOTEL
NEWS
KOLYNOS
CANADA
1901
MULLINS AND SONS
FURNITURE
USED CLOTHING
20
EAT

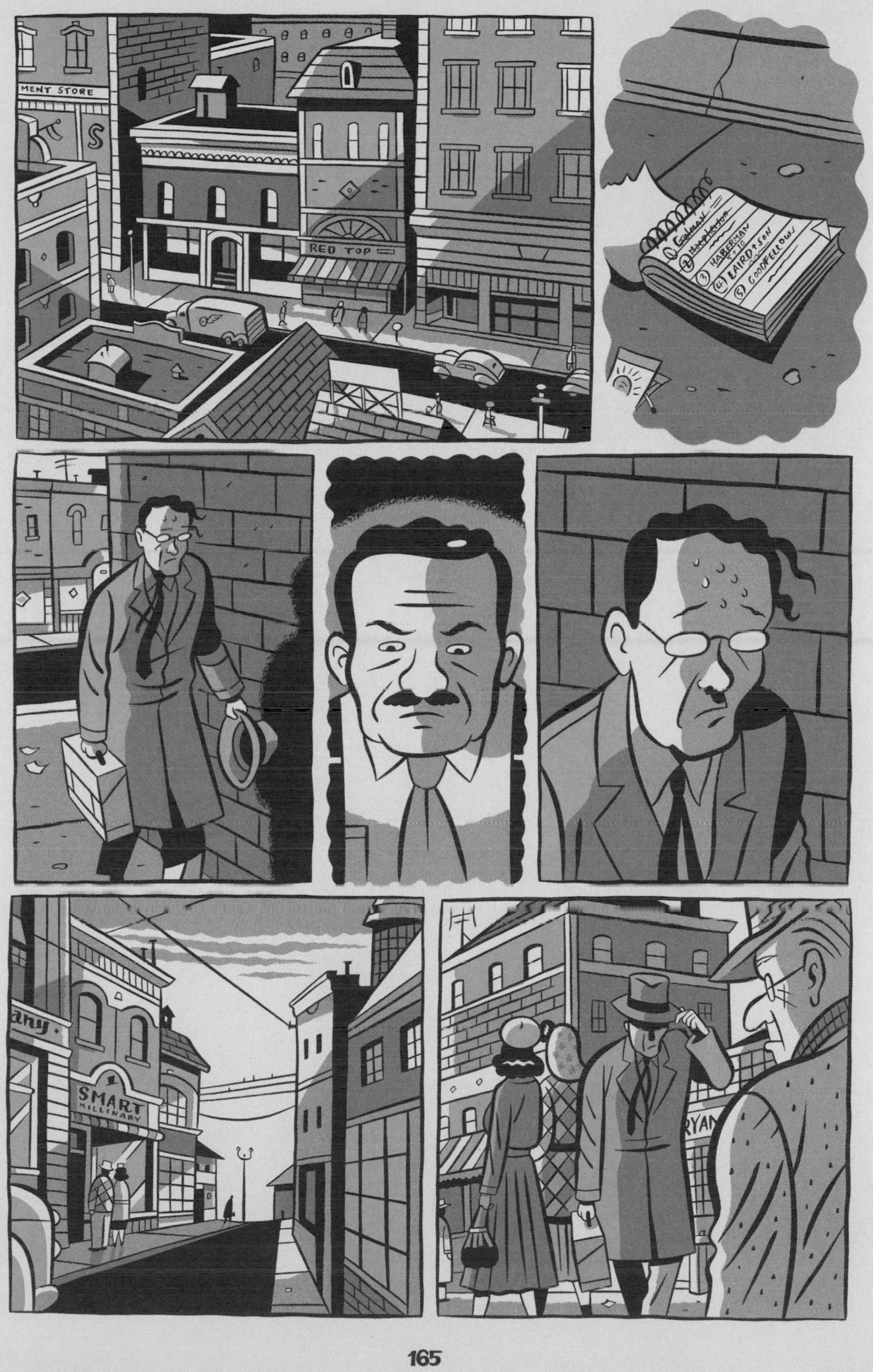
MENT STORE
RED TOP
HABERMAN
5+10
LAIRD+SON
GOODFELLOWS
SMART
MILLINARY

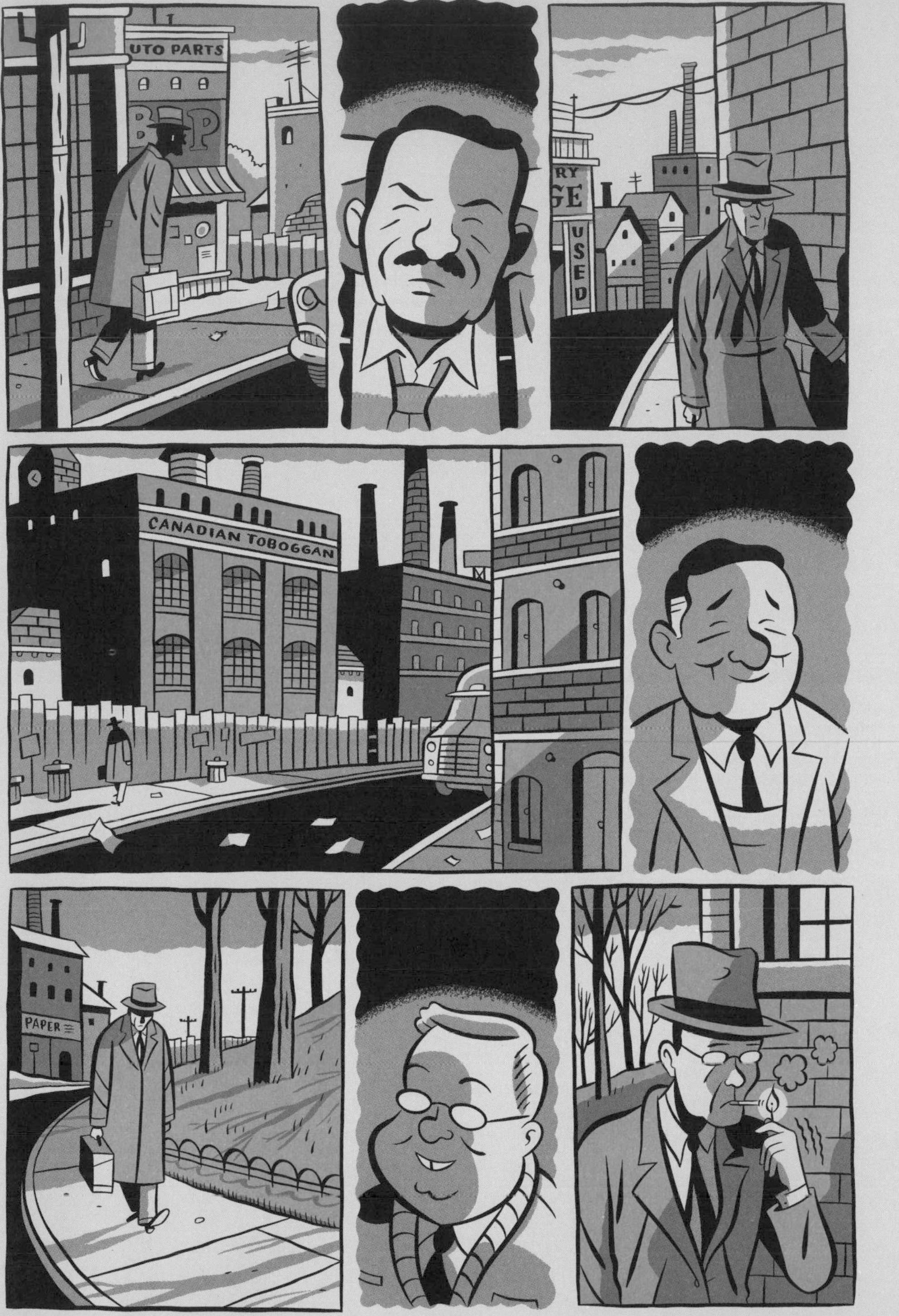
UTO PARTS
USED
CANADIAN TOBOGGAN
PAPER

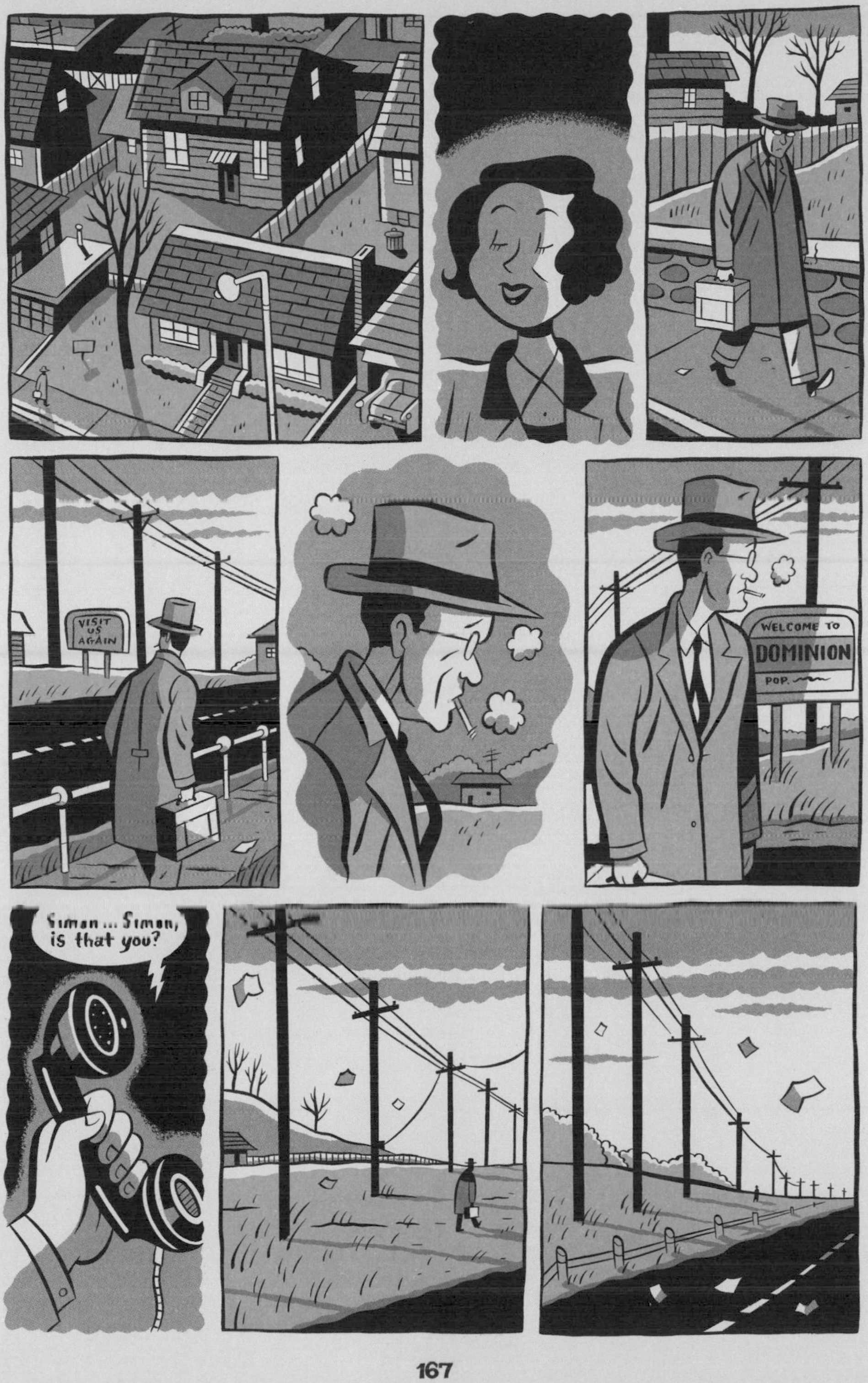
VISIT US AGAIN
WELCOME TO
DOMINION
POP.
Simon ... Simon, is that you?

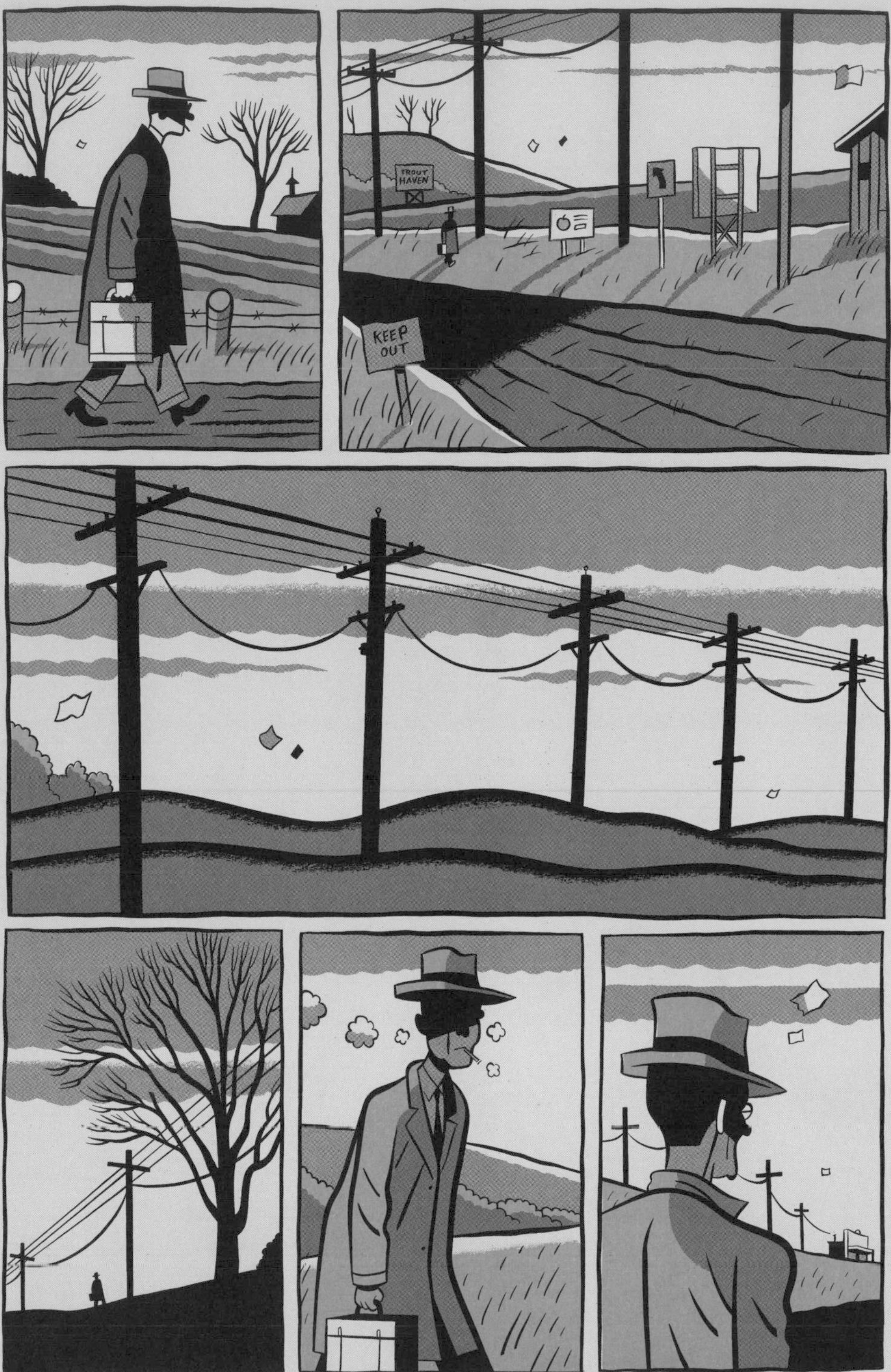
TROUT HAVEN
KEEP OUT

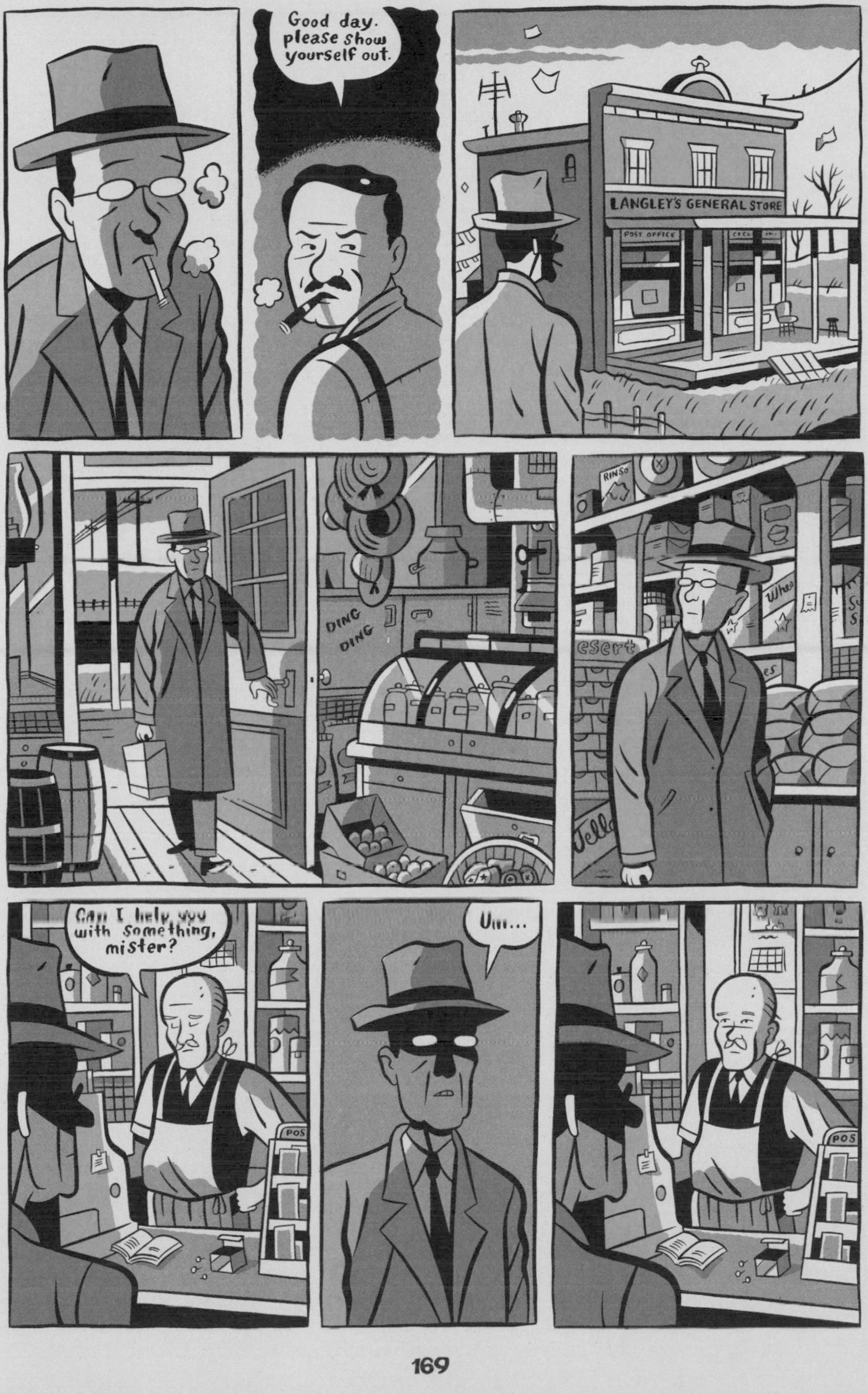
Good day. please show yourself out.
LANGLEY'S GENERAL STORE
POST OFFICE
RINSO
DING DING
esert
Can I help you with something, mister?
Um...

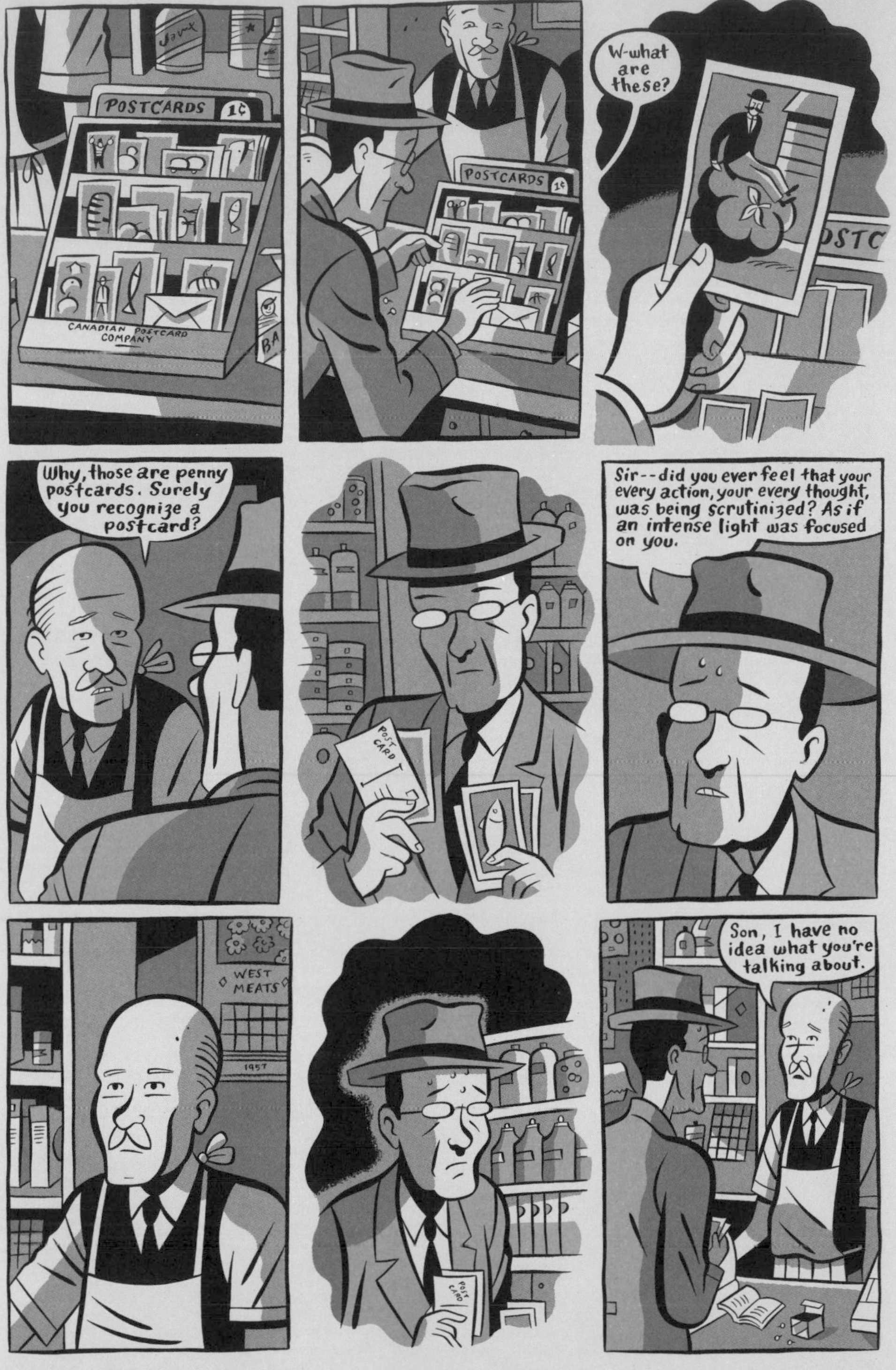
POSTCARDS 1¢
CANADIAN POSTCARD COMPANY
POSTCARDS 1¢
W-what are these?
Why, those are penny postcards. Surely you recognize a postcard?
POST CARD
Sir--did you ever feel that your every action, your every thought, was being scrutinized? As if an intense light was focused on you.
WEST MEATS
1957
POST CARD
Son, I have no idea what you're talking about.

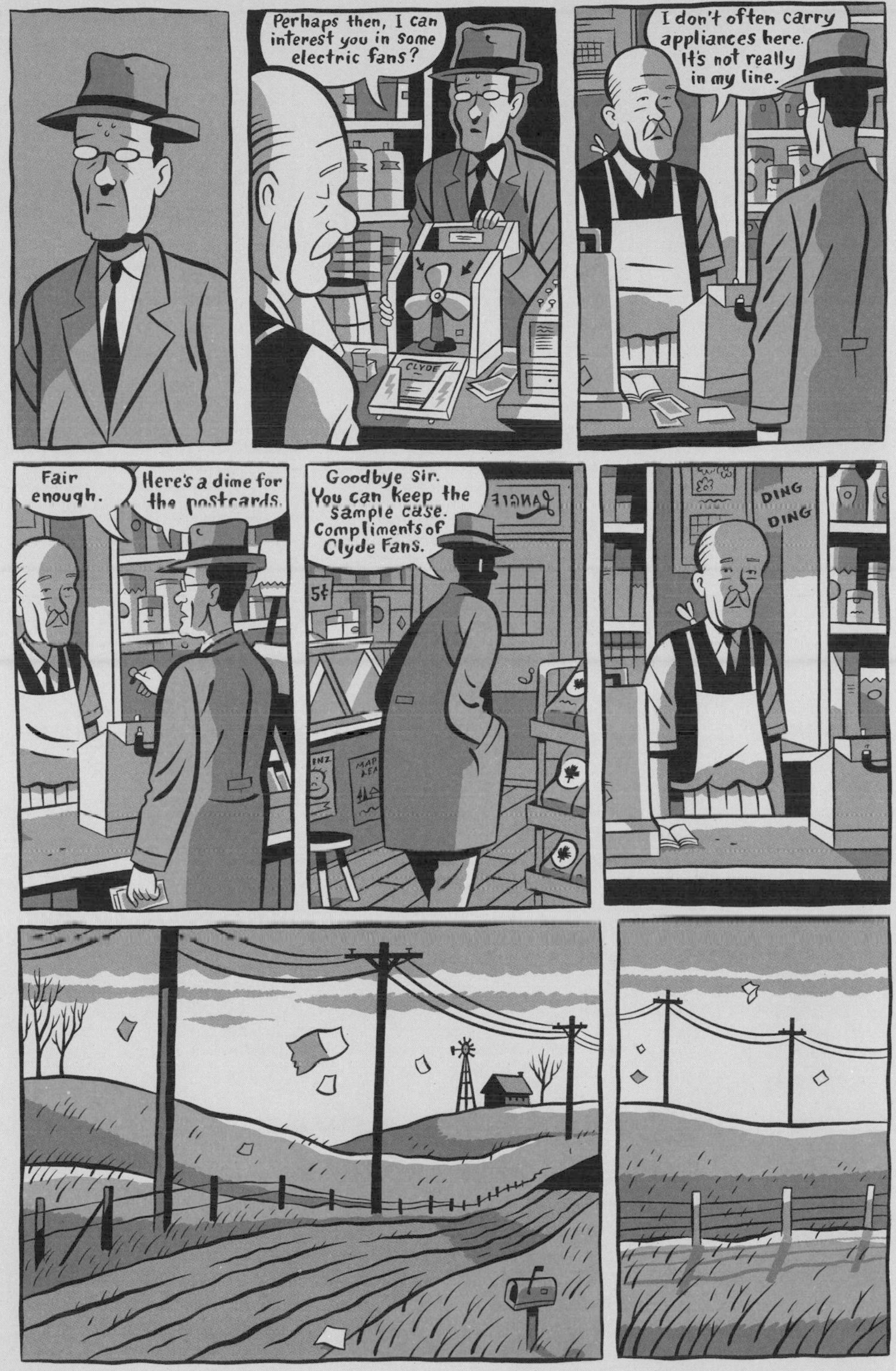
Perhaps then, I can interest you in some electric fans?
CLYDE
I don't often carry appliances here. It's not really in my line.
Fair enough.
Here's a dime for the postcards.
Goodbye sir. You can keep the sample case. Compliments of Clyde Fans.
5¢
DING
DING

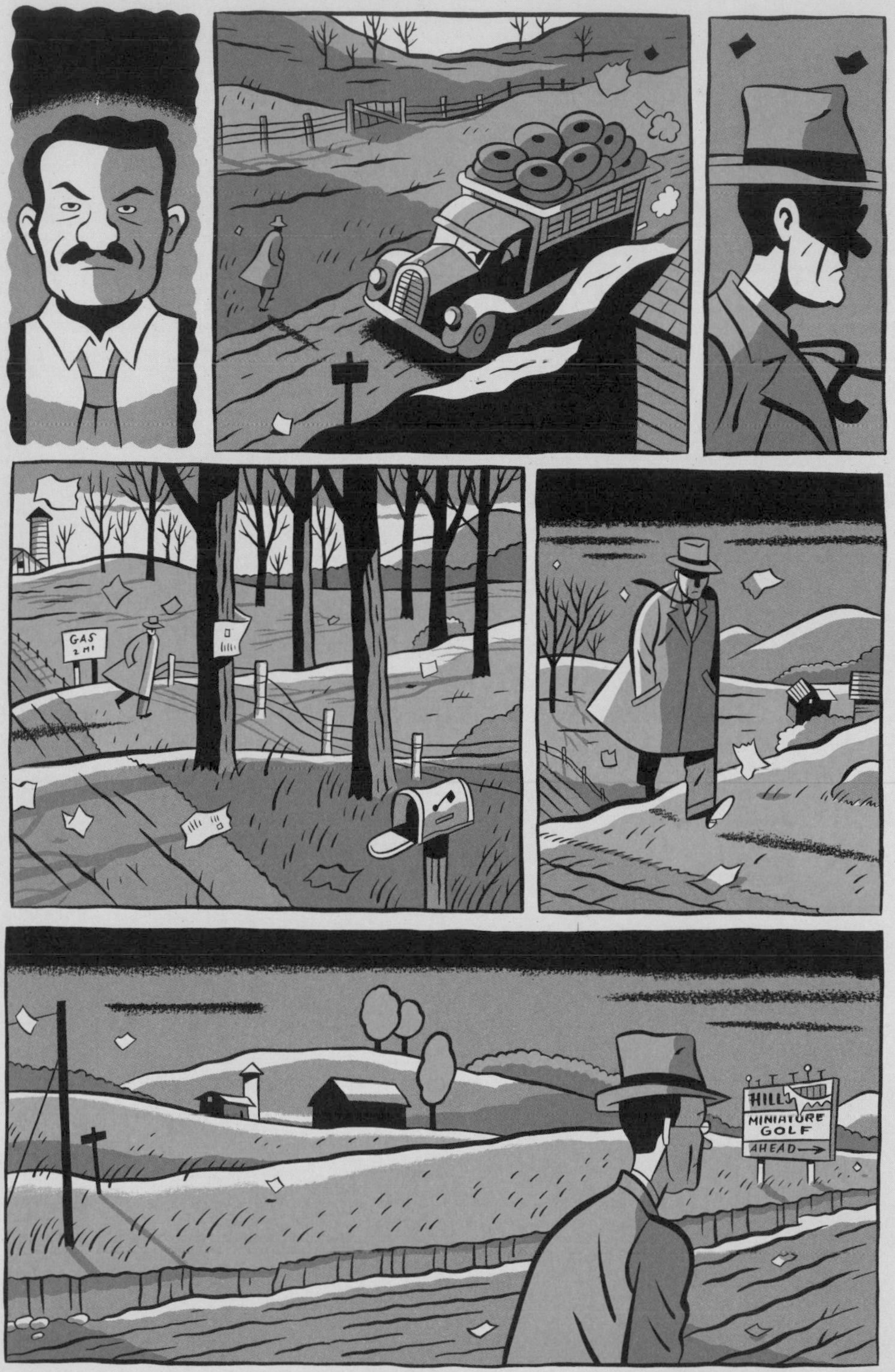
GAS 2 MI
HILL
MINIATURE GOLF
AHEAD

Simon?

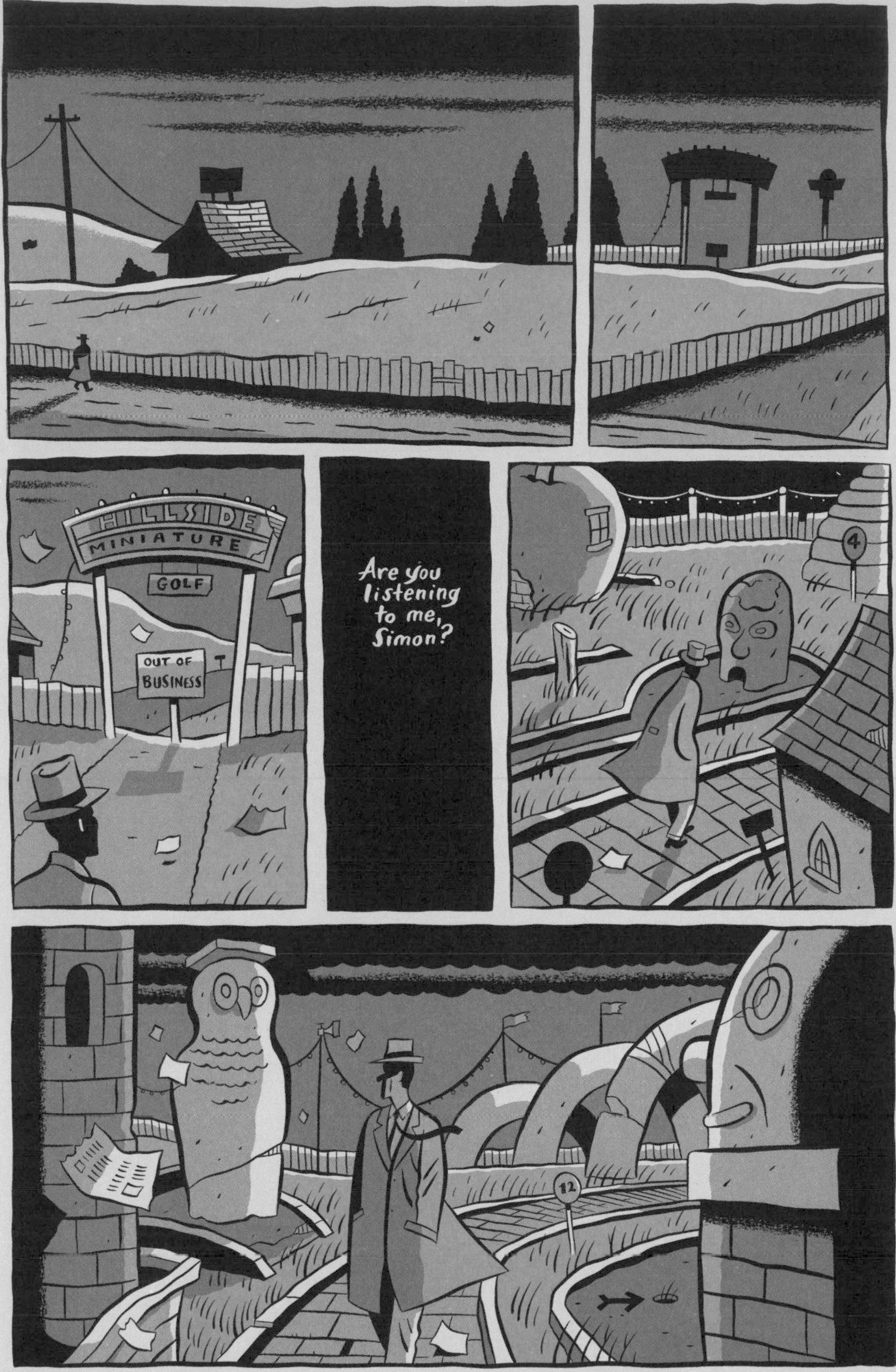
HILLSIDE
MINIATURE
GOLF
OUT OF BUSINESS
Are you listening to me, Simon?
4
12

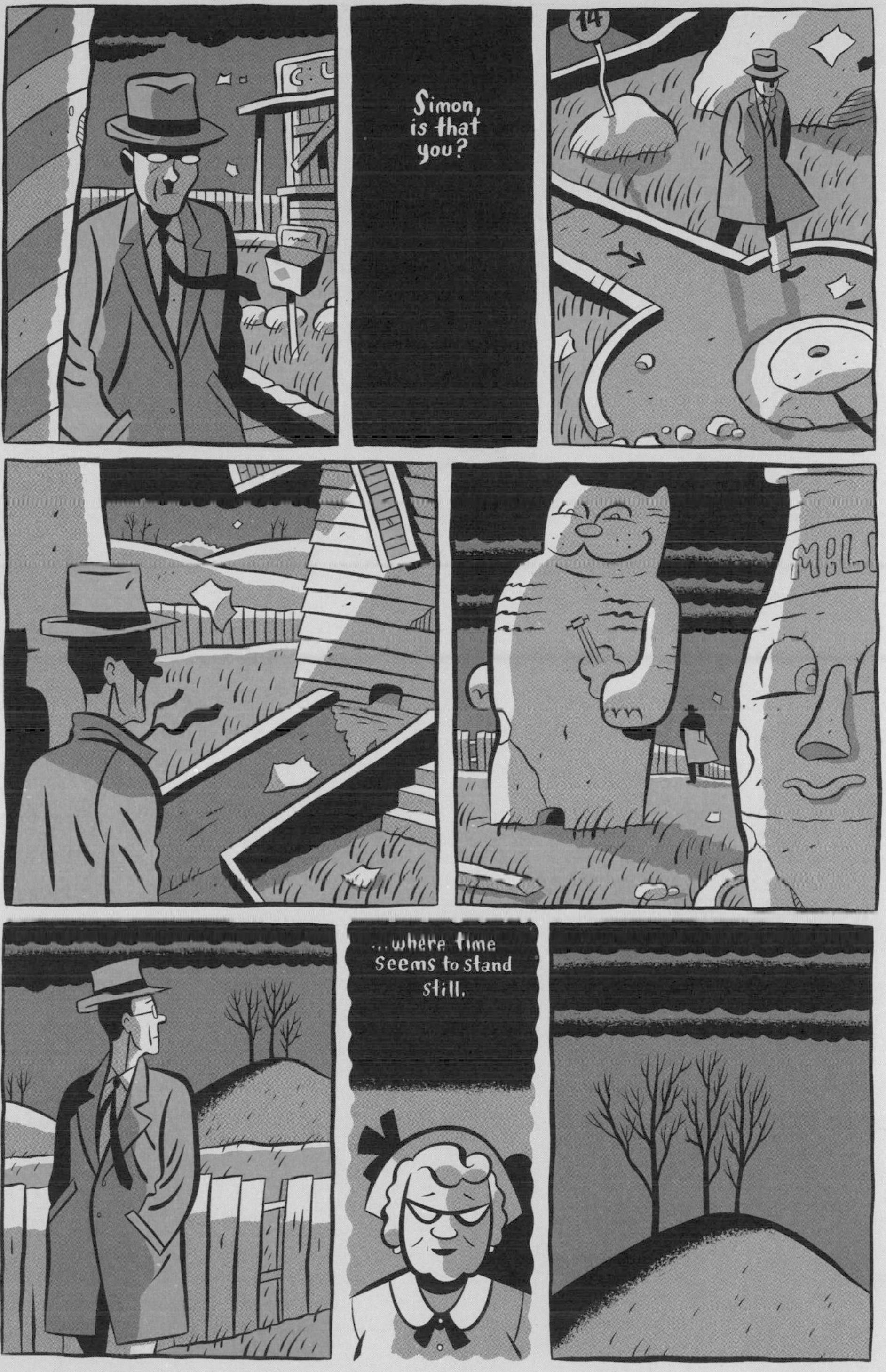
C.U
Simon, is that you?
14
MILL
...where time seems to stand still.

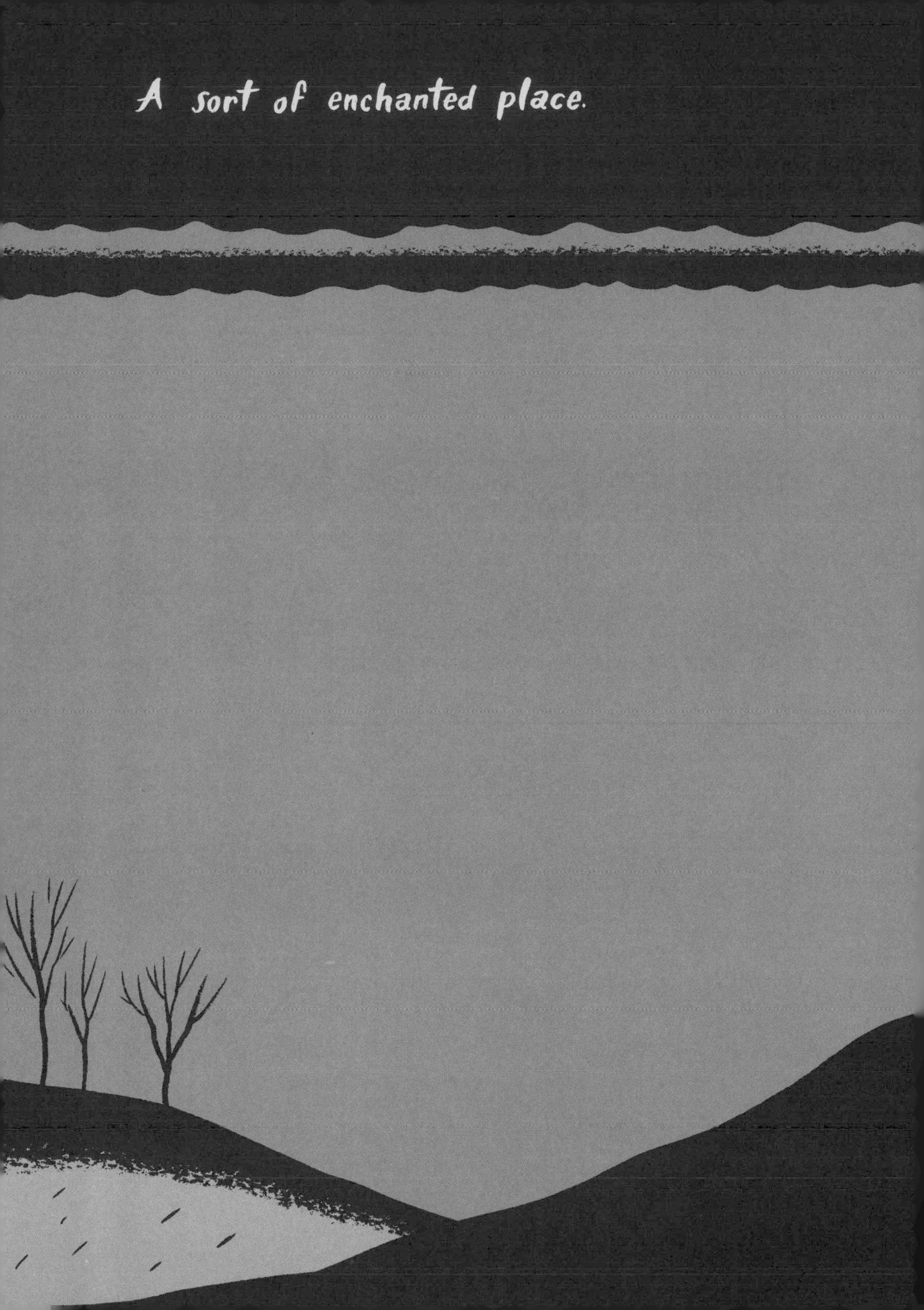
A sort of enchanted place.

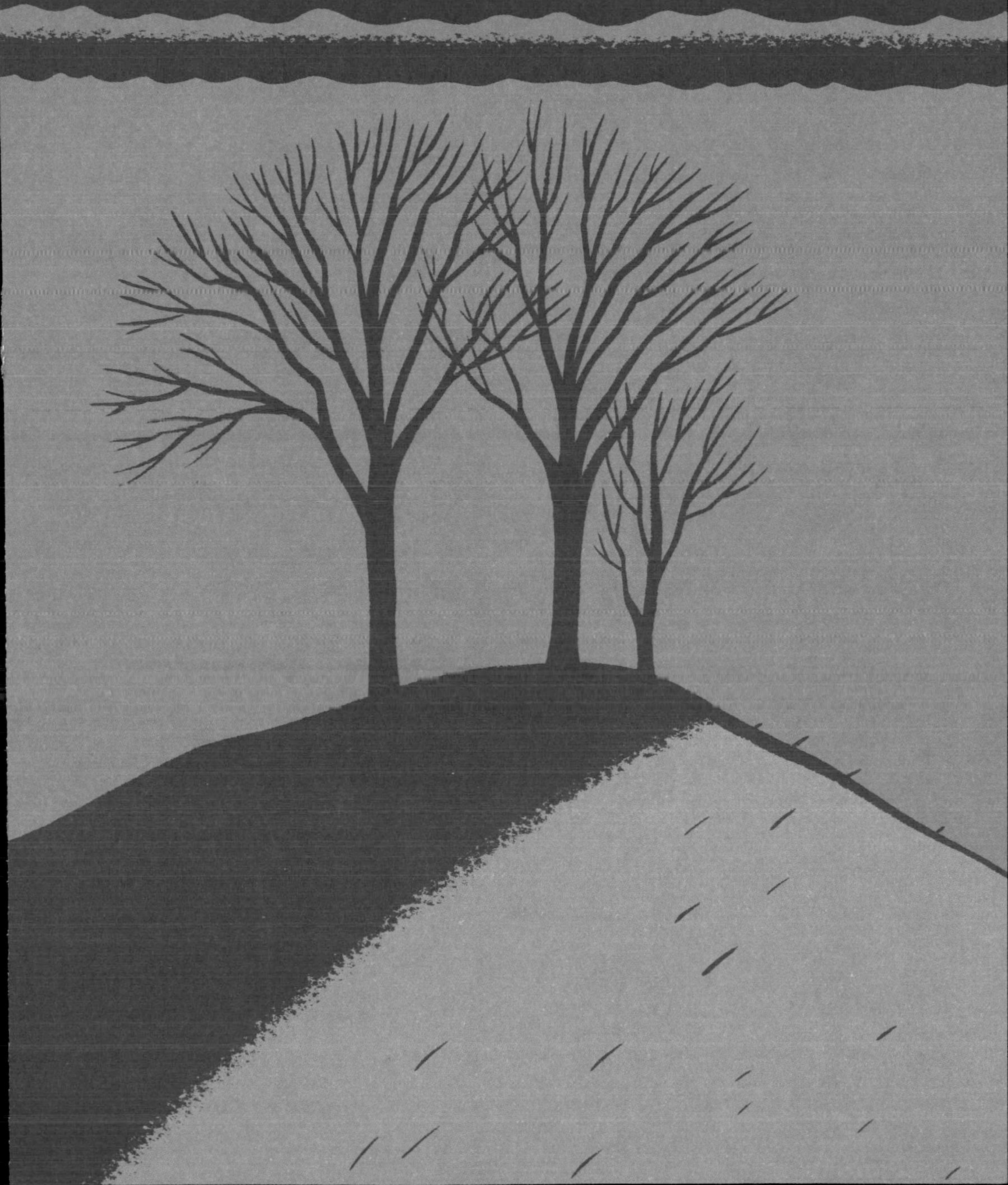

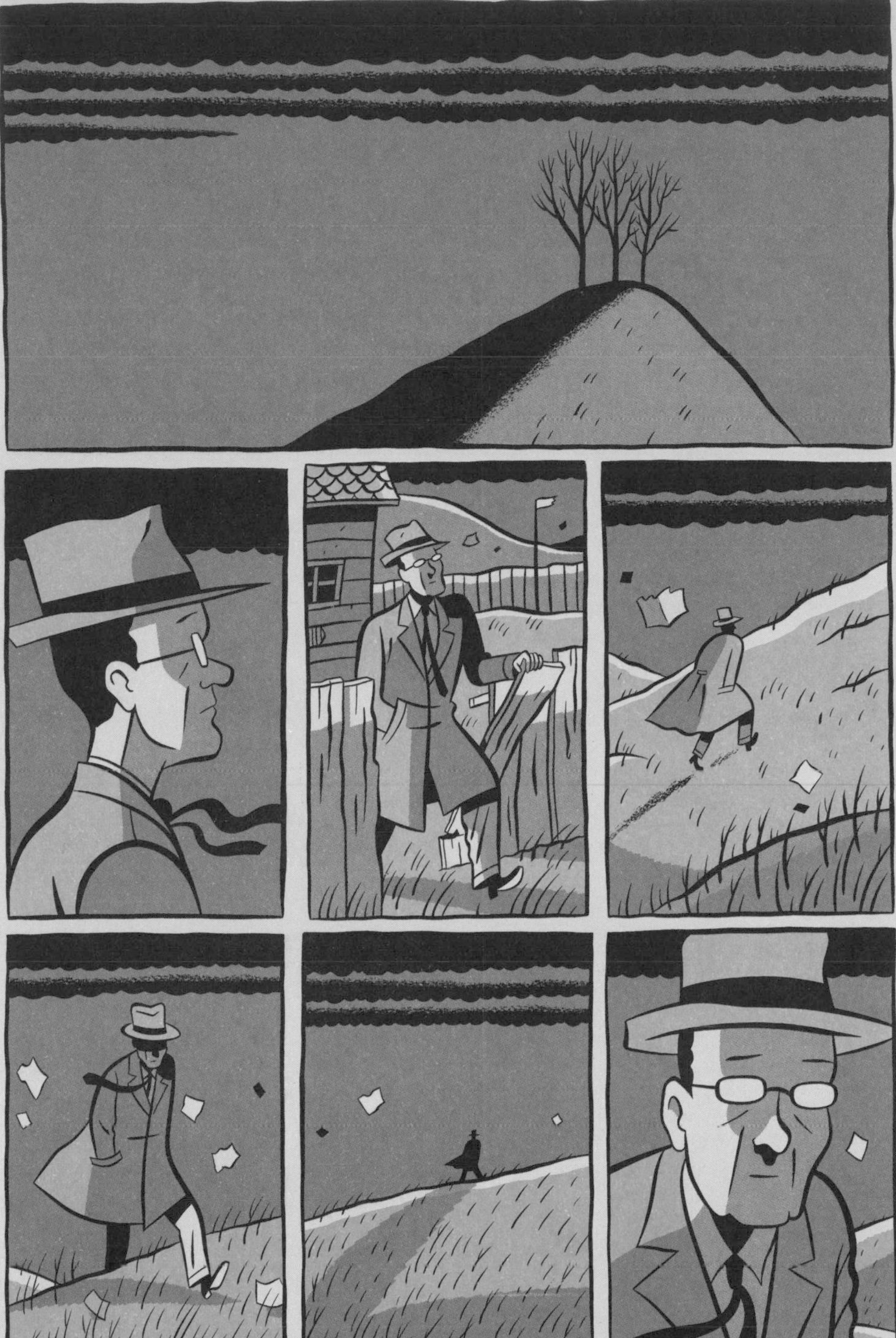

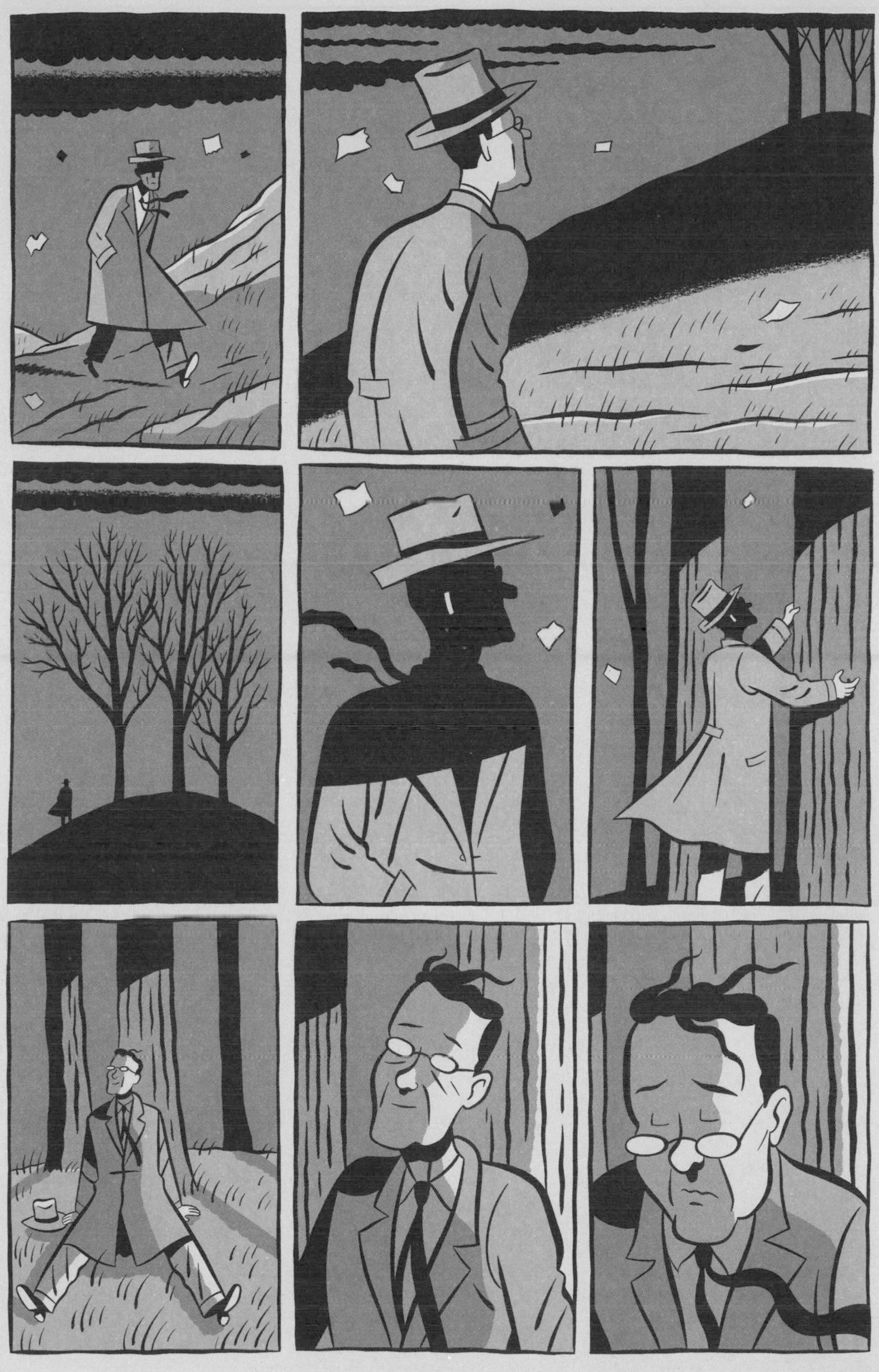

1966

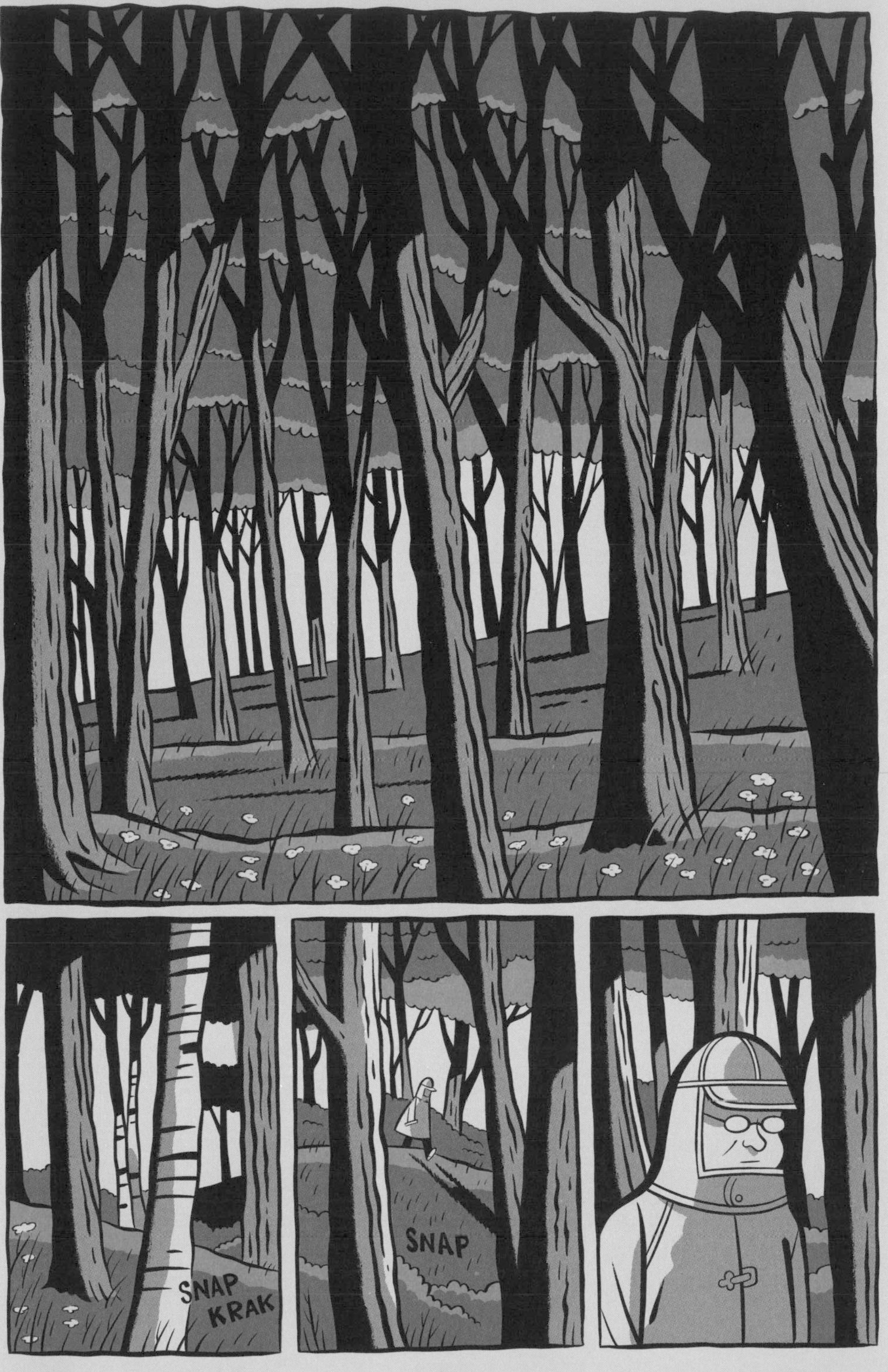
SNAP
KRAK
SNAP

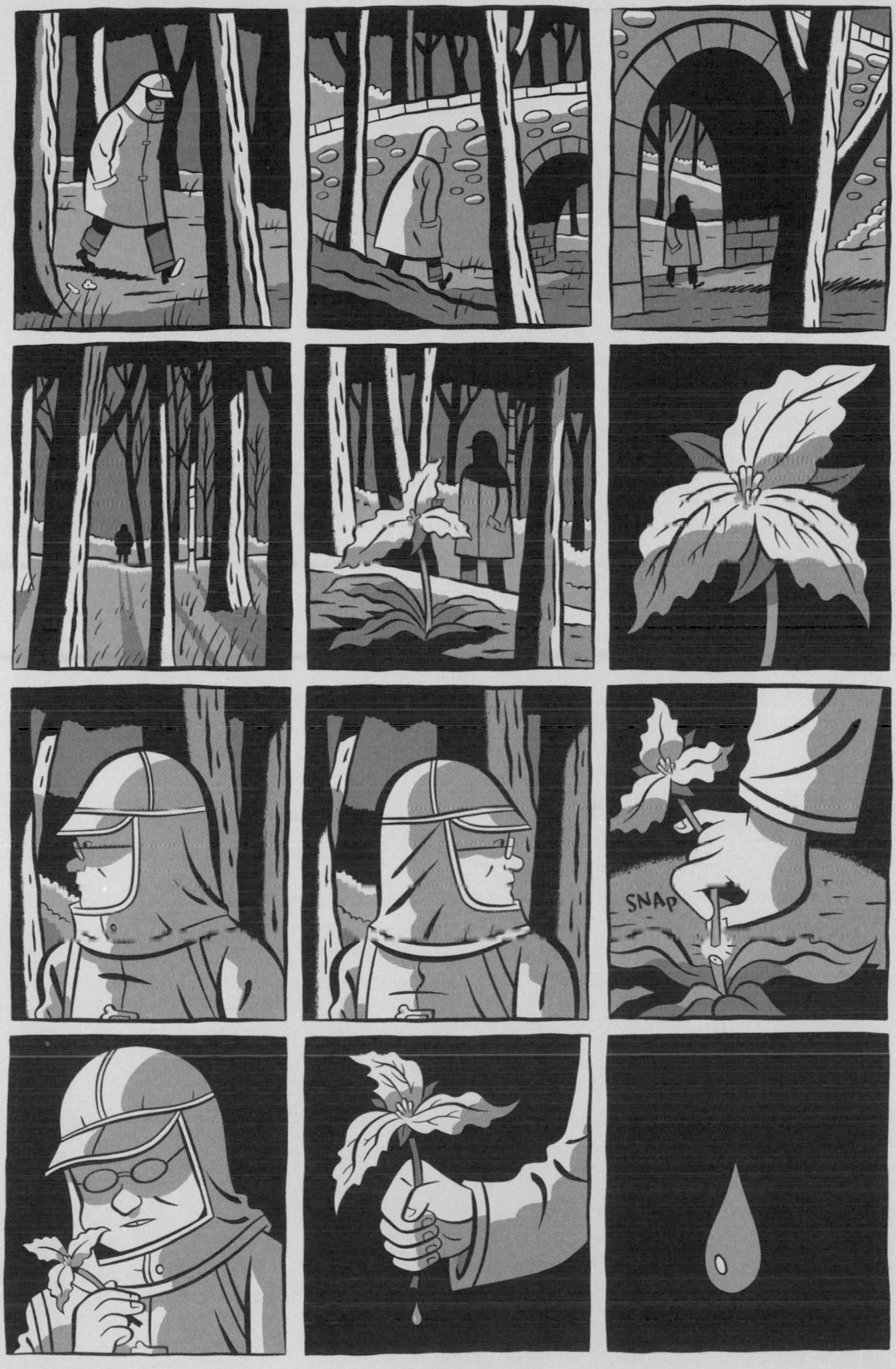
SNAp

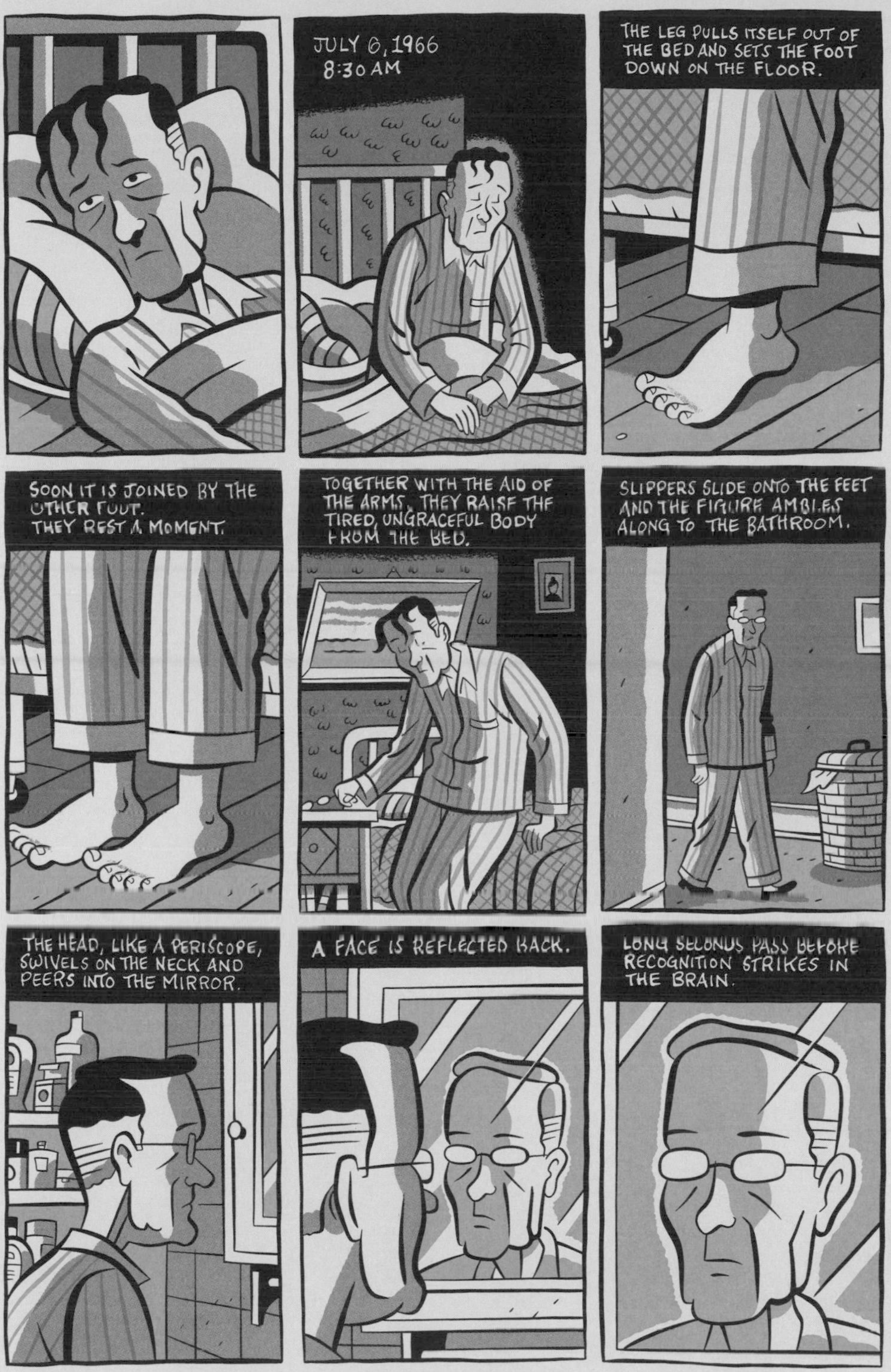
JULY 6, 1966
8:30 AM
THE LEG PULLS ITSELF OUT OF THE BED AND SETS THE FOOT DOWN ON THE FLOOR.
SOON IT IS JOINED BY THE OTHER FOOT.
THEY REST A MOMENT.
TOGETHER WITH THE AID OF THE ARMS, THEY RAISE THE TIRED, UNGRACEFUL BODY FROM THE BED.
SLIPPERS SLIDE ONTO THE FEET AND THE FIGURE AMBLES ALONG TO THE BATHROOM.
THE HEAD, LIKE A PERISCOPE, SWIVELS ON THE NECK AND PEERS INTO THE MIRROR.
A FACE IS REFLECTED BACK.
LONG SECONDS PASS BEFORE RECOGNITION STRIKES IN THE BRAIN.

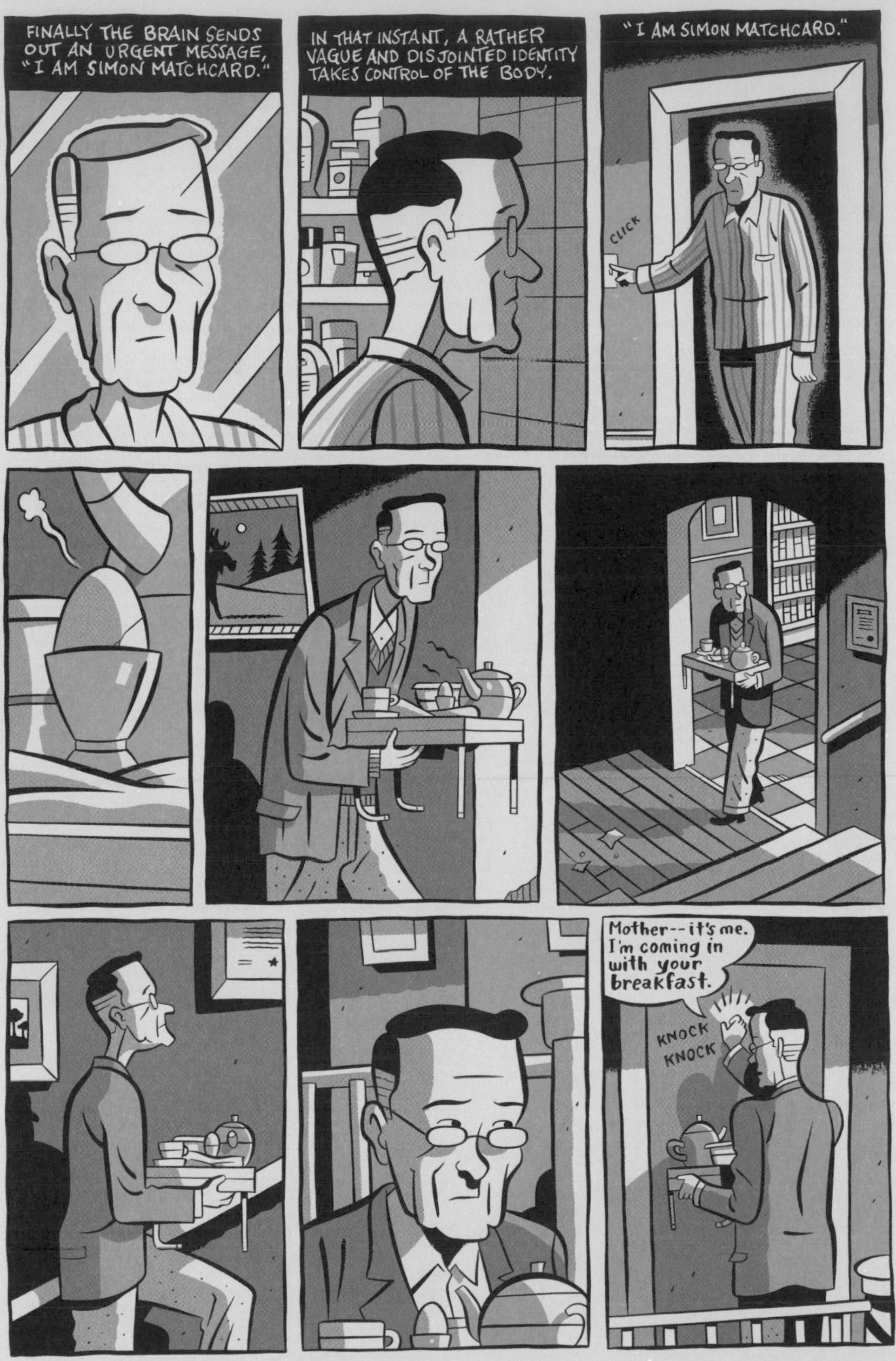
FINALLY THE BRAIN SENDS OUT AN URGENT MESSAGE, "I AM SIMON MATCHCARD."
IN THAT INSTANT, A RATHER VAGUE AND DISJOINTED IDENTITY TAKES CONTROL OF THE BODY.
"I AM SIMON MATCHCARD."
CLICK
Mother--it's me. I'm coming in with your breakfast.
KNOCK KNOCK

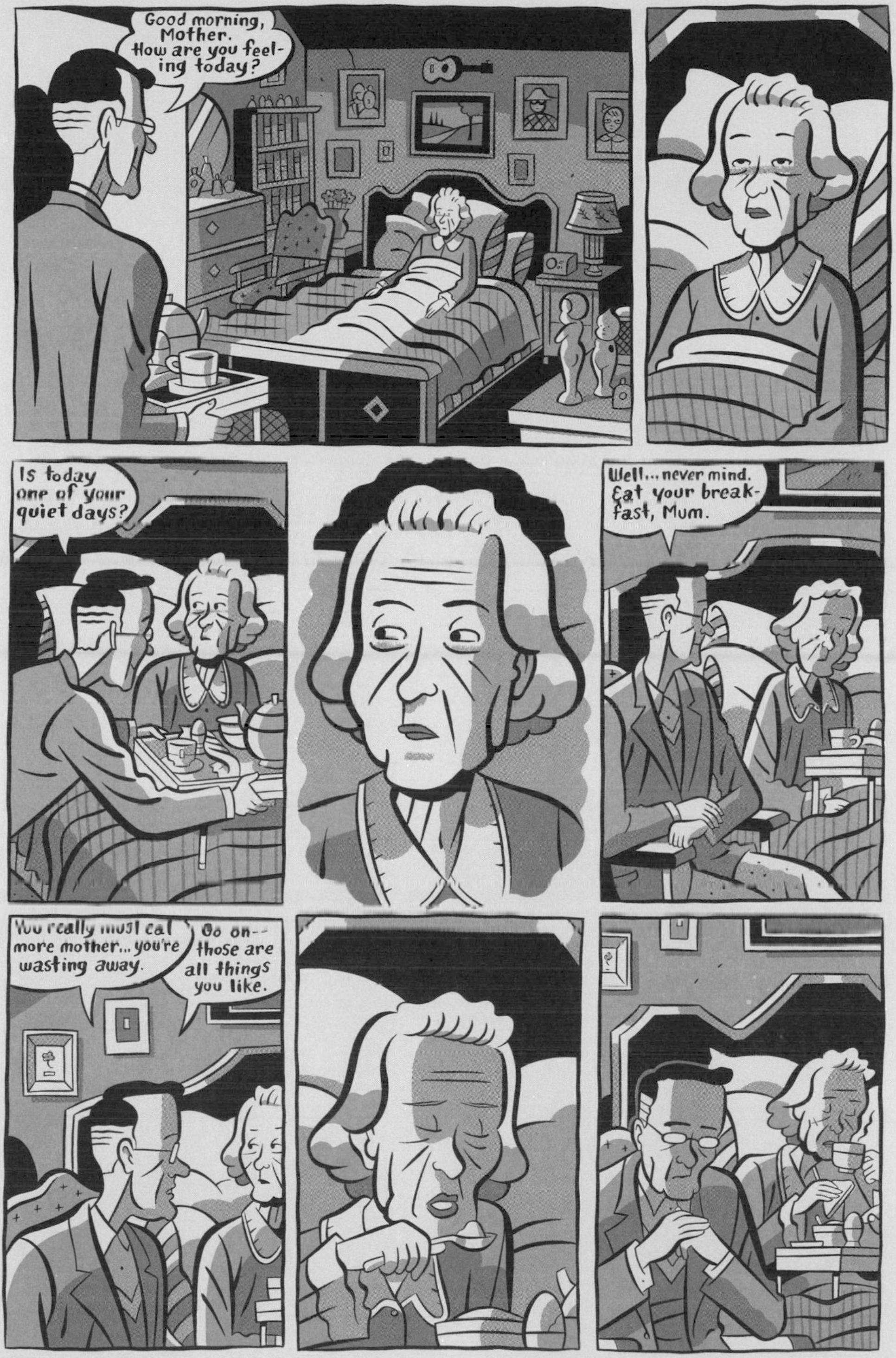
Good morning, Mother. How are you feeling today?
Is today one of your quiet days?
Well... never mind. Eat your breakfast, Mum.
You really must eat more mother... you're wasting away.
Go on-- those are all things you like.

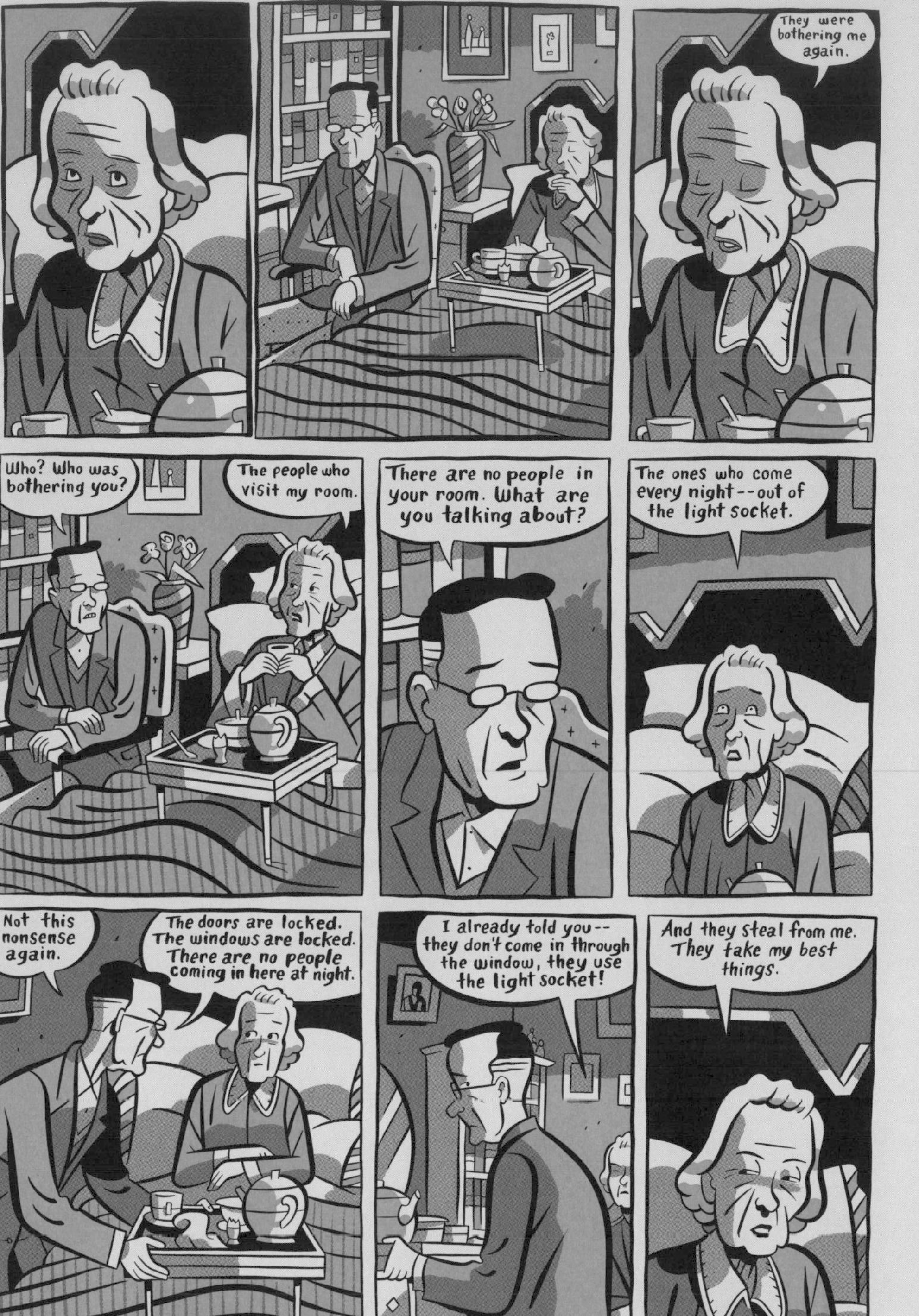
They were bothering me again.
Who? Who was bothering you?
The people who visit my room.
There are no people in your room. What are you talking about?
The ones who come every night--out of the light socket.
Not this nonsense again.
The doors are locked. The windows are locked. There are no people coming in here at night.
I already told you-- they don't come in through the window, they use the light socket!
And they steal from me. They take my best things.

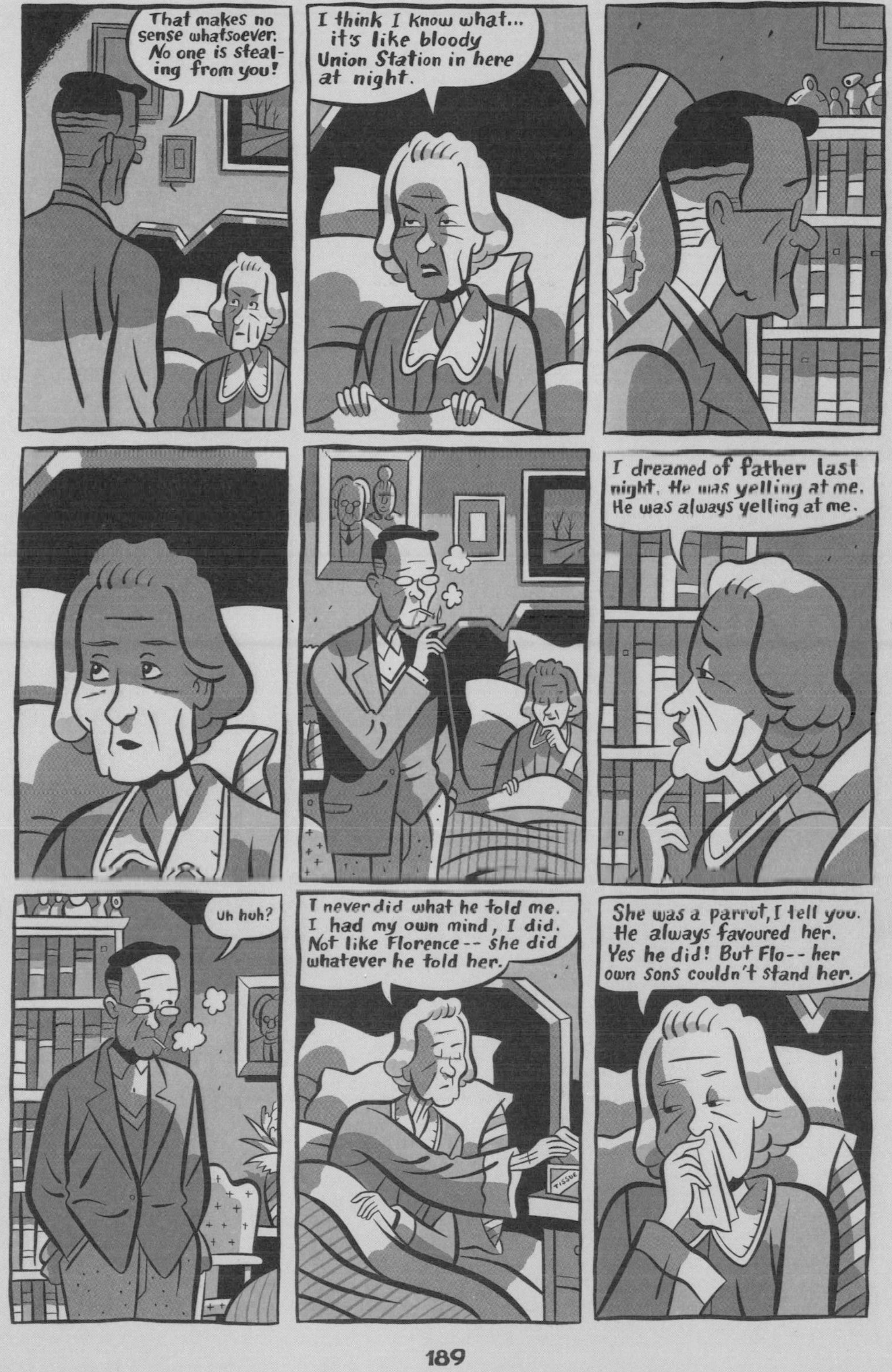
That makes no sense whatsoever. No one is stealing from you!
I think I know what... it's like bloody Union Station in here at night.
I dreamed of father last night. He was yelling at me. He was always yelling at me.
Uh huh?
I never did what he told me. I had my own mind, I did. Not like Florence -- she did whatever he told her.
She was a parrot, I tell you. He always favoured her. Yes he did! But Flo-- her own sons couldn't stand her.
TISSUE

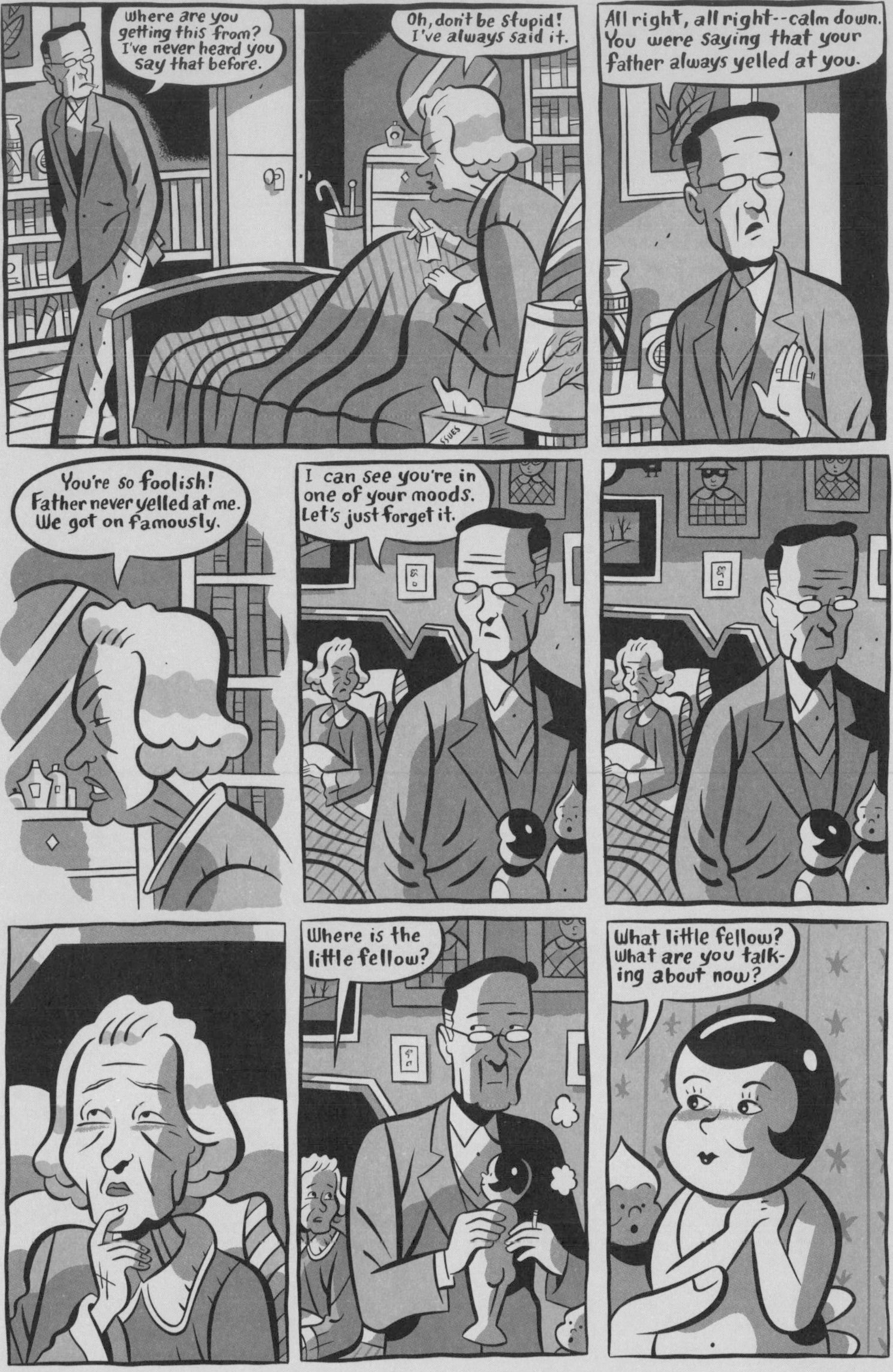
Where are you getting this from? I've never heard you say that before.
Oh, don't be stupid! I've always said it.
All right, all right--calm down. You were saying that your father always yelled at you.
You're so foolish! Father never yelled at me. We got on famously.
I can see you're in one of your moods. Let's just forget it.
Where is the little fellow?
What little fellow? What are you talking about now?

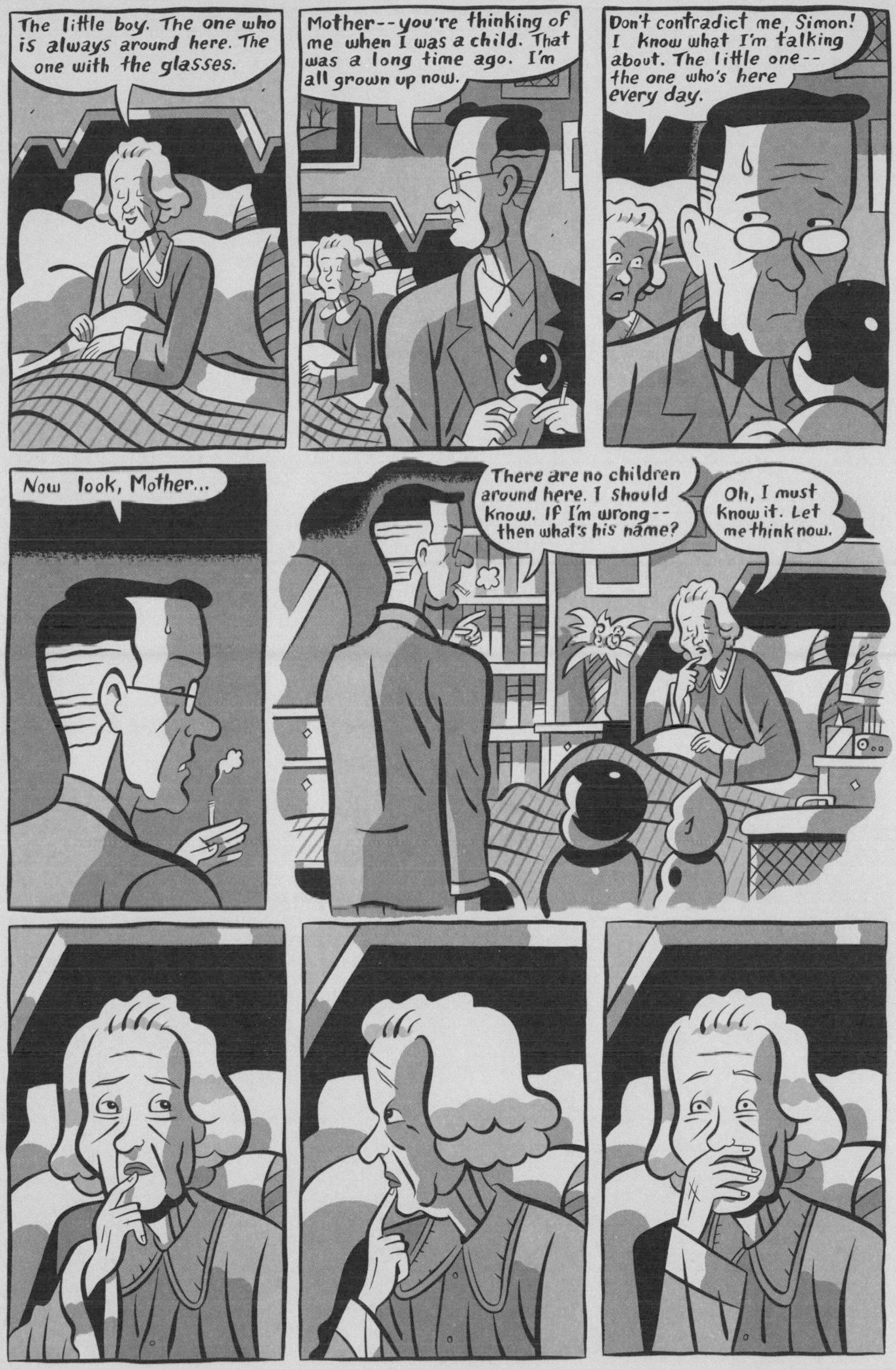
The little boy. The one who is always around here. The one with the glasses.
Mother--you're thinking of me when I was a child. That was a long time ago. I'm all grown up now.
Don't contradict me, Simon! I know what I'm talking about. The little one--the one who's here every day.
Now look, Mother...
There are no children around here. I should know. If I'm wrong--then what's his name?
Oh, I must know it. Let me think now.

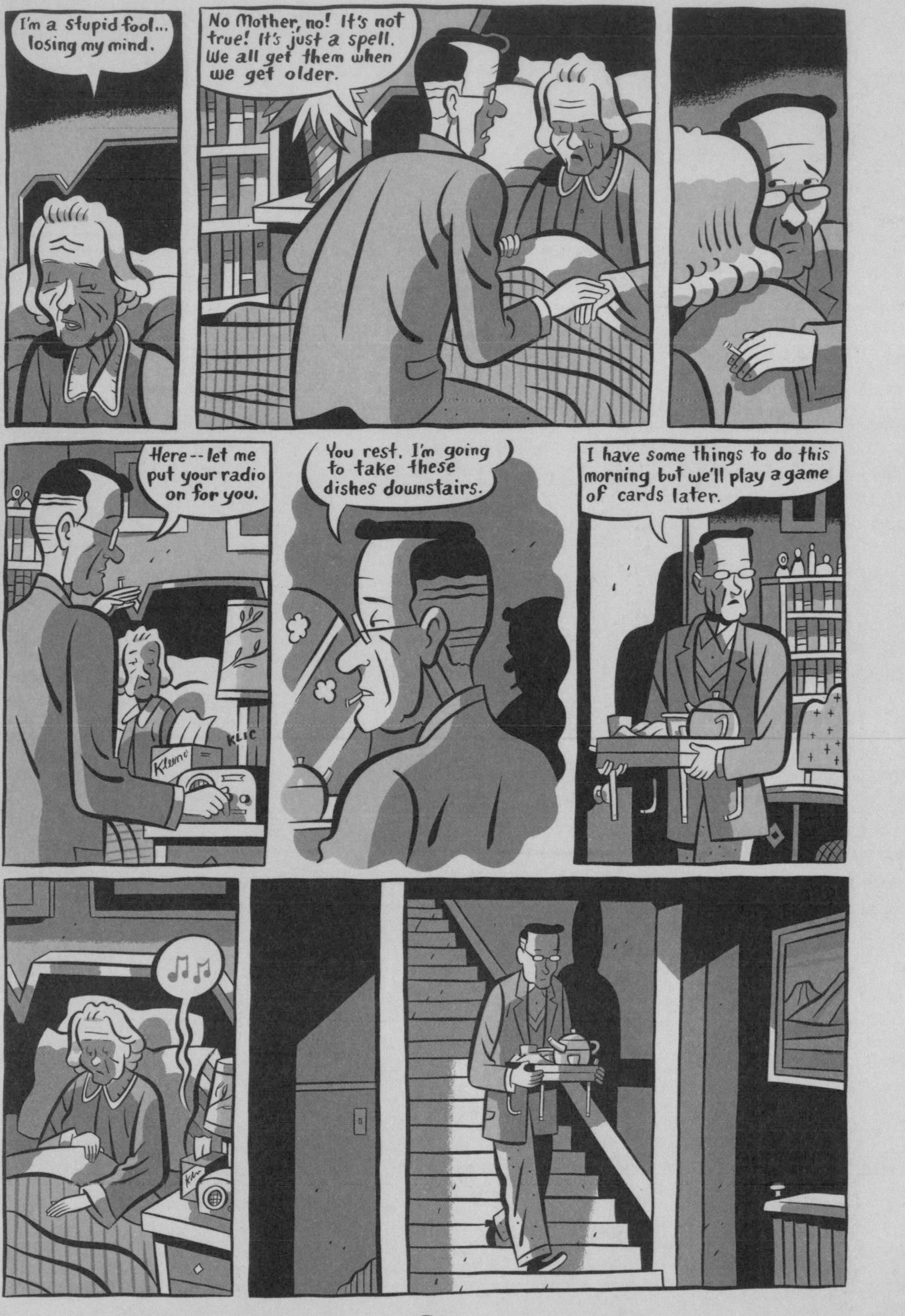
I'm a stupid fool... losing my mind.
No Mother, no! It's not true! It's just a spell. We all get them when we get older.
Here--let me put your radio on for you.
KLIC
You rest. I'm going to take these dishes downstairs.
I have some things to do this morning but we'll play a game of cards later.

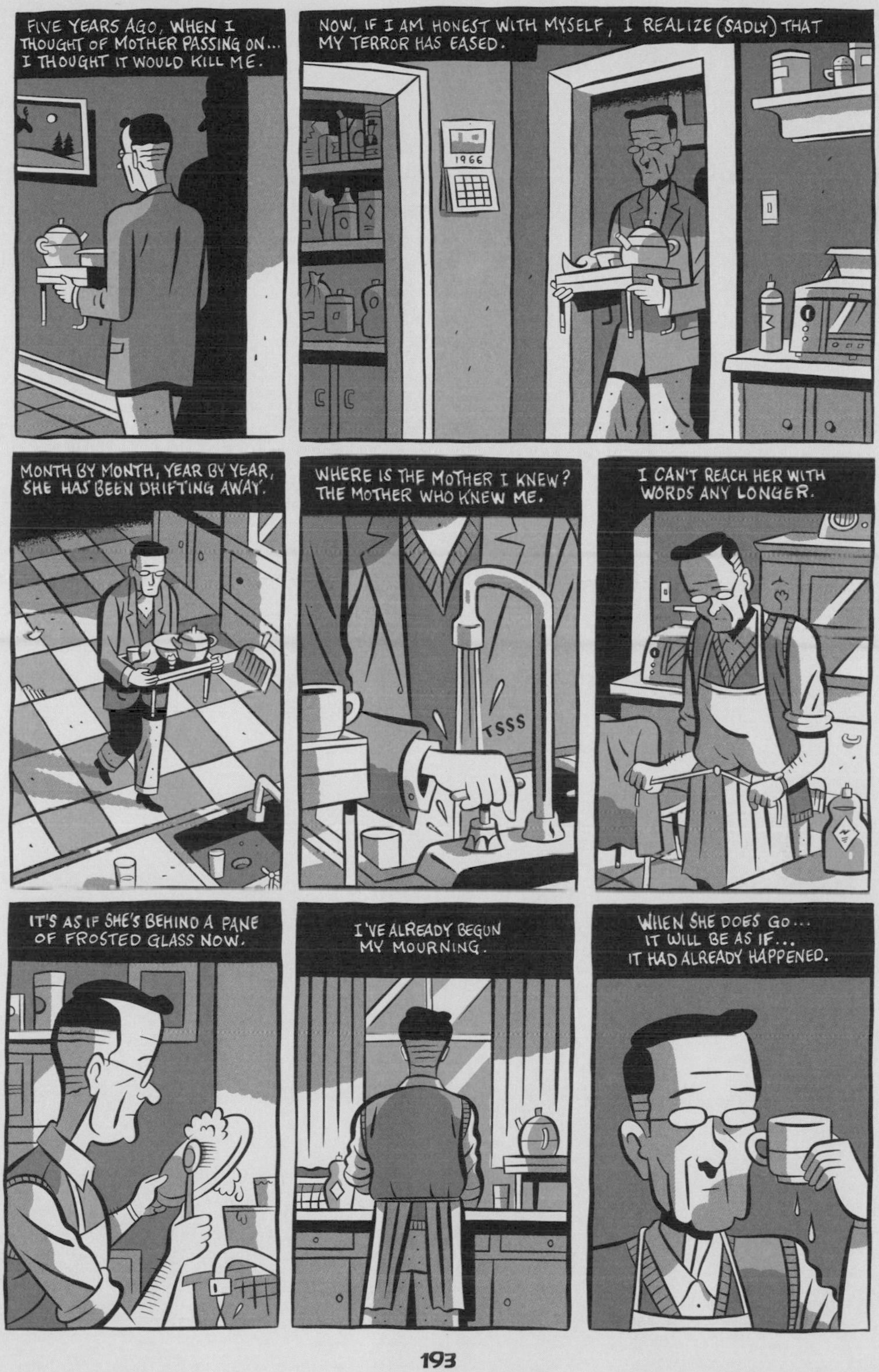

FIVE YEARS AGO, WHEN I THOUGHT OF MOTHER PASSING ON... I THOUGHT IT WOULD KILL ME.
NOW, IF I AM HONEST WITH MYSELF, I REALIZE (SADLY) THAT MY TERROR HAS EASED.
1966
MONTH BY MONTH, YEAR BY YEAR, SHE HAS BEEN DRIFTING AWAY.
WHERE IS THE MOTHER I KNEW? THE MOTHER WHO KNEW ME.
TSSS
I CAN'T REACH HER WITH WORDS ANY LONGER.
IT'S AS IF SHE'S BEHIND A PANE OF FROSTED GLASS NOW.
I'VE ALREADY BEGUN MY MOURNING.
WHEN SHE DOES GO... IT WILL BE AS IF... IT HAD ALREADY HAPPENED.

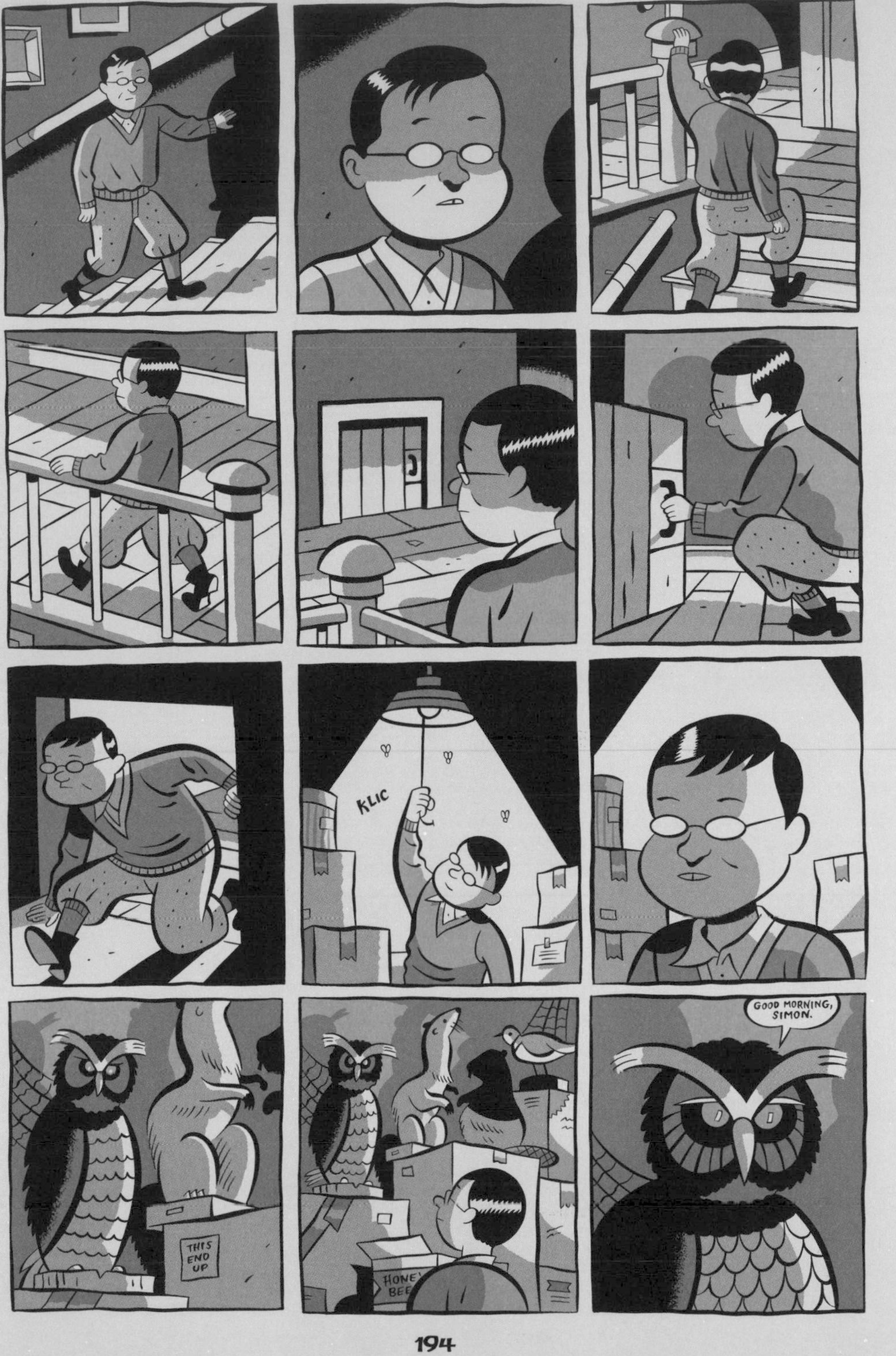
KLIC
THIS END UP
HONEY BEE
GOOD MORNING, SIMON.

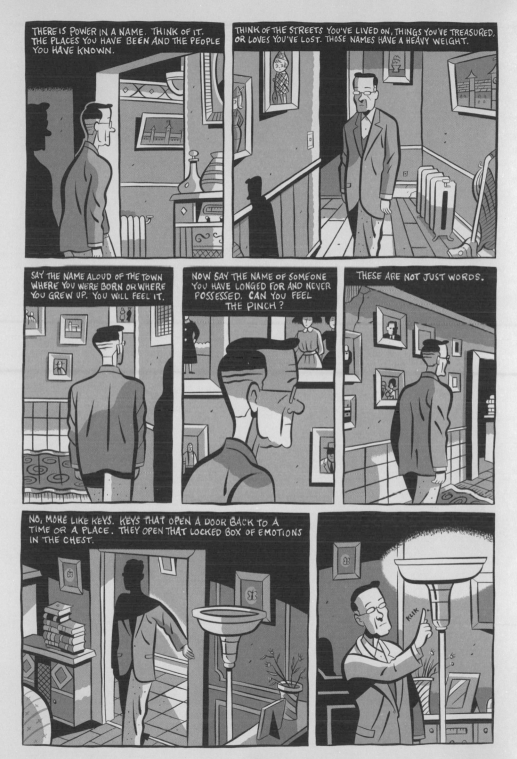

THERE IS POWER IN A NAME. THINK OF IT. THE PLACES YOU HAVE BEEN AND THE PEOPLE YOU HAVE KNOWN.

THINK OF THE STREETS YOU'VE LIVED ON, THINGS YOU'VE TREASURED, OR LOVES YOU'VE LOST. THOSE NAMES HAVE A HEAVY WEIGHT.

SAY THE NAME ALOUD OF THE TOWN WHERE YOU WERE BORN OR WHERE YOU GREW UP. YOU WILL FEEL IT.

NOW SAY THE NAME OF SOMEONE YOU HAVE LONGED FOR AND NEVER POSSESSED. CAN YOU FEEL THE PINCH?

THESE ARE NOT JUST WORDS.

NO, MORE LIKE KEYS. KEYS THAT OPEN A DOOR BACK TO A TIME OR A PLACE. THEY OPEN THAT LOCKED BOX OF EMOTIONS IN THE CHEST.

KLIK

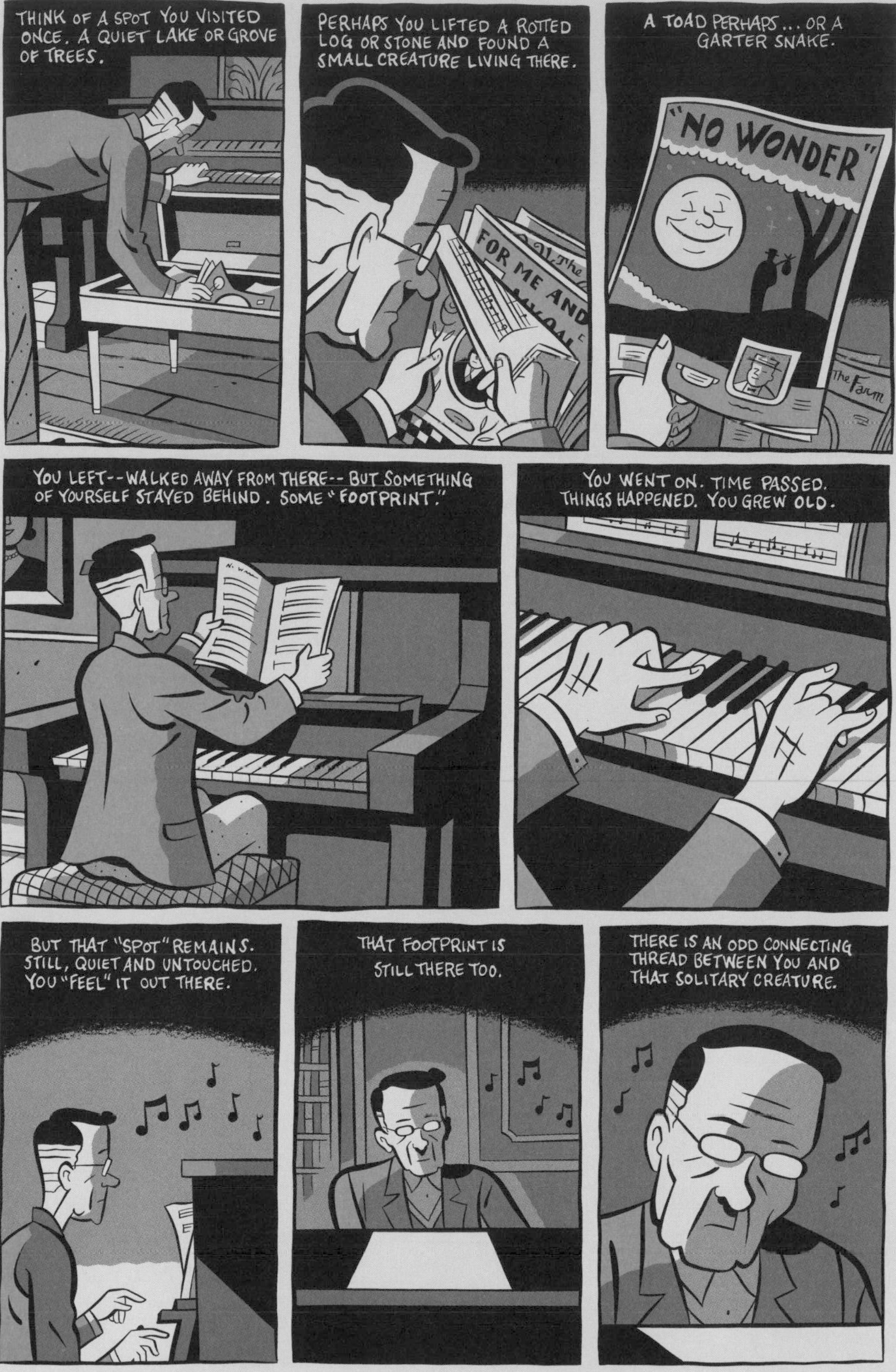
THINK OF A SPOT YOU VISITED ONCE. A QUIET LAKE OR GROVE OF TREES.
PERHAPS YOU LIFTED A ROTTED LOG OR STONE AND FOUND A SMALL CREATURE LIVING THERE.
FOR ME AND
A TOAD PERHAPS... OR A GARTER SNAKE.
"NO WONDER"
The Farm
YOU LEFT--WALKED AWAY FROM THERE--BUT SOMETHING OF YOURSELF STAYED BEHIND. SOME "FOOTPRINT."
YOU WENT ON. TIME PASSED. THINGS HAPPENED. YOU GREW OLD.
BUT THAT "SPOT" REMAINS. STILL, QUIET AND UNTOUCHED. YOU "FEEL" IT OUT THERE.
THAT FOOTPRINT IS STILL THERE TOO.
THERE IS AN ODD CONNECTING THREAD BETWEEN YOU AND THAT SOLITARY CREATURE.

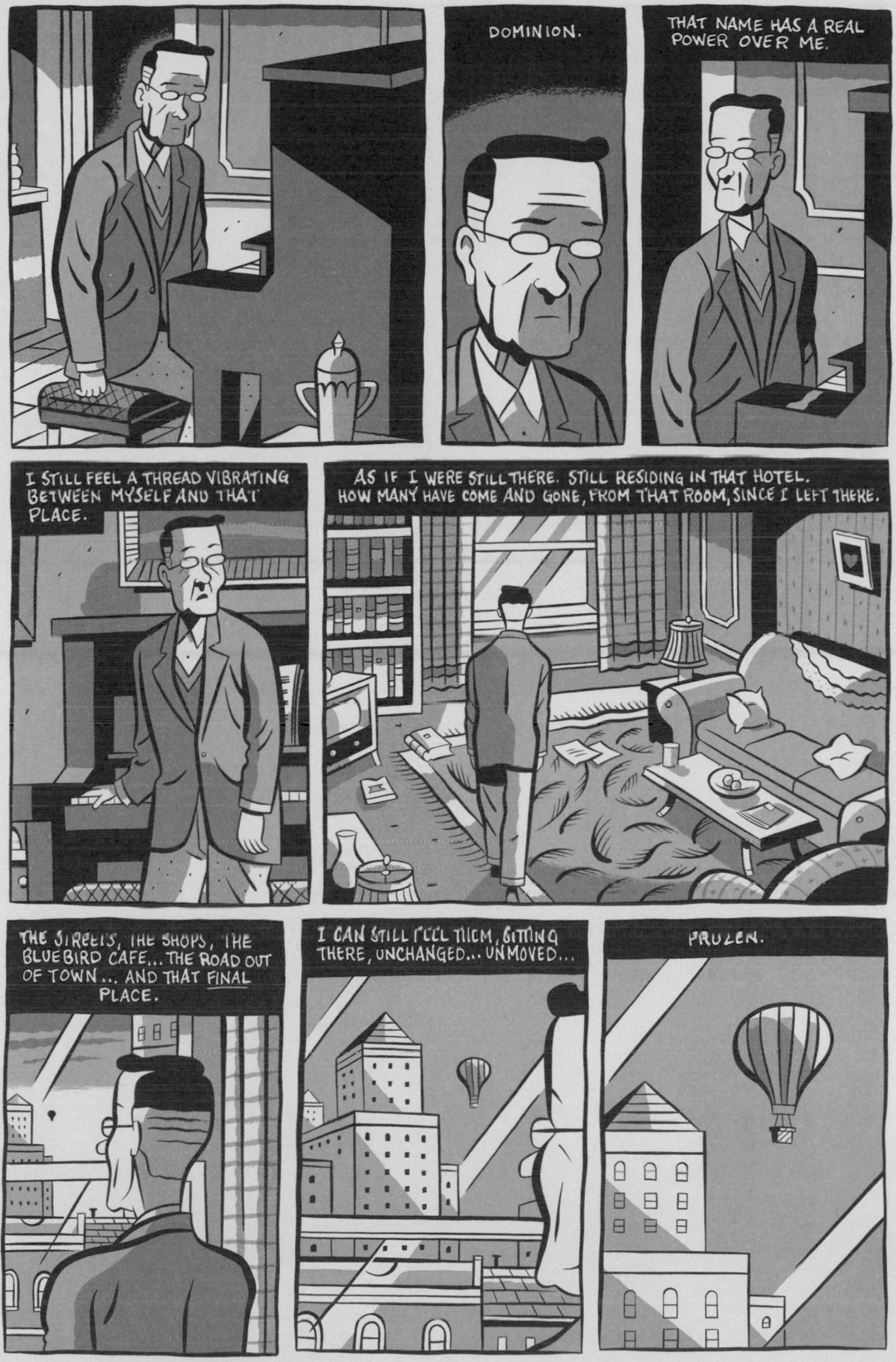
DOMINION.
THAT NAME HAS A REAL POWER OVER ME.
I STILL FEEL A THREAD VIBRATING BETWEEN MYSELF AND THAT PLACE.
AS IF I WERE STILL THERE. STILL RESIDING IN THAT HOTEL. HOW MANY HAVE COME AND GONE, FROM THAT ROOM, SINCE I LEFT THERE.
THE STREETS, THE SHOPS, THE BLUEBIRD CAFE... THE ROAD OUT OF TOWN... AND THAT FINAL PLACE.
I CAN STILL FEEL THEM, SITTING THERE, UNCHANGED... UNMOVED...
FROZEN.

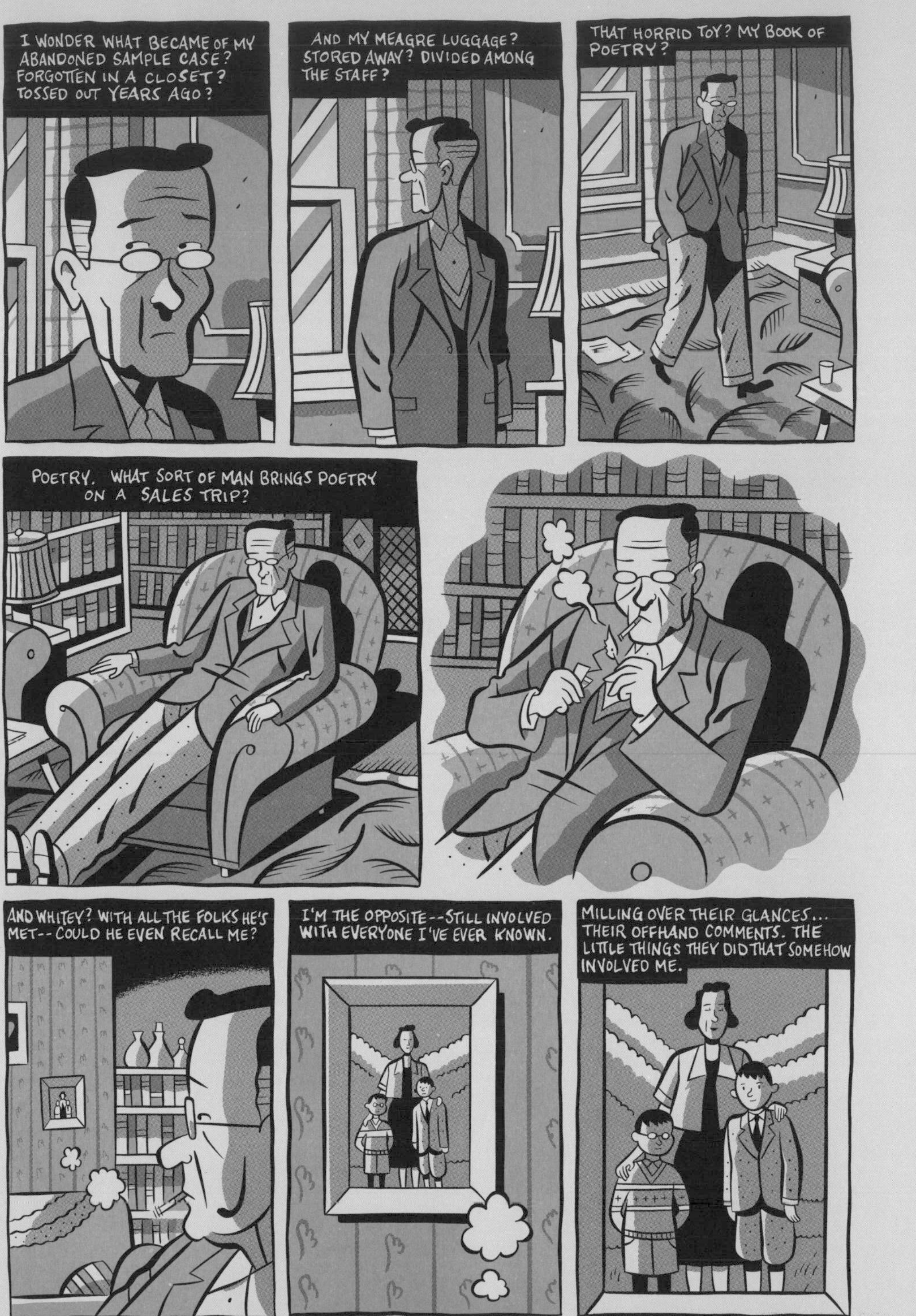
I WONDER WHAT BECAME OF MY ABANDONED SAMPLE CASE? FORGOTTEN IN A CLOSET? TOSSED OUT YEARS AGO?
AND MY MEAGRE LUGGAGE? STORED AWAY? DIVIDED AMONG THE STAFF?
THAT HORRID TOY? MY BOOK OF POETRY?
POETRY. WHAT SORT OF MAN BRINGS POETRY ON A SALES TRIP?
AND WHITEY? WITH ALL THE FOLKS HE'S MET--COULD HE EVEN RECALL ME?
I'M THE OPPOSITE--STILL INVOLVED WITH EVERYONE I'VE EVER KNOWN.
MILLING OVER THEIR GLANCES... THEIR OFFHAND COMMENTS. THE LITTLE THINGS THEY DID THAT SOMEHOW INVOLVED ME.

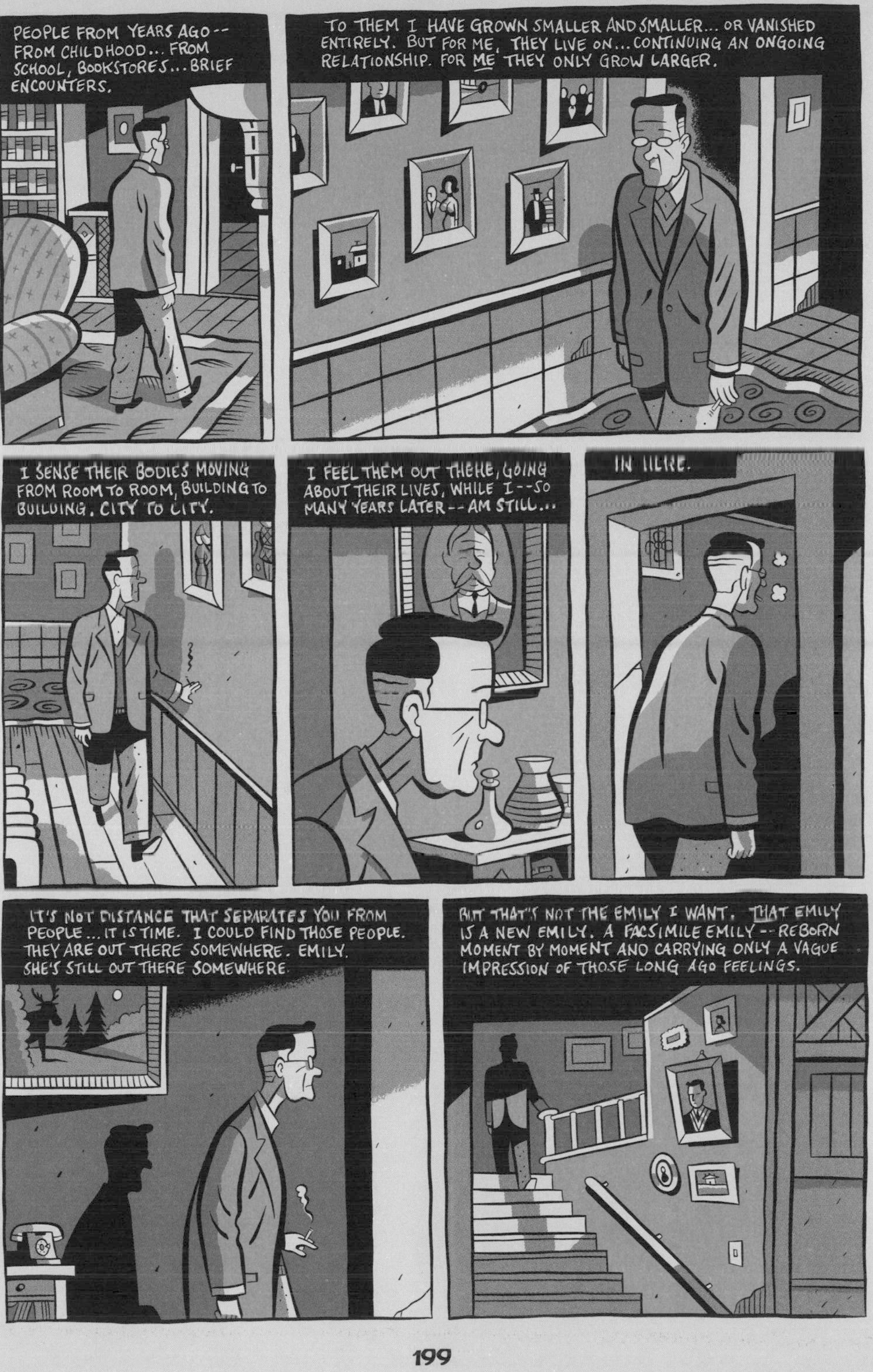
PEOPLE FROM YEARS AGO-- FROM CHILDHOOD... FROM SCHOOL, BOOKSTORES... BRIEF ENCOUNTERS.
TO THEM I HAVE GROWN SMALLER AND SMALLER... OR VANISHED ENTIRELY. BUT FOR ME, THEY LIVE ON... CONTINUING AN ONGOING RELATIONSHIP. FOR ME THEY ONLY GROW LARGER.
I SENSE THEIR BODIES MOVING FROM ROOM TO ROOM, BUILDING TO BUILDING. CITY TO CITY.
I FEEL THEM OUT THERE, GOING ABOUT THEIR LIVES, WHILE I--SO MANY YEARS LATER--AM STILL...
IN HERE.
IT'S NOT DISTANCE THAT SEPARATES YOU FROM PEOPLE... IT IS TIME. I COULD FIND THOSE PEOPLE. THEY ARE OUT THERE SOMEWHERE. EMILY. SHE'S STILL OUT THERE SOMEWHERE.
BUT THAT'S NOT THE EMILY I WANT. THAT EMILY IS A NEW EMILY. A FACSIMILE EMILY--REBORN MOMENT BY MOMENT AND CARRYING ONLY A VAGUE IMPRESSION OF THOSE LONG AGO FEELINGS.

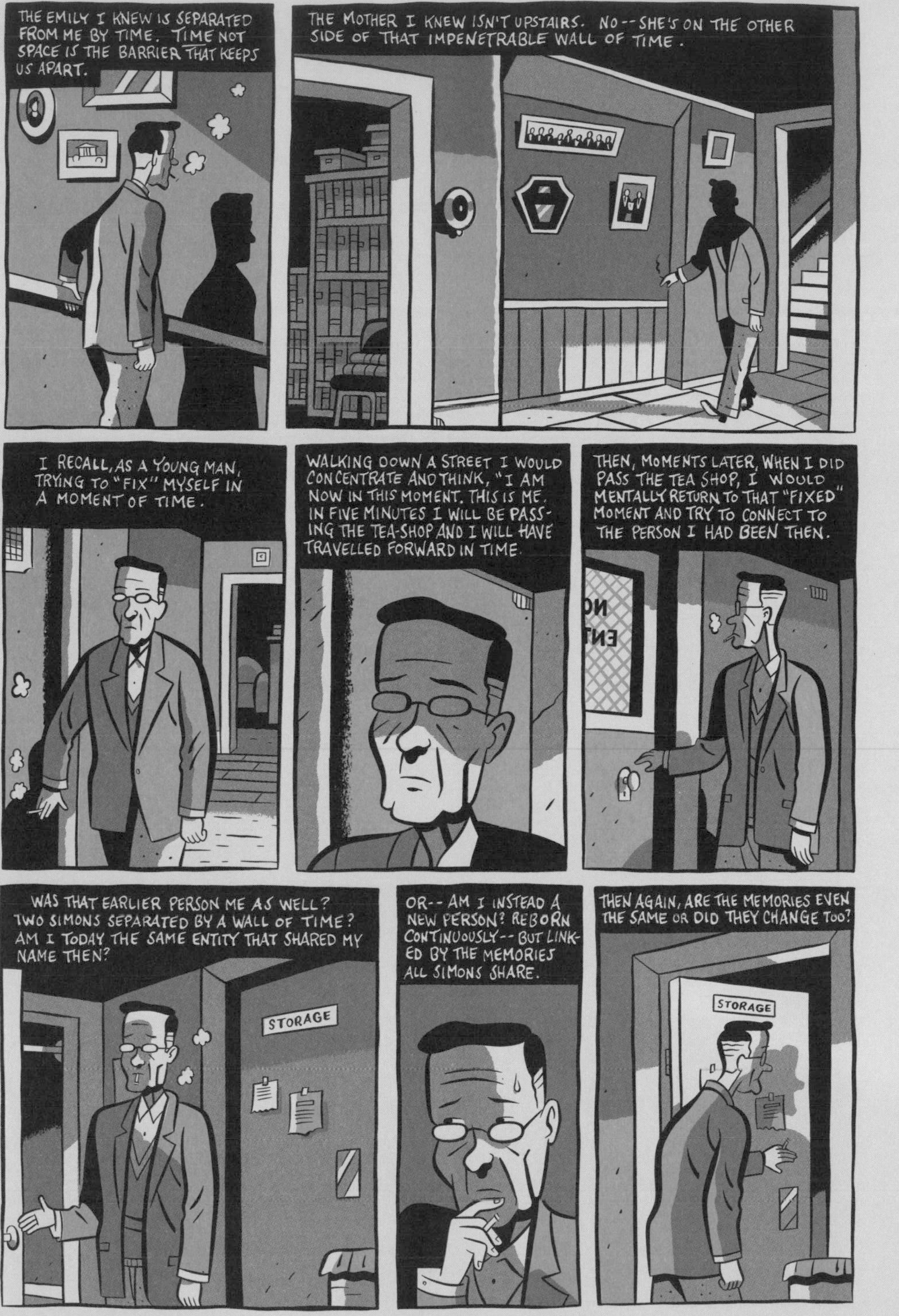
THE EMILY I KNEW IS SEPARATED FROM ME BY TIME. TIME NOT SPACE IS THE BARRIER THAT KEEPS US APART.
THE MOTHER I KNEW ISN'T UPSTAIRS. NO--SHE'S ON THE OTHER SIDE OF THAT IMPENETRABLE WALL OF TIME.
I RECALL, AS A YOUNG MAN, TRYING TO "FIX" MYSELF IN A MOMENT OF TIME.
WALKING DOWN A STREET I WOULD CONCENTRATE AND THINK, "I AM NOW IN THIS MOMENT. THIS IS ME. IN FIVE MINUTES I WILL BE PASSING THE TEA-SHOP AND I WILL HAVE TRAVELLED FORWARD IN TIME.
THEN, MOMENTS LATER, WHEN I DID PASS THE TEA SHOP, I WOULD MENTALLY RETURN TO THAT "FIXED" MOMENT AND TRY TO CONNECT TO THE PERSON I HAD BEEN THEN.
WAS THAT EARLIER PERSON ME AS WELL? TWO SIMONS SEPARATED BY A WALL OF TIME? AM I TODAY THE SAME ENTITY THAT SHARED MY NAME THEN?
STORAGE
OR--AM I INSTEAD A NEW PERSON? REBORN CONTINUOUSLY--BUT LINKED BY THE MEMORIES ALL SIMONS SHARE.
THEN AGAIN, ARE THE MEMORIES EVEN THE SAME OR DID THEY CHANGE TOO?
STORAGE

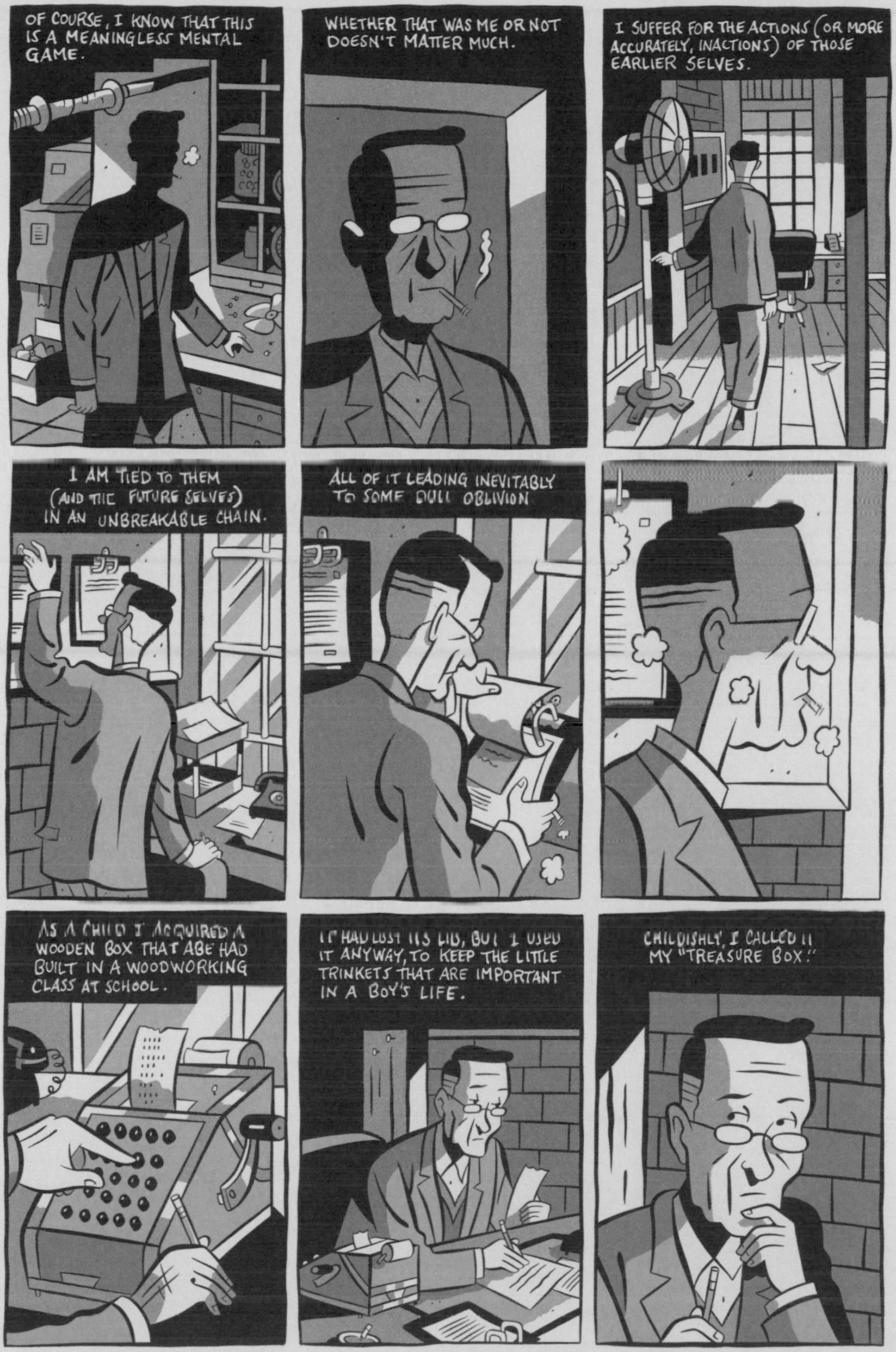
OF COURSE, I KNOW THAT THIS IS A MEANINGLESS MENTAL GAME.
WHETHER THAT WAS ME OR NOT DOESN'T MATTER MUCH.
I SUFFER FOR THE ACTIONS (OR MORE ACCURATELY, INACTIONS) OF THOSE EARLIER SELVES.
I AM TIED TO THEM (AND THE FUTURE SELVES) IN AN UNBREAKABLE CHAIN.
ALL OF IT LEADING INEVITABLY TO SOME DULL OBLIVION
AS A CHILD I ACQUIRED A WOODEN BOX THAT ABE HAD BUILT IN A WOODWORKING CLASS AT SCHOOL.
IT HAD LOST ITS LID, BUT I USED IT ANYWAY, TO KEEP THE LITTLE TRINKETS THAT ARE IMPORTANT IN A BOY'S LIFE.
CHILDISHLY, I CALLED IT MY "TREASURE BOX."

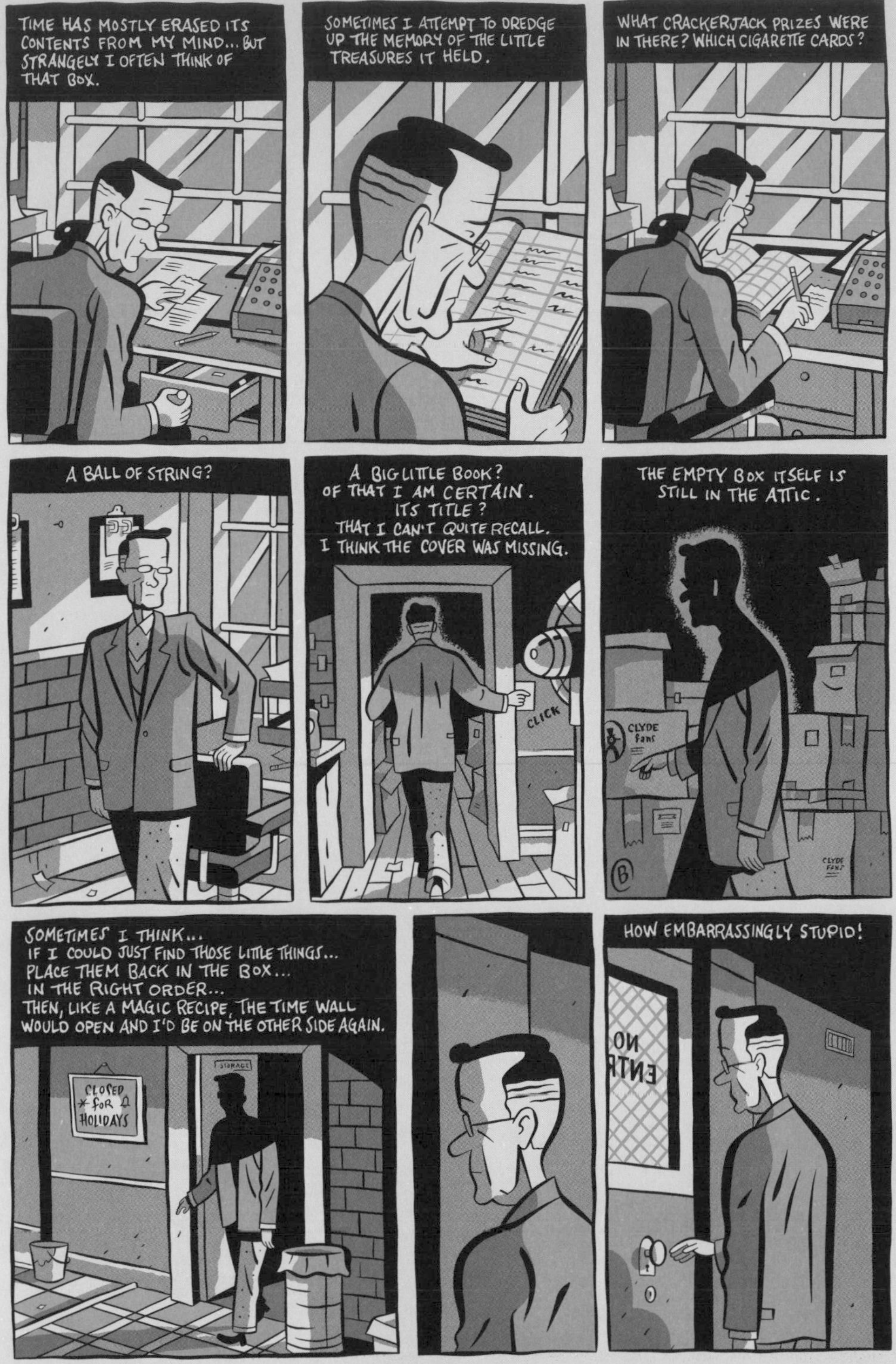
TIME HAS MOSTLY ERASED ITS CONTENTS FROM MY MIND... BUT STRANGELY I OFTEN THINK OF THAT BOX.
SOMETIMES I ATTEMPT TO DREDGE UP THE MEMORY OF THE LITTLE TREASURES IT HELD.
WHAT CRACKERJACK PRIZES WERE IN THERE? WHICH CIGARETTE CARDS?
A BALL OF STRING?
A BIG LITTLE BOOK? OF THAT I AM CERTAIN. ITS TITLE? THAT I CAN'T QUITE RECALL. I THINK THE COVER WAS MISSING.
CLICK
THE EMPTY BOX ITSELF IS STILL IN THE ATTIC.
CLYDE fans
SOMETIMES I THINK... IF I COULD JUST FIND THOSE LITTLE THINGS... PLACE THEM BACK IN THE BOX... IN THE RIGHT ORDER... THEN, LIKE A MAGIC RECIPE, THE TIME WALL WOULD OPEN AND I'D BE ON THE OTHER SIDE AGAIN.
CLOSED FOR HOLIDAYS
STORAGE
HOW EMBARRASSINGLY STUPID!

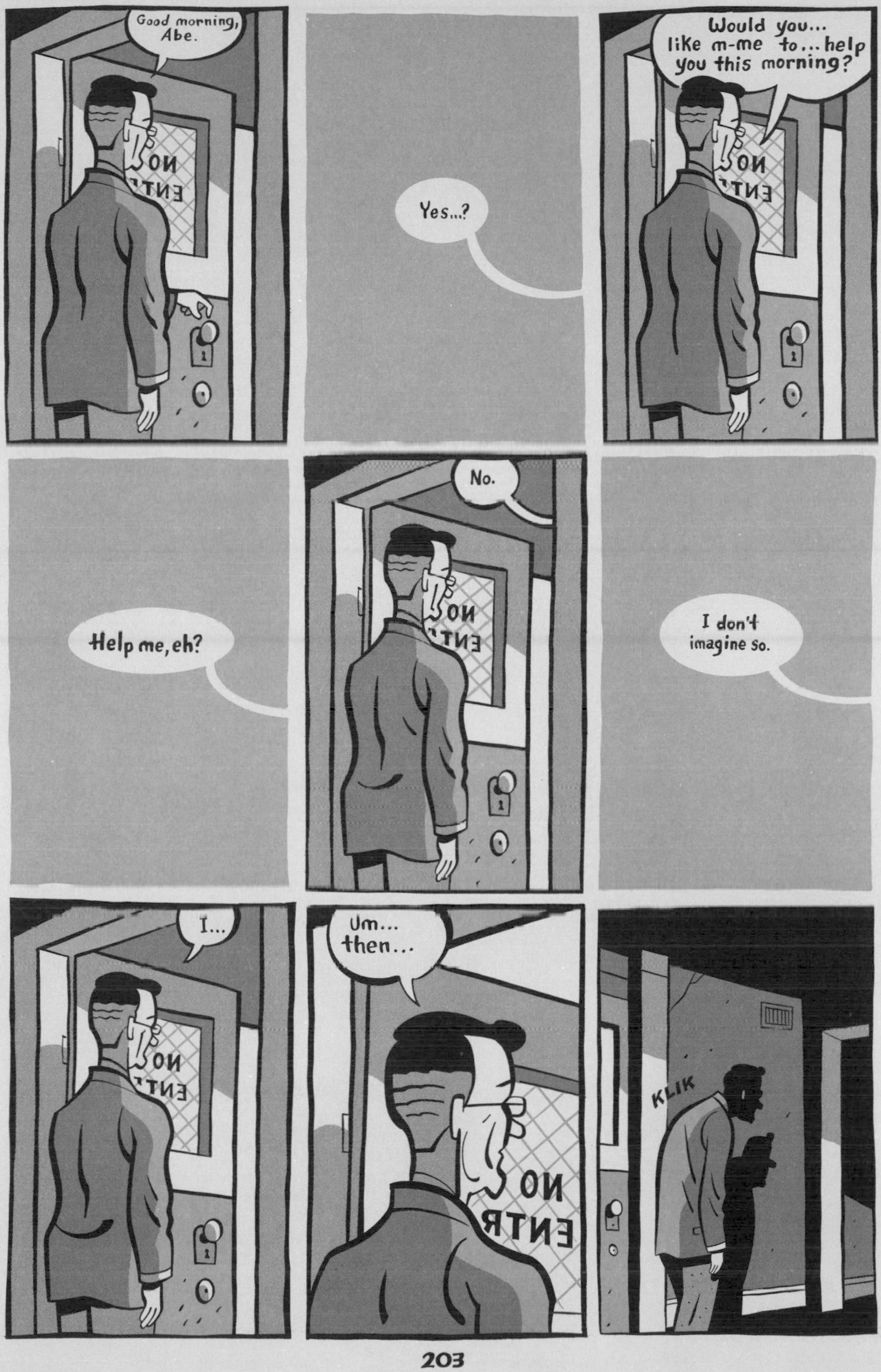
Good morning, Abe.
Yes...?
Would you... like m-me to... help you this morning?
Help me, eh?
No.
I don't imagine so.
I...
Um... then...
KLIK

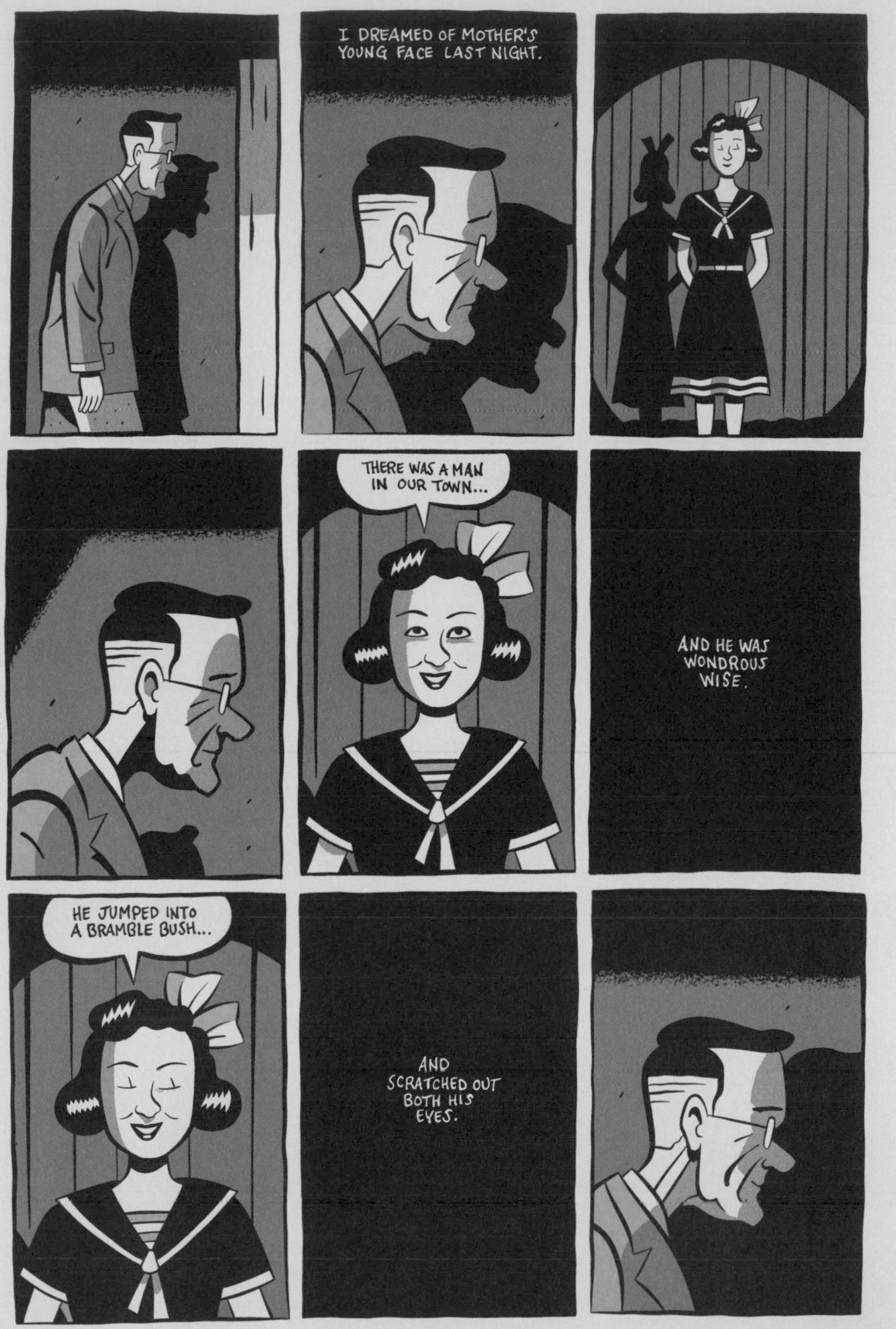

I DREAMED OF MOTHER'S YOUNG FACE LAST NIGHT.
THERE WAS A MAN IN OUR TOWN...
AND HE WAS WONDROUS WISE.
HE JUMPED INTO A BRAMBLE BUSH...
AND SCRATCHED OUT BOTH HIS EYES.

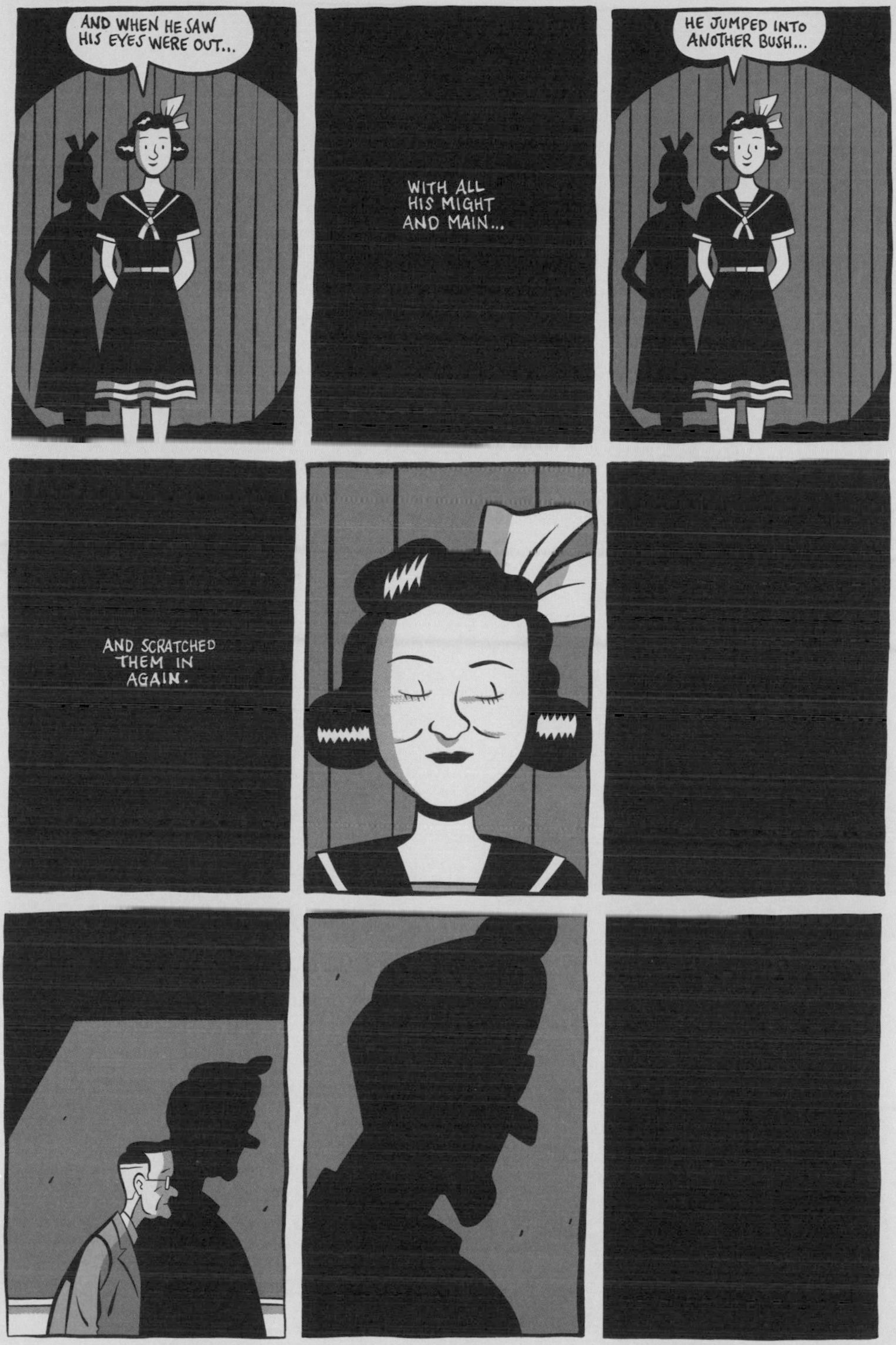
AND WHEN HE SAW HIS EYES WERE OUT...
WITH ALL HIS MIGHT AND MAIN...
HE JUMPED INTO ANOTHER BUSH...
AND SCRATCHED THEM IN AGAIN.

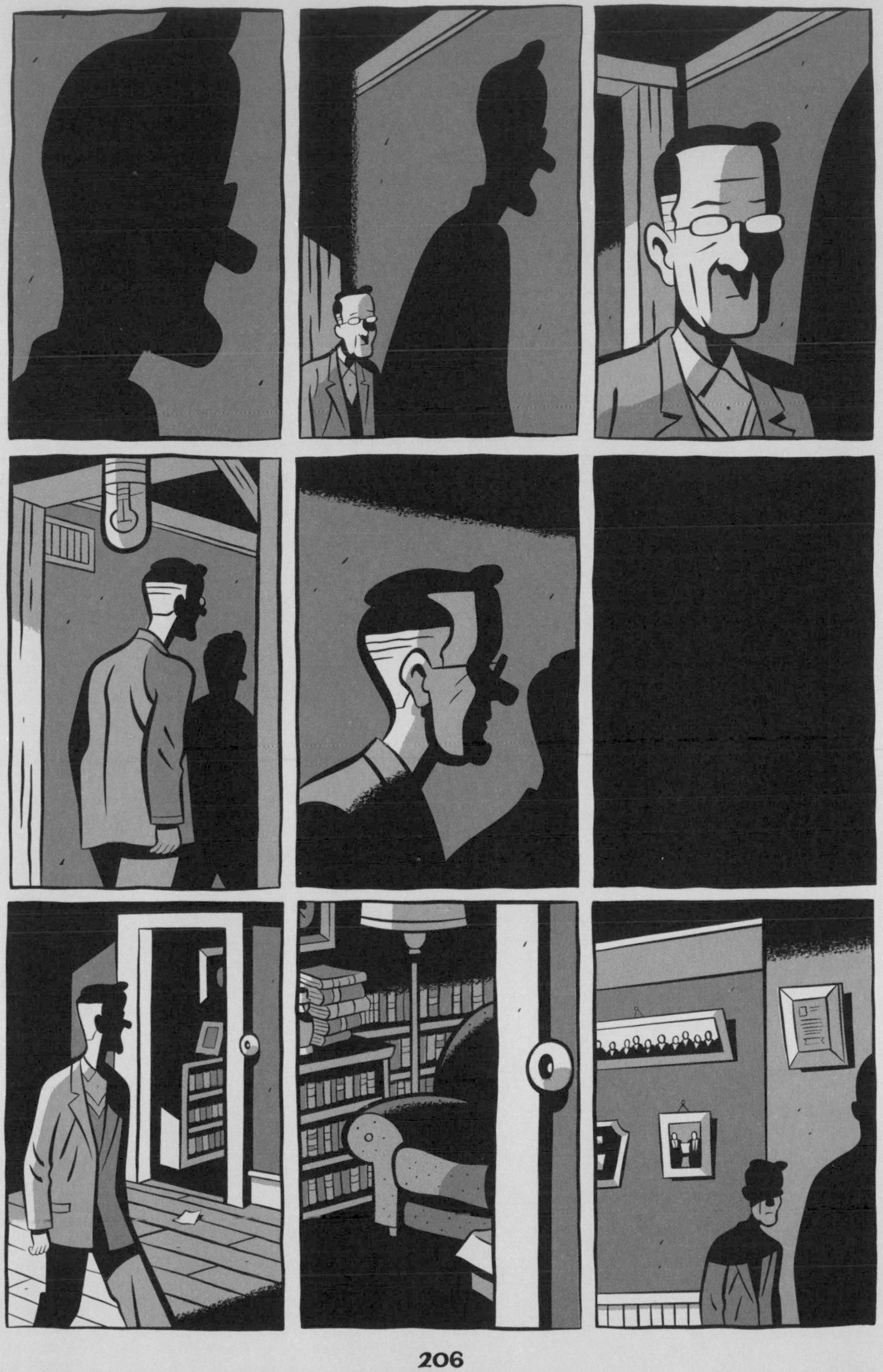

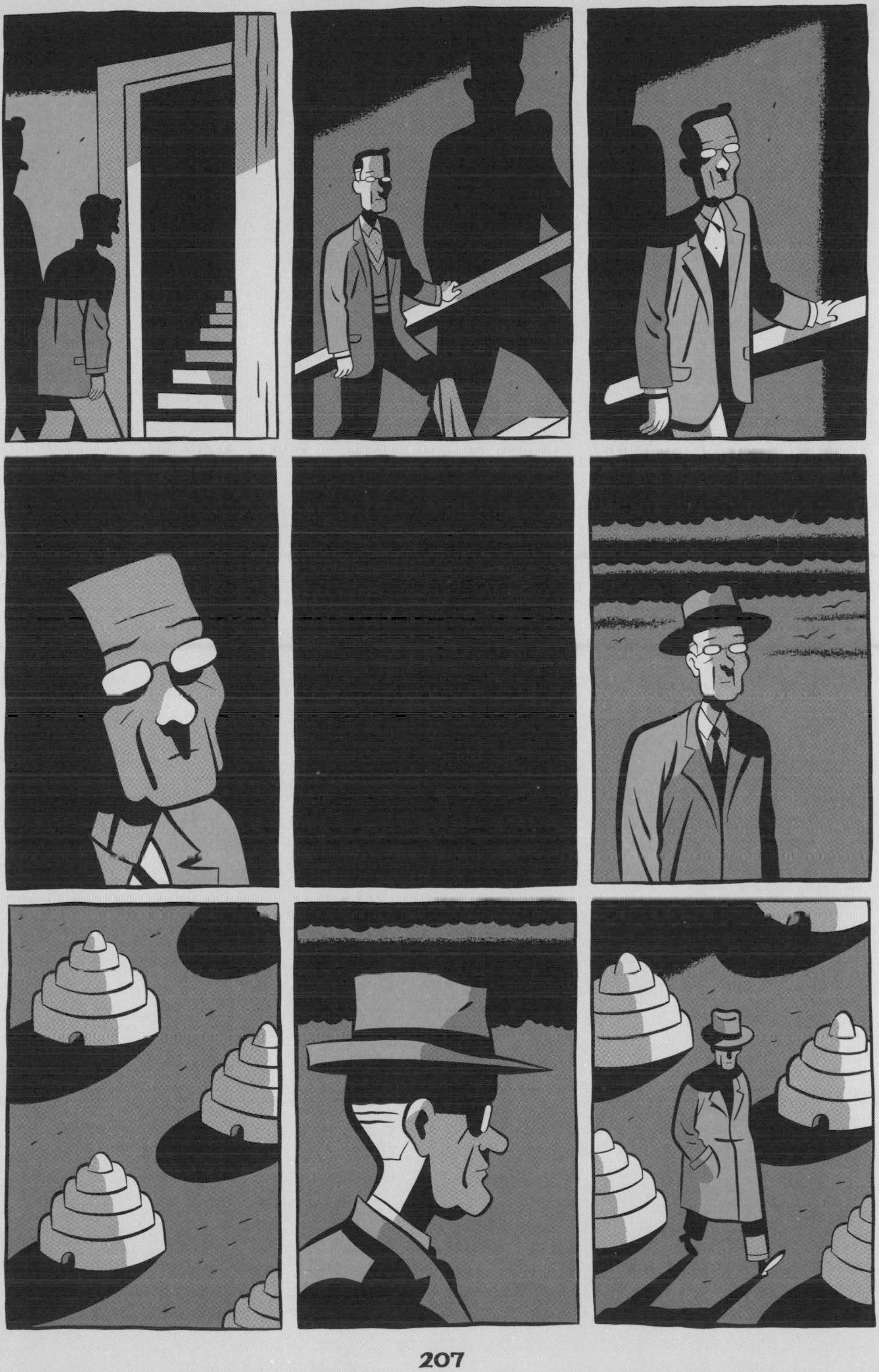

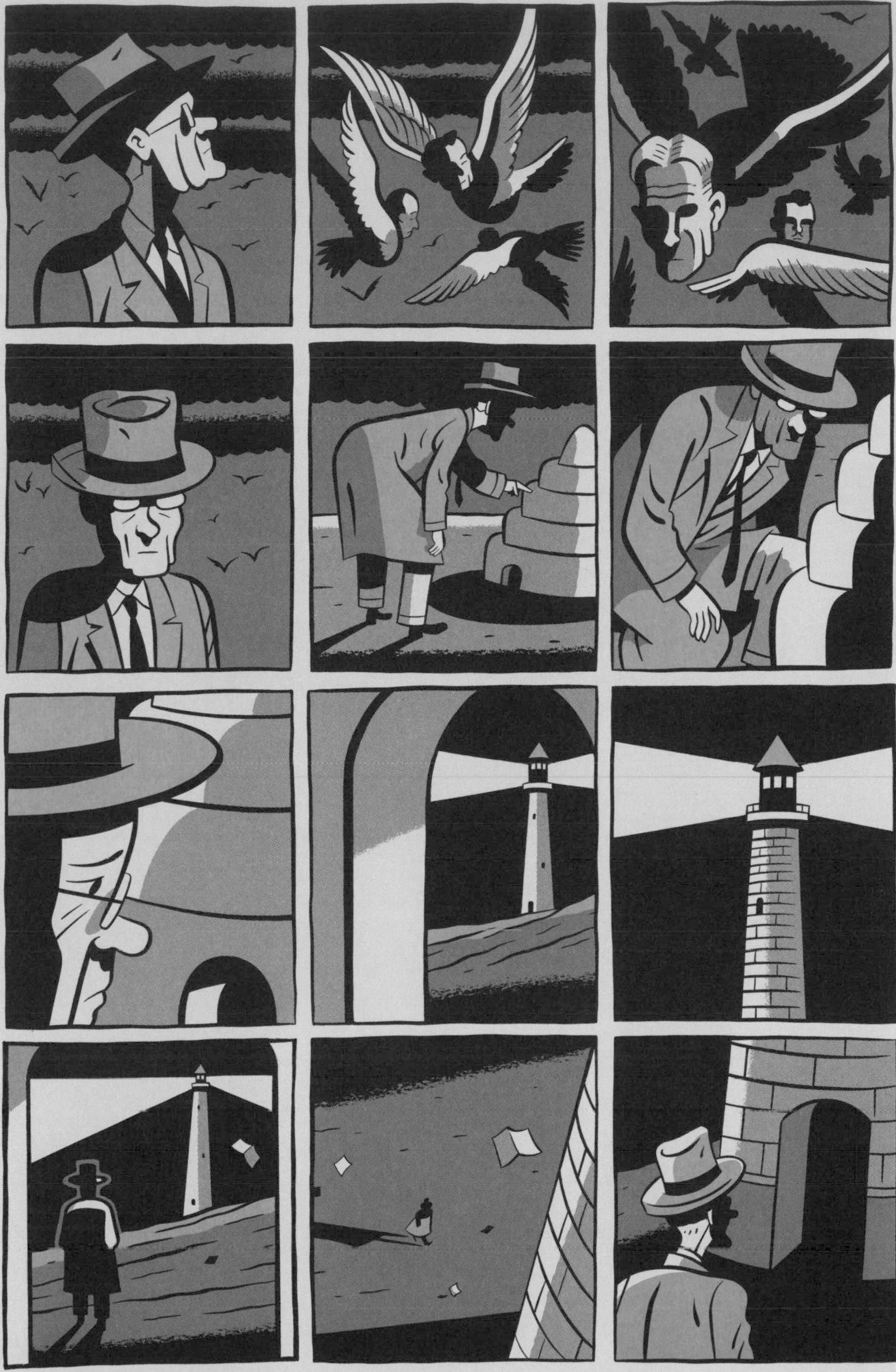

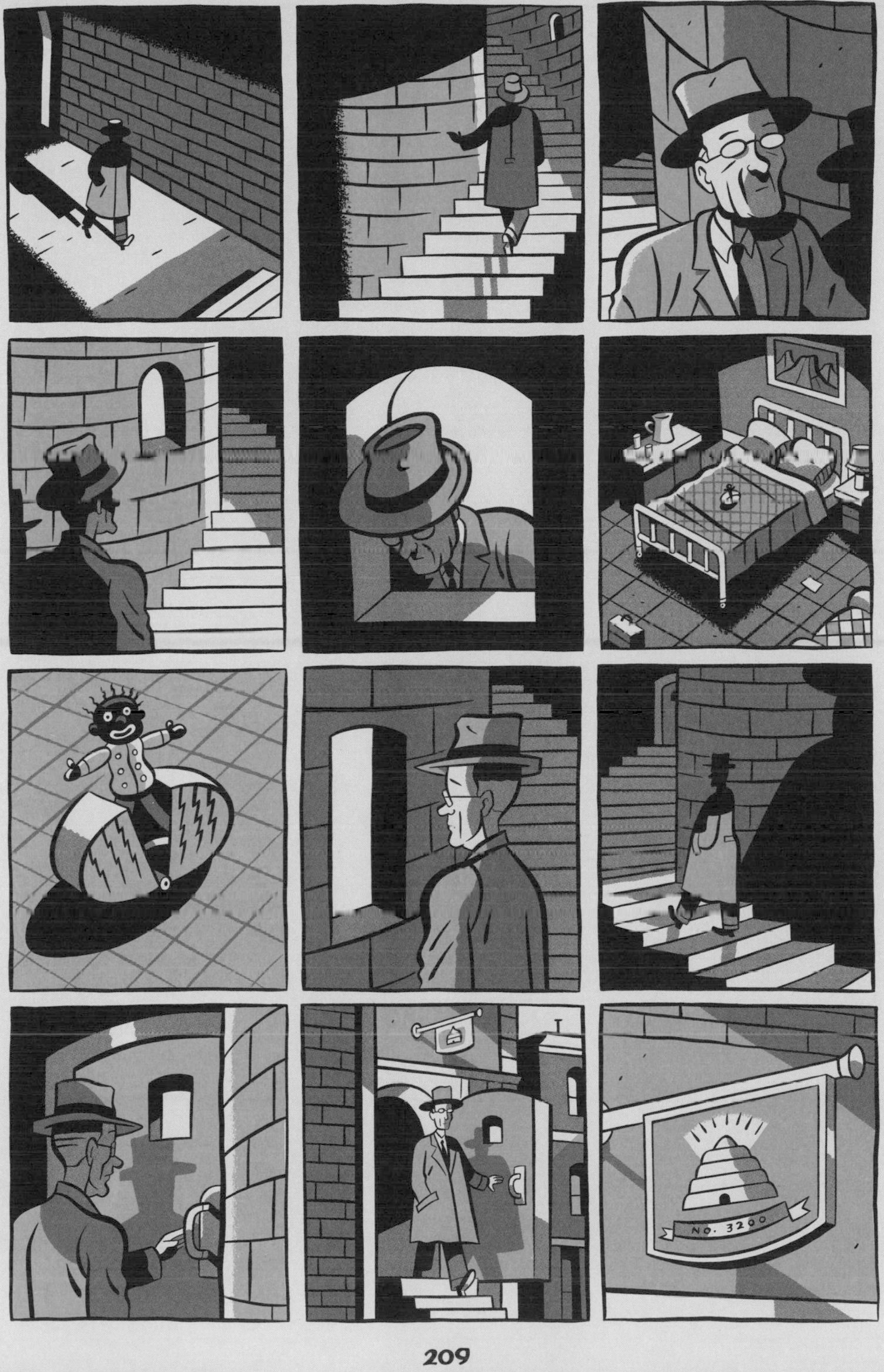

NO. 3200

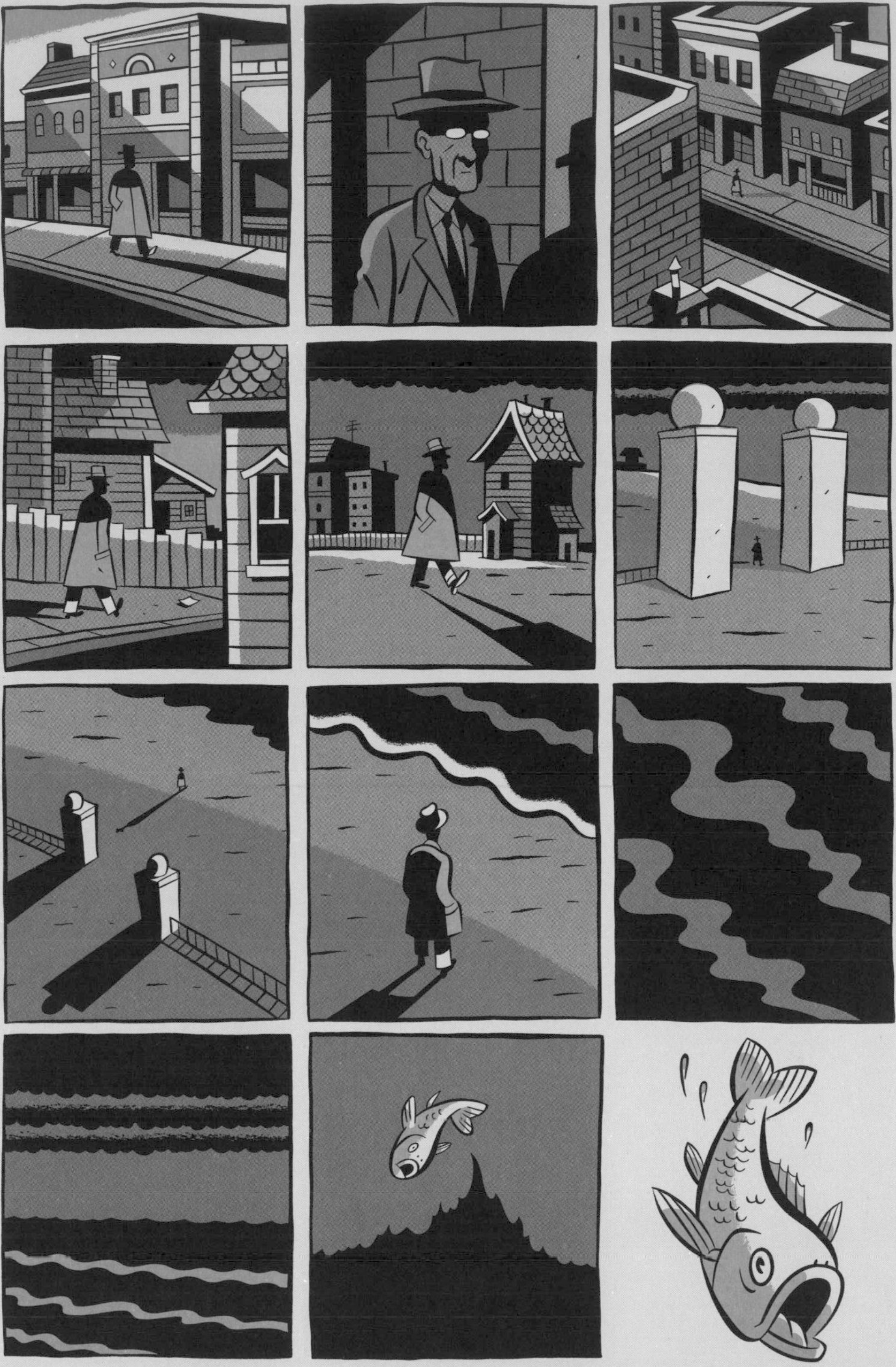

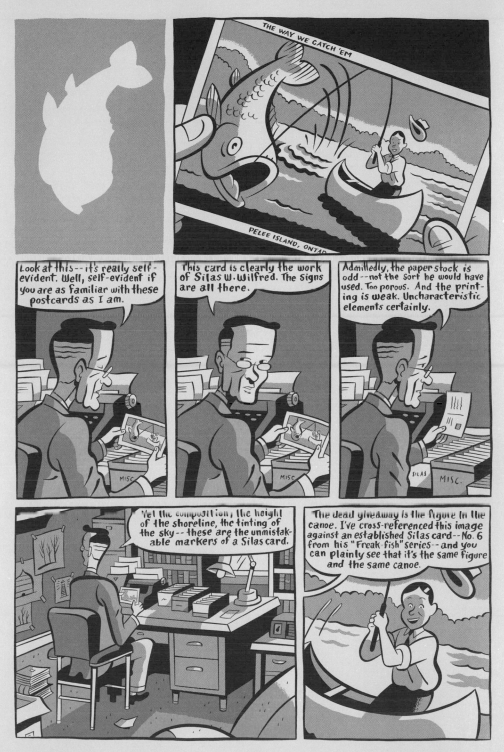

THE WAY WE CATCH 'EM

PELEE ISLAND, ONTA...

Look at this -- it's really self-evident. Well, self-evident if you are as familiar with these postcards as I am.

This card is clearly the work of Silas W. Wilfred. The signs are all there.

Admittedly, the paper stock is odd -- not the sort he would have used. Too porous. And the printing is weak. Uncharacteristic elements certainly.

MISC

MISC

SILAS   MISC.

Yet the composition, the height of the shoreline, the tinting of the sky -- these are the unmistakable markers of a Silas card.

The dead giveaway is the figure in the canoe. I've cross-referenced this image against an established Silas card -- No. 6 from his "Freak-fish" series -- and you can plainly see that it's the same figure and the same canoe.

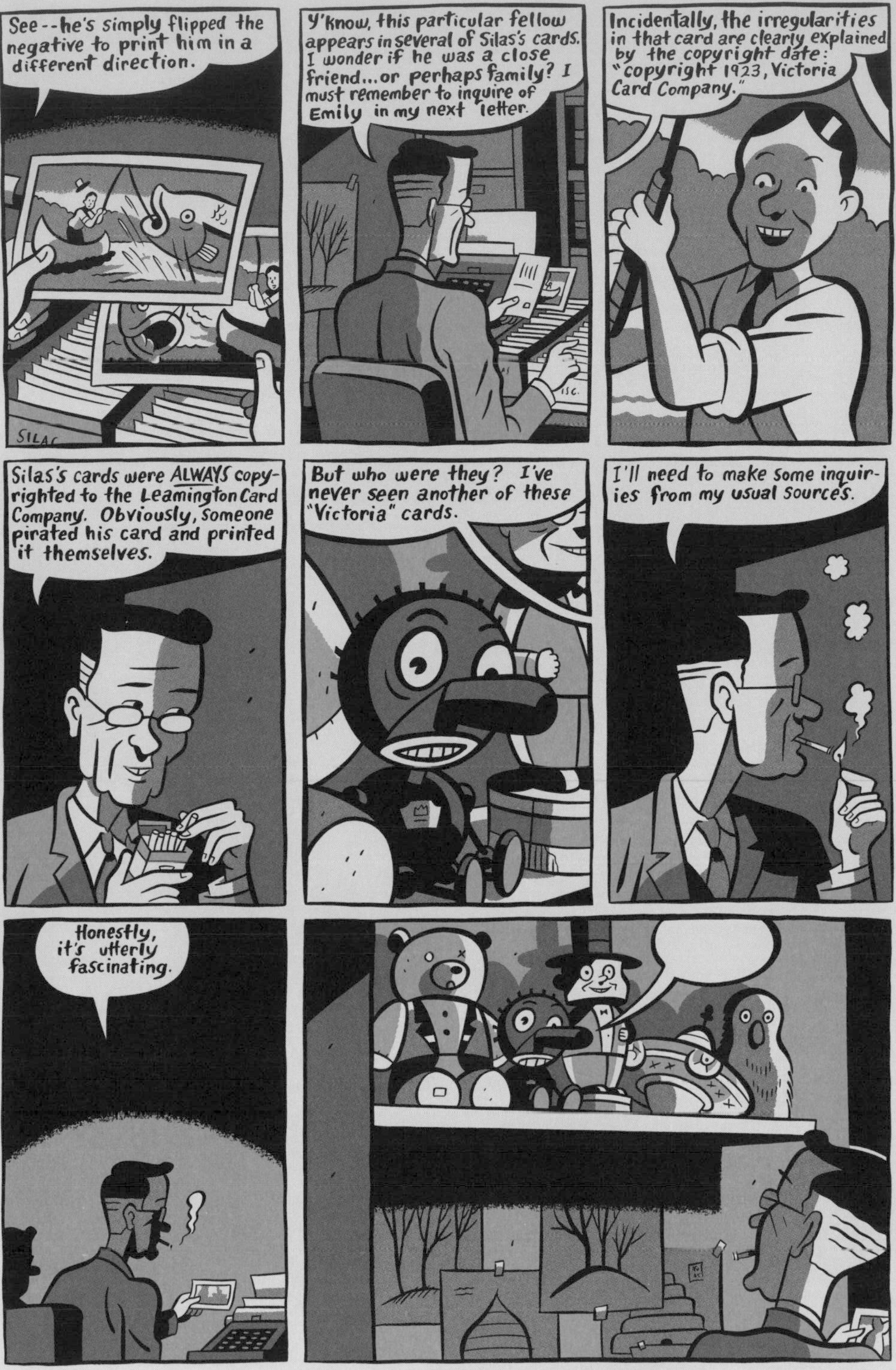

See--he's simply flipped the negative to print him in a different direction.
SILAS
Y'know, this particular fellow appears in several of Silas's cards. I wonder if he was a close friend...or perhaps family? I must remember to inquire of Emily in my next letter.
Incidentally, the irregularities in that card are clearly explained by the copyright date: "copyright 1923, Victoria Card Company."
Silas's cards were ALWAYS copyrighted to the Leamington Card Company. Obviously, someone pirated his card and printed it themselves.
But who were they? I've never seen another of these "Victoria" cards.
I'll need to make some inquiries from my usual sources.
Honestly, it's utterly fascinating.

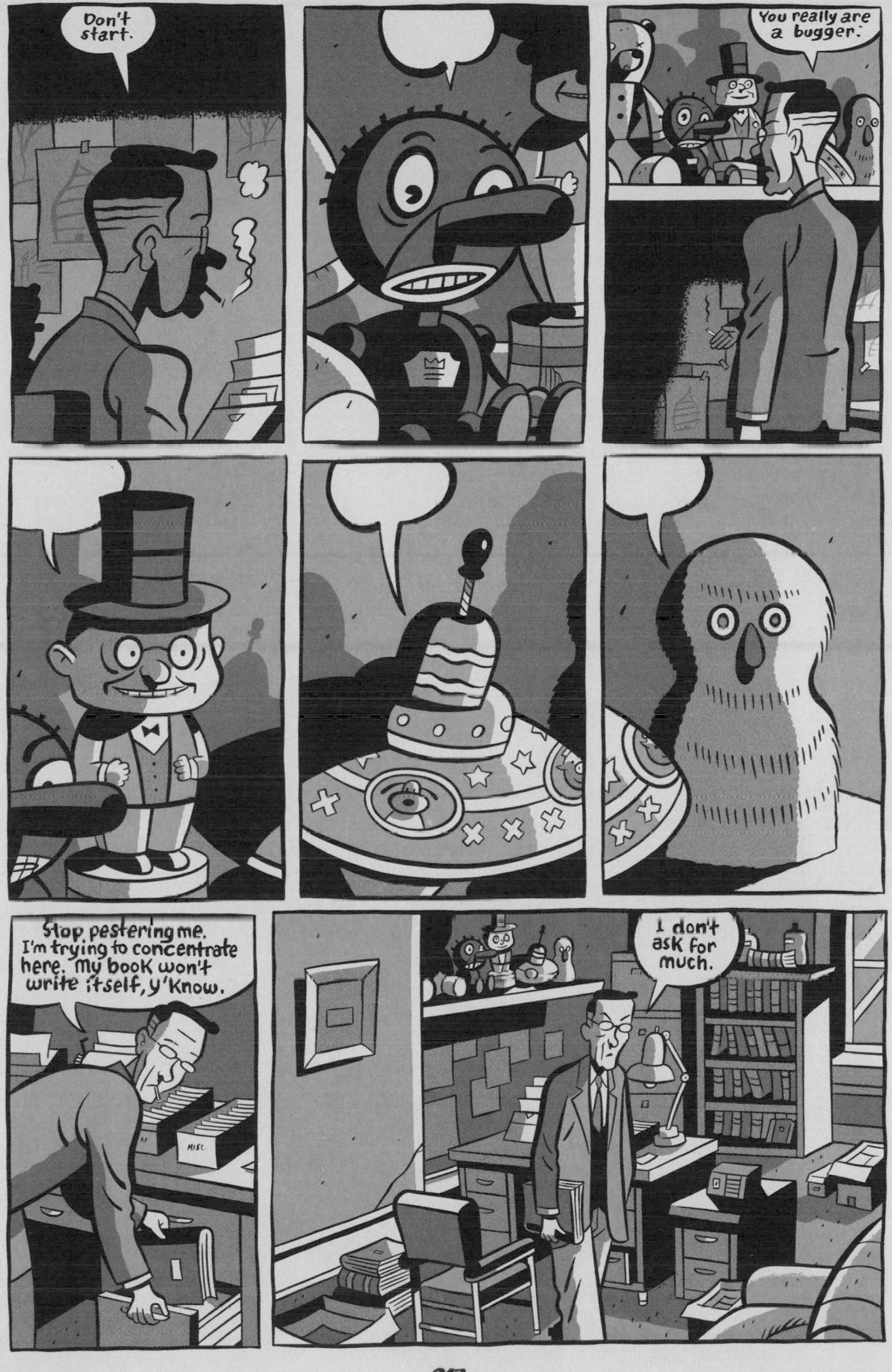
Don't start.
You really are a bugger.
Stop pestering me. I'm trying to concentrate here. My book won't write itself, y'know.
MISC.
I don't ask for much.

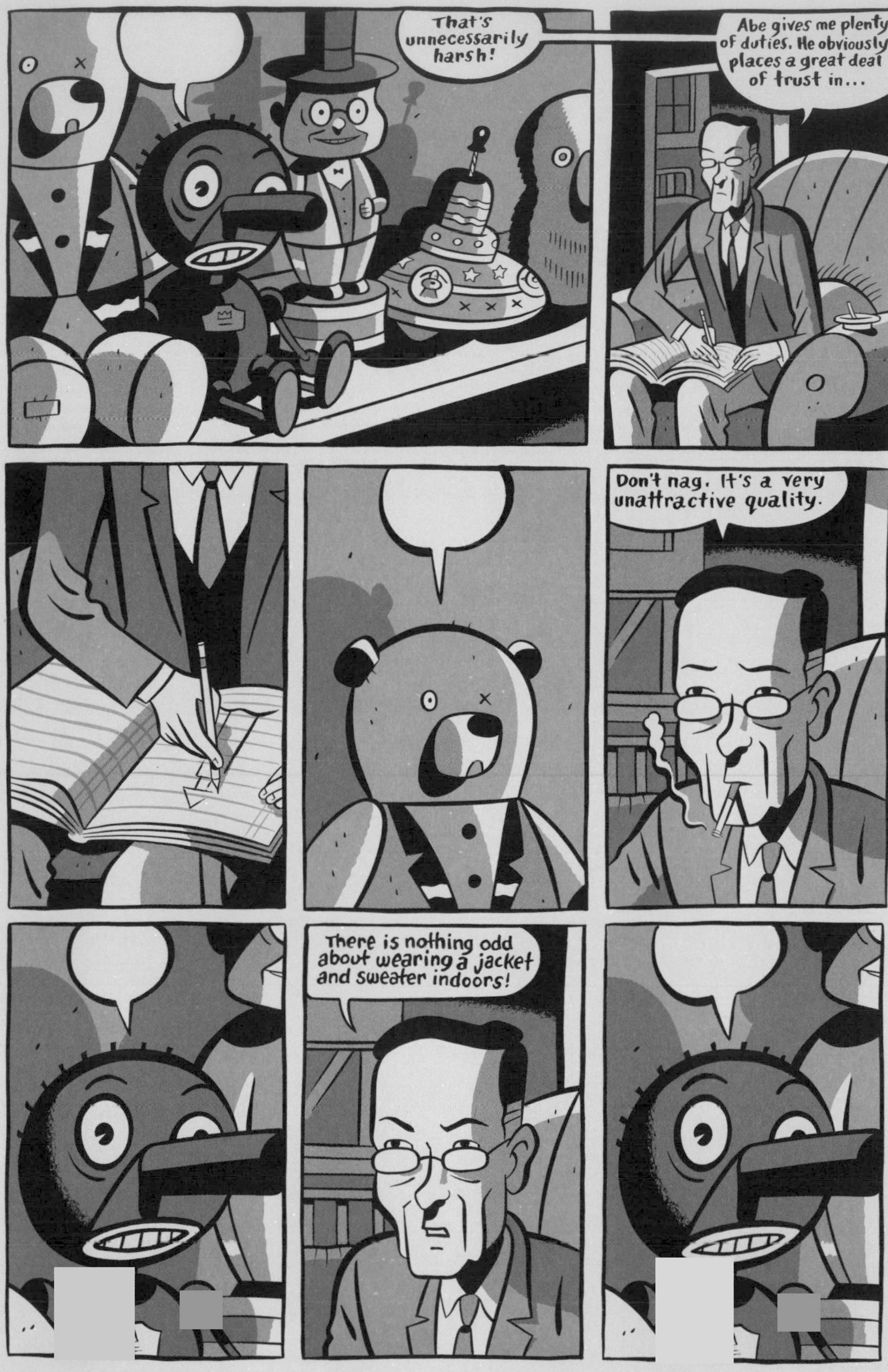
That's unnecessarily harsh!
Abe gives me plenty of duties. He obviously places a great deal of trust in...
Don't nag. It's a very unattractive quality.
There is nothing odd about wearing a jacket and sweater indoors!

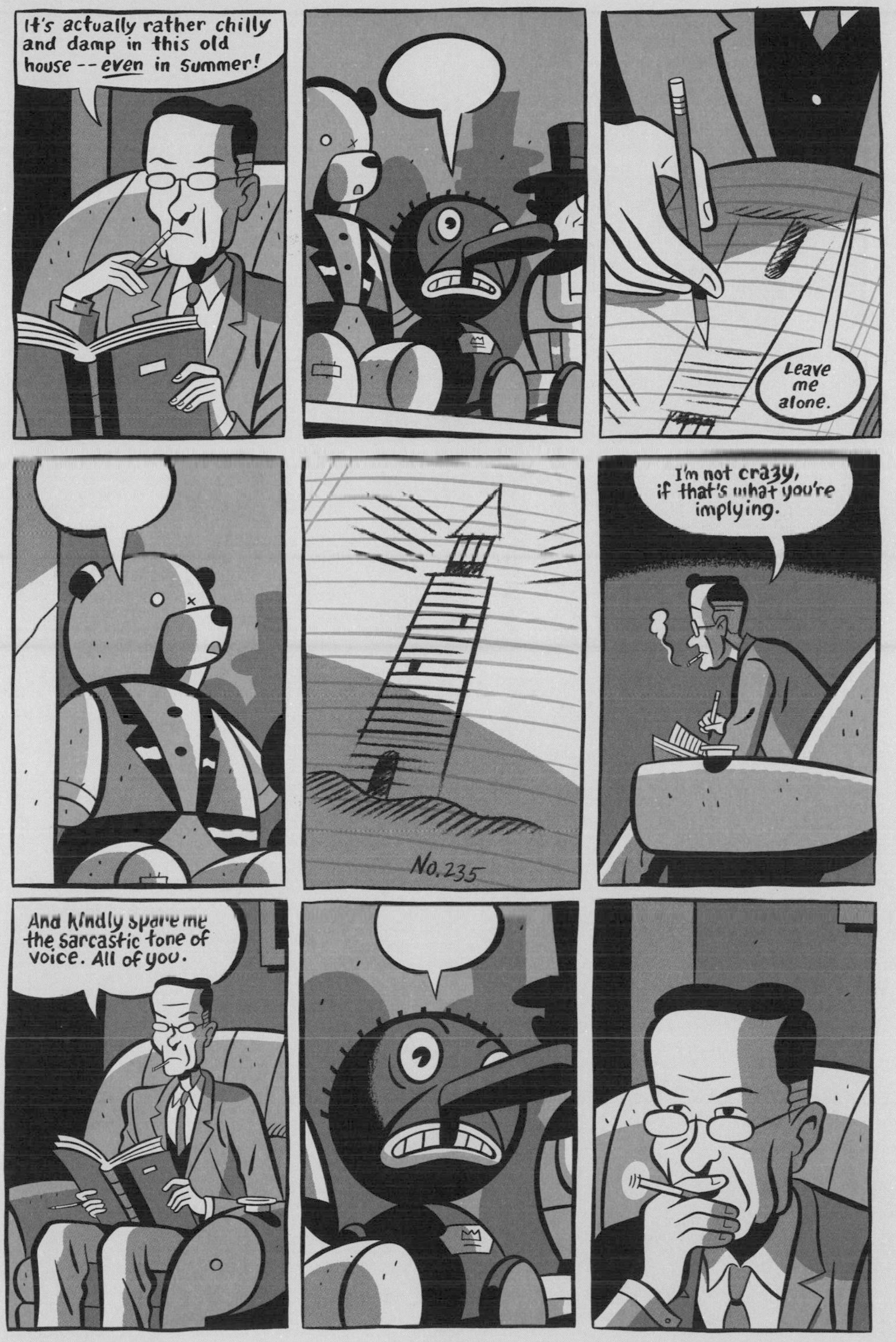
It's actually rather chilly and damp in this old house -- even in summer!
Leave me alone.
No. 235
I'm not crazy, if that's what you're implying.
And kindly spare me the sarcastic tone of voice. All of you.

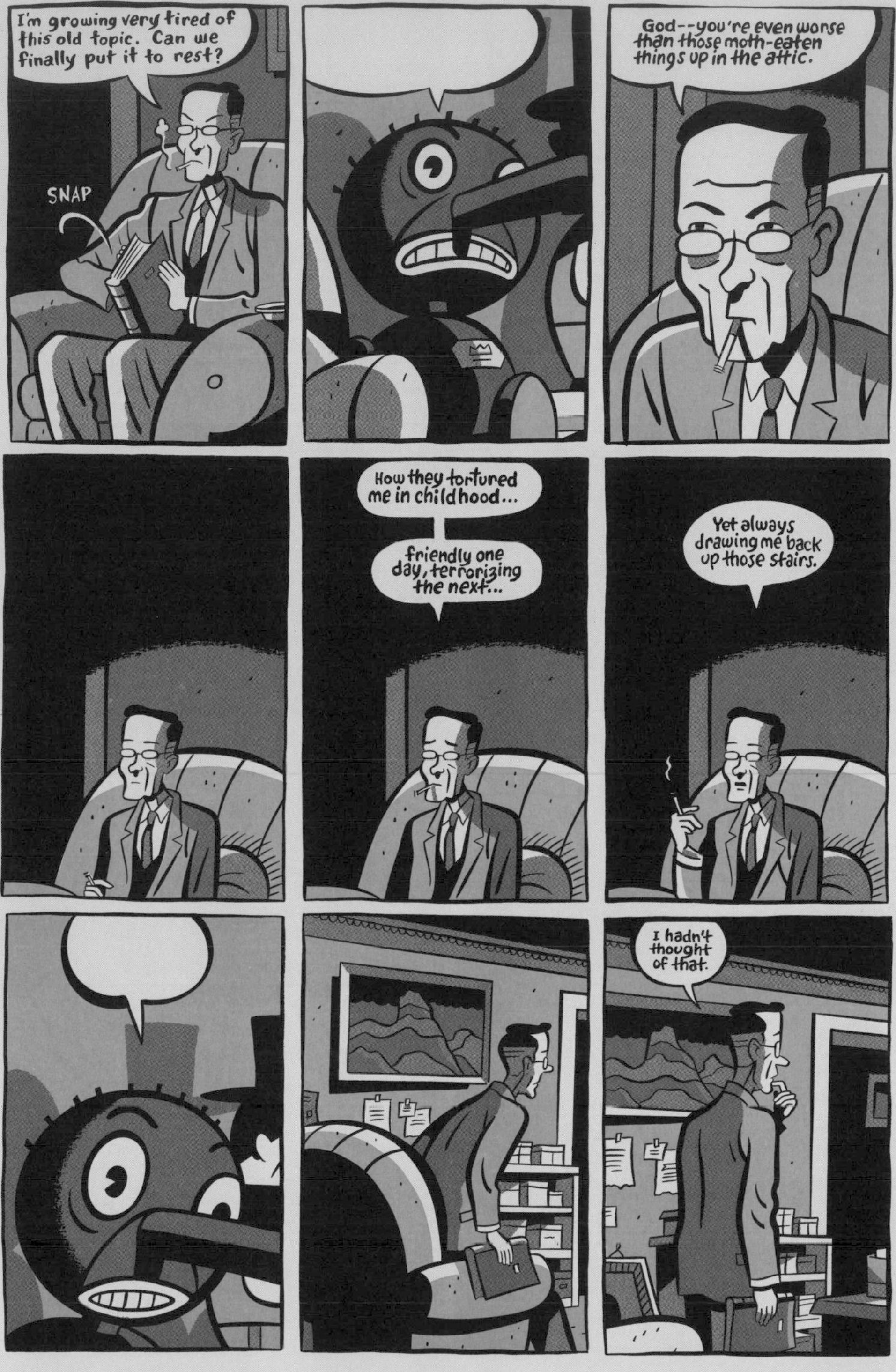
I'm growing very tired of this old topic. Can we finally put it to rest?
SNAP
God--you're even worse than those moth-eaten things up in the attic.
How they tortured me in childhood...
friendly one day, terrorizing the next...
Yet always drawing me back up those stairs.
I hadn't thought of that.

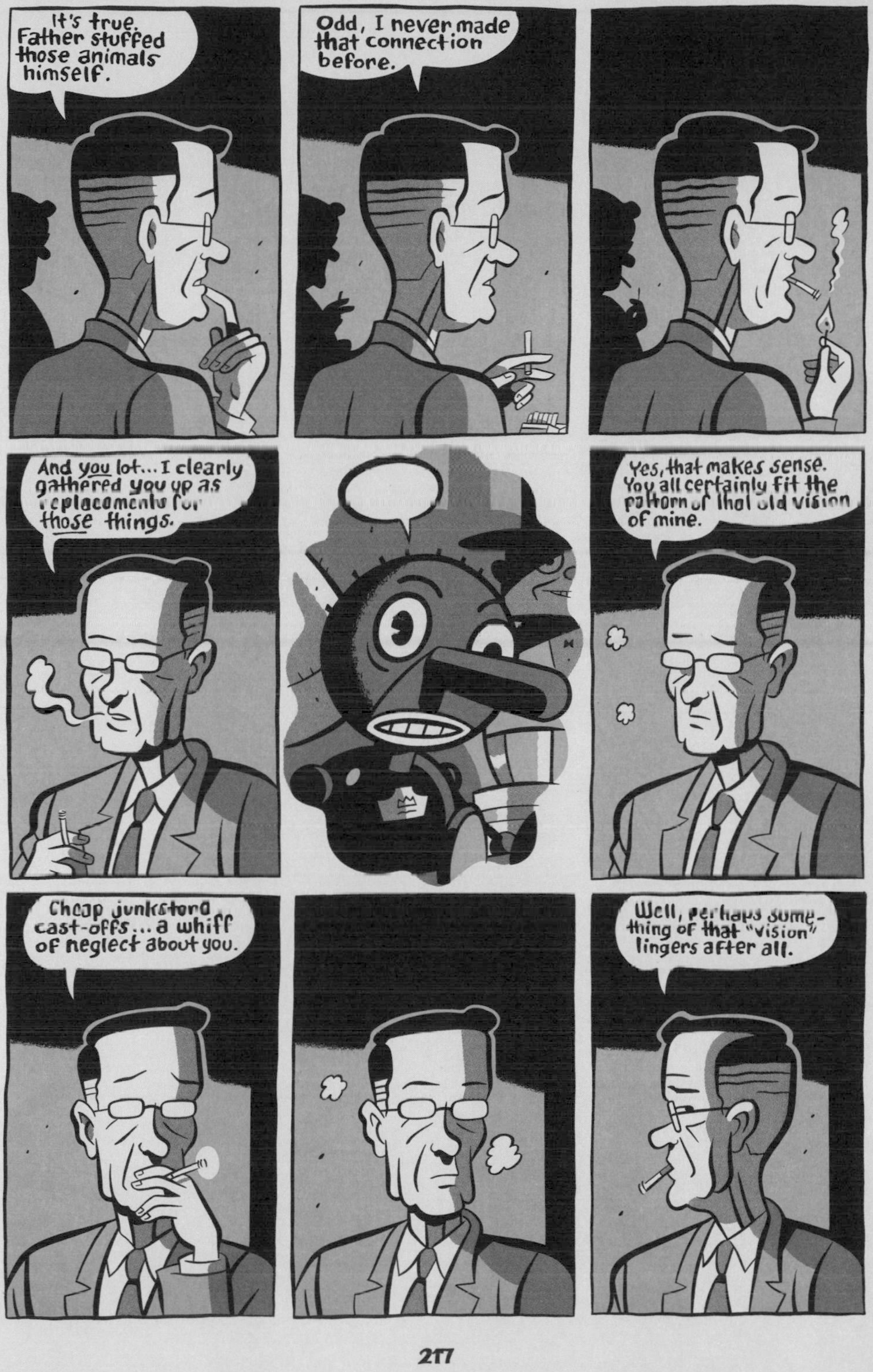
It's true. Father stuffed those animals himself.
Odd, I never made that connection before.
And you lot... I clearly gathered you up as replacements for those things.
Yes, that makes sense. You all certainly fit the pattern of that old vision of mine.
Cheap junkstore cast-offs... a whiff of neglect about you.
Well, perhaps some-thing of that "vision" lingers after all.

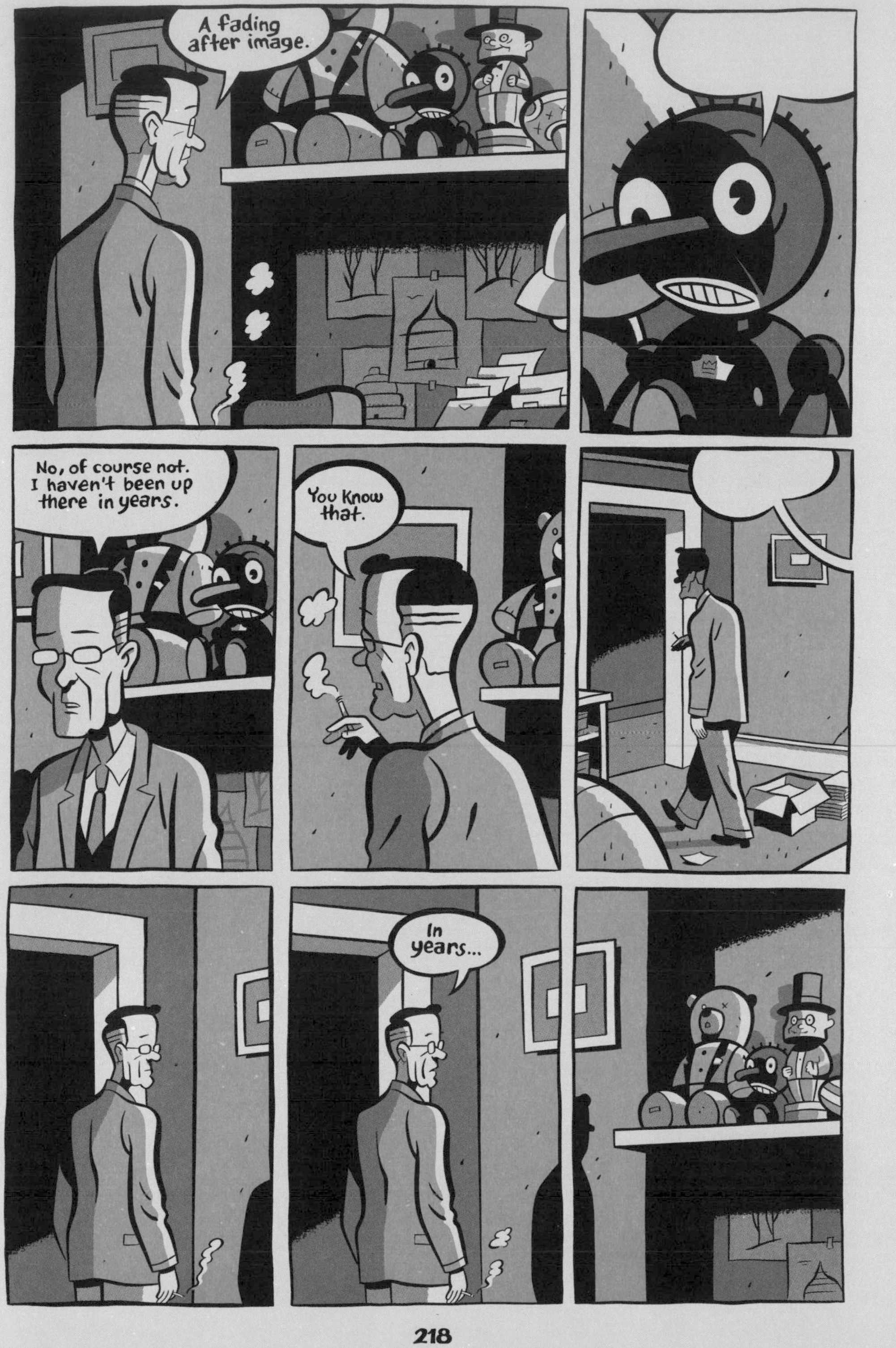
A fading after image.
No, of course not. I haven't been up there in years.
You know that.
In years...

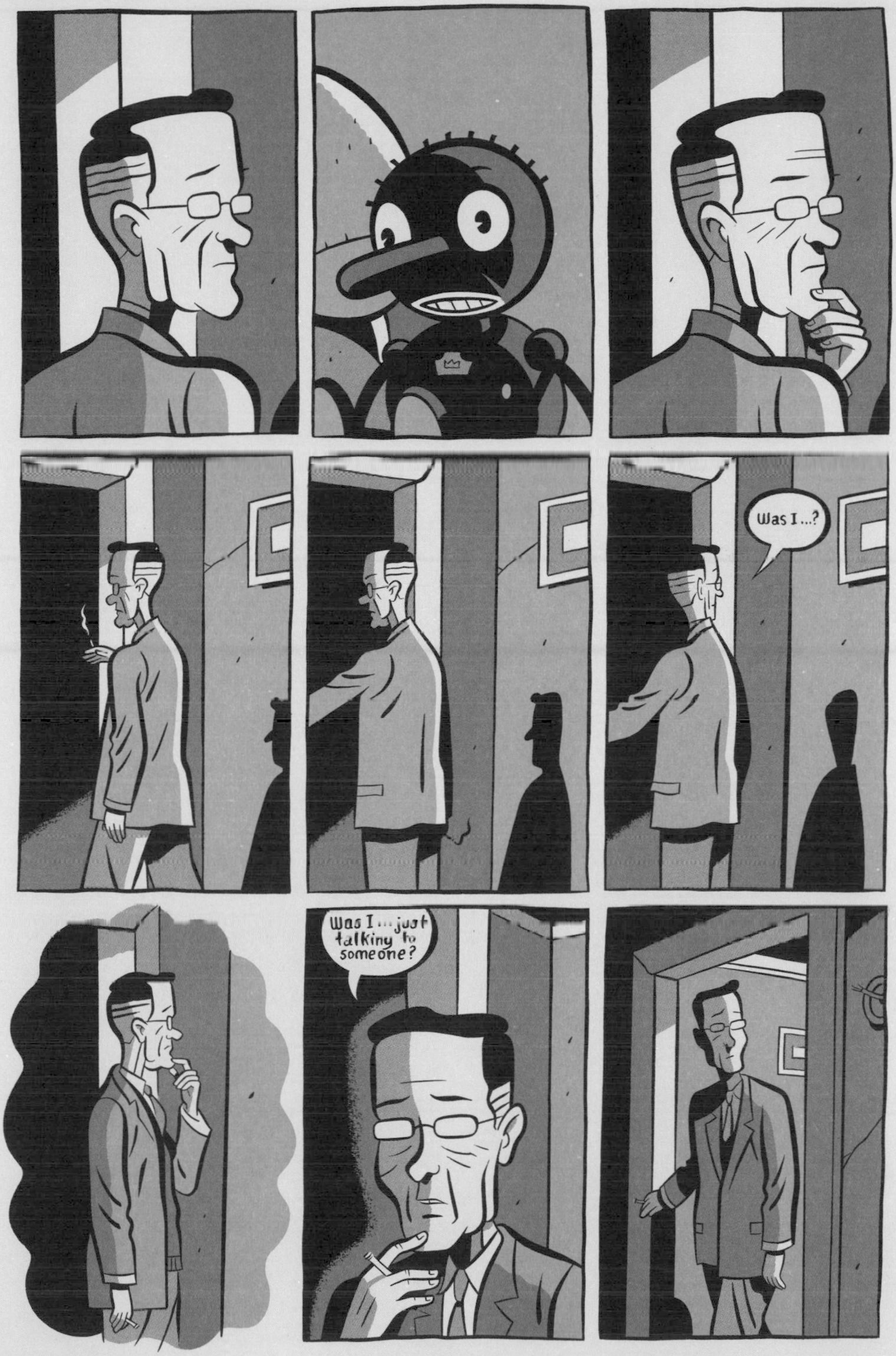
Was I...?
Was I... just talking to someone?

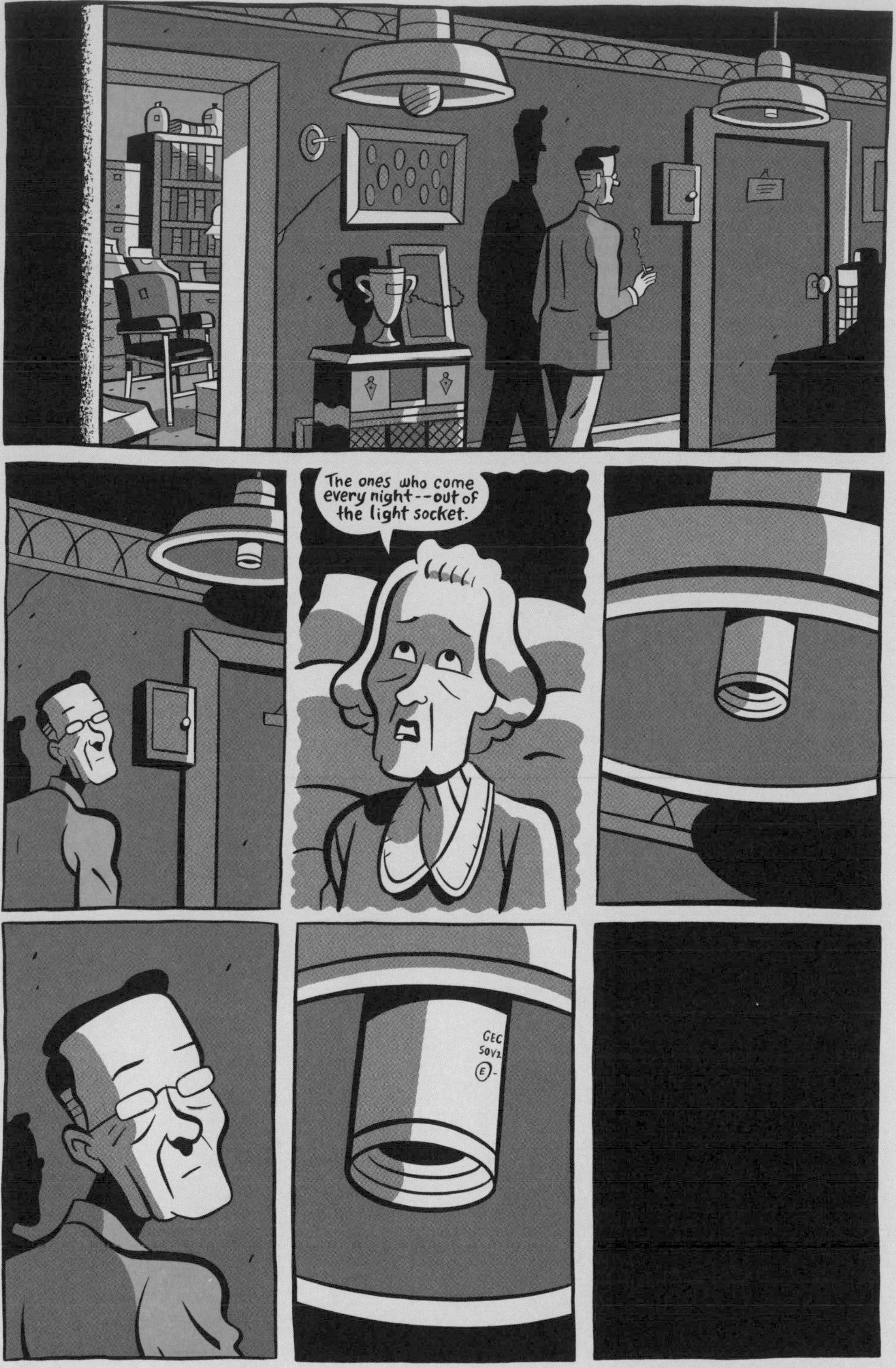
The ones who come every night--out of the light socket.
GEC
50V2
E

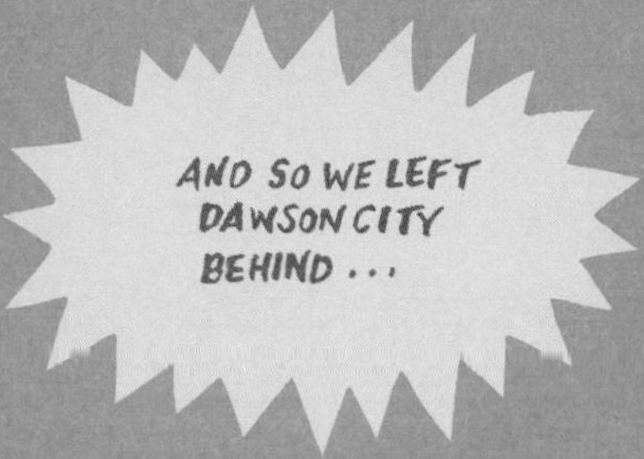
AND SO WE LEFT DAWSON CITY BEHIND . . .

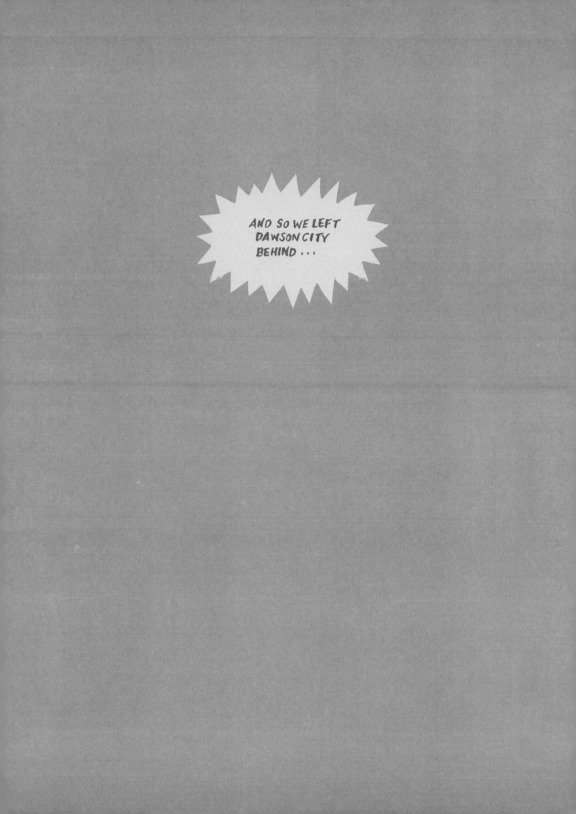

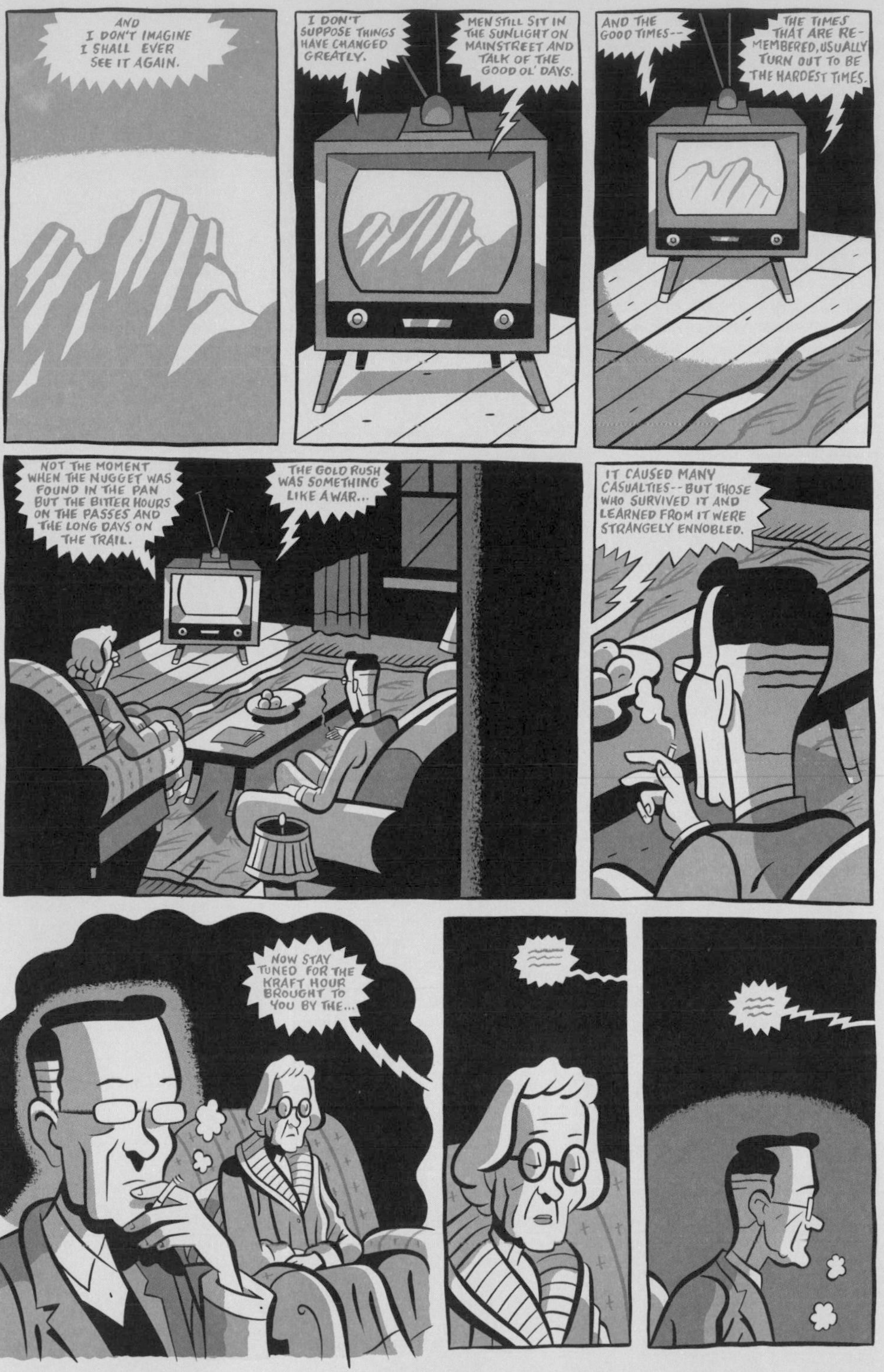
AND I DON'T IMAGINE I SHALL EVER SEE IT AGAIN.
I DON'T SUPPOSE THINGS HAVE CHANGED GREATLY.
MEN STILL SIT IN THE SUNLIGHT ON MAINSTREET AND TALK OF THE GOOD OL' DAYS.
AND THE GOOD TIMES--
THE TIMES THAT ARE REMEMBERED, USUALLY TURN OUT TO BE THE HARDEST TIMES.
NOT THE MOMENT WHEN THE NUGGET WAS FOUND IN THE PAN BUT THE BITTER HOURS ON THE PASSES AND THE LONG DAYS ON THE TRAIL.
THE GOLD RUSH WAS SOMETHING LIKE A WAR...
IT CAUSED MANY CASUALTIES--BUT THOSE WHO SURVIVED IT AND LEARNED FROM IT WERE STRANGELY ENNOBLED.
NOW STAY TUNED FOR THE KRAFT HOUR BROUGHT TO YOU BY THE...

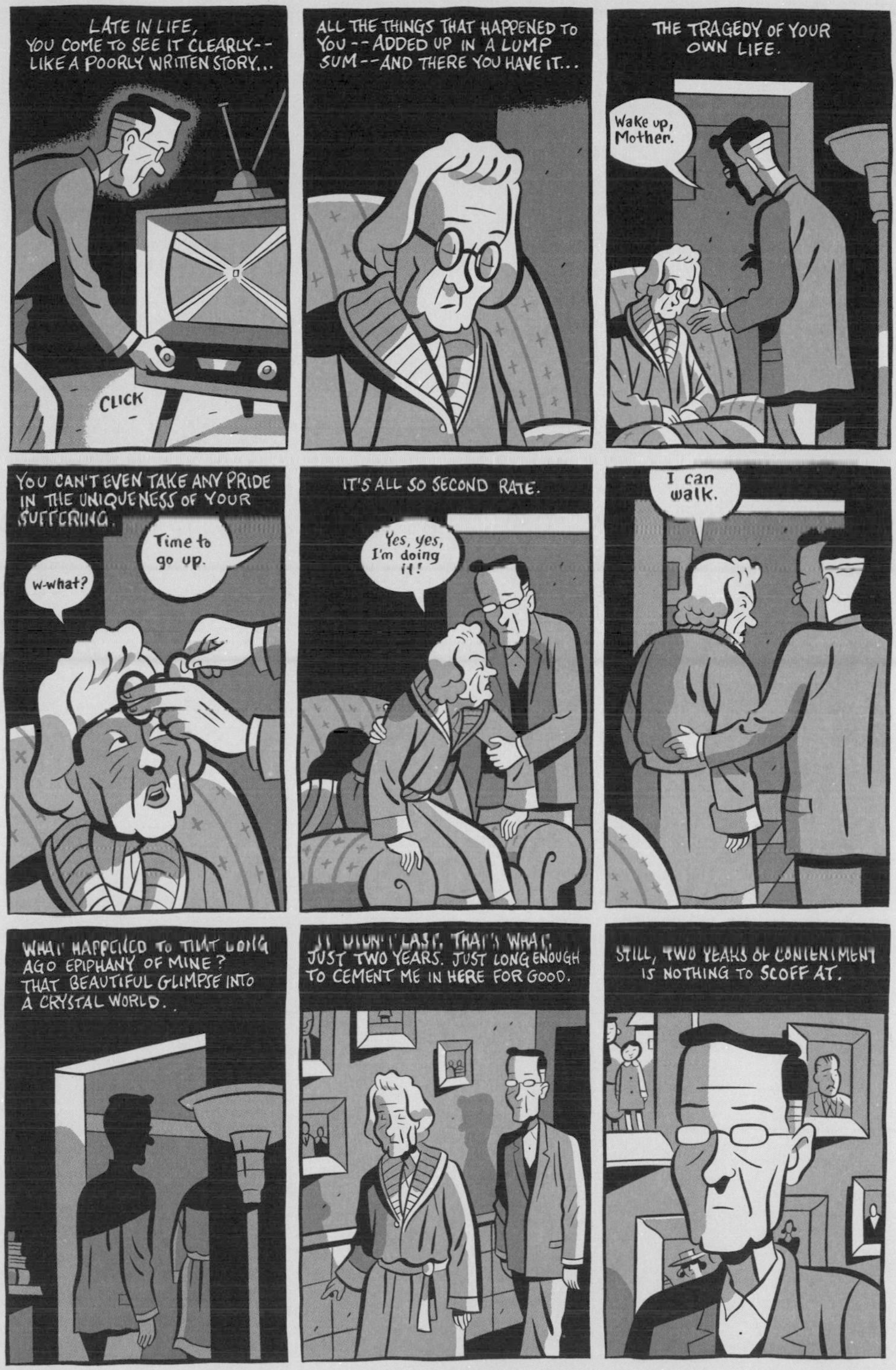
LATE IN LIFE, YOU COME TO SEE IT CLEARLY-- LIKE A POORLY WRITTEN STORY...
CLICK
ALL THE THINGS THAT HAPPENED TO YOU -- ADDED UP IN A LUMP SUM -- AND THERE YOU HAVE IT...
THE TRAGEDY OF YOUR OWN LIFE.
Wake up, Mother.
YOU CAN'T EVEN TAKE ANY PRIDE IN THE UNIQUENESS OF YOUR SUFFERING.
Time to go up.
W-what?
IT'S ALL SO SECOND RATE.
Yes, yes, I'm doing it!
I can walk.
WHAT HAPPENED TO THAT LONG AGO EPIPHANY OF MINE? THAT BEAUTIFUL GLIMPSE INTO A CRYSTAL WORLD.
IT DIDN'T LAST, THAT'S WHAT. JUST TWO YEARS. JUST LONG ENOUGH TO CEMENT ME IN HERE FOR GOOD.
STILL, TWO YEARS OF CONTENTMENT IS NOTHING TO SCOFF AT.

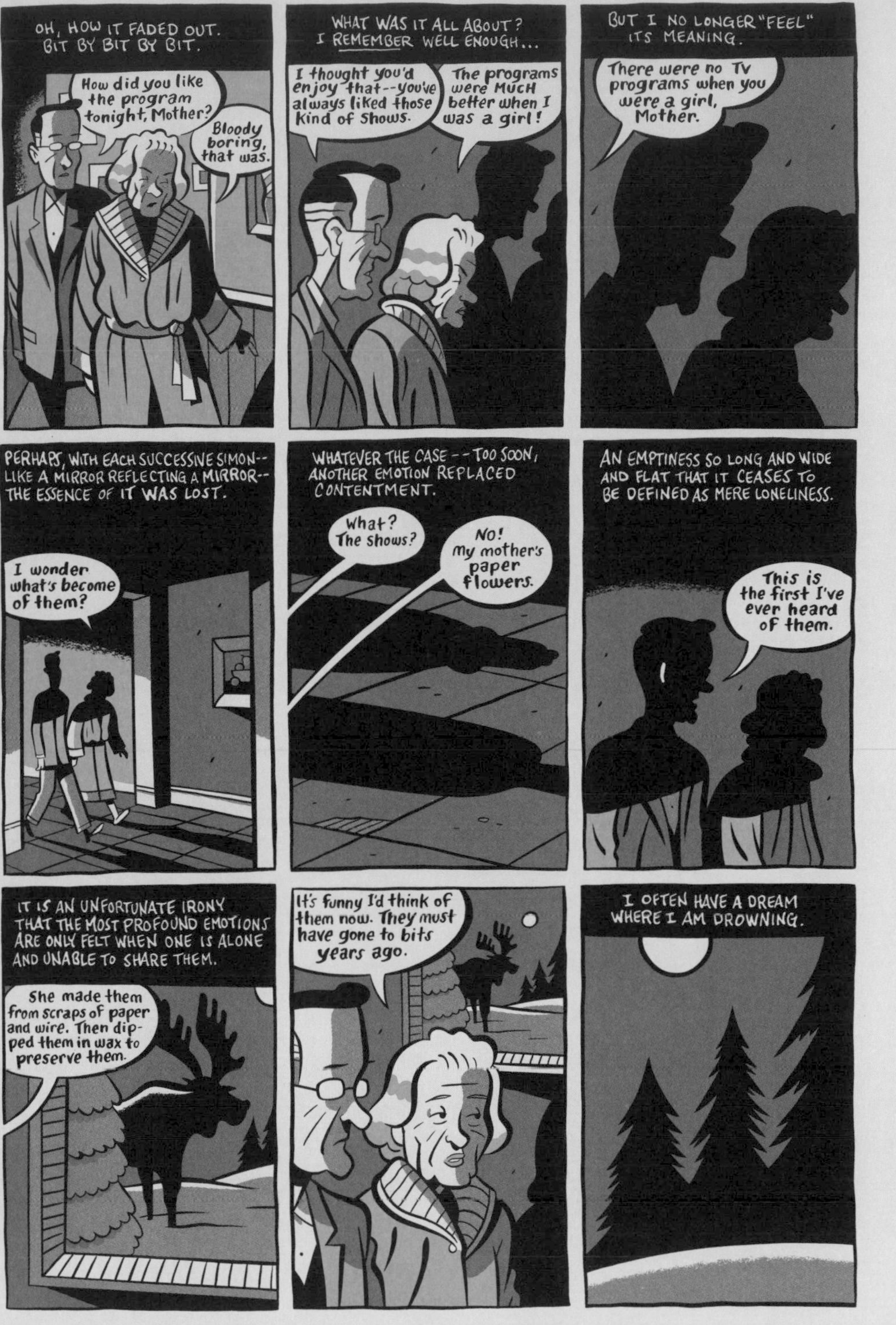

OH, HOW IT FADED OUT. BIT BY BIT BY BIT.
How did you like the program tonight, Mother?
Bloody boring, that was.
WHAT WAS IT ALL ABOUT? I REMEMBER WELL ENOUGH...
I thought you'd enjoy that--you've always liked those kind of shows.
The programs were MUCH better when I was a girl!
BUT I NO LONGER "FEEL" ITS MEANING.
There were no TV programs when you were a girl, Mother.
PERHAPS, WITH EACH SUCCESSIVE SIMON-- LIKE A MIRROR REFLECTING A MIRROR-- THE ESSENCE OF IT WAS LOST.
I wonder what's become of them?
WHATEVER THE CASE--TOO SOON, ANOTHER EMOTION REPLACED CONTENTMENT.
What? The shows?
No! my mother's paper flowers.
AN EMPTINESS SO LONG AND WIDE AND FLAT THAT IT CEASES TO BE DEFINED AS MERE LONELINESS.
This is the first I've ever heard of them.
IT IS AN UNFORTUNATE IRONY THAT THE MOST PROFOUND EMOTIONS ARE ONLY FELT WHEN ONE IS ALONE AND UNABLE TO SHARE THEM.
She made them from scraps of paper and wire. Then dipped them in wax to preserve them.
It's funny I'd think of them now. They must have gone to bits years ago.
I OFTEN HAVE A DREAM WHERE I AM DROWNING.

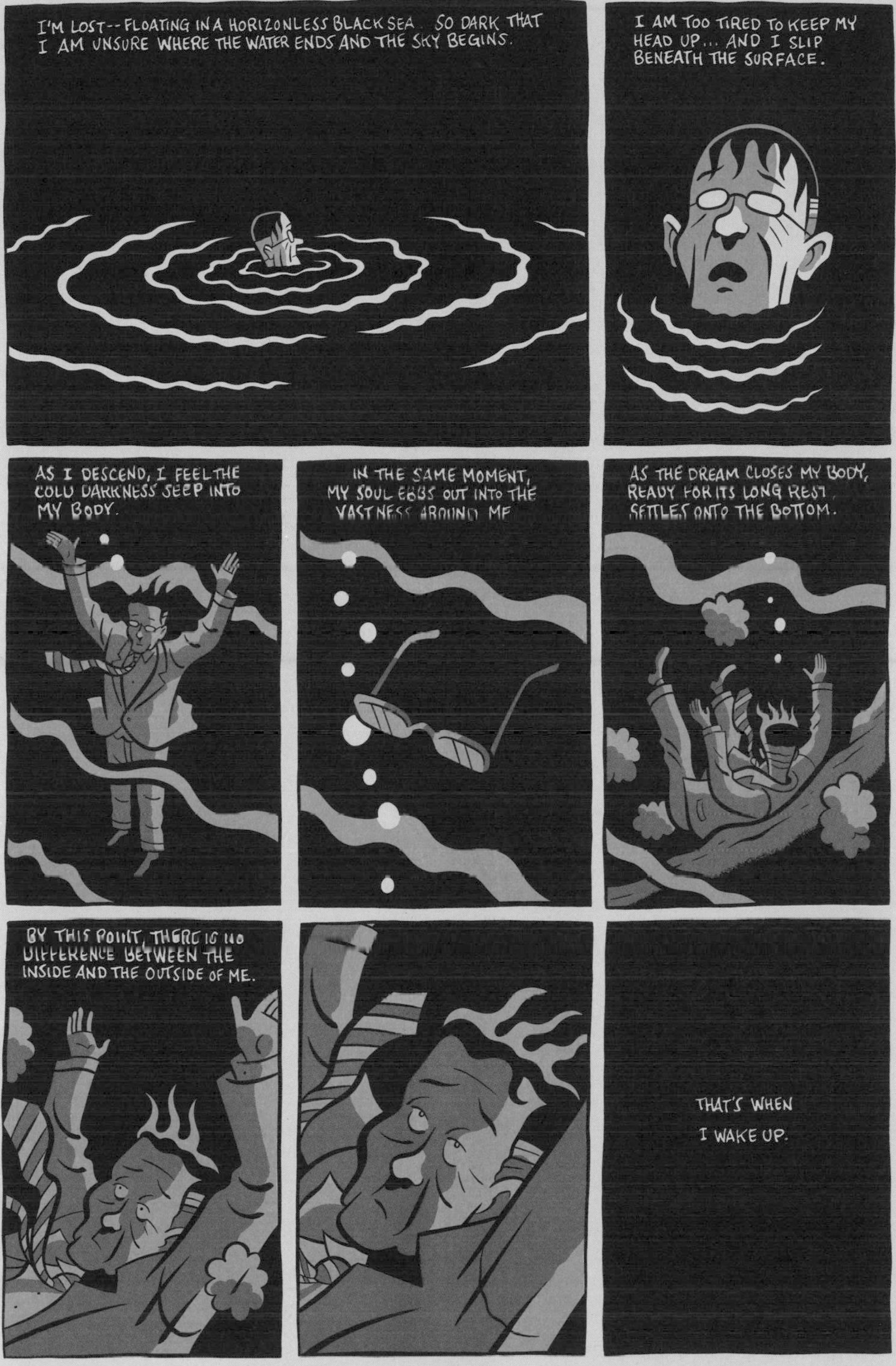
I'M LOST--FLOATING IN A HORIZONLESS BLACK SEA. SO DARK THAT I AM UNSURE WHERE THE WATER ENDS AND THE SKY BEGINS.
I AM TOO TIRED TO KEEP MY HEAD UP... AND I SLIP BENEATH THE SURFACE.
AS I DESCEND, I FEEL THE COLD DARKNESS SEEP INTO MY BODY.
IN THE SAME MOMENT, MY SOUL EBBS OUT INTO THE VASTNESS AROUND ME.
AS THE DREAM CLOSES MY BODY, READY FOR ITS LONG REST, SETTLES ONTO THE BOTTOM.
BY THIS POINT, THERE IS NO DIFFERENCE BETWEEN THE INSIDE AND THE OUTSIDE OF ME.
THAT'S WHEN I WAKE UP.

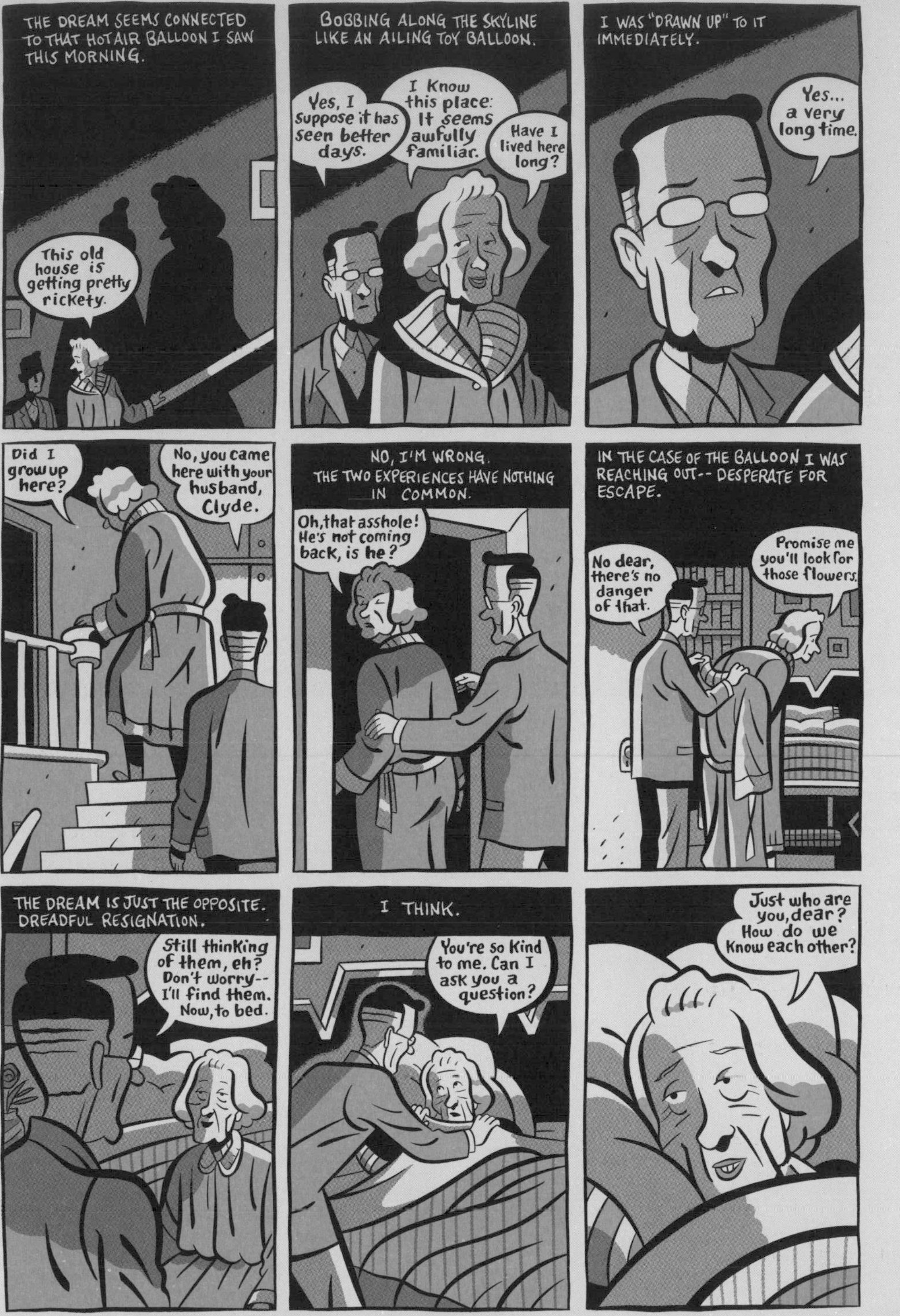
THE DREAM SEEMS CONNECTED TO THAT HOT AIR BALLOON I SAW THIS MORNING.
This old house is getting pretty rickety.
BOBBING ALONG THE SKYLINE LIKE AN AILING TOY BALLOON.
Yes, I suppose it has seen better days.
I Know this place: It seems awfully familiar.
Have I lived here long?
I WAS "DRAWN UP" TO IT IMMEDIATELY.
Yes... a very long time.
Did I grow up here?
No, you came here with your husband, Clyde.
NO, I'M WRONG. THE TWO EXPERIENCES HAVE NOTHING IN COMMON.
Oh, that asshole! He's not coming back, is he?
IN THE CASE OF THE BALLOON I WAS REACHING OUT-- DESPERATE FOR ESCAPE.
No dear, there's no danger of that.
Promise me you'll look for those flowers.
THE DREAM IS JUST THE OPPOSITE. DREADFUL RESIGNATION.
Still thinking of them, eh? Don't worry-- I'll find them. Now, to bed.
I THINK.
You're so Kind to me. Can I ask you a question?
Just who are you, dear? How do we Know each other?

THIS BRINGS ME TO A
RECENT INSIGHT.

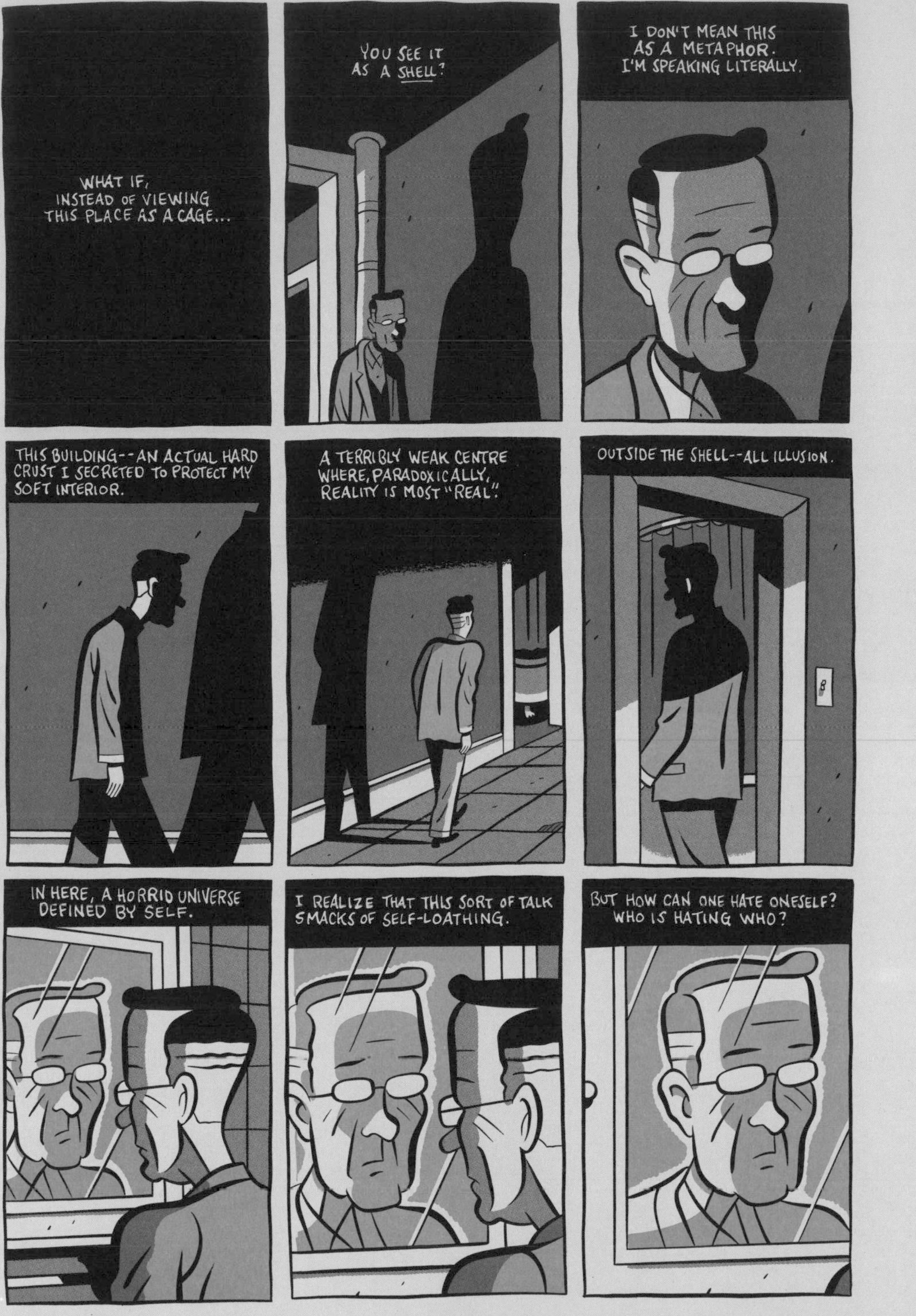
WHAT IF, INSTEAD OF VIEWING THIS PLACE AS A CAGE...
YOU SEE IT AS A SHELL?
I DON'T MEAN THIS AS A METAPHOR. I'M SPEAKING LITERALLY.
THIS BUILDING--AN ACTUAL HARD CRUST I SECRETED TO PROTECT MY SOFT INTERIOR.
A TERRIBLY WEAK CENTRE WHERE, PARADOXICALLY, REALITY IS MOST "REAL".
OUTSIDE THE SHELL--ALL ILLUSION.
IN HERE, A HORRID UNIVERSE DEFINED BY SELF.
I REALIZE THAT THIS SORT OF TALK SMACKS OF SELF-LOATHING.
BUT HOW CAN ONE HATE ONESELF? WHO IS HATING WHO?

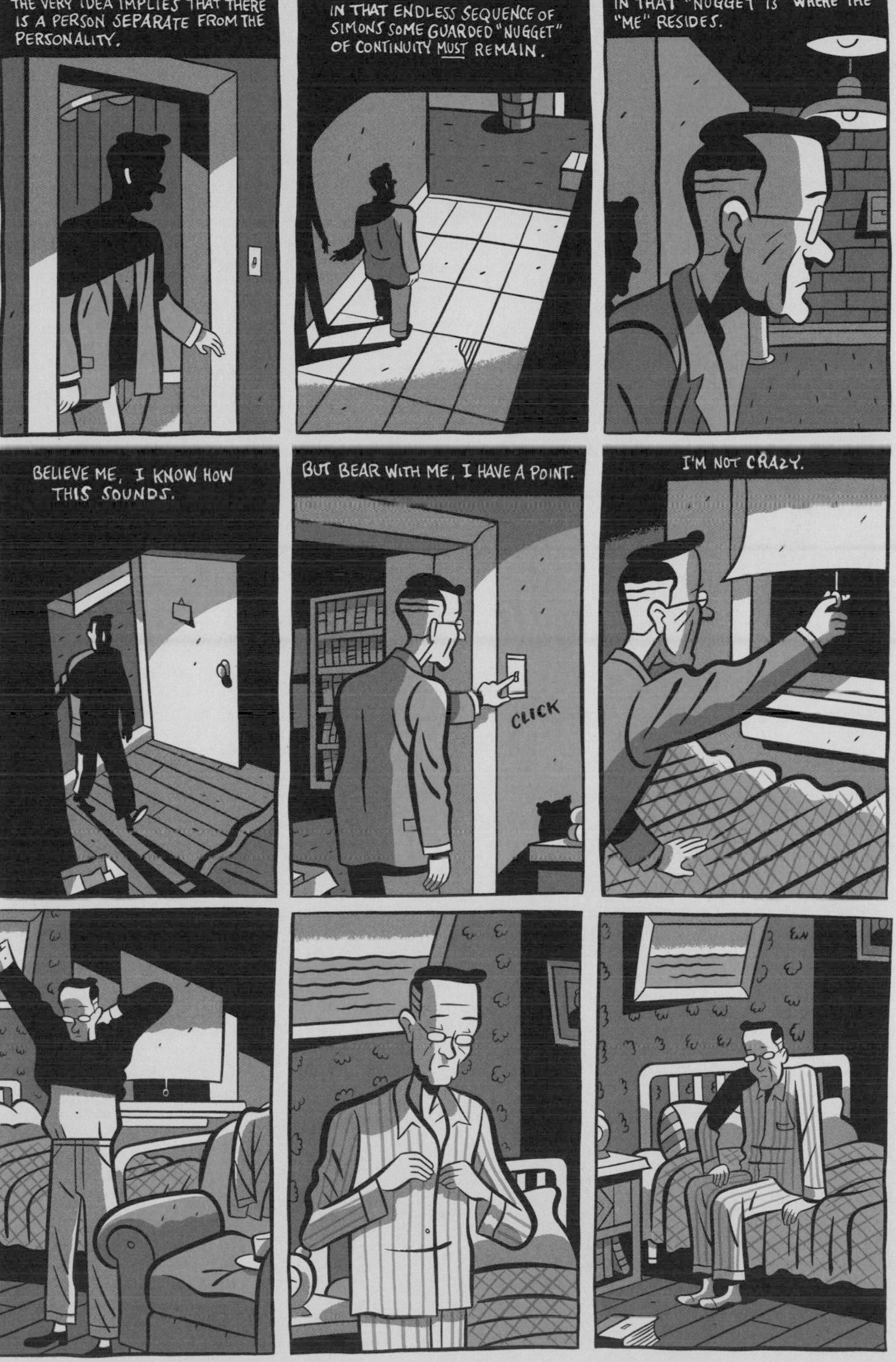
THE VERY IDEA IMPLIES THAT THERE IS A PERSON SEPARATE FROM THE PERSONALITY.
IN THAT ENDLESS SEQUENCE OF SIMONS SOME GUARDED "NUGGET" OF CONTINUITY MUST REMAIN.
IN THAT "NUGGET" IS WHERE THE "ME" RESIDES.
BELIEVE ME, I KNOW HOW THIS SOUNDS.
BUT BEAR WITH ME, I HAVE A POINT.
CLICK
I'M NOT CRAZY.

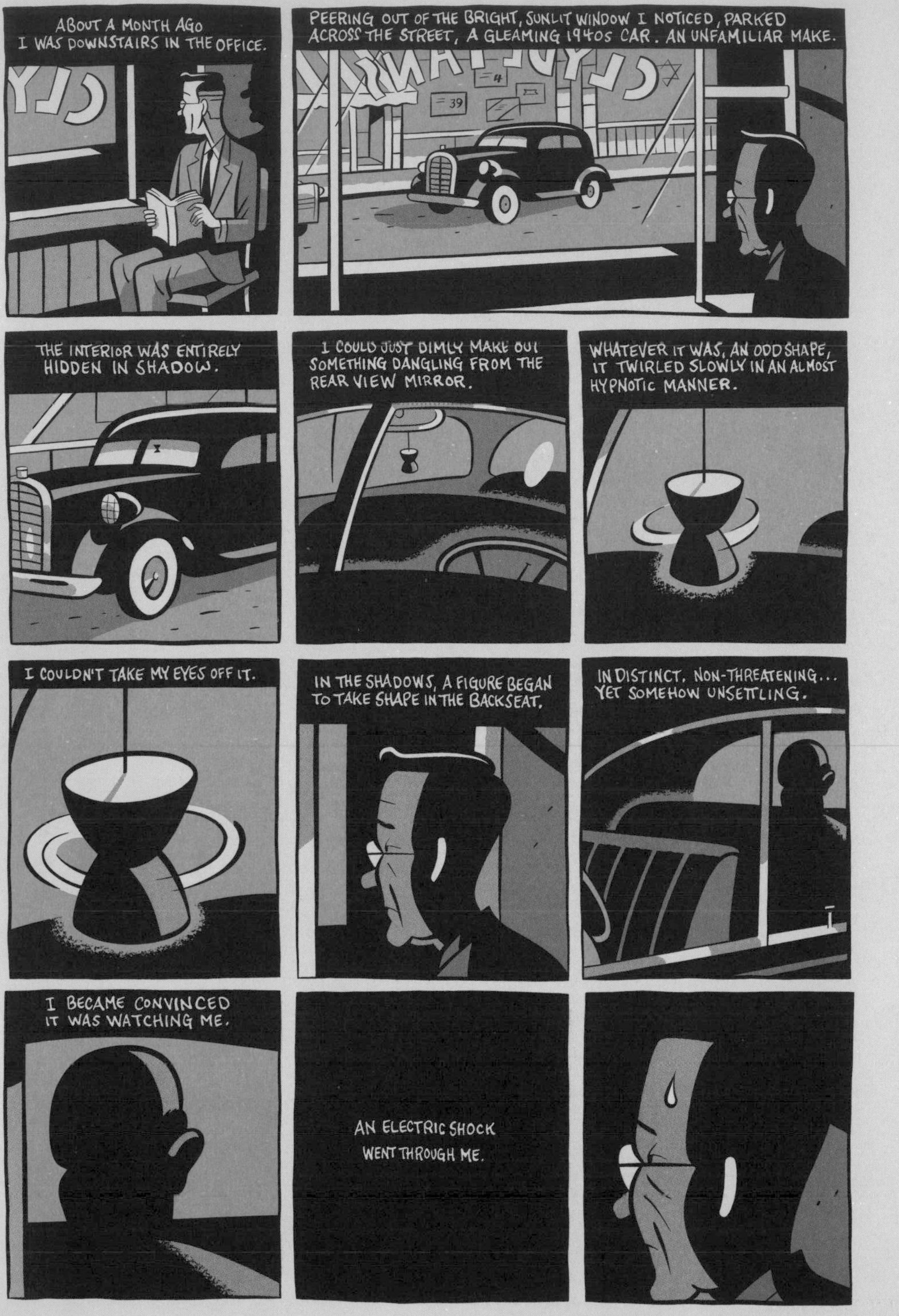
ABOUT A MONTH AGO I WAS DOWNSTAIRS IN THE OFFICE.
PEERING OUT OF THE BRIGHT, SUNLIT WINDOW I NOTICED, PARKED ACROSS THE STREET, A GLEAMING 1940s CAR. AN UNFAMILIAR MAKE.
THE INTERIOR WAS ENTIRELY HIDDEN IN SHADOW.
I COULD JUST DIMLY MAKE OUT SOMETHING DANGLING FROM THE REAR VIEW MIRROR.
WHATEVER IT WAS, AN ODD SHAPE, IT TWIRLED SLOWLY IN AN ALMOST HYPNOTIC MANNER.
I COULDN'T TAKE MY EYES OFF IT.
IN THE SHADOWS, A FIGURE BEGAN TO TAKE SHAPE IN THE BACKSEAT.
INDISTINCT. NON-THREATENING... YET SOMEHOW UNSETTLING.
I BECAME CONVINCED IT WAS WATCHING ME.
AN ELECTRIC SHOCK WENT THROUGH ME.

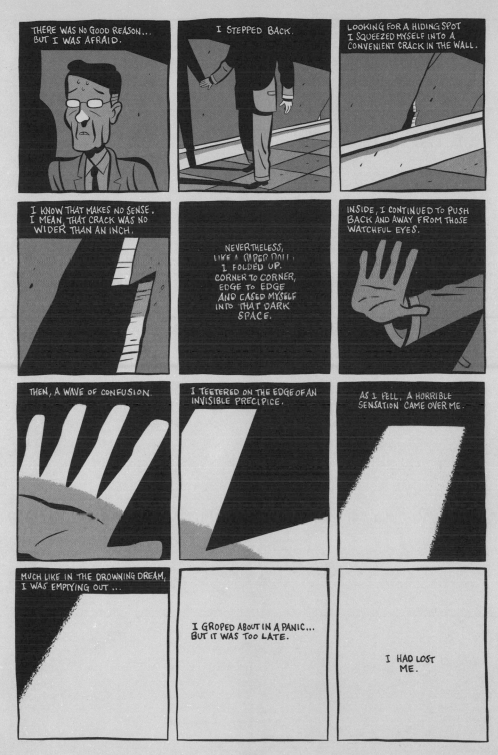

THERE WAS NO GOOD REASON...
BUT I WAS AFRAID.

I STEPPED BACK.

LOOKING FOR A HIDING SPOT
I SQUEEZED MYSELF INTO A
CONVENIENT CRACK IN THE WALL.

I KNOW THAT MAKES NO SENSE.
I MEAN, THAT CRACK WAS NO
WIDER THAN AN INCH.

NEVERTHELESS,
LIKE A PAPER DOLL,
I FOLDED UP,
CORNER TO CORNER,
EDGE TO EDGE
AND EASED MYSELF
INTO THAT DARK
SPACE.

INSIDE, I CONTINUED TO PUSH
BACK AND AWAY FROM THOSE
WATCHFUL EYES.

THEN, A WAVE OF CONFUSION.

I TEETERED ON THE EDGE OF AN
INVISIBLE PRECIPICE.

AS I FELL, A HORRIBLE
SENSATION CAME OVER ME.

MUCH LIKE IN THE DROWNING DREAM,
I WAS EMPTYING OUT...

I GROPED ABOUT IN A PANIC...
BUT IT WAS TOO LATE.

I HAD LOST
ME.

LOOK

233

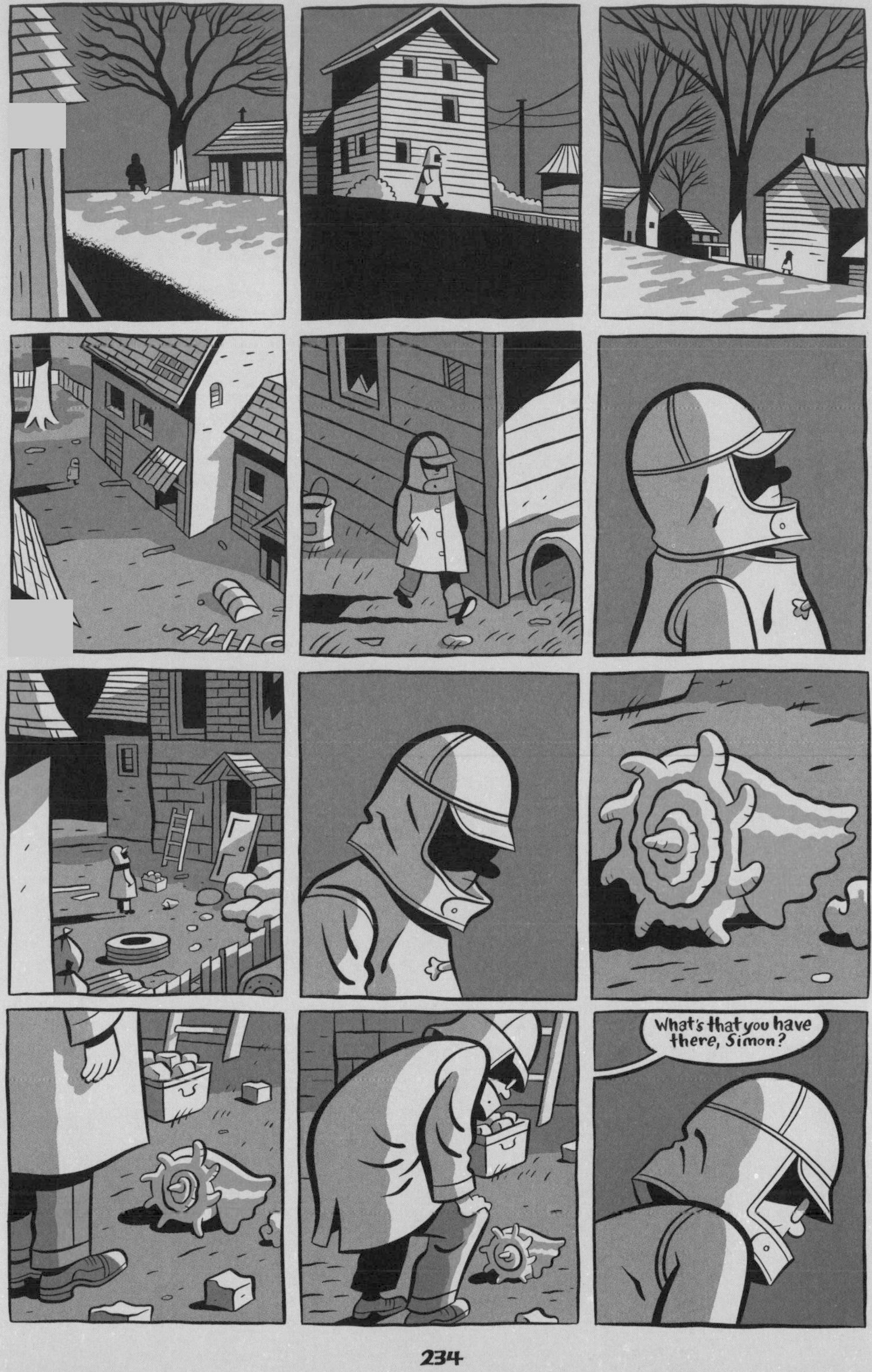
What's that you have there, Simon?

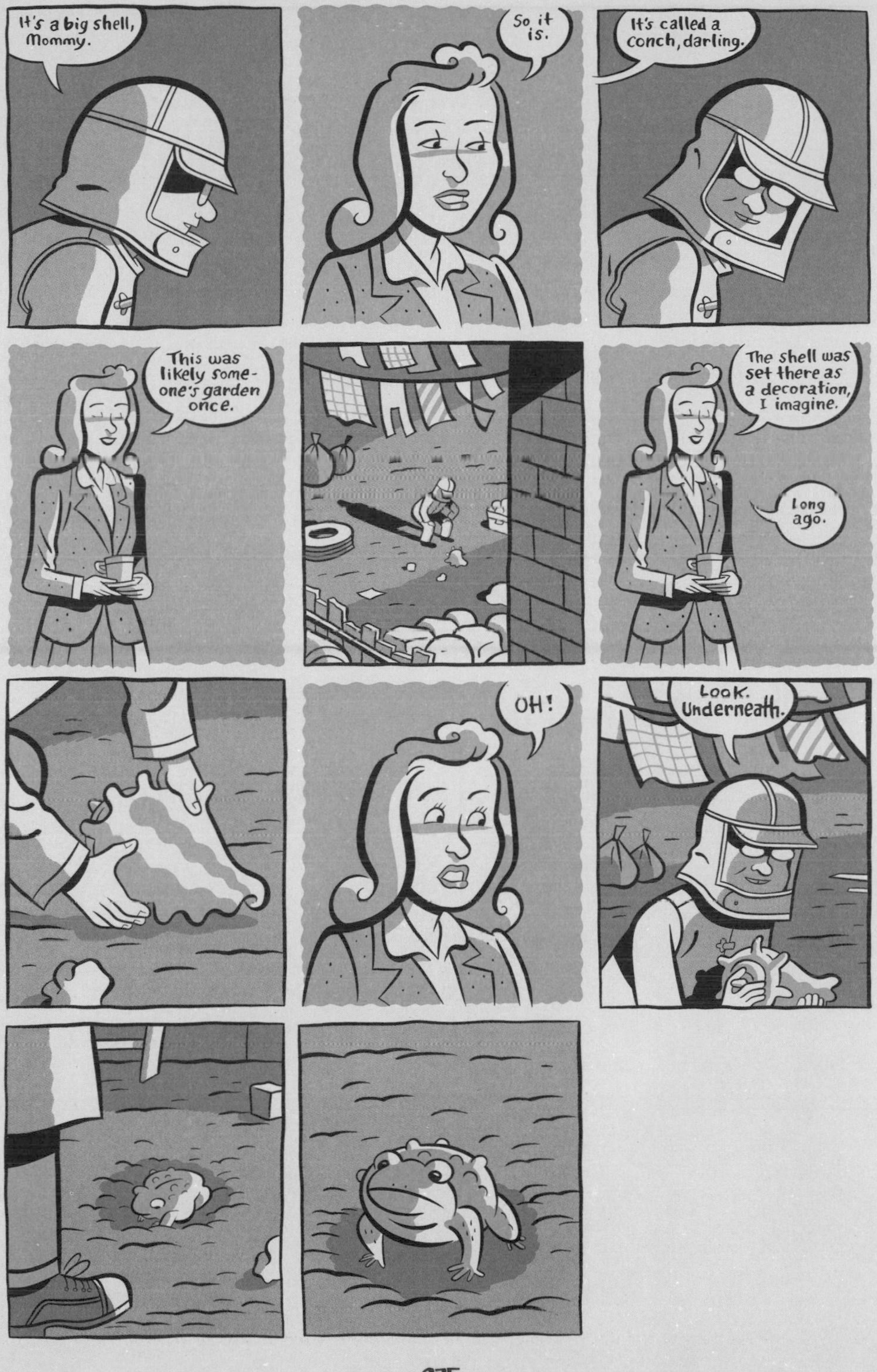

It's a big shell, Mommy.
So it is.
It's called a conch, darling.
This was likely some-one's garden once.
The shell was set there as a decoration, I imagine.
Long ago.
OH!
Look. Underneath.

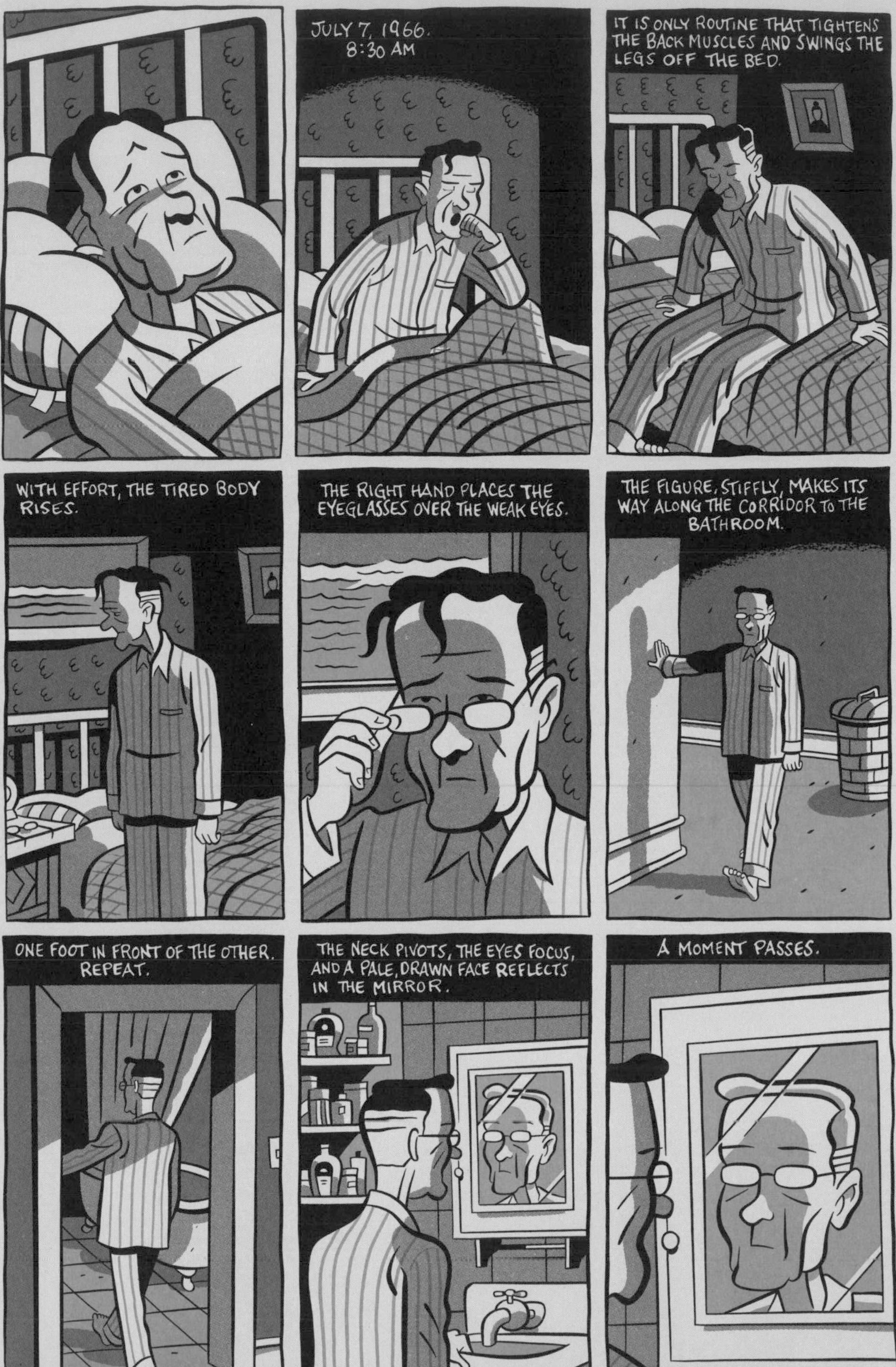
JULY 7, 1966.
8:30 AM
IT IS ONLY ROUTINE THAT TIGHTENS THE BACK MUSCLES AND SWINGS THE LEGS OFF THE BED.
WITH EFFORT, THE TIRED BODY RISES.
THE RIGHT HAND PLACES THE EYEGLASSES OVER THE WEAK EYES.
THE FIGURE, STIFFLY, MAKES ITS WAY ALONG THE CORRIDOR TO THE BATHROOM.
ONE FOOT IN FRONT OF THE OTHER. REPEAT.
THE NECK PIVOTS, THE EYES FOCUS, AND A PALE, DRAWN FACE REFLECTS IN THE MIRROR.
A MOMENT PASSES.

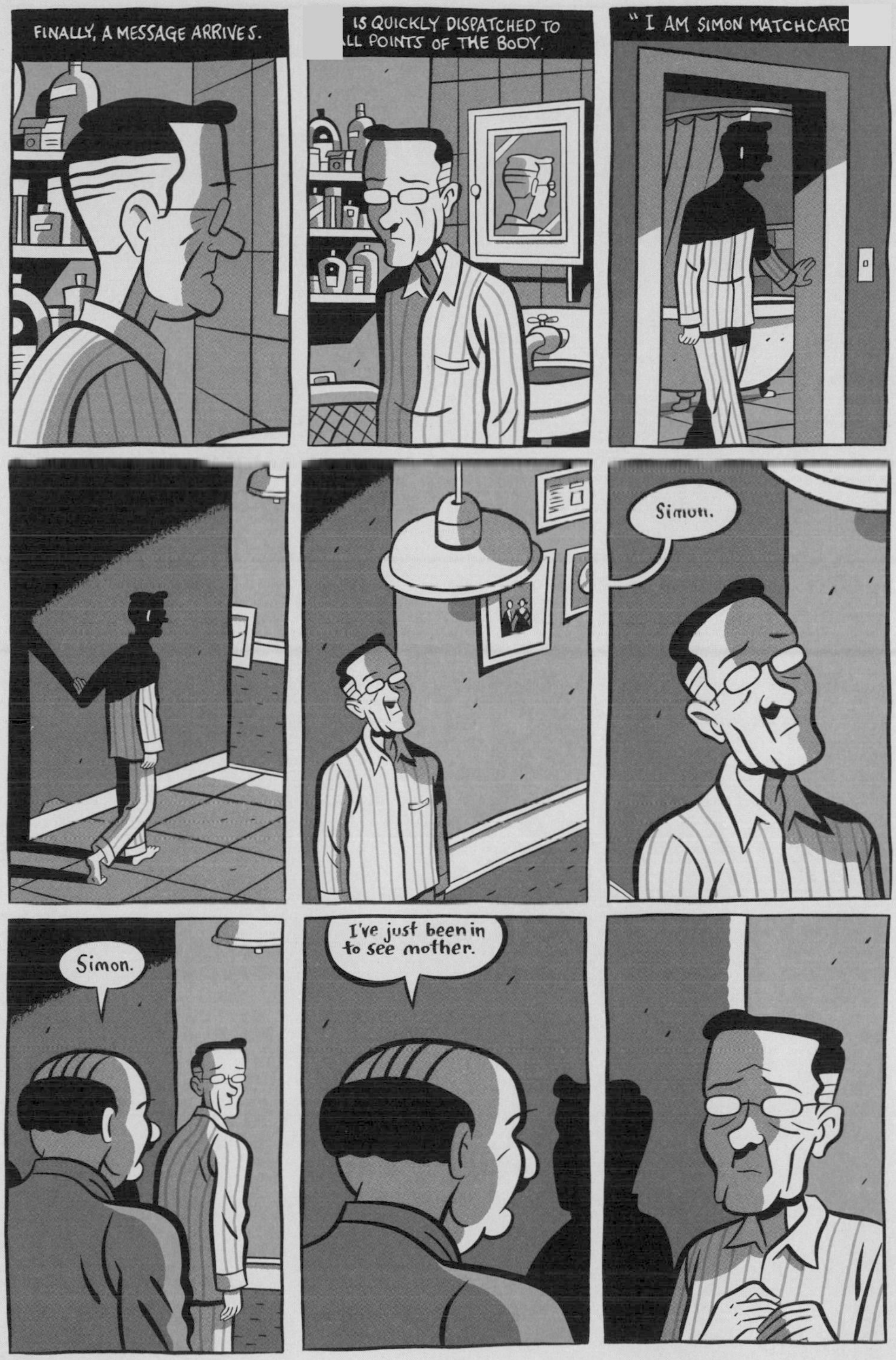
FINALLY, A MESSAGE ARRIVES.
IS QUICKLY DISPATCHED TO
LL POINTS OF THE BODY.
"I AM SIMON MATCHCARD
Simon.
Simon.
I've just been in to see mother.

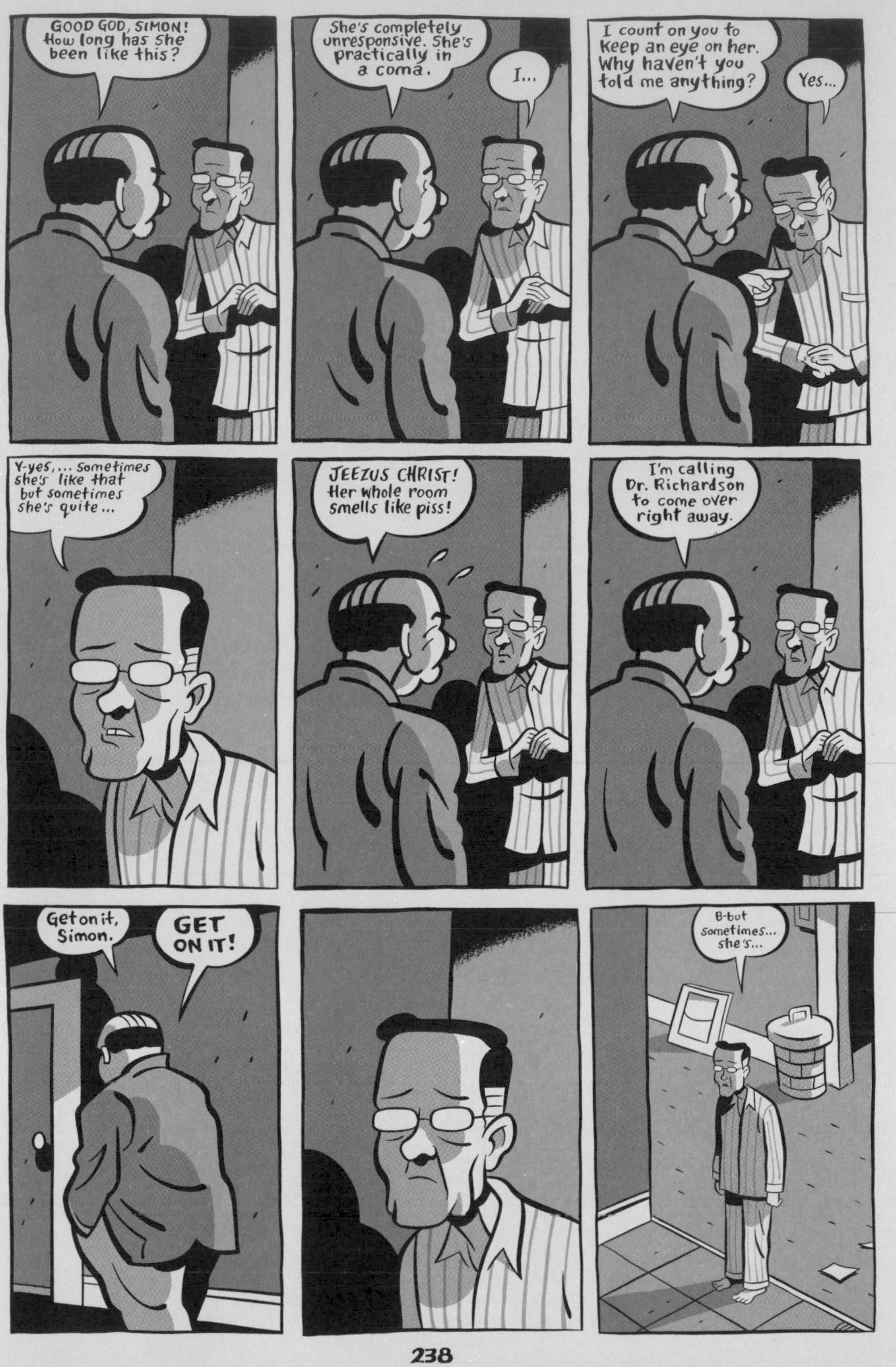
GOOD GOD, SIMON! How long has she been like this?
She's completely unresponsive. She's practically in a coma.
I...
I count on you to keep an eye on her. Why haven't you told me anything?
Yes...
Y-yes, ... sometimes she's like that but sometimes she's quite ...
JEEZUS CHRIST! Her whole room smells like piss!
I'm calling Dr. Richardson to come over right away.
Get on it, Simon.
GET ON IT!
B-but sometimes... she's...

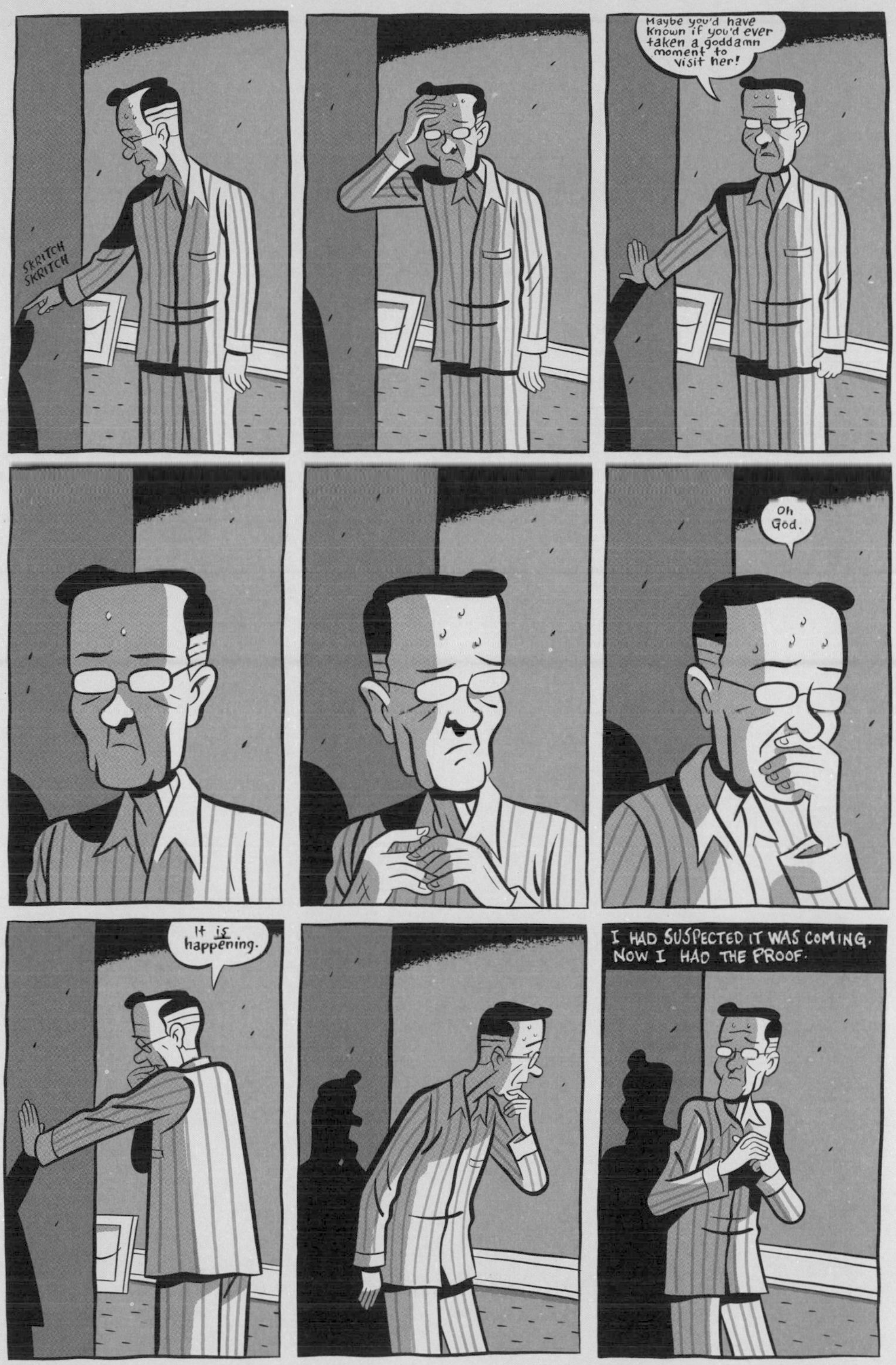
SKRITCH
SKRITCH
Maybe you'd have known if you'd ever taken a goddamn moment to visit her!
Oh God.
It is happening.
I HAD SUSPECTED IT WAS COMING. NOW I HAD THE PROOF.

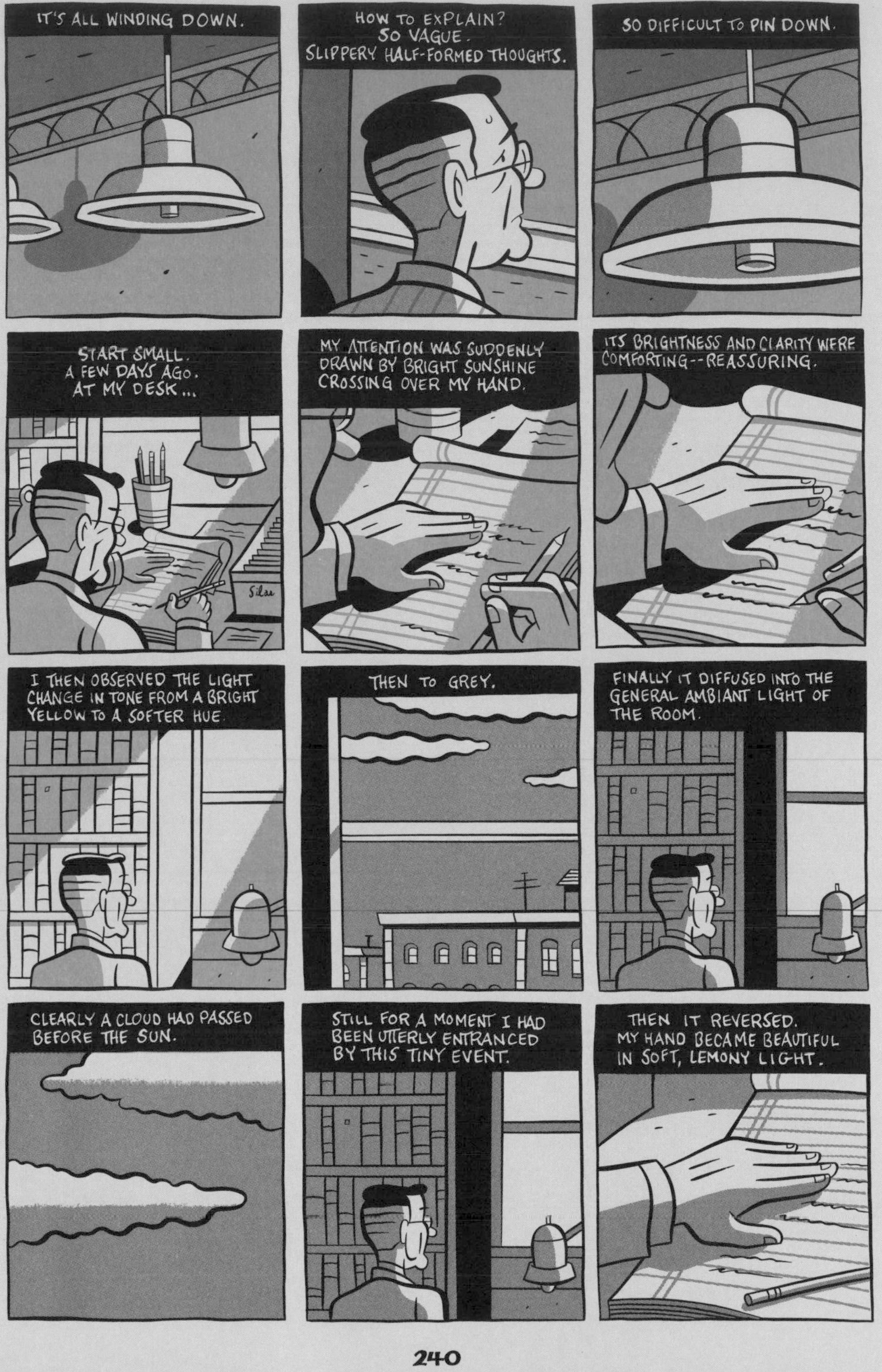
IT'S ALL WINDING DOWN.
HOW TO EXPLAIN? SO VAGUE. SLIPPERY HALF-FORMED THOUGHTS.
SO DIFFICULT TO PIN DOWN.
START SMALL. A FEW DAYS AGO. AT MY DESK...
Silas
MY ATTENTION WAS SUDDENLY DRAWN BY BRIGHT SUNSHINE CROSSING OVER MY HAND.
ITS BRIGHTNESS AND CLARITY WERE COMFORTING--REASSURING.
I THEN OBSERVED THE LIGHT CHANGE IN TONE FROM A BRIGHT YELLOW TO A SOFTER HUE.
THEN TO GREY.
FINALLY IT DIFFUSED INTO THE GENERAL AMBIANT LIGHT OF THE ROOM.
CLEARLY A CLOUD HAD PASSED BEFORE THE SUN.
STILL FOR A MOMENT I HAD BEEN UTTERLY ENTRANCED BY THIS TINY EVENT.
THEN IT REVERSED. MY HAND BECAME BEAUTIFUL IN SOFT, LEMONY LIGHT.

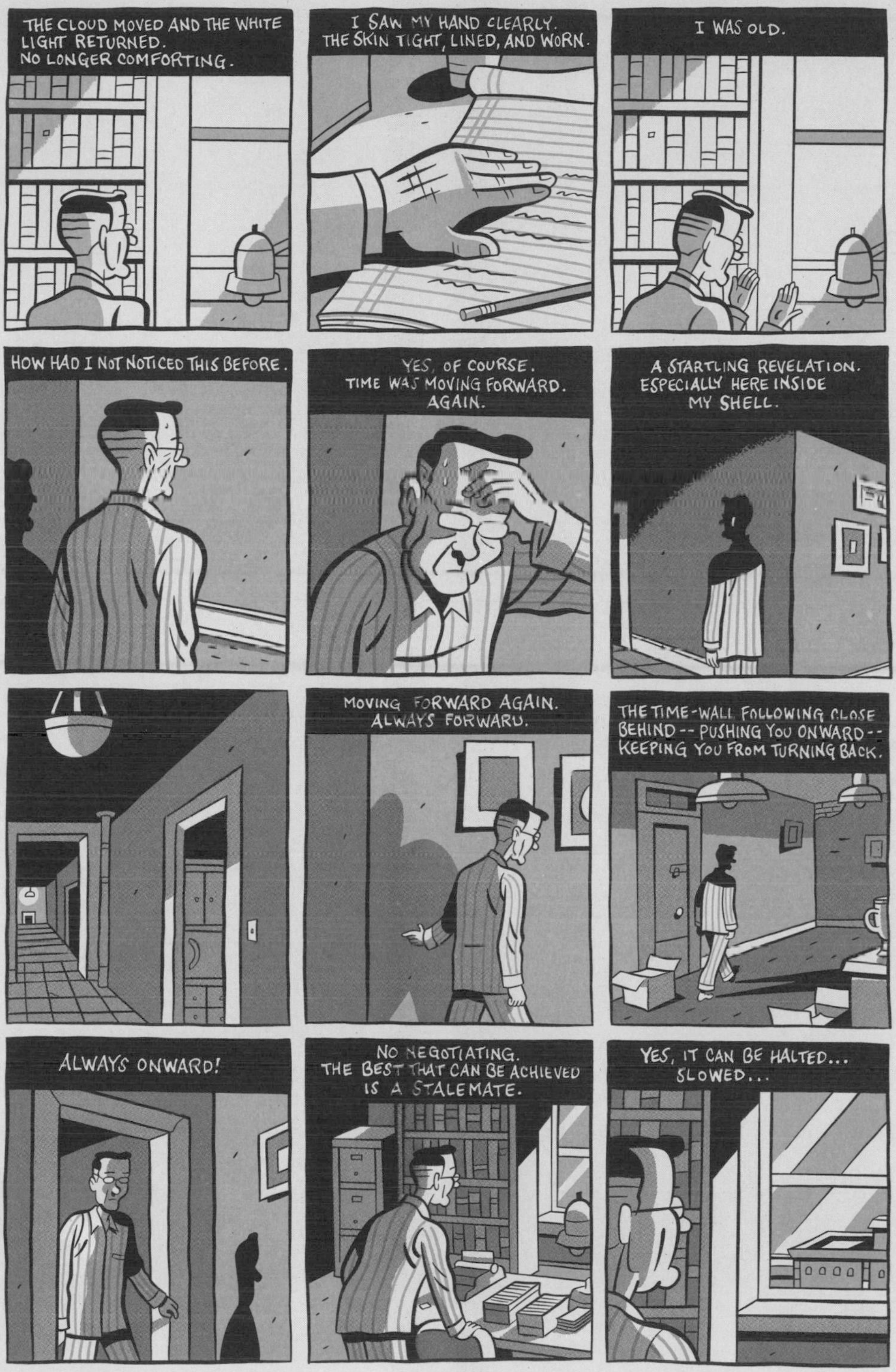
THE CLOUD MOVED AND THE WHITE LIGHT RETURNED. NO LONGER COMFORTING.
I SAW MY HAND CLEARLY. THE SKIN TIGHT, LINED, AND WORN.
I WAS OLD.
HOW HAD I NOT NOTICED THIS BEFORE.
YES, OF COURSE. TIME WAS MOVING FORWARD. AGAIN.
A STARTLING REVELATION. ESPECIALLY HERE INSIDE MY SHELL.
MOVING FORWARD AGAIN. ALWAYS FORWARD.
THE TIME-WALL FOLLOWING CLOSE BEHIND -- PUSHING YOU ONWARD -- KEEPING YOU FROM TURNING BACK.
ALWAYS ONWARD!
NO NEGOTIATING. THE BEST THAT CAN BE ACHIEVED IS A STALEMATE.
YES, IT CAN BE HALTED... SLOWED...

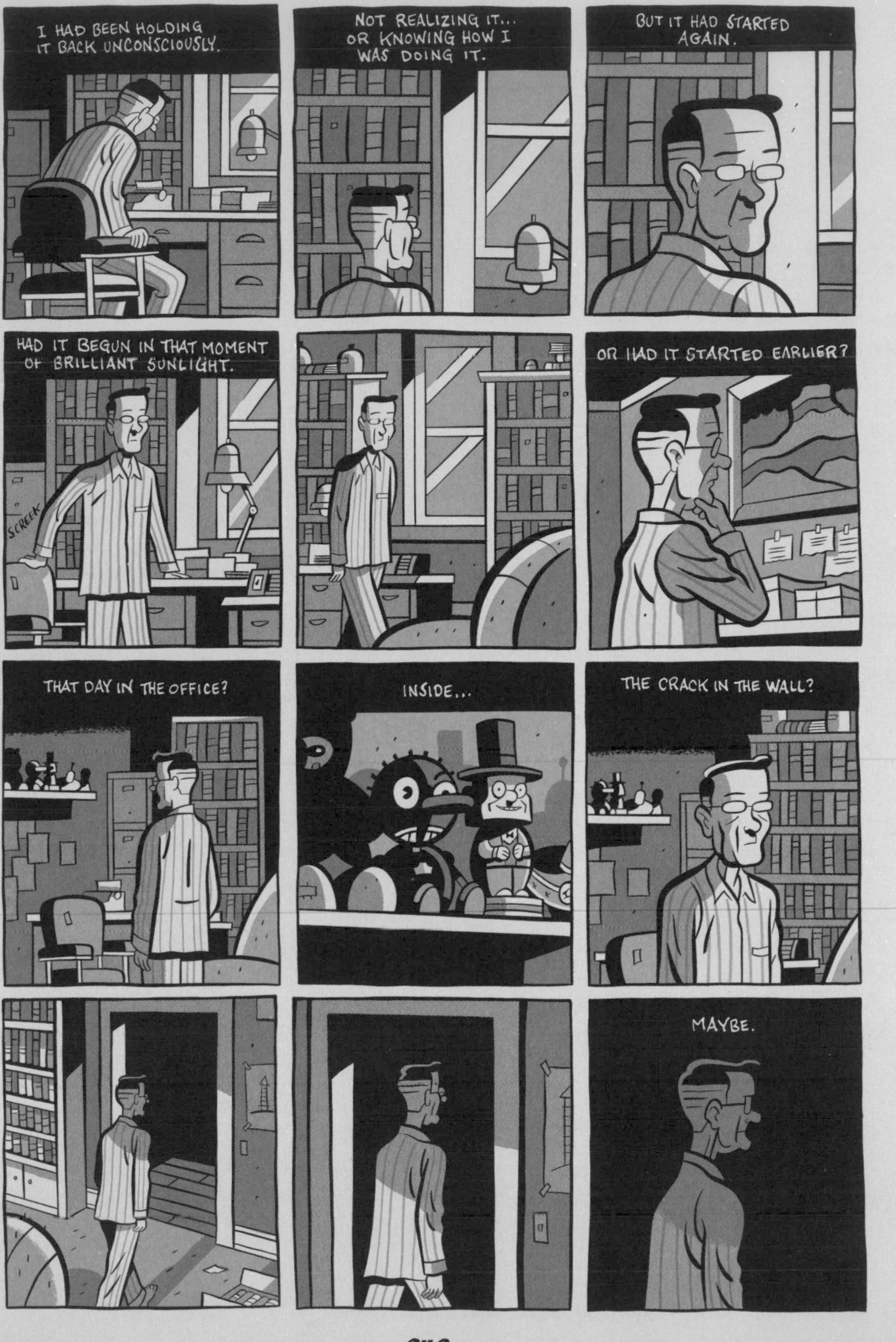
I HAD BEEN HOLDING IT BACK UNCONSCIOUSLY.
NOT REALIZING IT... OR KNOWING HOW I WAS DOING IT.
BUT IT HAD STARTED AGAIN.
HAD IT BEGUN IN THAT MOMENT OF BRILLIANT SUNLIGHT.
SCREEK
OR HAD IT STARTED EARLIER?
THAT DAY IN THE OFFICE?
INSIDE...
THE CRACK IN THE WALL?
MAYBE.

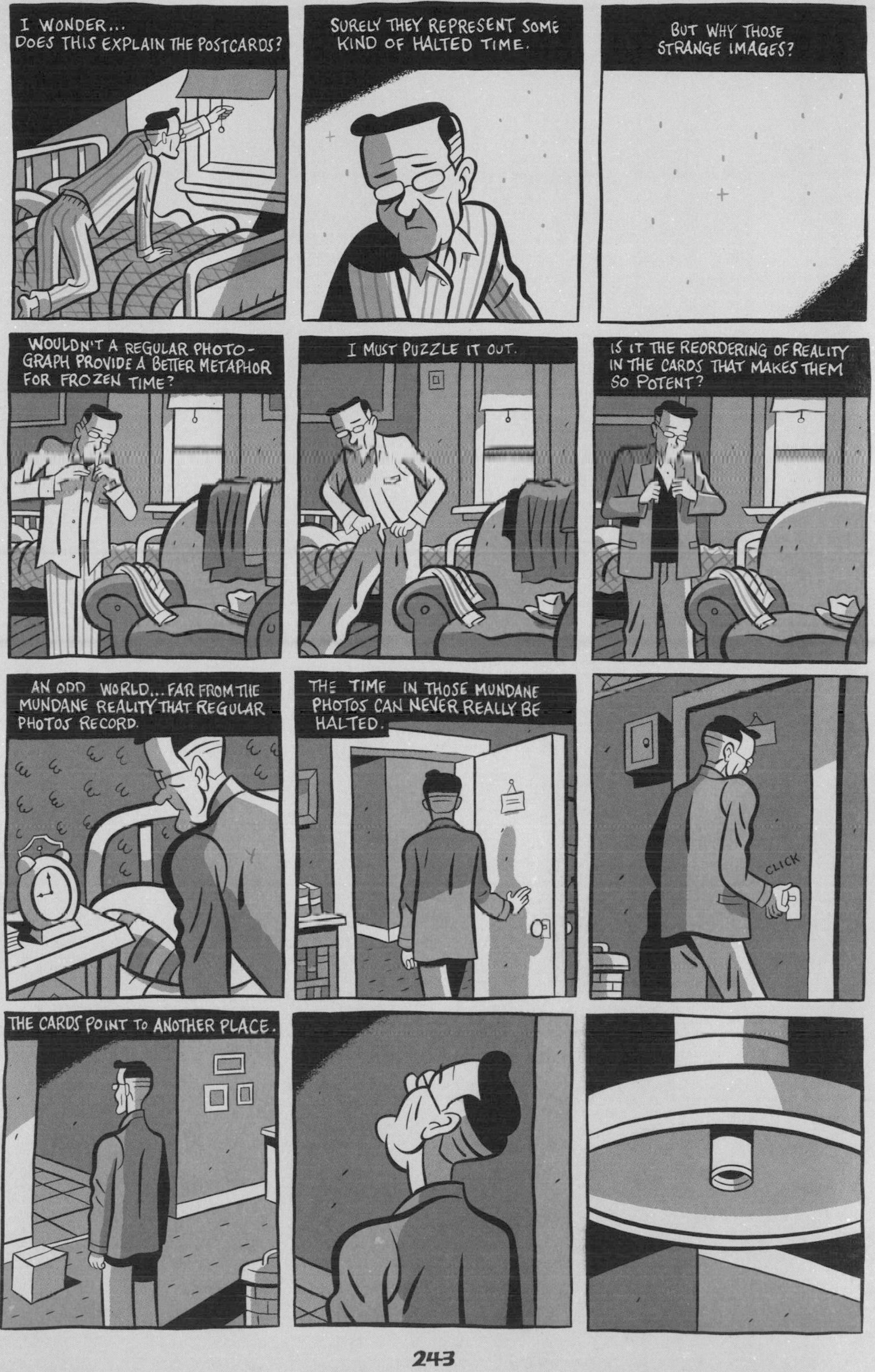
I WONDER...
DOES THIS EXPLAIN THE POSTCARDS?
SURELY THEY REPRESENT SOME KIND OF HALTED TIME.
BUT WHY THOSE STRANGE IMAGES?
WOULDN'T A REGULAR PHOTOGRAPH PROVIDE A BETTER METAPHOR FOR FROZEN TIME?
I MUST PUZZLE IT OUT.
IS IT THE REORDERING OF REALITY IN THE CARDS THAT MAKES THEM SO POTENT?
AN ODD WORLD... FAR FROM THE MUNDANE REALITY THAT REGULAR PHOTOS RECORD.
THE TIME IN THOSE MUNDANE PHOTOS CAN NEVER REALLY BE HALTED.
CLICK
THE CARDS POINT TO ANOTHER PLACE.

Just up here, Doctor.

I'm afraid she won't be much help.

Well, that is to be expected.

Honestly, I was quite surprised by her condition.

From what you describe, it sounds likely to be dementia.

Hmm

CLICK

244

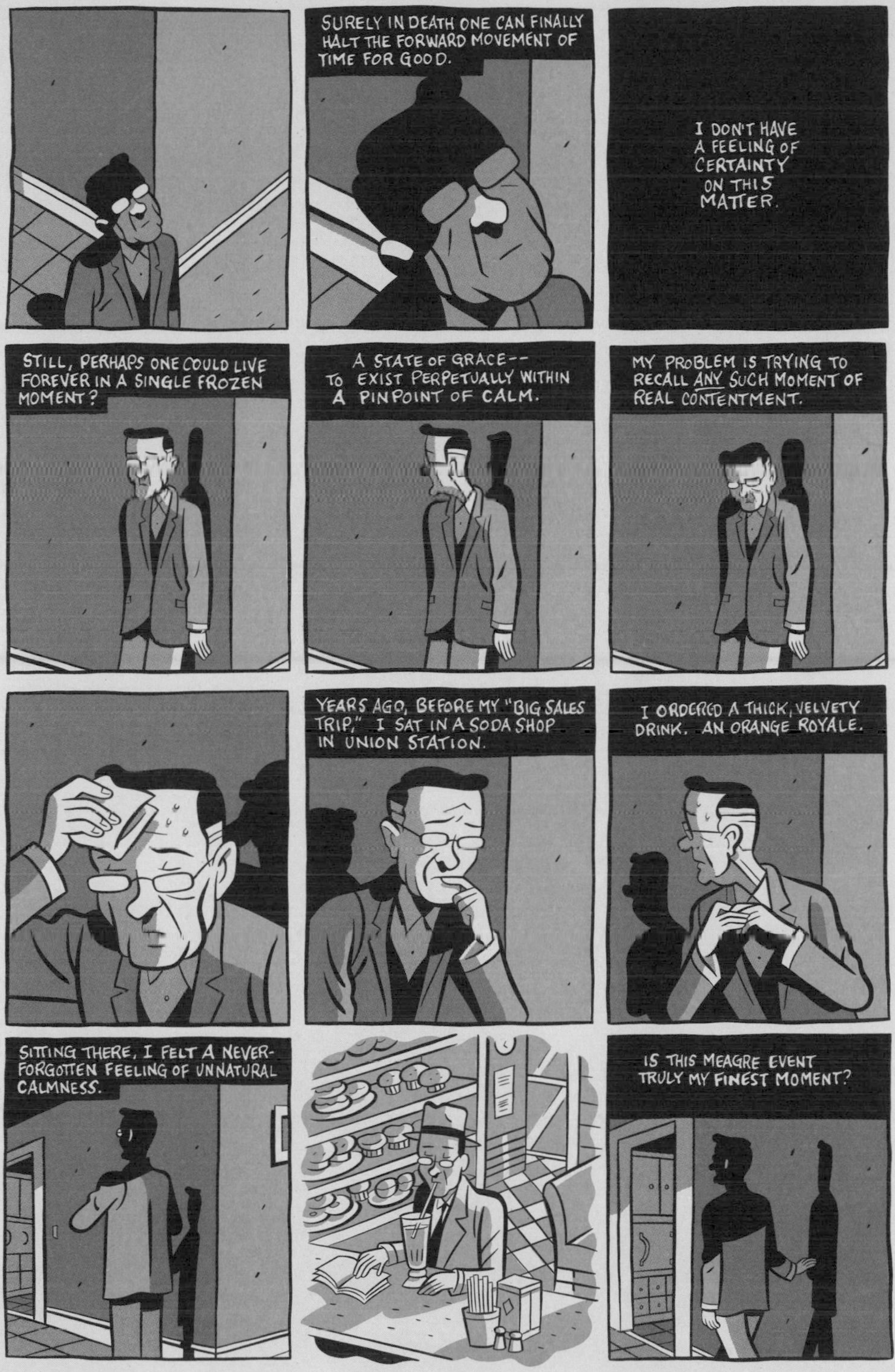

SURELY IN DEATH ONE CAN FINALLY HALT THE FORWARD MOVEMENT OF TIME FOR GOOD.
I DON'T HAVE A FEELING OF CERTAINTY ON THIS MATTER.
STILL, PERHAPS ONE COULD LIVE FOREVER IN A SINGLE FROZEN MOMENT?
A STATE OF GRACE-- TO EXIST PERPETUALLY WITHIN A PINPOINT OF CALM.
MY PROBLEM IS TRYING TO RECALL ANY SUCH MOMENT OF REAL CONTENTMENT.
YEARS AGO, BEFORE MY "BIG SALES TRIP," I SAT IN A SODA SHOP IN UNION STATION.
I ORDERED A THICK, VELVETY DRINK. AN ORANGE ROYALE.
SITTING THERE, I FELT A NEVER-FORGOTTEN FEELING OF UNNATURAL CALMNESS.
IS THIS MEAGRE EVENT TRULY MY FINEST MOMENT?

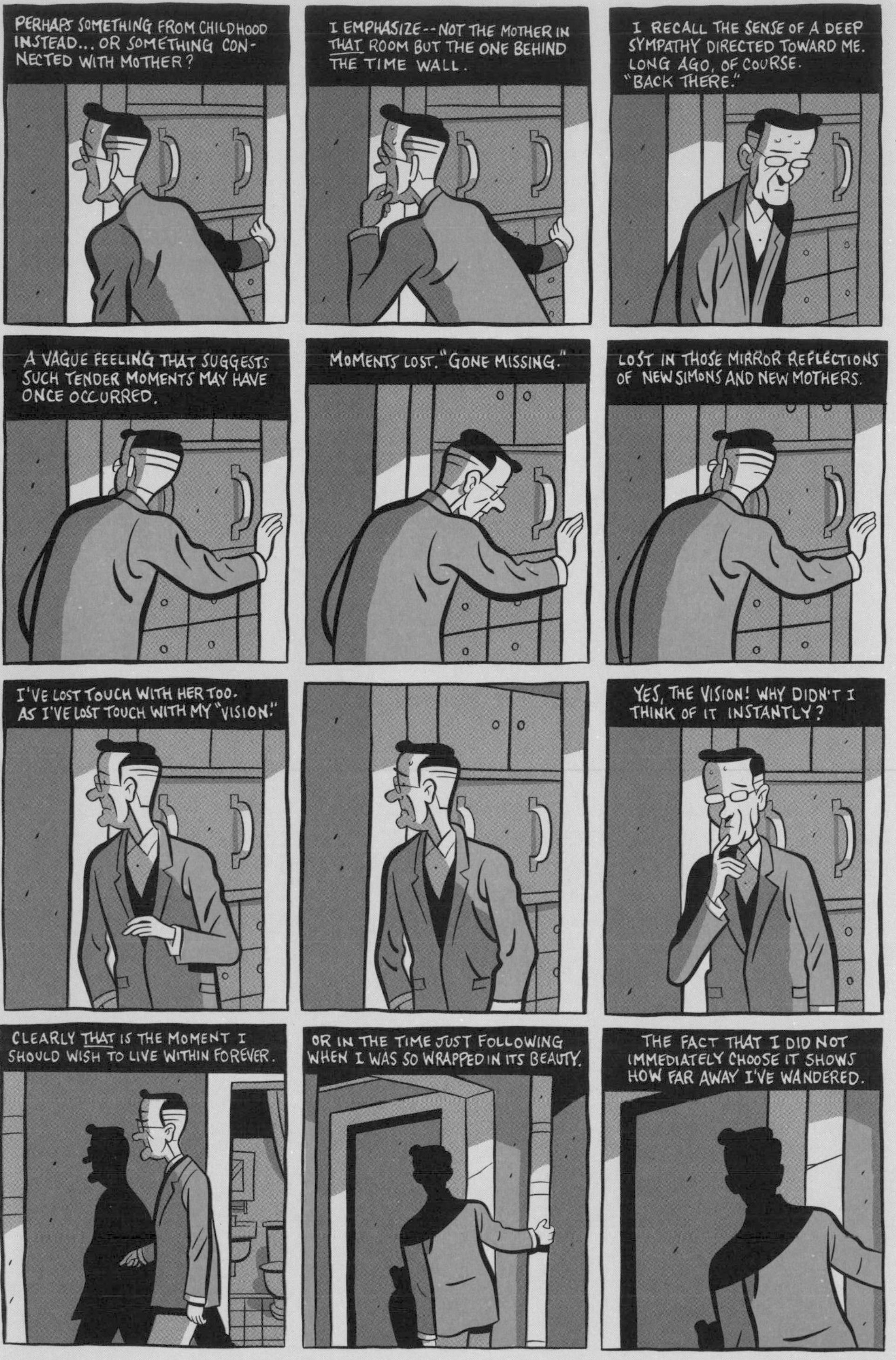
PERHAPS SOMETHING FROM CHILDHOOD INSTEAD... OR SOMETHING CONNECTED WITH MOTHER?
I EMPHASIZE--NOT THE MOTHER IN THAT ROOM BUT THE ONE BEHIND THE TIME WALL.
I RECALL THE SENSE OF A DEEP SYMPATHY DIRECTED TOWARD ME. LONG AGO, OF COURSE. "BACK THERE."
A VAGUE FEELING THAT SUGGESTS SUCH TENDER MOMENTS MAY HAVE ONCE OCCURRED.
MOMENTS LOST. "GONE MISSING."
LOST IN THOSE MIRROR REFLECTIONS OF NEW SIMONS AND NEW MOTHERS.
I'VE LOST TOUCH WITH HER TOO. AS I'VE LOST TOUCH WITH MY "VISION."
YES, THE VISION! WHY DIDN'T I THINK OF IT INSTANTLY?
CLEARLY THAT IS THE MOMENT I SHOULD WISH TO LIVE WITHIN FOREVER.
OR IN THE TIME JUST FOLLOWING WHEN I WAS SO WRAPPED IN ITS BEAUTY.
THE FACT THAT I DID NOT IMMEDIATELY CHOOSE IT SHOWS HOW FAR AWAY I'VE WANDERED.

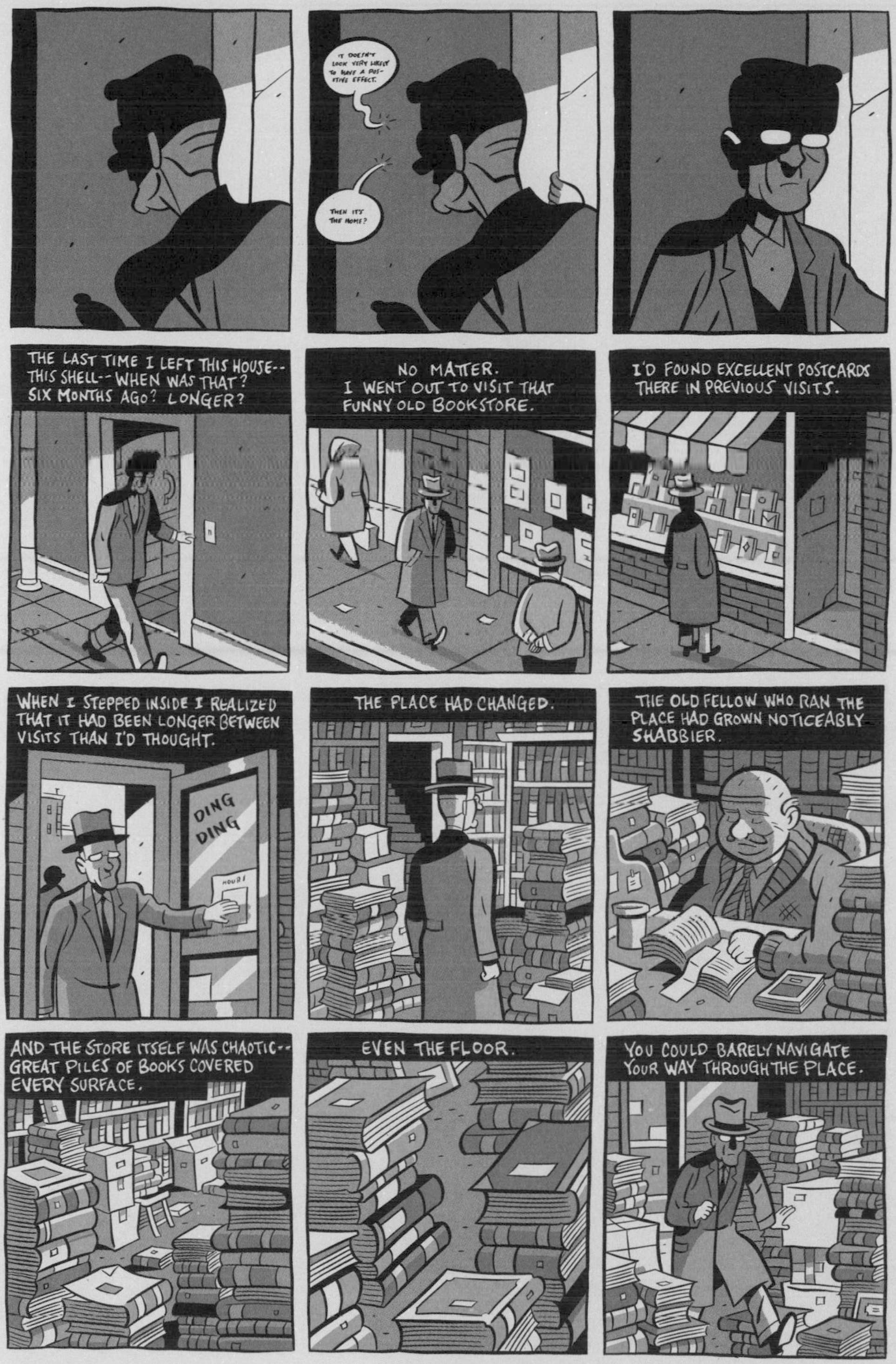
IT DOESN'T LOOK VERY LIKELY TO HAVE A POS-ITIVE EFFECT.
THEN IT'S THE HOME?
THE LAST TIME I LEFT THIS HOUSE-- THIS SHELL-- WHEN WAS THAT? SIX MONTHS AGO? LONGER?
NO MATTER. I WENT OUT TO VISIT THAT FUNNY OLD BOOKSTORE.
I'D FOUND EXCELLENT POSTCARDS THERE IN PREVIOUS VISITS.
WHEN I STEPPED INSIDE I REALIZED THAT IT HAD BEEN LONGER BETWEEN VISITS THAN I'D THOUGHT.
DING DING
HOURS
THE PLACE HAD CHANGED.
THE OLD FELLOW WHO RAN THE PLACE HAD GROWN NOTICEABLY SHABBIER.
AND THE STORE ITSELF WAS CHAOTIC-- GREAT PILES OF BOOKS COVERED EVERY SURFACE.
EVEN THE FLOOR.
YOU COULD BARELY NAVIGATE YOUR WAY THROUGH THE PLACE.

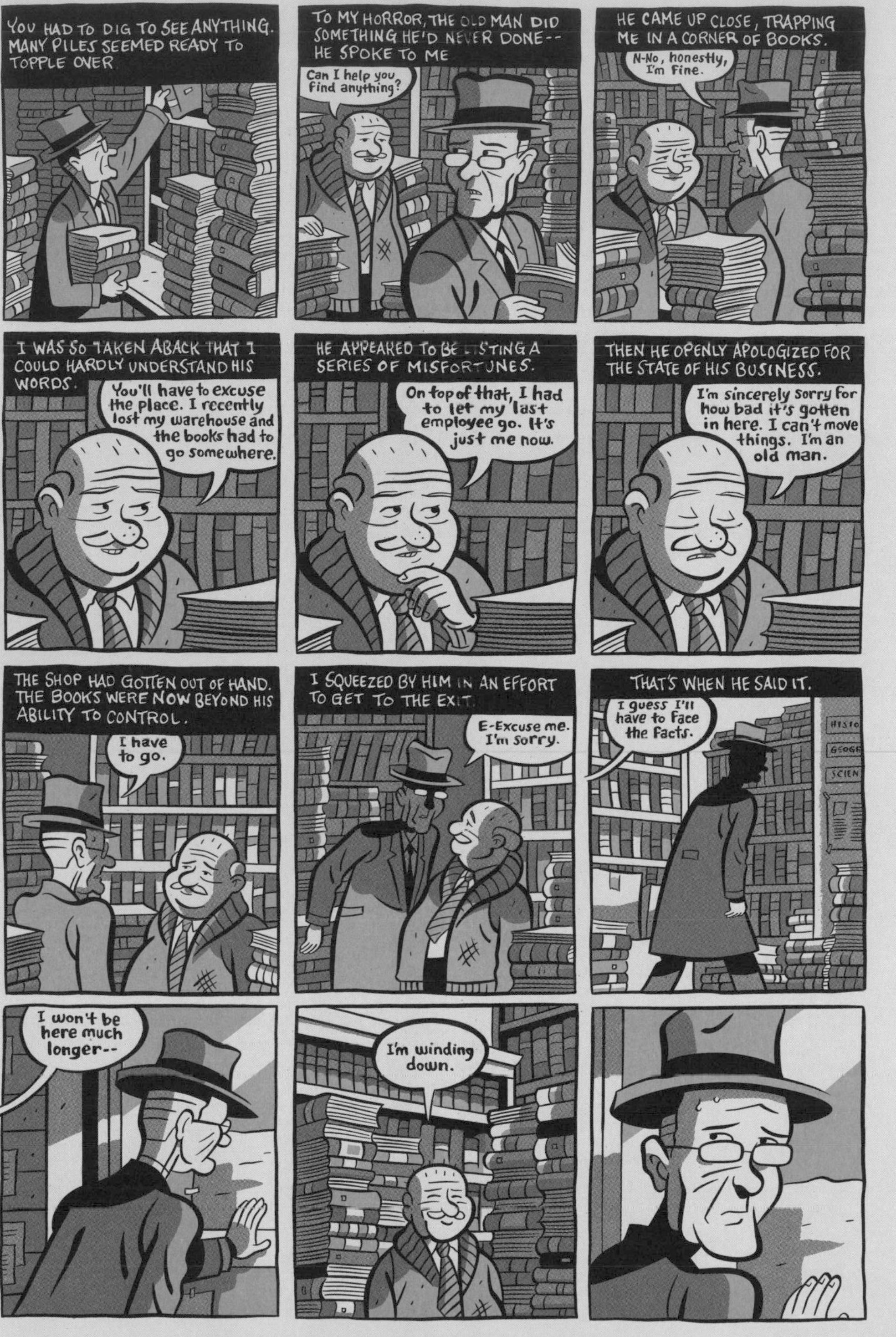
YOU HAD TO DIG TO SEE ANYTHING. MANY PILES SEEMED READY TO TOPPLE OVER.
TO MY HORROR, THE OLD MAN DID SOMETHING HE'D NEVER DONE-- HE SPOKE TO ME.
Can I help you find anything?
HE CAME UP CLOSE, TRAPPING ME IN A CORNER OF BOOKS.
N-No, honestly, I'm fine.
I WAS SO TAKEN ABACK THAT I COULD HARDLY UNDERSTAND HIS WORDS.
You'll have to excuse the place. I recently lost my warehouse and the books had to go somewhere.
HE APPEARED TO BE LISTING A SERIES OF MISFORTUNES.
On top of that, I had to let my last employee go. It's just me now.
THEN HE OPENLY APOLOGIZED FOR THE STATE OF HIS BUSINESS.
I'm sincerely sorry for how bad it's gotten in here. I can't move things. I'm an old man.
THE SHOP HAD GOTTEN OUT OF HAND. THE BOOKS WERE NOW BEYOND HIS ABILITY TO CONTROL.
I have to go.
I SQUEEZED BY HIM IN AN EFFORT TO GET TO THE EXIT.
E-Excuse me. I'm sorry.
THAT'S WHEN HE SAID IT.
I guess I'll have to face the facts.
I won't be here much longer--
I'm winding down.

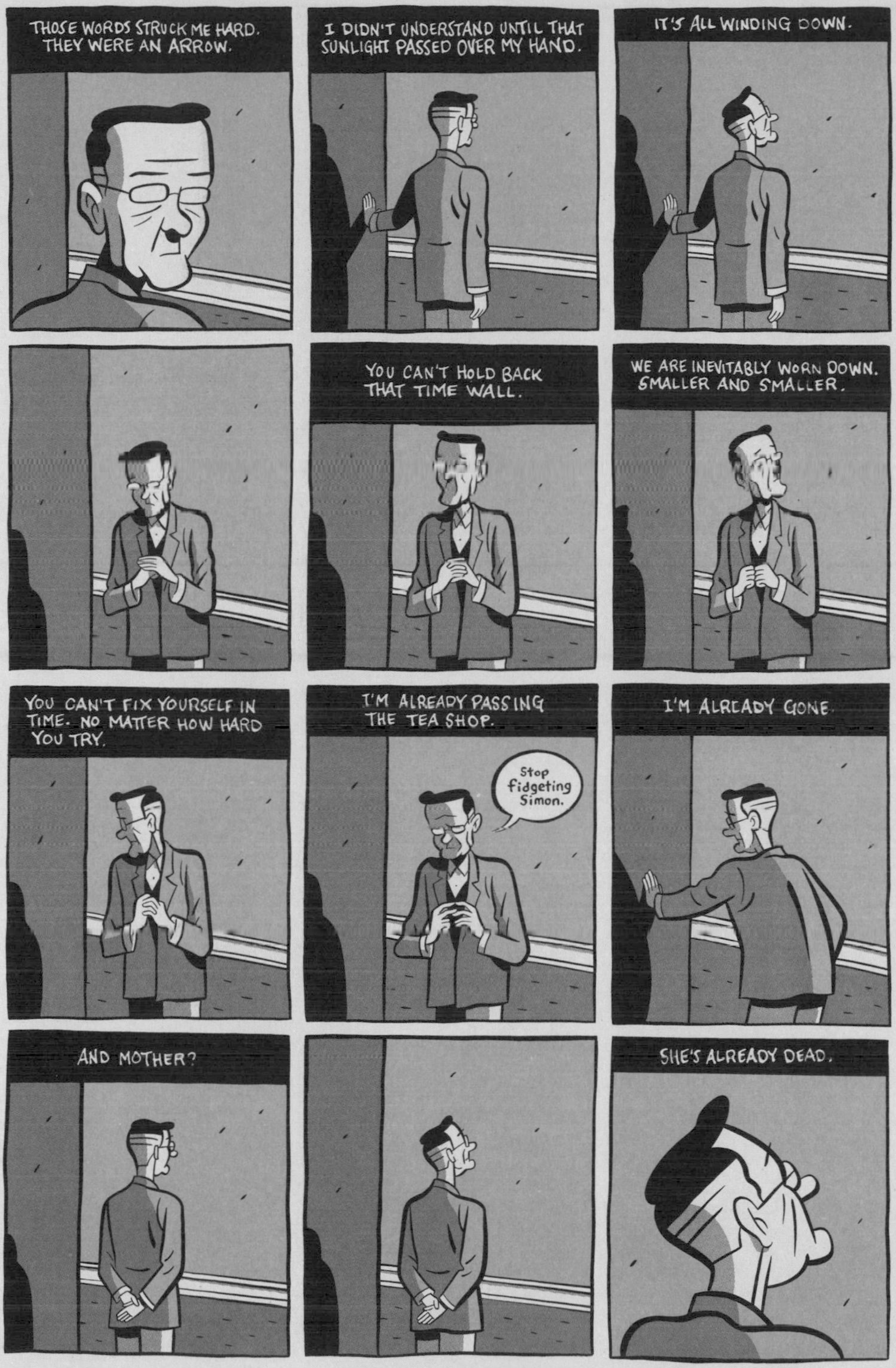
THOSE WORDS STRUCK ME HARD. THEY WERE AN ARROW.
I DIDN'T UNDERSTAND UNTIL THAT SUNLIGHT PASSED OVER MY HAND.
IT'S ALL WINDING DOWN.
YOU CAN'T HOLD BACK THAT TIME WALL.
WE ARE INEVITABLY WORN DOWN. SMALLER AND SMALLER.
YOU CAN'T FIX YOURSELF IN TIME. NO MATTER HOW HARD YOU TRY.
I'M ALREADY PASSING THE TEA SHOP.
Stop fidgeting Simon.
I'M ALREADY GONE.
AND MOTHER?
SHE'S ALREADY DEAD.

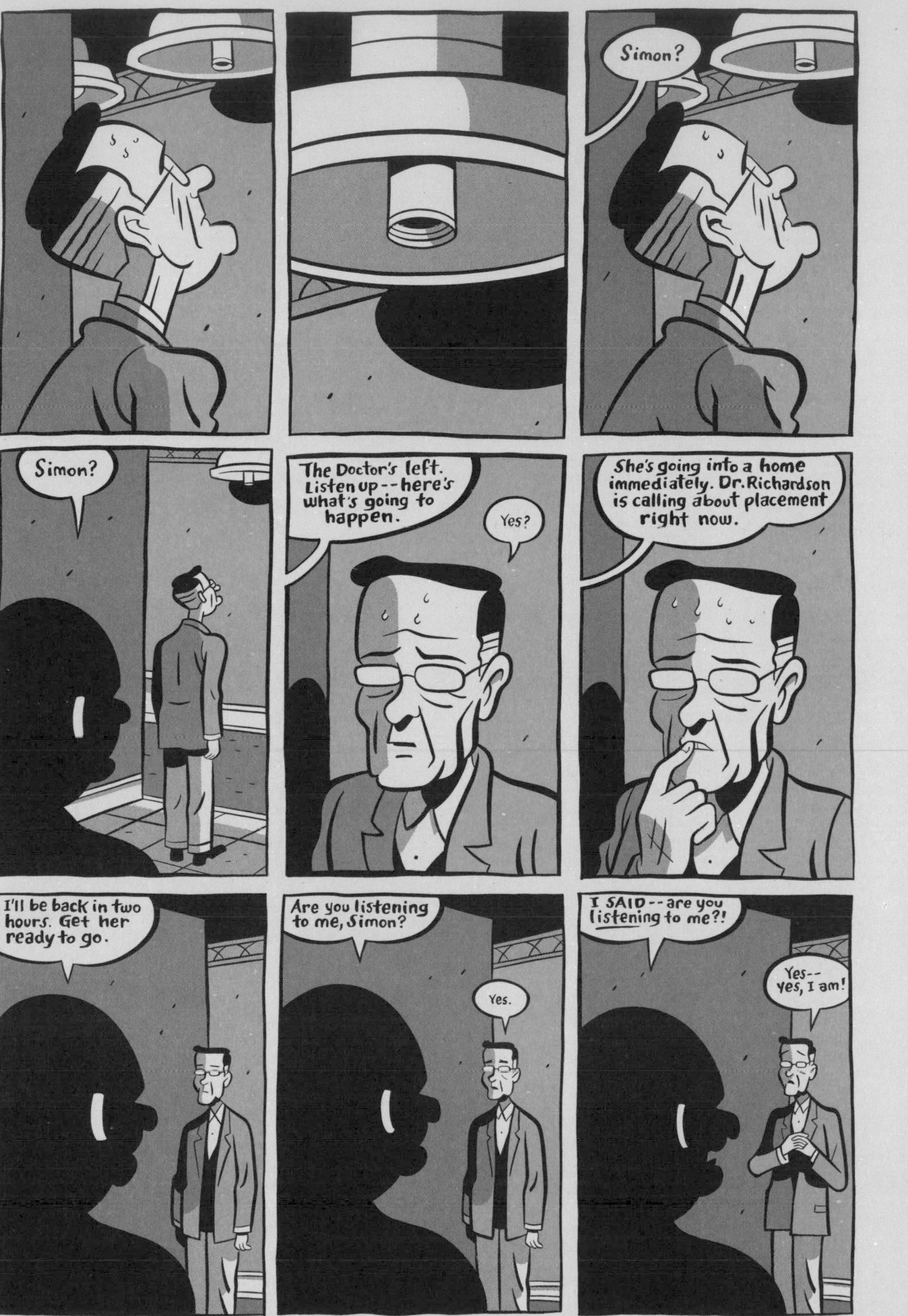
Simon?
Simon?
The Doctor's left. Listen up--here's what's going to happen.
Yes?
She's going into a home immediately. Dr. Richardson is calling about placement right now.
I'll be back in two hours. Get her ready to go.
Are you listening to me, Simon?
Yes.
I SAID--are you listening to me?!
Yes--yes, I am!

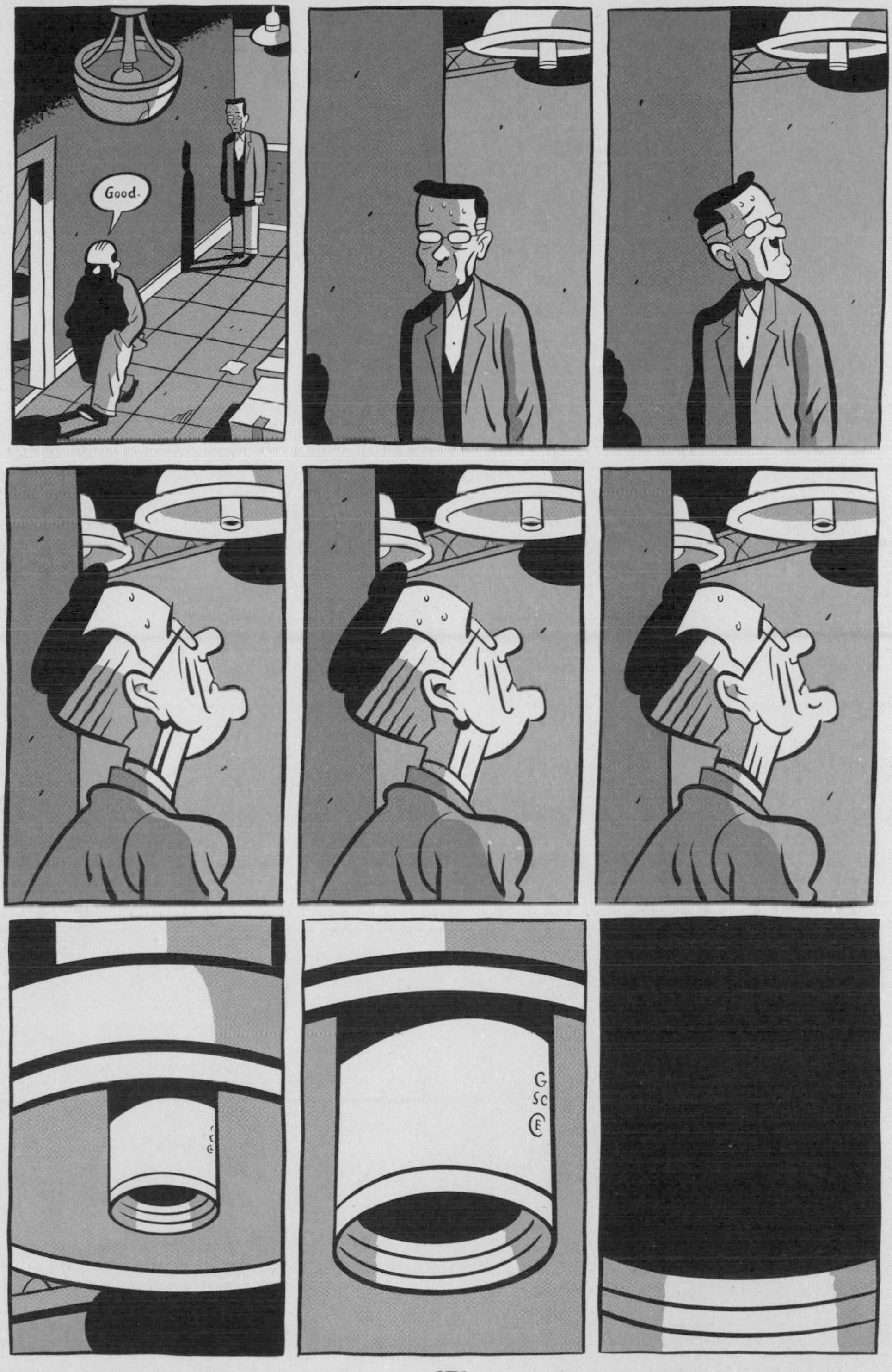
Good.

LOOK.

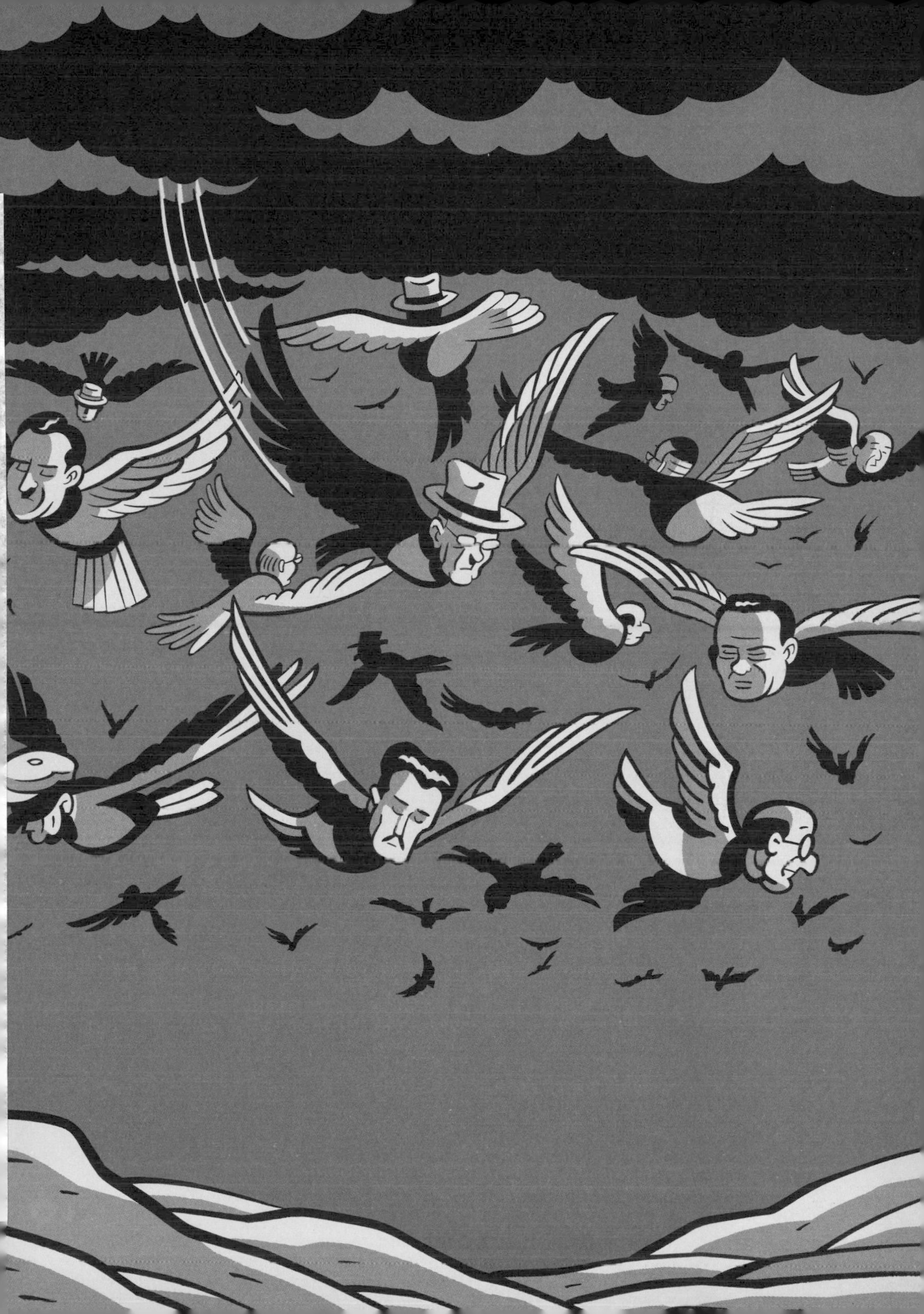

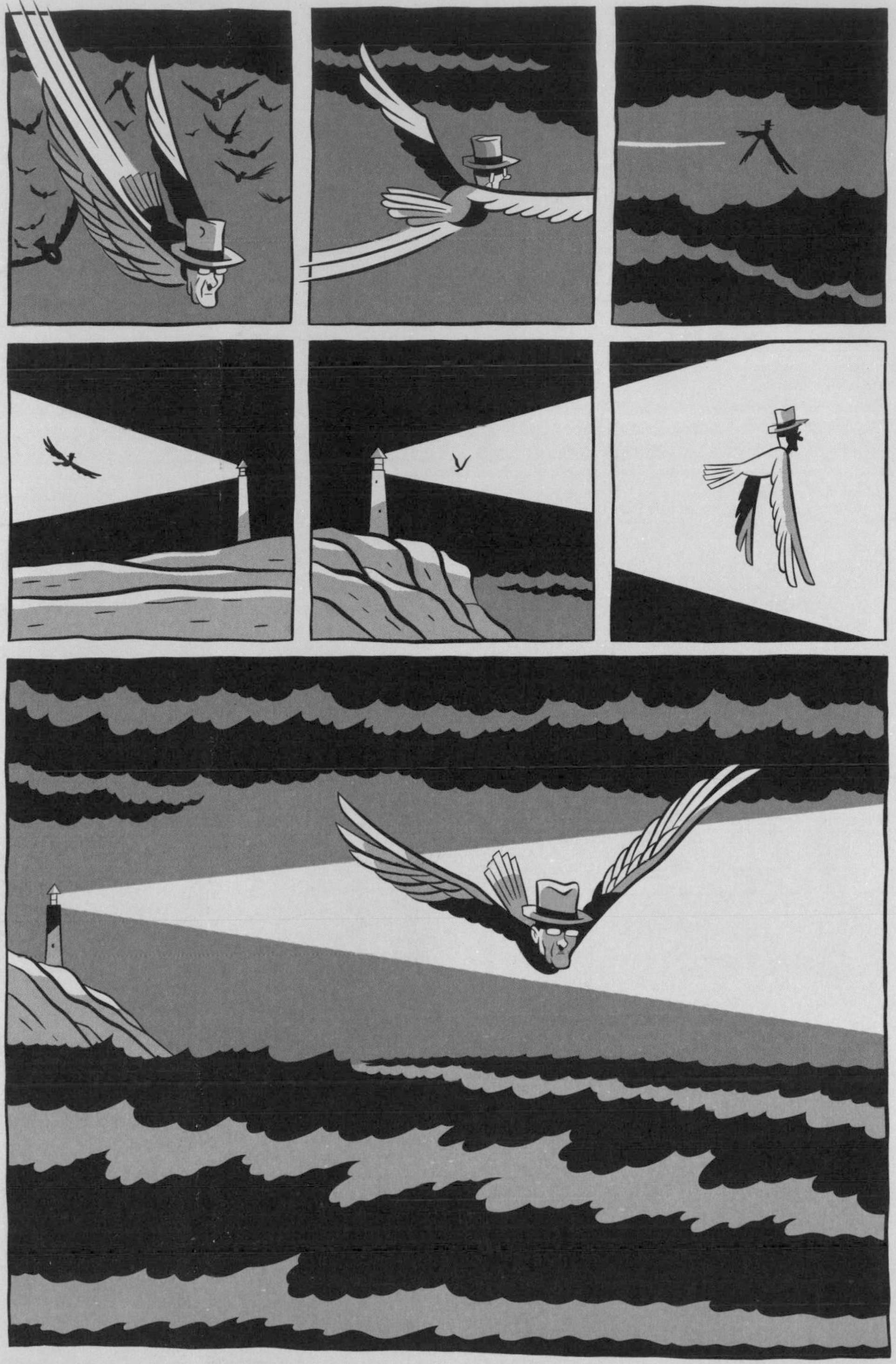

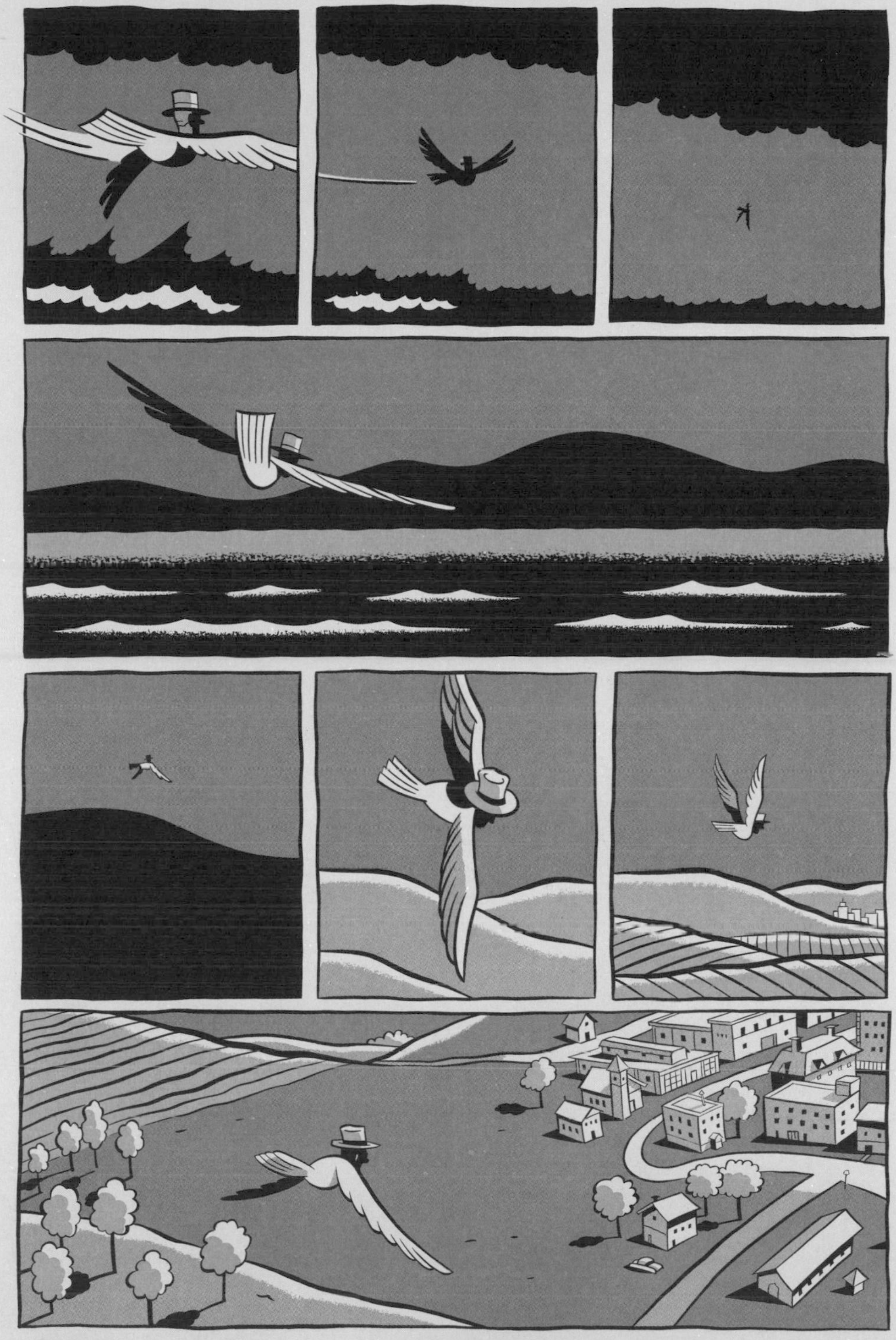

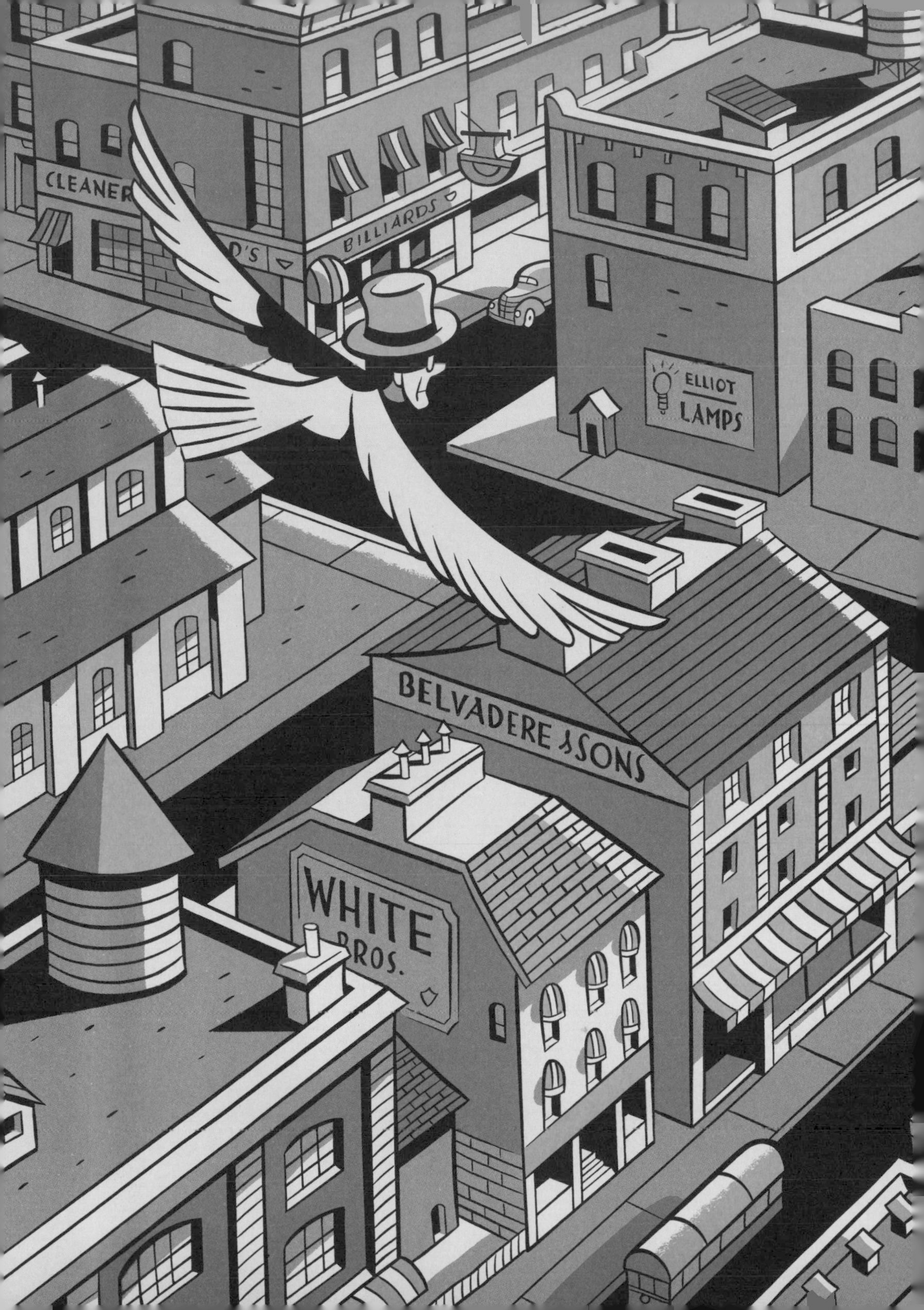
CLEANER
BILLIARDS
ELLIOT
LAMPS
BELVADERE & SONS
WHITE
BROS.

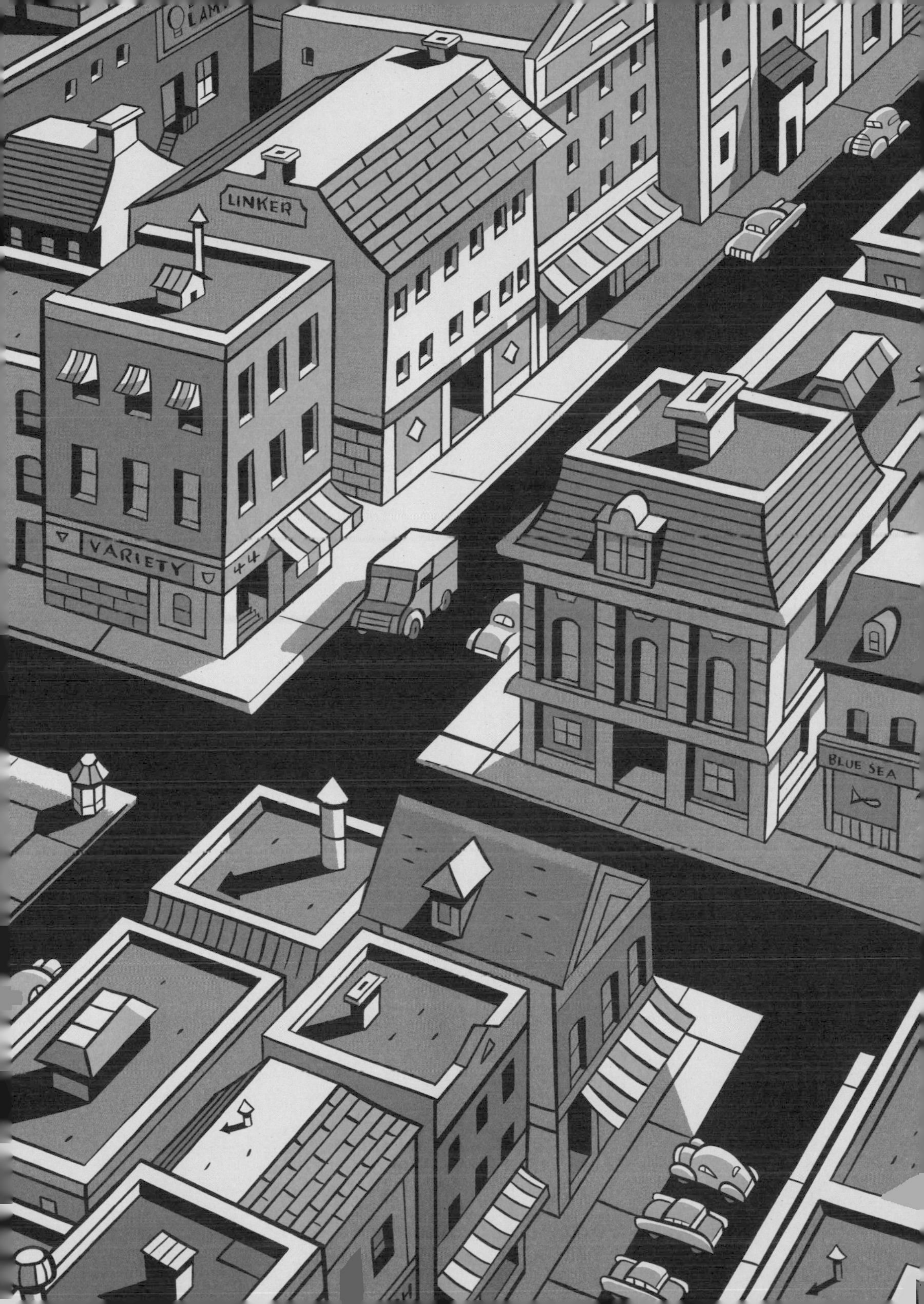
LINKER
VARIETY
44
BLUE SEA

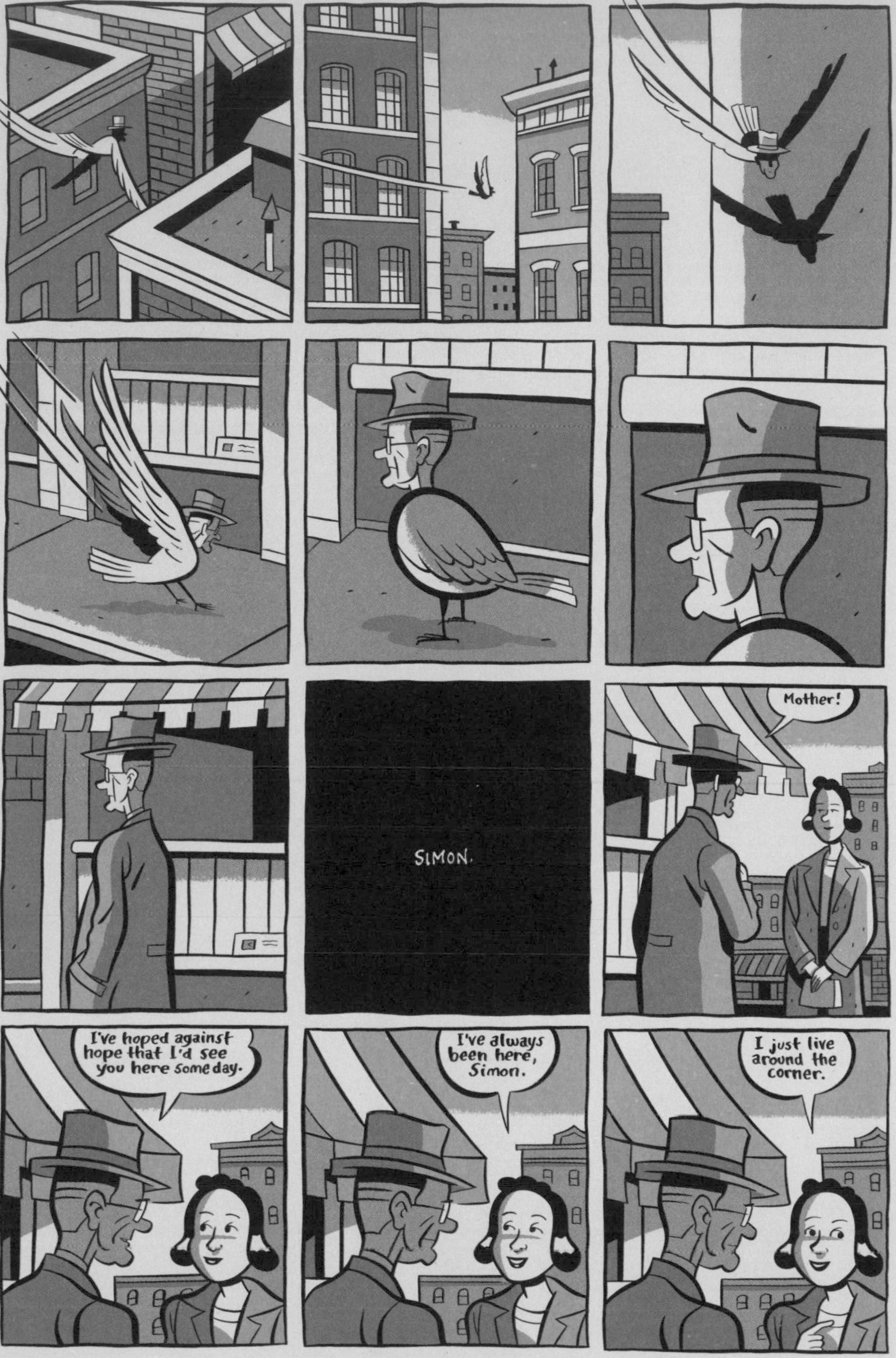
SIMON.
Mother!
I've hoped against hope that I'd see you here some day.
I've always been here, Simon.
I just live around the corner.

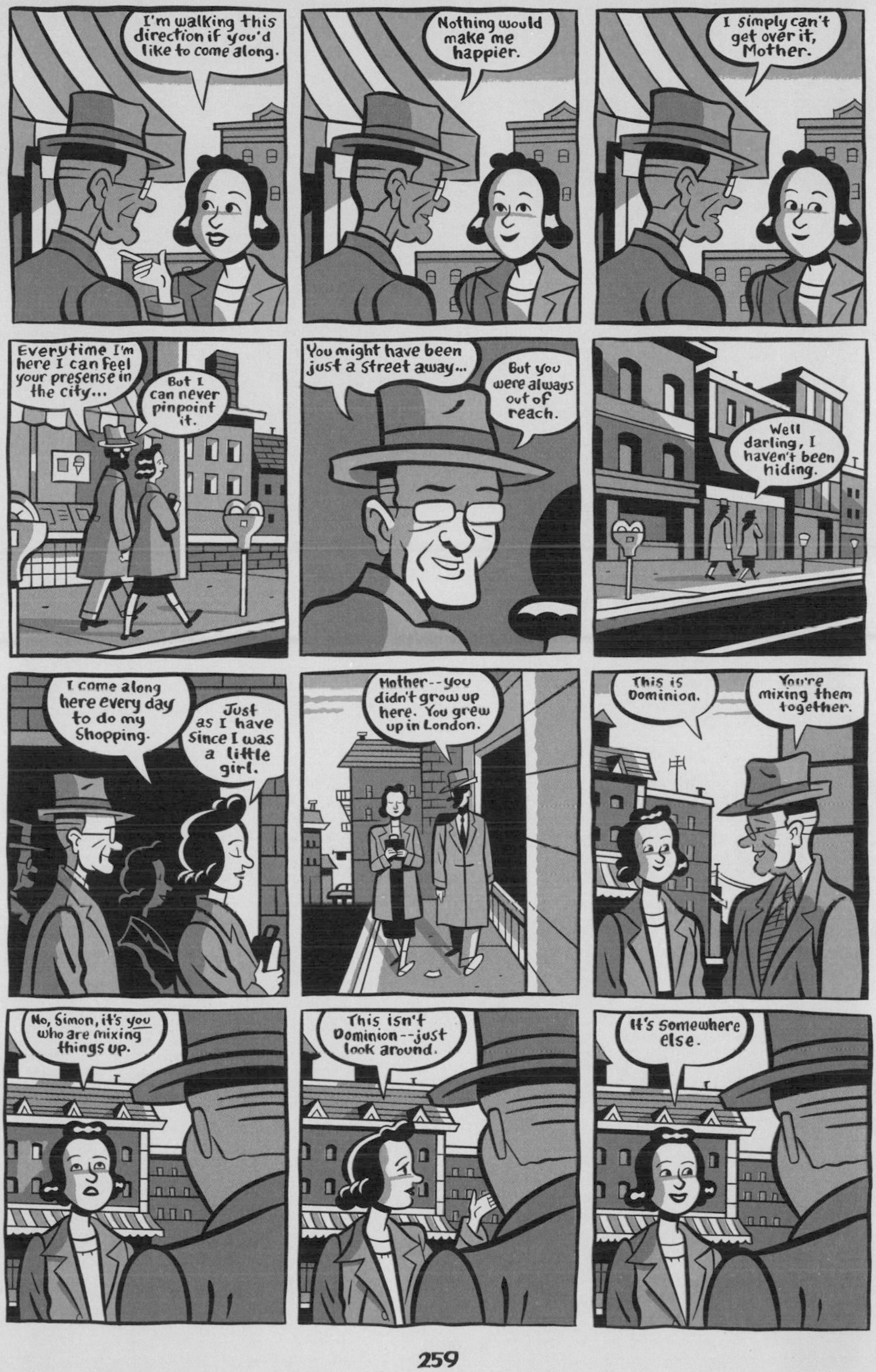

I'm walking this direction if you'd like to come along.
Nothing would make me happier.
I simply can't get over it, Mother.
Everytime I'm here I can feel your presense in the city...
But I can never pinpoint it.
You might have been just a street away...
But you were always out of reach.
Well darling, I haven't been hiding.
I come along here every day to do my shopping.
Just as I have since I was a little girl.
Mother--you didn't grow up here. You grew up in London.
This is Dominion.
You're mixing them together.
No, Simon, it's you who are mixing things up.
This isn't Dominion--just look around.
It's somewhere else.

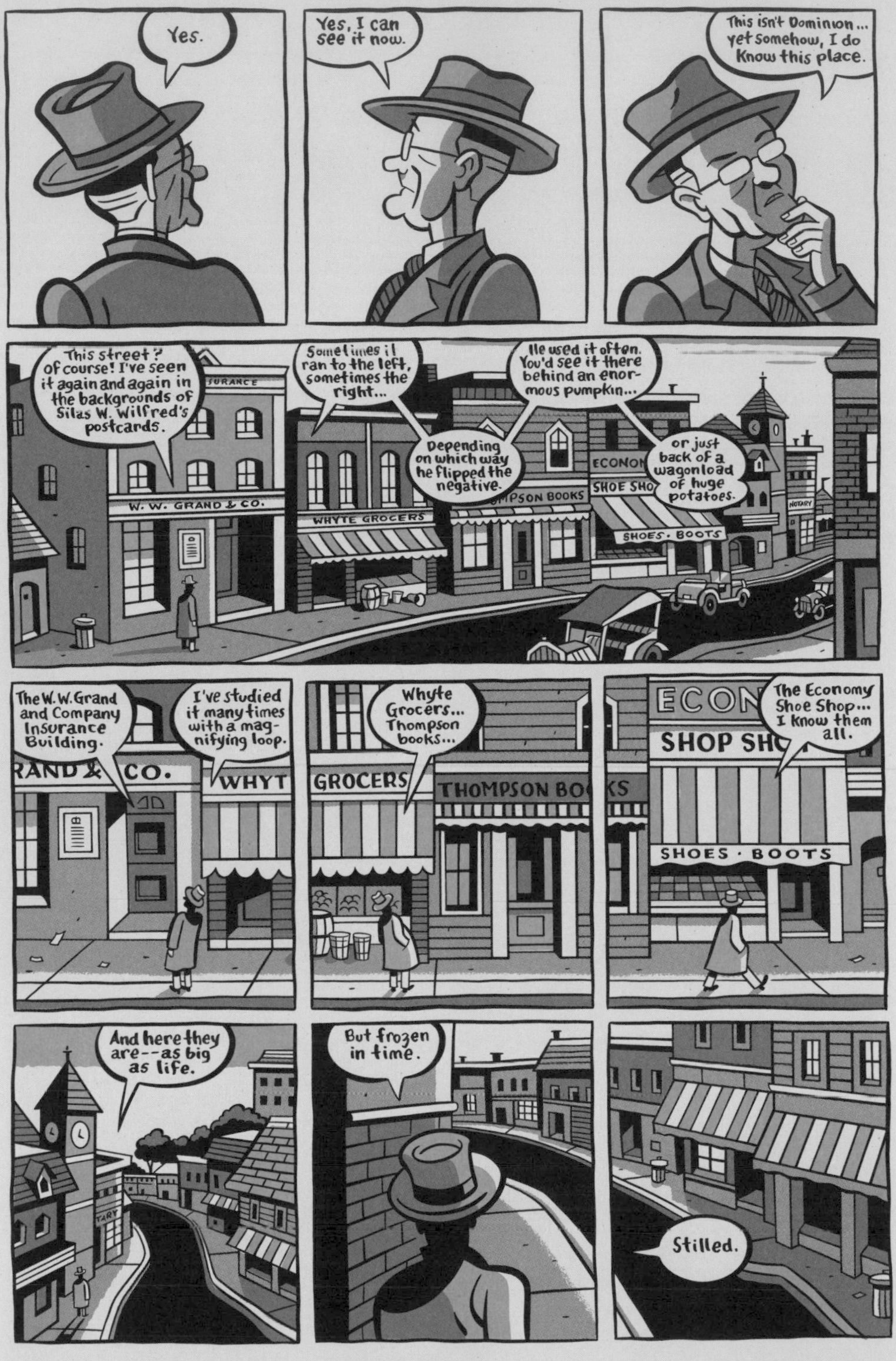
Yes.
Yes, I can see it now.
This isn't Dominion... yet somehow, I do know this place.
This street? Of course! I've seen it again and again in the backgrounds of Silas W. Wilfred's postcards.
Sometimes it ran to the left, sometimes the right...
Depending on which way he flipped the negative.
He used it often. You'd see it there behind an enormous pumpkin...
or just back of a wagonload of huge potatoes.
W. W. GRAND & CO.
WHYTE GROCERS
THOMPSON BOOKS
ECONOM
SHOE SHO
SHOES · BOOTS
NOTARY
The W. W. Grand and Company Insurance Building.
I've studied it many times with a magnifying loop.
Whyte Grocers... Thompson books...
The Economy Shoe Shop... I know them all.
SHOP SHO
And here they are--as big as life.
But frozen in time.
Stilled.

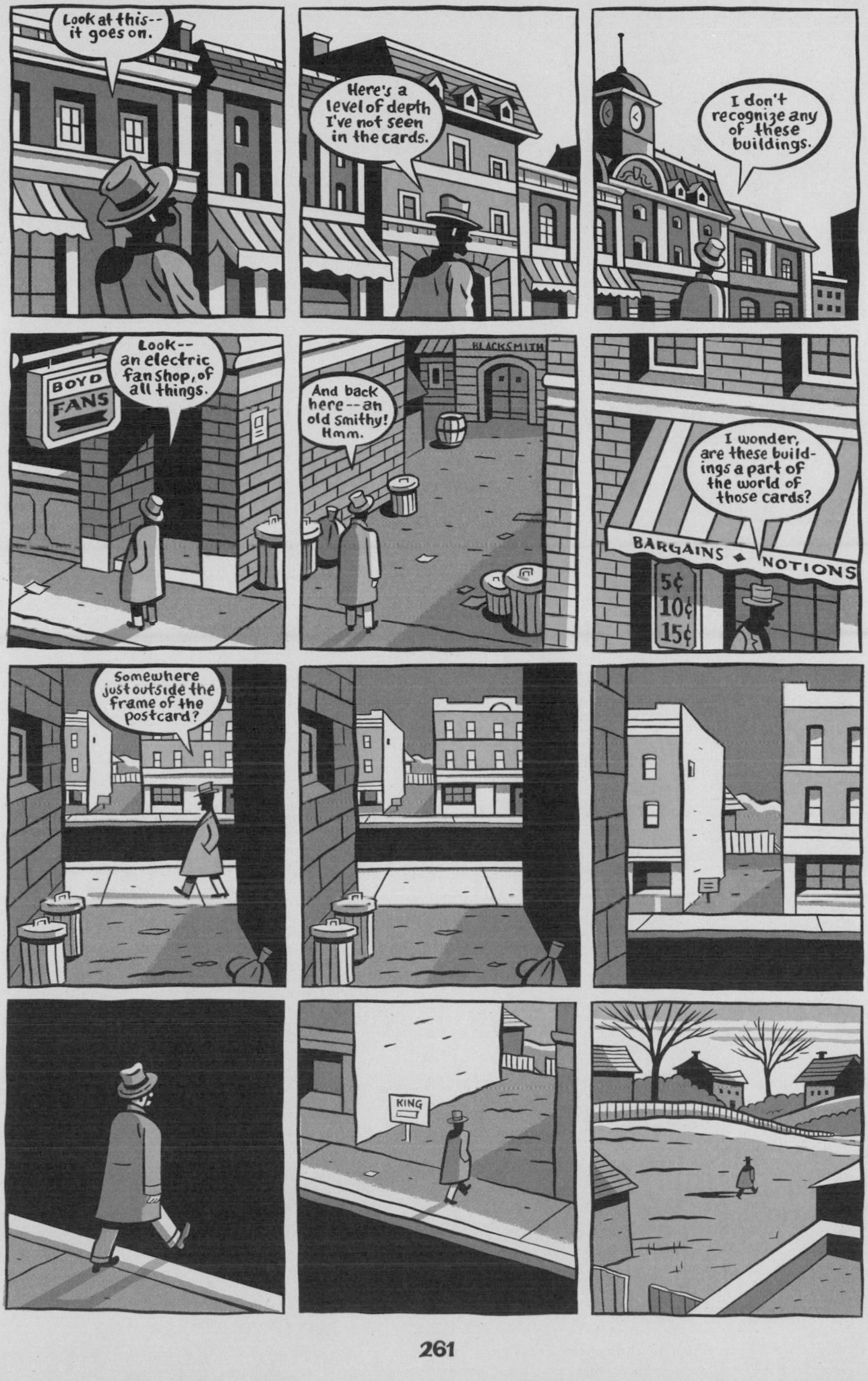
Look at this--
it goes on.
Here's a level of depth I've not seen in the cards.
I don't recognize any of these buildings.
BOYD
FANS
Look-- an electric fan shop, of all things.
BLACKSMITH
And back here--an old smithy! Hmm.
I wonder, are these buildings a part of the world of those cards?
BARGAINS ◆ NOTIONS
5¢
10¢
15¢
Somewhere just outside the frame of the postcard?
KING

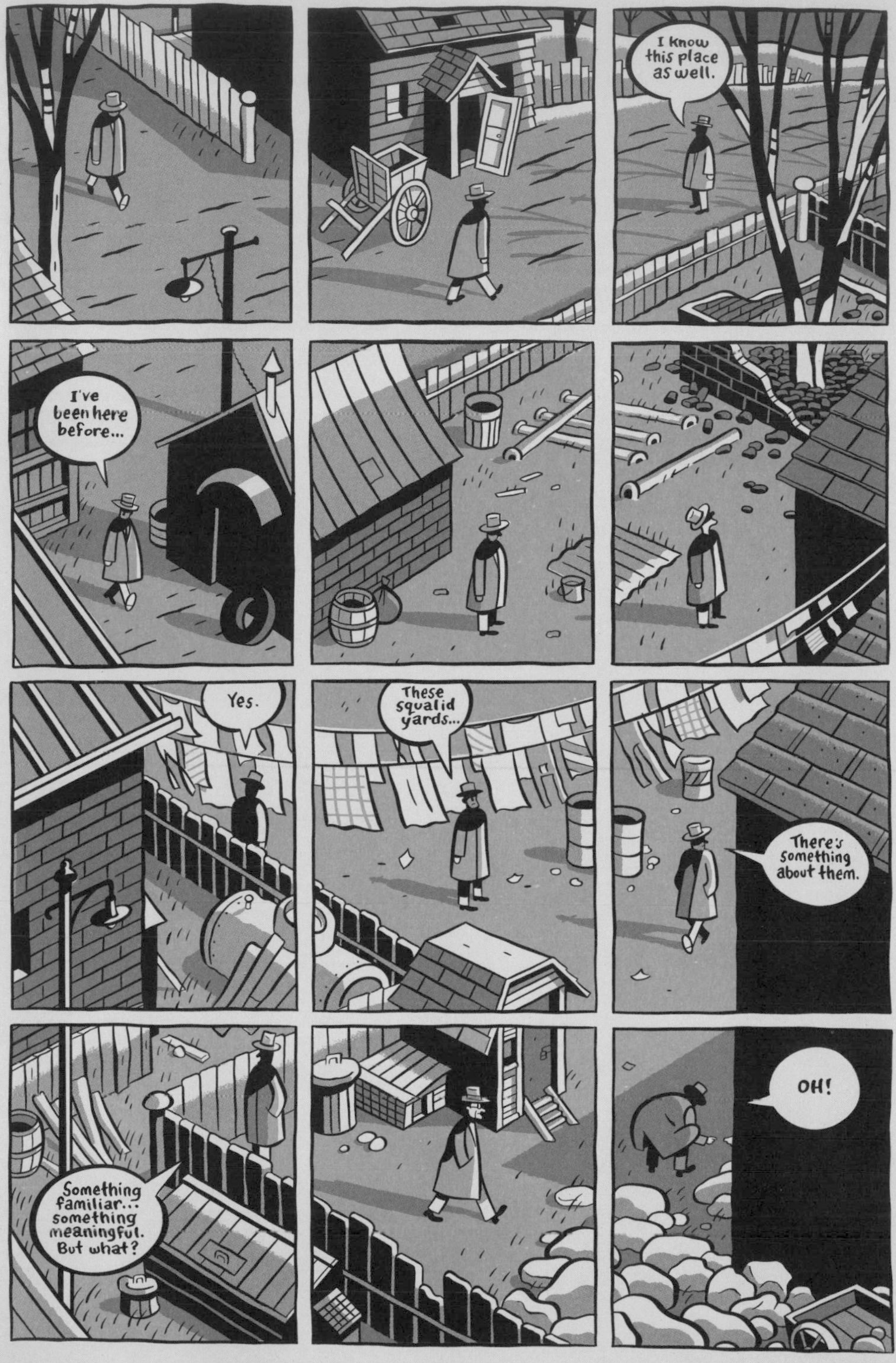
I know this place as well.
I've been here before...
Yes.
These squalid yards...
There's something about them.
Something familiar... something meaningful. But what?
OH!

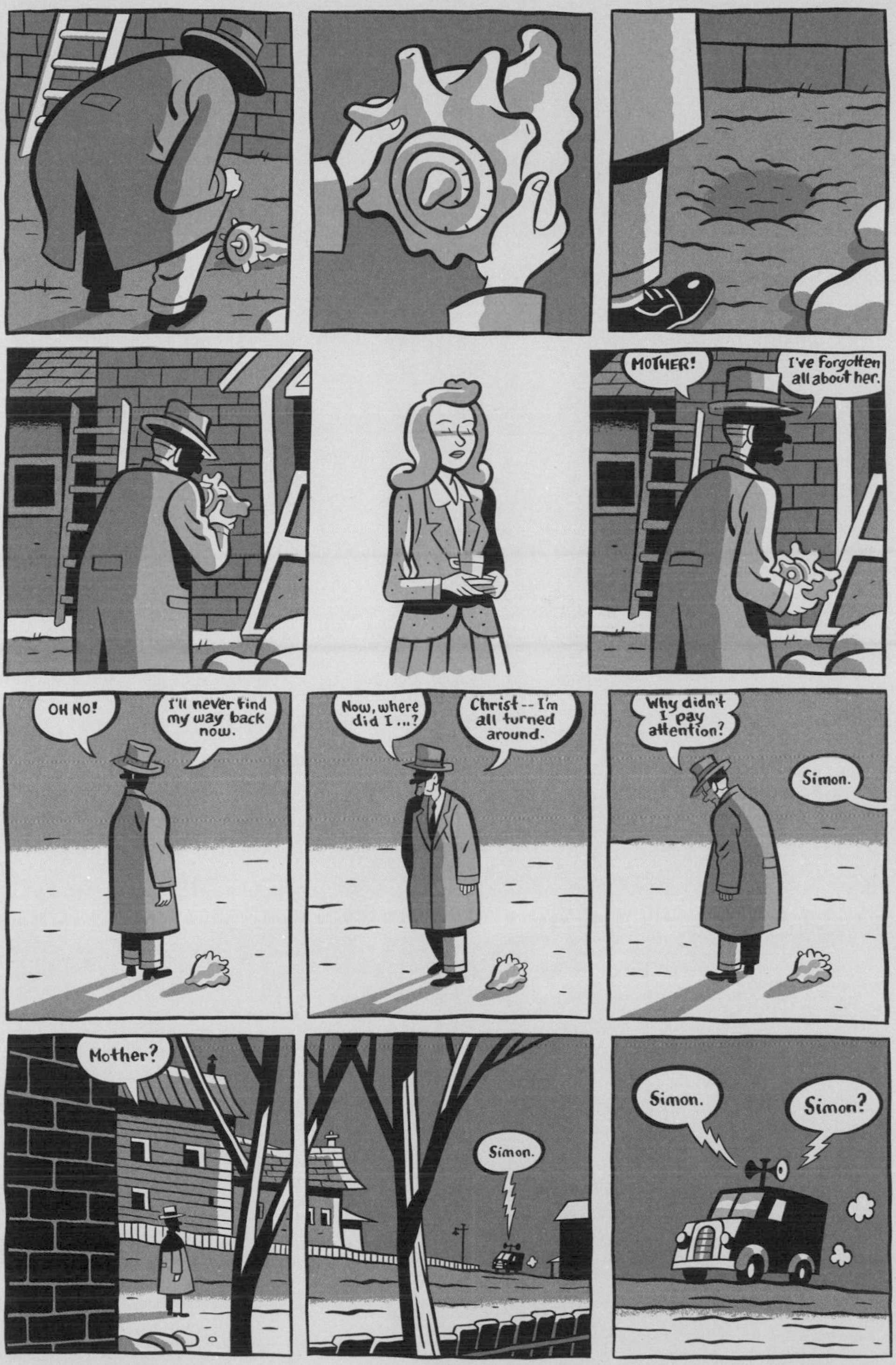
MOTHER!
I've Forgotten all about her.
OH NO!
I'll never find my way back now.
Now, where did I...?
Christ -- I'm all turned around.
Why didn't I pay attention?
Simon.
Mother?
Simon.
Simon.
Simon?

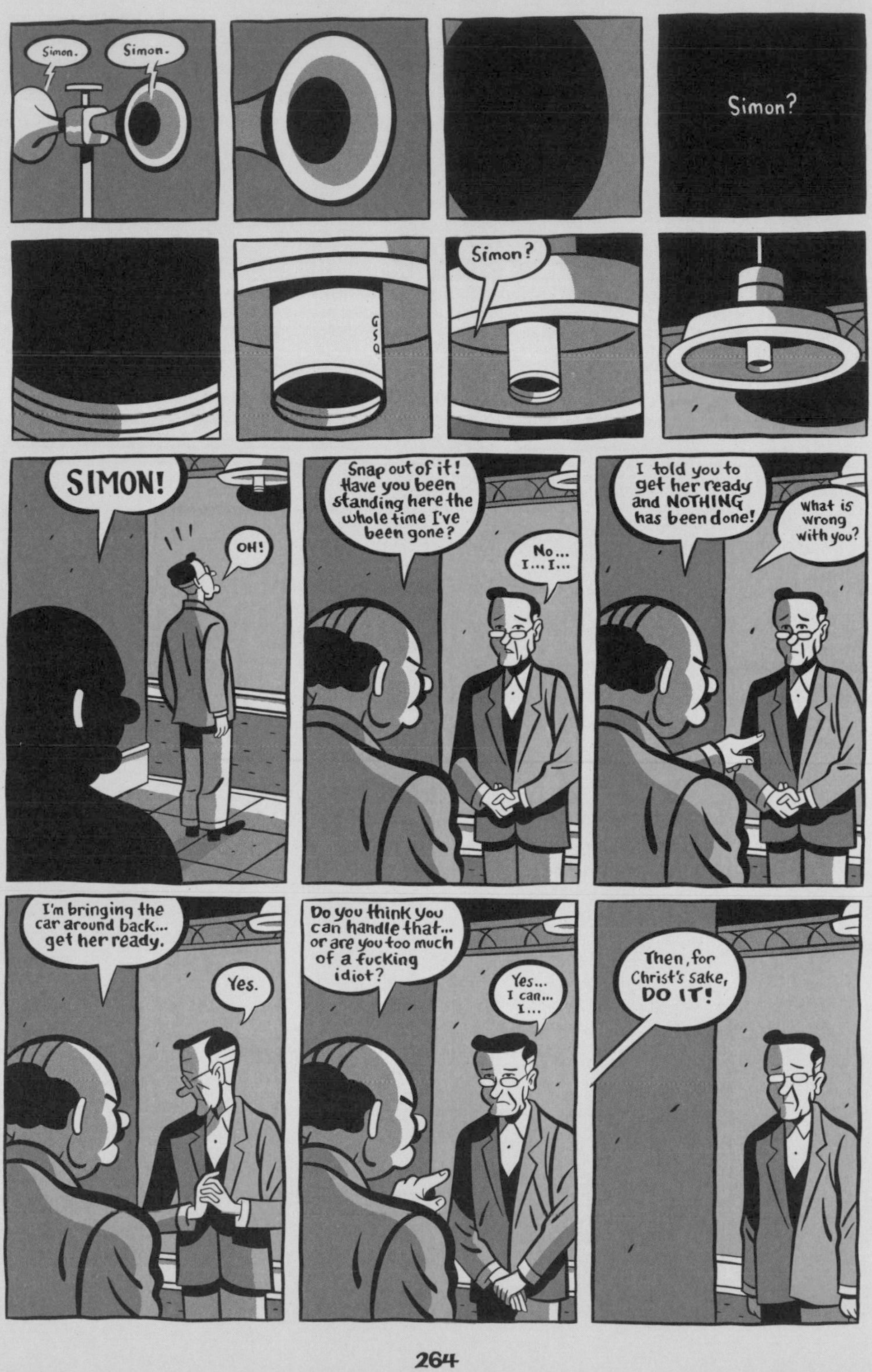
Simon.
Simon.
Simon?
Simon?
SIMON!
OH!
Snap out of it! Have you been standing here the whole time I've been gone?
No... I... I...
I told you to get her ready and NOTHING has been done!
What is wrong with you?
I'm bringing the car around back... get her ready.
Yes.
Do you think you can handle that... or are you too much of a fucking idiot?
Yes... I can... I...
Then, for Christ's sake, DO IT!

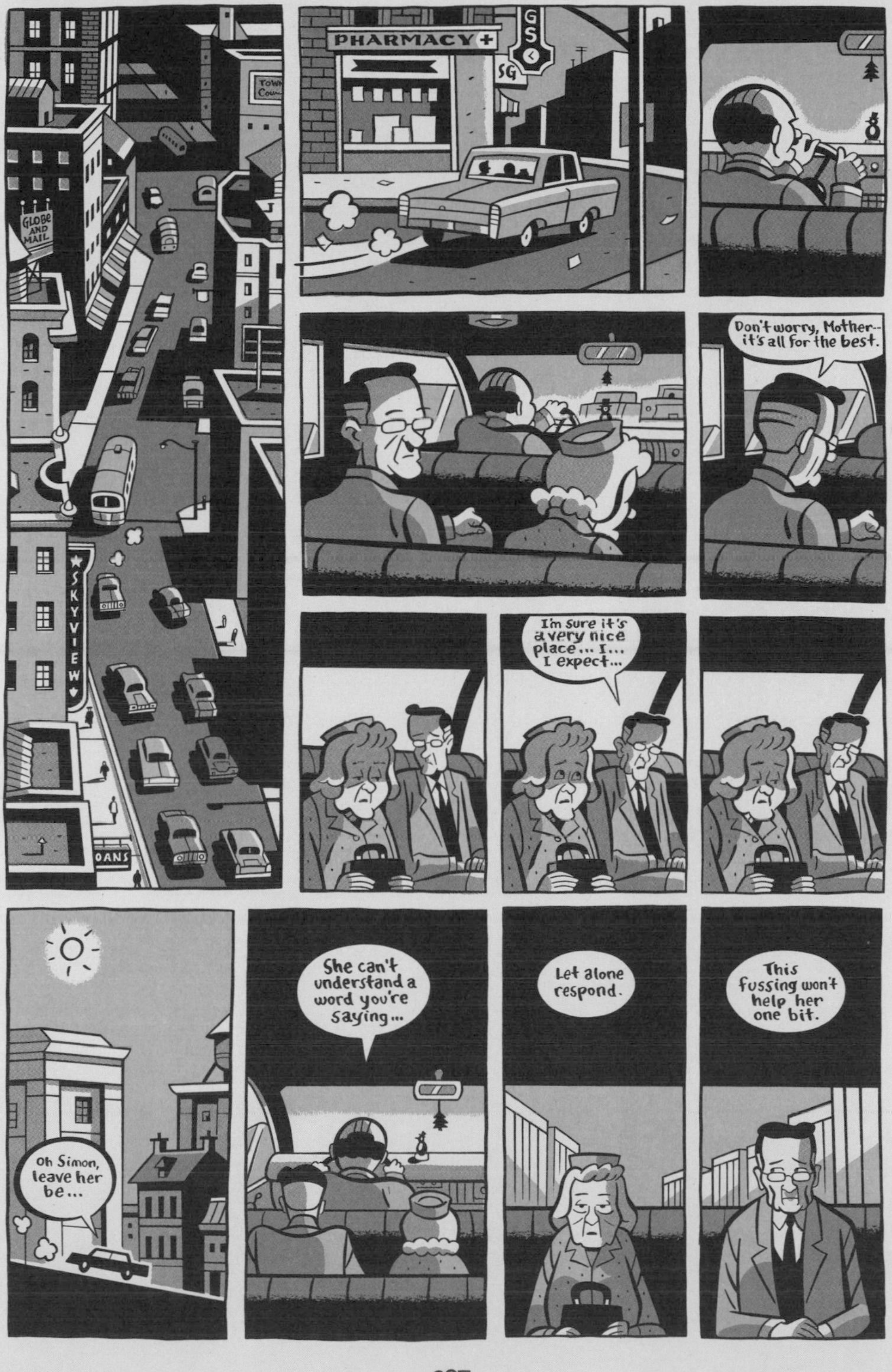

GLOBE AND MAIL
PHARMACY
SKYVIEW
OANS
Don't worry, Mother-- it's all for the best.
I'm sure it's a very nice place... I... I expect...
Oh Simon, leave her be...
She can't understand a word you're saying...
Let alone respond.
This fussing won't help her one bit.

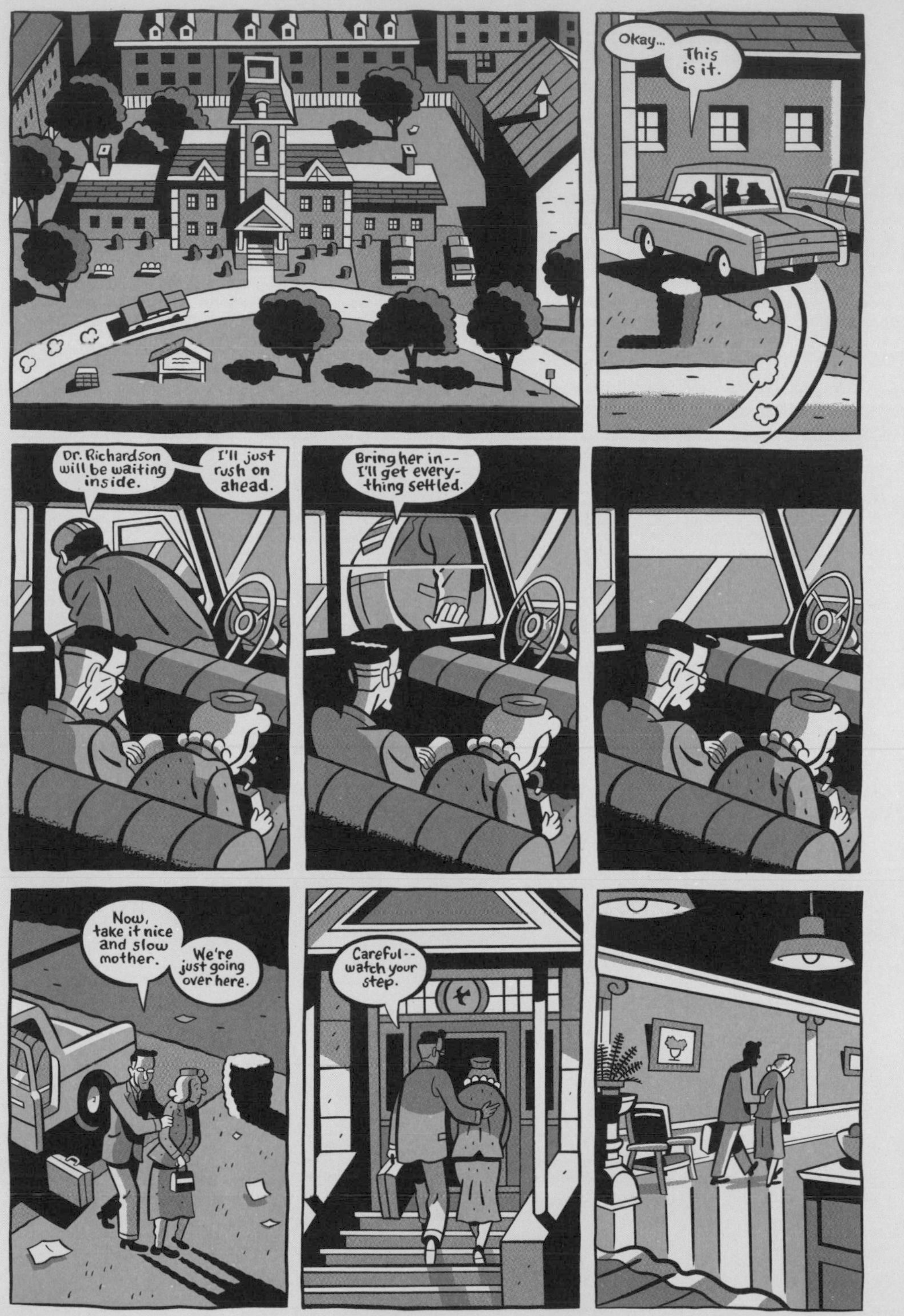
Okay...
This is it.
Dr. Richardson will be waiting inside.
I'll just rush on ahead.
Bring her in-- I'll get every-thing settled.
Now, take it nice and slow mother.
We're just going over here.
Careful-- watch your step.

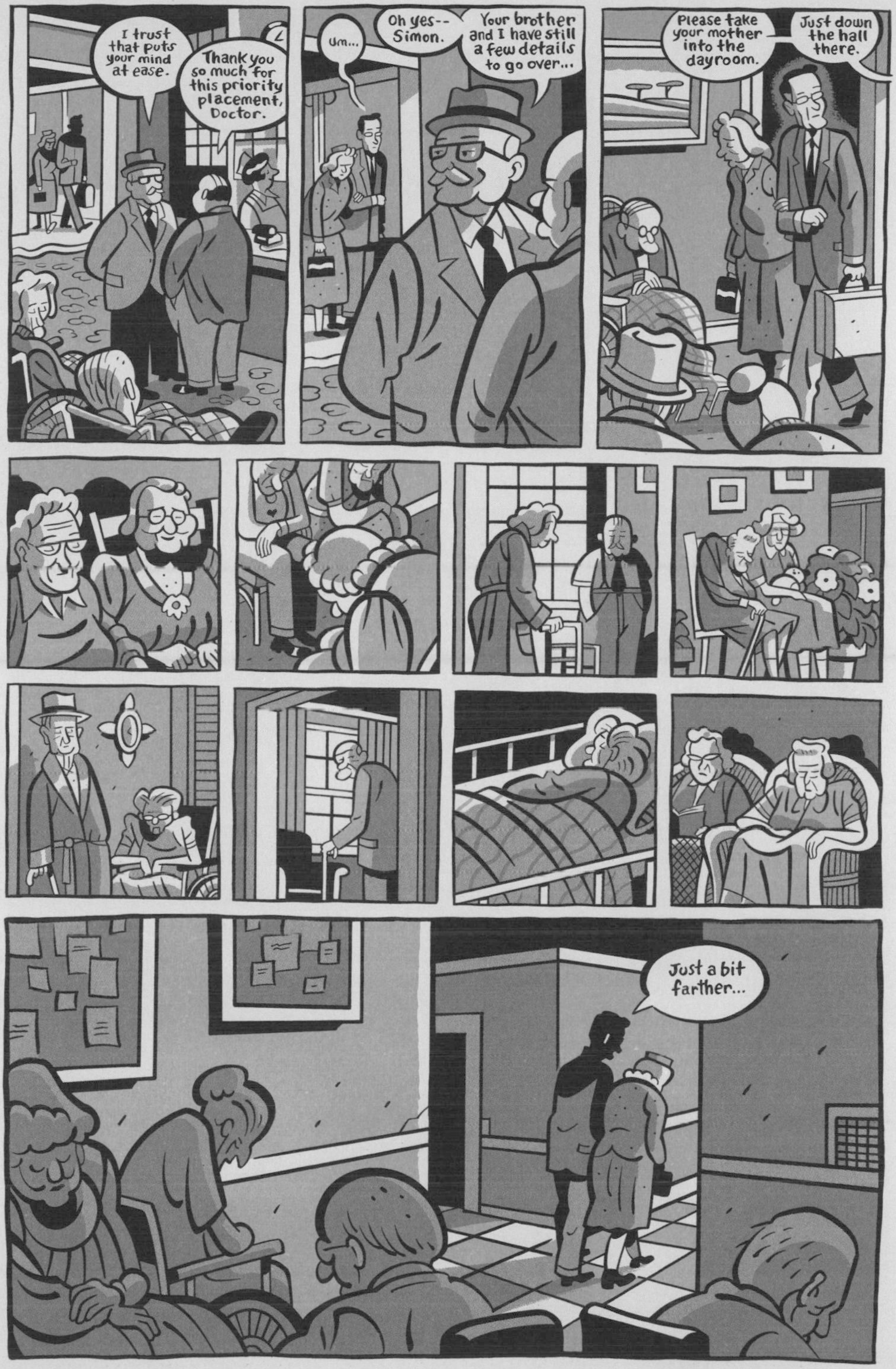
I trust that puts your mind at ease.
Thank you so much for this priority placement, Doctor.
Um...
Oh yes-- Simon.
Your brother and I have still a few details to go over...
Please take your mother into the dayroom.
Just down the hall there.
Just a bit farther...

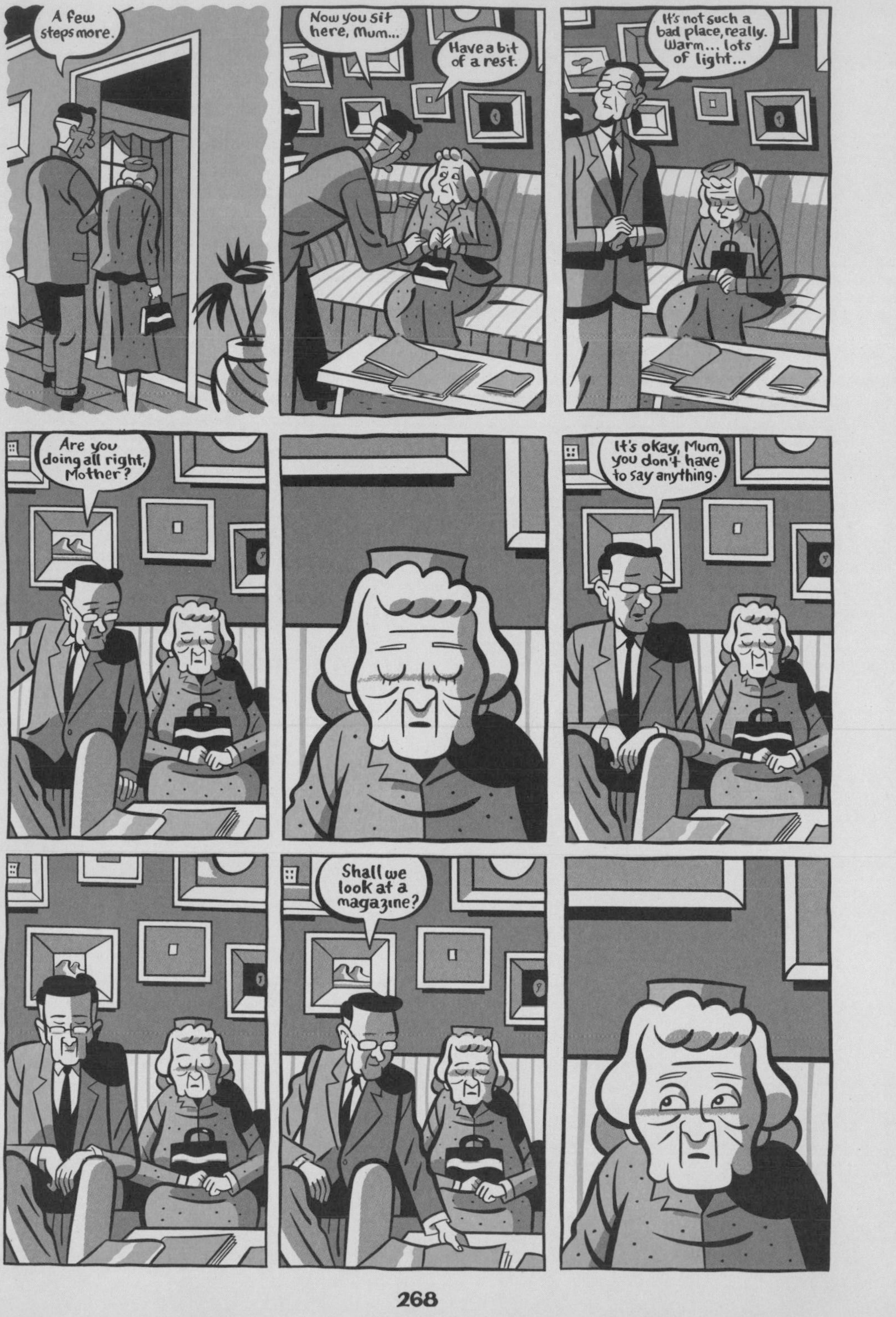
A few steps more.
Now you sit here, Mum...
Have a bit of a rest.
It's not such a bad place, really. Warm... lots of light...
Are you doing all right, Mother?
It's okay, Mum, you don't have to say anything.
Shall we look at a magazine?

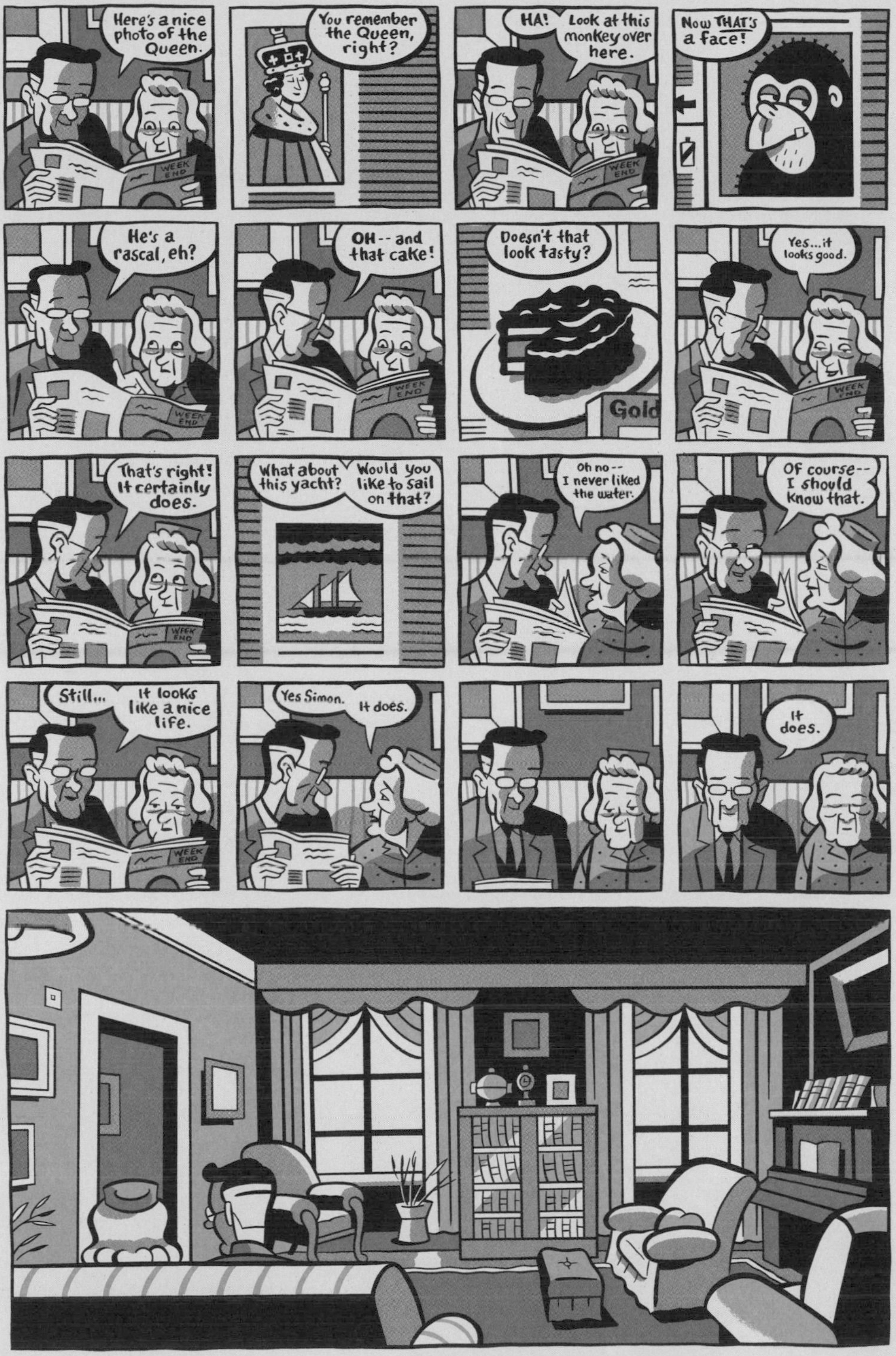
Here's a nice photo of the Queen.
WEEK END
You remember the Queen, right?
HA!
Look at this monkey over here.
WEEK END
Now THAT'S a face!
He's a rascal, eh?
WEEK END
OH -- and that cake!
WEEK END
Doesn't that look tasty?
Gold
Yes... it looks good.
WEEK END
That's right! It certainly does.
WEEK END
What about this yacht?
Would you like to sail on that?
Oh no -- I never liked the water.
Of course -- I should know that.
Still...
It looks like a nice life.
WEEK END
Yes Simon.
It does.
It does.

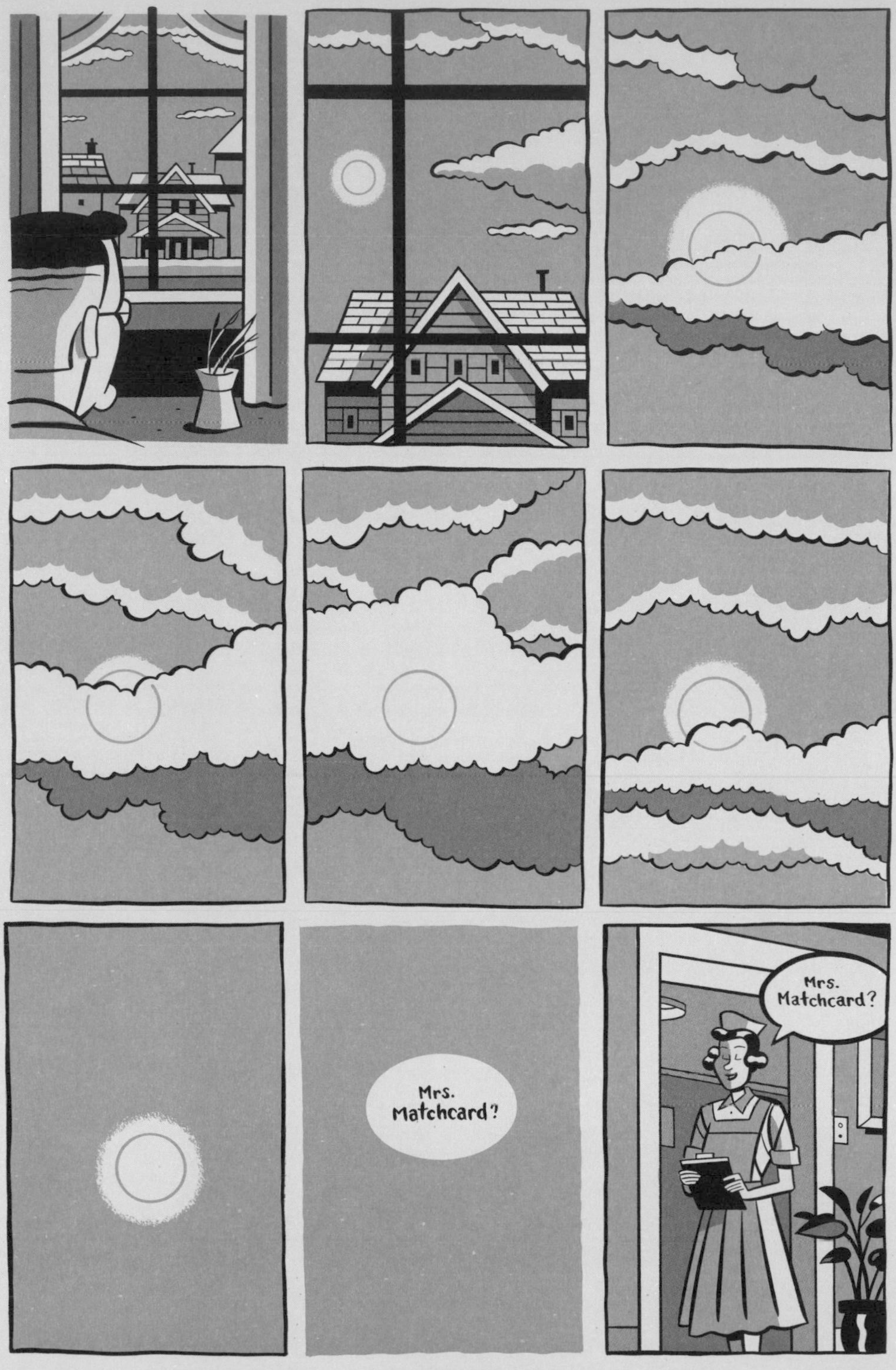
Mrs.
Matchcard?
Mrs.
Matchcard?

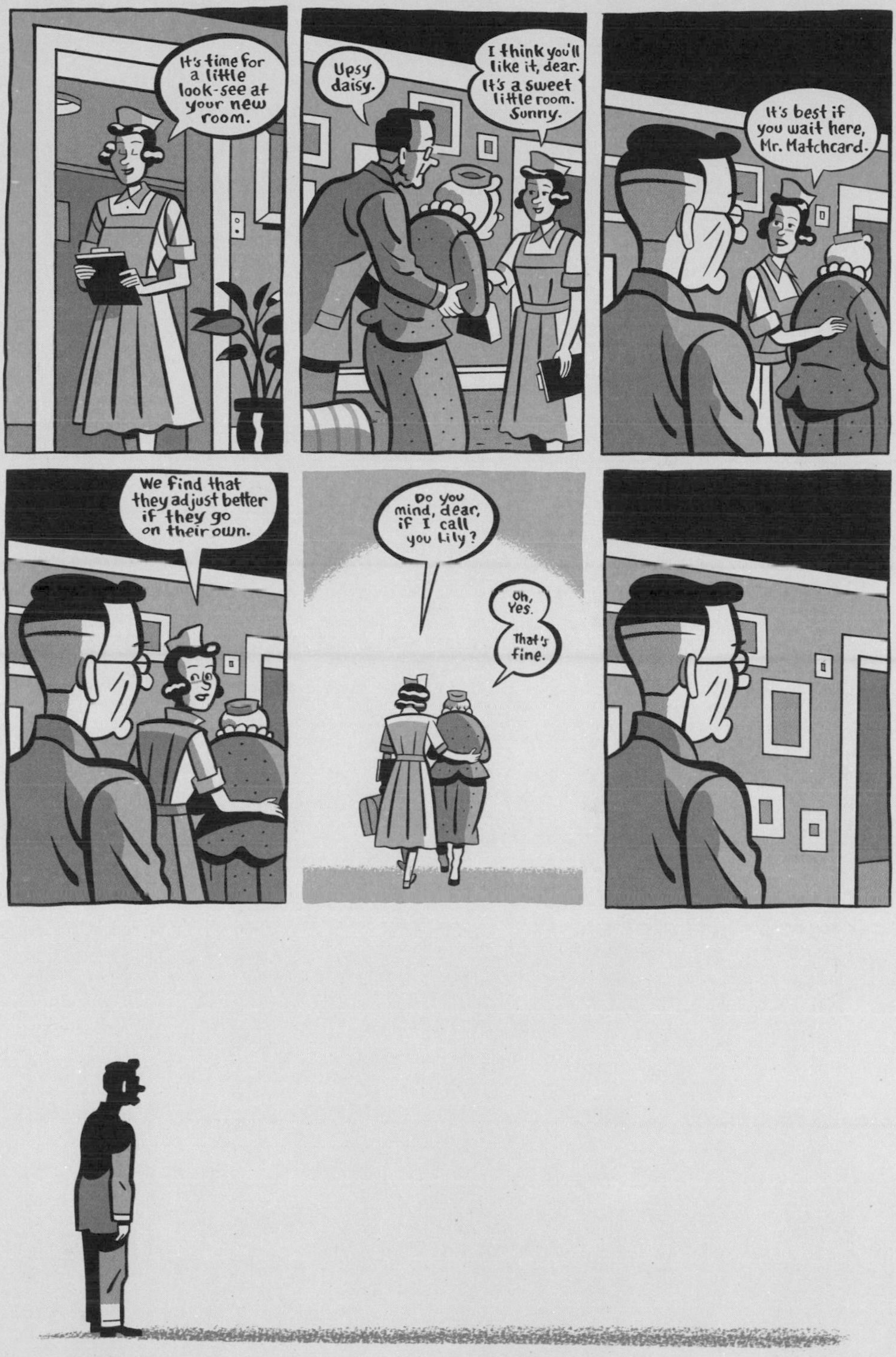
It's time for a little look-see at your new room.
Upsy daisy.
I think you'll like it, dear. It's a sweet little room. Sunny.
It's best if you wait here, Mr. Matchcard.
We find that they adjust better if they go on their own.
Do you mind, dear, if I call you Lily?
Oh, Yes.
That's fine.

UP
MY LITTLE
BOY...

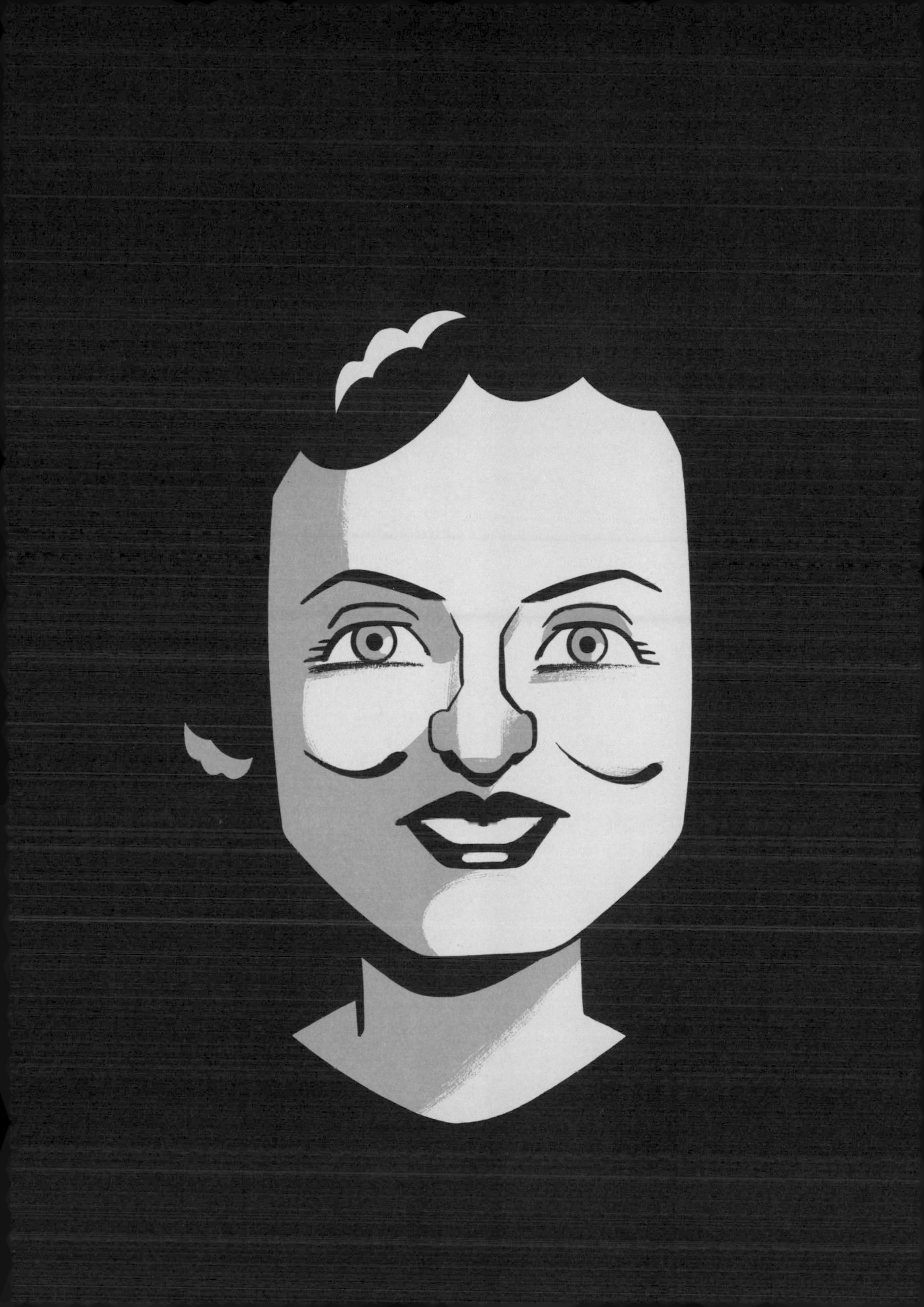

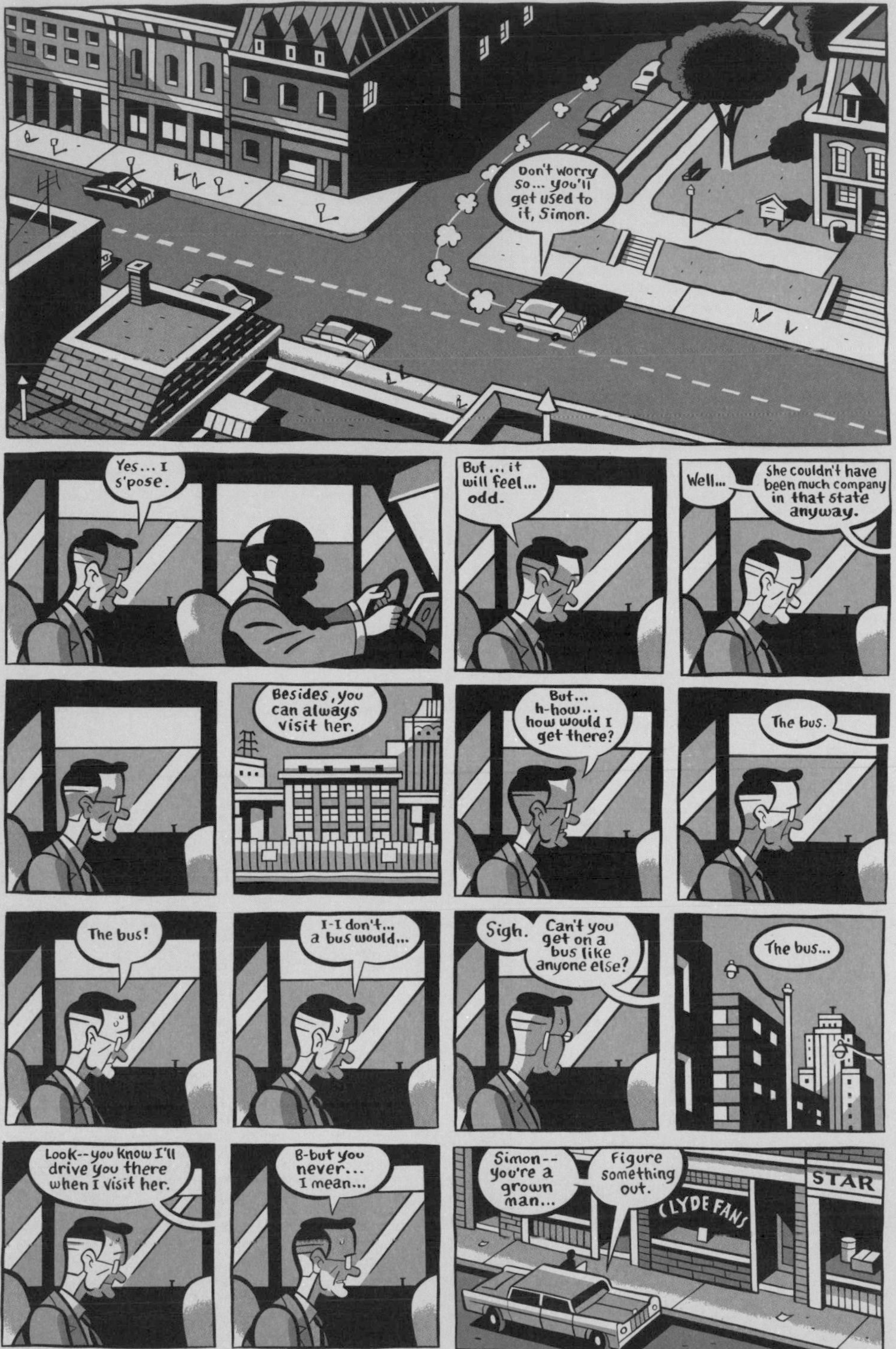
Don't worry so... you'll get used to it, Simon.
Yes... I s'pose.
But... it will feel... odd.
Well...
She couldn't have been much company in that state anyway.
Besides, you can always visit her.
But... h-how... how would I get there?
The bus.
The bus!
I-I don't... a bus would...
Sigh.
Can't you get on a bus like anyone else?
The bus...
Look--you know I'll drive you there when I visit her.
B-but you never... I mean...
Simon-- you're a grown man...
Figure something out.
CLYDE FANS
STAR

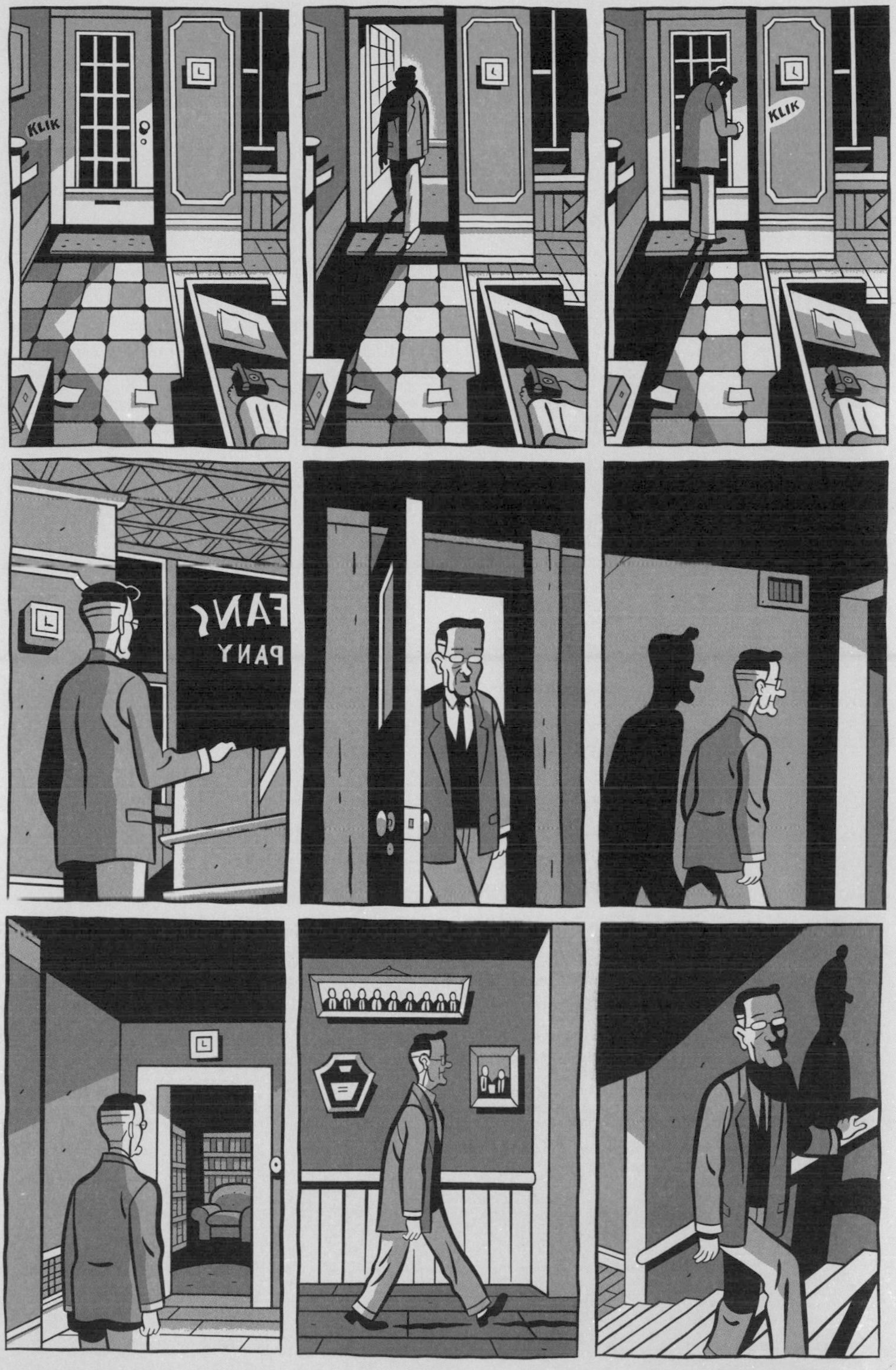
KLIK
KLIK

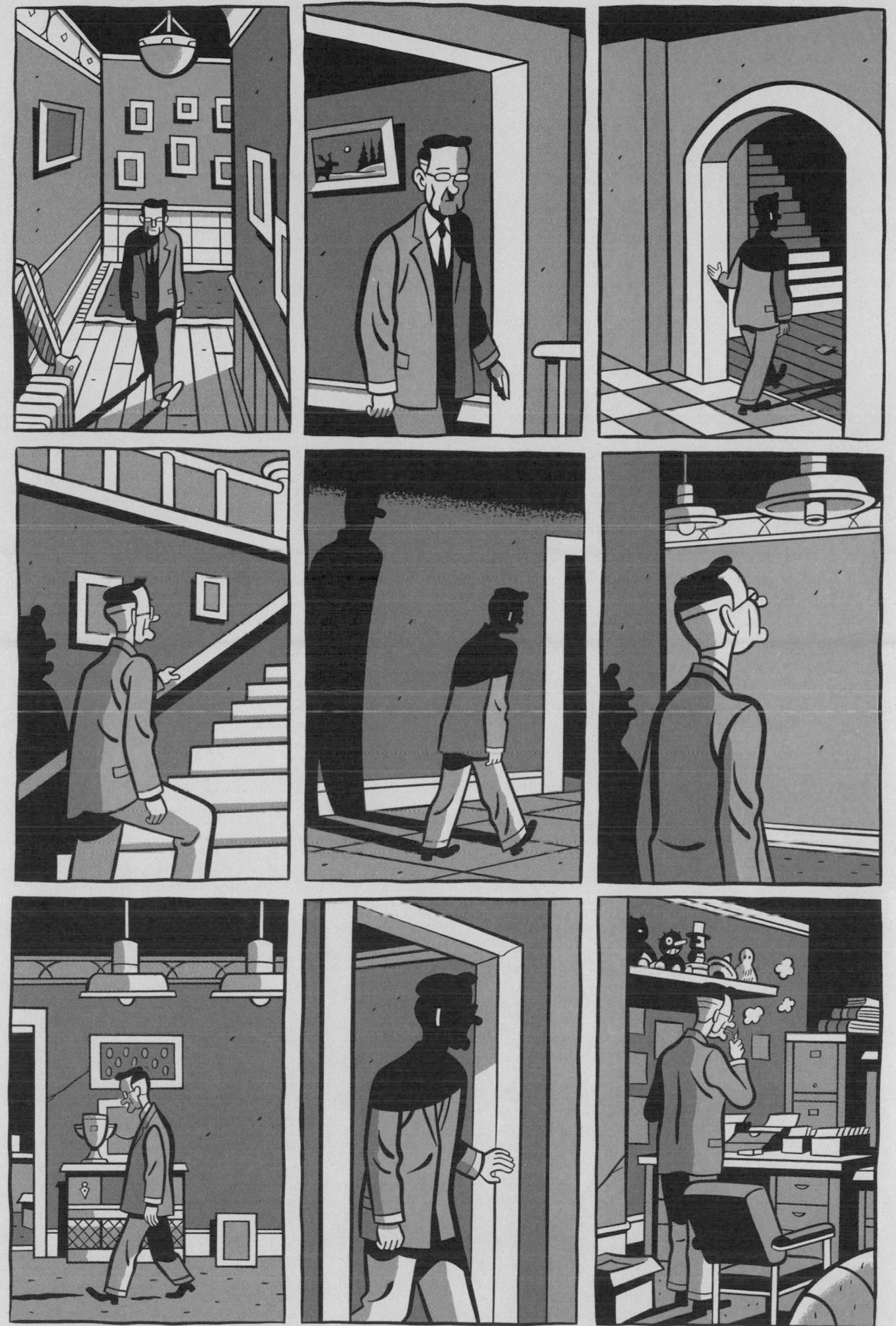

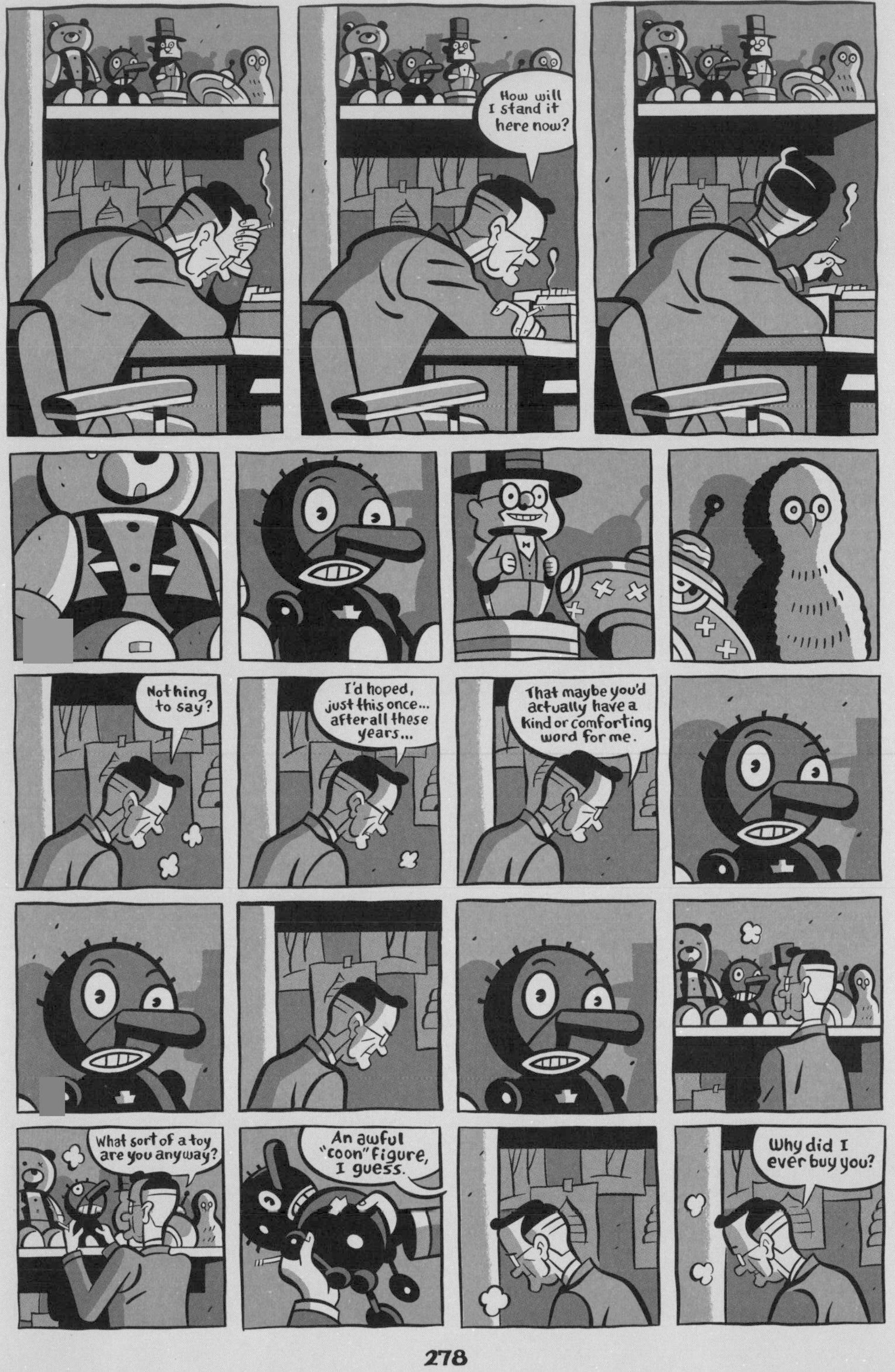
How will I stand it here now?
Nothing to say?
I'd hoped, just this once... after all these years...
That maybe you'd actually have a kind or comforting word for me.
What sort of a toy are you anyway?
An awful "coon" figure, I guess.
Why did I ever buy you?

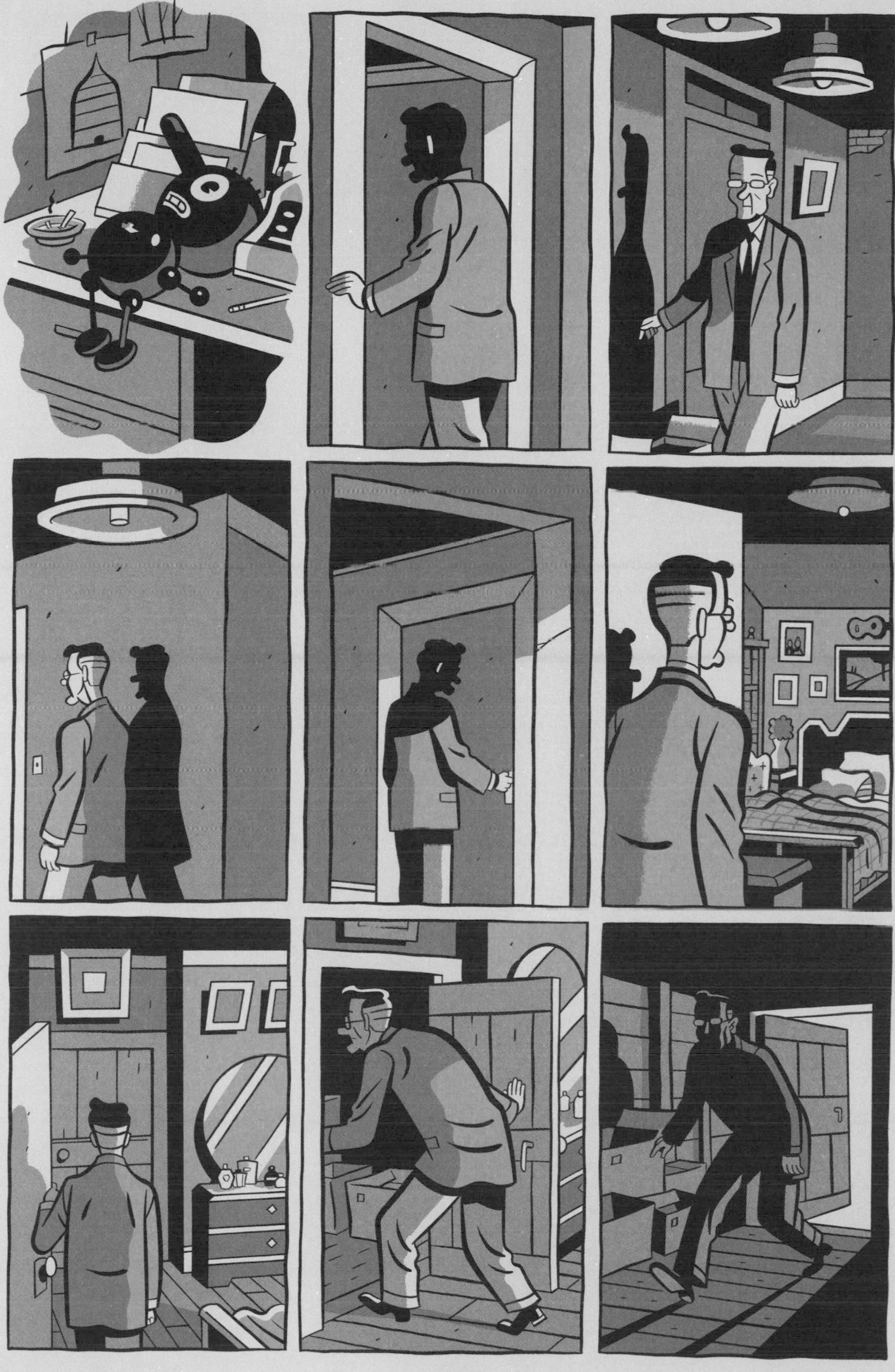

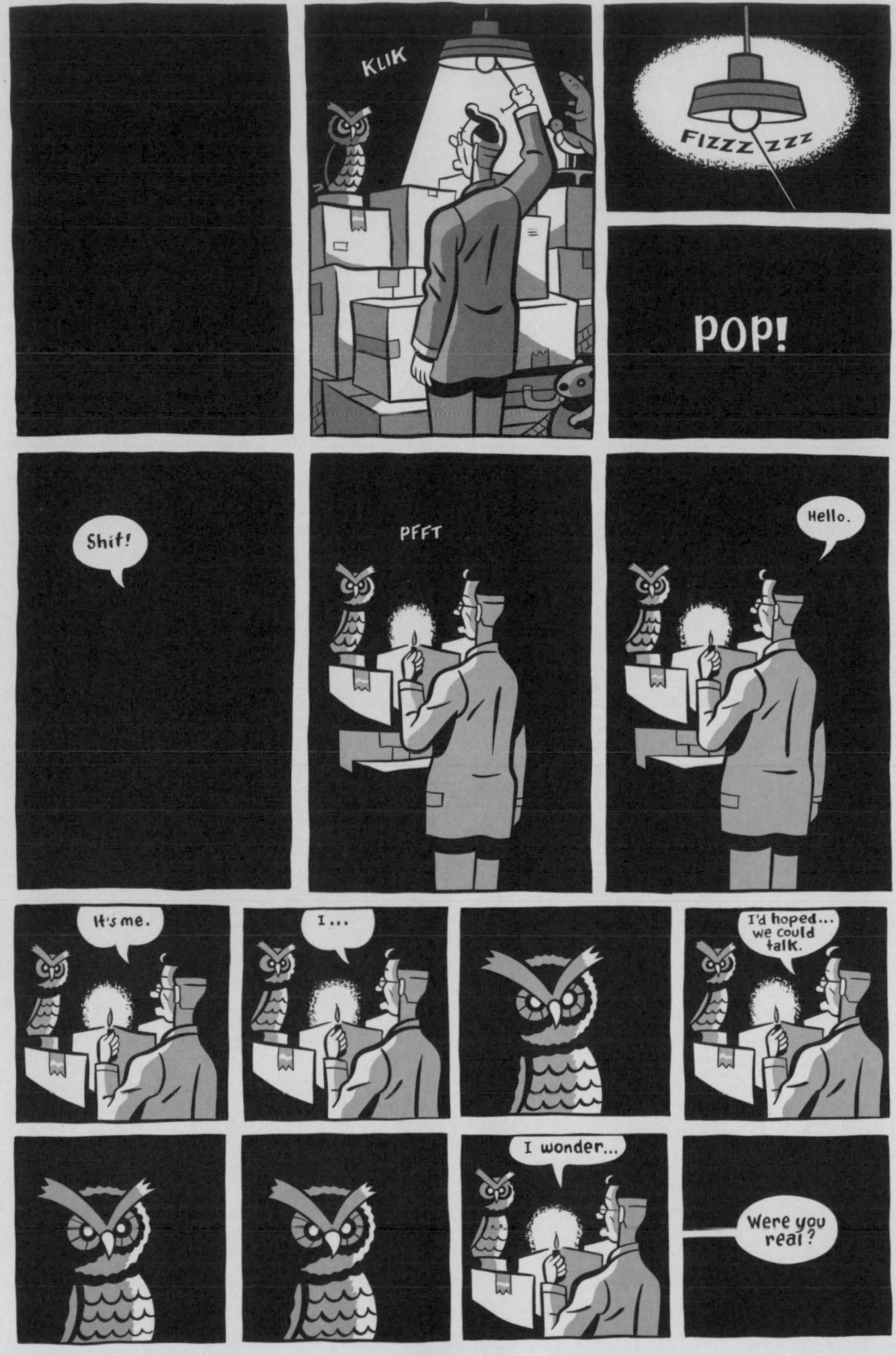

KLIK
FIZZZ ZZZ
POP!
Shit!
PFFT
Hello.
It's me.
I...
I'd hoped... we could talk.
I wonder...
Were you real?

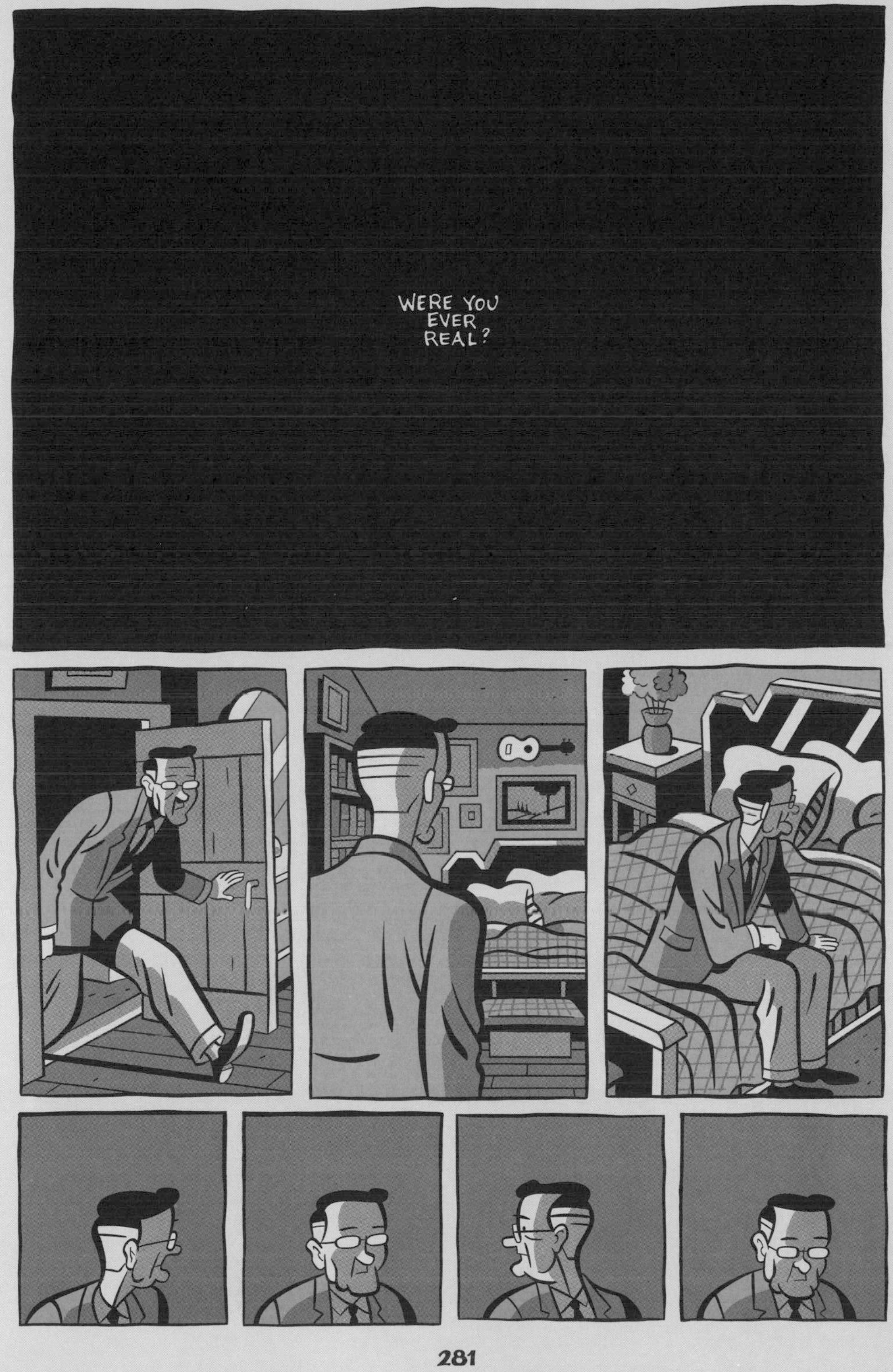
WERE YOU EVER REAL?

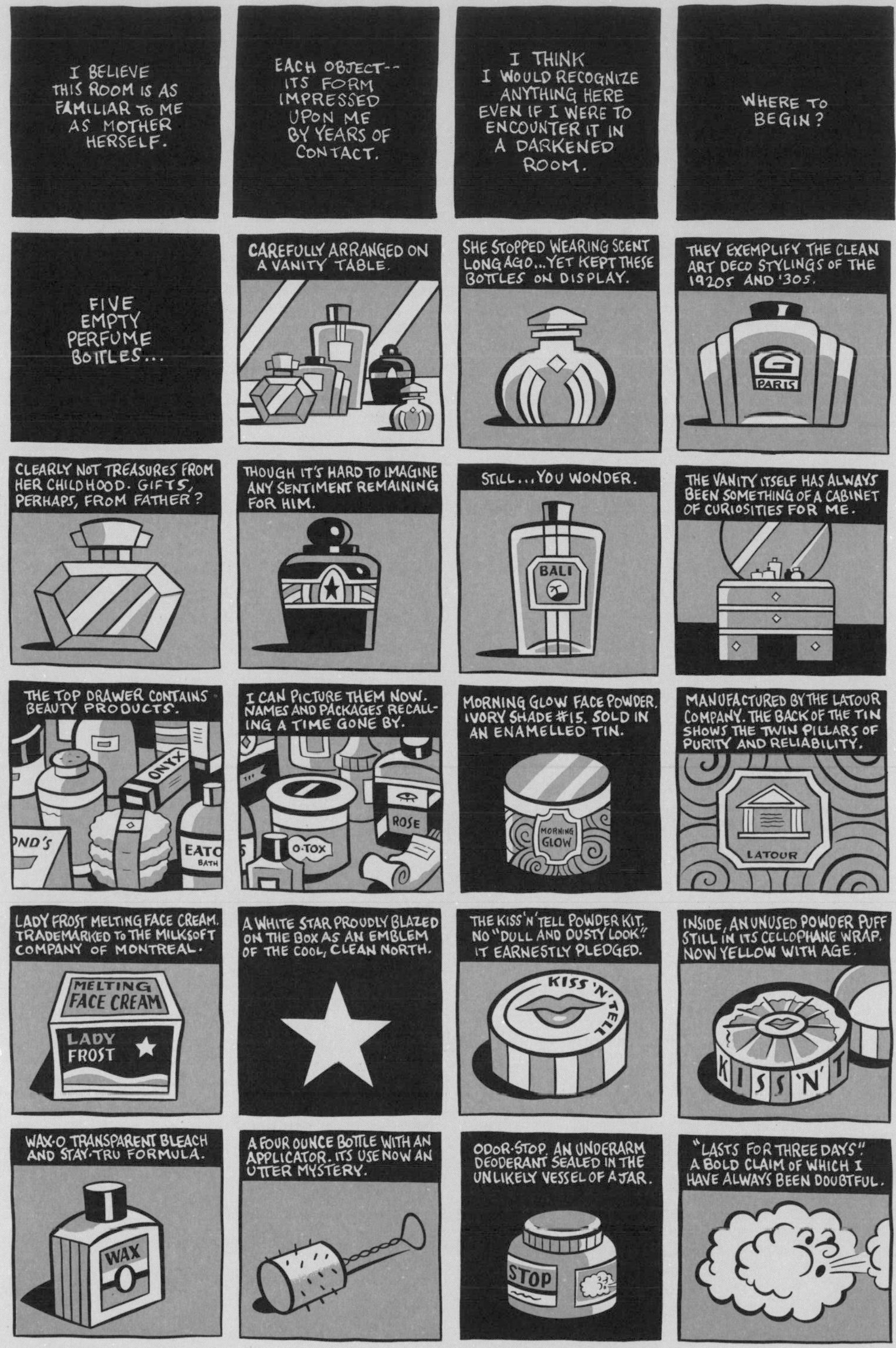
I BELIEVE THIS ROOM IS AS FAMILIAR TO ME AS MOTHER HERSELF.
EACH OBJECT-- ITS FORM IMPRESSED UPON ME BY YEARS OF CONTACT.
I THINK I WOULD RECOGNIZE ANYTHING HERE EVEN IF I WERE TO ENCOUNTER IT IN A DARKENED ROOM.
WHERE TO BEGIN?
FIVE EMPTY PERFUME BOTTLES...
CAREFULLY ARRANGED ON A VANITY TABLE.
SHE STOPPED WEARING SCENT LONG AGO... YET KEPT THESE BOTTLES ON DISPLAY.
THEY EXEMPLIFY THE CLEAN ART DECO STYLINGS OF THE 1920S AND '30S.
G
PARIS
CLEARLY NOT TREASURES FROM HER CHILDHOOD. GIFTS, PERHAPS, FROM FATHER?
THOUGH IT'S HARD TO IMAGINE ANY SENTIMENT REMAINING FOR HIM.
STILL... YOU WONDER.
BALI
THE VANITY ITSELF HAS ALWAYS BEEN SOMETHING OF A CABINET OF CURIOSITIES FOR ME.
THE TOP DRAWER CONTAINS BEAUTY PRODUCTS.
ONYX
ND'S
EATO
BATH
I CAN PICTURE THEM NOW. NAMES AND PACKAGES RECALLING A TIME GONE BY.
ROSE
O-TOX
MORNING GLOW FACE POWDER. IVORY SHADE #15. SOLD IN AN ENAMELLED TIN.
MORNING GLOW
MANUFACTURED BY THE LATOUR COMPANY. THE BACK OF THE TIN SHOWS THE TWIN PILLARS OF PURITY AND RELIABILITY.
LATOUR
LADY FROST MELTING FACE CREAM. TRADEMARKED TO THE MILKSOFT COMPANY OF MONTREAL.
MELTING FACE CREAM
LADY FROST
A WHITE STAR PROUDLY BLAZED ON THE BOX AS AN EMBLEM OF THE COOL, CLEAN NORTH.
THE KISS'N'TELL POWDER KIT. NO "DULL AND DUSTY LOOK" IT EARNESTLY PLEDGED.
KISS 'N' TELL
INSIDE, AN UNUSED POWDER PUFF STILL IN ITS CELLOPHANE WRAP. NOW YELLOW WITH AGE.
KISS'N'T
WAX-O TRANSPARENT BLEACH AND STAY-TRU FORMULA.
WAX O
A FOUR OUNCE BOTTLE WITH AN APPLICATOR. ITS USE NOW AN UTTER MYSTERY.
ODOR-STOP. AN UNDERARM DEODERANT SEALED IN THE UNLIKELY VESSEL OF A JAR.
STOP
"LASTS FOR THREE DAYS." A BOLD CLAIM OF WHICH I HAVE ALWAYS BEEN DOUBTFUL.

OF COURSE, THIS IS JUST A SMALL SAMPLING OF A MUCH LARGER ASSORTMENT.

NEXT TO THESE ITEMS IS A SHALLOW CARDBOARD BOX.

CANADA

CONTAINING A VARIETY OF ODD RUBBER HOSES, BOTTLES, BULBS, AND PADS.

40P

ALL OF WHICH I HAVE AVOIDED LOOKING CLOSELY UPON IN FEAR OF DISCOVERING THEIR PURPOSES.

IN THE DRAWER BELOW THERE IS ANOTHER BOX.

BEAVER SHOES

INSIDE ARE THE PAPERS THAT MAKE A LIFE-- BIRTH CER-TIFICATES, INSURANCE FORMS, WARRANTEES, PHOTOGRAPHS.

THE HOME DOCTOR

CAN LIF

I OFTEN POKED INTO THIS BOX AS A CHILD-- METHODICALLY PLACING THEM IN SEVERAL NEAT LITTLE STACKS.

SNAPS

AMONG THESE PAPERS THERE IS A REFRIGERATOR PAMPHLET.

HURONIA 1936

CIL

CARELESSLY DOODLED ON ITS TITLE PAGE ARE A FEW SMALL FACES. PROFILES.

HURONIA
REFRIDGERATION
SALES & SERVICE

MOTHER MUST HAVE CASUALLY JOTTED THEM DOWN LONG AGO WHEN SHE WAS A YOUNG WIFE.

WHEN I THINK OF THAT LOST OLD WOMAN, HERE IN THIS BED... OH HOW SAD THOSE LITTLE SCRIBBLES SEEM.

THE CHILDLIKE SWEETNESS OF THOSE FIVE TINY, RAGGED PEOPLE...

CARRYING ON...

TO THE RIGHT OF THAT BOX LIES A HAIRBRUSH PURCHASED IN 1937 FROM THE HAIR-RITE BRUSH COMPANY.

ITS BRISTLES ARE A SIMULATED PIG-BRISTLE MADE FROM A THEN-NEW FORM OF NYLON.

THE DESIGN OF THE BRUSH, AND ITS MATCHING MIRROR, SPEAK OF THE CRAZE IN THE 1920S FOR ALL THINGS EGYPTIAN.

THEY WERE ALREADY OUT OF STYLE WHEN MANUFACTURED. ALREADY OLD FASHIONED WHEN PURCHASED.

THE REST OF THE DRAWER CONTAINS A VARIETY OF ITEMS BUT MOSTLY GLOVES. MOTHER LOVED GLOVES.

THERE IS ONE PAIR, ELBOW LENGTH, MADE OF AN ELEGANT WHITE CALF. THREE IVORY BUTTONS AT THE WRIST.

THE BUTTONS FEATURE A TINY ENGRAVING OF A FOUR-LEAF CLOVER.

ANOTHER PAIR IS BLACK AND FLARED AT THE WRIST. ZIGZAG STITCHING ADORNS THE CUFF.

PURCHASED AT THE HUDSON'S BAY COMPANY IN 1946. A LUXURY AFTER THE PRIVA-TIONS OF THE WAR YEARS.

THE SALESGIRL HAD COMMENTED ON MOTHER'S DELICATE HANDS.

A REMARK MOTHER ALWAYS RECALLED.

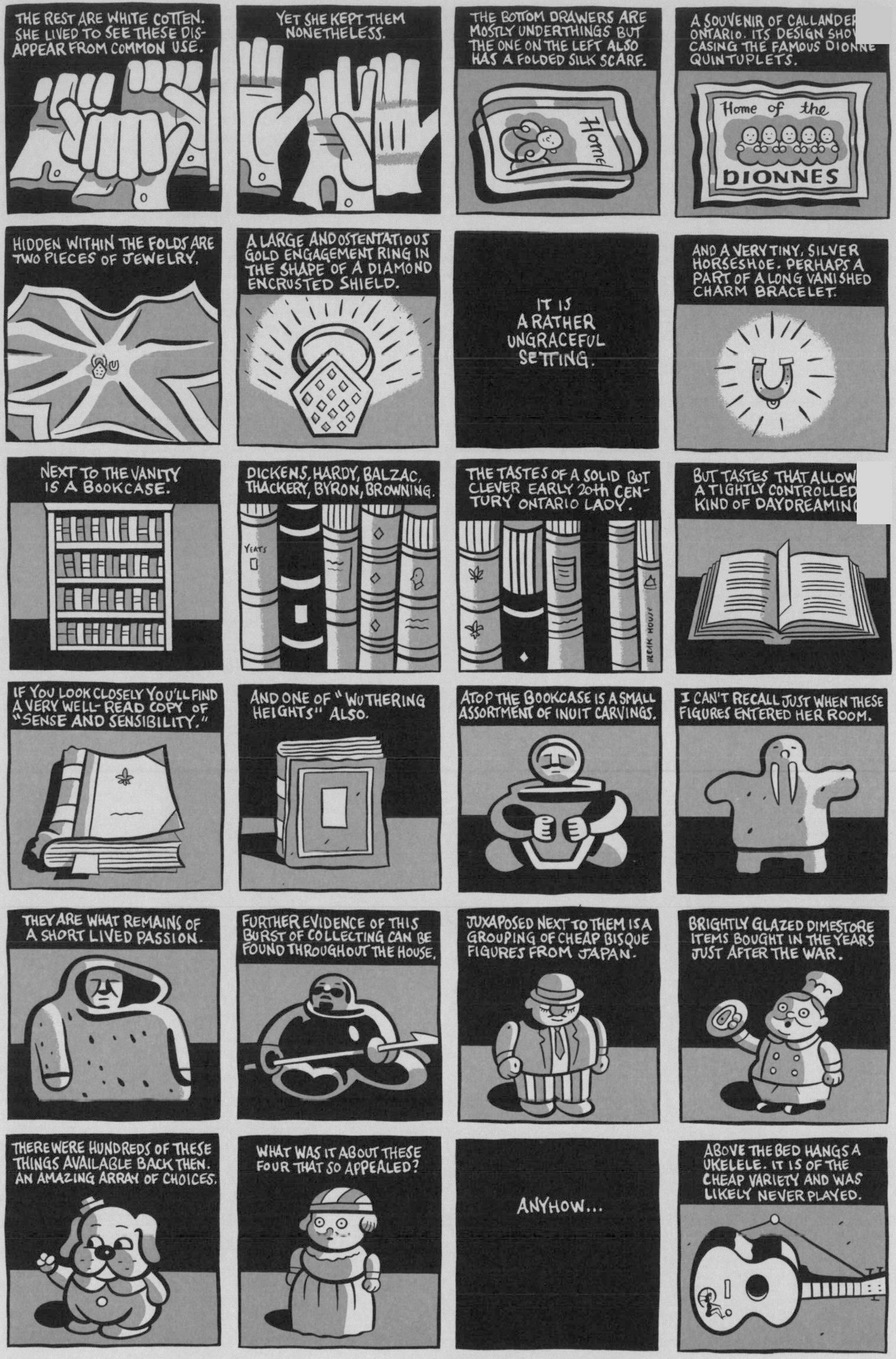
THE REST ARE WHITE COTTEN. SHE LIVED TO SEE THESE DIS-APPEAR FROM COMMON USE.
YET SHE KEPT THEM NONETHELESS.
THE BOTTOM DRAWERS ARE MOSTLY UNDERTHINGS BUT THE ONE ON THE LEFT ALSO HAS A FOLDED SILK SCARF.
Home
A SOUVENIR OF CALLANDE ONTARIO. ITS DESIGN SHOW CASING THE FAMOUS DIONNE QUINTUPLETS.
Home of the
DIONNES
HIDDEN WITHIN THE FOLDS ARE TWO PIECES OF JEWELRY.
A LARGE AND OSTENTATIOUS GOLD ENGAGEMENT RING IN THE SHAPE OF A DIAMOND ENCRUSTED SHIELD.
IT IS A RATHER UNGRACEFUL SETTING.
AND A VERY TINY, SILVER HORSESHOE. PERHAPS A PART OF A LONG VANISHED CHARM BRACELET.
NEXT TO THE VANITY IS A BOOKCASE.
DICKENS, HARDY, BALZAC, THACKERY, BYRON, BROWNING.
YEATS
THE TASTES OF A SOLID BUT CLEVER EARLY 20th CENTURY ONTARIO LADY.
BLEAK HOUSE
BUT TASTES THAT ALLOW A TIGHTLY CONTROLLED KIND OF DAYDREAMIN
IF YOU LOOK CLOSELY YOU'LL FIND A VERY WELL-READ COPY OF "SENSE AND SENSIBILITY."
AND ONE OF "WUTHERING HEIGHTS" ALSO.
ATOP THE BOOKCASE IS A SMALL ASSORTMENT OF INUIT CARVINGS.
I CAN'T RECALL JUST WHEN THESE FIGURES ENTERED HER ROOM.
THEY ARE WHAT REMAINS OF A SHORT LIVED PASSION.
FURTHER EVIDENCE OF THIS BURST OF COLLECTING CAN BE FOUND THROUGHOUT THE HOUSE.
JUXAPOSED NEXT TO THEM IS A GROUPING OF CHEAP BISQUE FIGURES FROM JAPAN.
BRIGHTLY GLAZED DIMESTORE ITEMS BOUGHT IN THE YEARS JUST AFTER THE WAR.
THERE WERE HUNDREDS OF THESE THINGS AVAILABLE BACK THEN. AN AMAZING ARRAY OF CHOICES.
WHAT WAS IT ABOUT THESE FOUR THAT SO APPEALED?
ANYHOW...
ABOVE THE BED HANGS A UKELELE. IT IS OF THE CHEAP VARIETY AND WAS LIKELY NEVER PLAYED.

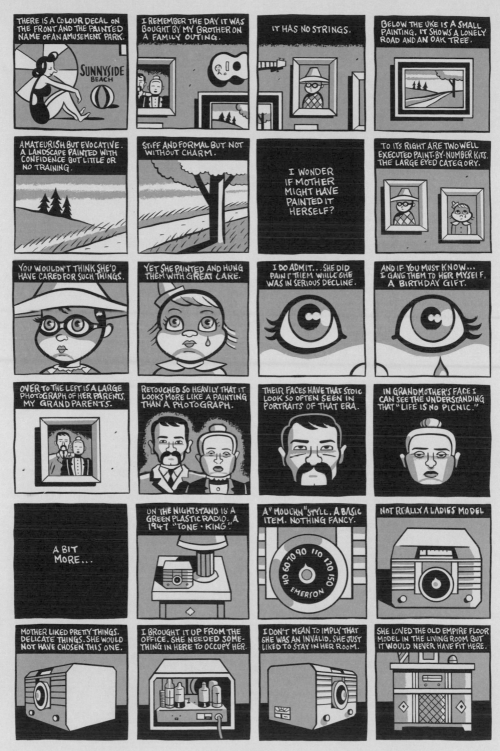

THERE IS A COLOUR DECAL ON THE FRONT AND THE PAINTED NAME OF AN AMUSEMENT PARK.

SUNNYSIDE BEACH

I REMEMBER THE DAY IT WAS BOUGHT BY MY BROTHER ON A FAMILY OUTING.

IT HAS NO STRINGS.

BELOW THE UKE IS A SMALL PAINTING. IT SHOWS A LONELY ROAD AND AN OAK TREE.

AMATEURISH BUT EVOCATIVE. A LANDSCAPE PAINTED WITH CONFIDENCE BUT LITTLE OR NO TRAINING.

STIFF AND FORMAL BUT NOT WITHOUT CHARM.

I WONDER IF MOTHER MIGHT HAVE PAINTED IT HERSELF?

TO ITS RIGHT ARE TWO WELL EXECUTED PAINT-BY-NUMBER KITS. THE LARGE EYED CATEGORY.

YOU WOULDN'T THINK SHE'D HAVE CARED FOR SUCH THINGS.

YET SHE PAINTED AND HUNG THEM WITH GREAT CARE.

I DO ADMIT... SHE DID PAINT THEM WHILE SHE WAS IN SERIOUS DECLINE.

AND IF YOU MUST KNOW... I GAVE THEM TO HER MYSELF. A BIRTHDAY GIFT.

OVER TO THE LEFT IS A LARGE PHOTOGRAPH OF HER PARENTS, MY GRANDPARENTS.

RETOUCHED SO HEAVILY THAT IT LOOKS MORE LIKE A PAINTING THAN A PHOTOGRAPH.

THEIR FACES HAVE THAT STOIC LOOK SO OFTEN SEEN IN PORTRAITS OF THAT ERA.

IN GRANDMOTHER'S FACE I CAN SEE THE UNDERSTANDING THAT "LIFE IS NO PICNIC."

A BIT MORE...

ON THE NIGHTSTAND IS A GREEN PLASTIC RADIO. A 1947 "TONE · KING."

A "MODERN" STYLE. A BASIC ITEM. NOTHING FANCY.

60 70 90 110 120 150
EMERSON

NOT REALLY A LADIES MODEL

MOTHER LIKED PRETTY THINGS. DELICATE THINGS. SHE WOULD NOT HAVE CHOSEN THIS ONE.

I BROUGHT IT UP FROM THE OFFICE. SHE NEEDED SOMETHING IN HERE TO OCCUPY HER.

I DON'T MEAN TO IMPLY THAT SHE WAS AN INVALID. SHE JUST LIKED TO STAY IN HER ROOM.

SHE LOVED THE OLD EMPIRE FLOOR MODEL IN THE LIVING ROOM BUT IT WOULD NEVER HAVE FIT HERE.

285

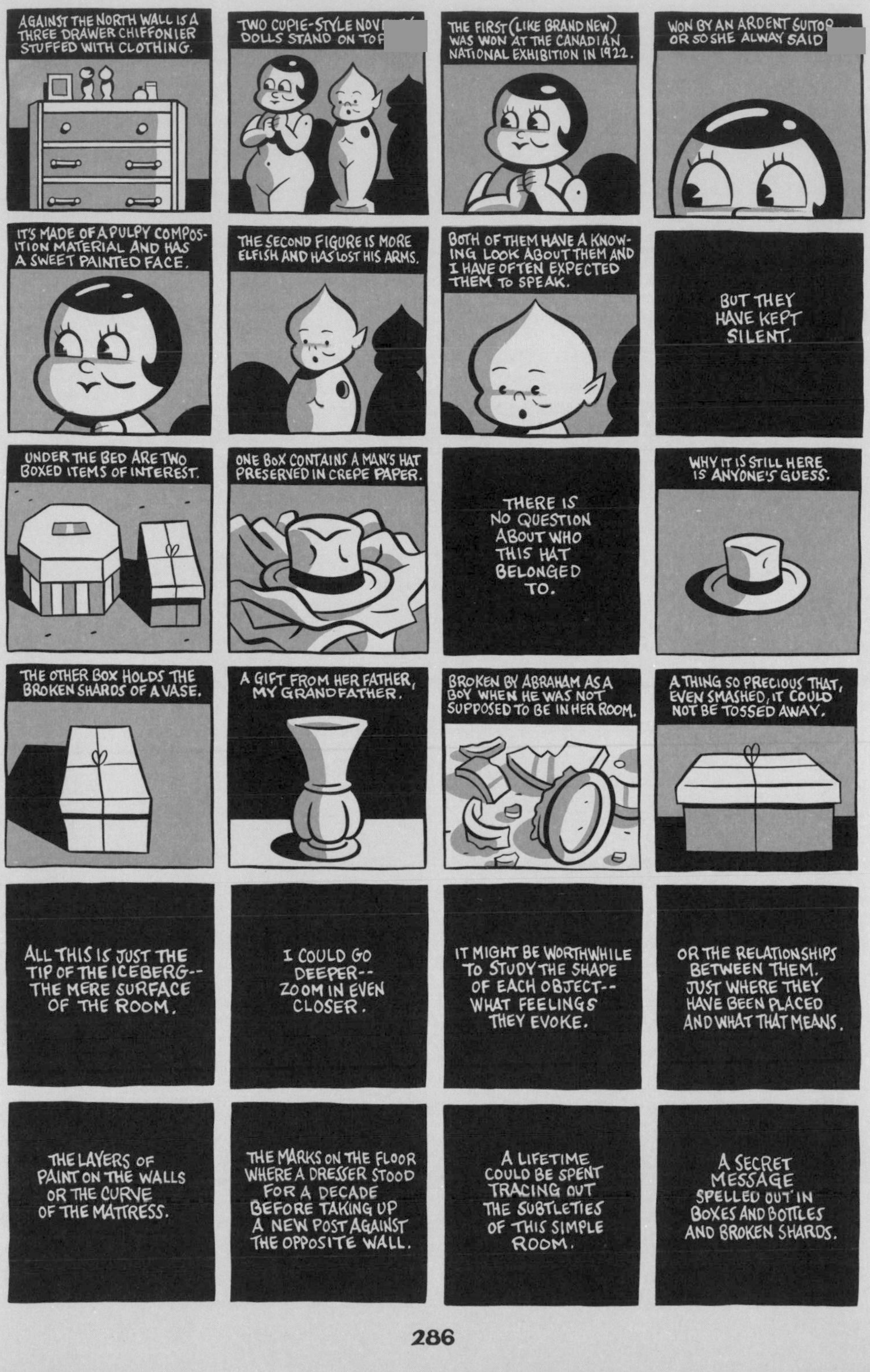

AGAINST THE NORTH WALL IS A THREE DRAWER CHIFFONIER STUFFED WITH CLOTHING.
TWO CUPIE-STYLE NOV[redacted] DOLLS STAND ON TOP
THE FIRST (LIKE BRAND NEW) WAS WON AT THE CANADIAN NATIONAL EXHIBITION IN 1922.
WON BY AN ARDENT SUITOR[redacted] OR SO SHE ALWAY SAID
IT'S MADE OF A PULPY COMPOSITION MATERIAL AND HAS A SWEET PAINTED FACE.
THE SECOND FIGURE IS MORE ELFISH AND HAS LOST HIS ARMS.
BOTH OF THEM HAVE A KNOWING LOOK ABOUT THEM AND I HAVE OFTEN EXPECTED THEM TO SPEAK.
BUT THEY HAVE KEPT SILENT.
UNDER THE BED ARE TWO BOXED ITEMS OF INTEREST.
ONE BOX CONTAINS A MAN'S HAT PRESERVED IN CREPE PAPER.
THERE IS NO QUESTION ABOUT WHO THIS HAT BELONGED TO.
WHY IT IS STILL HERE IS ANYONE'S GUESS.
THE OTHER BOX HOLDS THE BROKEN SHARDS OF A VASE.
A GIFT FROM HER FATHER, MY GRANDFATHER.
BROKEN BY ABRAHAM AS A BOY WHEN HE WAS NOT SUPPOSED TO BE IN HER ROOM.
A THING SO PRECIOUS THAT, EVEN SMASHED, IT COULD NOT BE TOSSED AWAY.
ALL THIS IS JUST THE TIP OF THE ICEBERG-- THE MERE SURFACE OF THE ROOM.
I COULD GO DEEPER-- ZOOM IN EVEN CLOSER.
IT MIGHT BE WORTHWHILE TO STUDY THE SHAPE OF EACH OBJECT-- WHAT FEELINGS THEY EVOKE.
OR THE RELATIONSHIPS BETWEEN THEM. JUST WHERE THEY HAVE BEEN PLACED AND WHAT THAT MEANS.
THE LAYERS OF PAINT ON THE WALLS OR THE CURVE OF THE MATTRESS.
THE MARKS ON THE FLOOR WHERE A DRESSER STOOD FOR A DECADE BEFORE TAKING UP A NEW POST AGAINST THE OPPOSITE WALL.
A LIFETIME COULD BE SPENT TRACING OUT THE SUBTLETIES OF THIS SIMPLE ROOM.
A SECRET MESSAGE SPELLED OUT IN BOXES AND BOTTLES AND BROKEN SHARDS.

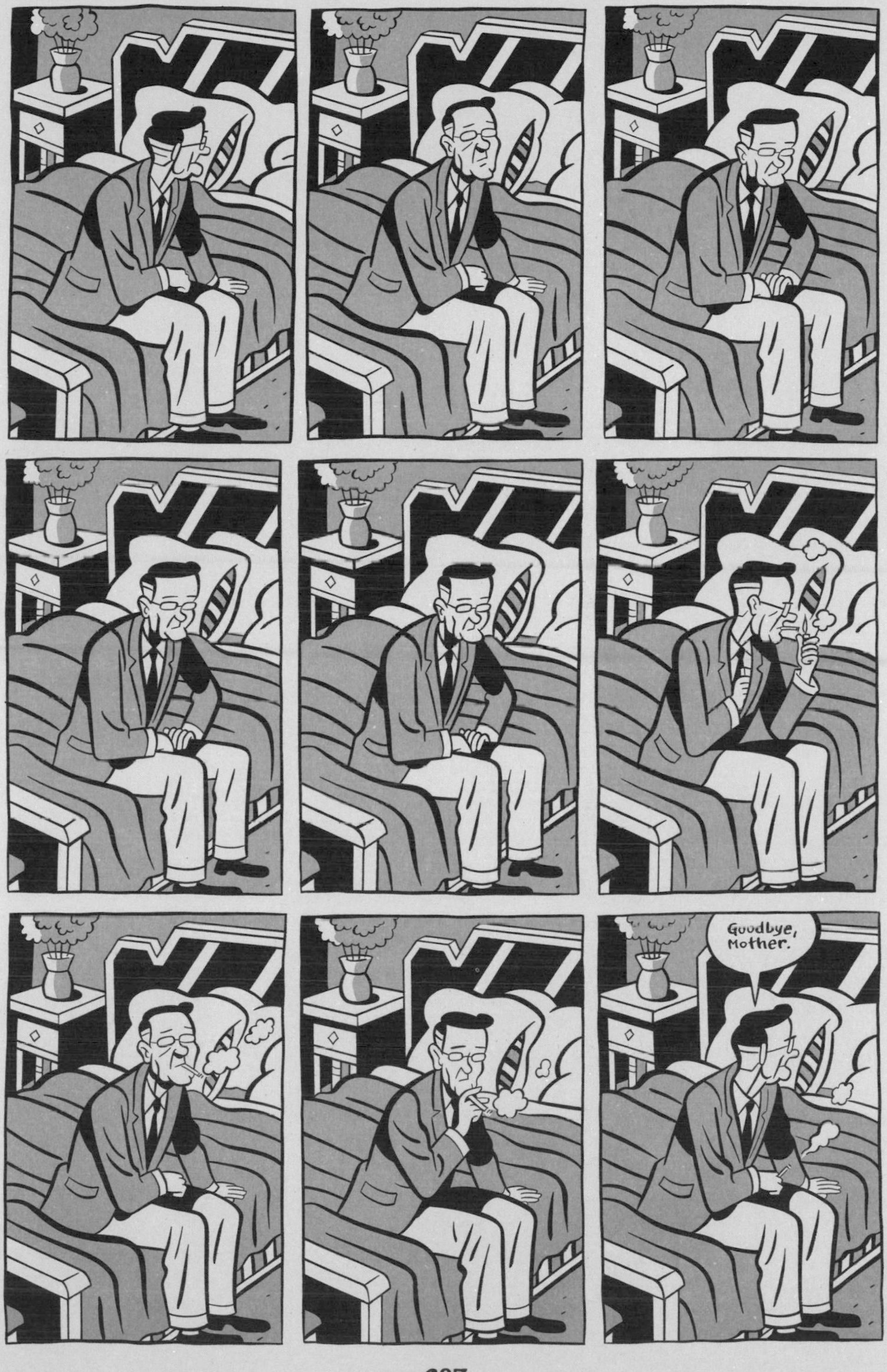
Goodbye, Mother.

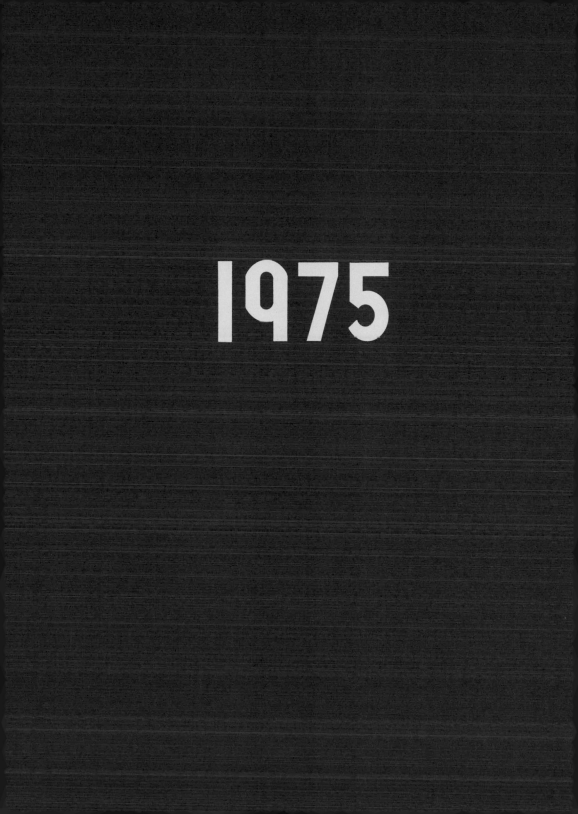

1975

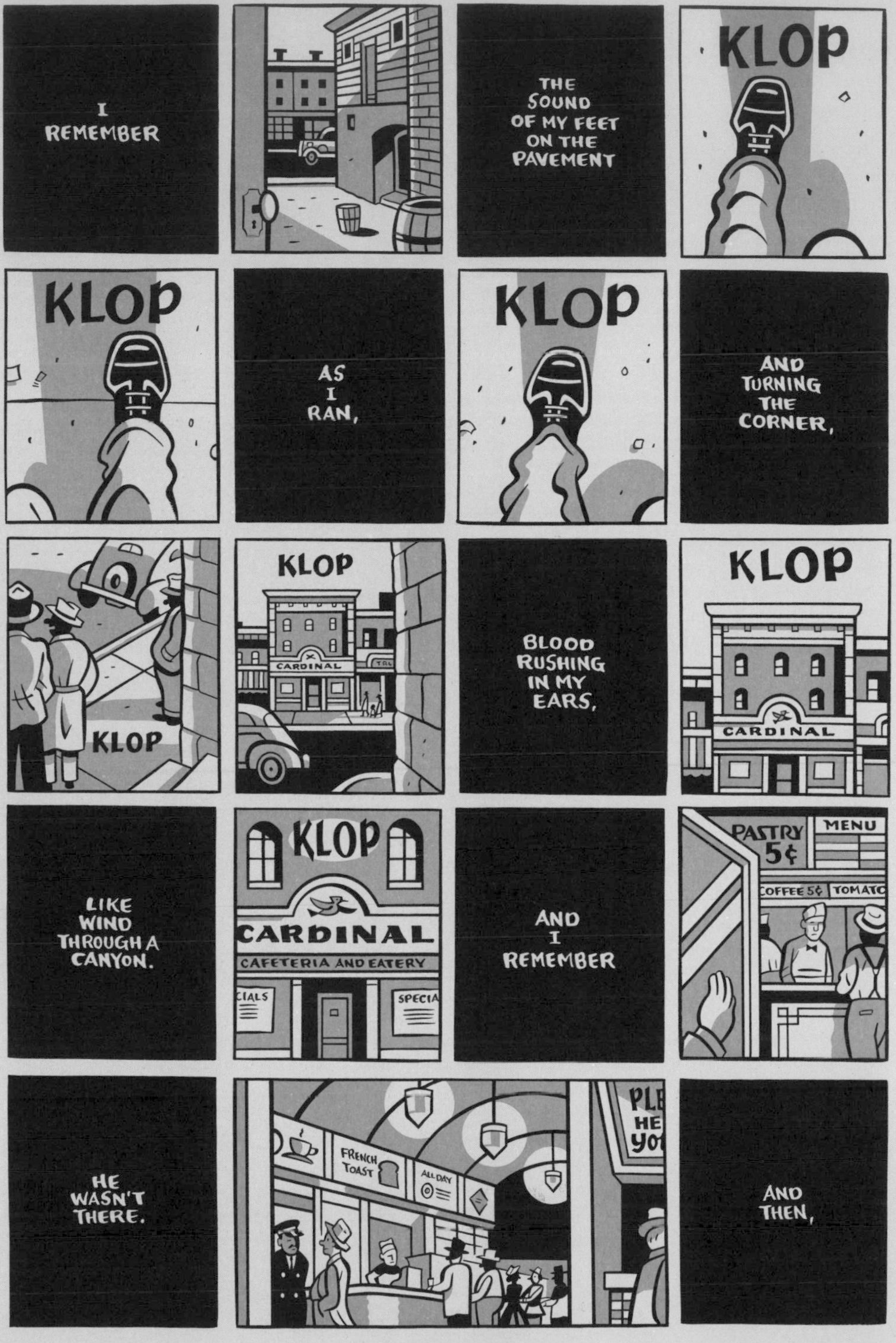
I REMEMBER
THE SOUND OF MY FEET ON THE PAVEMENT
KLOP
KLOP
AS I RAN,
KLOP
AND TURNING THE CORNER,
KLOP
KLOP
CARDINAL
BLOOD RUSHING IN MY EARS,
KLOP
CARDINAL
LIKE WIND THROUGH A CANYON.
KLOP
CARDINAL
CAFETERIA AND EATERY
AND I REMEMBER
PASTRY 5¢
MENU
COFFEE 5¢
TOMATO
HE WASN'T THERE.
FRENCH TOAST
ALL DAY
AND THEN,

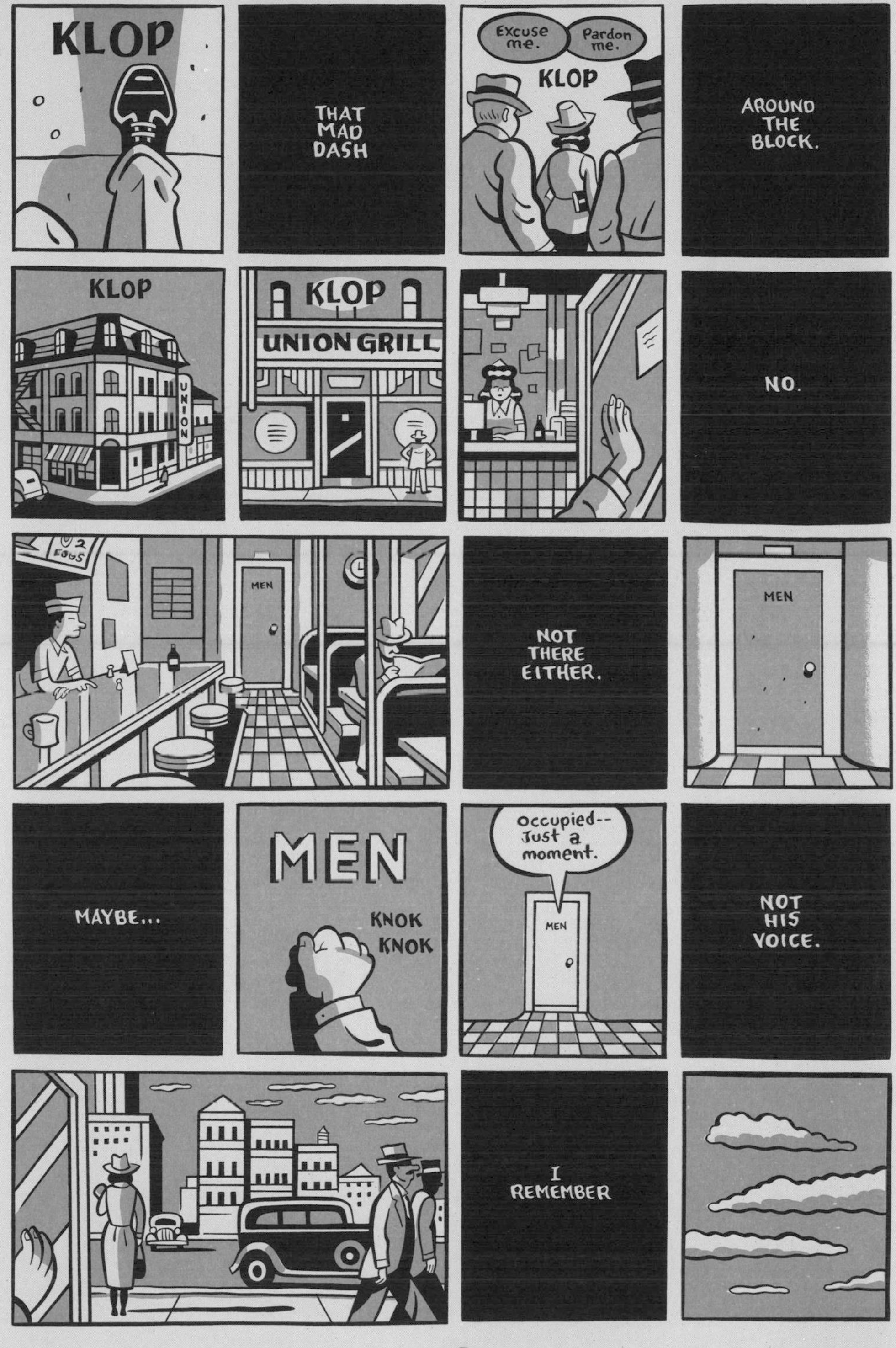
KLOP
THAT MAD DASH
Excuse me.
Pardon me.
KLOP
AROUND THE BLOCK.
KLOP
UNION
KLOP
UNION GRILL
NO.
2 EGGS
MEN
NOT THERE EITHER.
MEN
MAYBE...
MEN
KNOK KNOK
Occupied-- Just a moment.
MEN
NOT HIS VOICE.
I REMEMBER

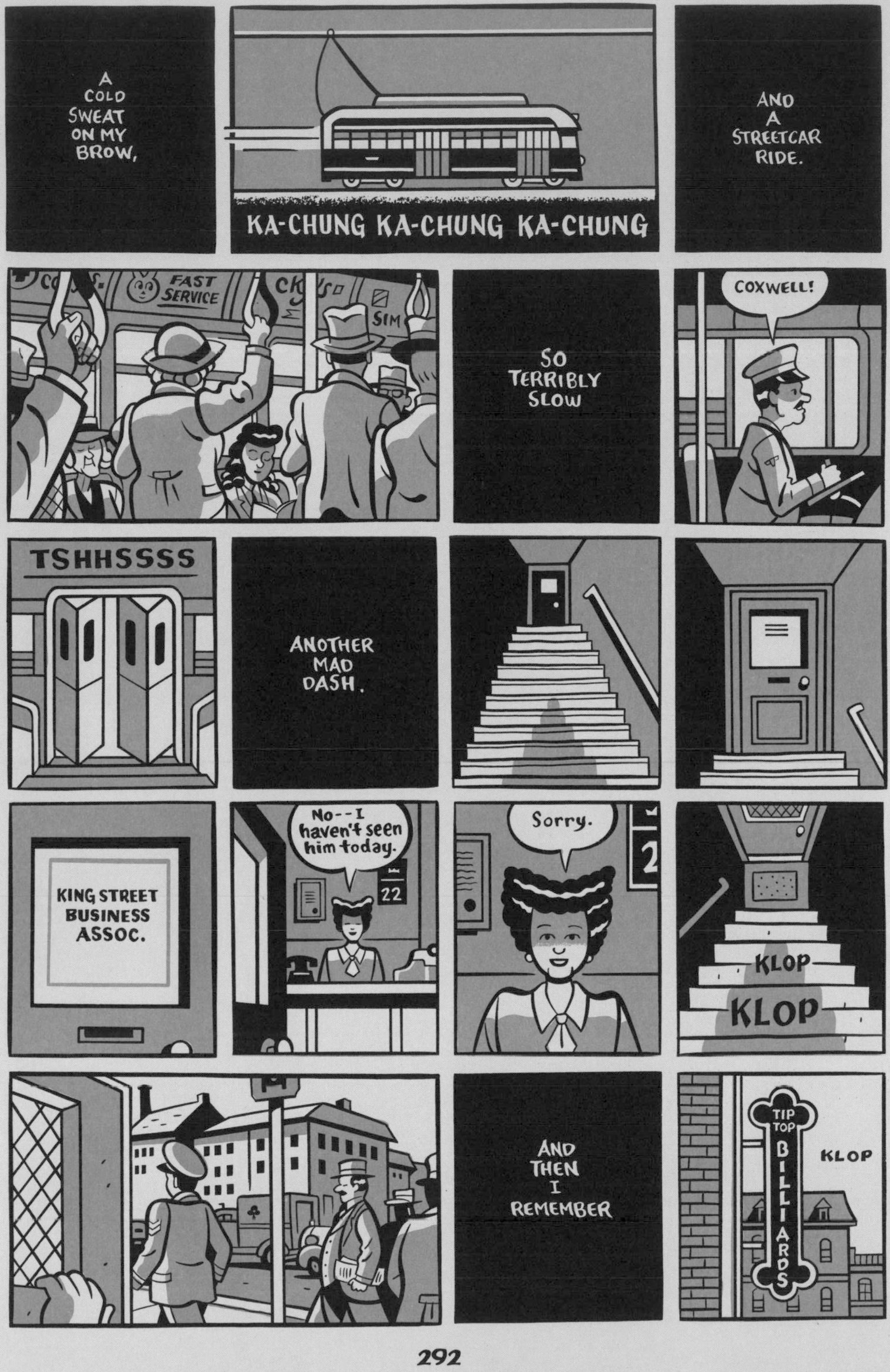
A COLD SWEAT ON MY BROW,
KA-CHUNG KA-CHUNG KA-CHUNG
AND A STREETCAR RIDE.
FAST SERVICE
SO TERRIBLY SLOW
COXWELL!
TSHHSSSS
ANOTHER MAD DASH.
KING STREET BUSINESS ASSOC.
No--I haven't seen him today.
22
Sorry.
KLOP
KLOP
AND THEN I REMEMBER
TIP TOP BILLIARDS
KLOP

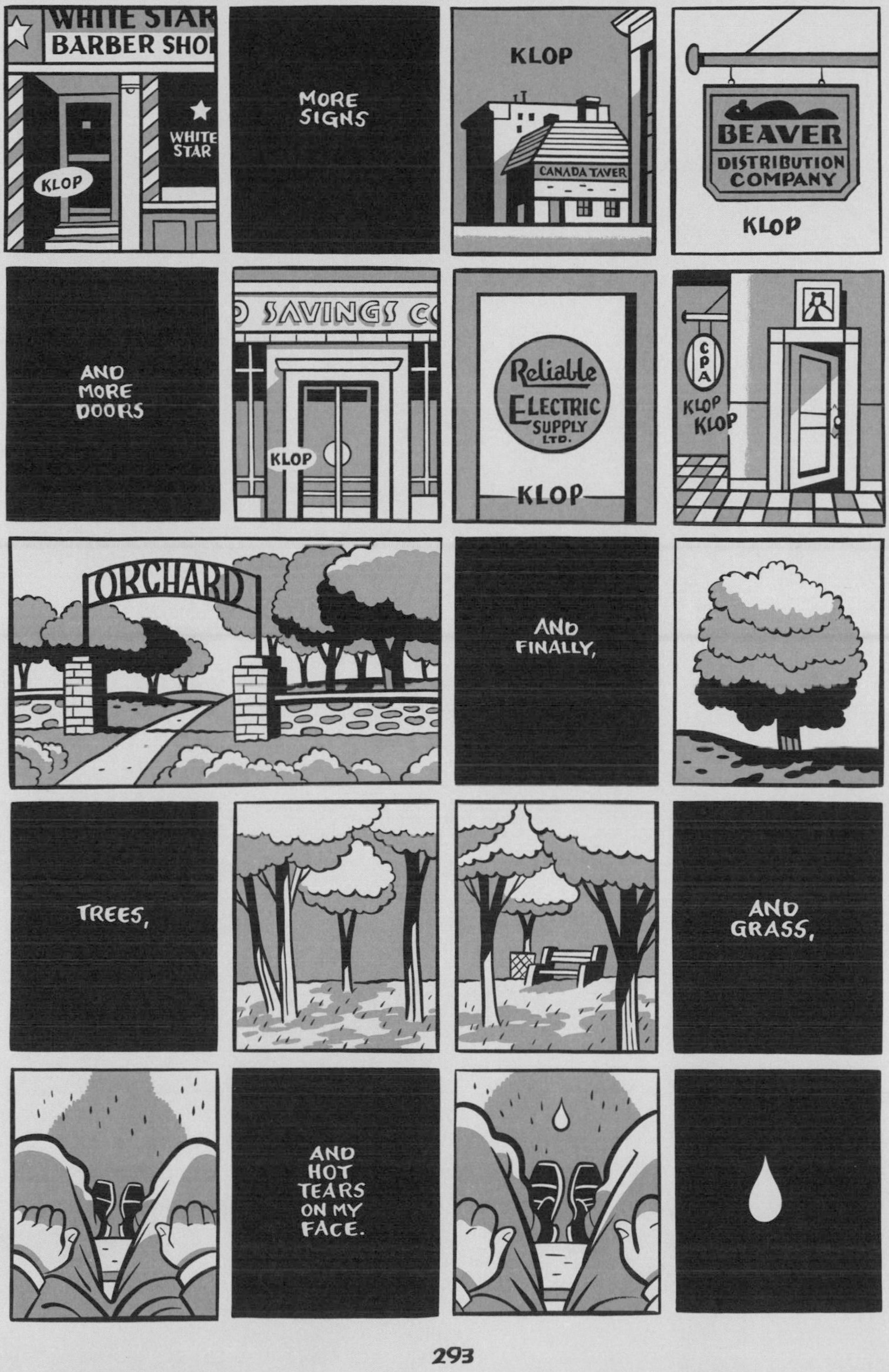
WHITE STAR
BARBER SHO
WHITE STAR
KLOP
MORE SIGNS
KLOP
CANADA TAVER
BEAVER
DISTRIBUTION COMPANY
KLOP
AND MORE DOORS
SAVINGS C
KLOP
Reliable ELECTRIC SUPPLY LTD.
KLOP
CPA
KLOP
KLOP
ORCHARD
AND FINALLY,
TREES,
AND GRASS,
AND HOT TEARS ON MY FACE.

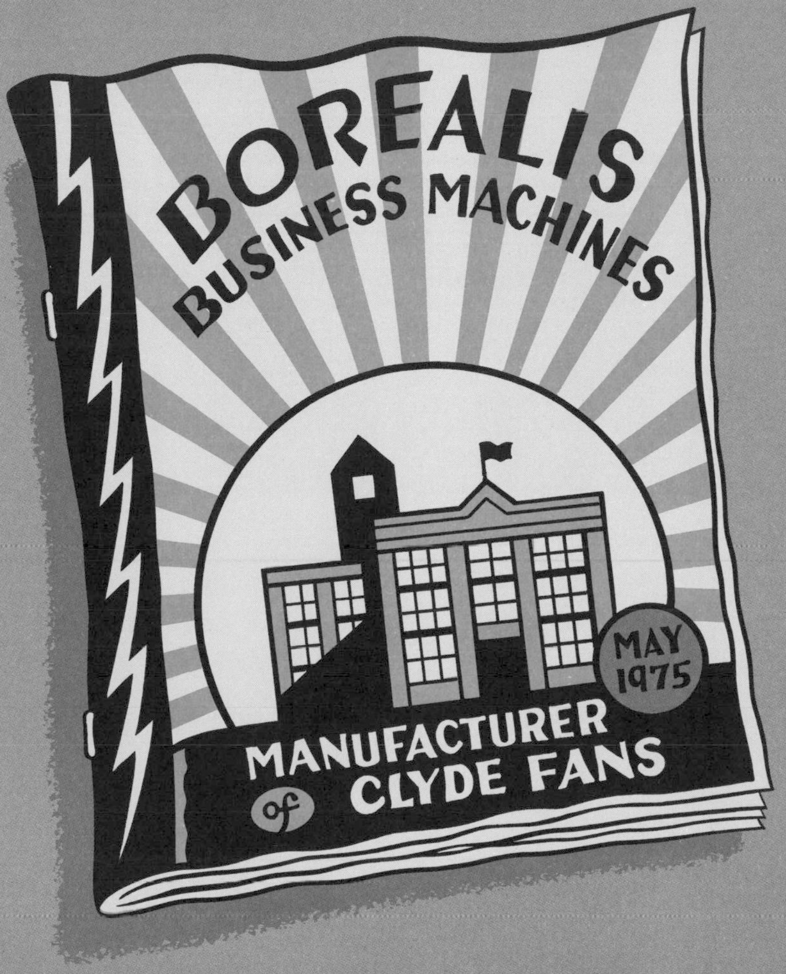
BOREALIS
BUSINESS MACHINES
MAY 1975
MANUFACTURER of CLYDE FANS

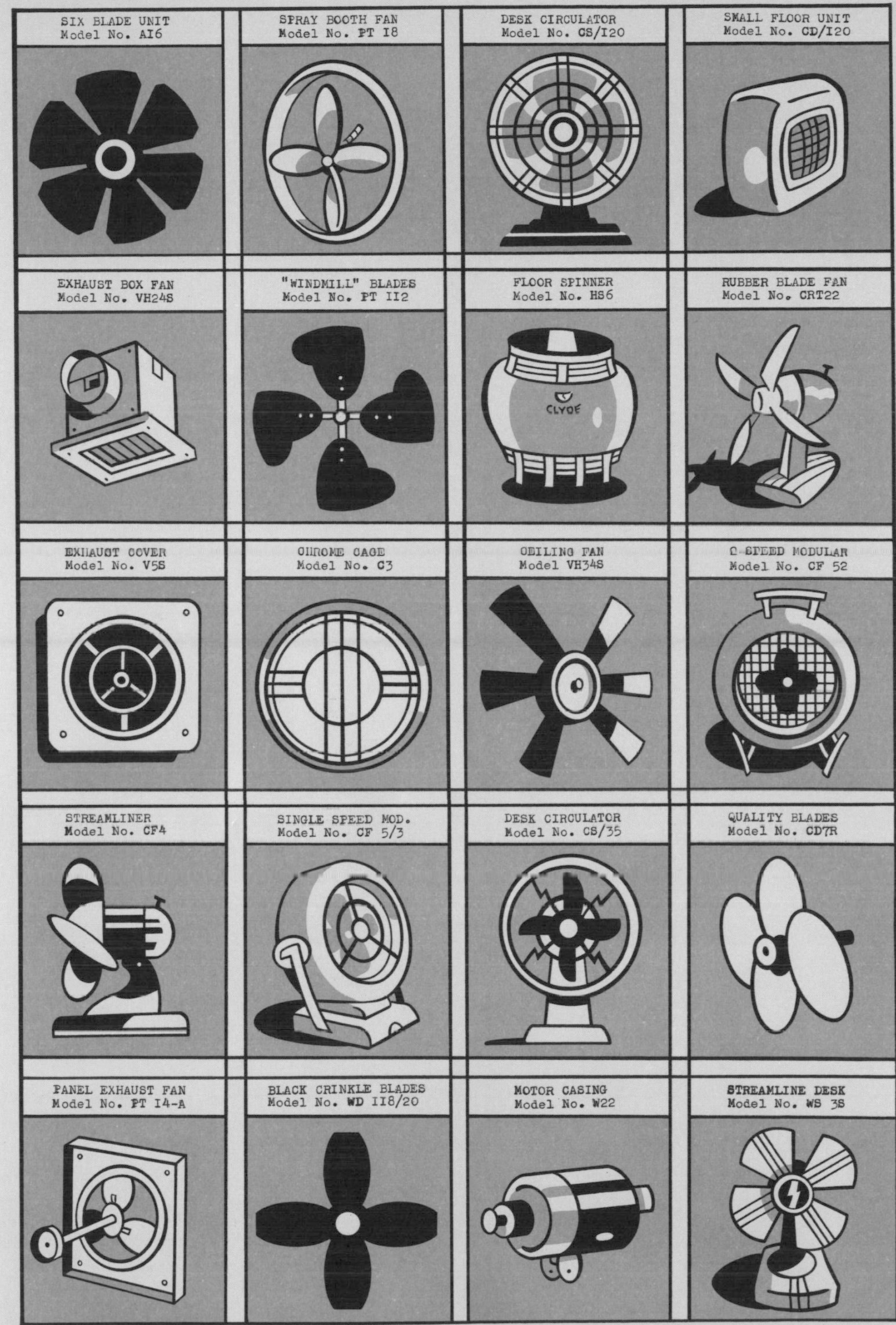
SIX BLADE UNIT
Model No. AI6
SPRAY BOOTH FAN
Model No. PT I8
DESK CIRCULATOR
Model No. CS/I20
SMALL FLOOR UNIT
Model No. CD/I20
EXHAUST BOX FAN
Model No. VH24S
"WINDMILL" BLADES
Model No. PT II2
FLOOR SPINNER
Model No. HS6
CLYDE
RUBBER BLADE FAN
Model No. CRT22
EXHAUST COVER
Model No. V5S
CHROME CAGE
Model No. C3
CEILING FAN
Model VH34S
2 SPEED MODULAR
Model No. CF 52
STREAMLINER
Model No. CF4
SINGLE SPEED MOD.
Model No. CF 5/3
DESK CIRCULATOR
Model No. CS/35
QUALITY BLADES
Model No. CD7R
PANEL EXHAUST FAN
Model No. PT I4-A
BLACK CRINKLE BLADES
Model No. WD II8/20
MOTOR CASING
Model No. W22
STREAMLINE DESK
Model No. WS 3S

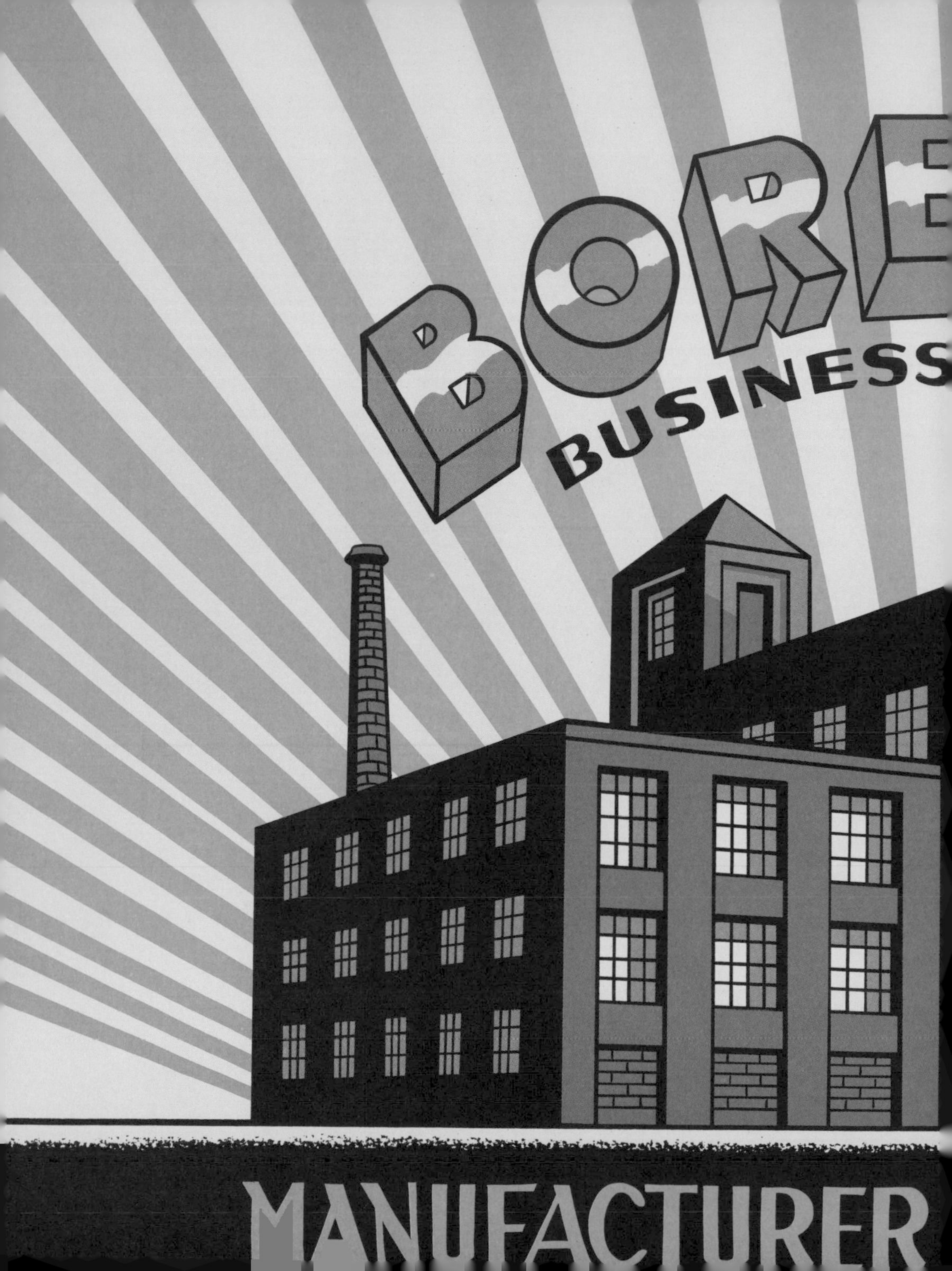
BORE
BUSINESS
MANUFACTURER

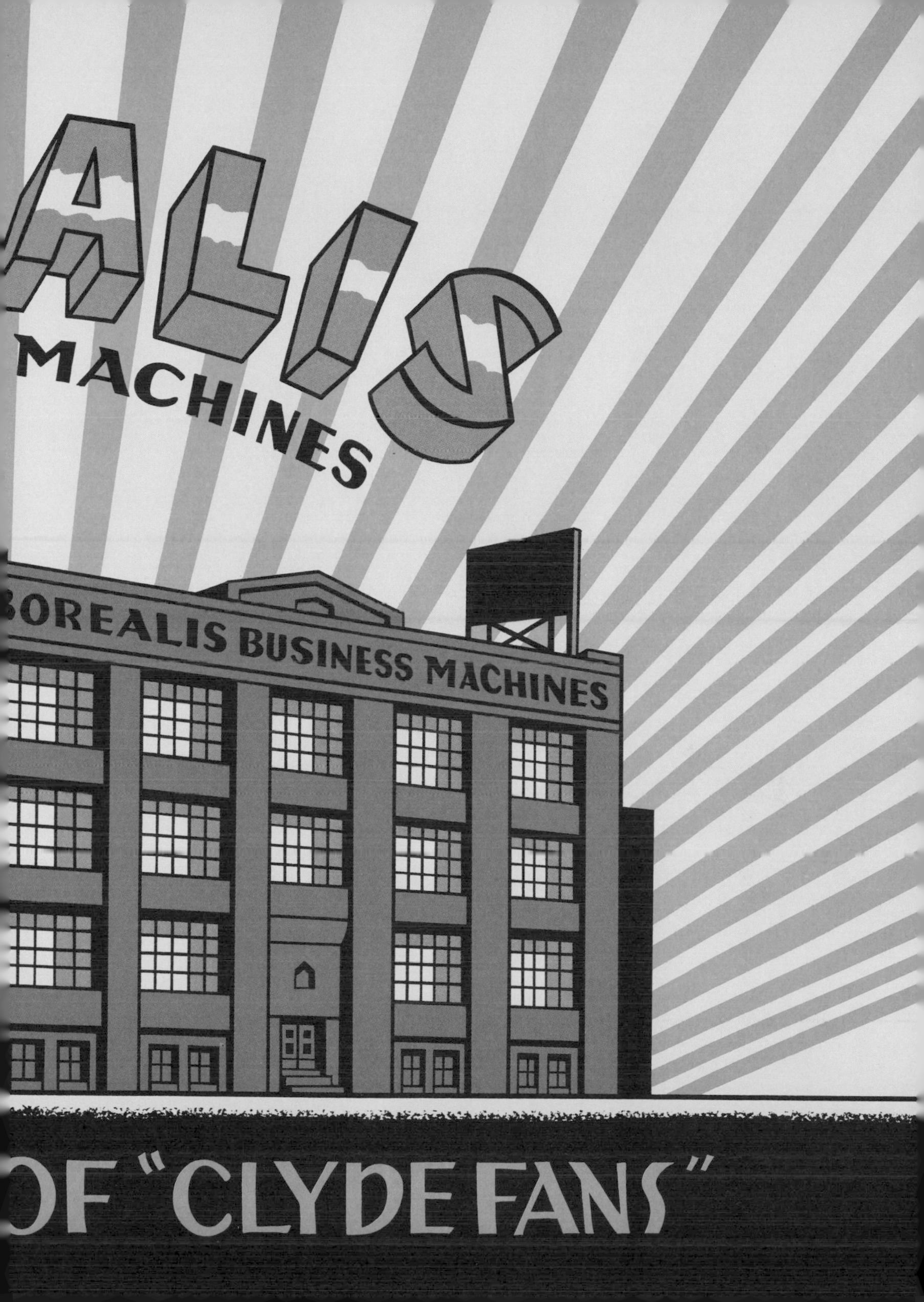
ALIS
MACHINES
BOREALIS BUSINESS MACHINES
OF "CLYDE FANS"

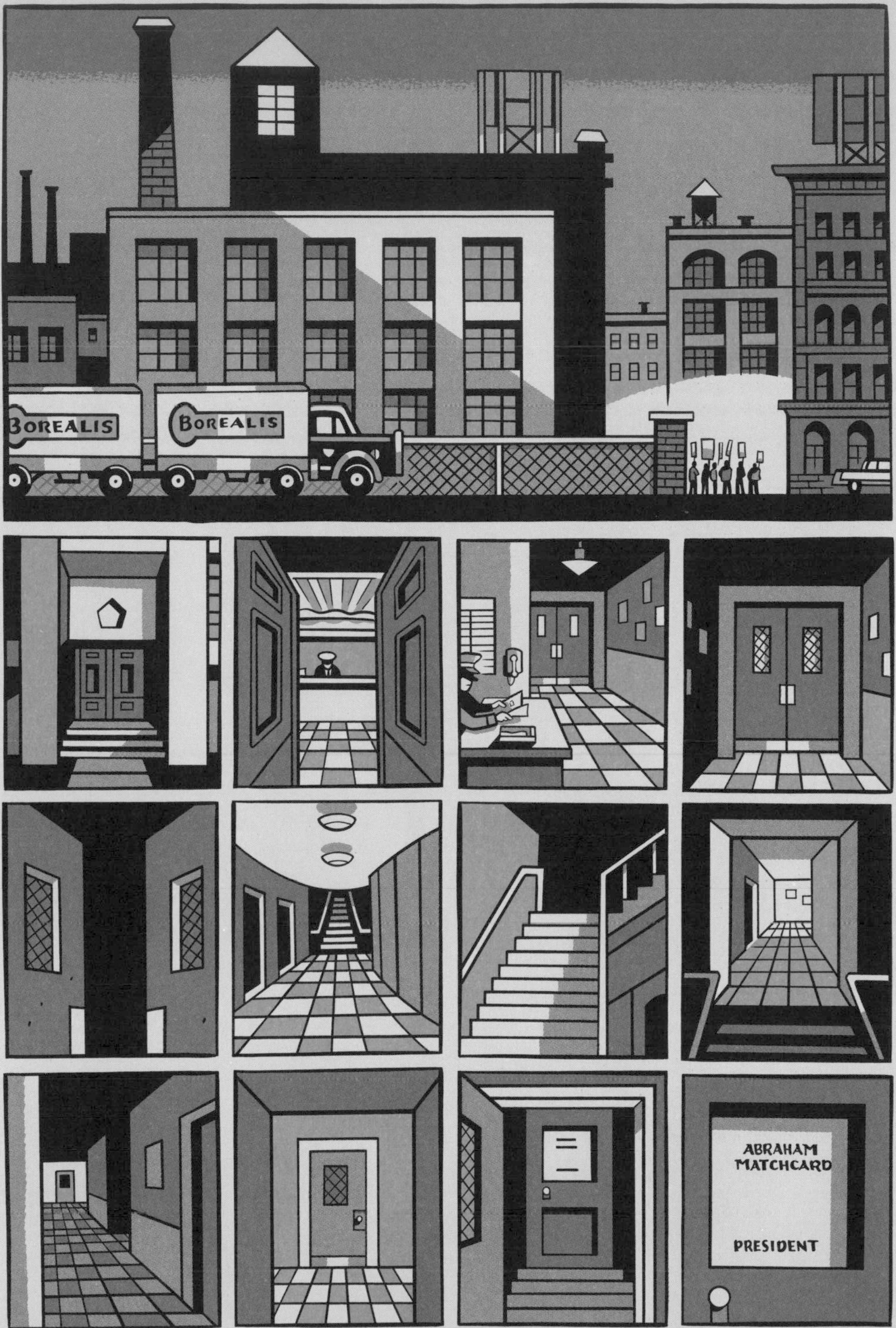
BOREALIS
BOREALIS
ABRAHAM MATCHCARD
PRESIDENT

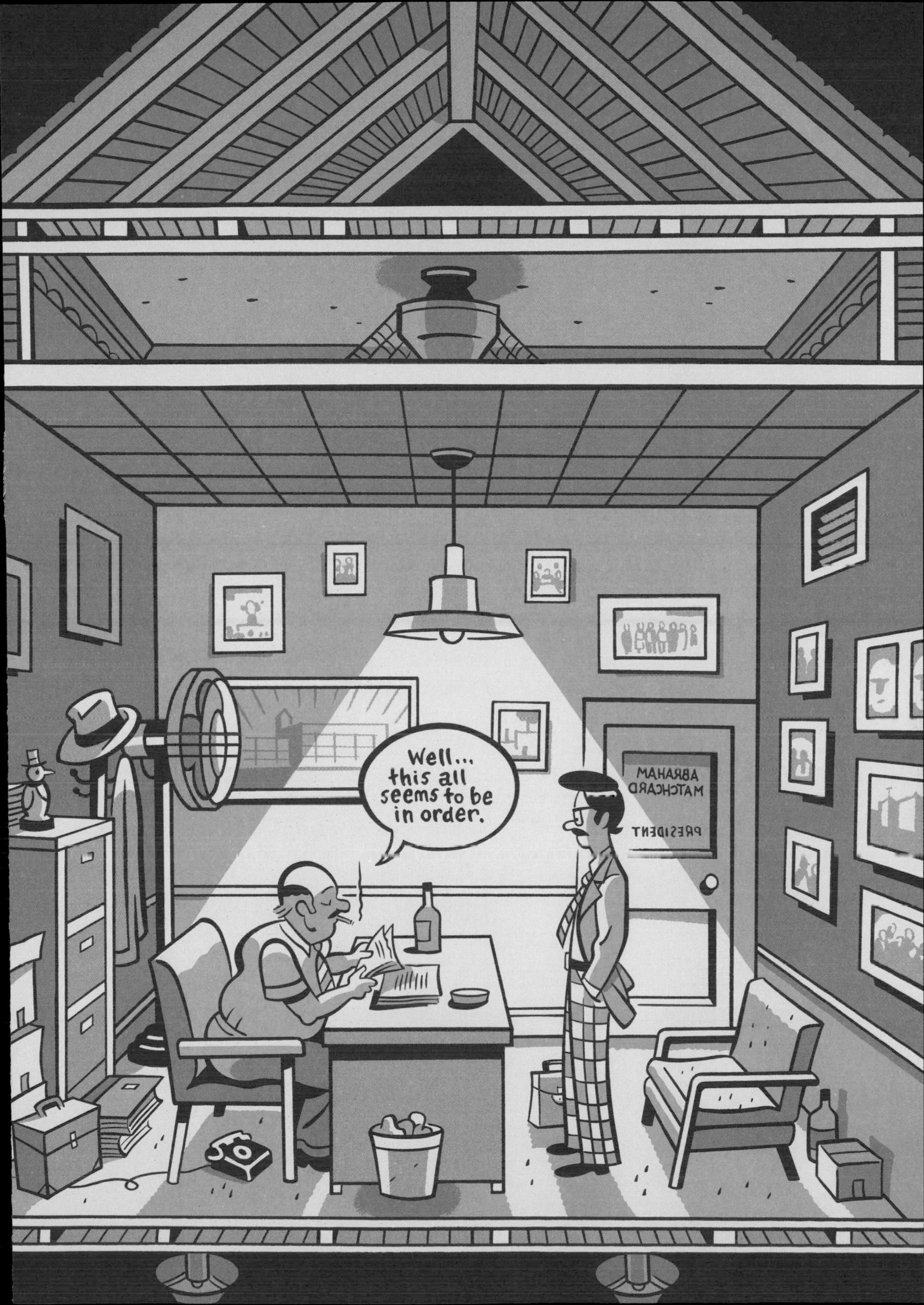
ABRAHAM MATCHCARD
PRESIDENT
Well... this all seems to be in order.

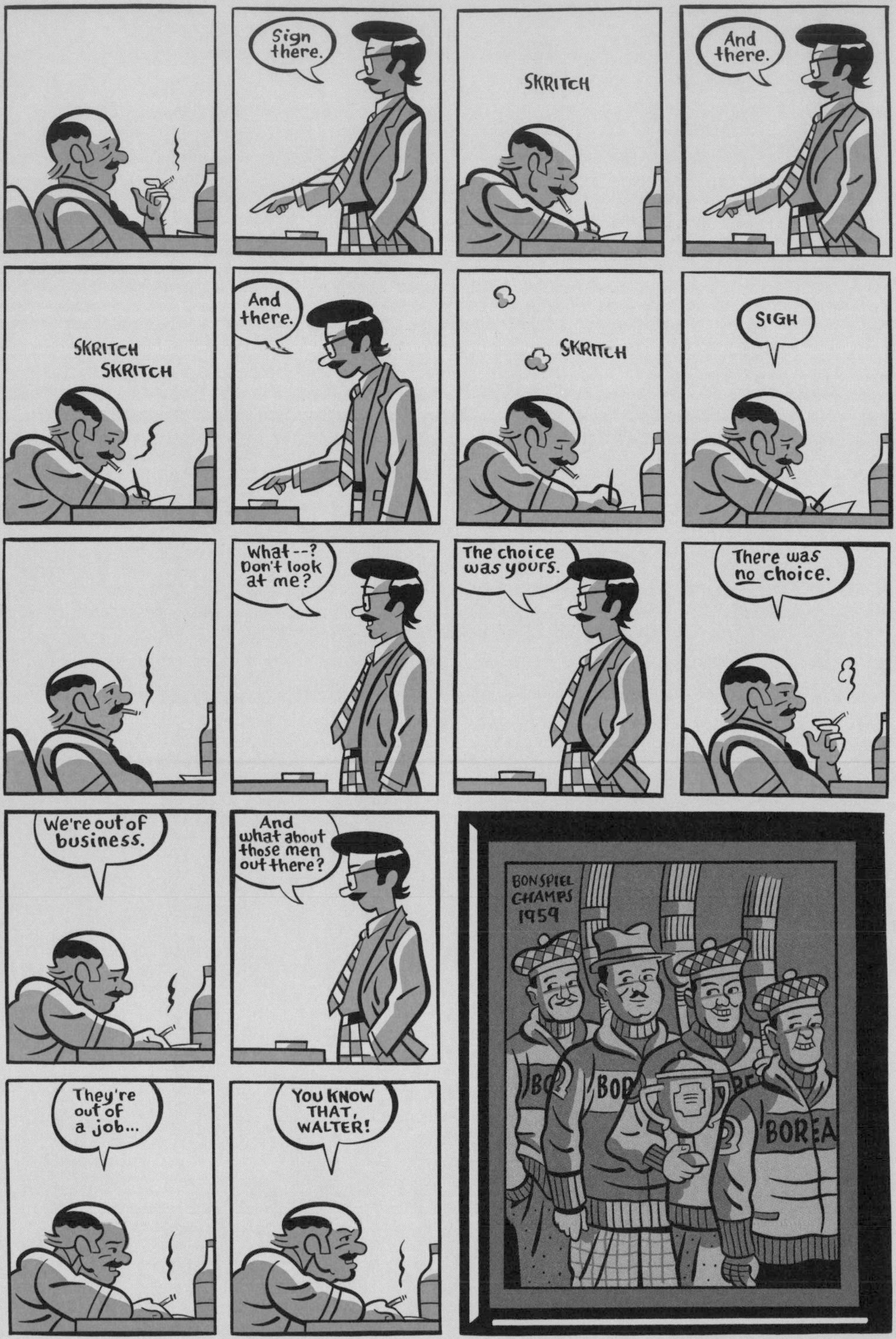
Sign there.
SKRITCH
And there.
SKRITCH
SKRITCH
And there.
SKRITCH
SIGH
What--? Don't look at me?
The choice was yours.
There was no choice.
We're out of business.
And what about those men out there?
BONSPIEL CHAMPS 1959
They're out of a job...
YOU KNOW THAT, WALTER!

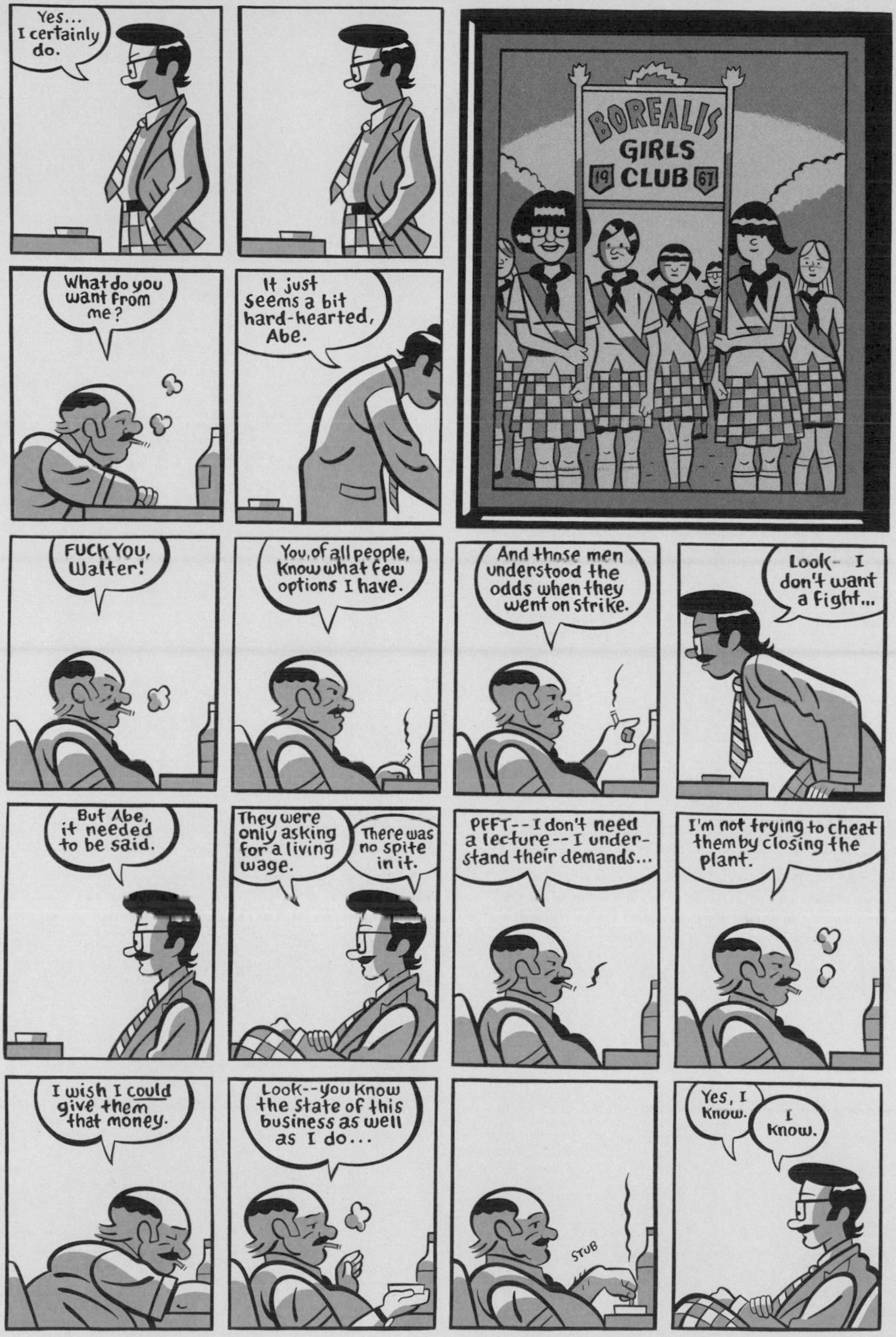
Yes... I certainly do.
BOREALIS GIRLS 19 CLUB 67
What do you want from me?
It just seems a bit hard-hearted, Abe.
FUCK YOU, Walter!
You, of all people, know what few options I have.
And those men understood the odds when they went on strike.
Look- I don't want a fight...
But Abe, it needed to be said.
They were only asking for a living wage.
There was no spite in it.
PFFT--I don't need a lecture--I understand their demands...
I'm not trying to cheat them by closing the plant.
I wish I could give them that money.
Look--you know the state of this business as well as I do...
STUB
Yes, I know.
I know.

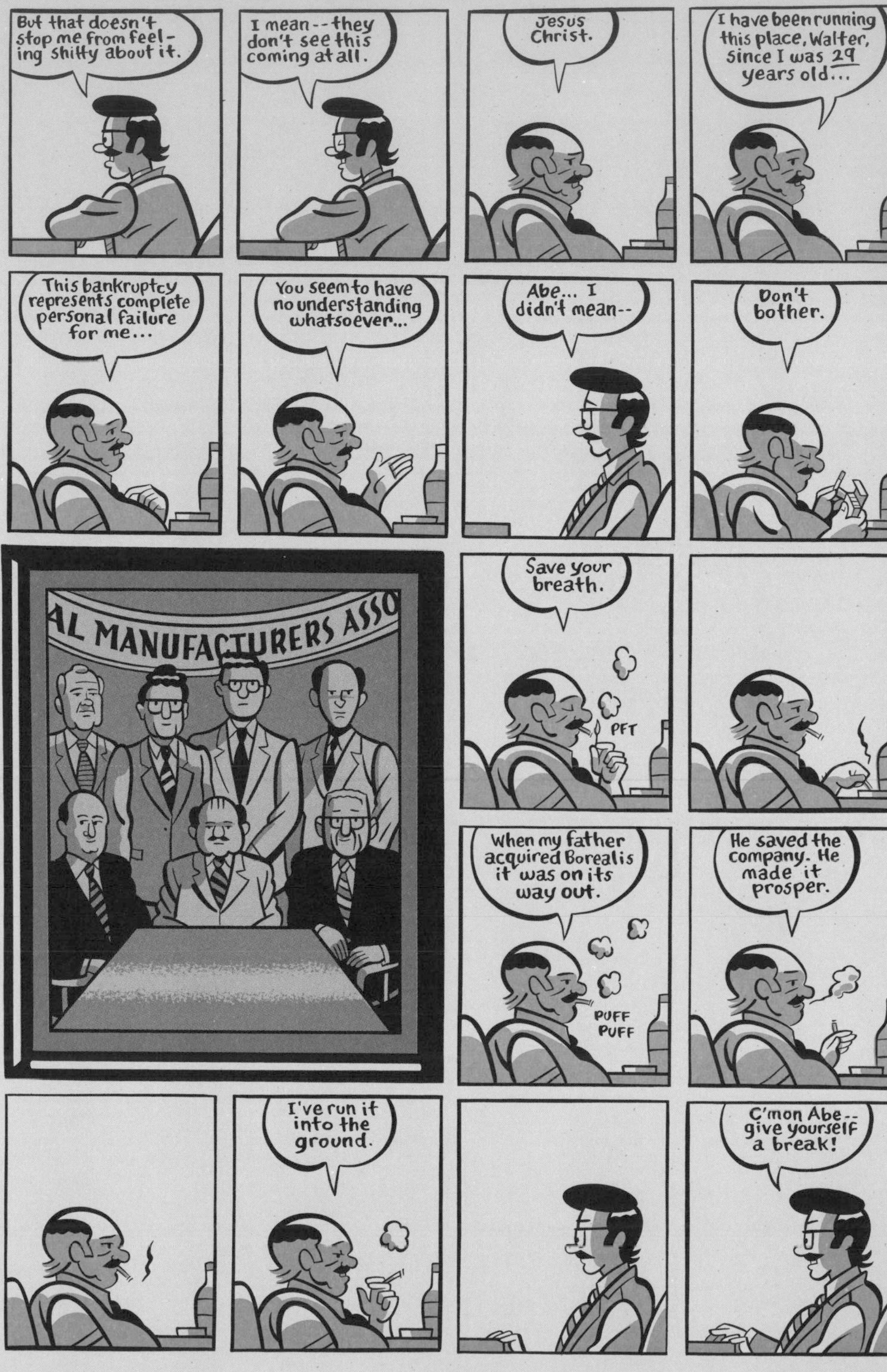
But that doesn't stop me from feel-ing shitty about it.
I mean -- they don't see this coming at all.
Jesus Christ.
I have been running this place, Walter, since I was 29 years old...
This bankruptcy represents complete personal failure for me...
You seem to have no understanding whatsoever...
Abe... I didn't mean--
Don't bother.
AL MANUFACTURERS ASSO
Save your breath.
PFT
When my father acquired Borealis it was on its way out.
PUFF PUFF
He saved the company. He made it prosper.
I've run it into the ground.
C'mon Abe -- give yourself a break!

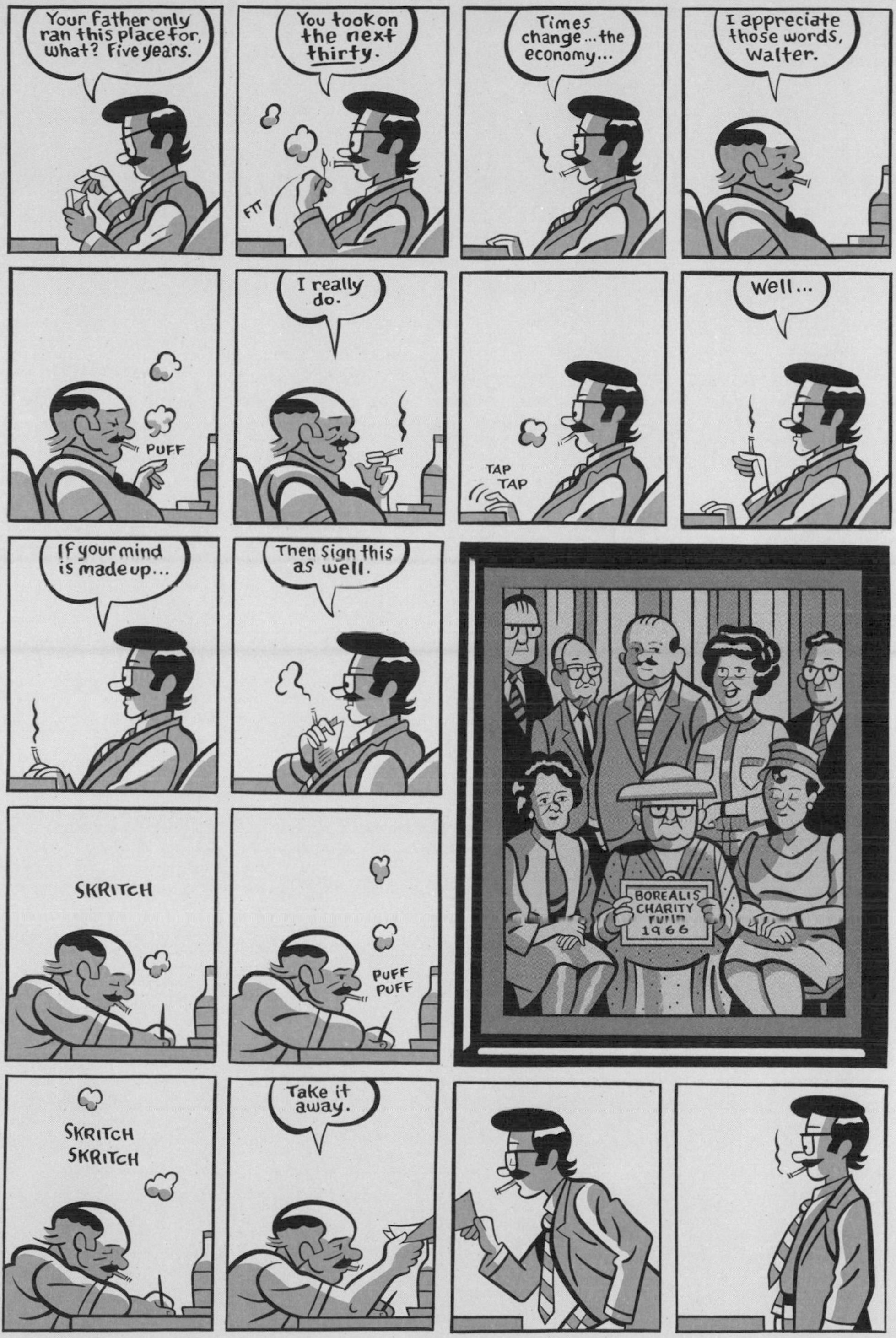
Your father only ran this place for, what? Five years.
You took on the next thirty.
FTT
Times change ... the economy...
I appreciate those words, Walter.
PUFF
I really do.
TAP TAP
Well...
If your mind is made up...
Then sign this as well.
BOREALIS CHARITY
1966
SKRITCH
PUFF PUFF
SKRITCH SKRITCH
Take it away.

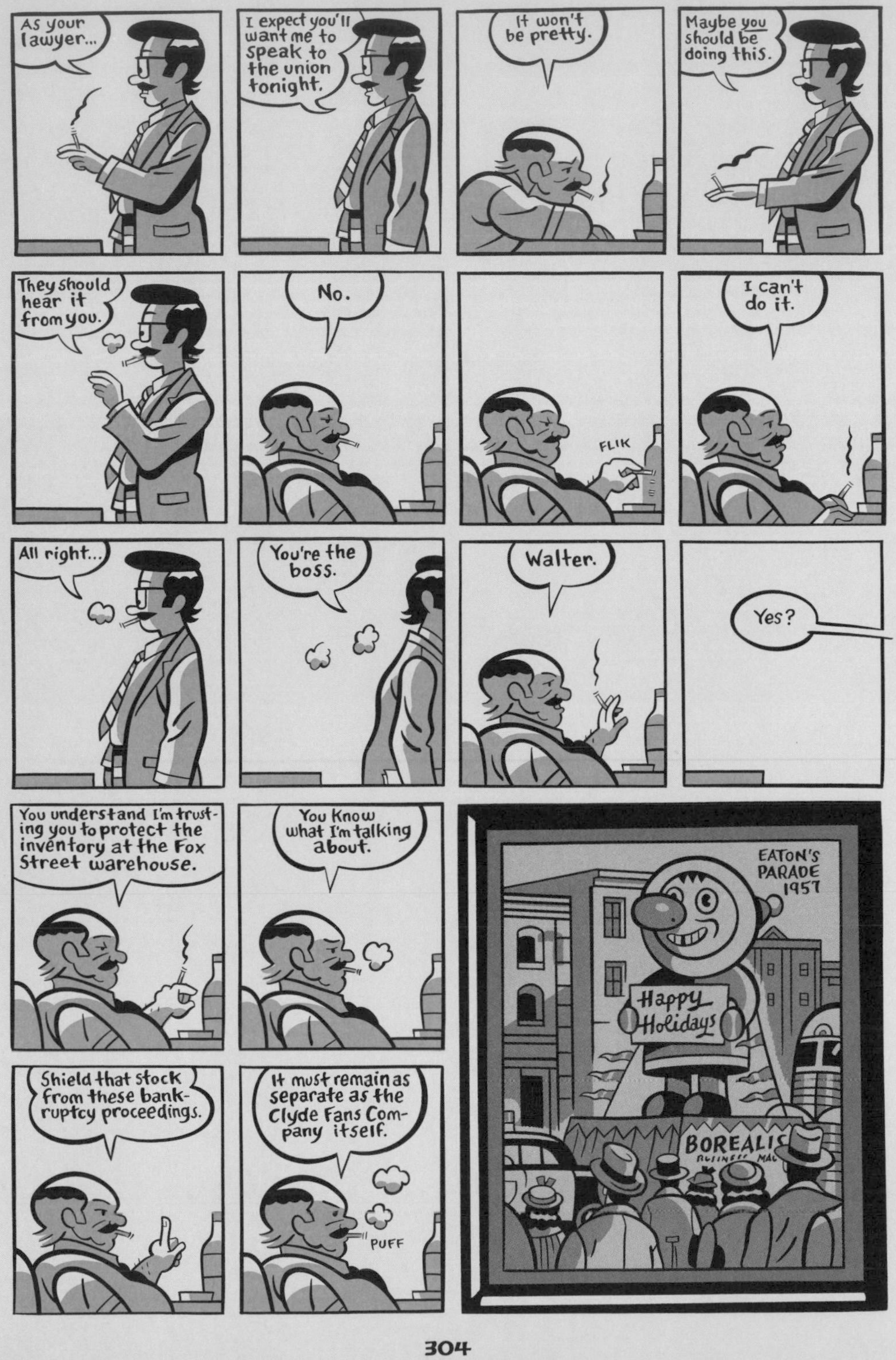
As your lawyer...
I expect you'll want me to speak to the union tonight.
It won't be pretty.
Maybe you should be doing this.
They should hear it from you.
No.
FLIK
I can't do it.
All right...
You're the boss.
Walter.
Yes?
You understand I'm trusting you to protect the inventory at the Fox Street warehouse.
You know what I'm talking about.
EATON'S PARADE 1957
Happy Holidays
BOREALIS
Shield that stock from these bankruptcy proceedings.
It must remain as separate as the Clyde Fans Company itself.
PUFF

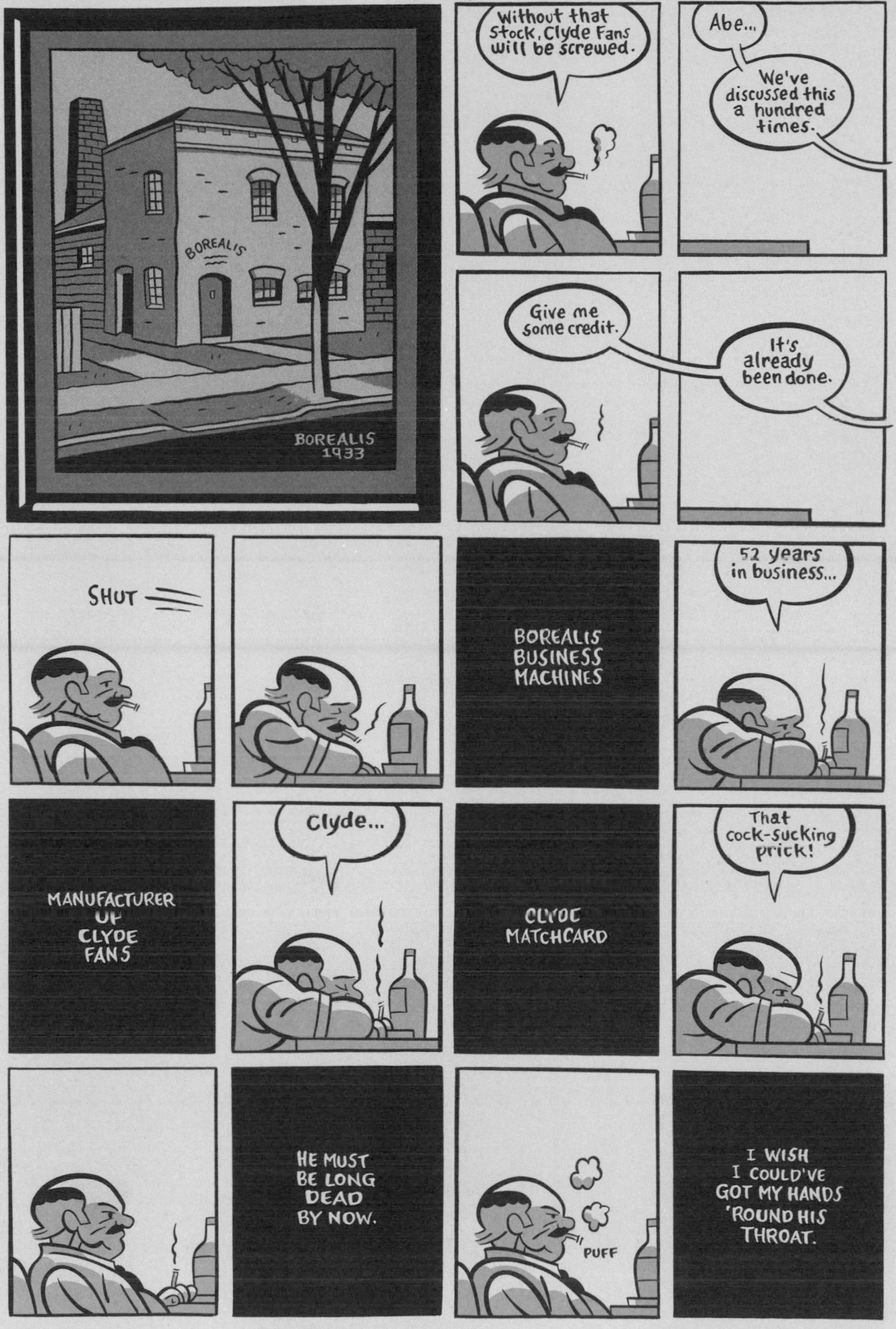
BOREALIS
BOREALIS 1933
Without that Stock, Clyde Fans will be screwed.
Abe...
We've discussed this a hundred times.
Give me some credit.
It's already been done.
SHUT
BOREALIS BUSINESS MACHINES
52 years in business...
MANUFACTURER OF CLYDE FANS
Clyde...
CLYDE MATCHCARD
That cock-sucking prick!
HE MUST BE LONG DEAD BY NOW.
PUFF
I WISH I COULD'VE GOT MY HANDS 'ROUND HIS THROAT.

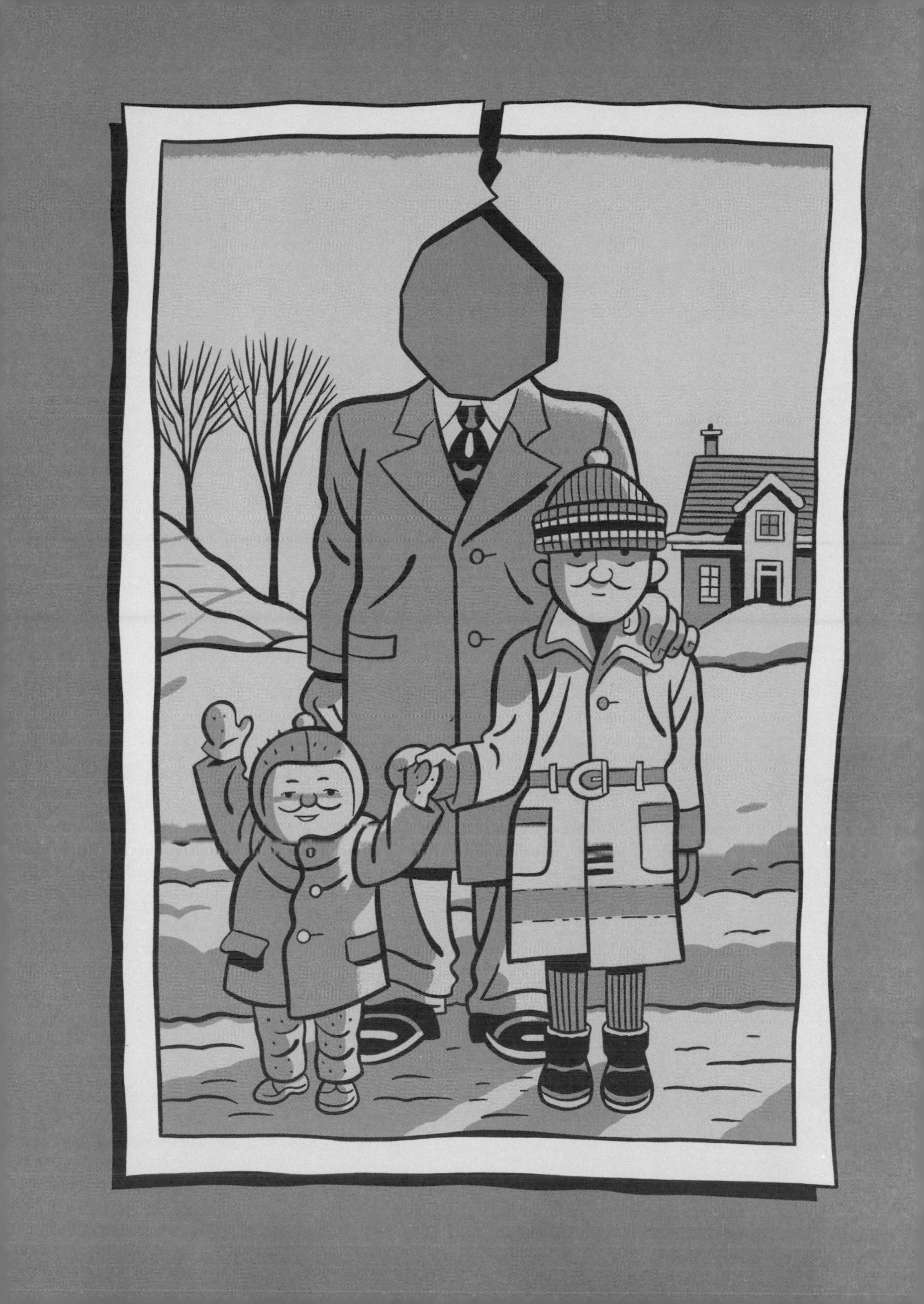

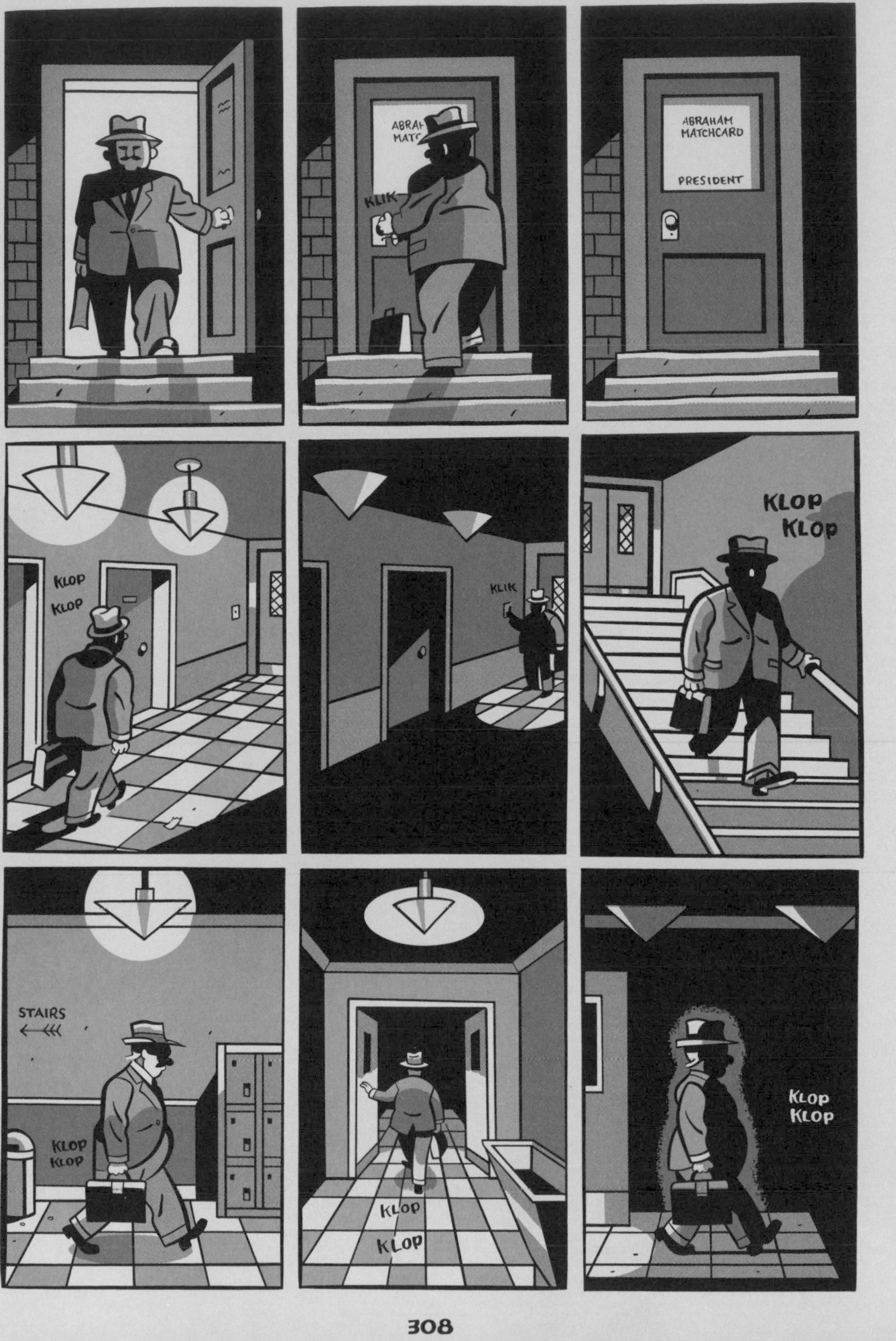
ABRAH
MATC
KLIK
ABRAHAM
MATCHCARD
PRESIDENT
KLOP
KLOP
KLIK
KLOP
KLOP
STAIRS
KLOP
KLOP
KLOP
KLOP
KLOP
KLOP

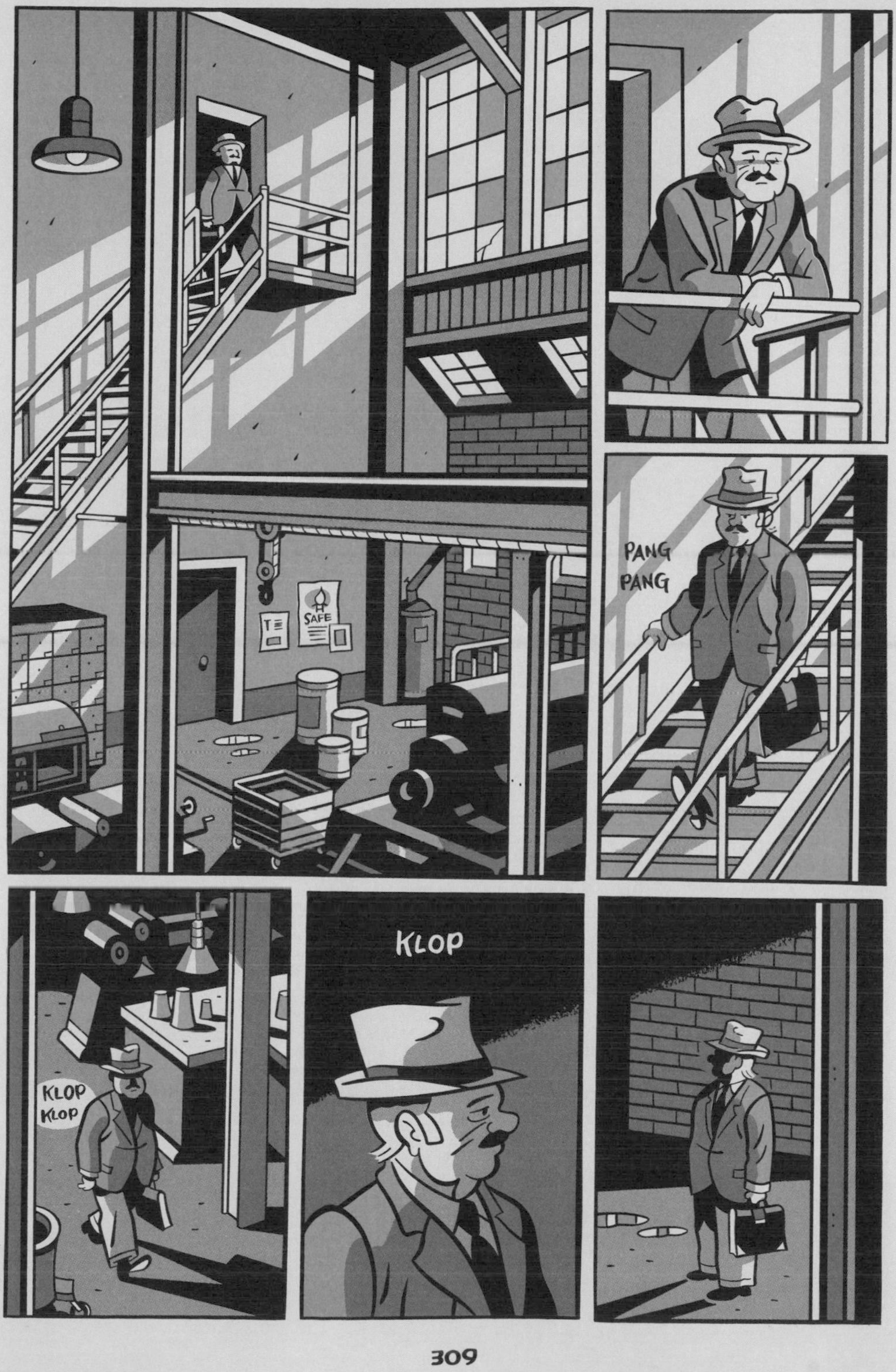
SAFE
PANG
PANG
KLOP
KLOP
KLOP

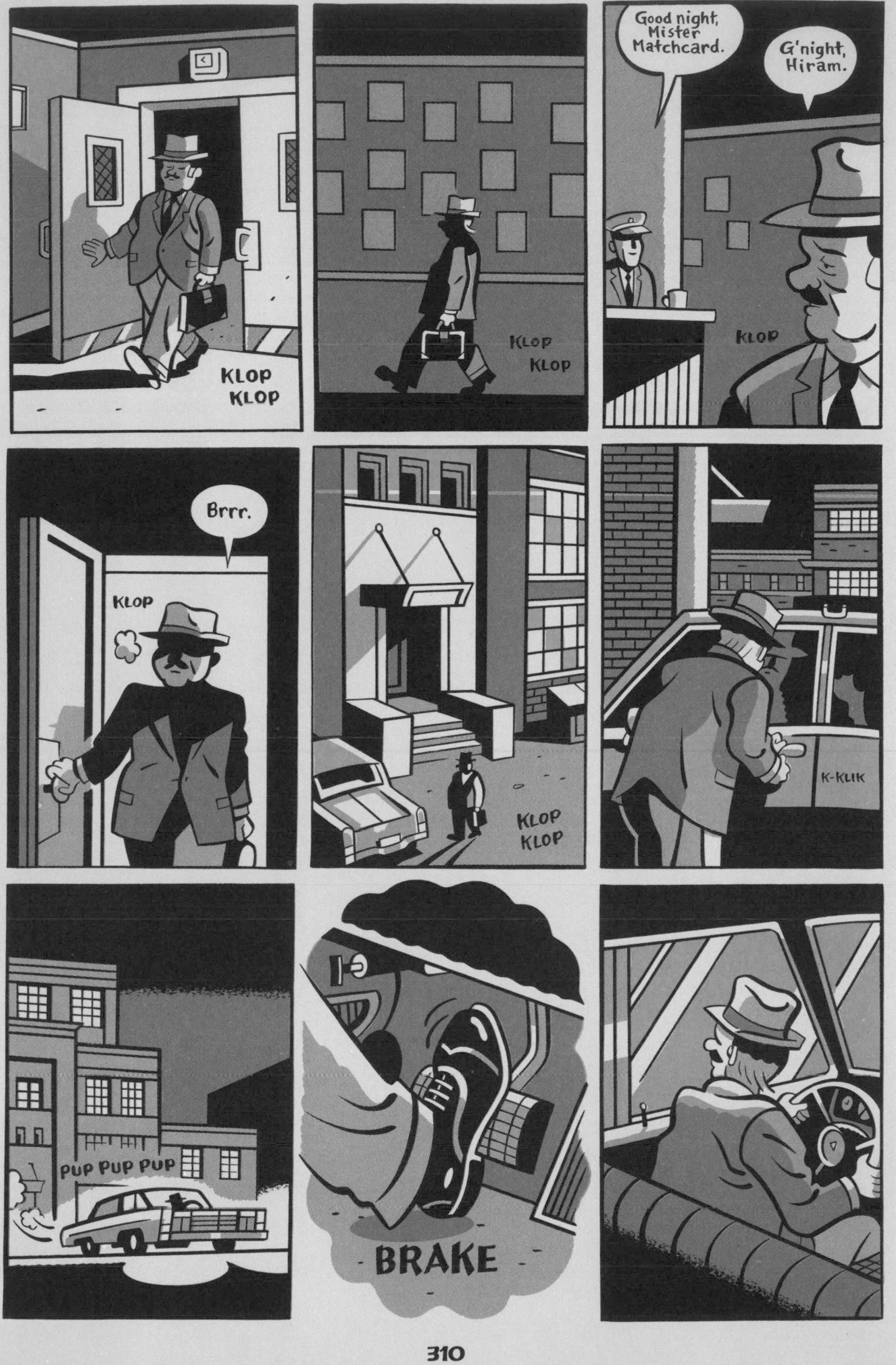
KLOP
KLOP
KLOP
KLOP
Good night, Mister Matchcard.
G'night, Hiram.
KLOP
Brrr.
KLOP
KLOP
KLOP
K-KLIK
PUP PUP PUP
BRAKE

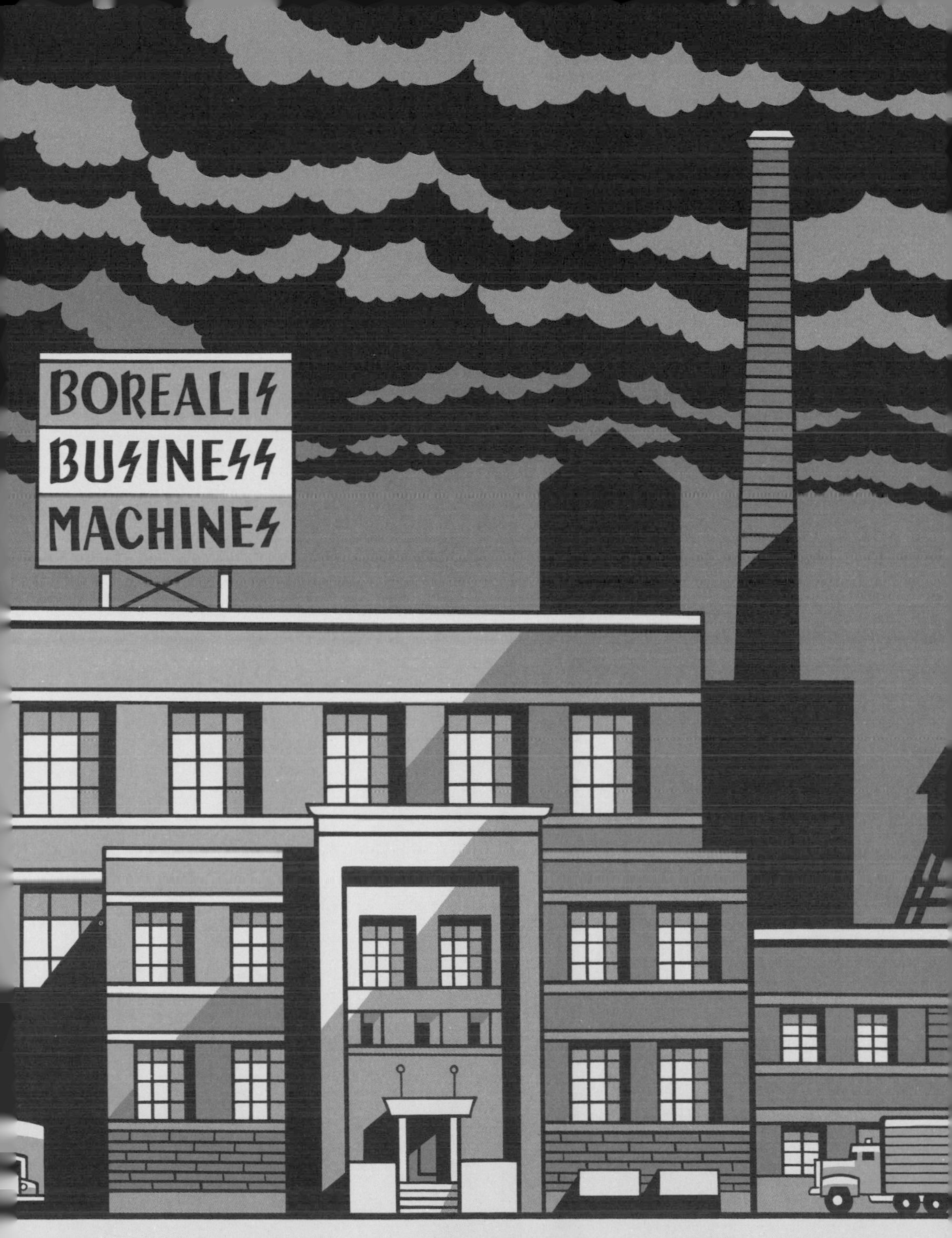
BOREALIS
BUSINESS
MACHINES

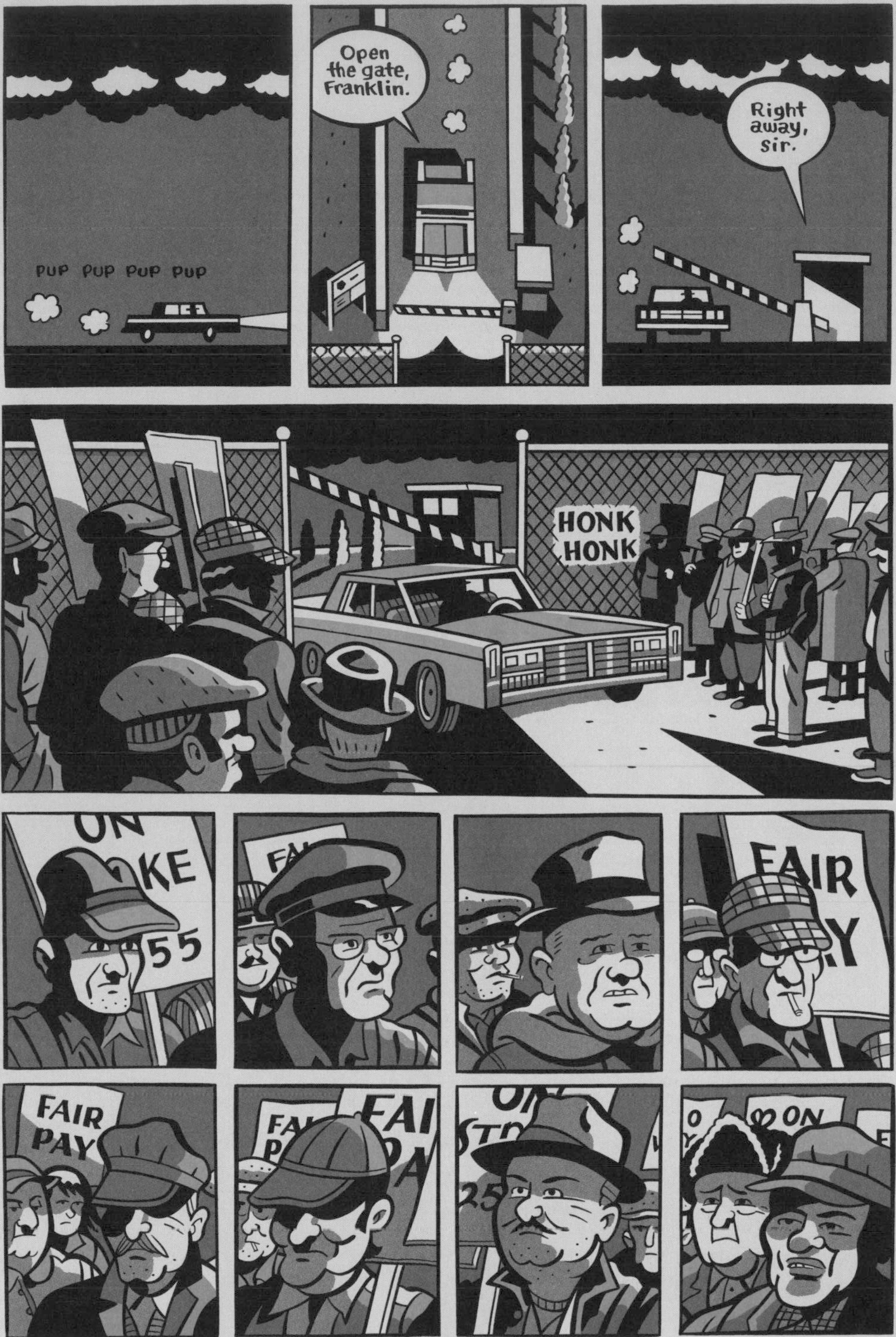
PUP PUP PUP PUP
Open the gate, Franklin.
Right away, sir.
HONK HONK
55
FAIR
FAIR PAY
ON

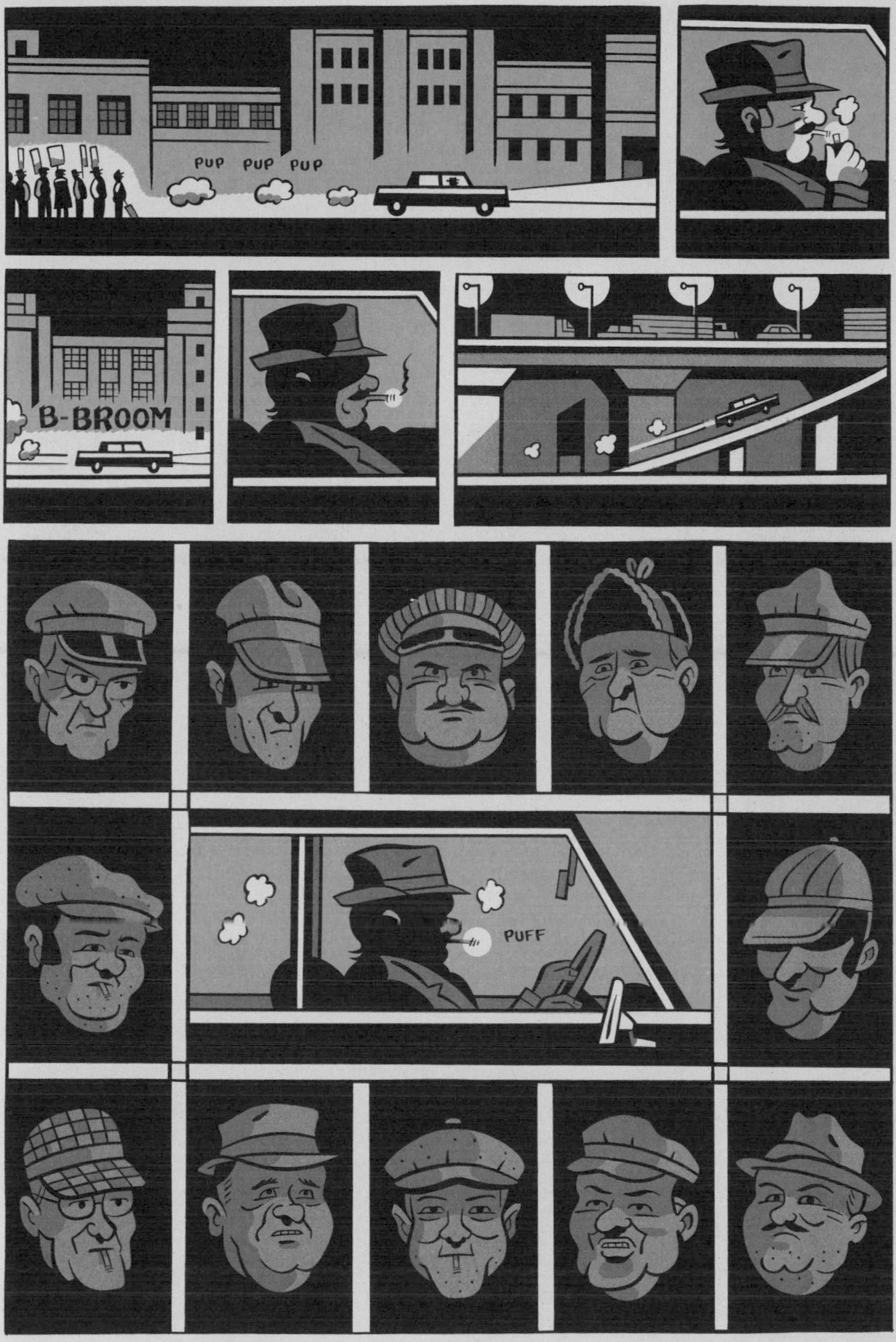
PUP PUP PUP
B-BROOM
PUFF

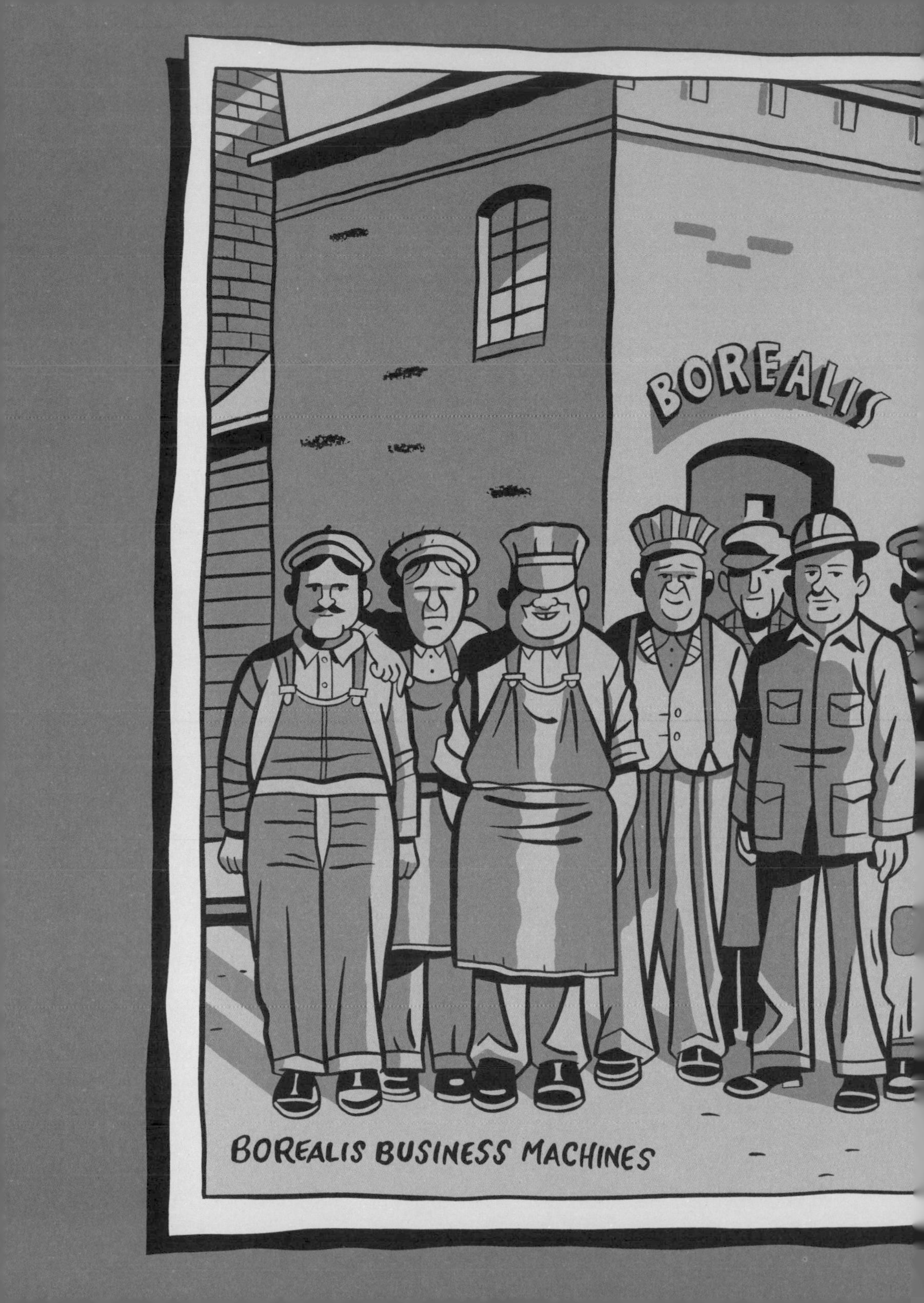
BOREALIS
BOREALIS BUSINESS MACHINES

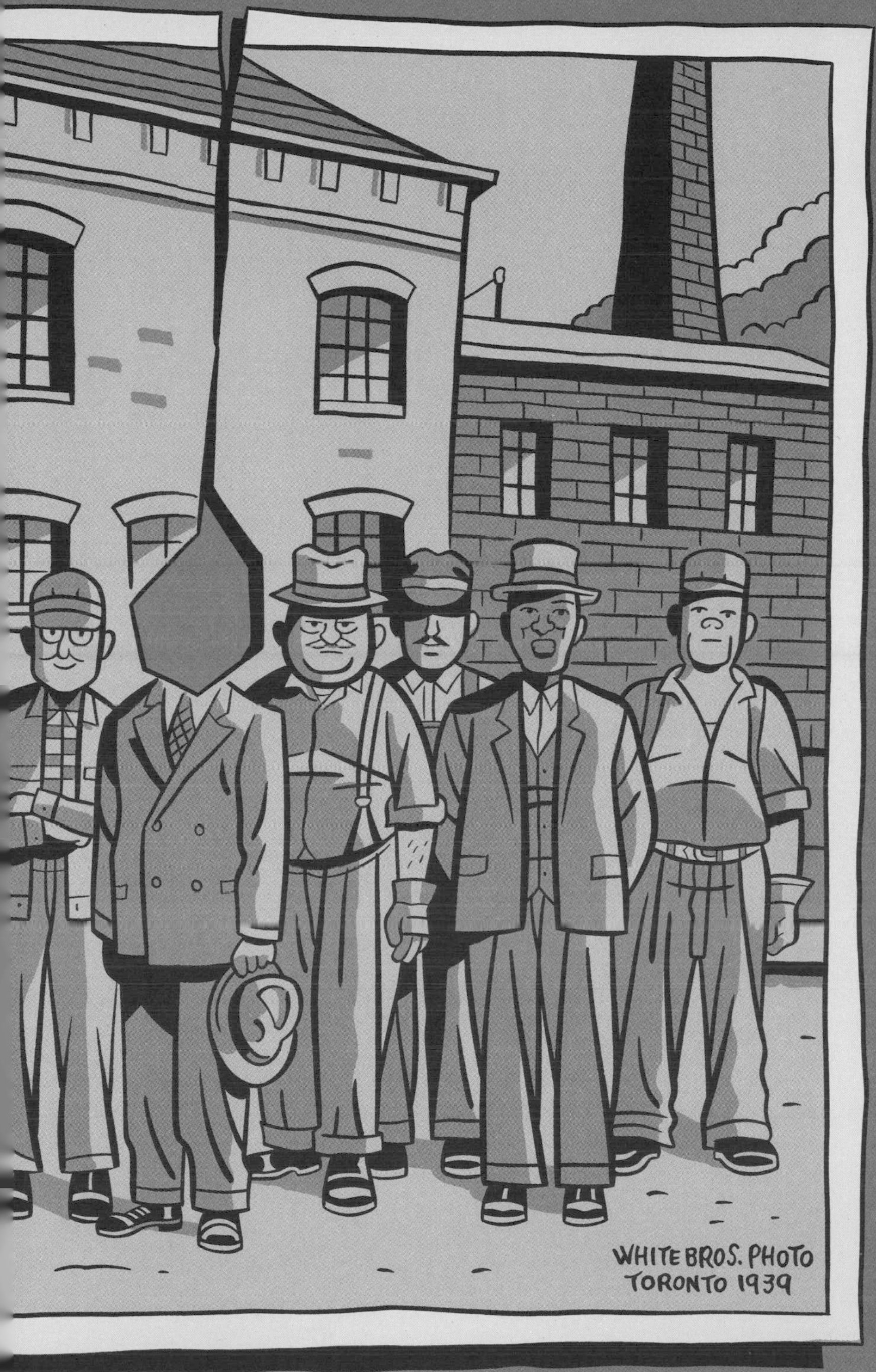
WHITE BROS. PHOTO
TORONTO 1939

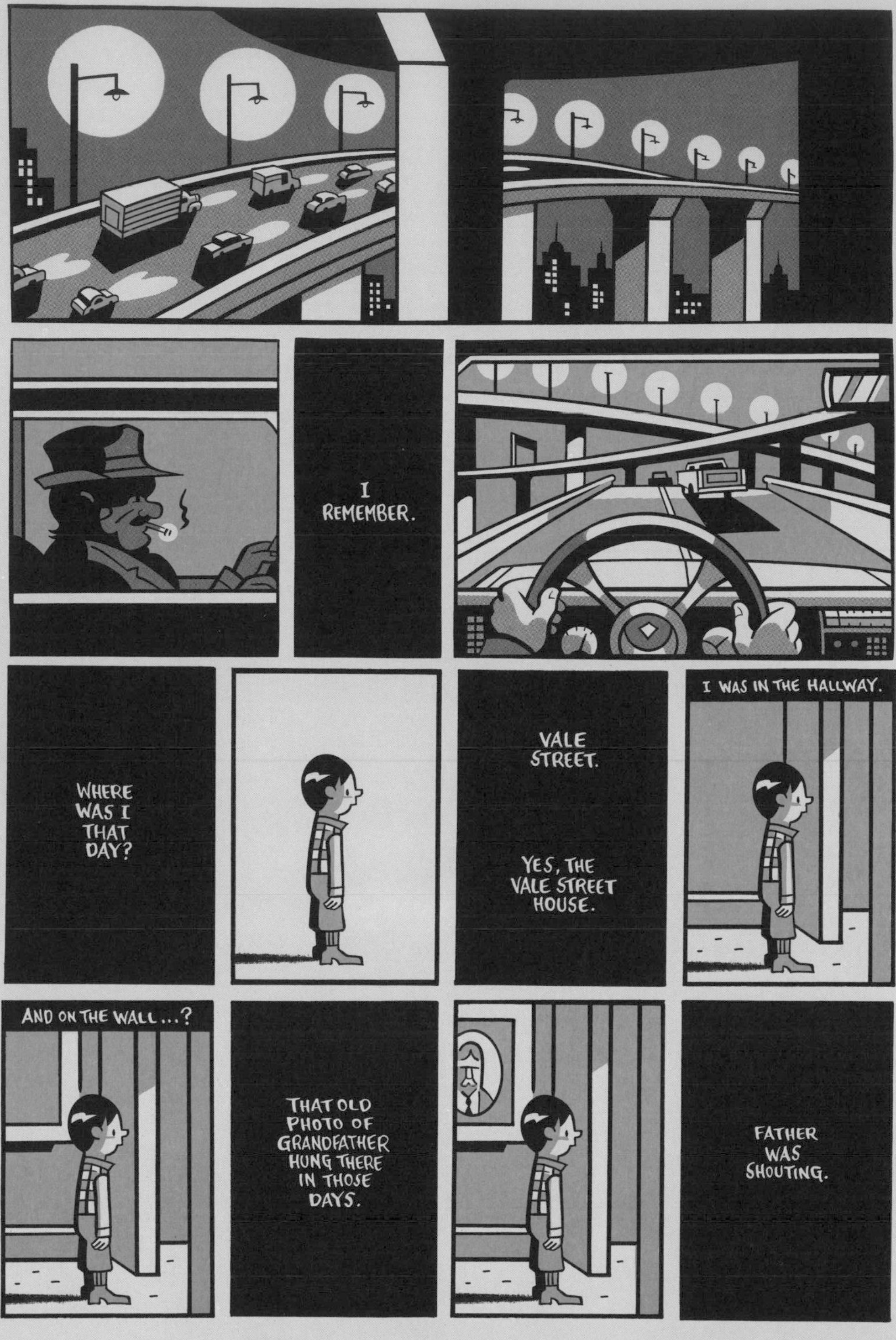
I REMEMBER.
WHERE WAS I THAT DAY?
VALE STREET.
YES, THE VALE STREET HOUSE.
I WAS IN THE HALLWAY.
AND ON THE WALL...?
THAT OLD PHOTO OF GRANDFATHER HUNG THERE IN THOSE DAYS.
FATHER WAS SHOUTING.

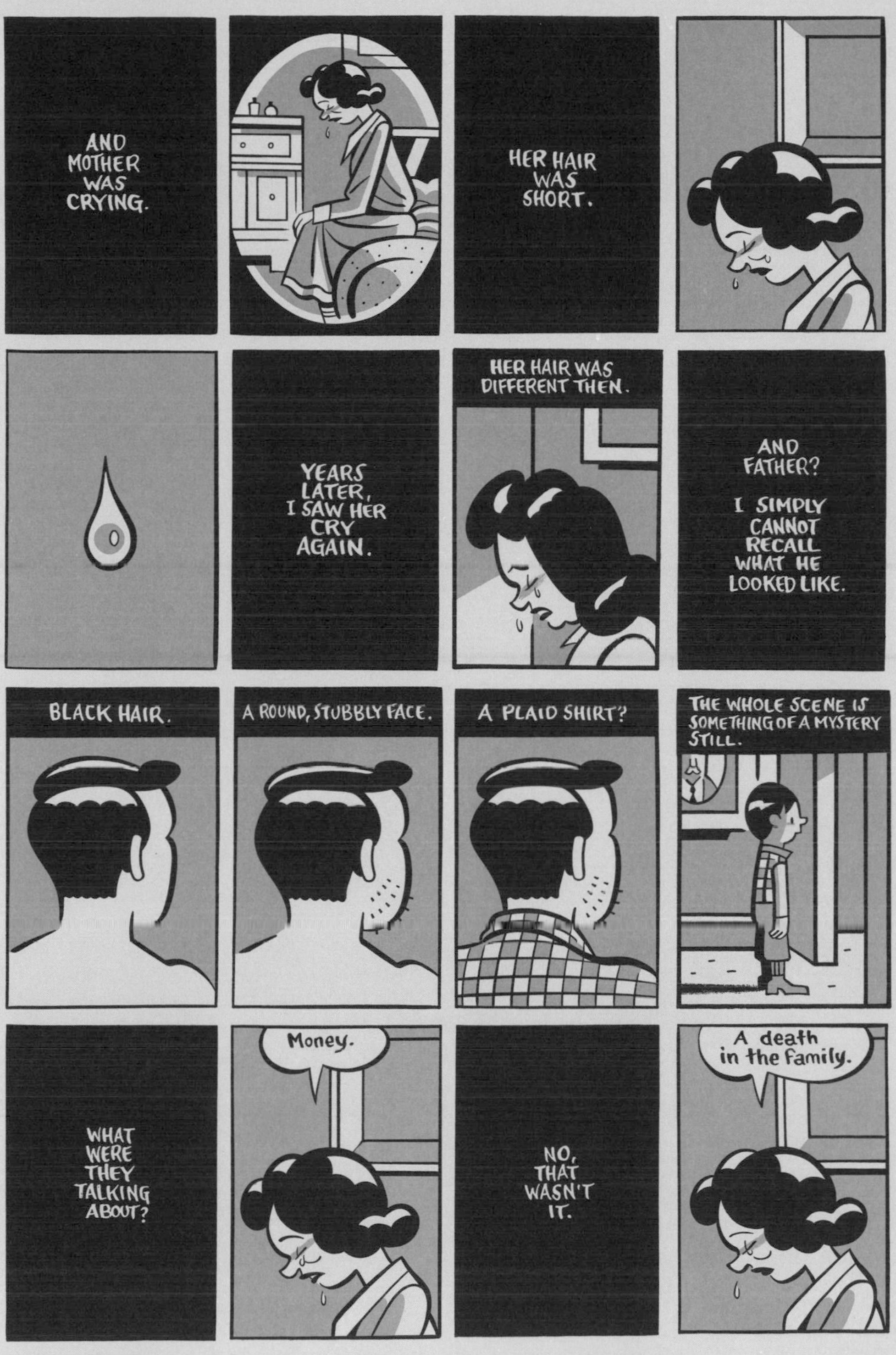
AND MOTHER WAS CRYING.
HER HAIR WAS SHORT.
YEARS LATER, I SAW HER CRY AGAIN.
HER HAIR WAS DIFFERENT THEN.
AND FATHER?
I SIMPLY CANNOT RECALL WHAT HE LOOKED LIKE.
BLACK HAIR.
A ROUND, STUBBLY FACE.
A PLAID SHIRT?
THE WHOLE SCENE IS SOMETHING OF A MYSTERY STILL.
WHAT WERE THEY TALKING ABOUT?
Money.
NO, THAT WASN'T IT.
A death in the family.

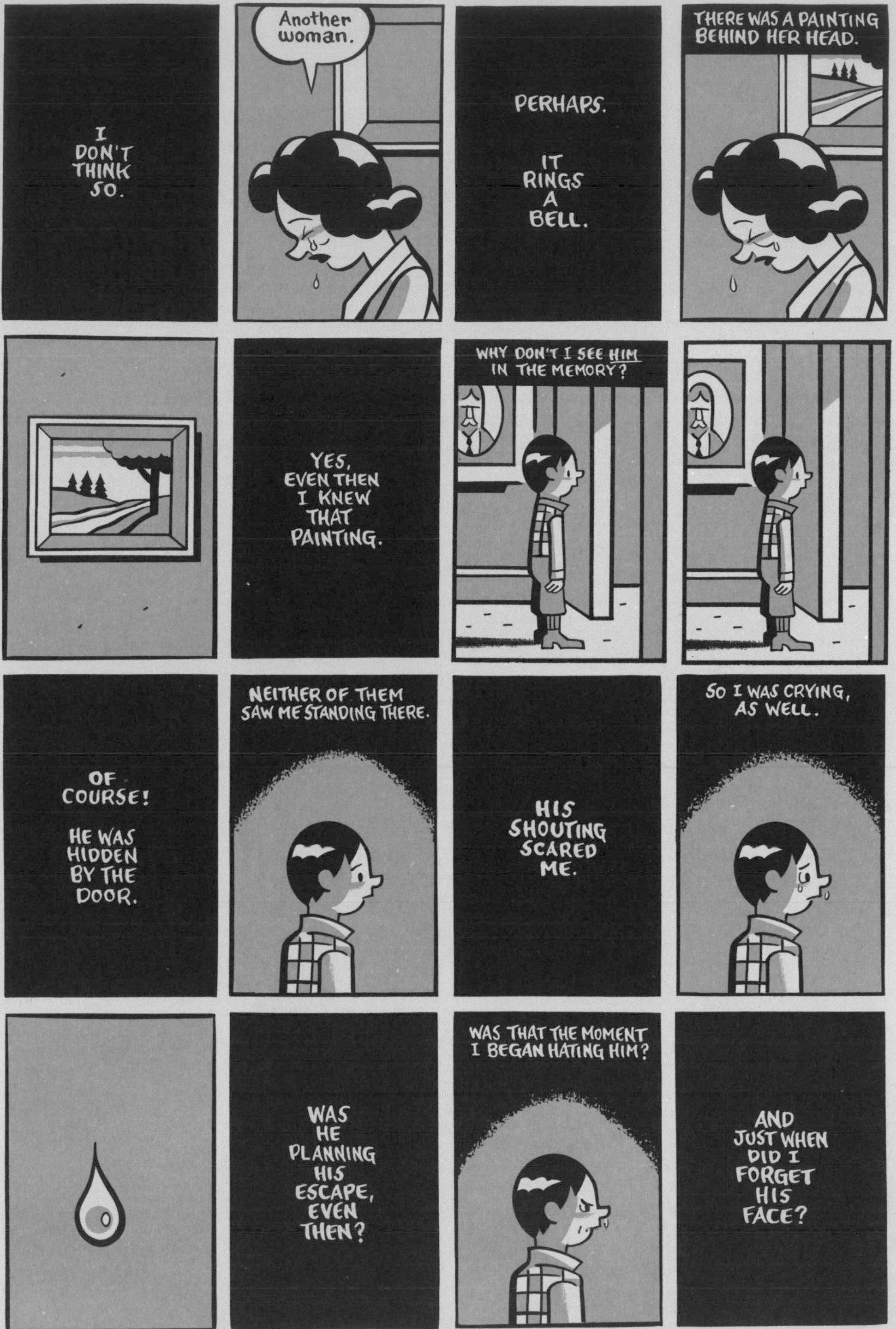
I DON'T THINK SO.
Another woman.
PERHAPS.
IT RINGS A BELL.
THERE WAS A PAINTING BEHIND HER HEAD.
YES, EVEN THEN I KNEW THAT PAINTING.
WHY DON'T I SEE HIM IN THE MEMORY?
OF COURSE!
HE WAS HIDDEN BY THE DOOR.
NEITHER OF THEM SAW ME STANDING THERE.
HIS SHOUTING SCARED ME.
SO I WAS CRYING, AS WELL.
WAS HE PLANNING HIS ESCAPE, EVEN THEN?
WAS THAT THE MOMENT I BEGAN HATING HIM?
AND JUST WHEN DID I FORGET HIS FACE?

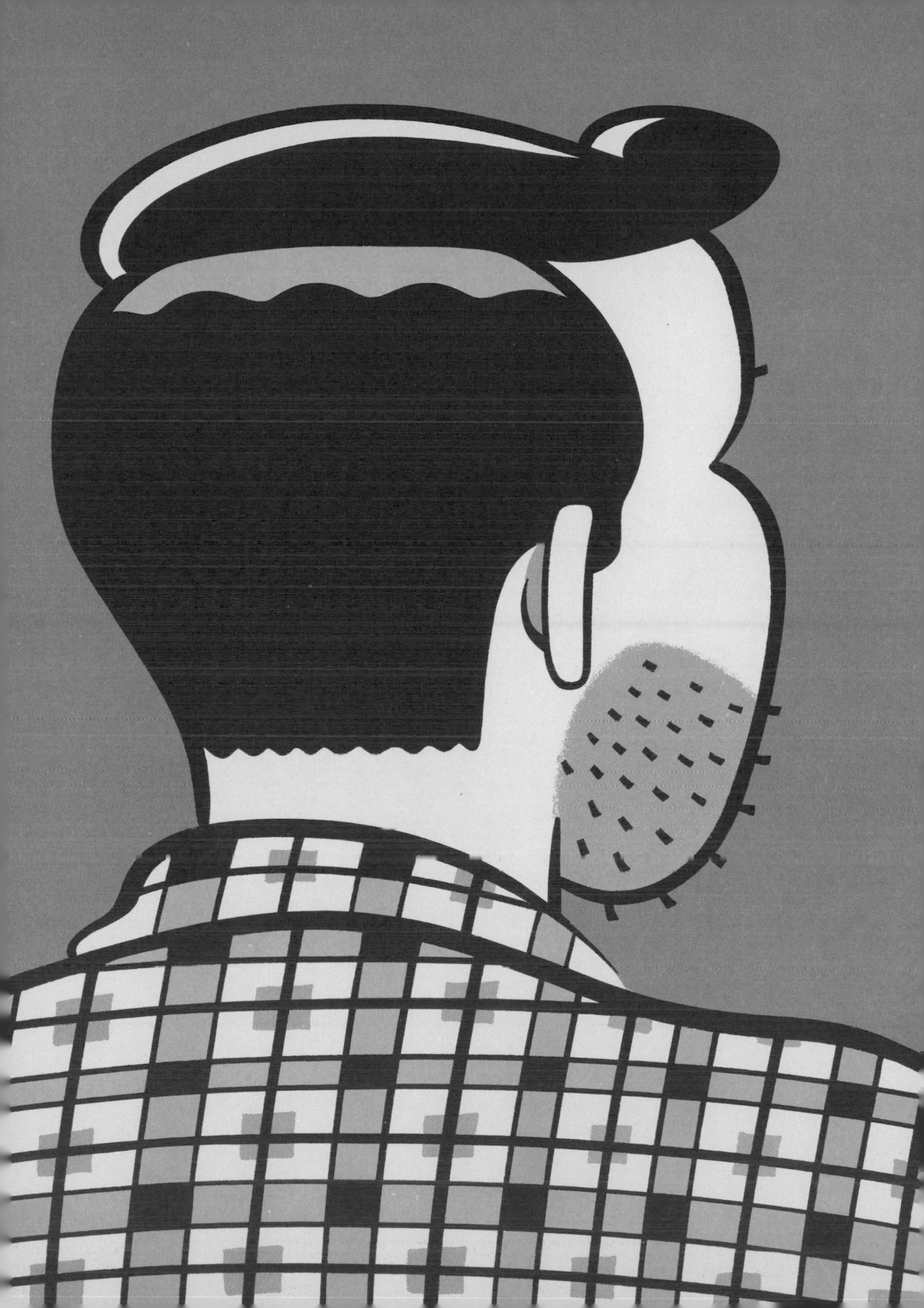

"BE HONEST."

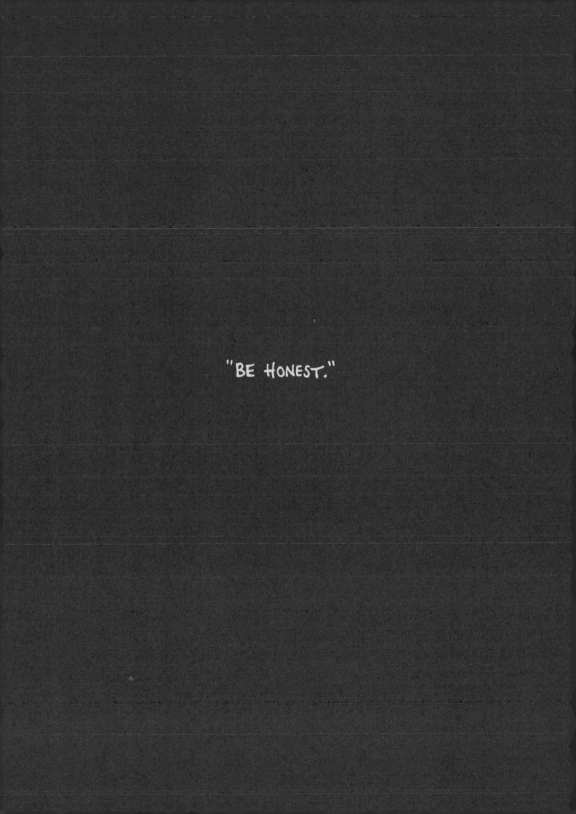

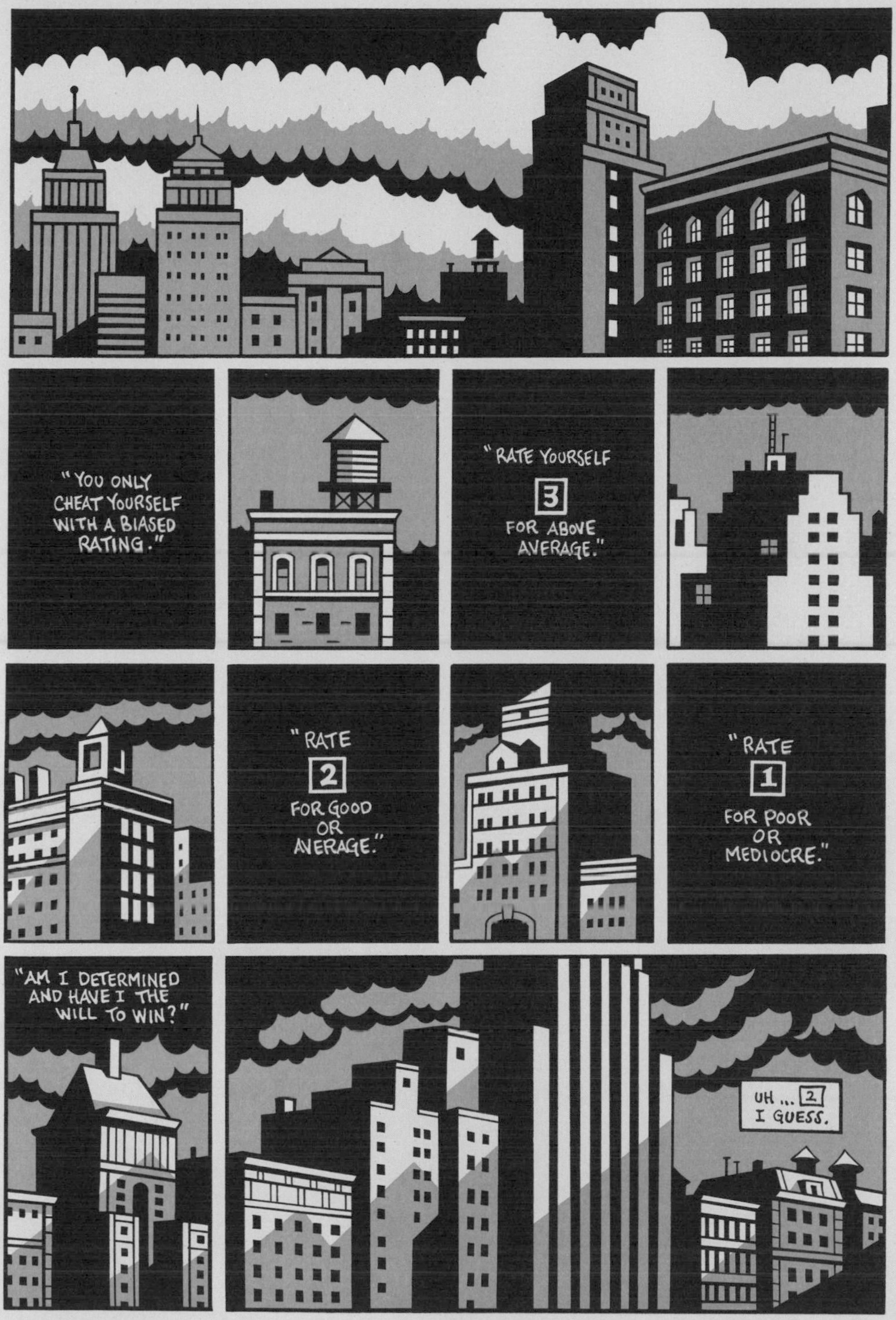
"YOU ONLY CHEAT YOURSELF WITH A BIASED RATING."
"RATE YOURSELF 3 FOR ABOVE AVERAGE."
"RATE 2 FOR GOOD OR AVERAGE."
"RATE 1 FOR POOR OR MEDIOCRE."
"AM I DETERMINED AND HAVE I THE WILL TO WIN?"
UH ... 2 I GUESS.

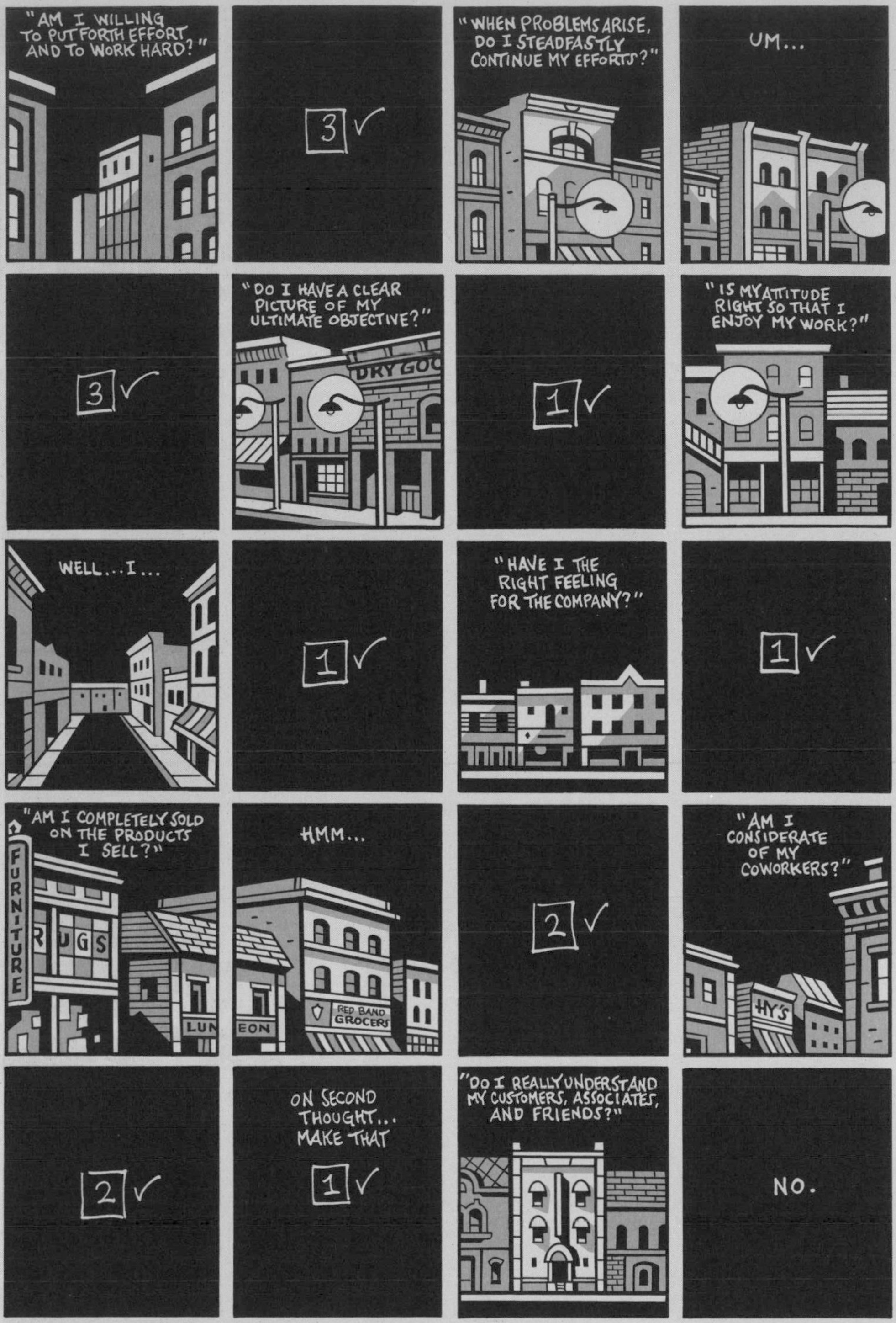
"AM I WILLING TO PUT FORTH EFFORT AND TO WORK HARD?"
3 ✓
"WHEN PROBLEMS ARISE, DO I STEADFASTLY CONTINUE MY EFFORTS?"
UM...
3 ✓
"DO I HAVE A CLEAR PICTURE OF MY ULTIMATE OBJECTIVE?"
1 ✓
"IS MY ATTITUDE RIGHT SO THAT I ENJOY MY WORK?"
WELL...I...
1 ✓
"HAVE I THE RIGHT FEELING FOR THE COMPANY?"
1 ✓
"AM I COMPLETELY SOLD ON THE PRODUCTS I SELL?"
FURNITURE
RUGS
HMM...
RED BAND GROCERS
2 ✓
"AM I CONSIDERATE OF MY COWORKERS?"
HY'S
2 ✓
ON SECOND THOUGHT... MAKE THAT
1 ✓
"DO I REALLY UNDERSTAND MY CUSTOMERS, ASSOCIATES, AND FRIENDS?"
NO.

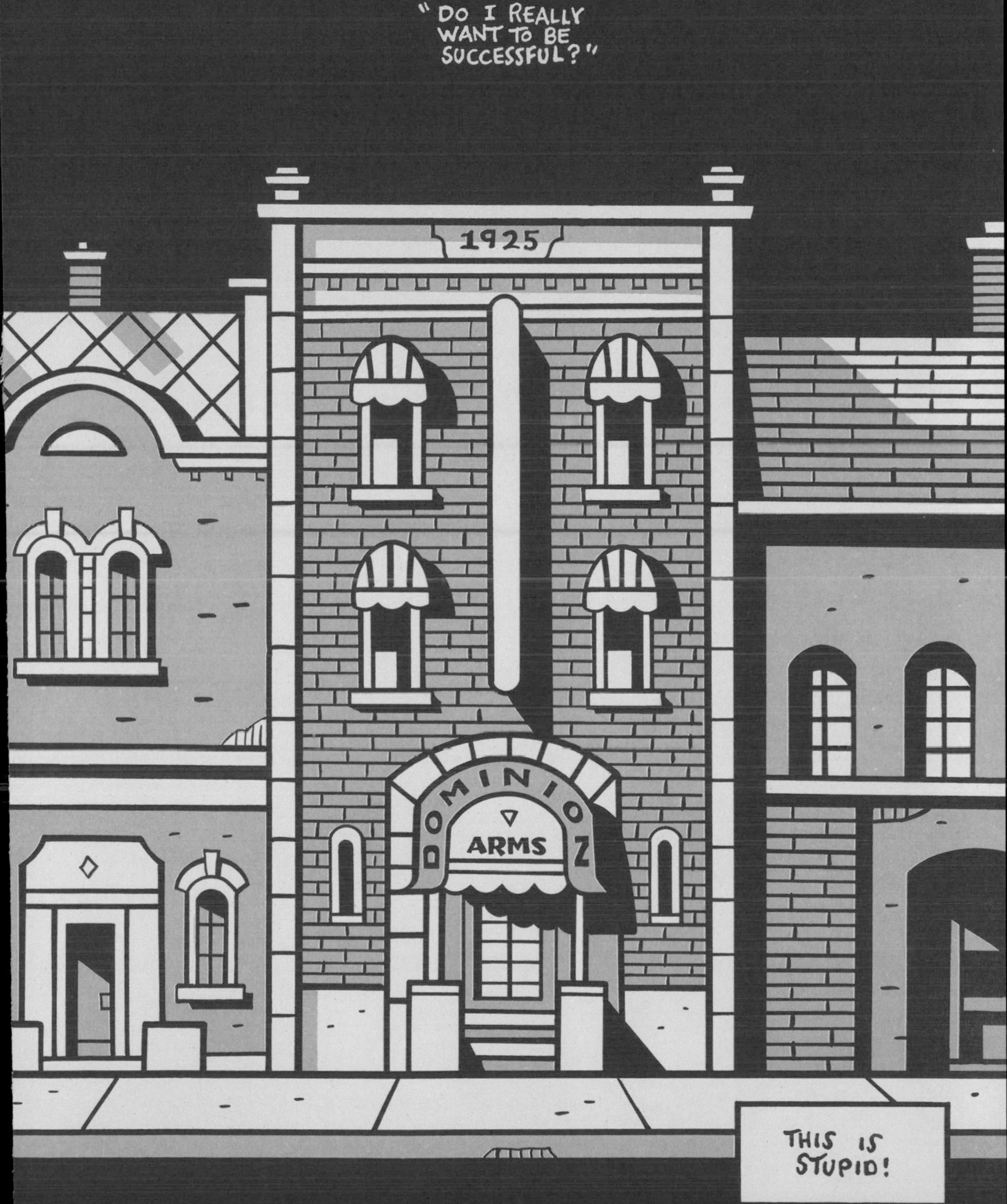
"DO I REALLY WANT TO BE SUCCESSFUL?"
1925
DOMINION
ARMS
THIS IS STUPID!

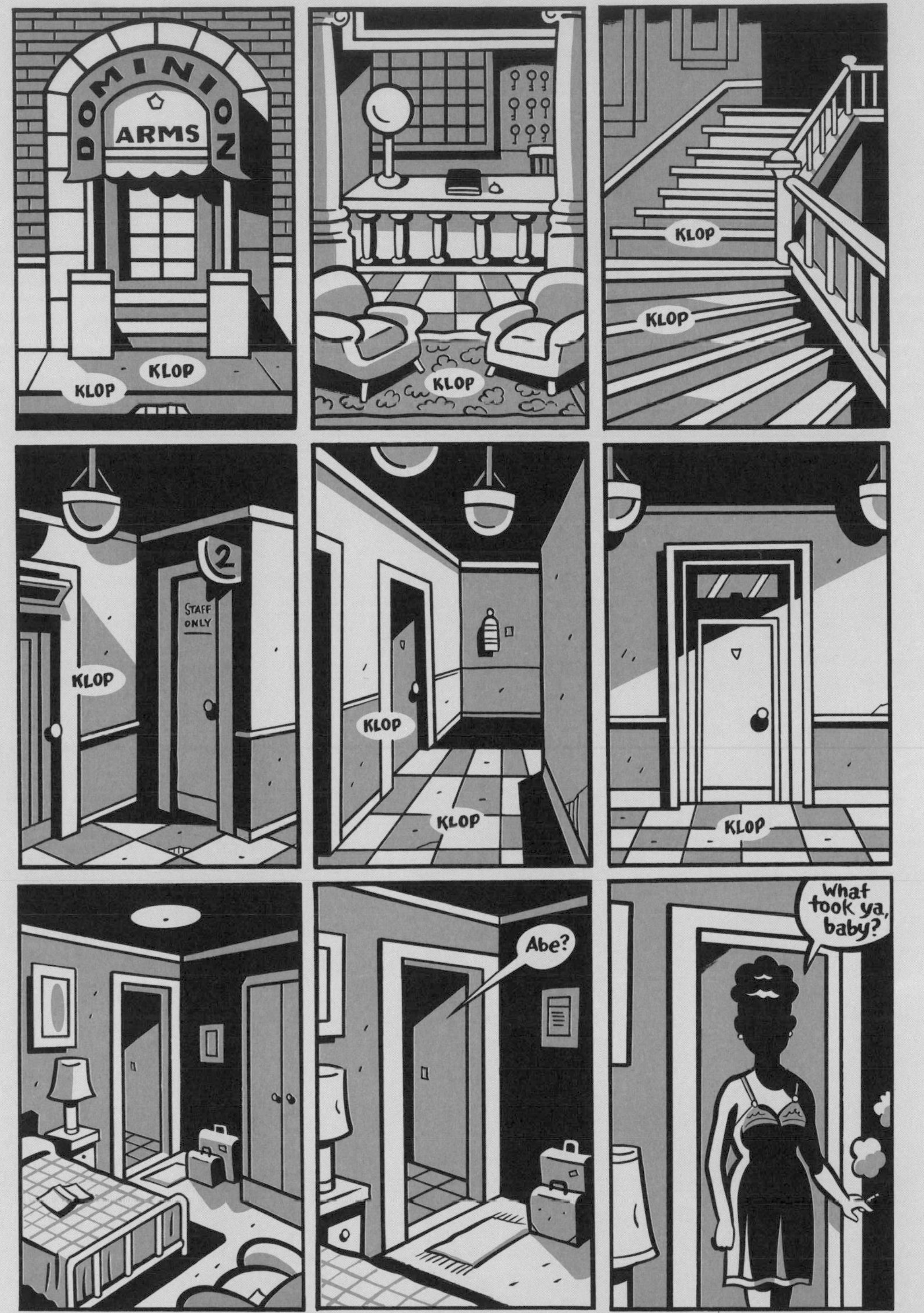
DOMINION
ARMS
KLOP
KLOP
KLOP
KLOP
KLOP
KLOP
STAFF ONLY
KLOP
KLOP
KLOP
KLOP
Abe?
What took ya, baby?

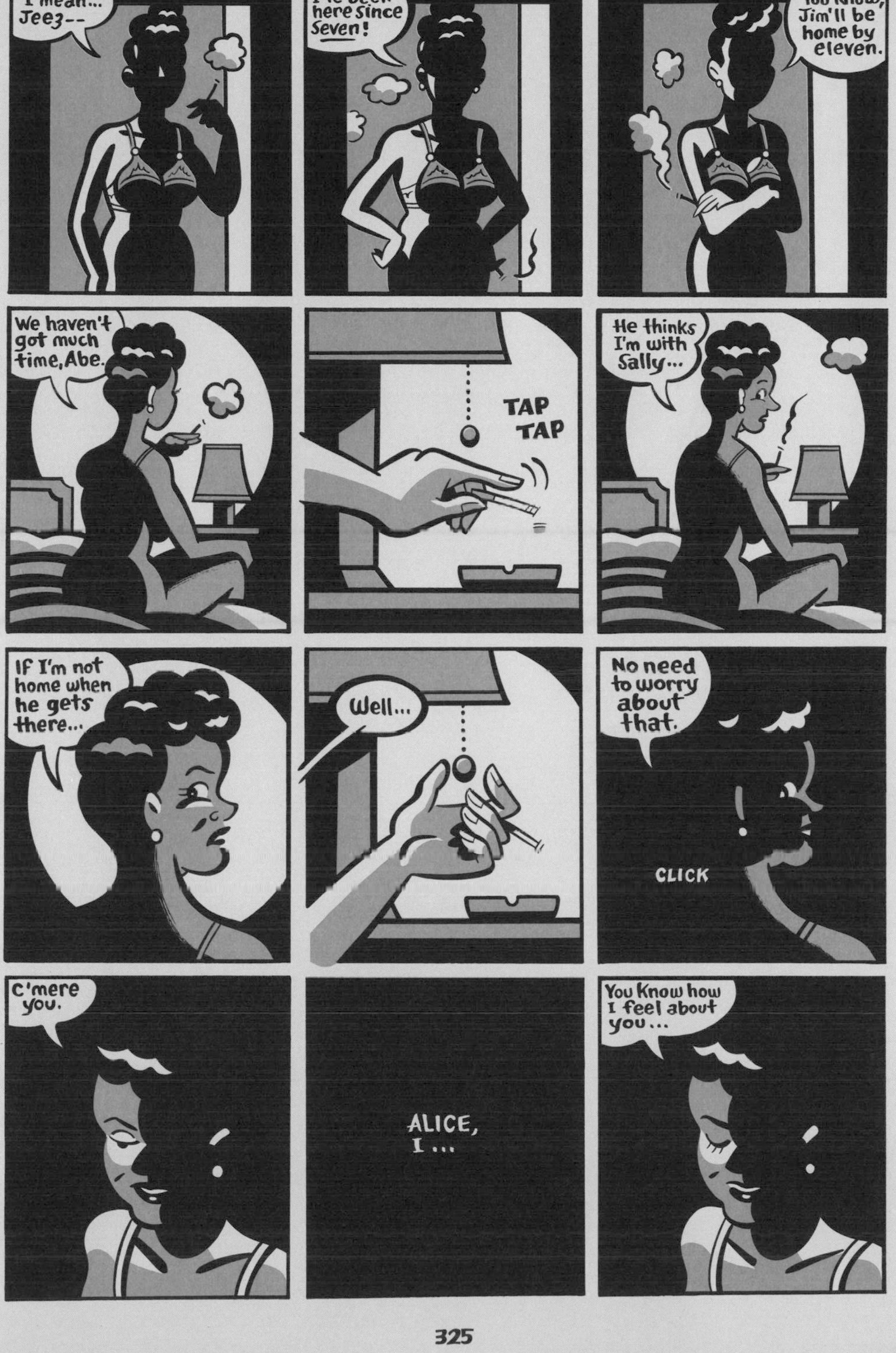
I mean... Jeez--
I've been here since Seven!
You know, Jim'll be home by eleven.
We haven't got much time, Abe.
TAP TAP
He thinks I'm with Sally...
If I'm not home when he gets there...
Well...
No need to worry about that.
CLICK
C'mere you.
ALICE, I...
You know how I feel about you...

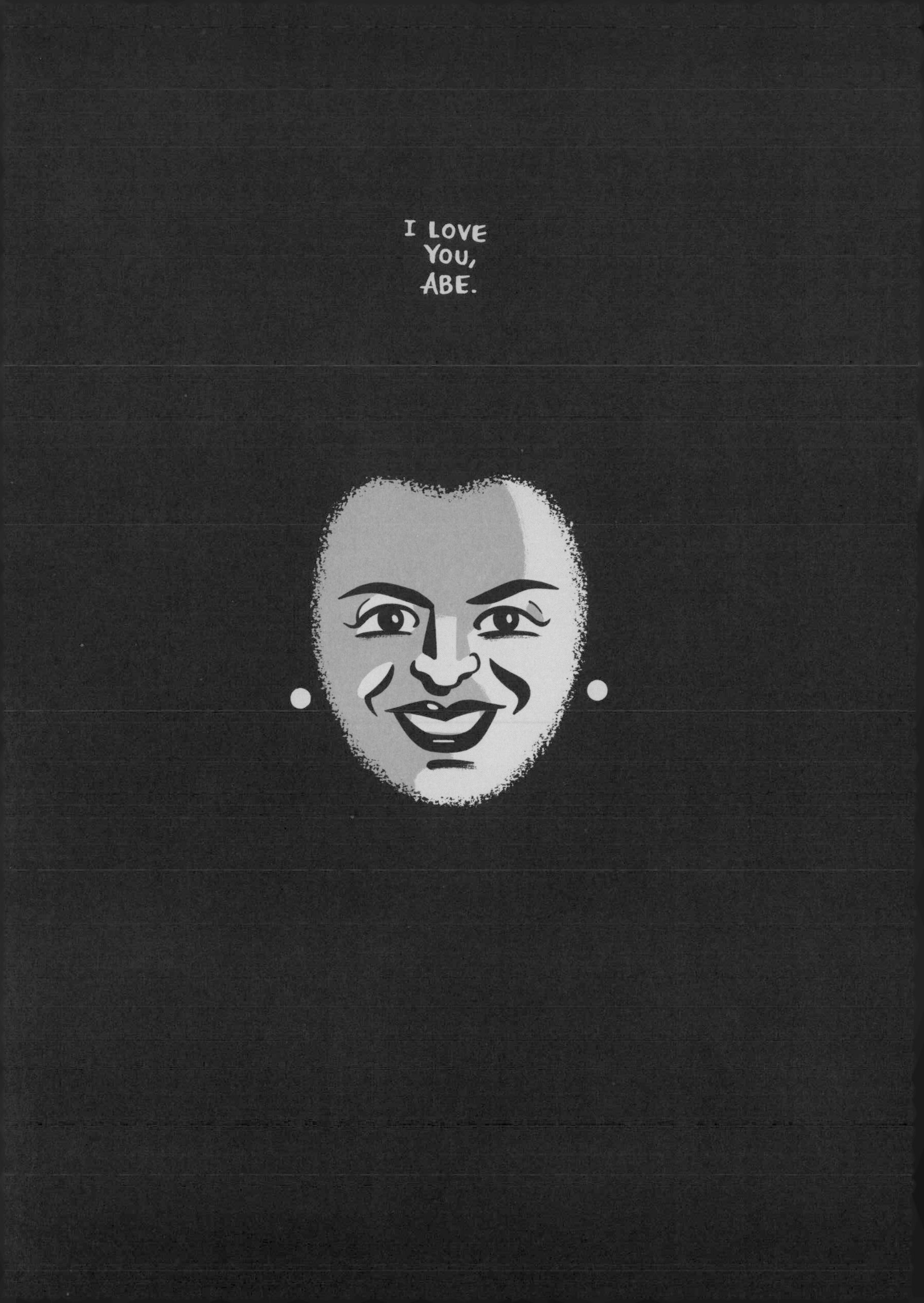
I LOVE YOU, ABE.

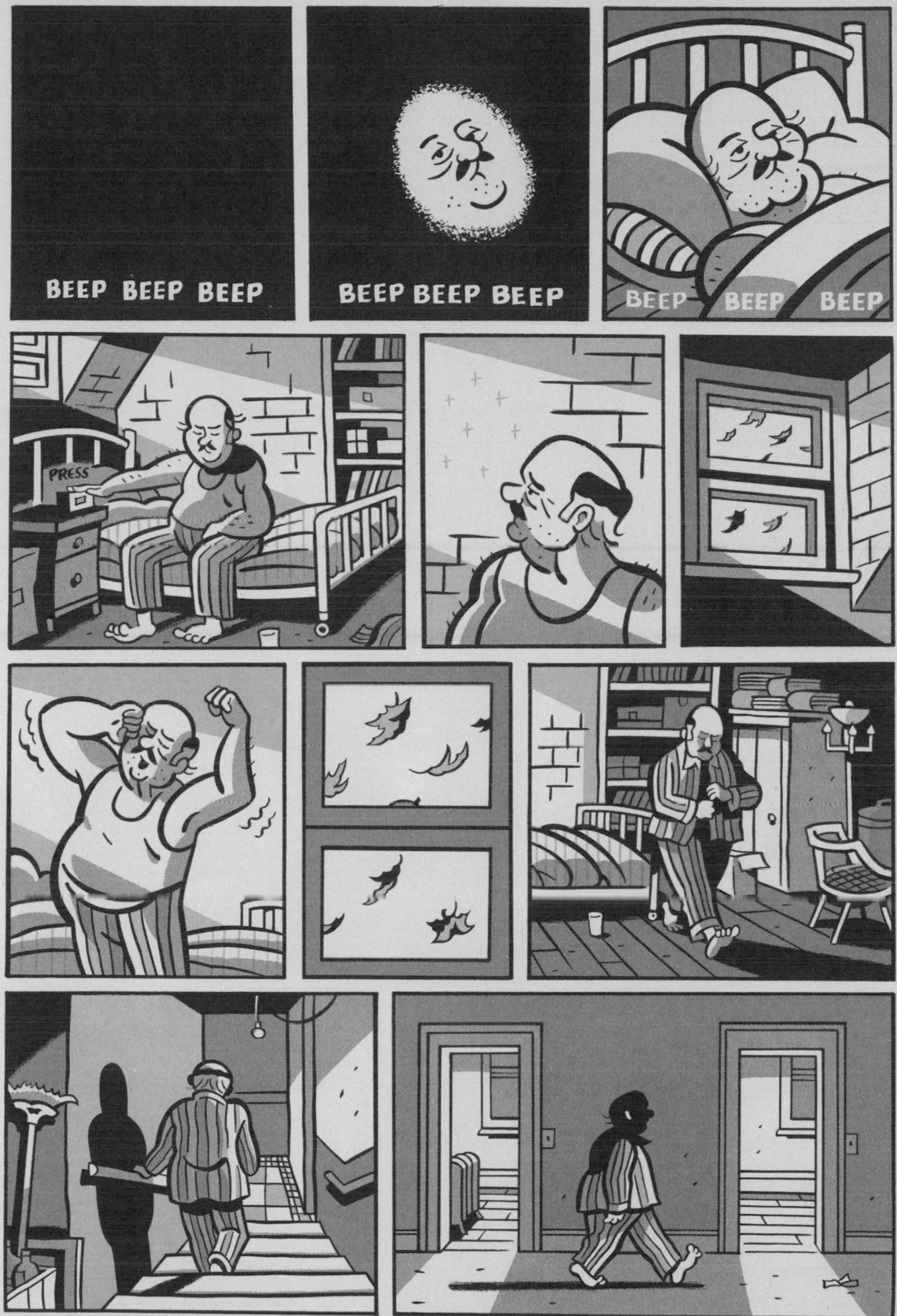
BEEP BEEP BEEP
BEEP BEEP BEEP
BEEP BEEP BEEP
PRESS

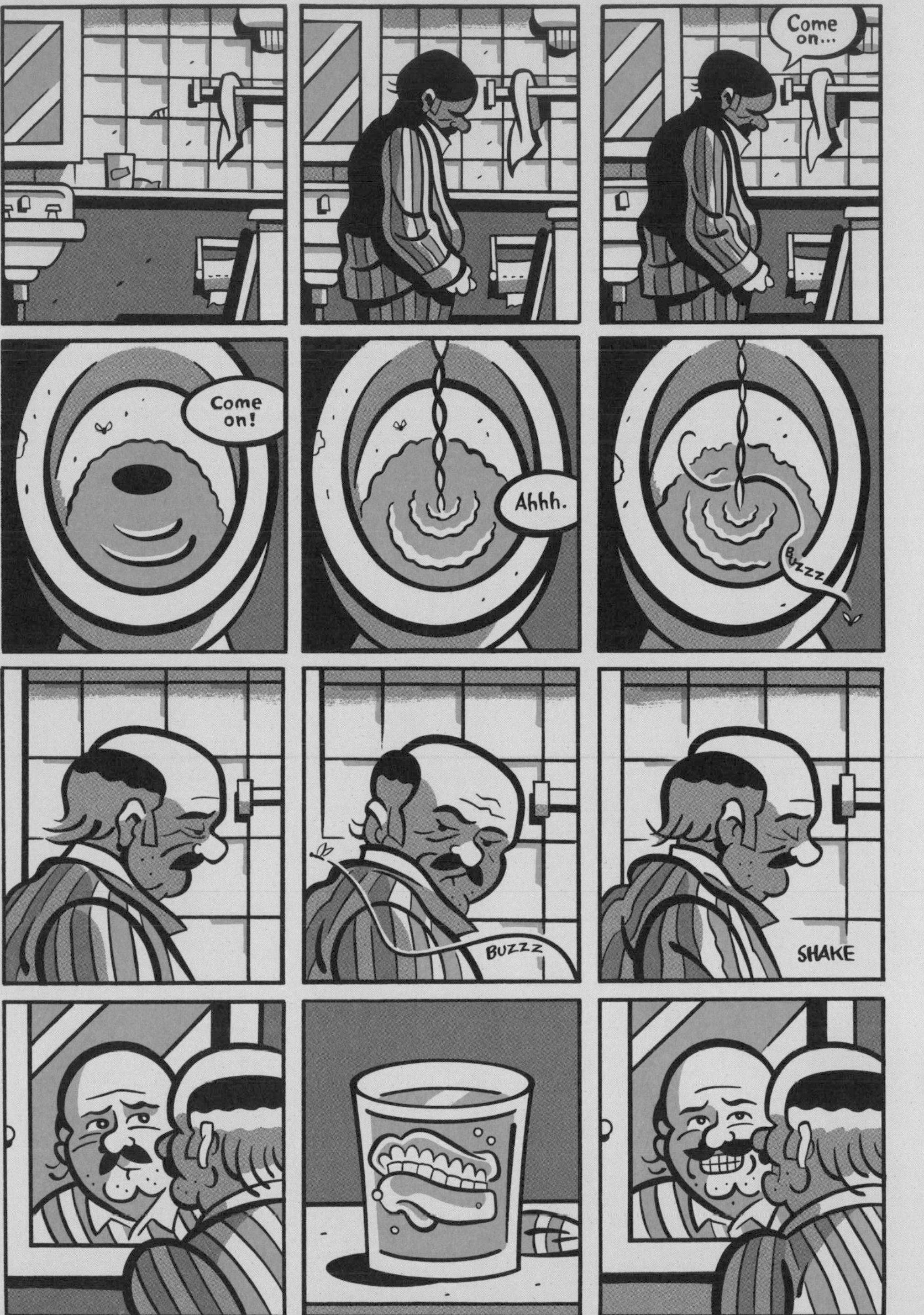
Come on...
Come on!
Ahhh.
BUZZZ
BUZZZ
SHAKE

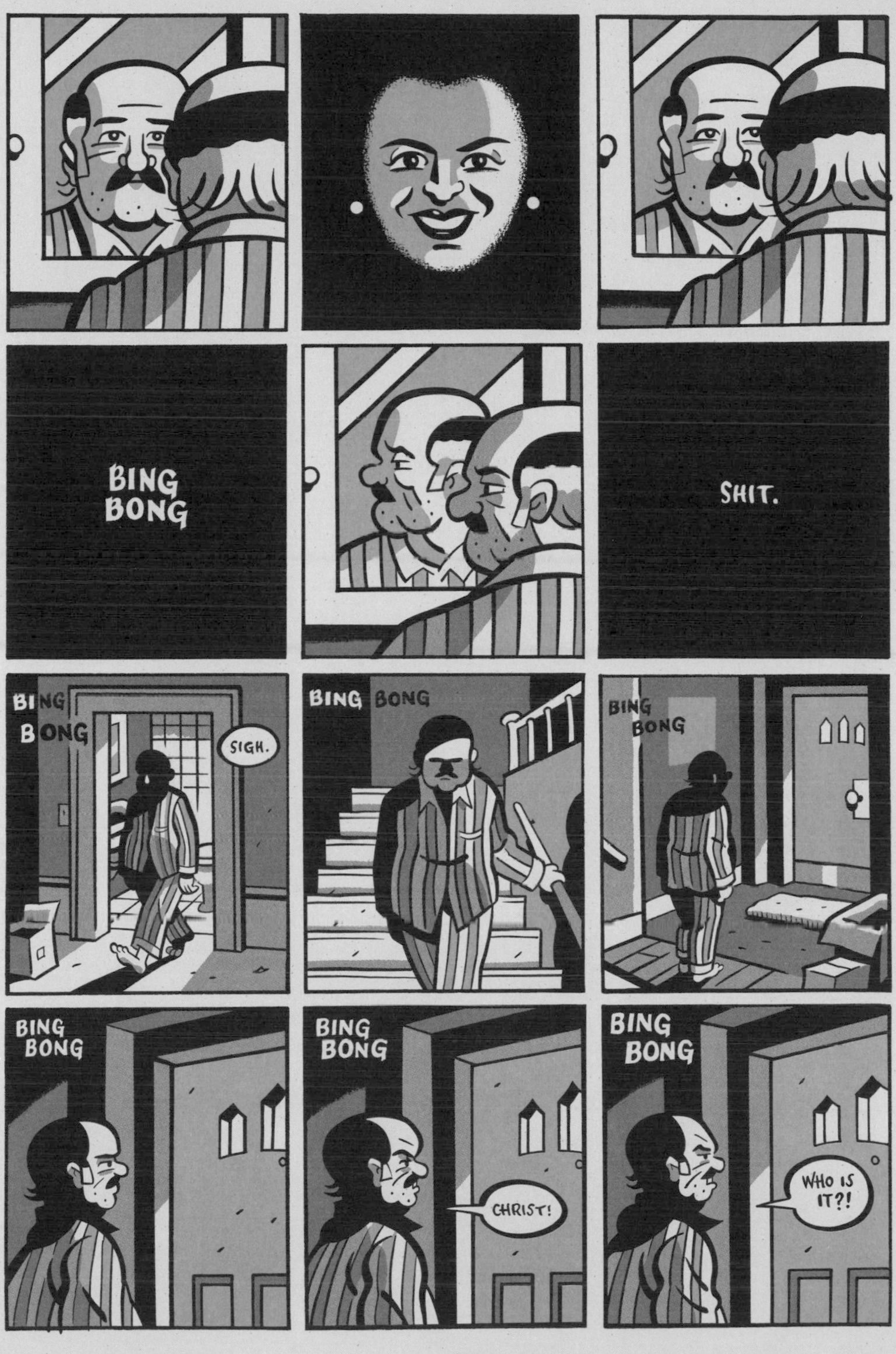
BING
BONG
SHIT.
BING
BONG
SIGH.
BING BONG
BING
BONG
BING
BONG
BING
BONG
CHRIST!
BING
BONG
WHO IS
IT?!

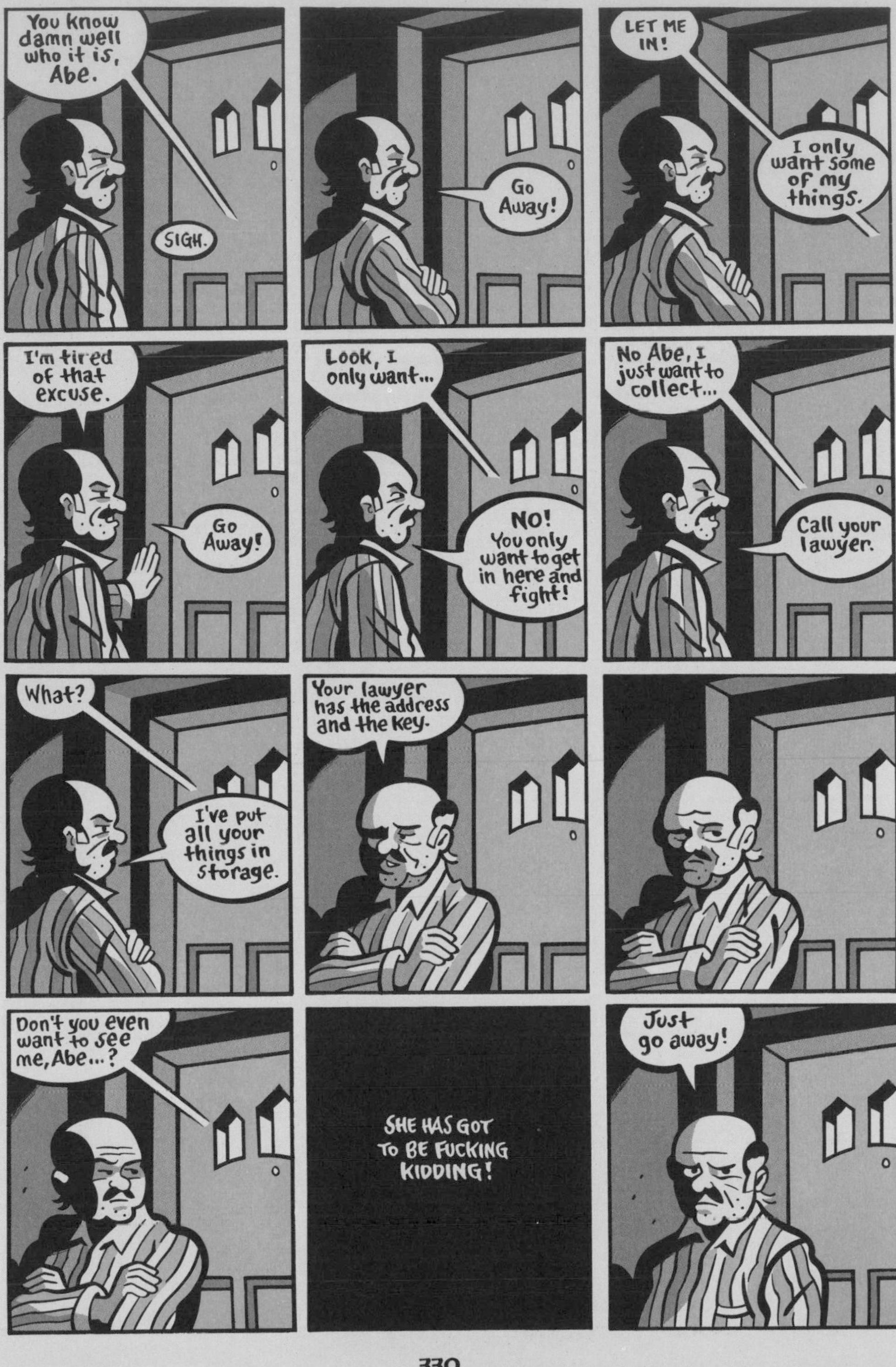
You know damn well who it is, Abe.
SIGH.
Go Away!
LET ME IN!
I only want some of my things.
I'm tired of that excuse.
Go Away!
Look, I only want...
NO! You only want to get in here and fight!
No Abe, I just want to collect...
Call your lawyer.
What?
I've put all your things in storage.
Your lawyer has the address and the key.
Don't you even want to see me, Abe...?
SHE HAS GOT TO BE FUCKING KIDDING!
Just go away!

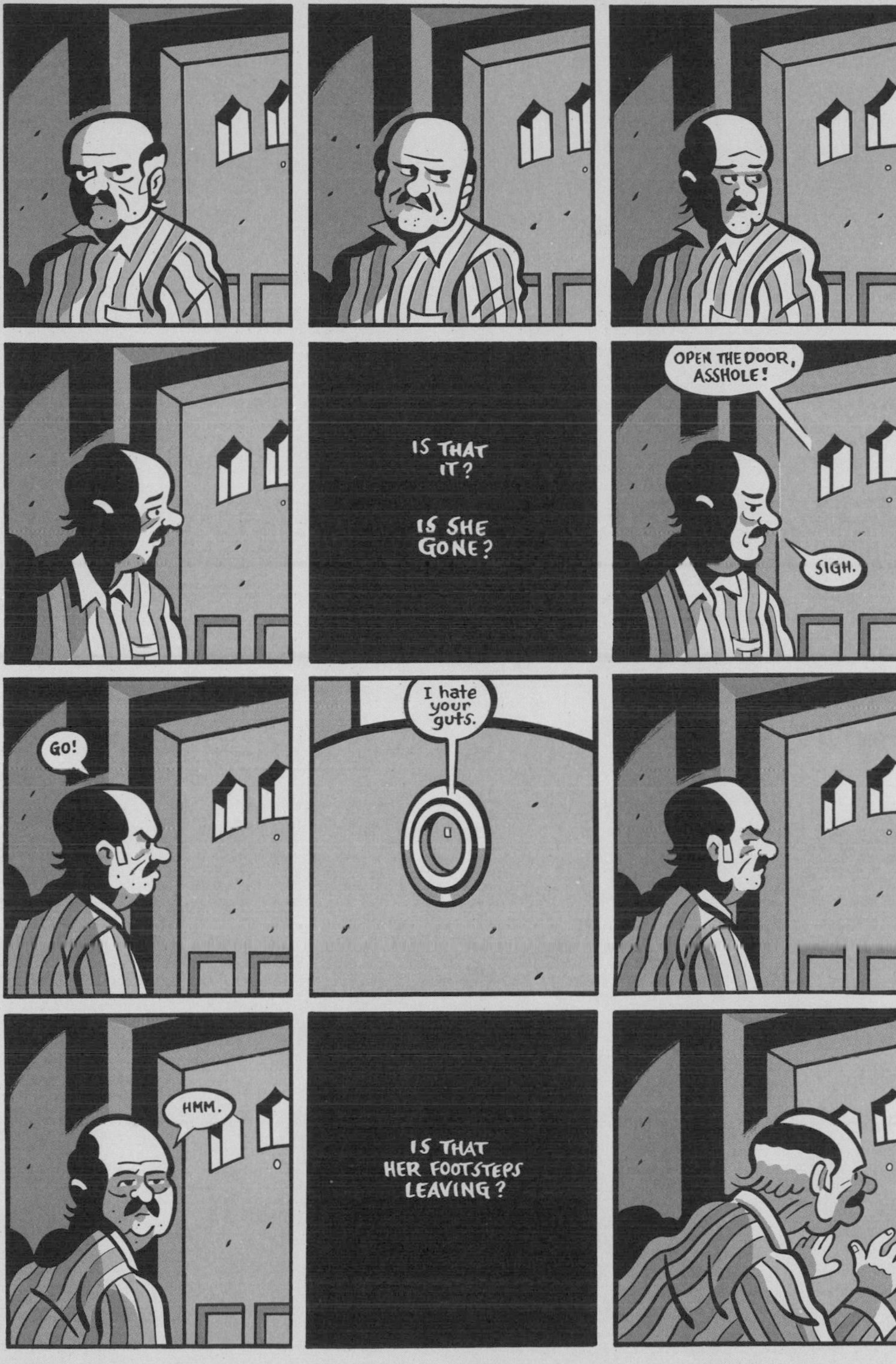
IS THAT
IT?
IS SHE
GONE?
OPEN THE DOOR,
ASSHOLE!
SIGH.
GO!
I hate
your
guts.
HMM.
IS THAT
HER FOOTSTEPS
LEAVING?

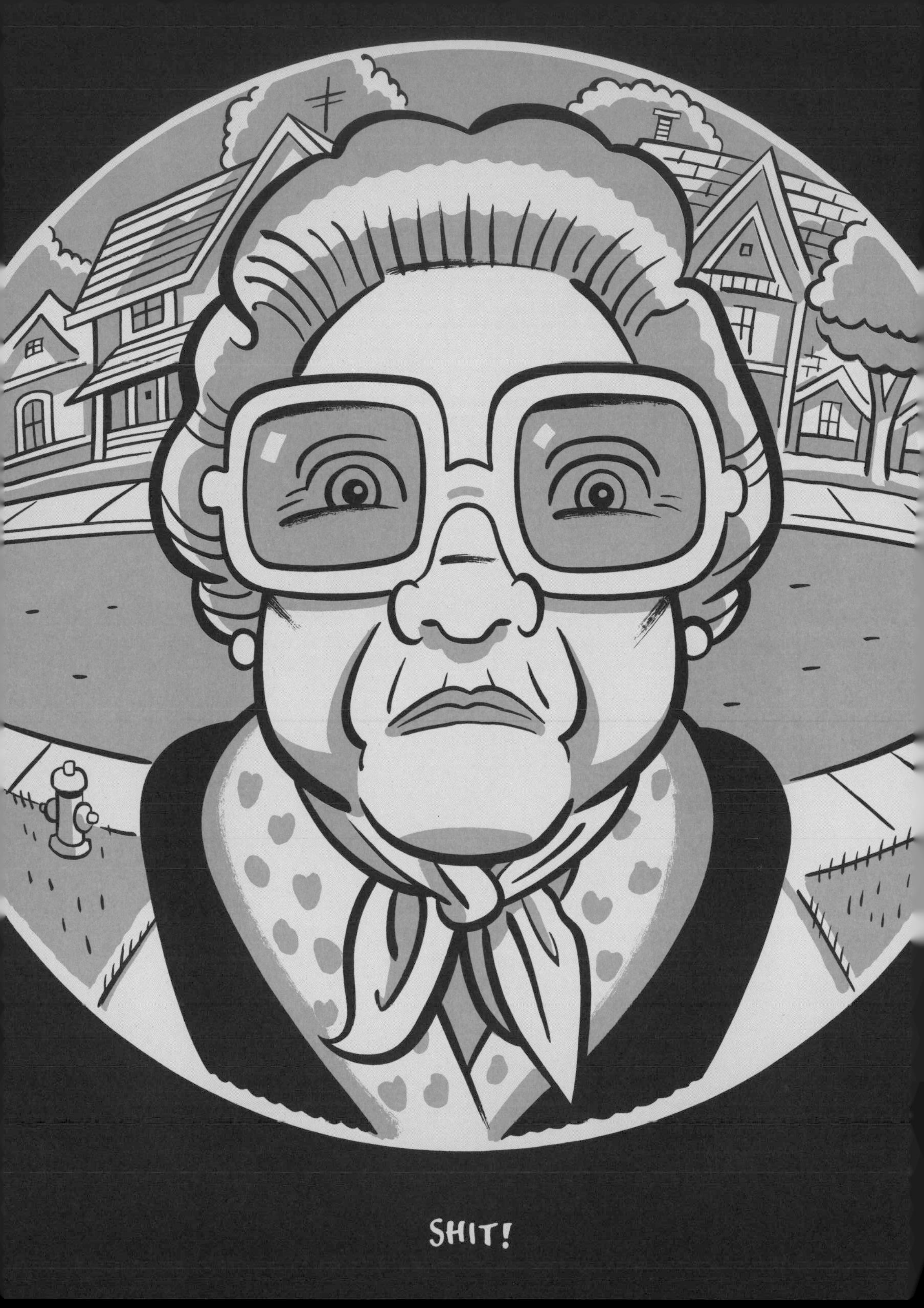
SHIT!

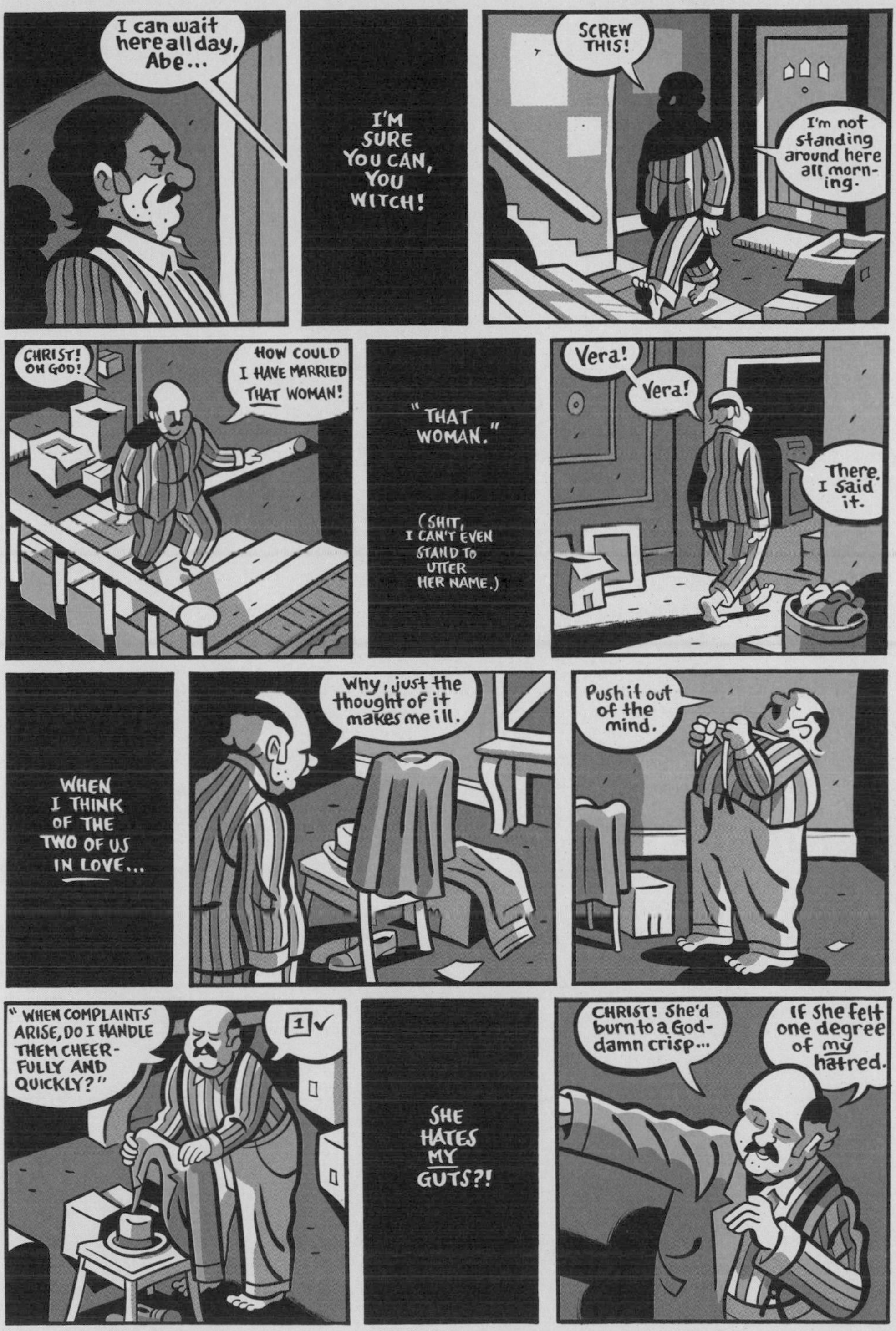
I can wait here all day, Abe...
I'M SURE YOU CAN, YOU WITCH!
SCREW THIS!
I'm not standing around here all morning.
CHRIST! OH GOD!
HOW COULD I HAVE MARRIED THAT WOMAN!
"THAT WOMAN."
(SHIT, I CAN'T EVEN STAND TO UTTER HER NAME.)
Vera!
Vera!
There, I said it.
WHEN I THINK OF THE TWO OF US IN LOVE...
Why, just the thought of it makes me ill.
Push it out of the mind.
"WHEN COMPLAINTS ARISE, DO I HANDLE THEM CHEERFULLY AND QUICKLY?"
1 ✓
SHE HATES MY GUTS?!
CHRIST! She'd burn to a God-damn crisp...
If she felt one degree of my hatred.

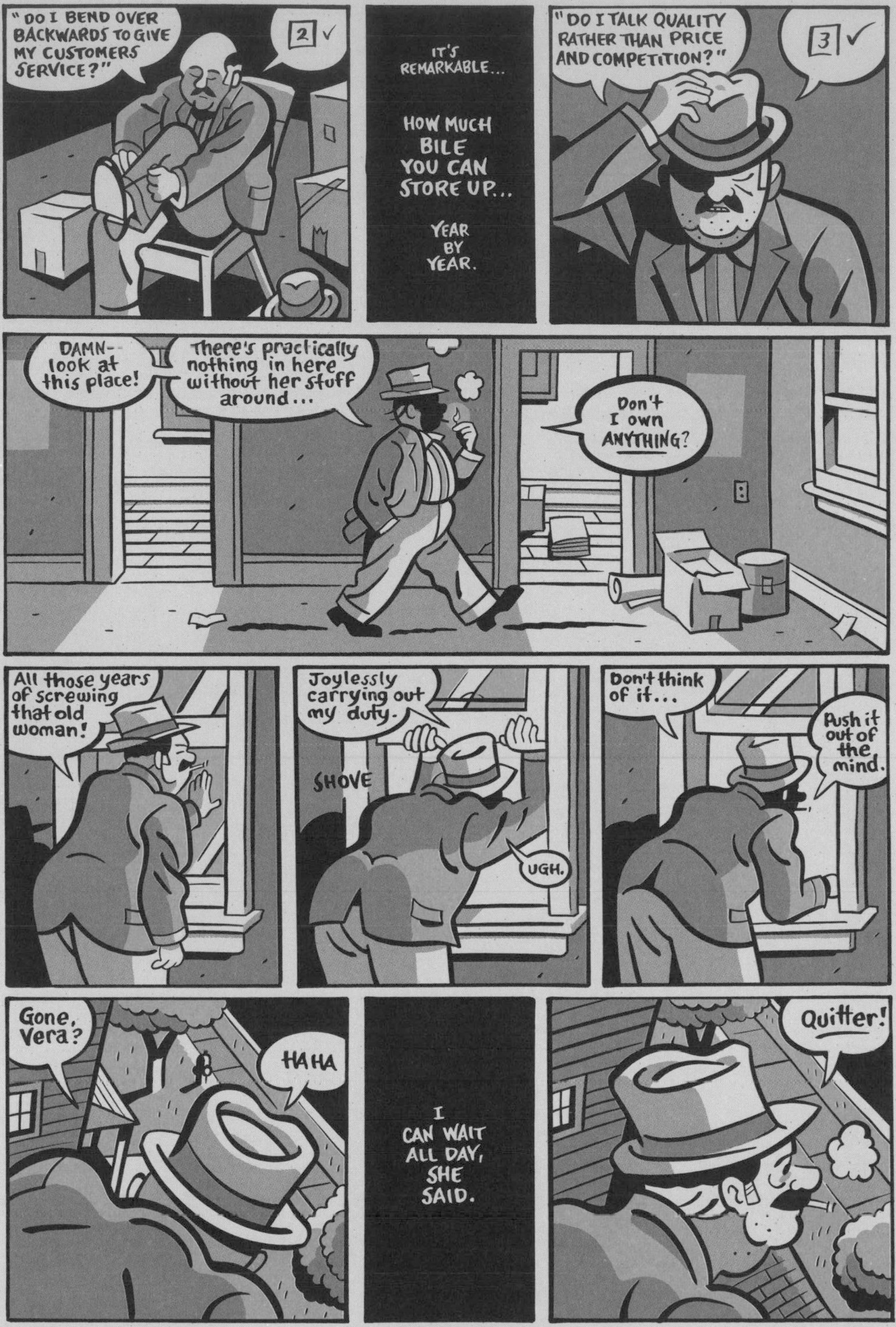

"DO I BEND OVER BACKWARDS TO GIVE MY CUSTOMERS SERVICE?"
2 ✓
IT'S REMARKABLE...
HOW MUCH BILE YOU CAN STORE UP...
YEAR BY YEAR.
"DO I TALK QUALITY RATHER THAN PRICE AND COMPETITION?"
3 ✓
DAMN-- look at this place!
There's practically nothing in here without her stuff around...
Don't I own ANYTHING?
All those years of screwing that old woman!
Joylessly carrying out my duty.
SHOVE
UGH.
Don't think of it...
Push it out of the mind.
Gone, Vera?
HAHA
I CAN WAIT ALL DAY, SHE SAID.
Quitter!

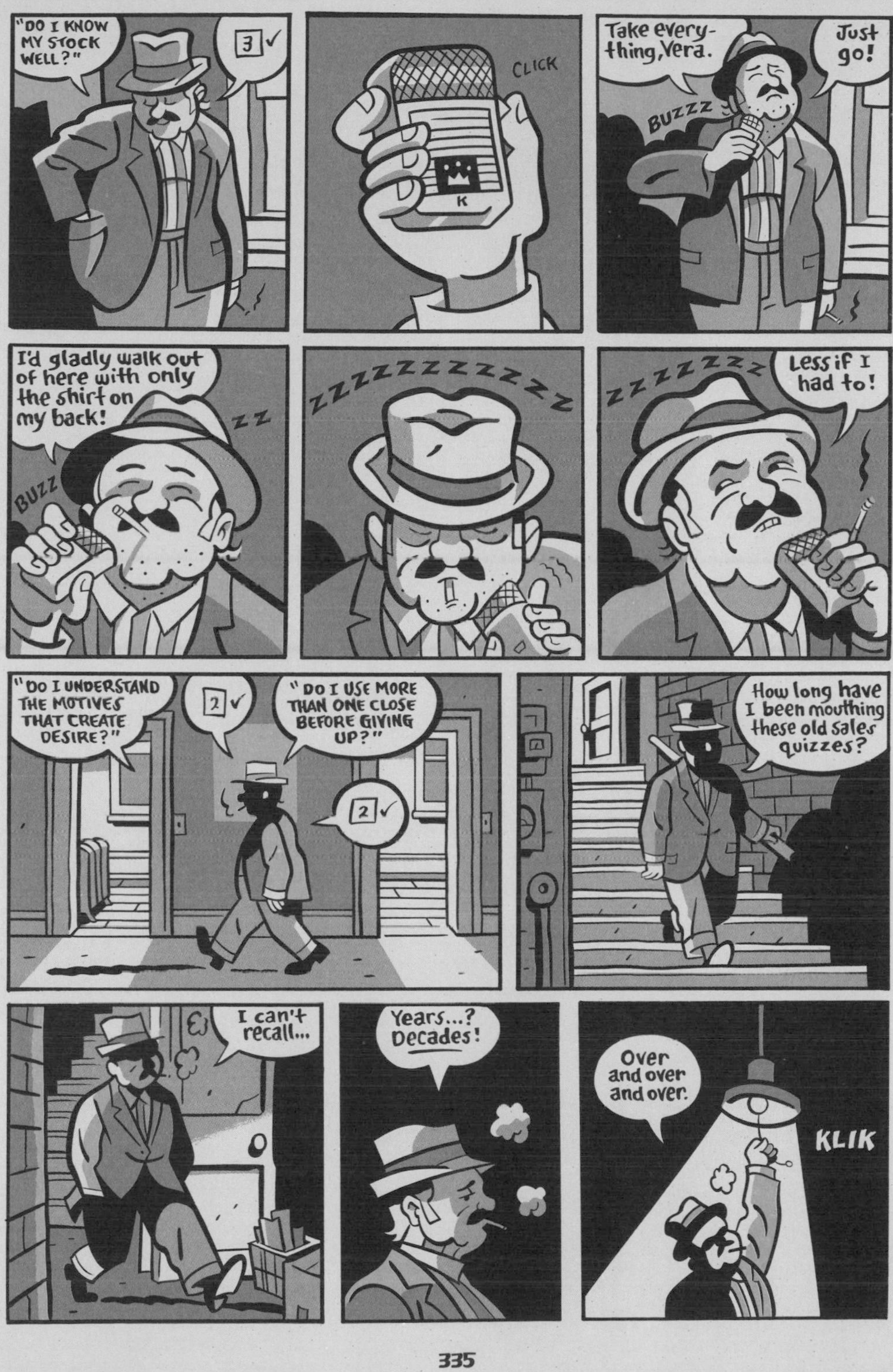
"DO I KNOW MY STOCK WELL?"
3 ✓
CLICK
Take every-thing, Vera.
Just go!
BUZZZ
I'd gladly walk out of here with only the shirt on my back!
ZZ
BUZZ
ZZZZZZZZZZZZZ
ZZZZZZZ
Less if I had to!
"DO I UNDERSTAND THE MOTIVES THAT CREATE DESIRE?"
2 ✓
"DO I USE MORE THAN ONE CLOSE BEFORE GIVING UP?"
2 ✓
How long have I been mouthing these old sales quizzes?
I can't recall...
Years...? Decades!
Over and over and over.
KLIK

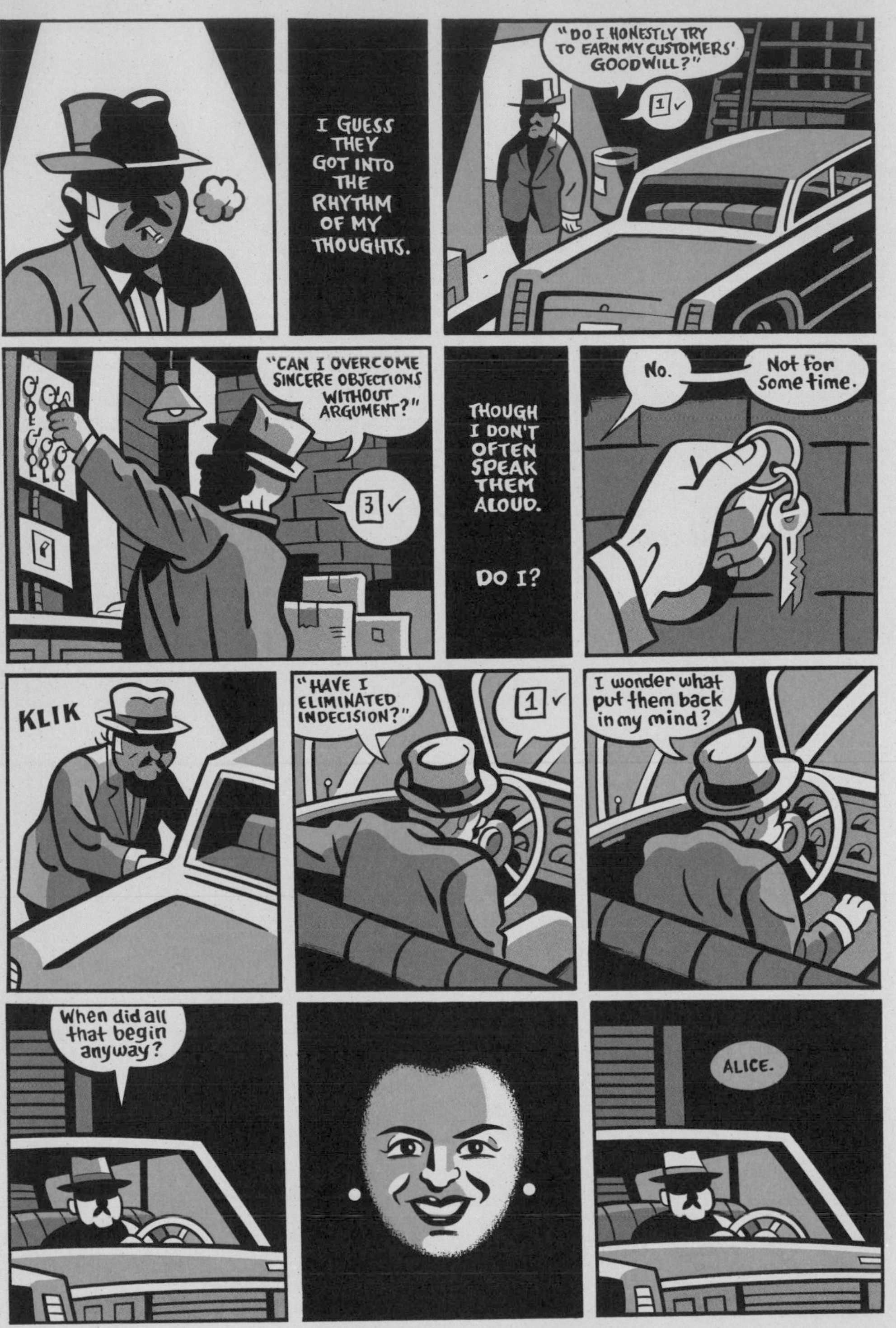
I GUESS THEY GOT INTO THE RHYTHM OF MY THOUGHTS.
"DO I HONESTLY TRY TO EARN MY CUSTOMERS' GOODWILL?"
1 ✓
"CAN I OVERCOME SINCERE OBJECTIONS WITHOUT ARGUMENT?"
3 ✓
THOUGH I DON'T OFTEN SPEAK THEM ALOUD.
DO I?
No.
Not for some time.
KLIK
"HAVE I ELIMINATED INDECISION?"
1 ✓
I wonder what put them back in my mind?
When did all that begin anyway?
ALICE.

I LOVE
YOU,
ABE.

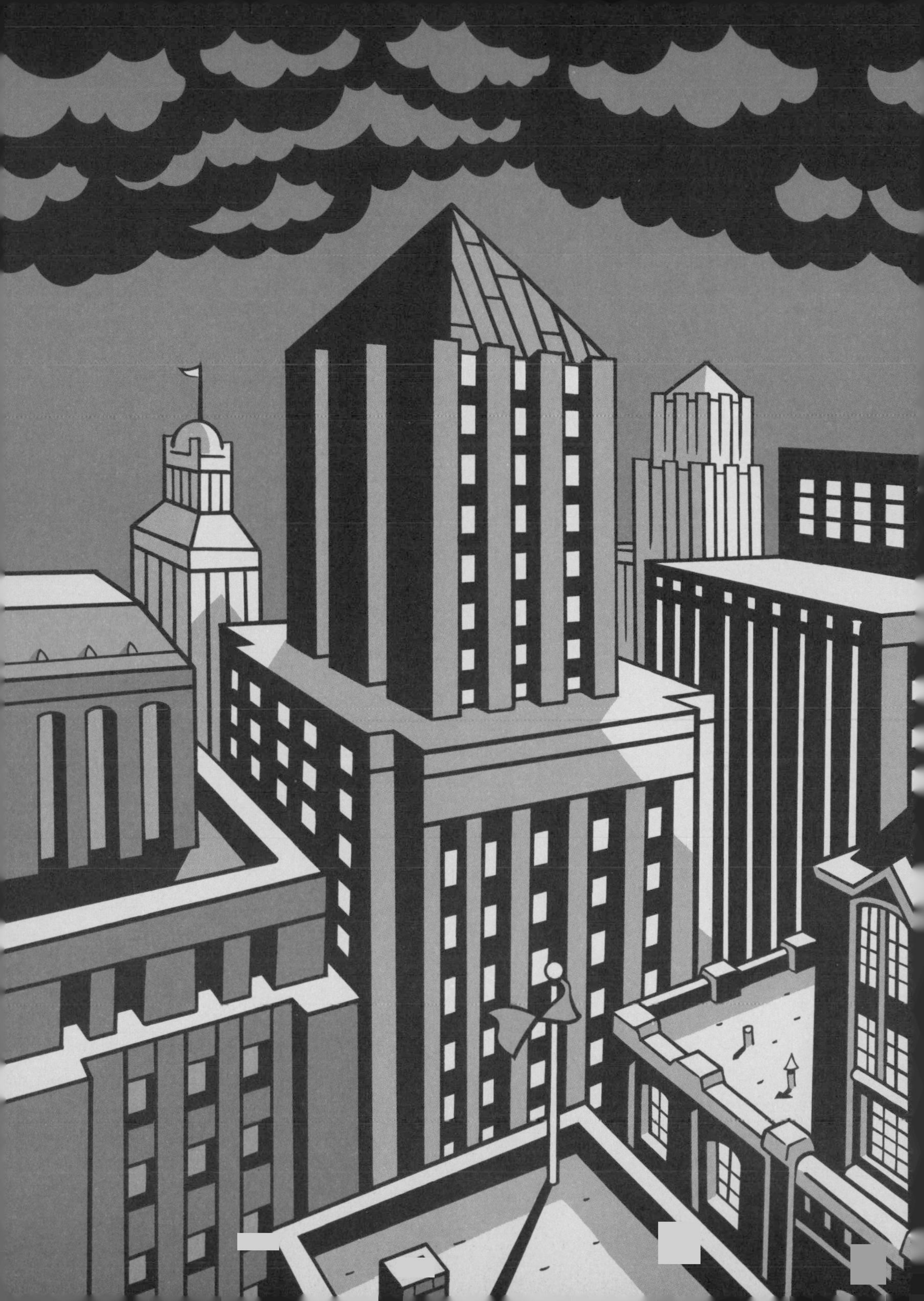

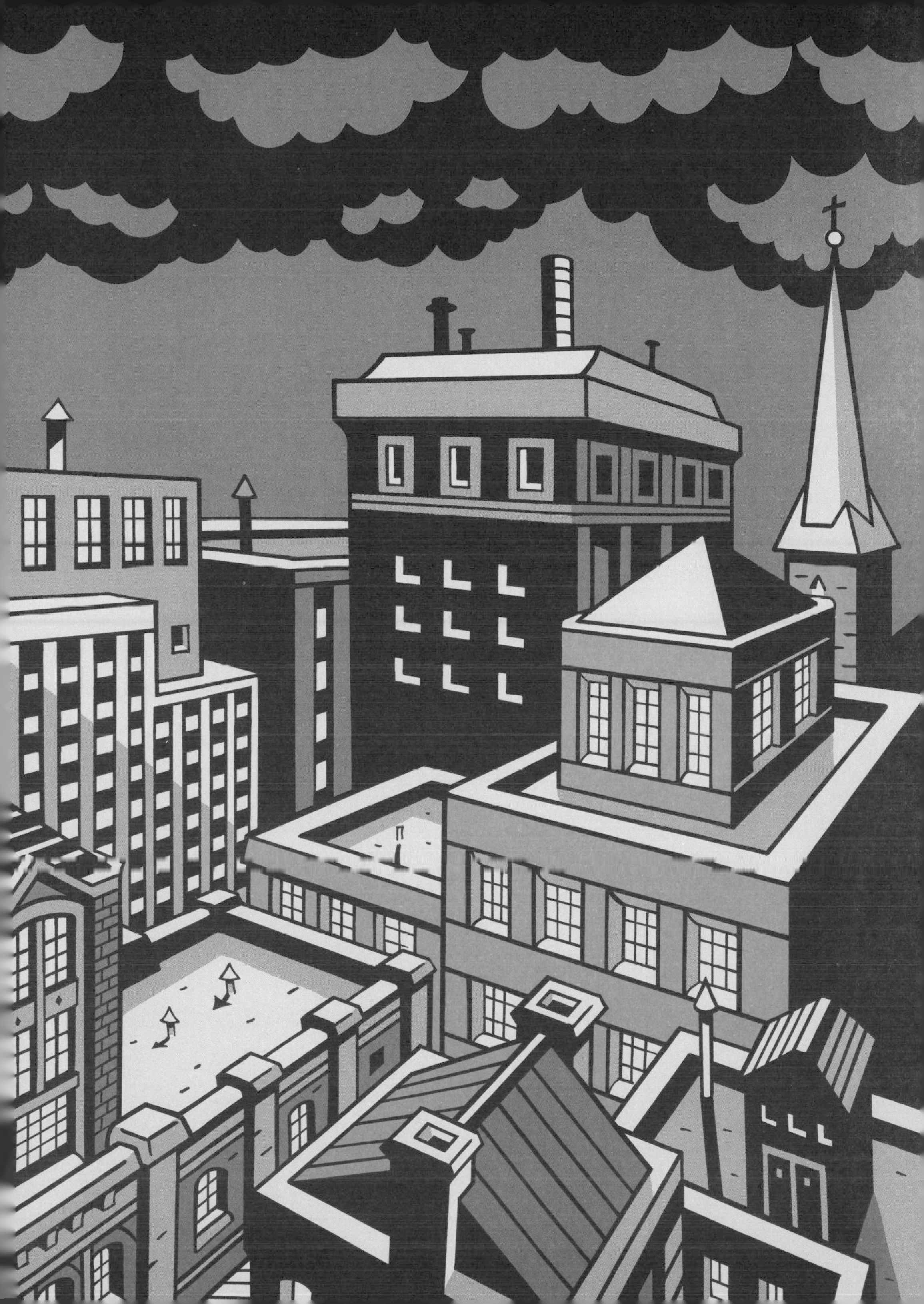

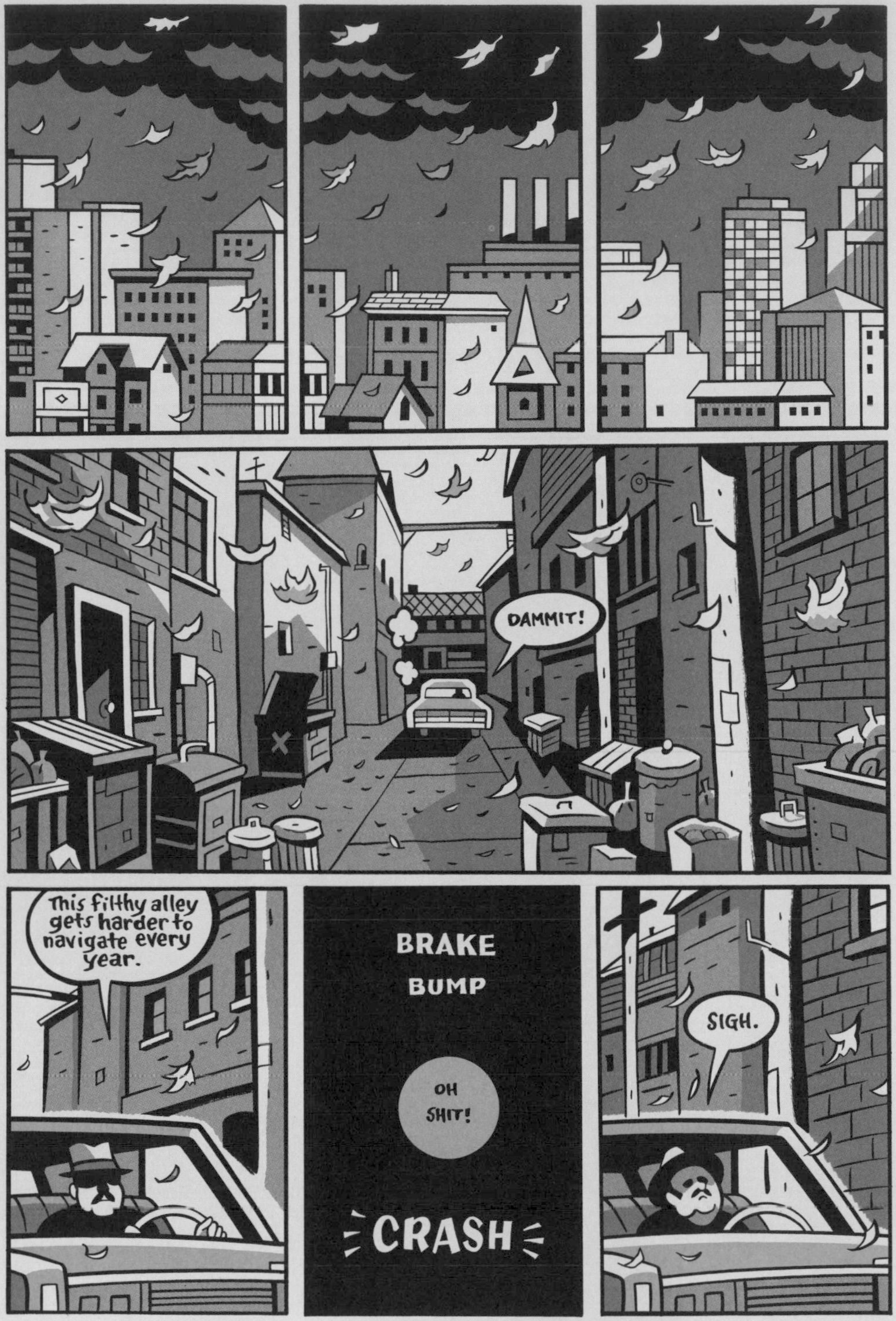
DAMMIT!
This filthy alley gets harder to navigate every year.
BRAKE
BUMP
OH SHIT!
CRASH
SIGH.

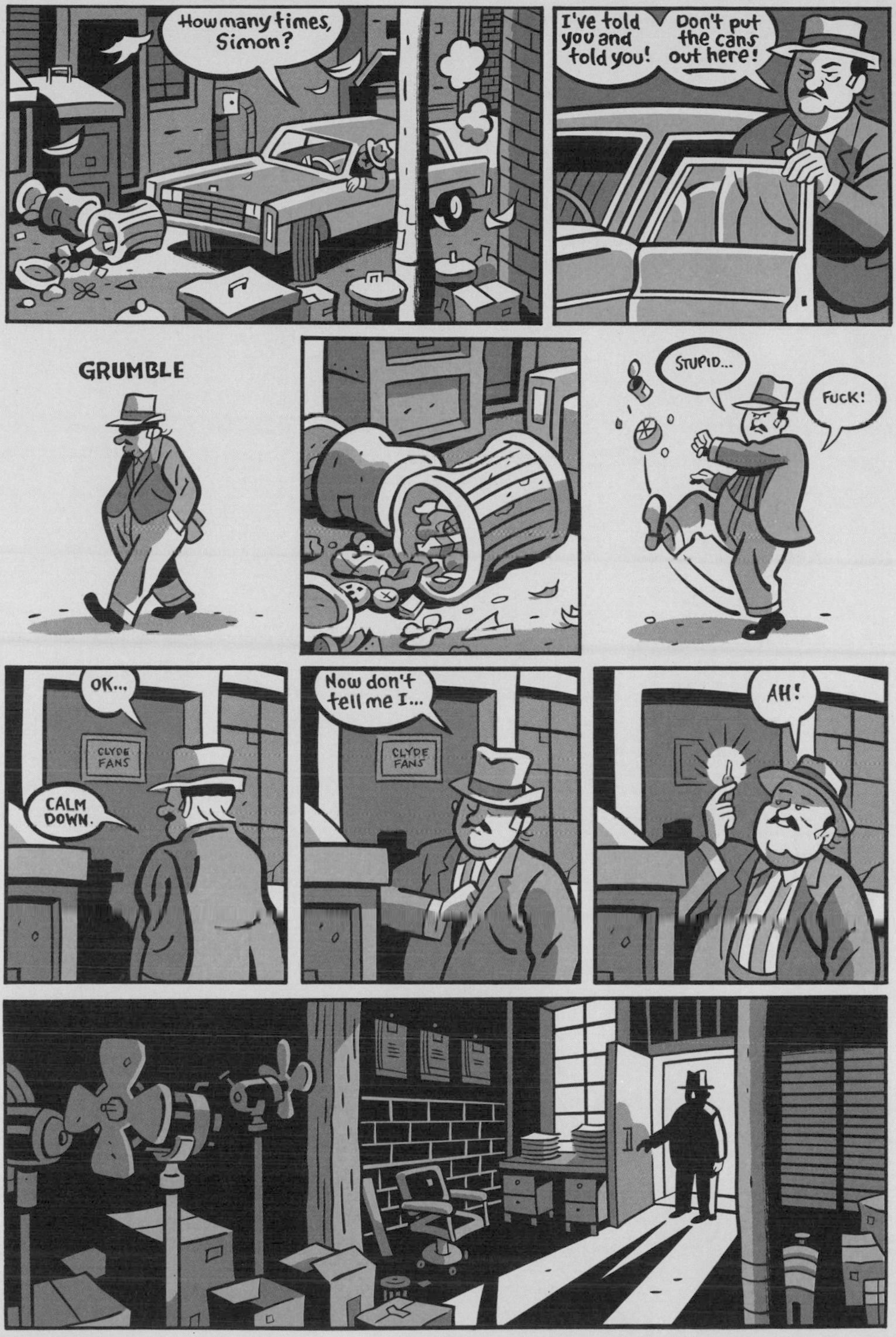
How many times, Simon?
I've told you and told you!
Don't put the cans out here!
GRUMBLE
STUPID...
FUCK!
OK...
CALM DOWN.
Now don't tell me I...
AH!
CLYDE FANS

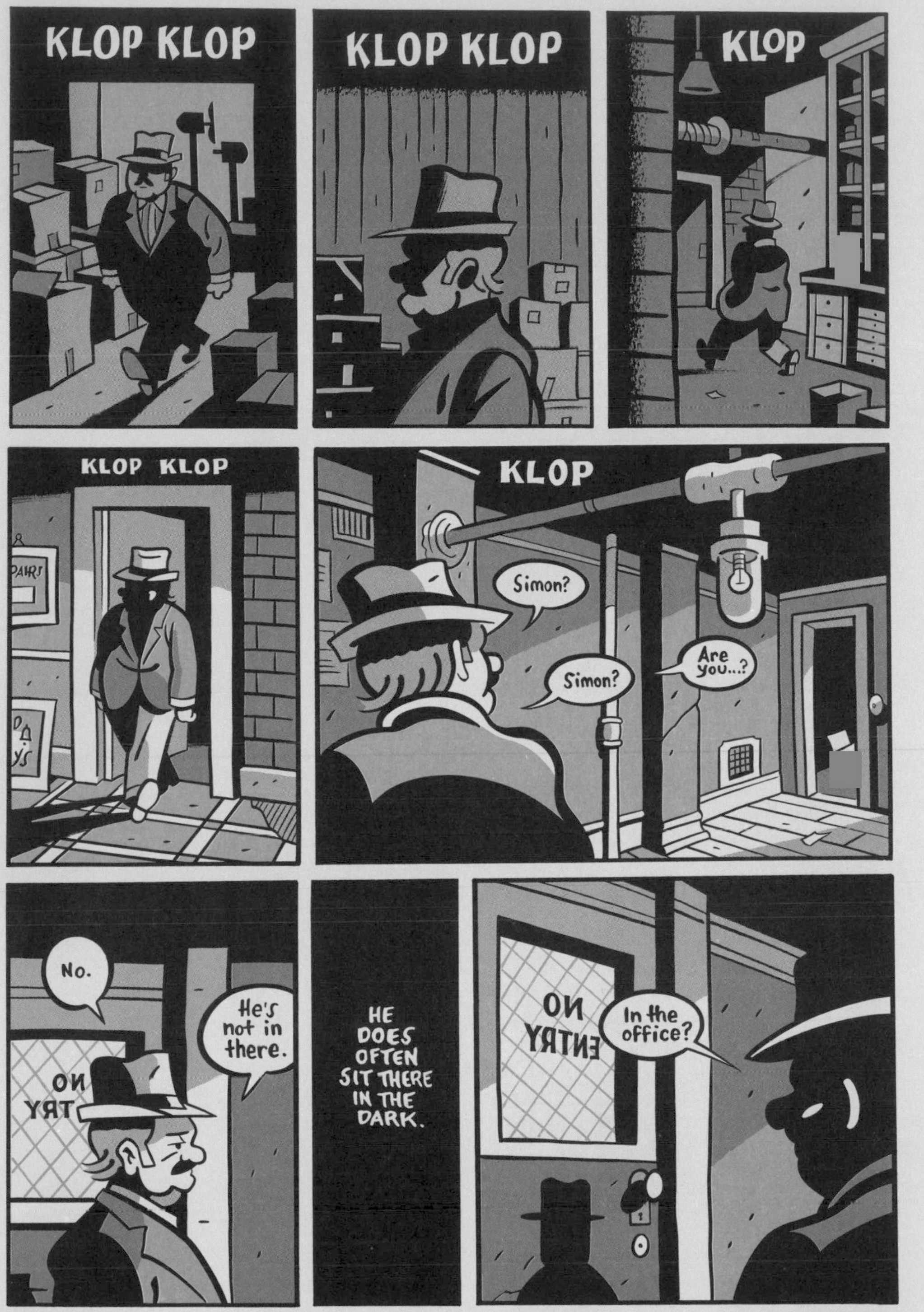

KLOP KLOP
KLOP KLOP
KLOP
KLOP KLOP
KLOP
Simon?
Simon?
Are you...?
No.
He's not in there.
HE DOES OFTEN SIT THERE IN THE DARK.
In the office?

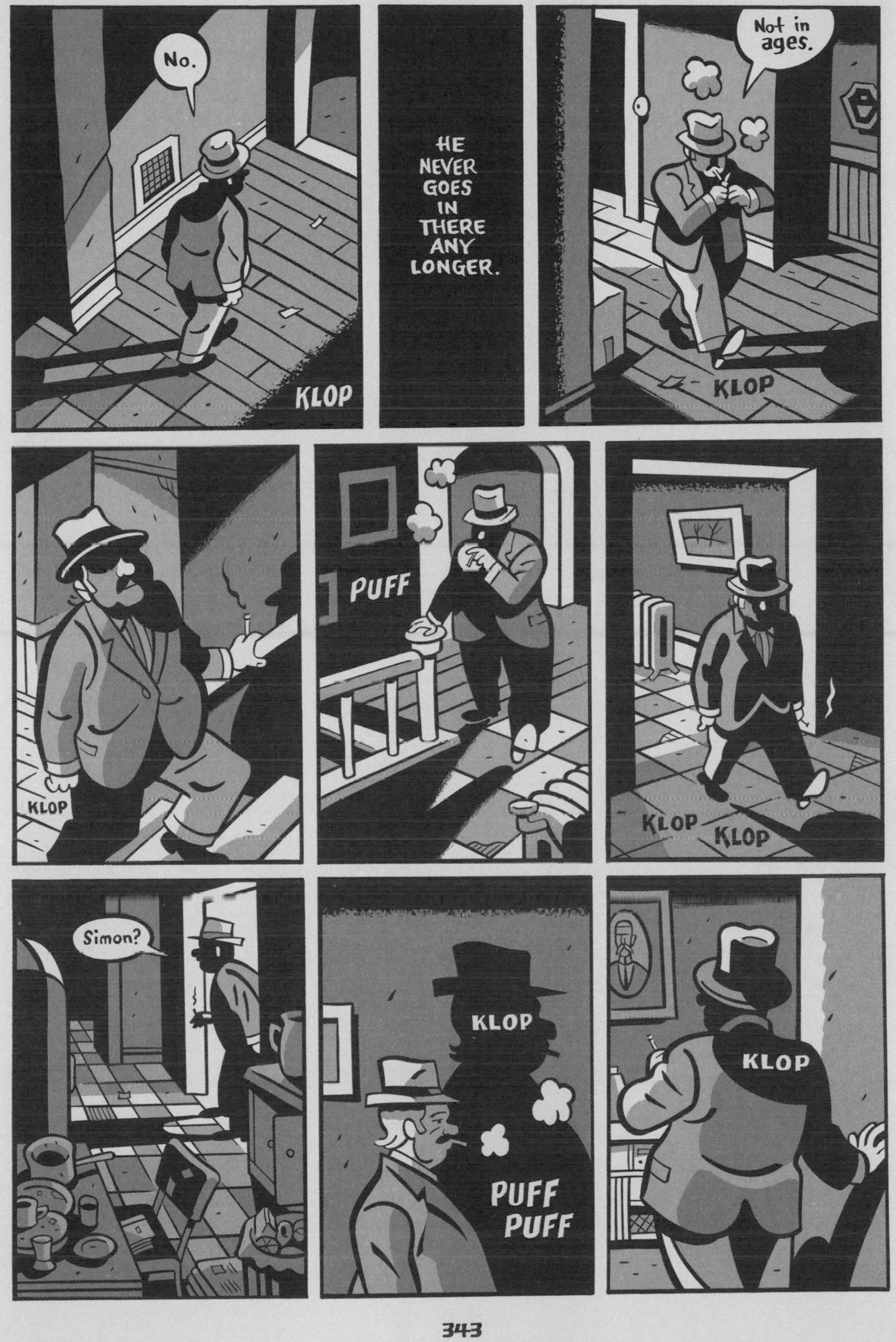
No.
KLOP
HE NEVER GOES IN THERE ANY LONGER.
Not in ages.
KLOP
KLOP
PUFF
KLOP
KLOP
Simon?
KLOP
PUFF
PUFF
KLOP

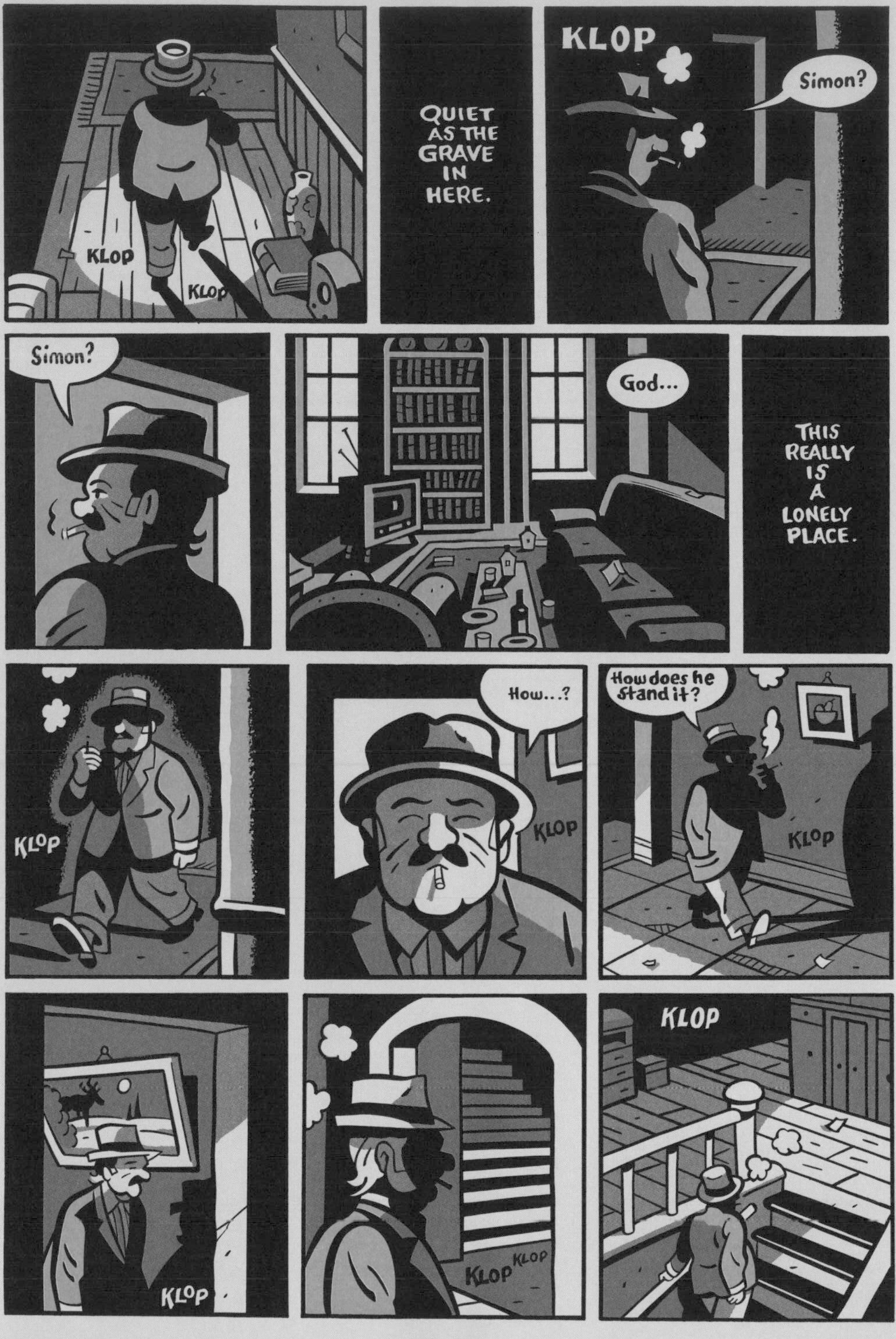
KLOP
KLOP
QUIET AS THE GRAVE IN HERE.
KLOP
Simon?
Simon?
God...
THIS REALLY IS A LONELY PLACE.
KLOP
How...?
KLOP
How does he stand it?
KLOP
KLOP
KLOP
KLOP
KLOP

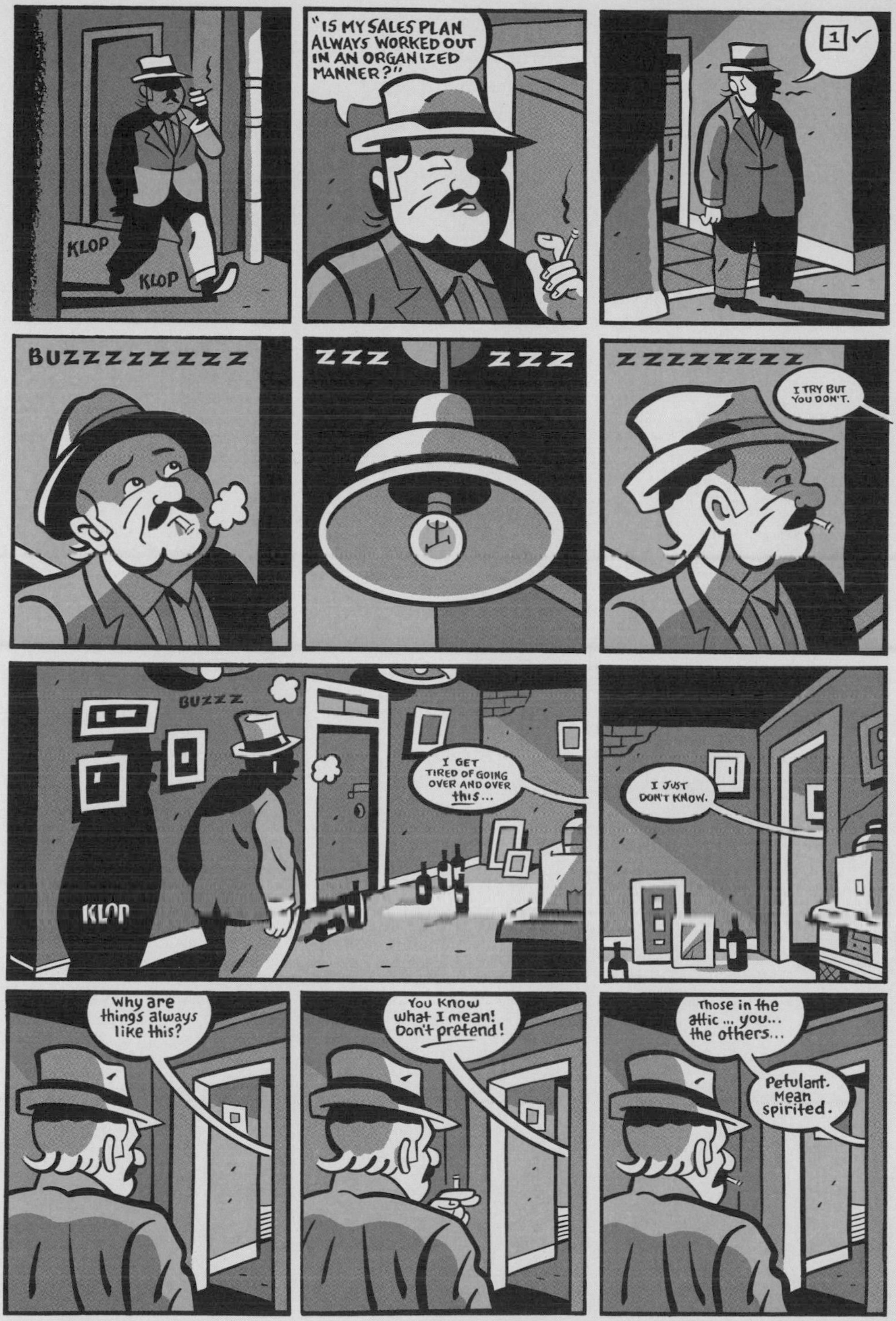
KLOP
KLOP
"IS MY SALES PLAN ALWAYS WORKED OUT IN AN ORGANIZED MANNER?"
1 ✓
BUZZZZZZZZZ
ZZZ ZZZ
ZZZZZZZZZ
I TRY BUT YOU DON'T.
BUZZZ
KLOP
I GET TIRED OF GOING OVER AND OVER this...
I JUST DON'T KNOW.
Why are things always like this?
You know what I mean! Don't pretend!
Those in the attic ... you... the others...
Petulant. Mean spirited.

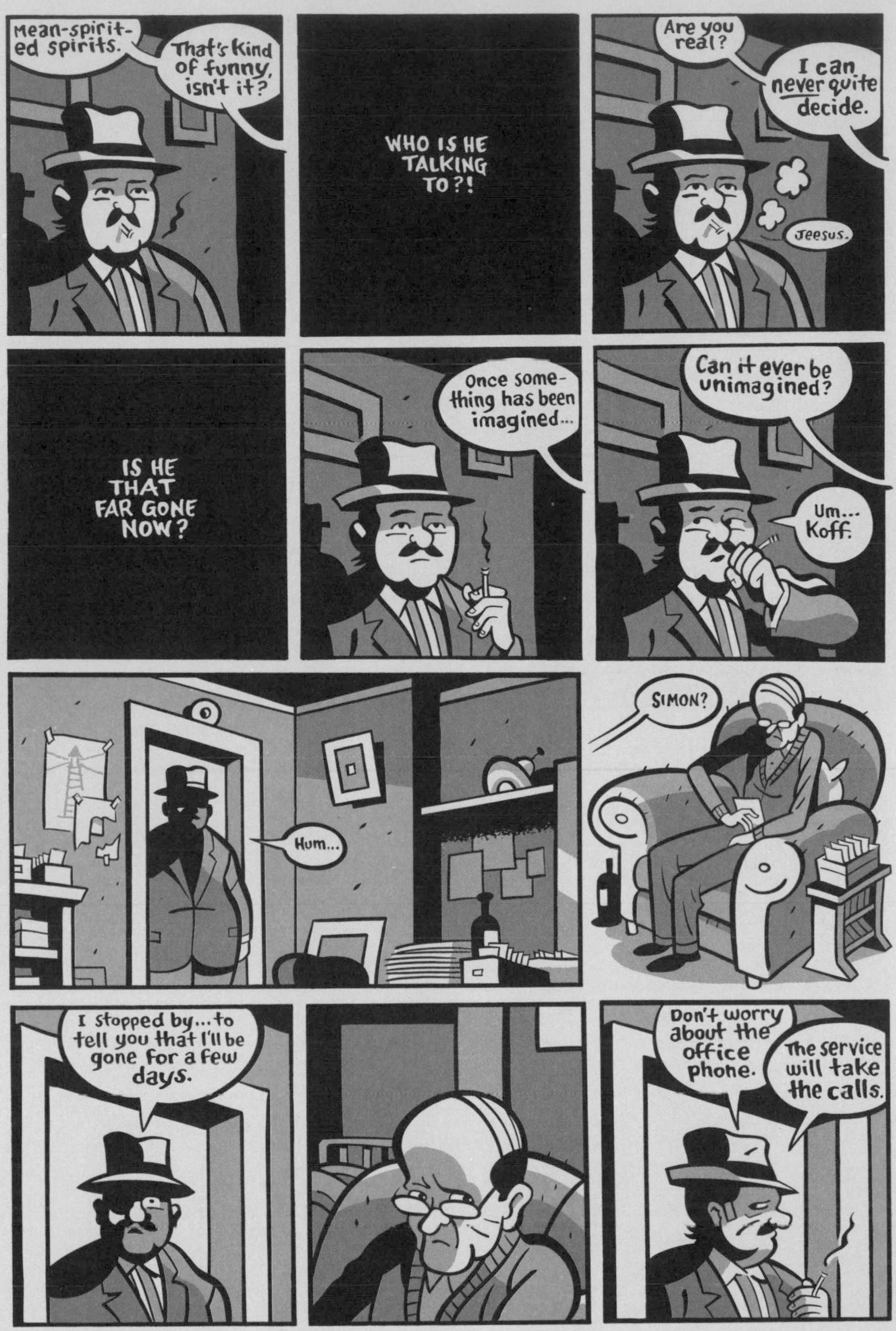
Mean-spirited spirits.
That's kind of funny, isn't it?
WHO IS HE TALKING TO?!
Are you real?
I can never quite decide.
Jeesus.
IS HE THAT FAR GONE NOW?
Once something has been imagined...
Can it ever be unimagined?
Um... Koff.
Hum...
SIMON?
I stopped by... to tell you that I'll be gone for a few days.
Don't worry about the office phone.
The service will take the calls.

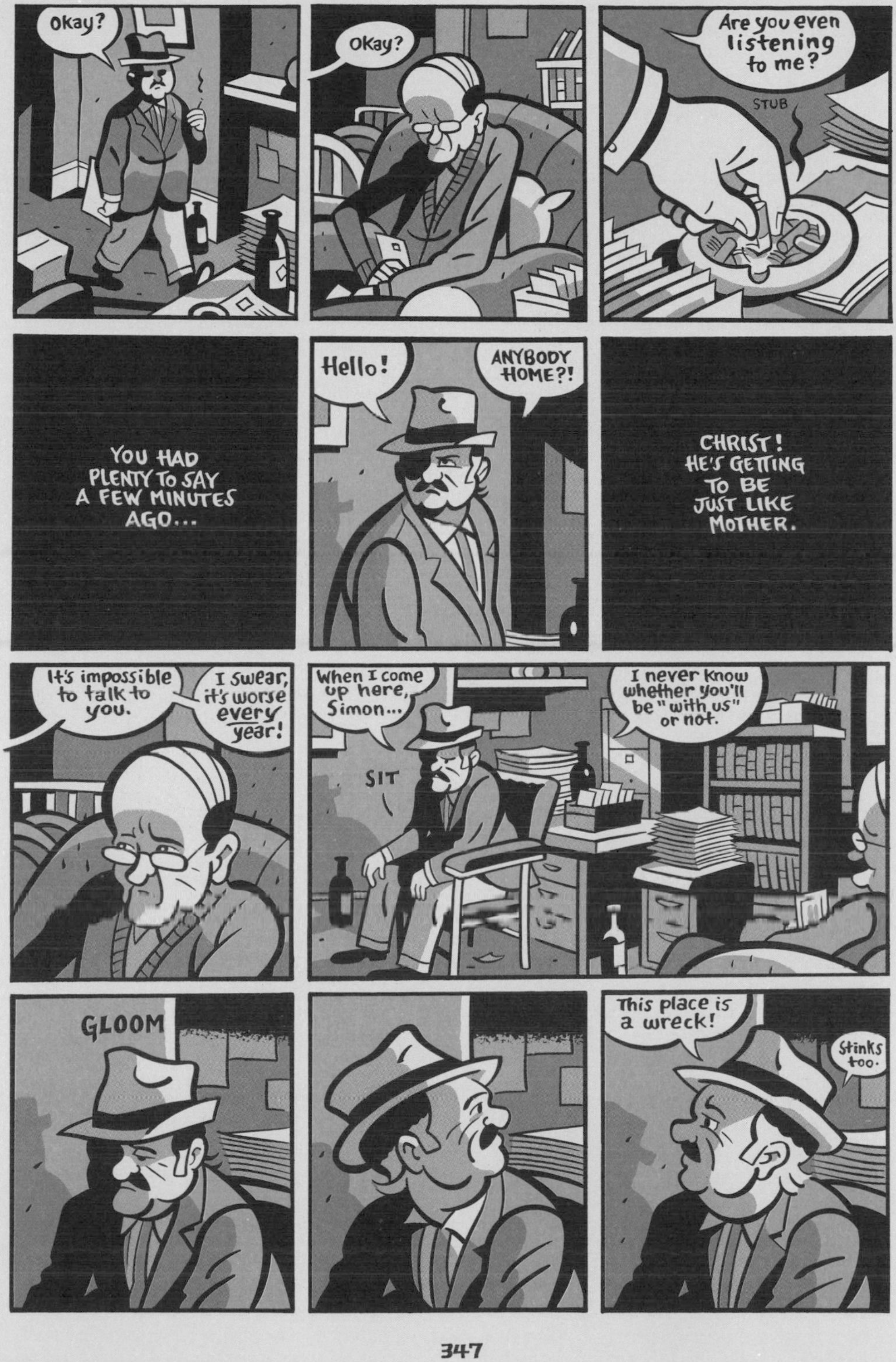
Okay?
Okay?
Are you even listening to me?
STUB
YOU HAD PLENTY TO SAY A FEW MINUTES AGO...
Hello!
ANYBODY HOME?!
CHRIST! HE'S GETTING TO BE JUST LIKE MOTHER.
It's impossible to talk to you.
I swear, it's worse every year!
When I come up here, Simon...
SIT
I never know whether you'll be "with us" or not.
GLOOM
This place is a wreck!
Stinks too.

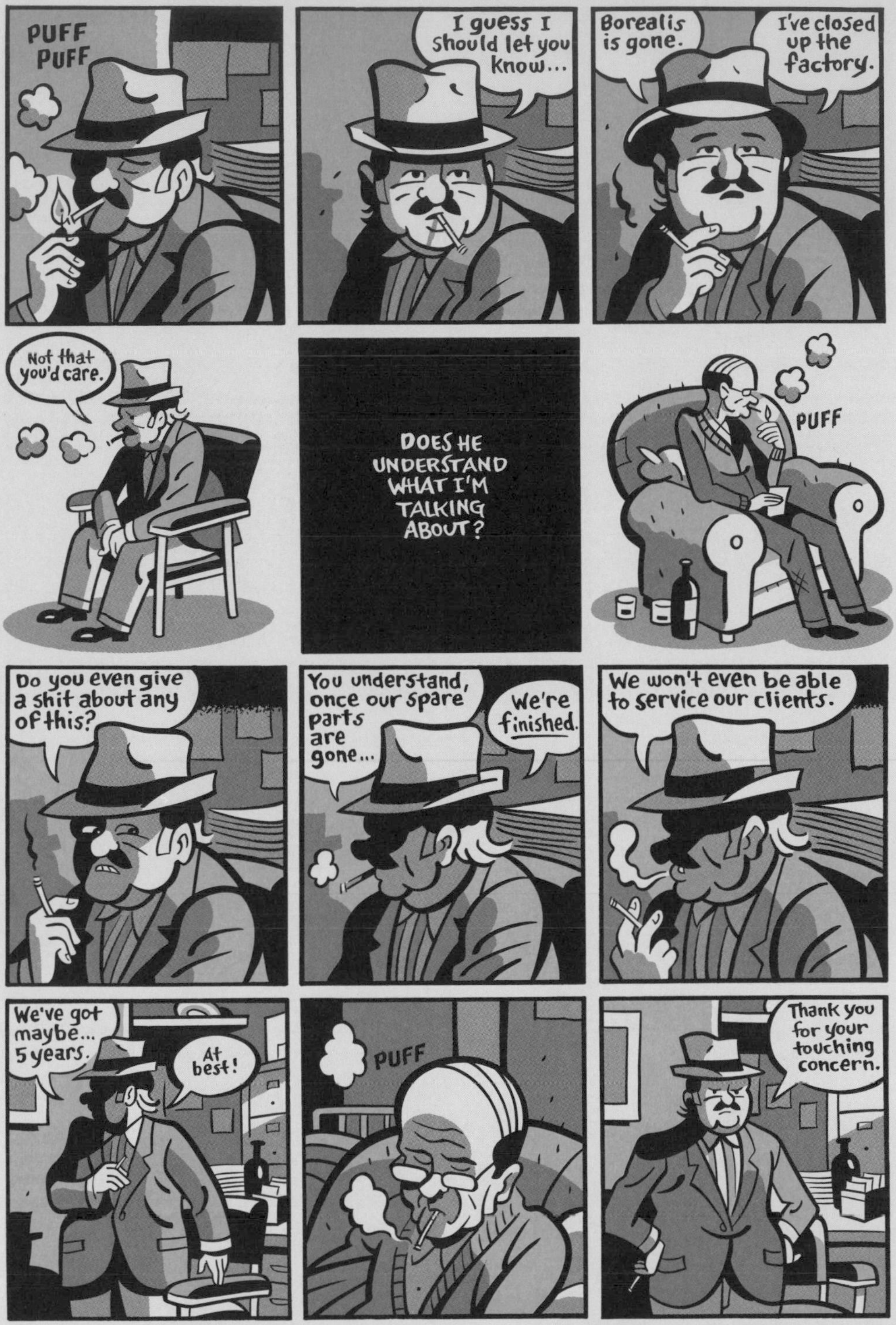
PUFF
PUFF
I guess I should let you know...
Borealis is gone.
I've closed up the factory.
Not that you'd care.
DOES HE UNDERSTAND WHAT I'M TALKING ABOUT?
PUFF
Do you even give a shit about any of this?
You understand, once our spare parts are gone...
We're finished.
We won't even be able to service our clients.
We've got maybe... 5 years.
At best!
PUFF
Thank you for your touching concern.

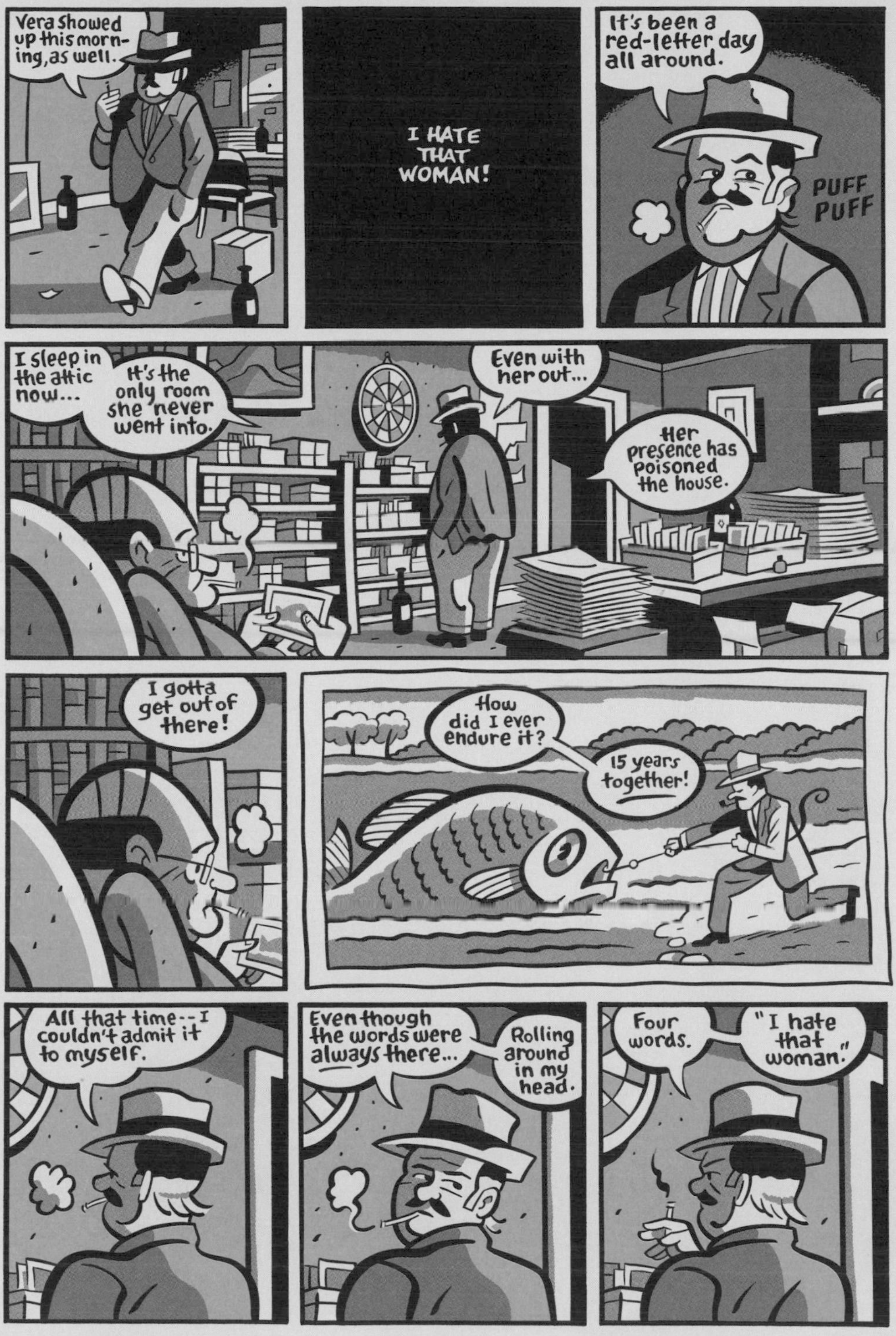
Vera showed up this morning, as well.
I HATE THAT WOMAN!
It's been a red-letter day all around.
PUFF PUFF
I sleep in the attic now...
It's the only room she never went into.
Even with her out...
Her presence has poisoned the house.
I gotta get out of there!
How did I ever endure it?
15 years together!
All that time-- I couldn't admit it to myself.
Even though the words were always there...
Rolling around in my head.
Four words.
"I hate that woman."

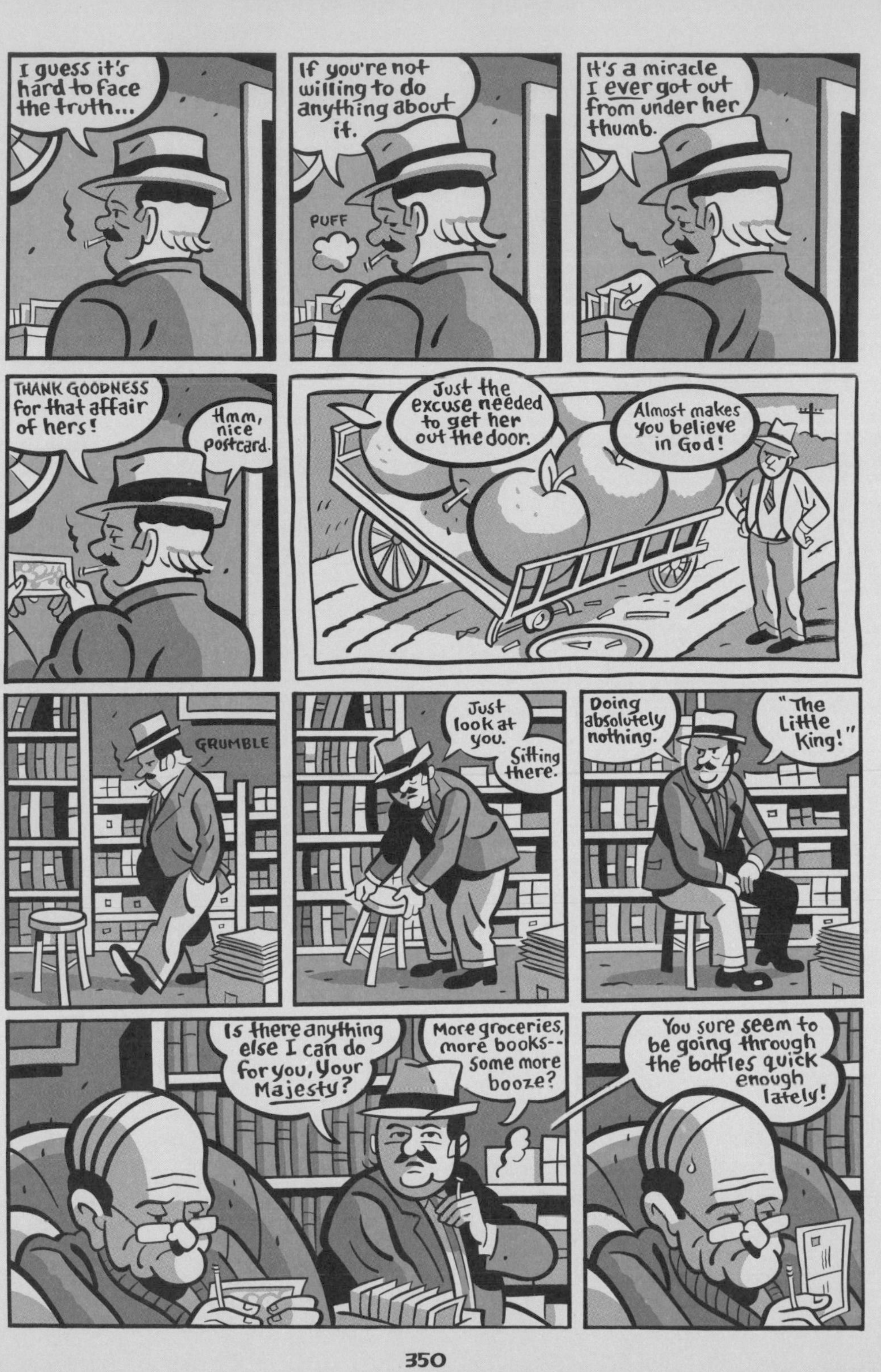

I guess it's hard to face the truth...
If you're not willing to do anything about it.
PUFF
It's a miracle I ever got out from under her thumb.
THANK GOODNESS for that affair of hers!
Hmm, nice postcard.
Just the excuse needed to get her out the door.
Almost makes you believe in God!
GRUMBLE
Just look at you.
Sitting there.
Doing absolutely nothing.
"The Little King!"
Is there anything else I can do for you, Your Majesty?
More groceries, more books-- some more booze?
You sure seem to be going through the bottles quick enough lately!

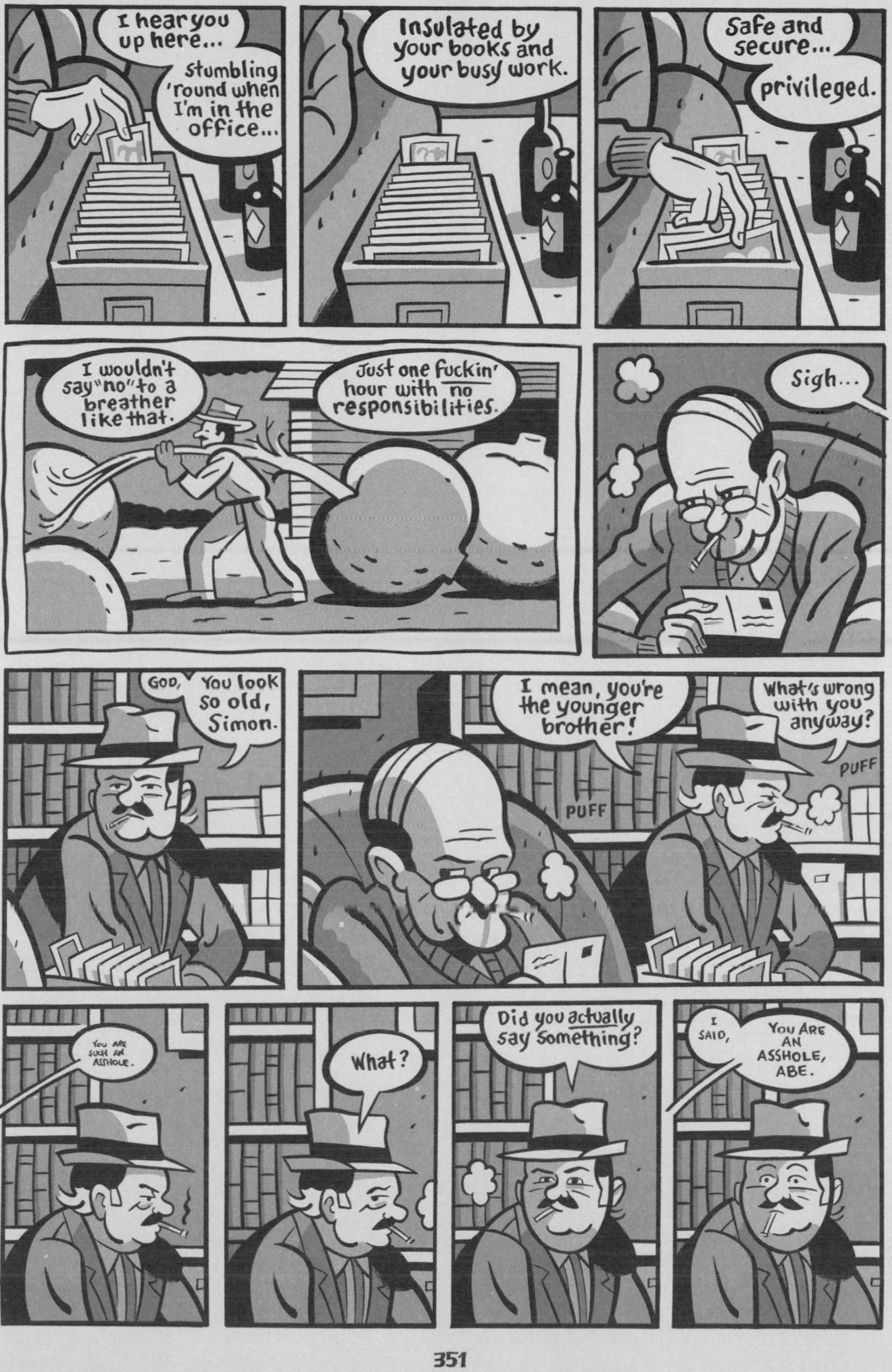

I hear you up here...
stumbling 'round when I'm in the office...
Insulated by your books and your busy work.
Safe and secure...
privileged.
I wouldn't say "no" to a breather like that.
Just one fuckin' hour with no responsibilities.
Sigh...
GOD,
You look so old, Simon.
I mean, you're the younger brother!
What's wrong with you anyway?
PUFF
PUFF
YOU ARE SUCH AN ASSHOLE.
What?
Did you actually say something?
I SAID,
YOU ARE AN ASSHOLE, ABE.

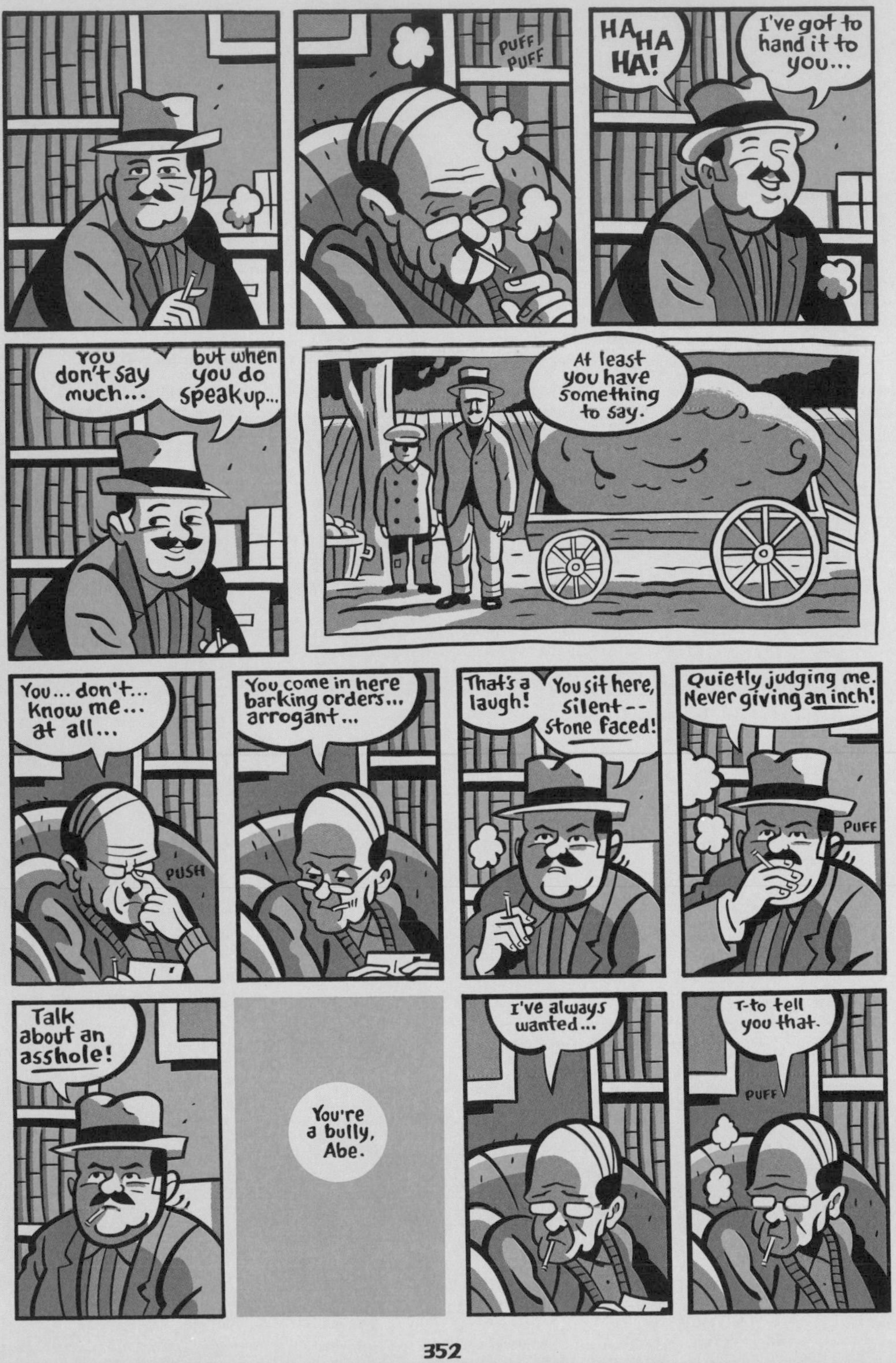
PUFF PUFF
HA HA HA!
I've got to hand it to you...
You don't say much...
but when you do speak up...
At least you have something to say.
You... don't... know me... at all...
PUSH
You come in here barking orders... arrogant...
That's a laugh!
You sit here, silent -- stone faced!
Quietly judging me. Never giving an inch!
PUFF
Talk about an asshole!
You're a bully, Abe.
I've always wanted...
T-to tell you that.
PUFF

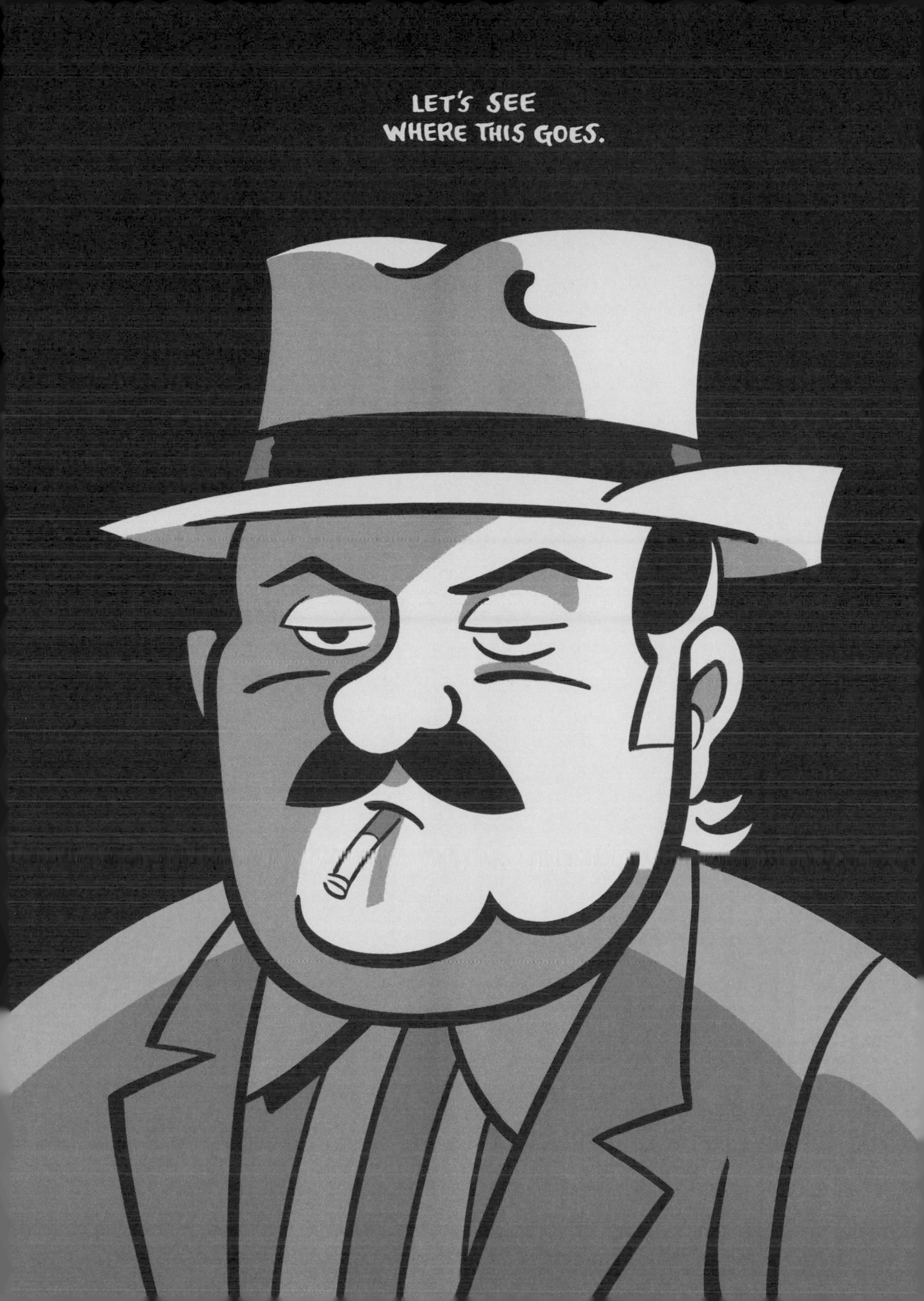
LET'S SEE
WHERE THIS GOES.

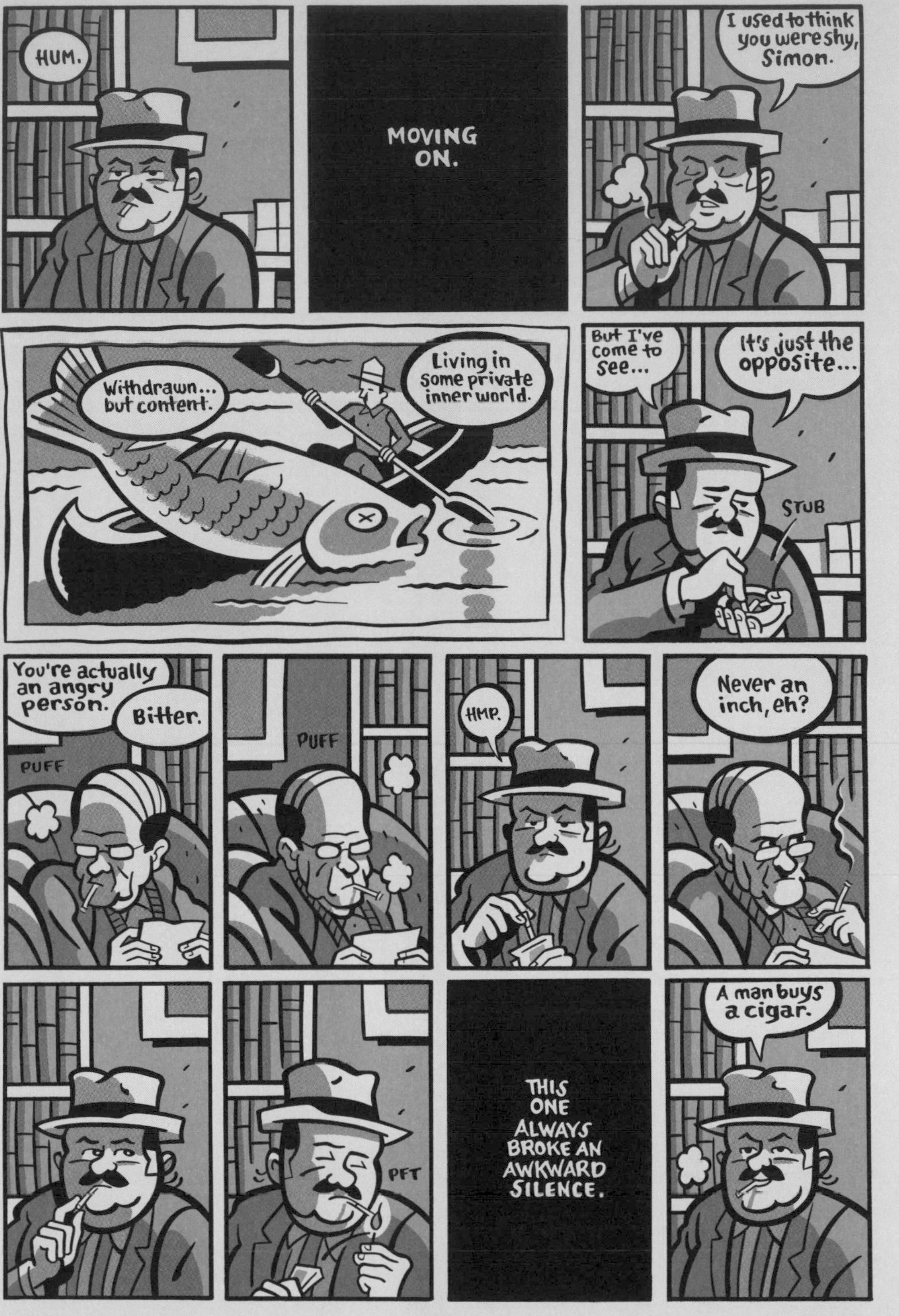
HUM.
MOVING ON.
I used to think you were shy, Simon.
Withdrawn... but content.
Living in some private inner world.
But I've come to see...
It's just the opposite...
STUB
You're actually an angry person.
Bitter.
PUFF
PUFF
HMP.
Never an inch, eh?
PFT
THIS ONE ALWAYS BROKE AN AWKWARD SILENCE.
A man buys a cigar.

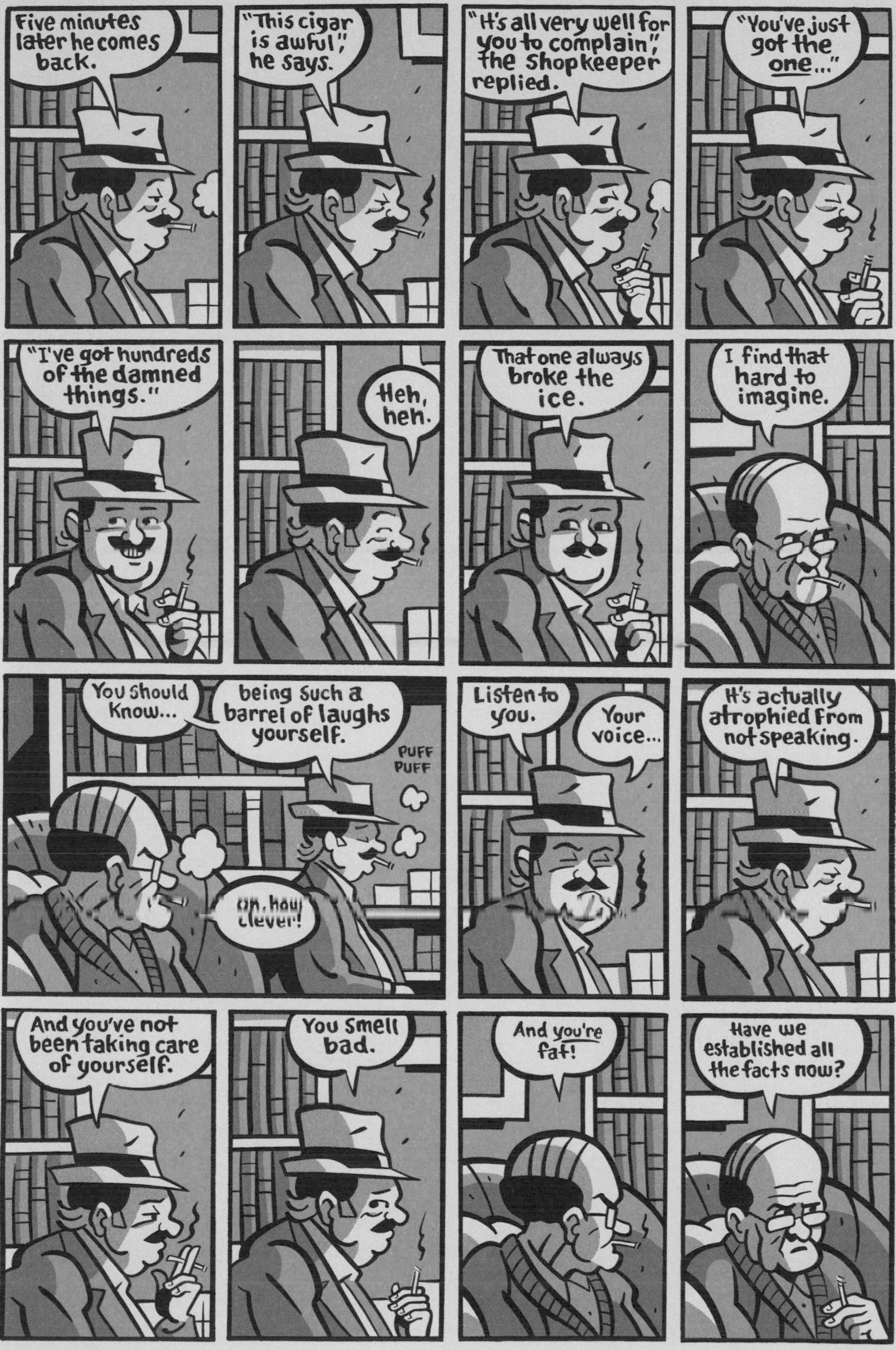
Five minutes later he comes back.
"This cigar is awful," he says.
"It's all very well for you to complain," the shopkeeper replied.
"You've just got the one..."
"I've got hundreds of the damned things."
Heh, heh.
That one always broke the ice.
I find that hard to imagine.
You should know...
being such a barrel of laughs yourself.
PUFF PUFF
Oh, how clever!
Listen to you.
Your voice...
It's actually atrophied from not speaking.
And you've not been taking care of yourself.
You smell bad.
And you're fat!
Have we established all the facts now?

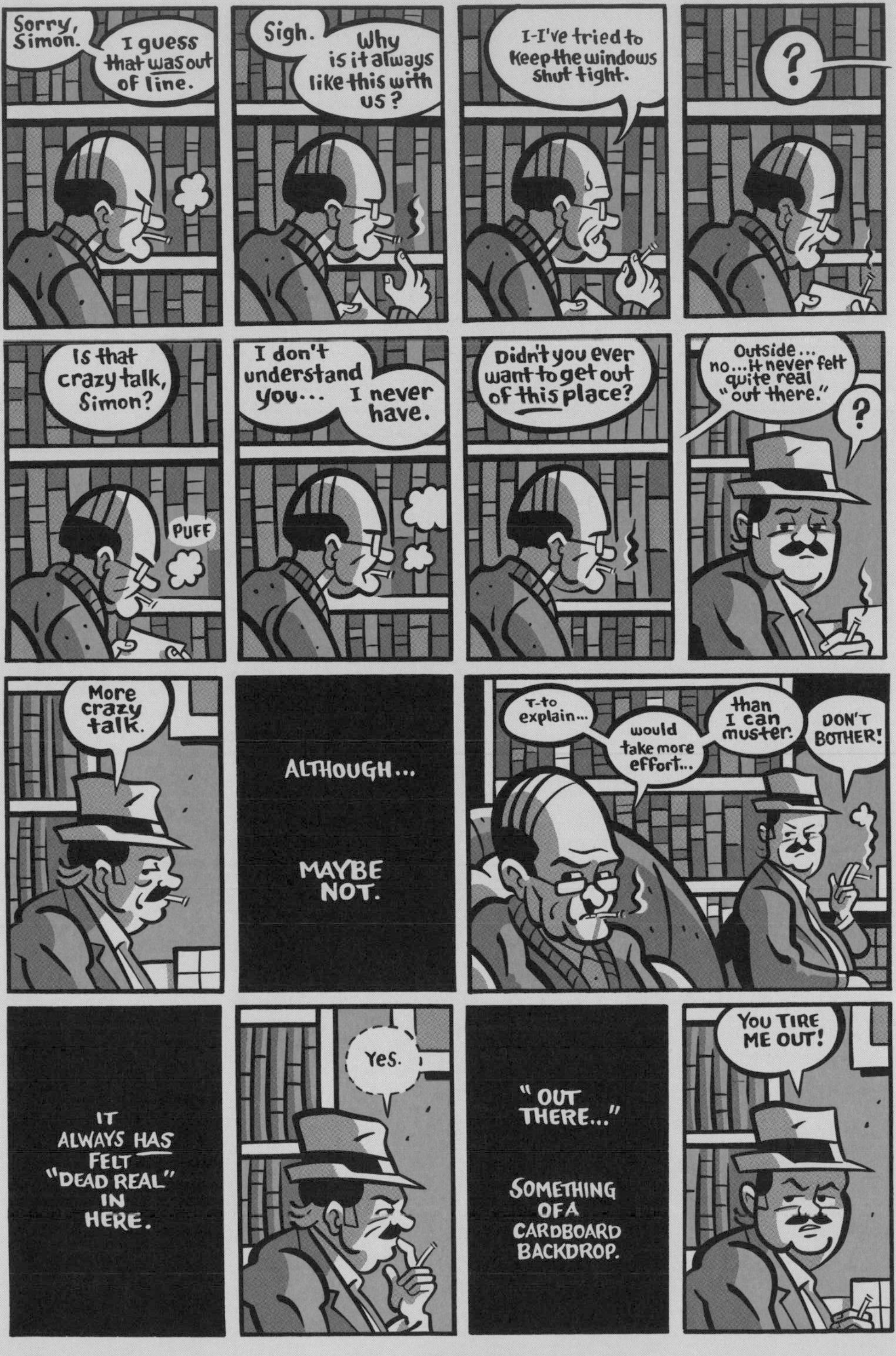
Sorry, Simon.
I guess that was out of line.
Sigh.
Why is it always like this with us?
I-I've tried to keep the windows shut tight.
?
Is that crazy talk, Simon?
I don't understand you...
I never have.
Didn't you ever want to get out of this place?
Outside... no... it never felt quite real "out there."
?
PUFF
More crazy talk.
ALTHOUGH...
MAYBE NOT.
T-to explain...
would take more effort...
than I can muster.
DON'T BOTHER!
IT ALWAYS HAS FELT "DEAD REAL" IN HERE.
Yes.
"OUT THERE..."
SOMETHING OF A CARDBOARD BACKDROP.
YOU TIRE ME OUT!

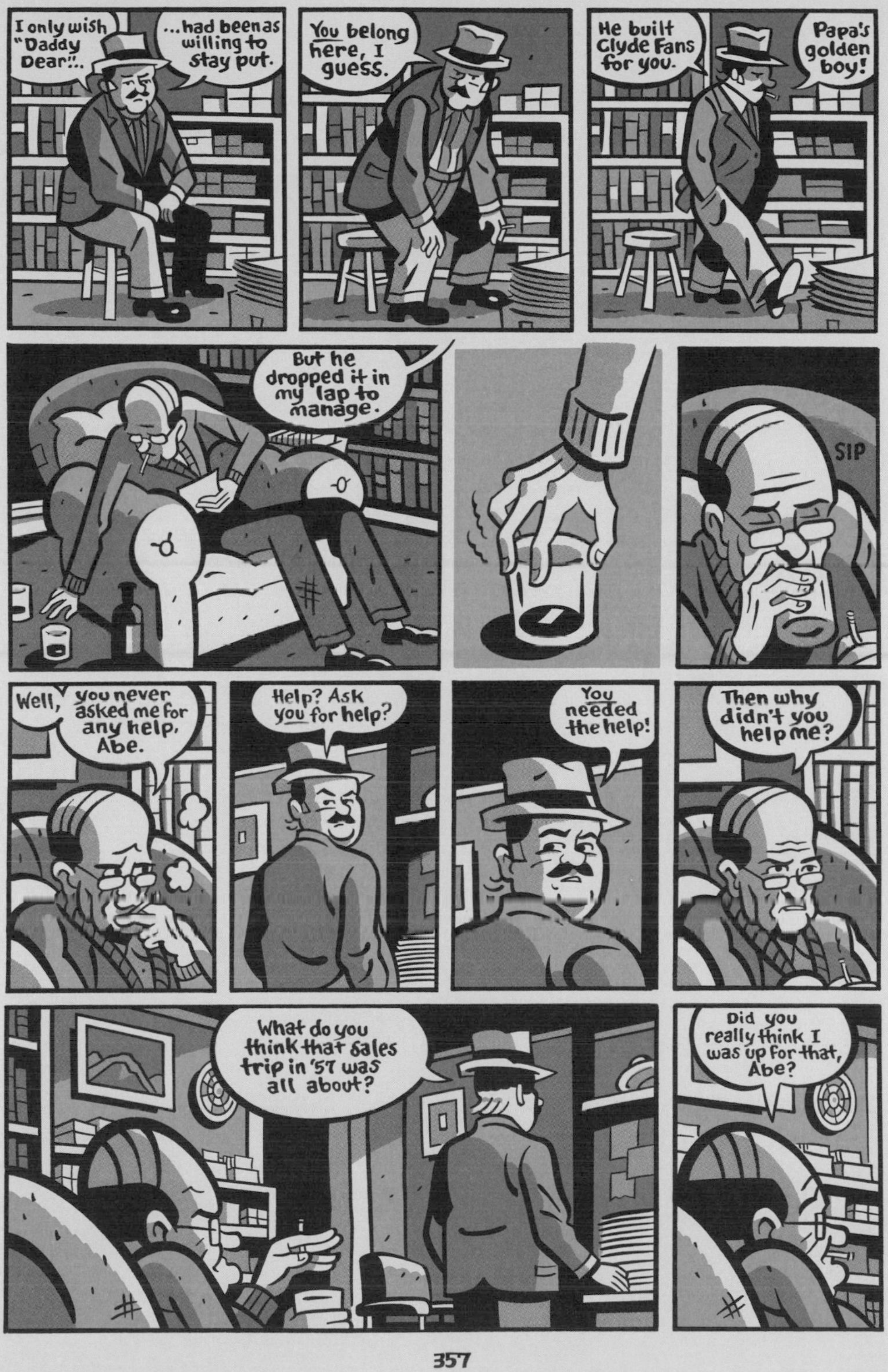
I only wish "Daddy Dear"...
...had been as willing to stay put.
You belong here, I guess.
He built Clyde Fans for you.
Papa's golden boy!
But he dropped it in my lap to manage.
SIP
Well,
you never asked me for any help, Abe.
Help? Ask you for help?
You needed the help!
Then why didn't you help me?
What do you think that sales trip in '57 was all about?
Did you really think I was up for that, Abe?

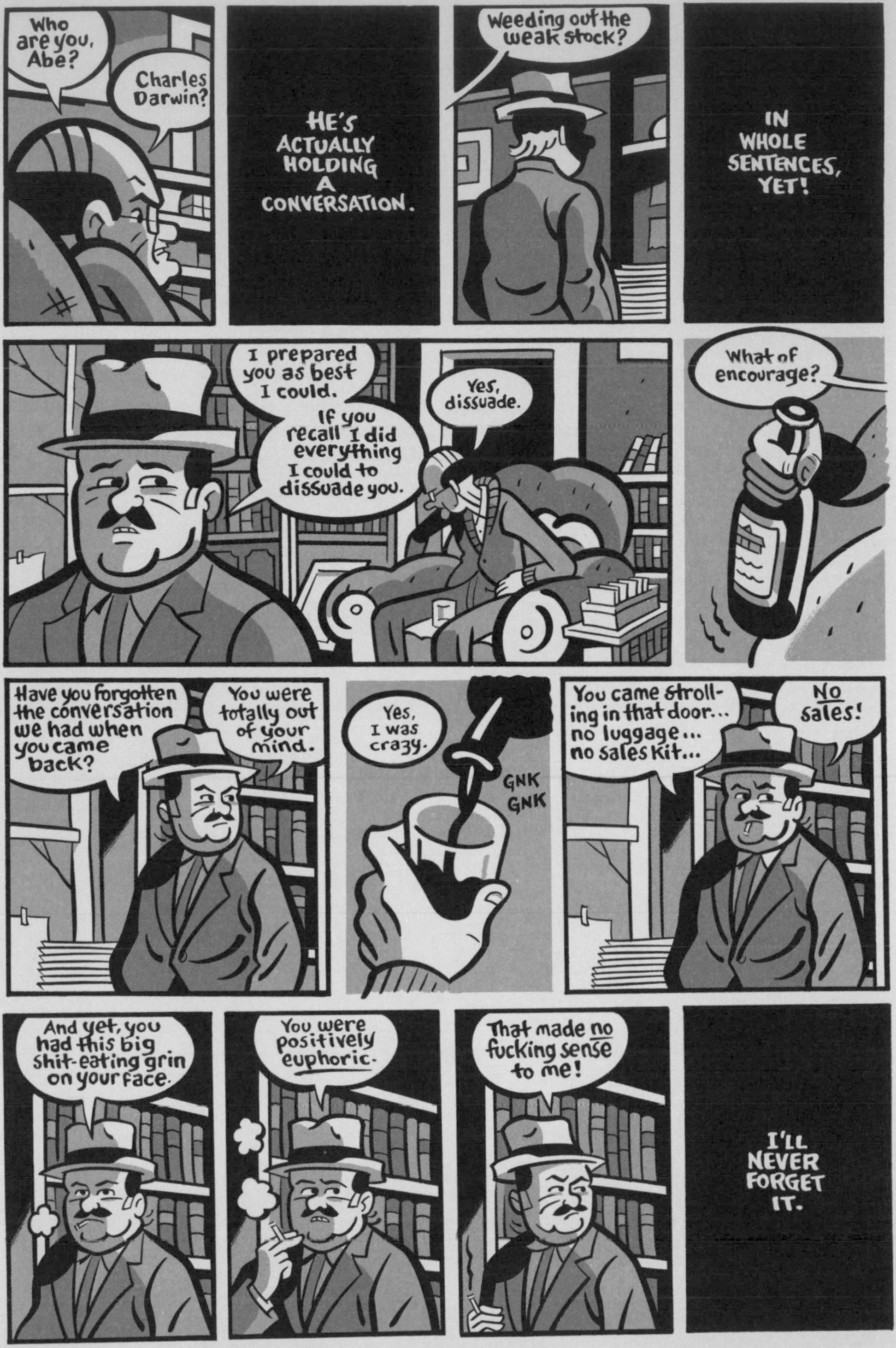

Who are you, Abe?
Charles Darwin?
HE'S ACTUALLY HOLDING A CONVERSATION.
Weeding out the weak stock?
IN WHOLE SENTENCES, YET!
I prepared you as best I could.
If you recall I did everything I could to dissuade you.
Yes, dissuade.
What of encourage?
Have you forgotten the conversation we had when you came back?
You were totally out of your mind.
Yes, I was crazy.
GNK GNK
You came strolling in that door... no luggage... no sales kit...
No sales!
And yet, you had this big shit-eating grin on your face.
You were positively euphoric.
That made no fucking sense to me!
I'LL NEVER FORGET IT.

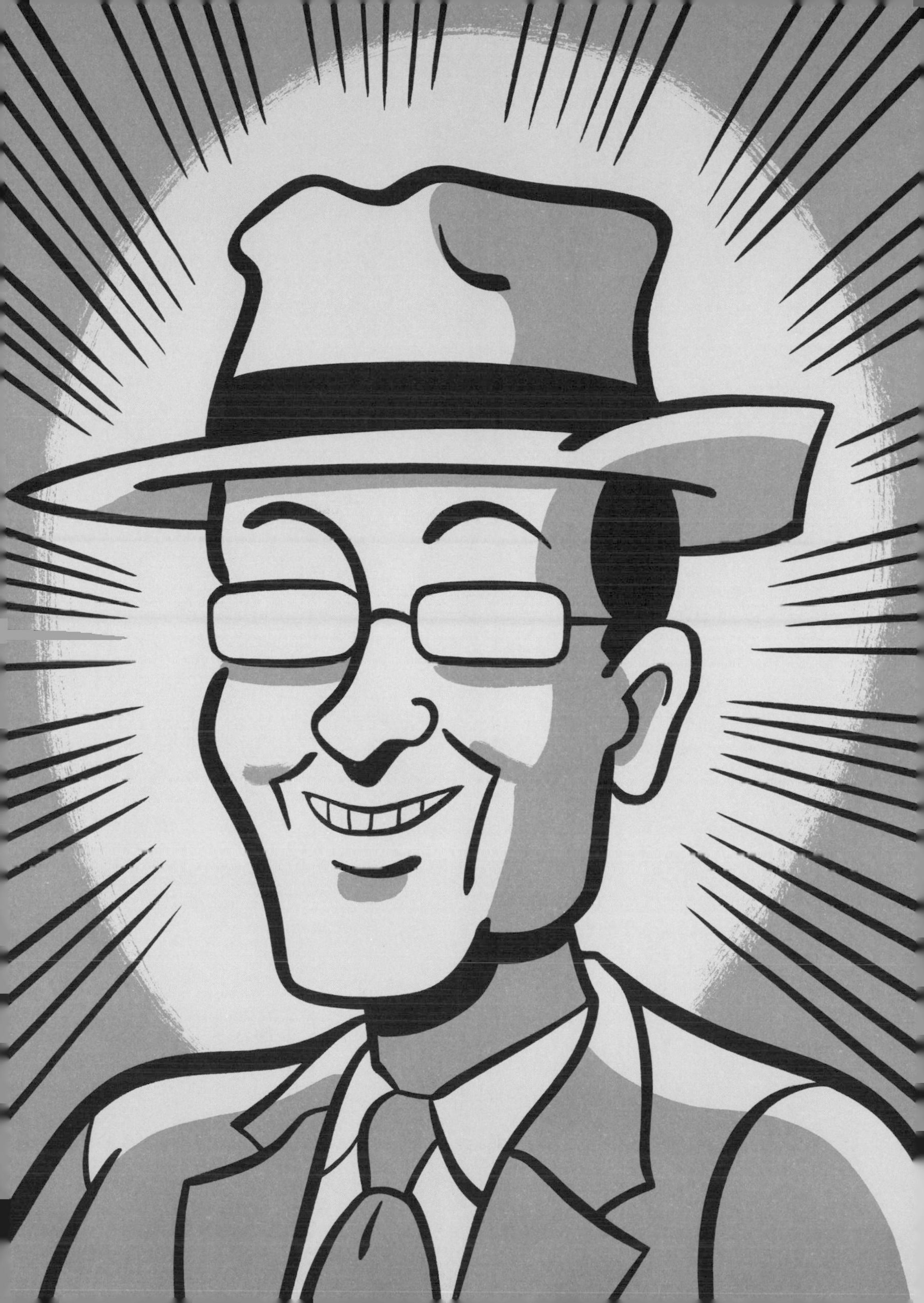

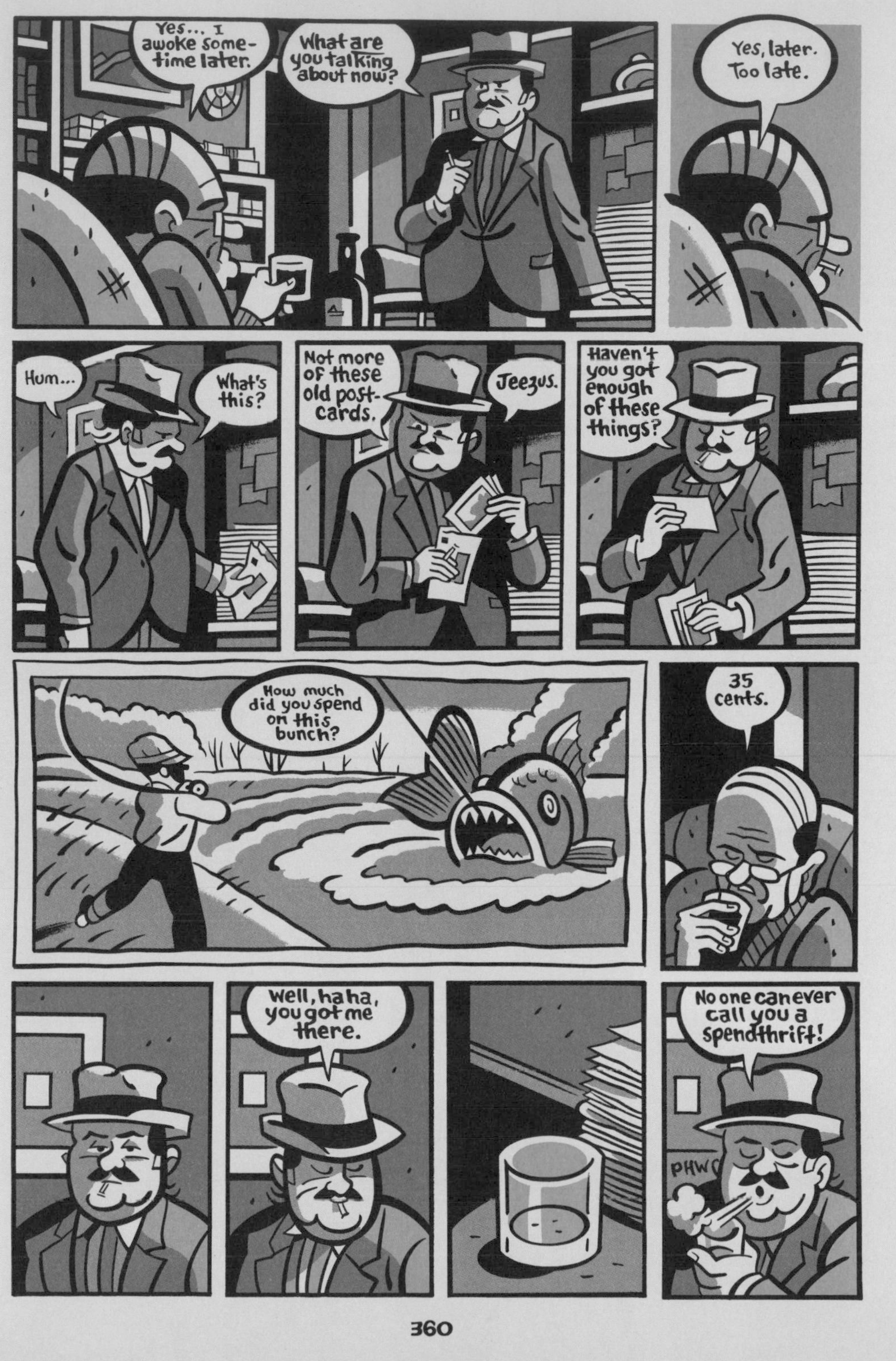

Yes... I awoke sometime later.
What are you talking about now?
Yes, later. Too late.
Hum...
What's this?
Not more of these old postcards.
Jeezus.
Haven't you got enough of these things?
How much did you spend on this bunch?
35 cents.
Well, haha, you got me there.
No one can ever call you a spendthrift!
PHWO

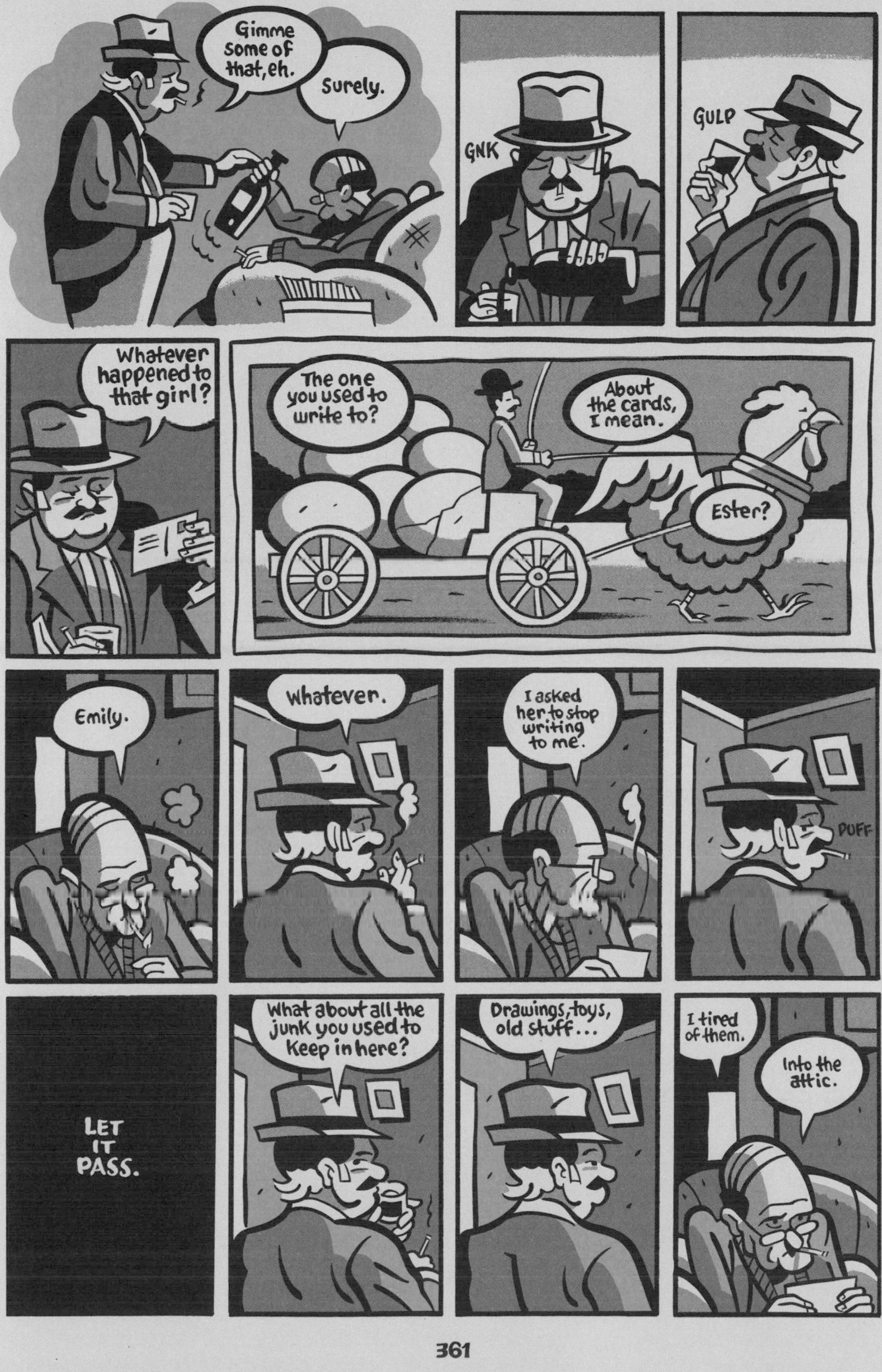
Gimme some of that, eh.
Surely.
GNK
GULP
Whatever happened to that girl?
The one you used to write to?
About the cards, I mean.
Ester?
Emily.
Whatever.
I asked her to stop writing to me.
PUFF
LET IT PASS.
What about all the junk you used to keep in here?
Drawings, toys, old stuff...
I tired of them.
Into the attic.

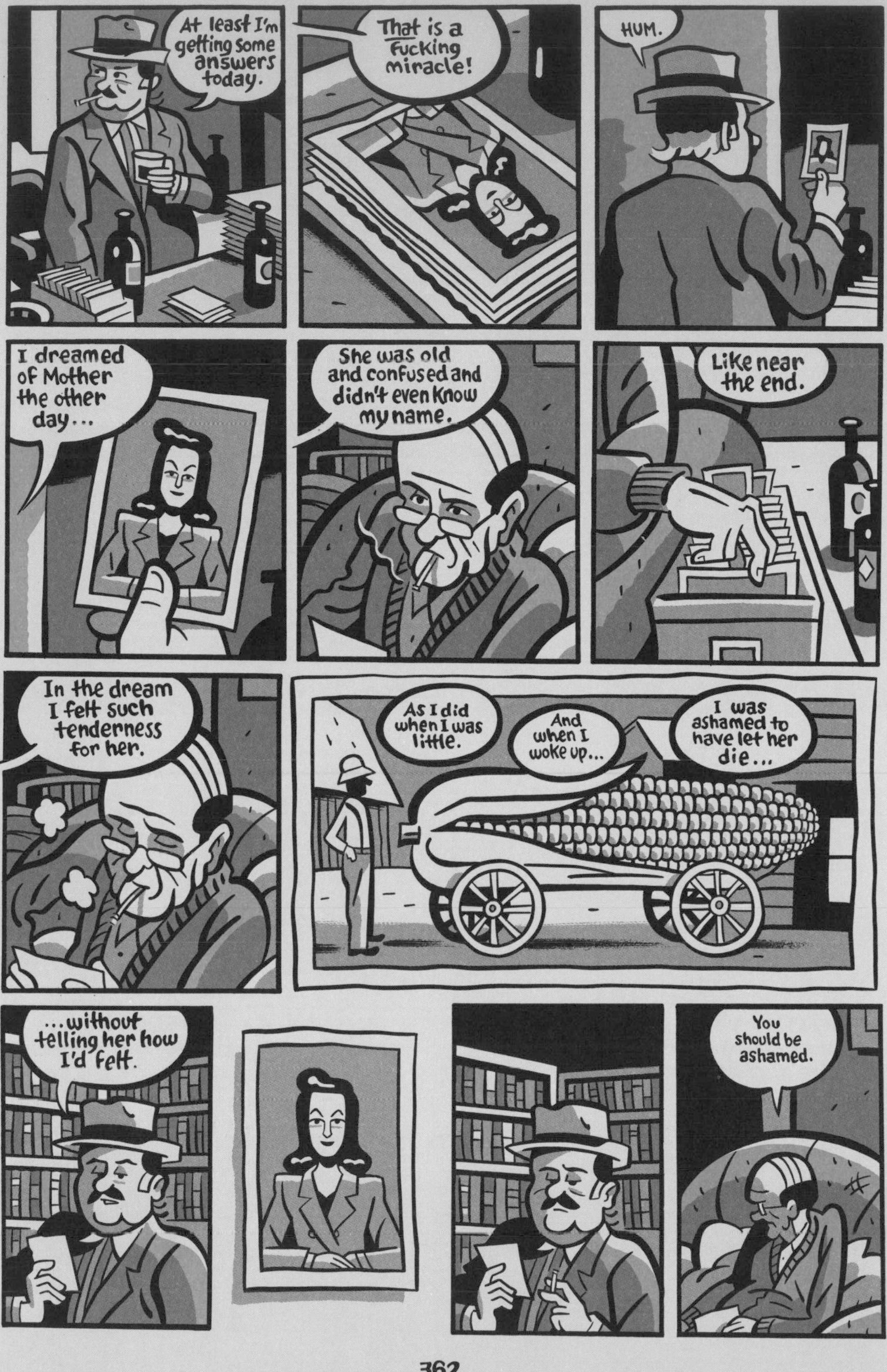
At least I'm getting some answers today.
That is a Fucking miracle!
HUM.
I dreamed of Mother the other day...
She was old and confused and didn't even know my name.
Like near the end.
In the dream I felt such tenderness for her.
As I did when I was little.
And when I woke up...
I was ashamed to have let her die...
...without telling her how I'd felt.
You should be ashamed.

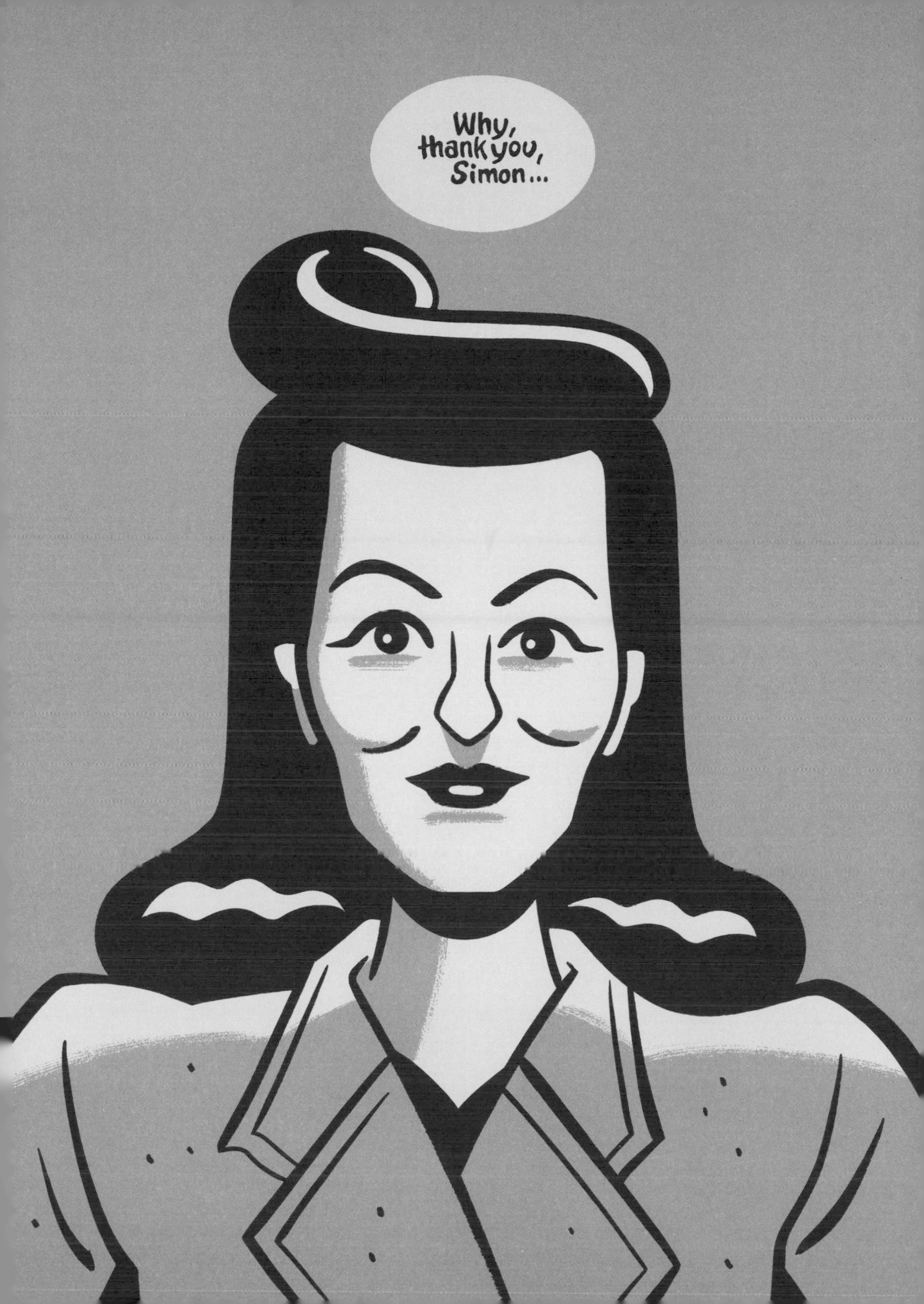
Why, thank you, Simon...

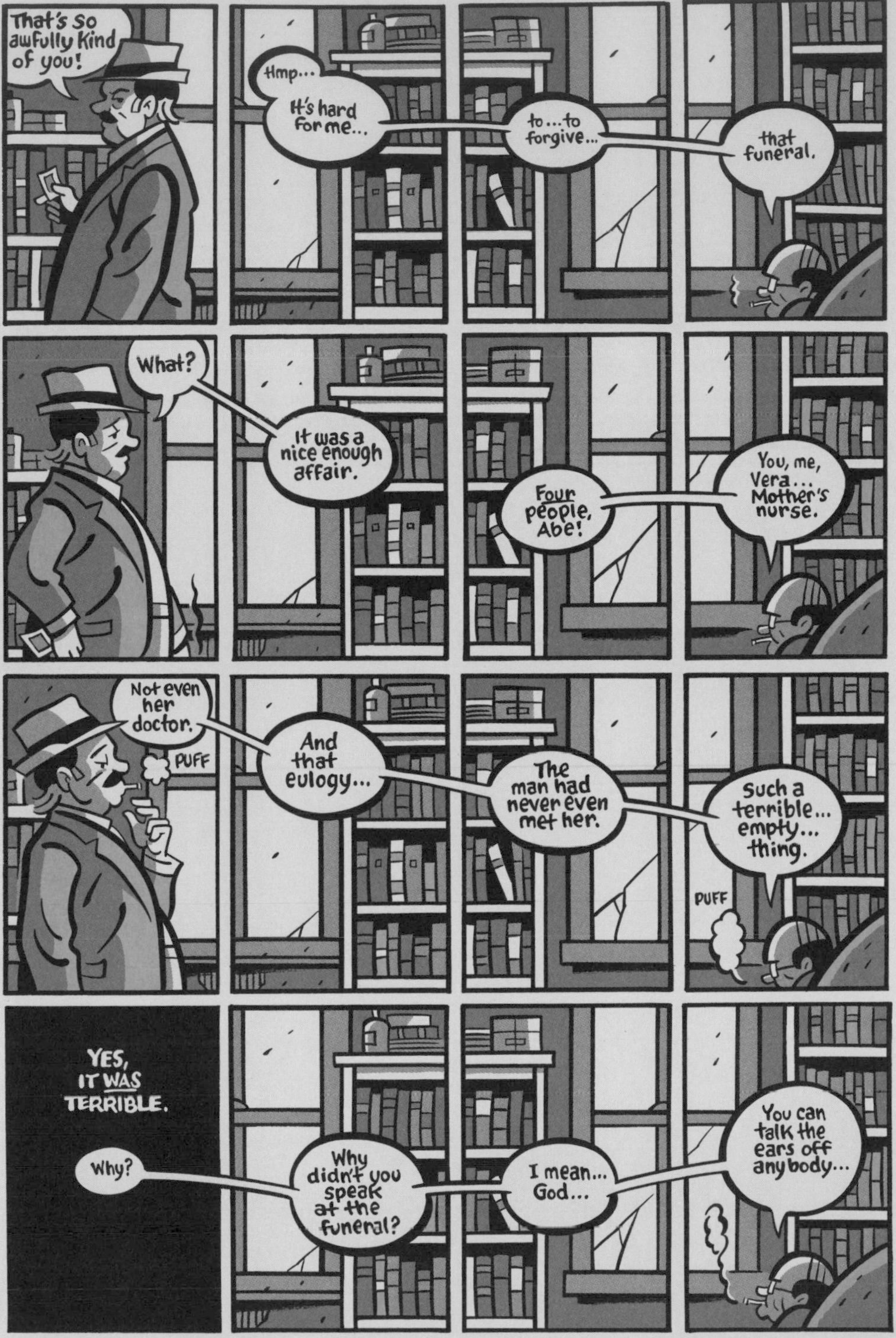
That's so awfully kind of you!
Hmp...
It's hard for me...
to... to forgive...
that funeral.
What?
It was a nice enough affair.
Four people, Abe!
You, me, Vera... Mother's nurse.
Not even her doctor.
PUFF
And that eulogy...
The man had never even met her.
Such a terrible... empty... thing.
PUFF
YES, IT WAS TERRIBLE.
Why?
Why didn't you speak at the funeral?
I mean... God...
You can talk the ears off anybody...

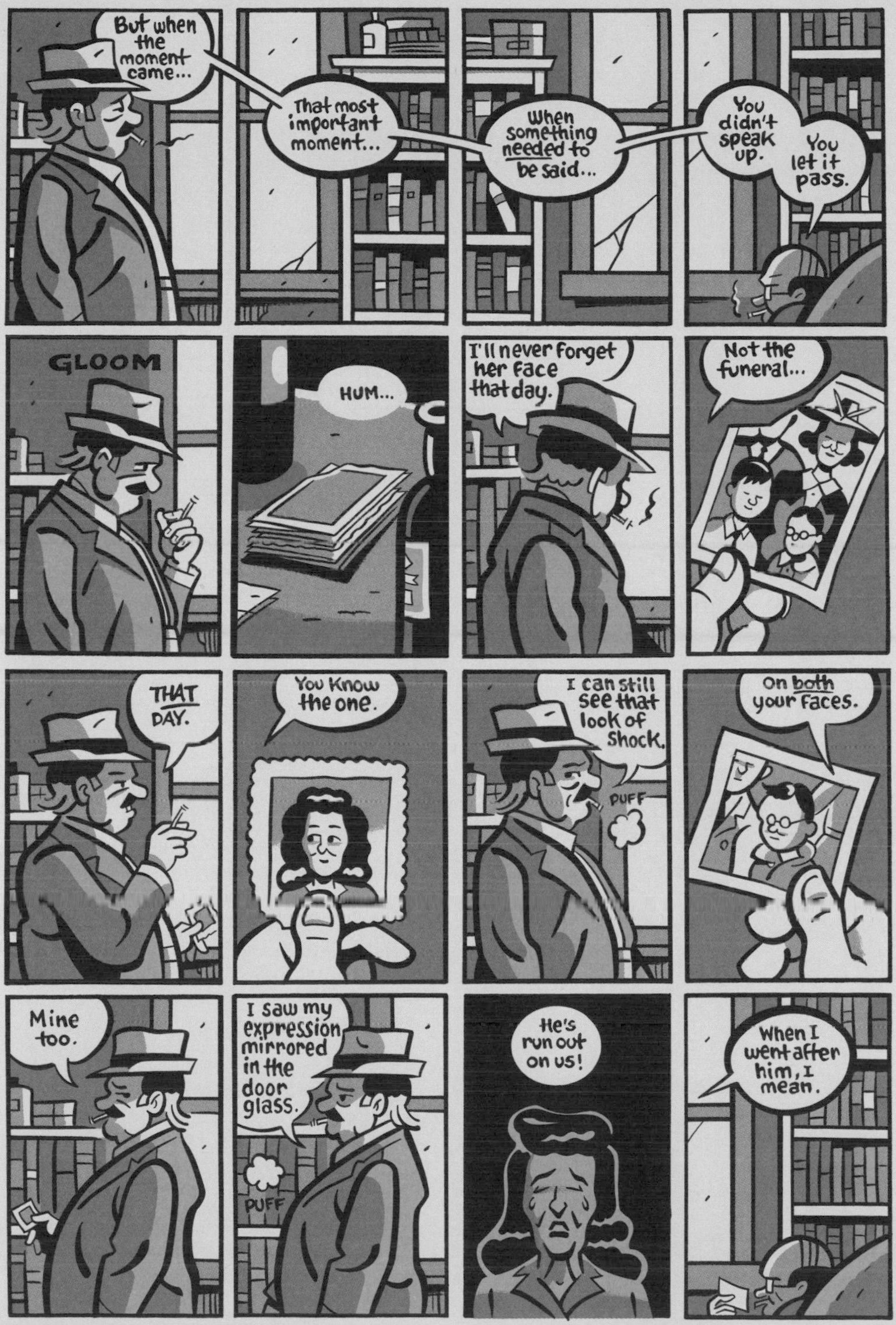
But when the moment came...
That most important moment...
When something needed to be said...
You didn't speak up.
You let it pass.
GLOOM
HUM...
I'll never forget her face that day.
Not the funeral...
THAT DAY.
You know the one.
I can still see that look of shock.
PUFF
On both your faces.
Mine too.
I saw my expression mirrored in the door glass.
PUFF
He's run out on us!
When I went after him, I mean.

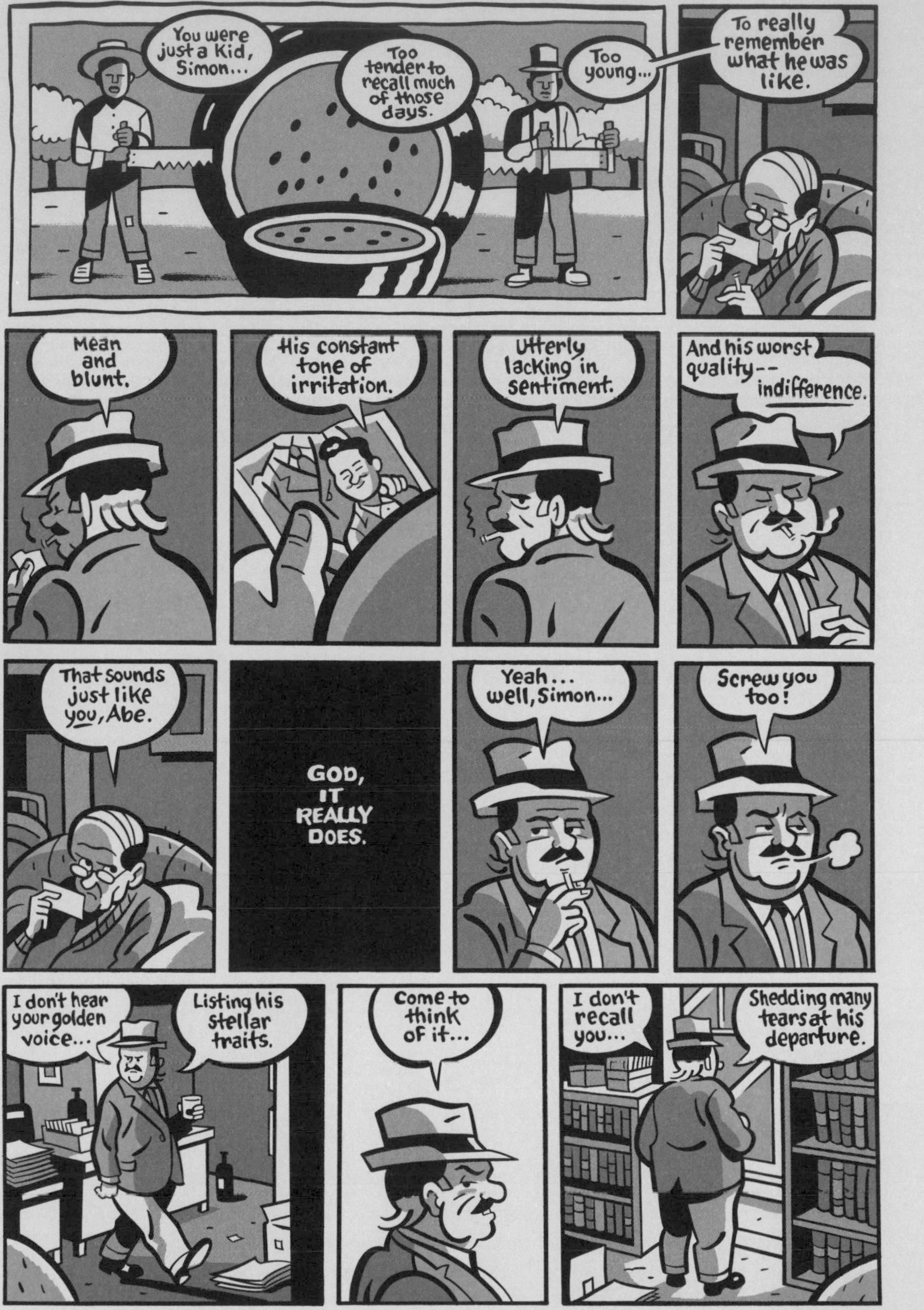

You were just a Kid, Simon...
Too tender to recall much of those days.
Too young...
To really remember what he was like.
Mean and blunt.
His constant tone of irritation.
Utterly lacking in sentiment.
And his worst quality-- indifference.
That sounds just like you, Abe.
GOD, IT REALLY DOES.
Yeah... well, Simon...
Screw you too!
I don't hear your golden voice...
Listing his stellar traits.
Come to think of it...
I don't recall you...
Shedding many tears at his departure.

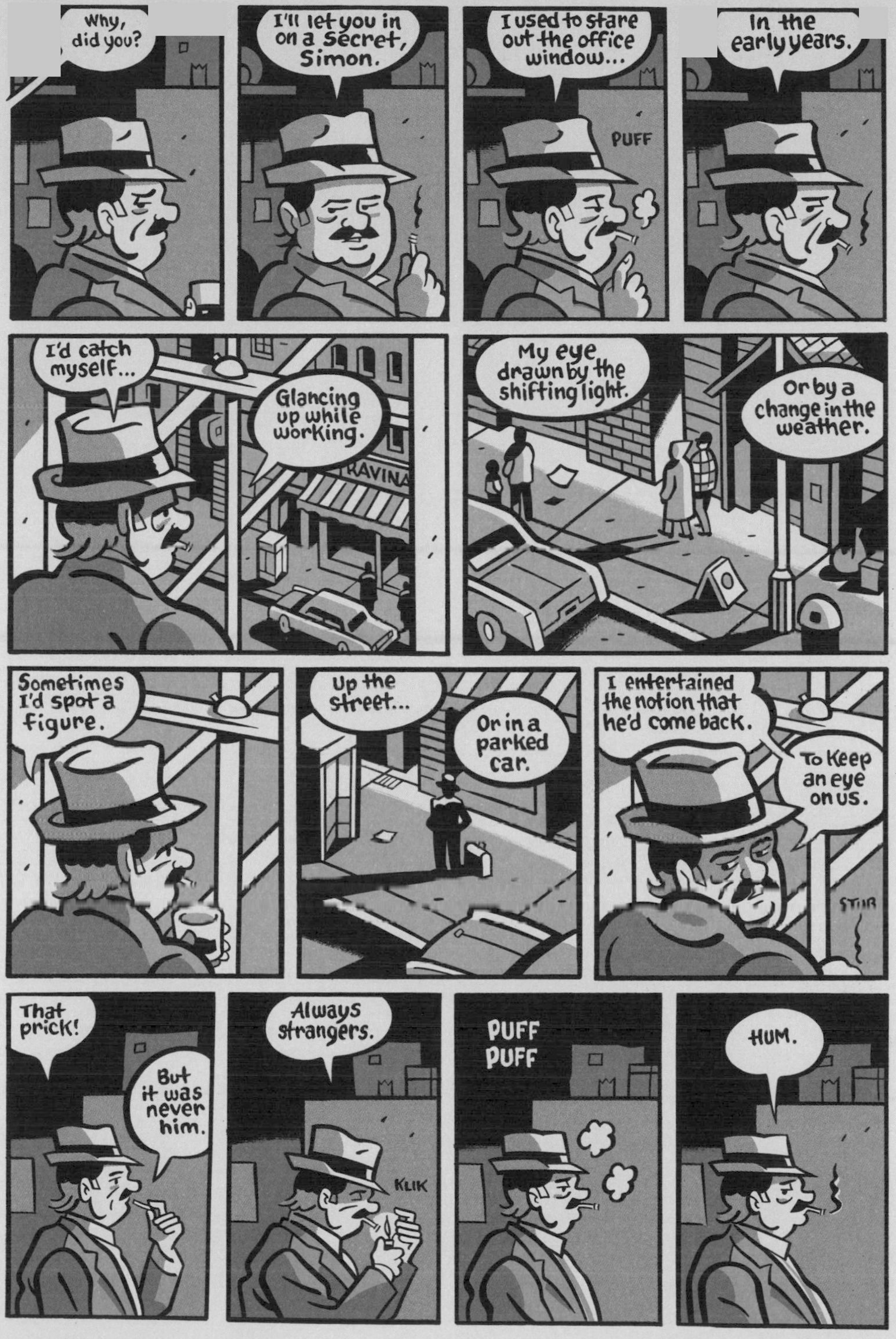
Why, did you?
I'll let you in on a secret, Simon.
I used to stare out the office window...
PUFF
In the early years.
I'd catch myself...
Glancing up while working.
RAVINA
My eye drawn by the shifting light.
Or by a change in the weather.
Sometimes I'd spot a figure.
Up the street...
Or in a parked car.
I entertained the notion that he'd come back.
To keep an eye on us.
STIR
That prick!
But it was never him.
Always strangers.
KLIK
PUFF PUFF
HUM.

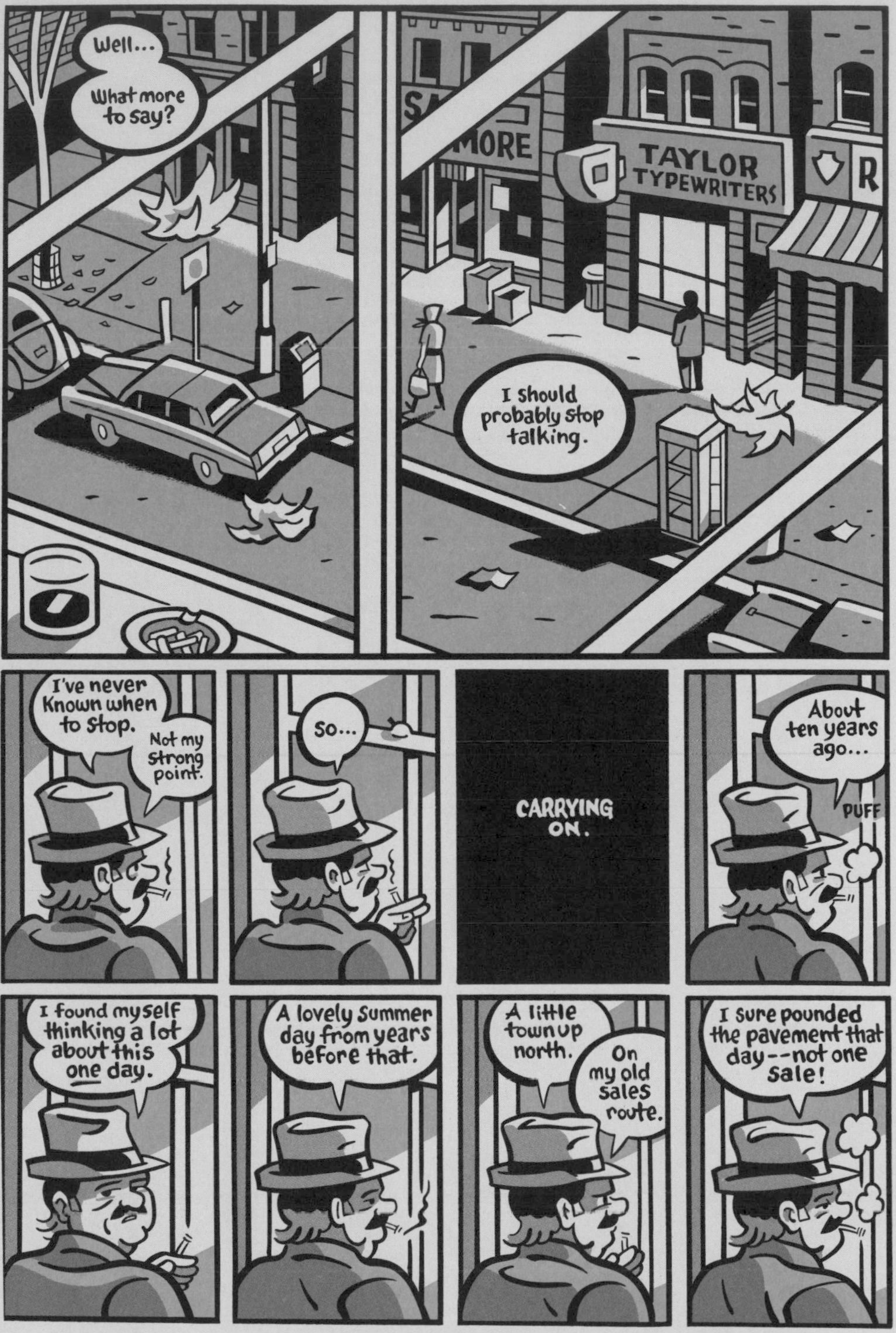
Well...
What more to say?
SA
MORE
TAYLOR TYPEWRITERS
R
I should probably stop talking.
I've never Known when to stop.
Not my strong point.
So...
CARRYING ON.
About ten years ago...
PUFF
I found myself thinking a lot about this one day.
A lovely summer day from years before that.
A little town up north.
On my old sales route.
I sure pounded the pavement that day--not one sale!

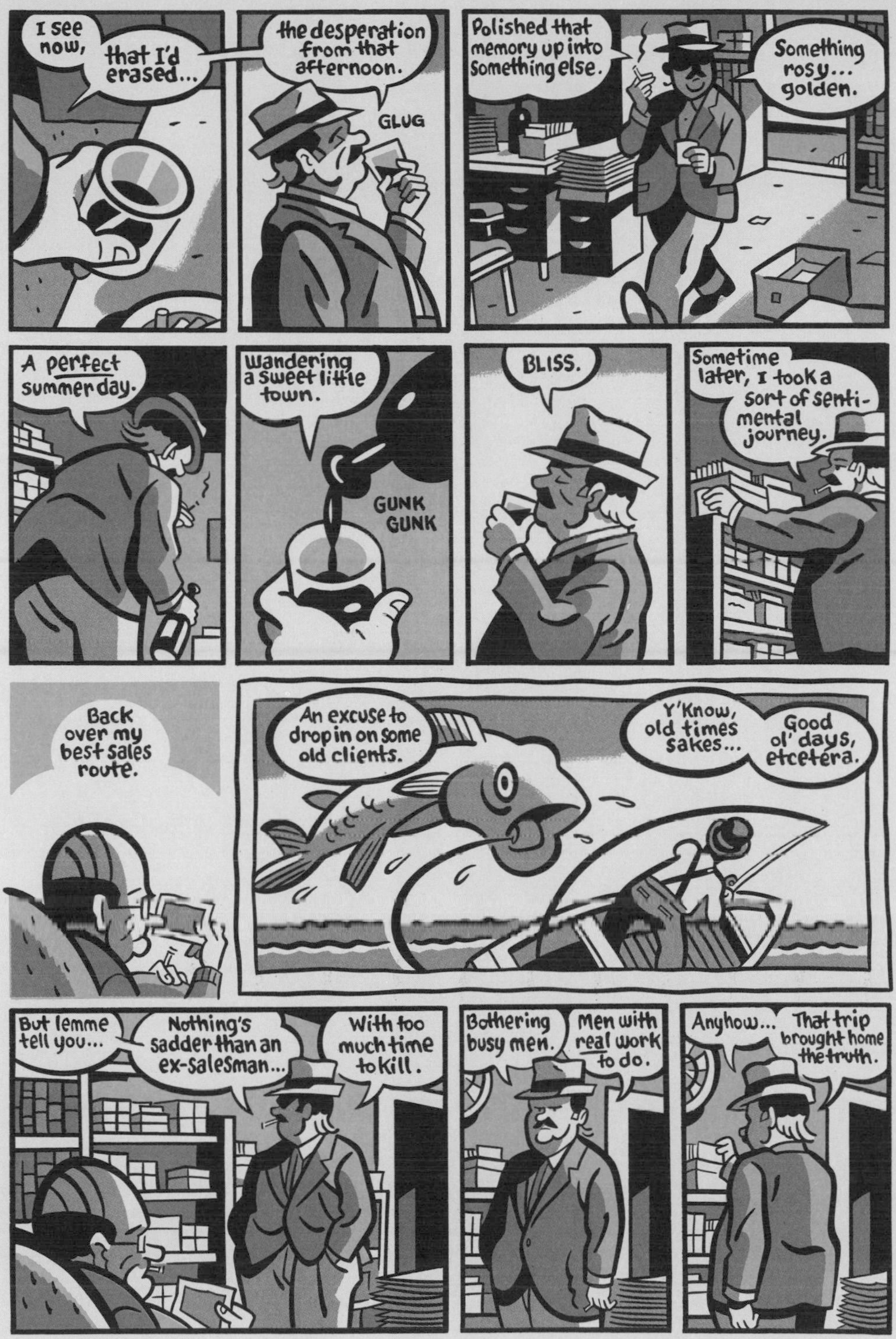

I see now,
that I'd erased...
the desperation from that afternoon.
GLUG
Polished that memory up into something else.
Something rosy... golden.
A perfect summer day.
Wandering a sweet little town.
GUNK GUNK
BLISS.
Sometime later, I took a sort of senti-mental journey.
Back over my best sales route.
An excuse to drop in on some old clients.
Y'Know, old times sakes...
Good ol' days, etcetera.
But lemme tell you...
Nothing's sadder than an ex-salesman...
With too much time to kill.
Bothering busy men.
Men with real work to do.
Anyhow...
That trip brought home the truth.

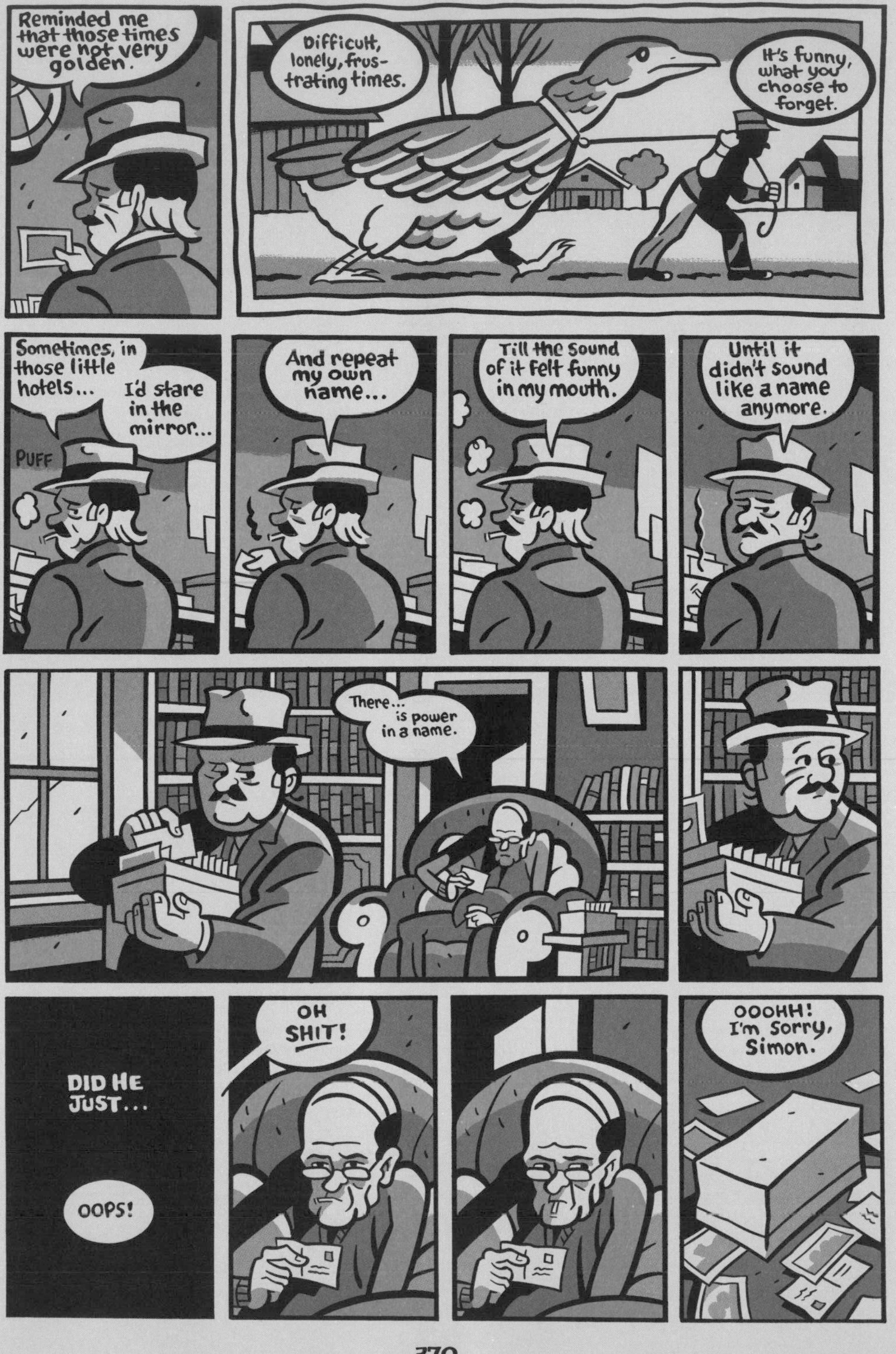
Reminded me that those times were not very golden.
Difficult, lonely, frustrating times.
It's funny, what you choose to forget.
Sometimes, in those little hotels...
I'd stare in the mirror...
PUFF
And repeat my own name...
Till the sound of it felt funny in my mouth.
Until it didn't sound like a name anymore.
There... is power in a name.
DID HE JUST...
OOPS!
OH SHIT!
OOOHH! I'm sorry, Simon.

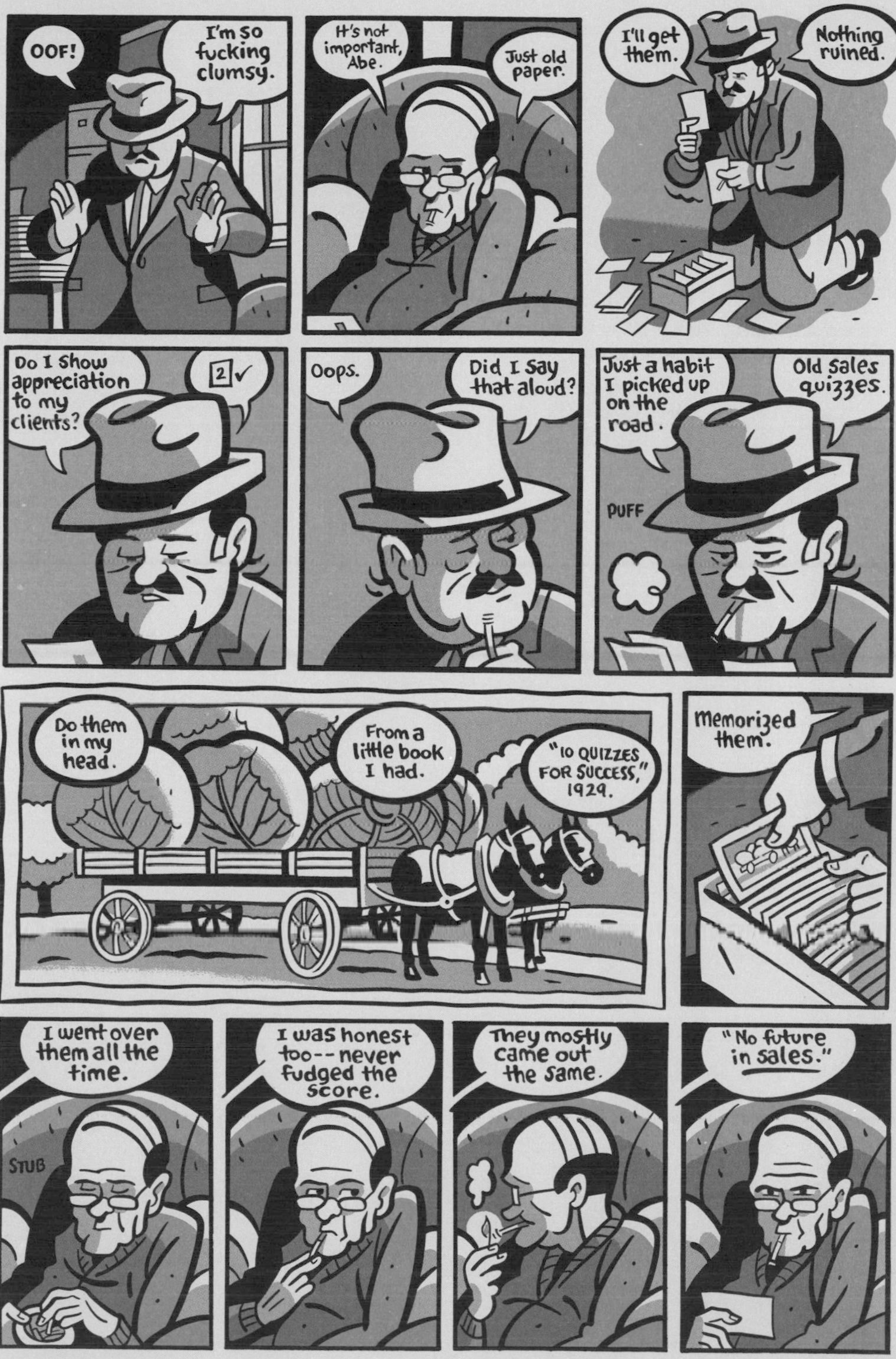
OOF!
I'm so fucking clumsy.
It's not important, Abe.
Just old paper.
I'll get them.
Nothing ruined.
Do I show appreciation to my clients?
2 ✓
Oops.
Did I say that aloud?
Just a habit I picked up on the road.
Old sales quizzes.
PUFF
Do them in my head.
From a little book I had.
"10 QUIZZES FOR SUCCESS," 1929.
Memorized them.
I went over them all the time.
STUB
I was honest too-- never fudged the score.
They mostly came out the same.
"No future in sales."

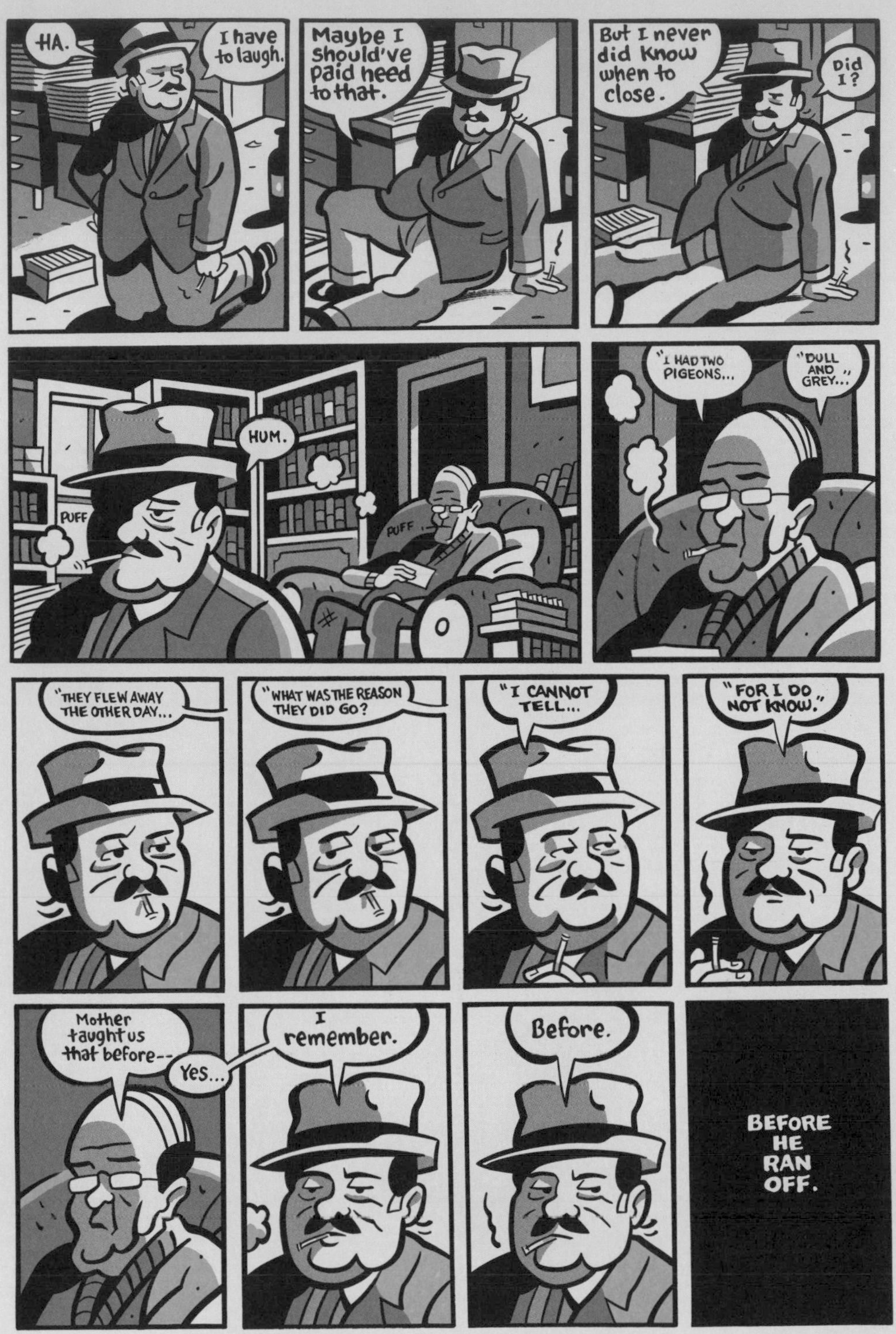
HA.
I have to laugh.
Maybe I should've paid need to that.
But I never did Know when to close.
Did I?
HUM.
PUFF
PUFF
"I HAD TWO PIGEONS...
"DULL AND GREY..."
"THEY FLEW AWAY THE OTHER DAY...
"WHAT WAS THE REASON THEY DID GO?
"I CANNOT TELL...
"FOR I DO NOT KNOW."
Mother taught us that before--
Yes...
I remember.
Before.
BEFORE HE RAN OFF.

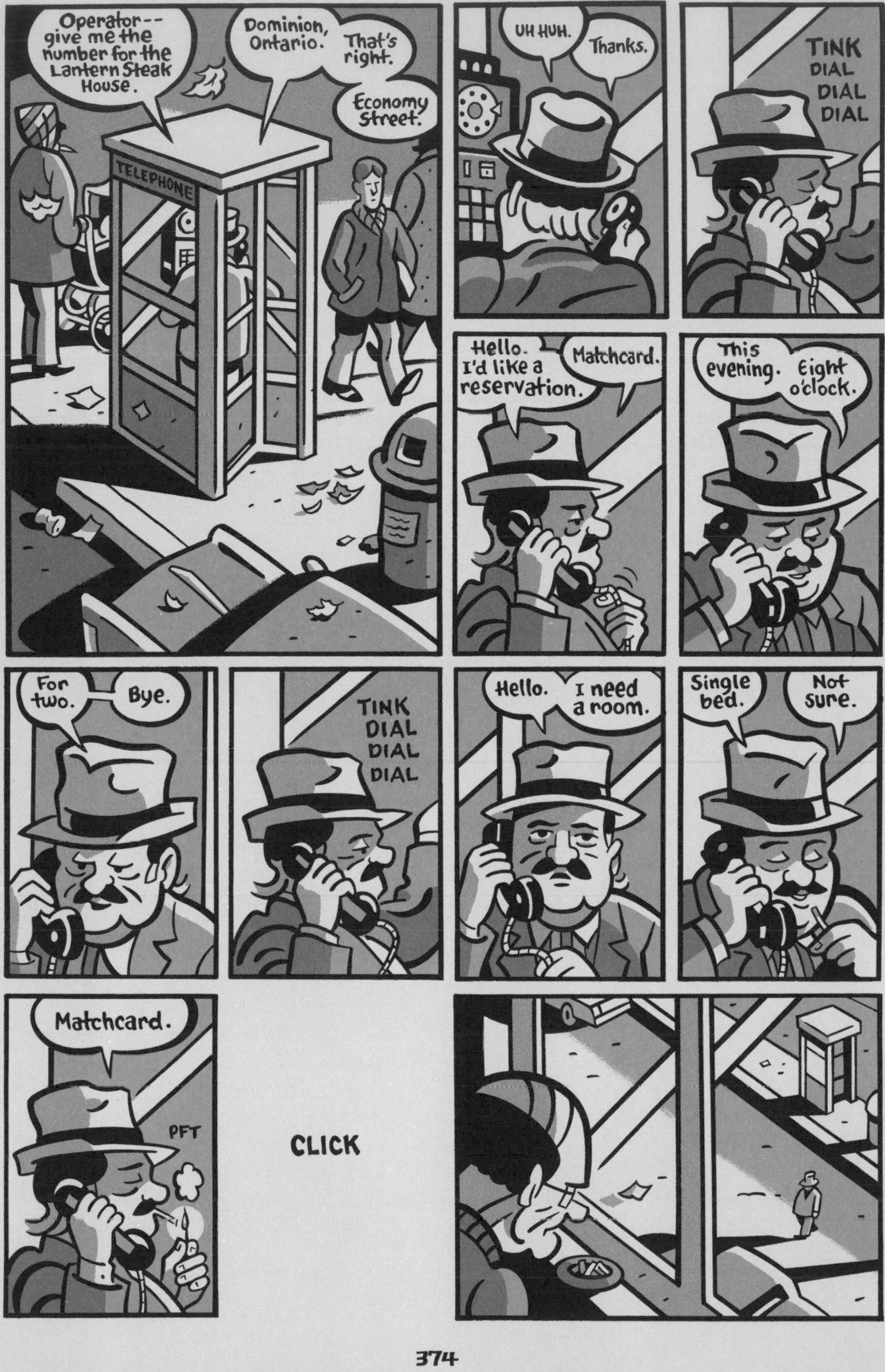
Operator-- give me the number for the Lantern Steak House.
Dominion, Ontario.
That's right.
Economy Street.
TELEPHONE
UH HUH.
Thanks.
TINK
DIAL
DIAL
DIAL
Hello. I'd like a reservation.
Matchcard.
This evening.
Eight o'clock.
For two.
Bye.
TINK
DIAL
DIAL
DIAL
Hello.
I need a room.
Single bed.
Not sure.
Matchcard.
PFT
CLICK

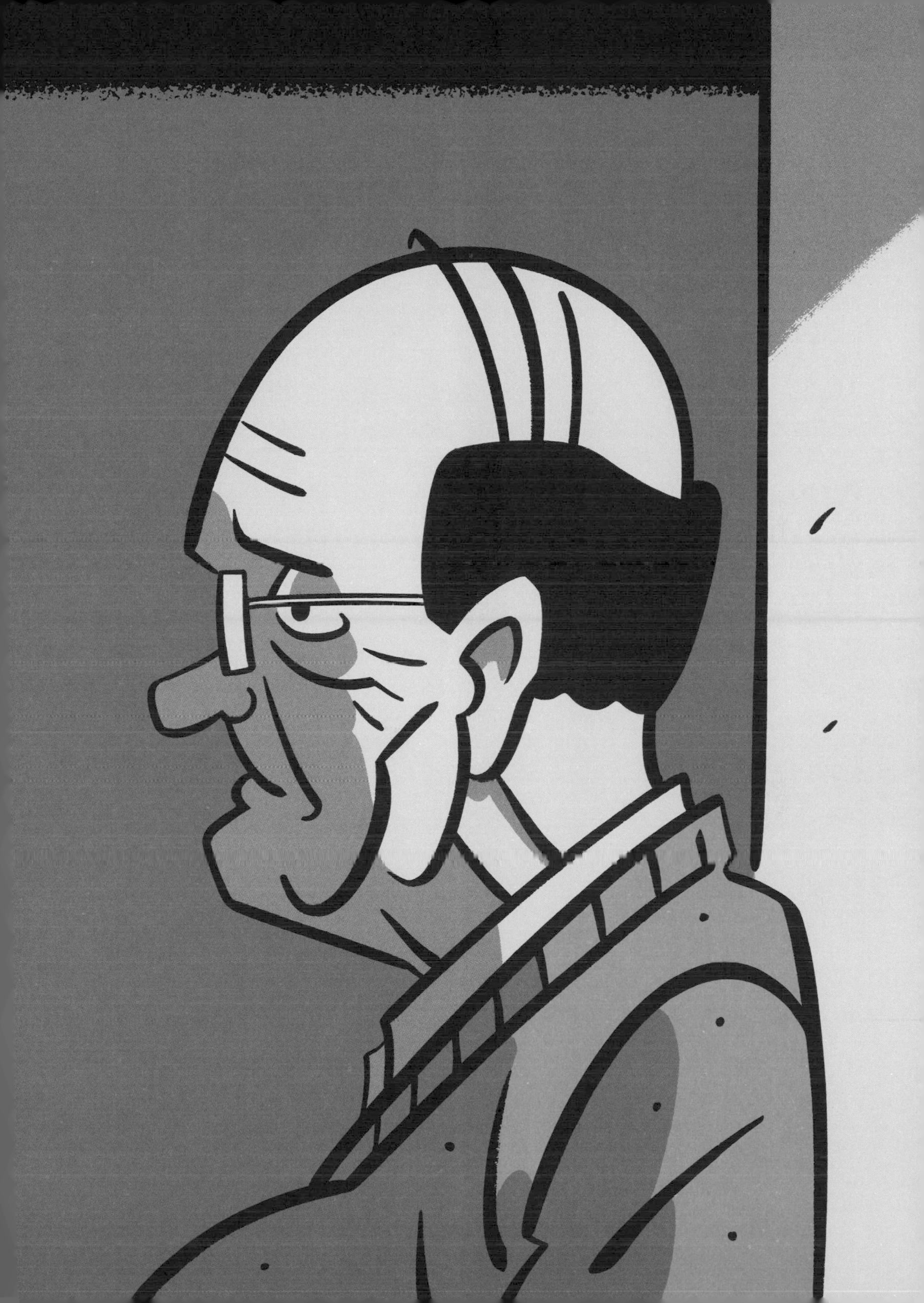

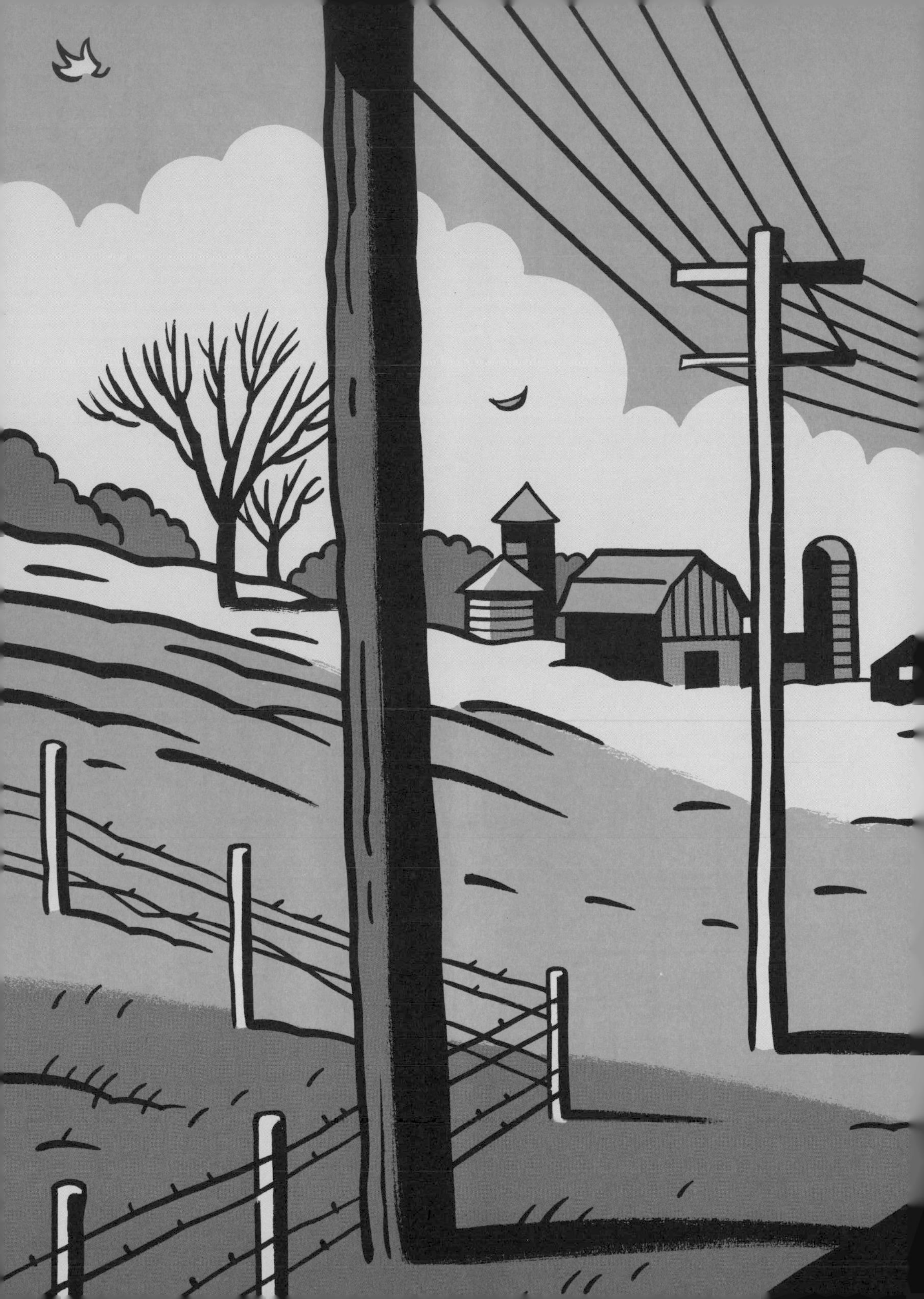

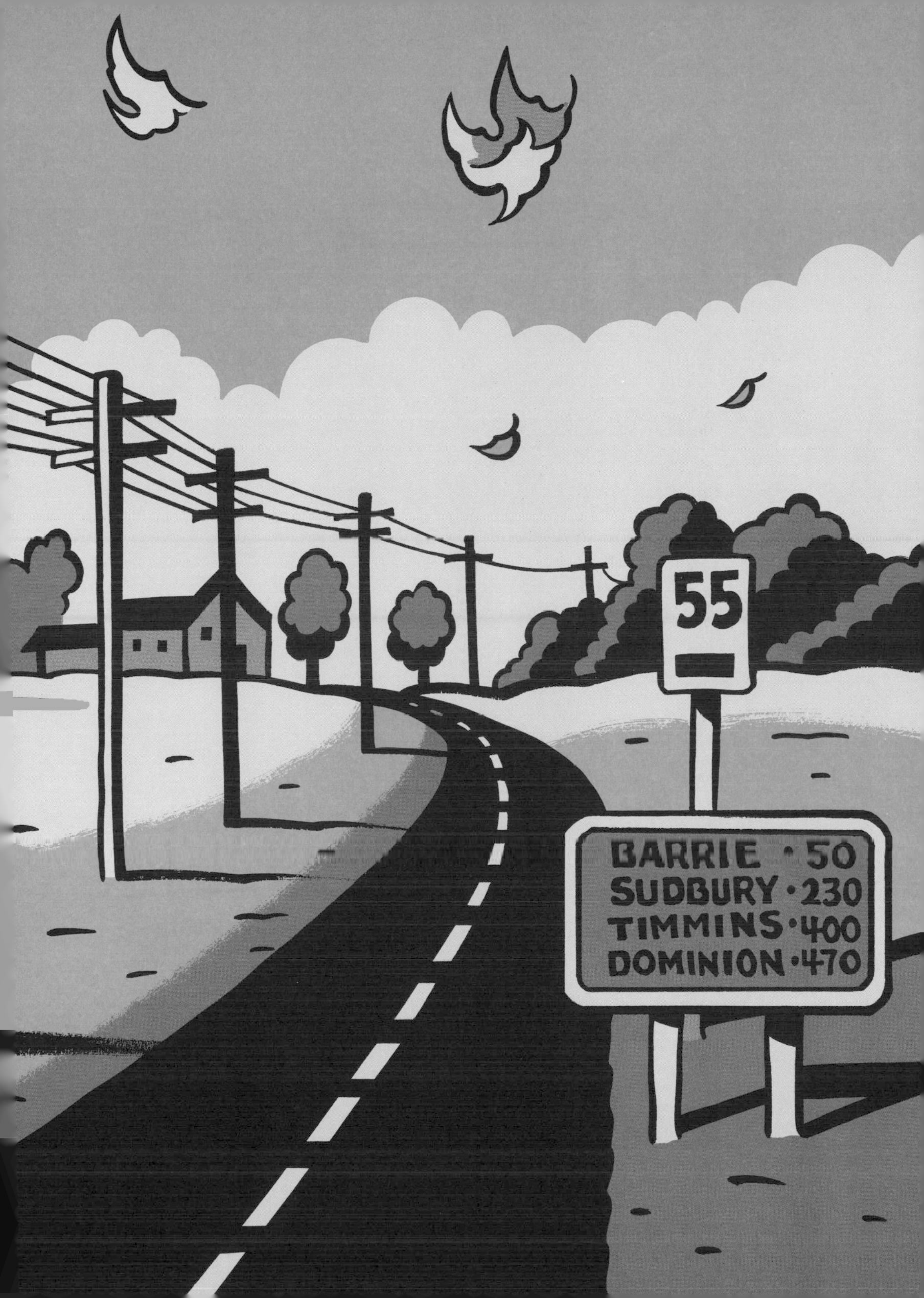
55
BARRIE • 50
SUDBURY • 230
TIMMINS • 400
DOMINION • 470

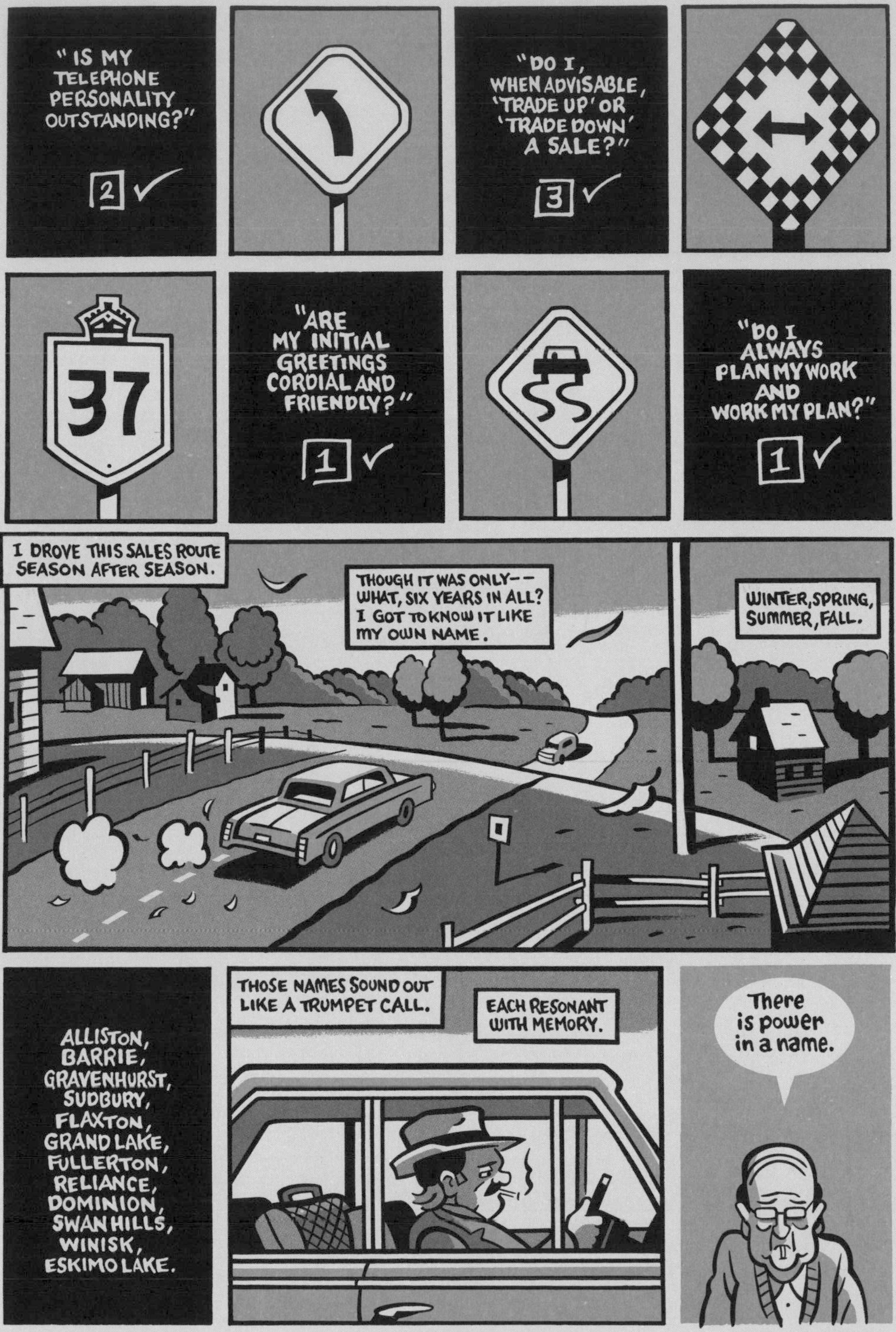

"IS MY TELEPHONE PERSONALITY OUTSTANDING?"
2 ✓
"DO I, WHEN ADVISABLE, 'TRADE UP' OR 'TRADE DOWN' A SALE?"
3 ✓
37
"ARE MY INITIAL GREETINGS CORDIAL AND FRIENDLY?"
1 ✓
"DO I ALWAYS PLAN MY WORK AND WORK MY PLAN?"
1 ✓
I DROVE THIS SALES ROUTE SEASON AFTER SEASON.
THOUGH IT WAS ONLY-- WHAT, SIX YEARS IN ALL? I GOT TO KNOW IT LIKE MY OWN NAME.
WINTER, SPRING, SUMMER, FALL.
ALLISTON, BARRIE, GRAVENHURST, SUDBURY, FLAXTON, GRAND LAKE, FULLERTON, RELIANCE, DOMINION, SWAN HILLS, WINISK, ESKIMO LAKE.
THOSE NAMES SOUND OUT LIKE A TRUMPET CALL.
EACH RESONANT WITH MEMORY.
There is power in a name.

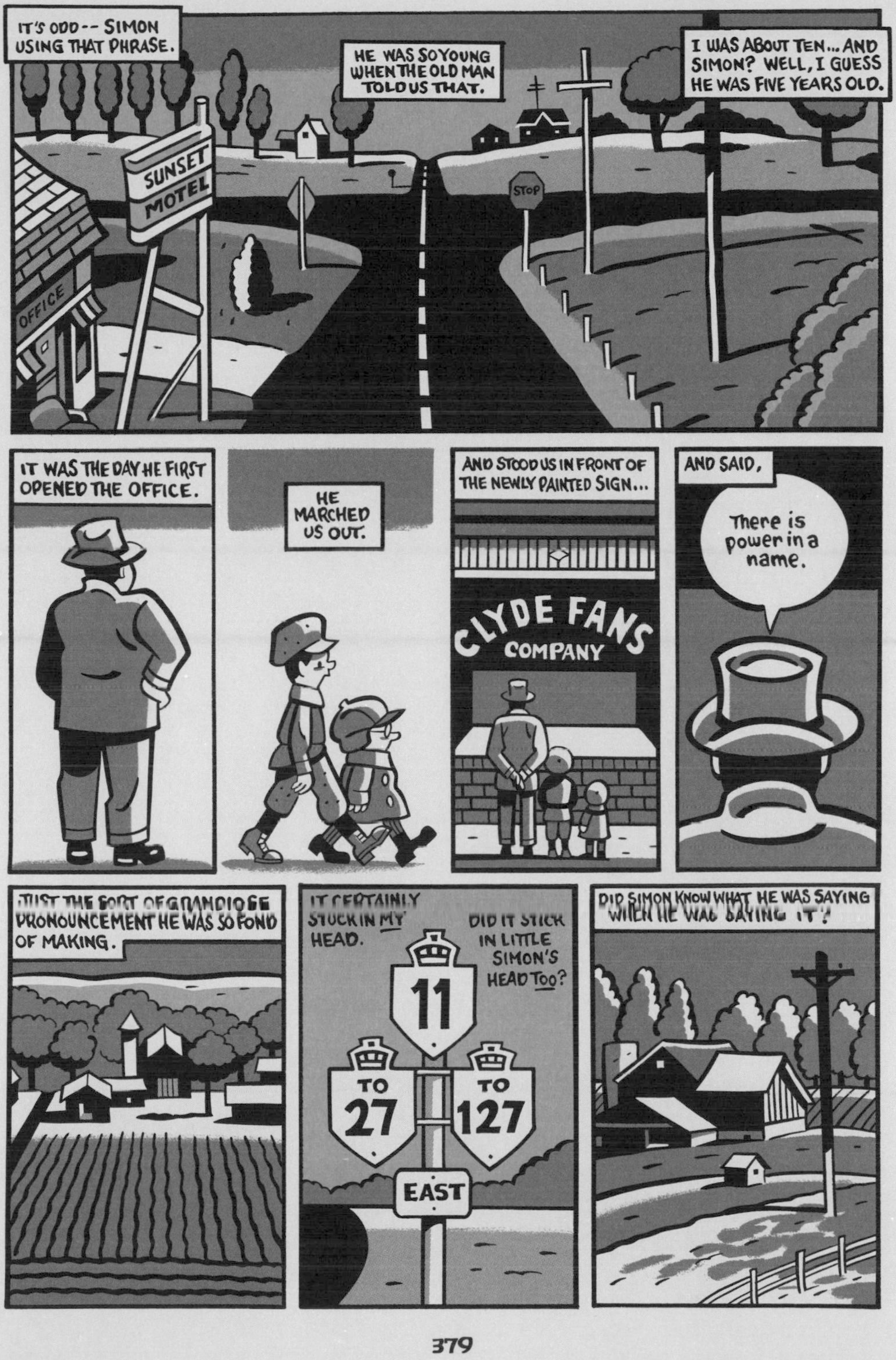

IT'S ODD -- SIMON USING THAT PHRASE.
HE WAS SO YOUNG WHEN THE OLD MAN TOLD US THAT.
I WAS ABOUT TEN... AND SIMON? WELL, I GUESS HE WAS FIVE YEARS OLD.
SUNSET MOTEL
STOP
OFFICE
IT WAS THE DAY HE FIRST OPENED THE OFFICE.
HE MARCHED US OUT.
AND STOOD US IN FRONT OF THE NEWLY PAINTED SIGN...
CLYDE FANS
COMPANY
AND SAID,
There is power in a name.
JUST THE SORT OF GRANDIOSE PRONOUNCEMENT HE WAS SO FOND OF MAKING.
IT CERTAINLY STUCK IN MY HEAD.
DID IT STICK IN LITTLE SIMON'S HEAD TOO?
11
TO 27
TO 127
EAST
DID SIMON KNOW WHAT HE WAS SAYING WHEN HE WAS SAYING IT?

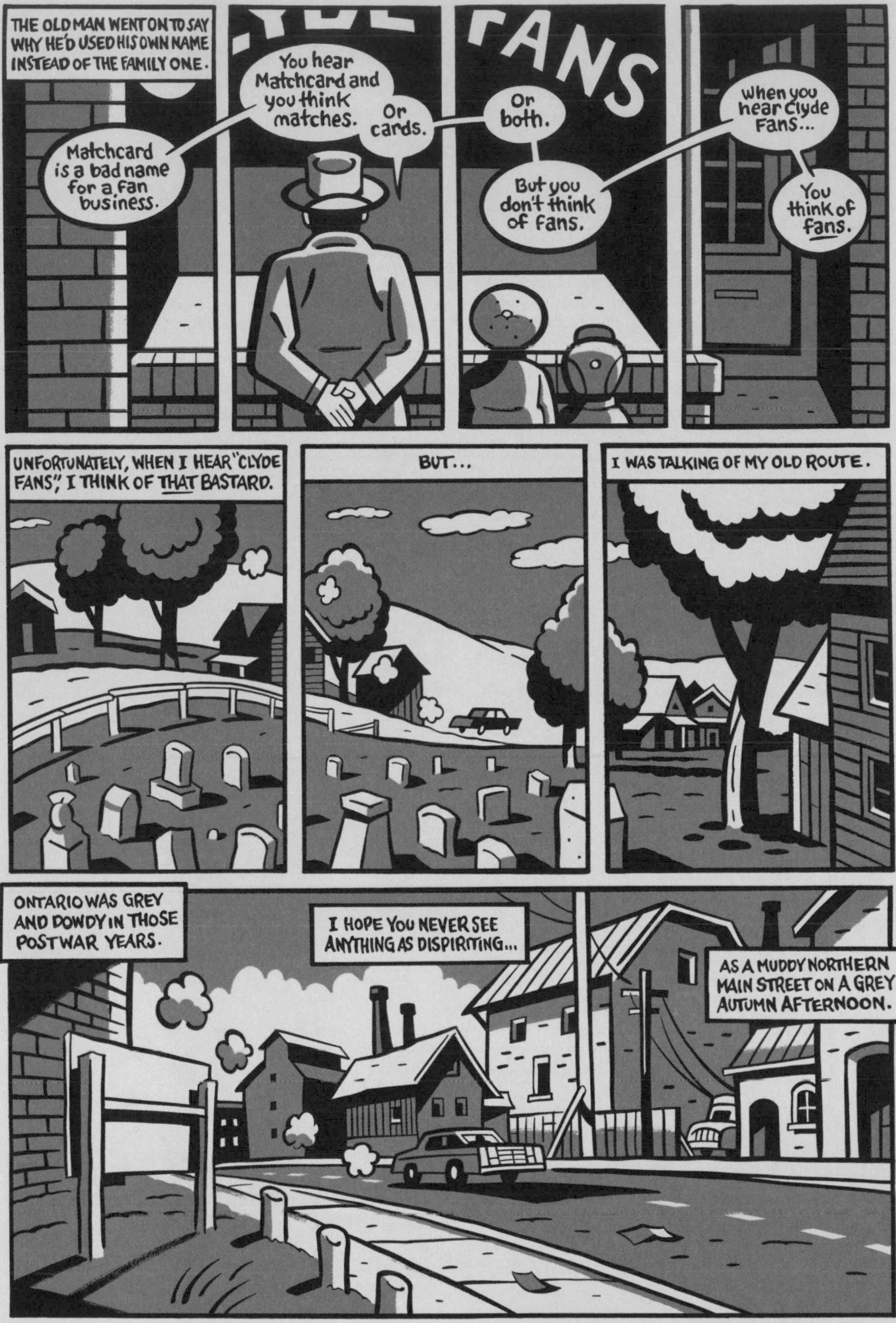
THE OLD MAN WENT ON TO SAY WHY HE'D USED HIS OWN NAME INSTEAD OF THE FAMILY ONE.
Matchcard is a bad name for a fan business.
You hear Matchcard and you think matches.
Or cards.
Or both.
But you don't think of fans.
When you hear Clyde Fans...
You think of fans.
UNFORTUNATELY, WHEN I HEAR "CLYDE FANS", I THINK OF THAT BASTARD.
BUT...
I WAS TALKING OF MY OLD ROUTE.
ONTARIO WAS GREY AND DOWDY IN THOSE POSTWAR YEARS.
I HOPE YOU NEVER SEE ANYTHING AS DISPIRITING...
AS A MUDDY NORTHERN MAIN STREET ON A GREY AUTUMN AFTERNOON.

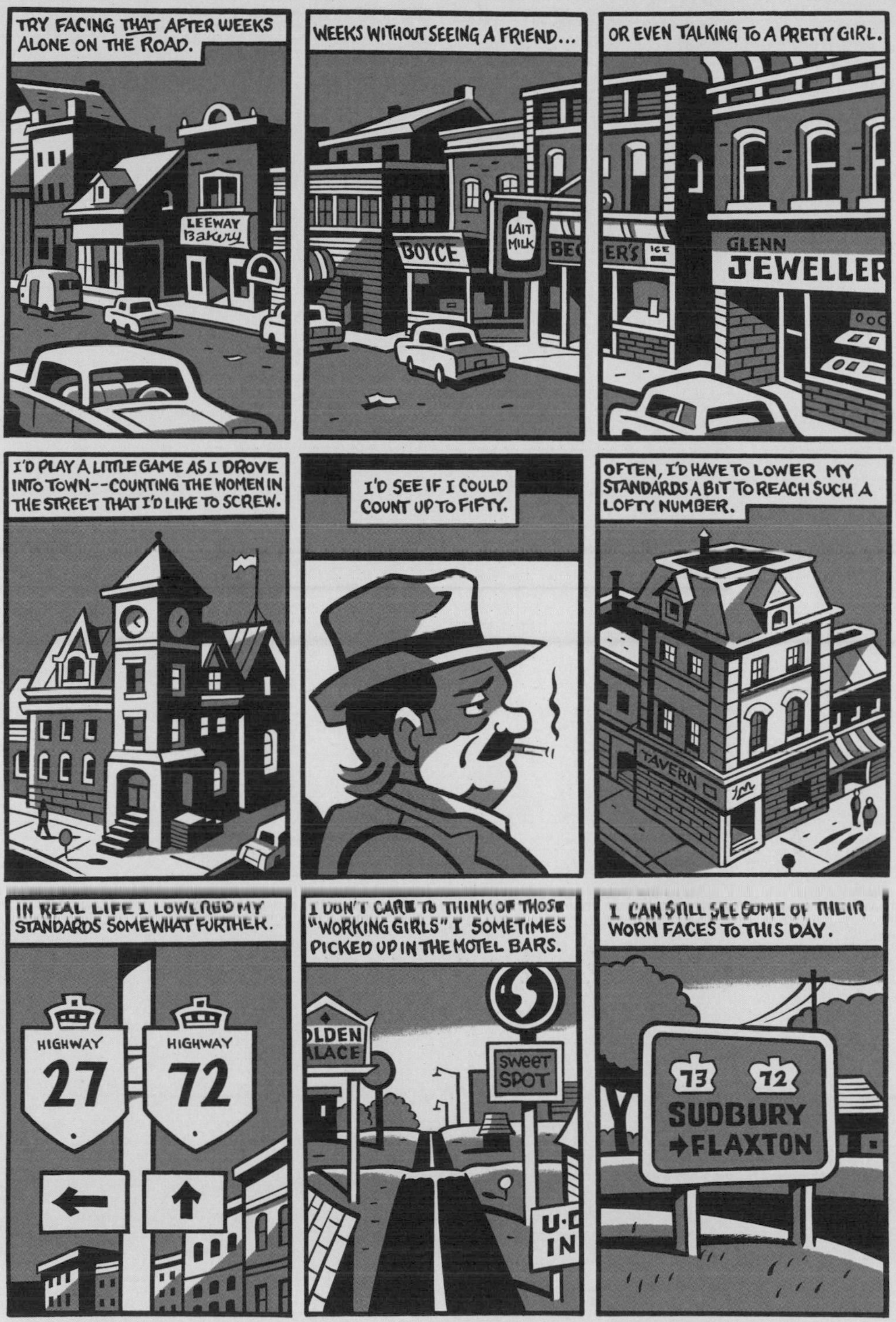
TRY FACING THAT AFTER WEEKS ALONE ON THE ROAD.
LEEWAY Bakery
WEEKS WITHOUT SEEING A FRIEND...
LAIT MILK
BOYCE
OR EVEN TALKING TO A PRETTY GIRL.
ICE
GLENN JEWELLER
I'D PLAY A LITTLE GAME AS I DROVE INTO TOWN--COUNTING THE WOMEN IN THE STREET THAT I'D LIKE TO SCREW.
I'D SEE IF I COULD COUNT UP TO FIFTY.
OFTEN, I'D HAVE TO LOWER MY STANDARDS A BIT TO REACH SUCH A LOFTY NUMBER.
TAVERN
IN REAL LIFE I LOWERED MY STANDARDS SOMEWHAT FURTHER.
HIGHWAY 27
HIGHWAY 72
I DON'T CARE TO THINK OF THOSE "WORKING GIRLS" I SOMETIMES PICKED UP IN THE MOTEL BARS.
SWEET SPOT
I CAN STILL SEE SOME OF THEIR WORN FACES TO THIS DAY.
73 72
SUDBURY
→FLAXTON

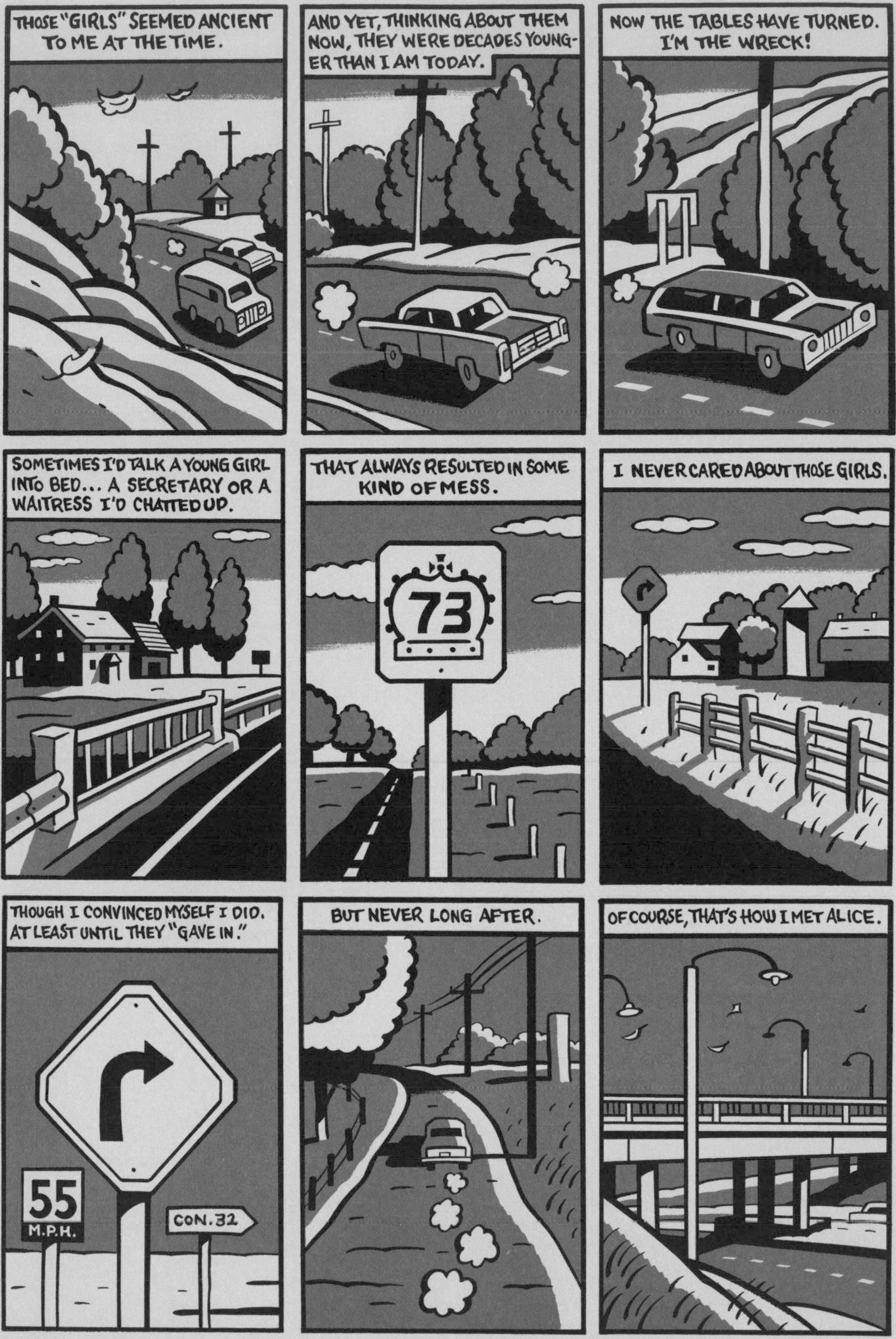
THOSE "GIRLS" SEEMED ANCIENT TO ME AT THE TIME.
AND YET, THINKING ABOUT THEM NOW, THEY WERE DECADES YOUNGER THAN I AM TODAY.
NOW THE TABLES HAVE TURNED. I'M THE WRECK!
SOMETIMES I'D TALK A YOUNG GIRL INTO BED... A SECRETARY OR A WAITRESS I'D CHATTED UP.
THAT ALWAYS RESULTED IN SOME KIND OF MESS.
73
I NEVER CARED ABOUT THOSE GIRLS.
THOUGH I CONVINCED MYSELF I DID. AT LEAST UNTIL THEY "GAVE IN."
55
M.P.H.
CON. 32
BUT NEVER LONG AFTER.
OF COURSE, THAT'S HOW I MET ALICE.

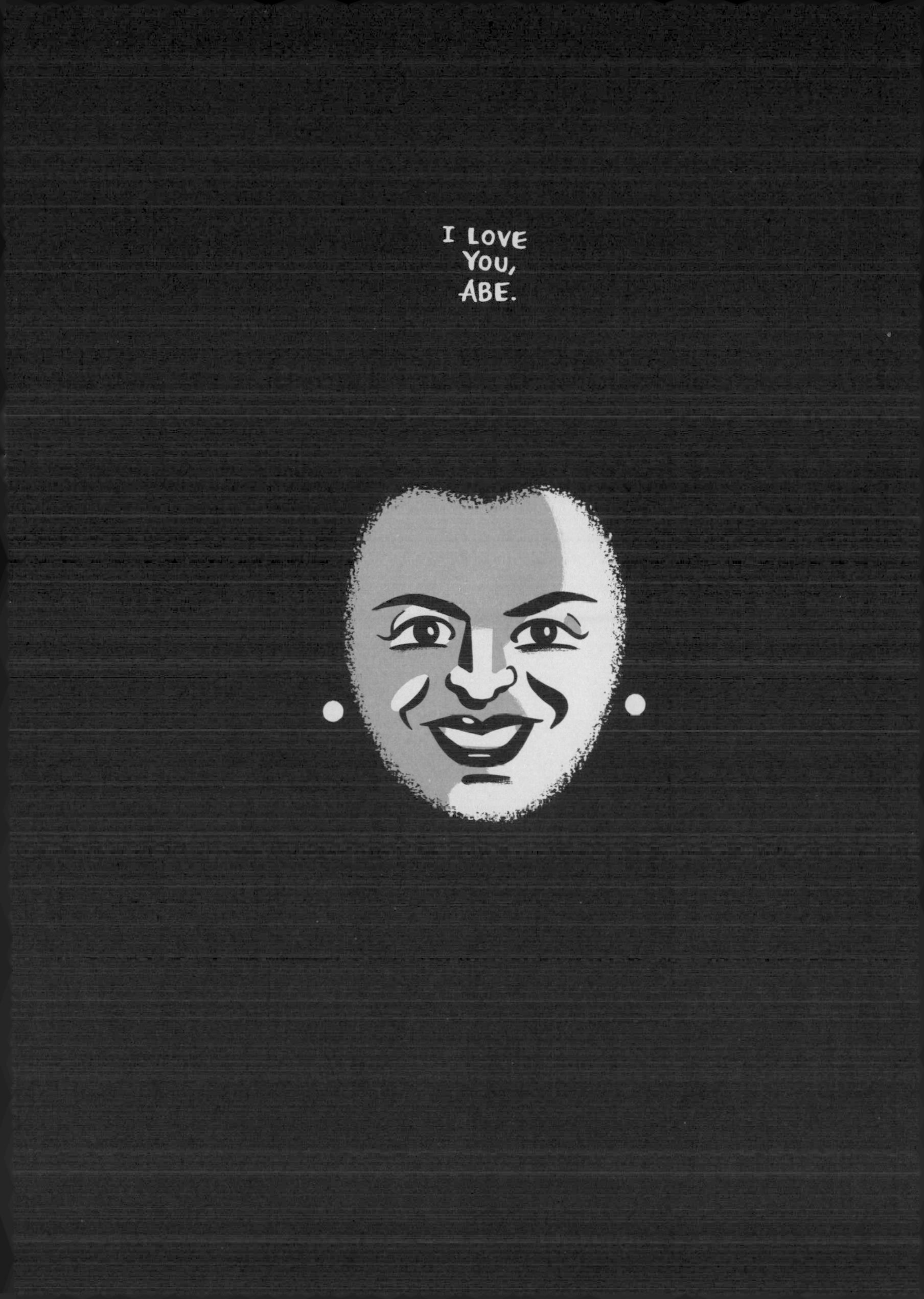
I LOVE YOU, ABE.

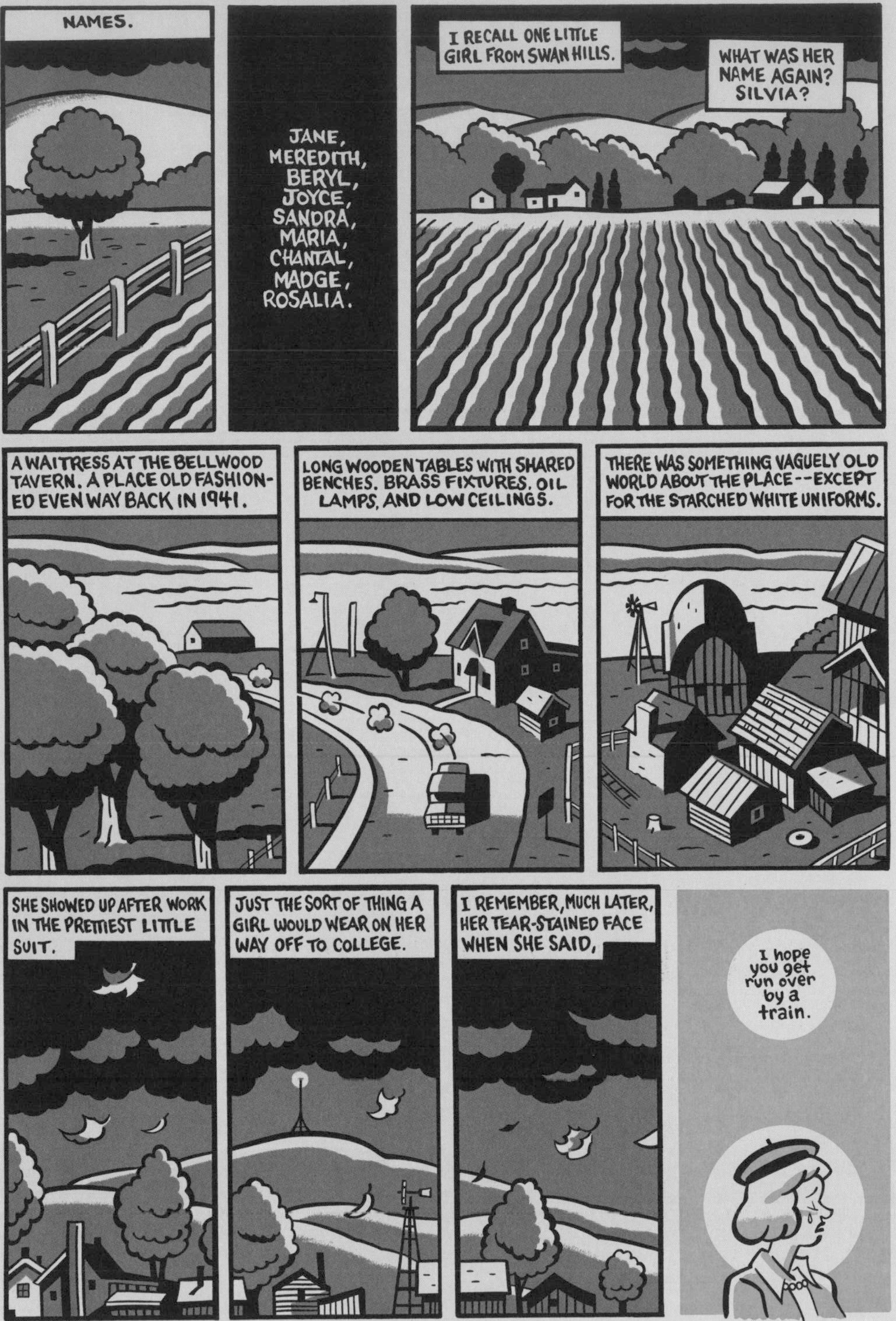
NAMES.
JANE, MEREDITH, BERYL, JOYCE, SANDRA, MARIA, CHANTAL, MADGE, ROSALIA.
I RECALL ONE LITTLE GIRL FROM SWAN HILLS.
WHAT WAS HER NAME AGAIN? SILVIA?
A WAITRESS AT THE BELLWOOD TAVERN. A PLACE OLD FASHIONED EVEN WAY BACK IN 1941.
LONG WOODEN TABLES WITH SHARED BENCHES. BRASS FIXTURES. OIL LAMPS, AND LOW CEILINGS.
THERE WAS SOMETHING VAGUELY OLD WORLD ABOUT THE PLACE--EXCEPT FOR THE STARCHED WHITE UNIFORMS.
SHE SHOWED UP AFTER WORK IN THE PRETTIEST LITTLE SUIT.
JUST THE SORT OF THING A GIRL WOULD WEAR ON HER WAY OFF TO COLLEGE.
I REMEMBER, MUCH LATER, HER TEAR-STAINED FACE WHEN SHE SAID,
I hope you get run over by a train.

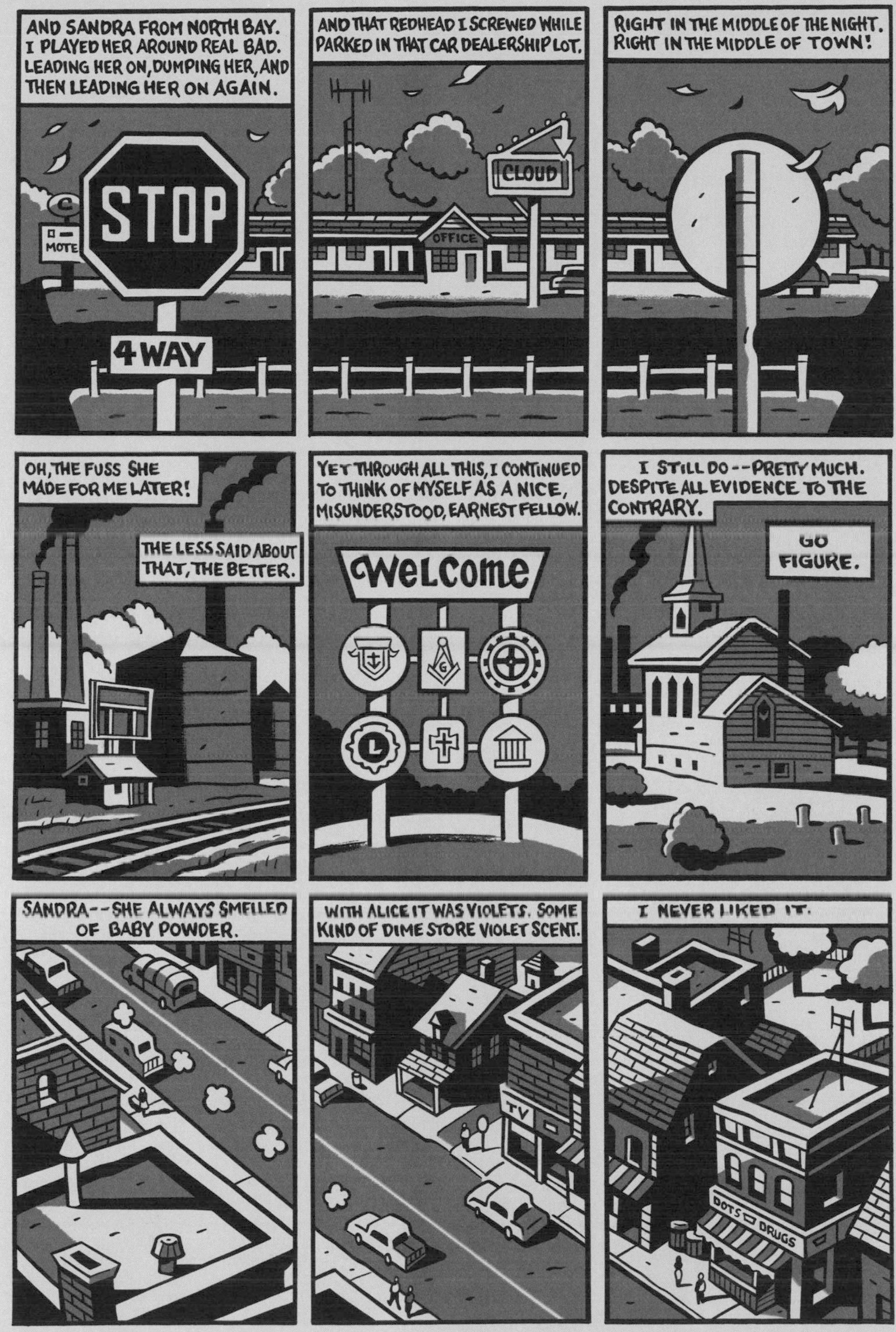
AND SANDRA FROM NORTH BAY. I PLAYED HER AROUND REAL BAD. LEADING HER ON, DUMPING HER, AND THEN LEADING HER ON AGAIN.
MOTE
STOP
4 WAY
AND THAT REDHEAD I SCREWED WHILE PARKED IN THAT CAR DEALERSHIP LOT.
CLOUD
OFFICE
RIGHT IN THE MIDDLE OF THE NIGHT. RIGHT IN THE MIDDLE OF TOWN!
OH, THE FUSS SHE MADE FOR ME LATER!
THE LESS SAID ABOUT THAT, THE BETTER.
YET THROUGH ALL THIS, I CONTINUED TO THINK OF MYSELF AS A NICE, MISUNDERSTOOD, EARNEST FELLOW.
Welcome
I STILL DO--PRETTY MUCH. DESPITE ALL EVIDENCE TO THE CONTRARY.
GO FIGURE.
SANDRA--SHE ALWAYS SMELLED OF BABY POWDER.
WITH ALICE IT WAS VIOLETS. SOME KIND OF DIME STORE VIOLET SCENT.
TV
I NEVER LIKED IT.
DOTS DRUGS

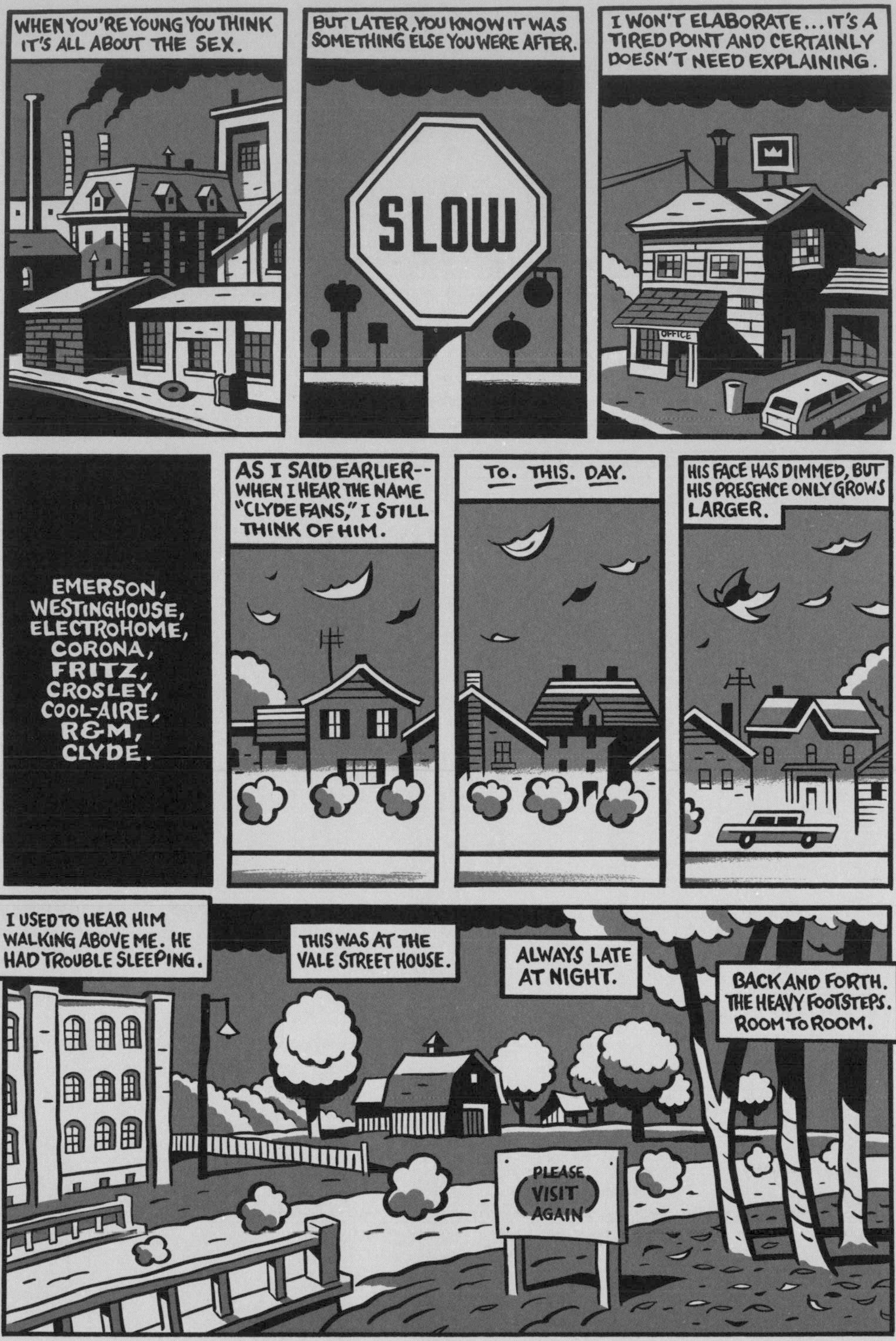
WHEN YOU'RE YOUNG YOU THINK IT'S ALL ABOUT THE SEX.
BUT LATER, YOU KNOW IT WAS SOMETHING ELSE YOU WERE AFTER.
SLOW
I WON'T ELABORATE... IT'S A TIRED POINT AND CERTAINLY DOESN'T NEED EXPLAINING.
OFFICE
EMERSON, WESTINGHOUSE, ELECTROHOME, CORONA, FRITZ, CROSLEY, COOL-AIRE, R&M, CLYDE.
AS I SAID EARLIER-- WHEN I HEAR THE NAME "CLYDE FANS," I STILL THINK OF HIM.
TO. THIS. DAY.
HIS FACE HAS DIMMED, BUT HIS PRESENCE ONLY GROWS LARGER.
I USED TO HEAR HIM WALKING ABOVE ME. HE HAD TROUBLE SLEEPING.
THIS WAS AT THE VALE STREET HOUSE.
ALWAYS LATE AT NIGHT.
BACK AND FORTH. THE HEAVY FOOTSTEPS. ROOM TO ROOM.
PLEASE VISIT AGAIN

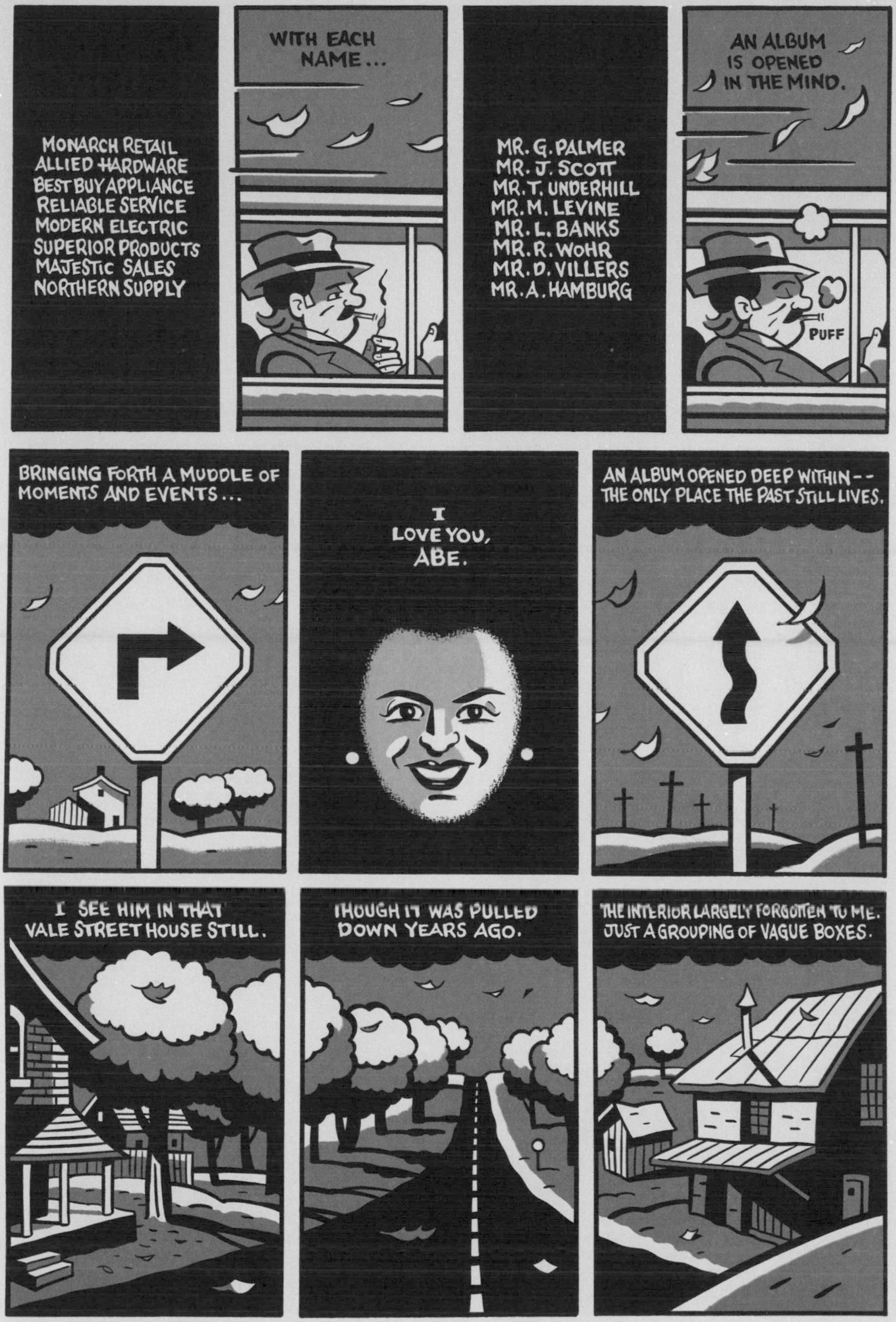
MONARCH RETAIL
ALLIED HARDWARE
BEST BUY APPLIANCE
RELIABLE SERVICE
MODERN ELECTRIC
SUPERIOR PRODUCTS
MAJESTIC SALES
NORTHERN SUPPLY
WITH EACH NAME...
MR. G. PALMER
MR. J. SCOTT
MR. T. UNDERHILL
MR. M. LEVINE
MR. L. BANKS
MR. R. WOHR
MR. D. VILLERS
MR. A. HAMBURG
AN ALBUM IS OPENED IN THE MIND.
PUFF
BRINGING FORTH A MUDDLE OF MOMENTS AND EVENTS...
I LOVE YOU, ABE.
AN ALBUM OPENED DEEP WITHIN-- THE ONLY PLACE THE PAST STILL LIVES.
I SEE HIM IN THAT VALE STREET HOUSE STILL.
THOUGH IT WAS PULLED DOWN YEARS AGO.
THE INTERIOR LARGELY FORGOTTEN TO ME. JUST A GROUPING OF VAGUE BOXES.

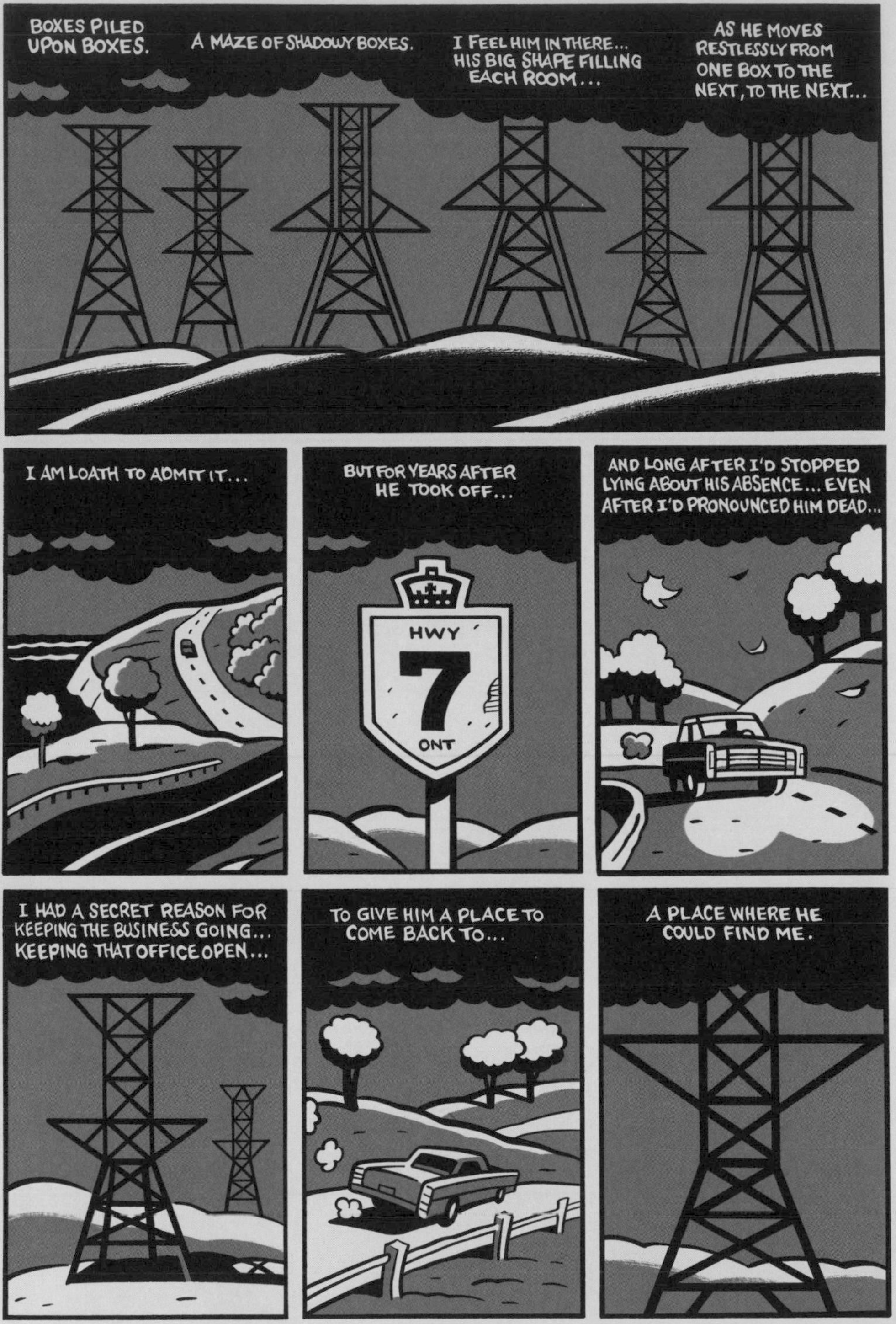
BOXES PILED UPON BOXES.
A MAZE OF SHADOWY BOXES.
I FEEL HIM IN THERE... HIS BIG SHAPE FILLING EACH ROOM...
AS HE MOVES RESTLESSLY FROM ONE BOX TO THE NEXT, TO THE NEXT...
I AM LOATH TO ADMIT IT...
BUT FOR YEARS AFTER HE TOOK OFF...
HWY
7
ONT
AND LONG AFTER I'D STOPPED LYING ABOUT HIS ABSENCE... EVEN AFTER I'D PRONOUNCED HIM DEAD...
I HAD A SECRET REASON FOR KEEPING THE BUSINESS GOING... KEEPING THAT OFFICE OPEN...
TO GIVE HIM A PLACE TO COME BACK TO...
A PLACE WHERE HE COULD FIND ME.

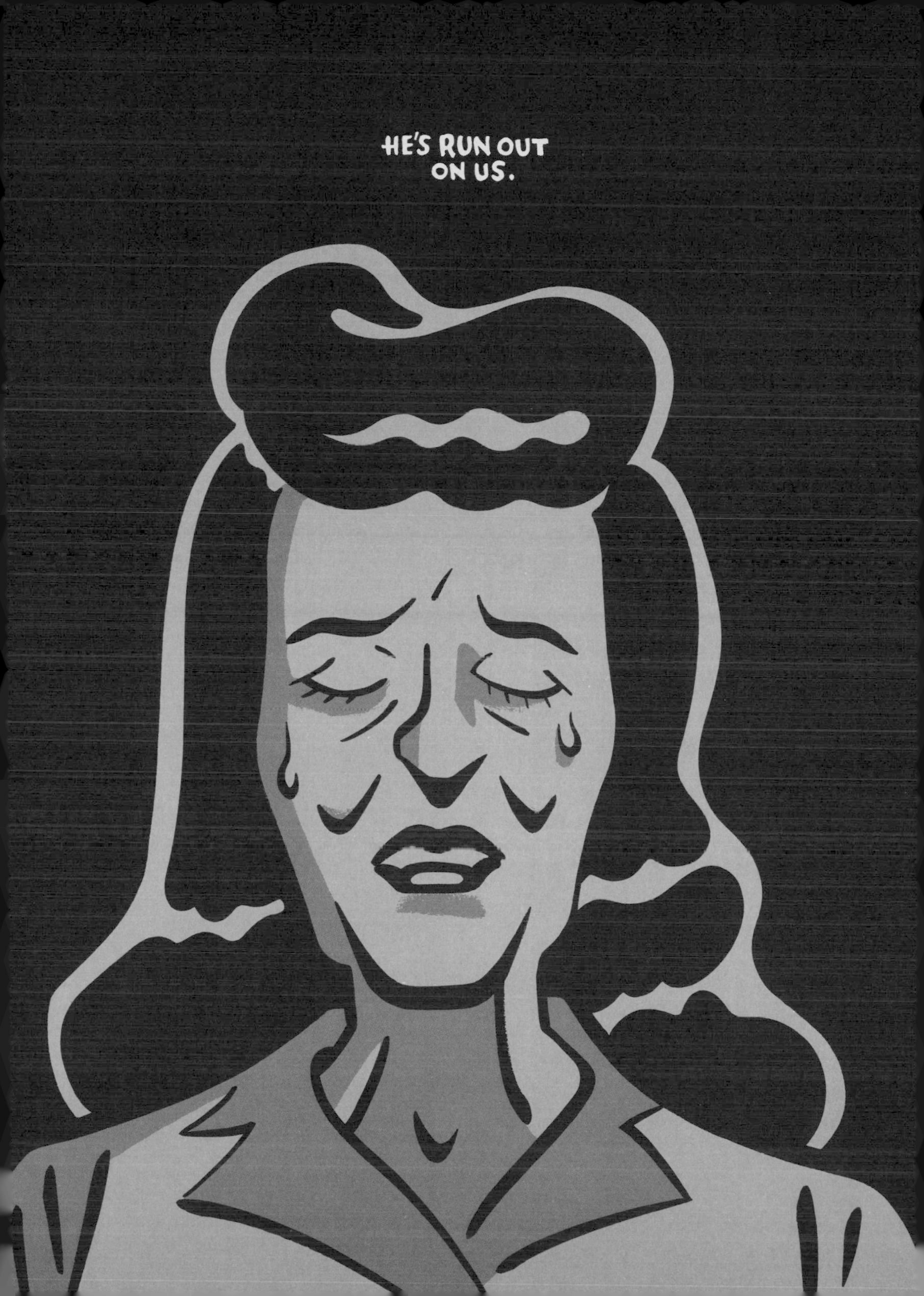
HE'S RUN OUT ON US.

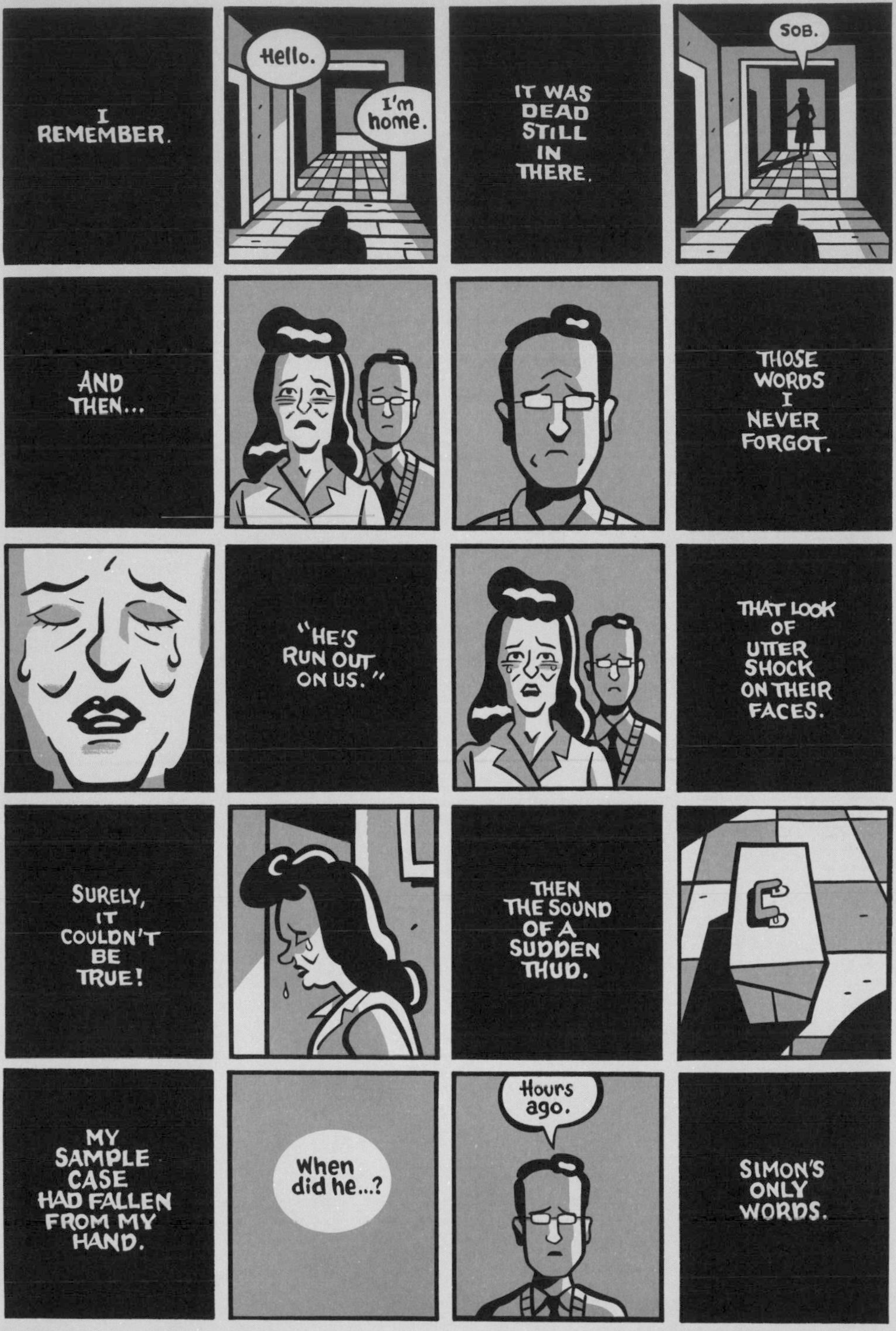
I REMEMBER.
Hello.
I'm home.
IT WAS DEAD STILL IN THERE.
SOB.
AND THEN...
THOSE WORDS I NEVER FORGOT.
"HE'S RUN OUT ON US."
THAT LOOK OF UTTER SHOCK ON THEIR FACES.
SURELY, IT COULDN'T BE TRUE!
THEN THE SOUND OF A SUDDEN THUD.
MY SAMPLE CASE HAD FALLEN FROM MY HAND.
When did he...?
Hours ago.
SIMON'S ONLY WORDS.

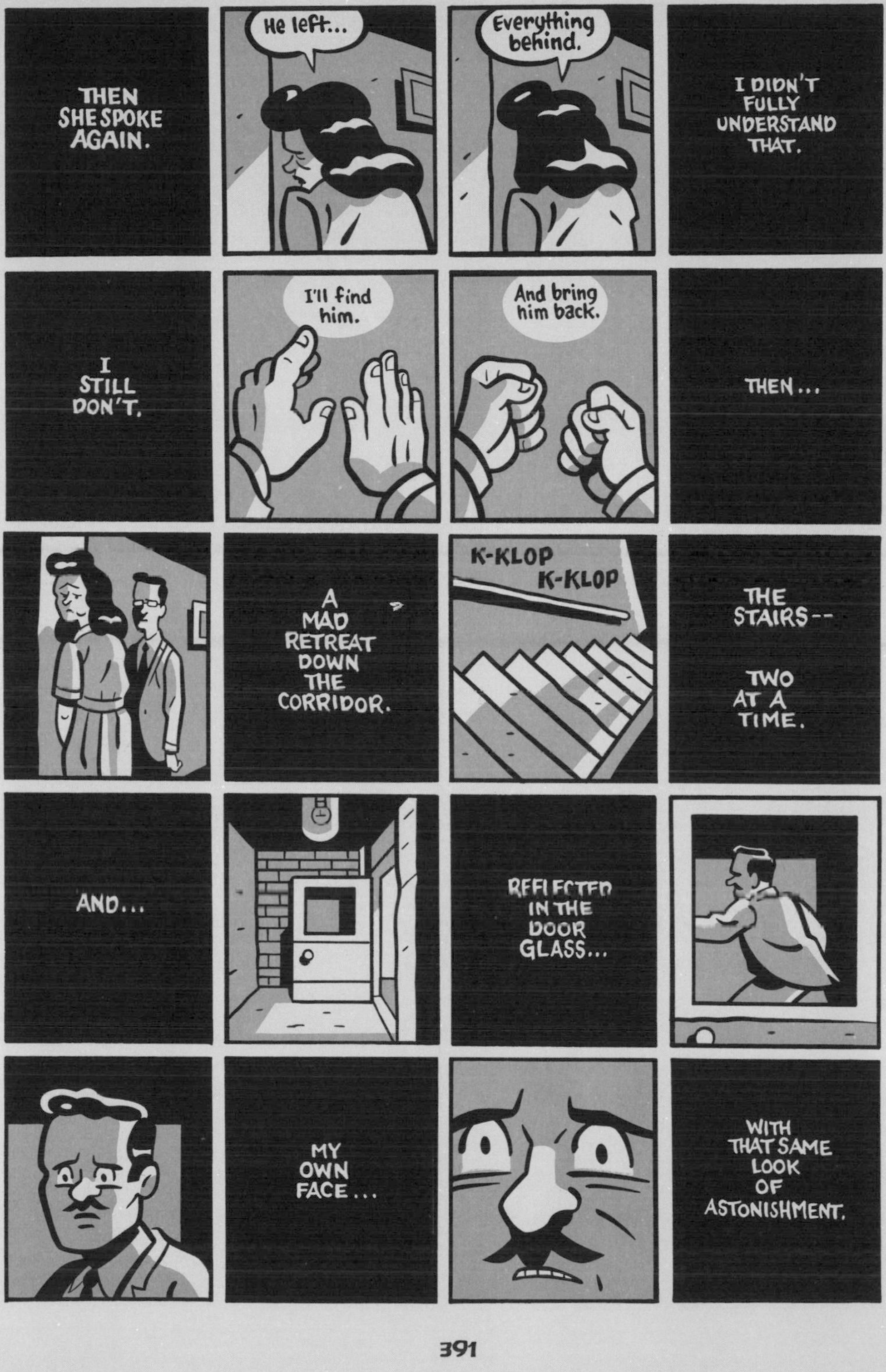
THEN SHE SPOKE AGAIN.
He left...
Everything behind.
I DIDN'T FULLY UNDERSTAND THAT.
I STILL DON'T.
I'll find him.
And bring him back.
THEN...
A MAD RETREAT DOWN THE CORRIDOR.
K-KLOP K-KLOP
THE STAIRS--
TWO AT A TIME.
AND...
REFLECTED IN THE DOOR GLASS...
MY OWN FACE...
WITH THAT SAME LOOK OF ASTONISHMENT.

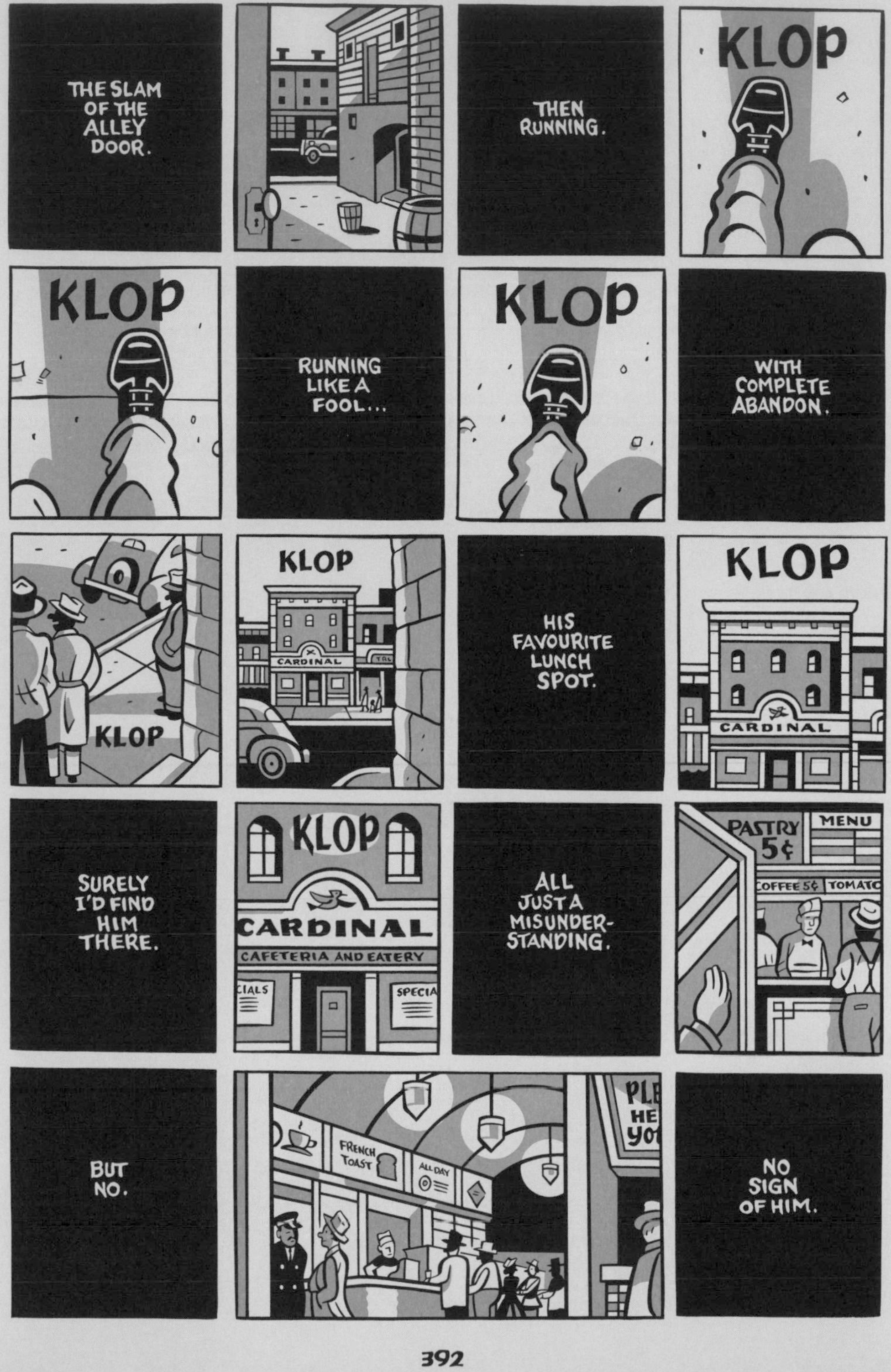
THE SLAM OF THE ALLEY DOOR.
THEN RUNNING.
KLOP
KLOP
RUNNING LIKE A FOOL...
KLOP
WITH COMPLETE ABANDON.
KLOP
KLOP
CARDINAL
HIS FAVOURITE LUNCH SPOT.
KLOP
CARDINAL
SURELY I'D FIND HIM THERE.
KLOP
CARDINAL
CAFETERIA AND EATERY
CIALS
SPECIA
ALL JUST A MISUNDER-STANDING.
PASTRY 5¢
MENU
COFFEE 5¢
TOMATO
BUT NO.
FRENCH TOAST
ALL DAY
NO SIGN OF HIM.

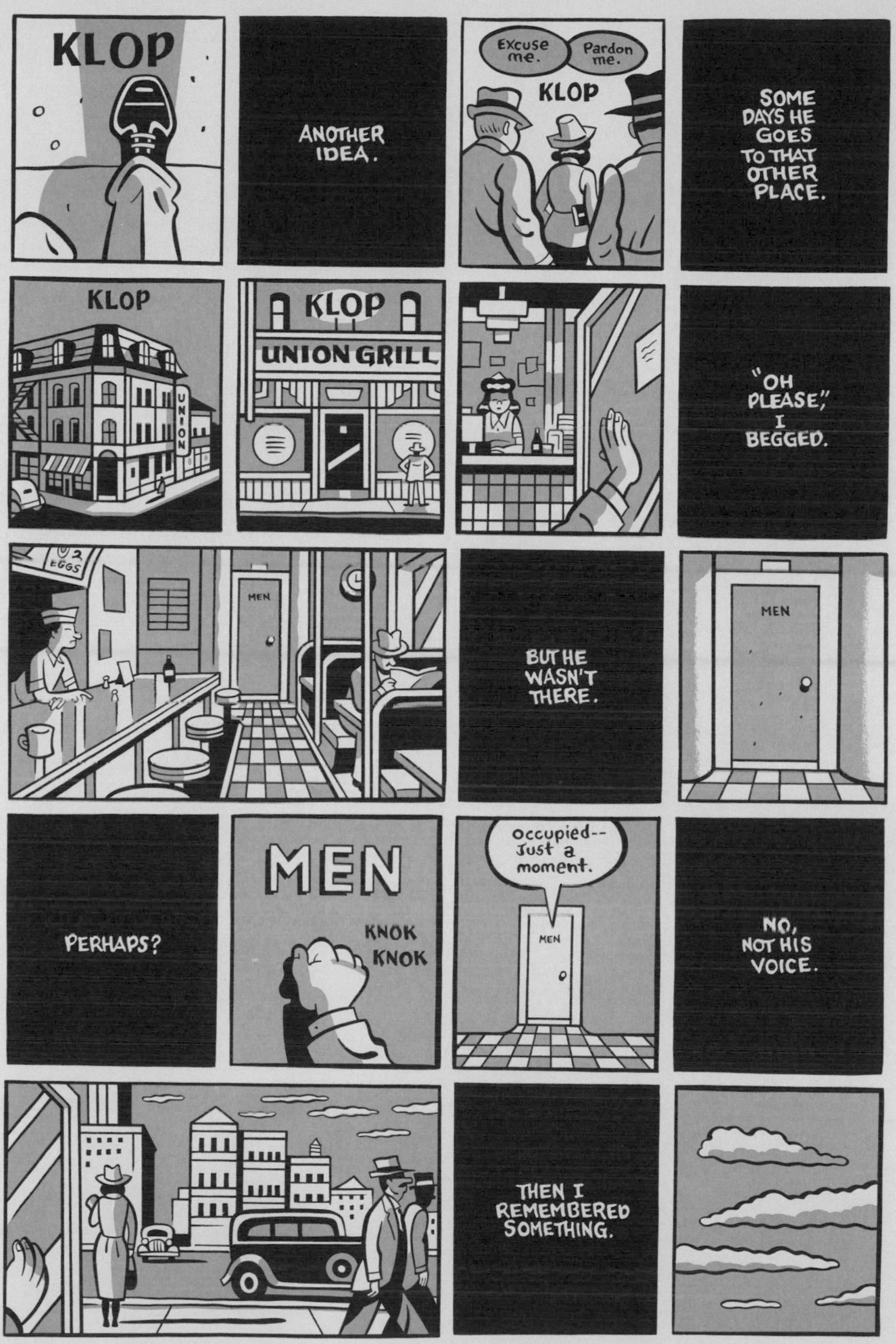
KLOP
ANOTHER IDEA.
Excuse me.
Pardon me.
KLOP
SOME DAYS HE GOES TO THAT OTHER PLACE.
KLOP
UNION
KLOP
UNION GRILL
"OH PLEASE," I BEGGED.
2 EGGS
MEN
BUT HE WASN'T THERE.
MEN
PERHAPS?
MEN
KNOK KNOK
Occupied-- Just a moment.
MEN
NO, NOT HIS VOICE.
THEN I REMEMBERED SOMETHING.

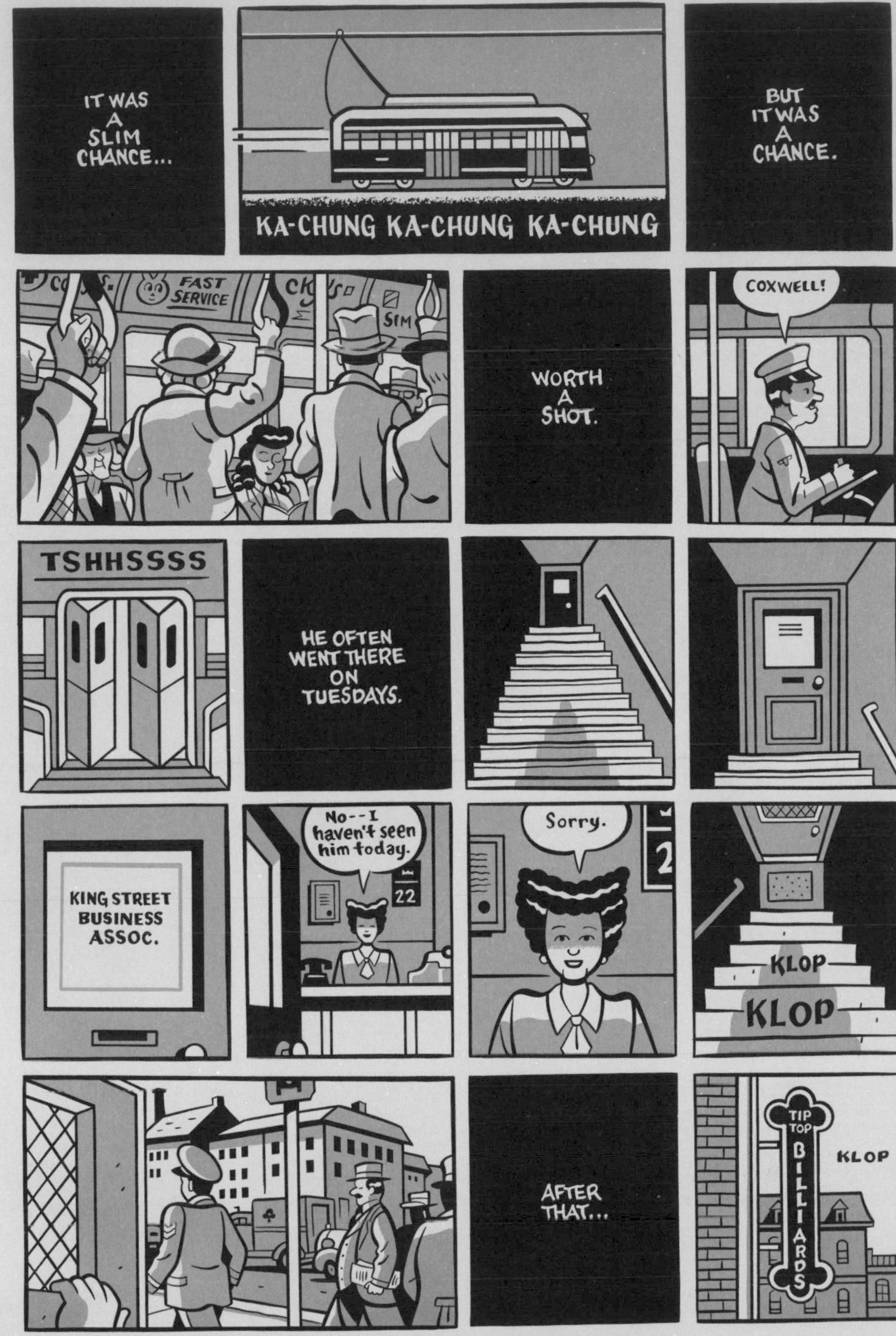
IT WAS A SLIM CHANCE...
KA-CHUNG KA-CHUNG KA-CHUNG
BUT IT WAS A CHANCE.
FAST SERVICE
WORTH A SHOT.
COXWELL!
TSHHSSSS
HE OFTEN WENT THERE ON TUESDAYS.
KING STREET BUSINESS ASSOC.
No--I haven't seen him today.
22
Sorry.
KLOP
KLOP
AFTER THAT...
TIP TOP BILLIARDS
KLOP

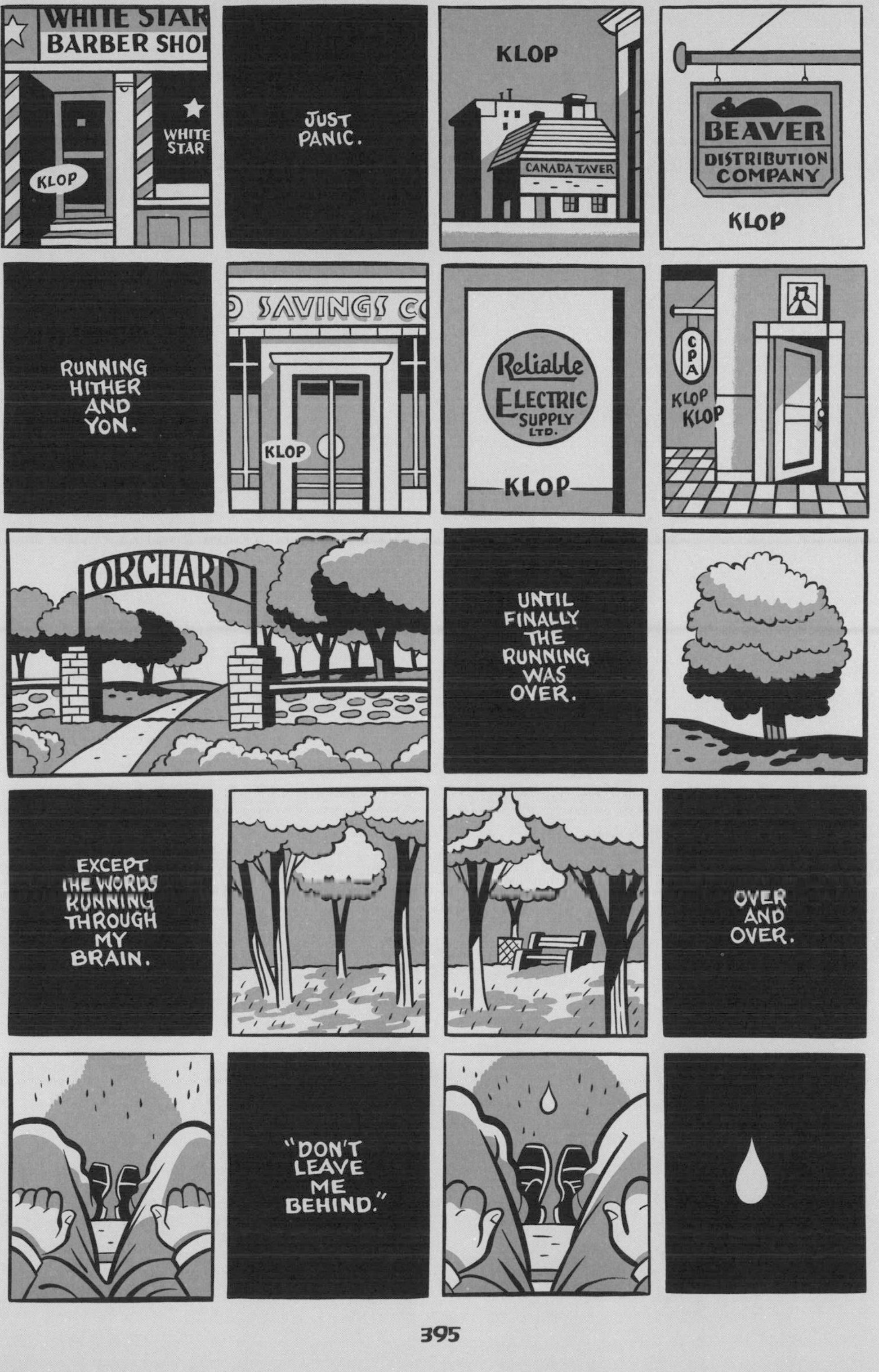
WHITE STAR
BARBER SHO
WHITE STAR
KLOP
JUST PANIC.
KLOP
CANADA TAVER
BEAVER
DISTRIBUTION COMPANY
KLOP
RUNNING HITHER AND YON.
SAVINGS C
KLOP
Reliable
ELECTRIC
SUPPLY
LTD.
KLOP
CPA
KLOP
KLOP
ORCHARD
UNTIL FINALLY THE RUNNING WAS OVER.
EXCEPT THE WORDS RUNNING THROUGH MY BRAIN.
OVER AND OVER.
"DON'T LEAVE ME BEHIND."

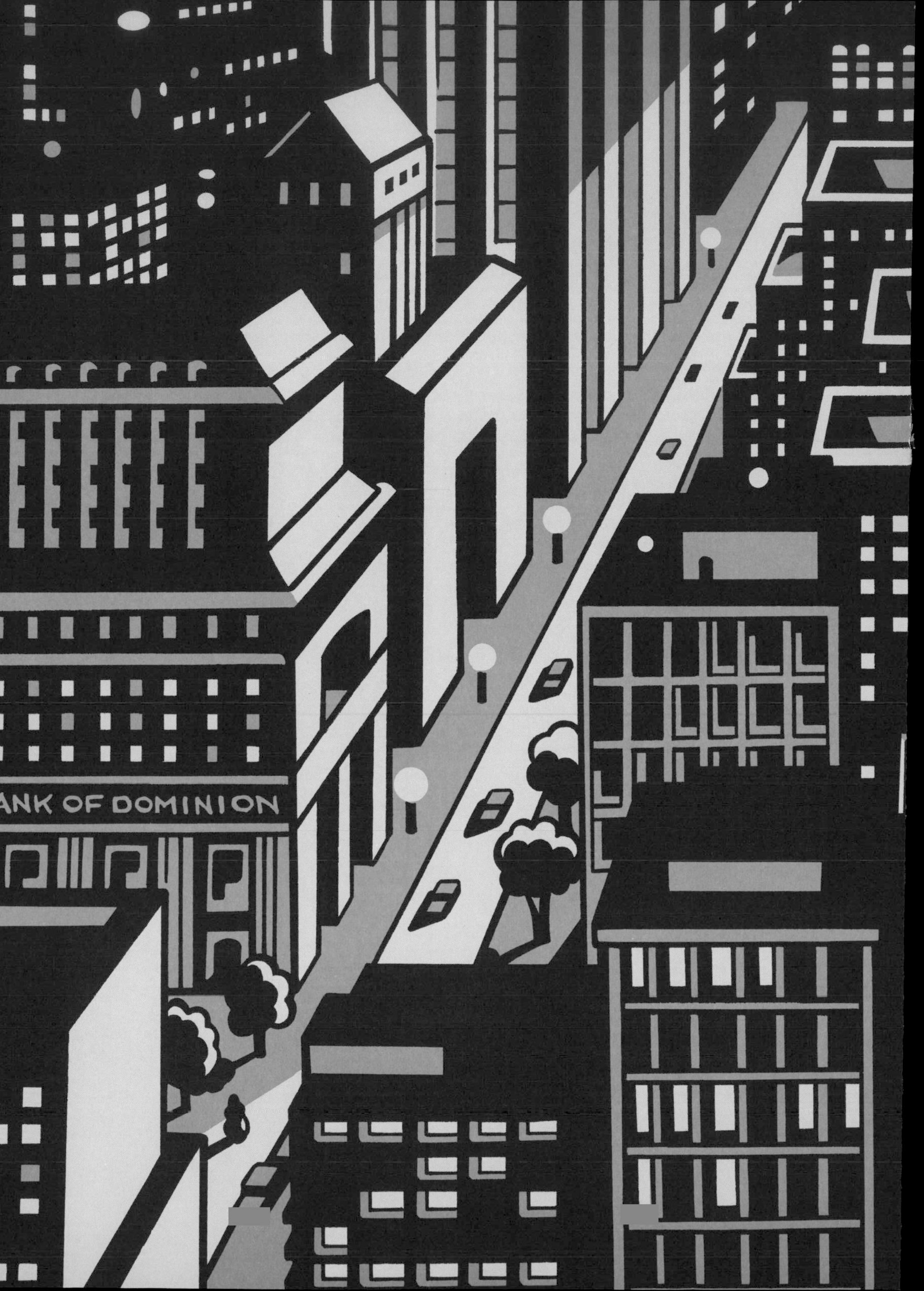
ANK OF DOMINION

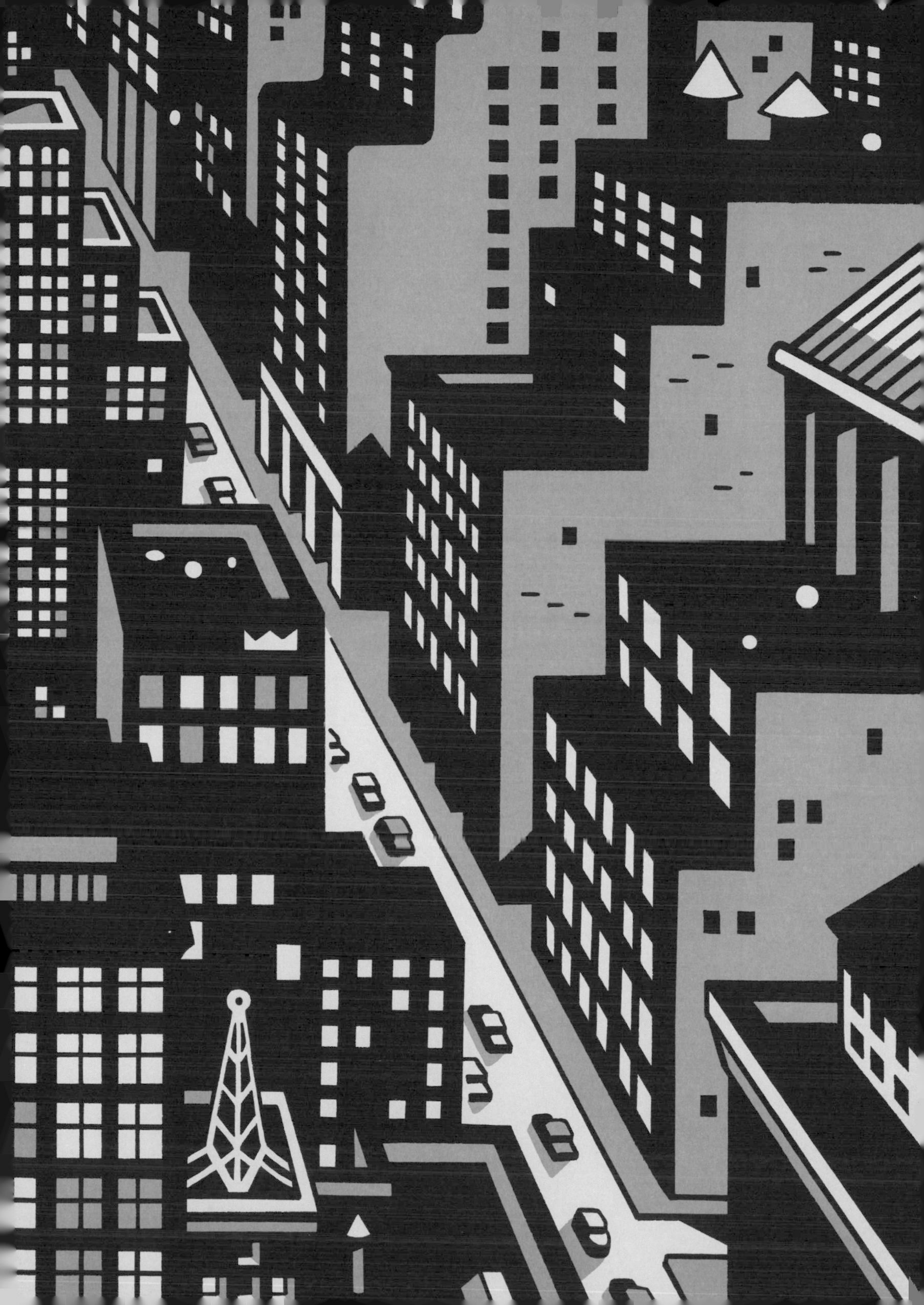

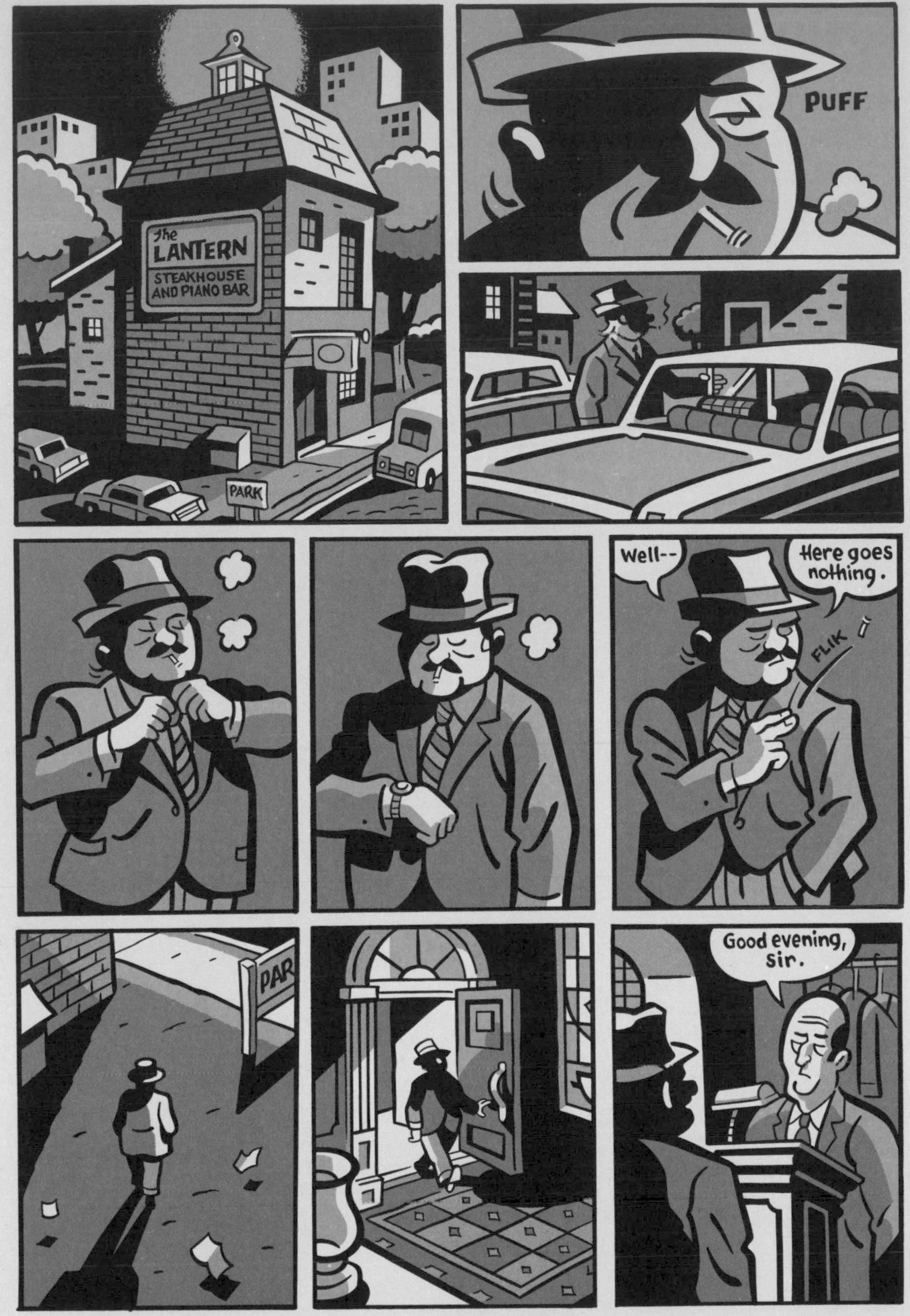
The LANTERN
STEAKHOUSE AND PIANO BAR
PARK
PUFF
Well--
Here goes nothing.
FLIK
PAR
Good evening, sir.

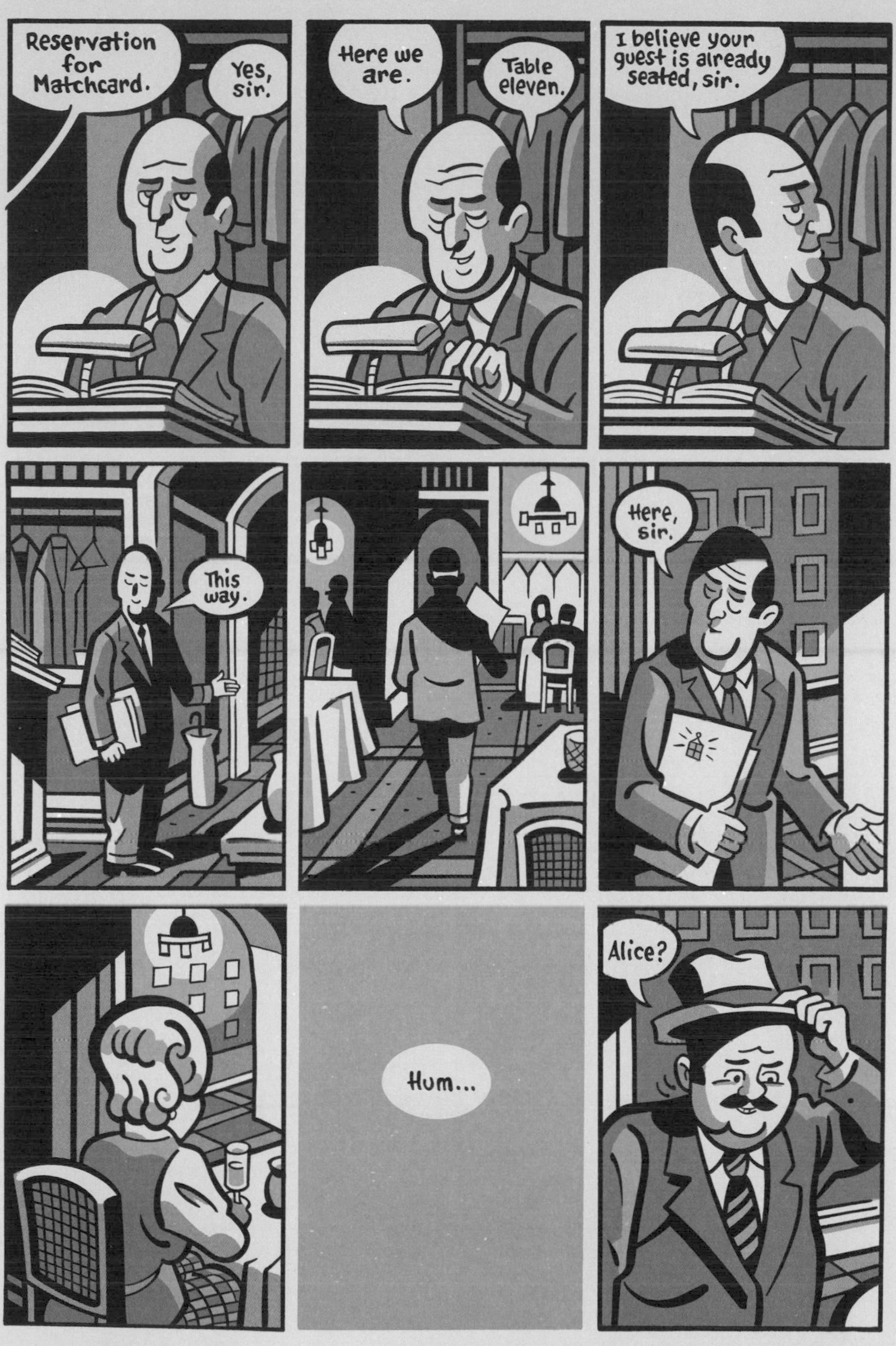
Reservation for Matchcard.
Yes, sir.
Here we are.
Table eleven.
I believe your guest is already seated, sir.
This way.
Here, sir.
Hum...
Alice?

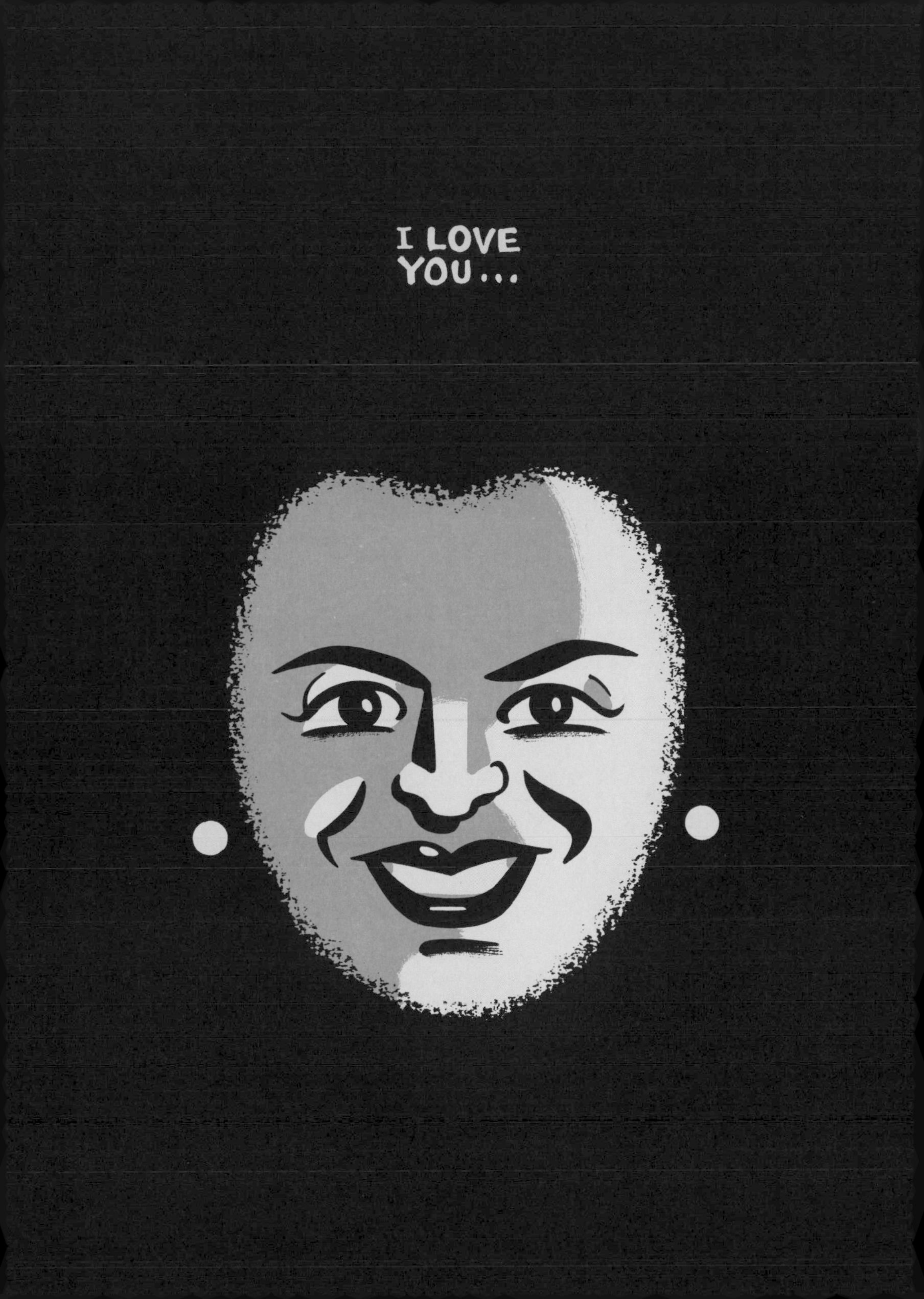
I LOVE YOU...

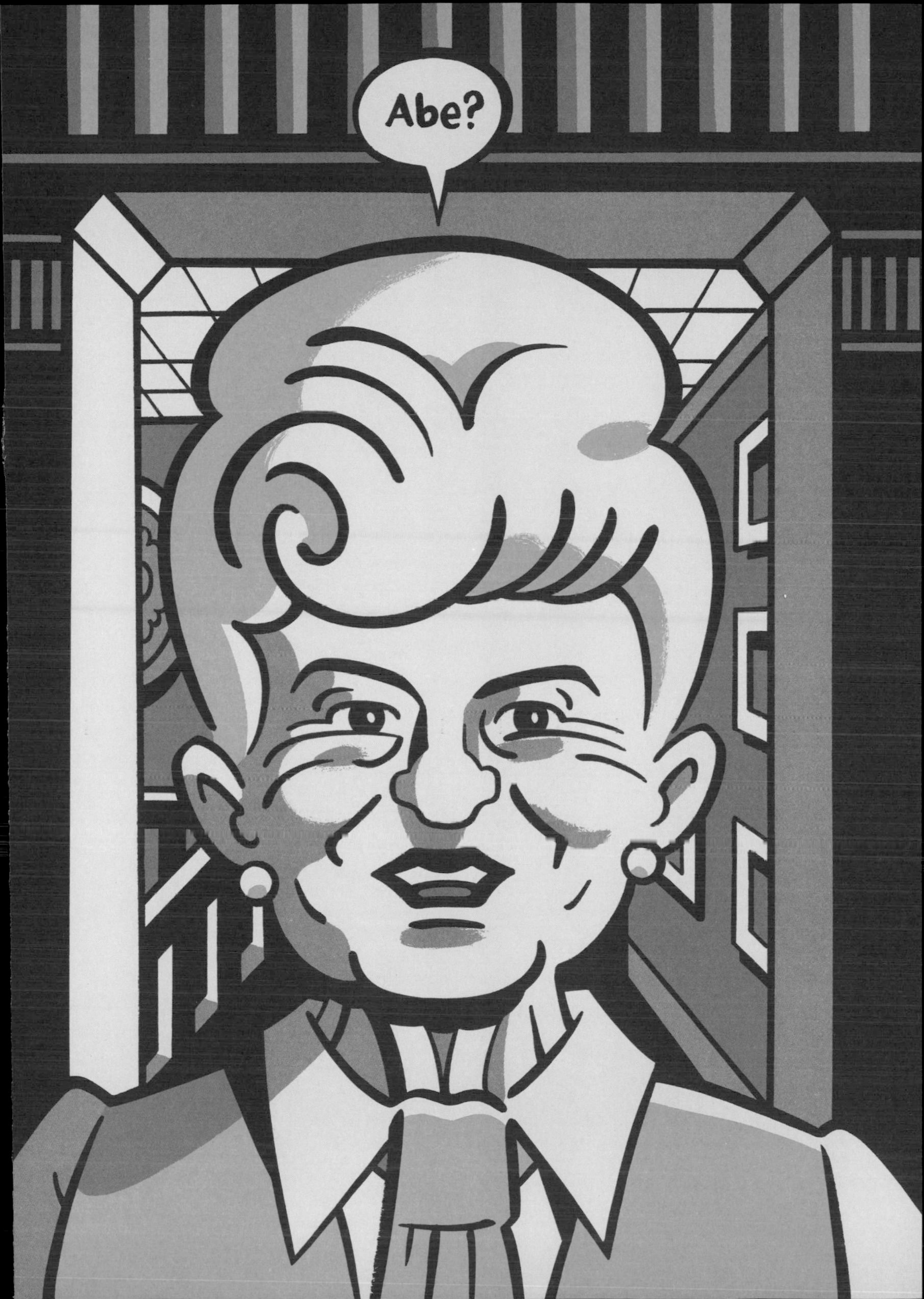
Abe?

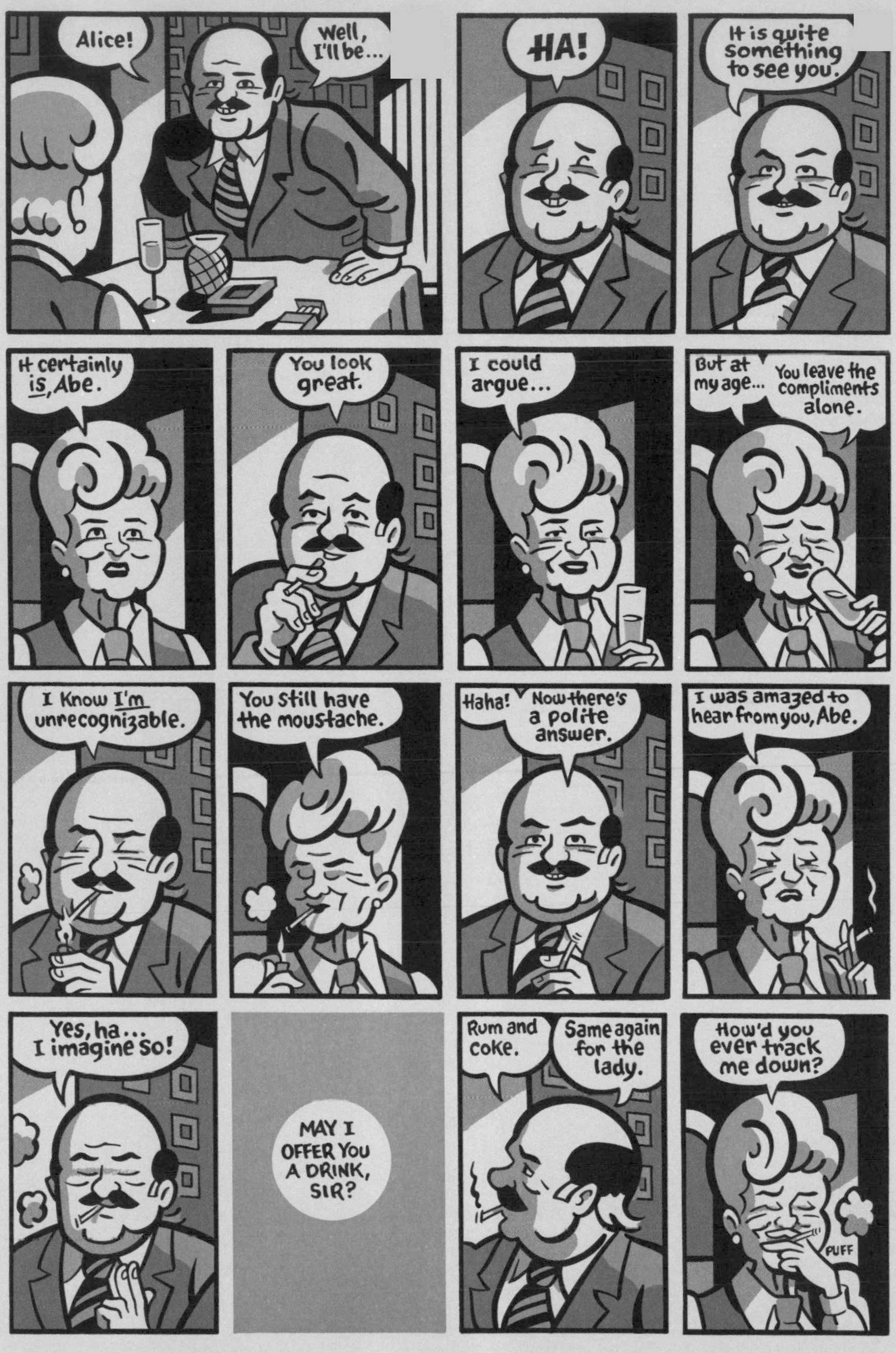
Alice!
Well, I'll be...
HA!
It is quite something to see you.
It certainly is, Abe.
You look great.
I could argue...
But at my age...
You leave the compliments alone.
I know I'm unrecognizable.
You still have the moustache.
Haha!
Now there's a polite answer.
I was amazed to hear from you, Abe.
Yes, ha... I imagine so!
MAY I OFFER YOU A DRINK, SIR?
Rum and coke.
Same again for the lady.
How'd you ever track me down?
PUFF

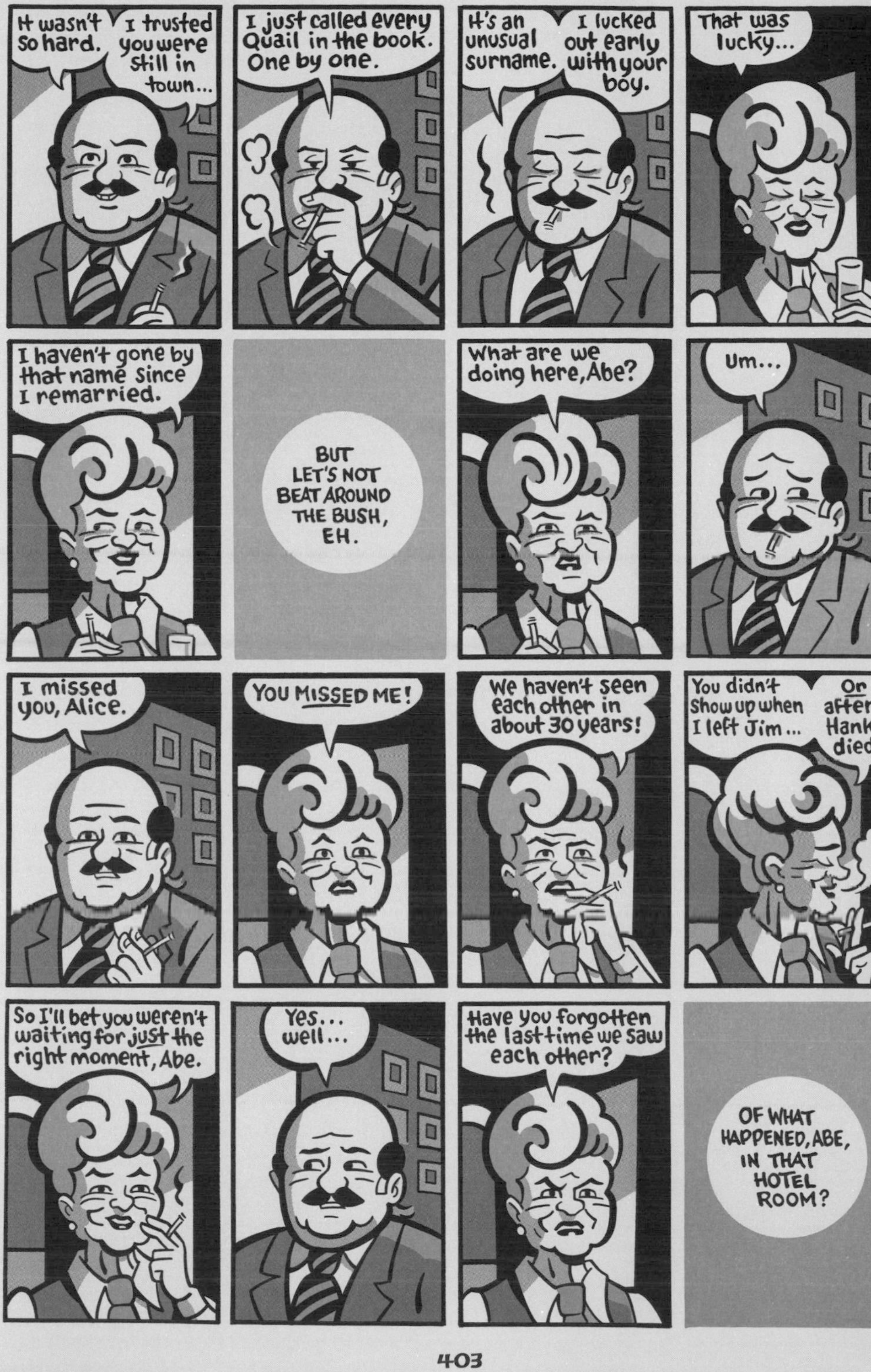
It wasn't so hard.
I trusted you were still in town...
I just called every Quail in the book. One by one.
It's an unusual surname.
I lucked out early with your boy.
That was lucky...
I haven't gone by that name since I remarried.
BUT LET'S NOT BEAT AROUND THE BUSH, EH.
What are we doing here, Abe?
Um...
I missed you, Alice.
YOU MISSED ME!
We haven't seen each other in about 30 years!
You didn't show up when I left Jim...
Or after Hank died.
So I'll bet you weren't waiting for just the right moment, Abe.
Yes... well...
Have you forgotten the last time we saw each other?
OF WHAT HAPPENED, ABE, IN THAT HOTEL ROOM?

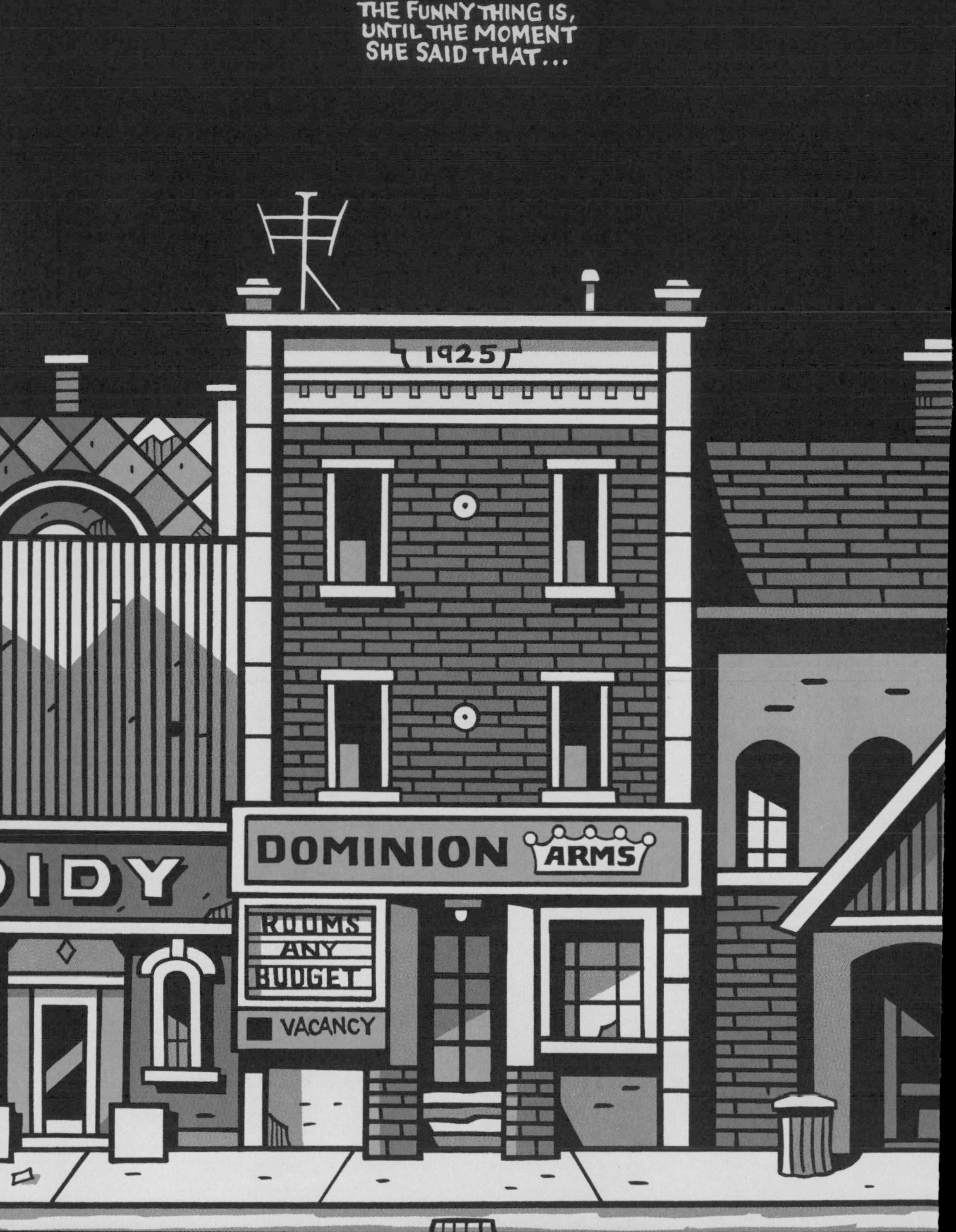
THE FUNNY THING IS, UNTIL THE MOMENT SHE SAID THAT...
1925
DOMINION ARMS
ROOMS ANY BUDGET
VACANCY

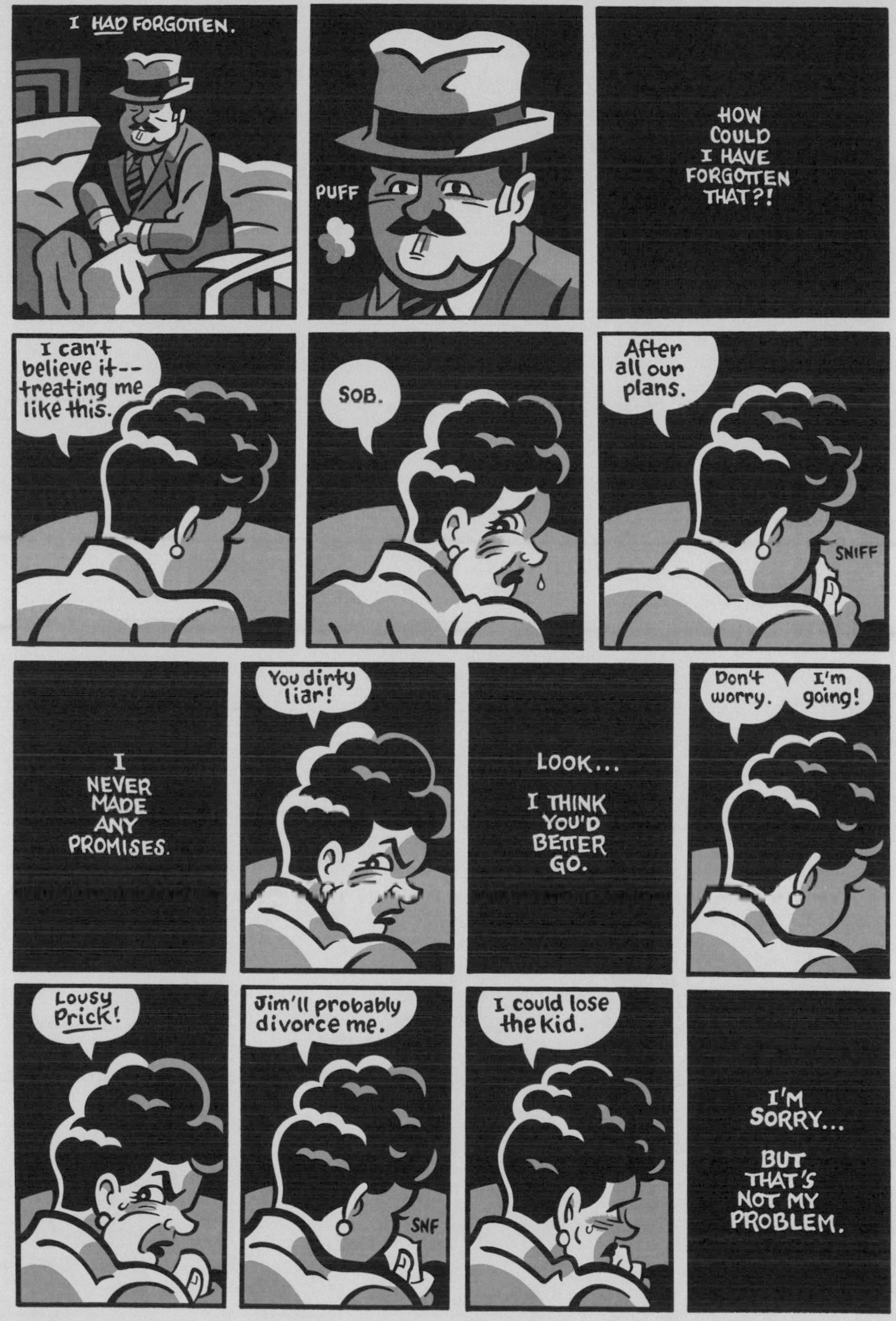
I HAD FORGOTTEN.
PUFF
HOW COULD I HAVE FORGOTTEN THAT?!
I can't believe it-- treating me like this.
SOB.
After all our plans.
SNIFF
I NEVER MADE ANY PROMISES.
You dirty liar!
LOOK... I THINK YOU'D BETTER GO.
Don't worry.
I'm going!
Lousy Prick!
Jim'll probably divorce me.
SNF
I could lose the kid.
I'M SORRY... BUT THAT'S NOT MY PROBLEM.

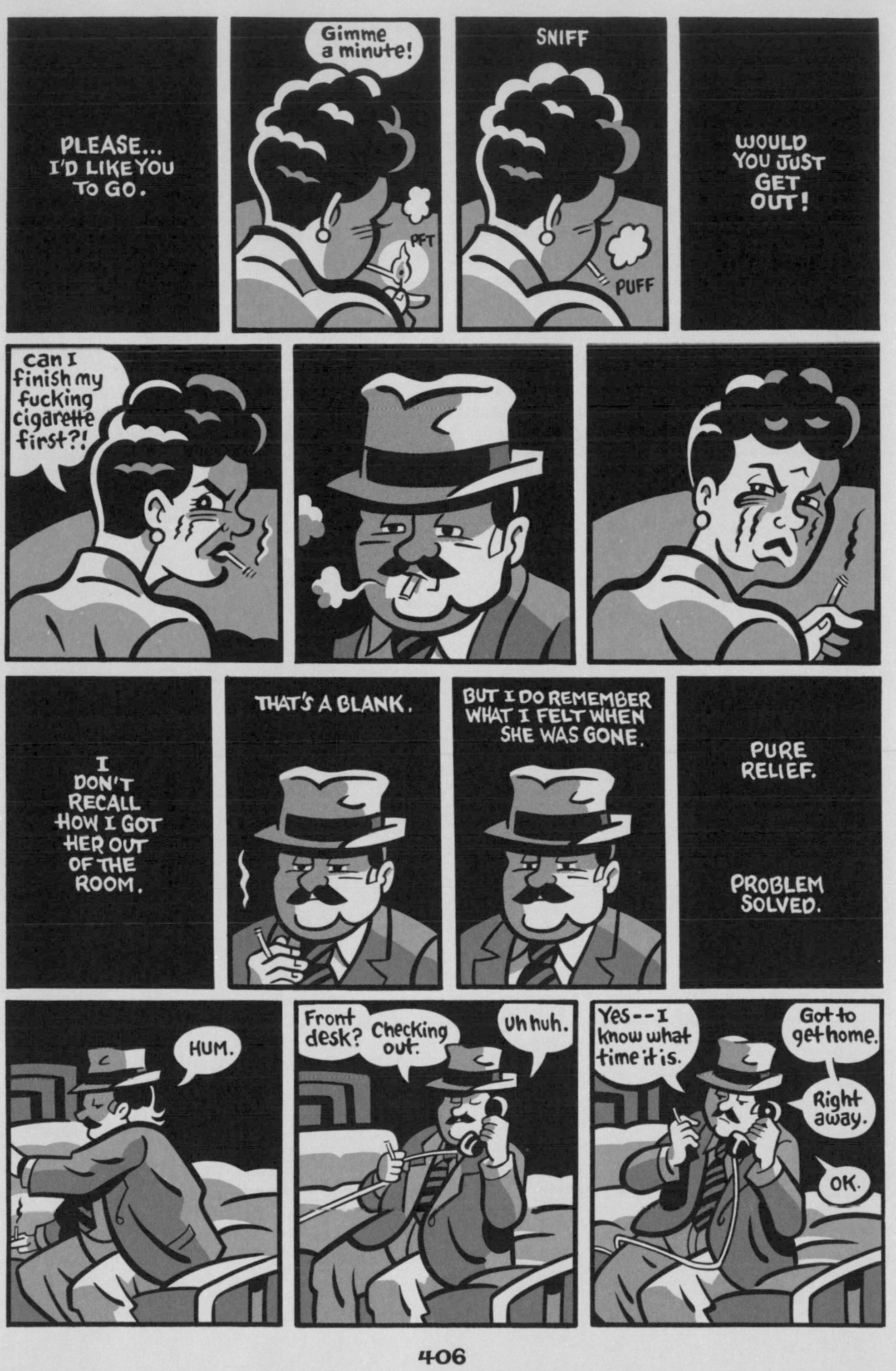
PLEASE... I'D LIKE YOU TO GO.
Gimme a minute!
PFT
SNIFF
PUFF
WOULD YOU JUST GET OUT!
Can I finish my fucking cigarette first?!
I DON'T RECALL HOW I GOT HER OUT OF THE ROOM.
THAT'S A BLANK.
BUT I DO REMEMBER WHAT I FELT WHEN SHE WAS GONE.
PURE RELIEF.
PROBLEM SOLVED.
HUM.
Front desk?
Checking out.
Uh huh.
Yes--I know what time it is.
Got to get home.
Right away.
OK.

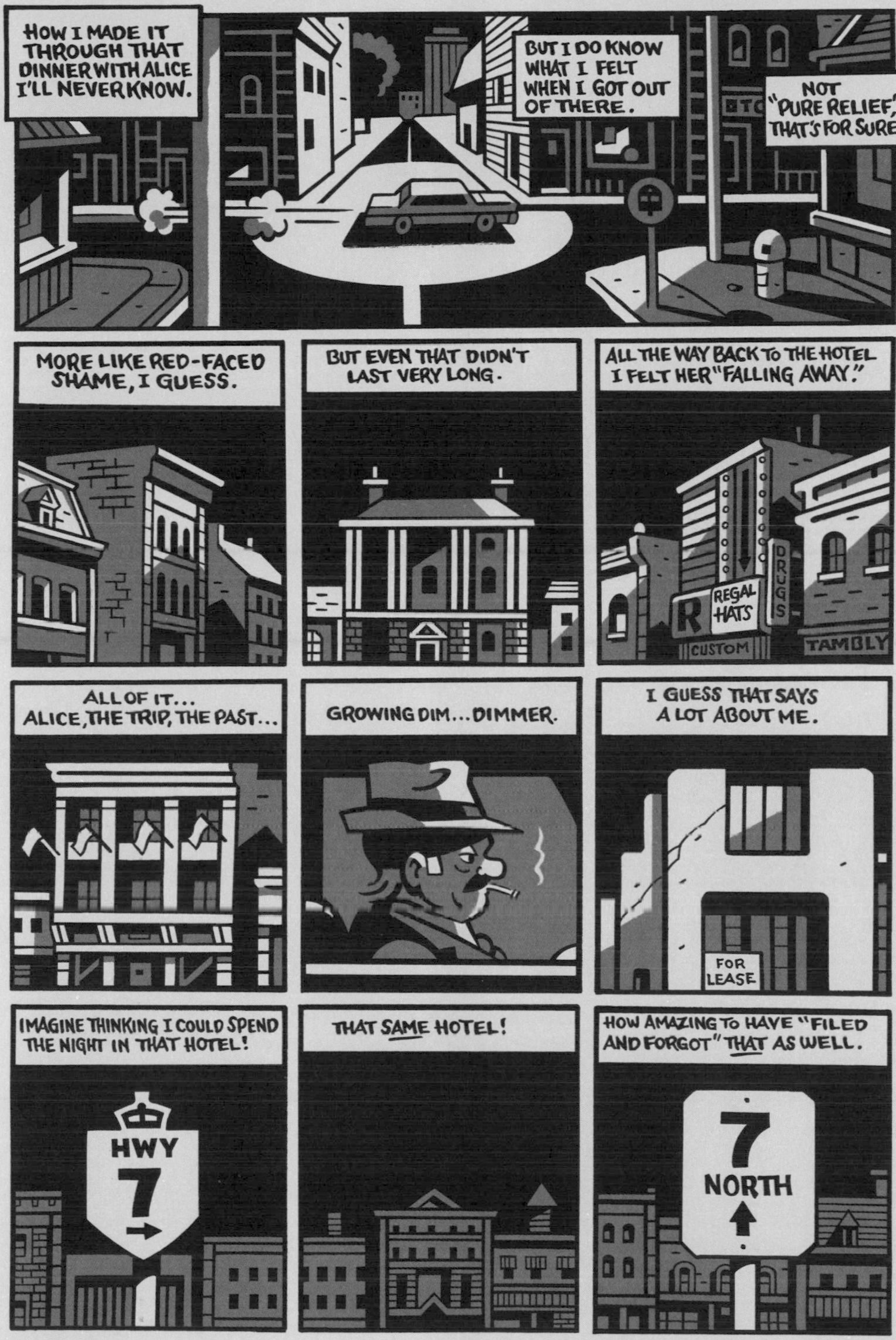
HOW I MADE IT THROUGH THAT DINNER WITH ALICE I'LL NEVER KNOW.
BUT I DO KNOW WHAT I FELT WHEN I GOT OUT OF THERE.
NOT "PURE RELIEF," THAT'S FOR SURE.
MORE LIKE RED-FACED SHAME, I GUESS.
BUT EVEN THAT DIDN'T LAST VERY LONG.
ALL THE WAY BACK TO THE HOTEL I FELT HER "FALLING AWAY."
REGAL HATS
DRUGS
CUSTOM
TAMBLY
ALL OF IT... ALICE, THE TRIP, THE PAST...
GROWING DIM... DIMMER.
I GUESS THAT SAYS A LOT ABOUT ME.
FOR LEASE
IMAGINE THINKING I COULD SPEND THE NIGHT IN THAT HOTEL!
HWY 7
THAT SAME HOTEL!
HOW AMAZING TO HAVE "FILED AND FORGOT" THAT AS WELL.
7 NORTH

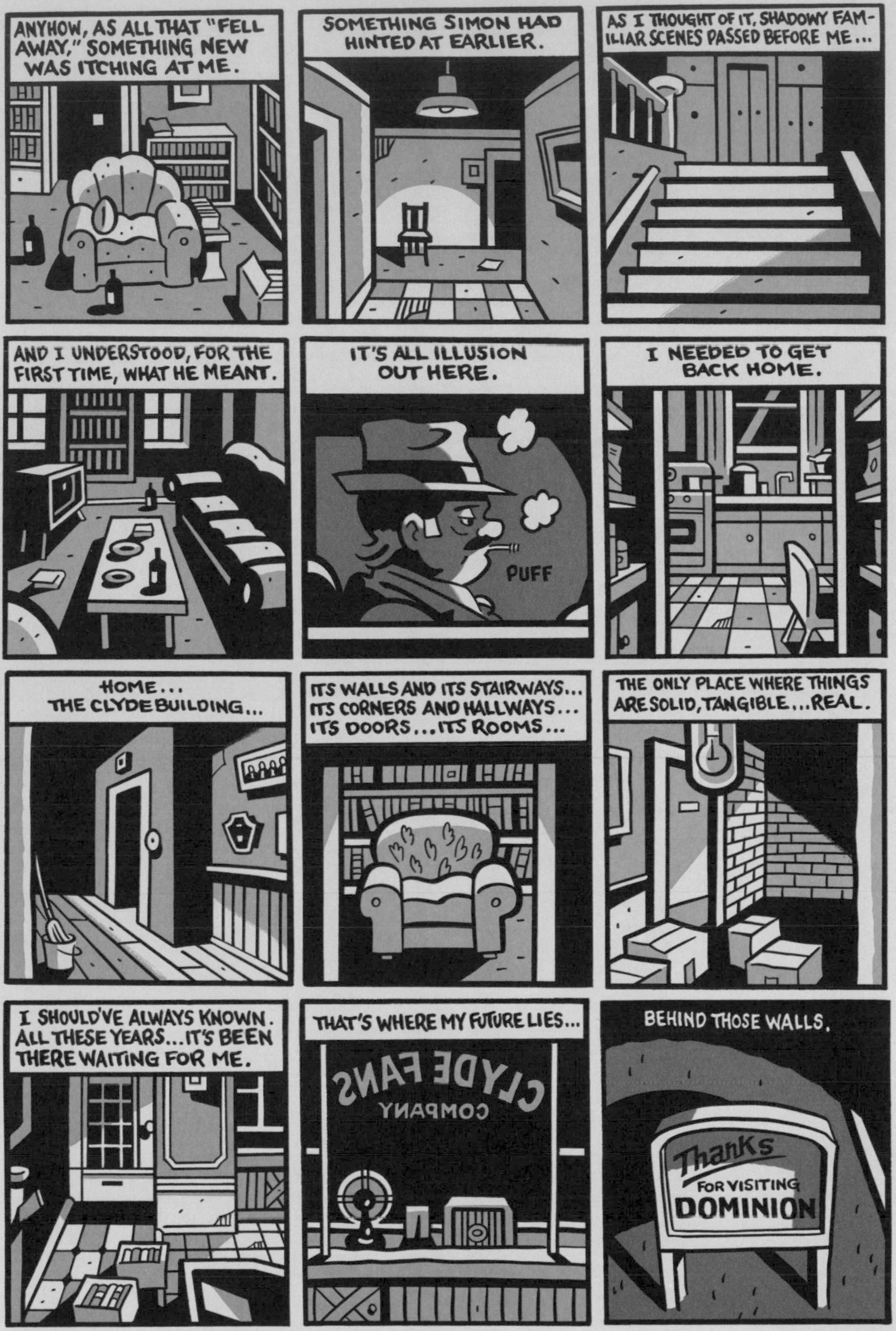
ANYHOW, AS ALL THAT "FELL AWAY," SOMETHING NEW WAS ITCHING AT ME.
SOMETHING SIMON HAD HINTED AT EARLIER.
AS I THOUGHT OF IT, SHADOWY FAMILIAR SCENES PASSED BEFORE ME...
AND I UNDERSTOOD, FOR THE FIRST TIME, WHAT HE MEANT.
IT'S ALL ILLUSION OUT HERE.
PUFF
I NEEDED TO GET BACK HOME.
HOME... THE CLYDE BUILDING...
ITS WALLS AND ITS STAIRWAYS... ITS CORNERS AND HALLWAYS... ITS DOORS... ITS ROOMS...
THE ONLY PLACE WHERE THINGS ARE SOLID, TANGIBLE... REAL.
I SHOULD'VE ALWAYS KNOWN. ALL THESE YEARS... IT'S BEEN THERE WAITING FOR ME.
THAT'S WHERE MY FUTURE LIES...
CLYDE FANS
COMPANY
BEHIND THOSE WALLS.
Thanks FOR VISITING DOMINION

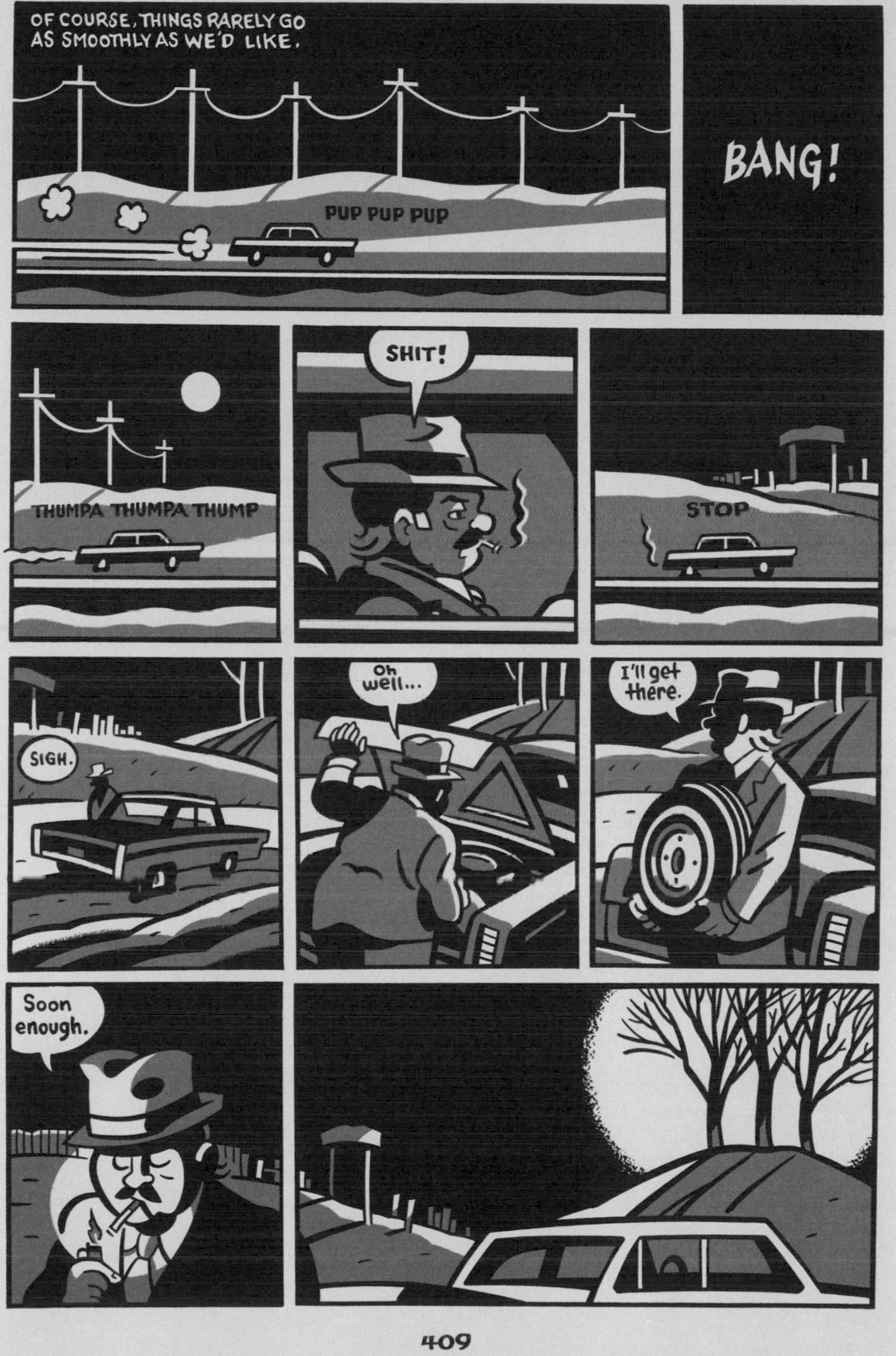
OF COURSE, THINGS RARELY GO AS SMOOTHLY AS WE'D LIKE.
PUP PUP PUP
BANG!
THUMPA THUMPA THUMP
SHIT!
STOP
SIGH.
Oh well...
I'll get there.
Soon enough.

1957

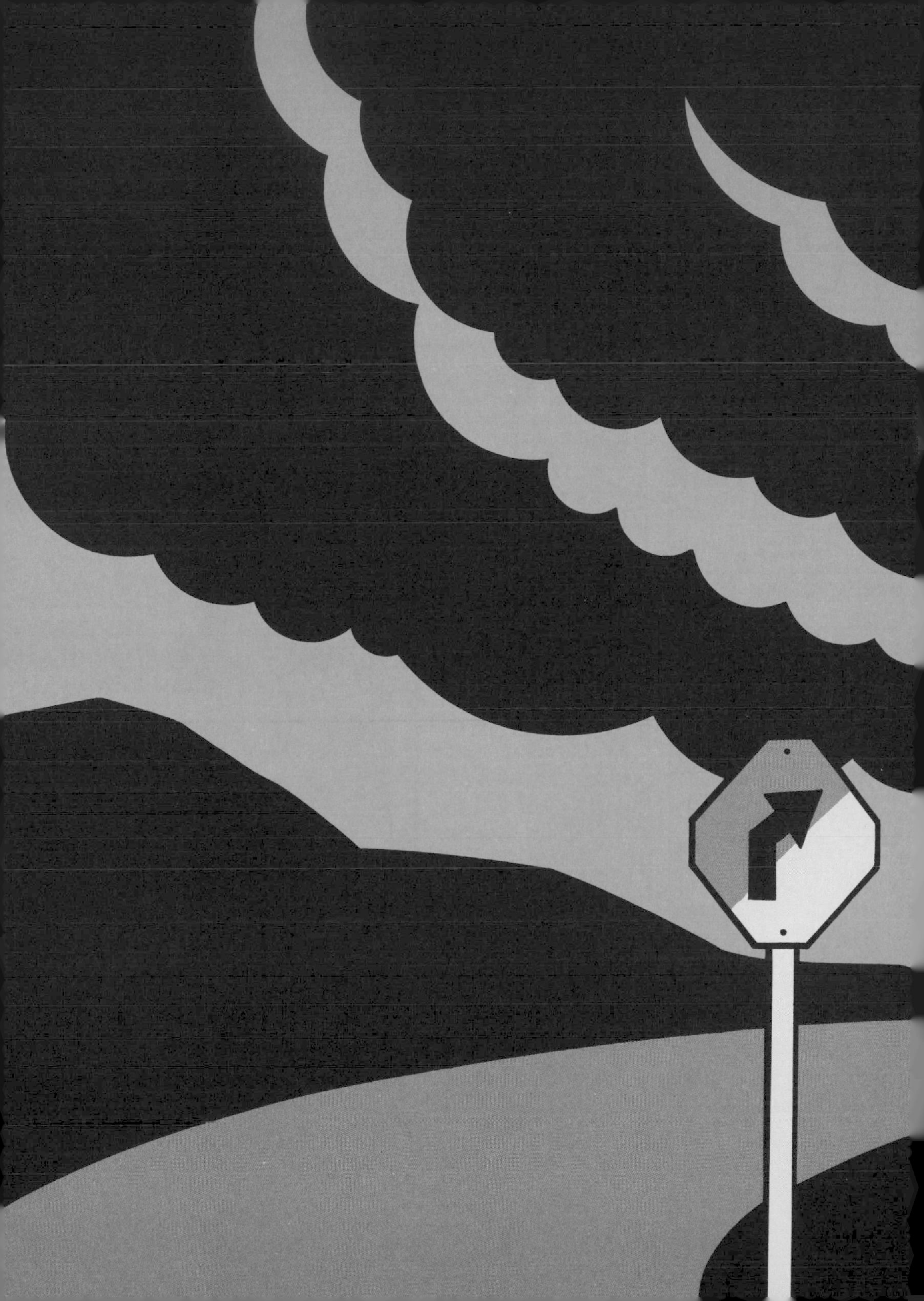

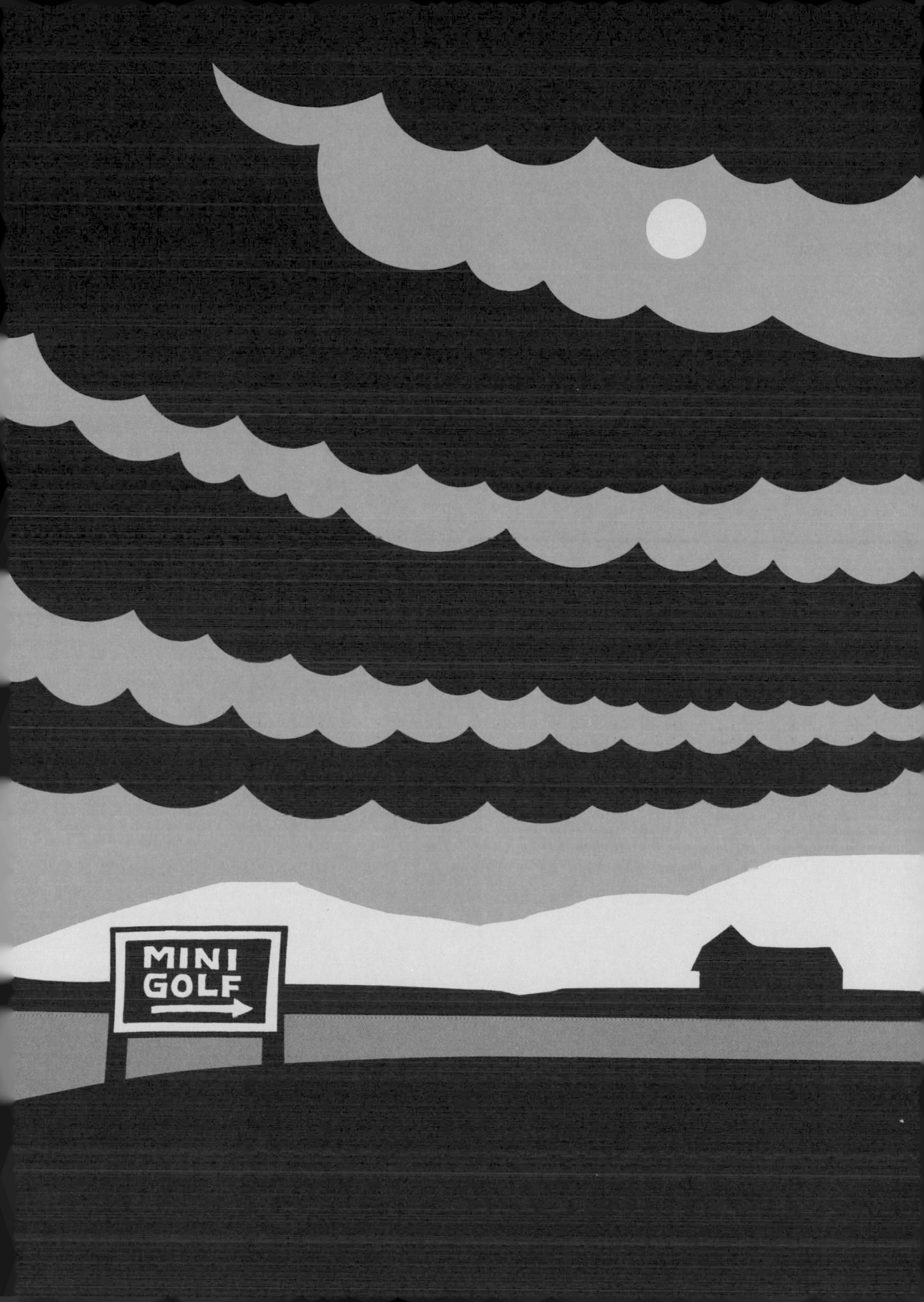
MINI
GOLF

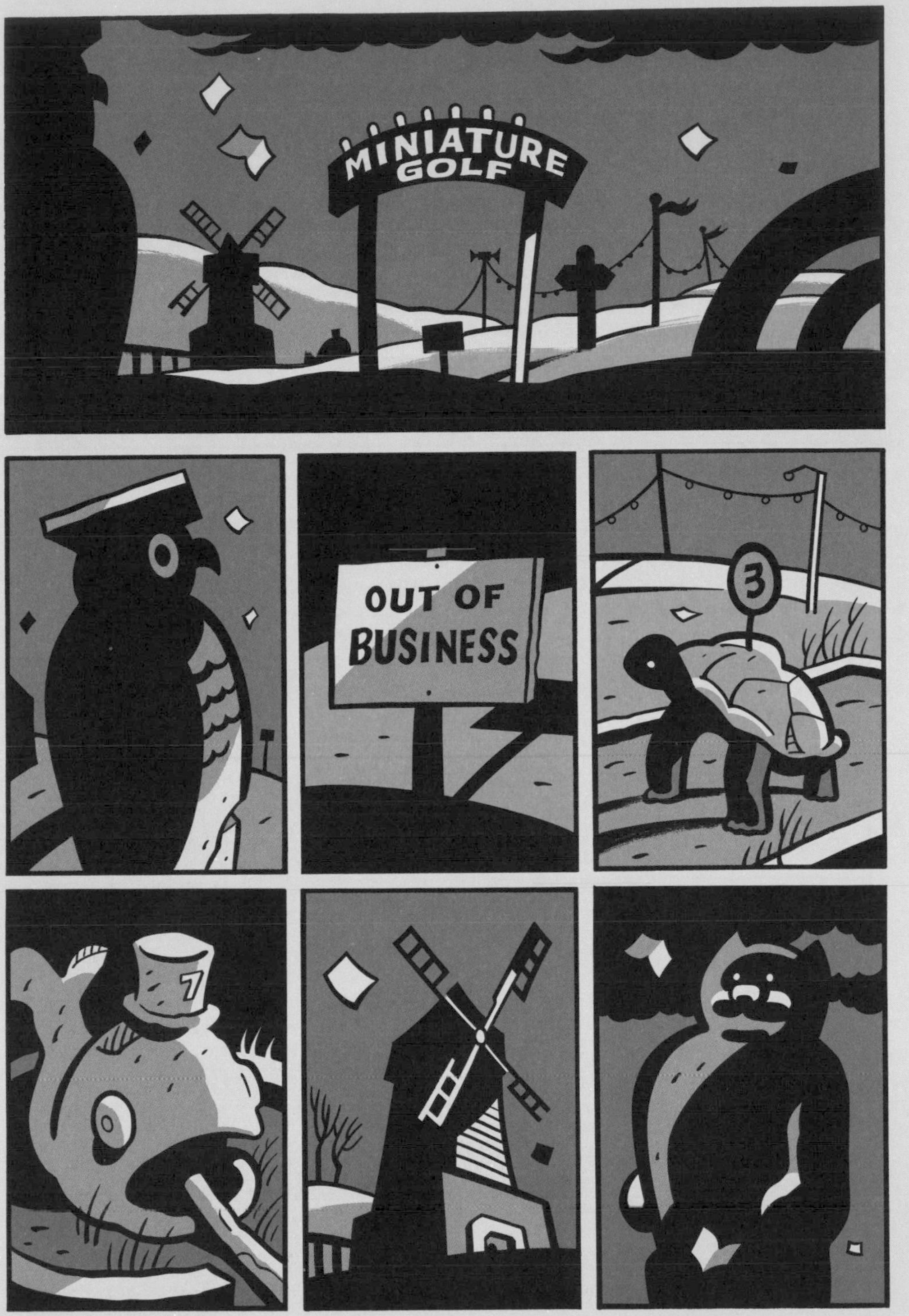
MINIATURE GOLF
OUT OF BUSINESS
3
7

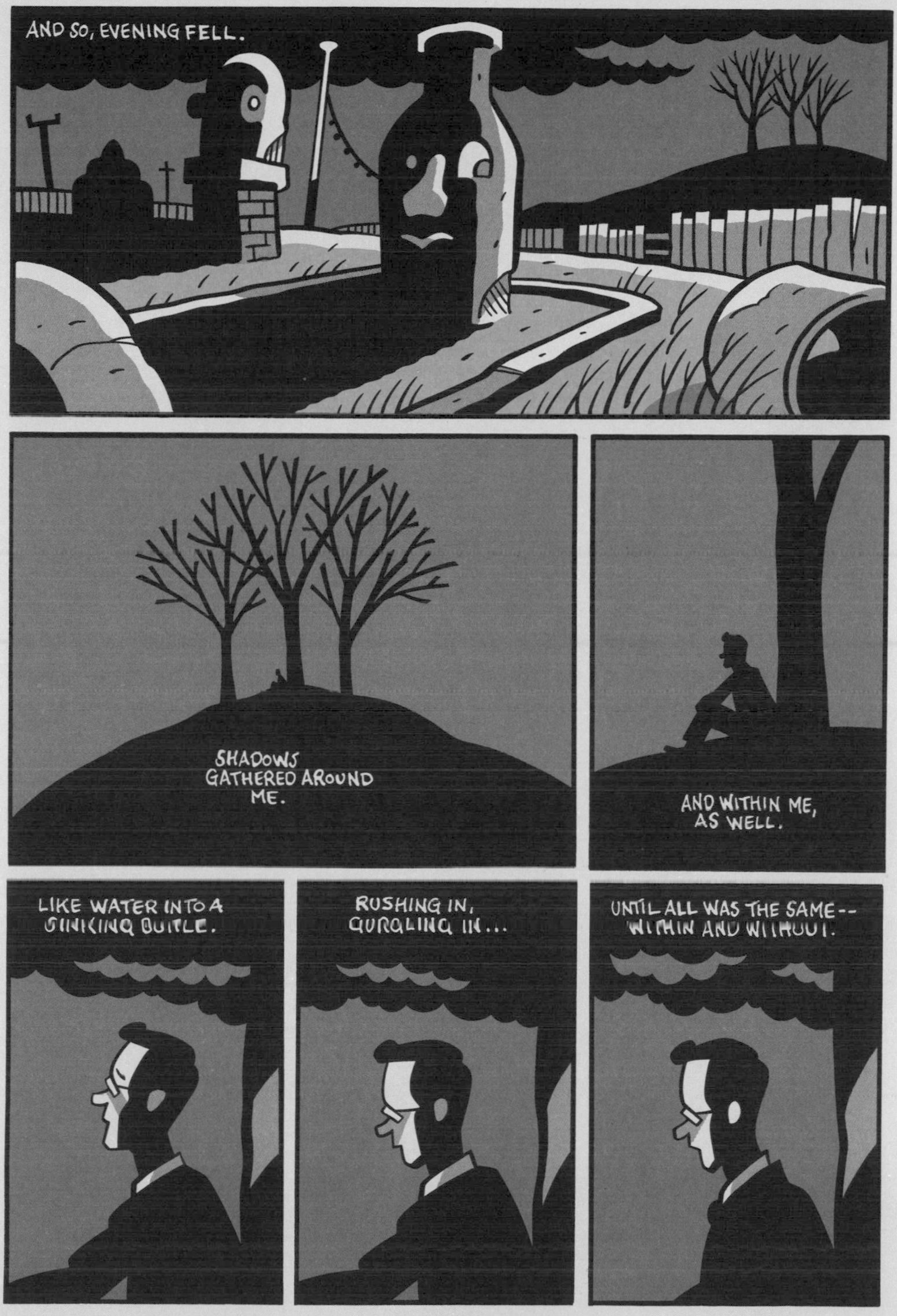
AND SO, EVENING FELL.
SHADOWS GATHERED AROUND ME.
AND WITHIN ME, AS WELL.
LIKE WATER INTO A SINKING BOTTLE.
RUSHING IN, GURGLING IN...
UNTIL ALL WAS THE SAME-- WITHIN AND WITHOUT.

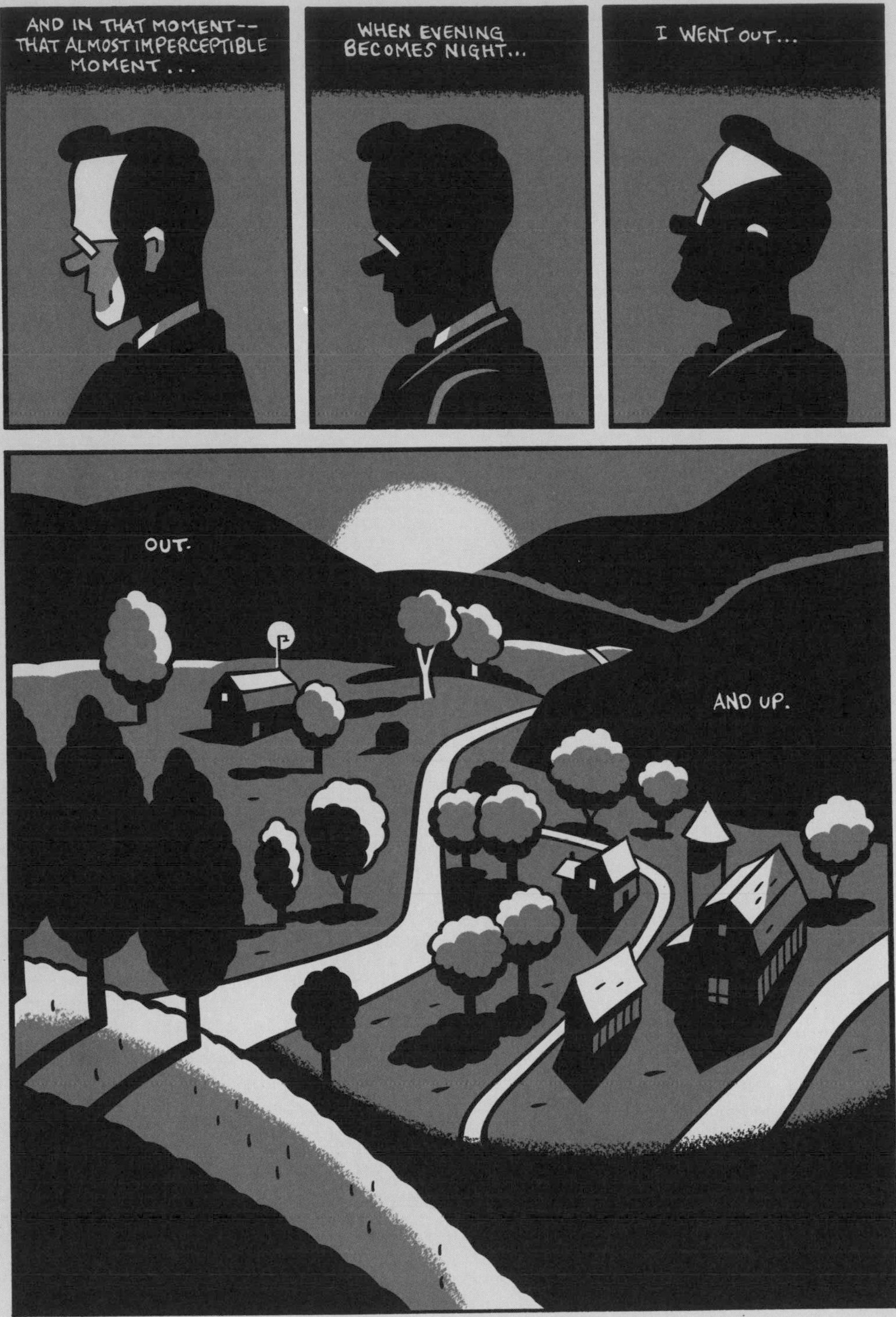
AND IN THAT MOMENT-- THAT ALMOST IMPERCEPTIBLE MOMENT...
WHEN EVENING BECOMES NIGHT...
I WENT OUT...
OUT.
AND UP.

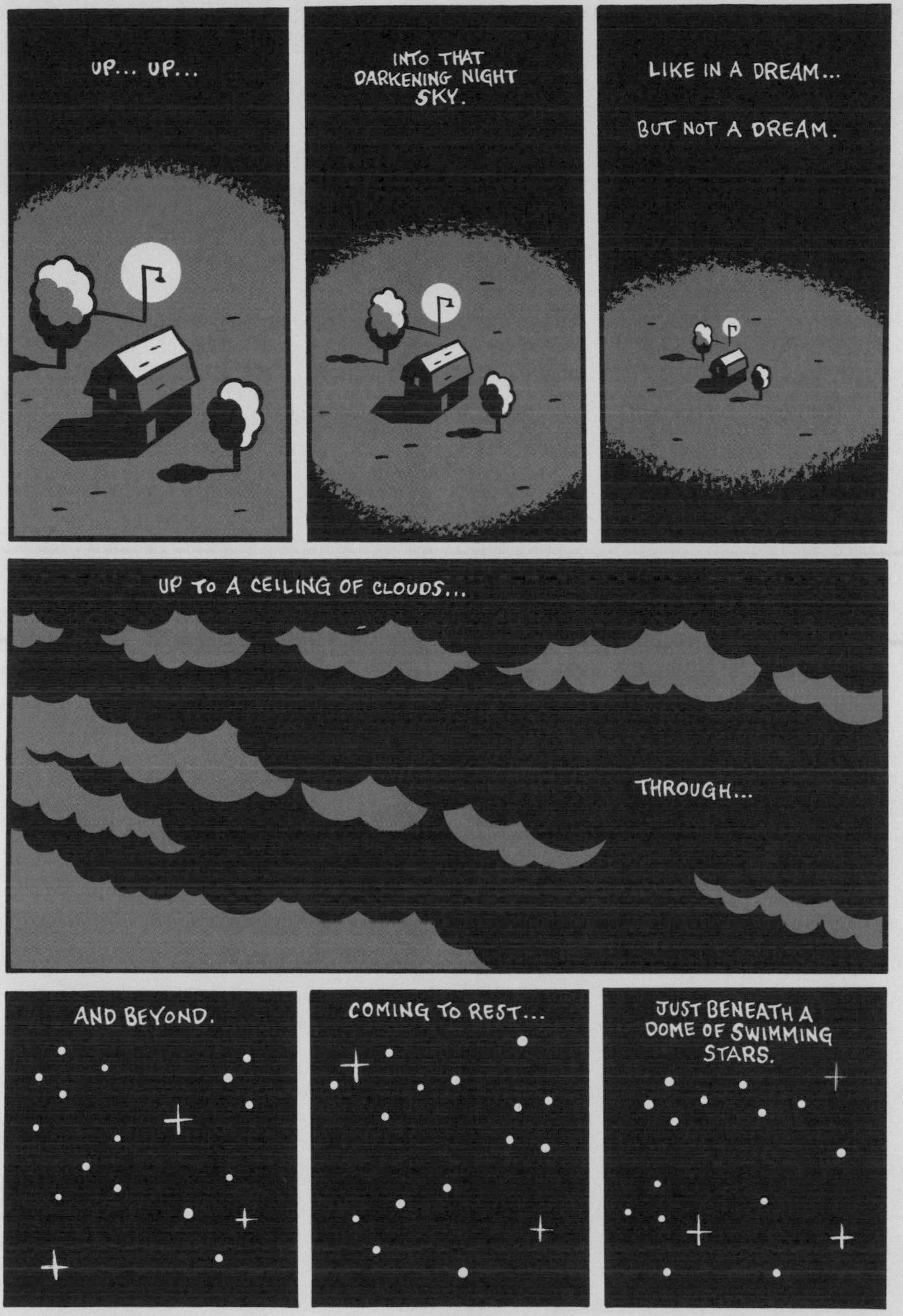
UP... UP...
INTO THAT DARKENING NIGHT SKY.
LIKE IN A DREAM...
BUT NOT A DREAM.
UP TO A CEILING OF CLOUDS...
THROUGH...
AND BEYOND.
COMING TO REST...
JUST BENEATH A DOME OF SWIMMING STARS.

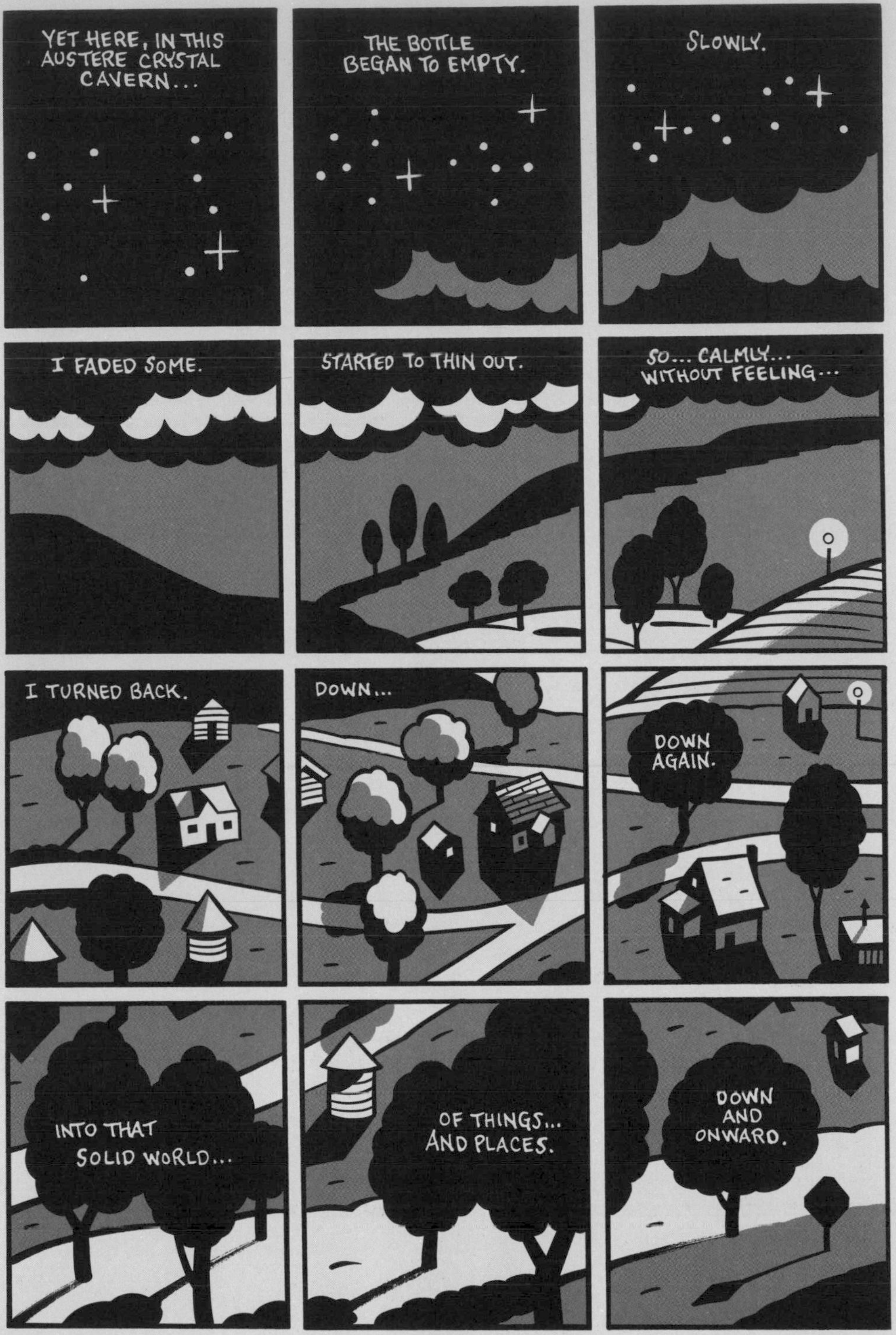
YET HERE, IN THIS AUSTERE CRYSTAL CAVERN...
THE BOTTLE BEGAN TO EMPTY.
SLOWLY.
I FADED SOME.
STARTED TO THIN OUT.
SO... CALMLY... WITHOUT FEELING...
I TURNED BACK.
DOWN...
DOWN AGAIN.
INTO THAT SOLID WORLD...
OF THINGS... AND PLACES.
DOWN AND ONWARD.

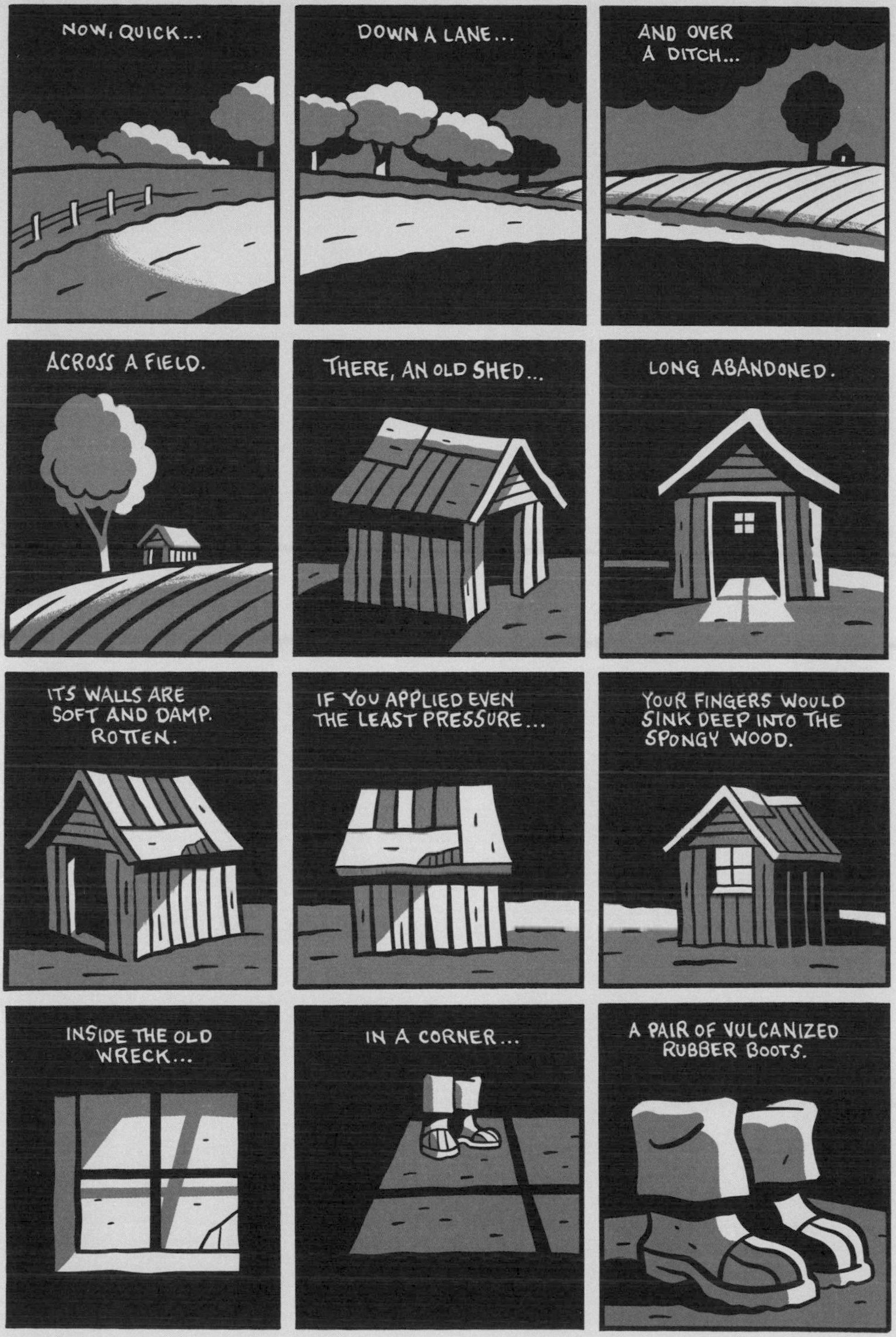
NOW, QUICK...
DOWN A LANE...
AND OVER A DITCH...
ACROSS A FIELD.
THERE, AN OLD SHED...
LONG ABANDONED.
ITS WALLS ARE SOFT AND DAMP. ROTTEN.
IF YOU APPLIED EVEN THE LEAST PRESSURE...
YOUR FINGERS WOULD SINK DEEP INTO THE SPONGY WOOD.
INSIDE THE OLD WRECK...
IN A CORNER...
A PAIR OF VULCANIZED RUBBER BOOTS.

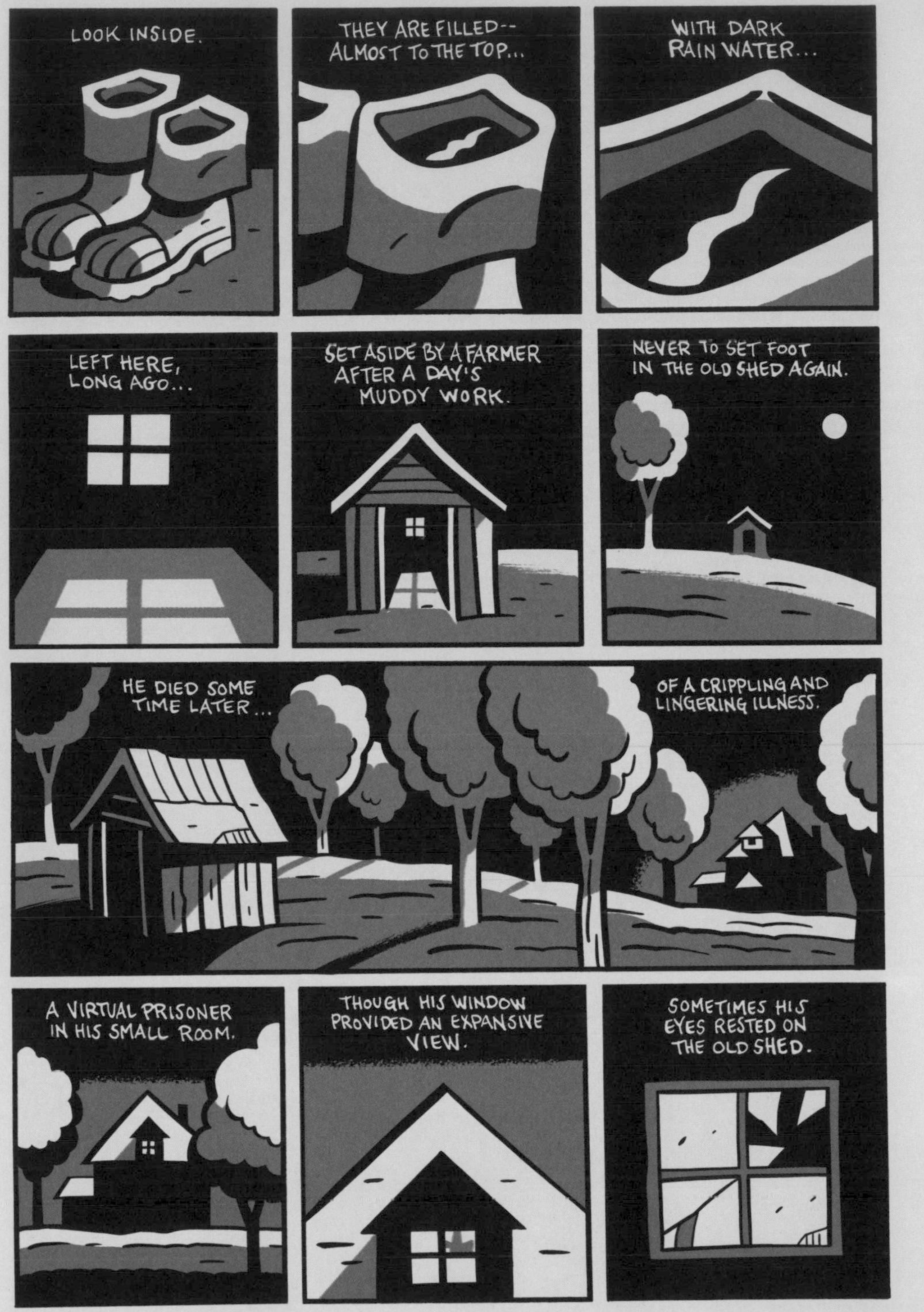
LOOK INSIDE.
THEY ARE FILLED-- ALMOST TO THE TOP...
WITH DARK RAIN WATER...
LEFT HERE, LONG AGO...
SET ASIDE BY A FARMER AFTER A DAY'S MUDDY WORK.
NEVER TO SET FOOT IN THE OLD SHED AGAIN.
HE DIED SOME TIME LATER...
OF A CRIPPLING AND LINGERING ILLNESS.
A VIRTUAL PRISONER IN HIS SMALL ROOM.
THOUGH HIS WINDOW PROVIDED AN EXPANSIVE VIEW.
SOMETIMES HIS EYES RESTED ON THE OLD SHED.

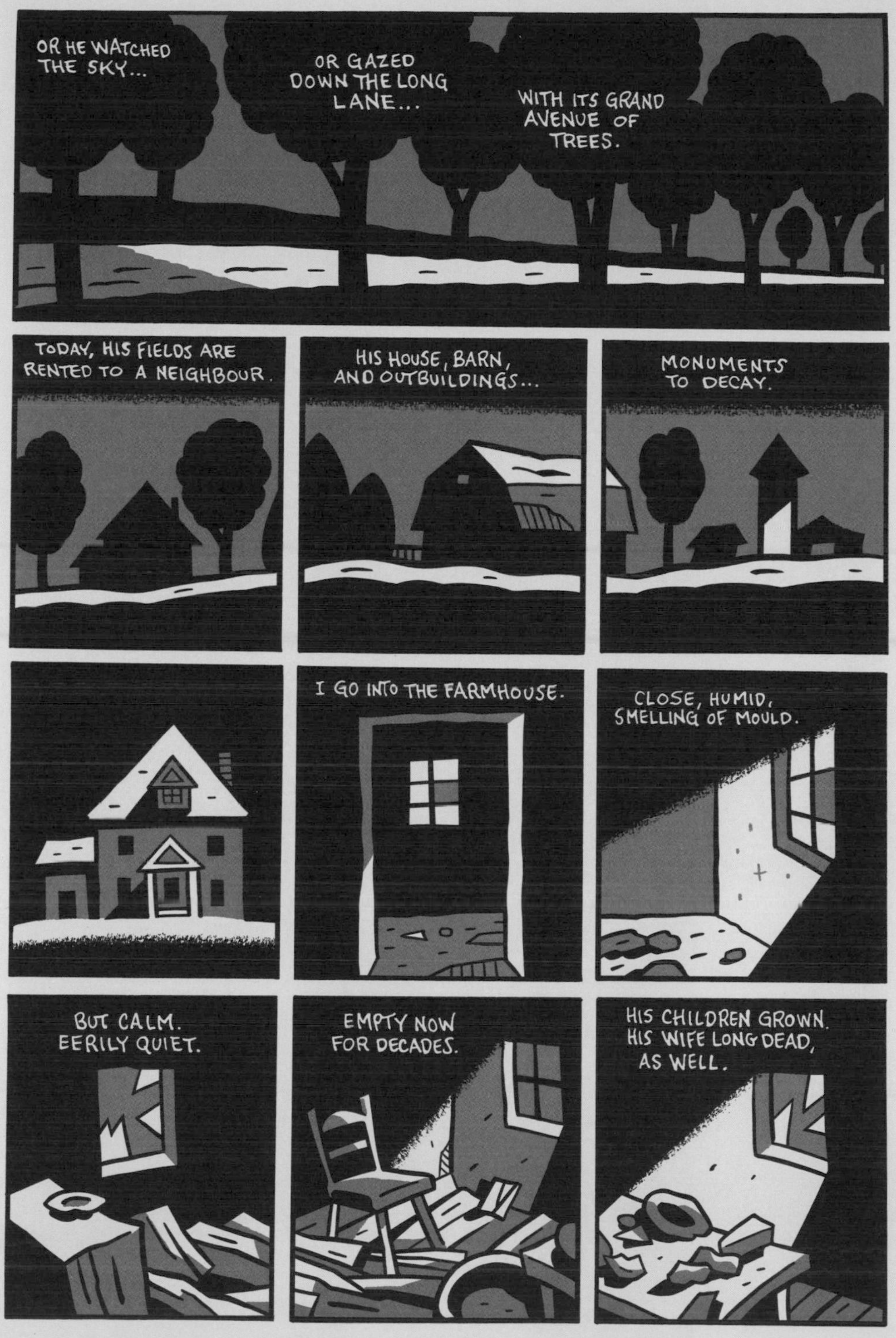
OR HE WATCHED THE SKY...
OR GAZED DOWN THE LONG LANE...
WITH ITS GRAND AVENUE OF TREES.
TODAY, HIS FIELDS ARE RENTED TO A NEIGHBOUR.
HIS HOUSE, BARN, AND OUTBUILDINGS...
MONUMENTS TO DECAY.
I GO INTO THE FARMHOUSE.
CLOSE, HUMID, SMELLING OF MOULD.
BUT CALM. EERILY QUIET.
EMPTY NOW FOR DECADES.
HIS CHILDREN GROWN. HIS WIFE LONG DEAD, AS WELL.

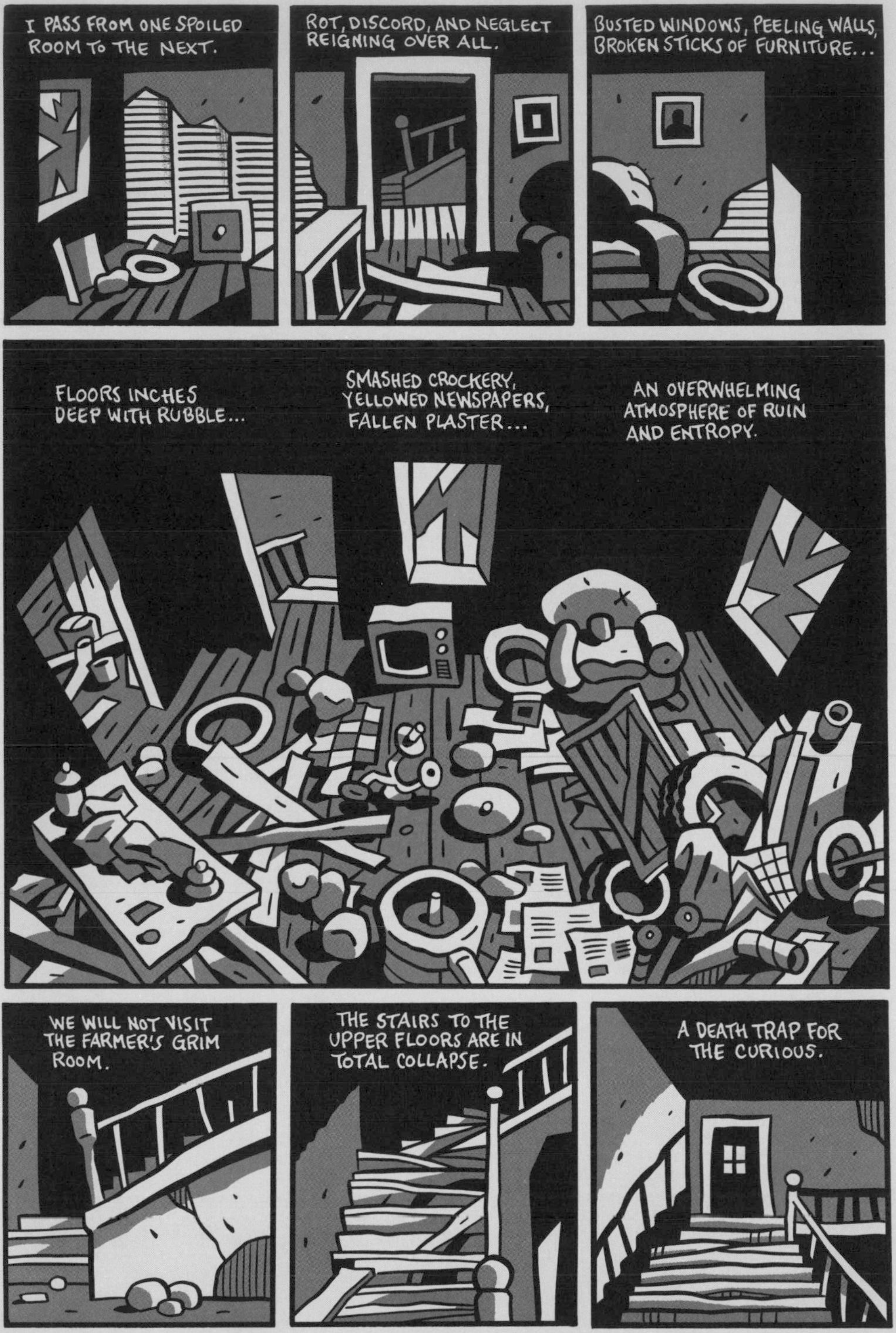
I PASS FROM ONE SPOILED ROOM TO THE NEXT.
ROT, DISCORD, AND NEGLECT REIGNING OVER ALL.
BUSTED WINDOWS, PEELING WALLS, BROKEN STICKS OF FURNITURE...
FLOORS INCHES DEEP WITH RUBBLE...
SMASHED CROCKERY, YELLOWED NEWSPAPERS, FALLEN PLASTER...
AN OVERWHELMING ATMOSPHERE OF RUIN AND ENTROPY.
WE WILL NOT VISIT THE FARMER'S GRIM ROOM.
THE STAIRS TO THE UPPER FLOORS ARE IN TOTAL COLLAPSE.
A DEATH TRAP FOR THE CURIOUS.

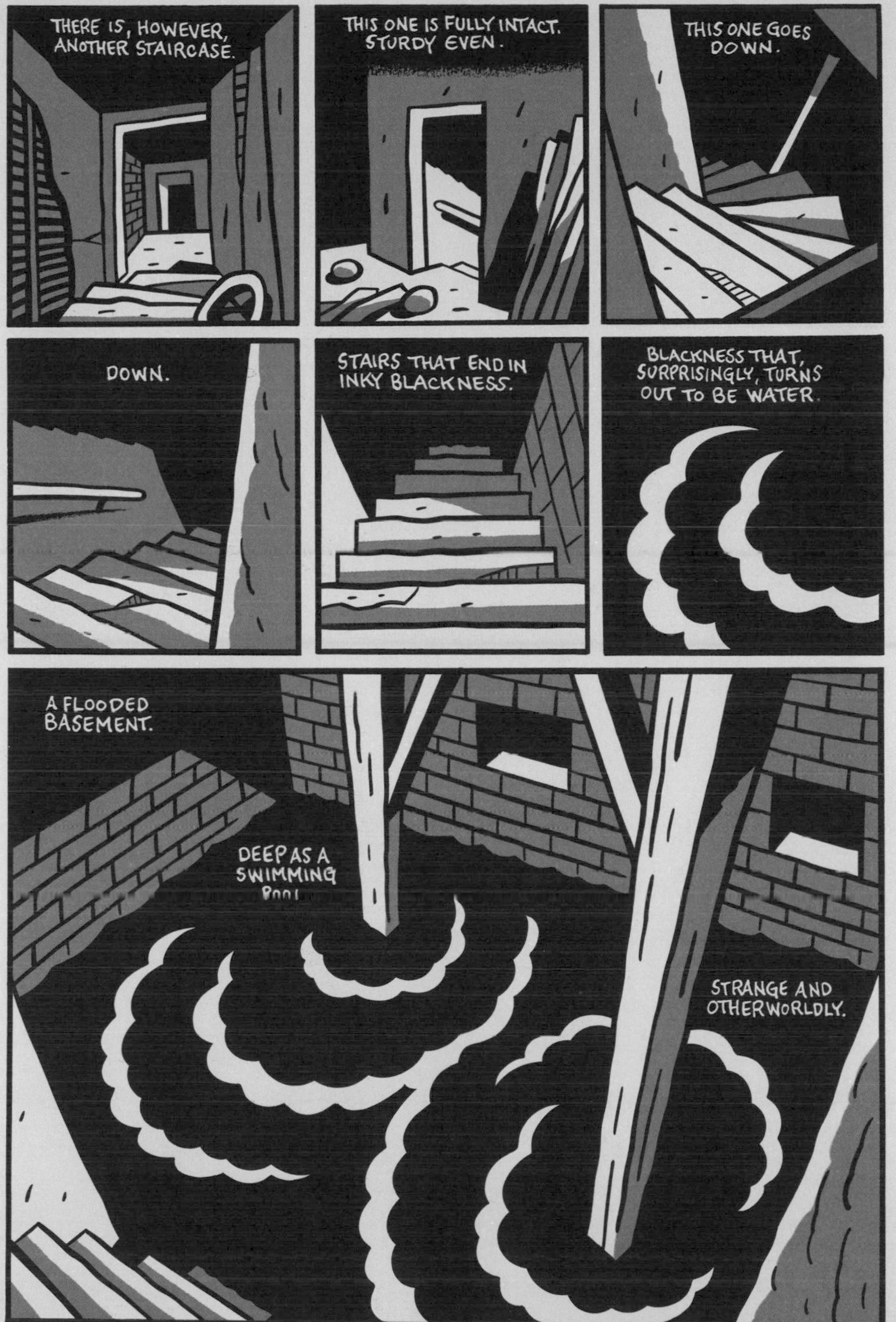
THERE IS, HOWEVER, ANOTHER STAIRCASE.
THIS ONE IS FULLY INTACT. STURDY EVEN.
THIS ONE GOES DOWN.
DOWN.
STAIRS THAT END IN INKY BLACKNESS.
BLACKNESS THAT, SURPRISINGLY, TURNS OUT TO BE WATER.
A FLOODED BASEMENT.
DEEP AS A SWIMMING POOL.
STRANGE AND OTHERWORLDLY.

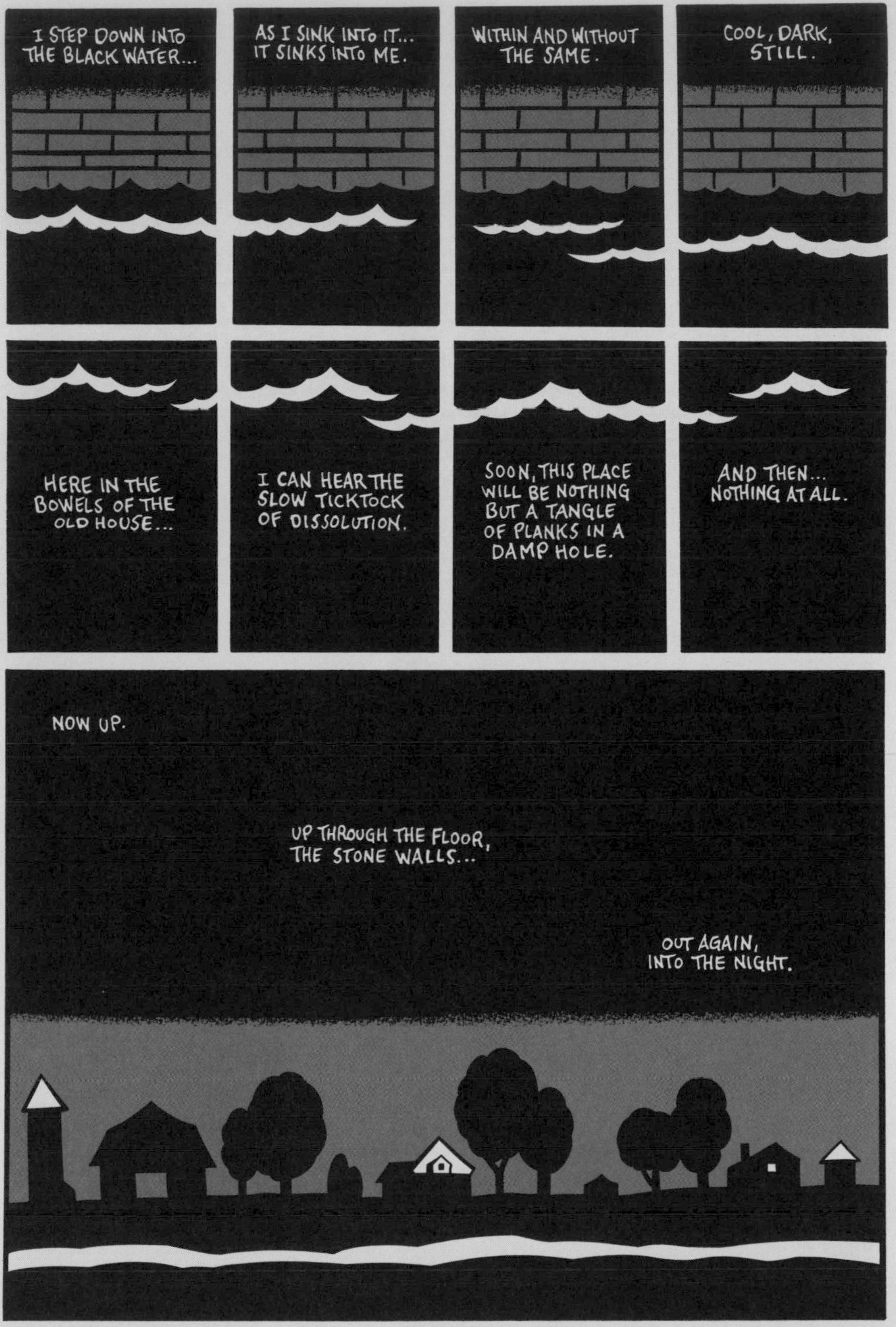
I STEP DOWN INTO THE BLACK WATER...
AS I SINK INTO IT... IT SINKS INTO ME.
WITHIN AND WITHOUT THE SAME.
COOL, DARK, STILL.
HERE IN THE BOWELS OF THE OLD HOUSE...
I CAN HEAR THE SLOW TICKTOCK OF DISSOLUTION.
SOON, THIS PLACE WILL BE NOTHING BUT A TANGLE OF PLANKS IN A DAMP HOLE.
AND THEN... NOTHING AT ALL.
NOW UP.
UP THROUGH THE FLOOR, THE STONE WALLS...
OUT AGAIN, INTO THE NIGHT.

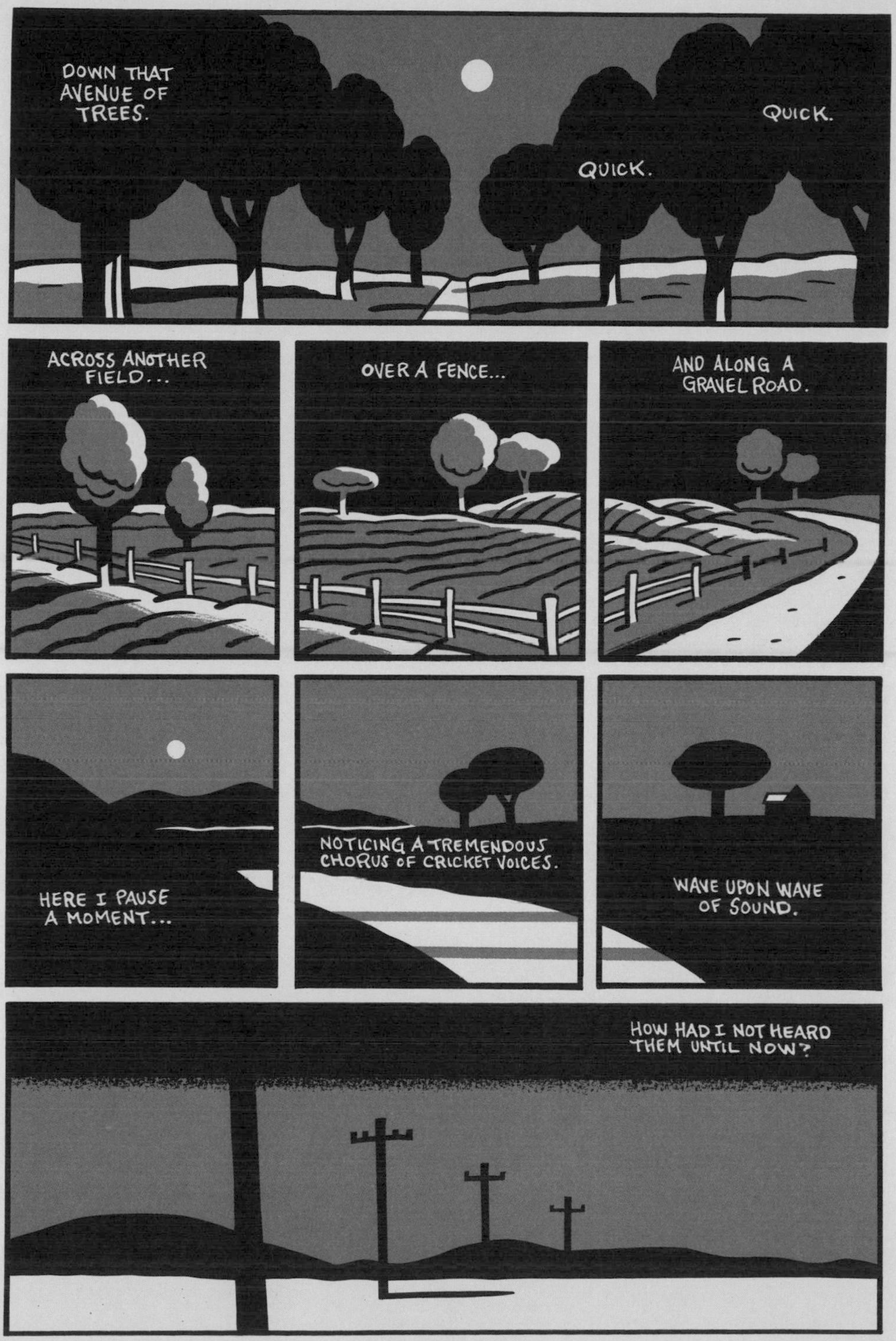
DOWN THAT AVENUE OF TREES.
QUICK.
QUICK.
ACROSS ANOTHER FIELD...
OVER A FENCE...
AND ALONG A GRAVEL ROAD.
HERE I PAUSE A MOMENT...
NOTICING A TREMENDOUS CHORUS OF CRICKET VOICES.
WAVE UPON WAVE OF SOUND.
HOW HAD I NOT HEARD THEM UNTIL NOW?

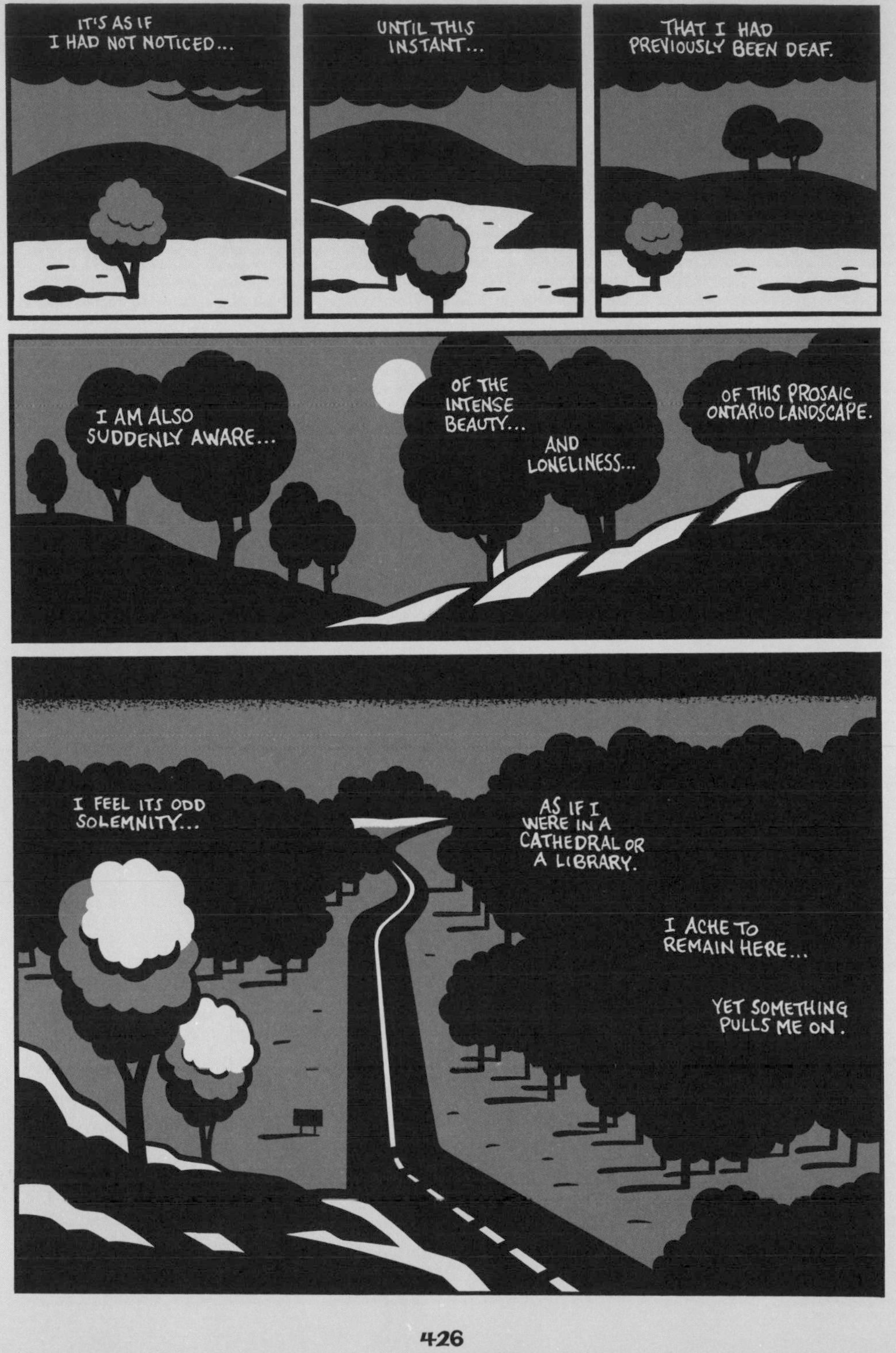
IT'S AS IF
I HAD NOT NOTICED...
UNTIL THIS
INSTANT...
THAT I HAD
PREVIOUSLY BEEN DEAF.
I AM ALSO
SUDDENLY AWARE...
OF THE
INTENSE
BEAUTY...
AND
LONELINESS...
OF THIS PROSAIC
ONTARIO LANDSCAPE.
I FEEL ITS ODD
SOLEMNITY...
AS IF I
WERE IN A
CATHEDRAL OR
A LIBRARY.
I ACHE TO
REMAIN HERE...
YET SOMETHING
PULLS ME ON.

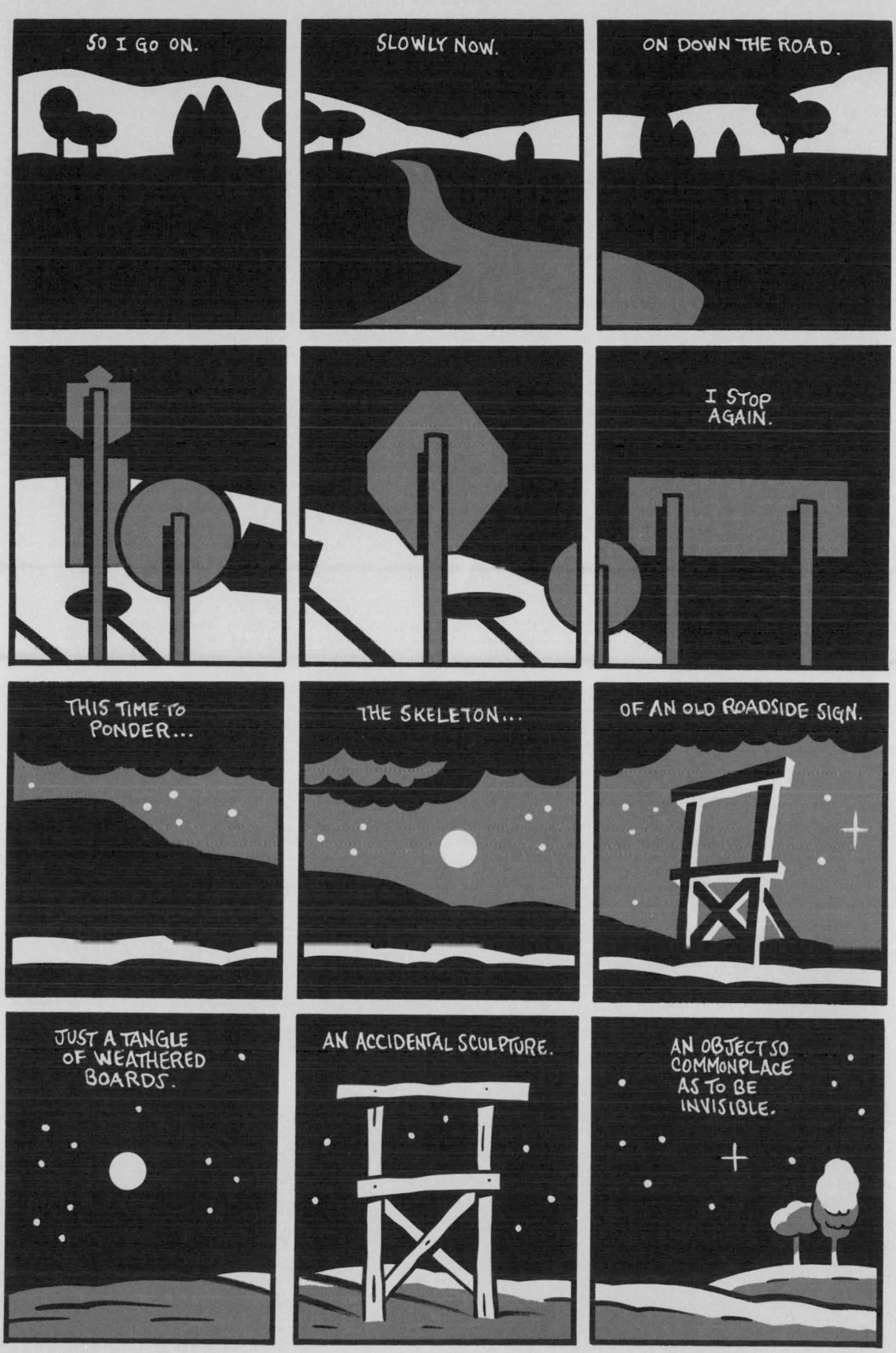
SO I GO ON.
SLOWLY NOW.
ON DOWN THE ROAD.
I STOP AGAIN.
THIS TIME TO PONDER...
THE SKELETON...
OF AN OLD ROADSIDE SIGN.
JUST A TANGLE OF WEATHERED BOARDS.
AN ACCIDENTAL SCULPTURE.
AN OBJECT SO COMMONPLACE AS TO BE INVISIBLE.

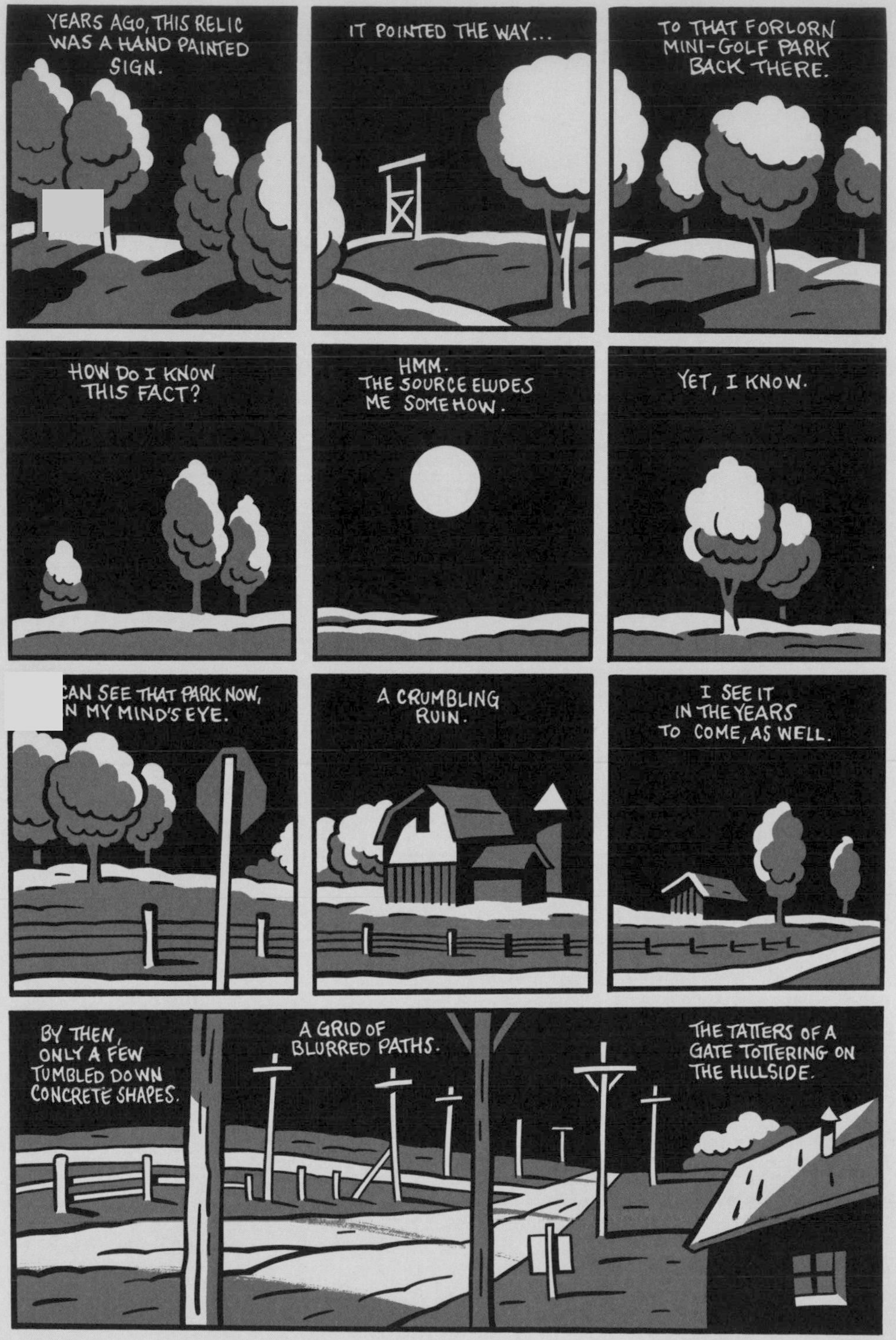
YEARS AGO, THIS RELIC WAS A HAND PAINTED SIGN.
IT POINTED THE WAY...
TO THAT FORLORN MINI-GOLF PARK BACK THERE.
HOW DO I KNOW THIS FACT?
HMM. THE SOURCE ELUDES ME SOMEHOW.
YET, I KNOW.
CAN SEE THAT PARK NOW, N MY MIND'S EYE.
A CRUMBLING RUIN.
I SEE IT IN THE YEARS TO COME, AS WELL.
BY THEN, ONLY A FEW TUMBLED DOWN CONCRETE SHAPES.
A GRID OF BLURRED PATHS.
THE TATTERS OF A GATE TOTTERING ON THE HILLSIDE.

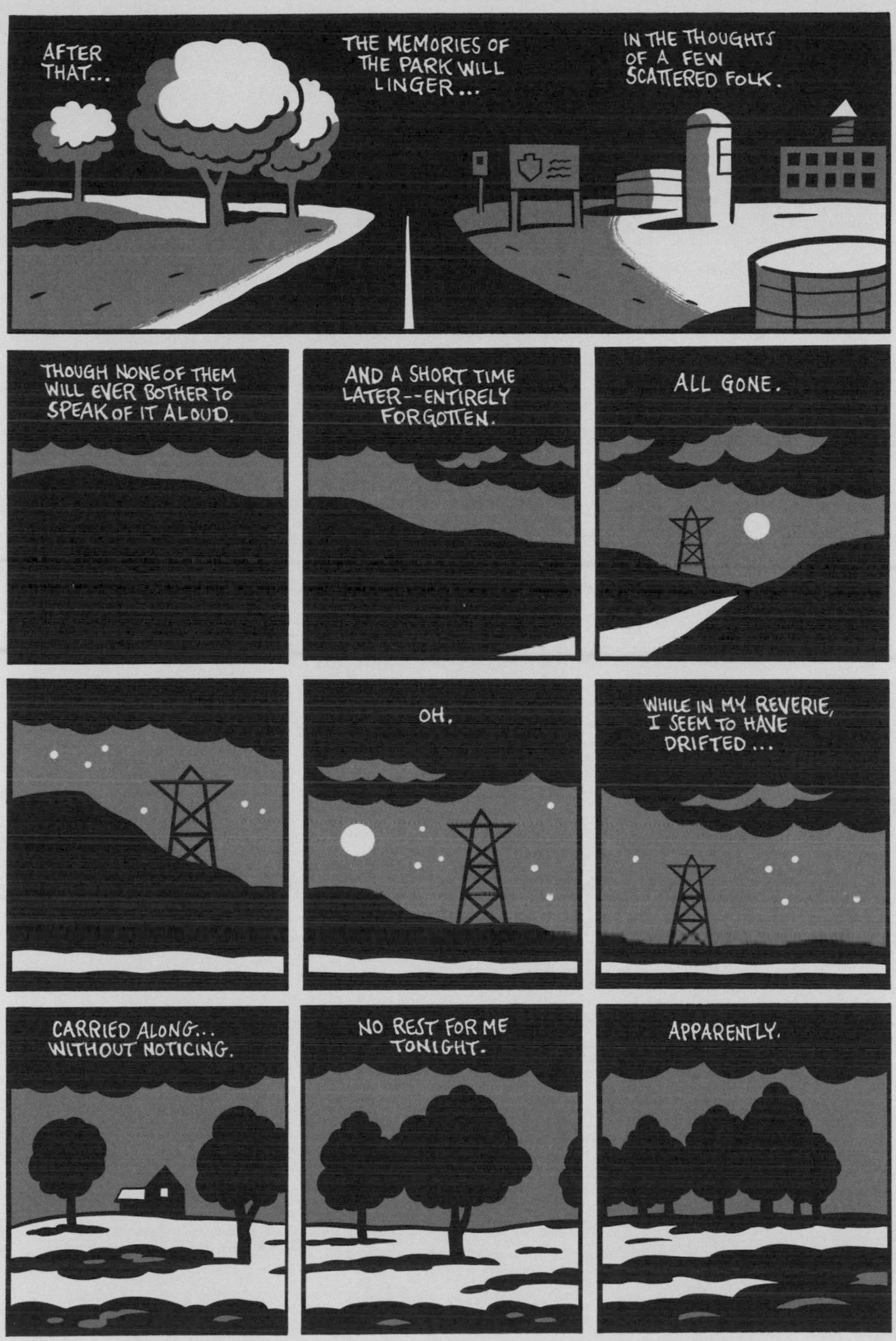
AFTER THAT...
THE MEMORIES OF THE PARK WILL LINGER...
IN THE THOUGHTS OF A FEW SCATTERED FOLK.
THOUGH NONE OF THEM WILL EVER BOTHER TO SPEAK OF IT ALOUD.
AND A SHORT TIME LATER--ENTIRELY FORGOTTEN.
ALL GONE.
OH.
WHILE IN MY REVERIE, I SEEM TO HAVE DRIFTED...
CARRIED ALONG... WITHOUT NOTICING.
NO REST FOR ME TONIGHT.
APPARENTLY.

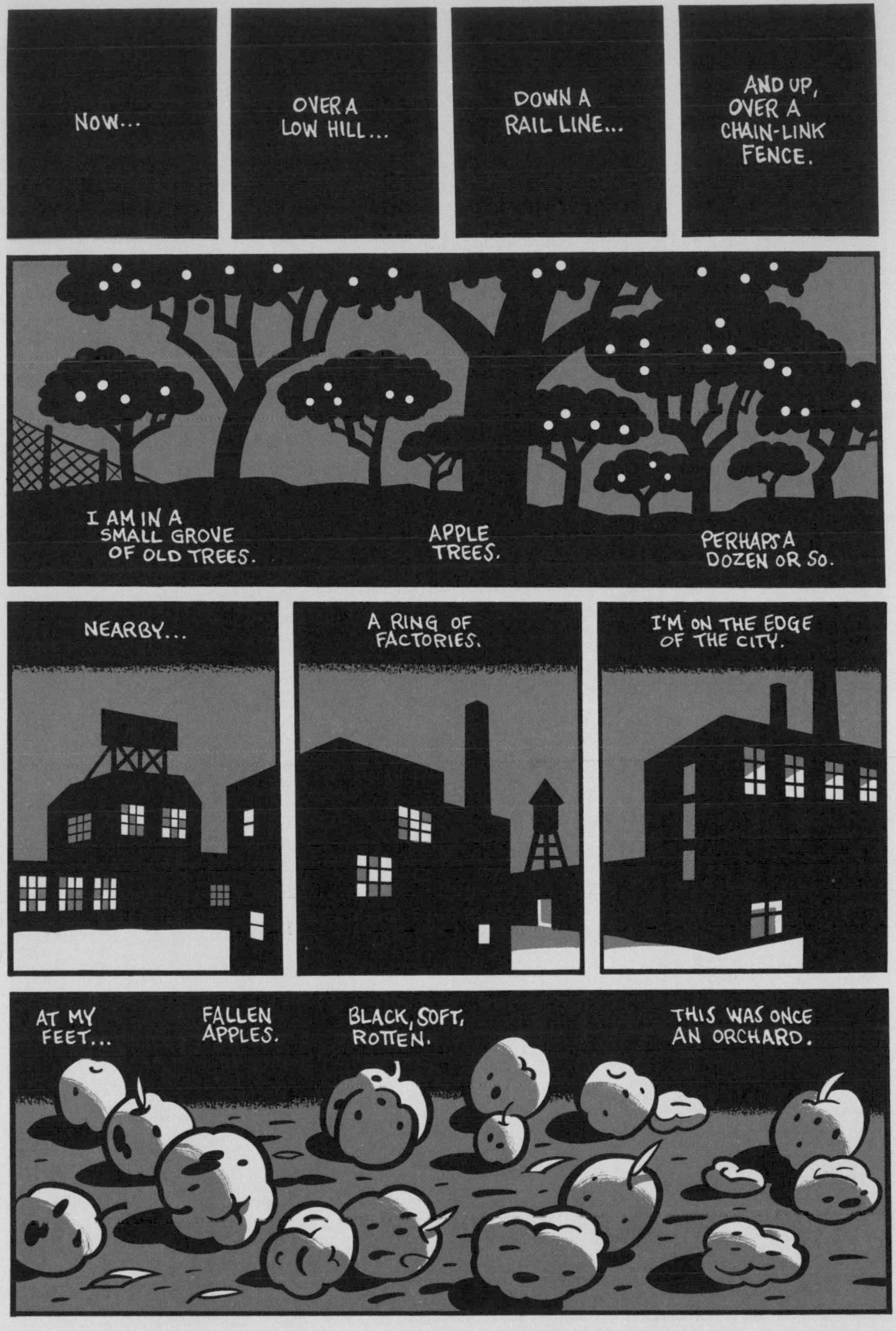
NOW...
OVER A LOW HILL...
DOWN A RAIL LINE...
AND UP, OVER A CHAIN-LINK FENCE.
I AM IN A SMALL GROVE OF OLD TREES.
APPLE TREES.
PERHAPS A DOZEN OR SO.
NEARBY...
A RING OF FACTORIES.
I'M ON THE EDGE OF THE CITY.
AT MY FEET...
FALLEN APPLES.
BLACK, SOFT, ROTTEN.
THIS WAS ONCE AN ORCHARD.

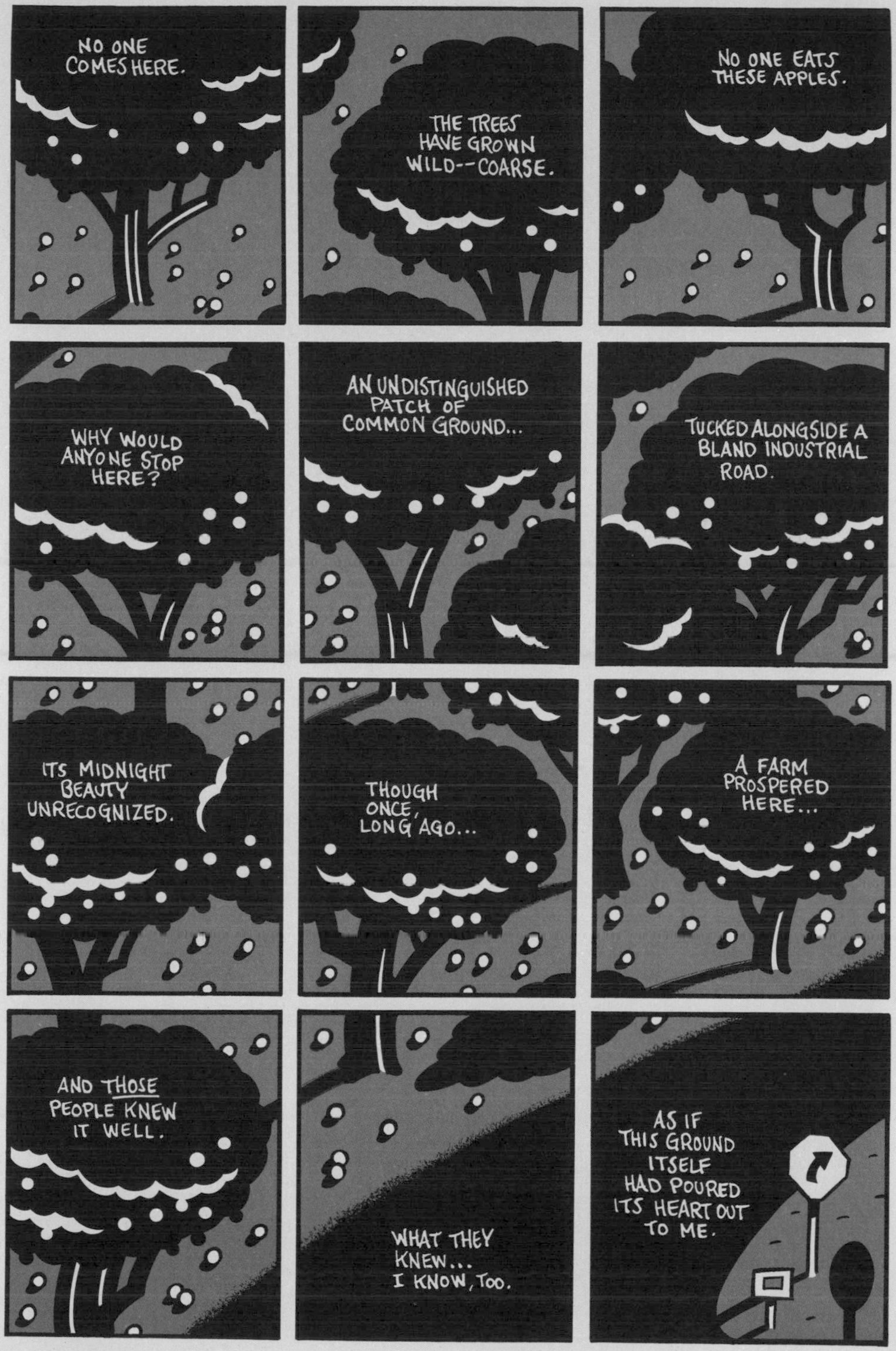
NO ONE COMES HERE.
THE TREES HAVE GROWN WILD--COARSE.
NO ONE EATS THESE APPLES.
WHY WOULD ANYONE STOP HERE?
AN UNDISTINGUISHED PATCH OF COMMON GROUND...
TUCKED ALONGSIDE A BLAND INDUSTRIAL ROAD.
ITS MIDNIGHT BEAUTY UNRECOGNIZED.
THOUGH ONCE, LONG AGO...
A FARM PROSPERED HERE...
AND THOSE PEOPLE KNEW IT WELL.
WHAT THEY KNEW... I KNOW, TOO.
AS IF THIS GROUND ITSELF HAD POURED ITS HEART OUT TO ME.

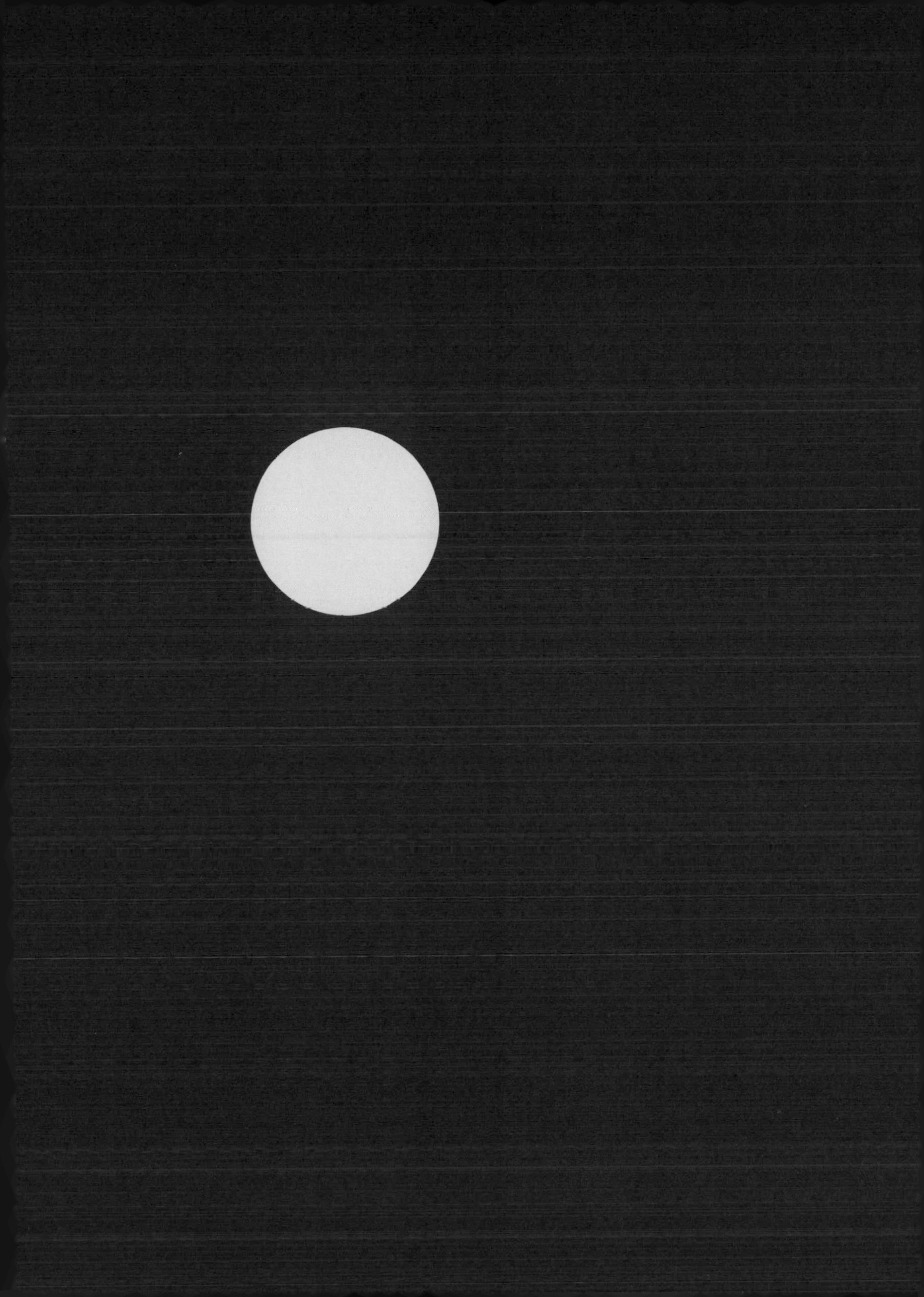

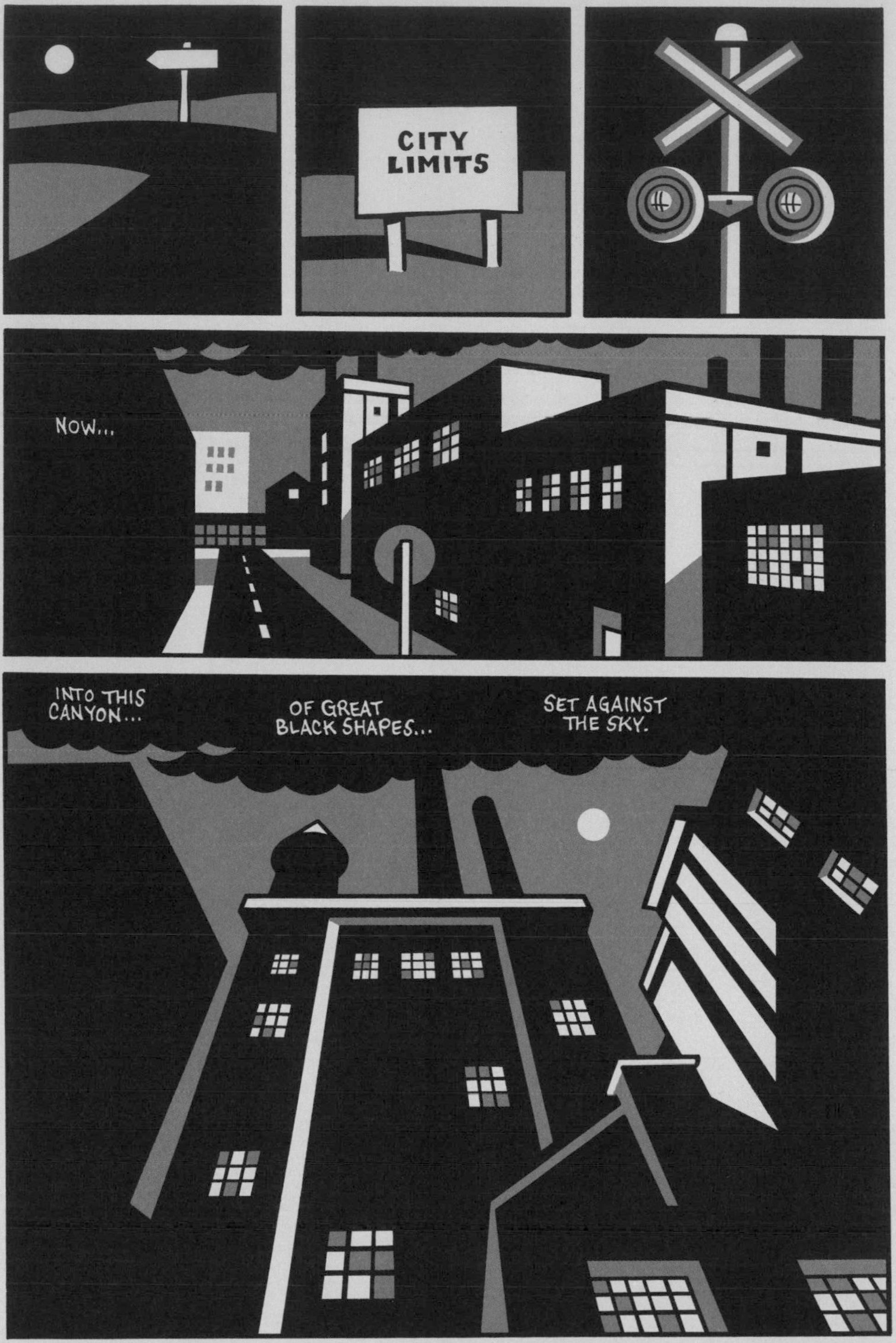
CITY
LIMITS
NOW...
INTO THIS CANYON...
OF GREAT BLACK SHAPES...
SET AGAINST THE SKY.

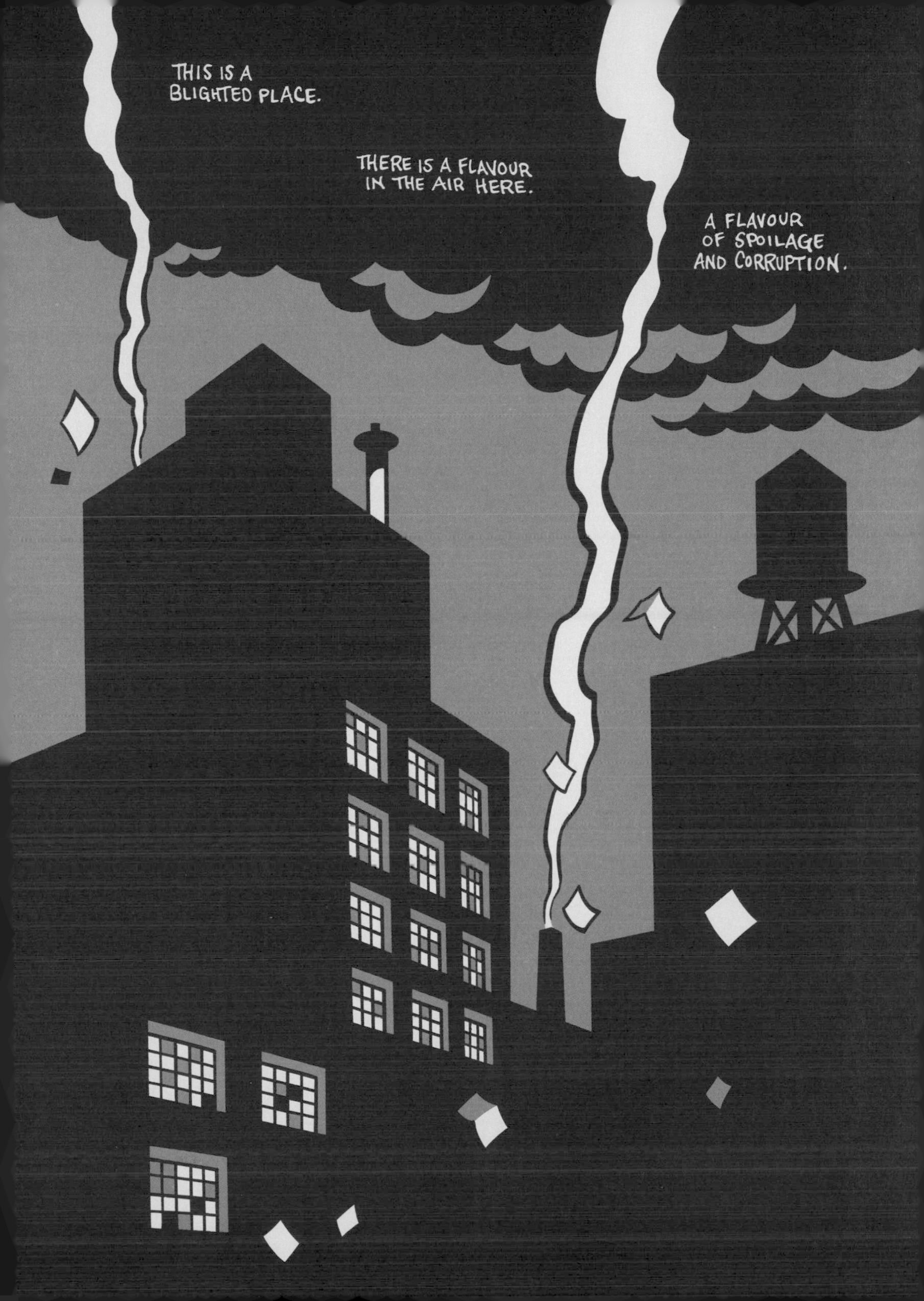
THIS IS A BLIGHTED PLACE.
THERE IS A FLAVOUR IN THE AIR HERE.
A FLAVOUR OF SPOILAGE AND CORRUPTION.

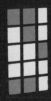

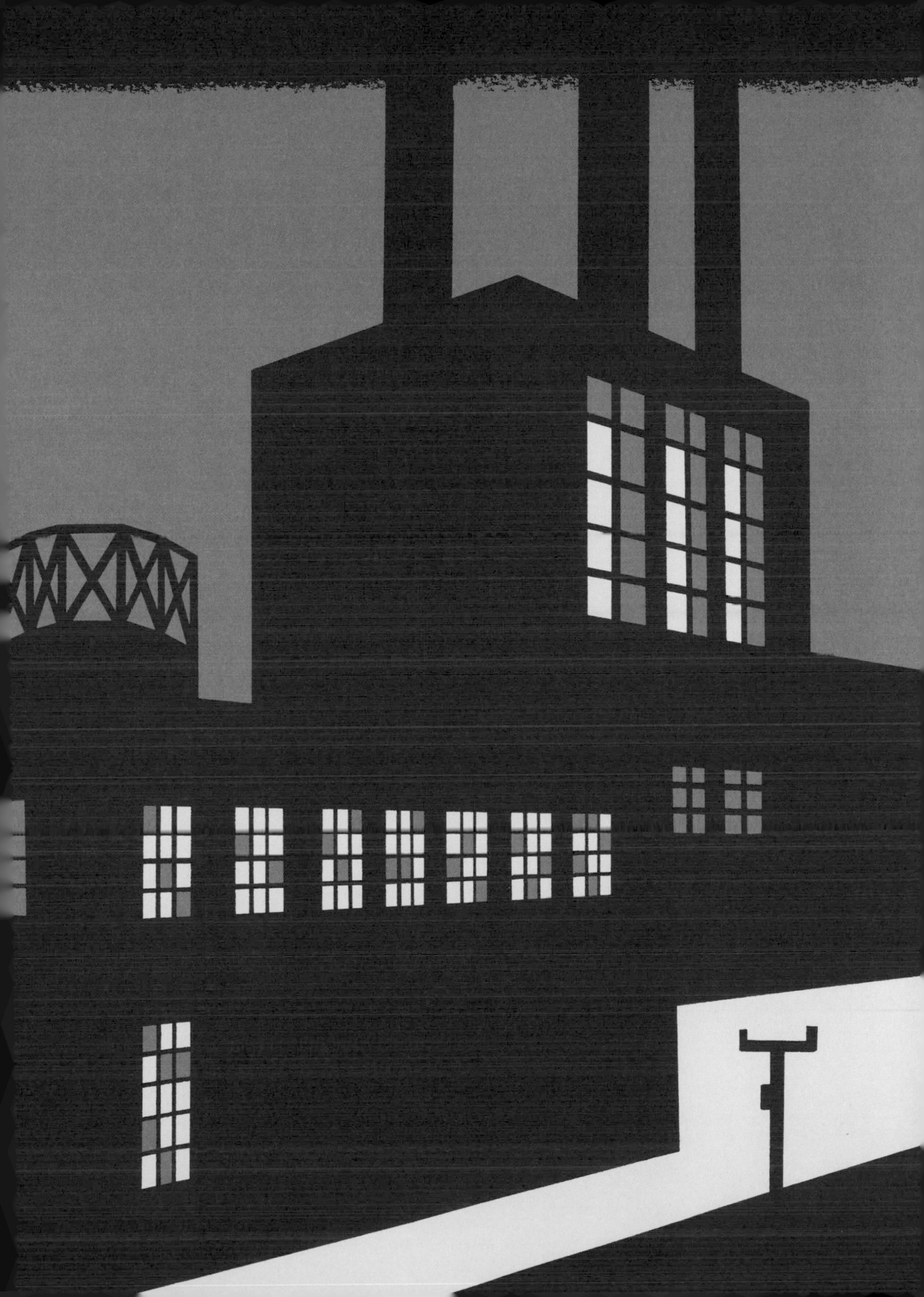

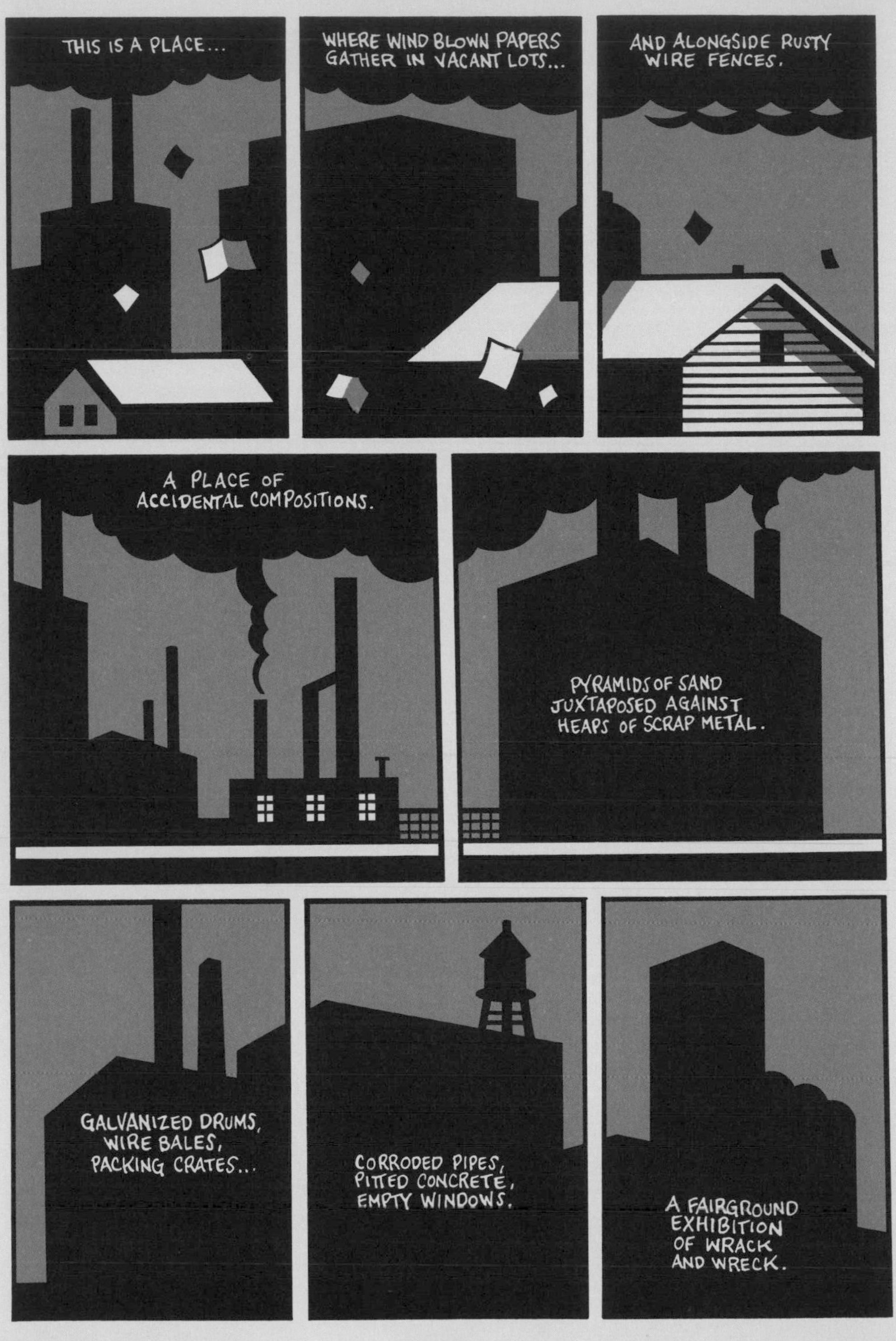

THIS IS A PLACE...
WHERE WIND BLOWN PAPERS GATHER IN VACANT LOTS...
AND ALONGSIDE RUSTY WIRE FENCES.
A PLACE OF ACCIDENTAL COMPOSITIONS.
PYRAMIDS OF SAND JUXTAPOSED AGAINST HEAPS OF SCRAP METAL.
GALVANIZED DRUMS, WIRE BALES, PACKING CRATES...
CORRODED PIPES, PITTED CONCRETE, EMPTY WINDOWS.
A FAIRGROUND EXHIBITION OF WRACK AND WRECK.

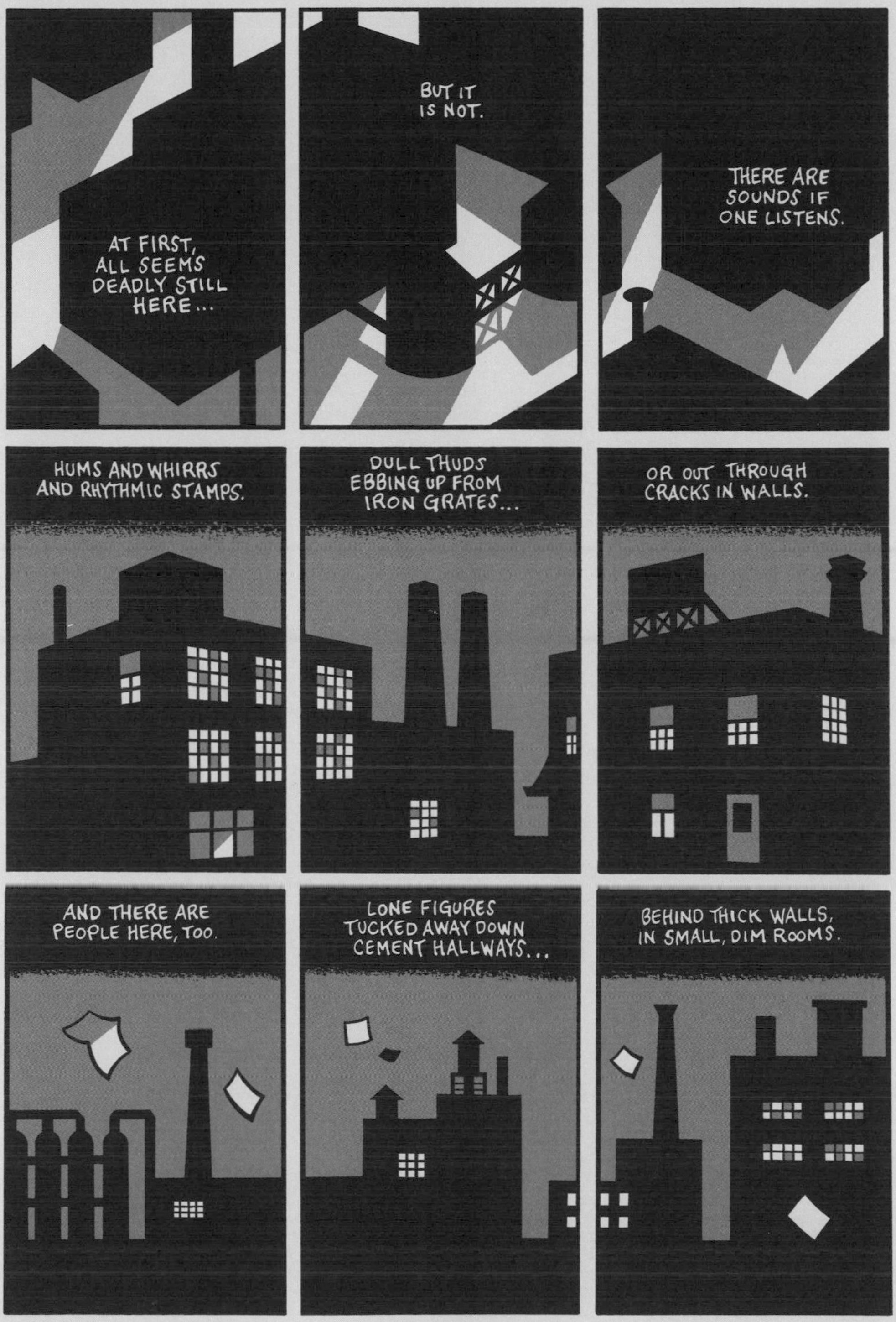
AT FIRST, ALL SEEMS DEADLY STILL HERE...
BUT IT IS NOT.
THERE ARE SOUNDS IF ONE LISTENS.
HUMS AND WHIRRS AND RHYTHMIC STAMPS.
DULL THUDS EBBING UP FROM IRON GRATES...
OR OUT THROUGH CRACKS IN WALLS.
AND THERE ARE PEOPLE HERE, TOO.
LONE FIGURES TUCKED AWAY DOWN CEMENT HALLWAYS...
BEHIND THICK WALLS, IN SMALL, DIM ROOMS.

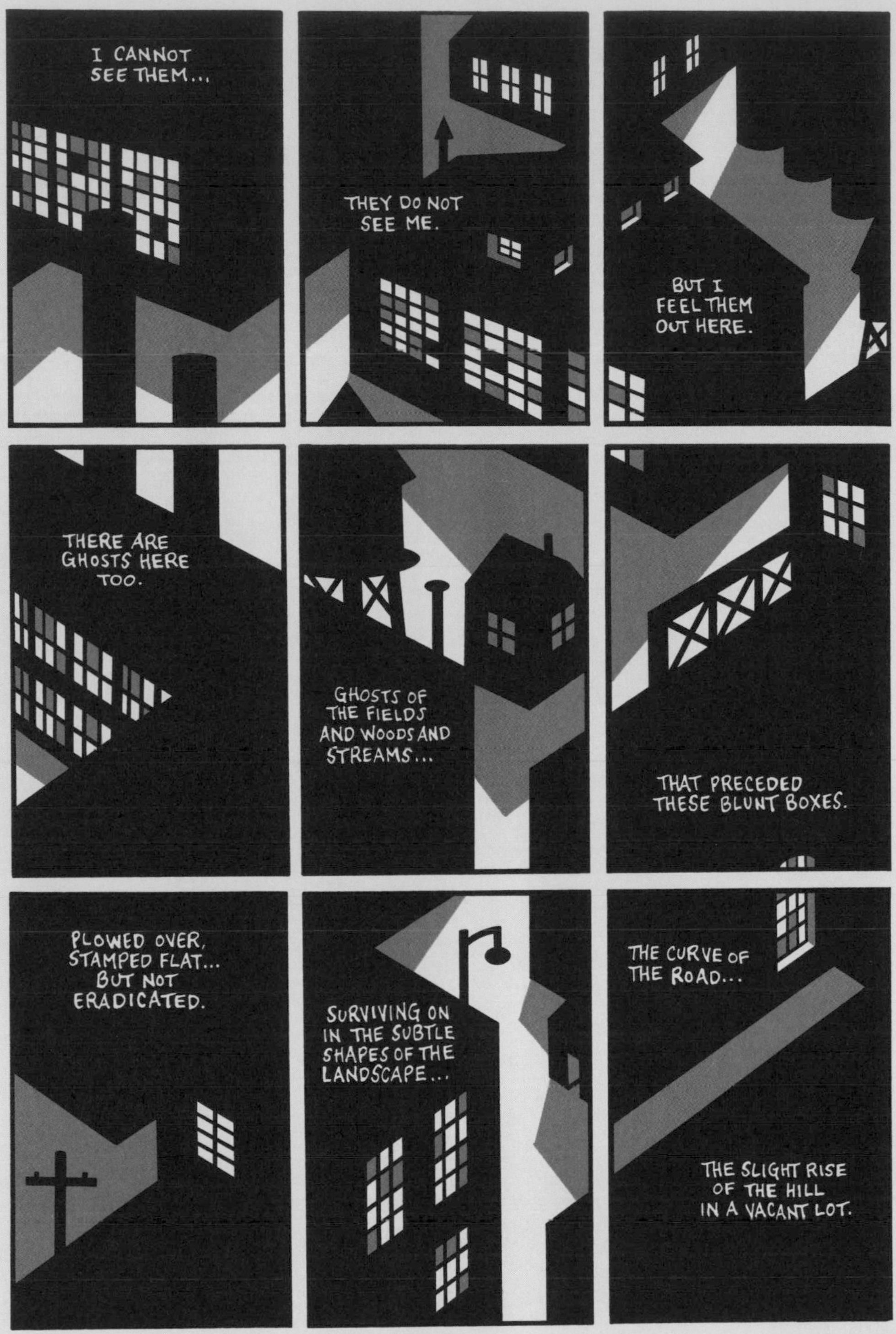
I CANNOT SEE THEM...
THEY DO NOT SEE ME.
BUT I FEEL THEM OUT HERE.
THERE ARE GHOSTS HERE TOO.
GHOSTS OF THE FIELDS AND WOODS AND STREAMS...
THAT PRECEDED THESE BLUNT BOXES.
PLOWED OVER, STAMPED FLAT... BUT NOT ERADICATED.
SURVIVING ON IN THE SUBTLE SHAPES OF THE LANDSCAPE...
THE CURVE OF THE ROAD...
THE SLIGHT RISE OF THE HILL IN A VACANT LOT.

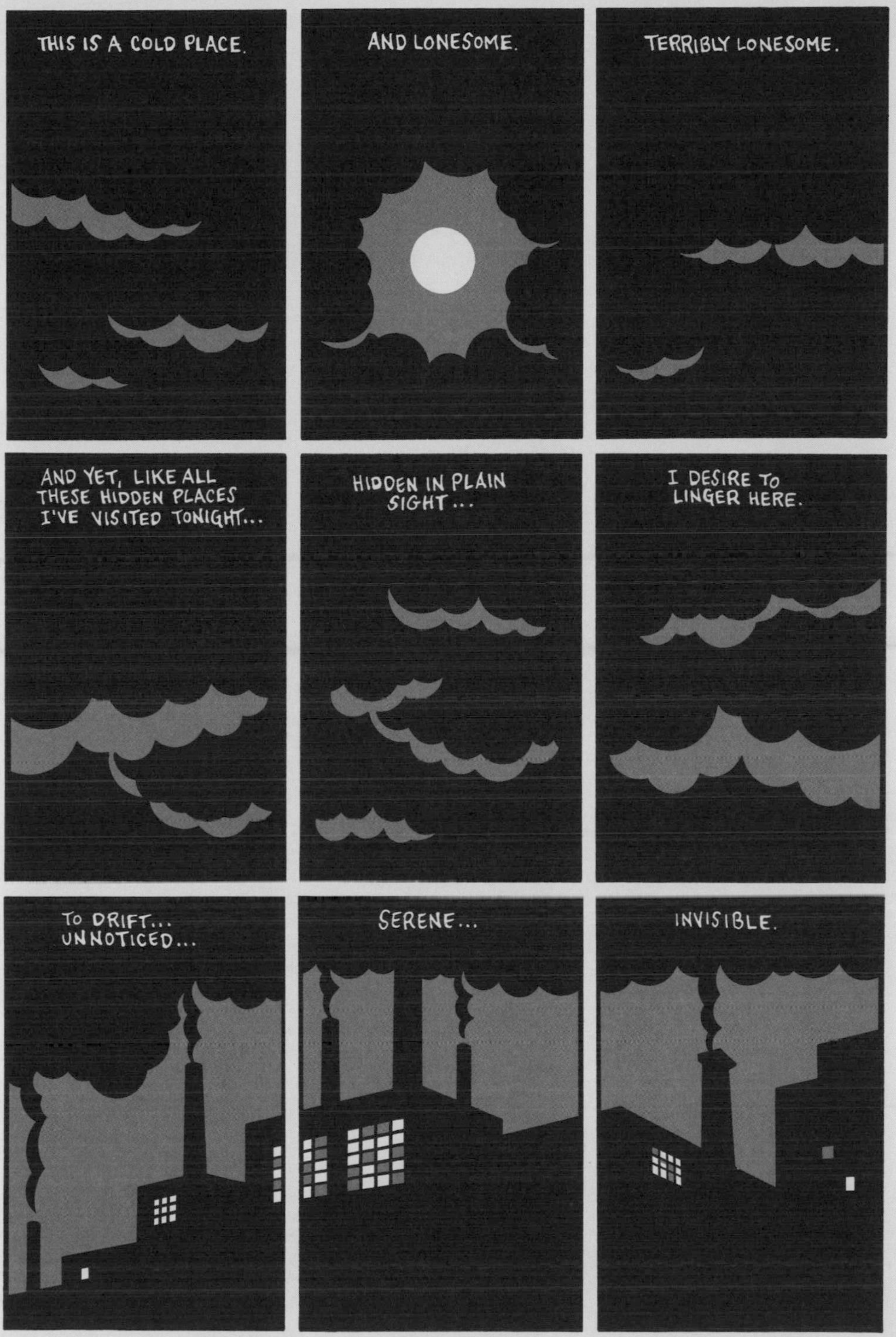
THIS IS A COLD PLACE.
AND LONESOME.
TERRIBLY LONESOME.
AND YET, LIKE ALL THESE HIDDEN PLACES I'VE VISITED TONIGHT...
HIDDEN IN PLAIN SIGHT...
I DESIRE TO LINGER HERE.
TO DRIFT... UNNOTICED...
SERENE...
INVISIBLE.

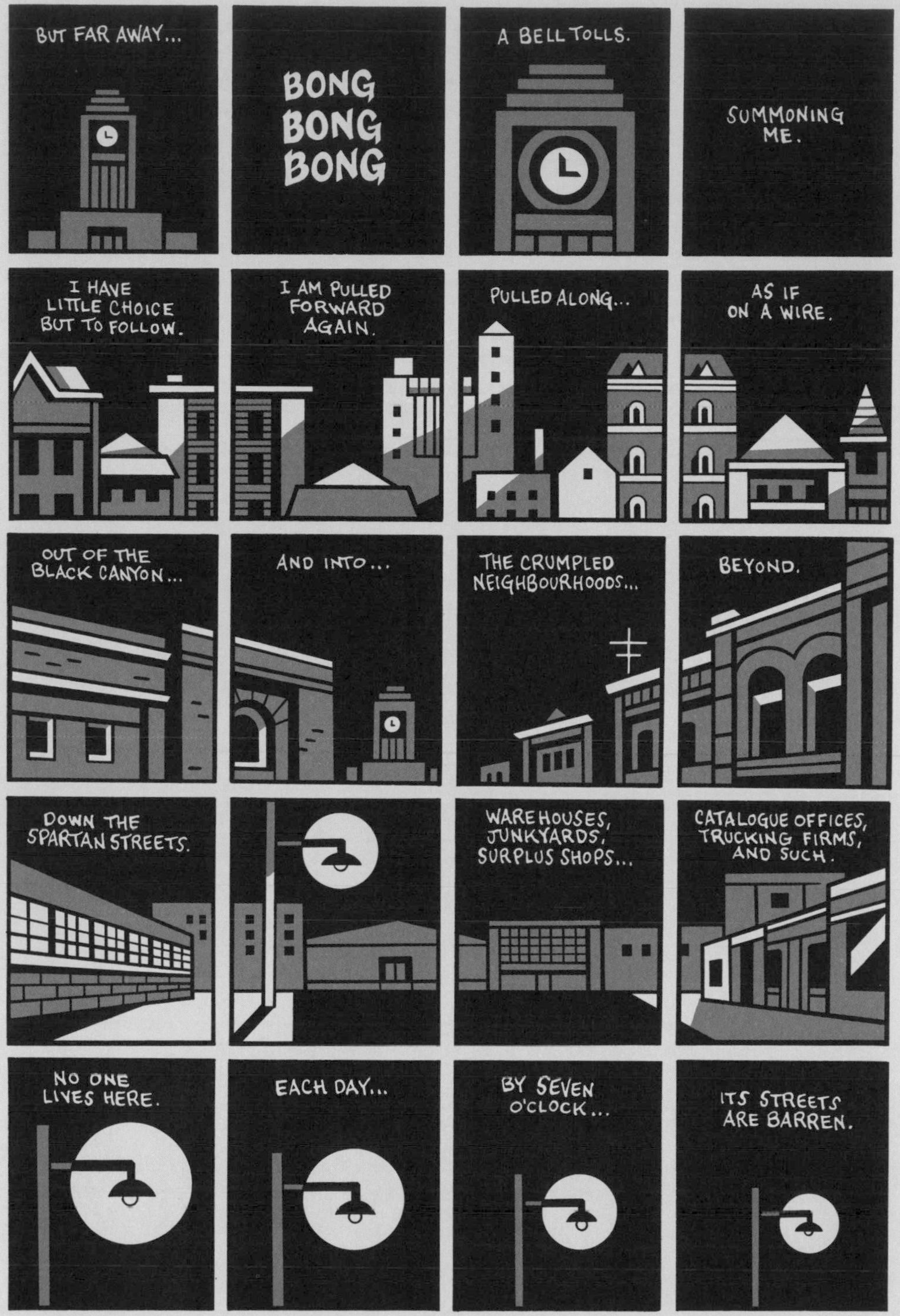
BUT FAR AWAY...
BONG BONG BONG
A BELL TOLLS.
SUMMONING ME.
I HAVE LITTLE CHOICE BUT TO FOLLOW.
I AM PULLED FORWARD AGAIN.
PULLED ALONG...
AS IF ON A WIRE.
OUT OF THE BLACK CANYON...
AND INTO...
THE CRUMPLED NEIGHBOURHOODS...
BEYOND.
DOWN THE SPARTAN STREETS.
WAREHOUSES, JUNKYARDS, SURPLUS SHOPS...
CATALOGUE OFFICES, TRUCKING FIRMS, AND SUCH.
NO ONE LIVES HERE.
EACH DAY...
BY SEVEN O'CLOCK...
ITS STREETS ARE BARREN.

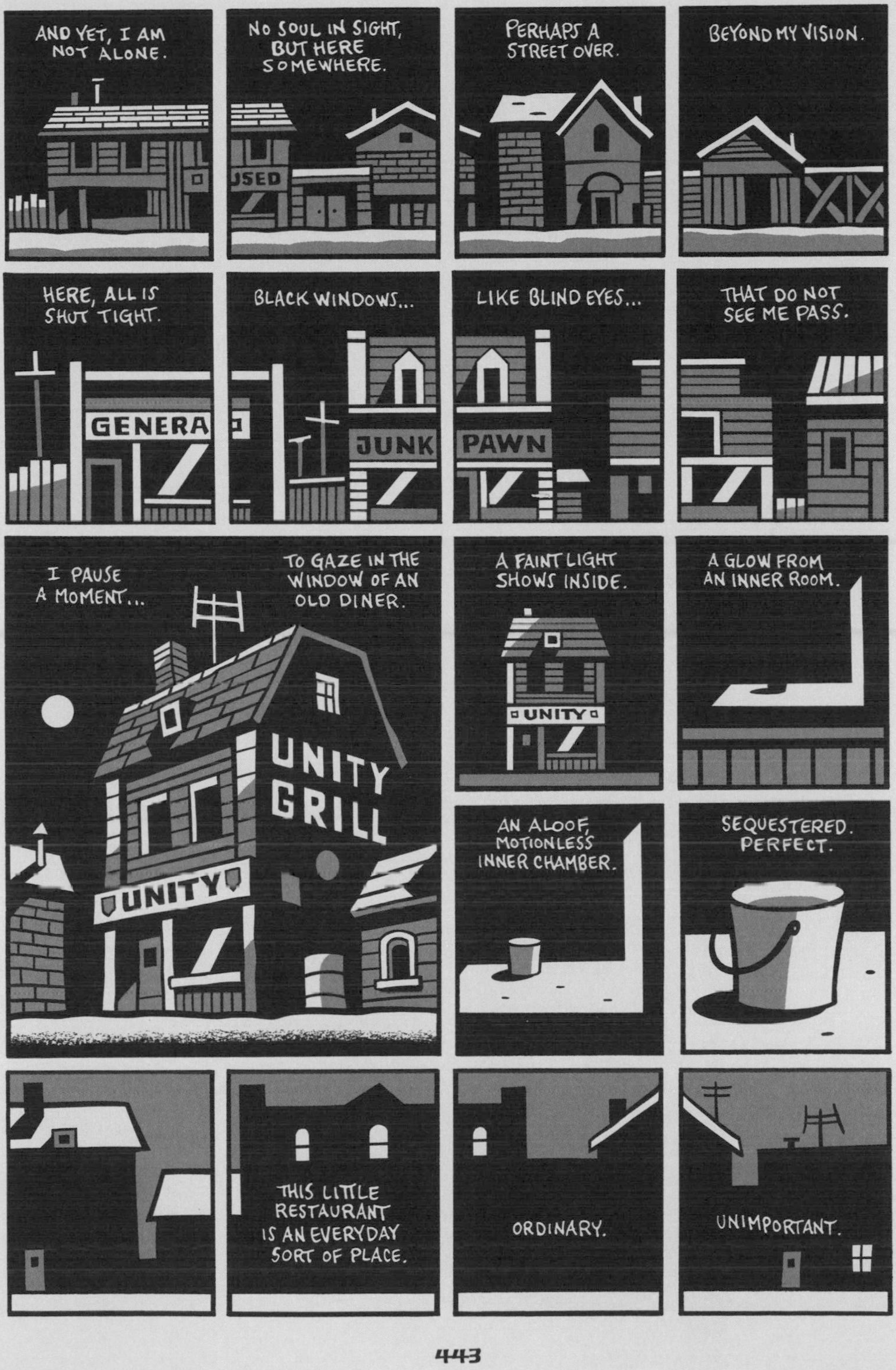
AND YET, I AM NOT ALONE.
NO SOUL IN SIGHT, BUT HERE SOMEWHERE.
PERHAPS A STREET OVER.
BEYOND MY VISION.
HERE, ALL IS SHUT TIGHT.
GENERA
BLACK WINDOWS...
JUNK
LIKE BLIND EYES...
PAWN
THAT DO NOT SEE ME PASS.
I PAUSE A MOMENT...
TO GAZE IN THE WINDOW OF AN OLD DINER.
UNITY GRILL
UNITY
A FAINT LIGHT SHOWS INSIDE.
UNITY
A GLOW FROM AN INNER ROOM.
AN ALOOF, MOTIONLESS INNER CHAMBER.
SEQUESTERED. PERFECT.
THIS LITTLE RESTAURANT IS AN EVERYDAY SORT OF PLACE.
ORDINARY.
UNIMPORTANT.

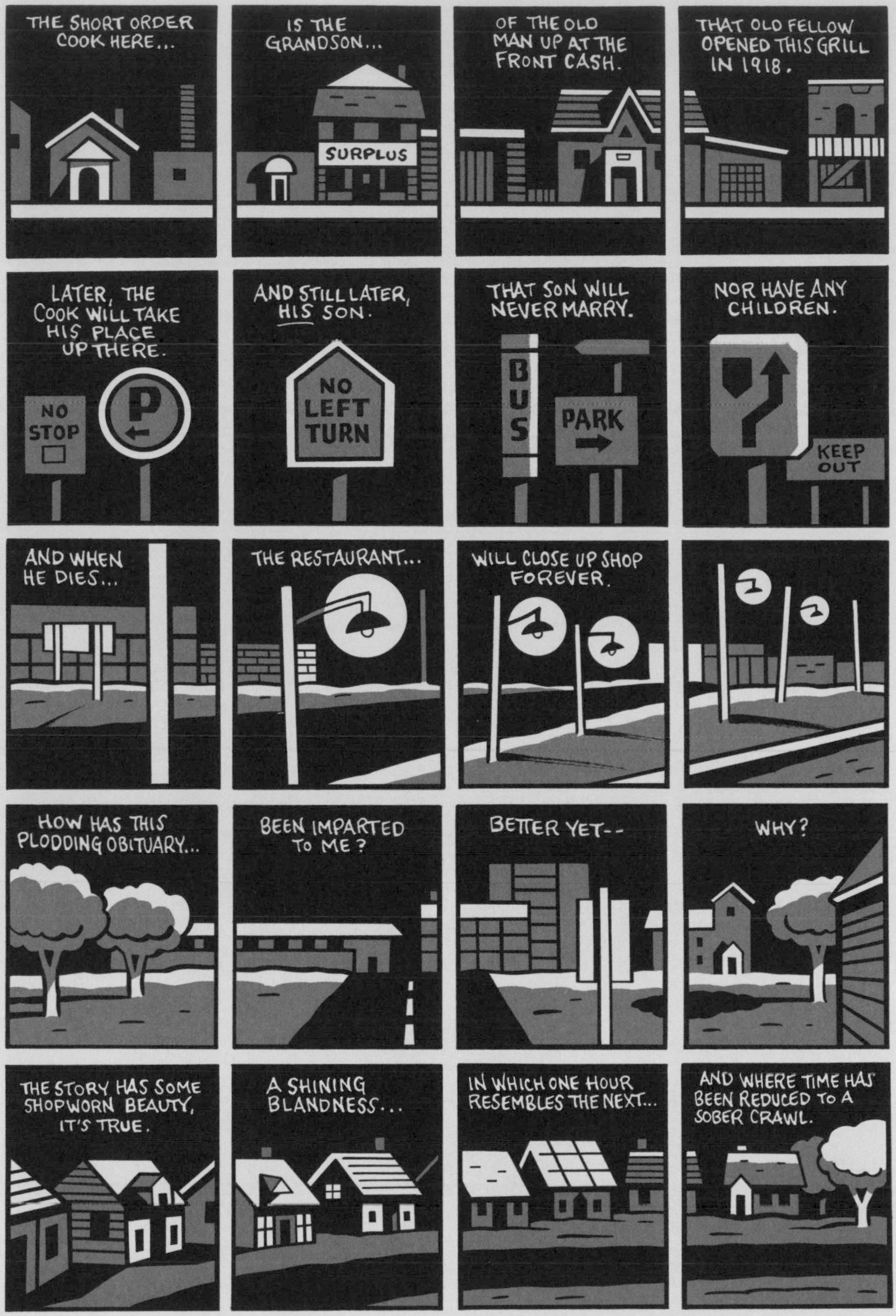
THE SHORT ORDER COOK HERE...
IS THE GRANDSON...
SURPLUS
OF THE OLD MAN UP AT THE FRONT CASH.
THAT OLD FELLOW OPENED THIS GRILL IN 1918.
LATER, THE COOK WILL TAKE HIS PLACE UP THERE.
NO STOP
P
AND STILL LATER, HIS SON.
NO LEFT TURN
THAT SON WILL NEVER MARRY.
BUS
PARK
NOR HAVE ANY CHILDREN.
KEEP OUT
AND WHEN HE DIES...
THE RESTAURANT...
WILL CLOSE UP SHOP FOREVER.
HOW HAS THIS PLODDING OBITUARY...
BEEN IMPARTED TO ME?
BETTER YET--
WHY?
THE STORY HAS SOME SHOPWORN BEAUTY, IT'S TRUE.
A SHINING BLANDNESS...
IN WHICH ONE HOUR RESEMBLES THE NEXT...
AND WHERE TIME HAS BEEN REDUCED TO A SOBER CRAWL.

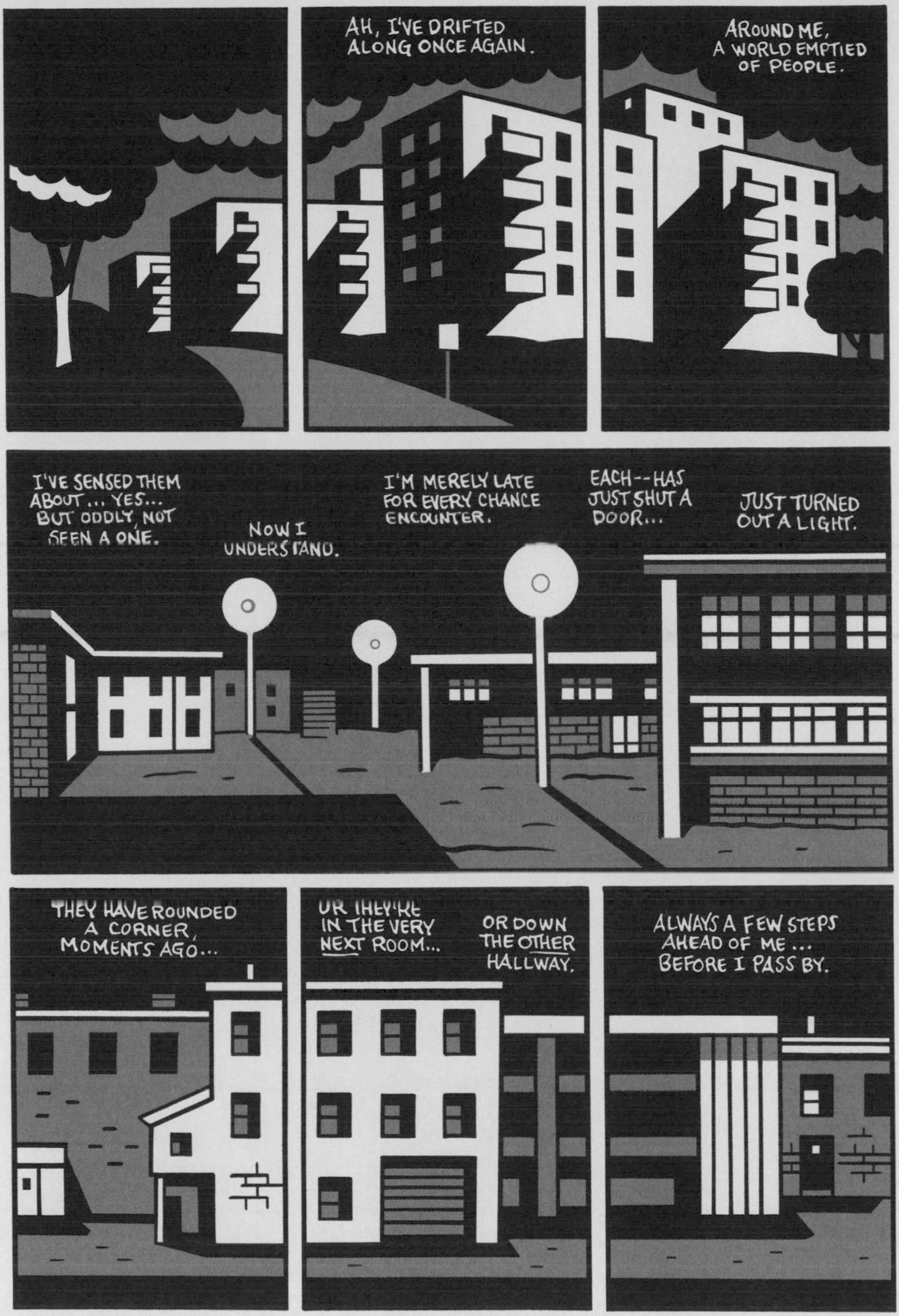
AH, I'VE DRIFTED ALONG ONCE AGAIN.
AROUND ME, A WORLD EMPTIED OF PEOPLE.
I'VE SENSED THEM ABOUT... YES... BUT ODDLY, NOT SEEN A ONE.
NOW I UNDERSTAND.
I'M MERELY LATE FOR EVERY CHANCE ENCOUNTER.
EACH--HAS JUST SHUT A DOOR...
JUST TURNED OUT A LIGHT.
THEY HAVE ROUNDED A CORNER, MOMENTS AGO...
OR THEY'RE IN THE VERY NEXT ROOM...
OR DOWN THE OTHER HALLWAY.
ALWAYS A FEW STEPS AHEAD OF ME... BEFORE I PASS BY.

NOW...

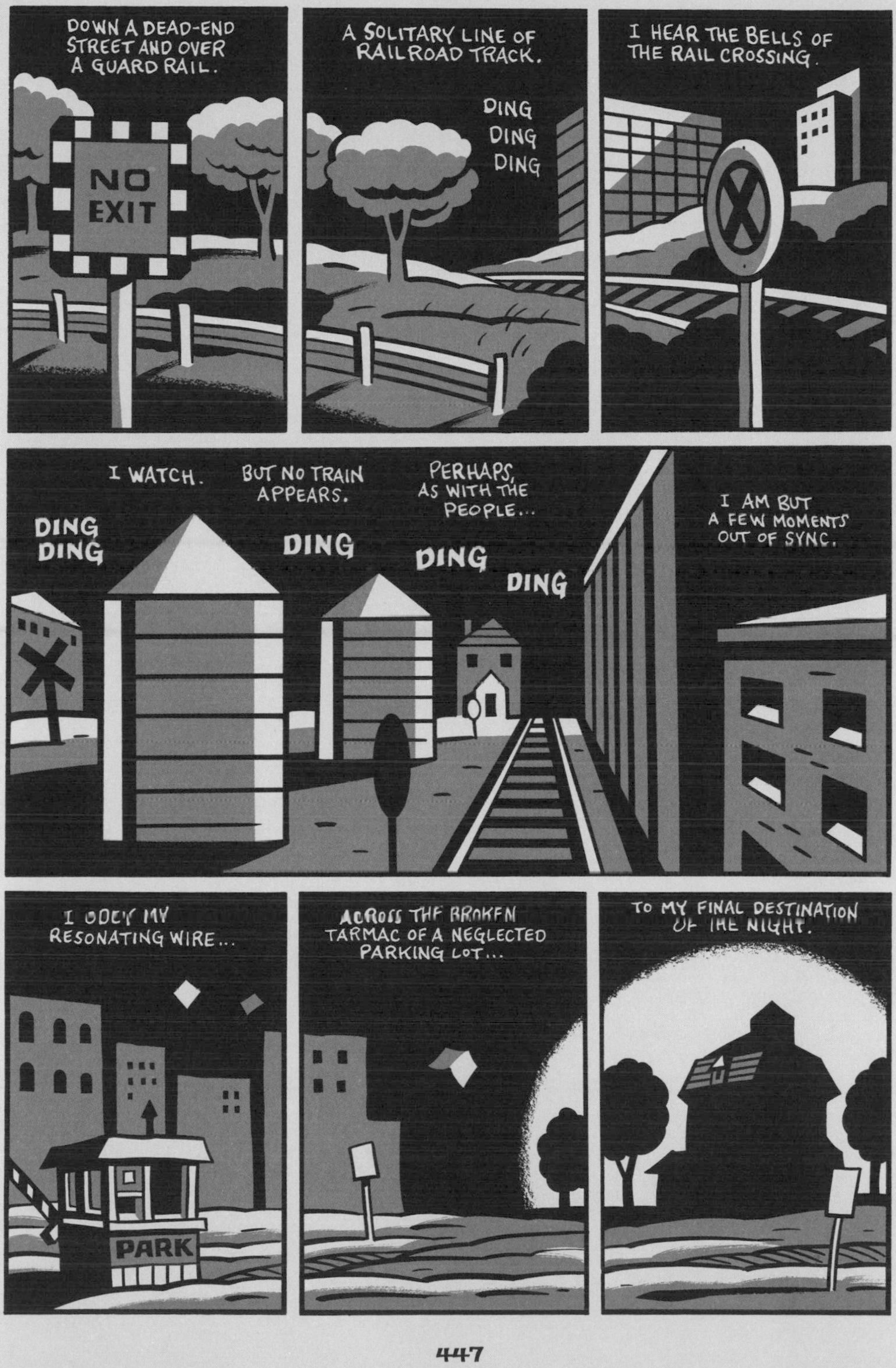
DOWN A DEAD-END STREET AND OVER A GUARD RAIL.
NO EXIT
A SOLITARY LINE OF RAILROAD TRACK.
DING DING DING
I HEAR THE BELLS OF THE RAIL CROSSING.
I WATCH.
DING DING
BUT NO TRAIN APPEARS.
DING
PERHAPS, AS WITH THE PEOPLE...
DING
DING
I AM BUT A FEW MOMENTS OUT OF SYNC.
I OBEY MY RESONATING WIRE...
PARK
ACROSS THE BROKEN TARMAC OF A NEGLECTED PARKING LOT...
TO MY FINAL DESTINATION OF THE NIGHT.

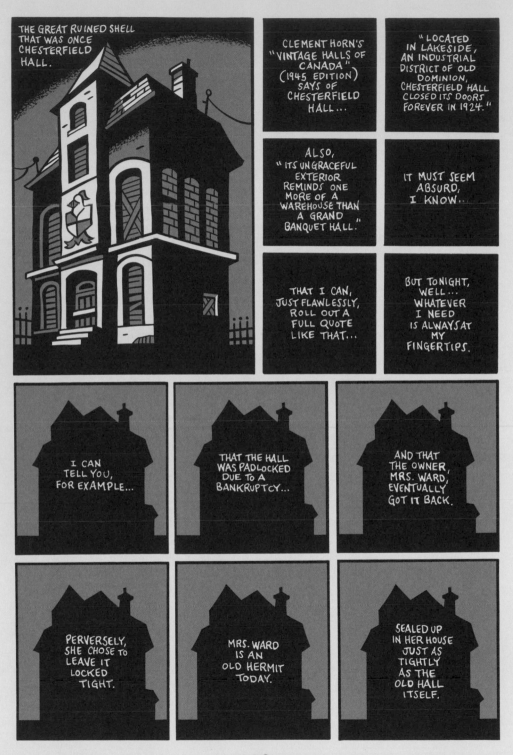

THE GREAT RUINED SHELL THAT WAS ONCE CHESTERFIELD HALL.

CLEMENT HORN'S "VINTAGE HALLS OF CANADA" (1945 EDITION) SAYS OF CHESTERFIELD HALL...

"LOCATED IN LAKESIDE, AN INDUSTRIAL DISTRICT OF OLD DOMINION, CHESTERFIELD HALL CLOSED ITS DOORS FOREVER IN 1924."

ALSO, "ITS UNGRACEFUL EXTERIOR REMINDS ONE MORE OF A WAREHOUSE THAN A GRAND BANQUET HALL."

IT MUST SEEM ABSURD, I KNOW...

THAT I CAN, JUST FLAWLESSLY, ROLL OUT A FULL QUOTE LIKE THAT...

BUT TONIGHT, WELL... WHATEVER I NEED IS ALWAYS AT MY FINGERTIPS.

I CAN TELL YOU, FOR EXAMPLE...

THAT THE HALL WAS PADLOCKED DUE TO A BANKRUPTCY...

AND THAT THE OWNER, MRS. WARD, EVENTUALLY GOT IT BACK.

PERVERSELY, SHE CHOSE TO LEAVE IT LOCKED TIGHT.

MRS. WARD IS AN OLD HERMIT TODAY.

SEALED UP IN HER HOUSE JUST AS TIGHTLY AS THE OLD HALL ITSELF.

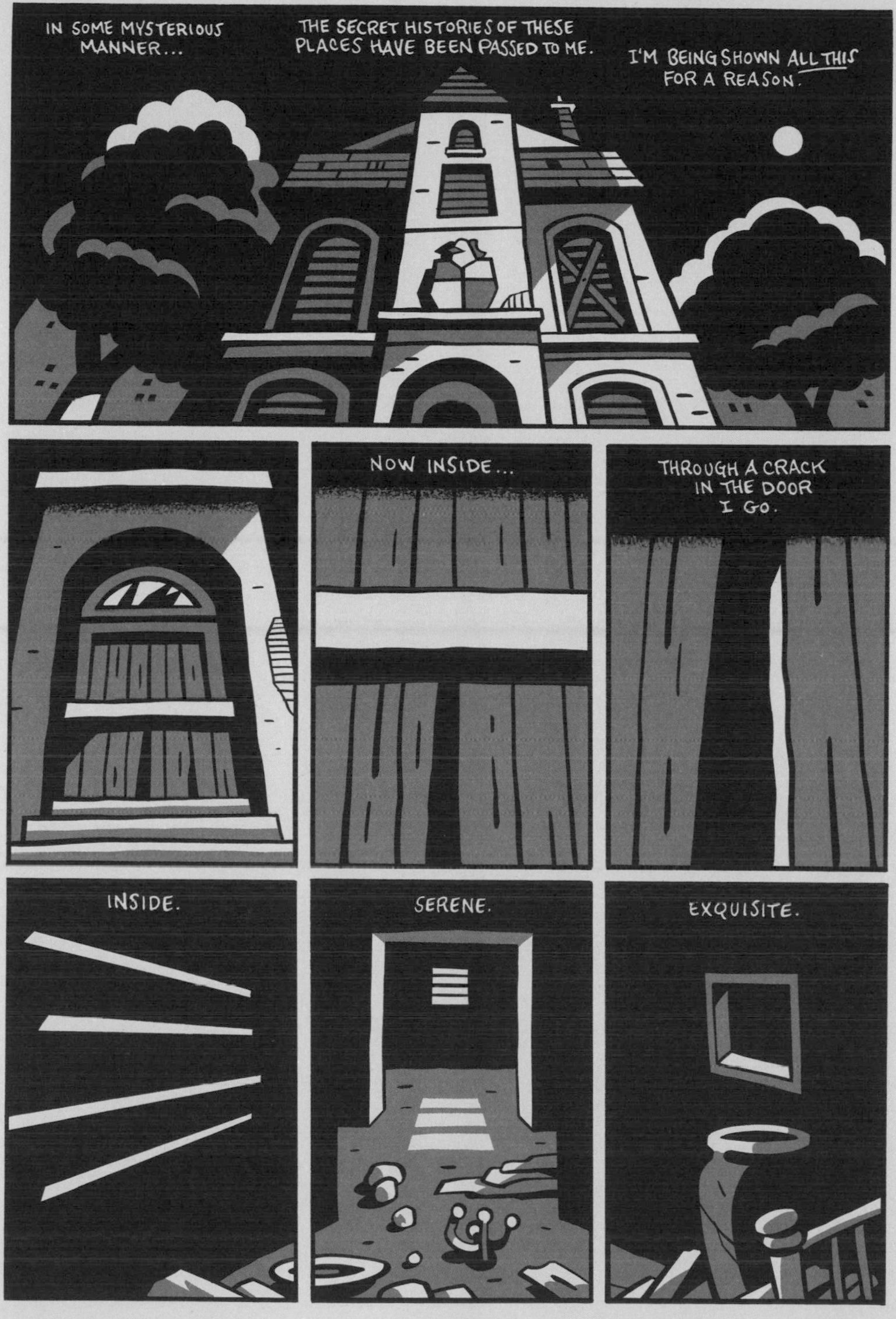
IN SOME MYSTERIOUS MANNER...
THE SECRET HISTORIES OF THESE PLACES HAVE BEEN PASSED TO ME.
I'M BEING SHOWN ALL THIS FOR A REASON.
NOW INSIDE...
THROUGH A CRACK IN THE DOOR I GO.
INSIDE.
SERENE.
EXQUISITE.

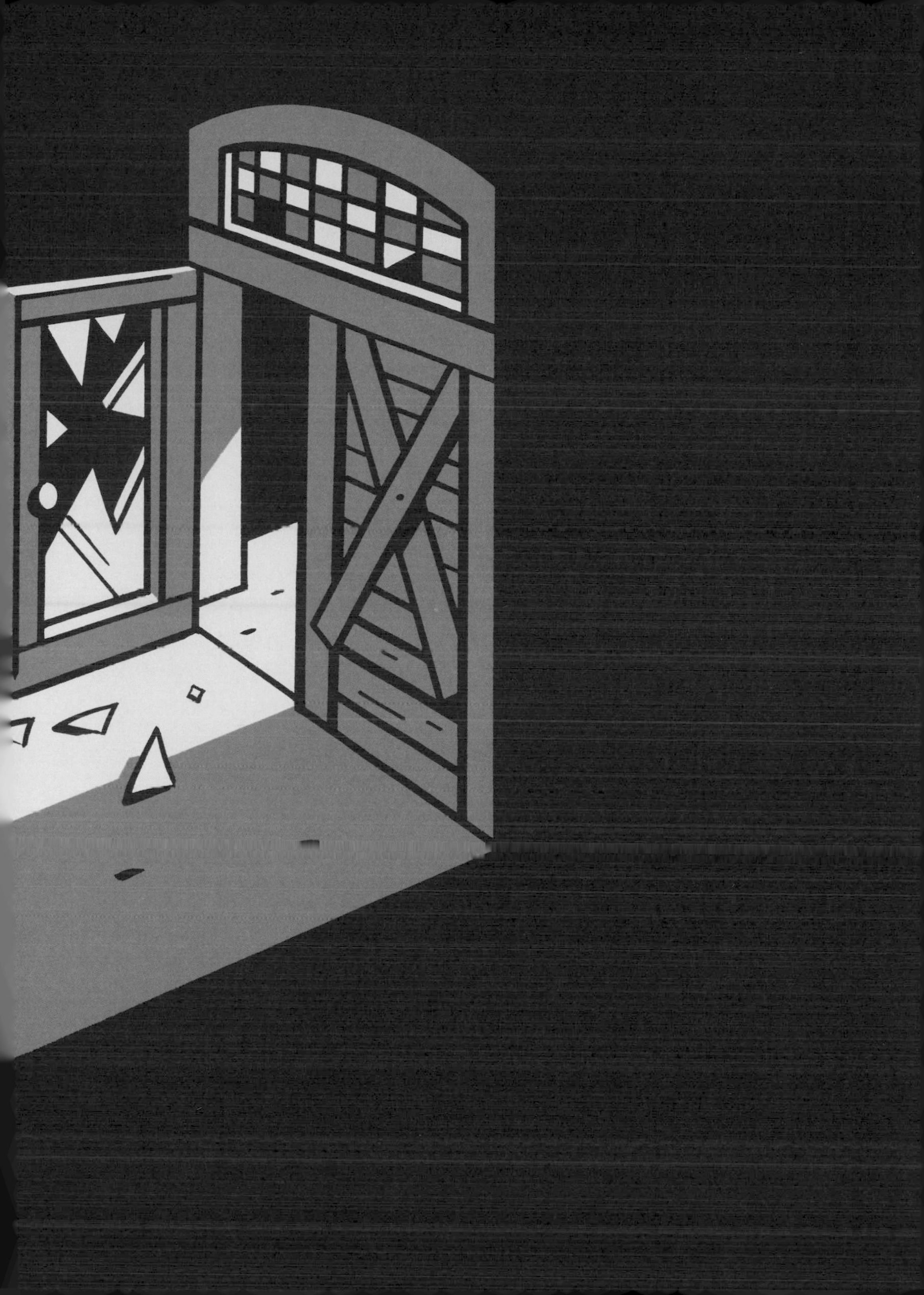

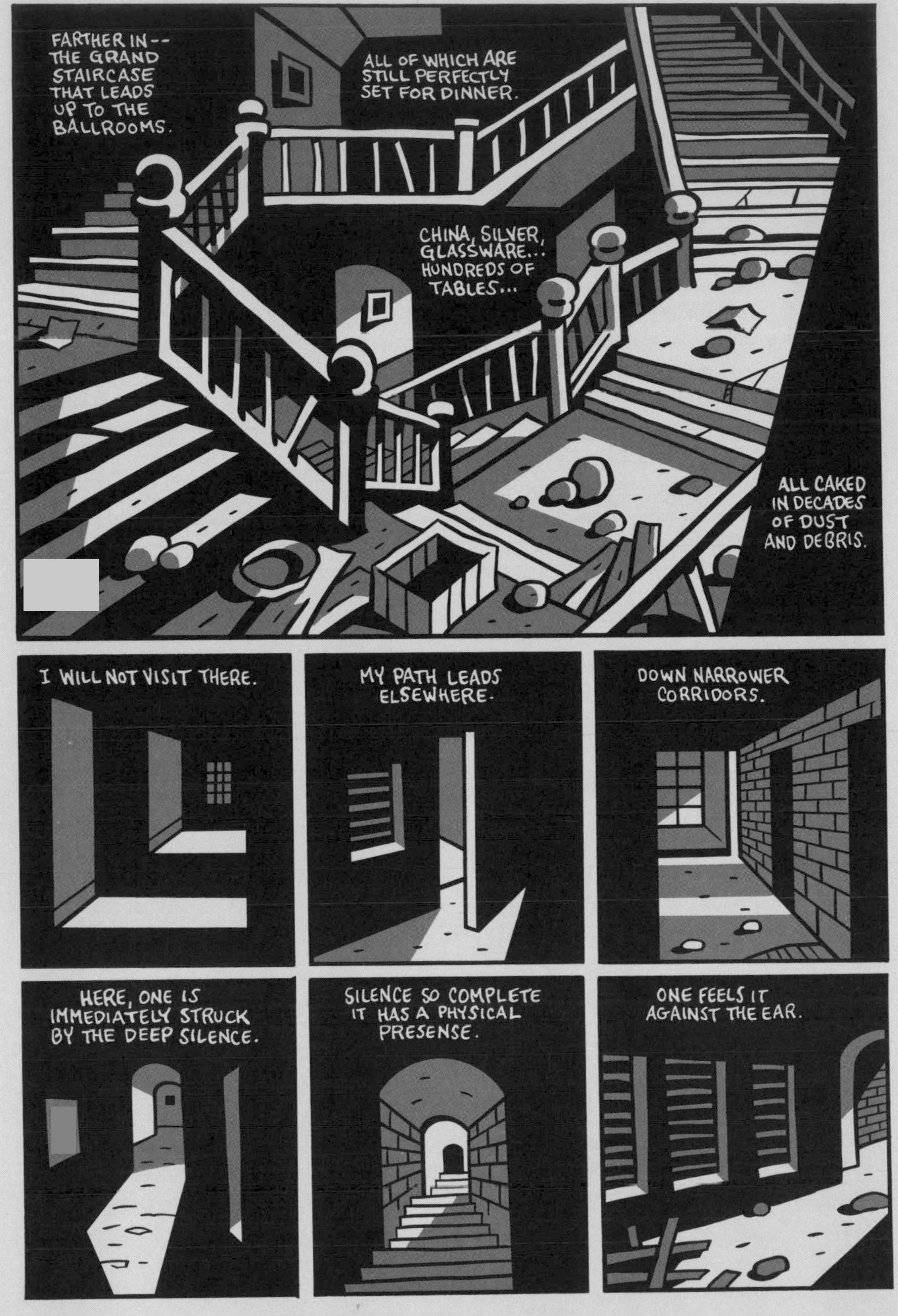
FARTHER IN-- THE GRAND STAIRCASE THAT LEADS UP TO THE BALLROOMS.
ALL OF WHICH ARE STILL PERFECTLY SET FOR DINNER.
CHINA, SILVER, GLASSWARE... HUNDREDS OF TABLES...
ALL CAKED IN DECADES OF DUST AND DEBRIS.
I WILL NOT VISIT THERE.
MY PATH LEADS ELSEWHERE.
DOWN NARROWER CORRIDORS.
HERE, ONE IS IMMEDIATELY STRUCK BY THE DEEP SILENCE.
SILENCE SO COMPLETE IT HAS A PHYSICAL PRESENSE.
ONE FEELS IT AGAINST THE EAR.

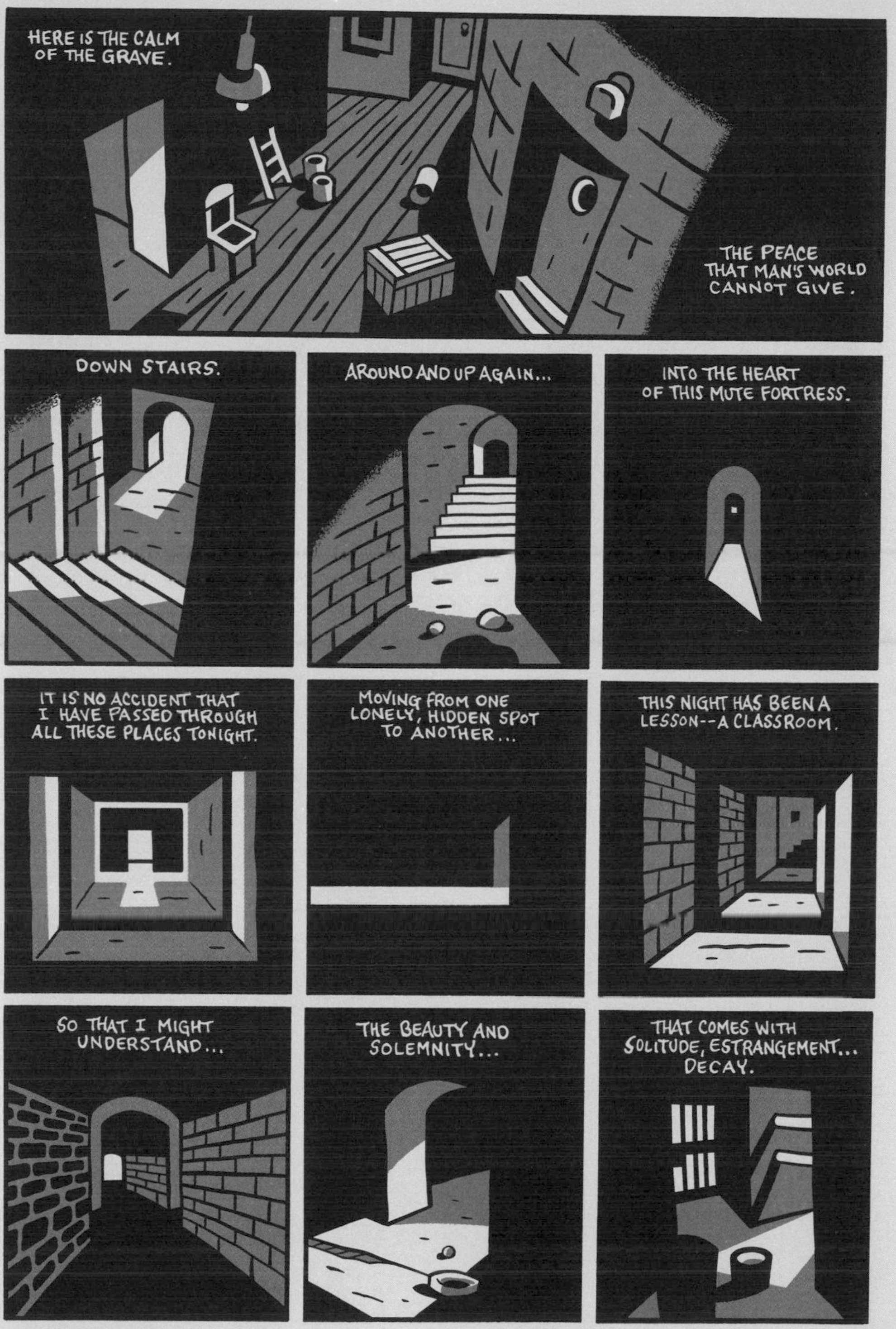
HERE IS THE CALM OF THE GRAVE.
THE PEACE THAT MAN'S WORLD CANNOT GIVE.
DOWN STAIRS.
AROUND AND UP AGAIN...
INTO THE HEART OF THIS MUTE FORTRESS.
IT IS NO ACCIDENT THAT I HAVE PASSED THROUGH ALL THESE PLACES TONIGHT.
MOVING FROM ONE LONELY, HIDDEN SPOT TO ANOTHER...
THIS NIGHT HAS BEEN A LESSON--A CLASSROOM.
SO THAT I MIGHT UNDERSTAND...
THE BEAUTY AND SOLEMNITY...
THAT COMES WITH SOLITUDE, ESTRANGEMENT... DECAY.

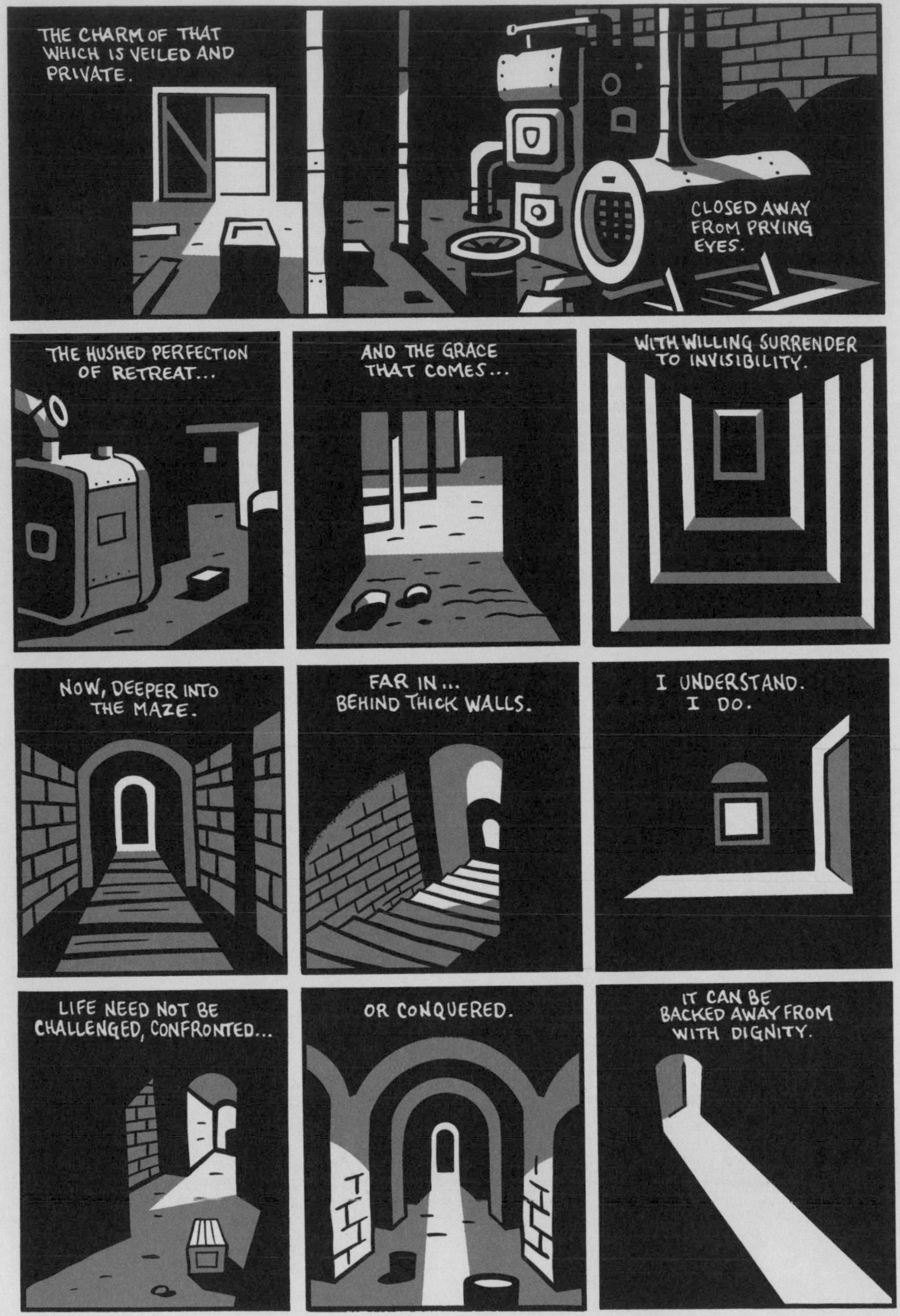
THE CHARM OF THAT WHICH IS VEILED AND PRIVATE.
CLOSED AWAY FROM PRYING EYES.
THE HUSHED PERFECTION OF RETREAT...
AND THE GRACE THAT COMES...
WITH WILLING SURRENDER TO INVISIBILITY.
NOW, DEEPER INTO THE MAZE.
FAR IN... BEHIND THICK WALLS.
I UNDERSTAND. I DO.
LIFE NEED NOT BE CHALLENGED, CONFRONTED...
OR CONQUERED.
IT CAN BE BACKED AWAY FROM WITH DIGNITY.

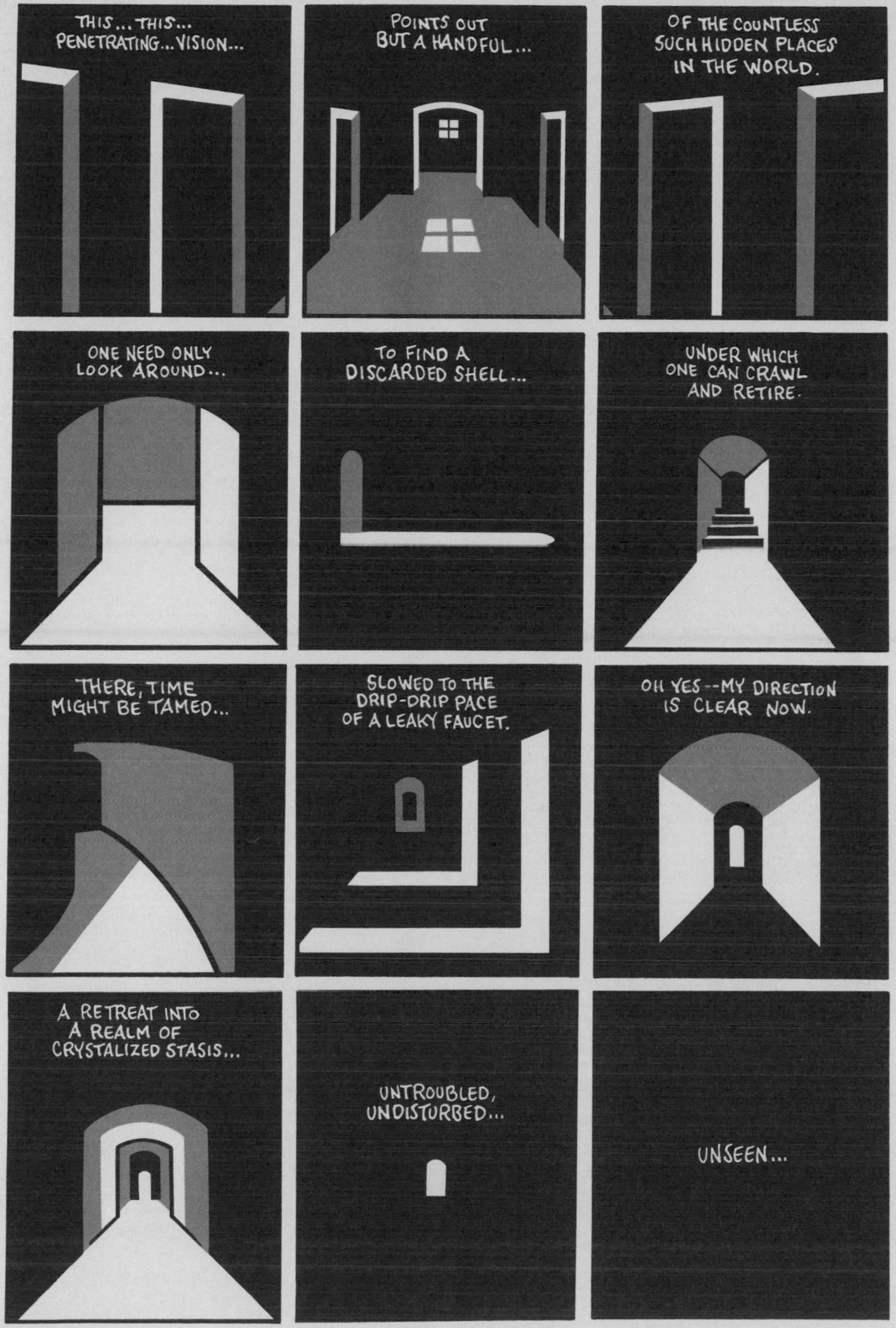
THIS... THIS...
PENETRATING... VISION...
POINTS OUT
BUT A HANDFUL...
OF THE COUNTLESS
SUCH HIDDEN PLACES
IN THE WORLD.
ONE NEED ONLY
LOOK AROUND...
TO FIND A
DISCARDED SHELL...
UNDER WHICH
ONE CAN CRAWL
AND RETIRE.
THERE, TIME
MIGHT BE TAMED...
SLOWED TO THE
DRIP-DRIP PACE
OF A LEAKY FAUCET.
OH YES--MY DIRECTION
IS CLEAR NOW.
A RETREAT INTO
A REALM OF
CRYSTALIZED STASIS...
UNTROUBLED,
UNDISTURBED...
UNSEEN...

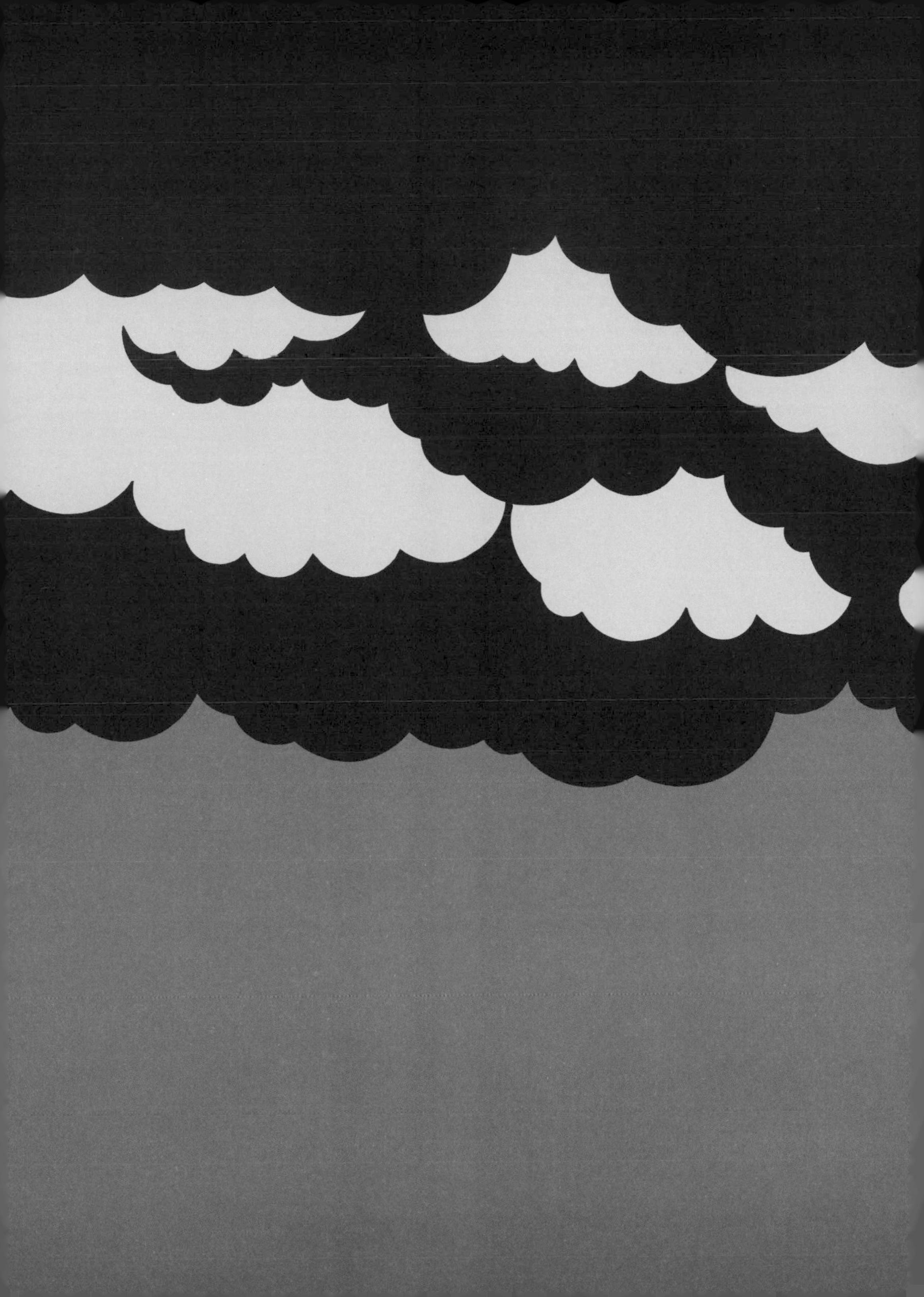

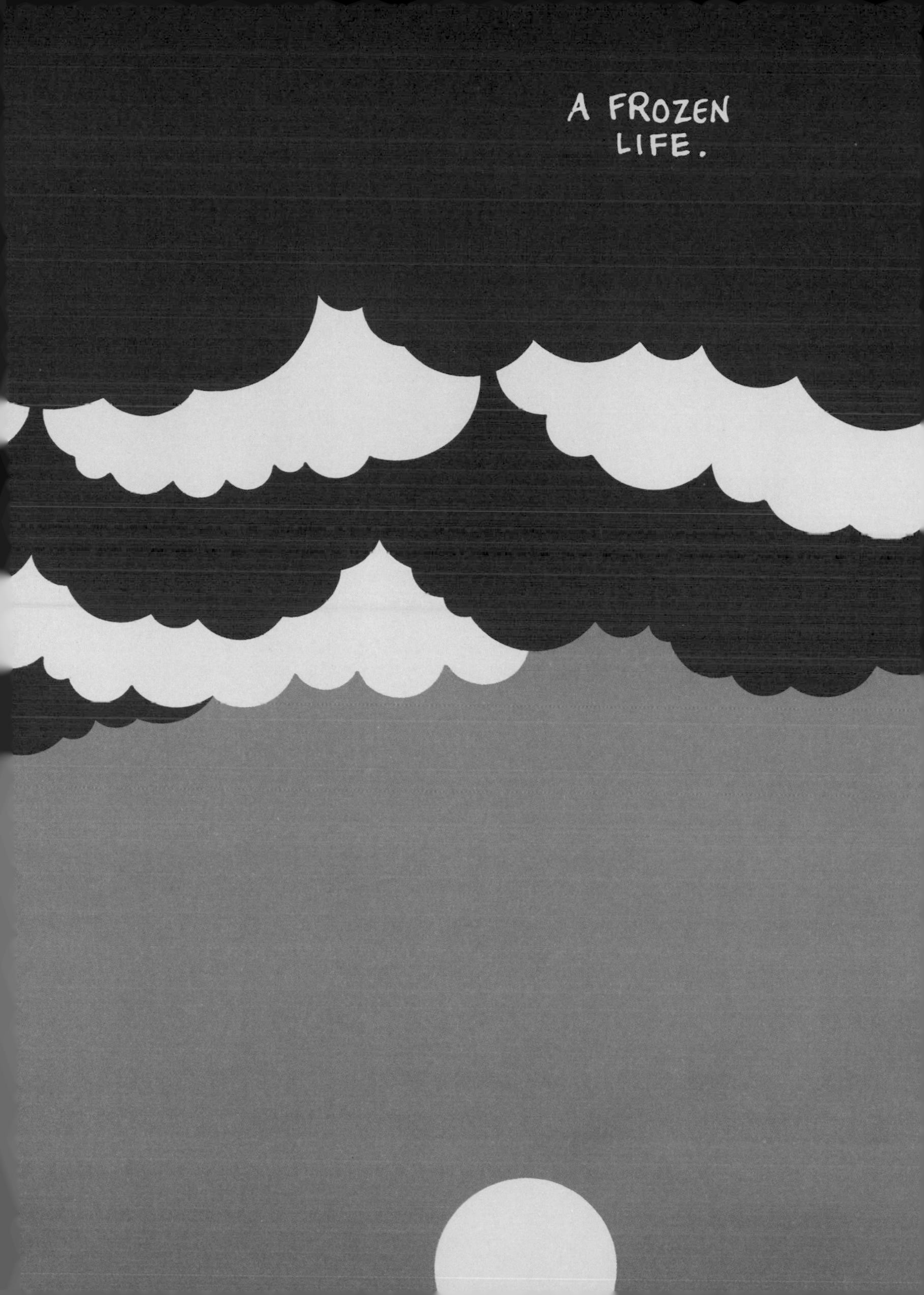

A FROZEN
LIFE.

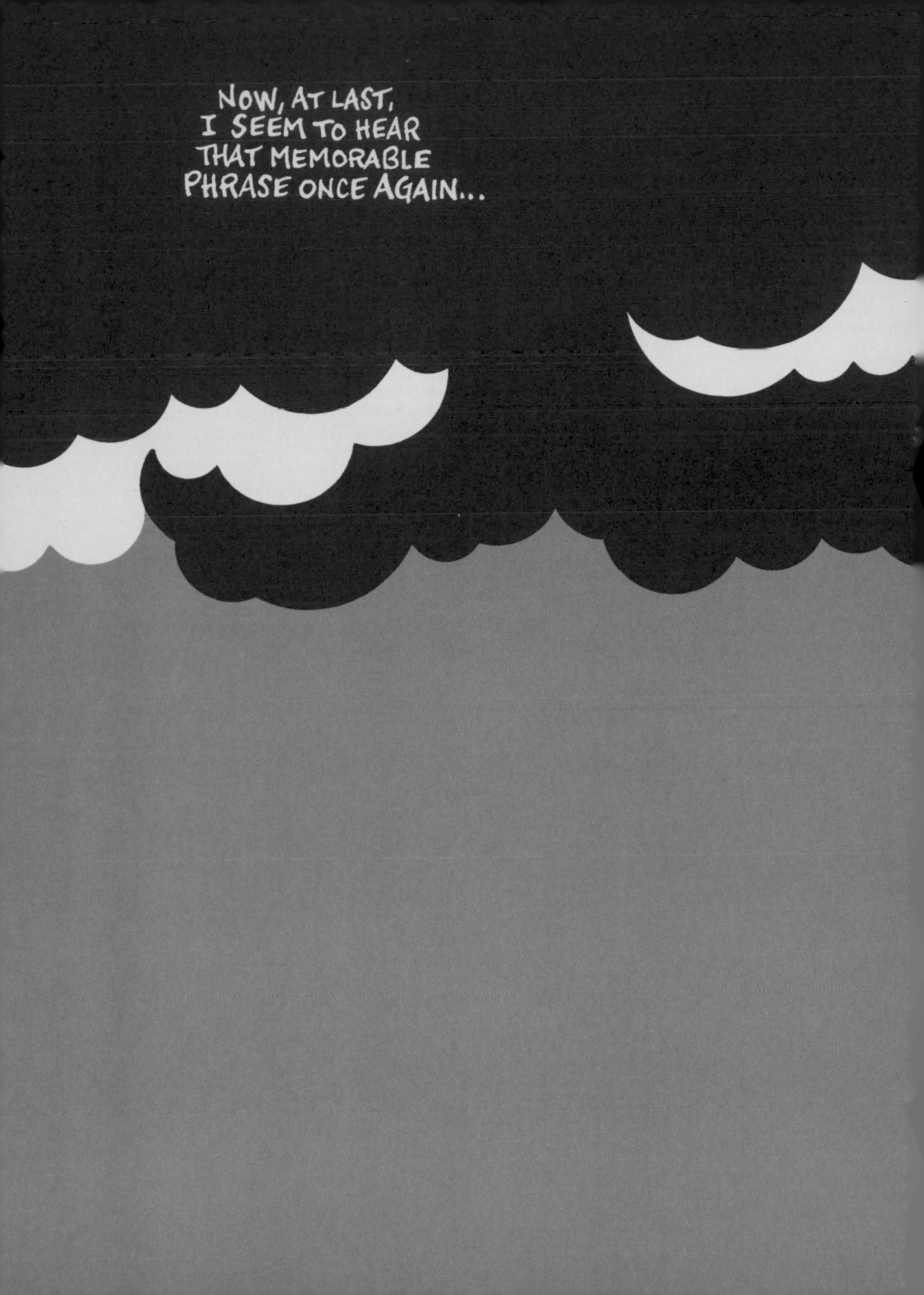
NOW, AT LAST, I SEEM TO HEAR THAT MEMORABLE PHRASE ONCE AGAIN...

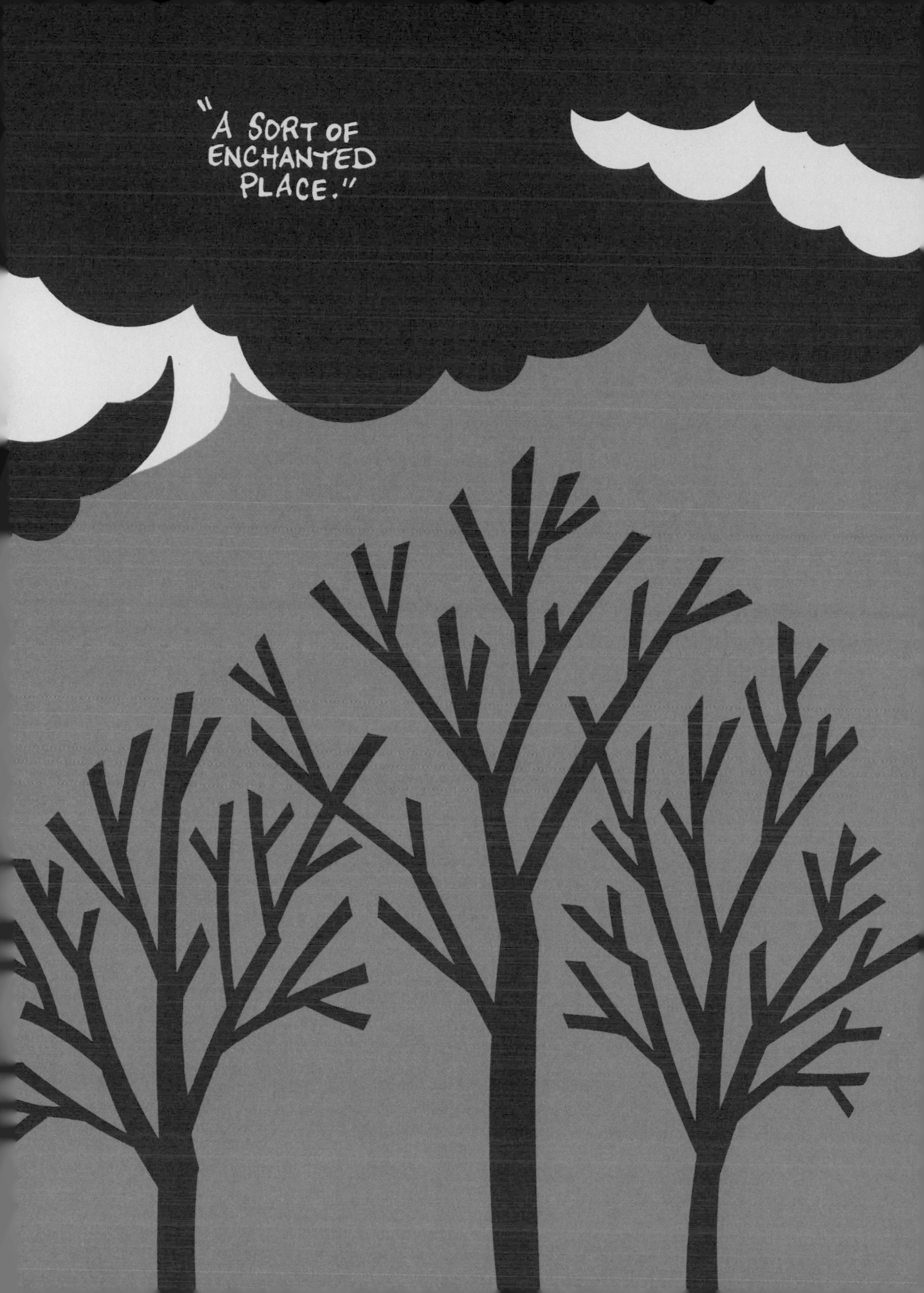
"A SORT OF ENCHANTED PLACE."

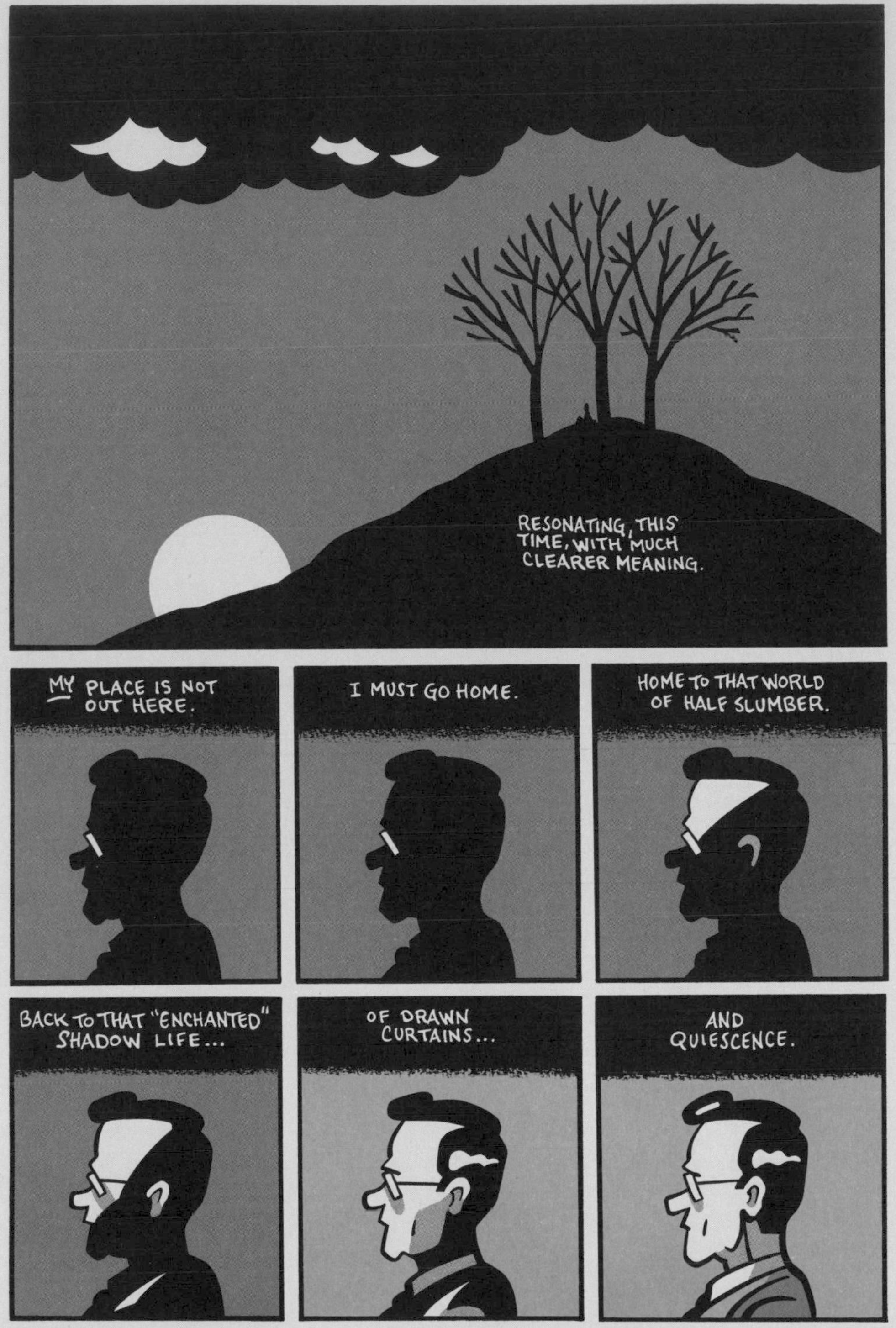
RESONATING, THIS TIME, WITH MUCH CLEARER MEANING.
MY PLACE IS NOT OUT HERE.
I MUST GO HOME.
HOME TO THAT WORLD OF HALF SLUMBER.
BACK TO THAT "ENCHANTED" SHADOW LIFE...
OF DRAWN CURTAINS...
AND QUIESCENCE.

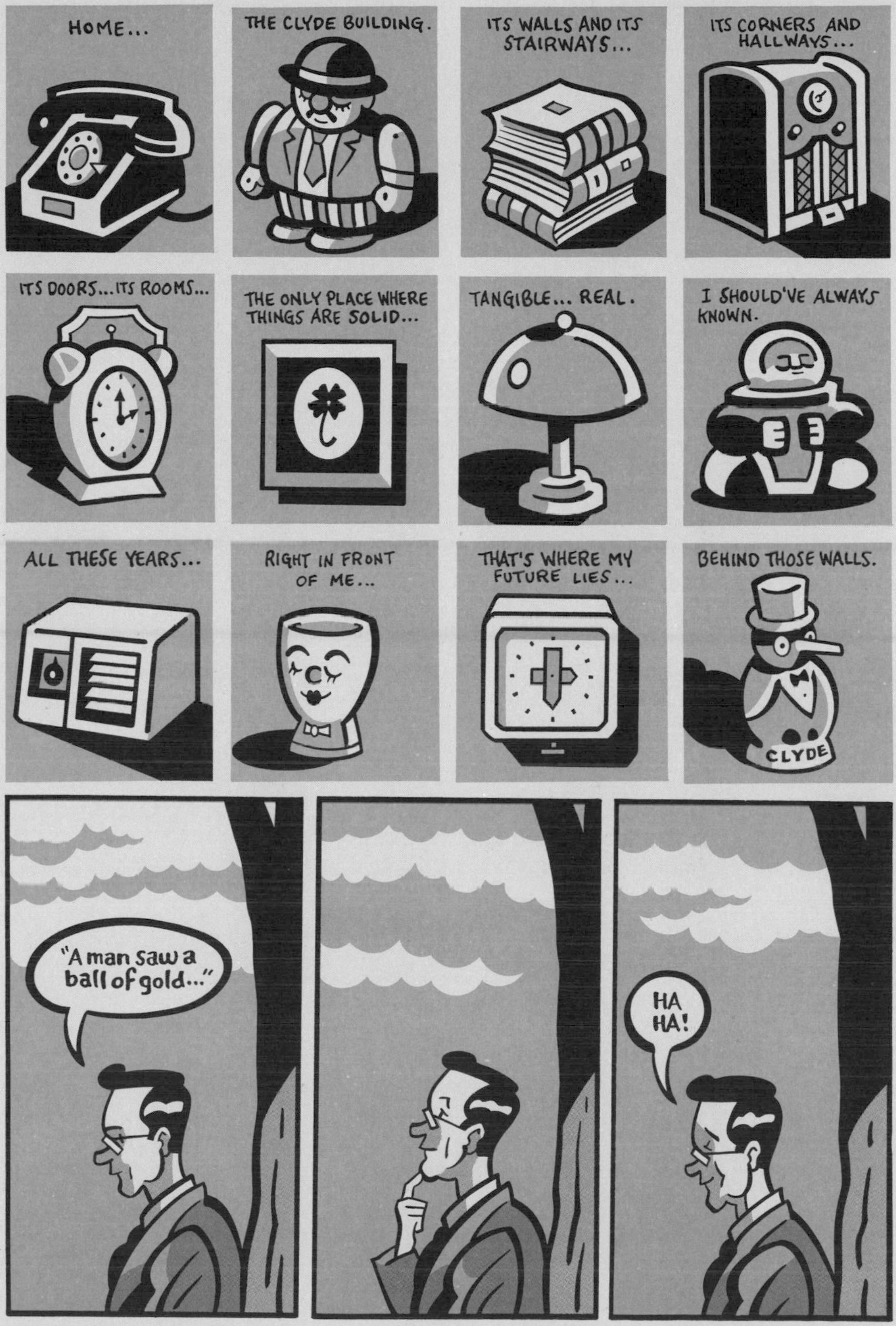

HOME...
THE CLYDE BUILDING.
ITS WALLS AND ITS STAIRWAYS...
ITS CORNERS AND HALLWAYS...
ITS DOORS... ITS ROOMS...
THE ONLY PLACE WHERE THINGS ARE SOLID...
TANGIBLE... REAL.
I SHOULD'VE ALWAYS KNOWN.
ALL THESE YEARS...
RIGHT IN FRONT OF ME...
THAT'S WHERE MY FUTURE LIES...
BEHIND THOSE WALLS.
CLYDE
"A man saw a ball of gold..."
HA HA!

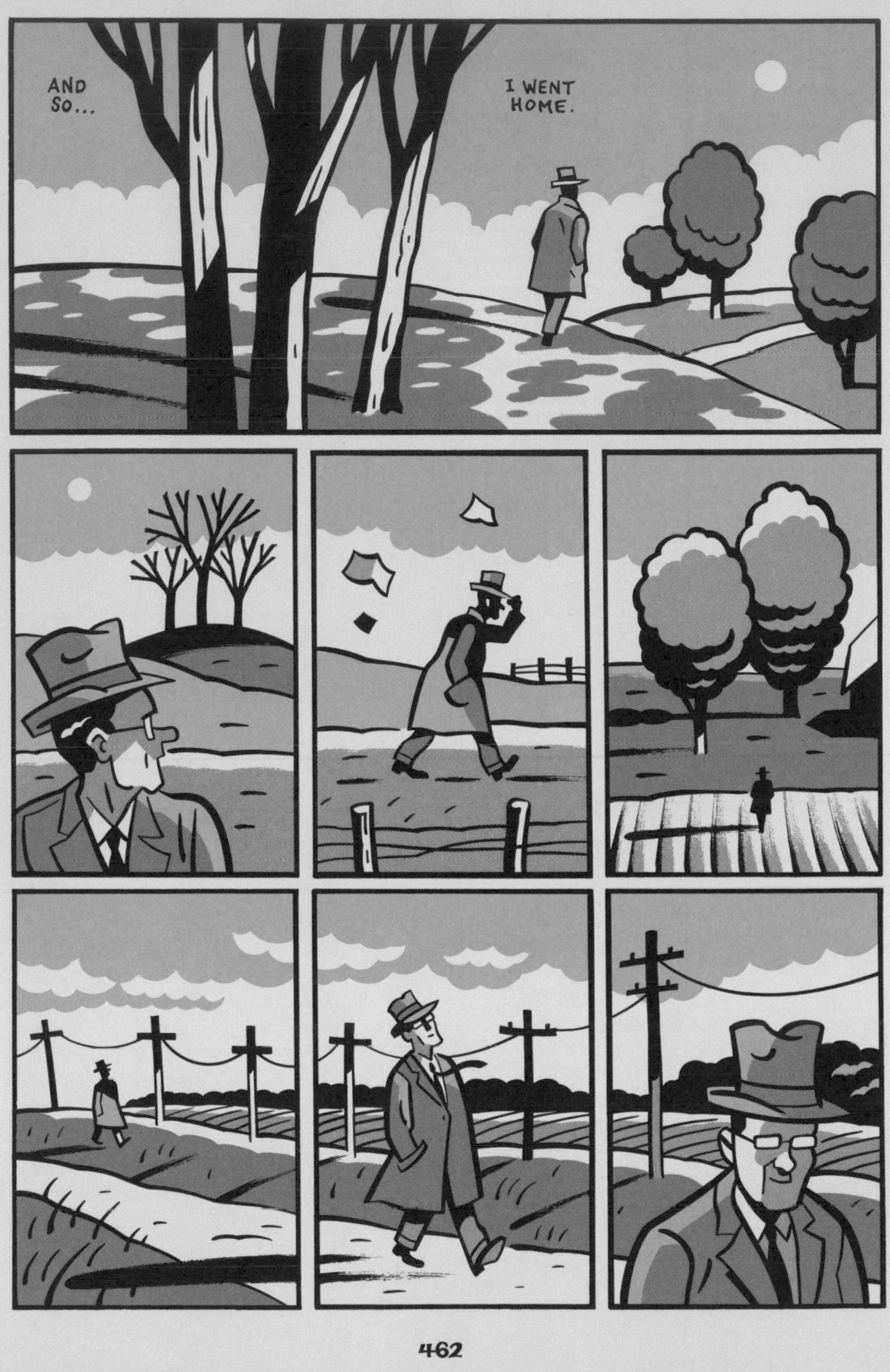
AND SO...
I WENT HOME.

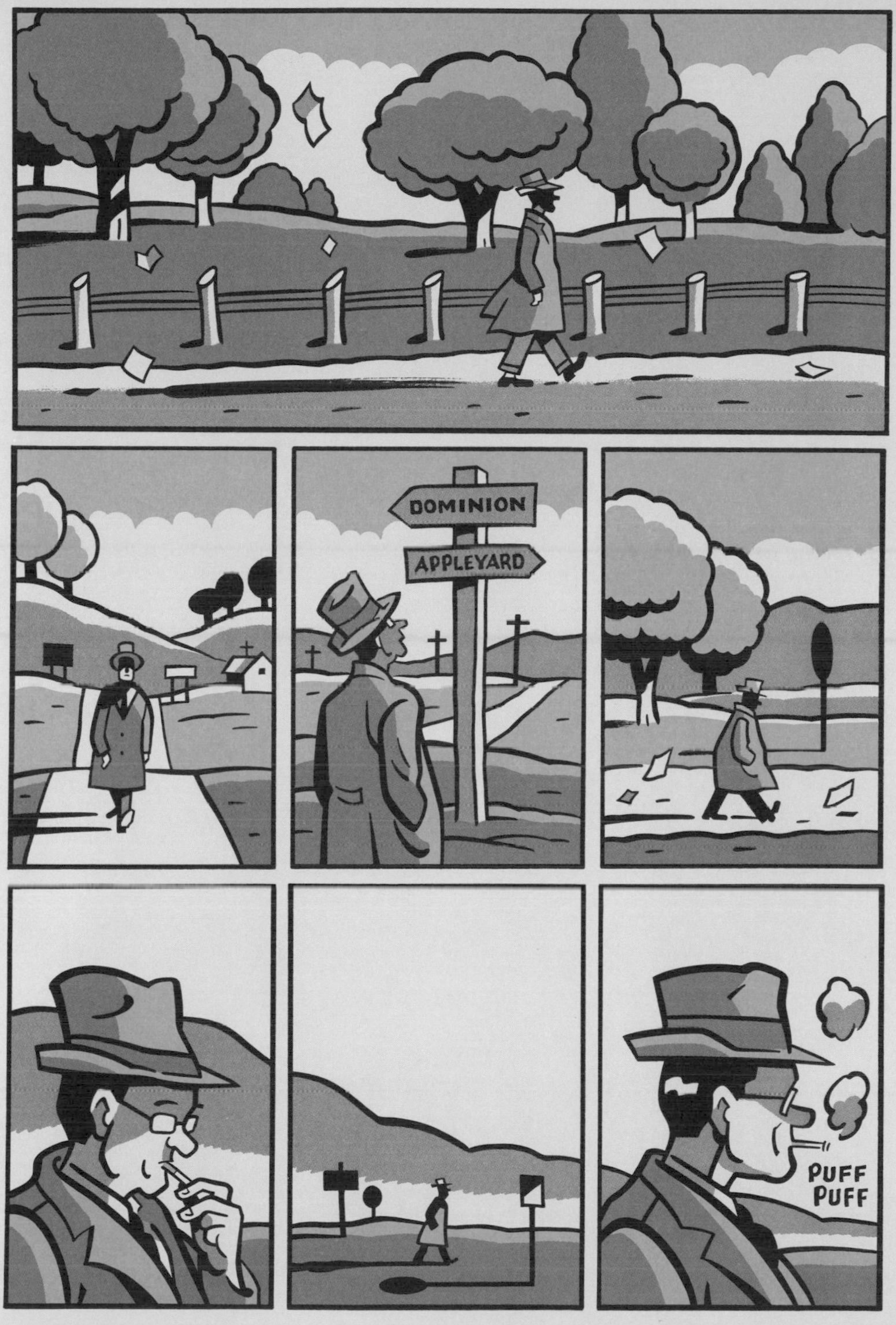
DOMINION
APPLEYARD
PUFF
PUFF

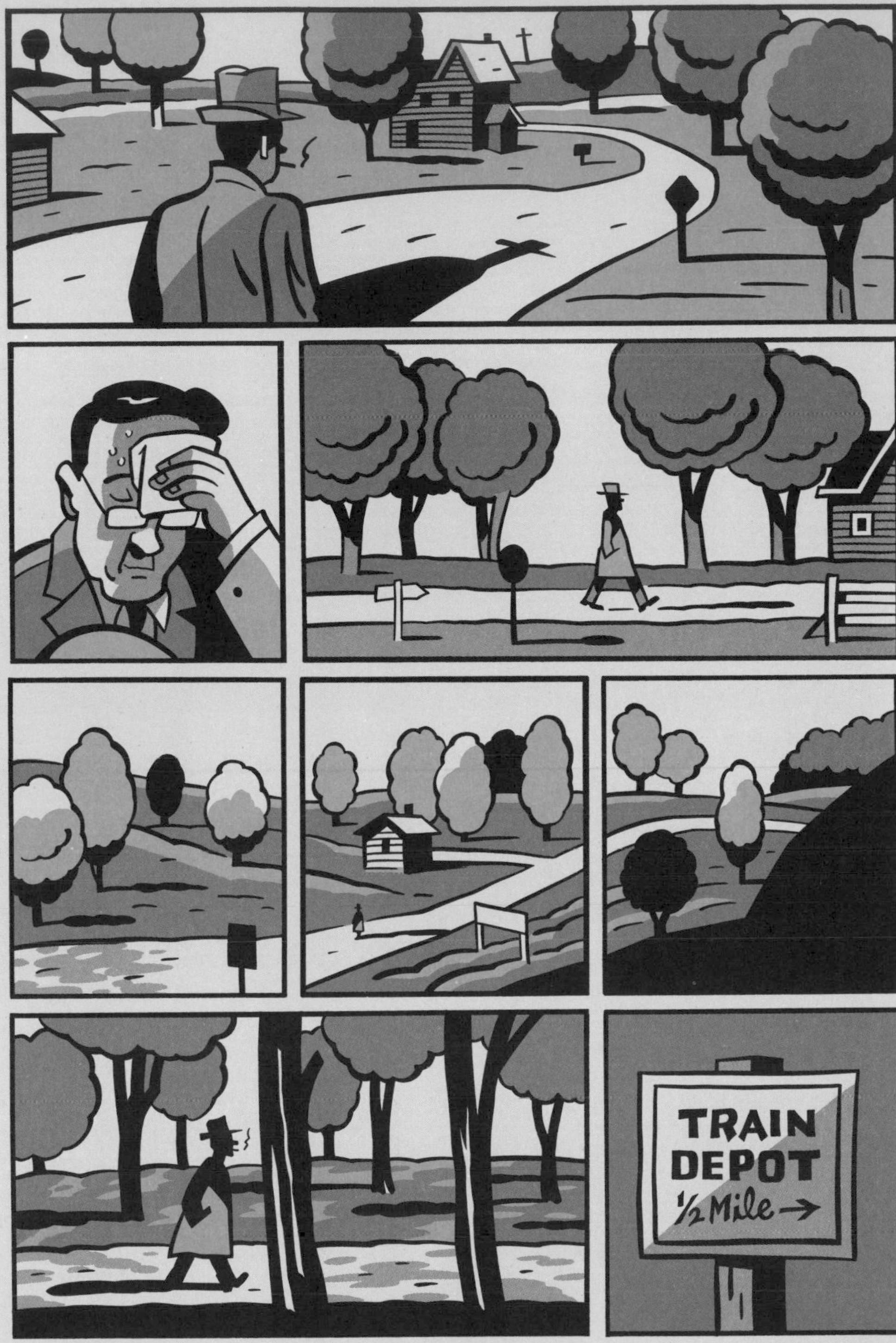
TRAIN
DEPOT
1/2 Mile →

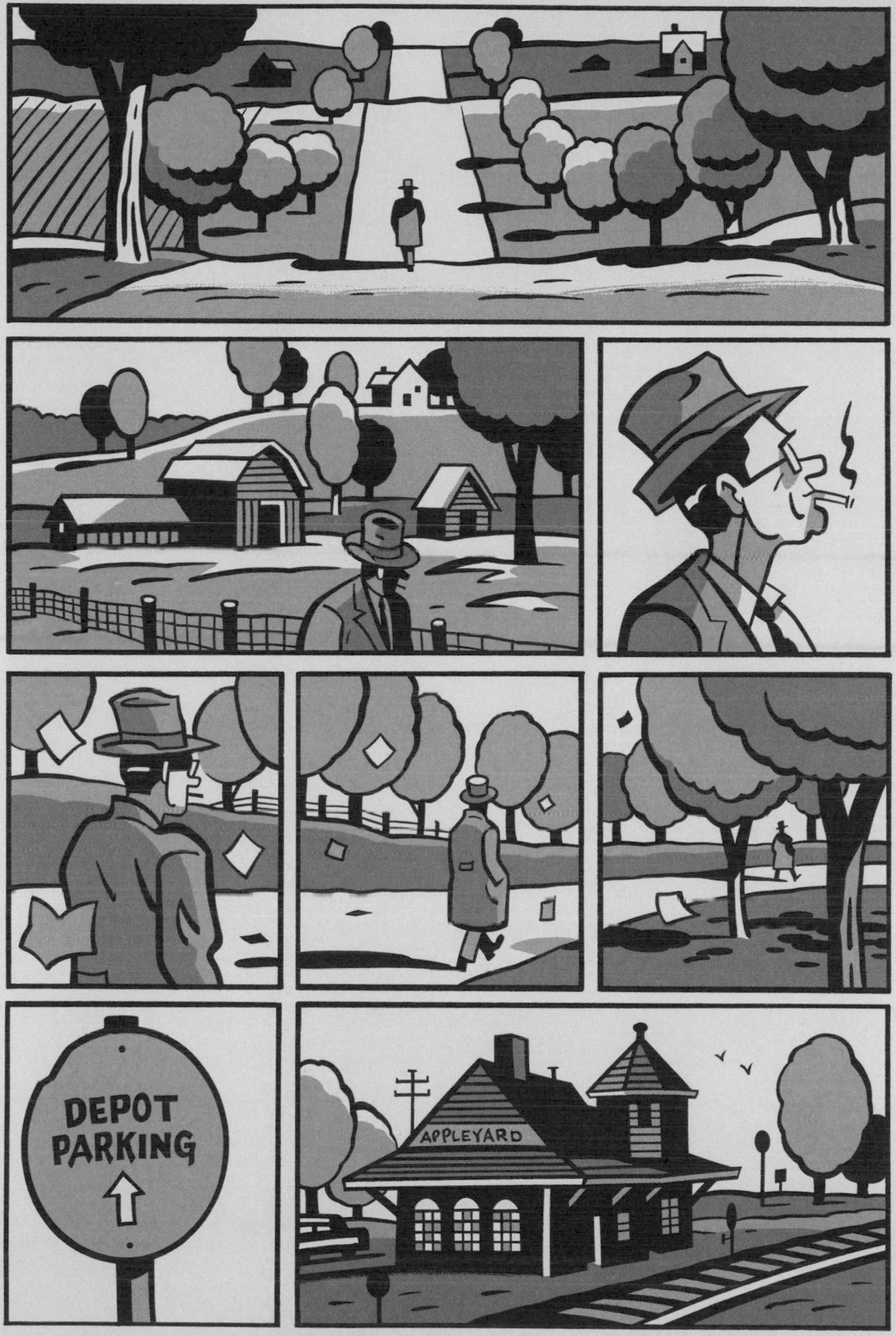
DEPOT
PARKING
APPLEYARD

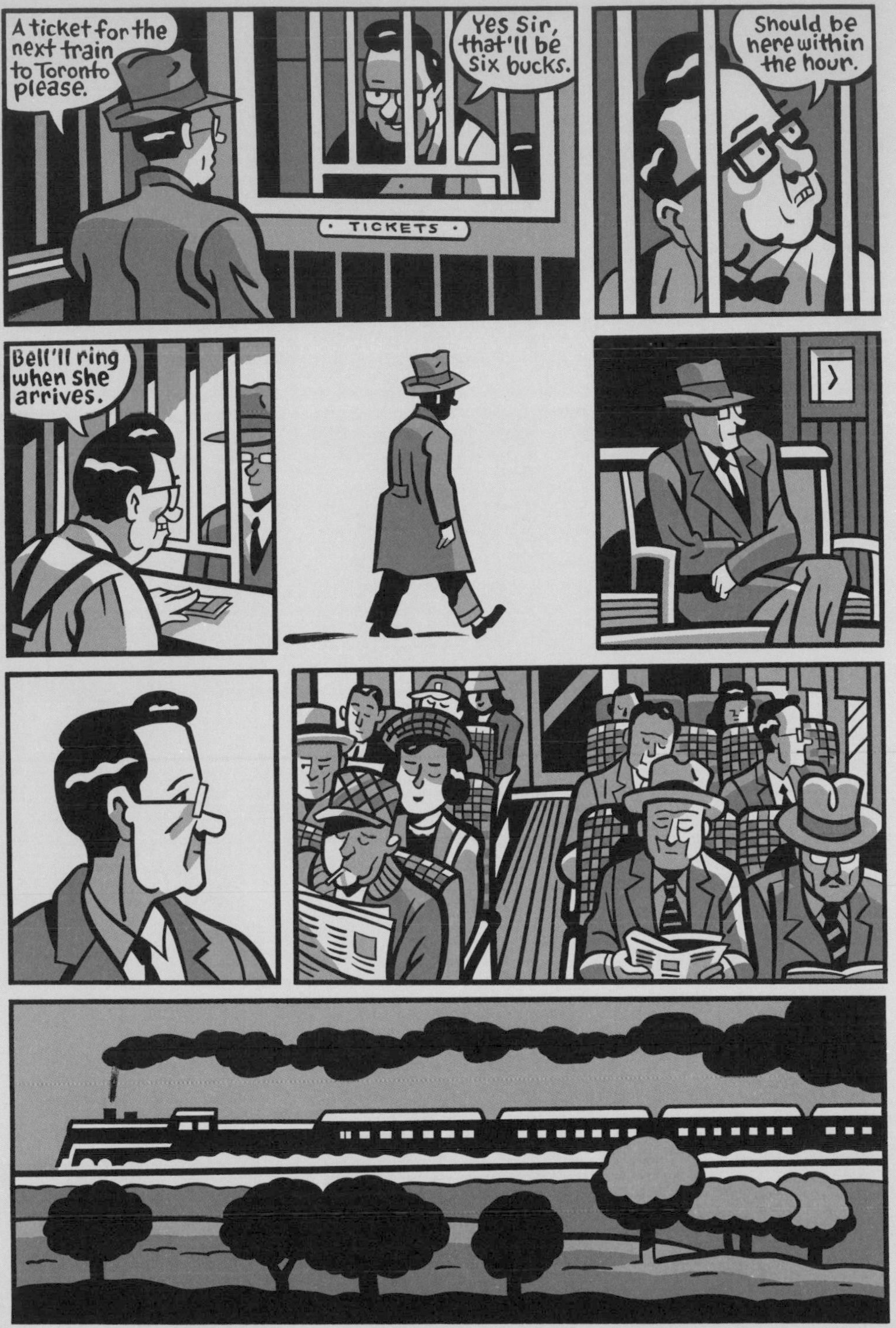
A ticket for the next train to Toronto please.
Yes Sir, that'll be six bucks.
TICKETS
Should be here within the hour.
Bell'll ring when she arrives.

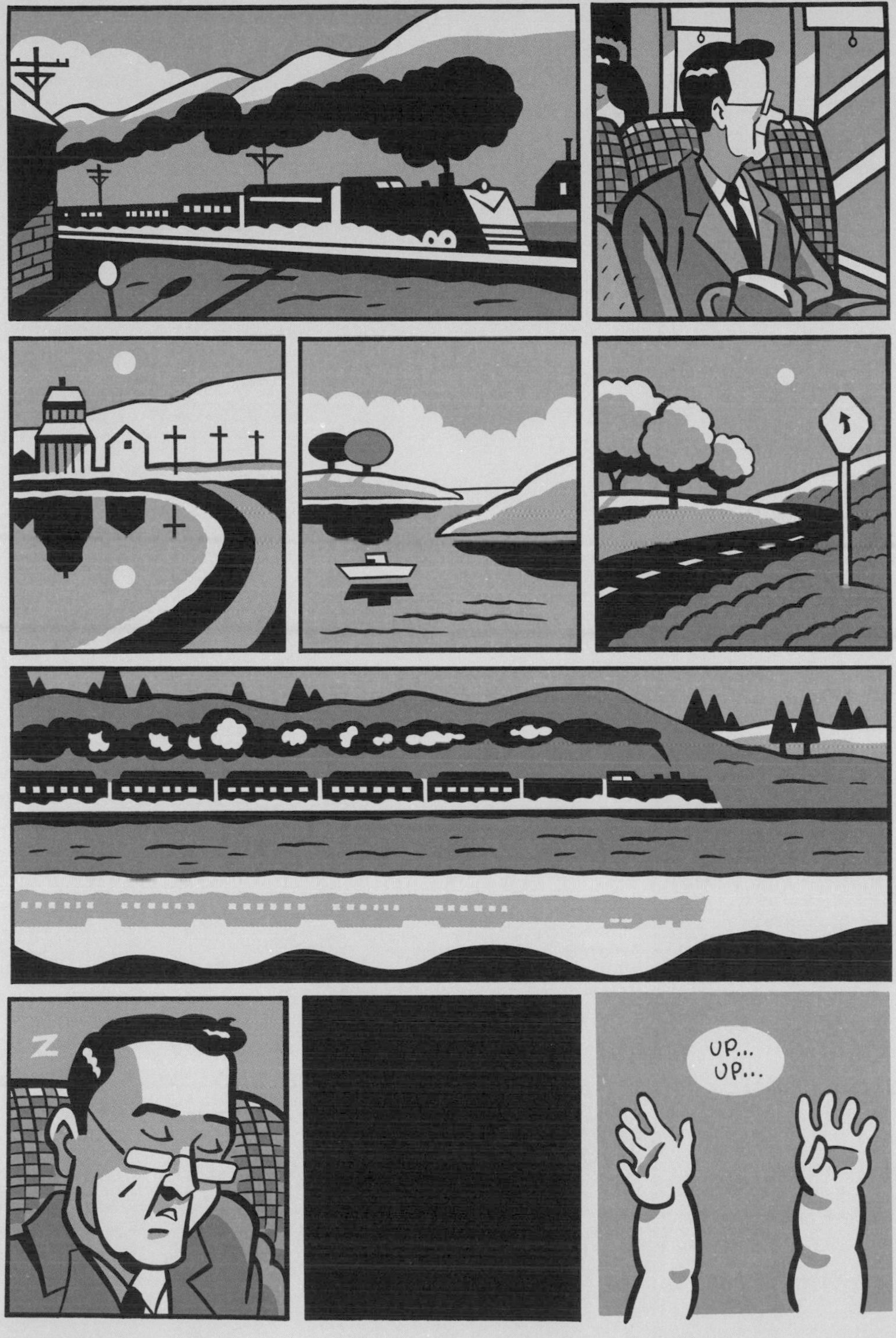
Z
UP...
UP...

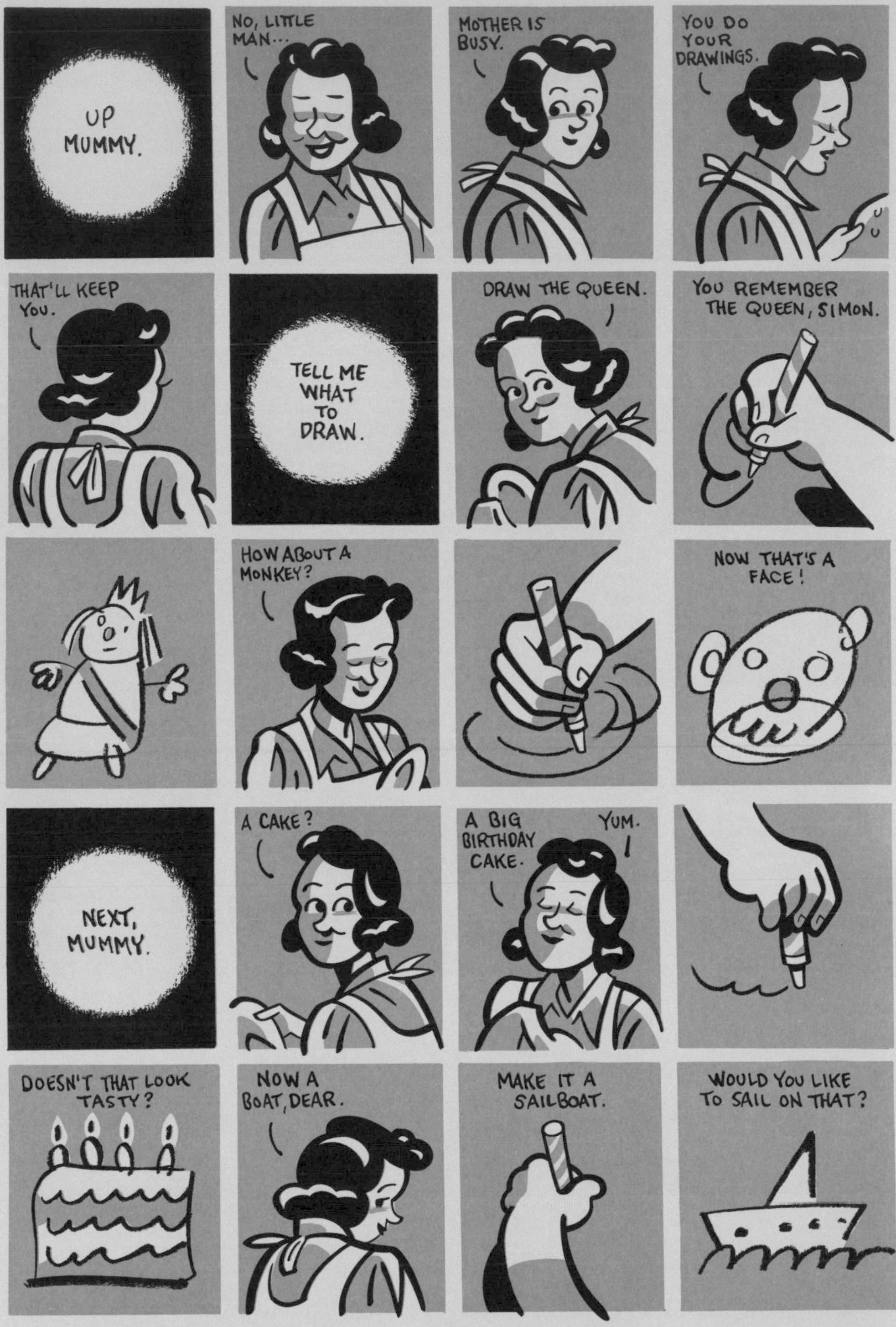
UP MUMMY.
NO, LITTLE MAN...
MOTHER IS BUSY.
YOU DO YOUR DRAWINGS.
THAT'LL KEEP YOU.
TELL ME WHAT TO DRAW.
DRAW THE QUEEN.
YOU REMEMBER THE QUEEN, SIMON.
HOW ABOUT A MONKEY?
NOW THAT'S A FACE!
NEXT, MUMMY.
A CAKE?
A BIG BIRTHDAY CAKE.
YUM.
DOESN'T THAT LOOK TASTY?
NOW A BOAT, DEAR.
MAKE IT A SAILBOAT.
WOULD YOU LIKE TO SAIL ON THAT?

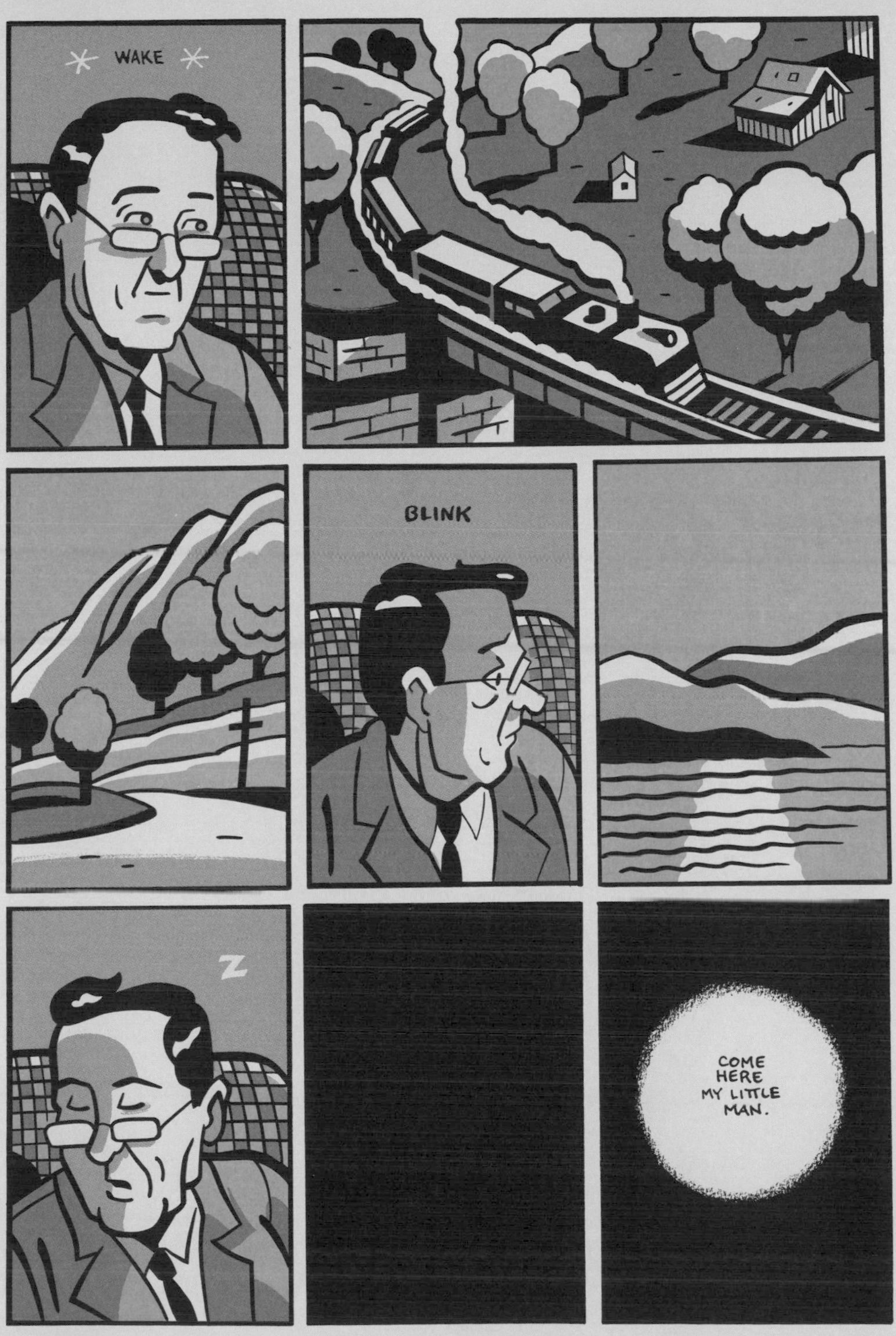
WAKE
BLINK
Z
COME HERE MY LITTLE MAN.

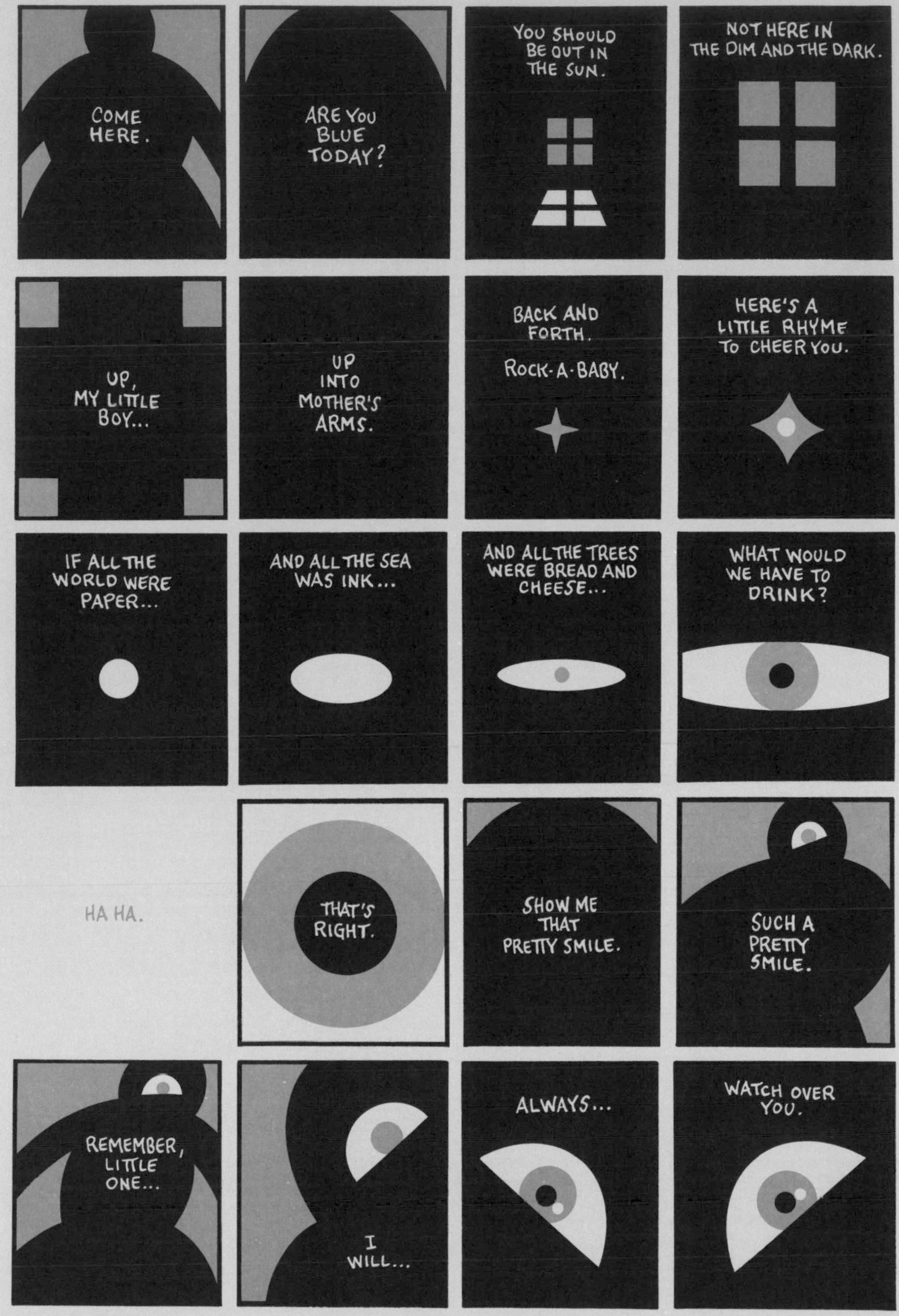
COME HERE.
ARE YOU BLUE TODAY?
YOU SHOULD BE OUT IN THE SUN.
NOT HERE IN THE DIM AND THE DARK.
UP, MY LITTLE BOY...
UP INTO MOTHER'S ARMS.
BACK AND FORTH.
ROCK-A-BABY.
HERE'S A LITTLE RHYME TO CHEER YOU.
IF ALL THE WORLD WERE PAPER...
AND ALL THE SEA WAS INK...
AND ALL THE TREES WERE BREAD AND CHEESE...
WHAT WOULD WE HAVE TO DRINK?
HA HA.
THAT'S RIGHT.
SHOW ME THAT PRETTY SMILE.
SUCH A PRETTY SMILE.
REMEMBER, LITTLE ONE...
I WILL...
ALWAYS...
WATCH OVER YOU.

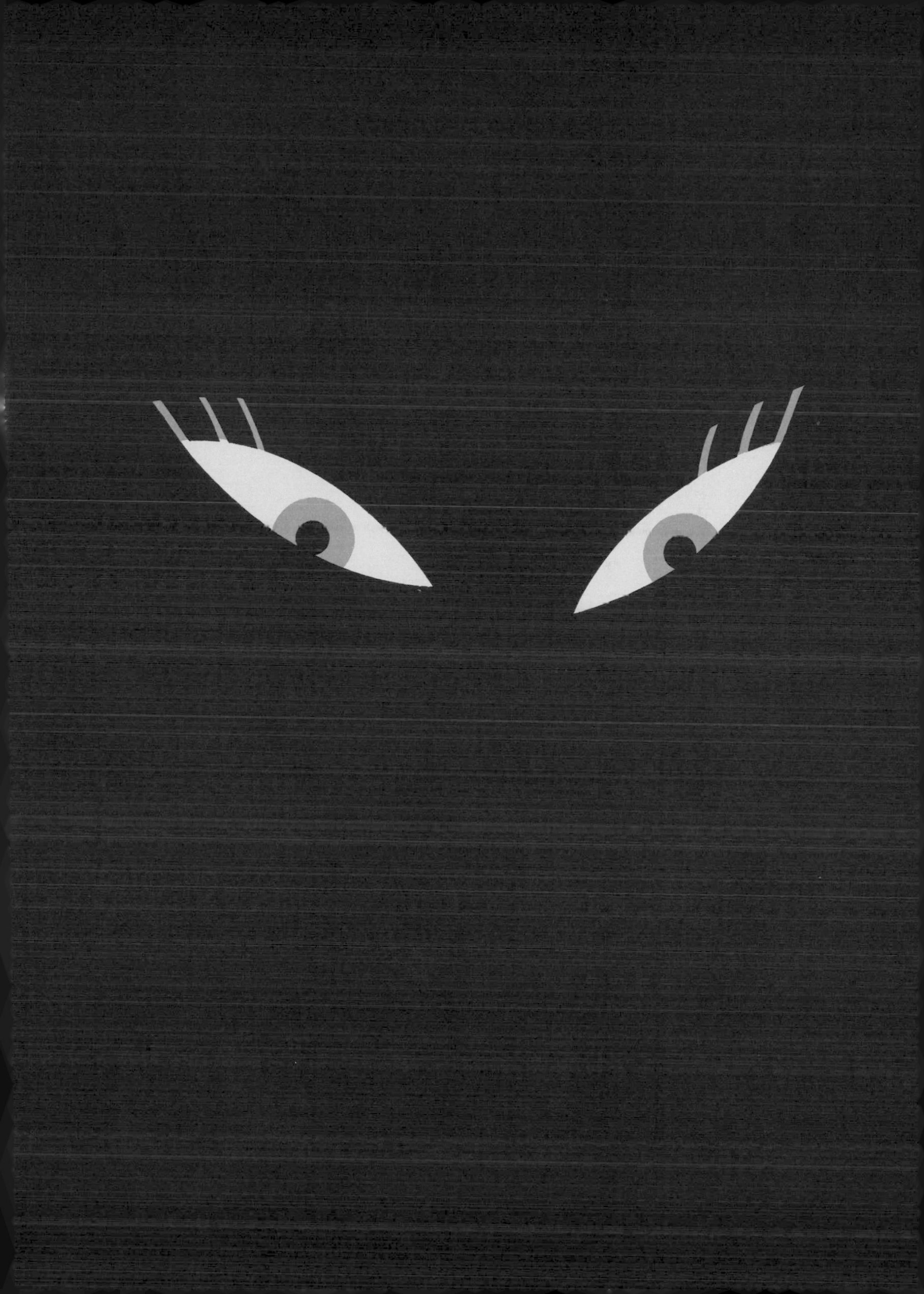

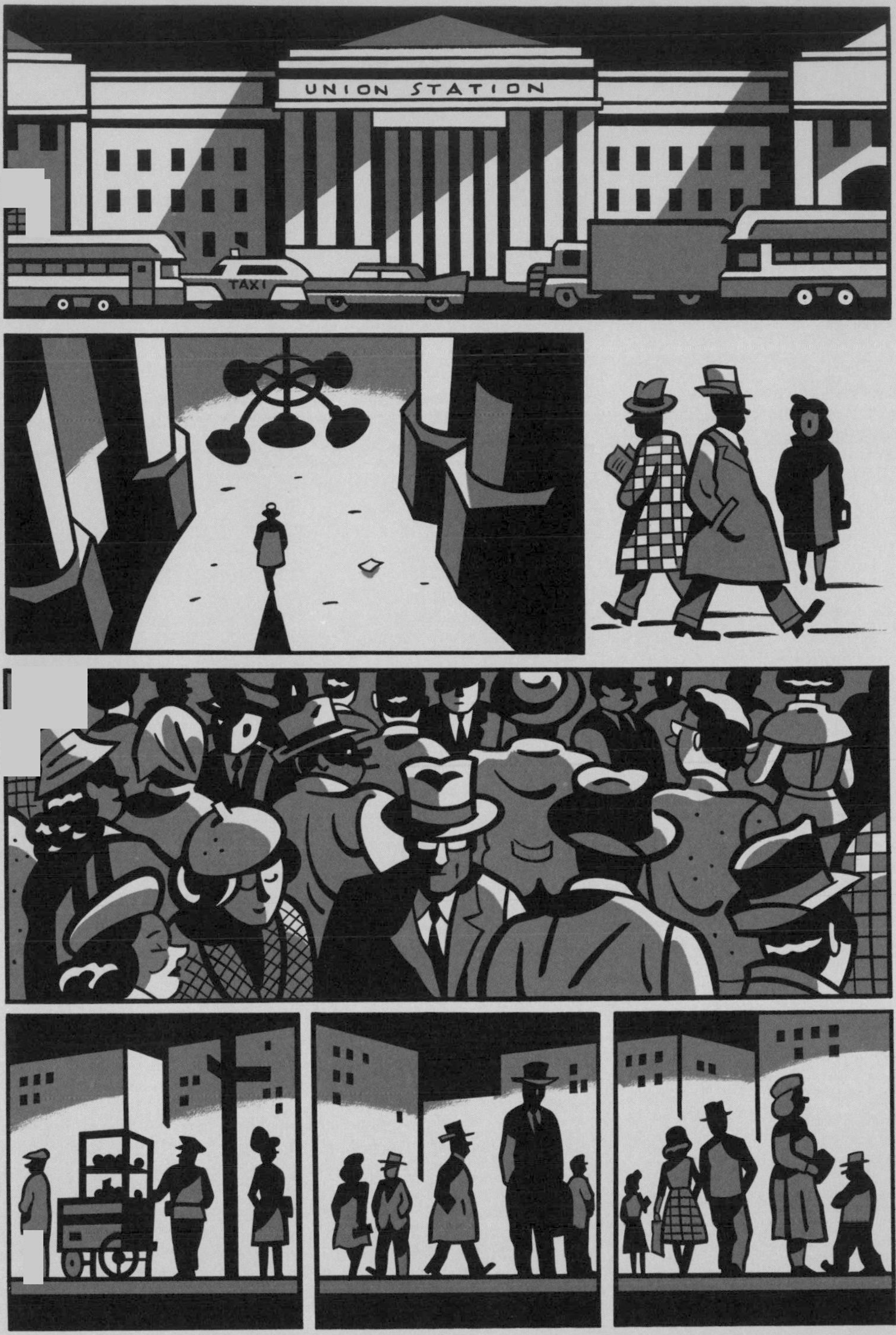
UNION STATION
TAXI

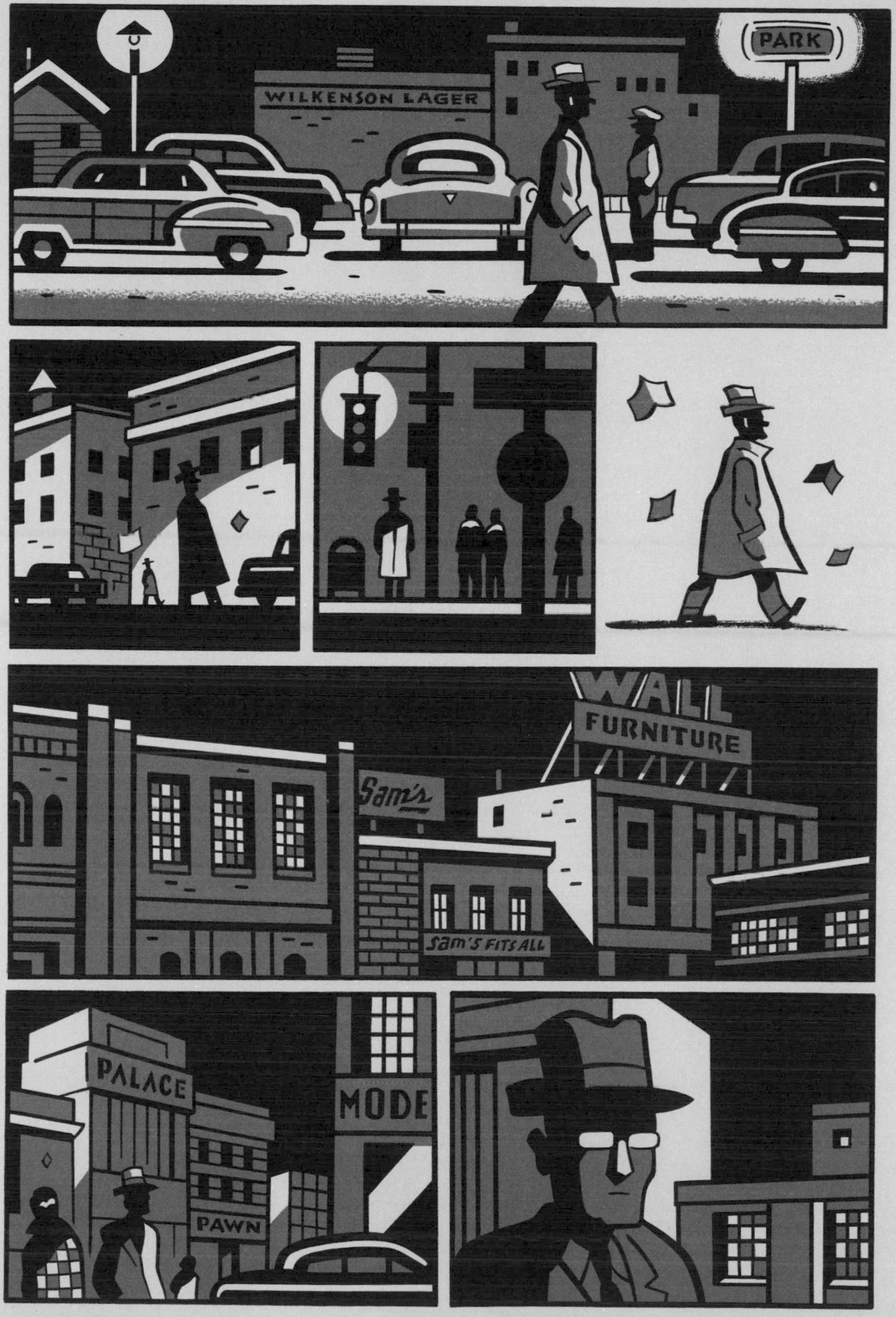
PARK
WILKENSON LAGER
WALL
FURNITURE
Sam's
Sam's FITS ALL
PALACE
MODE
PAWN

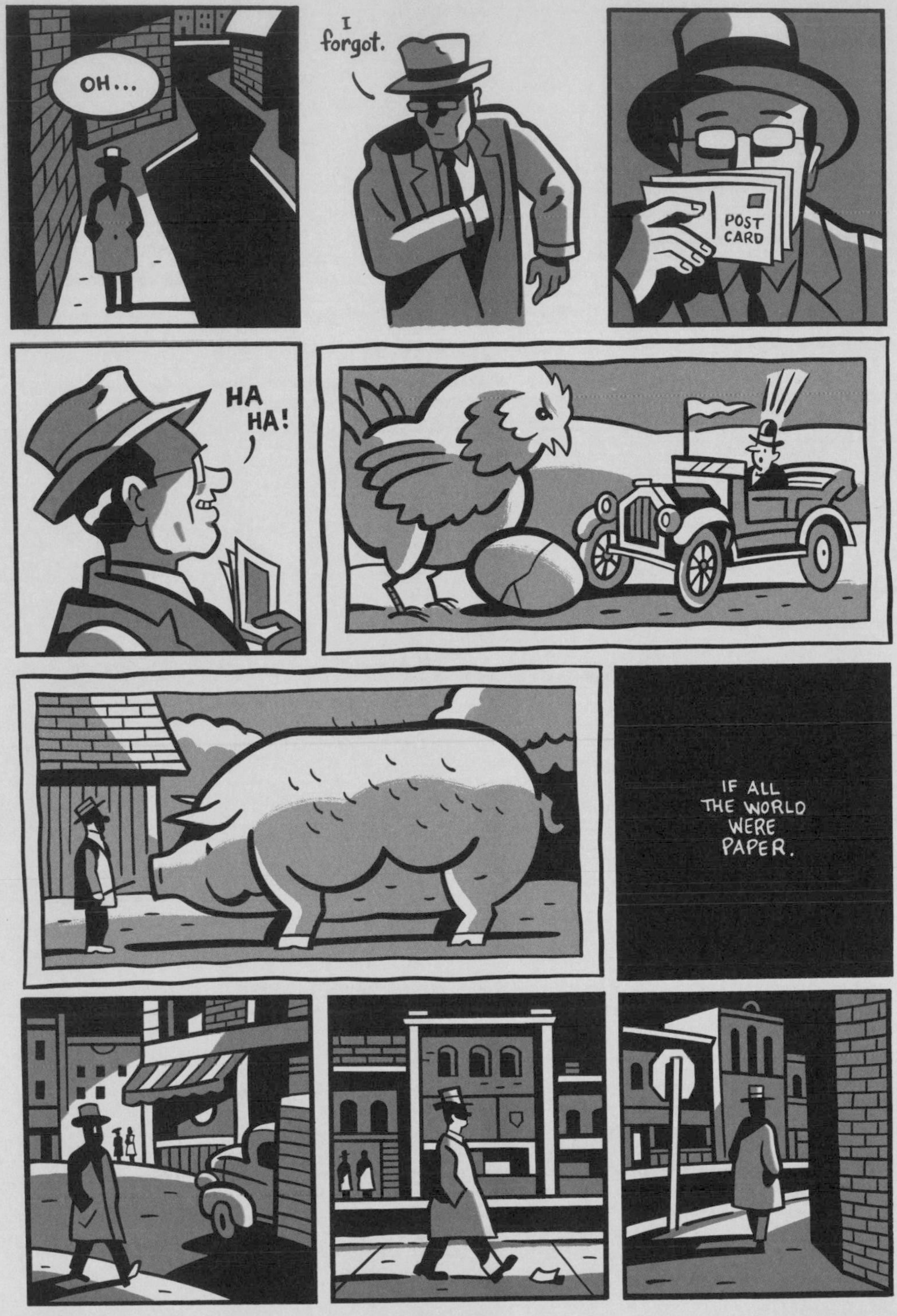
OH...
I forgot.
POST CARD
HA HA!
IF ALL THE WORLD WERE PAPER.

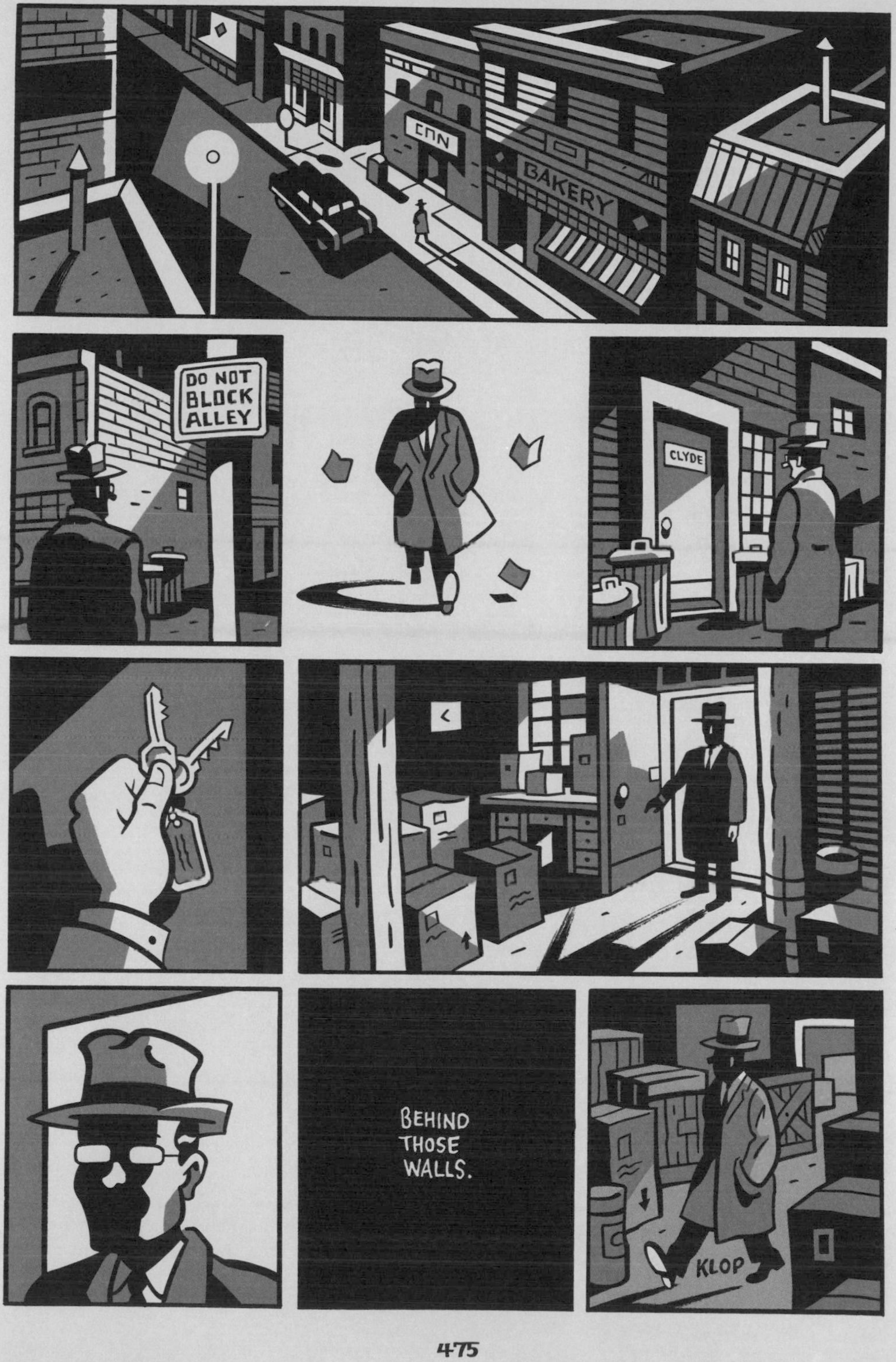

CMN
BAKERY
DO NOT BLOCK ALLEY
CLYDE
BEHIND THOSE WALLS.
KLOP

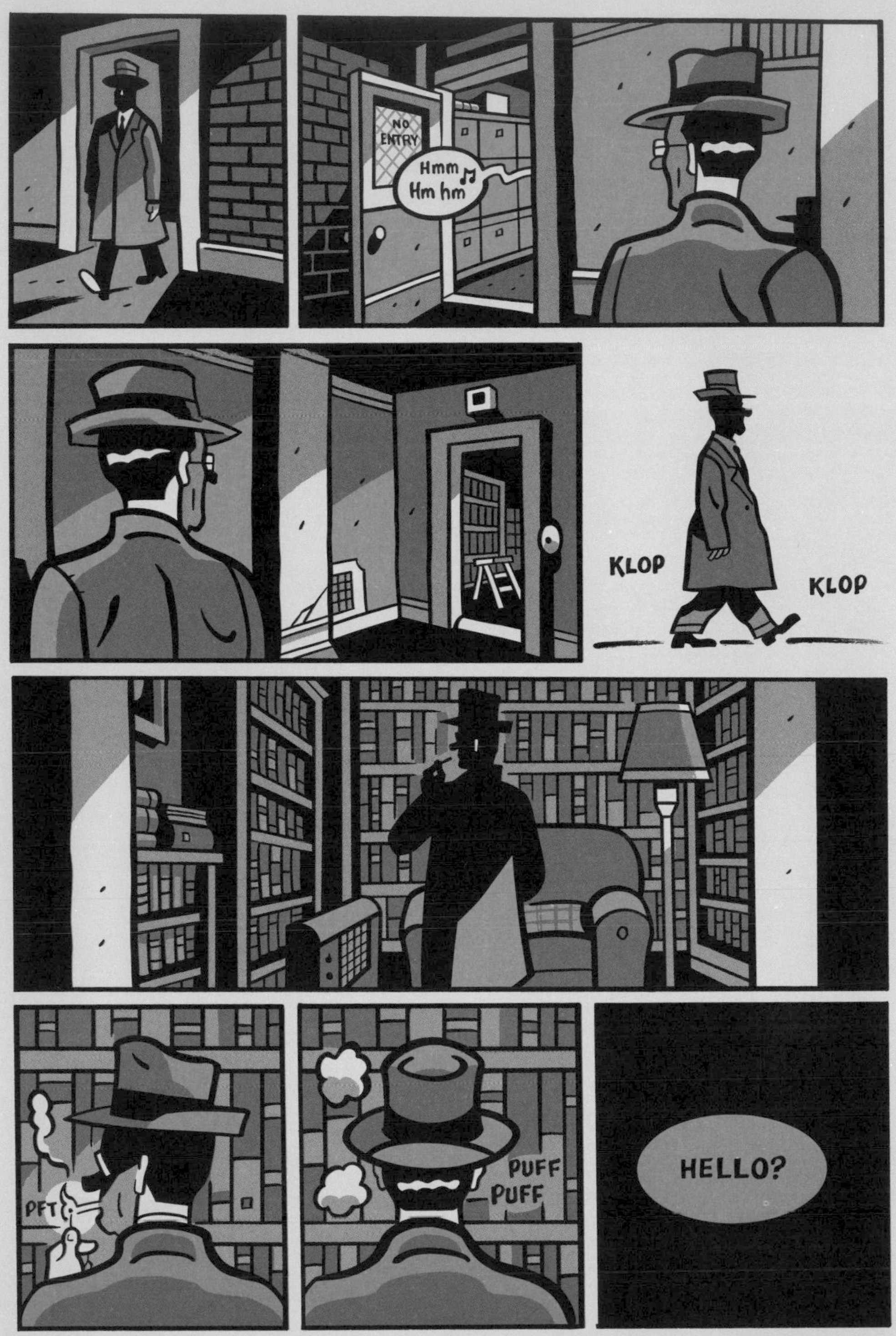
NO ENTRY
Hmm Hm hm
KLOP
KLOP
PFT
PUFF
PUFF
HELLO?

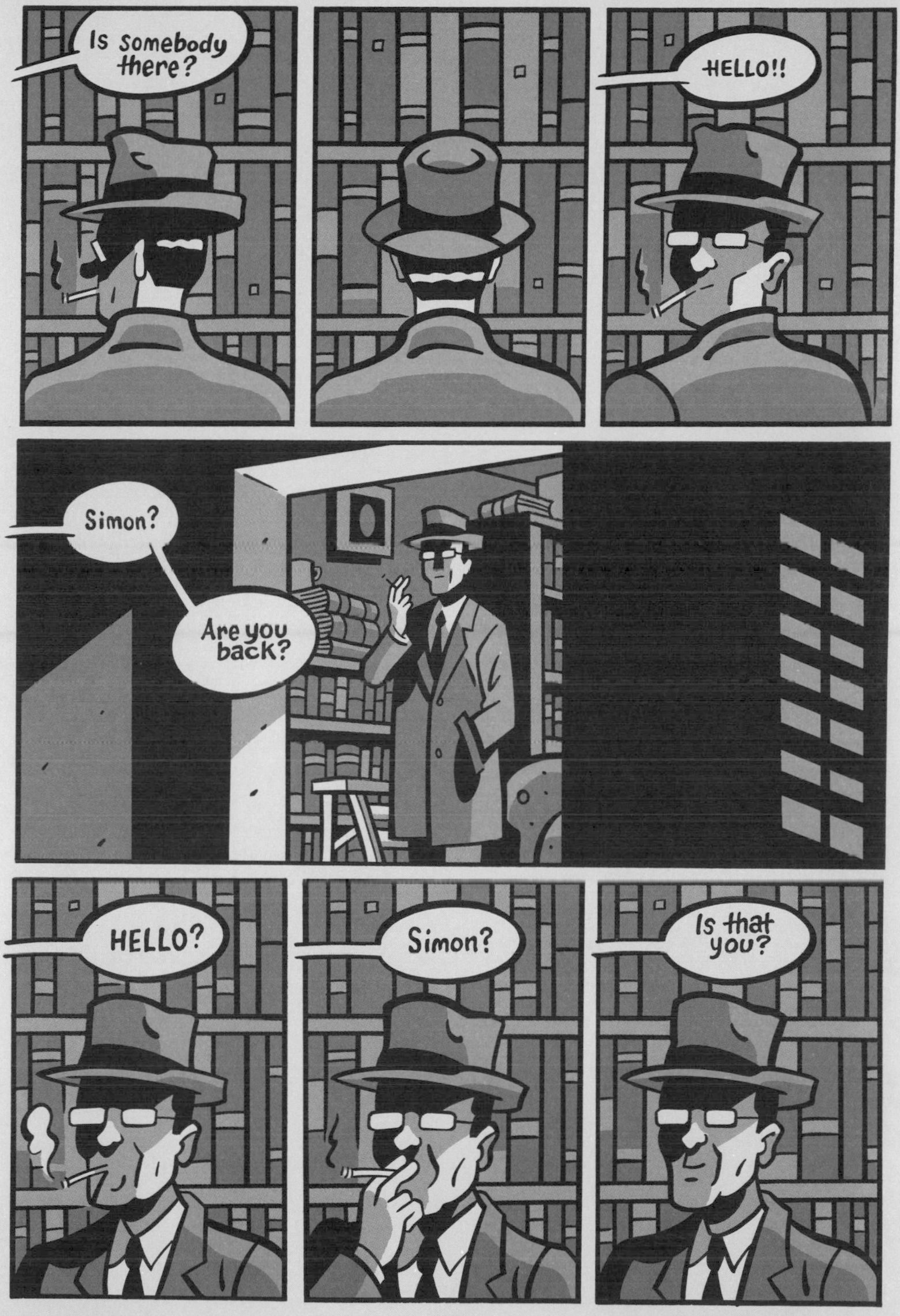
Is somebody there?
HELLO!!
Simon?
Are you back?
HELLO?
Simon?
Is that you?

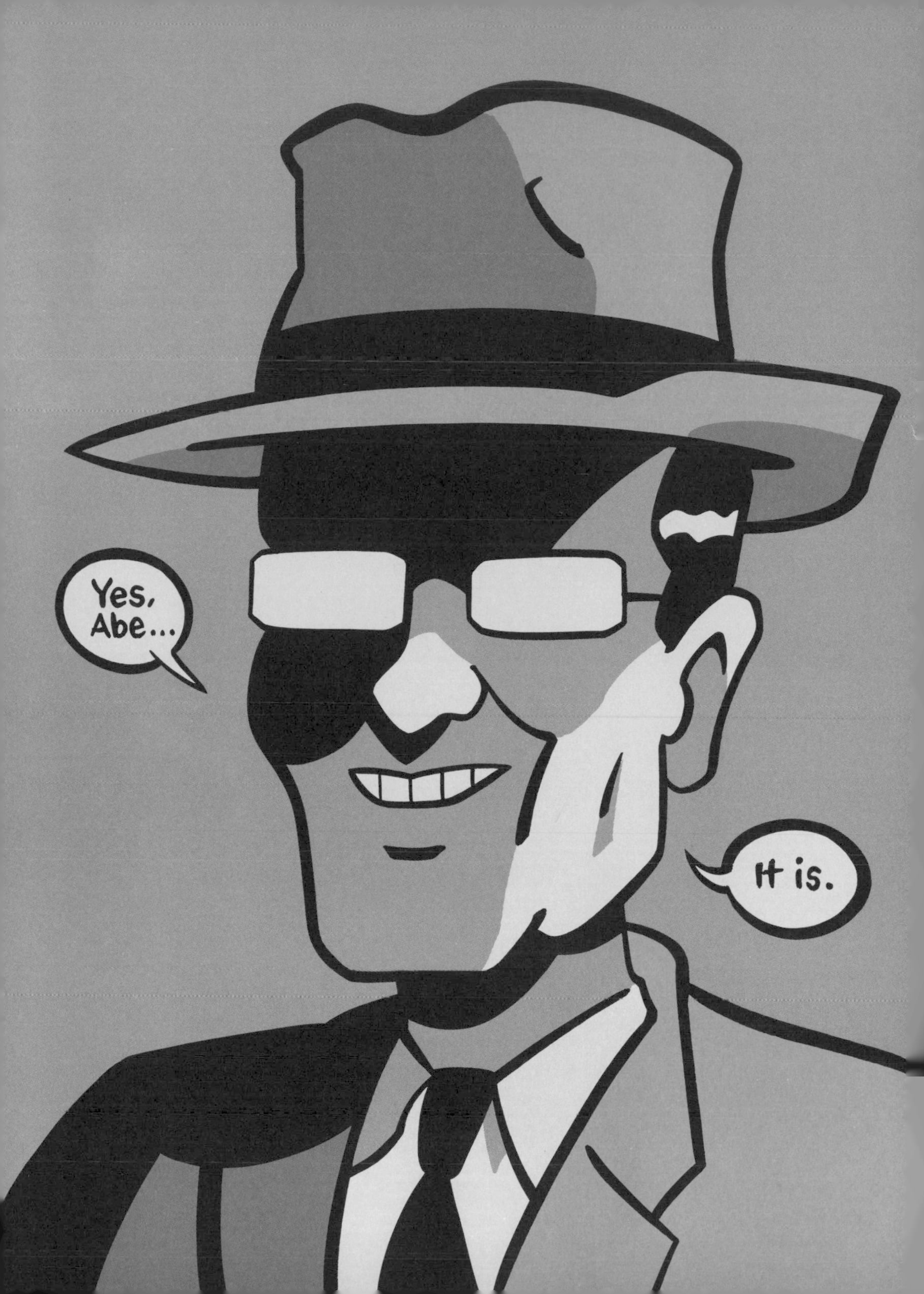
Yes, Abe...
It is.

The END

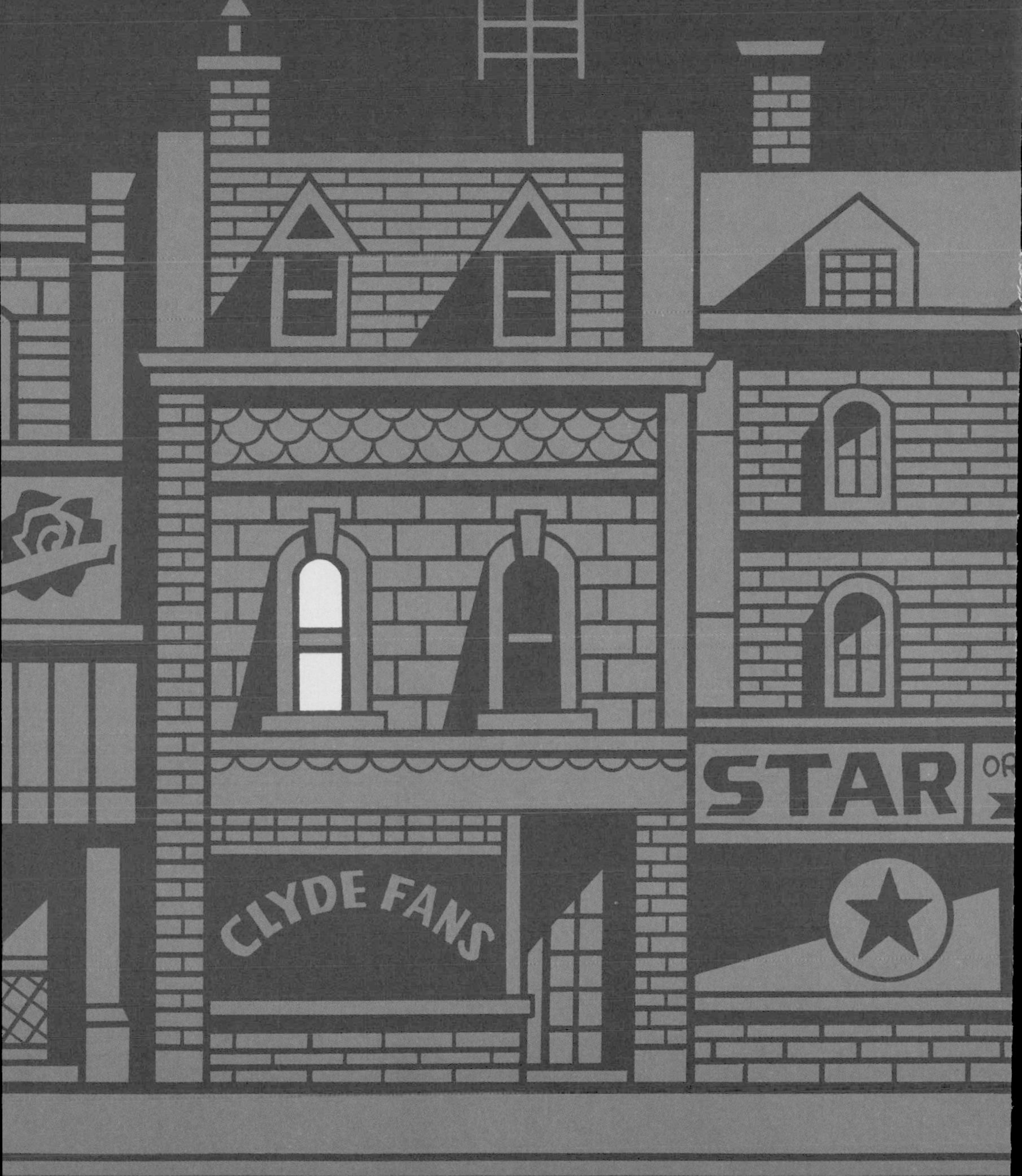
CLYDE FANS
STAR

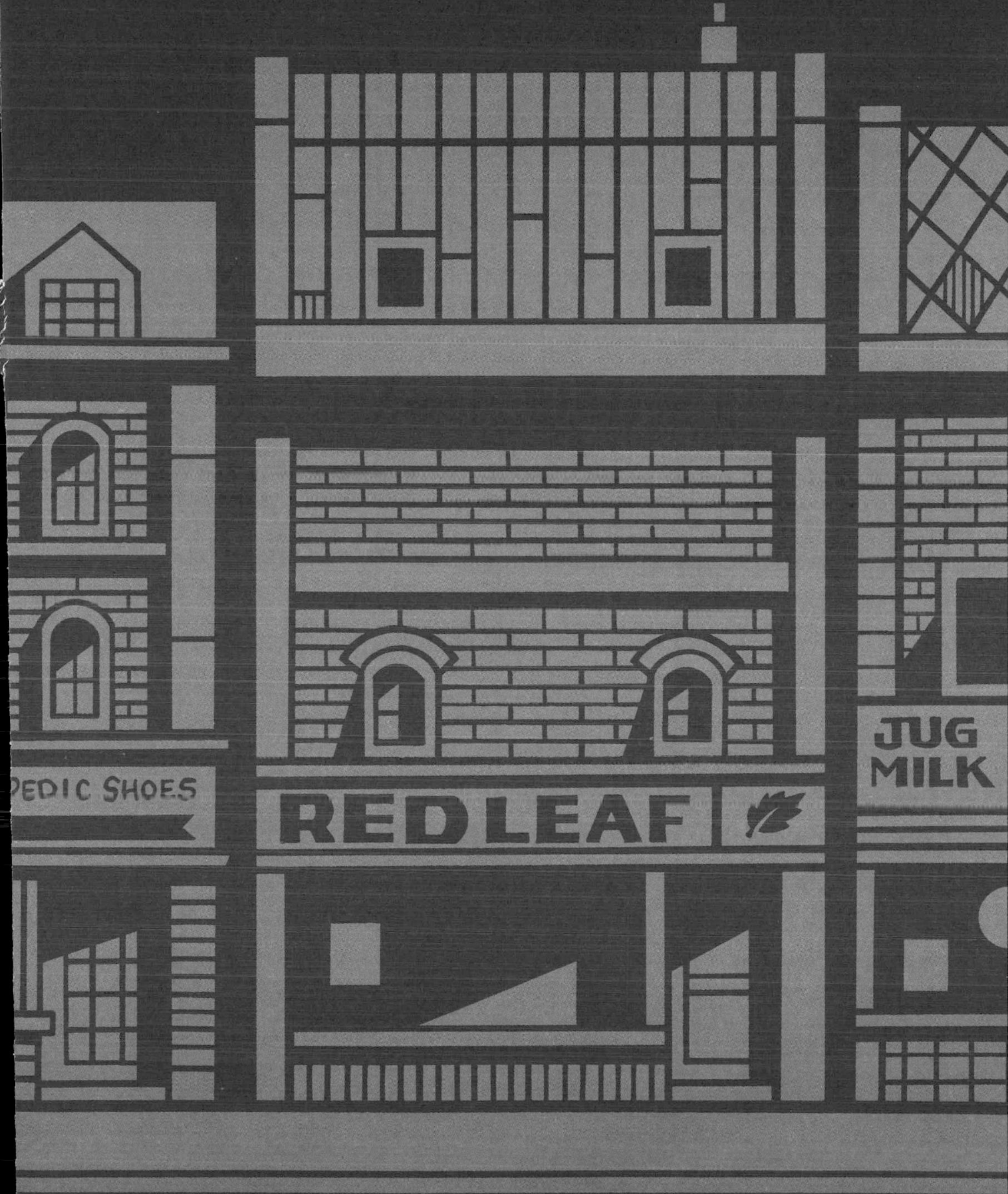
PEDIC SHOES
RED LEAF
JUG
MILK

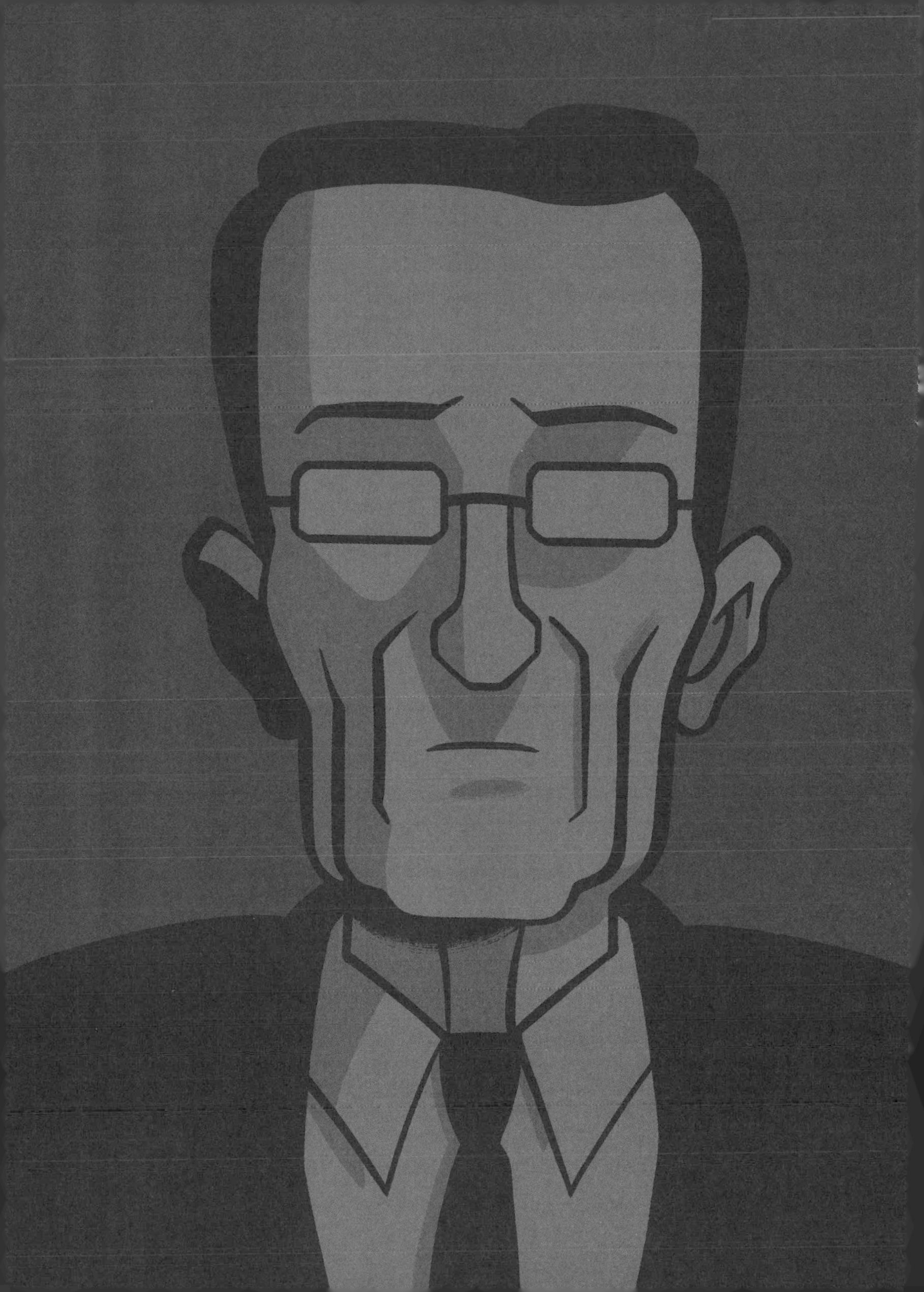

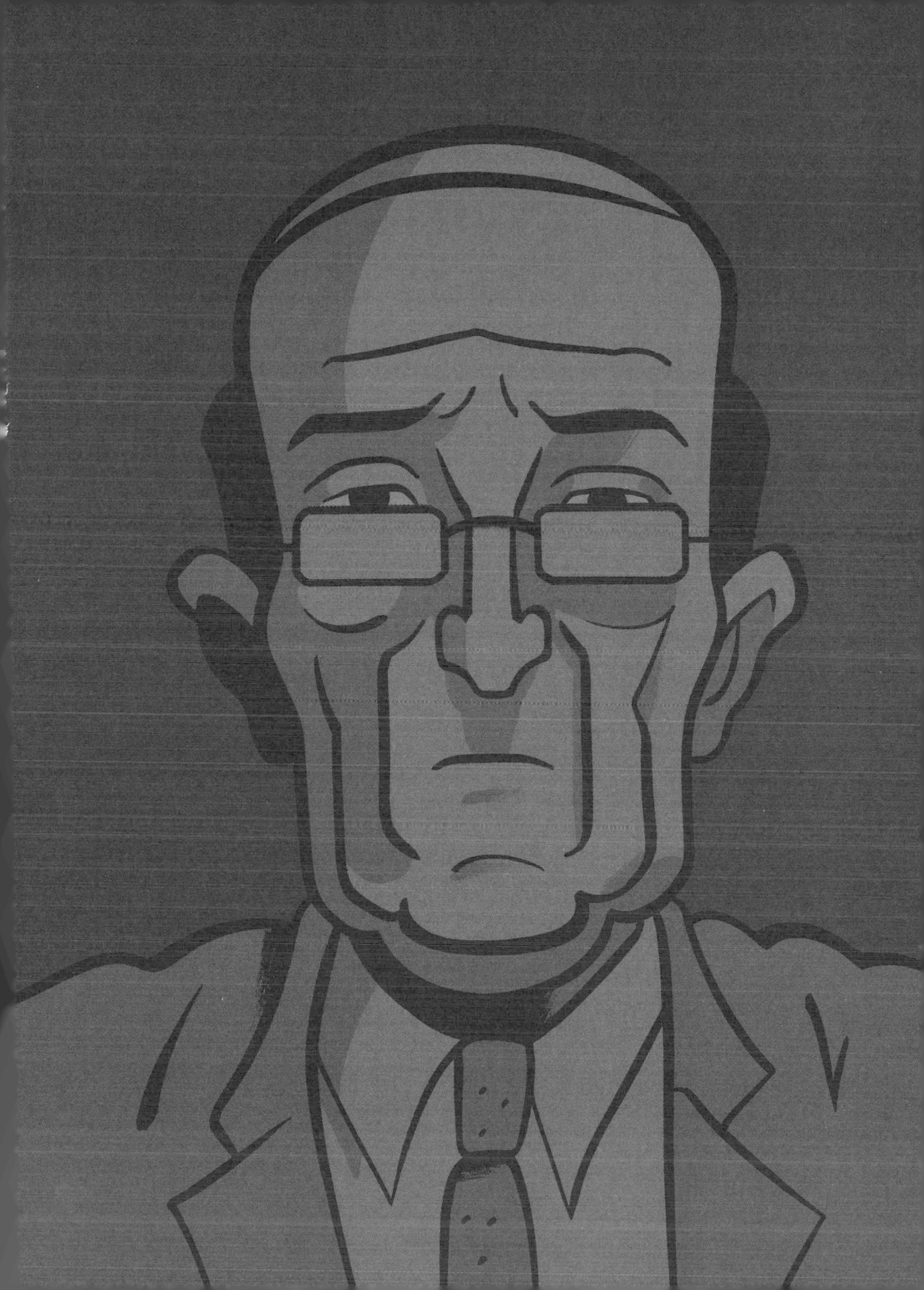

AUTHOR'S NOTE

It must be twenty-five or thirty years now since I first looked into the dark storefront window of the Clyde Fans building at King and Sherbourne. Yes, it was a real business. An old business. Already out of business. Back then, it was the kind of lingering Toronto storefront you walked past without noticing. Just another dilapidated grey building. I don't think that would be so true in today's much shiner Toronto. No, that faded old storefront would stand out like a sore thumb.

For some reason I took a deeper notice that day and stopped to really look. I pressed my nose to the glass and peered into the dark office for the first time. There wasn't much to see. A tin ceiling, a desk, a couple of rotary phones. Almost exactly as I've drawn the office in this book. And, like my fictional office, the real one had two framed portraits on the rear wall. Standard black and white business photos from the late fifties. Too dark to make out details but clear enough to see the faces of two middle-aged men. They stuck in my mind.

Just when those portraits took on a fictional life of their own I don't recall. I only know that by the time I had finished my first graphic novel (*It's a Good Life, If You Don't Weaken*), the Matchcard brothers were ready to be the subject of my second. Why do we pick what we pick? Then, I might have said I picked that storefront because I was interested in the past, or perhaps because it made me think about progress and failure. Looking back now, it is obvious to me that it was simpler. I was seduced by the closed world of that bygone business.

What I saw in there, and ultimately what sustained my interest through this long project, was a self-contained universe. A quiet, dimly lit, isolated little world furnished with the leftovers of the drab, postwar era of my parents. A lonely world, perhaps, but enticing to me because it seemed to exist separately from the hustle-bustle of "our" world. An inner place where time appeared to be moving slower. Very appealing to someone like me—someone who generally retreats rather than advances. I didn't know all this back then of course, but now, it's obvious—I mean, this is what *all* my work is about. I began the book thinking I was writing a mundane, everyday story but finished up recognizing it was more about the mystic side of things. Making art is always a surprise.

I used the term "second book" a moment ago. *Clyde Fans* was certainly meant to be my second book. I figured it might take a few years to complete. Maybe five. I certainly didn't plan on twenty years. Even now, I'm flabbergasted writing that down.

Somehow, like the old storefront, the book just lingered on well past it's time.

Now, it's not like I worked on it for twenty solid years. Of course not. I worked on it here and there, completing other projects, other books, in the meantime. *Clyde Fans* plodded along year by year. After a decade, I grew ashamed of myself. When people asked about the book, I would change the subject. In recent years, I was mortified to have it mentioned at all—like a large blemish on your face you'd rather not have pointed out. Only when finally completed did I breathe again. In fact, I've started bragging about how long it took—making it sound like an accomplishment rather than a testament to *letting things slide*.

Besides the delay, the biggest surprise about *Clyde Fans* is how little the story changed over two decades. Essentially the book was finished almost exactly as it was envisioned. Oh, little things changed—ideas sharpened, scenes omitted—but all in all, it is the story I set out to write. In fact, it ends on the very line of dialogue I planned in 1997. The saving grace was that my methods were flexible enough for that enormous lag time. I didn't write a script. I don't work that way. I plotted, of course, and knew what scenes would be where and who said what. I knew the overall arc of the thing, but it was in the drawing that each scene came to life. That's where the real writing happened and that's why, in subtle ways, the book could grow with me. Had I written that final chapter twenty years ago, the same things would have happened, but I suspect it would have had quite different words and images.

Now the elephant in the room—the drawing itself. The early chapters look much different from the later ones. Drawing style changes over time. It is inevitable. It pains me to look at the early pages, full of drawing choices I would not make today. I did consider redrawing them. For about a second. But no—*more years?*—impossible. It had to finish. Like children, sometimes you just have to push a book out of the nest.

And so it is done. I'm grateful to set it free. I feel as if I am Sisyphus and have finally found a way to keep that rock at the top of the hill. I have a renewed affection for the book. Free of obligation, I am allowed to enjoy it. One thing you can be assured of—this is the biggest book I will ever make. No more twenty year projects for me. And, without doubt, my life will surely be divided into two clear periods: before and after *Clyde*.

—Seth, 2019

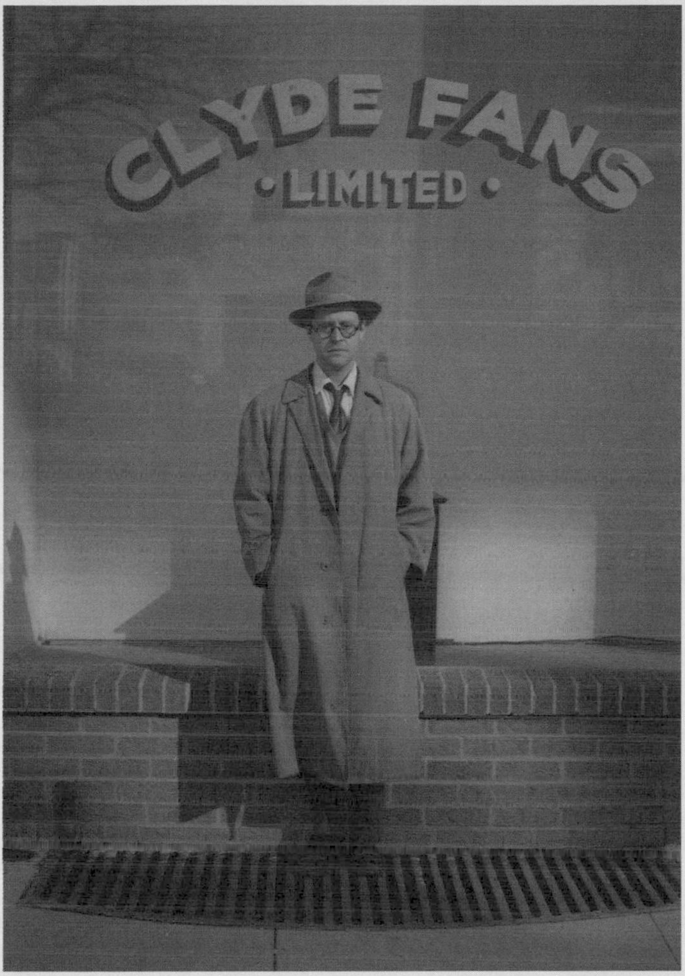
CLYDE FANS
·LIMITED·

SETH (CIRCA MID 1990) IN FRONT OF THE OLD CLYDE FANS STOREFRONT.

Seth is a cartoonist and designer. In the past three decades, he has drawn graphic novels, designed books, illustrated magazines, made sculptures, written articles, and exhibited in galleries. He is the subject of a recent National Film Board documentary, *Seth's Dominion.* He lives in Guelph, Ontario, with his wife, Tania, in a house named Inkwell's End.

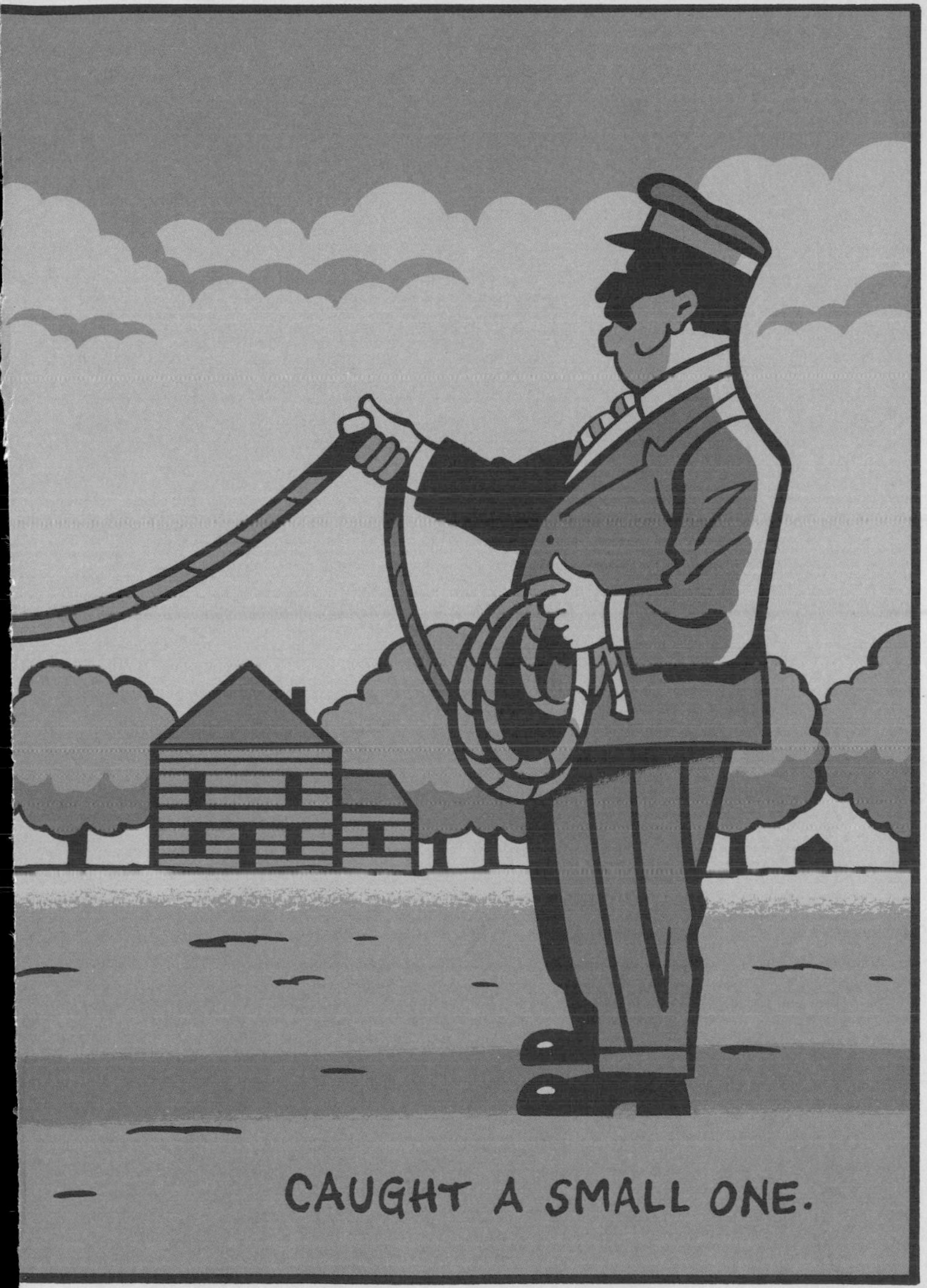
CAUGHT A SMALL ONE.

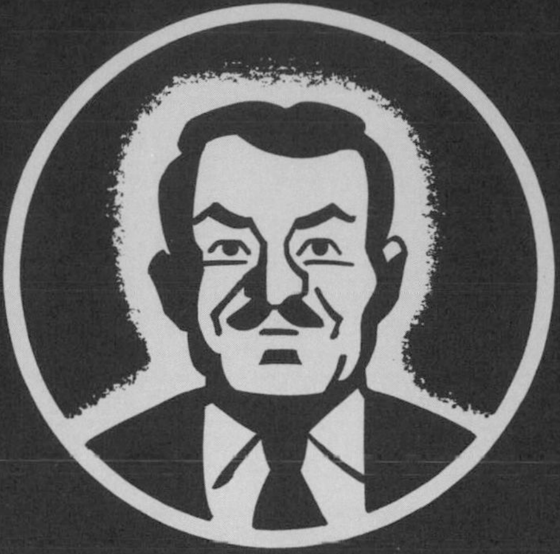

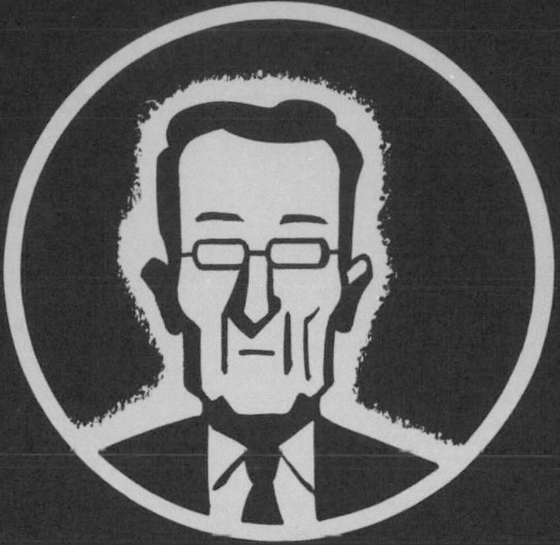

OTHER BOOKS BY SETH

- IT'S A GOOD LIFE, IF YOU DON'T WEAKEN
- VERNACULAR DRAWINGS
- BANNOCK, BEANS AND BLACK TEA
- FORTY CARTOON BOOKS OF INTEREST
- WIMBLEDON GREEN
- GEORGE SPROTT 1894–1975
- THE GREAT NORTHERN BROTHERHOOD OF CANADIAN CARTOONISTS
- ABOUT LOVE, 3 STORIES BY CHEKHOV
- SUNSHINE SKETCHES OF A LITTLE TOWN
- PALOOKAVILLE 20–23
- SETH'S DOMINION

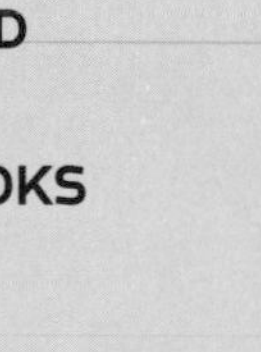

Photo on page 485 by M. Mortimer.

drawnandquarterly.com

ISBN 978-1-77046-357-8 | First edition: April 2019
Printed in China | 10 9 8 7 6 5 4 3 2 1

Cataloguing data available from Library and Archives Canada.

Published in the USA by Drawn & Quarterly, a client publisher of Farrar, Straus and Giroux. Orders: 888.330.8477. Published in Canada by Drawn & Quarterly, a client publisher of Raincoast Books. Orders: 800.663.5714. Published in the United Kingdom by Drawn & Quarterly, a client publisher of Publishers Group UK. Orders: info@pguk.co.uk.

Canada Drawn & Quarterly acknowledges the support of the Government of Canada and the Canada Council for the Arts for our publishing program.

DRAWN & QUARTERLY

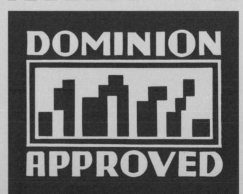

DOMINION APPROVED

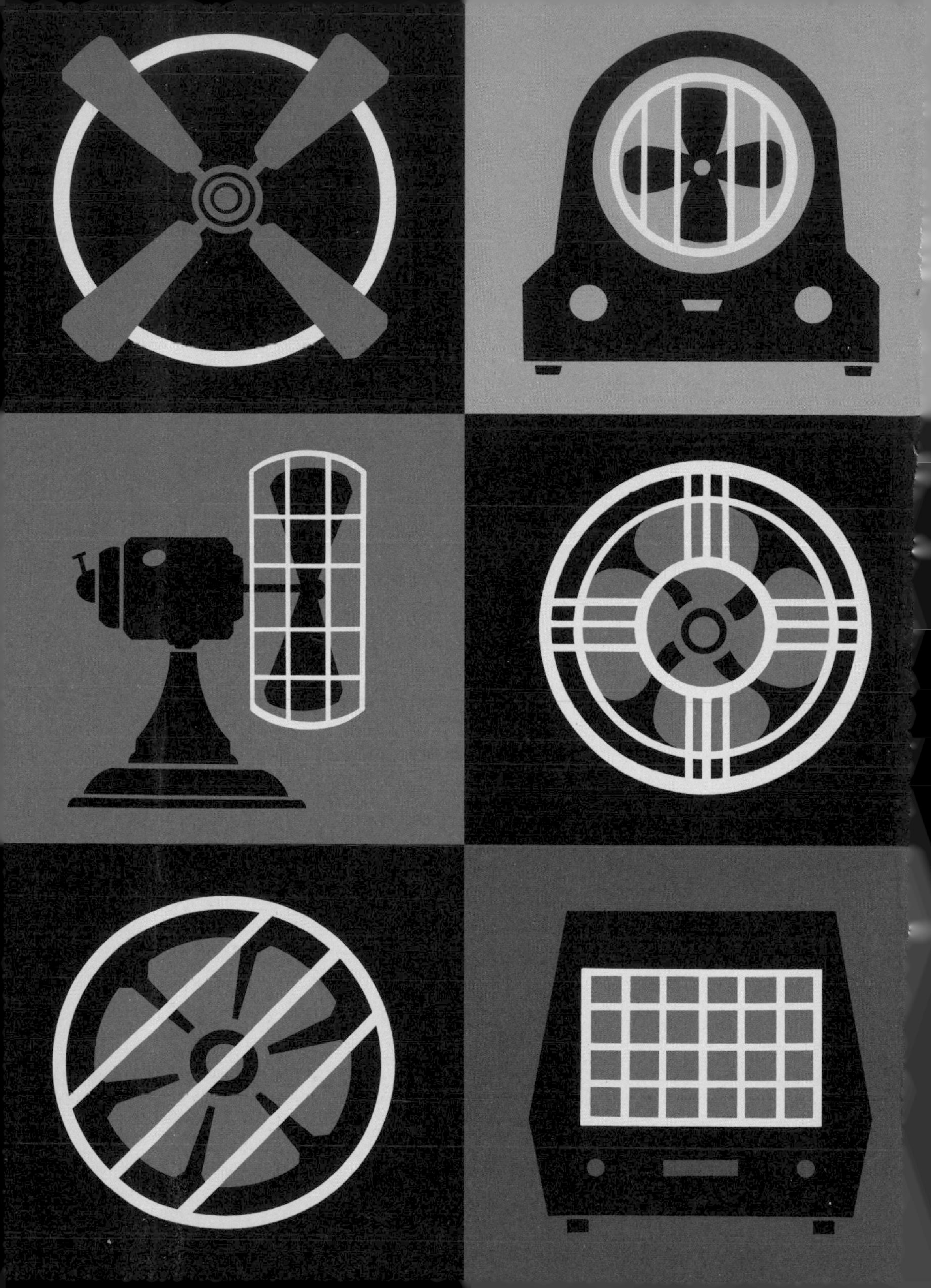